1 MONTH OF
FREE
READING

at

www.ForgottenBooks.com

By purchasing this book you are eligible for one month membership to ForgottenBooks.com, giving you unlimited access to our entire collection of over 1,000,000 titles via our web site and mobile apps.

To claim your free month visit:

www.forgottenbooks.com/free906940

ISBN 978-0-265-90139-7
PIBN 10906940

FORT WAYNE CITY

AND

ALLEN COUNTY

DIRECTORY

1895-6.

CONTAINING

AN ALPHABETICALLY ARRANGED LIST OF BUSINESS FIRMS AND PRIVATE
CITIZENS IN FORT WAYNE—A MISCELLANEOUS DIRECTORY OF CITY AND
COUNTY OFFICERS, PUBLIC AND PRIVATE SCHOOLS, CHURCHES,
BANKS, INCORPORATED INSTITUTIONS, SOCIETIES AND BENEVO-
LENT SOCIETIES, ETC., ETC.—A CLASSIFIED LIST OF ALL
TRADES, PROFESSIONS AND PURSUITS—A DIRECTORY
OF ALLEN COUNTY.

SOLD ONLY BY SUBSCRIPTION.

VOLUME XXVII.

R. L. Polk & Co., Publishers,

38 Bass Block, Fort Wayne.

INTRODUCTORY.

In presenting this, the seventeenth volume of the Fort Wayne City and Allen County Directory, we note with pleasure the increase in population, notwithstanding the depression during the last two years. The Directory of 1894 contained 15,904 names; this contains 16,154 names, multiplied by three, shows the total population to be 48,462.

The Directory, in accuracy, is as nearly perfect as the most unceasing vigilance could make it. The publication of a directory is a work of great difficulty and labor of which the public have no conception, because if they had we should suppose that many of our merchants, store keepers and others who use it a great deal during the year, besides having their business represented from year to year in both the alphabetical and classified portion of the Directory without any cost to them, would give up the practice of borrowing and purchase a copy for their own use. The taking of names was completed about the 1st of March, and it is hoped that anyone who has changed his business location or residence since that date whose name, business or profession is not properly inserted will not censure the publishers, as communications appeared in the daily papers requesting such to send in their addresses for correction, the frequency of removals rendering it impossible for the publishers to make a correct directory without such assistance. To find a name you must know how to spell it. It is not uncommon for members of the same family to spell their names differently, preserving the pronunciation—a few instances as follows: Baar Bahr, Barr, Beyer; Maher, Maier, Mayer, Meier, Meyer, Mier, Myer Schaefer, Schäfer, Shafer, Shaffer. We have in our office a library containing directories of all the principal cities of the United States for the free use of our patrons and strangers visiting our city. In addition to the benefits which our citizens derive from this valuable library, our "Exchange System," which places the Fort Wayne City Directory in all directory libraries throughout the country, serves as an excellent advertisement for a prosperous city, for no other publication can convey such an idea of a city, its growth, its people, with their trades and professions; its schools, churches, societies, banks and railroads, and all the various institutions and organizations.

The wide circulation of the Directory enables capitalists and business men in every locality to communicate with our citizens and to note the progress and improvements the Directory annually records. Attention is directed to the city map, corrected up to date, and street guide attached thereto indicating by letter and number where each street may easily be found. We have at great expense and labor acquired this information, which we feel no hesitation in placing before you. In our County list for 1895 we make a new feature, giving the name of every male over 21 years of age. With accurate Post Office address, we found many of our patrons who regard the acreage and valuation following each farmers's name, as unimportant, they only requiring the accurate address.

We extend our thanks to the patrons of the Directory for their continued confidence and support. 		THE PUBLISHERS.

GENERAL INDEX.

INDEX TO ADVERTISEMENTS.

3816

NAMES AND CHANGES OF ADDRESS RECEIVED TOO LATE FOR REGULAR INSERTION.

Adair Mrs Carrie, bds 163 E Jefferson.

Albers & Wagner, Insurance, Loans and Real Estate, 5 and 6 Foellinger Blk.

Alden Frank W, moved to Delaware, O.

Allen John T. carpenter, res 312 Clay.

Anderson Philip A, clerk, bds 21 Pine.

Anderson Wm. laborer, res 41 Hench.

Bade Frederick, truckman, res 11 N Calhoun.

Baer Frank E. bds 128 W Main.

Baker George, cabtmkr Ft Wayne Furn Co, bds 34 W Superior.

Barnett Walter W, Physician and Surgeon, Sec Fort Wayne College of Medicine, 2 and 3 White Blk, res 43 W DeWald. Tel 457.

Barney Arthur E, trav agt, bds 220 W Wayne.

Bayless Gustave E, trav agt, bds 164 Brackenridge.

Bell Clothing House, Epstein & Sons, 18 Calhoun

Bell James W, res 170 W Main.

Bellamy Frank A, circulator Ft Wayne Journal bds 250 Calhoun.

Bender Willard L, teamster, res 16 Lasselle.

Berg Peter, teamster, res 171 Taber.

Biegel Julius T, painter, res 526 E Wayne.
Bisel Elmer E, hoseman, res 171 VanBuren.
Blair Solon K, res 225 W Wayne.
Boese Dora (wid Frederick), res 600 E Lewis.
Bower George B M, physician, res 90 E Berry.
Bradbury Ollie, domestic 21 Lincoln av.
Bradley Jessie L, Stenogr A Grindle, bds 233 E Lewis.
Braithwaite Wm H, fireman, bds 112 Howell.
Bramigk Werner, physician, 174 Broadway, res 12 Wilt.
Brimmer Joseph H, Painter and Wall Paper
    33 W Main, res e s West Leo road rear of Centlivre
    Brewery.   Tel 164.
Brittingham John S, wood turner, res 164 W Creighton av.
Brown Petrus Z, bds 57 W Wayne.
Brown & Purcell (A L Brown, Frank E Purcell), props
    Hotel Rich Calhoun n w cor Douglas av.   Tel 226.
Bulson Albert E jr, physician. res 55 W Wayne.
Callaghan Patrick D, flagman, res 44 Hoagland av.
Chadwick Samuel W, molder, res 95 Wall.
Conrad George, bds 135 Madison.
Cooper Wm P, Special Agent New York Life
    Insurance Co, 33 E Berry, res 182 W Washington.
    (*See p* 496.)
Croft Harry H, bds 260 Clinton.
Cutler George W, res cor Howell and Rumsey.
Cutler Wm M, grocer, res 3 Oak.
Davis Willard T, helper Ft W Elec Ry Co, res 721 E
    Washington.
Denter Michael, bds 15 N Calhoun.
Dewey Charles. laborer, res 419 W Main.
Dickey Joseph H, res 511 E Lewis.
Dishong C, moved to Yakima, Wash.
Dunifan George W, res 6 Reed.
Eberwein E F, res 260 Clinton.
Ebner George, car bldr Penn Co, res 228 Hugh.
Ehrman Charles F (Ehrman & Geller), res 152 Griffith.
Eiter John, bds 252 Clinton.
Elliott Finnimore F, engr, res 82 4th.
Epstein Hart (Epstein & Sons), res 248 W Wayne.
Epstein Samuel H (Epstein & Sons), bds 248 W Wayne.
Epstein Simon (Epstein & Sons). bds 248 W Wayne.
Epstein & Sons (Hart, Samuel H and Simon),
    props The Bell Clothing House, 18 Calhoun.
Feldheiser Andrew, motorman, res 511 E Lewis.

Fitch Wm S, clk Penn Co, res 77 E Butler.
Flick Clara Belle, Mngr Chestnut Slope Green-
    houses. 132 Thompson av. Tel 455. Store 33 W
    Berry. Tel 467, res 132 Thompson av.
Franz August. res 128 Madison.
Gross Lodema (wid Thomas), res cor Lafayette and Madison
Gross Wm O (Gross & Pellens), res 152 Ewing.
Grote Frederick H, bds 245 W Washington.
Grote Herman, bds 245 W Washington.
Haley John P, brakeman, bds 266 Calhoun.
Hapner G R, bds 9 Winch.
Harris Elwood E, teamster, res 89 St Joe boulevard.
Hartstein Paul, lab, res 99 Shawnee av.
Hedges John, trav agt, res 210 Lafayette.
Heilbroner Louis E, wines and cigars. 24 E Columbia.
Hood Emily W. stenogr R G Dun & Co, bds 247 W Berry
Holmes Wm A, moved to Chicago.
Jacobs John, res 2 Hanover.
Koch Mrs F, boarding house, 24 W Wayne.
Lallow Charles, carp, res 12 Custer av.
Lallow Louis J, carp, res 232 St Mary's av.
Lanoir Mary, domestic 22 W Wayne.
Lowe Charles, fireman E L & P Co, bds A A Fratenberg.
Mc Ilvaine Louise, bds 256 E Lewis.
Marc Charles P, bds 14 Brandriff.
McNutt L D, res 84 W Main.
Maxwell Edwin, propr St. James Hotel.
Meller Frederick H, res 24 W Williams.
Monahan Dennis, 86 Calhoun.
Moore Clara (wid Christopher), res 3 Bass.
Myers Wm C, res 707 Broadway.
Neff Elmer H, res 145 Griffith.
Ostermann Annie M (wid Lambert), res 239 E Washington
Overbulzer Frank J, brakeman N Y, C & St. L R R, bds
    206 W Superior.
Pinney Charles A, conductor, res 701 Hanna.
Remmert Mrs J H, res. 39 Wefel.
Rhine Wm, helper Kerr Murray Mnfg Co, res cor Creigh-
    ton av and Winter.
St Hair Wm S, blacksmith, res 161 Barr.
St James Hotel, Edwin Maxwell Propr, 233 and
    235 Calhoun.
Segur Charles A, res 159 Holman.
Smith Henry I, lawyer, 23 Court, rms 76 Montgomery.
Thompson Thomas, carpenter, res 123 Walton av.
Wagner John T (Albers & Wagner), res 4 University.

R. L. POLK & CO.'S
FORT WAYNE DIRECTORY.
1895-96.

MISCELLANEOUS DEPARTMENT.

STREETS AND AVENUES.

Abbott, from Pontiac south, second east of Walton av.

Aboit, from Sherman west beyond Franklin av, first south of Spring.

Adams, from Manford north, third east of Hartman.

Alexander, from Pontiac south, first east of Walton av.

Allen (East), from Calhoun east to Lafayette, first north of Pontiac.

Allen (West), from Calhoun west to Hoagland av, first north of Pontiac.

Alliger, from Maumee road south to Pioneer av, second east of Walton av.

Andrew, from Huffman north to Archer av, third west of Wells.

Andrew av, from Pioneer av east to Coombs, first south of New Haven av.

Anna, from Shawnee av west to Miner, second south of W Creighton av.

Antoinette, from Walton av east, first north of Pontiac.

Archer av, from Wells west to Gertrude av, second north of Huffman.

Baker, from Calhoun west to Fairfield av, second north of Wabash R R.

Baker av, from St Joseph boulevard east, second north of Elmwood av.

Baltes, from Spy Run av east to St Joseph river, second north of St Mary's river.

Barnett, from Spy Run av east to St Joseph river, second north of Prospect av.

Barr, from E Superior south to Pontiac, second east of Calhoun.

Barr (North), from E Superior north to Burgess av, second east of N Calhoun.

Barthold, from L S & M S Ry north beyond W Fourth, fourth west of Wells.

Basin, from N Y, C & St L R R north to High, first west of St Mary's av.

Bass, from Hoagland av west to Fairfield av, first south of Wabash R R.

Beaver av, from Home av south to Rudisill av, first east of Broadway.

Begue, from E Wayne north to N Y, C & St L R R, third east of Hanna.

Belle, from Shawnee av west, first south of W Creighton av.

Bequette, from W Main north, first west of Runnion av.

Berry (East), from Calhoun east to Monroe, first south of E Main.

Berry (West), from Calhoun west to St Mary's river, first south of W Main.

Boltz, from Lafayette east, second south of Pontiac.

Bond, from New Haven rd south to Wabash R R, second east of toll gate.

Boone, from Cherry west to L S & M S Ry. first north of W Main.

Bowser, from Wells west to Clark, first north of High.

Brackenridge, from Calhoun west to Broadway, third north of Wabash R R.

Brandriff, from Webster west to Hoagland av, third south of Wabash R R.

Breck, from St Mary's av west, first north of N Y, C & St L R R.

Broadway, from N Y, C & St L R R south beyond Rudisill av, sixth west of Calhoun.

Brooklyn, from P, Ft W & C Ry south to Ontario, first west of St Mary's river.

Brooklyn av, a continuation of Brooklyn from Ontario south to Little River turnpike.

Brookside, from Taylor south to Leland, first west of Broadway.

Brown, from St Mary's river west beyond Paul, second south of P, Ft W & C Ry.

Buchanan, from Lafayette east to Winter, third north of E Creighton av.

Burgess, from St Mary's av west to L S & M S Ry, first north of Breck.

Burgess av, from Spy Run av west, first north of Elizabeth.

Burnett av, from Indiana av east to Fairfield av, first north of Rudisill av.

Bush, from Hicksville State road north, first east of St Joseph Gravel road.

Butler (East), from Clinton east to Lafayette, second north of E Creighton av.

Butler (West), from Calhoun west to Fairfield av, second north of W Creighton av.

Calhoun, from Superior south to Rudisill av.

Calhoun (North), from Superior north to city limits, first east of N Harrison.

Canal, from E Wayne north to Maumee river, fifth east of Hanna.

Caroline, from Suttenfield south to Pontiac, first east of Lafayette.

Carson av, from Parnell av east to St Joe Gravel rd, first north of Charlotte av.

Case, from L S & M S Ry north to E Sixth, first east of Wells.

Cedar, from Maumee rd south to E Lewis, first east of Ohio.

Centlivre, from Spy Run av west, third north of Elizabeth.

Centre, from Fair north to N Y, C & St L R R, first west of St Mary's river.

Charles, from Lafayette east to Hanna, fourth south of E DeWald.

Charlotte av, from Baker av east to St Joe Gravel rd, first north of Hicksville State rd.

Cherry, from St Mary's river north to N Y, C & St L R R, first west of the river.

Chestnut, from Calhoun east to Clinton, first south of Holman.

Chestnut, from Roy west beyond Warren, second south of Wabash R R.

Chicago, from Calhoun west, first north of P, Ft W & C Ry.

Chute, from Maumee road south to Wabash R R, second east of Harmer.

Clara av, from Spy Run av east to St Joseph river, first north of St Mary's river.

Clark, from High north to Bowser, third west of Wells.

Clay, from E Columbia south to Lasselle, fourth east of Calhoun.

Clay (North), from E Sixth north to Spy Run, third east N Clinton.

Cleveland, from junction of W Main and Runnion av northeast.

Clifton, from Manford north, second east of Hartman.

Clinton, from E Superior south to Pontiac, first east of Calhoun.

Clinton (North), from E Superior north to Seventh, first east of N Calhoun.

Cochran, from Maumee river east to canal, first north of N Y, C & St L R R.

Cody, from Garfield west to city limits, second south of Columbia av.

Colerick, from Hoagland av west to Fairfield av second south of Wabash R R.

College, from Berry south to Stophlet, fifth west of Broadway.

Columbia (East), from Calhoun east to Maumee river, first north of E Main.

Columbia (West), from Colhoun west to Harrison, first north of W Main.

Columbia av, a continuation east to city limits of E Columbia from Maumee river.

Comparet, from E Wayne south to Maumee road, fourth east to Hanna.

Coombs, from E Wayne north to Maumee river, fourth east of Hanna.

Coombs, from Pioneer av northeast to Curtice av, second south of New Haven av.

Cottage av, from South Wayne av to Beaver av, first south of Home av.

Cour, from Webster east to Piqua av, second south of Killea av.

Court, from E Main south to E Berry, first east of Calhoun.

Creighton av (East), from Calhoun east to Walton av, sixth south of Wabash R R.

Creighton av (West), from Calhoun west to Broadway, sixth south of Wabash R R.

Crescent, from Fairfield av west to South Wayne av, second south of W Creighton av.

Crescent av, from Maumee river north to Elmwood av, first west of Beulah lake.

Curtice av, from Coombs south to Slataper, first east of Wayne Trace.

Custer av, from Burgess north to High, third west of St Mary's av,

Dawson, from Calhoun west to Hoagland av, third south
of Wabash R R.

Dayton. from Fairfield av west to Indiana av, second north
of Rudisill av.

Dearborn, from Edgewater av north to St Joseph boulevard, third east of Maumee river.

De Groff, from Burgess north to High, first west of St
Mary's av.

Delta boulevard, from Edgewater av north to Lake av,
first east of Crescent av.

De Wald (East), from Calhoun east to Hanna, first north
of E Creighton av.

De Wald (West), from Calhoun west to Broadway, first
north of W Creighton av.

Diamond, from Walton av east, third north of Pontiac.

Dinnen av, from Thompson av south to Hartnett av, first
west of Broadway.

Division, from Maumee road south to Hayden, first east of
Harmer.

Dock, from Harrison east to Barr, first south of N Y,
C & St L R R.

Dodge av, from St Joe Gravel road east to Malcolm,
second north of Hicksville State road.

Dougall, from Dwenger av north and south, third east of
Glasgow av.

Douglas av, from Calhoun west to McClellan, sixth south
of W Main.

Dubois, from Maumee road south to Wabash R R, third
east of Walton av.

Duck, from Calhoun east to Barr, first north of E Superior.

Duryea, from Hoagland av west to Fairfield av, second
north of W Creighton av.

Dwenger av, from Glasgow av east to city limits, first
north of N Y, C & St L R R.

Eagle, from Taylor south to Ida av, second west of Broadway.

Eckart lane, from Hanna east to Smith, third south of
Pontiac.

Eden av, from Oneida northwest, north of Elmwood av.

Edgerton, from Walton av west to Winter, first south of
P, F W & C Ry.

Edgewater av, from Columbia av east to city limits, first
north of Maumee river.

Edith av, from Spring north to Margaret av, third west of
St Mary's av.

Edna, from Spy Run av west, fourth north of Elizabeth.

Edsall av, from New Haven av north to New Haven and
    Fort Wayne turnpike, fifth east of Pioneer av.
Edward, first north of Orchard av, running west.
Elenora, from Viola av west, first south of Spring.
Eliza, from Francis east to Winter, and from Walton av to
    Alliger, second south of E Lewis.
Eliza av, from Parnell av east, first south of Hicksville
    State rd.
Elizabeth, from Spy Run av west to N Barr, first north of
    Emily.
Ellen av, from Jesse av west to Gertrude av, first north of
    Spring.
Elm, from St Mary's river west to same, first south of W
    Main.
Elmwood av, from St Joseph boulevard east to Crescent
    av, third north of Columbia av.
Emily, from Spy Run av west, first south of Elizabeth.
Emily, from Thomas east to Gay, second south of E
    Creighton av.
Erie, from Francis east to Walton av, second north of E
    Washington.
Euclid, from Antoinette north beyond Diamond, first east
    of Walton av
Eva, from Huestis av south to Maple av, first west of
    Broadway.
Evans, from Queen east to Hartman, third south of
    Pontiac.
Ewing, from W Superior south to Baker, third west of
    Calhoun.
Fair, from St Mary's river west to same, third south of
    W Main.
Fairfield av, from Brackenridge south to Rudisill av, fifth
    west of Calhoun.
Fairview, from New Haven and Fort Wayne turnpike
    south to Highland av, third east of Lumbard.
Ferguson, from Broadway east to Miner, second south of
    W Creighton av.
Fifth (East), from Wells east to N Calhoun, fifth north of
    St Mary's river.
Fifth (West), from Wells west to Orchard, second south
    of canal feeder.
First, from Wells east to L S & M S Ry, first north of St
    Mary's river.
Fisher, from Thomas east to Holton av, second south of E
    Creighton av.
Fisher, from Dwenger av north and south, fourth east of
    Glasgow av.

Fletcher av, from Maumee rd south to Pioneer av, first east of Walton av.

Force, from P, Ft W & C Ry south to Tenth, first east of Hanna.

Fourth (East), from Wells east to N Calhoun, fourth north of St Mary's river.

Fourth (West), from Wells west, third north of High.

Fox, from W Creighton av north to Taylor, second east of Broadway.

Fox av, from Pontiac north to P, Ft W & C Ry, second west of Wayne Trace.

Francis, from Maumee river south to Wabash R R, first east of Hanna.

Franklin, from Holton av west to Smith, fourth south of Pontiac, and from Alexander east to Simon, first south of Pontiac.

Franklin av, from L S & M S Ry north to High and from canal feeder north to Archer av, first west of St Mary's av.

Frederick, from Herman south to N Y, C & St L R R, first west of St Mary's av.

Frederick, from Holton av west beyond Smith, second south of Pontiac.

French, from Hoagland av east to Webster, first north of Rudisill av.

Fry, from W Main north to Boone, fifth east of St Mary's river.

Fulton, from W Superior south to Brackenridge, first east of Broadway.

Garden, from Taylor north to St Mary's river, second west of Broadway.

Garfield, from Wines north to Lake av, first west of Walton av.

Gay, from E Lewis south to Tenth, third east of Hanna.

Geary, south of Manford, running north and south.

Gerke, from Holton av west beyond Smith, first south of Pontiac.

Gertrude av, from Spring north to Margaret av, first south of G R & I R R.

Gladstone, from McDougall north to Eliza av, first east of Parnell av.

Glasgow av, from Maumee river south to Maumee rd, second east of Walton av.

Grace, from Calhoun east to Lafayette, second south of Pontiac.

✗Grace av, from Broadway east to Shawnee av, third south of W Creighton av.

Grand, from Calhoun west to Hoagland av, first south of
  Wabash R R.
Grant, from Gay east to P, F W & C Ry, first south of
  Wallace.
Grant av, from E Wayne south to Maumee rd, first east of
  Walton av.
Greeley, from Webster west to Jackson, first north of N
  Y, C & St L R R.
Greene, from Smith east to Winter, first north of E
  Creighton av.
Griffith, from W Superior south to Brackenridge, second
  east of Broadway.
Griswold av, from Parnell av west to St Joseph river,
  first north of Eliza av.
Gumpper av, from Webster east to Piqua av, first north of
  Rudisill av.
Guthrie, from junction of Broadway and Michigan av
  southwest to Thompson av.
Haidee, from Orff av west to Lindenwood av, third north
  of Orchard av.
Hamilton, from Calhoun east to Lafayette, second south of
  Wabash R R.
Hanna, from Maumee river south to city limits, sixth east
  of Calhoun.
Hanna (North), from Prospect av south to St Mary's river,
  second east of Spy Run av.
Hanover, from E Washington north to Seneca, second
  west of Walton av.
Harmer, from Maumee river south to Hayden, second east
  of Hanna.
Harmony court, from W Main south to W Berry, first
  west of Calhoun.
Harrison, from Superior south to Rudisill av, first west of
  Calhoun.
Harrison (North), from W Superior north to E Sixth, first
  west of N Calhoun.
Hartman, from Pontiac south beyond Evans, fifth east of
  Walton av.
Hartnett, from Broadway west to St Mary's river, first
  south of Thompson av.
Hayden, from Francis east to Walton av, third south of E
  Lewis.
Hendricks, from Fairfield av west to Martin, first north of
  G R & I R R.
Henry, from Holton av west beyond Smith, fifth south of
  Pontiac.

Hensch, from Huffman north to Archer av, second west of
Wells.

Herman, from St Mary's av east to St Mary's river, first
north of N Y, C & St L R R.

Hicksville State road, from Parnell av east beyond city
limits.

High, from Wells west beyond canal feeder, first north of
St Mary's river.

Highland, from Calhoun west to Webster, second south of
Wabash R R.

Highland av, from Lumbard east to Edsall av, first south of
New Haven and Fort Wayne turnpike.

Hillsdale av, from Eliza av south beyond Baker av, first
east of St Joseph boulevard.

Hoagland av, from Wabash R R south to Rudisill av,
fourth west of Calhoun.

Holman, from Calhoun east to Hanna, seventh south of E
Main.

Holton av, from P, F W & C Ry south to city limits,
seventh east of Hanna.

Home, from Pennsylvania south, first east of Wayne Trace.

Home av, from Fairfield av west to Thompson av, first
south of W Creighton av.

Horace, from John east to Holton av, second south of
Wallace.

Hough, from Clay east to Hanna, first north of P, F W
& C Ry.

Howard, from E Washington north to Erie, first west of
Walton av.

Howell, from G R & I R R east to canal feeder, fifth south
of Spring.

Huestis av, from Broadway west to Thompson av, second
south of W Creighton av.

Huffman, from Wells west to Jesse av, first north of canal
feeder.

Hugh, from Hanna east to Gay, from Ohio to Winter and
from Walton av to Alliger, first south to E Lewis.

Humphrey, from Grant av to Glasgow av, first south of
E Washington.

Hurd, from Holton av east to Winter, first south of E
Creighton av.

Huron, from St Mary's river west to same, second south
of W Main.

Ida av, from Metz west to city limits, third north of
Wabash R R.

Indiana av, from Grace av south to Rudisill av, first west
of Broadway.

Jackson, from N Y, C & St L R R south to G R & I R R, second west of Broadway.

James, from Leith south, first east of Calhoun.

Jane, from Leith south, second east of Calhoun.

Jefferson (East), from Calhoun east to Division, fourth south of E Main.

Jefferson (West), from Calhoun west to Garden, fourth south of W Main.

Jenison, from Holton av east to Winter, second south of E Creighton av.

Jesse, from G R & I R R east, first north of Howell.

Jesse av, from Spring north beyond Margaret av, second west of St Mary's av.

John, from Wallace south to Tenth, third east of Hanna.

Johns av, from Hoagland av east to Lafayette, second south of Pontiac.

Jones, from Rockhill west beyond Nelson, third south of W Jefferson.

Julia, from Thomas east to Holton av, first south of E Creighton av.

Kansas, from Wabash R R south to Melita, first east of Hoagland av.

Killea av, from Calhoun west to Hoagland av, second south of Pontiac.

King, from E Wayne south to Maumee road, third east of Hanna.

Kinnaird, from Fairfield av west to Indiana av, second south of Home av.

Knode, from Pontiac south, first east of Hartman.

Koch, from Archer av south, first west of Wells.

Koenig, from Meehan north, first west of Hanna.

Lafayette, from E Superior south to city limits, third east of Calhoun.

Lafayette (North), from E Sixth north, second east of N Clinton.

Lahmeyer, from Winter east to Lillie, second north of Pontiac.

Lake, from St Mary's av west, first north of canal feeder.

Lake av, from St Joseph boulevard east beyond city limits, first north Columbia av.

Lantermier, from Walton av west to Winter, second south of Wabash R R.

Lasselle, from Lafayette east to Hanna, fourth north of E Creighton av.

Lavina, from Broadway east to Fairfield av, third south of W Jefferson.

Lavinia av, from Taylor south, fourth west of Broadway.

Lee, from Wayne Trace northeast, third south of Coombs.

Leesburg road, from end of W Main north.

Leith, from Calhoun east and west, first south of Pontiac.

Leland, from Metz west, first south of Taylor.

Lewis (East) from Calhoun east to Walton av, fifth south of E Main.

Lewis, (West), from Calhoun west to Ewing, fifth south of W Main.

Liberty, from Harmer east to canal, first south of N Y, C & St L R R.

Lillie, from Maumee rd south to Simons av and from Edgerton south to Pontiac, first west of Walton av.

Lima Plank road, continuation of Wells from Archer av north.

Lincoln, from Dwenger av north and south, first east of Glasgow av.

⨯ Lincoln av, from Broadway east to Shawnee av, fourth south of W Creighton av.

Lindenwood av, from Orchard north to N Y, C & St L R R, second west of Leesburg rd.

Little River turnpike, from south end of Broadway southwest across St Mary's river.

Locust, from Fairfield av west, first north of Wabash R R.

Locust, from Calhoun west to Harrison, first south of St Mary's river.

Loree, from Edgewater av north to Rivermet av, second east of Maumee river.

⤩ Lukens av, from Fairfield av west to Indiana av, first south of Home av.

Lumbard, from New Haven and Fort Wayne turnpike south to Wayne Trace, first east of Glasgow av.

Lynn av, from St Joe Gravel road east to Malcolm, first north of the Hicksville State road.

Mc Clellan, from W Lewis south to Chicago, third west of Calhoun.

Mc Culloch, from Maumee road south to Hayden av, fourth east of Harmer.

Mc Donald, from Lumbard east beyond Prospect, first north of Wabash R R.

Mc Dougall, from St Joseph boulevard east to Hillside av, first north of Baker av.

Mc Lachlan, from Leith south, third east of Calhoun.

Madison, from Barr east to Division, fifth south of E Main.

Misden lane, from Pearl south to W Berry, first west of Harrison.

Main (East), from Calhoun east to Clay, second south of E Superior.

Main (West), from Calhoun west to city limits, first north of W Berry.

Malcolm, from Hicksville State road north, second east of St Joe Gravel road.

Manford, from Abbott east to Simon and from Hartman to Wayne Trace, second south of Pontiac.

✠ Maple av, from Broadway west to Thompson av, third south of W Creighton av.

Margaret av, from St Mary's av west to Gertrude av, fifth north of Spring.

Maria, from G R & I R R east beyond Rumsey av, second south of Spring.

Marion, from High north to W Third and from St Joseph north to canal feeder, first west of Wells.

Marion, from Miller south to Wabash R R, first west of Brooklyn av.

Marshall, from Webster east to Piqua av, first south of Killea av.

Martin, from junction of Broadway and Lavina south to P, Ft W & C Ry.

Mary, from Runnion av west to G R & I R R, first north of W Main.

Masterson, from Calhoun east to Lafayette, third south of Wabash R R.

Maud, from Thomas east to Holton av, first north of Pontiac.

Maumee road, from junction of Washington and Harmer southeast to Glasgow av.

Meadow, from St Mary's river west to Paul, first south of P, Ft W & C Ry.

Mechanic, from Fair north, third west of St Mary's river.

Meehan, from Hanna west, first south of Pontiac.

Melita, from Harrison west to Hoagland av, second south of Wabash R R.

Mercer, from Walton av east, second north of Pontiac.

Meridian, from Archer av south, fourth west of Wells.

Metz, from Taylor south to Wabash R R, second west of Broadway.

Meyer, from Holton av west beyond Smith, third south of Pontiac.

Miami, first south of Pioneer av, near P, F W & C Ry Co's yards.

Michael av, from Ross west, first north of W Superior.

Michigan av, from Broadway west to Metz, second north of Wabash R R.

Milan, from Walton av west to Winter, first south of E Creighton av.

Mill road, from junction of Elizabeth and N Barr across Spy Run west to L S & M S Ry.

Miller, from Brooklyn av west, second north of Wabash R R.

x Miner, from W De Wald south to Grace av, first east of Broadway.

Monroe, from E Berry south to Lasselle, fifth east of Calhoun.

Monroe (North), from Baltes north to Prospect av, first east of Spy Run av.

Montgomery, from Calhoun east to Hanna, fifth south of E Main.

Morrison, from Runnion av east to Park, first north of W Main.

Morton, from Edgewater av north to Lake av, east of Crescent av.

Murray, from Calhoun east to Lafayette, first south of Wabash R R.

Nelson, from W Berry south to Taylor, sixth west of Broadway.

Ne-wee-ah av, from Spy Run av east, third north of Prospect av.

New Haven av, from Pioneer av east, fourth east of Walton av.

New Haven and Fort Wayne turnpike, a continuation of Maumee rd from Glasgow av east beyond city limits.

Ninth, from Hanna east to Gay, first south of Pontiac.

Nirdlinger av, from Broadway west to Swinney av, second south of P, F W & C Ry.

x Nutman av, from Fairfield av west to Indiana av, third north of Rudisill av.

Oak, from Division east to Ohio, second south of E Washington.

Oakland, from Aboit north to Archer av, first east of St Mary's av.

Oakley, from Taylor south to W DeWald, first west of Fairfield av.

Ohio, from Maumee rd south to Wabash R R, third east of Harmer.

Old Fort, from Edgewater av north to Lake av, first west of Maumee river.

Oliver, from P, F W & C Ry south to Meyer. fifth east of Hanna.

Oneida, from Edgewater av north to St Joseph boulevard, fourth east of Maumee river.

Ontario, from Brooklyn av west beyond Paul, third south of P, F W & C Ry.

Orchard, from High north to W Third, and from W Fifth
to canal feeder, second west of Wells.

Orchard av, from Leesburg rd west to Lindenwood av,
first north of W Main.

Orff av, from Orchard av north to N Y, C & St L R R,
first west of Leesburg rd.

Organ av, from Hoagland av west to Indiana av, and from
Beaver av west to Broadway, first south of Pontiac.

Osage, from W Main north, fifth west of St Mary's river.

Packard, from Organ av south, first west of Hoagland av.

Packard av, from Fairfield av west to Indiana av, third
south of Home av and from Beaver av west to
Broadway.

Pape av, from St Mary's av east across St Mary's river to
Van Buren.

Park, from Dwenger av north and south, fifth east of
Glasgow av.

Park av, from Broadway west to Thompson av, fourth
south of W Creighton av.

Park av, from Cleveland av north, first east of Runnion av.

Park place, see Allen (West).

Parnell av, from St Joseph river north, first west of
Gladstone.

Paul, from Meadow south to Ontario, second west of St
Mary's river.

Pearl, from Harrison west to Broadway, first north of W
Main.

Pelican, from Wayne Trace northeast, fourth south of
Coombs.

Penn, from Alliger east beyond Dubois, first south of
Maumee rd.

Pennsylvania, from Wayne Trace northeast, second south
of Coombs.

Perth, from Pennsylvania south, second east of Wayne
Trace.

Phillips, from Broadway east to Miner, first south of W
Creighton av.

Pierce av, from Fairfield av west to South Wayne av, first
south of E Creighton av.

Pine, from Taylor north, first west of Fairfield av.

Pioneer av, from Walton av southeast to Coombs, first
south of Wabash R R.

Piqua av, from junction of Calhoun and Grace south to
Rudisill av.

Pitt, from Curtice av northeast to Texas.

Pittsburgh, from Winch east beyond Edsall av, first south
of Penn.

Pittsburgh, from Clay east to Hanna, first north of P, F W & C Ry.

Polk, from Custer av east, first north of L S & M S Ry.

Pontiac (East), from Calhoun east to Wayne Trace, first south of E Creighton av.

Pontiac (West), from Calhoun west to Fairfield av, first south of W Creighton av.

Poplar, from Fairfield av west to Oakley, second north of W Creighton av.

Prince, from Bass south to Colerick, first east of Fairfield, av.

Pritchard, from Fairfield av west to Rockhill, second south of W Jefferson.

Prospect, from New Haven and Fort Wayne turnpike south to Wabash R R, first east of Lumbard.

Prospect av, from Spy Run av east to St Joseph river, fourth north of St Mary's river.

Purman, from Warsaw west, first north of Pontiac.

Putnam, from Wells west to Jesse av, first north of Huffman.

Queen, from Pontiac south, third east of Walton av.

Railroad, from Calhoun east to Clinton, first north of P, Ft W & C Ry.

Ramsey av, from Nutman av south to Dayton av, first east of Indiana av.

Randall, from Grant av east to Glasgow av, second south of E Washington.

Randolph, from Spy Run av west, second north of Elizabeth.

Raymond, from Lee east beyond Perth, first north of Wayne Trace.

Rebecca, from G R & I R R east beyond Rumsey av, third north of Spring.

Reed, from Buchanan south to Pontiac, third west of Walton av.

Reynolds, from Edsall av west beyond Roy, first south of Wabash R R.

Richardson, from Runnion av east and west, first north of N Y, C & St L R R.

Rivermet av, from St Joseph boulevard east to Crescent av, second north of Columbia av.

Riverside av, from Spy Run av east to St Joseph river, first north of Prospect av. ◆

Rockhill, from W Main south to G R & I R R, fourth west of Broadway.

Romy av, from Parnell av east to Gladstone, second south of Hicksville State rd.

Ross, from W Superior north, first east of Van Buren.

Roy, from New Haven av north to Wabash R R, fourth east of Pioneer av.

Rudisill av, from south end of Broadway east to Piqua av, first south of Home av.

Rumsey av, from N Y, C & St L R R north to Spring, first east of Runnion av.

Runnion av, from W Main north to Spring, second east of G R & I R R.

Ruth, from Spy Run av west, second south of Elizabeth.

St Joe Gravel road, from Hicksville State rd northeast, first east of Baker av.

St Joseph, from Wells west to Orchard, first south of canal feeder.

St Joseph boulevard, from Columbia av north to Parnell av, on east bank of St Joseph river.

St Martin's, from Lafayette east to Hanna, second north of E Creighton av.

St Mary's av, from N Y, C & St L R R north to Margaret av. sixth west of Wells.

Sand, from N Y, C & St L R R north to Maumee river, first east of Walton av.

Savannah, from E Creighton av south to E Pontiac, second east of Walton av.

Savilla av, from Broadway east to Indiana av, fifth south of W Creighton av.

Schaper, from Holton av west, sixth south of Pontiac.

Schele av, from Lumbard east and west, first south of New Haven av.

Schick, from N Y, C & St L R R, south to Maumee rd, first east of canal.

Scholes, from St Mary's av east, first north of High.

Schroeder, from Pontiac north to P, F W & C Ry, first west of Wayne Trace.

Scott av, from Broadway west to Thompson av, first south of W Creighton av.

Second, from Wells east, second north of St Mary's river.

Selden, from Walton av west to Winter, first south of Wabash R R.

Seneca, from canal east to Hanover, first north of N Y, C & St L R R.

Seventh, from N Clinton east to N Clay, first north of Sixth.

Shawnee av, from W Creighton av south to Home av, second east of Broadway.

Sherman, from W Fourth north to Archer av, second east of St Mary's av.

Short, from Huffman north to Archer av, first west of Wells.

Siemon, from Pontiac south to Leith, first east of Calhoun.

Simon, from Pontiac south to Manford, fourth east of Walton av.

Simons, from Walton av west to Winter, second north of P, F W & C Ry.

Sinclair av, from St Mary's av west, first north of High.

Sixth, from Wells east, first south of canal feeder.

Slataper, from Wayne Trace northeast, first south of Coombs.

Smith, from P, F W & C Ry south to city limits, fourth east of Hanna.

✗ South Wayne av, from W Creighton av south to Rudisill av, fifth west of Calhoun.

Spring, from Sherman west beyond G R & I R R, first south of Huffman.

Spring, from Mary south to Wabash R R, first west of Runnion av.

Spy Run av, from E Superior north to city limits, first east of Barr.

Stophlet, from Broadway west to Garden, third south of P, Ft W & C Ry.

Sturgis, from Fulton west, first south of W Jefferson.

Summer, from New Haven av north to Pittsburgh, second east of Pioneer av.

Summit, from Division east to Winter, first north of E Lewis.

Superior (East), from Calhoun east beyond Lafayette, second north of N Y, C & St L R R.

Superior (West), from Calhoun west to Jackson, second north of N Y, C & St L R R.

Suttenfield, from Webster east to Hanna, second south of W Creighton av.

Swinney av, a continuation of Nirdlinger av west from College.

Swinney Park, end of W Jefferson.

Sylvan, from Wines east to city limits, third south of Columbia av.

Taber, from Webster east to Hanna, first south of W Creighton av.

Tam, between Walton av and Winter, first south of Simons.

Taylor, from Fairfield av west to Lavinia, fourth north of W Creighton av.

Tecumseh, from Edgewater av north to city limits, fifth east of Maumee river.

Tenth, from Hanna east to Gay, second south of Pontiac.

Texas, from Pitt northwest and southeast.

Theresa av, from New Haven av south to Wayne Trace, first east of Pioneer av.

Third (East), from Wells east, third north of St. Mary's river.

Third (West), from Wells west to St. Mary's av, second north of High.

Thomas, from P, F W & C Ry south to Meyer, sixth east of Hanna.

Thomasetta, from Thomas west to Gay, first south of E Creighton av.

Thompson av, from Scott av south to Broadway, first west of same.

Tilden av, from Delta boulevard west to city limits, first north of Columbia av.

Toledo, from Lafayette east to Monroe, first south of Wabash R R.

Tons, from Dwenger av north and south, second east of Glasgow av.

Trentman av, from Beaver av to Broadway, first south of Home av.

Turpie, from Manford north to Wayne Trace, fourth east of Hartman.

Tyler av, from Spring south to Howell, first east of G R & I R R.

Union, from W Main south to G R & I R R, third west of Broadway.

University, from E Wayne south to Maumee rd, fifth east of Hanna.

Van Buren, from St Mary's river south to Pritchard, first west of Broadway.

Vermilyea av, from Fairfield av west to South Wayne av, third south of W Creighton av.

Victoria av, from Piqua av south to Rudisill av, first east of Calhoun.

Viola av, from Spring south to Elenora, first west of G R & I R R.

Virginia, from Lafayette east to Monroe, second south of Wabash R R.

Wabash av, from E Washington south to Maumee rd, first west of Glasgow av.

Wagner, from Spy Run on east to St Joseph river, third north of St Mary's river.

Wall, from Broadway west to Garden, first south of P, F W & C Ry.

Wallace, from Lafayette east to Smith, third south of P, F W & C Ry.

Walnut, from Fairfield av west to Wabash R R, third
    north of W Creighton av.

Walter, from E Wayne south to Maumee rd, sixth east of
    Hanna.

Walton av, from Maumee river north to Lake av, south to
    E Washington and from Maumee rd south to Pontiac,
    tenth east of Hanna.

Warren, from New Haven av north to Pittsburgh, first
    east of Pioneer av.

Warsaw, from Lasselle south to E DeWald and from E
    Creighton av south to Pontiac, first east of Lafayette.

Washington (East), from Calhoun east to Glasgow av,
    third south of E Main.

Washington (West), from Calhoun west to city limits, third
    south of W Main.

Watkins, from W Main north, first east of L S & M S Ry.

Wayne (East), from Calhoun east to Glasgow av, second
    south of W Main.

Wayne (West), from Calhoun west to College, second south
    of W Main.

Wayne Trace, a continuation of Pioneer av from Coombs
    beyond city limits.

Webster, from St Mary's river south to Rudisill av, sec-
    ond west of Calhoun.

Wefel, from High north, first west of Barthold.

Wells, from W Superior north across St Mary's river to
    Archer av, third west of Calhoun.

Wheeler, from Rumsey av west to G R & I R R, first south
    of N Y, C & St L R R.

Whitmore, from Brooklyn av west, first north of Wabash
    R R

Wiebke, from Lafayette east, third south of Pontiac.

Will, from Orff av west to Lindenwood av, second north
    of Orchard av.

Williams (East), from Calhoun east to Lafayette, fourth
    south of Wabash R R.

Williams (West), from Calhoun west to Fairfield av, fourth
    south of Wabash R R.

Wilt, from Broadway west to Nelson, first south of W
    Jefferson.

Winch, from Penn south to Pioneer av, third east of Wal-
    ton av.

Wines, from Walton av northwest to Edgewater av, first
    north of Maumee river.

Winter, from Lewis south to city limits, second west of
    Walton av.

Wright, from G·R & I R R east beyond Rumsey av, first
    south of Spring.
Zollars av, from Metz west, second north of Wabash R R.
Zollinger, from Glasgow av east to Lincoln, second north of
    N Y, C & St L R R.

WARD BOUNDARIES.

Ward 1. (Including Lakeside addition.) Bounded on
the north by St Mary's river between Lafayette and
Hanna, on the east by Hanna, on the south by the P, Ft
W & C Ry, and on the West by Lafayette.

Ward 2. Bounded on the north by St Mary's river
between Calhoun and Lafayette, on the east by Lafayette,
on the south by the P, Ft W & C Ry, and on the west by
Calhoun.

Ward 3. Bounded on the north by St Mary's river
between Calhoun and Webster, on the east by Calhoun, on
the south by the P, Ft W & C Ry, and on the west by
Webster.

Ward 4. Bounded on the north by St Mary's river
between Webster and the continuation of Broadway to N
Y, C & St L R R, thence northwest to Van Buren st
bridge, on the east by Webster, on the south by the P Ft
W & C Ry, and on the west by Broadway.

Ward 5. Bounded on the north by St Mary's river and
the canal basin, on the east by Broadway, on the south by
the Wabash R R, on the west by the city line.

Ward 6. Bounded on the north by the P, Ft W & C Ry,
on the east by Calhoun, on the south by Killea and
Creighton avs, on the west by Hoagland av, Broadway and
the Wabash R R.

Ward 7. Bounded on the north by the P, Ft W & C Ry,
on the east by Hanna, on the south by Boltz and Grace,
and on the west by Calhoun.

Ward 8. Bounded on the north by the N Y, C & St L
R R, on the east by the city line, on the south by Pioneer
av, P, Ft W & C Ry and Wabash R R, and on the west by
Hanna.

Ward 9. Bounded on the north by Archer av, canal
feeder and Spy Run, on the east and south by the St
Mary's river and the canal basin, and on the west by the
city line.

Ward 10. Bounded on the north by the P, Ft W & C
Ry, on the east by Walton av, on the south by Pontiac and
south line of Industrial Park addition, and on the west by
Hanna.

South Wayne. Bounded on the east by Hoagland av, on the north by W Creighton av to the river, on the west by St Mary's river, and on the south by Rudisill av.

CITY GOVERNMENT.

Municipal Election, first Tuesday in May.

Regular sessions of the Common Council, second and fourth Tuesdays of each month.

Council Chamber, City Hall. cor Barr and E Berry sts.

OFFICERS

CITY OF FORT WAYNE, IND.,

1895.

Chauncey B Oakley, Mayor.
Wm T Jefferies, Clerk.
James H Simonson, Comptroller.
John M Evans, Deputy Comptroller.
Clarence W Edsall, City Auditor.
Lewis C Hunter, City Treasurer.
B F Ninde, City Attorney.
F M Randall, Civil Engineer.
James Ligget, Superintendent Police.
Wm Borgmann, Captain Police.
Henry Lapp, Lieutenant Police.
Fred Daseler, Sargeant Police.
Henry Hilbrecht jr, Chief of Fire Department.
Ferd Schroeder, Captain Fire Company No 1.
Michael Connors, Captain Fire Company No 2.
Louis Steup, Captain Fire Company No 3.
John Stahlhut, Captain Fire Company No 4.
John Baker, Captain Fire Company No 5.
John Zent, Captain Fire Company No 6.
C A Doswell, Custodian of Parks.
Nelson Thompson, Street Superintendent.
James Brice, Foreman Street Repairs.
L C Hollenbacher, Weighmaster.
Wm Ropa, Marketmaster.
W H Brown, Poundmaster.

TRUSTEES OF WATER WORKS.

Charles McCulloch,   Henry C Graffe,
                    Wm Bittler.
P J McDonald, Clerk.   Frank Iten, Inspector.

TRUSTEES OF PUBLIC SCHOOLS.

John M Moritz,   Oliver P Morgan,   A E Hoffman,
John S Irwin, Superintendent.

COUNCIL DIRECTORY.

COUNCILMEN AT LARGE.

R J Fisher,   Charles Griebel,
     E H McDonald,   John Mohr jr.
          Charles Waltemath.

COUNCILMEN.

Ward.		Ward.	
1.	Wm H Tigar.	6.	Wm M Glenn.
2.	H G Sommers.	7.	P J Scheid.
3.	G H Loesch.	8.	P E Wolf.
4.	A Kelker.	9.	T J Young.
5.	H Hild.	10.	B Borkenstein.

STANDING COMMITTEES.

Finance—Wolf, Loesch, Hild, Fisher, Mohr jr.
Rules, Regulations and Ordinances—Loesch, Kelker, Waltemath.
Judiciary—Kelker, Scheid, Waltemath.
Printing—Young, Hild, Sommers.
Elections—Hild, Young, Griebel.
Contracts and Franchises—Glenn, Wolf, Young, McDonald, Scheid.
Fees and Salaries—Mohr jr, Tigar, Glenn.
Street Lights—Griebel, Borkenstein, Glenn.
Education—McDonald, Tigar, Loesch.
Streets and Alleys—Fisher, Young, Waltemath.
Water Works—Scheid, Tigar, Glenn.
Parks—Kelker, Sommers, Scheid.
Public Health—Loesch, Sommers, Waltemath.
Public Property—Fisher, Young, Wolf.

MEMBERS OF OFFICIAL BOARDS.

(Board of Public Works, Room No 2.)

Thomas D De Vilbiss, Chairman.
Levi Griffith.
Willis Hattersley.
      Meets Monday, 3 p m; Friday, 7.30 p m.

BOARD OF PUBLIC SAFETY.
(Room No 8)

Charles S Bash, Chairman.
Rudolph Steger.
Rudolphus B Rossington.
Meets Wednesday, 3 p m.

BOARD OF HEALTH AND CHARITIES.
(Room No 6)

G B Stemen, Secretary.
Jacob Hetrick.
Aaron E Van Buskirk.
Meets Tuesday, 4 p m.
Each day for professional business from 11 to 12 a m.
A J You, Clerk of the Official Boards.

FIRE DEPARTMENT.

Chief Engineer—Henry Hilbrecht jr, office Central Station, E Main.
Steamer No 1, Central Station.
Hook and Ladder Co No 1, Central Station.
Hose Co No 1, Central Station.
Engine Co No 2, Wallace bet Clay and Lafayette.
Hook and Ladder Co No 2, Wallace bet Clay and Lafayette.
Hose Co No 2, Wallace bet Clay and Lafayette.
Chemical Engine Co No 3, W Washington bet Harrison and Webster.
Hose Co No 3, W Washington bet Harrison and Webster.
Engine Co No 4, Maumee rd bet Ohio and Schick.
Hose Co No 4, Maumee rd bet Ohio and Schick.
Engine Co No 5, Broadway bet Lavina and Hendricks.
Hose Co No 5, Broadway bet Lavina and Hendricks.
Engine Co No 6, n w cor Wells and 3rd.
Hose Co No 6, n w cor Wells and 3rd.

FIRE ALARM TELEGRAPH STATIONS.

6—S E Corner Calhoun and Columbia streets.
7—Corner St Mary's avenue and Spring streets.
8—   "   Wells and Huffman streets.
9—   "   St. Mary's avenue and Burgess street.
12—   "   Wells street and Lake Shore Ry.
13—   "   High and Clark streets.
14—   "   Superior and Ewing streets.
15—   "   Calhoun and Jefferson streets.
16—   "   Calhoun and Chicago streets.

17—Corner Calhoun and Williams streets.
18—   "   Calhoun and Leith streets.
23—   "   Washington and Clay streets.
24—   "   Washington and Harmer streets.
25—   "   Lewis and Hanna streets.
26—   "   Summit and Division streets.
27—   "   Maumee rd and Schick street.
28—   "   Hayden and Francis streets.
31—   "   Douglas avenue and Webster street.
32—   "   Jefferson and Griffith streets.
34—   "   Broadway and Jefferson street.
35—   "   Washington and VanBuren streets.
36—   "   Union and Pritchard streets.
37—   "   Broadway and Wall street.
38—   "   Washington and College streets.
41—Olds & Sons' Works.
42—No 2 Engine House.
43—Corner Hanna and Wallace streets.
45—   "   Grant and Smith streets.
46—   "   Hanna street and Creighton avenue.
47—   "   Lafayette and De Wald streets.
48—   "   Creighton avenue and Thomas street.
51—   "   Berry and Webster streets.
52—   "   Main and Griffith streets.
53—   "   Main and Van Buren streets.
54—   "   Main and Cherry streets.
56—   "   Boone and Osage streets.
61—   "   Berry and Court streets.
62—   "   Harrison and Columbia streets.
63—   "   Columbia and Barr streets.
64—   "   Barr and Madison streets.
65—   "   Lafayette and Holman streets.
67—Pittsburg Round House.
71—Corner Fairfield avenue and Bass street.
72—   "   Butler street and Hoagland avenue.
73—   "   Broadway and Taylor street.
74—   "   Fox and De Wald streets.
81—   "   Wayne and Walter streets.
82—   "   Lewis and Lillie streets.
83—   "   Washington street and Grant avenue.
93—Jenney Electric Light and Power Co, Spy Run ave.
114—No 6 Engine House.
121—Central Engine House.
124—Corner Lake avenue and Oneida street.
127—No 4 Engine House.
132—No 3 Engine House.
135—No 5 Engine House.
136—Fort Wayne Electric Corporation, Broadway.

POLICE DEPARTMENT.

Headquarters, City Hall, s e cor Barr and E Berry.
Superintendent—James Ligget.
Captain—Wm F Borgmann.
Lieutenant—Henry Lapp.
Sergeants—F G Daseler, Frank Jewell.
Patrolmen—Wm F Knock, Robert Dickson, Henry J
Harkenrider, Jacob M Bower, Charles F Spillner,
Frank A Vachon, Ernest Paul, James A Richardson,
Edward Grim, Abraham Goeglein, George Coling,
George J Strodel, M Wm Somers, Benjamin H Elliott,
John Greer jr, Frederick J Buechner, Henry F San-
der, Jesse Patton, Albert G Foulks, Theodore Har-
dendorf, Adolphus J Hines, Robert Phipps, John W.
Flickinger, Frederick W Gallmeier, Lot F Sharp,
John W Aiken, Elijah E Tanner.

RATES OF FARE,

AS ESTABLISHED BY CITY ORDINANCES, RELATIVE TO PUB-
LIC CARRIAGES.

SEC. 7. The prices to be charged by the owner or driver
of any vehicle, except an omnibus, for the conveyance of
passengers for hire, within said city, shall be as follows, to
be regulated and estimated by the distance on the most
direct routes, namely:

For conveying a passenger not exceeding one mile 50c
For conveying a passenger any distance over a mile
and less than two miles..........................$1.00

For conveying children between five and fourteen years
of age, half the above prices may be charged for like dis-
tances, but for children under five years of age no charge
shall be made, unless such child is the only passenger, in
which case full charge may be made.

The distance from any railroad depot or hotel to any
other railroad or hotel shall, in all cases, be estimated as
not exceeding one mile.

For the use of coaches drawn by two horses, with one
or more passengers, by the day...................$8.00

For the use of any vehicle by the hour, with one or more
passengers, with the privilege of going from place to
place, and stopping when required, as follows:

For the first hour..............................$1.50
For each succeeding hour........................ 1.00

Every passenger shall be allowed to have conveyed upon such vehicle, without charge, his ordinary traveling baggage, not exceeding in any case one trunk.

Sec. 13. Any person who shall violate any or either of the provisions of this chapter, or any section, clause or provision of any section of this chapter, or who shall fail or neglect to comply with any or either of the requirements thereof, shall, upon conviction, pay a fine of not more than one hundred dollars.

STREET RAILWAYS.

Fort Wayne Electric Railway Co, southeast cor Main and Court.
President—John H Bass.
Vice-President and Treasurer—M S Robison jr.
Secretary—J M Barrett.
Superintendent—L D McNutt.

Lakeside Street Railway Co, office The Wayne.
Directors—R T McDonald, H J Miller, A D Guild.
Superintendent—J D McDonald.

FEDERAL OFFICERS.

GOVERNMENT BUILDING.

Postmaster—W W Rockhill.
Collector of Internal Revenue — Wm H Bracken, (Lawrenceburg, Ind.)
Division Deputy Collector Internal Revenue — Charles Reese.
U S Gauger—Charles Goodman.
U S Pension Officers—Board of Medical Examiners—Dr. Wm H Meyers, Pres ; Dr J L Smith, Hoagland, Ind ; Dr. Miles E Porter. Special Examiners—A P Ingram and Walter N Campbell.

U. S. COURTS.

District Court of the United States—Second Tuesdays in June and December. Hon J H Baker, Judge ; Noble C Butler, Clerk ; Frank B Burke, U S District Attorney, Indianapolis ; Elmer Leonard, U S Commissioner ; T J Logan, Resident Deputy Clerk ; Wm H Hawkins, Marshal, Rochester ; Thomas A Wilkinson, Resident Deputy Marshal.

Circuit Court of United States—Second Tuesdays in June and December. James E Jenkins, Judge; Noble C Butler, Clerk; T J Logan, Resident Deputy Clerk; Wm H Hawkins, Marshal, Rochester; T A Wilkinson, Resident Deputy Marshal.

COUNTY BOARD OF TRUSTEES WITH POST-OFFICE ADDRESSES.

Aboit—James H Stouder, Fort Wayne.
Adams—Christian Schlaudroff, Fort Wayne.
Cedar Creek—Martin Moudy, Hursh.
Eel River—W A Johnson, Churubusco.
Jackson—Wm M Keller, Monroeville.
Jefferson—Frederick Fry, Maples.
Lafayette—Christopher C Young, Zanesville.
Lake—A P Cook, Arcola.
Madison—W H Bauserman, Monroeville.
Marion—George Shookman, Hoagland.
Maumee—John Small, Woodburn.
Milan—Joseph F Wertz, Chamberlain.
Monroe—A S Robinson, Monroeville.
Perry—James E Ballou, Huntertown.
Pleasant—Benjamin H Webster, Nine Mile.
St Joseph—Martin Bloom Jr, Fort Wayne.
Scipio—Milo R Gorrell, Hall's Corners.
Springfield—Wm B Daniels, Harlan.
Washington—Benjamin McQuiston, Fort Wayne.
Wayne—M F Schmetzer, Fort Wayne.

COURTS.

Circuit Court—2d floor Court House. Hon Edward O'Rourke, Judge; Newton D Doughman, Prosecuting Attorney. Terms of Court—First Monday in February, third Monday in April, first Monday in September and third Monday in November.

Superior Court—2d floor Court House. Hon C M Dawson, Judge. Terms of Court—Second Monday in January, first Monday in April, second Monday in September and second Monday in November.

JUSTICES OF PEACE FOR ALLEN COUNTY.

Township.	Name	P O Address.	Term Ex.
Aboit	David H Kelsey ....,	Kelseyville.........	April16,'96
Adams	James A Crippen....	New Haven	Nov. 9, '98
	Valentine Linker ...	Fort Wayne........	Oct. 28, '98
Cedar Creek	Christian J Schlaker	Leo................	Nov. 9, '98
Eel River .	Alva C Disler.......	Ari.	
Jackson	Timothy Baldwin...	Baldwin	April18,'96
Jefferson ...	Henry C Martin.....	Maples....	Mar. 14,'99
Lafayette...	Edmund Wickliffe..	Zanesville	Nov. 9, '98
Lake.......	George W Keim.....	Arcola	Nov. 9, '98
Madison ...	John Shaffer.......	Monroeville........	Nov. 9, '98
Marion	Solomon Snider	Poe.................	Nov. 9, '98
Maumee ...	Wm W Driver	Woodburn	Nov. 9, '98
	Eli Ringwalt........	Chamberlain........	May 16, '96
Milan	James M Nuttle.....	Chamberlain........	May 9, '98
Monroe	John D Allegar......	Monroeville........	Nov. 9, '98
	J D McCormick.....	Monroeville	Nov. 9, '98
Perry	Stephen Thornton...	Huntertown........	Nov.18, '98
Pleasant ...	John M Shives	Nine Mile..........	Dec. 6, '98
St Joseph ..	Theodore H Ashley.	Fort Wayne........	Nov. 9, '98
Scipio......	Daniel Porter.......	Hall's Corners	Nov. 15, '05
Springfield.	John H Eckles......	Harlan	Nov. 18, '98
Washingt'n	Alexand'r McDaniels	Fort Wayne........	Nov. 9, '98
Wayne.....	Harry F France.....	Fort Wayne........	Oct. 24, '99
	Michael Tancey.....	Fort Wayne........	Nov. 9, '98
	Michael H Bohen....	Fort Wayne........	Nov. 13,'98
	Louis P Huser......	Fort Wayne........	Nov. 9, '98
	Charles A Hays.....	Fort Wayne........	Mar. 13,'96

OFFICERS OF ALLEN COUNTY.

Court House, between Calhoun and Court, E Berry and E Main

Judge of the Circuit Court—Hon Edward O'Rourke.

Judge of the Superior Court—Hon Charles M Dawson.

Clerk—H M Metzger.

Prosecuting Attorney—Newton D Doughman.

Sheriff—Edward F Clausmeier.

Recorder—George W Fickel.

Treasurer—L C Hunter.

Auditor—C W Edsall.

Surveyor—Charles W Branstator.

Supt of Bridges—Wm H Goshorn.

Coroner—Morse Harrod.

Commissioners—Jasper W Jones, Chairman; John H Stellhorn, Matthew Ferguson, Sylvanus F Baker.

Attorneys for County Commissioners—Morris, Bell, Barrett & Morris.
School Supt—Flavius J Young.
Assessor—Stephen A Heath.

TOWNSHIP ASSESSORS WITH POSTOFFICE ADDRESSES.

Aboit—F C W Klaehn, Fort Wayne.
Adams—Wm Eggeman, Fort Wayne.
Cedar Creek—John Metcalf, Cedarville.
Eel River—Jeremiah Heffelfinger, Hellers Corners.
Jackson—Benjamin F Eick, Monroeville.
Jefferson—George J Miller, Monroeville.
Lafayette—Henry P Hays, Zanesville.
Lake—James D Butts, Arcola.
Madison—Silas Miller, Hoagland.
Marion—Charles Meyers, Soest.
Maumee—George Husted, Antwerp, Ohio.
Milan—John M Lake, Harlan.
Monroe—Eli D Bauserman, Monroeville.
Pleasant—W E Dalman, Nine Mile.
Perry—G E Rickett, Huntertown.
St Joseph—Joseph T Fonkel, Cedarville.
Scipio—Wallace G Deatsman, Hicksville, Ohio.
Springfield—Henry A Walter, Harlan.
Washington—H F E Kruse, Fort Wayne.
Wayne—Michael V Walsh, Fort Wayne.

BANDS OF MUSIC.

First Regiment Light Artillery Band and Orchestra, 82 Calhoun. Gart Shober, Bandmaster.
Fort Wayne City Band. 70 Calhoun. Prof Philip Keinz, Leader.
Fort Wayne Cornet Band, St John's Lutheran School Hall. Meets Monday and Thursday evenings of each week. Jacob Stumpf, Leader and Pres ; Wm Brown, Vice-Pres and Treas ; E A Bittler, Sec.
Reineke's Orchestra, 70 Calhoun and 41 E Main. Organized, 1872. F J Reineke, Director and Manager.
Wayne Orchestra, 103 Broadway. C L Kaiser, Leader.

BANKS AND BANKERS.

First National Bank, 73-77 Calhoun. Organized May,
1863; reorganized May, 1882. Capital, $300,000; sur-
plus, $175,000. John H Bass, Pres; M W Simons,
Vice-Pres; L R Hartman, Cash; W L Pettit, Asst
Cash.

Hamilton National Bank, 44 Calhoun. Organized 1879.
Capital, $200,000; surplus, $250,000. Charles McCul-
loch, Pres; John Mohr jr, Cash; C W Orr, Asst Cash;
Frank H Poole, 2d Asst Cash.

Nuttman & Co (Private), 32 E Main. Organized 1883.
O S Hanna, Cash.

Old National Bank, s w cor Calhoun and Berry. Capital
$350,000; surplus, $125,000. Organized January,
1885. S B Bond, Pres; O P Morgan, Vice-Pres;
J D Bond, Cash; J C Woodworth, Asst Cash.

White National Bank, n w cor Wayne and Clinton. Organized April 25, 1892. Capital, $200,000; surplus,
$25,000. J W White, Pres; T B Hedekin, Vice-Pres;
H A Keplinger, Cash; G G Detzer, Asst Cash.

BUILDING, LOAN AND SAVING ASSOCIATIONS.

Allen County Loan and Savings Association, 32 E Berry.
Organized April 7, 1890. Capital Stock, $2,000,000.
Managers meet every Monday; directors 3d Tuesday
of each month; annual meeting 3d Tuesday in May.
Gottlieb Haller, Pres; D C Fisher, Vice-Pres; Thomas
C Rogers, Sec; H A Keplinger, Treas; O N Heaton,
Attorney.

Concordia Building and Loan Association.—Saengerbund.
Organized January, 1891. Meets fourth Wednesday
of each month. Charles Kaiser, Pres; Charles H
Buck, Sec; Charles Stellhorn, Treas.

Fort Wayne Building, Loan-Fund and Savings Association.—Sons of Columbus Hall. Organized April 11,
1884. Capital stock, $1,000,000. Meets first Tuesday
after the 18th of each month. Annual meeting, second Wednesday in May. O E Bradway, Pres; F W
Wilson, Vice-Pres; P J McDonald, Sec; Christopher
Hettler, Treas; Wm Stephan, D J Shaw, A J Glutting, C R Higgins, F H Fink, G Muhlenbruch, W L
Moellering, T J Rodabaugh and G H Judy, Directors.

German Allen Building, Loan and Savings Association.—
47 W Main. Organized November, 1887. Capital
stock, $100,000. Meets first Wednesday of each

month. A M Schmidt, Pres; Otto Herbst, Sec; George Motz, Treas.

German Columbus Building and Loan Association.—Custer House. Capital $100,000. Meets fourth Thursday of each month. F H Fink, Pres; J H Pranger, Sec; Charles Stellhorn, Treas.

German Jackson Building, Loan and Savings Association. —47 W Main. Organized June, 1890. Capital stock, $100,000. Meets third Thursday of each month. C W Jacobs, Pres; Otto Herbst, Sec: George Motz, Treas.

Germania Building and Loan Association—Rogers Hall, 26 W Main. Meets every third Thursday. Otto. Nichter, Pres; Henry Zurmuehlen, Sec; Anselm Fuelber, Treas.

Indiana Farmers' Savings and Loan Association—32 E Berry. Organized November, 1892. Authorized capital, $25,000,000. Meets every Monday evening. Hon'R S Peterson (Decatur, Ind), Pres; Hon R C Bell, Vice-Pres; Wm Miller, Treas; C E Rhoades, Sec; H P Moses, Asst Sec.

Jefferson Building, Loan and Savings Association—47 W Main. Organized January, 1889. Capital stock, $300,000. Meets third Tuesday of each month. Peter G Hohnhaus, Pres; Otto Herbst, Sec; George Motz, Treas.

Phœnix Building and Savings Union—39 and 40 Bank Block. Organized August, 1894. Authorized capital, $1,000,000. Meets 1st and 3d Monday of each month. Dr Carl Schilling, Pres; Henry C Berghoff, Treas; J F Bickel, Sec; T N Roach, Supt Agencies.

Teutonia Building and Loan Association.—47 W Main. Organized March 22, 1893. Capital stock, $1,000,000. Meets fourth Wednesdays. August M Schmidt, Pres; Otto Herbst, Sec; George Motz, Treas.

Tri-State Building and Loan Association Nos 2 and 3.— Tri-State Bldg. Incorporated. George W. Pixley, Pres; D N Foster, Vice-Pres; C A Wilding, Sec; Joseph W Bell, Treas; W J Vesey, Atty.

Washington German, Building, Loan-Fund and Savings Association—Custer House. Organized December, 1887. Capital, $100,000. Meets first Tuesday of each month. Otto Nichter, Pres; John H Pranger, Sec; Henry Suedhoff, Treas.

Wayne Building, Loan and Savings Association—47 W Main. Organized October 24, 1887. Capital, $100,-000. Meets third Friday of each month. H W Martin, Pres; Otto Herbst, Sec; George Motz, Treas.

CEMETERIES.

Achduth Veshalom Congregation (Jewish), e s Broadway
bet Wabash R R and P, F W & C Ry.

Concordia, n s Maumee rd e of Concordia College. Wm
Meinzen, Supt.

German Lutheran (St John's), Bluffton rd 3 miles s w of
city.

Lindenwood, Huntington rd one-half mile w of city limits.
J H Doswell, Supt.

New Catholic, Hicksville State rd 2½ miles e of Columbia
st bridge.

CHURCHES.

BAPTIST.

Beaver Chapel, n w cor Indiana and Cottage avs. Sunday
school 9 a m. Preaching 2 p m.

First Baptist Church, "The Tabernacle of the People,"
W Jefferson bet Harrison and Webster. Rev Stephen
A Northrop, D D, pastor. Sunday services 10.30 a
m and 7.30 p m ; Sunday school 12.15 p m. Prayer
meeting Wednesday, 7.30 p m.

CHRISTIAN.

Central Christian Church, w s Harrison 1 s of Wayne. Rev
Thomas L Cooksey, pastor. Sunday services 11 a m
and 7.30 p m ; Sunday school 10 a m. Prayer meeting Wednesday, 7.30 p m.

First Church of Christ, s e cor W Jefferson and Griffith.
Elder Perry J Rice, pastor. Sunday services 10.45
a m and 7.30 p m ; Sunday school 9.30 a m. Y P S
C E 6.15 p m.

CHURCH OF GOD.

Cor Hoagland av and De Wald.

CONGREGATIONAL.

Plymouth Congregational Church, s e cor W Jefferson and
Harrison. Rev James S Ainslie, pastor. Sunday
services 10.30 a m and 7.30 p m ; Sunday school 9.30
a m ; Y P S C E 7.30 p m.

South Congregational Church, n e cor De Wald and Hoagland av. Rev James S Ainslie, pastor. Services Sunday 10.30 a m and 7.30 p m ; Sunday school 9.15 a m ;
Y P S C E 6.45 p m ; Thursday Junior Y P S C E
at 4.15. Prayer meeting at 7.30 p m.

EPISCOPAL.

St Andrew's Mission, Shawnee av. In charge of the Brotherhood of St Andrew's Church.

Trinity Church, s w cor Fulton and W Berry. Rev A W Seabrease, rector. Sunday services 10.45 a m and 7.30 p. m; Sunday school 9.30 a m; Week services, Wednesday 7.30 p m; Friday 9 a m.

GERMAN EVANGELICAL.

German Evangelical Church, n e cor Holman and Clinton. Rev Samuel H Baumgartner, pastor. Sunday services 10.30 a m and 7.30 p m; Sunday school 9.30 a m. Prayer meeting Thursday 7.30 p m.

HEBREW.

Achduth Veshalom Temple, s w cor Harrison and W Wayne. Samuel Hirschberg, rabbi. Services Friday 7.30 p m; Saturday 10 a. m. Children's instruction Saturday 9 to 10 a m; Sunday 9 to 11 a m.

LUTHERAN.

Christ's Evangelical Lutheran Church. Meets in Y M C A Hall. Rev A A Hundley, pastor. Services 10.30 a m and 7.30 p m; Sunday school 9 a m; Y P S C E 6.30 p m.

Emanuel German Church, s s W Jefferson bet Union and Jackson. Rev Charles Gross, pastor. Sunday services 10 a m and 7.30 p m; Sunday school 2 p m.

English Lutheran. Meets in Y M C A Hall. Sunday services 10.30 a m and 7.30 p m; Sunday school 9.30 a m.

Evangelical Lutheran Zion's Congregational Church, s e cor E Creighton av and Hanna. Rev Henry Juengel, pastor. Services 10 a m and 2 p m.

Grace Church (German Evangelical), s e cor Gay and Pontiac Rev Theodore J C Stellhorn, pastor. Services 10 a m and 2 p m; Sunday school 2 p m.

Lutheran Church of the Redeemer, n w cor Washington and Fulton. Rev C F Wm Meyer, pastor. Services 10.30 a m and 7.30 p m; Sunday school at 2.30 p m.

St John's Evangelical Lutheran Church (German), s e cor W Washington and Van Buren. Rev Henry P Dannecker, pastor. Sunday services 10 a m, 2.30 p m (in German), 7.30 p m (in English).

St Paul's Church (German), w s Barr bet E Jefferson and E Lewis. Rev Henry G Sauer, pastor; Rev Joseph A Bohn, asst pastor. Sunday services 10 a m, 2.30 and 7.30 p m; Sunday school 2.30 p m.

5

Trinity Church (English Lutheran), s e cor E Wayne and
Clinton. Rev Samuel Wagenhals, pastor. Sunday
services 10.30 a m and 7.30 p m ; Sunday school 2.30
p m ; Y P S C E 6.45 p m.

METHODIST EPISCOPAL.

African Church, n e cor E Wayne and Francis. Rev G
W Brown, pastor. Sunday services 10.30 a m and
7.30 p m. Sunday school 2.30 p m.
Berry Street Church, n e cor Berry and Harrison. Rev
M S Marble, pastor. Services 10.30 a m and 7.30 p
m; Sunday school 2.15 p m. Prayer meeting Wednes-
day 7.30 p m.
Free Methodist, 270 E Creighton av. Rev W T Loring,
pastor. Services 10.30 and 7.30 p m ; Sunday school
2.30 p m.
St Paul's Church, s w cor Walton av and Selden. Rev
John W Paschall, pastor. Services 10.30 a m and
7.30 p m ; Sunday school 2 p m. Prayer meeting
Thursday 7.30 p m.
Simpson Church, s e cor Dawson and Harrison. Rev Ray
J Wade, pastor. Sunday services 10.30 a m and 7.30
p m ; Sunday school 9.30 a m ; Epworth Leagues 3
and 4.30 p m ; Class meeting 11.30 a m.
Trinity Church, n e cor Cass and 4th. Rev H M Johnson,
pastor. Sunday services 10.30 a m and 7.30 p m
(summer 8 p m) ; Sunday school 9.30 a m. Prayer
meeting Wednesday 7.30 p m.
Wayne Street Church, s w cor Broadway and W Wayne.
Rev George N Eldridge, pastor. Sunday services
10.30 a m and 7.30 p m ; Sunday school 2.15 p m.
Prayer meeting Wednesday 7.30 p m.

PRESBYTERIAN.

Bethany, s w cor Boone and Fry. Rev G E Davies,
pastor. Sunday services 10.30 a m and 7.30 p m ;
Sunday school 3 p m ; Prayer meeting Thursday
7.30 p m:
First, n e cor Clinton and E Washington. Rev D W
Moffat, pastor. Sunday services 10.30 a m and 7.30
p m ; Sunday school 9.30 a m ; Prayer meeting
Wednesday 7.30 p m.
Third, n e cor Calhoun and Holman. Rev J M Boggs,
pastor. Sunday services 10.30 a m and 7.30 p m ;
Sunday school 11.45 a m. Prayer meeting Wednesday
7.30 p m.

United Presbyterian, Lafayette near Pontiac. Rev A McDowell, pastor. Preaching 2 p m and 7 p m ; Sunday school 3 p m.

Westminster Presbyterian, s s of Berry bet Webster and Ewing. Rev James L Leeper, pastor. Sunday services 10.30 a m and 7.30 p m ; Sunday school 12 noon. Prayer meeting Wednesday 7.30 p m.

REFORMED

Grace Church (English), s s E Washington bet Barr and Lafayette. Rev. A K Zartman, pastor. Sunday services 10.30 a m and 7.30 p m ; Sunday school 9.30 a m. Service Wednesday 7.30 p m.

St John's Reformed (German), s e cor W Washington and Webster. J H Bosch, pastor. Sunday services 10 a m, 7 p m ; Sunday school 8.30 a m.

Salem Church (German), e s Clinton bet E Wayne and Berry. Rev John Kuelling, pastor. Sunday services 10.30 a m and 7.30 p m ; Sunday school 2 p m (winter) and 9 a m (summer).

ROMAN CATHOLIC.

Cathedral of the Immaculate Conception, Cathedral Square, Calhoun bet Lewis and Jefferson. Right Rev Joseph Rademacher, V G, Bishop ; Very Rev Joseph H Brammer, Rev J R Quinlan and Rev Charles B Guendling. Sunday services 6, 8, 8.30 (children's service) and 10.30 a m ; Vespers 3 p m ; Sunday school 2 p m.

St Joseph's Chapel (in connection with St Joseph's Hospital), Rev Thomas Eisenring, C S S, Chaplain. Sunday services 8 a m and 4 p m. Weekday services 8 a m.

St Mary's Church (German), s e cor Lafayette and Jefferson. Rev John H Oechtering pastor ; assistant, Rev Rudolph Denk.. Sunday services 8 and 10 a m and 2.30 p m ; Sunday school 2 p m.

St Patrick's Church, n w cor De Wald and Harrison. Rev Joseph F Delaney, pastor. Sunday services, Mass, 8 and 10 a m ; Vespers, 3 p m ; Sunday school, 2.15 p m.

St Paul's Church (German), Rev Edward Koenig, pastor, n e cor Griffith and W Washington. Services 10 a m and 2 p m.

St Peter's Church (German), s e cor E De Wald and Warsaw. Rev A Messman, pastor. Sunday services 8 and 10 a m and 3 p m ; Sunday school 2 p m.

UNITED BRETHREN.

First, s e cor E Lewis and Harmer. Rev Amos W Ballinger, pastor. Sunday services 10.30 a m and 7.30 p
m ; Prayer meeting Wednesday 8 p m.

HOSPITALS AND ASYLUMS.

Allen County Asylum, n s Bluffton road nr the bridge.
Herman W Felts, Supt.

Allen County Orphans' Home, 114 Pritchard. T E Ellison, Pres ; E A K Hackett, Sec ; J D Bond, Treas.

Hope Hospital, s w cor Barr and Washington. Miss
Nancy Mayhew, Supt.

Indiana School for Feeble-Minded Youth, Hicksville State
rd bet Parnell av and St Joe Gravel rd. E A K
Hackett, Pres, Ft Wayne ; Mrs Laura H Bass, Sec,
Ft Wayne ; Dr A H Shaffer, Treas, Huntington ;
Alexander Johnson, Supt.

Orphan's Home of the Reformed Church in the U S,
located 1½ miles n e of city limits. Established 1883.
Rev John Rettig, Supt.

St Joseph's Hospital, s w cor W Main and Broadway.
Sister Secunda, Superioress.

St Vincent's Orphan Asylum, e s Wells n of Putnam. Sister Maria Eudoxia, Superioress.

INCORPORATED INSTITUTIONS.

Anthony Wayne Mnfg Co The, s w cor Lafayette and
Wabash R R. Incorporated January 27, 1886. Cap-
ital, $18,000. John Rhinesmith, Pres ; J H Simonson,
Sec and Treas ; A C F Wichman, Supt.

Bash S & Co, 22--24 W Columbia. Incorporated June 4,
1890. Capital, $100,000. Solomon Bash, Pres ;
Charles S Bash, Vice-Pres ; Peter D Smyser, Treas ;
Daniel F Bash, Sec.

Bass Foundry and Machine Works, Hanna south of
Wabash R R. Established 1853. Incorporated 1873.
Capital, $500,000. J H Bass, Pres ; J I White, Sec ;
R J Fisher, Treas.

Berghoff Herman Brewing Co The, e s Grant av nr E
Washington. Incorporated April, 1887. Capital,
$100,000. Herman J Berghoff, Pres ; Hubert Berg-
hoff, Sec and Treas.

Brenzinger Bread Baking Co, 14 W Washington. Incorporated. Wm F Brenzinger, Pres ; D McCutcheon,
Sec and Treas.

Brookside Farm Co. 1½ miles west of city, Incorporated March, 1884. John H Bass, Pres.

Carnahan W L Co The, 13 W Jefferson. Incorporated 1894. W L Carnahan, Pres; W E Hood, Sec and Treas.

Cook Automatic Boiler Cleaner Co, 54 E Columbia. Incorporated 1892. Jerome Q Cook, Supt.

Dreibelbiss Abstract of Title Co The, Tri-State Bldg. Incorporated January 1, 1887. Capital, $10,000. John Dreibelbiss, Pres; Robert B Dreibelbiss, Sec and Treas.

Fay M W Warehouse Co, 135 Calhoun. Incorporated 1893. Capital, $10,000. M W Fay, Pres and Treas; H C Rockhill, Sec.

Fidelity Benevolent Association, 7-8-9 Pixley & Long Bldg. Incorporated 1894. Carl Sauer, Pres; Dr. John Schilling, Vice-Pres and Med Director; A L Schroeder, Sec.

Fort Wayne Artificial Ice and Cold Storage Co, cor Wells and L S & M S Ry. R T McDonald, Pres; C R Higgins, Sec and Treas.

Fort Wayne Athletic Association, 18 W Berry. Incorporated November 15, 1892. Capital, $15,000. H M Diehl, Pres; J E Miller, Vice-Pres; Louis Heilbroner, Sec and Treas.

Fort Wayne Catholic Circulating Library and Association, n e cor Calhoun and E Lewis. Incorporated August 4, 1874. Kilian Baker, Pres; P J McDonald, Sec; George A Litot, Treas.

Fort Wayne City Band, 70 Calhoun. Organized 1871. Incorporated1879. Capital, $3,000. H P Scherer, Pres; Byron Stopher, Sec; F J Reineke, Treas; Philip Keinz, Leader. Regular meetings every Friday evening.

Fort Wayne Club, 71–73 Harrison. Incorporated March 30, 1892. Capital, $20,000. S R Alden, Pres; James H. Fry, Sec; J W White, Treas.

Fort Wayne Commercial Exchange, 28-29 Bass Blk. Incorporated 1893. G E Bursley, Pres; W L Carnahan, Vice-Pres; Frank L Smock. Sec; E H McDonald, Treas.

Fort Wayne Conservatory of Music, 22-26 E Main. Incorporated 1871. Judge L M Ninde, Pres; Fred J Hayden, Sec; C F W Meyer, Director.

Fort Wayne Cycling Club, 54 W Wayne. Frank S. Lightfoot, Pres; F W Urbahns, Sec; A L Randall, Treas.

Fort Wayne District Telegraph Co, 15 W Columbia. Incorporated. Capital, $20,000. R T McDonald, Pres; Edward Gilmartin, Vice-Pres; W P Breen, Treas; C R Higgins, Sec and Mngr.

Fort Wayne Electric Corporation, Broadway s e cor G R & I R R. Incorporated. R T McDonald, Pres; C S Knight, Vice-Pres; Charles C Miller, Sec and Treas.

Fort Wayne Electric Railway Co, s e cor Main and Court. Incorporated 1887. Capital, $1,000,000. J H Bass, Pres; M S Robison Jr, Vice-Pres and Treas; J M Barrett, Sec; L D McNutt, Supt.

Fort Wayne Furniture Co The, office and factory e end of Columbia. Incorporated November, 1887. Capital, $75,000. D N Foster, Pres; P A Randall, Vice-Pres; W E Mossman, Sec; D B Kehler, Treas.

Fort Wayne Gas Co, 50 Clinton, 9 Court. Charles F Dieterich (N Y), Pres; Henry C Paul, assistant to Pres; E J Jerzmanowski (N Y), Vice-Pres; A B Proal, (N Y), Treas; F E W Scheimann, Sec; G Max Hofmann, Supt.

Fort Wayne Harrison Telephone Co, White Bank Bldg. Incorporated January, 1895. Capital, $100,000. George P Haywood, Pres; E G Leysenki, Vice-Pres; W P Breen, Treas; E H Andrews, Sec; I N Woods, Promoter.

Fort Wayne Insurance Co, 22 Bank Blk. Organized September, 1891. John J Jacobs, Pres; J E Beahler, Sec.

Fort Wayne Land and Improvement Co, 3-4 Pixley & Long Bldg. Incorported February, 1890. Capital, $250,000. R T McDonald, Pres; D N Foster, Vice-Pres; Aaron B Howey, Sec; G W Pixley, Treas.

Fort Wayne Mercantile Accident Association, 12 E Berry. Incorporated March, 1894. Geo A Durfee, Pres; Frederick E Nash, Sec and Treas.

Fort Wayne Newspaper Union (eastern branch Chicago Newspaper Union), 76-80 Clinton. J F Cramer, Pres, C E Strong, Treas; Charles D Tillo, Mngr.

Fort Wayne Organ Co, office and factory e s of Fairfield av s of Creighton. Incorporated 1871. S B Bond, Pres; A S Bond, Sec, Treas and Supt.

Fort Wayne Relief Union, 144 Pritchard. Incorporated 1882. Mrs E H McDonald, Pres; Miss Helen Moffat, Sec; Miss C M Fowler, Supt.

Fort Wayne Variable Saw Mill Feed Co, 15-17 E Superior. Henry C Zollinger, Pres and Sec; Louis Zollinger, Treas; Walter G Burns, Gen'l Mngr; Charles Bowman, Supt.

Fort Wayne Water Power Co, office in First National Bank ; power house w s Spy Run av near Burgess av. J H Bass, Pres ; H J Miller, Sec ; Lem R Hartman, Treas.

Foster D N Furniture Co, 11-13 Court. Incorporated August 9, 1884. Capital, $80,000. D N Foster, Pres ; L G Hamilton, Sec ; Wm J Kettler, Treas.

Hoffman Lumber Co, 200 W Main. Incorporated 1887. A E Hoffman, Pres ; Wm H Hoffman, Vice-Pres ; John W Sale, Sec and Treas.

Hoosier Mnfg Co, 28-30 E Berry. Incorporated April, 1882. Capital, $30,000. Amos S Evans, Pres ; Geo P Evans, Sec ; John P Evans, Treas.

Hope Hospital, s w cor Barr and Washington. Incorporated November 2, 1878. H C Paul, Pres ; W D Page, Sec ; Otto Gross, Treas ; Miss N A Mayhew, Supt.

Horton Mnfg Co, w s Osage n of W Main. Incorporated August, 1883. Capital, $30,000. Henry C Paul, Pres ; Wm A Bohn, Sec and Treas ; John C Peters, Mngr.

Indiana Furniture Co, 166 Calhoun. Incorporated May, 1890. Capital, $15,000. John V Reul, Pres ; Wm F Graeter, Sec and Treas.

Indiana Machine Works, Osage n of Main, Incorporated September 29, 1888. Capital, $75,00. John C Peters, Pres ; P A Randall, Vice-Pres ; John M Landenberger, Sec, Treas and Mngr.

Indiana Mining Co, 32 W Berry. Incorporated. Capital Stock, $500,000, D C Fisher, Sec and Treas.

Indiana Oil and Land Co, Tri-State Bldg. Incorporated April, 1895. J H Grier, Sec and Treas.

Jenney Electric Light and Power Co, 43 E Berry. Incorporated 1883. Capital, $50,000. Henry C Graffe, Pres ; R T McDonald, Vice-Pres ; George W Pixley, Treas ; Charles G Guild, Sec and Treas.

Journal Co The, 30 E Main. Incorporated May 12, 1884. Capital, $10,000. H C Rockhill, Pres and Genl Mngr; A J Moynihan, Sec and Treas,

Kerr Murray Mnfg Co, n e cor Murray and Calhoun. Incorporated 1881. Capital, $100,000. Alfred D Cressler, Pres and Genl Mngr ; G A Schust, Sec ; G L Hackius, Treas.

Lakeside Street Railway Co, office The Wayne. Incorporated 1892. Capital, $50,000. R T McDonald, H J Miller, A D Guild, Directors ; J D McDonald, Supt.

Lindenwood Cemetery Association, Tri-State Bldg. Incorporated February 12, 1885. Oliver P. Morgan, Pres; Charles A Wilding, Sec and Treas.

Masonic Temple Association, n e cor Clinton and Wayne. Incorporated February, 1878. Capital, $50,000. A Hattersley, Pres; W W Rockhill, Sec; W H Mordhurst, Treas.

Mayflower Milling Co, 20 W Columbia. Incorporated October 1, 1889, Capital, $20,000. C S Bash, Pres; J W Orr, Sec and Treas; H E Bash, Genl Mngr.

Old Fort Mnfg Co, 35-36 Bank Blk. Incorporated September 14, 1888. Capital, $20,000. N D Doughman, Pres; P A Randall, Vice-Pres and Treas; A M Beugnot, Sec.

Old Fort Spice and Extract Co, 29 E Columbia. Incorporated March 10, 1894. Capital, $10,000. J D Williams, Pres and Treas; John Fitzgerald, Sec.

Olds' Wagon Works, s s Murray bet Calhoun and Lafayette. Incorporated 1882. Capital, $200,000. H G Olds, Pres; S C Lumbard, Vice-Pres; John Mohr Jr, Sec; W H Olds, Treas.

Paul Mnfg Co, cor 6th and Calhoun. Incorporated 1892, Capital, $22,500. Henry C Paul, Pres; Wm Paul Jr, Vice-Pres and Treas; Charles A Paul, Sec,

Peters Box and Lumber Co, 79-105 High. Established 1870. Incorporated November 26, 1873. Capital, $50,000. Charles Pape, Pres and Genl Mngr; W H Murtaugh, Vice-Pres; Carl F Siemon Jr, Sec.

Pottlitzer Bros Fruit Co, 8 Harrison. Incorporated December 1, 1891. Capital, $30,000. Leo Pottlitzer, Pres; Isidore Pottlitzer, Sec; Herman Pottlitzer, Treas.

Riverview Farm Co, office Broadway and P, Ft W & C Ry, Incorporated 1892. Capital, $100,000. R T McDonald, H J Miller, A D Guild, Directors.

Ryan Trucking Co The, 19-23 Wells. Incorporated 1891. Capital $15,000. P A Randall, Pres; R T McDonald, Vice-Pres; S W Cook, Sec; John A Coy, Mngr.

Skelton B W Co The, 209 Calhoun. Incorporated April 28, 1891. Capital, $25,000. B W Skelton, Pres; C S Bash, Vice-Pres; J B Franke, Sec and Treas.

Sperry Pelton Manufacturing Co, 28 E Berry. Incorporated March 12, 1895. Capital, $10,000. C W Sperry, Pres; George P Evans, pSec; J P Evans, Treas; Leander Pelton, Supt.

Standard Medical and Surgical Institute, 135 Calhoun. Incorporated 1890. Capital, $100,000. Dr N R Wenger, Pres and Mngr; R A Lantz, sec.

Standard Wheel Co of Illinois. Incorporated 1891. Capital, $2,000,000. Crawford Fairbanks, Pres, (Terre Haute, Ind). Charles Minshall, Vice-Pres and Treas, (Terre Haute, Ind); E M France, Sec, (Terre Haute, Ind); D E Allen, Genl Mngr, (Terre Haute, Ind); C M Crim, Mngr, (Ft Wayne, Ind). Works and Office s e cor Lafayette and Wabash R R.

Star Iron Tower Company, s end Wells on N Y, C & St L R R. Incorporated February, 1884. Capital $62,500. J H Bass, Pres; H G Olds, Vice-Pres; P A Randall, Sec; R T McDonald, Treas.

Taylor Bros Piano Co, 19 W Wayne. Incorporated January, 1895. Capital, $4,000. Samuel R Taylor, Pres; I N Taylor, Sec.

Wayne Knitting Mills, east side Park av nr W Main. Organized 1891. Capital, $100,000. Henry C Paul, Pres; Othniel H Larwill, Treas; Theodore H Thieme, Sec and Mngr.

Wayne Oil Tank Co, 201 Lafayette. Capital, $15,000. C S Bash, Pres; W E Hunter, Sec and Treas.

Western Gas Construction Co, Buchanan between Holton av and Winter. Incorporated 1890. Capital, $50,000. O N Guldlin, Pres; Ernest F Lloyd, Sec; Gordon W Lloyd, Treas.

Younge's Medical and Surgical Institute, 176 Calhoun, Incorporated. J W Younge, M D, Pres.

LABOR ORGANIZATIONS.

Barbers' Union, No 14, K of L Hall—Meets second and fourth Mondays of each month. E B Robinson, Pres; A L Lichtenwalter, Sec.

Bricklayers' and Masons' Union, No 2—Meets every Monday evening at No 7 E Main. Fred Kohlmeyer, Pres; H C Ehle, Sec.

Brotherhood of Carpenters and Joiners, No 153, A O U W Hall Court—Meets every Saturday at 7.30 p m. E E Cummings, Pres; H L Mollet, Sec.

Brotherhood of Locomotive Firemen, A G Porter Lodge No 141—Meets every Monday evening at 70 Calhoun. Mathew Walker, Master; Wm Dexter, Sec.

Cigarmakers' Union, No 37—Meets first and third Thursday evenings of each month, at Saengerbund Hall. Levi Bender, Pres; L P Sanders, Sec.

Fort Wayne Brewers' Union, No 62—54 E Main, Nimrod
   Hall. Meets second and fourth Saturday of each
   month. Adolph Laemmermann, Pres ; John Leh-
   mann, Sec.
Fort Wayne Division No 12 (Locomotive Engineers)—
   Meets every Sunday at 2 p m, at 136 Calhoun.
   J G Bechtol, Chief Engineer ; Marion Teagarden, Sec.
Fort Wayne Pressmen's Union No 58—Meets first Friday
   of each month at 64 E Main. Wm Carroll, Pres ;
   Martin App, Sec.
Fort Wayne Trades and Labor Council—Meets second and
   last Fridays of each month at K of L Hall. Rezin
   Orr, Pres ; S J Roberts, Sec.
Fort Wayne Typographical Union No 78—Meets first
   Sunday of each month at K of L Hall. F E Lanter-
   man, Pres ; H L Williamson, Sec.
International Association of Machinists, Friendship Lodge
   No 70—Foster's Block. Meets second and last day of
   each month. L Seibt, Pres; Wm Brennan, Sec.
John Groof Lodge, No 67 (Railway Car Men)—Meets at
   K of L Hall, Bank Blk, second and fourth Tuesday of
   each month. Frank Frisby, Chief Car Man; P E
   Mills, Sec.
Journeymen Butchers' Labor Union No 6463—K of L
   Hall. Meets second and fourth Sunday of each
   month, Herman Strodel, Pres, C E Hartshorn, Sec.
Junior Order of American Mechanics Wayne Council No
   35, Jr O U A M—106 Calhoun. Meets every Wednes-
   day evening. L Y Geiss, Counsellor; A A Jacobs, R C.
Liberty Assembly K of L No 2315—Meets every Thurs-
   day evening at K of L Hall, Bank Blk. Clark
   Hanren, M W; A H Hague, Foreman; George E
   Rhein, Rec Sec; Philip Rapp, Fin Sec.
Local Union No 46 (Tinworkers)—Meets first and third
   Thursday evenings of each month at K of L Hall.
   Charles Siemon, Pres; Wm Bohn, Sec.
Musicians' Protective Union No 44—Meets first Sunday of
   each month at 12 W Main. Gart Shober, Pres; W
   D Kyle, Sec.
Stone Masons' Union No 7—Roeger's Hall, 26 W Main.
   Meets first and third Tuesday of each month. Alois
   Hoffman, Pres; John Schmidt, Sec.
Summit City Lodge No 34 (Boilermakers)—Meets third
   Wednesday in each month at K of L Hall. Edward
   Litot, Pres; A K Fahlsing, Sec.
Wayne Division No 119 (Railway Conductors)—Meets every
   Sunday at 2 p m at 106 Calhoun. Charles Ziegler,
   Chief Condr; C N Taylor, Sec and Treas.

Wheelmakers' Union No 5323—Meets first and third Wednesday of each month at K of L Hall. Theodore M Cutshall, Pres; Edward Morris, Sec.

LIBRARIES.

Allen County Teachers' Library, 12 Bass Blk. Established 1888; 2,000 volumes. F J Young, Acting Librarian.

Apollo Musical Library, 97½ Calhoun.

Catholic Young Men's Reading Hall and Club Rooms, Library Hall. Open every evening. Rev J R Quinlan, Director.

Concordia College (1,500 volumes).

Emerline J Hamilton Library, 23½ W Wayne, 2,100 volumes. Margaret E Hamilton, Pres and Sec.

Fort Wayne Catholic Circulating Library and Association, Library Hall, n e cor Calhoun and E Lewis. Kilian Baker, Pres; P J McDonald, Sec; George A Litot, Treas; Rev J R Quinlan, Director. Association meets first Thursday of each month. Library open Sundays from 3 to 5 and 7 to 9 p m.

Polk's Directory Library, containing directories of principal cities and states, 38 Bass Blk.

Public Library (Room 8), City Hall. Board of Trustees, John Moritz, A E Hoffman, O P Morgan. Committee, Mrs E R Dryer, Miss Merica Hoagland, Miss Margaret Hamilton, Mrs A S Lauferty, John H Jacobs, Col R S Robertson, C T Lane, Rev Samuel Wagenhals, Miss Katherine Hamilton, Alternate. Mrs Susan C Hoffman, Librarian.

Y M C A Association, 103 and 105 Calhoun.

MILITARY.

Fort Wayne Grays—Armory n w cor Broadway and Jefferson. Meets Wednesday and Friday of each week. H W Hageman, Capt; C G Pape, 1st Lieut; C Borgman, 2d Lieut.

Fort Wayne Rifles—Randall Hall. C E Reese, Capt; P A Thompson, 1st Lieut; J W Thompson, 2d Lieut.

Rifles' Cadet Corps The—Randall Hall. Meets Friday evening of each week. Charles Reese Capt; P A Thompson 1st Lieut.

Wayne True Blues—Armory Randall Hall. Meets Thursday evening of each week. J B Fonner, Capt; H C Mains, 1st Lieut; W A Spice, 2d Lieut; Otto Meyer, Sergt.

Third Battalion, 3rd Regiment, Infantry—Headquarters,
Randall Hall. J E Miller, Major; J E Gaskins,
Adjt.

Zollinger Battery—27 Calhoun. Organized 1888. Wm F
Ranke, Capt; C A Teagarden, 1st Lieut; H C Nie-
meyer. 2nd Lieut; W F Alderman, 1st Sergt; O S
Jones, Pres; Ed Schoch, Sec.

Alabama Club—140 Calhoun. W W Clarke, Pres; Frank
Getz, Sec.

MISCELLANEOUS SOCIETIES.

Allen County Bible Society. Called meetings, meets at
residences of members. Dr Wm T Ferguson, Pres;
H C Schrader, Sec.

Allen County Licensed Liquor Dealers' Protective Association, 64 E Main. Meets first Tuesday of each
month. Jacob Hartman, Pres; G J Ortleib, Sec.

Allen County Medical Society. No regular meetings. Dr
G L Greenawalt, Pres; Dr A P Buchanan, Sec.

Ancient Order Hibernians, Allen County Division No 1.
Meets second Thursday and fourth Sunday each
month at Hibernia Hall, White Blk. Rev J R Quinlan, Spiritual Director; J H Rohan, Pres; Daniel
McKendry, Sec; M F Belger, County Pres.

Annie Besant Theosophical Society, Ninde Blk. Meets
every Thursday at 8 p m. Hon Edward O'Rourke,
Pres; Mrs. Julia B Taylor, Sec.

Bobolink Club, 195¼ Calhoun. Meets second and fourth
Sundays of each month. John P O'Rourke, Pres;
Fred G Krebs, Sec.

Bruederlicher Unterstuetzungs Verein, Harmony Hall.
Meets third Sunday of each month. Frederick
Schmetzer, Pres; W C Baade, Sec.

Butchers' Association, 54 E Main, Nimrod Hall. Meets
first Tuesday of each month. Gottlieb Haller, Pres;
David J Shaw, Sec.

Caledonian Society, 76 Calhoun. Meets first and third
Mondays of each month. J B White, Pres; D McKay,
1st Vice-Pres; Francis Burgess, 2d Vice-Pres; Thomas
Duncan, Sec; R Dickie, Treas.

Catholic Knights of America, St Bernard Branch, No 3,
Library Hall, n e cor Calhoun and E Lewis. Meets
first and third Sundays of each month. Very Rev J
H Brammer, Spiritual Director; F H Fink, Pres;
Patrick Ryan, Sec; J H Welch, Treas.

Catholic Knights of America, Father Delaney Branch, No 715, St Patrick's School Hall. Meets first and third Fridays of each month. Rev J F Delaney, Spiritual Director.

Catholic Knights of America, St John's Branch, No 566, St Mary's School Hall. Meets second Sunday. Rev J H Oechtering, Spiritual Director; Joseph Suelzer, Pres.

Catholic Knights of America, Supreme Secretary's office 27-28 Bass Blk. Most Rev W A Gross (Portland, Ore), S S D; M T Shine (Covington, Ky), S P; Charles E Hannauer (St Louis, Mo), S V P; Wm S O'Rourke, S S; Charles J Kirschner (Toledo, O), S T.

Catholic Knights of America, Uniform Rank, No 103, Library Hall. Meets first and third Sundays of each month. John Houser, Capt.

Catholic Young Men's Amusement Society, Library Hall. Rooms open from 8 a m to 10 p m. Rev J R Quinlan, Director.

Columbian Reading Circle. Meets Sons of Columbus Hall, 10-12 W Wayne, Tuesday 8 p m. Edward Schele, Pres; Mamie Hutzell, Sec.

Deutscher Landwehr Verein, Saengerbund Hall. Meets third Sunday of each month. Paul Drinkwitz, Pres; M Truebenbach, Sec,

Euphonia Double Quartette, 138 Calhoun, Organized July, 1887. August Schmidt, Pres; Wm C Baade, Sec.

Father Edward Council, No 237, C B L, St Paul's School. Meets first and fifteenth of each month. Henry Huber, Pres; Cornelius Brunner, Sec.

Father O'Leary Council, No 327, C B L, Library Hall. Meets first and third Mondays of each month. Victor A Sallot, Pres; Wm H Ronan, Sec.

Fort Wayne Athletic Association, 18 W Berry. H M Diehl, Pres; Louis Heilbroner, Sec.

Fort Wayne Board of Underwriters, 23 Bass Blk. Organized, 1882. D L Harding, Pres ; C E Graves, Sec and Treas.

Fort Wayne Club, 71-73 Harrison. Annual meeting, January 1st ; Governor's meeting once a month. Rooms open daily. Membership, 425. R J Fisher, Pres ; R T McDonald, 1st Vice-Pres ; S C Lumbard, 2d Vice-Pres ; H C Paul, 3d Vice-Pres ; Ben Rothschild, 4th Vice-Pres ; James H Fry, Sec ; Louis Fox, Treas.

Fort Wayne Commercial Exchange, 29-30 Bass Blk. Chartered January 17, 1894. G E Bursley, Pres ; Wm Beck, Sec. Meets every Tuesday evening.

Fort Wayne Cycling Club, 54 W Wayne.   Organized 1892.
    F S Lightfoot, Pres ; F W Urbans, Sec ; A L Ran-
    dall, Treas.   Meetings first Tuesday of each month.
Fort Wayne Driving Club, 30 E Main.   Meets July 3 to 5
    and August 27 to September 1.   W H Watt, Pres ;
    H C Rockhill, Sec.
Fort Wayne Occult Science Society, A O U W Hall,
    Court st.   Meets every Sunday and Thursday even-
    ings.   J M Stonder, Pres ; Mrs M B Gorsline, Sec.
Fort Wayne Relief Union, 14 Arcade and 144 Pritchard.
    Mrs E H McDonald, Pres ; Miss Helen Moffat, Sec ;
    Miss Catherine Hamilton, Treas.
Fort Wayne Saengerbund, Saengerbund Hall, 55 W Main.
    Organized February 9, 1869.   Meets first Tuesday of
    each month.   Paul Richter, Pres ; Conrad Bauss, Vice-
    Pres ; August Langhorst, Sec ; Frank Rahe, Fin Sec ;
    Gottlieb Unger, Treas ; Prof A J Rager, Director.
Fort Wayne Turn Verein, Saengerbund Hall.   Meets sec-
    ond Sunday of each month.   Henry Weist, Pres ;
    August Langhorst, Vice-Pres ; Paul Weitzman, Sec ;
    Otto Herbst, Treas.
German Soldiers' Benefit Society, 26 W Main.   Meets
    first and third Sunday of each month.   Wm Ohlers-
    meyer, Pres ; Charles Roegers, Sec.
Home for Emergencies, 144 Pritchard.   Mrs W D Page,
    Pres ; Mrs L A Thayer, Sec ; Miss Catherine Hamil-
    ton, Treas.
Humane Society.   Organized January 1888.   Meets first
    Monday of each month, 23 Bank Blk.   George H Wil-
    son Pres ; Charles Archer, Sec ; Louis Schlaudroff,
    officer.
Isaac Knapp Dental Coterie.   Organized January 20, 1891.
    Meets at members offices.   Dr S B Brown, Pres ; Dr.
    M A Mason, Sec.
Knights of St Charles.   Meets St Mary's School Hall sec-
    ond Tuesday of each month.   Edward Leeuw, Pres ;
    Michael Etching, Capt.
Knights of St John, Emmett Commandary, No 17.   Meets
    Library Hall every Wednesday evening.   E J Len-
    non, Capt ; Dennis Gorman, Pres ; V J Baker, Sec ;
    S J Gardt, Treas.
Knights of St John, Indiana Commandary, No 173.   Jacob
    Hartman, Capt ; Henry Wiegand, Sec.
Knights of St John, Wayne Commandary, No 148.   St
    Paul's School Hall.   Meets Friday night of each
    week.   Joseph Kopp, Capt ; John Kohrman, Sec.

Ladies' Auxiliary of the Fort Wayne Caledonia Society.
Mrs James Cairns, Pres ; Mrs Ellen Dickey, Sec.

Parliamentary Coterie Club, 14 Arcade. Meets first and
third Mondays of each month at 4 p m. Miss Merica
Hoagland, Pres ; Mrs Fairbank, Sec.

Philharmonic Club, 138 Calhoun. Organized May, 1891.
Meets second Monday evening of each month. Fred
Scheimann, Pres ; Daniel Krapf, Sec.

Q & O Club, 41½ W Main. Meets first Tuesday of each
month. E F Heine, Pres ; Dan Auer, Sec.

St Bernard Benevolent Society, 103, C K of A. Meets
first Sunday of each month. James Woulfe, Pres ;
Patrick Ryan, Sec ; F H Fink, Treas.

St Boniface Benevolent Society of St Paul's Catholic
Church. Meets each fourth Sunday. Erasmus Stork,
Pres ; Michael Gruber, Sec.

St Carl· Boromaus Benevolent Society, St Mary's School
Hall. Meets first Sunday of each month. Henry
Brink, Pres ; H W Kohrmann, Sec.

St Joseph Benevolent Association. Meets at St Patrick's
School Hall second Sunday of each month. Frank W
Bennett, Pres ; Michael Shea, Sec ; G P Gordon,
Treas.

St Joseph's Catholic Benevolent Society, Library Hall,
n e cor Calhoun and E Lewis. Meets second Sunday
of each month. G P Gordon, Pres ; Patrick Ryan,
Sec ; C F Graffe, Treas.

St Paul's Evangelical Lutheran Young Men's Society.
Meets cor Barr and Madison first Monday of each
month. George Dannenfelser, Pres ; Henry Eberline, Sec.

St Julian Council, No 87, C B L, Library Hall, n e cor
Calhoun and E Lewis. Meets first and third Tuesdays
of each month. Peter Braun, Pres ; John Ryan, Sec ;
Frank Voirol. Collector.

St Paul's Young Men's Society (Catholic). Meets fourth
Sunday of each month at St Paul's School Hall.
Michael Gruber, Pres ; Frank Bott, Sec.

St Vincent De Paul Society. Meets at St Patrick's School
Hall fourth Sunday of each month. Mrs Max Grove,
Pres ; Frank Mungovan, Sec ; Mrs James Finnell,
Treas.

St Vincent De Paul Society, Cathedral of the Immaculate Conception. Meets Chapel, fourth Sunday of each
month. Rev J R Quinlan, Spiritual Director ; Mrs
H F Fleming, Pres.

Saxonia Aid Society, 6 Force. Meets third Sunday of
each month. Charles Fiedler, Pres ; Wm Becker,
Sec.
Schroeder's Dramatic Co, 97 Broadway. Louis S C
Schroeder, Business Mngr; Harry Leland, Stage Mngr.
Schwaben Unterstuetzungs Verein, Saengerbund Hall.
Wm Hahn, Pres ; Herman Weipert. Sec.
Soldiers' Sons and Citizens' Club, 14 Arcade. Meets sec-
ond and fourth Saturdays of each month. A R Wal-
ter, Pres ; A W Pierce, Sec.
Standard Club, 42 W Berry. Regular meeting first
Thursday of each month. Charles Falk, Pres ; Louis
Frankel, Sec.
Three Rivers Rod and Reel Club, 54 E Main. Organized
1888. Meets first Sunday of each month. H Baker,
Pres ; Robert Mayer, Sec.: F Belchin, Treas.
Traveling Men's Protective Assn, Post A, 29 Calhoun.
Meets last Saturday of each month. L J Bobilya,
Pres ; Charles J Bulger. Sec.
West Lake Fishing Club, 27 Calhoun. Meets first of each
month. Samuel Alexander, Pres ; Wm Kehler, Sec
and Treas.
Young Men's Christian Association (City Department),
105 Calhoun. Organized March 18, 1886. A H Pol-
hamus, Chairman ; C H Newton, Rec Sec ; W F
McCaughey, Genl Sec.
Young Men's Christian Association (Railroad Department),
245 Calhoun. Amos Sine, Chairman ; J W Burns,
Genl Sec.

NEWSPAPERS.

Business Guide The, 76-80 Clinton. Established 1887.
Clarence G Smith, publr. Issued monthly at 50c per
annum.
Fort Wayne Dispatch (Ind), 88 Clinton. Established 1878.
James, Mitchell, propr. Issued weekly. Terms, $1
per annum.
Fort Wayne Freie Presse (German, daily, Dem), 24 Clin-
ton. Established 1888. Incorporated 1895. Ft Wayne
Freie Presse Co, publrs. Issued daily except Sunday.
Terms, 10c a week.
Fort Wayne Gazette (daily, weekly and Sunday, Rep), 41
E Berry. R N Leonard, propr. Issued every morn-
ing at 10 cents per week ; issued weekly on Thursday,
$1 per annum.
Fort Wayne Journal (daily, Dem), 30 E Main. Estab-
lished 1880. The Journal Co, publrs. Issued every
morning at 10 cents per week.

Fort Wayne Weekly Journal (Dem), 30 E Main. Established 1868. The Journal Co, publrs. Issued Thursdays, $1 per annum.
Fort Wayne News (Ind). 19 E Main. Wm D Page, propr.
Issued every evening. Terms, daily $3 per year ;
weekly, issued Fridays, $1 per year.
Fort Wayne Sentinel (daily and weekly, Dem), 107 Calhoun. Established 1833. E A K Hackett, propr.
Terms, daily by mail, $4.80, by carrier, 10 cents per
week ; weekly $1 per annum.
Indiana Staats Zeitung (daily and weekly, Democratic), 37
E Columbia. Established 1857. John Sarnighausen,
propr and, editor-in chief. Daily $4 per annum.
weekly $2 per annum.
Journal of The Medical Science (monthly), 30 E Main.
The Journal Co, publrs. C B Stemen, editor-in-
chief. Subscription, $1 per year.
Monday Morning Times (Ind), 47 E Berry. Established
1892. Gart Shober, propr. Issued every Monday
morning. Rates, $2 per year.
Woechenliche Freie Presse, 24 Clinton. Ft Wayne Freie
Presse Co. publrs.

PARKS.

Allen County Fair Grounds, end of W Washington bet St
Mary's river and P, Ft W & C Ry.
Anthony Wayne Park. on n s of Maumee river e of Main
st bridge. A summer resort for parties, picnics, etc.
Centlivre Park, west side Spy Run av, north of canal
feeder. A summer resort for parties, picnics, etc.
City Park, cor Broadway and Taylor.
Hayden Park, e s Harmer bet Maumee av and E Jefferson.
League Park (Base Ball), e s Calhoun n of E Superior.
McCulloch Park, Broadway opp Nirdlinger av.
North Side Park, e s N Clinton bet 5th and 6th.
Swinney Park, see *Allen County Fair Grounds*.
Vordermark's Grove, s s Maumee rd, 1 e of Glasgow av.
Williams' Park, s s Creighton av bet Webster and Hoag-
land av.

POSTOFFICE.

Southeast cor Berry and Clinton.
Postmaster--W W Rockhill.
Assistant Postmaster--F E D Keplinger.
Office Hours—Week days, 7.15 a m to 9 p m ; Sundays, 9
to 10 a m. Corridors open until 11 p m daily.

Money Order Department--Clerk, C A Beuret; office
hours, 8 a m to 5 p m.
Orders are issued in sums of not more than $100. Larger
amounts may be transmitted to the same person by
additional orders.

FEES CHARGED FOR MONEY ORDERS.

For Orders for sums not exceeding $	2.50	3 cents
Over $ 2.50 and not exceeding	5.00	5 cents
Over 5.00 and not exceeding	10.00	8 cents
Over 10.00 and not exceeding	20.00	10 cents
Over 20.00 and not exceeding	30.00	12 cents
Over 30.00 and not exceeding	40.00	15 cents
Over 40.00 and not exceeding	50.00	18 cents
Over 50.00 and not exceeding	60.00	20 cents
Over 60.00 and not exceeding	75.00	25 cents
Over 75.00 and not exceeding	100.00	30 cents

Rates on all International Money Orders—Not exceeding
$10, ten cents; over $10 and not exceeding $20,
twenty cents; over $20 and not exceeding $30, thirty
cents; over $30 and not exceeding $40, forty cents;
over $40 and not exceeding $50, fifty cents.
Mailing Department—Supt of Mails, W W Kerr; Night
Clerk, R A McCulloch; Chief Clerk, Thos W Blair;
Assistants, George Humphrey; Stamper, Jesse S
Braden.
General Delivery Department—Chief Clerk, F J Drake.
Registered Letter Department--Clerk, George R Craw.
Office Hours, 8 a m to 5 p m.
Stamp Department—Clerk, M C Baade. Office Hours,
7.15 a m to 7.30 p m.
Day Distributing Clerk—J W Eggemann.
Night Distributing Clerk—W D Seaton.
Free Delivery Department—Superintendent of Letter
Carriers, C F Kettler.

Carriers:

No 1—George D Piepenbrink.
No 2—Harry Zwahlen.
No 3—C D Bourie
No 4—Amos K Mehl.
No 5—W A Ross.
No 6—Paul Richter.
No 7—Wm Zimmerly.
No 8—H W Martin.
No 9—Thomas Davis.
No 10—Charles A Stockbridge.

No 11—C M Rouzer.
No 12—Wm Kanning.
No 13—Frank A Manuel.
No 14—Wm Stahl.
No 15—Frederick R Reiling.
No 16—Wm De Hart.
No 17—F Huguenard.
Substitutes—Elmer E Banks, Ernest Scheiman.
Custodian Force—W W Rockhill, Custodian; Patrick
Ryan, Janitor; R H Kaough, Fireman; John Mooney,
Laborer; Henry Stoll, Laborer; Julia Lauer, Char-
woman.
Five deliveries daily in the business portion of the city,
viz : At 7 a m, 1, 2, 4.15 and 10 p m.
Two deliveries daily outside the business portion of the
city, viz : 7 a m and 2 p m.
Factory deliveries, viz : 7 a m and 1 and 2 p m.
Sundays, office open from 9 to 10 a m. Three city collec-
tions by the carriers are made at 4, 5 and 10 p m.
One collection outside business portion at 6 p m.
Postage—The postage on letters to be forwarded in the
mails to any part of the United States, is two cents
per ounce, prepaid by stamp. The postage for letters
dropped in this office for delivery in the city, two
cents per ounce, prepaid by stamp.
Canada and the British Provinces—Two cents per ounce ;
prepayment compulsory.
Postage to all countries included in Universal Postal Union
—For prepaid letters, five cents per half ounce ; for
unpaid letters received, ten cents per half ounce ; for
postal cards, two cents each ; for newspapers, if not
over two ounces in weight, one cent for each ; for
books, other printed matter, legal and commercial
documents, pamphlets, music, visiting cards, photo-
graphs, prospectuses, announcements and notices of
various kinds, whether printed, engraved or litho-
graphed, one cent per each weight of two ounces or
fraction of two ounces ; merchandise, ten cents for
each eight ounces or fraction thereof, and parcel not
to exceed that weight.
Registration—Valuable letters to any part of the United
States and Canada and the Universal Postal Union
will be registered on application, for which a charge
of eight cents (in addition to postage) will be made.

PUBLIC BUILDINGS, HALLS, ETC.

Allen County Jail, w s Calhoun n of Superior.
Anderson's Blk and Hall, n w cor Broadway and Jefferson.
A O U W Hall, Bank Blk.
Arcade Bldg, s s Berry bet Calhoun and Harrison.
Arion Hall, cor Main and Harrison.
Auger Blk, 65 E Main.
Barr Street Market House, s e cor Barr and Berry.
Bank Blk, s e cor Main and Court.
Bass Blk, 73–77 Calhoun.
B of L E Hall, 136 Calhoun.
Broadway Theater, 97 Broadway.
Bursley Blk, e s Calhoun bet Washington and Jefferson.
Caledonian Hall, 76 Calhoun.
Carpenters' Union Hall, 7 Bank Blk.
Centennial Blk, 197–199 Broadway.
Certia Blk, w s Calhoun bet Wayne and Berry.
City Hall, s e cor Barr and W Berry.
Colerick's Hall, over 49–53 Columbia.
County Jail, w s N Calhoun n of Superior.
Court House, e s Calhoun bet Main and Berry.
Driscoll's Hall, s e cor Calhoun and Wabash R R.
Esmond Blk, 298 Calhoun.
Eureka Hall, 43 W Superior.
Evans Blk, s s Berry bet Calhoun and Clinton.
Ewing Blk, s w cor W Main and Harrison.
Fleming Blk, e s Calhoun bet Washington and Jefferson.
Foellinger's Blk, 34 and 36 Calhoun.
Fort Wayne Club, e s Harrison bet Berry and Wayne.
Foster Blk, e s Court bet Main and Berry.
Government Bldg, s e cor Berry and Clinton.
G A R Hall, n w cor Calhoun and Main.
Hackett Blk, e s Calhoun bet Wayne and Washington.
Hamilton Homestead, s e cor Clinton and Lewis.
Harmony Hall, 20 W Berry.
Herrington Blk, e s Fairfield av bet Williams and Bass.
Hibernia Hall, 176 Calhoun.
Hope Hospital, s w cor Barr and Washington.
Kane's Blk, s s Main bet Calhoun and Harrison.
Keystone Blk, s w cor Calhoun and Columbia.
Knights of the Golden Eagle Hall, 52½ Calhoun.
K of L Hall, Bank Blk.
Library Hall, n e cor Calhoun and E Lewis.
Mc Dougall's Blk, n w cor Calhoun and Berry.
Masonic Hall, n e cor Wayne and Clinton.
Masonic Temple, cor Wayne and Clinton.

Miller Blk, w s Clinton bet Berry and Main.
Miner Blk, n e cor Clinton and Main.
Myer's Blk, 108 Fairfield av
Nestel Blk, s w cor Broadway and W Jefferson.
New Aveline House Blk. s e cor Calhoun and Berry.
Nierman's Blk, 5 and 7 N Harrison.
Nill's Hall, 80 Calhoun,
Nimrod Hall, 54 E Main.
Odd Fellows' Bldg, n e cor Calhoun and Wayne.
Odd Fellows' Hall, Bank Blk.
Odd Fellows' Hall (new), n s Berry bet Calhoun and Harrison.
Old National Bank Bldg, s w cor Calhoun and Berry.
Philharmonic Hall. 108 Calhoun.
Phœnix Blk, w s Calhoun n of Main.
Pixley & Long Bldg, s s E-Berry bet Calhoun and Clinton.
Postoffice, s e cor Berry and Clinton.
Princess Roller Rink, s e cor Main and Fulton.
Remmell's Blk, s w cor Broadway and Washington.
Rich Blk, e s Calhoun bet Washington and Jefferson.
Saengerbund Hall, 51-53 W Main.
Schmitz Blk, 116 and 118 Calhoun.
Schott's Blk, n w cor Barr and Washington.
Schroeder's Blk (old), 242 Calhoun.
Schroeder's Blk (new), s e cor Broadway and W Washington.
Schroeder's Hall, 97-105 Broadway.
Seidel Blk, 52 Calhoun.
Shuman Blk, n s Main bet Barr and Clinton.
South Wayne Hall, cor Lincoln and Indiana avs.
St Joseph's Hospital, s w cor Broadway and W Main.
St Mary's Hall, s w cor Lafayette and Jefferson.
Standard Hall, 40-44 W Berry.
Studer Blk, 228 W Main.
Swinney Blk. 11, 13 and 15 E Main.
Temperance Hall, 94 Harrison.
Trades and Labor Hall, s e cor Wayne and Calhoun.
Trentman Blk, e s Calhoun between Berry and Wayne.
Tri-State Bldg, Berry between Court and Clinton.
Union Blk, n w cor Main and Clinton.
Verth's Hall, 267 E Wayne.
White Bank Bldg, n w cor Clinton and Wayne.
White's Blk, s e cor Wayne and Calhoun.
Wolke Blk, s w cor Calhoun and Wayne.
Young Men's Christian Association Bldg, 105 Calhoun.
Zelt's Hall, s e cor E Creighton and Gay.

RAILROADS.

Cincinnati, Richmond & Fort Wayne, leased and operated by the Grand Rapids & Indiana.

Findlay, Fort Wayne and Western (Tangent Line), offices Tri-State Bldg. C M Bissell, Genl Mngr ; J H Russell, Genl Freight and Passenger Agt : C H Roser, Comptroller ; R G Thompson, Passenger and Ticket Agt ; R F Douglas, Asst Passenger and Ticket Agt ; C H Newton, Freight Agt. Passenger and Freight Depot, cor Calhoun and Wabash R R.

Fort Wayne, Cincinnati & Louisville, leased and operated by the Lake Erie & Western. Depot cor Cass and Railroad.

Grand Rapids & Indiana, offices, freight and passenger depots with Pittsburgh, Ft Wayne & Chicago Ry. W R Shelby, Vice-Pres and Treas ; J H P Hughart, Genl Mngr ; F A Gorham, Auditor ; E C Leavenworth, Genl Freight Agt ; C L Lockwood, Genl Passenger Agt ; W B Stimson, Supt Northern Division. General Offices, Grand Rapids, Mich. P S O'Rourke, Supt Southern Division—Office, Ft Wayne, Ind. R B Rossington, Freight Agt ; John E Ross, Ticket Agt.

Lake Erie & Western R R, freight office cor 1st and Railroad, depot cor Cass and Railroad. E S Philley, Freight and Ticket Agt.

Lake Shore & Michigan Southern, freight office, cor First and Railroad. Depot. cor Cass and Railroad. D W Caldwell, Pres and Genl Mngr, Cleveland, O ; H A Worcester, Division Supt, Hillsdale, Mich ; E S Philley, Freight and Ticket Agt, Fort Wayne, Ind.

New York, Chicago & St Louis R R (Western Division), offices. Odd Fellows' Bldg. This division extends from Chicago to Bellvue, O, 275 miles. C D Gorham, Supt ; G W Vaughn, Engineer, Cleveland, O ; S K Blair, Trainmaster ; D H Caldwell, Chief Train Dispatcher ; Melvin C Baker, District Passenger and Ticket Agt ; H C Moderwell, Local Freight Agt. (*See opposite inside back cover.*)

Pennsylvania Company, operating the P, Ft W & C Ry, office, e s Clinton bet Holman and Railroad ; passenger depot, n e cor Calhoun and Railroad ; freight depot, n e cor Clinton and Railroad. Joseph Wood, Genl Mngr, Pittsburgh, Pa ; E B Taylor, Genl Supt Transportation, Pittsburgh, Pa ; Charles Watts, Genl Supt, Pittsburgh, Pa ; C D Law, Supt Western

Division ; G L Potter, Supt Motive Power ; R B Rossington, Freight Agt, Ft Wayne, Ind ; John E Ross,
Ticket Agent.

Pittsburgh, Fort Wayne & Chicago, leased and operated
by Pennsylvania Company.

Wabash, general offices, St Louis, Mo ; Master Mechanic's
office, cor Fairfield av and Wabash R R ; passenger
depot, s e .cor Calhoun and Wabash R R; freight
depot, s w cor Calhoun and Wabash R R. Charles M
Hays, Genl Mngr ; H L Magee, Genl Supt ; C S
Crane, Genl Passenger Agt ; M Knight, Freight
Traffic Mngr, St Louis, Mo ; S B Knight, Genl
Freight Agt, St Louis, Mo ; E A Gould, Supt, Peru,
Ind ; W A Sprott, Division Freight Agt, Toledo, O ;
C H Newton, Local Freight Agt, office Freight
Depot ; R G Thompson, Passenger and Ticket Agt;
R F Douglas, Asst Passenger Agt, Fort Wayne, Ind.

SCHOOLS—PUBLIC.

BOARD OF SCHOOL TRUSTEES.

President—John M Moritz.
Secretary—A Ely Hoffman.
Treasurer—Oliver P Morgan.
Superintendent—John S Irwin, M D, LL D.
Clerk and Librarian—Miss Mary Irwin.
Janitor in Chief—James A Gavin.

SPECIAL TEACHERS.

Music—Miss Mary Belle Clark.
Writing—John L Tyler.

BLOOMINGDALE SCHOOL.

N W CORNER MARION AND BOWSER STREETS.

Principal, Miss Margaret M McPhail.
Teachers—Miss Sarah E McKean, Miss Margaret I Mur-
phy, Mrs Mabel E Clayton, Miss Grace C Glenn, Miss
Alice L Hamil, Miss Zeruiah E McLain, Miss Nellie
L Markey, Miss Elizabeth J Bowman, Miss Victoria
Carter, Miss Olive D Brosius, Miss Martha Stumpf.
Janitor—Miss Catherine Sheridan.

CLAY SCHOOL.

N W CORNER CLAY AND WASHINGTON STREETS.

Principal—Miss Mary McClure.
Teachers—Miss Emma Stanley, Miss Emma L Armstrong.
  Miss Anna G Habecker, Miss Annette A Gaskins,
  Miss Rose E Kohn, Miss Ewa L Beebe, Miss Euretta
  C Banister, Miss Belle Geake, Miss Mary E Markey,
  Miss Nellie M McKay, Mrs Jennie S Woodward,
  Miss Katharine A Ersig.
Janitor—Michael L Brannan.

EAST GERMAN SCHOOL.

IN HARMER SCHOOL BUILDING.

Principal—Miss Emma C Weber.
Teacher—Miss Bertha Ritter.

FRANKLIN SCHOOL.

N E CORNER FRANKLIN AVENUE AND HUFFMAN STREET.

Principal—Miss Mary E Freeman.
Teachers—Miss Mary E Shoaff, Miss Minnie L Ortman.
Janitor—Mrs Mary Hedges.

HAMILTON SCHOOL.

N E CORNER PONTIAC AND CLINTON STREETS.

Principal—Miss Anna M Fairfield.
Teachers—Miss Addie Durnell, Miss Lida A Spalding,
  Mrs Delia F Wilson.
Janitor—Mrs Jennie Bryan.

HANNA SCHOOL.

S W CORNER HANNA AND WALLACE STREETS.

Principal—Miss Isabel R Lloyd.
Teachers—Mrs Marian H Brenton, Miss Margaret A
  Wade, Miss Addie H Williams, Miss Anna Maude
  Lipes, Mrs Eva M Baughman, Miss Louise C Heller,
  Miss Emma M Hebert, Miss May W Daugherty, Miss
  Martha E Wohlfort, Mrs Elizabeth O Collins, Miss
  Anna Boss.
Janitor—Mrs Maria Perrett.

HARMER SCHOOL.

N W CORNER HARMER AND JEFFERSON STREETS.

Principal—Mrs Mary S Waldo.
Teachers—·Mrs Sarah J Stahl, Miss M Georgina Wadge, Miss Mary E Christie, Miss Fannie Kohn, Miss Edith Holsworth, Miss Katharine M Scherer, Miss Emma H Ersig, Miss Henrietta M Winbaugh.
Janitor—Mrs Anna J Clarke.

HIGH SCHOOL.

E WAYNE STREET BETWEEN CALHOUN AND CLINTON STREETS.

Principal—Chester T Lane, A M.
Teachers—Harvey O Wise, A B; Albert B Crowe, A B; Miss Mary L Jay, Miss Caroline Colvin, A B; Miss Mary A Pyle, Miss Ellen McKeag, Miss Emma Louise Hamilton, Miss Katharine H Blynn, A B.
Janitor—Conrad Leidolf.

HOAGLAND SCHOOL.

N W CORNER HOAGLAND AVENUE AND BUTLER STREET.

Principal—Miss Frances Hamilton.
Teachers—Miss ·Mary A Abel, Miss Mary E Dick, Miss Elizabeth M Biegler, Miss Mary E Orff, Miss Matilda E Knight, Miss Maude F Hendricks, Miss Carrie A Snively, Miss Etta C Brooks, Miss Leora Miner, Miss Minnie I Newell. Miss Mary E McClure, Miss Lillie B Beaber.
Janitor—Mrs Ann O'Callahan.

HOLTON AVENUE SCHOOL.

S W CORNER HOLTON AND CREIGHTON AVENUES.

Principal—Miss Edith M Brewster.
Teachers—Miss Laura D Muirhead, Miss Bertha Stahl, Miss Sophia C Nix.
Janitor—Miss Catherine Clear.

JEFFERSON SCHOOL.

S W CORNER JEFFERSON AND GRIFFITH STREETS.

Principal—Miss Harriet E Leonard.
Teachers—Miss Clara Phelps, Miss Janet A McPhail, Miss Elizabeth E Chapin, Miss Helen Brenton, Miss Grace M Waldo, Miss Elizabeth Collins, Miss Anna M Trenam, Miss Mary I Smith, Miss Mary M Brokaw, Miss Cora A Conover, Miss Ella R Williard, Miss Gertrude E Clark.
Janitor—John Immel.

LAKESIDE SCHOOL.

N W CORNER LAKE AVENUE AND DEARBORN STREET.

Principal—Miss Louvie E Strong,

McCULLOCH SCHOOL.

N W CORNER McCULLOCH AND ELIZA STREETS.

Principal—Miss Cecilia C Foley.
Teachers—Miss Fannie R Conover, Miss Emma S Gutermuth, Miss Anna Zucker.
Janitor—Mrs Mary E Dolan.

MINER STREET SCHOOL.

S W CORNER MINER AND DE WALD STREETS.

Principal—Miss Alice M Habecker.
Teachers—Miss Martha M Clark, Miss M Kate Abel, Miss Fannie M Lowry, Miss Minnie B Seibt, Miss M Frank Muirhead, Miss Lillian Fisk, Miss Katharine C Beebe, Mrs Elsie A Hall.
Janitor—Mrs Orpha Clippinger.

NEBRASKA SCHOOL.

S E CORNER BOONE AND FRY STREETS.

Principal—Miss Susan S Sinclair.
Teachers—Miss Lillie V Bowen, Miss Carrie B Schrader, Miss Prudence L Bowman,
Janitor—Mrs Anna Renzer.

WASHINGTON SCHOOL.

S W CORNER WASHINGTON AND UNION STREETS.

Principal—Miss Margaret S Cochrane.
Teachers—Miss Jessie L Humphrey, Miss Mary Smyser, Miss Mabel Robertson, Miss Edna M Alderman, Miss Blanche Blynn, Miss Ada M Griffiths, Miss Daisy K Beaber, Miss Marina J Geake, Miss Effie Lumbard.
Janitor—Mrs Sophie Kellermeyer.

WEST GERMAN SCHOOL.

E S WEBSTER STREET SOUTH OF WASHINGTON STREET.

Principal—Carl Schwarz.
Teacher—Miss Sarah C Schaaf.
Janitor—Mrs Frederika Bierbaum.

SUBSTITUTES.

Miss Caroline Biddle, Miss Maude Biegler, Miss May L Fisk, Miss Ethel K Jenness, Miss Annie L Miller, Mrs Martha J Moderwell, Miss Catherine E Murphy.

SCHOOLS AND COLLEGES.

MISCELLANEOUS.

Academy of Our Lady of the Sacred Heart. Conducted by the Sisters of the Holy Cross, Mother Arserne, Superioress. P O Address, Academy, Allen Co, Ind.

Cathedral Schools, in charge of the Brothers of the Holy Cross. Rev J R Quinlan, Director; Brother Engelbert, Superior. Cathedral square s w cor Clinton and E Jefferson.

Concordia College (German Lutheran). e s Schick bet E Washington and Maumee rd. Organized in Missouri in 1839. Established in Fort Wayne in 1861. Joseph Schmidt, Pres.

Emanuel's (German Lutheran), n e cor Union and Wilt. Rev Charles Gross, Principal.

European School of Art, 16 Rockhill.

Fort Wayne Art School, s w cor E Lewis and Barr. Wm Forsyth, Instructor.

Fort Wayne Business College, n w cor Calhoun and Berry. G W Lahr, Pres.

Fort Wayne College of Medicine, 160 W Superior. C B Stemen, M D, Dean; W W Barnett, M D, Sec.

Fort Wayne Conservatory of Music, Bank Blk. C F W Meyer, Director.

Grace (German Evangelical Lutheran) s e cor Gay and Pontiac. Rev Theodore J C Stellhorn, Principal.

International Business College and School of Shorthand and Typewring, cor Calhoun and Washington. T L Staples, Proprietor.

Plymouth Church Kindergarten, s w cor Jefferson and Harrison. Mrs Kate H Ainslie and Miss Lena Hiler, Kindergartners.

St Augustine's Academy (for girls), under the direction of the Sisters of Providence. Cathedral square s e cor Calhoun and E Jefferson. Sister M Cyril, Superioress.

St John's (German Lutheran). s e cor W Washington and Van Buren. Jacob Stumpf, Principal.

St Mary's (German Catholic, for boys), s w cor E Jefferson and Lafayette; St Mary's (for girls), s e cor E Jefferson and Lafayette. Conducted by the Sisters of Notre Dame. Rev J H Oechtering, Director.

St Patrick's School, n w cor DeWald and Webster. Sister Mary Catherine, Principal.

St Paul's (German Catholic), s e cor W Washington and Griffith. J Hauk, Director.

St Paul's (German Lutheran), n e cor Barr and Madison.
  . Rev Henry G Sauer, Director; John H Ungemach,
    Principal.
St Peter's (German Catholic), s s St Martin's bet War-
    saw and Hanna. Conducted by the Sisters of Notre
    Dame. Rev A Messman, Director.
Trinity German Lutheran School, s w cor Huffman and
    Oakland av. Henry Nehrenz, Principal.
Westminster Seminary (for young ladies), 251 W Main.
    Mrs D B Wells and Miss Carrie B Sharp, Principals.
Zion (German Lutheran), s w cor E Creighton av and
    Force. Frederick A Klein, Principal.; John Man-
    gelsdorf, W Wolf, Teachers

SECRET AND BENEVOLENT SOCIETIES.

MASONIC.

Hall northeast cor Clinton and E Wayne.

Wayne Lodge, No 25' F & A M. Meets first Saturday on
    or before full moon. J C Craig, W M; D L Harding,
    Sec.
Summit City Lodge, No 170, F & A M. Meets first Fri-
    day of each month. Edgar S Young, W M; Frank E
    Stouder, Sec.
Sol D Bayless Lodge, No 359, F & A M. Meets second
    Monday of each month. C L Carter, W M; Wm E
    Hood, Sec.
Home Lodge, No 342, F & A M. Meets first Tuesday of
    each month. Joseph E Sunderland, W M; T C War-
    ner, Sec.
Fort Wayne Chapter, No 19, R A M. Meets first Wednes-
    day of each month. R A Ligget, H P; W J Pro-
    basco, Sec.
Fort Wayne Council, No 4, R & S M. Meets second
    Wednesday of each month. A M Tower, Ill M; W J
    Probasco. Sec.
Fort Wayne Commandery, No 4, K T. Meets third Tues-
    day of each month. Wm Geake, E C; H G Granger,
    Rec.
Fort Wayne Grand Lodge of Perfection, A & A S Rite, N
    M J. Meets first and third Tuesdays of each month.
    Wm Geake, T P G M; C B Fitch, Sec.
Darius Council Princes of Jerusalem, A & A S Rite, N M
    J. Meets second and fourth Tuesdays of each month.
    C M Dawson, S P G M; C B Fitch, Sec.

MASONIC (COLORED).

St Mary's Lodge, No 14, F & A M, 254 Calhoun. Meets first Monday of each month. I E Jones, W M; Soloman Raines, Sec.

St Paul's Chapter, No 8, R A M, 254 Calhoun. Meets second Tuesday of each month. W H Brown, H P; Charles Raines, Sec.

Lincoln Commandery, No 8, K T, 254 Calhoun. Meets third Tuesday of each month. S M Raines, E C; James Smith, Rec.

Matchless Chapter, O E S, No 8, 254 Calhoun. Meets first Friday of each month. Sarah Wallace, A M; Ollie Brown, Sec.

AMERICAN SONS OF COLUMBUS.

Fort Wayne Colony. Meets every Friday evening at No 1 Hackett Bldg. F X Schuhler, Noble Admiral; Robert M Reilly, Noble Sec.

American Daughters of Isabella. Meets first and third Saturdays in each month at Columbus Hall, 11 and 12 W Wayne. Carrie Viberg, W P; Mary Brannan, W S; Mrs F X Schuhler, W T.

A. O. U. W.

Fort Wayne Lodge, No 19; Bank Blk. Meets every Friday evening. L L Miller, M W; J J Bauer, Recorder.

Summit City Lodge, No 36; s w cor Calhoun and Superior. Meets every Thursday evening. M S Wilson, M W; N Conover, Recorder.

Maumee Lodge, No 50; Bank Blk. Meets every Wednesday evening. John W Brown, M W; J M Culver, Recorder.

Summit City Lodge, No 2, D of H. Meets every Tuesday evening in A O U W Hall, No 3 Bank Blk. Mrs E B Gordon, C of H; Mrs Jeannette France, Recorder.

Fort Wayne Lodge, No 11, D of H; Bank Blk. Meets every Tuesday evening. Mrs E B Smith, C of H; Lena Bleibtreu, L of H.

B. P. O. E.

Fort Wayne Lodge, No 155; Trentman Bldg. Meets every Tuesday evening. O B Wiley, E R; Sid Hubbard, Sec.

G. A. R.

Anthony Wayne Post, No 271; Trentman Blk. Meets first and third Fridays of each month. C C Miller, P C; Joseph Lombard, Adjutant.

Union Veteran Legion, Encampment No 51, s e cor Calhoun and Wayne. Meets first and third Thursdays of each month. H C Zollinger, Col Com ; E B Moore, Adjutant.

Colonel E S Walker Camp, Sons of Veterans, No 159. Meets every Tuesday at G A R Hall. H A Bricker, Capt ; D E Bricker, Sergt.

Sion S Bass Post, No 40 ; Nills Hall, 80 Calhoun. Meets second and fourth Fridays of each month. M R Johnson, Com ; Charles Beam, Adjt.

Tri-State Veterans' Association, 176 Calhoun. Gov Wm McKinley, Pres ; Col J W Young, Adj Genl.

Ladies' Aid Society, Auxiliary to Colonel E S Walker Camp S of V ; G A R Hall. Meets first and third Thursdays of each month. Sibyl A Niedhammer, Pres ; Nettie Rice, Sec.

I. O. R. M.

Me-che-can-noch-qua Tribe, No 106, Harmony Hall. Meets every Wednesday evening. J T Leach, Sachem ; L E Brown, C of R.

INDEPENDENT ORDER OF B'NAI B'RITH.

B'nai B'rith Lodge, Harmony Hall. Organized April 15, 1865. Meets first and third Sundays of each month. Theodore Frank, Pres ; Charles Young, Sec.

I. O. O. F.

Court Kekionga, No 1,539, Harmony Hall. Meets second and fourth Fridays of each month. G B Taylor, C R ; H G Granneman, Sec.

Fort Wayne Lodge, No 14, Odd Fellows' Hall, n e cor Calhoun and Wayne. Meets every Monday evening. J F Uebelhoer, N G ; Duncan McLeish, Sec.

Harmony Lodge, No 19, Harmony Hall. Meets every Thursday evening. J N Pfeiffer, N G ; J N Kelsey, Sec.

Concordia Lodge, No 228, Harmony Hall. Meets every Wednesday evening. John Wackmuller, N G ; Karl Bahlinger, Sec.

Summit Encampment, No 16, Harmony Hall. Meets first and Third Fridays of each month. P Pfleger, C P ; A L Bond, Scribe.

Fort Wayne Encampment, No 152, Odd Fellows' Hall, n e cor Calhoun and Wayne. Meets second and fourth Fridays of each month. J W Frederick, C P ; D L Harding, P S.

Deborah Lodge, No 110, D of R, Harmony Hall. Meets second and fourth Tuesdays of each month. Susan Zimmer, N G ; Mrs Wm Windsor, Sec.

Concordia Lodge, No 41, D of R, Harmony Hall. Meets second and fourth Fridays of each month. Mrs Sophie Schulz, N G ; Miss Mary Krause, Sec.

Queen Esther Lodge, No 324, D of R, Odd Fellows' Hall. Meets first and third Saturdays of each month. Mrs. J M Singmaster, N G ; Minnie Bittner, R C.

Canton Fort Wayne, No 17, Patriarchs Militant, Harmony Hall. Meets first and third Tuesdays of each month. C A Stolte, Capt ; C H Mayer, Sec.

I. O. O. F. (COLORED.)

Allen Lodge, No 3505 ; 254 Calhoun. Meets second Wednesday of each week. Wm Brown, N G ; F Dickerson, Sec.

KNIGHTS OF HONOR.

Fort Wayne Lodge, No 1547 ; 30 Calhoun. Meets second and fourth Wednesdays of each month. W L Pettit, Dictator ; A G Barnett, Reporter.

KNIGHTS OF PYTHIAS.

Phœnix Lodge. No 101 ; Aldine Bldg. Meets every Monday evening. Oscar Lingloff, C C ; J Shaw, K of S.

Fort Wayne Lodge, No 116. Meets every Tuesday evening, Odd Fellows' Hall, cor Calhoun and Wayne. Chauncey Miller, C C ; J F Naylor, K of R.

Rathbone Temple, No 31 ; Aldine Bldg. Meets every Tuesday evening. Althico Foster, E C ; Ella Fessender, Sec.

Summit City Uniform Rank, Randall Hall. Meets second and fourth Wednesdays of each month. W A Lichtenwalter, Capt ; Marshall Commincavish, Rec Sec.

KNIGHTS OF THE GOLDEN EAGLE.

Wayne Castle, No 2 ; 142 Calhoun. Meets every Wednesday evening. A C Schmuck, N C ; G A Kiefer, M R.

K. O. T. M.

Wayne Tent, No 54 ; Odd Fellows' Hall. Meets every Thursday. P J Lebeck, Com ; A E Thomas, R K ; L S Williams, P C.

Fort Wayne Hive, No 6, L O T M, Harmony Hall. Meets second and fourth Mondays of each month. Alice McClelland, L C ; Miss Stella Mulqueen, L R K.

ORDER OF CHOSEN FRIENDS.

Columbian Council, No 3; 81 Calhoun. Meets every
Thursday. Mrs L A Hauss, Counsellor; D F Hauss,
Sec.

PATRIOTIC ORDER SONS OF AMERICA.

Washington Camp, No 38; Trentman Blk. Meets every
Wednesday. E G Davis, Pres; Frank Lechler, R C.

ROYAL ARCANUM.

Howard Council, No 246; Harmony Lodge Hall. Meets
first and third Fridays of each month. George J
Worth, Regent; H C Moderwell, Sec.

SONS OF ST GEORGE.

Robin Hood Lodge, No 248; Harmony Hall. Meets second and fourth Tuesdays of each month. John Slater,
Pres; John T Leach, Sec.

TELEGRAPH AND TELEPHONE COMPANIES.

Central Union Telephone Co, office Tri-State Bldg.
Edgar L Taylor, Mngr.
Fort Wayne District Telegraph Co, 15 W Columbia. C R
Higgins, Sec and Mngr.
Fort Wayne Harrison Telephone Co, White Bank Bldg.
I N Woods, Promoter.
Postal Telegraph Co, 15 W Columbia. C E Stettler,
Mngr.
Western Union Telegraph Co, New Aveline House Blk.
Oscar L Perry, Mngr.

City Directory Office
Library,
38 Bass Blk.

Directories and Gazetters on file for the use
of our patrons.
List of names furnished on application.

R. L. POLK & CO.'S
FORT WAYNE DIRECTORY.
1895-96.

ABBREVIATIONS.

adv	advertisement	mnfr	manufacturer
agt	agent	mngr	manager
appr	apprentice	n	north or north of
assn	association	n e cor	northeast corner
asst	assistant	nr	near
av	avenue	n s	north side
bds	boards	n w cor	northwest corner
bel	below	opp	opposite
bet	between	p o	postoffice
bldg	building	pres	president
blk	block	propr	proprietor
blksmith	blacksmith	publr	publisher
bkkpr	bookkeeper	R M S	Railway Mail Service
carp	carpenter	res	residence
cash	cashier	Rev	Reverend
clk	clerk	rd	road
col'd	colored	s	south or south of
collr	collector	s e cor	southeast corner
condr	conductor	sec	secretary
cor	corner	s s	south side
e	east or east of	supt	superintendent
e s	east side	tel opr	telegraph operator
engr	engineer	treas	treasurer
inspr	inspector	w	west or west of
lab	laborer	w s	west side
mach	machinist	wid	widow
mkr	maker		
mnfg	manufacturing		

The word "street" is always understood.

RAILROADS.

F F W & W Ry	Findlay, Fort Wayne & Western
G R & I R R	Grand Rapids & Indiana
L E & W R R	Lake Erie & Western
L S & M S Ry	Lake Shore & Michigan Southern
Penn Co	Pittsburg, Fort Wayne & Chicago
Wabash R R	Wabash

ALPHABETICAL LIST OF NAMES.

Abbott Hettie, domestic 17 W Creighton.
Abbott Mattie C, bds 172 E Berry.
Abbott Wm T, real estate, Foster Blk, res 172 E Berry.

Abdon George, Plumber, Yard Hydrants, Street Washers and Pumps, Steam and Hot Water Heating, 30 Clinton, res same.

Abel, *see also Ebel and Habel.*

Abel John C, lawyer, 3 and 4 Bank Blk, res 405 Calhoun.

Abel Mary A, teacher Hoagland School, bds 405 Calhoun.

Abel M Kate, teacher Miner School, bds 405 Calhoun.

Abell Adelaide, sec Y M C A, rms 19 W Wayne.

Abercrombie John engr G R & I R R, rms 28 Brackenridge.

Aborn Thomas E, printer Archer Ptg Co, res 43 W Berry.

Abrams Sherman W, brakeman Penn Co, res 31 Lasselle.

Abstract Office The (Kuhne & Co), 19 Court.

Academy of Our Lady of the Sacred Heart, 6 miles n of Court House.

Achduth Veshalom (Jewish) Cemetery, e s Broadway bet Wabash and P, F W & C R R's.

Achduth Veshalom (Jewish) Temple, s w cor Harrison and W Wayne

Achenbach Harry A (Ft Wayne Music Co), res 340 E Washington.

Acker, *see also Aker and Eicher.*

Acker Alphonso C, removed to Syracuse, N Y.

Acker Wm J, paperhanger, res 86 Organ av.

Ackerman Charles, lab Penn Co, res 64 Summit.

Ackerman John, car repairer Penn Co, res 77 Summit.

Ackermann Herbert, fresco painter, bds Hoffmann House.

Ackermann Margaret, bds 88 Hanna.

Ackermann Martin, laborer, res 88 Hanna.

Ackermann Theresa (wid Wolfgang), bds 56 Maumee rd

Acrolf Abraham, shoemaker, 174 Calhoun, bds 112 Wall.

Adair John, Carp, res s s E Leith 2 e of Lafayette.

Adams Charles C, engineer Penn Co. res 110 Hanna.

Adams Elizabeth B, bds 111 Brackenridge.

Adams Express Co, Wm Geiger Agent, 10 W Wayne. Tel 622.

Adams George D, telegraph operator, res 165 Griffith.

Adams Israel B, engr Penn Co, res 111 Brackenridge.

Adams Israel J R, mach E B Kunkle & Co, res n s Huntington rd nr Lindenwood Cemetery.

Adams John H, dentist, 106 Calhoun, res 32 Lake av.

Adams Joseph H, res 70 Harrison.

Adams Louisa, music teacher, bds 111 Brackenridge.

Adams Mary, died October 5, 1894.

Adams Mary O, artist, bds 111 Brackenridge.

Adams Minnie, bds 165 Griffith.

Adams Oscar S, molder E B Kunkle & Co, res 98 Ewing.

Adams Thomas H (col'd), brakeman Penn Co, res 104 Hayden.

Adams Township School No 3, cor Pioneer av and Winch.

Adams Walter W, appr Bass F & M Wks, bds 110 Hanna.

Adams Wilbur H, brakeman G R & I R R, rms 223 Lafayette.

Adams Wm, painter Penn Co, res 131 Union.

Adams Wm A, died August 27, 1894.

Adams Wm N, toolmaker Ft Wayne Electric Corp, res 42 Michigan av.

Adamson May (wid Louis), res 63 Brackenridge.

Adelmann Mary E (wid Joseph), bds 242 E Lewis.

Adfield James, laborer, res 535 E Washington.

Adkins Albert C, helper, res 48 Lasselle.

Adler Anna (wid Andrew), res 61 Wall.

Adler Fredericka R, presser Hoosier Mnfg Co, bds 61 Wall.

Adler Hugo C, foreman Wayne Knitting Mills, res 270 W Jefferson.

Aehnett Adelbert, grocer, 567 E Washington, res 565 same.

Aehnett Isabella, bds 565 E Washington.

Aehnett Johanna, seamstress, bds 565 E Washington.

Aehnett Otilie, seamstress, bds 565 E Washington.

Ætna Insurance Company, of Hartford, Conn. Charles W Orr, Agt, 312 W Washington.

Affolder John, laborer, bds 76 Smith.

Affolder Louis, laborer, res 76 Smith.

Affolder Louis jr, laborer, bds 76 Smith.

Affolder Minnie W, seamstress, bds 76 Smith.

African M E Church, n e cor Wayne and Francis.

Agenbroad Henry, hostler Winkelmeyer & Hans, rms 44 W Main.

Agenbroad John F, driver City Trkg Co, rms 40 Monroe.

Agster Anna M (wid Gottlieb), res 42 W Jefferson.

Agster Charles A, foreman Wabash R R, res 206 Hoagland av.

Ahern Dennis F, bartender W E Hatch, bds 2 Baker.

Ahern Dennis F, switchman, bds 148 Holman.

Ahern Edward E, fireman Wabash R R, bds 148 Holman.

Ahern James, died September 19, 1894.

Ahern Johanna, (wid Eugene), res 148 Holman.

Ahern Mamie, opr S M Foster, bds 148 Holman.

Ahern Mary E, stenographer, bds 83 Wagner.

Pixley-Long Block, Fort Wayne.

Old National Bank, Fort Wayne.
Tri-State Building, and
Elektron ✦ ✦ ✦

Court House, Whitley County.
Government Building, Kalamazoo.
Court House, Kalamazoo.

WM. GEAKE,

STEAM STONE WORKS,

DEALER AND CONTRACTOR IN
ALL KINDS OF . . . . .

CUT AND ORNAMENTAL STONE WORK,

Nos. 76, 78, 80 AND 82 PEARL STREET.

TELEPHONE 94.

Ahern Patrick T, tel opr Postal Tel Co, bds 148 Holman.
Ahern Thomas, contractor, 83 Wagner, res same.
Ahern Wm, line repairer, res 65 E De Wald.
Ahlersmeyer Wilhelm, contractor, n e cor Winch and Pioneer av. res same.
Ahner Charles, car builder Penn Co, res 118 Smith.
Abner Jacob, car builder Penn Co, res 251 Walton av.
Aichele August, marble cutter, bds 231 St Mary's av.
Aichele Clarence A, barber Louis Uplegger, bds 231 St Mary's av.
Aichele George F, marble, 510 W Main, res 231 St Mary's av.
Aiken, *see also Eaken.*
Aiken, Charles, yardmaster L S & M S Ry, res 30 W 4th.
Aiken H Margaret (wid Wm N), bds 310 Hanna.
Aiken John H, Lawyer, 9 and 11 W Main, res 11 Wall.
Aiken John W, policeman, res 310 Hanna.
Aiken Wm A, roaster G E Bursley & Co, res 113 Lake av.
Aikens Henry W J, insurance 3 Arcade Bldg, res s s Pontiac opp Holton av.
Ainslie Rev James S, pastor Plymouth Congregational Church. res 309 W Jefferson.
Ainsworth Effie, operator S M Foster, bds 76 Wells.
Ainsworth Wm N, buyer, res 76 Wells.
Ake Elias, chemist Old Fort Spice and Extract Co, res 12 Savilla av.
Ake John S, laborer. res 221 Madison.
Ake Rosanna H (wid Zedekiah), bds 16 Lincoln av.
Aker Ambrose B, laborer, res 196 Sherman.
Aker Aurilla A, bds 196 Sherman.
Aker Charles H, lab Hoffman Bros, res 65 Howell.
Aker Charles L, clk A A Lowry, bds 196 Sherman.
Aker Minnie I, bds 196 Sherman.
Akers Carrie, student, bds 278 W Creighton av.
Akers Florence I, bds 261 W Wayne.
Akey Edward J, cabinetmaker Ft Wayne Furn Co, res 54 Begue.
Akroyd Mark, lab, res w s Edgewater av 1 n of bridge.
Akster Annie M (wid Gottlieb), res 42 W Jefferson.
Albach Louis, laborer, bds 43 Walnut.
Albaugh Eliza A, domestic, res 111 Wells.
Albers Edith M, bds 378 Calhoun.
Albers Elizabeth (wid Herman), res 69 Force.

Albers Herman J, molder Bass F & M Wks, res 298 E Creighton av.

Albers Mary, seamstress, bds 69 Force.

Albers Peter R, condr Ft W E Ry Co, res 378 Calhoun.

Albers Philip E, lab Penn Co, res 428 E Wayne

Albersmeyer Charles, molder Bass F & M Works, bds 192 Madison

Albersmeyer Christian H, clerk Martin Detzer, bds 192 Madison.

Albersmeyer Elizabeth, opr Hoosier Mnfg Co, bds 192 Madison.

Albersmeyer Frederick, carpenter, res 419 E Lewis.

Albersmeyer Hannah, bds 192 Madison.

Albersmeyer Lisetta, seamstress, bds 192 Madison.

Albert Josephine A, teacher Westminster Seminary, bds 164 E Lewis.

Albert Mary L (wid Julius), res 164 E Lewis.

Albrecht Anton, cigarmkr A N Ehle, res 516 E Lewis.

Albrecht Dorothy (wid Martin), res 1 Liberty.

Albrecht Edward, removed to Roanoke, Ind.

Albrecht Frank, driver Hose Co No 4, res 38 Oak.

Albrecht Frank L, died September 18, 1894.

Albrecht John D, photo-printer Miner & Dexter, bds 14 Elm.

Albrecht Julia S, candymkr J H Meyer, bds 14 Elm.

Albrecht Mary, bds 516 E Lewis.

Albrecht Otto, painter Olds Wagon Wks, res 182 Smith.

Albrecht Pauline (wid John), res 57 Hendricks.

Albrecht Peter, clk Ft Wayne Gas Co, bds 14 Elm.

Albrecht Samuel W, bkkpr Nuttman & Co, res 126 E Wayne.

Albright Thomas J, fireman N Y, C & St L R R, bds 52 Runnion av.

Alden Frank W, insurance agt, res 115 W Washington.

Alden Samuel R, Lawyer, 17 and 18 Bank Blk, res 135 E Washington. Tel 214.

Alderman Dayton H, agtl implts, 4 and 6 Harrison, res 220 W Washington.

Alderman Edna M, teacher Washington School, bds 220 W Washington.

Alderman Frank, mngr Rocker Washer Co, res 303 W Washington. Tel 234.

Alderman Wm F, bds 303 W Washington.

Aldine Printing House, Clarence F Cook Propr, Job, Copperplate and Steel Die Printing and Rubber Stamp Making, 63 E Berry. Tel 414. (*See p. 89.*)

Aldrich Bessie E, dressmaker, bds 150 Maumee rd.

†Aldrich Elisha M, res 301 Fairfield av.

Aldrich George B, bds 150 Maumee rd.

Aldrich George W, sausage mnfr, 198 Broadway, res 150 Maumee rd.

†Ale Frederick W, printer The Journal, bds 274 Hoagland av.

Alexander Charles C, music teacher, 54 E Washington, res same.

Alexander Edward H, clk H C Graffe, bds 51 W Berry.

Alexander Frank E, car bldr Penn Co, res 60 Columbia av.

Alexander Lucius F, advance agt, bds 54 E Washington.

Alexander Reece H, foreman Bond Cereal Mills, res 54 E Washington.

Alexander Samuel M, cigar mnfr, 7 E Main, res 45 1st.

Alfelt Emil, helper G H Seabold, bds 22 W Main.

Algier Henry, propr Algier Manufacturing Co, res 262 E Washington.

Algier Mnfg Co, Henry Algier propr, tinners. 252 E Lewis.

Algier Mary, domestic, rms 264 E Washington.

Alleger, *see also Allgeier.*

Alleger Frank J, driver Powers & Barnett, res 39 W Jefferson.

Allen Albert S, painter, 158 Calhoun, res 112 W Creighton av.

Allen Claud (col'd), porter, rms 96 Melita.

Allen County Asylum, Herman W Felts, supt; n s Bluffton rd 1 w of bridge.

Allen County Jail, w s Calhoun 1 n of Superior.

Allen County Loan and Savings Association, Gottlieb Haller Pres, D C Fisher Vice-Pres, T C Rogers Sec, Harry A Keplinger Treas, O N Heaton Attorney, 32 E Berry. Tel 46.

Allen County Orphans' Home, 144 Pritchard.

Allen County Teachers' Library, 12 Bass Blk.

Allen Cyrus, fireman N Y, C & St L R R, bds 52 Runnion av.

Allen Cyrus W, carpenter, res 256 W Creighton av.

Allen Ethan, asst G B M Bower, bds 256 W Creighton av.

Allen Frank F, architect, bds 256 W Creighton av.

Allen George H, clk F C Cratsley, rms 324 Calhoun.

Allen George I, bds 256 W Creighton av.
Allen Jennie M, teacher, bds 256 W Creighton av.
Allen Jennie R (col'd), domestic, bds 69 Melita.
Allen John B, bds 256 W Creighton av.
Allen John T, carpenter Penn Co, res 94 Thomas.
Allen Louis P, cigarmkr John C Eckert, res 11 McClellan.
Allen Lyman P, laborer Rastetter & Son, res 155 Union.
Allen Margaret, bds 112 W Creighton av.
Allen Richard, porter White National Bank, res Lake av e of city limits.
Allen Thomas H, painter A S Allen, bds 112 W Creighton av.
Allen Usiford S, painter A S. Allen, bds 112 W Creighton av.
Allen Wm W, painter J W Brimmer, bds 155 Union.
Aller Isaac N, winder Ft Wayne Electric Corp, res 51 Huestis av.
Allgeier, *see also Alleger.*
Allgeier Anthony. drayman, 162 E Taber, res same.
Allgeier Frank J, tinsmith L E & W R R, res 115 N Harrison.
Allison Mina (Smalley & Allison), res 206 W Washington.
Allway, *see Alway.*
Alonzo Clara, bds 36 Hayden.
Alringer Isadore, clk J B White, res 168 Griffith.
Alringer May, bds 168 Griffith.
Alspach Harry, laborer, bds Windsor Hotel.
Alt Anton, laborer, res 149 Suttenfield.
Altekruse Emma L (wid Henry R), res s w cor Reynolds and Warren.
Altekruse Ernest F, candymaker Fox Branch U S B Co, bds s w cor Reynolds and Warren.
Altekruse Henry R, died May 19, 1894.
Altekruse Wm E, carpenter Rhinesmith & Simonson, res 31 N Calhoun
Altenau Charles C. plasterer, res 33 Charles.
Altenburger Basilius, res 183 Montgomery.
Alter Albert C. newsdealer, bds 175 Madison.
Alter Barbara N (wid Nicholas), res 175 Madison.
Alter Frances. opr S M Foster, bds 27 John.
Alter George J, clk Philip Graf, res 18 Buchanan.
Alter George J jr, clk Wm Hahn & Co, bds 18 Buchanan.
Alter Henry A, painter, res 60 Summit.
Alter Jacob A, painter, res 20 Wilt.
Alter Jacob A jr, painter, res 19 Pritchard.

Alter John, clerk, bds 167 Harmer.
Alter John H, painter, bds 20 Wilt.
Alter Lizzie, opr S M Foster, bds 27 John.
Alter Peter, carpenter, res 27 John.
Alter Peter jr, res 27 John.
Altevogt Henry F, clk F P Wilt & Co, bds 38 W Allen.
Altevogt Herman F, res 38 W Allen.
Altevogt Lizzie F, bds 38 W Allen.
Altevogt Louis W, mach Bass F & M Wks, res 590 Calhoun
Altevogt Wm R, mach Bass F & M Wks, res 42 W Allen.
Alvord Charlotte, bds 154 W Berry.
Alvord Frances D (wid Alvin A), res 154 W Berry.
Alway Edward, car inspr N Y, C & St L R R, res 89 Richardson.
Aman, *see also Amon.*
Aman Celia M, clk J O Seibert, bds 215 E Washington.
Aman Francis A, carp Penn Co, res 28 E Leith.
Aman John H, molder Bass F & M Wks, bds 215 E Washington.
Aman Joseph F, clk Root & Co, bds 215 E Washington.
Aman Louis, plasterer, res 215 E Washington.
Amans Ida, domestic 98 E Berry.
Ambler Dora, domestic Union House.
Ambler Emmett E, inspr Ft Wayne Gas Co, res 143 Griffith.
American Electrical Directory, Star Iron Tower Co, publrs, foot of Wells and Nickel Plate R R.
American Express Co, Loyal P Hulburd Agt, 24 E Main. Tel 141.
Amerman James B, painter, rms 58 W Main.
Ames Edward T, electrical engineer, bds The Randall.
Ames Fredous H, bds 15 Hamilton.
Ames George W, bds 15 Hamilton.
Ames Georgiana, bds 15 Hamilton.
Ames Julius, carpenter, rms 183 E Lewis.
Ames Milo E, engr G R & I R R, res 199 E Lewis.
Ames Rufus, engineer, res 15 Hamilton.
Amon, *see also Aman.*
Amon Charles, res Bluffton rd of city limits,
Amon Frank C, bds Charles Amon.
Amon Maude, bds Charles Amon.
Amrhein Andrew, laborer, bds 145 E Lewis.
Amstutz Peter, laborer, res 35 John.
Ancient Order United Workmen Hall, Bank Blk.

Anderson Allen, bender L Rastetter & Son, bds 95 Franklin av.

Anderson Andrew, condr N Y, C & St L R R, res 137 W Superior.

Anderson Block Hall, n w cor Broadway and Jefferson.

Anderson Calvin, bds 123 W Wayne.

Anderson Charles, laborer, bds 95 Franklin av.

Anderson Christopher C, bds 21 Calhoun.

Anderson Claes A, machinist, res 90 N Harrison.

Anderson Clarence E, porter, bds 137 W Superior.

Anderson Columbus C, brakeman, res 9 Herman.

Anderson Eli G, cashier Penn Co, res 123 W Wayne.

Anderson Ella, bds 123 W Wayne.

Anderson Florence M, domestic 44 W Washington.

Anderson F Everett, clerk, res 76 Lake av.

Anderson George, engineer Rastetter & Son, res 96 Wall.

Anderson George, fireman Penn Co, bds 219 Lafayette.

Anderson George, laborer, res 95 Franklin av.

Anderson George D, clk Penn Co, res 31 Bass.

Anderson Harry A, traveling agt, res 149 Spy Run av.

Anderson Ingvar, (Waterhouse & Anderson), bds 309 Lafayette.

Anderson James R, engineer G R & I R R, res 411 Calhoun.

Anderson John H, laborer, res 6 Bush.

Anderson John N (col'd), died July 17, 1894.

Anderson John W, driver Dittoe's Grocery Co, bds 85 W Superior.

Anderson John W, laborer, res 22 Fairfield av.

Anderson Joseph, engineer, bds 55 Barr.

Anderson Julia (wid James), dressmaker, n w cor Wells and Superior, res same.

Anderson Lillian A, domestic 251 W Main.

Anderson Matilda, bds 448 Lafayette.

Anderson Olga, seamstress, bds 448 Lafayette.

Anderson Peter, hammersmith Bass F & M Wks, res 300 E Washington.

Anderson Peter, machinist, res 448 Lafayette.

Anderson Philip A, clerk, bds 5 Bass.

Anderson Robert E, machinist, res 43 Lasselle.

Anderson Thorwald A, bds 448 Lafayette

Anderson Wm E, laborer, bds 94 Franklin av.

Anderson Wm W, laborer, res 94 Franklin av.

Anderson Wilson D, bds 51 Hendricks.

Anderton Mrs Alma D, bds 70 Douglas av.

Andofer George, laborer, res 139 W 3rd.

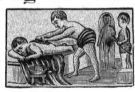

Andre Amelia M, clk T H McCormick, bds 127 Harrison.
Andrew David, died August 5, 1894.
Andrew Jeannette, bds 201 Barr.
Andrew Lizzie, milliner, 311¼ W Main, bds 201 Barr.
Andrew Nancy (wid David), res 201 Barr.
Andrews Annie, waitress The Randall.
Andrews Cary, res 290 E Lewis.
Andrews James, condr Ft W E Ry Co, res No 42 Clay.
Andrews James C, boilermkr, res 592 Calhoun.
Andrews John, Resident Manager Ft Wayne City
  Directory, 38 Bass Blk, res 109 Edgewater av.
Andrews L Richmond, carpenter, bds 37 Eliza.
Andrews Reginald J, bds 109 Edgewater av.
Andrews Reynolds E, clerk, res Lake av nr Crescent av.
Andrick Elizabeth, domestic Theresa Swinney.
Andrus Cora A, bds 78 Douglas av.
Andrus George H, engineer, res 78 Douglas av.
Angelbeck Augusta, domestic 48 Brackenridge.
Angell Byron D, res 242 W Berry.
Angell John J, res 12 Pape av.
Angell Mary C (wid Orange), res 166 W Berry.
Angevine George E, blksmith, 35 Pearl, res 20 Miner.
Angevine Wm E (Kretsinger & Angevine), res 82 Force.
Angove Arthur C (Princess Cash Store), res 216 W Wayne.
Angove Arthur C jr (Princess Cash Store), bds 216 W
  Wayne.
Angove Arthur C and Arthur C Jr,
  Proprs Princess Cash Store, 111 Calhoun.
Angove James H, cashier Princess Cash Store, bds 216 W
  Wayne.
Angst Anna, opr S M Foster, bds 56 Madison.
Angst Joseph B, clk Root & Co, bds 56 Madison.
Angst Kate, opr S M Foster, bds 56 Madison.
Angst Theresa (wid Lenhart), res 56 Madison.
Ankenbruck Benjamin, appr H C Franke & Son, bds
  30 Erie.
Ankenbruck Frank M, saloon, 267 E Wayne, res same.
Ankenbruck John B, carpenter, res 249 E Wayne.
Ankenbruck Joseph T (Hartman & Ankenbruck), res
  30 Erie.
Ankenbruck Louis, driver People's Store, bds 172 Harmer.
Ankenbruck Martin H (Ankenbruck & Potthoff), res 126
  E Washington.
Ankenbruck & Potthoff (Martin H Ankenbruck, Wm Pott-
  hoff), grocers, 126 E Washington. Tel 100.

Annie Besant Theosophical Society, Ninde Blk.
Anstett George B, driver F S Tinkham, res 22 Burgess.
Anthony Joseph A, res 108 Jackson.
Anthony Lydia A (wid Abraham), res 68 Gay.
Anthony Senes S, bartender, bds 42 W Main.
Anthony Wayne Mnfg Co The, John Rhinesmith Pres, James H Simonson Sec-Treas, A C F Wichman Supt, Mnfrs Washing Machines, s w cor Lafayette and Wabash R R. Tel 27.
Antrup Frederick W, res 79 W Main.
Antseidel Adam, blacksmith Olds' Wagon Wks, res 69 Stophlet.
Anweiler George W, mach hd Penn Co, bds 172 Ewing.
Anweiler Wm G, helper Wabash R R, res 166 W Creighton av.
Apollo Musical Library, 97½ Calhoun.
App, see also Happ.
App Anna, bds 104 W Washington.
App Blk, 106 Calhoun.
App Bros (Henry J and George J), shoe mnfrs, 46 W Main.
App Clement P, clk Matthias App, bds 104 W Washington.
App George J (App Bros), res 318 E Washington.
App Henry J (App Bros), res 362 E Washington.
App Martin, pressman The Journal, res 360 E Washington.
App Matthias, shoes, 106 Calhoun, res 104 W Washington.
Applegate Bergen W, city editor Ft Wayne Sentinel, res 22 E Butler.
Arantz Emma, bds 58 E Washington.
Arantz Philip, res 58 E Washington.
Arantz Simon P, car repr Penn Co, res 447 Lafayette.
Arcade Bldg, 9–17 W Berry.
Arcade Music Store, I H Case Mngr, Pianos and Organs, 2–6 Arcade. Tel 306.
Archbold Chellis H, clk E B Archbold, bds 114 Richardson.
Archbold Ezra B, grocer, 114 Richardson, res same.
Archbold Julia A, domestic 270½ Calhoun.
Archbold Maurice J, lab Ft Wayne Electric Corp, bds 114 Richardson.
Archer Carl W, stripper, bds 74 South Wayne av.
Archer Charles E, mngr Archer Printing Co, res 213 Wells.
Archer David L, lab S Bash & Co, res 45 2nd.
Archer Fred R, bds 45 2nd.
Archer John H, real estate, res 35 Putnam.
Archer J Frank, fireman Penn Co, res 297 Harrison.

WM. MILLER,
BRICK MANUFACTURER.

**OFFICE AND WORKS, East Side of Hanna St.,
South of City Limits,**

Fort Wayne,   -   Ind.

ALVIN MARTIN,

Livery, Sale, Boarding
And Feed Stable.

Rigs at Reasonable Rates.
Sample Wagons for Commercial Men.

CLINTON ST., N. E. Cor. Nickel Plate
Railroad.

Fort Wayne, Ind.

CHRISTIAN J. ULMER,
PROPRIETOR OF THE

Belmont Stables.
LIVERY,

New and Latest Improved 'Bus, **The Belmont,** for Excursions,
Parties, Etc., Seating Ten Couples.

SALE AND BOARDING.

83 E. Main St., near Barr.   FORT WAYNE, IND.

William Ruchel,
General Carpenter,

BUILDER AND
CONTRACTOR.

Estimates Furnished upon
application.
Jobbing Promptly Attended to.

Shop and Residence :

209 East Lewis St ,

FORT WAYNE,   ,   -   -   INDIANA.

Archer Mary J, dressmaker, bds 176 Huffman.

Archer Mary L, clk Archer Printing Co, bds 35 Putnam.

Archer Olive E, bkkpr Archer Ptg Co, bds 35 Putnam.

Archer Perry J (Coverdale & Archer), res 75 Wells.

Archer Printing Co, Charles E Archer Mngr, W Sherman Archer Supt, Printers and Publishers, 82 Clinton. Tel 55.

Archer W Sherman, supt Archer Printing Co, res 74 South Wayne av.

Archibald Abraham F, clk Wabash R R, res 27 Hanna.

Archibald James L, trimmer Olds' Wagon Wks, bds 312 E Creighton av.

Arehart James R, engr N Y, C & St L R R, res 296 W Main.

Arens Bernard, mach hd Standard Wheel Co, res 90 John.

Arens Catherine, opr S Freiburger & Bro, bds 90 John.

Arens Henry, lab L Rastetter & Son, bds 90 John.

Arens Herman, bellowsmkr Ft Wayne Organ Co, res 330 Force.

Arens Herman J, bellowsmaker, bds 90 John.

Arens John, res 124 Madison.

Arens Mary, trimmer S Freiburger & Bro, bds 90 John.

Arens Matilda (wid Anton), res 330 Force.

Argerbright James M, clk Pickard Bros, res 213 E Wayne.

Arieon, *see also Irion.*

Arieon James L, wheelmaker, res 10 Locust.

Arieon Louis, bricklayer, res 10 Locust.

Arion Hall, cor Main and Harrison.

Arlington Hotel, M S Wickliffe Propr, 107 and 109 E Columbia.

Armack Benjamin J, gang foreman Penn Co, res 18 Hough.

Armack Dorothea (wid Albert A), bds 73 W Jefferson.

Armack Frederick W, mach Ft Wayne Iron Wks, bds 221 Lafayette.

Armbruster Lawrence, laborer, res 136 Horace.

Armel Charles C, carpenter, res 95 Wagner.

Armel Walter, mach hd Paul Mnfg Co, res 24 Wagner.

Armel Wm H, switchman, res 479 Lafayette.

Armfield John C, trav agt The W L Carnahan Co, rms 24 W Berry.

Armstrong Charles E, laborer, bds 11 Marion.

Armstrong Emma L, teacher Clay School, bds 113 W Wayne.

Armstrong Franklin, laborer, bds 17 Wabash av.

Armstrong James, rms 63 W Superior.

Armstrong James A, (James A Armstrong & Co), rms 115 E Berry. Tel 474.

The accompanying cut represents the RAYON, a Sketching Camera for Artists, set up in position for making an enlarged sketch from any photograph or object that can be placed inside of the Camera.

The RAYON can also be used for Sketching from nature, for making Bromide Prints from any photograph for Magic Lantern purposes and for making your own Lantern Slides from any other slide, or from a Photograph, negative or any object. We make different styles at $6.00, $10.00. $12.00, and $25.00. Artists in Fort Wayne and vicinity are invited to call at our office, 16 West Columbia street, up stairs, and make a sketch from any photograph free of charge. JENNE CAMERA MANUFACTURING CO.,

FORT WAYNE,   -   -   INDIANA.

JOHN H. JOHNSON,
CONTRACTOR OF ALL KINDS OF
Artificial Stone Work,
Sidewalks and Basement Floors.
Coping for Lawns and Curbing for Streets.
ESTIMATES FURNISHED FREE.

FORT WAYNE,   -   INDIANA.

LOUIS F. HORSTMAN,
MANUFACTURER OF
BUGGY TOPS,
BOOTS, TOE PADS, STORM APRONS,
CUSHIONS, DASHES, ETC.
No. 9 East Superior Street,

Fort Wayne,   -   Ind.

J. F. FLETCHER,
LIVERY,
SALE, AND
Boarding Stable.
A Great Variety of Turnouts Always Ready.

32 BARR STREET.

FORT WAYNE, IND.

Armstrong James A & Co, (James A Armstrong, Charles T Pidgeon, W S Turner), whol millinery 31–35 W Berry. Tel 474.

Arneson Julia, bds 405 W Main.

Arney Sarah J, bds 225 E Wayne.

Arnold Anthony, cabinetmaker, res 478 Harrison.

Arnold Anthony A, Mach Bass F & M Wks, bds 478 Harrison.

Arnold David A, cabinetmkr Ft Wayne Furn Co, res 444 Lafayette.

Arnold Emma, bds 135 Broadway.

Arnold Emma A, bds 478 Harrison.

Arnold Harry A, trav agt Klotz & Haller, bds 478 Harrison.

Arnold Henry, res 176 W Jefferson.

Arnold James H, car repr Penn Co, res 138 Shawnee av.

Arnold John J, expressman, res 200 E Washington.

Arnold Lizzie, domestic 286 W Wayne.

Arnold Mary E, clk J O Seibert, bds 200 E Washington.

Arnold Montgomery, bds 176 W Jefferson.

Arnold Scott E, waiter Ft Wayne Club, rms 56 E Main.

Arnold Sophia, domestic 39 W Washington.

Arnold Wilhelmina, (wid Clements), forelady Wayne Knitting Mills, res 29 Boone.

Arns, *see Arens.*

Arp Charles, sausagemaker Fred Eckart Packing Co, bds 250 E Wayne.

Arter Ephraim, teamster David Tagtmeyer, res s w cor High and Franklin av.

Arter Joseph, teamster David Tagtmeyer, res 51 Oakley.

Artis George (col'd), waiter, res 31 Pearl.

Artis Susan (col'd), laundress, res 49 Hayden.

Ash Emma L, bds 104 E Main.

Ash Frederick H, clk H J Ash, bds 104 E Main.

Ash Henry J, Wholesale and Retail Stoves, Tinners' Stock, Tinware and Hardware, 16 E Columbia, res 104 E Main, Tel 142.

Ash Ida C, res 288 E Wayne.

Ash James W, clerk, bds 288 E Wayne.

Ash Lillian G, bds 104 E Main.

Ash Louella F, bkkpr H J Ash, bds 104 E Main.

Ashley Joseph, clerk, bds 28 Scott av.

Ashley Joseph, laborer Ft Wayne Electric Corp, bds 24 Scott av.

Ashley Leona, bds 28 Scott av.

Askins Verna, bds 108 W De Wald.
Astry George A, dep State Commander K O T M, res 232 Fairfield av.
Astry Jonas, car J M Henry, res 54 Hendricks.
Atchison Millard F, barber, 131 Buchanan, res same.
Atkins Harry, brakeman, bds 20 Cass.
Atkinson Elizabeth (wid John), res 93 Gay.
Atterbury Wm W, master mechanic Penn Co, res 122 E Main.
Atwood Jesse A, miller City Mills, rms 58 W Berry.
Aubrey Alfred J (Aubrey Bros), res 56 Thomas.
Aubrey Bros (Alfred J and John J), grocers, 56 Thomas.
Aubrey Frank J, meats, 129 Buchanan, bds 34 Smith.
Aubrey John J (Aubrey Bros), bds 136 Horace.
Aubrey Joseph W, lab, res 2 rear Leikauf's Packing House.
Aubry Joseph J, mach hd Rhinesmith & Simonson, res 17 Hough.
Auer Charles H, clerk, bds 17 Nirdlinger av.
Auer Conrad, wiper Penn Co. res 17 Nirdlinger av.
Auer Daniel, laborer, res 108 Wells.
Auer Daniel jr, tailor, bds 108 Wells.
Auer Emma, bds 17 Nirdlinger av.
Auer Frank X, bartender, J M Himbert, bds 108 Wells.
Auer George, tinner, bds 108 Wells.
Auer George C, conductor, bds 17 Nirdlinger av.
Auer Jacob, mach hd Olds' Wagon Wks, res 49 E Williams.
Auer John, laborer, res w s Walton av 3 s of Pontiac.
Auer John H, bartender J H Auth, bds 108 Wells.
Auer John R, lab Penn Co, res n s New Haven av 2 e of Pioneer av.
Auer Louis J, slater, bds w s Lumbard 3 n of Chestnut.
Auer Sophie, bds 108 Wells.
Auer Wm H, brakeman, bds 17 Nirdlinger av.
Auger Bird L, clk B L Auger, bds 16 E Washington.
Auger Blk, 65 E Main.
Auger B Louis, Florist, 16 E Washington, res same.
Auger Charles M, florist, res 453 E Wayne.
Aumann Charles, laborer, res 28 Orchard.
Aumann Charles W, clk Louis Wolf & Co, bds 16 Orchard.
Aumann Conrad F, mach hd Penn Co, res 118 Gay.
Aumann Henry E W, lab Ft Wayne Elecric Corp, bds 16 Orchard.
Aumann Henry F (Gerding & Aumann Bros), bds 118 Gay.
Aumann Lizzie C, dressmaker, bds 16 Orchard.

Aumann Lizzie M, clk Root & Co, bds 28 Orchard.
Aumann Louis F. cigarmaker F J Gruber, bds 118 Gay.
Aumann Louise A, bds 118 Gay.
Aumann Minnie P, dressmaker, bds 118 Gay.
Aumann Wm, res 16 Orchard.
Aumann Wm H (Gerding & Aumann Bros), res 123 John.
Aumann Wm H F, bkkpr J B White, bds 16 Orchard.
Aumick Jesse D, brakeman Penn Co, bds 206 Walton av.
Aurentz Anna P, bds 129 W Main.
Aurentz Augustus C, confectioner, 109 Calhoun, bds 129 W Main.
Aurentz Emma S, bds 129 W Main.
Aurentz Frank W, clerk, bds 129 W Main.
Aurentz Robert J, clk S A Aurentz, bds 129 W Main.
Aurentz Skelly P, clk S A Aurentz, bds 129 W Main.
Aurentz Solomon A, grocer, 31 W Main, res 129 same.
Austin Birdie M, teacher, bds 72 Brackenridge.
Austin Carrie M, clk W B Phillips, bds 275 Webster.
Austin Clarence R, laborer, bds 27 Grand.
Austin Daniel S, teacher Adams Twp School No 3, res 156 Horace.
Austin Emma N, bds 72 Brackenridge.
Austin E Jennie (wid Hieronymus B), res 72 Brackenridge.
Austin Frank, boilercleaner Cook A B C Co, bds 72 Brackenridge.
Austin Harry E, laborer, bds 27 Grand.
Austin Louise M (wid John C), res 27 Grand.
Austin Nellie M, bds 27 Grand.
Auth Catherine (wid Peter), res 23 W 4th.
Auth John H, saloon, 138 Calhoun, res 123 W Washington.
Auth Joseph, brakeman N Y, C & St L R R, bds 23 W 4h.
Auth Veronica, domestic 181 W Wayne.
Avels Mrs Mary, attendant School for Feeble-Minded Youth.
Avery Frederick S, rms 70 Harrison.
Avis John W, motorman, res 110 Grant av.
Axt August W, res e s Abbott 1 s of Pontiac.
Axt Charles W, molder Bass F & M Wks, res 154 E Lewis.
Axt Moritz, res 129 Francis.
Axt Wm H, car repr Penn Co, res 212 Madison.
Ayers George F, clk Bowersock & Gooden, bds 6 Pape av.
Ayers Gertrude, teacher, bds 6 Pape av.
Ayers Glenn, clk Root & Co, bds 108 South Wayne av.
Ayers Philip G, traveling agt, res 108 South Wayne av.

B

Baade, *see also Bade.*
Baade Christian, res e s Broadway 1½ miles s city limits.
Baade Ernst, car bldr Penn Co, res 69 Hugh.
Baade Fred C, clk Ft Wayne Gas Co, res 261 E Jefferson.
Baade Frederick H, ice, 129 Broadway, res 7 Huestis av.
Baade Henry, car repairer, res 17 Barthold.
Baade Henry C (Kayser & Baade), res 157 Broadway.
Baade Henry F, clk V Gutermuth, bds 17 Barthold.
Baade Lizzie C, bds 263 E Jefferson.
Baade Martha, clk Kayser & Baade, bds 157 Broadway.
Baade Martin W, bds Christian Baade.
Baade Sophia, bds Christian Baade.
Baade Wm, truckman, res 263 E Jefferson.
Baade Wm C, stamp clerk P O, res 251 E Jefferson.
Baals August (Baals & Co), res 94 W Main.
Baals Clara H, bds 94 W Main.
Baals Emma A. nurse, bds 302 W Jefferson.
Baals Metha M, bds 94 W Main.
Baals Mina A, clk A Mergentheim, bds 302 W Jefferson.
Baals Robert F, clk Baals & Co, bds 94 W Main.
Baals Rosanna (wid John L), res 302 W Jefferson.
Baals Sadie C, clerk, bds 302 W Jefferson.
Baals Wm G, farmer, res 110 Home av.
Baals & Co (August Baals), furniture storage, 59 E Main.
Baatz Ernest J, laborer, res 68 Hendricks.
Baatz Wm, polisher, bds 68 Hendricks.
Babb Carl H, foreman A Kalbacher, bds 263 Calhoun.
Babcock Edwin B, car repr Penn Co, res 23 Oak.
Babcock Mary (wid John F), res w s Harrison 1 s of Butler.
Babcock Oliver L, laborer, res 68 Charles.
Babcock Thomas Z, mgr Ft Wayne Electric Corp, res 107 Fairfield av.
Babcock Wm H, bds 23 Oak.
Bach, *see also Beck.*
Bach John, car builder, Penn Co, bds 594 Lafayette.
Bach Susanna, died January 28, 1895.
Bachman Wm C, laborer Keller & Braun, res 78 Wall.
Bachon Joseph, bds 57 Barr.
Backes, *see also Beckes.*
Backes Jacob, boilermaker Penn Co, bds 30 E 3d.
Backes John J, boilermaker Penn Co, res 129 Wilt.
Backes Anna, bds 23 Nirdlinger av.
Backes Mrs Mary, res 23 Nirdlinger av.

MARTIN & FITZSIMMONS,

Merchant Tailors.

Suits to Order, $15.00 and Upwards.
Perfect Fit and Workmanship Guaranteed.
Cleaning and Repairing a Specialty.

172 West Jefferson St., FORT WAYNE, IND.

F. W. GRONAU,

Carriage *AND* Buggy Painter

No. 91 East Superior St.,

FORT WAYNE, INDIANA.

Greek Candy Manufactory,

Wholesale and Retail Manufacturer of the

Greek and Russian Candy, French Chewing Candy, Turkish Nougat, Peanut, Cocoanut, Etc.

Also, a Full Line of Chocolate and Cream Bonbons and Fine Caramels
Made Fresh Every Day.

Fine Ice Cream Parlor ! Ice Cream Soda Water, Milk Shake. Lemonade Etc. A Full Line of Cigars kept
A. KUTCHE, Propr, 154 Calhoun St. constantly on hand.

JOHN A. WATKINS,

Carpenter and Builder!

JOBBING PROMPTLY ATTENDED TO.

200 Broadway, - Fort Wayne, Ind.

Backes Wm. boilermaker Penn Co. bds 129 Wilt.

Backman, *see Beckman.*

Bacome Frank E, foreman Aldine Printing House, res 113 Lafayette.

Bacon Adeline E, bds 241 W Washington.

Bacon Frederick, opr Wayne Knitting Mills, bds 14 Runnion av.

Bacon Leonora J, domestic s w cor Allen and Webster.

Bade, *see also Baade.*

Bade Frederick, truckman B W Skelton Co, res 21 Pine.

Bade Minnie, domestic 157 W Wayne.

Bade Wm C F, sawyer Hoffman Bros, res 162 W 3rd.

Badiac Eva J, stenographer, bds 63 Elizabeth.

Badiac Josephine E, bds 63 Elizabeth.

Badiac Louis T, laborer, res 63 Elizabeth.

Badker Sarah, domestic 126 E Berry.

Baer, *see also Baier, Bair, Bayer, Bear, Beyer and Boyer.*

Baer Alvin E, engr N Y, C & St L R R, res 323 W Washington.

Baer August J, tailor J H Grimme & Sons, res 40 Oak.

Baer Bertha, bds 323 W Washington.

Baer Essie C, opr S M Foster, bds 401 Barr.

Baer Frances J, opr S M Foster, bds 401 Barr.

Baer Joseph G, actionmkr Ft Wayne Organ Co, bds 401 Barr.

Baer Mary (wid George J), res 401 Barr.

Baer Mary E, milliner, bds 401 Barr.

Baer Wm M, cabinetmkr, bds 401 Barr.

Bagby Albert L, res 85 W Superior.

Bahlinger Karl, mach Penh Co, res 339 Lafayette.

Bahr Minnie, domestic 76 E Butler.

Bahret, *see also Barrett.*

Bahret Christian, mach Ft Wayne Electric Corp, res 38 James.

Baier, *see also Baer, Bair, Bayer, Bear, Beyer and Boyer.*

Baier John N, mach hd Rhinesmith & Simonson, res 67 Rockhill.

Bail Anthony, mach hd Rhinesmith & Simonson, bds 198 Reed.

Bail Emily, seamstress, bds 198 Reed.

Bail Joseph, carp Rhinesmith & Simonson, res 198 Reed.

Bail Joseph F, turner Anthony Wayne Mnfg Co, bds 198 Reed.

Bailer Jacob (Jacob Bailer & Son), res 38 Maumee rd.

Bailer Jacob & Son (Jacob and Samuel), grocers, 38 Maumee rd.

H. A. TARMON,
Contractor & Builder.

JOB WORK PROMPTLY ATTENDED TO.

LEAVE ORDERS AT CHICAGO BAKERY.

Residence 83 E. Wayne St.
Shop No. 191 Brackenridge St.

Fort Wayne,   -   Indiana.

JOSEPH METKER,

CONTRACTOR FOR PLAIN AND ORNAMENTAL
PLASTERING.

Contracts Taken Complete. Twenty-Eight years Experience.
CORRESPONDENCE SOLICITED.

Rear of Washington and   Fort Wayne, Indiana.
Comparet Streets,

Misses Smalley & Allison,
Fashionable
DRESSMAKING.

206 W. Washington Street,   Fort Wayne, Ind.

9

Bailer Moritz, clk J Bailer & Son, bds 38 Maumee rd.
Bailer Samuel (Jacob Bailer & Son), bds 38 Maumee rd.
Bailey Alexander, lab Penn Co, res 157 Holman.
Bailey August, helper Penn Co, bds 157 Holman.
Bailey Elizabeth, bds 200 Broadway.
Bailey Frank, laborer, res n s Baltes av 5 e of Spy Run av.
Bailey Frank M, condr N Y, C & St L R R, res 120
    Greeley.
Bailey Harriet, bds 76 W Creighton av.
Bailey Isaac M, driver, res 110 Erie.
Bailey Josephine (wid Francis), bds 97 Wagner.
Bailey Millie B, domestic 330 W Washington.
Bailey Pearl S, messenger N Y, C & St L R R, bds 36
    Thomas.
Bailey Richard, bell boy New Aveline House.
Bailey Sylvanus, bds 110 Erie.
Bailey T Emanuel, printer, res 36 Baker.
Baillie Andrew, hoseman Hose Co No 5, rms same.
Baillie George S, mach Ft Wayne Electric Corp, bds 166
    Jackson.
Baillie Helen J, presser Hoosier Mnfg Co, bds 166 Jackson.
Baillie John D, blksmith Wabash R R, res 166 Jackson.
xBaillie John W, blksmith Wabash R R, res 22 Huestis av.
Baillie Thomas S, engr N Y, C & St L R R, bds 166
    Jackson.
Baily Alpheus H, harnessmaker, res 98 Wagner.
Baily Ella F, bds 98 Wagner.
Baily Frank C, stereotyper, bds 98 Wagner.
Baily James A, printer, res 104 Madison.
Bain John E, driver F L Jones & Co, rms 94 W Main.
Bainbridge Wm K, foreman Kerr Murray Mnfg Co, bds
    Windsor Hotel.
Bair, *see also* Baer Baier, Bayer, Bear, Beyer and Boyer.
Bair Allen, harnessmaker, 134 Broadway, res same.
yBair Cora I, bds 81 Home av.
Baird Clarence H, express messenger, bds 301 Calhoun.
Baird Julius W, died September 21, 1894.
Baird Sarah L (wid Julius W), res 386 Calhoun.
Baker, *see also* Becker.
Baker Agnes C, bds 98 E Main.
Baker Albert, rms 295 W Wayne.
Baker Alice, dressmaker, rms 302 Hoagland av.
Baker Ambrose C, Mnfr of Fine Havana Cigars ;
    Brands—"Electric Spark" 10c ; "Red Seal," "Jim
    and Fatty" 5c ; 31 E Main, res 10 Baker av.

H. C. FRANKE & SON

PRACTICAL

Sanitary Plumbers,
Steam ✼ Gas Fitters

Contracts taken complete.
Estimates cheerfully furnished
upon application.
Correspondence solicited.
Also Water Works and Sewer-
age.

**Jobbing Promptly
Attended To.**

Old Water Works Office,   **68 BARR STREET.**

A New Process for Cleaning Clothes.

✼ **GUST. SCHUBERT** ✼

ELECTRICAL DYER

The Only Place Like It in the Country.

Ladies' Silk or Woolen Dresses, Curtains,
Blankets, Ostrich Plumes, Etc., Cleaned
and Pressed. Gentlemen's Clothing
Cleaned. Dyed, Pressed and Repaired.

**No. 65 EAST MAIN ST.,
FORT WAYNE, IND.**

FREDERICK KORTE.
WILLIAM H KORTE.

KORTE & SON,
GENERAL

Contractors and Builders

PUBLIC BUILDINGS AND RESIDENCES,
(Wood, Stone or Brick.)
BRIDGES AND CISTERNS
Estimates cheerfully furnished.
Give us your bid.
Jobbing promptly attended to.
Office and Shop. 65 MAUMEE AVE.,
Fort Wayne, Ind.

Baker Amelia E, bds 139 Clinton.
Baker Andrew J, capt Engine No 5; res 41 Lavina.
Baker Benjamin A, driver L H McAfee, res 62 W 5th.
Baker Barnard H, wagonmaker, 18 Lafayette, res 139 Clinton.
Baker Clara L, domestic 211 W Berry.
Baker Claud F, printer Ft Wayne Gazette, res 18 Wagner.
Baker C Lewis, carpenter, res 134 E Taber.
Baker Edward J, blacksmith, bds 139 Clinton.
Baker Eldon S, printer The Journal, bds 274 Hoagland av.
Baker Frank D, motorman Ft W E Ry Co, res 104 E Wayne.
Baker Frank J, res 75 W De Wald.
Baker George, laborer, bds 62 W 5th.
Baker Grace L, bds 134 E Taber.
Baker Henry F, carp Wiegmann & Franke, res 3 Jones.
Baker Henry J, electrician, res 157 E Wayne.
Baker Ira, molder Kerr Murray Mnfg Co, bds Windsor Hotel.
Baker Isaac W, car bldr Penn Co, res 102 W Butler.
Baker Jacob, res St Joseph boulevard nr Baker av.
Baker John, res 139 Clinton.
Baker John, roofer, res 18 Lasselle.
Baker John G, lumberman, res 347 E Wayne.
Baker Jonas E, carp, res s e cor Leith and Harrison.
Baker Joseph J, cashier U S Express Co, res 128 E Main.
Baker Joseph L, saloon, 34 E Columbia, res same.
Baker Josiah C M, ticket recr Penn Co, res 636 Calhoun.
Baker Kilian, Mnfr Hardwood Lumber and Wagon Stock, cor E Superior and Lafayette, res 92 E Main.
Baker Lawrence A, cigarmkr, A C Baker, bds 10 Baker av.
Baker Mrs Lillie, attendant School for Feeble-Minded Youth.
Baker Maggie, bds 10 Baker av.
Baker Margaret A, bds 92 E Main.
Baker Mary, domestic 92 W Jefferson.
Baker Mary J (wid Henry), res 10 Baker av.
Baker Melvin C, District Passenger and Ticket Agt N Y, C & St L R R, bds 24 W Berry.
Baker Nellie A, bds 10 Baker av.
Baker Noah A, lab Ft Wayne Electric Corp, res 48 W Leith.
Baker Rosella M, bds 92 E Main.
Baker Thomas J, attendant School for Feeble-Minded Youth.

SCHONE & VEITH,

Undertakers AND

Embalmers.

Calls attended to Day or Night.

53 E. Berry St.

[Aldine Block.]

FORT WAYNE, IND.

TELEPHONES:
Office, 837, Residence, 304.

Mrs. L. A. Hauss,

Ladies' Hair Dressing

Parlors.

Shampooing and Children's Hair
Cutting a Specialty.

Fashionable Dress and Cloak Making.

105-107 Broadway,

Fort Wayne, Indiana.

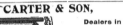

CARTER & SON,

Dealers in

Hot Air

Furnaces,

Mantels of Tile,

Wood, Slate and Iron.

Tile Facings and

Vestibules.

29 CLINTON ST.,

Fort Wayne, Ind,

Baker Vincent J, plumber A Hattersley & Sons, bds 17 Ross.
Bakofen Julius G, lab Horton Mnfg Co, res w s St Mary's av 2 n of Lake.
Baldock Harry C, bds 150 Fulton.
Baldock Lida, res 21 Eliza.
Baldock Wm R, printer, Fort Wayne News, res 150 Fulton.
Baldwin D H & Co, Philemon Dickinson Mngr, Pianos, Organs and Musical Merchandise, 98 Calhoun. (*See p 93.*)
Baldwin Elbert D, bookkeeper, bds 189 W Berry.
Baldwin Frances H (wid Elbert D), res 189 W Berry.
Baldwin George H, switchman, res 210 W Superior.
Baldwin John, coachman 122 W Wayne.
Baldwin Mrs Mary, res 170 Greeley.
Baldwin Merchant H, train dispatcher N Y, C & St L R R, res 189 W Berry.
Baldy Jacob T, laborer, bds 4 Mary.
Bales Charles H, trav agt S Bash & Co, bds 31 Cass.
Ball, *see also Boll.*
Ball Emma, bds 172 W Main.
Ball Magdalena (wid Rudolph), res 172 W Main.
Ballard Levi, painter Penn Co, res 212 E Jefferson.
Ballinger Rev Amos W, pastor First United Brethren Church, res 292 E Lewis.
Ballmann, *see also Bolman.*
Ballmann Carrie, bds 28 Nirdlinger av.
Ballmann Catherine M, bds 28 Nirdlinger av.
Ballmann Francis J, res 28 Nirdlinger av.
Ballou Lillie, student, rms 43 W Lewis.
Balsiger Gottfried, coremkr Bass F & M Wks, res 19 Guthrie.
Baltes, *see also Boltz.*
Baltes Clara A, bds 57 W Berry.
Baltes Edward M, mngr Western Lime Co, 3 Harrison, bds 57 W Berry.
Baltes Jacob, contractor, res cor Spy Run av and Wagner.
Baltes John, bricklayer, res 67 Force.
Baltes Michael, res 57 W Berry. Tel 417.
Baltes Peter P, bricklayer, res St Joseph boulevard nr Baker av.
Balthasar Louis, reporter Freie Presse, bds 154 Harrison.
Baltzell Dayton, st car conductor, res 36 Walton av.
Balzer Charles, laborer, bds 213 Hayden.
Balzer Louis, engr N Y, C & St L R R, res 193 W Superior.

Balzer Rose, bds 162 Hayden.
Balzer Valentine, laborer, res 213 Hayden.
Balzer Valentine, watchman, res 162 Hayden.
Banard John, carpenter, res 121 Gay.
Bandau Frederick, watchman Penn Co, res 27 Pritchard.
Bandau Henry C, lab Ft Wayne Electric Corp, bds 27 Pritchard.
Baudau Theodore C, boilermaker, bds 27 Pritchard.
Bandelier August, laborer Penn Co, res 17 Gay.
Bandil Nancy, died August 16, 1894.
Bandt Frederick W, cigarmkr Kasten & Kohlmeyer, bds 87 W De Wald.
Bandt Frederick W, contractor, 87 W De Wald, res same.
Bandtel George F, clk Pfeiffer & Schlatter, res 358 E Wayne.
Bandweg Gustave, laborer, res 27 Smith.
Bandweg Wm, laborer, bds 27 Smith.
Banet Alexander E, watchman, res 55 E Columbia.
Banet Louis E, saloon, 72 E Columbia, res 11 Riverside av.
Baugert Bonifacius, grocer, 34 Fairfield av, res same.
Baugert Clara, bds 34 Fairfield av.
Baugert Joseph, bds 34 Fairfield av.
Banister Euretta C, teacher Clay School, bds 49 W Berry.
Banister Mrs L Webb, Principal Banister School of Music, 49 W Berry, res same. Tel 540.
Banister School of Music, Mrs L Webb Banister Principal, 49 W Berry. Tel 540.
Bank Blk, W Main s e cor Court.
Banks Creed T, physician, res 219 W Washington.
Banks Elmer E, letter carrier P O, res 39 2d.
Banks Harvey S, bds 219 W Washington.
Banks Homer M, removed to Chicago, Ill.
Banks Ollie, bds 28 Chicago.
Bante, see Bente.
Barnum Selina (wid George), res cor St Joe Gravel rd and Charlotte av.
Barber Asphalt Paving Co The, J M Wright superintendent, 7 and 9 Vordermark Bldg.
Barber Harlow E, fireman Penn Co, res 26 E Butler.
Barber Wm H, brakeman, res 29 Charles.
Barbier Alfred, painter Penn Co, res s s Maumee rd 1 e of Lumbard.
Barbier George, baker L P Scherer, bds 260 E Wayne.
Barbour Dolly S, bds 132 E Berry.

Barbour George K, mach Penn Co, res 365 Lafayette.
Barbour Myron F, res 90 E Berry.
Barcus Edith M, bds 238 Calhoun.
Barcus Ira O, canvasser, res 168 W De Wald.
Barcus Henry H, Baker and Wholesale Manufacturing Confectioner, 238 Calhoun, res same. Tel 535.
Bard Samuel, res 39¼ W Berry.
Barden Wm N, engr Penn Co, res 28 W Creighton av.
Bargain Store The, Wm Rockhill propr, s w cor Harrison and Main.
Bargdill George R, clk J A Armstrong & Co, bds 220 W Wayne.
Barhand Augusta, domestic 96 W Berry.
Barlow Mrs Jennie, res 361 W Main.
Barman Wm, boilermaker, res 65 Oliver.
Barnard, *see Bernard.*
Barner Addie H, bds 155 Montgomery.
Barner Charles F, patternmkr Bass F & M Wks, res 155 Montgomery.
Barner Emma K, dressmaker, bds 155 Montgomery.
Barner Henry C, tinsmith H J Ash, res 153 Montgomery.
Barner Lillian L, bds 155 Montgomery.
Barnes Charles A, fireman N Y, C & St L R R, res 436 W Main.
Barnes Charles E, boltmkr Penn Co, res 12 Fox.
Barnes Edward A, chief inspr Ft Wayne Electric Corp, bds The Wayne.
Barnes Frank J, collector, bds 165 E Lewis.
Barnes Georgianna E (wid Edward R), bds The Wayne.
Barnes James W, res 21 Archer av.
Barnes Joseph, lather, res 165 E Lewis.
Barnes Joseph L, lather, bds 159 Hanna.
Barnes Wm, lather, bds 165 E Lewis.
Barnett Abraham G (Powers & Barnett), res 18 E Wayne.
Barnett Byron H, transfer agt Powers & Barnett, bds 18 E Wayne.
Barnett Charles E, physician, 2 White Blk, bds 43 W De Wald.
Barnett James W, clk Powers & Barnett, bds 18 E Wayne.
Barnett Walter W, sec Ft Wayne College of Medicine; physician, 94 Calhoun, res 43 W De Wald. Tel 57.
Barney Arthur E, traveling agt, bds 51 W Berry.
Barnfield Dr John H, removed to Logansport, Ind.
Barr Ernest J, hostler G Seabold, bds same.
Barr Frank J, bds 22 W Main.

Barr Margaret E (wid Thomas J), removed to Kansas City, Mo.

Barr Mary A (wid Thomas), res 330 W Jefferson.

Barr St Market House, s e cor Barr and Berry.

Barr Wm J, grocer, 32 W Main, res 63 W De Wald. Tel 547.

Barrand Eugene J, lather, bds 106 Riverside av.

Barrand John B, supt L Diether & Bro, res 30 Oak.

Barrand Frank, lather, res 106 Riverside av.

Barrand Julian L, lather, bds 106 Riverside av.

Barrand Mary F, bds 106 Riverside av.

Barrand Peter J, lather, bds 106 Riverside av.

Barrett, *see also Bahret.*

Barrett Florence (F Barrett & Co), bds 409 W Main.

Barrett Frederick C (F Barrett & Co), res 409 W Main.

Barrett F & Co (Florence and Frederick C Barrett), grocers, 380 W Main.

Barrett Harriet M (wid James), bds 20 Murray.

Barrett Isaiah, res 277 E Wayne.

Barrett James M (Morris, Bell, Barrett & Morris), sec Ft Wayne Electric Ry Co, res 255 Fairfield av.

Barrett John W, brakeman N Y, C & St L R R, res 337 W Main.

Barrey, *see also Barry.*

Barrey Frank L, laborer, bds 73 Gay.

Barrey John H, lab Standard Wheel Co, res 73 Gay.

Barron Lew W, clk M Frank & Co, res 181 Griffith.

Barrow Henry C, helper Penn Co, res 75 John.

Barrow John (Soliday & Barrow), res 71 E Main.

Barrows Frank R, photographer, 23 W Berry, res 242 W Wayne.

Barrows Lulu G, bds 242 W Wayne.

Barrows Raymond H, bds 242 W Wayne.

Barrus Timothy, contractor, 14 Winch, res same.

Barry, *see also Barrey.*

Barry Edward J, bell boy, bds 110 Hayden.

Barry Owen, hammerman Penn Co, res 110 Hayden.

Bartel Robert, with Keller, Edmunds & Law Electric Construction Co, bds St James Hotel.

Bartele Michael, physician, 207 E Jefferson, res same.

Bartels, *see also Bertels.*

Bartels Henry C, mach hd Standard Wheel Co, res 181 Gay.

Bartels Lizzie, domestic 281 Webster.

Bartels Mary (wid Wm), res 263 Gay.

Bartels Wm, lab Standard Wheel Co, bds 263 Gay.

Bartels Wm C, molder, res 58 Hayden.
Barth Cyrenius, coachman 130 W Berry.
Barthold Frederick L, insurance agt, res 80 Franklin av.
Bartholomew Frank P, stair builder Rhinesmith & Simonson, res 467 Lafayette.
Bartholomew Rillman, foreman Rhinesmith & Simonson, res 108 Wallace.
Bartlett Edward, switchman, bds Summit City Hotel.
Bartlett Laura E, seamstress, rms 205 Madison.
Bartley Frank, attendant School for Feeble-Minded Youth.
Barton Daniel, conductor, rms 30 Baker.
Barts Albert, car builder Penn Co, res 303 Lafayette.
Bartzell Marie, cook, bds 263 Calhoun.
Baschelier Christina (wid George), bds 366 W Main.
Base Christina (wid Amand) res 150 E Jefferson.
Base Frank, helper, bds 150 E Jefferson.
Basey Lizzie, dressmaker, rms 232 E Jefferson.
Bash Charles S, pres Mayflower Milling Co and Wayne Oil Tank Co and vice-pres S Bash & Co, res 280 W Wayne. Tel 148.
Bash Daniel F, sec S Bash & Co, res 24 W Berry.
Bash Harry E, genl mngr Mayflower Milling Co, bds 240 W Berry.
Bash Solomon, pres S Bash & Co, res 240 W Berry. Tel 10.
Bash S & Co, Solomon Bash Pres, Charles S Bash Vice-Pres, Daniel F Bash Sec, Peter D Smyser Treas, Produce and Commission, 22 and 24 W Columbia. Tel 63.
Bash Willis B, bds 240 W Berry.
Bash Winfield S, collector. res 183 W Berry. Tel 442.
Bashara Salem, notions, 43½ E Columbia, res same.
Bashelier Cora A (wid Philip), res 85 Cass.
Bashelier Frederick H, lab L Rastetter & Son, res 59 Walnut.
Basil Ida C, bur-cutter Keller Dental Co, bds 133 Holman.
Bass Blk, 73–77 Calhoun.
Bass Emma (col'd; wid Alfred), res 489 E Wayne.
Bass Foundry and Machine Works (Capital $500,000), John H Bass Pres, J I White Sec, R J Fisher Treas, Car Wheels, Railroad Ties and General Machinery, Hanna s of Wabash R, R. Tel 193.
Bass John H, pres Bass Foundry & Machine Wks, First National Bank, Ft Wayne Electric Ry Co and Star Iron Tower Co, res 113 W Berry. Tel 24.
Bass John H jr, bds 113 W Berry.

Bass Laura G. bds 113 W Berry.
Bass Ollie (col'd), domestic 18 W Washington.
Bass Wm H (col'd), shoemkr S Fischmann, res 489 E Wayne.
Bassett Cora A, stenographer, bds 109 Madison.
Bassett Elias (col'd), cook The Randall, res 43 Hayden.
Bassett Isaiah (col'd), cook The Randall, rms 71 Monroe.
Bassett John M, purchasing agent Standard Wheel Co, res 118 Jackson.
Bassett Wm O, mach Penn Co, res 109 Madison,
Bastian Ida C, domestic 14 Clay.
Bastian Jacob, driver L P Scherer, res 28 Lillie.
Bastues Christian (wid Michael), res 222 Hugh.
Bastues John M, molder Bass F & M Wks, res 399 E Lewis
Batchelder Jesse S, confectioner, 29 W Main, res 206 E Lewis.
Batchelder Jesse S jr, candymkr, bds 206 E Lewis.
Batchelder Katie M, clk J S Batchelder, bds 206 E Lewis.
Batchelder Nicholas, helper Penn Co, bds 206 E Lewis.
Bates Arthur, cook Wm Seidel & Bro, bds same.
Bates Christina, seamstress, bds 92 Summit.
Bates Eva G (wid Wm H), bds 409 Calhoun.
Bates Geary S, bds 156 E Taber.
Bates Henry L, stonecutter, res 129 W 3d.
Bates John F, agent, res 92 Summit.
Bates Lycurgus E, carp Penn Co, res 156 E Taber.
Bates Maggie, bds 156 E Taber.
Bates Mrs Sarah, domestic 54 W 4th.
Bates Theodore F, peddler, res 79 Winch.
Bates Will G, circulator Ft Wayne Gazette, res 41 E Berry.
Bathest J Henry, boilermkr Penn Co, res 13 Summit.
Batmann Martin, laborer, bds 137 Force.
Battenberg George F, carpenter, res 13 Elm.
Battershall Jennie, attendant School for Feeble-Minded Youth.
Baty Wm E, machine hand, res 224 W Superior.
Bauch Edward C, cabinetmaker, bds 203 Taylor.
Bauch Henry G, helper, bds 203 Taylor.
Bauch Oscar L, laborer, bds 203 Taylor.
Baucher Benjamin, teamster W H Brown, bds 73 Holman.
Bauer, *see also Bougher and Bower.*
Bauer Albertina (wid August), bds 85 Shawnee av.
Bauer Annie, bds 38 Douglas av.
Bauer Frederick, helper Fleming Mnfg Co, res 15 Pape av.
Bauer Henry, shoes, 321 Lafayette, res same.

Bauer John J, foreman Ft Wayne Electric Corp, res 232 W De Wald.

Bauer John J, molder, res 117 Force.

Bauer Joseph A, student, bds 38 Douglas av.

Bauer Kajetan J (Glutting, Bauer & Hartnett), res 38 Douglas av.

Bauer Mary L, bds 321 Lafayette.

Bauer Theodore, butcher Wilkens Bros, res 110 Richardson.

Bauer Tracy W, lab Ft Wayne Electric Corp, bds 232 W De Wald.

Baughman, *see also Bowman.*

Baughman Bert, engr N Y, C & St L R R, res 82 W 3d.

Baughman Eva M (wid Harvey M), teacher Hanna School, res 31 Charles.

Baughman Jeremiah S, carp Jacob Klett & Sons, res 63 W 4th.

Baughman John E, asst B H Mommer. res rear 63 W 4th.

Baughman Newton J, engineer, res 82 W 3d.

Baum Harry E, bds 121 Boone.

Baum Milton E, conductor, res 121 Boone.

Bauman Mrs Minnie, housekeeper 188 W De Wald.

Baumann Paul, dyer, res Spy Run av n e cor Baltes.

Baumann Sophia (wid John), bds 546 Calhoun.

Baumeister Charles, helper, rms 65 John.

Baumeister Frederick W, molder, res 65 John.

Baumeister Mary, domestic 94 Wells.

Baumgard Max, baker, res s s Eckart lane 2 e of Hanna.

Baumgartner Rev Samuel H, pastor Evangelical Assn, res n e cor Holman and Clinton.

Baumgratz Charles, brickmkr, res n s Boltz 1 e of Lafayette.

Baun Frederick J, blacksmith, res 3 Marion.

Baur Frederick, miller, res 65 High.

Baus Adam, lab L Rastetter & Son, bds 211 St Mary's av.

Baus Adam jr, laborer, bds 211 St Mary's av.

Baus Mrs Barbara, res 89 E Lewis.

Baus Hulda E, cutter S M Foster, bds 89 E Lewis.

Bauss Conrad, saloon, 91 John, res same.

Baxter Alexander M (Baxter & Tarmon), res 30 Columbia av.

Baxter Isabella, seamstress, bds 9 Emily.

Baxter James, mach Keller Dental Co, bds 9 Emily.

Baxter Joseph, electrician Jenney E L & P Co, res 7th s e cor Barr.

Baxter Lillian R, waitress 270½ Calhoun.

Baxter Phœbo (wid Joseph), res 9 Emily.
Baxter Thomas, chief engr Ft Wayne Water Wks, res 90 Wilt.
Baxter Witter F, Agt Connecticut Mutual Life Insurance Co of Hartford, Conn, 33 Bass Blk, bds 108 E Berry.
Baxter & Tarmon (Alexander M Baxter, Harry W Tarmon), machinists, 16 W Columbia.
Bayer, *see also Baer, Baier, Bair, Bear, Beyer and Boyer.*
Bayer Agnes, seamstress, bds 163 Hayden.
Bayer Bros (Frederick and John), horse collar mnfrs, 28 Clinton.
Bayer Charles, well digger, bds 43 Cass.
Bayer Charles C A, cigarmaker, res 28 Hanna.
Bayer Frederick (Bayer Bros), bds 34 Sherman.
Bayer Jacob, shoemaker, Lake av nr city limits, bds Wm E Miller.
Bayer John (Bayer Bros), bds 34 Sherman.
Bayer John M, carpet weaver, res 34 Sherman.
Bayer Joseph, laborer, res 163 Hayden.
Bayer Wm A, cigar mnfr, 98 W Main, res 94 same.
Bayha Lydia, teacher Westminister Seminary, bds 251 W Main.
Bayless Frank O, mach Ft Wayne Electric Corp, res 28 Stophlet.
Bayless Gustavus E, traveling agt, res 171 Van Buren.
Bayless Leah E (wid Gustavus), res 160 W Superior.
Bayliss Absalom, teamster, res 207 Gay.
Beaber, *see also Bieber.*
Beaber Abraham W, student, bds 109 Fairfield av.
Beaber Bertha A, milliner, bds 109 Fairfield av.
Beaber Daisy K, teacher Washington School, bds 342 Broadway.
Beaber Daniel, carpenter, res 15 W DeWald.
Beaber D Lafayette, carpenter, res 109 Fairfield av.
Beaber Goldie M, bds 15 W De Wald.
Beaber Jacob, carp J M Henry, res 342 Broadway.
Beaber Lillie B, teacher Hoagland School, bds 342 Broadway.
Beach August, painter, 444 Broadway, res same.
Beach Edward A, bds 133 E Berry.
Beach Elizabath (wid Wm), bds 375 Lafayette.
Beach Frederick, died April 7th, 1895.
Beach Frederick E, checker L S & M S Ry, res s e cor Harrison and canal feeder.

Beach Frederick J, confectioner, 290 Calhoun, res same.
Beach Frederick W, clk Morgan & Beach, bds 133 E Berry.
Beach Henry, shoemaker, 375 Lafayette, res same.
Beach John H, laborer, res 26 Cass.
Beach Magdalene (wid Frederick) res 133 E Berry. Tel. 450.
Beadell Eva, domestic 35 W Washington.
Beadell Henry (Beadell & Co), res 111 E Washington.
Beadell Nathaniel E, printer Ft Wayne Sentinel, res 214 E Jefferson.
Beadell & Company, (Henry Beadell, John Porteous, Archibald Mitchell), Proprs People's Store; Dry Goods, Notions and Men's Furnishings, 20 and 22 E Berry. Tel 313.
Beagle Elva, medical student, bds 119 W Washington.
Beahler John E, insurance and sec Ft Wayne Ins Co, 22 Bank Blk, res 166 Columbia av. Tel 214.
Beahrs Charles E, laborer, bds 324 Maumee rd.
Beahrs John A, watchman, res 324 Maumee rd.
Beall Frank D, tel opr N Y, C & St L R R, bds 190 W Berry.
Beals Melvin M, watchman, res 402 E Wayne.
Beals Thomas C, mach Penn Co, res 115 Barr.
Beam Calvin, packer Ft Wayne Furn Co, res 128 E Lewis.
Beam Della, bds 128 E Lewis.
Beam John, res 3 Bass.
Beam Lydia A (wid Peter), bds 303 Calhoun.
Beam Mattie A, bds 3 Bass.
Beam Rebecca (wid David), res 128 E Lewis.
Beamer Louis O, real estate, res 33 Lincoln av.
Bear, see also Baer, Baier, Bair, Bayer, Beyer and Boyer.
Bear Edward, brakeman, res 30 Baker.
Bear John H, helper Wabash R R, res 11 Bass.
Bear Ora (wid Michael), seamstress, bds 301 W Washington.
Bearaeisen Amelia, domestic J V Fox.
Beard Charles G, driver L Diether & Bro, res 17 Michael av.
Beard Harry, clk J A Ryan, bds 418 Clinton.
Bearinger Bessie L, bds 55 W De Wald.
Bearinger George W, check clk Penn Co, res 55 W DeWald.
Bearinger Harry L, clk Penn Co, bds 55 W De Wald.
Bearinger Josie L, candymaker, bds 55 W De Wald.
Bearman Frederick H, clk F H Dicke, bds 22 Oliver.
Beaston Amy H (wid Harry S), res 43 Wagner.
Beaston Emma H (wid Harry), res 43 Wagner.

Beaston Willard S, mach hd Ft Wayne Furn Co, bds 43 Wagner.

Beattie Joseph, laborer, bds 55 W 5th.

Beattie Lizzie C, student, bds 595 Calhoun.

Beattie Maggie V, bds 595 Calhoun.

Beattie Neal McL, porter J B White, bds 595 Calhoun.

Beattie Wm, boilermaker, res 595 Calhoun.

Beattie Wm A, appr Ft Wayne Iron Wks, bds 595 Calhoun

Beaver Augustus C, genl mngr Ft Wayne Lumber Co, res 815 Broadway.

Beaver Chapel, n w cor Cottage and Indiana av.

Beaver Charles B, agt United States and Pacific Express Cos, 79 Calhoun, res 119 Columbia av.

Beaver Edwin L, traveling agt, res 115 Columbia av.

Beaver Florence E, bds 815 Broadway.

Beaver Harry S, clk Dittoe's Grocery Co, bds 119 Columbia av.

Beaver Hugh M, clk U S Express Co, bds 119 Columbia av

Beaver Minnie A, bds 305 W Washington.

Beaver Montgomery G, Asst Mngr Ft Wayne Lumber Co, res 365 Broadway.

Beberstine Fredericka (wid Abraham), bds w s Piqua av 3 s of Rudisill av.

Beberstine George W, contractor, res s s Rudisill av 2 e of Calhoun.

Bechtol John G, engr Penn Co, res 354 W Washington.

Bechtold Louis, grocer, 152 Maumee rd, res same.

Beck, see Bach.

Beck Abraham R, laborer, bds 10 Ewing.

Beck Charles J, laborer, res 124 Wilt.

Beck Henry, patternmkr Penn Co, res 157 Rockhill.

Beck James, hostler J C Brinsley, bds 25 W Columbia.

Beck Leopold, carpet weaver, 136 Barr, res same.

Beck Minnie C, dressmkr, bds 157 Rockhill.

Beck Pauline M, dressmkr, bds 157 Rockhill.

Beck Peter, res 174 Fairfield av.

Beck Rhoda, domestic New Aveline House.

Beck Susannah C (wid Wm L), res 10 Ewing.

Beck Wm G, engineer Penn Co, res 153 Rockhill.

Beck Wm P, bkkpr Geo DeWald & Co, res 30 Pritchard.

Becker, see also Baker.

Becker Abbott Z, engr N Y, C & St L R R, res 69 High.

Becker Abraham M, brakeman N Y. C & St L R R, res 47 W Main.

Becker Anna E, died March 18, 1895.

Becker Anthony A, mach hd Anthony Wayne Mnfg Co, bds 94 Lasselle.

Becker August, driver Fort Wayne Artificial Ice Co, res 19 Pritchard.

Becker August E C, grocer, 158 Fairfield av, res 107 W Williams. Tel 352.

Becker Charles, horse shoer Fred Becker, bds 11 E Washington.

Becker Charles E, clk Ft Wayne Electric Corp, bds 168 Holman.

Becker Charles M, foreman George Jaap, res 31 Lillie.

Becker Conrad, butcher Eckart Pkg Co, res 80 Buchanan.

Becker Emma L, clk M Frank & Co, bds 220 W Berry.

Becker Frederick, bds w s Winter 2 s of Pontiac.

Becker Frederick, horseshoer, 13 E Washington, res 11 same.

Becker George E, clk Adams Express Co, res 315 E Wayne

Becker Harry V, traveling agt, res 109 E Washington.

Becker Henry W, marble cutter, res 134 Francis.

Becker John J, supt Wayne Oil Tank Co, res 168 Holman.

Becker John L, bds 249 Gay.

Becker Joseph F, clk Geo De Wald & Co, bds 249 Gay.

Becker Josephine, bds 249 Gay.

Becker Lorenz, helper Kerr Murray Mnfg Co, res 94 Lasselle.

Becker Louis, res 249 Gay.

Becker Louis C, painter Olds Wagon Wks, bds 80 Buchanan.

Becker Mamie, bds 94 Lasselle.

Becker Mary, bds 11 E Washington.

Becker Mary, trimmer Freiburger & Bro, bds 80 Buchanan.

Becker Michael, laborer, res 66 Alliger.

Becker Minnie, bds 11 E Washington.

Becker Sophia K, bds 220 W Berry.

Becker Theresa, domestic 261 W Berry.

Becker Wilhelmina (wid Christian), res 220 W Berry.

Becker Wm T, tinner Freiburger & Suelzer, res w s Winter 2 s of Pontiac.

Beckes, *see also Backes.*

Beckes Amelia, rms Henry Oswalt.

Beckes Jacob, saloon, 221 Lafayette, res same.

Beckes John, driver C L Centlivre Brwg Co, res 24 Randolph.

Beckes Peter, rms Henry Oswalt.

10

Beckett Wm, driver, res e s Spy Run av 2 n of canal bridge.

Beckman Edward, res St Vincent, Washington twp.

Beckman Edward H, dep county treasurer, bds 70 Harrison.

Beckman Ellen (wid John), res 21 Taylor.

Beckman Frederick, laborer Bass F & M Wks, res 173 Gay.

Beckman George, saloon, 101 Force, res 103 same.

Beckman Lizzie, domestic 71 Walnut.

Beckstein John, res 32 Lake av.

Beckstein George J, fireman G R & I R R, res 176 Jackson.

Bedson Clarence W, timekpr N Y, C & St L R R, bds 25 Brackenridge.

Bedson Ernest M, fireman N Y, C & St L R R, bds 25 Brackenridge.

Bedson John H, foreman N Y, C & St L R R, res 25 Brackenridge. Tel 439.

Bedson Mary (wid James) bds 25 Brackenridge.

Bedson Percy W, clk Pixley & Co, bds 25 Brackenridge.

Beebe Charles H, res 44 Brackenridge.

Beebe DeWitt C, conductor, res 78 E Butler.

Beebe Eva L, teacher Clay School, bds 44 Brackenridge.

Beebe Katherine C, teacher Miner St School, bds 44 Brackenridge.

Beekner Charlotte C, starcher F L Jones & Co, bds 19 Cochran.

Beekner Conrad, carpenter, res 19 Cochran.

Beerbaum, see Bierbaum.

Beermann Emma J, dressmaker, bds 39 Boone.

Beermann Frederick, teamster E Gilmartin, res 39 Boone.

Beers George W, contractor, 17 Pixley & Long Bldg, res 110 E Berry. Tel 506.

Beers Henry C, winder Ft Wayne Electric Corp, bds 266 W Jefferson.

Beezley Edwin J, conductor, res 304 Harrison.

Begue Mary (wid John), res 162 E Wayne.

Behler Adam, shoemaker, res 81 Montgomery.

Behn Charles, car builder Penn Co, bds Windsor Hotel.

Behren Christian, coremkr Bass F & M Wks, res 18 Guthrie.

Behren Lizzie, domestic 286 W Wayne.

Behrendt Tena, domestic 154 Griffith.

Behrendt Wilhelm, laborer, res 243 John.

Behrens Ferdinand H, carpenter, res 68 Nelson.

Behrens Herman H, lab Bass F & M Wks, res 84 Gay.

Beidler Wm S, brakeman N Y, C & St L R R, res 194 W Superior.

Beierlein, see also Beyerlein.

Beierlein George J, carp J M Henry, res 52 Huffman.

✝Beighler John, farmer, res 109 Home av.

Beigler, see Biegler.

Beindel George, laborer, res 204 Smith.

Beinder Jacob, truckman Penn Co, rms rear 179 Clinton.

Beier Emma E, domestic 120 Boone.

Bierline John, lab City Parks, res 107 Cass.

Beitzell Rosa A, domestic 251 W Main.

Beitzell Wm, trucker L S & M S Ry, res 35 W 5th.

Belchin Frank, saloon, 54 E Main, res same.

Belchner Frederick, packer Empire Mills, res n s Orchard av nr Leesburg rd.

Belden Edward H, electrician, rms 25 W Creighton av.

Belger Michael F (Belger & Lennon), res 19 W De Wald.

Belger & Lennon (Michael F Belger, Edwin J Lennon), saloon, 140 Calhoun.

Belknap Catherine (wid James), bds 195 W Wayne.

Bell Alice, domestic 125 E Main.

Bell Charles W, conductor, bds 80 W 3d.

Bell Dora, seamstress, bds 14 Lafayette.

Bell Edgar L, trav agt J W Bell, res 28 St Joseph boulevard.

Bell George A, clk J W Bell, rms 8 St Joseph boulevard.

Bell George E, clk N Y, C & St L R R, res 80 W 3d.

Bell Horace L, buyer Fred Eckart Pckg Co, res 438 W Main.

Bell Jacob, laborer, res 237 Lafayette.

Bell James W, res 123 Harrison.

Bell Joseph W, saddlery hardware, 13 E Columbia, res 285 W Wayne. Tel 275, res 254.

Bell Julia A (wid Wm M), res 80 W 3d.

Bell Louis, fireman N Y, C & St L R R, bds 71 Boone.

Bell Margaret E (wid Wm E), housekeeper 349 W Jefferson.

Bell Maud, housekeeper 152 W Main.

Bell Robert C (Morris, Bell, Barrett & Morris), res 132 W Wayne. Tel 346.

Bell Thomas H, conductor, res 78 W 3d.

Bell Wm F, conductor, res 180 Montgomery.

Bellamy Ada A, clk Louis Wolfe & Co, bds 135 Cass.

Bellamy Elizabeth (wid Albert F), res 135 Cass.

Bellamy Frank A, circulator Ft Wayne Journal, bds 135 Cass.

Bellamy John D, lab N Y, C & St L R R, res 253 St Mary's av.

Bellamy Mary E, bds 135 Cass.

Belling Nicholas A, cutter Hoosier Mnfg Co, res St Joseph boulevard nr Baker av.

Belmont Stable, C J Ulmer Propr, 88 E Main. *(See p 97.)*

Beloe Dora, domestic A H Hamilton.

Beloe Mary, domestic A H Hamilton.

Belot Frank J, deputy county clerk, bds 80 Wagner.

Belot John C, clk C W Cook, res 80 Wagner.

Belott George E, Cigars and Tobacco, 82 Calhoun, res 225 W Main.

Belshner Frederick, miller, res 45 Orchard av.

Beman Wm G, laborer Ft Wayne Electric Corp, res 54 Harrison.

Benadum Charles F, bartender, rms 214 Calhoun.

Bender Albert G, winder Ft Wayne Electric Corp, bds 20 Poplar.

Bender Caroline (wid John), res 169 Force.

Bender Charles, mach hd Olds Wagon Wks, bds 4 Melita.

Bender Charles H W, laborer, bds 206 Francis.

Bender Christopher P, woodwkr Charles Ehrmann, res 343 E Creighton av.

Bender Cyrus, helper, bds 4 Melita.

Bender Dennis, bds 259 E Washington.

Bender Edward, cigarmkr Ward & Mahoney, bds 4 Melita.

Bender Edward L W, barber John H Kabisch, bds 22 Miner.

Bender Elizabeth, bds 18 Chicago.

Bender Elizabeth, stripper J C Eckert, bds 4 Melita.

Bender Emilie (wid Philip), res 115 Taylor.

Bender Frank H, cigarmkr L Bender, bds 168 E Washington.

Bender Frank W, bds 169 Force.

Bender George, clerk, res 25 Smith.

Bender George J, clk Frederick Oetting, bds 127 Eliza.

Bender Henry, laborer, res 29 Bass.

Bender Henry, teamster, res Brooklyn av s of Ontario.

Bender John F, cabinetmaker, bds 115 Taylor.

Bender Laura, bds 206 Francis.

Bender Laura, domestic Y W C A, bds 94 Walton av.

Bender Levi H, cigarmkr H W Ortmann, res 4 Melita.

Bender Levi H, gasfitter, res 356 Calhoun.
Bender Louis, Cigar Manufacturer, 168 E Washington, res same.
Bender Louis jr, painter, bds 168 E Washington.
Bender Milton, teamster, res 174 W Superior.
Bender Minnie C, domestic 194 E Washington.
Bender Reuben, died September 6th, 1894.
Bender Rosa (wid Reuben), res 4 Melita.
Bender Samuel, switchman, res 69 Gay.
Bender Sophia (wid George), res 206 Francis.
Bender Ursula (wid Adam), res 20 Poplar.
Bender Willard L, teamster, res rear 88 Madison.
Bender Wm C, fireman Penn Co, res 34 Wall.
Bender Wm H, clk G E Bursley & Co, bds 343 E Creighton av.
Bender Wm L, trucker Wabash R R, res 88 Madison.
Bendorf Herman, cigarmaker, bds 69 Charles.
Bendure Wm H, fitter Ft Wayne Furn Co, res 48 Harmer.
Benedict Ambrose H, mach Penn Co, bds 15 W Butler.
Benedict Charlotte L (wid Leslie R), res 304 E Creighton av.
Benedict Edward R, conductor, res 11 Hough.
Benedict Jacob, saloon, 36 W Main, res same.
Benedict Mary E, bds 15 W Butler.
Benedict Wm, carpenter, res 15 W Butler.
Benedict Wm L, conductor, res 7 Edgerton.
Beneke Frederick W, carbldr Penn Co, res 225 W Creighton av.
Beneke Gustave, teamster Wm Miller, bds same.
Beneke Herman, lab Penn Co, res 225 W Creighton av.
Beneke Wm F, drugs, 443 Broadway, res same. Tel 338.
Bengs Gustave, boilermkr Bass F & M Wks, bds 155 John.
Bengs Herman, stonecutter, res 155 John.
Bengs Martha M, domestic 298 E Jefferson.
Bengs Otto F, carpenter, 175 John, res same.
Bengs Robert, carpenter, bds 155 John.
Benke Christian F, res 155 Harrison.
Benner Annie (wid Conrad) bds Carl Skattula.
Bennett Asa, car bldr Penn Co, res 95 Hough.
Bennett Atha, bds 82 Lake av.
Bennett Fannie M, dressmaker, bds 336 W Main.
Bennett Joseph F, expressman, res 287 E Lewis.
Bennett Rosanna (wid Winton), bds n e cor Oliver and Buchanan.
Bennett Winona E, bds 43 Lavina.

Bennigen Joseph, laborer, res 168 Hayden.
Bennigin Bertha M, bds 155 E Creighton av.
Bennigin Charles F, res 155 E Creighton av.
Bennigin Edward P, caller G R & I R R, bds 155 E. Creighton av.
Bennigin Hugh, molder, res 201 E Lewis.
Bennigin Marcelena, clk Geo DeWald & Co, bds 201 E Lewis.
Benninghoff Daniel R, barber, 300 Calhoun, res 37 Hugh.
Benoy Charles W, mach Bass F & M Wks, res 155 Force.
Benoy Frank T, foreman Bass F & M Wks, res 72 E DeWald.
Bensman Catherine M (wid Rudolph), res 92 Madison.
Bensman Elizabeth (wid Rudolph), res 76 Madison.
Bensman Wm H, clk Bass F & M Wks, bds 92 Madison.
Bensman Wm J, boilermkr Wabash R R, res 76 Madison.
Bente Charles W, painter Wabash R R, res 26 Poplar.
Bente Frank, machinist, bds 155 Griffith.
Bente George F, painter Wabash R R, bds 155 Griffith.
Bente Harry F, hostler, bds 155 Griffith.
Bente Herman F, fireman Wabash R R, res 155 Griffith.
Bente Wm, hostler, bds 155 Griffith.
Bentley Ellis, bds 100 E Jefferson.
Benton Thomas B, lab N Y, C & St L R R, res 71 Howell.
Bentz Elizabeth, domestic 144 Maumee rd.
Benward John E, helper Penn Co, res 190 W Superior.
Benway Eliza (wid Wm), res 32 Winch.
Benway Henry A, driver, bds 32 Winch.
Benz Charles F, cigarmkr, res 393 E Washington.
Benz Charles F, shoes, 111 Maumee rd, res 25 same.
Benz Daniel, truckman Penn Co, res 77 Cass.
Benz Henry, check clk Penn Co, res 73 Scott av.
Benz Nicholas, res 79 Cass.
Benz Otto M, mach hd Horton Mnfg Co, bds 169 Holman.
Bequette Elizabeth (wid John B), res 498 W Main.
Bequette Elizabeth, opr Wayne Knitting Mills, bds 498 W Main.
Bequette Henry G, machinist, bds 498 W Main.
Bequette John A, clk Falk & Lamley, res 498 W Main.
Bequette Theresa, bds 498 W Main.
Berch Lydia, typewriter, bds 135 E Washington.
Bercot Ella F, dressmaker, bds 18 Wagner.
Bercot Felix, teamster John Draker, res Spy Run av n e cor Baltes.

Bercot Frank J, Road House and Saloon, n w cor Spy Run av and Randolph, res same.

Berdelmann Ernst H, car repr N Y, C & St L R R, res 66 Barthold.

Berdelmann John H, printer, bds 66 Barthold.

Berdelmann, Minnie L, bds 66 Barthold.

Berdelmann Wm H R, boxmkr Empire Box Factory, bds 66 Barthold.

Berg, *see also Borg and Burg.*

Berg Anna M (wid Christopher), res 556 Hanna.

Berg Kate, seamstress, bds w s Spy Run av 3 n of bridge.

Berg Peter, helper Penn Co, res 34 Buchanan.

Berg Philip J, molder Indiana Mach Wks, bds w s Spy Run av 3 w of bridge.

Bergel Franklin J, harnessmkr A L Johns & Co, bds 107 Walton av.

Bergel Melinda (wid Valentine), res 107 Walton av.

Berger, *see also Boerger and Burger.*

Berger Paul, blksmith Standard Wheel Co, bds 553 E Wayne.

Berger Valentine, carp Penn Co, res 203 Taylor.

Berghoff Gustav A, propr Summit City Soap Wks, res 467 E Washington.

Berghoff Henry C, Propr Globe Spice Mills, Treas Phœnix Building and Savings Union, res 95 E Jefferson. Tel 476.

Berghoff Herman Brewing Co The, Herman J Berghoff Pres. Hubert Berghoff Sec and Treas, e s Grant av nr E Washington. Tel 105. (*See right top lines.*)

Berghoff Herman J, Pres The Herman Berghoff Brewing Co, res 50 E Washington.

Berghoff Hubert, Sec and Treas The Herman Berghoff Brewing Co, res 312 E Jefferson.

Berghoff John A, clk Summit City Soap Wks, bds 467 E Washington.

Berghorn Frederick, car builder Penn Co, res 34 Hugh.

Berghorn Frederick, helper Penn Co, res 169 Holman.

Berghorn Frederick jr, clk C Schwier & Son, bds 34 Hugh.

Berghorn Louis H F, tailor F Hardung, res 169 Holman.

Berghorn Louisa C W, bds 34 Hugh.

Bergk Carl, Physician and Surgeon, 74 Calhoun, res 52 W 4th.

Bergmann, *see also Borgmann.*

Bergmann Annie S L, bds w s Calhoun 1 s of Rudisill av.

Bergmann Henry P, res w s Calhoun 1 s of Rudisill av.

Berkler John, dyer Wayne Knitting Mills, bds 16 Maiden lane.

Berlin Henry J, packer Empire Mills, res 45 Boone.

Berlin Minnie L, died July 17, 1894.

Bernard Mrs Nancy J, bds 16 Brackenridge.

Bernard Simon B, res 88 W Superior.

Berndt Charles A, cigarmaker, res 145 John.

Berndt Martha, bds 145 John.

Berner May, domestic 158 W Berry.

Bernhard Frederick, music teacher, res 104 E Lewis.

Bernhard Gustave A, molder Bass F & M Wks, bds 104 E Lewis.

Bernhard Newman, trav agt S M Foster, bds 136 W Wayne.

Bernhardt Frank F, mason. res 391 Force.

Bernhardt John C, helper Penn Co. res 29 John.

Bernhardt May, dressmaker, bds 29 John.

Bernhardt Wm J, tailor W H Blondoit, bds 29 John.

Berning Amelia, domestic 244 W Wayne.

Berning Charlotte (wid Conrad), res 420 E Washington.

Berning Conrad, laborer, res 90 Summit.

Berning Conrad jr, butcher F Parrot, bds 90 Summit.

Berning Dora M, clk Seaney Millinery Co, bds 90 Summit.

Berning Henry, helper Bass F & M Wks, res 50 Smith.

Berning Louise M, domestic 98 E Berry.

Berning Wm, mach Penn Co, res 22 Eliza.

Bernius Catherine M, domestic 245 E Lewis.

Berns, *see Burns.*

Berr Edward, brakeman, bds 38 Brackenridge.

Berry, *see also Barrey and Barry.*

Berry Arthur J, storekpr School for Feeble-Minded Youth.

Berry Street M E Church, n e cor W Berry and Harrison.

Bersch George, carpenter, res 66 W 3d.

Bertels, *see also Bartels.*

Bertels John, contractor, 160 Harmer, res same.

Berthold, *see also Barthold.*

Berthold Christina J (wid John F), res 156 Gay.

Berthold Louis E, baker, bds 156 Gay.

Bertrand Arthur J, cigarmkr John C Eckart, rms 190 E Wayne.

Besancon Alexander L, plasterer, res w s Parnell av 1 n of Griswold av.

Besancon Frank, lather, res 20 Riverside av.

Besancon Frank A, lather, w s Parnell av 1 n of Griswold av.

Besancon Henry, luther, res 11 Romy av.
Besancon Josephine (wid Frank), res Parnell av n w cor Griswold av.
Beschur Theresa, domestic 54 W Berry.
Besson Ellen, bds 136 Monroe.
Besson Eugene, coppersmith, bds 136 Monroe.
Besson Frank, stonecutter Keller & Braun, bds 136 Monroe.
Besson Hortense (wid John), res 136 Monroe.
Besson James, plumber Penn Co, bds 136 Monroe.
Besson Joseph J, clerk, res 22 Summit.
Besson Mary, res 136 Monroe.
Bethany Presbyterian Church, s w cor Boone and Fry.
Betts Ella A, bds 121 W Washington.
Betts Ellen (wid John), res 121 W Washington.
• Betts Kate, cook Hotel Rich.
Betts Mazzie, clk Paragon Mnfg Co, bds 121 W Wash-ington.
Betz Anna L, pack'r B W Skelton Co, bds 50 Nird-linger av.
Betz Emma M, dressmaker, bds 50 Nirdlinger av.
·Betz Frederick A, baker Zoeller & Merz, res 52 Nird-linger av.
Betz George A, lab Ft Wayne Electric Corp, res 203 Metz.
Betz John F, lab Hoffman Bros, res 50 Nirdlinger av,
Betz Samuel J, carpet layer D N Foster Furn Co, res Illi-nois rd 3 miles n of city limits.
Betzler Creszens (wid George), bds 296 Broadway.
Betzler George A, finisher Ft Wayne Organ Co, res 296 Broadway.
Beuch *see also Beach.*
Beuchel Otto, carpenter, res 514 E Lewis.
Beuchel Robert, carpenter, res 142 Madison.
Beuchel Wm, carp Charles Wermuth, res 514 E Lewis.
Beugnot Alice M, sec Old Fort Mnfg Co, bds 162 E Wayne.
Beugnot Aline, bds 25 Hough.
Beugnot Ann (wid Paul), res 30 Runnion av.
Beugnot Clara F, bds 30 Runnion av.
Beugnot John J, helper Penn Co, bds 18 Madison.
Beugnot Justine (wid Augustus), res 25 Hough.
Beugnot Theodore, laborer, bds 25 Hough.
Beuke Arthur, clerk, bds 155 Harrison.
Beuke Christian F, truckman, res 155 Harrison.
Beuke Edith O, bds 155 Harrison.

Beuke Gertrude, student, bds 155 Harrison.
Beuret Cecilia, bds 34 2d.
Beuret Charles A, money order clk P O, bds 31 W De Wald.
Beuret Charles A, wheelmaker, bds 34 2nd.
Beuret Frank L, bds 34 2d.
Beuret Henry J (Beuret & Co), res 146 E De Wald.
Beuret John B, res 34 2d.
Beuret M Philomene, opr S M Foster, bds 34 2d.
Beuret Sylvester, wheelmaker, bds 34 2d.
Beuret & Co (Henry J Beuret), Wholesale Carriage and Wagon Material, 23 W Columbia.
Beuttel, *see Buettel.*
Bevelhaimer Daniel, carpenter, res 167 W De Wald.
Bevelhaimer Edward P, clk Wm J Riethmiller, bds 167 W De Wald.
Bevelhaimer Wm D, carp bridge dept Penn Co. res 492 Harrison.
Beverforden August, asst steward The Randall, bds same.
Beverforden August H, clk H F Beverforden, res 286 Calhoun.
Beverforden Henry F, Depot Drug Store, 286 Calhoun, res 26 E De Wald. Tel 286.
Beverforden Hugo F, clk H F Beverforden, res 286 Calhoun.
Beverforden Rudolph, Saloon, 288 Calhoun, res 11 Brandriff.
Beverforden Wm H D, traveling agt, res 29 Jane
Bevington Sheridan, motorman Ft W E Ry Co, res 245 Webster.
Bewlah George F, brakeman, bds 97 Taylor.
Beyer, *see also Baer, Baier, Bair, Bayer and Bear.*
Beyer Charles, cigarmaker, res 29 Hanna.
Beyer Paul, removed to Grand Rapids, Mich.
Beyerle Henry G, teamster, res 85 Summit.
Beyerlein, *see also Beierlein.*
Beyerlein Anna B (wid Frederick). rms 8 Wheeler.
Beyerlein Charles F, clk F M Smaltz, res 65 Boone.
Beyerlein Clara, former Wayne Knitting Mills, bds 8 Wheeler.
Beyerlein Frederick, car bldr Penn Co, bds 34 Jones.
Beyerlein George M, lab Penn Co, res 34 Jones.
Beyerlein John L, painter, bds 34 Jones.
Beyerlein Julius H, clk F M Smaltz, res 59 Boone.
Beyerlein Lulu, opr Wayne Knitting Mills, bds 8 Wheeler.
Beyerlein Wm H, helper Bass F & M Wks, bds 34 Jones.
Beyrau August F, slater, res 226 John.

Beyrau Wm, removed to Danville, Ill.
Biber Marie R, domestic Charles A Hoffmann.
Bice Mrs Margaret, domestic, rms 20 W Lewis.
Bickel Jacob, bd: 218 Broadway.
Bickel Joseph F, sec Phœnix Building and Savings Union, res Huntington, Ind.
Bickford John D, res 45 1st..
Bickford J H, pastor Wayne M E Church, res 195 W Wayne.
Bickford Wm I, carpenter, res 24 Wagner.
Bicknell Wm W, clk People's Store, bds 38 Baker.
Bicknese Christian, laborer, bds 73 W Williams.
Bicknese Frederick C, saloon, 86 Barr, res 171 E Lewis.
Bicknese Frederick W E, clk Princess Cash Store, res 73 W Williams.
Bicknese Herbert, molder, bds 171 E Lewis.
Bicknese Minnie, bds 73 W Williams.
Bicknese Sophia, bds 73 W Williams.
Bicknesse Henry, mach hd Penn Co, res 18 Madison.
Biddle Catherine, subteacher Public Schools, bds 166 Ewing.
Biddle C I, perfume mnfr, 169 Ewing, bds same.
Biddle Edward F, trav agt C I Biddle, bds 169 Ewing.
Biddle Frank M, physician, 169 Ewing, bds same.
Biddle Hannah (wid James F), bds 169 Ewing.
Biddle Helen, bds 169 Ewing.
Biddle Mary, bds 169 Ewing.
Biddle Thomas M, trav agt C I Biddle, bds 169 Ewing.
Bidwell Wm P, carpenter, bds 26 South Wayne av.
Bidwell Wm S, carpenter, res 26 South Wayne av.
Bieber, *see also Beaber.*
Bieber Wm H, foreman Ft Wayne Lumber Co, res 40 Thompson av.
Bieberick Annie, opr Wayne Knitting Mills, bds 146 W 3d.
Bieberick Susan, opr Wayne Knitting Mills, bds 146 W 3d.
Biedenweg Gottfried, res 27 Smith.
Biedenweg Martha, domestic 126 E Main.
Biedenweg Wm F C, lab Bass F & M Wks, bds 27 Smith.
Biederman Gottfried, saloon, 150 Barr, bds 106 same.
Biegel, *see also Beegle.*
Biegel Julius T, painter, res 79 Hanna.
Biegler Daniel, salesman, res 78 South Wayne av.
Biegler Elizabeth M, teacher Hoagland School, bds 78 South Wayne av.
Biegler George P, appr Wabash R R, bds 78 South Wayne av

Biegler Maude, sub teacher Public Schools, bds 78 South Wayne av.
Bieker Daniel, tailor, bds 28 Wells.
Biemer George, blksmith, 7 Clay, res 9 same.
Biemer George A, bds 9 Clay.
Biemer Joseph A, clerk, bds 9 Clay.
Biemer Julian, plater, bds 9 Clay.
Bierbaum Frederick G, teamster James Wilding, res 53 Taylor.
Bierbaum Frederick R, car repr N Y, C & St L R R, res 24 Breck.
Bierbaum Fredericka (wid Hermann), res 53 Taylor.
Bierbaum Wm F, laborer, res 184 Greeley.
Bierbaum Wm H, machinist, bds 53 Taylor.
Bierline. see Beirline.
Bierman, see Beerman.
Bies Margaret (wid Frank), res 20 W Lewis.
Bies Mary, dressmaker, bds 20 W Lewis.
Biewend Mrs Celestine N, res 57 Douglas av.
Biewend Maud N, bds 57 Douglas av.
Biggs Rebecca, dressmaker, 58 W Berry, res same.
Bignon Adolph, upholsterer Penn Co, res 298 Hanna.
Bignon Charles A, laborer, bds 298 Hanna.
Bikel Charles, cabinetmaker, res rear 178 E Washington.
Bilcer Elmore, teamster, bds Jacob Bilcer.
Bilcer Jacob, teamster, res s s Wright 1 w of Tyler av.
Bilcer John, teamster, bds Jacob Bilcer.
Bilderback Blanche B, stenogr M W Fay, bds 247 E Wayne.
Bilderback Joseph H, special agt C E Everett, res 247 E Wayne.
Bilderback Louise, bkkpr C E Everett, bds 247 E Wayne.
Bilgerig Andrew, gardener, res 74 Murray.
Bill Jacob, laborer, res 180 Hanna.
Bill Jacob jr, druggist, 285 E Creighton av, res 86 Oakley.
Billheimer Cora, clk Wm Rockhill, bds 160 Greeley.
Billings George, brakeman, rms 96 Boone.
Billings Wm, condr N Y, C & St L R R, rms 359 W Main.
Billman Jesse F, agent, res 132 Thomas.
Billman Matilda (wid Ray), res 33 Monroe.
Billman Mrs Rose, res 36 Hayden.
Bimer Charles, setter David Tagtmeyer, res 58 Barthold.
Binder Otto W, appr C W Bruns & Co, bds Orphans Reformed Home.
Binkley Frank C, insurance agt, 320 Broadway, bds same.
Binkley Mary (wid Jacob), rms 241 E Wayne.

Birbeck Helen B, student, bds 97 W De Wald.
Birbeck Wm, mach Wabash R R, res 97 W De Wald.
Birbeck Wm D, stenogr Kerr Murray Mnfg Co, bds 97 W De Wald.
Birchman John E, candymaker, res 64 E Columbia.
Bird James S, car builder Penn Co, res n s New Haven av 2 e of Edsall av.
Bird Thomas S, molder, bds James S Bird.
Bireley Wm W, helper Penn Co, res 143 Wallace.
Birk, see Bork and Burke.
Birkenbeul Henry, helper Bass F & M Wks, res 40 Charles.
Birkhold Mattheu, meats, 13 Highland, res 41 E Williams.
Bischoff Mrs Delilah. bds 40 W Superior.
Bischoff Mrs Fredericka, res 104 St Mary's av.
Bischoff Rudolph A, professor Concordia College, res College Grounds.
Bischoff Wm, cigarmaker, res 156 Huffman.
Bisel Elmer E, horseman Hose Co No 5, res 207 Broadway
Bishop Charles B, butcher, bds 13 Erie.
Bishop Martha (wid Martin), res 13 Erie.
Bishop Mary (wid Jacob), res 201 Calhoun.
Bishop Nellie D, bookbinder Ft Wayne Sentinel, bds 13 Erie.
Bishop Wm C, brakeman N Y, C & St L R R, res 24 Boone.
Bissell Charles M, General Manager Findlay, Ft Wayne and Western Ry, bds The Randall.
Bisson Michael, potash mnfr, w s Glasgow av 2 n of N Y, C & St L R R, res 2 Glasgow av.
Bitler Samuel D, tress hoop mnfr, 421 E Wayne, res 319 same.
Bitner Alonzo J, molder Penn Co, res 31 Lincoln av.
Bitner Charles, brakeman N Y, C & St L R R, bds 75 Boone.
Bitner Clark A, molder Penn Co, res 67 E De Wald.
Bitner Clark E, clk D W Bitner, bds 616 Calhoun.
Bitner David W, grocer, 616 Calhoun, res same. Tel 424.
Bitner John R, mach Penn Co, res 175 E Lewis.
Bitner Minnie P, opr S M Foster, bds 31 Lincoln av.
Bitsberger Emanuel F, teamster, res 102 Wallace.
Bitsberger Mrs E F, dressmaker, 102 Wallace, res same.
Bitsberger Hal E, mach hd Olds Wagon Wks, bds 102 Wallace.
Bitsberger Wm H, mach hd Olds Wagon Wks, bds 102 Wallace.

Bittenger Jacob R, lawyer, 26 Court, res 262 W Washington.

Bittenger Marcia M, bds 262 W Washington.

Bittenger Lawrence E, clk Penn Co, res 36 Montgomery.

Bittikoffer Catherine (wid John), res 12 Highland.

Bittikoffer John F, nickel plater Ft Wayne Electric Corp, bds 12 Highland.

Bittikoffer Louis H, driver A Kalbacher, bds 12 Highland.

Bittikoffer Rose D, coremkr Ft Wayne Electric Corp, bds 12 Highland.

Bittinger Adam H (Bittinger & Edgerton), res 44 Archer av.

Bittinger & Edgerton (Adam H Bittinger, Dixon Edgerton), Lawyers, 27 and 28 Bank Blk. Tel 214.

Bittler Edmund A G, clk P O, bds 301 W Jefferson.

Bittler Wm S, pump repr Penn Co, res 301 W Jefferson.

Bitzinger Henry, helper Bass F & M Wks, res 438 E Wayne.

Bitzinger Jehn, laborer, bds 438 E Wayne.

Bitzinger John G, mach hd Anthony Wayne Mnfg Co, res 112 Summit.

Bitzler, see Betzler.

Bixler T Isaac, laborer, res n s Spring 1 w of Franklin av.

Bixler Levi A L, carp Fort Wayne Electric Corp, bds 145 Shawnee av.

Bixler Wm G, farmer, res n s Pennsylvania av 2 e of Bond.

Black Edith A, rms 15 Vordermark Bldg.

Black Edward F (col'd), waiter The Wayne, rms 93 E Lewis.

Black John A, janitor N Y, C & St L R R, res 49 Eliza.

Black Marion, traveling agt, bds 17 W Lewis.

Blackburn Anna (wid Thomas K), bds 51 E De Wald.

Blackburn Anna, opr F L Jones & Co, bds 94 Montgomery.

Blackburn Charles, brakeman N Y, C & St L R R, bds 312 W Main.

Blackburn Emmet, machinist, bds 25 Gay.

Blackburn George, conductor, res 25 Gay.

Blackburn Harry S, fireman N Y, C & St L Ry, res 67 Boone.

Blackburn James H, brakeman, res 51 E De Wald.

Blackburn Uriah, tinner, bds 25 Gay.

Blain Charles S, brakeman, bds 27 Baker.

Blain Mary J (wid Robert A), res 34 Chicago.

Blaine Harley M, brakeman Penn Co, res 226 Calhoun.

Blair Henry B, fireman Jenney E L and P Co, bds Camilla Schilling.
Blair Solon K, train master western, division N Y, C & St L R R, Oddfellows Bldg, res 185 W Wayne. Tel 5.
Blair Thomas W, chief mailing clk P O, res 220 E Wayne.
Blaising John B, meats, 269 E Washington, res same.
Blaising Philip J, st car conductor, res 44 Grant av.
Blake Alfred L, appr Penn Co, bds 120 Harrison.
Blake Catherine, domestic 156 W Wayne.
Blake James R, laborer, bds 178 W De Wald.
Blakely Elizabeth (wid Wm), res 107 Fletcher av.
Blakely Eva M, stenographer, bds 326 Harrison.
Blakely Homer H, clk Penn Co, bds 326 Harrison.
Blakely John F, printer Archer Ptg Co, bds 107 Fletcher av.
Blakely Mary C (wid Wm), res 326 Harrison.
Blakesley James E, conductor, res 53 Holton av.
Blanchard Eber, fireman Penn Co, res 38 W Williams.
Bland Louis (col'd), waiter, bds 51 W Su erior.
Bland Samuel A (col'd), waiter Ft Wayne Club, rms 51 W Superior.
Blank John, boilerwasher Penn Co, res 161 E Taber.
Blankenship Nancy (wid John), res 16 Sturgis.
Blase Louisa, bds 82 E Washington.
Blase Minnie, bds 82 E Washington.
Blase Wilhelmina (wid Louis), res 82 E Washington.
Blauser Addie, domestic Columbia House.
Bledsoe Nathaniel H, trav agt S F Bowser & Co, res 35, Columbia av.
Bledsoe Valerie E, bds 35 Columbia av.
Blee John M, bds 338 W Main.
Blee John A, lab Standard Wheel Co, bds 96 Clay.
Bleeke Christina F, dressmaker, bds 417 E Wayne.
Bleibtreu Frederick H, toolmkr Fort Wayne Electric Corp, res 13 Poplar.
Bleibtreu Lena M, stenographer, bds 13 Poplar.
Bleich Emil, laborer, res 47 Smith.
Bleich Henry S, lab Bass F & M Wks, res 74 Gay.
Bleich Herman W, molder, bds 45 Smith.
Bleich John, coremkr Bass F & M Wks, res 45 Smith.
Bleke Diedrich L, laborer Penn Co, res 131 Madison.
Bleke Frederick D, upholsterer, bds 131 Madison.
Bley, see also Bly.
Bley George W, car bldr Penn Co, res 173 Montgomery.
Bley Henry L, conductor Penn Co, res 7 Savannah.
Bley Joseph F, insurance agt, res 114 Hayden.

Bley Theodore, asst yardmaster Penn Co, res s s Wayne Trace 1 w of P, F W & C Ry.

Blitz Maximillian J, Cut Rate Ticket Broker and Steamship Agt, 82 Calhoun, res New Aveline House. Tel 479.

Bloch George A, carp Olds Wagon Wks, bds 60 Prince.

Block see also Plock.

Block Annie, domestic The Wayne.

Block Elizabeth, domestic 119 W Wayne.

Block Frederick H, apprentice Bass F & M Wks, bds 87 Maumee rd.

Block Frederick, laborer Penn Co, res 135 Gay.

Block Mary (wid Frederick), bds 87 Maumee rd.

Block Mary, domestic The Wayne.

Block Sophia, domestic 302 W Washington.

Block Wm, laborer, res 87 Maumee rd.

Block Wm H, gas fitter, bds 87 Maumee rd.

Bloemker Henry E, carpenter, res 80 Organ av.

Bloemker John, carpenter, bds 80 Organ av.

Bloemker Lisette C (wid Frederick), res 55 Baker.

Blombach Charles, plasterer, bds 172 Smith.

Blombach Hugo, saloon, s e cor E Creighton and Gay, res 179 Gay.

Blombach Louis, res 172 Smith.

Blombach Otto, plasterer, res 131 Gay.

Blomenberg Christian E (Huser & Blomenberg), res 123 Union.

Blondell August E, shaper Ft Wayne Organ Co, res w s Webster 1 n of Johns av.

Blondoit Abel, sawfiler, res s s New Haven av 4 e of Pioneer av.

Blondoit Wm H, tailor, 47 E Lewis, res same.

Blood John L, laborer, res e s Piqua av 5 s of Rudisill av.

Bloom John A, junk, 227 Calhoun, res n s Columbia av 1 w of Oneida.

Bloom John F, clk B Lehman, bds 127 Oliver.

Bloom Nathan W (Kerlin & Bloom), res 183 Columbia av.

Bloomfield Mrs Clemence C, res 208 W De Wald.

Bloomfield Frederick A, clk Penn Co, res 208 W De Wald.

Bloomhuff Anna, music teacher, res 45 W Main.

Bloomingdale Fruit House, A L Dodane propr, 92 Wells.

Bloomingdale School, n w cor Marion and Bowser.

Bloor, see also Ploor.

Blossom Maud L, bds 5 Marion.

Blotkamp Emma, bds 26 Bass.

Blotkamp Frank J, mach hd Penn Co, res 26 Bass.

†Blount Ambrose C, storekpr L E & W R R, res 48 Huestis av.

Blount James A, driver, res 9 N Calhoun.

Blue John, molder Kerr Murray Mnfg Co, bds 20 Murray.

Blue Leonard, molder Kerr Murray Mnfg Co, res 75 W Williams.

Blum Caroline, bds 1 Liberty.

Blum Charles J, lab Penn Co, bds 11 Erie.

Blum Henry, bds 19 Walnut.

Blum Katherina (wid Henry), res 19 Walnut.

Blum Nicholas, stonemason, res 11 Erie.

Blum Nicholas jr. molder Bass F & M Wks, bds 11 Erie.

Blum Peter J, laboror, bds 11 Erie.

Blust Ignatius, driver, res 16 Sturgis.

Blust Louisa J, bds 16 Sturgis.

Bly, *see also Bley.*

Bly Kittie Oppelt, bds 156 Calhoun, res same.

Blynn Blanche, teacher Washington School, bds 155 W Wayne.

Blynn Katherine H, teacher High School, bds 155 W Wayne.

Blynn Harriet A (wid Wm), dressmaker, res 155 W Wayne.

Blystone Carl A, bds 53 High.

Blystone Isaac, res 16 Holman.

Blystone Oliver A, contractor, 53 High, res same.

Blythe Samuel W, grocer, e s Leesburg rd 3 n of N Y, C & St L R R, res same.

Boaeuf Julian A, carp, res 179 St Mary's av.

Boag Mary L, bds 69 W Lewis.

Boag Wm G, mach Penn Co, res 69 W Lewis.

Board of Health and Charities, Room 6 City Hall.

Board of Public Safety, room 8 City Hall.

Board of Public Works, Room 2, City Hall.

Bobay Ferdinand F, machine hand, res 124 Union.

Bobay Frank, motorman Ft W E Ry Co, bds 53 Baker.

Bobay Laura, domestic 25 W Washington.

Bobilya Louis J (Romy & Bobilya), res 51 Columbia av.

Bobolink Club, 195½ Calhoun.

Bobs Christopher, finisher Horton Mnfg Co, res 221 St Mary's av.

Boch Charles, student, bds 197 W Superior.

Bock, *see also Buck and Buuck.*

Bock Wm C, carpenter, 35 Nirdlinger av, res same.

Bock Wm F, res 39 Nirdlinger av.

Bockeloh Mrs Emma, res 78 Dawson.

Bockeloh Lizzie, bds 83 W Washington.
Bockhoff Louis F, removed to Indianapolis, Ind.
Bocksburger Louis, barber Louis Uplegger, res 36 Koch.
Bode, *see also Bohde*.
Bode Frank H, bds 1 Monroe.
Bode Henry F, teamster, res 1 Monroe.
Bode Rosa, domestic 134 Montgomery.
Bodine John, brakeman N Y, C & St L R R, bds 34 Runnion av.
Bodine Tisby A (wid Allen), bds 66 Elizabeth.
Body Carrie, domestic 91 W Berry.
Boecker, *see Baker and Becker*.
Boedecker Herman, lab Bass F & M Wks, bds 85 Holman.
Boedeker Gustav, driver Pottlitzer Bros, res 172 Francis.
Bordeker Wm, packer Pottlitzer Bros, res 195 High.
Boegel Emma L, bds 70 Webster.
Boegel Ernest, lab Hoffman Bros, res 70 Webster.
Boegel Frederick E, molder F H Borcherding, res 33 John.
Boegel Henry H, laborer, bds 70 Webster.
Boegli Peter, ruler Ft Wayne Book Bindery, res 130 Wells.
Boehlen Frederick, jeweler A Bruder, rms 270 W Jefferson.
Boehm Barnett W, plasterer, res 10 Winch.
Boehm Charles O, painter, bds 10 Winch.
Boehm Christian F, plumber, 120 Rockhill, res same.
Boehm Hattie L, milliner, res 10 Winch.
Boehm Jennie, bds 10 Winch.
Boehrer Alexis, molder Bass F & M Wks, res 147 Force.
Boenker Frederick, carp Indiana Mach Wks, res n w cor Holton av and Fisher.
Boerger, *see also Berger and Burger*.
Boerger Anna J, domestic 290 Fairfield av.
Boerger Charles R (C R Berger & Bro), bds 194 E Washington.
Boerger C R & Bro (Charles R and Wm H), house movers, 312 Hanna and 194 E Washington.
Boerger Emma, bds 194 E Washington.
Boerger Florenz J, boiler flanger Penn Co, bds 183 E Washington.
Boerger Gustav W, Real Estate and Insurance (Fire and Life), 215 E Wayne, res same.
Boerger Rudolph, res 183 E Washington.
Boerger Sarah, bds 183 E Washington.

Boerger Simon J, bds 183 E Washington.

Boerger Wm, res 194 E Washington.

Boerger Wm H (C R Boerger & Bro), res 312 Hanna.

Boerschinger Henry J, driver The Herman Berghoff Brewing Co, res St Joseph boulevard nr Baker av.

Boerschinger Henry L, gardener, res St Joseph boulevard nr Baker av.

Boes Louis, molder Bass F & M Wks, res 510 E Lewis.

Boese Anna, domestic 164 E Berry.

Boese Christina (wid Amond), res 150 E Jefferson.

Boese Clara, seamstress, bds 135 Montgomery.

Boese Dora F, clk Root & Co, bds 135 Montgomery.

Boese Frank A, clk Root & Co, bds 150 E Jefferson.

Boese Frederick, meats, 139 Force, res 135 same.

Boese Frederick A. res s e cor Penn and Dubois.

Boese Frederick W, lab Penn Co, res 97 Pennsylvania av.

Boese John F C, clerk, bds 12 Hough.

Boese Lizzie, domestic 172 Hanna.

Boese Otto F W. hostler, bds 12 Hough.

Boese Richard, truckman Penn Co, res 250 Calhoun.

Boese Wm, carpenter, res 26 Wallace.

Boese Wm C, car bldr Penn Co, res 15 Hough.

Boester Ernest L, clk Geo De Wald & Co, bds 164 Griffith

Boester Frederick H, contractor, 164 Griffith, res same.

Boester Henry F, student, bds 164 Griffith.

Boester John G, carpenter F H Boester, bds 164 Griffith.

Boester Mary L, bds 164 Griffith.

Boettcher Charles F, forgeman Bass F & M Wks, res 227 Gay.

Boettcher Ernest, opr Wayne Knitting Mills, res 20 Howell.

Bogart Wm W, barber Edward Schele, bds 324 Calhoun.

Bogash Frank H, trainer C L Centlivre Brewing Co, res e s Spy Run av 2 n of canal bridge.

Bogenschuetz Charles, bartender F Belchin, res 164 Harmer.

Bogenschuetz Joseph, bartender C Entemann, bds 204 Lafayette.

Boger George H, lab Ind Mach Wks, bds 164 Wells.

Boger Margaret A (wid Samuel), bds 33 Randolph.

Boger Mary I, opr S M Foster, bds 33 Randolph.

Boggs Rev John M, pastor Third Presbyterian Church, res 46 Brackenridge.

Bogler Anna, opr S M Foster, bds 103 Madison.

Bohde, see also Bode.

+Bohde Charles H, dipper Ft Wayne Electric Corp, res 57
    Home av.
Bohde Frederick W, driver, bds 400 E Lewis.
Bohde John W, sawyer Standard Wheel Co, bds 168 Sut-
    tenfield.
Bohde Wm, driver. bds 103 Erie.
Bohen, *see also Bowen.*
Bohen Cecelia (wid Michael), res 245 E Jefferson.
Bohen Michael H, Justice of the Peace, Law
    and Collections, 23 E Main, res 245 E Jefferson.
Bohen Thomas H, slater J H Welch, bds 245 E Jefferson.
Bohen Wm C, slater J H Welch, res 147 Madison.
Bohley George J, painter, res 78 Swinney av.
Bohling Henry F C, ruler G W Winbaugh, bds 157 E Force.
Bohling Mary D, packer Bond's Cereal Mills, bds 157
    Force.
Bohling Wm, laborer, res 157 Force.
Bohling Wm F, cashier L S & M S Ry, res 126 W 3d.
Bohman, *see Baughman, Bauman and Bowman.*
Bohn Adolph T, printer Archer Ptg Co, bds 20 W Allen.
Bohn August H, lab Olds Wagon Wks, bds 20 W Allen.
Bohn Charles J P, electrician, bds 20 W Allen.
Bohn Christian P, printer The Journal, res 20 W Allen.
Bohn Clara M, bds 20 W Allen.
Bohn Edward W, student, bds 178 Barr.
Bohn Rev Joseph A, second pastor St Paul's Lutheran
    Church, res 178 Barr.
Bohn Louisa R, seamstress, bds 20 W Allen.
Bohn Philipp H, student, bds 178 Barr.
Bohn Theodore, clk J M Neufer, bds 20 W Allen.
Bohn Wm A, sec-treas Horton Mnfg Co, res 285 W Berry.
Bohne Carl H, foreman Kerr Murray Mnfg Co, res 34 W
    Creighton av.
Bohne Frederick H, clk Wm Meyer & Bro, res 25 Boone.
Bohne Louis, clk F M Smith & Co, bds 25 Boone.
Bohner Elizabeth (wid Adam), bds 116 Fulton.
Bohner Henry, farmer County Poor Farm, bds same.
Bohner Jacob C, bartender R Beverforden, res s e cor
    Reed and Jenison.
Bohrer Savina (wid Henry), bds 182 W Williams.
Boisnet Louis A, laborer, res 316 E Creighton av.
Boland Anna, housekeeper McKinnie House.
Boland Asa H, plasterer, res 56 E Leith.
Boland Hubert T C, clk A L Dodane, bds 72 Cass.
Boland Mrs Mary J, res 72 Cass.

Bolei Elizabeth (wid George), bds 79 Swinney av.
Bolender Levi, bds 49 E Jefferson.
Boles, *see also Boltz.*
Boles Edward, trav agt Beuret & Co, bds 36 W Wayne.
Boles Rachel C, bds 36 W Wayne.
Boley Francis, res w s Hillside av 2 s of Baker av.
Boley Josephine M, opr A L Johns & Co, bds Francis Boley.
Boley Louis C, cigarmkr A C Baker, bds Francis Boley.
Boling Edward, cigarmaker, bds 17 Cass.
Boling Lemuel R, painter, res 17 Cass.
Bolinger Mrs Anna A, rms 24 Harrison.
Boll, *see also Ball.*
Boll Victor, tuner D H Baldwin & Co, rms 98 Calhoun.
Bolmahn Charles, lab Olds Wagon Wks, bds head Pennsylvania.
Bolmahn Ernst, engineer, res head of Pennsylvania.
Bolmahn John, laborer, bds head of Pennsylvania.
Bolman, *see also Ballmann.*
Bolman Albert F, saloon, 36 Fairfield av, res 75 Scott av.
Bolman August F, helper Indiana Mach Wks, res 60 Elm.
Bolman Christian D, mach hd Olds Wagon Wks, bds 47 W Lewis.
Bolman Christian E, foreman Olds Wagon Wks, res 47 W Lewis.
Bolman Fredrrick A, conductor, res 188 Jackson.
Bolman Frederick C, asst foreman Olds Wagon Wks, bds 47 W Lewis.
Bolman Henry G, clk H D Niemann, bds 47 W Lewis.
Bolman Minnie, domestic 104 E Main.
Bolman Otto F, brakeman, bds 147 Union.
Bolman Theodore, lab L Rastetter & Son, bds 147 Union.
Bolman Wm A, gate tender Olds Wagon Wks, bds 47 W Lewis.
Boltz, *see also Baltes and Boles.*
Boltz Frederick C, res 87 Cass.
Boltz Frederick G, clerk, bds 87 Cass.
Boltz George C, bds 87 Cass.
Boltz Peter S, Supt Metropolitan Life Insurance Co of New York, 1 and 2 White Bank Blk, res 70 W Wayne.
Bolyard Daniel, fireman Penn Co, res 59 W Williams.
Bon Daniel, insurance agt, res 11 Huffman.
Bona Julius A, res 97 Glasgow av.
Bond Albert L, photographer, res 43 W Butler.

✝Bond Albert S, treas and supt Ft Wayne Organ Co, res 362 Fairfield av.

Bond Cereal Mills, H W Bond propr, 65 E Columbia. Tel 178.

Bond Charles E, teller Old National Bank, res 289 Fairfield av. Tel 170.

Bond Charles Z, machinist, bds 122 Fairfield av.

Bond Frank D, clk Old National Bank, bds 322 Fairfield av

Bond Frank J, barnman A L Martin, bds 14 Clinton.

Bond Henry W, propr Bond Cereal Mills, 65 E Columbia, res 104 W Berry. Tel 178. res 530.

Bond Herbert W, clk Ft Wayne Organ Co, bds 322 Fairfield av.

Bond Hugh Mc C, bds 256 Fairfield av.

Bond Jared D, cash Old National Bank, res 3 W De Wald.

Bond Jennie M (wid Alonzo S), res 122 Fairfield av.

Bond Jessie A, bds 322 Fairfield av.

Bond Lavinia A (wid Charles W), res 256 Fairfield av. Tel 201.

Bond Lucretia F (wid Wm J), res 26 Mc Clellan.

Bond Milo, condr N Y, C & St L R R, rms 32 Calhoun.

Bond Stephen B, pres Old National Bank and Ft Wayne Organ Co, res 322 Fairfield av. Tel 1.

Bonfield Lizzie, opr Wayne Knitting Mills, bds 275 E Lewis.

Bonfield Mary (wid Kennedy), res 180 E Wayne.

Bonillon Jennie, demestic 61 Broadway.

Bonner Ray R, lab S F Bowser & Co, bds 118 Smith.

Bonner Theodore H, brakeman, bds 118 Smith.

Bonnet J George, helper, res 104 E Wayne.

Bonneville Earl S, clk The Wayne, bds same.

Bonter George W P, conductor, res 73 W De Wald.

Bookwalter Clyde, street car conductor, bds 15 W Williams.

Bookwalter Elias H, pressman Ft Wayne Gazette, res 15 W Williams.

Bookwalter John A, iron fences, 213 E Wayne, res same.

Bookwalter & Son, mnfrs printers' roller composition, 15 W Williams.

Boone Agnes J, bds 76 Chicago.

Boone Charles A, brakeman, bds 76 Chicago.

Boone Joseph L, laborer, bds 76 Chicago.

Boone Mary C, bds 76 Chicago.

Boone Wm N, huckster, res 76 Chicago.

Boorman George E, fireman N Y, C & St L R R, res 41 Elm.

Boose Rudolph, bds 27 Baker.
Bopp, *see also Popp.*
Bopp Charles A, cigarmkr W A Bayer, bds Henry C Bopp.
Bopp George, painter J H Brimmer, res 130 Hayden.
Bopp Henry C, wagonmkr Fleming Mnfg Co, res e s Hillside av 2 s of Baker av.
Bopp Maggie M, domestic The Wayne.
Bopp Peter J, clk Penn Co, bds 520 E Lewis.
Borcherding Ferdinand H, foundry, e s N Barr 1 n of Superior, res 35 Liberty.
✦Borchert Frederick A, painter, res 59 Indiana av.
Borg, *see also Berg and Burg.*
Borg Rev Theodore B, chaplain St Vincent Orphan Asylum.
Borgmann, *see also Bergman.*
Borgmann August C. teamster, res 17 Lavina.
Borgmann Christian W, laborer, bds 200 Ewing.
Borgmann Christopher F, clk Wm Hahn & Co, res 35 Lavina.
Borgmann Elizabeth S C, seamstress, bds 35 Lavina.
Borgmann Fredericka (wid Christian), res 35 Lavina.
Borgmann Fredericka C (Borgmann & Leeser), bds 35 Lavina.
Borgmann Marie C, clk Geo DeWald & Co, bds 35 Lavina.
Borgmann Wm, contractor, 200 Ewing, res same.
Borgmann Wm F, captain of police, res 22 W 4th.
Borgmann & Leeser The Misses, (Fredericka C Borgmann, Pauline A H Leeser), Fine Millinery Goods, 137 Broadway.
Borhek Herman S, rms 294 Calhoun.
Bork, *see also Burke.*
Bork August, laborer, bds 252 Gay.
Bork Charles, laborer, bds 252 Gay.
Bork Emma, domestic Herman Berghoff.
Bork Julius, laborer, res 252 Gay.
Bork Wm R, lab L Rastetter & Son, bds 252 Gay.
Borkenstein Bernhard, carpenter 222 John, res same.
Bornemann Charles, sexton, res 98 Harrison.
Bornemann Frederick C, guns, 58 E Main, bds 98 Harrison.
Bornkamp Frederick W, bricklayer, res 7 Gay.
Bort Frank, laborer Ligget Bros, rms 5 N Harrison.
Bortner Thella, stenographer S M Hench, bds 222 Madison
Borton Club Room, 24 Arcade Bldg.
Borts Albert, car bldr Penn Co, bds 303 Lafayette.
Bosch Rev John H, Pastor St John's Reformed Church, res 59 W Washington.

Boschet Gottlieb, lab N Y, C & St L R R, res 81 Barthold.
Boschet Henry, carpenter, bds 163 Wells.
Boschet John, machine hand, bds 81 Barthold.
Boschet Sophia, domestic 88 W Berry.
Bosecker Frederick F, lab Ft Wayne Electric Corp, bds 104 Wall.
Bosecker Louise M, bds 104 Wall.
Bosecker Wm G, planer Horton Mnfg Co, res 104 Wall.
Bosecker Wm L V, appr Kerr Murray Mnfg Co, bds 102 Wall.
Bosecker A Lincoln, conductor, res 290 W Main.
Bosecker Charles F, carpenter, res n w cor Runnion av and Richardson.
Boseker Christian, contractor, res 37 Brackenridge.
Boseker Frank H, carpenter res 131 Shawnee av.
Boseker Gottfried, coremaker, res 19 Guthrie.
Boseker Harry C, clerk, bds 37 Brackenridge.
Boseker Henry traveling agent, res 66 W De Wald.
Boshler Charles W, mngr J C Peters & Co, res 70 W Butler.
Boss Anna, teacher Hanna School, bds 138 E Main.
Boss Mary (wid Henry), bds 138 E Main.
Bosselman Kate, domestic 88 E Berry.
Bosselmann Diedrich, boilermaker, res 233 Madison.
Bossler Henry H, real estate, res w s Spy Run av 1 n of bridge.
Bossler Joseph, helper Penn Co. res 22 Gay.
Bossler Joseph jr, molder, bds 18 Bass.
Bossler Kittie A, dressmaker, bds w s Spy Run av 1 n of bridge.
Bossler Maggie, cook J C Hinton, rms 20 W Lewis.
Bostick Addie F, bds 170 E Wayne.
Bostick Harriet (wid Emanuel), res 170 E Wayne.
Bostick John W, res 130 E Wayne.
Bostick Samuel W, clk Penn Co, bds 130 E Wayne.
Bostick Wm D (E B Kunkle & Co), bds 170 E Wayne.
Boswell Andrew J, physician, n w cor E Wayne and Barr, res 132 Fairfield av. Tel 205.
Bosworth Percy B, foreman Fort Wayne Electric Corp, res 338 Broadway.
Bothner Annie E, bds 136 Calhoun.
Bothner John G, saloon, 136 Calhoun, res same.
Bott Charles V, laborer, bds 46 Taylor.
Bott Clements J, student, bds 46 Taylor.

Bott Edward U, patternmkr Kerr Murray Mnfg Co, bds 26 Walnut.
Bott Elizabeth, seamstress Ella H Kenlin, bds 36 Taylor.
Bott Frank J, clk Fox br U S Bkg Co, bds 26 Walnut.
Bott Innocence, blksmith Penn Co, res 26 Walnut.
Bott John, bartender Jordan Bros, rms 67 Harrison.
Bott Kate, bds 27 E 3d.
Bott Nellie G, dressmaker, bds 46 Taylor.
Bott Theresa M, dressmaker, bds 46 Taylor.
Bott Urban, mach Wabash R R, res 46 Taylor.
Bottenberg Andrew J. res 13 Liberty.
Botteron Emma, domestic 336 W Main.
Bottger John E, engr N Y, C & St L R R, res 296 W Jefferson.
Bougher, *also Bauer and Bower*.
Bougher Frank E (Riegel & Bougher), res 12 Calhoun.
Boulton Edward A, driver, bds 129½ W 3d.
Bourie A Ophelia. stenographer Olds Wagon Wks and notary public, bds 97 Edgewater av.
Bourie Brutus A (Bourie, Cook & Co), res 18 W DeWald.
Bourie Clinton D, letter carrier, res 142 Columbia av.
Bourie, Cook & Co, (Brutus A Bourie, John M Cook, A Trentman), Cigar Mnfrs, 358 Calhoun.
Bourie Desdemona F, bds 18 W De Wald.
Bourie George W, clk Pixley & Co, bds 97 Edgewater av.

Bourie Louis T, res 97 Edgewater av.
Bouvier Rosetta, domestic 195 W Berry.
Bovine David F, trucker Wabash R R, res n s Cottage av 2 w of Indiana av.
Bowden Walter A, tel opr, res 160 Ewing.
Bowen, *see also Bohen*.
Bowen Daniel W, lawyer, res 229 E Washington.
Bowen Franklin J, driver W F Geller, res 71 Garden.
Bowen George R, res 108 Barr.
Bowen George W, physician 12 W Main, res 232 E Washington.
Bowen Lillie V, teacher Nebraska School, bds 229 E Washington.
Bower, *see also Bauer and Bougher*.
Bower Claude A, clerk, bds 35 E 4th.
Bower Cora H, bds 586 Calhoun.
Bower George B M, Physician; Nervous and Skin Diseases, 72 Harrison, res 100 W Berry. Tel 357.
Bower Harry, flagman. res 237 Walton av.

Bower Jacob M. policeman, res 35 E 4th.

Bower John F, teacher Adams Township School, bds 210 Fairfield av.

Bowers Alfaretta, bds 306 Maumee rd.

Bowers Charles A, watchman Olds Wagon Wks, res 168 W Williams.

Bowers David B, farmer, res 306 Maumee rd.

Bowers David L, carpenter, 57 Prospect av, res same.

Bowers Emma S, bds 20 Stophlet.

Bowers Harry H, student, bds 306 Maumee rd.

Bowers Ida B, bds 57 Prospect av.

Bowers Jacob, fireman G R & I R R, bds rear 57 W Williams.

Bowers John E, student, bds 306 Maumee rd.

Bowers Joht W, painter J H Brimmer, res 129 Home av.

Bowers Margaret, domestic 96 E Berry.

Bowers Maria (wid James), bds 44 Lavina.

Bowers Wm E, student, bds 306 Maumee rd,

Bowers Wm L, painter, res 44 Lavina.

Bowersock Andrew (Bowersock & Gooden), res 13 Michael av.

Bowersock & Gooden (Andrew Bowersock, Isaac Gooden), grocers, 45 W Main.

Bowley Edwin J, opr Wayne Knitting Mills, bds 52 Runnion av,

Bowling Thomas J, lampman Penn Co, res 183 Jackson.

Bowman, *see also Baughman. Bauman and Bohman.*

Bowman Arthur F, clk J D Gumpper, res 39 Shawnee av.,

Bowman Bessie F, student, bds 9 Boone.

Bowman Charles, Machinist; Saw Repairing a Specialty, 37 Pearl, res 39 1st. (*See right side lines and card in classified Saw Works.*)

Bowman Charles A, brakeman N Y, C & St L R R, bds 9 Boone.

Bowman Clarence H, painter Penn Co, res 337 Harrison.

Bowman Clyde F, clk Shepler & Noble, bds 263 Calhoun.

Bowman Cyrenius A, canvasser Singer Mnfg Co, res 241 Clay,

Bowman Elizabeth, teacher Bloomingdale Schools, bds 15 Michael av.

Bowman Elma, bds 9 Boone.

Bowman Emeline D (wid Alfred), res 15 Michael av.

Bowman Hattie, domestic 77 E Berry.

Bowman John E, carpenter, res 9 Boone.

Bowman Prudence L, teacher Nebraska Schools, bds 15 Michael av.

Bowman Sarah (wid Benjamin), removed to Angola, Ind.

Bowser Alexander, res 264 E Creighton av.

Bowser Allen A (S F Bowser & Co), res 264 E Creighton av

Bowser Charles W, painter, bds Sylvester S Bowser.

Bowser Cora E, bds Sylvester S Bowser.

Bowser Daisy, bds 95 Summit.

Bowser Ernest M, watchman S F Bowser & Co. bds 55 Charles.

Bowser Etta, dressmaker 334 Calhoun, res same.

Bowser Frank M, farmer county poor farm, bds same.

Bowser George W, fireman Penn Co, res 284 Walton av.

Bowser Isaiah, res 266 E Creighton av.

Bowser Lafayette, foreman, bds 264 E Creighton av.

Bowser Lola D, seamstress, bds 334 Calhoun.

Bowser Margaret (wid Samuel), res 95 Summit.

Bowser Mary K (wid George W), res 55 Charles.

Bowser Nelson J, bds 13 Chestnut.

Bowser Nettie, bds Sylvester S Bowser.

Bowser Orra J, painter 266 E Creighton av, res same.

Bowser Raymond E, bds 55 Charles.

Bowser Sylvanus F (S F Bowser & Co), res 252 E Creighton av.

Bowser Sylvester S, carpenter S F Bowser & Co, res w s Winter 2 n of Pontiac.

Bowser S F & Co, (Sylvanus F and Allen A Bowser), Patentees and Mnfrs of High Grade Specialties, cor E Creighton av and Thomas. Tel 374. (See page 4.)

Bowser Waldo P, bds 334 Calhoun.

Bowsher Amos, mail agent, res 55 E Butler.

Bowsher Nellie V, stenographer, bds 55 E Butler.

Boyce Benjamin, engr Bass F & M Wks, res 286 Hanna.

Boyd Seymour D, clk Bass F & M Wks, res 361 Hanna.

Boyd Thomas L, laborer, res 141 W Wayne.

Boyer, see also Baer, Baier, Bair and Bear.

Boyer Ida F, nurse, 172 Holman, bds same.

Boyer J Louise, nurse, bds 172 Holman.

Boyes Charles H, cutter S Freiburger & Bro, bds 104 Barr.

Boylan Mrs M Etta, housekeeper Jewel House.

Boyle John P, lab, res s s New Haven av, 2 e of Pontiac.

Boyles Anna D, bds 35 Miner.

Boyles Grace H, bds 35 Miner.

Boyles Robert C, finisher, bds 35 Miner.

Boyles Robert D, patternmaker Bass F & M Wks, res 35 Miner.

Brabandt Ernest R, molder Bass F & M Wks, res 99 John.

Brabandt Henry B, molder Bass F & M Wks, res 168 John.

Bracht Charles, porter The Wayne.

Bracht Joseph C, engr N Y, C & St L R R, res 33 W Butler. Tel 421.

Bracht Wm F, engineer, res 83 Boone.

Brackenridge Charles S, civil engr 144 W Wayne, res same.

Brackenridge Eliza J (wid Joseph), bds 77 W Wayne.

Brackenridge George W, Trustee Wayne Township, 9 Arcade Up Stairs, res 31 Douglas av. Tel 326.

Brackenridge Wm T, mngr Old Fort Chemical Co, res 77 W Wayne.

Bradbury Frank C, trucker Penn Co, res 15 Zollars av.

Bradbury James L, lab Rastetter & Son, bds 122 Chicago.

Bradbury Ollie, domestic 33 Miner.

Braddock Wm A, carp George Young, res 101 Franklin.

Brademeyer, *see Bredemeyer.*

Braden Charles, porter The Randall.

Braden David, teamster, res 271 W Creighton av.

Braden Frank, bell boy The Randall.

Braden Ida, cook, rms 146 Holman.

Braden Jesse S, clk Post Office, bds 271 W Creighton av.

Bradley Edgar O, engineer Penn Co, res 38 E Williams.

Bradley George O, carpenter, res 33 W Williams.

Bradley Harry J, architect, bds 101 Calhoun.

Bradley James K, mach Penn Co, res 233 E Lewis.

Bradley Jessie L, bds 233 E Lewis.

Bradley Nelson L, designer, 36 Bass Blk, res 149 E Jefferson.

Bradley Robert A, draughtsman Wing & Mahurin, bds 33 W Williams.

Bradley Sarah A, propr Grand Central Hotel, 101 Calhoun.

Bradley Viola M, bds 101 Calhoun.

Bradley Wm N, res 101 Calhoun.

Bradshaw Canalda (col'd), res 47 Hayden.

Bradshaw Eliza (col'd), domestic, bds 47 Hayden.

Bradshaw Frank (col'd), hostler, bds 47 Hayden.

Bradshaw Samuel H (col'd), barber S G Hubbard, res 19 Francis.

Bradshaw Wm W (col'd), laborer, bds 47 Hayden.

Bradtmueller Charles H C, blacksmith 6 Calhoun, res 172 Madison.

Bradtmueller Gottlieb, carp Penn Co, res 59 Douglas av.
Bradtmueller Henry W, clk Root & Co, bds 172 Madison.
Bradtmueller Herman W, driver Geo DeWald & Co, bds 172 Madison.
Bradtmueller Louisa C, milliner, bds 172 Madison.
Bradtmueller Matilda E, bds 105 Wall.
Bradtmueller Wm, res 127 Francis.
Bradway Orlando E, foreman Penn Co, res 216 E Lewis.
Brady Edward, brakeman, res 67 Smith.
Brady Jesse D, clk Root & Co, bds 170 W Wayne.
Brady Wm H (Root & Co), res 170 W Wayne.
Braeuer, *see also Breuer and Bruer.*
Braeuer Conrad, shoemkr, 358 Broadway, res same.
Braeuer John C, shoemkr C Braeuer, res 184 Griffith.
Braeuer John W, bds 358 Broadway.
Brahs Anna (wid John), res e s Calhoun 2 s of Marshall.
Braithwait Charles F, engr N Y, C & St L R R, res 224 High.
Braithwait Charles L, driver F Barrett & Co, bds 224 High.
Braithwait George W, fireman, bds 224 High.
Braithwait N Elijah, lab Hoffman Bros, bds 224 High.
Braithwaite Wm H, fireman, bds n s Jesse 1 e of Runnion av.
Brake Henry, painter, res 180 Maumee rd
Brake Ulrich G, lab J C Jahn & Co, res 189 Maumee rd.
Brake Ulrich G jr, fireman, res 182 Maumee rd.
Brames Anna E, bds 162 E Jefferson.
Brames Louis (L Brames & Co), res 162 E Jefferson.
Brames L & Co (Louis Brames), Proprs Summit City Bottling Works, 123-127 Clay. Tel 257, (*See p 3.*)
Brames Margaret, domestic 72 W Wayne.
Brammer, *see also Bremer.*
Brammer Very Rev Joseph H, Vicar-General Diocese of Fort Wayne, res 172 Clinton.
Branard Annie, dressmaker, 78 W Main, res same.
Brandenburger Fred C, hostler C E Rippe, bds 113 Broadway.
Brandenburger Gustave H, car repr, res n s Poplar 2 e of Fox.
Brandenburger Rosina (wid Samuel), res 113 Broadway.
Brandt Ada, opr Wayne Knitting Mills, bds 15 Boone.
Brandt Amelia, clk Wm Hahn & Co, bds 34 Mc Clellan.
Brandt August C, cigar mnfr, 158 Harrison, bds same,
Brandt Bertha E, student, bds 34 Mc Clellan.

154   R. L. POLK & CO.'S

Brandt Catherine (wid Frederick), res 158 Harrison.
Brandt Charles, grain buyer, res 34 Mc Clellan.
Brandt Christian, lathe hd Ind Mach Wks, res 15 Boone.
Brandt Christian A, billposter Ft Wayne City Bill Posting Co, bds 104 Mechanic.
Brandt Clara, bds 158 Harrison.
Brandt Diedrich, coremkr Bass F & M Wks, res 142 John.
Brandt Dora, bds 172 Hayden.
Brandt Gottlieb F, sawyer, res 7 Marion.
Brandt Henry, lab J A Bloom, res 172 Hayden.
Brandt Herman, foreman Rhinesmith & Simonson, res 187 E Taber.
Brandt Lena. domestic 316 W Jefferson.
Brandt Louise, bds 34 Mc Clellan.
Brandt Minnie. clk J M Kane, bds 34 Mc Clellan.
Brandt Theodore, finisher Ft Wayne Organ Co, bds 172 Hayden.
Brandt Theodore W, clk Wm Meyer & Bro, bds 45 W Jefferson.
Brandt Wm J, cigarmaker, res 152 Harrison.
Branican Beverly (col'd), porter, res 100 Indiana av.
Braning Henry E, carpenter, res 1 Victoria av.
Brannan, see also Brennan.
Brannan Bridget, housekeeper Rev Joseph F Delaney.
Brannan Celia M, bds 195 E Lewis.
Brannan Elizabeth, res 199 E Lewis.
Brannan John H, bridge contractor, res 195 E Lewis.
Brannan Mary, teacher, bds 195 Lewis.
Brannan Michael L, janitor Clay School, res 171 E Washington.
Brannan Richard B, plumber, bds 195 E Lewis.
Branstator Charles W, county surveyor Allen County, office Court House, bds 29 E Main.
Branstator John A, painter, res 74 Fletcher av.
Branstrator Walter T, laborer, bds 106 Barr.
Brasch Charles, porter The Wayne, rms 60 W Berry.
Brase August C, grocer, 73 W Jefferson, res same.
Brase Frederick C, teamster, res 75 W Jefferson.
Brase Theodore F, driver, res 202 Fairfield av.
Braun, see also Brown.
Braun Barbara (wid John), res 78 Wall.
Braun Catherine, clk Louis Wolf & Co, bds 151 Hanna.
Braun Charles G (Keller & Braun), res 157 Van Buren.
Braun Charles M, harnersmkr F Hilt, bds 78 Wall.
Braun Clara C, clk George Braun, bds 135 Fairfield av.

C. P. TINKHAM, D. D. S. 21, 22, 23, 24 Arcade Block,
West Berry Street,
Office Telephone   Residence Telephone   FORT WAYNE, IND.

FORT WAYNE DIRECTORY.   155

Braun Frederick, helper, bds 6 Winch.
Braun Frederick C, cigarmkr P O Drinkwitz, bds 233 John.
Braun George, baker, 135 Fairfield av, res same.
Braun George J, bds 54 Lavina.
Braun Henry, stereotyper, bds 6 Winch.
Braun Jacob F, res 3 Marion.
Braun John, carpenter, res 6 Winch.
Bräun Lena. domestic 254 W De Wald.
Braun Louis, laborer, res e s Fletcher av 3 n of Wabash R R.
Braun Louise, domestic 378 Hanna.
Braun Lulu, bds 151 Hanna.
Braun Martin, boilermkr Bass F & M Wks, res 70 Summit.
Braun Martin, clerk, bds 135 Fairfield av.
Braun Mary (wid Matthias), res 151 Hanna.
Braun Peter M, patternmkr Bass F & M Wks, res 387 E Lewis.
Braun Wm, pressfeeder Ft Wayne Newspaper Union, bds 6 Winch.
Braun Wm, student, bds 135 Fairfield av.
Braungart George, mach hd Ft Wayne Furn Co, res 158 Fairfield av.
Brauneisen Joseph, grocer, 146 Wells, res same.
Brauntmeyer Charles H. brass finisher A Hattersley & Sons, res 176 Ewing.
Brauntmeyer Frederick W, molder, res 168 Ewing.
Brazier Henry, brakeman, bds 208 E Lewis.
Bredemyer Anna, bds 8 Marion.
Bredemyer Anna (wid Wm), died July 12, 1894.
Bredemyer Henry E, watchman Hamilton Bank, res 38 E 4th.
Bredemyer H Wm, painter, res 8 Marion.
Bredemyer Wm, lab Standard Wheel Co, bds 24 Force.
Breen Ellen N, dressmaker, bds 15 Bass.
Breen Henry, laborer, bds 15 Bass.
Breen James E, conductor, res 71 E De Wald.
Breen Maria (wid Michael), res 15 Bass.
Breen Michael, night clk Penn Co, bds 15 Bass.
Breen Wm P (Breen & Morris), res 121 W Main.
Breen & Morris (Wm P Breen, John Morris jr), Lawyers, 44 Calhoun. Tel 151.
Breene Edward G, flagman, bds 63 Boone.
Breer Ferdinand, carver Ft Wayne Furn Co, res 53 Rivermet av.
Breese Edward S, painter, res 42 Harmer.

Breese George H, helper, res 60 Wall.

Breese Randolph, appr Penn Co, bds 126 Harrison.

Brehm Mrs Anna, res 599 Calhoun.

Brehm Charles, clk Ankenbruck & Potthoff), bds 170 E Washington.

Brehm Wm, barber S G Hubbard, res 170 E Washington.

Breidenstein Daniel, clk G H Seabold, bds same.

Breidenstein Simpson, real estate, res w s Spy Run av 2 n of canal bridge.

Breimeier Clara A, bds 219 W Jefferson.

Breimeier Ernest, res 221 W Creighton av.

Breimeier Ernest H F, Contractor and Builder 207 W DeWald, res same.

Breimeier Frederick H E, carpenter, res 225 W Jefferson.

Breimeier Gustav A, mach Ft Wayne Electric Corp, bds 221 W Creighton av.

Breimeier Henry C, res 219 W Jefferson.

Breimeier Herman H F, bricklayer, bds 221 W Creighton av.

Breimeier Louis C, clk A E C Becker, res 101 W Williams.

Breimeier Margaret, domestic 131 E Wayne.

Breimeier Minnie L, bds 219 W Jefferson.

Bremer, *see also Brammer.*

Bremer Henry H, clk J B White, res 47 Archer av.

Bremer Henry H jr, driver, bds 47 Archer av.

Bremer Wm, laborer, bds 156 Shawnee av.

Bremer Wm F, clk F Kreibaum, res 124 W 3d.

Brenckant Doynie, shoemaker, res 14 Nirdlinger av.

Brenckant Lizzie, bds 14 Nirdlinger av.

Brennan, *see also Brannan.*

Brennan Bernard T, cigarmkr W A Bayer, res 120 St Mary's av.

Brennan Michael, laborer, bds 419 W Main.

Brennan Wm T, mach Fort Wayne Electric Corp, res 182 E Lewis.

Brenner Charles F, mach Kerr Murray Mnfg Co, bds 78 Wilt.

Brenner George, printer Freie Presse, bds 55 Madison.

Brenner Mary (wid John) res 78 Wilt.

Brenner Mollie B, dressmaker, bds 78 Wilt.

Brenton Edith, bds 19 Madison.

Brenton Helen E, teacher Jefferson School, res 220 W Wayne.

Brenton Marian H (wid Milton H), teacher Hanna School, bds 19 Madison.

Brenzinger Bread Baking Co The, Wm F Brenzinger Pres, Frederick D Mc Cutcheon Sec and Treas, Wholesale and Retail Bakers, 14 W Washington. Tel 548.

Brenzinger Wm F, pres Brenzinger Bread Baking Co, res Toledo, O.

Bresch George T, laborer, bds 22 Wefel.

Bresler Albert W, farmer, res e s Huntington rd opp Lindenwood Cemetery.

Bresler James M, lab Killian Baker, bds 38 Wall.

Bresnahan John, wiper, bds 206 Lafayette.

Bresnahan John J, fireman N Y, C & St L R R, res 206 Lafayette. Tel 448.

Bresnahan Mary E, tailoress G Scheffler, bds 206 Lafayette.

Bresnahan Patrick E, mach Penn Co, bds 206 Lafayette.

Bresnahan Thomas F, clerk, bds 206 Lafayette.

Breuer, see also Braeuer and Bruer.

Breuer Wm, foreman The Herman Berghoff Brewing Co, res 574 E Washington.

Brewer Wm L, trav agt, res 238 W Wayne.

Brewster Edith M, principal Holton Avenue School, bds 141 E De Wald.

Briant, see also Bryant.

Briant Lucinda A (wid Wm H), res 228 W Creighton av.

Brice James F, foreman street repairs, res 159 W Superior

Brick Christiana L (wid Adam), bds 122 W Jefferson.

Bricker Conrad, engr Penn Co, res cor Thomas and Green.

Bricker David, engr G R & I R R, res 22 Oliver.

Bricker D Edwin, mngr S M Foster, res 299 E Lewis.

Bricker Homer A, clk D N Foster Furn Co, bds 74 Thomas.

Bricker John M, feed barn, 97 and 99 E Columbia, res 78 same.

Brickmakers' Association, 55 Clinton.

Brickner Charles H, carp The Paul Mnfg Co, res 256 Gay

Brickner John, bds 16 Maiden lane.

Brickuer Clement O, stonemason, bds 141 Erie.

Brickuer Herman, stonemason, res 141 Erie.

Brickuer Oswald, dyer, bds 141 Erie.

Brielmeier Joseph, stonecutter Keller & Braun, res 4 Huron.

Briggemann Henry A, piano tuner, bds 328 E Wayne.

Briggemann Wm, meats, 281 E Creighton av, res 21 Euclid av.

12

158 R. L. POLK & CO.'s

Briggemann Wm F, driver City Trucking Co, bds 159 Harrison.

Briggs Frances A (wid Martin), res 250 Calhoun.

Briggs Frank W, clk Root & Co, bds 161 W Main.

Briggs Mrs Harriet, res 161 W Main.

Briggs Lilian M, clk Root & Co, bds 161 W Main.

Briggs Martin E, clk St James Hotel, bds same.

Bright Benjamin W, molder Bass F & M Wks, res 337 Hanna.

Bright Laura M, bds 229 E Wayne.

Bright Wm J, carbldr Penn Co, res 229 E Wayne.

Brill Henry F, conductor, res 301 E Creighton av.

Brillhart Andrew J, lab Ft Wayne Electric Corp, res 10 Ida av.

Brimmer Joseph H, House and Sign Painting, Wall Paper and Paper Hanging, 33 W Main, res 265 W Jefferson. Tel 164.

Brindle Henry, plasterer, res 11 Indiana av.

Brink Henry H, foreman Rhinesmith & Simonson, res 298 E Washington.

Brink John J, druggist, 44 Wells, res same. Tel 331.

Brink Mamie H, bkkpr Wm Hahn & Co, bds 320 E Washington.

Brinker Ella, domestic 152 W Washington.

Brinker Theodore, checker N Y C & St L R R, res 312 W Jefferson.

Brinker Theodore A, clk A Mergentheim, bds 312 W Jefferson.

Brinkman Frederick J B, mach hd Penn Co, res 80 Oliver.

Brinkman Henry F, mason 177 Gay, res same.

Brinkman Wm E, painter, res 222 Gladstone.

Brinkman Wm H, mason, bds 177 Gay.

Brinkroeger Herman P W, grocer, 48 Harrison, bds 63 High. Tel 190.

Brinkroeger John F W, clerk, res 63 High.

Brinneng Ernest, farmer, res Fairfield av s w cor Rudisill av.

Brinsley Charles E, molder, res 33 Wells.

Brinsley George C (George C Brinsley & Son), res 264 W Washington.

Brinsley George C jr (George C Brinsley & Son), res 85 W Main.

Brinsley George C & Son (George C and George C jr), oils, 28 Pearl.

Brinsley John C, livery, 28 Pearl, res 110 W Main. Tel 225.

Brinsley J Clifford, condr Wabash R R, res 128 Rockhill.
Brintzenhofe, Ammon S, mach Wasbash R R, res w s Brooklyn av 3 s of Ontario.
Bristol Abons, laborer, bds 98 E Columbia.
Bristol Mrs Irene, bds 64 E Columbia.
Britcher Edward M, res 12 E 3d.
Britcher Edward P, laborer, res 20 Lafayette.
Brittingham John S, wood turner L Diether & Bro, res 469 Harrison.
Britton Charles M, fireman Penn Co, res 178 Hanna.
Brittone Maude, domestic 15 W Jefferson.
Broach Elizabeth, dressmkr, bds 19 Michael av.
Broach Lulu, seamstress M L Sherin, bds 19 Michael av.
Broadway Theater, Schroeder Bros mngrs, 97 Broadway.
Brock, see Bracht.
Brockerman Ethel B, bds 12 Marion.
Brockerman Jacob R, plasterer, res 12 Marion.
Brockerman Leonard S, plasterer, res 48 South Wayne av.
Brockerman Rudy L, bds 48 South Wayne av.
Brockerman Thomas W, removed to Huntertown, Ind.
Brockmann Henry, lab Bass F & M Wks, res 23 Julia.
Brockmeyer Edward G, molder Bass F & M Wks, bds 87 Wall.
Brockway Jennie (wid Clarence M), res 11 Melita.
Brockway Louis C, driver T Ryan, bds 11 Melita.
Brockway Nellie M, clk H H G Upmeyer, bds 11 Melita.
Brodt Frederick, canvasser, res 51 Liberty.
Broegemeyer Henry, bds 173 Ewing.
Brocking Augusta, bds Charles Broeking.
Broeking Carrie, bds Charles Broeking.
Broeking Charles, grocer, n e cor Gay and E Creighton av, res same.
Broeking Charles jr, painter Olds Wagon Wks, bds Charles Broeking.
Broeking Wm, painter Olds Wagon Wks, bds Charles Broeking.
Brokaw Frances B, stenogr J A Armstrong & Co, bds 20 W Creighton av.
Brokaw James H, condr G R & I R R, res 20 W Creighton av
Brokaw Lee, porter The Randall.
Brokaw Mary M, teacher Jefferson School, bds 20 W Creighton av.
Brokaw Oscar R, bds 20 W Creighton av.
Brokaw Samuel, sanitary policeman, res 70 Charles.

Bromelmeier Charles H, engineer N Y, C & St L R R, res 356 W Main.
Bron Wm E, lab Winkelmeyer & Hans, bds 16 W 3d.
Bronson Drusilla (wid Abraham), res 5 Brandriff.
Brooks Abraham B C, cabinetmaker, res 488 Fairfield av.
Brooks Alonzo A, brakeman N Y, C & St L R R, res 3 Centre.
Brooks Charlotte (wid Henry), bds 269 W De Wald.
Brooks Ernest, barber W A Lichtenwalter, bds 122 Clay.
Brooks Etta C, teacher Hoagland School, bds 269 W DeWald.
Brooks George H, carpenter, res 3 E Superior.
Brooks Gilbert E, fireman Penn Co, res 26 W Jefferson.
Brooks Henry, driver, bds 382 E Washington.
Brooks Henry, printer Ind Staats Zeitung, res 72 Webster
Brooks Henry C, contractor, res 269 W De Wald.
Brooks Kate (wid Walter), bds 28 Lake av.
Brooks Michael, fireman, bds 324 Calhoun.
Brooks Olive M, student, bds 269 W De Wald.
Brooks Oscar H, bkkpr Olds Wagon Wks, res 169 E Berry
Brooks Wm, carpenter, res 136 Jackson.
Brooks Wm H, died Oct 13th, 1894.
Broom Harry E, helper, bds 31 Gay.
Broom John N, foreman S F Bowser & Co, res 31 Gay.
Broom John W, mach hd Anthony Wayne Mnfg Co, bds 31 Gay.
Broom Theresa, opr Hoosier Mnfg Co, bds 31 Gay.
Brosius Aaron, timber, res 178 Wells.
Brosius Andrew, attendant School for Feeble-Minded Youth.
Brosius A D, route agt Adams Express Co, res 81 Griffith.
Brosius Jesse, clk R M S, res 176 Wells.
Brosius Olive D, teacher Bloomingdale School, bds 178 Wells.
Brosowski Edward, laborer, bds 490 Hanna.
Brosowski Ernst, laborer, bds 490 Hanna.
Brosowski Martin, lab Bass F & M Works, res 490 Hanna.
Brosowski Rudolph, mach hd L Rastetter & Son, bds 490 Hanna.
Brossard Clara T, dressmaker, bds 82 Wells.
Brossard Frank E, clk M Frank & Co, bds 82 Wells.
Brossard George, res 18 W 5th.
Brossard George, machinist, bds 82 Wells.

Brossard John, blacksmith Western Gas Cons Co, res 82 Wells.
Brossard Josephine C, bds 33 Wefel.
Brossard Theresa, dressmaker, 33 Wefel, bds same.
Brossard Wm, blksmith Penn Co, res 33 Wefel.
Brossard Wm G, wrapper Louis Wolf & Co, bds 33 Wefel.
Brotherhood of Locomotive Engineers' Hall, 136 Calhoun.
Brotherhood of Locomotive Firemen's Hall, 70 Calhoun.
Brothers of the Holy Cross, s w cor Clinton and Jefferson.
Brothers Rosa, bds 263 Calhoun.
Browand Frances M, milliner, bds 287 Harrison.
Browand Mary J (wid Michael), res 287 Harrison.
Browand Michael S, agent, rms rear 41½ W Main.
Browand Norman C (Browand & Heldt), bds 287 Harrison.
Browand Reuben M, barber Browand & Heldt, bds 287 Harrison.
Browand Wm A, barber Browand & Heldt, bds 287 Harrison.
Browand & Heldt (Norman C Browand, John M Heldt), barbers, 103 Calhoun.
Brower Cain, sawyer Ft Wayne Furn Co, res 47 N Calhoun.
Brower Charles S, teamster, bds 266 South Wayne av.
Brower Delphine A, opr S M Foster. bds 47 N Calhoun.
Brower George W, carpenter, res 266 South Wayne av.
Brower Stella, bds 47 N Calhoun.
Brown, see also Braun.
Brown Alexander, switchman, res 100 W Superior.
Brown Alice (wid Thomas), res 180 E Lewis.
Brown Arthur, bds 213 Broadway.
Brown Augustus C, foreman L S & M S Ry, res 40 E 3d.
Brown Bert R, apprentice Penn Co, bds 270 E Lewis.
Brown Burt A, clk Penn Co, bds 71 Holman.
Brown Charles L, clerk, rms 28 Douglas av.
Brown Charley R (col'd), porter bds 125 Eliza.
Brown Charles S, barber, 9 Maumee rd, bds 164 Walton av.
Brown Christina (wid John), res 110 Van Buren.
Brown David, horse dealer, res 16 W 3d.
Brown David E, lab Penn Co, res 272 E Creighton av.
Brown Edward, lab N Y, C & St L R R, bds rear 198 Lafayette.
Brown Edward H, well driver Robert Spice, res 17 Richardson.
Brown Edyth, bds 40 E 3d.
Brown Emanuel, res 26 Winch.
Brown Eva A (col'd), bds 31 Grand.

Brown Flora (wid John), res 29 Prince.
Brown Frank, res 60 W Pontiac.
Brown Frank, bartender John Condon, rms 17 Baker.
Brown Frank D, painter, bds 91 Huestis av.
Brown Frank G, res 13 Poplar.
Brown Frank I, timber inspr N Y, C & St L R R, bds 113 W Wayne.
Brown Frank L, barber 178½ and 498 Broadway, res 498 same.
Brown Fred S (Underwood & Brown), res 1 Elm.
Brown George H, fireman Penn Co, res 288 Calhoun.
Brown George H, saloon, 60½ Calhoun, res 99 E Jefferson.
Brown George W (col'd), res 273 E Wayne.
Brown Harry (col'd), waiter, bds 125 Eliza.
Brown Harry S, fireman, bds 40 E 3d.
Brown Harvey H, molder Bass F & M Wks, res 269 E Jefferson.
Brown Haswell S, fireman, bds s w cor Baker and Harrison.
Brown Hattie J, bds 270 E Lewis.
Brown Henry J, hostler, bds 110 Van Buren.
Brown James, laborer, res 172 Montgomery.
Brown James A, fireman Jenney Electric L & P Co, bds e s Spy Run av 5 n of Riverside av.
Brown James D, propr St James Hotel, 233 and 235 Calhoun.
Brown James E, condr N Y, C & St Louis R R, res 270 E Lewis.   Tel 165.
Brown James H, brakeman G R & I R R, res 335 Harrison.
Brown John, blacksmith, res 71 Holman.
Brown John, laborer, bds Edward Connett.
Brown John, lab Ft Wayne Electric Ry Co, res rear 198 Lafayette.
Brown John, pump repr, res 29 Prince.
Brown John A, messenger U S Express Co, bds 110 Van Buren.
Brown John B, iron inspr Penn Co, res 18 E Williams.
Brown John E, clk Penn Co, bds 166 W Berry.
Brown John O, carpenter, res 414 W Main.
Brown John S, sect foreman Penn Co, res 164 Walton av.
Brown John W, barber, 42 E Columbia, res 181 Columbia av.
Brown John W (col'd), cook, res 31 Grand.
Brown John W, teamster, res 57 Franklin av.
Brown Kate, seamstress, bds 37 E De Wald.
Brown Laura E G (col'd), musician, bds 273 E Wayne.

Brown Louis E, helper Penn Co, bds 38 Baker.
Brown Margaret (wid Joseph), res 4 Kansas.
Brown Mary, bds 26 Wagner.
Brown Mary, bds 287 W Washington.
Brown Mary E (wid John), res 287 W Washingten.
Brown Mary L, bds 110 Van Buren.
Brown Mattie, domestic 441 Broadway.
Brown Nettie, attendant School for Feeble-Minded Youth.
Brown Ollie M (col'd), music teacher, bds 31 Grand.
Brown Rufus R, res 324 Hanna.
Brown Sarah A, bds 172 Montgomery.
Brown Sarah F (wid Orson B), res 38 Baker.
Brown Seneca B, dentist, 15 Bank Blk, res 102 W Berry.
Brown Stephen M, mach Bass F & M Wks, res 252 E Lewis.
Brown Thomas J, stock buyer, res 312 Lafayette.
Brown Wm, laborer, bds 16 W 3d.
Brown Wm jr, boilermaker Bass F & M Wks, bds 40 Pritchard.
Brown Wm E, hostler Winkelmeyer & Hans, bds s e cor Cass and 2d.
Brown Wm H (col'd), pound master and city scavenger, res 125 Eliza.
Brown Wm H, Heavy Moving and General Transfer, 73 and 75 Holman, res same. Tel 73. (*See page 91.*)
Brown Wm M, laborer Penn Co, res 19 Dubois.
Browne Robert, flagman, res 213 Broadway.
Browne Wm C, helper, bds 213 Broadway.
Brownfield David C, tanner, bds 231 Calhoun.
Browning Oscar G, foreman Standard Wheel Co. bds 101 Wallace.
Brownsberger Charles, cigarmkr, bds 177 Calhoun.
Brownsberger Charles E, flagman, res 55 Taylor.
Brownsberger George W, res 97 Taylor.
Brownsberger Samuel W, lab Fort Wayne Electric Corp, res 97 Taylor.
Brownsberger Wm, driver Powers & Barnett, res 177 Calhoun.
Bruce Agnes, cook 25 E Main.
Brucker Charles J, molder Bass F & M Wks, bds 277 W Washington.
Brucker Frank X, cooper, res 277 W Washington.
Brucker Michael, cooper, res 62 Nelson.
Bruder August, Watches and Jewelry, 93 Calhoun, rms 19 W Wayne.
Brudi Henry E, baker Brenzinger Baking Co, res 29 W 5th.

Brudi J George (W H Brudi & Bro), res 233 Wells.

Brudi Wm H (W H Brudi & Bro), res 165 Wells.

Brudi W H & Bro (Wm H and J George), flour mill, n e cor Wells and 6th. Tel 319.

Bruebach Amelia E (wid George T), res 134 Montgomery.

Bruebach Harry J, brakeman, bds 134 Montgomery

Bruebach Edward J, clerk, bds 134 Montgomery.

Brueck Theodore J, coremkr Bass F & M Wks, res 155 Hayden.

Bruening, see Brunning.

Bruer, see also Braeuer and Brewer.

Bruer Mary J (wid Martin), res 312 W Main.

Bruer Wm E, fireman, bds 312 W Main.

Bruggemann Henry, saloon, 272 Hanna, res 291 same.

Brumbaugh Harry S, condr N Y, C & St L R R, rms 345 W Main.

Brumfiel Wilbert A, fireman N Y, C & St L R R, bds 296 W Jefferson.

Brummer Emilie B, bds 47 Lavina.

Brummer Katherine (wid John), res 47 Lavina.

Brune Wm, lab Hoffman Bros, res 156 Greeley.

Bruner Alexander, cigarmaker, res 58 Huestis av.

Bruner Angeline (wid Owen), bds 58 Huestis av.

Bruner Louisa M (wid Martin), res 152 Union.

Bruner Martin, died November 25, 1894.

Brunett Andrew, carpenter, bds 51 W 4th.

Brunett Charles, engr Jacob Klett & Sons, bds 51 W 4th.

Brunett Mary (wid Joseph), res 51 W 4th.

Brunka Anna S, opr Hoosier mnfg Co, bds 558 Lafayette.

Brunka Wilhelm H C, painter, bds 558 Lafayette

Brunka Wm H, helper Wabash R R, res 558 Lafayette.

Brunner Anna M, bds 184 W Main.

Brunner Cornelius (Brunner & Haag), res 184 W Main.

Brunner John. shoemaker, res 47 Pritchard.

Brunner Joseph A, watchmkr H C Graffe, res 39 Hendricks.

Brunner Louis J, painter, 79 Swinney av, res same.

Brunner Rosa A, packer G E Bursley & Co, bds 184 W Main.

Brunner & Haag (Cornelius Brunner, Charles Haag), marble works, 124 W Main.

Bruns Anna E (wid Christian F), res 224 E Jefferson.

Bruns Caroline M (wid Christian F), res 158 Griffith.

Bruns Christian, blksmith Penn Co, res 152 Wallace.

Bruns Christian H E, car bldr Penn Co, res 332 Harrison.

Bruns C W & Co (Frederick J Zimmerly), Plumbers, Gas and Steam Fitters, 135 Calhoun. Tel 207.

Bruns George W, butcher Gottlieb Haller, bds 332 Harrison

Bruns Herman, fireman, bds 9 Edgerton.

Bruns John W, real estate, rms 72 Barr.

Bruns Philip C, bds 224 E Jefferson.

Bruns Wm C. laborer, res 9 Edgerton.

Brunskill James, laborer, res 3 Mc Lachlan.

Brunskill James jr, laborer, bds 3 Mc Lachlan.

Brunskill John S, barber, 318 Lafayette, bds 27 Jane.

Brunson Allen, motorman Ft W E Ry Co, res 33 Michigan av.

Brush Edward, brakeman G R & I R R, rms 28 Douglas av

Bryan Eliza P (wid Henry), bds 15 Mc Lachlan.

Bryan Jane (wid Ervin), janitress Hamilton School, res 406 Calhoun.

Bryant, see also Briant.

Bryant George W, mach hand, res 111 Fox av.

Bryant John O, molder Penn Co, bds 216 E Lewis.

Bryant Joseph H, flue cleaner Penn Co, bds 111 Fox av.

Bryant Wm H, messenger Penn Co, res 113 Fox av.

Brysland Mrs Lillian, domestic School for Feeble-Minded Youth.

Bryson Charles B, barber H H Stites, bds 36 Hendricks.

Bryson Wm F, pension agt, 36 Hendricks, res same.

Bube Frank, porter New Aveline House.

Bucey Clarence, insurance agt, bds 180 Lafayette.

Buchanan Lawrence A, brakeman N Y, C & St L R R, res 289 W Washington.

Buchart Matthew, painter, res 88 Home av.

Buche, see Bueche and Bush.

Buchel Robert E, carpenter, res 142 Madison.

Bucher Adam F, carbuilder Penn Co, res 15 Ross.

Bucher Grace A, bds Dimon L Carpenter.

Buchheit Adam, carpenter, res 142 Union.

Buchheit Alois J, bkkpr Glutting, Bauer and Hartnett, bds 142 Union.

Buchheit Lizzie A, bds 142 Union.

Buchheit Salome M, bds 142 Union.

Buchman Alfred O, insurance agt, res 242 Smith.

Buchman Alpheus P, Physician, 18 W Washington, Office hours, 1 to 4 and 7 to 8 p m; res same. Tel 361.

Buchman Emma M, bds 18 W Washington.

Buchsbaum Maurice, Patentee and Mnfr Permanent Invoice-File-Journal, 92 and 94 E Columbia, bds 335 E Wayne. (*See front cover.*)

Buck, *see also Bock and Buuck.*

Buck Charles H, grocer, 141 Broadway, res 29 Nirdlinger av

Buck Charles W, res 188 Hanna.

Buck Edwin C, clerk, bds 269 W Jefferson.

Buck George H, clerk, bds 82 W 3d.

Buck Henry W, clk McDonald & Watt, res 290 W Jefferson.

Buck Herbert C, driver U S Exp Co, bds 269 W Jefferson.

Buck Nellie M, bds 269 W Jefferson.

Buck Sophia (wid Diederick), bds 290 W Jefferson.

Buck Wilson S, Sec and Treas Fort Wayne Mercantile Accident Assn and Agent Equitable Life Assurance Society, 3 Arcade Bldg, res 269 W Jefferson. (*See back cover and page 4.*)

Buckels George T, foreman Kilian Baker, res 102 E Superior.

Buckels Wm T, signwriter, 16 W Columbia, bds 100 Calhoun.

Buckley, *see also Bulkley.*

Buckley Charles E, printer Monday Morning Times, bds 27 Baker.

Buckley Frederick, lab city waterworks, bds 209 Lafayette.

Buckley Henry S, blksmith Wabash R R, res 29 Baker.

Buckley Joseph H, heater, bds 29 Baker.

Buckley Mary M, bds 29 Baker.

Buckley Patrick, laborer, bds 27 Bass.

Buckwalter, *see also Bookwalter.*

Buckwalter Louis R, mach Penn Co, res 54 W Jefferson.

†Budd Francis F, supt Hoosier Mnfg Co, res 406 Broadway

Budde John F C, barber, 333½ Lafayette, bds 43 St Martins

Budde Magdalena (wid Herman), res 43 St Martins.

Buddemeyer Ernst, died August 14th, 1894.

Bueche, *see also Busche and Bush.*

Bueche Frederick, foreman City Mills, bds 15 Clark.

Bueche George, res 15 Clark.

Buechner Conrad, carp John Suelzer, bds same.

Buechner Frederick J, policeman, res n s Herman 4 e of St Mary's av.

Buehfink Isabel (wid George), res 67 High.

Buehfink John G, mach hd Rhinesmith & Simonson, res 69 High.

Buehfink Mary A, bds 67 High.

Buehler John H A, clk Sam, Pete & Max, bds 22 Oak.
Buehler Minnie, domestic 212 W Berry.
Buehler Samuel E, blksmith Jacob A Spereisen, bds 56 Taylor.
Buehler Wm C, springmkr Penn Co, res 22 Oak.
Bueker Henry E (City Carriage Wks), res 409 E Washington.
Buell Lena, stenographer S Freiburger & Bro, bds 28 W Creighton av.
Buell R Raymond, traveling agt, res 426 E Washington.
Buelow Frederick, lab Bass F & M Wks, res 232 Smith.
Buelow John C, res 149 Wells.
Buesching, see also Busching.
Buesching Henry, boilermkr, res 41 Carson av.
Buesching Minnie, opr S M Foster, bds 41 Carson av.
Buesking Conrad, shoes, 302 Hanna, res same.
Buesking Henry, shoemkr, 316 E Washington, res same.
Buettel Adam C (Pape Furniture Co), bds 234 Francis.
Buettel Dora (wid George), midwife, 234 Francis, res same.
Buettel Henry W, watchman, res 1 Eliza.
Buetter Henry H, clerk, bds 340 E Wayne.
Buff Julian, feed, 24 Wells, res 179 St Mary's av.
Buffalo German Insurance Co, of Buffalo N Y, Edward Seidel Agent, 52½ Calhoun.
Buffington Ella V, opr Hoosier Mnfg Co, bds J C Buffington
Buffington Jesse C, res e s Piqua av 3 s of Marshall.
Buford Edward, stave jointer, bds 90 E Main.
Buford Edward, well driver, res 216 St Mary's av.
Buford John C, well driver, bds 216 St Mary's av.
Buford Logan, laborer, rms 216 St Mary's av.
Buford Norman G, laborer, bds 216 St Mary's av.
Buford Royal H, laborer, bds 216 St Mary's av.
Bugbee John, lab Penn Co, res Pittsburgh s w cor Bond.
Bugert Adam, clerk, bds 135 Force.
Bugert George, car bldr Penn Co, res 135 Force.
Bugert Matthew, painter 176 Broadway, res 88 Home av.
Buhr Catherine, (wid Nicholas), housekpr 38 Douglas av.
Buhr Charles H, clk Pfeiffer & Schlatter, res 62 Maumee rd.
Buhr Elizabeth, domestic 115 E Berry.
Buhr Frederick, clk W Doehrmann, bds 26 Oak.
Buhrkuhl Henry, res 87 Monroe.
Builders' Lime Association, Fred Miller Pres and Treas, Frederick Rippe Vice-Pres, all kinds Building Material, 257 Calhoun, yard between Chestnut and Railroad. Tel 511. (See right bottom lines.)

Bulger Charles J, traveling agt, bds 176 Griffith.
Bulger George J, bds 176 Griffith.
Bulger Ida E, milliner, bds 176 Griffith.
Bulger John H, bds 176 Griffith.
Bulger Martin L, bds 132 W Main.
Bulger Nellie, stenographer Smith Credit Rating Co, bds 176 Griffith.
Bulger Patrick J, truckman, res 176 Griffith.
Bullerman Charles, blacksmith, bds 286 W Jefferson.
Bullerman Charlotte, tailoress, bds 286 W Jefferson.
Bullerman Henry F, teamster, res 286 W Jefferson.
Bullerman Louisa K, tailoress, bds 286 W Jefferson.
Bullermann Henry F, res 45 Rivermet av.
Bullermann Wm C, laborer, res 68 Burgess.
Bulmahn Frederick G, draughtsman, bds 90 Baker.
Bulmahn Henry C, printer, res 90 Baker.
Bulmahn Henry E, mach Ft Wayne Iron Wks, bds 90 Baker.
Bulmahn Lulu E, bds 90 Baker.
Bulow, see Buelow.
Bulson Albert E Jr, Physician and Surgeon; Practice Limited to Eye, Ear, Nose and Throat, 19, 20 and 21 Pixley & Long Bldg, res 213 W Berry. Tel office 413, res 409.
Bultemeyer Ernest H, car builder Penn Co, res 90 Wall.
Bultemeyer Frederick C, carp Wabash R R, res 121 Wall.
Bundy Joseph, carp, res e s Calhoun 5 s of Marshall.
Bunnell Wm R, brakeman, res 59 E 3d.
Burbank Harry H, asst ticket receiver Penn Co, res 20 Buchanan.
Burchard Ann, res 200 Lafayette.
Burchard Charles, asst foreman Penn Co, res 61 Madison.
Burchard George J C, helper Penn Co, res 196 Fairfield av.
Burchart Lewis W, blacksmith, bds 20 W Superior.
Burdett Samuel H, organ tuner, res 54 Nirdlinger av.
Burdick Josephine E B, opr Troy Steam Laundry, bds 224 E Jefferson.
Burg, see also Berg and Borg.
Burg Edward M, teamster, bds 235 Lafayette.
Burg Frederick P, laborer, bds 235 Lafayette.
Burg Jacob G, cigarmaker, bds 235 Lafayette.
Burg Nicholas, laborer, res 235 Lafayette.
Burg Nicholas jr, teamster, bds 235 Lafayette.
Burger, see also Berger and Boerger.
Burger A Louis, grocer, 81 Putnam, res same.

Burger Franz, supt Burger Gas Engine Co, res 16 W De Wald.

Burger Gas Engine Co, Franz Burger Supt, 36 E Berry, res 16 W De Wald.

Burger Gottlieb A, clk M Frank & Co, res 224 W Jefferson.

Burger Ira G, engineer Penn Co, bds 49 Baker.

Burger Johanna, bds 16 W De Wald.

Burger Joseph, photo-printer F Schanz, bds 16 W De Wald.

Burger Joseph A, barber S G Hubbard, res 135 Wells.

Burgess Elizabeth T, bkkpr Kuhne & Co, bds 178 W Jefferson.

Burgess Francis, mach Wabash R R, res 178 W Jefferson.

Burgett Harley I P, molder Bass F & M Wks, res 196 Smith.

Burgett Wm A, helper Western Gas Const Co, res 293 E Creighton av.

Burhenn Amelia, bds 122 W Creighton av.

Burhenn Camilla, bds 122 W Creighton av.

Burhenn Edward A, laborer, bds 122 W Creighton av.

Burhenn Jennie A, bds 122 W Creighton av.

Burhenn Mary A (wid Edward A), res 122 W Creighton av.

Burhenn Ollie E J, cigarmkr L Dessauer & Co, bds 122 W Creighton av.

Burk, see also Bork.

Burk Gertrude J, seamstress, bds 12 Orchard.

Burkas Albert C T, painter Penn Co, res 385 E Washington.

Burkas John A, bds 215 E Wayne.

Burkas Louis C, molder Bass F & M Wks, bds 215 E Wayne.

Burkas Minnie E, clk A Mergentheim, bds 215 E Wayne.

Burke Anne (wid Edward), res 83 Buchanan.

Burke Edward T, switchman, bds 83 Buchanan.

Burke Ella, bds 83 Buchanan.

Burke Jane (wid Robert), bds 301 Calhoun.

Burke Maggie, bds 301 Calhoun.

Burke Nellie, bds 301 Calhoun.

Burke Wm, clk O B Fitch, res 27 Elizabeth.

Burke Wm H, brakeman, rms 40 Boone.

Burket Frank W, brakeman, bds 137 Fletcher av.

Burkhard Ernst F, brewer The Herman Berghoff Brewing Co, res 62 Glasgow av.

Burkhard Sophia (wid Charles), bds 62 Glasgow av.

Burkholder Edgar O, bds 98 Baker.

Burkholder Elias P, painter, res 98 Baker.

Burkholder Walter S, agent, bds 98 Baker.
Burkmeyer Kate, bds 71 Lasselle.
Burlage Oliver C, cigarmkr A C Baker, bds 174 Maumee rd.
Burlager Ella, clerk, bds 210 E Washington.
Burlager Henry, laborer, bds 210 E Washington.
Burlager Henry H, polisher, res 163 E Washington.
Burlager Herman, lab Summit City Soap Wks, bds 210 E Washington.
Burlager John, laborer, bds 85 Summit.
Burlager John, wheelmaker, res 43 Summit.
Burlager John W, tinner, res 165 E Washington.
Burlager Susan, clerk, bds 210 E Washington.
Burlager Tena, opr Hoosier Mnfg Co, bds 210 E Washington.
Burlager Wm, laborer, res 210 E Washington.
Burlingame Rosamond M (wid Edward), res 15 E Leith.
Burnett Daniel (col'd), mach hd res w s Savannah, 1 n of Pontiac.
Burnett Eliza S, dressmaker, bds 90 Lake av.
Burnett Frank B, truckman Wabash R R, res 69 Scott av.
Burnett George W, boilermaker, bds 90 Lake av.
Burnett Samuel, teamster, res 90 Lake av.
Burnham Calvin, clk Ind Furn Co, res 67 Baker.
Burns Anna, domestic The Wayne.
Burns Arthur, plasterer, bds 41 Monroe.
Burns Charles, laborer, bds 2 Warsaw.
Burns Edward C, bds 381 Lafayette.
Burns Ella, domestic The Wayne.
Burns Ellen (wid Patrick), bds 43 W Willliams.
Burns Edward C, molder, bds 381 Lafayette.
Burns Frank J, mach Penn Co, res 41 W Williams.
Burns Ida M, dressmaker, 30 Thompson av, res same.
Burns James, helper Penn Co, res 381 Lafayette.
Burns James, engr Penn Co, res 61 Charles.
Burns James W, general secretary Young Men's Christian Assn (railroad dept), res 62 Brackenridge.
Burns John, mach hd L Rastetter & Son, bds 303 W Main.
Burns John J, laborer, res 30 Thompson av.
Burns John M, fireman F F Robacker, bds 45 E Main.
Burns John R, switchman, bds 30 Thompson av.
Burns Julia B, bds 381 Lafayette.
Burns Kate, waitress New Aveline House, bds same.
Burns Louisa A (wid Wm H), res 15 Mc Lachlan.
Burns Michael E, advertising mngr The Journal Co, res 529 Calhoun.

Burns Nancy (wid Arthur), bds 46 Force.

Burns Virgil R, helper Penn Co, res 47 Hendricks.

Burns Walter G, mechanical engineer, 14 Bass Blk, res 62 Brackenridge.

Burrell Duff G, lab Gerding & Aumann Bros, res 319 Lafayette.

Burrell Effie M, seamstress S M Foster, bds 319 Lafayette

Burrell Naomi, opr S M Foster, bds 319 Lafayette.

Burrowes Stephen A, bkkpr Morgan & Beach, res 377 Fairfield av. Tel 218.

Burrows Wm A, laborer, bds 57 Barr.

Burry Andrew G, bookbinder Ft Wayne Book Bindery, bds 130 Wells.

Bursley Blk, e s Calhoun bet Washington and Jefferson.

Bursley Gilbert E (G E Bursley & Co), res 301 Fairfield av. Tel 271.

Bursley G E & Co (Gilbert E Bursley, James M Mc Kay, Frank L Smock, Frank K Safford), wholesale grocers 129 Calhoun. Tel 64.

Bursley Joseph A, bds 301 Fairfield av.

Burt Alice, opr L F Horstman, bds 9 E Superior.

Burt Kate, seamstress bds 16 W 3d.

Burt Marion B, res 49 Miner.

Burt Wm E, brakeman, res 11 Summit.

Burtch Lydia S, stenogr S R Alden, bds 135 E Washington.

Burtsfield Wm L, clk Princess Cash Store, res 152 Wells.

Busch, see also Bush.

Busch Anton, wagonmaker, bds 46 E Columbia.

Busch Charles F, clk Charles Falk & Co, bds 75 Hoagland av.

Busch John W, inspector, res 72 Wilt.

Busch Lena, dressmaker, bds 75 Hoagland av.

Busch Martha L, dressmaker, bds 75 Hoagland av.

Busch Mary C, clk Wm Seidel & Bro, bds 107 E Main.

Busch Nicholas H, clk Charles Falk & Co, bds 75 Hoagland av

Busch Peter, res 75 Hoagland av.

Busche Anna C, bds 54 Charles.

Busche Catherine (wid Henry), res 54 Charles.

Busche Frederick J, painter Olds Wagon Wks, bds 54 Charles.

Busche Henry, butcher, res 190 Smith.

Busche Louise S, bds 54 Charles.

Busching, see also Bruesching.

Busching Fred (Wehrenberg & Busching). res Maysville rd nr Lake av beyond city Limits.

Busching Henry, res 148 Wallace.

Busching Mrs Wilhelmina, bds 148 Wallace.

Busching Wm, res Lake av beyond city limits.

Busching Wm, grocer, 124 Wallace, res same.

Buschle Theodore, laborer, bds 231 Barr.

Bush, *see also Bueche, Buesche, Busch and Busche.*

Bush Emanuel K, clerk, res 74 Douglas av.

Bush Frederica (wid Mortimer), res 11 Wall.

Bush Harvey A, printer, bds 38 Harrison.

Bush James L, electrician rms 18 E Columbia.

Bush Sarah (wid Isaac), bds Henry Oswalt.

Bush Sophia, laundress G H Seabold.

Bush Wm, laborer, rms 288 Calhoun.

Bushey Charles M, brakeman N Y, C & St L R R bds 405 W Main.

Bushman John, bds 29 E Main.

Bushor Mrs Fannie, boarding house 83 Holman.

Bushor Frederick G, harnessmkr A L Johns & Co, bds 83 Holman.

Bushor J Myrtle, bds 83 Holman.

Bushor Narcissus N, res 83 Holman.

Bushor Wm M, cook C Entermann, res 53 E Main.

Business Guide The, Clarence G Smith publr, 76 and 80 Clinton.

Buskirk Aaron E, physician, 80 Calhoun, res 416 same.

Busse Wm, helper Olds Wagon Wks, bds 121 Force.

Busse Amelia, bds 156 Ewing.

Busse Charles H, fireman L E & W R R, bds 156 Ewing.

Busse Charlotte (wid Wm), res 156 Ewing.

Busse Clara, cash Kayser & Baade, bds 156 Ewing.

Busse Elizabeth, bds 156 Ewing.

Busse Ferdinand W, painter Penn Co, res 202 Ewing.

Busse Frederick, foreman Olds Wagon Wks, res 161 Hanna

Busse Frederick C, blksmith Olds Wagon Wks, bds 156 Ewing.

Busse John H, clk Wm Hahn & Co, res 156 Ewing.

Busse Wm, helper Olds Wagon Wks, bds 161 Hanna.

Busse Wm, lab Penn Co, rms 168 Greeley.

Bussing Henry, confectioner, 138 Maumee rd, res same.

Butke Henry, clk Kasten & Kohlmeyer, bds 210 W Jefferson.

Butler Alexander W, laborer, res n e cor Edgerton and Winter.

Butler Ella M, packer, bds 44 E Pontiac.

Butler Franklin C, candymkr Fox br U S Baking Co, bds n e cor Edgerton and Winter.

Butler James P, barber, res 218 Broadway.
Butler Jennie E, bds 44 E Pontiac.
Butler Louis F, res 46 Wells.
Butt Clement, clk T D Gerow, bds 46 Taylor.
Butz Frederick, tailor, res s e cor Calhoun and Marshall.
Butz Jacob, tailor, res 145 Wells.
Buuck, *see also Bock and Buck.*
Buuck Charles, lab Penn Co, bds 10 Hough.
Buuck Conrad, shoemkr, 11 W Jefferson, res same.
Buuck Gustave, lab Bass F & M Wks, res 113 Smith.
Buuck Mary C, domestic 69 W Berry.
Buuck Minnie, opr S M Foster, bds 10 Hough.
Buuck Wm, carpenter Penn Co, bds 10 Hough.
Byall Carrie L, drugs, 238 E Creighton av, res same.
Byall Isaac A, postal clk, res 238 E Creighton av.
Byers Ada A, opr S M Foster, bds 57 Barr.
Byers Charity E (wid Hiram), boarding house, 57 Barr.
Byers Clara E, bds 57 Barr.
Byers Clifton J, bds 53 Huestis av.
Byers Dean L, carpenter, res 16 Huffman.
Byers Emma, bds 54 Force.
Byers George J, switchman, res 54 Force.
Byers George L, special agt C E Everett, res 53 Huestis av.
Byers Ida B, opr S M Foster, bds 57 Barr.
Byers Jacob C, winder, bds 53 Huestis av.
Byrd Ellis, porter The Wayne, rms 60 W Berry.

C

Cadwallader Charles H, tel opr W U Tel Co, bds 296 E Lewis.
Cadwallader Lizzie M, bds 296 E Lewis.
Cadwallader Thomas, truckman Penn Co, res 296 E Lewis.
Cady Ernest, fireman N Y C & St L R R, rms 354 W Main.
Caemmerer Selina, domestic 204 W Berry.
Caffery Mary (wid Cormack), bds 305 E Creighton av.
Cahill Edward, laborer, bds 34 W Superior.
Cahill John, bds 106 Barr.
Cahill John D, bds Arlington Hotel.
Cain, *see also Kain and Kane.*
Cain Charles, eng School for Feeble Minded Youth.
Cain James C, clk S F Swayne, bds 46 E Jefferson.
Cain John, fireman N Y, C & St L R R, bds 80 Boone.
Cain John C, clk E V Emerick, rms 19 E Jefferson.

13

Cain Martin J, appr Ind Mach Wks, bds 208 Thomas.
Cain Mary, domestic 160 Spy Run av.
Cain Michael, fireman N Y, C & St L R R, bds 80 Boone.
Cain Wm, laborer, res 208 Thomas.
Cairns, *see also Karns.*
Cairns Frank M, gang foreman Penn Co, res 499 Calhoun.
Cairns James G, mach Penn Co, res 430 Broadway.
Cairns James T, bander Ft Wayne Electric Corp, bds 430
    Broadway.
Cairns Mary E, clk J B White, bds 430 Broadway.
Calbetzor Franklin, removed to Wallen, Ind.
Calbetzor Sherman, laborer, bds 174 Huffman.
Caldwell David H, chief train dispatcher N Y, C & St L R
    R, res 281 Webster. Tel 75.
Caldwell Edward B, treas and mngr Ft Wayne Furn Co,
    res 231 W Berry.
Caldwell James, physician, 33 Calhoun, res 51 W Berry.
Caldwell Laura B, stenographer Ft Wayne Electric Corp,
    bds 51 W Berry.
Caldwell Sadie E, bds 51 W Berry.
Caledonian Hall, 76 Calhoun.
Calhoun David, erecter Kerr Murray Mnfg Co, bds Wind-
    sor Hotel.
Calhoun Jacob A, jeweler A Bruder, rms 89 W Jefferson.
Callaghan Daniel J, died Nov 12th, 1894.
Callaghan Elizabeth B, bds 78 Melita.
Callaghan John P, laborer, bds 78 Melita.
Callaghan Maurice P, brakeman N Y, C & St L R R, res
    171 High.
Callaghan Patrick D, flagman Penn Co, res 78 Melita.
Callahan Bernard J, plumber, bds 83 W Williams.
Callahan Esther, bds 32 Chicago.
Callahan James T, train despatcher N Y, C & St L R R,
    res 114 W Washington.
Callahan John, helper Penn Co, res 8 Bass.
Callahan Mary (wid John), bds 135 Lafayette.
Callahan May A, bds 83 W Williams.
Callahan Mary E, domestic 106 W Berry.
Callaway Cyrus, res 24 Jones.
Calmelat Helen M, bds 106 Spy Run av.
Cameron Glenn C, switchman Wabash R R, bds 40 W Wil-
    liams.
Cammeyer, *see Kammeyer.*
Campbell Alexander F, res 129 Wells.
Campbell Benjamin F, engr Penn Co, res 453 Webster.

Campbell Charles A, farmer, bds 47 John.
Campbell Charles H, ins agt, res 107 Wallace.
Campbell Daniel, fireman Wabash R R, res 53 Brackenridge.
Campbell Daniel A, cigar mnfr, 272 Calhoun, bds 53 Brackenridge.
Campbell Delbert F, lab Ft Wayne Electric Corp, bds 47 John.
Campbell Eliza M, bds 113 W Wayne.
Campbell Ella, laundress Harmon House.
Campbell Ellison T, shoemaker, res 47 John.
Campbell Emma J, operator, bds 47 John.
Campbell George E, clerk, bds 361 E Washington.
Campbell Hiel R, painter, bds 129 Wells.
Campbell Lydia (wid George B), res 361 E Washington.
Campbell Mervale F, polisher Olds Wagon Wks, bds 72 Brackenridge.
Campbell Vance, lineman, bds 29 E Main.
Campbell Walter N, special examiner U S Pension Office, res 113 W Wayne.
Campion Alice B, clerk, bds 24 E Butler.
Campion John J, clerk R M S, res 24 E Butler.
Campion Matthew, bds 24 E Butler.
Caplan Samuel, shoemaker, res 179 W Washington.
Carbaugh Alonzo W, helper Wabash R R, res 122 Chicago.
Carbaugh Oliver, turner Standard Wheel Co, res 19 Indiana av.
Carberry Henry P, lab N Y, C & St L R R, res 56 Burgess
Carey, *see also Carrey, Carry and Cary.*
Carey Charles W, conductor, res 240 Walton av.
Carey Edward, teamster James Wilding, bds 127 Fairfield av
Carey John S, conductor, res 59 Hugh.
Carey Mary (wid Thomas), res 127 Fairfield av.
Carey Mary C (wid Edward), res 284 E Jefferson.
Carey Michael, helper Penn Co, res 203 Lafayette.
Carier Clemence, res 178 E Berry.
Carier Helene, res 178 E Berry.
Carithers Zoe, opr S M Foster, bds cor Oak and Chute.
Carl, *see also Carrel and Carroll.*
Carl John, cigars, 259 Calhoun, res 9 Chestnut.
Carl John, laborer, res s s Rebecca 2 w of Tyler av.
Carl John D, laborer, bds 381 W Main.
Carl John M, clerk, bds 9 Chestnut.
Carling George, coppersmith, bds 122 Fairfield av.
Carll Ellen, clk J B White, bds 35 Walnut.

Carll George S, cabtmkr J M Miller, res 433 Lafayette.
Carll Harriet R (wid Hiram D), res 292 Hanna.
Carll Laura, student, bds 292 Hanna.
Carll Margaret (wid Patrick), res 35 Walnut.
Carll Margaret, dressmaker, bds 35 Walnut.
Carll Susan, bds 433 Lafayette.
Carman Frank C, engineer, res 17 Bass.
Carman Frank H, tinner S F Bowser & Co, bds 128 E De Wald.
Carman James G, engineer Penn Co. res 130 E De Wald.
Carmedy Catherine, removed to Columbus, O.
Carmedy John W, removed to Columbus, O.
Carmer George W, laborer, bds 120 Boone.
Carmer Wm A, caller, bds 120 Boone.
Carnahan Clara C, bds 119 E Wayne.
Carnahan Louise, bds 119 E Wayne.
Carnahan Robert H, vice-pres The W L Carnahan Co, bds 119 E Wayne.
Carnahan Wm L, pres The W L Carnahan Co, res 119 E Wayne. Tel 23.
Carnahan W L Co The, Wm Carnahan pres, W E Hodd sec and treas, whol shoes, 13 W Jefferson. Tel 42.
Carpenter Albert L, teamster, res n e cor Clinten and Duck.
Carpenter Mrs Amanda C, res 37 W Berry.
Carpenter Dimon L, carpenter Wabash R R, res s s New Haven rd 3 e of limits.
Carpenter Eliza (wid Martin J), nurse, bds 278 W Berry.
Carpenter Homer V, tel opr F W Elec. Corp bds 69 Cass.
Carpenter Warren, fireman Ft Wayne Electric Corp, res 30 Baker.
Carpenter Wesley, engr County Poor Farm.
Carpenter William H, fireman Penn Co, res 30 Melita.
Carpenters' Union Hall, 7 Bank blk.
Carr, see also Kerr.
Carr David W, horseshoer Wm Geary, rms Union House.
Carr Elizabeth, seamstress, bds 193 W Superior.
Carr Joseph W, mach hd Hoffman Bros, res 196 Broadway.
Carrel George, lab Penn Co, res n s Chestnut 3 e o Lumbard.
Carrey, see also Carey, Carry and Cary.
Carrey Frank J, helper Penn Co, res 294 E Creighton av.
Carrey John E, insurance agt, bds 294 E Creighton av.
Carrey Joseph A, blksmith Penn Co, res 160 Holman.
Carrey Lida, bds 294 E Creighton av.
Carroll, see also Carl and Carrel.

Carroll Albert E, bkkpr School for Feeble Minded Youth.
Carroll Denandy, carpenter, res 1 Bass.
Carroll Ella, bds 134 Fulton.
Carroll Harry, laborer, bds 96 W Superior.
Carroll John, engineer, res 111 Fairfield av.
Carroll John, mason, res 228 E Washington.
Carroll John M, insurance agt, res 193 Sherman.
Carroll J Joseph, student, bds 111 Fairfield av.
Carroll Julia, milliner, bds 69 Thomas.
Carroll Kate, bds 69 Thomas.
Carroll Margaret (wid Patrick), res 96 W Superior.
Carroll Margaret, bds 69 Thomas.
Carroll Patrick B, watchman, res 69 Thomas.
Carroll Robert E, Dealer in Pictures, Picture Frames and Moldings. Framing to order a Specialty, 14 E Berry, res 28 E Wayne.
Carroll Susan, domestic School for Feeble Minded Youth.
Carroll Wm J, pressman Monday Morning Times, res 96 W Superior.
Carry, *see also Carey. Carrey and Cary.*
Carry Benjamin, carpenter, bds 81 Lillie.
Carson John E, insurance agent, bds 104 Barr.
Carson John K, fish. 250 Calhoun, res same.
Carson Wm W, student Henry C Hanna, bds 135 E Berry.
Carter Benjamin F, conductor, res 171 Harrison.
Carter Charles L (Carter & Son), res 18 E Creighton av.
Carter Flora M, milliner, bds 194 E De Wald.
Carter James M, carpenter, res 187 Jackson.
Carter Josephine, stenogr Weil Bros & Co, bds 47 Maple av.
Carter Martha A (wid Isaac), bds 83 W Butler.
Carter Mary L, bds 187 Jackson.
Carter Oliver, bds 527 Calhoun.
Carter Peter, engineer Penn Co, res 194 E De Wald.
Carter Rebecca A (wid James W), res 47 Maple av.
Carter Rosa, clerk, bds 428 E Wayne.
Carter Samuel A, baker B Gutermuth, bds 29 W Columbia.
Carter Victoria, teacher Bloomingdale School, bds 47 Maple av.
Carter Wm (Carter & Son), res 127 E Main.
Carter Wm H, clk Carter & Son, bds 127 E Main.
Carter Wm H, bds 187 Jackson.
Carter & Son (Wm and Charles L), Hot Air Furnaces, Ranges, Wood and Tile Mantels and Grates, 29 Clinton. Tel 431. (*See bottom edge and p 113.*)
Carto Edward A, laborer, bds 155 Holman.

Carto James J, boilermkr L E & W R·R, res 35 N Calhoun,

Cartwright Blanche, teacher, bds 229 W Creighton av.

Cartwright Charles A, broommkr, 110 Hugh, res same.

Cartwright D Porter, baggageman G R & I R R, res 22 W De Wald.

Cartwright Ella (wid John), res 73 Baker.

Cartwright George W, section hand, res 39 Wall.

Cartwright James, res 23 Lillie.

Cartwright John F, bds 22 W De Wald.

Cartwright Samuel M P, lab, res s s French 8 w of Webster.

Cartwright Theodore S, trav agt Olds Wagon Wks, res Grinwell, Ia.

Cary, *see also Carey, Carrey and Carry.*

Cary David B, physician, 27 Clinton, res same.

Cary Dow, conductor, bds 40 E 5th.

Cary Ira L, motorman, res 53 Baker.

Cary Lavina (wid David), res 53 Madison.

Cary Norman E, clk District Tel Co, bds 53 Madison.

Cary Walter E, tel opr U U Tel Co, bds 53 Madison.

Case David, carpenter, res n s Jesse 2 e of Rumsey av.

Case Florence, bds 36 Colerick.

Case Ida M, bds 36 Colerick.

Case Isaac H, mngr Arcade Music Store, res 322 W Washington.

Case John W, bds 36 Colerick.

Case Vinnie, bds David Case.

Case Wm H, tinner Wabash R R, res 36 Colerick.

Case W F L, lab Wabash R R, bds 36 Colerick.

Casey Anna (wid Michael), bds 299 E Creighton av.

Casey Christopher, conductor, res 299 E Creighton av.

Casey Frank, teamster, bds 299 E Creighton av.

Casey Frank J, clk Wm Busching, bds same.

Casey John, mach Bass F & M Wks, res 159 Holman.

Casey Margaret (wid James), bds 13 Hamilton.

Cashman John W, Union Mutual Life Insurance Co of Portland, Me, 28 Bank Blk, res 41 E 4th.

Caskey Archey W, conductor, res 159 Force.

Cassady George M, brakeman Penn Co, res 35 Jane.

Cassady Mary J (wid Jacob), boarding house, 19 E Jefferson.

Cassady Marguerite, bkkpr Ind Furn Co. bds 19 E Jefferson.

Cassidy Patrick, laborer, bds 82 Montgomery.

Casso Frank A, fruits, 184 Calhoun, res same.

Casteel Mrs Birdie, res 28 Chicago.

Casteel Samuel W, baker Brenzinger Bread Co, bds 209 Lafayette.

Casteel Margaret, bds 209 Lafayette.

Casteel Mrs Mary, boarding house, 209 Lafayette.

Casteel Wm E, laborer, res 28 Chicago.

Castle Alfreda, domestic 15 Clay.

Castle Alice, domestic 252 E Creighton av.

Castle Calvin J, molder Bass F & M Wks, res 396 Hanna.

Castle Charles E, cabinetmaker, bds 566 Calhoun.

Castle Cora B, bds 566 Calhoun.

Castle Della E, domestic 162 E Berry.

Castle James F, turner, bds 566 Calhoun.

Castle Minnie V, domestic 18 McClellan.

Castle Robert S, teamster, res n e cor Dwenger av and Tons.

Castle Samuel L, carpenter Ft Wayne Organ Co, res 566 Calhoun.

Castle Wilda, domestic 59 E Berry.

Caston John E. foreman A L Johns & Co, bds 57 Barr.

Caston Lillian B, bds 134 Broadway.

Caswell Frank A, trav agt, res 50 W Superior.

Caswell Jerome O, dyer, 205 Calhoun, res same.

Catholic Cemetery Association, Library Hall, C F Muhler pres, Louis Fox sec.

Cathedral of the Immaculate Conception, Calhoun nr Lewis

Cathedral School (Catholic), s w cor Clinton and Jefferson

Catholic Knights of America, Wm S O'Rourke supreme sec, 27 Bass Blk.

Catholic Young Men's Reading Hall and Club Rooms, n e cor Calhoun and Lewis.

Catten Belle, domestic Columbia House.

Cattez Charles, bds 139 Buchanan.

Cattez Frank, fireman, bds 139 Buchanan.

Cattez John, helper Penn Co, bds 139 Buchanan.

Cattez Joseph, engineer, bds 139 Buchanan.

Cattez Julia (wid Joseph), res 139 Buchanan.

Cattez Julian J, driver The Herman Berghoff Brewing Co, bds 139 Buchanan.

Cattez Mary, bds 139 Buchanan.

Cattez Peter J, telegraph operator, bds 139 Buchanan.

Cavanaugh, see also Kavanaugh.

Cavanaugh James, insurance agt, bds 39 W Washington.

Cavanaugh Julia, opr Troy Steam Laundry, bds 18 Bass.

Cavanaugh Wm, agent, bds 5 Boone.

Cave Mac, brakeman, bds 313 Calhoun.

Centennial Block, 197 and 199 Broadway.

Center Spencer H, boilermkr Penn Co, res 100 Chicago.

Centlivre Charles F (C L Centlivre Brewing Co), res w s
    Spy Run av 2 n of Edna.

Centlivre Louis A (C L Centlivre Brewing Co), bds John
    B Reuss.

Centlivre C L Brewing Co (Louis A and
    Charles F Centlivre, J B Reuss), Brewers, Malsters and
    Bottlers, n end Spy Run av. Tel 62. (*See front edge
    and left side lines.*)

Centlivre's Park, w s Spy Run av n of canal
    feeder.

Central Chemical Co The, August Detzer mngr, 15 Doug-
    las av.

Central Christian Church, w s Harrison 1 s of Wayne.

Central Grammar School, E Wayne bet Calhoun and
    Clinton.

Central Union Telephone Co, Edgar
    L Taylor Mngr, Tri-State Bdg, n e cor Berry and
    Court. Tel 300.

Certia Block, w s Calhoun bet Wayne and Berry.

Certia Jacob B, res 114 Wells.

Certia Peter, saloon, 70 Calhoun, res 126 W Washington.

Chadwick John M, foreman Ft Wayne Electric Corp, res
    233 W Jefferson.

Chadwick Samuel W, molder Ft Wayne Electric Corp, res
    16 Bass.

Challenger Edward D, clk Penn Co, res 20 E Taber.

Challenger Frank C, res 50 W Superior.

Challenger Margaret A (wid Joseph W), res 50 W Superior.

Chamberlain Eva, removed to Portland, Ind.

Chamberlain James C, helper Penn Co, res 41 Baker.

Chamberlain Myrtle, bds 41 Baker.

Chamberlain Porter, engineer, res 71 W Butler.

Chamberlain Porter, fireman School for Feeble-Minded
    Youth.

Chamberlain Richard C, paperhanger, res 20 Chicago.

Chamberlain Sarah C R (wid Wm), bds 65 W Williams.

Chambers Mrs Jennie C, music teacher, 405 Calhoun, res
    same.

Chambers John D, physician, 16 Brackenridge, res same.

Chambers Mary L (wid Winfield S), dressmkr, 31 Pixley
    & Long Bldg, res same.

Chandler Charles, peddler, bds 29 E Main.

Chandler Clement W, carp L E & W R R, res 8 Emily.

Chandler Gilford A, carp L E & W R R, res 12 W 5th.
Chaney Harry L, clk The Randall, bds same.
Chapin Elizabeth E, teacher Jefferson School; bds 16 Douglas av.
Chapin Angeline F, stenogr Ft Wayne Electric Corp, bds 16 Douglas av.
Chapin Augustus A (Chapin & Denny), res 16 Douglas av.
Chapin Bertha M, ironer W B Phillips, bds 63 W Superior
Chapin Catherine B, bds 16 Douglas av.
Chapin Henry W, engineer, res 22 Boone.
Chapin Ralph W E, bds 16 Douglas av.
Chapin & Denny (Augustus A Chapin, Watts P Denny), Lawyers and Solicitors of Patents, 13–15 Bass Blk. (*See p 2.*)
Chapman Caroline A (wid Chauncey), res e s Oakland 2 s of Huffman.
Chapman Catherine (wid John V), res 100 E Lewis.
Chapman Charles H, chief clk trainmaster's office N Y, C & St L R R, res 316 Broadway.
Chapman Charles W, lab Wabash R R, bds 30 South Wayne av.
Chapman Eli, laborer, bds 30 South Wayne av.
Chapman Frank F, waiter, bds 124 E Berry.
Chapman Frank M, township assessor, res 150 Fairfield av
Chapman George W, lab Hoffman Bros, res 245 W Wayne.
Chapman Henry, laborer. res 141 E Lewis.
Chapman Jason S, conductor, res 42 Glasgow av.
Chapman J Clark, carp, res Spy Run av n e cor Baltes.
Chapman Lizzie M, bds 30 South Wayne av.
Chapman Mrs Maggie B, milliner, 150 Fairfield av. res same.
Chapman Minerva A, notions, 106 Broadway, res same.
Chapman Nathan E, res 30 South Wayne av.
Chapman Nathaniel L. engineer, res 10 Pritchard.
Chapman Wm, clerk, bds 141 E Lewis.
Charles Clyde A, conductor, res 8 Mechanic.
Charleswood Sheridan G, engineer, res 37 Elizabeth.
Chase Abbie F, bds 40 Garden.
Chase Emily B (wid Ira), bds 40 Garden.
Chase Oliver C, clk Penn Co, bds 76 Lake av.
Chase Reuben C, res 79 Hoagland av.
Chase Stephen W, real estate, res 176 Huffman.
Chaska Hannah M, bds 164 W Berry.
Chaska Samuel, trav agt Charles Falk & Co, res 164 W Berry.

Chaska Selina, bds 164 W Berry.

Chauvey Amelia F (wid Charles), res 29 Hough.

Chauvey Bros (Francis Chauvey), wagonmkrs, 35 E Superior.

Chauvey Charles E, blksmith Chauvey Bros, bds 35 E Superior.

Chauvey Francis (Chauvey Bros), res 35 E Superior.

Chauvey Frank A, blksmith Chauvey Bros, bds 35 E Superior.

Chauvey Jennie A, bds 29 Hough.

Chauvey John B, blksmith, res 223 E Wayne.

Chauvey Joseph, painter Chauvey Bros, bds 35 E Superior.

Chauvey Mary, bds 223 E Wayne.

Chauvey M Celeste, bds 29 Hough.

Chavene Joseph, saloon, 231 E Jefferson, res 249 same.

Cheney James, capitalist, bds 160 Spy Run av.

Cherry Charles P, clk Penn Co, res 109 W De Wald.

Cherry Clifford, painter, bds 160 E Washington.

Cherry Frank C, bds 157 E Washington.

Cherry Frank M, boilermkr Penn Co, res 157 E Washington

Cherry Hayden, stenogr Penn Co, bds 134 E Lewis.

Cherry Roland T, res 38 St Mary's av.

Cherry Wm H, boilermkr Penn Co, res 134 E Lewis.

Cherry Wm Y, machinist Penn Co, bds 134 E Lewis.

Cheviron Amelia M, bds 190 E Wayne.

Cheviron Louise T, res 190 E Wayne.

Cheyney Emma, attendant School for Feeble-Minded Youth

Chicago Carpet and Rug Factory The, S Reehling propr, n w cor Wells and Superior.

Chinworth Ida F, bds n e cor Spy Run and Prospect avs.

Chinworth Jane K (wid Robert), res n e cor Spy Run and Prospect avs.

Chisholm Arthur, brakeman, rms 15 Cass.

Choctaw Medicine Co, 15 Maple av.

Chodynski John, laborer, res 267 Hanna.

Cholvin Alphonsus, truckman, res 198 Metz.

Christ, see also Crist.

Christ Edward, molder, bds 206 John.

Christ Gottlieb A, barnman The Herman Berghoff Brewing Co, bds 75 Grant av.

Christ Otto G, molder Bass F & M Wks, res 206 John.

Christ Samuel D, fireman Penn Co, bds 209 Lafayette.

Christen Andrew F, clerk, bds 100 Calhoun.

Christen George A, clk Paragon Mnfg Co, bds 117 Hanna.

Christen, John, saloon, 100 Calhoun, res same. Tel 44.

Christen John C, boilermaker. bds 117 Hanna.

Christen Mary M, domestic 447 Lafayette.

Christen Wm, bartndr Jno Christen, res 15 W Washington

Christensen Christopher E, painter Olds Wagon Wks, res 15 St Martin.

Christian Chapel, s e cor W Jefferson and Griffith.

Christiansen C Peter, helper Penn Co, bds 82 Montgomery

Christie James K, molder Kerr Murray Mnfg Co, res 48 Walnut.

Christie Jane, opr S M Foster, bds 24 W Wayne.

Christie John N, gardener, res e s Spy Run av 1 n of Centlivre Brewing Co.

Christie Joseph, lab Penn Co, res 123 E De Wald.

Christie Mary E, teacher Harmer School, res n w cor Hoagland and Creighton avs.

Christie Wm P, machinist, res 45 Locust.

Christlieb John E, teamster, res w s Osage 1 n of Main.

Christy Lawrence J, agt C E Everett, res 40 Huestis av.

Church C Perry, res 111 Wells.

Cincinnati, Richmond & Fort Wayne Railroad, operated by Grand Rapids & Indiana Railroad.

Circuit Court, Hon Edward O'Rourke judge, 2d floor Court House.

Cissel Rev C C, pastor BerryS t M E Church, res 266 W Berry.

City Book Bindery, George W Winbaugh propr, 13 E Main. Tel 495.

City Carriage Works (George P Dudenhoefer, Henry E Bueker), Wholesale and Retail Manufacturers of Carriages, Buggies, Phaetons, Surreys, Sleighs, etc, n w cor Main and Barr. Tel 155. (*See left top lines.*)

City Clerk's Office, City Hall. Tel 113.

City Comptroller's Office, City Hall.

City Directory Library, R L Polk & Co, 38 Bass Blk.

City Engineer's Office, City Hall.

City Fire Department, Central Station, n s Main bet Barr and Lafayette.

City Hall, s e cor Barr and E Berry.

City Market, e s Barr bet E Wayne and City Hall.

City Mills, C Tresselt & Sons proprs, cor Clinton and N Y, C & St L R R. Tel 268.

City Park, e s Broadway bet Taylor and P, Ft W & C Ry.

City Steam Dye House, Frank F Robacker Mngr, 11 W Jefferson. (*See page 101.*)

City Treasurer's Office, Court House.

City Trucking Co, Jacobs & Neuhaus Proprs, 19 and 21 W Washington. Tel 122.

City Water Works. office city hall, reservoir bounded by Lafayette, Suttenfield, Clinton and E Creighton av.

City Weigh Scales, e end city hall.

Clapesattle George, clk A J Keller, rms 96 Broadway.

Clapham Edwin C, laborer Hoffman Bros, res s s Maria 1 e of G R & I R R.

Clapham Wm E, lawyer, 24 Bank Blk, rms 40 Madison.

Clark Alanson W, foreman Jacob Klett & Sons, res 21 Orchard.

Clark Alonzo K, clk M L Jones, res 53 Home av.

Clark Anna, student. bds 175 Rockhill.

Clark Anna J (wid Joseph), res 279 E Jefferson.

Clark Carrie, opr S M Foster, bds 69 E Creighton av.

Clark Charles C, rms 100 E Columbia.

Clark Clifford, mach hd S F Bowser & Co, res 68 Oakley.

Clark Ella, bds 186 Clay.

Clark George W, brakeman, res 138 W De Wald.

Clark Gertrude E, teacher Jefferson School, bds 175 Rockhill.

Clark Isabelle C, forewoman Hoosier Mnfg Co, bds 5 Brandriff.

Clark Jacob W, trainmaster Penn Co, res 15 Holman.

Clark Jarvis M, teamster, Mayflower Milling Co, res 67 College.

Clark Jesse H, bds 111 W Wayne.

Clark John H, electrician, bds 111 W Wayne.

Clark Joseph E, machinist, bds 279 E Jefferson.

Clark Louis N, laborer, res n e cor Brooklyn av and Ontario.

Clark Lydia M (wid John H), res 111 W Wayne.

Clark Martha M, teacher Miner Street School, bds 279 E Jefferson.

Clark Mary, matron Allen County Orphan's Home.

Clark Mary B, special music teacher Public Schools, bds 103 W Berry.

Clark Mary E (wid Marvin), res 92 Thomas.

Clark Mortimer, printer, bds 111 W Wayne.

Clark Oliver, clerk, bds 111 W Wayne.

Clark Samuel, res 5 Hamilton.

Clark Theodore, barber 352½ Broadway, res 358 same.

Clark Thomas, saloon, 102 E Columbia, res same.
Clark Victoria (wid James H), res 5 Brandriff.
Clark Wm W, mach Ft Wayne Electric Corp, res 5 Brandriff.
Clarke Boyd, traveling agent, res 498 Harrison.
Clary Dennis E, helper Penn Co, bds 313 Calhoun.
Clary Johanna (wid Patrick), bds 525 Calhoun.
Claude Joseph, bds 71 E Columbia.
Claus J August, carpet weaver 16 University, res same.
Claus Max J C, molder Bass F & M Wks, res 21 Gay.
Clausmeier Edward F, Sheriff Allen County, office Court House, res County Jail.
Claussner Charles, opr Wayne Knitting Mills, res 38 Watkins.
Claussner Charles jr, opr Wayne Knitting Mills, bds 38 Watkins.
Claussner Clara, bds 38 Watkins.
Claussner Mollie, opr Wayne Knitting Mills, res 38 Watkins.
Claussner Robert F, opr Wayne Knitting Mills, res 29 Elm.
Clay, *see also Klee and Kley.*
Clay School, n w cor Clay and Washington.
Claymiller Rudolph H, lab Ft Wayne Electric Corp, res 57 Grant.
Clayton George L, traveling agt, res 16 E De Wald.
Clayton Mabel E (wid Henry), teacher Bloomingdale School, bds 27 Prospect av.
Clayton Nettie, domestic 498 Harrison.
Clear Catherine (wid John), janitress Holton Av School, res 127 Oliver.
Clear Wm, bartender Lake Shore Hotel, bds same.
Cleary Edward, helper Penn Co, res 141 Shawnee av.
Cleary Johanna, waitress F J Lourent, bds same.
Cleary John J, boilermkr Penn Co, res 3 Eliza.
Cleary Josie, domestic 1 Calhoun.
Cleary Martin J, printer The Journal, bds 39 W Washington
Cleary Will C, tailor 118 Harrison, bds 39 W Washington.
Clem Isaiah, engineer G R & I R R, res 30 E Butler.
Clemens Annie, opr Wayne Knitting Mills, bds 15 Huron.
Clemens Charles, fireman N Y, C & St L R R, bds 354 W Main.
Clemens Daniel, lab Penn Co, bds 10 Elm.
Clemens Jacob, lab Ind Mach Wks, res 15 Huron.
Clements Wm, check clk Penn Co, bds 56 W Williams.
Clements Wm H, laborer, bds 54 W Williams.

Clemmer Benjamin R, carpenter, 183 Fairfield av, res 124 Chicago.
Cleveland Frank, brakeman G R & I R R, bds 231 Barr.
Clifford James E, coal dealer, res 7 Boone.
Clifford Thomas, watchman county poor farm.
Cline, *see also Klein and Kline.*
Cline James H, switchman Penn Co, res 288 E Creighton av.
Clinkman Rosa, waiter, bds 263 Calhoun,
Clippinger Charles L, teacher, res 537 Broadway.
Clippinger C Gertrude, bds 537 Broadway.
Clippinger Isaac D, lab Ft Wayne Electric Corp, bds 21 Miner.
Clippinger John A, bds 537 Broadway,
Clippinger Maria, bds 21 Miner.
Clippinger Orpha (wid Alexander), janitress Miner St School, res 21 Miner.
Clizbe Miss Azalea, bds 80 W Jefferson.
Clizbe Lemuel L, res 80 W Jefferson.
Clizbe Miss Lillabel, bds 80 W Jefferson.
Clock Ernest E, mach Bass F & M Wks, bds Webster Hotel.
Close Charles F, molder Bass F & M Wks, res 271 E Lewis
Close Edward C, clerk R M S, bds 271 E Lewis.
Close John W, laborer, res 99 Lasselle.
Close May E, bds 115 N Harrison.
Close Wm, coremkr Bass F & M Wks, bds 117 Hanna.
Closs Frank P, machine hand, res 205 Hanna.
Closs Lemuel, res 88 Fairfield av,
Cloud Daisy B, student, bds 7 Duryea.
Cloud Richard M, car bldr Penn Co, res 7 Duryea.
Clover Hill Stock Farm, 2 miles n of city limits on Lima Plank rd.
Clusserath Nicholas, clk Penn Co, bds 113 Force.
Clutter Sarah J (wid Ryan), res 228 Calhoun.
Coats Arthur F (col'd), waiter, bds 73 Grand.
Coats Wm H (col'd), cook, res 73 Grand, res same.
Coblentz Jacob W, physician, 63 Harrison, res same.
Cochoit Jules E, helper, res 74 Lasselle.
Cochran Phœbe J (wid George), bds 53 W De Wald.
Cochrane Agnes J, bds 258 W Berry.
Cochrane Margaret S, prin Washington School, res 258 W Berry.
Codd W W, car inspr Penn Co, rms McKinney House.
Coder Frank, asst supt Met Life Ins Co, res 16 W Jefferson
Cody Bridget (wid Maurice), res 71 E Superior.

Cody John H, foreman, res 288 W Main.
Cody Loretta, opr Wayne Knitting Mills, bds 288 W Main.
Cody Mary C, dressmaker, bds 288 W Main.
Cody Mary R, bds 71 E Superior.
Cody Maurice, died February 12, 1894.
Cody Nellie L, stenogr Paragon Mnfg Co, bds 288 W Main.
Coe Carrie, rms 85 Cass.
Coeurdevey Anna, domestic 152 E Berry.
Coeurdevey Edward R, bartender F J Bercot, bds n w cor Spy Run av and Randolph.
Coeurdevey Effie, domestic w s Spy Run av 3 n of Edna.
Coeurdevey Estelle, bds 158 Holman.
Coeurdevey Frank S, sawyer, res 60 Howell.
Couerdevey Henry, res 99 Wagner.
Coeurdevey Jerome F, helper Anthony Wayne Mnfg Co, res 168 Holman.
Coeurdevey John, barber J W Brown, bds 158 Holman.
Coeurdevey Seraphim, sawyer Standard Wheel Co, res 158 Holman.
Coffin Edwin O, painter, bds 179 W Washington.
Coffin John B, cook, bds 179 W Washington
Coffin Sarah A (wid Philander), res 179 Washington.
Cogshall Maggie (wid David), res 18 E Columbia.
Cohagan Alonzo W, cigarmkr G Reiter, bds 252 Calhoun.
Cohagan Wm E, clk Randall Cycle Co, res 82 Taylor.
Cohen, see also Coon, Koehn, Kohn and Kuhn.
Cohen Mrs. Fannie, res 3 Indiana av.
Cohen Henry, cigarmkr John C Eckert, bds 3 Indiana av.
Cohen Jacob, asst supt Met Life Ins Co, res 40 Walter.
Cohen Lee, caller Penn Co, bds 3 Indiana av.
Cohn David, peddler, bds 281 E Washington.
Cohn Joseph, tailor Goldstine & Pearlman, rms 55 E Wayne
Colbert Maude A, domestic 144 W Berry.
Colchin Wildia C, opr S Freiburger & Bro, bds 135 E Lewis
Colclesser Franklin P, car bldr Penn Co, res 249 Walton av
Cole, see also Koehl and Kuhl.
Cole Madge, res 10 Clinton.
Cole Peter, laborer, bds rear 196 Hanna.
Cole Rose, domestic 97 Pearl.
Coleman, see also Coolman and Kohlmann.
Coleman Addie B, bds 24 Michigan av.
Coleman Dora (wid John), res 90 E Lewis.
Coleman Frank, porter, bds 68 W Jefferson.
Coleman Henry, wagonmkr, res 90 E Lewis,
Coleman Mary A (wid Jacob), res 147 E Jefferson.

Coleman Sylvanus S, clk, res 410 E Washington.
Coleman Thomas, brakeman G R & I R R, res 389 E Lewis.
Colman Wm, laborer, res s s Maria 2 e of G R & I R R.
Colerick Bessie L, bds 193 W Berry.
Colerick Charles E, clk Penn Co, res 160 W Wayne.
Colerick Henry (Colerick & France), res 193 W Berry.
Colerick Margaret M, bds 266 W Wayne.
Colerick Maria A, res 85 E Jefferson.
Colerick Phil B, Attorney at Law, Tri-State Bldg res 93 E Berry.
Colerick Walpole G, Lawyer 22 Court, res 88 E Berry.
Colerick Will E, student and notary, 22 Court, bds 193 W Berry.
Colerick & France, (Henry Colerick, James E K France), Lawyers, 5 and 6 Pixley & Long Bldg.
Coling George policeman, res 160 Smith.
Goling J Charles, butcher Gottlieb Haller, bds 338 Harrison.
Coling Peter, shoemaker, res 338 Harrison.
Collar George W, died Feb 27, 1895.
Collett Arthur E, clk Wabash R R, res 40 Brackenridge.
Collie Willard A, tel opr N Y, C & St L R R, bds 121 E Main.
Collier, *see Colyer.*
Collins Anna B, bds 12 Brandriff.
Collins Charles C, winder, bds 12 Brandriff.
Collins Clara E, bds 12 Brandriff.
Collins Elizabeth, teacher Jefferson School, bds 42 Huestis av.
Collins Elizabeth O (wid Charles H), teacher Hanna School, bds 2 Monroe.
Collins John J, helper Penn Co, bds 111 Hanna.
Collins John W, helper Penn Co, bds 111 Hanna.
Collins Joseph A, cooper, res 81 Holman.
Collins Lizzie A, opr S M Foster, bds 10 Bass.
Collins Margaret, bds 111 Hanna.
Collins Martha (col'd), (wid Dennis), bds 31 Pearl.
Collins Mary M, dressmaker, bds 12 Brandriff.
Collins Melissa J (wid Lindley D), res 12 Brandriff.
Collins Michael J, blacksmith, bds 10 Bass.
Collins Nora, bds 10 Bass.
Collins Peter, laborer, bds 233 Webster.
Collins Thomas D, laborer Penn Co, res 10 Bass.

Collins Wm D, clerk, bds 10 Bass.
Collis Adam, machinist Penn Co, res 51 E Butler.
Collis John C, lab Olds Wagon Wks, bds 51 E Butler.
Collis Norman B, patternmkr Bass F & M Wks, res 391 Hanna.
Collopy John, fireman N Y, C & St L R R, bds 35 St Mary's av.
Colmey Charles D, fireman, bds 11 Suttenfield.
Colmey Christopher R, engr Penn Co, res 11 Suttenfield.
Colmey Mrs Lulu B (Colmey & Ripley), res 11 Suttenfield.
Colmey & Ripley (Lulu B Colmey, Elizabeth L Ripley), notions, 201 Calhoun.
Colson Charles D, engineer, res 329 W Main.
Columbia House, J P Ross propr, 25 and 27 W Columbia.
Columbia Machine Wks, L G Scholze propr, 54 E Columbia.
Colvin Albert, laborer, res 71 Wagner.
Colvin Caroline, teacher High School, bds 155 W Wayne.
Colvin Elbert, contractor, res 83 Franklin av.
Colvin Joseph, carpenter, res 25 Wagner.
Colvin Joseph, cabinetmaker, res 11 Wagner.
Colvin Mary A (wid John R), res 71 Wagner.
Colvin Wm, shoemaker 80 E Columbia, res 73 Baltes.
Colyer Arthur A, helper B W Skelton Co, bds 132 W De Wald.
Colyer Jacob A, cooper B W Skelton Co, res 132 W De Wald.
Combs, *see Coombs.*
Comer Mary A, domestic 306 Maumee rd.
Comer Wm O, brakeman, rms 30 Baker.
Comincavish Felix, res s s Bluffton rd 4 w of river bridge
Comincavish Marshall, mach S F Bowser & Co, res 150 Spy Run av.
Commeyer Sophia, opr S M Foster, bds 87 St Mary's av.
Comparet Charles M, shirt mnfr, 219 Madison, res same.
Comparet David F, produce, 76 E Columbia, res 59 Erie. Tel 375.
Comparet Thomas L, bkkpr Mc Donald & Watt, res 13 Liberty.
Compton Andrew J, conductor, res 133 Holman.
Compton Howard P, flagman, rms 133 Holman
Compton Wm S, del clk J D Gumpper, bds 382 Lafayette
Conahan John J, clk E W Lewis, res 123 St Mary's av.
Concordia Cemetery, n s Maumee rd e of Concordia College
Concordia Cemetery Association, Gottlieb Muhlenbruck sec, 39 W Main.

14

Concordia College (German Lutheran), n s Maumee rd e of Schick.

Condon John, saloon, 264 Calhoun, res 48 W Williams.

Conductors' Brotherhood, 106 Calhoun.

Congdon Bruce K, clk J G Mann, bds 104 Ewing.

Congdon Hattie E, bds 104 Ewing.

Congdon Johanna L (wid Joshua E), res 104 Ewing.

Conklin Charles S, engineer, bds 9 N Calhoun.

Conklin Eli B, agent, res 16 W Creighton av.

Conklin Elizabeth A (wid Thomas), res 207 W De Wald.

Conklin George W, clk Princess Cash Store, bds 278 W Creighton av.

Conklin Guy (Jacobs & Conklin), res 34 Wagner.

Conklin John J, engineer, res 278 W Creighton av.

Conklin Josie, teacher, bds 207 W De Wald.

Conklin Roy E, bill clk Wabash R R, bds 278 W Creighton av.

Conklin Wm E, engineer L E & W R R, res 4 E 5th.

Conlon Ellen (wid James), housekeeper 32 Hugh.

Conley Wm G, helper, bds 320 W Main.

Connecticut Mutual Life Insurance Company of Hartford, Conn, Witter F Baxter Agent, 33 Bass Blk.

Connelly, *see also Connolly.*

Connelly James, laborer, res 24 Brandriff.

Connelly James J, student, bds 24 Brandriff.

Connelly John J, lab Penn Co, bds 24 Brandriff.

Connelly John M, lab Wabash R R, res 110 W De Wald.

Connelly Margaret, res 13 Hoagland av.

Connelly Margaret, bds 371 W Main.

Connelly Margaret, dressmaker, bds 24 Brandriff.

Connelly Michael, laborer, res 371 W Main.

Connelly Thomas J, student, bds 24 Brandriff.

Connelly Wm, helper Horton Mnfg Co, bds 371 W Main.

Conners, *see also Connors and O'Connor.*

Conners Anna M, clk C H Waltemath & Sons, bds 43 Charles.

Conners Ella, bds 188 E Washington.

Conners Emma, domestic, 92 W Main.

Conners Frank B, machinist, bds 43 Charles.

Conners Hannah, mender Wayne Knitting Mills, bds 188 E Washington.

Conners James, brakeman N Y, C & St L R R, bds 75 Boone.

Conners Michael, capt Engine Co No 2, res 43 Charles.

Conners Walburga, bds 43 Charles.
Conners Wm H, mach Penn Co, bds 43 Charles.
Connett Alice B, bds 171 Holman.
Connett Allen, lab N Y, C & St L R R, bds Edward Connett.
Connett David S, lab Ft Wayne Electric Corp, res 1 w of Wabash R R 1 mile south of city limits.
Connett Edward, gardener, res Miller 4 w of Brooklyn av.
Connett Edward E, gardener, res s s Miller 5 w of Brook- -lyn av.
Connett George, laborer, bds Edward E Connett.
Connett John, Helper Wabash R R, res Brooklyn av s of Ontario.
Connett Mahlon T, carp. res s s Miller 1 w of Brooklyn av.
Connett Martin V, foreman Ft Wayne Electric Corp, res 171 Holman.
Connolly, see also Connelly.
Connolly James T, Prop The Wellington, 83 Calhoun, res 15 E Washington. Tel 249, res 227. (See right side lines.)
Connor. Elizabeth, student, bds 149 Fairfield av.
Connor Maggie (wid Patrick), removed to Chicago, Ill.
Connors, see also Conners and O'Connor.
Connors George W, stonecutter, bds 111 Putnam.
Connors Mary J E, clk People's Store, bds 138 Fulton.
Connors Thomas J, brakeman, bds 71 Boone.
Connors Wilhelmina (wid Clifton H), bds 111 Putnam.
Connors Wm, appr George Jaap, bds 111 Putnam.
Conover Alice E (wid Addison V D), res 130 W Jefferson.
Conover Cora A, teacher Jefferson School, bds 130 W Jefferson.
Conover Fanny R, teacher McCulloch School. bds 326 E Wayne.
Conover Grace L, teacher, bds 326 E Wayne.
Conover Lola, teacher, bds 326 E Wayne.
Conover Norton, foreman job room Ft Wayne Sentinel, res 326 E Wayne.
Conover Wm A, bill clk McDonald & Watt, res 7 Liberty.
Conrad, see also Coonrod.
Conrad Agnes, domestic 309 W Jefferson.
Conrad Christine, domestic 110 E Berry.
Conrad Elsie A, bds 170 E Creighton av.
Conrad George F, bds 105 Lafayette.
Conrad George H, molder Ft Wayne Electric Corp, bds 319 Harrison.
Conrad John C, lab N Y, C & St L R R, res 72 Franklin av.

Conrad Katie, cook County Poor Farm.
Conrad Mary, domestic 73 W Wayne.
Conrad Mary E (wid John), bds 105 Lafayette.
Conrad Theresa, bds 170 E Creighton av.
Conrad Thomas A, brakeman, bds 105 Lafayette.
Conrad Victor H, clk L S & M S Ry, rms 40 E 5th.
Conrad Wm, car bldr Penn Co, res 170 E Creighton av.
Conrad Wm, pressman, bds 72 Franklin av.
Conrady Frederick G, mach hd Penn Co, res 231 Harmer.
Conrady John G, car repr Penn Co, res 43 John.
Conrady Kate, dressmaker, bds 43 John.
Conrady Rose C, tailoress A F Schoch, bds 43 John.
Conrady Sophia, tailoress, bds 43 John.
Conroy Edward F, elevator opr Pixley & Long Bldg, bds 42 Melita.
Conroy James, blsmith Wabash R R, res 42 Melita.
Conroy James J, lab Ft Wayne Electric Corp, bds 42 Melita.
Conroy Nellie, bds 42 Melita.
Conroy Peter, helper Penn Co, bds 74 Montgomery.
Conroy Thomas M, student, bds 42 Melita.
Contant August C, mach Penn Co, res 72 Lasselle.
Converse Geneva, helper The Randall.
Conway Anthony, brakeman G R & I R R, rms 29 Melita.
Conway Bryan, lab Ft W E Ry Co, bds 11 Melita.
Conway Mrs Catherine, res 46 Hoagland av.
Conway Edward D, conductor, res 21 Hamilton.
Conway Frank O, saloon, 67 E Main, res same.
Conway Philip, bell boy The Wayne, bds 26 Hamilton.
Coogan Simon, engr N Y C & St L R R, bds 80 Boone.
Cook, see also Koch.
Cook Alba A, bkkpr Aldine Ptg House, bds 33 Madison.
Cook Albert H, res 33 Madison.
Cook Annie, seamstress, bds 34 John.
Cook Automatic Boiler Cleaner Co,
    Jerome Q Cook Supt, 59 E Columbia.
Cook Catherine (wid Adam), res 34 John.
Cook Charles F, lab Ft Wayne Electric Corp, bds 284 Harrison.
Cook Charles O, mach Penn Co, res 155 W Washington.
Cook Charles W, Farm Implements, 50 and 52 E Columbia, res New Haven, Ind
Cook Christian F, wheelmaker Olds Wagon Wks, res 48 W Lewis.
Cook Clarence F, Propr Aldine Printing House, 63 E Berry, res 194 W Creighton av.

Cook Edward C F, lab Ft Wayne Electric Corp, bds 48 W Lewis.

Cook Ernest W, sec Ryan Trucking Co and genl agt Allen County Loan & Savings Assn, 32 E Berry, res 70 Indiana av,

Cook Harry O, clerk, bds 284 Harrison.

Cook Jerome P, supt Cook Automatic Boiler Cleaner Co, mechanical engineer, 59 E Columbia, res 225 Madison.

Cook John M (Bourie, Cook & Co), res 85 W Butler,

Cook John S, brakeman G R & I R R, res 29 Melita.

Cook Robert, stripper H W Ortmann, bds 40 W Lewis.

Cook Rose L, bkkpr Tri-State Bldg and Loan Assn, bds 33 Madison.

Cook Sadie B, bds 284 Harrison.

Cook Susanna, bds 57 E De Wald.

Cook Walter E, clk Mossman, Yarnelle & Co, bds Ervin House.

Cook Wm W, clk Penn Co, bds 12 Harrison.

Cooke Harry B, helper Ryan Trucking Co, bds 188 Griffith.

Cooke John H, engr N Y, C & St L R R, res 430 W Main.

Cooksey Thomas L, pastor Central Christian Church, res 66 W Main.

Coolican Ellen A (wid Patrick), res 21 Poplar.

Coolican John J, winder, bds 21 Poplar.

Coolican Helen C, stenographer, bds 21 Poplar.

Coolican Margaret T, bds 21 Poplar.

Coolican Mary T, dressmaker, bds 21 Poplar.

Coolican Rose M, bds 21 Poplar.

Coolman, see also Coleman.

Coolman George W, carpenter, res 13 Wagner.

Coombes Eliza (wid John F), bds 164 Broadway.

Coombs Edmund H, iron and steel, 27 E Columbia, bds 186 W Berry. Tel 530.

Coombs Lillian M (wid John), res 186 W Berry. Tel 254.

Coombs Sarah A (wid Wm), res 35 W Main.

Coon, see also Cohen, Koehn and Kuhn.

Coon Alonzo, driver L Diether & Bro, res 147 Broadway.

Coon Hattie, tailoress A F Schoch, rms 19 Ross.

Coon Nathaniel B, trimmer Jenney E L & P Co, bds 88 Madison.

Cooney Patrick, bds 72 Thomas.

Coonrod, see also Conrad.

Coonrod Matthias C, laborer, res 320 E Jefferson.

Cooper, see also Kooper.

Cooper Cornelius G, mach Penn Co, res 6 Jones.

Cooper George J, engr N Y, C & St L R R, res 284 W Jefferson.
Cooper Lois A (wid Wm), res 44 W 3rd.
Cooper Mary (wid Cornelius), bds 6 Jones.
Cooper Wm, brakeman, rms 226 Calhoun.
Cooper Wm P, insurance agt, res 182 W Washington.
Cooper Winfield S, foreman Wabash R R, bds 122 Fairfield av.
Cope, see also Kopp.
Cope Abram. died January 20. 1895.
Cope Bert W, laborer, bds 55 Barr.
Cope Daniel C, laborer, res 55 Barr.
Cope David F. laborer, bds 146 E Lewis.
Cope Eva, bds 55 Barr.
Cope Josephine R, bkkpr S B Thing & Co, bds 146 E Lewis.
Copinus Albert, produce, 25 E Columbia, res 100 W Jefferson. Tel 492.
Copinus Louis W, clk A Copinus, bds 100 W Jefferson.
Coppen Ellen, domestic 260 Hoagland av.
Corbett Thomas, fireman N Y, C & St L R R, bds 80 Boone.
Corcoran Alice B, stenogr Weil Bros & Co, bds 120 High.
Corcoran Anthony, molder, bds 178 E Lewis.
Corcoran James, bds 120 High.
Corcoran James E, printer The Journal, bds 178 E Lewis.
Corcoran John, res 41 E De Wald.
Corcoran John J, printer The Journal, bds 178 E Lewis.
Corcoran Julia, bds 178 E Lewis.
Corcoran Mary (wid John), res 178 E Lewis.
Corcoran Mary M, bds 120 High.
Corcoran Owen H, clk Dreier & Bro, res 271 Harrison.
Corcoran Thomas, laborer, res 120 High.
Corlett Joseph E, photographer 71 Monroe, res same.
Corneille August L, patent medicines, 26 E Columbia, res 31 Duck.
Corneille Clara A, dressmaker, bds 41 E Superior.
Corneille Emma J, bds rear 45 E Superior.
Corneille Jennie, clk H A Howe, res 84 Calhoun.
Corneille John B, notary public, res rear 45 E Superior.
Corneille Louis J, died July 18th, 1894.
Corneille Mrs L J, Saddles, Harness, Collars, Etc, 69 E Main, res same.
Corneille Mrs Mary. res 41 E Superior.
Corneille Paul E, fireman Penn Co, res 41 E Superior.

Corneille Rosa, bds 22 Brackenridge.
Cornell Frederick W, trav agt G E Bursley & Co, res 338
   E Wayne.
Cornwall Frederick P, painter, res 251 W Wayne.
Cornyn Helen L (wid John W), bds 87 E Jefferson.
Corrigan Michael, cook Wayne Club, rms 58 E Wayne.
Cortwright, *see Cartwright.*
Corwin Lydia A (wid Theodore), bds 226 Fairfield av,
Cosgrove Frank K, traveling agent, res 103 W Superior.
Costello John, hostler C L Centlivre Brewing Co, bds w
   s Spy Run 2 n of Edna.
Costello Timothy J, train dispatcher Penn Co, res 152 E
   Taber.
Costigan Cecelia (wid Jacob), res 121 E Washington.
Costigan James V, clk Ft Wayne Electric Corp, res 147
   Shawnee av.
Costigan James W, winder Ft Wayne Electric Corp, bds
   147 Shawnee av.
Cothrell Andrew J, bds 65 Douglas av.
Cothrell James C, engr G R & I R R, bds 65 Douglas av.
Cothrell Ruth E, bds 65 Douglas av.
Cothrell Ruthette D (wid Jared E), res 65 Douglas av.
Cotner Edmund G, painter Penn Co, res 136 Walton av.
Couderat Frank, clk J H Hartman, bds 305 Hanna.
Couderat Jacob, machinist, bds 305 Hanna.
Couderat John, porter Ft Wayne Newspaper Union. res
   305 Hanna.
Couderat John jr, laborer, bds 305 Hanna.
Couderat Wm, lather, bds 305 Hanna.
Coulter Robert J, mngr Union Pacific Tea Co, rms 102
   Calhoun.
Councell Charles E, supt, res 161 Edgewater av.
Council Chambers, City Hall, s e cor Barr and E Berry.
Countryman George W, brakeman, res 104 N Harrison.
County Auditor's Office, C W Edsall auditor, Court House
County Clerk's Office, Harry M Metzger clerk, Court
   House.
County Commissioners' Office, Jasper
   W Jones Pres, J H Stellhorn Chairman, Matthias A
   Ferguson, Sylvanus F Baker, Office Court House.
County Jail, E C Clausmeier sheriff, w s Calhoun 1 n of
   Superior. Tel 168.
County Poor Farm, Herman W Felts supt. Bluffton road
   n of City limits. Tel 264.

County Recorder's office, George W Fickel recorder, Court House.

County Superintendent of Schools office, F J Young supt, 11 Bass Blk.

County Surveyor's office, C W Branstattor surveyor, Court House.

County Treasurer's Office, L C Hunter treas, Court House

Cour Claud A, res 261 E Washington.

Cour Eugene, died March 12, 1895.

Cour Frank, blksmith Ft W E Ry Co, res 330 E Jefferson.

Cour Frank V, bds 261 E Washington.

Cour George E, helper Penn Co, bds 261 E Washington.

Cour Henry, iron wkr Kerr Murray Mnfg Co, bds 261 E Washington.

Cour John H, helper Penn Co, bds 261 E Washington.

Cour Joseph P, boilermkr, bds 261 E Washington.

Cour Victorine (wid Eugene), res 19 Buchanan.

Cour Wm A, clerk Ft Wayne Newspaper Union, res 355 E Washington.

Cour Wm H, boilermaker Wabash R R, res 135 E Lewis.

Courdevey, see Coeurdevey.

Court House, bounded by Calhoun, Court, E Berry and E Main.

Cousar Charles, clk Bass F & M Wks, res 33 Elizabeth.

Coutts Viola, domestic 76 Murray.

Covault Emma, dressmaker, res 194 Lafayette.

Coverdale Asahel S (Coverdale & Archer), res 261 W Wayne.

Coverdale & Archer (Asahel S Coverdale, Perry J Archer), grocers. 24 Harrison.   Tel 395.

Covey Wm H, printer Ft Wayne Newspaper Union, bds 61 E Columbia.

Covington Mrs Thomas, res 47 Huestis av.

Cowden Harry M, tel opr Penn Co, res 408 Calhoun.

Cowdrey Adelbert, brakeman N Y, C & St L R R, res 103 Wilt.

Cowen M Robert, engr Penn Co, res 457 Lafayette.

Cowles Edwin N, bds 57 W Butler.

Cox, see also Koch and Kocks.

Cox Eliza, opr S M Foster, bds 183 Hanna.

Cox Elizabeth E (wid Joseph A), bds 17 Suttenfield.

Cox Emma (col'd) (wid Wm), res 54 Chicago.

Cox Enoch, storekper Penn Co, res 17 Suttenfield.

Cox James B, plumber P E Cox, bds 183 Hanna.

Cox John, helper Penn Co, res 183 Hanna.

Cox Lawrence, plumber P E Cox, bds 183 Hanna.

Cox Lizzie, nurse, 194 E Lewis, rms same.
Cox Patrick E, Plumber, Fort Wayne Electrical Construction Co,, 176 Calhoun, res 525 Calhoun. Tel 219.
Cox Thomas E, plumber P E Cox, bds 117 Hanna.
Cox Wm M, flagman, res 71 Smith.
Coy John A, mngr Ryan Trucking Co, res 212 W De Wald.
Coye John, bds 326 Hanna.
Coyle J David, dentist, 96 Calhoun, res same.
Coyle Philip, removed to Grand Rapids, Mich.
Crabbs Elizabeth (wid Joseph), res 64 W Main.
Crabill Levi, fireman Penn Co, res 402 Clinton.
Cragg Charles, carpet weaver, 121 Taber, res same,
Cragg Harry P, mach Ft Wayne Electric Corp, bds 121 Taber.
Cragg Robert V, clk S F Bowser & Co, bds 130 Wallace.
Cragg Thomas, trav agt S F Bowser & Co, res 130 Wallace.
Craig Andrew, carpenter, res 29 Boone.
Craig Atchison D, brakeman, res 141 Horace.
Craig Christian C, engr Penn Co, res 173 Harrison.
Craig Elwood, clerk, bds 27 Boone.
Craig James, mach hd Rhinesmith & Simonson, bds 96 Montgomery.
Craig James C, engineer, res 30 Masterson.
Craig James W, brakeman G R & I R R, res 142 Buchanan.
Craig Ralston H, fireman Penn Co, bds 231 Barr.
Craig Robert, stud groom J H Bass, Brookside.
Craig Sidney C, engr Penn Co, rms 94 Calhoun.
Craig Theodore L, mach Western Gas Constr Co, bds 141 Horace.
Craig Walter D, brakeman G R & I R R, bds 141 Horace.
Craigh Michael, engineer, res 110 Force.
Craine, see Crane.
Crall Charles E, Associated Press reporter Ft Wayne Sentinel, res 147 W Washington.
Crall Fred Le R, cash Hoosier Mnfg Co, res 210 W De Wald.
Cramer, see also Kramer.
Cramer Anna (wid Henry), bds 52 Grant av.
Cramer Mrs Augusta (Cramer & Neher), res 465 Lafayette
Cramer Edgar, laborer, res 86 E Lewis.
Cramer Francis, res 91 Lasselle.
Cramer Harry R, motorman Ft W E Ry Co, res 52 Grant av.
Cramer Henry E, laborer, res 393 E Lewis.
Cramer Jennie D, nurse. res 86 E Lewis.

Cramer John F, pres Ft Wayne Newspaper Union, res Milwaukee. Wis.

Cramer Lizzie, bds 92 Hanna.

Cramer Louise (wid Eli), bds 435 E Washington.

Cramer Stephen, brakeman N Y, C & St L R R, bds 22 Boone.

Cramer Theresa (wid Solomon K), bds 91 Lasselle.

Cramer Wm, laborer, bds 91 Laselle.

Cramer & Neher (Augusta Cramer, John V Neher), grocers, 527 Lafayette.

Cramp Wm S, clk People's Store, bds 22 Chicago.

Cran Annie (wid Charles), res 129 Holman.

Cran Charles, molder, res 158 Wallace.

Cran Charles W, patternmkr Western Gas Const Co, bds 158 Wallace.

Cran Mattie H, bds 129 Holman.

Cran Robert, foreman Bass F & M Wks, res 398 Calhoun.

Crance, see also Crantz and Krantz.

Crance Alice, bds 80 Thomas.

Crance Charles, cigarmkr, bds 80 Thomas.

Crance Cora, bds 508 Hanna.

Crance Ferdinand, laborer, res 132 John.

Crance Frank J, lather, bds 80 Thomas.

Crance George W, grocer s w cor Smith and E Creighton av, res 138. Smith.

Crance Harry E, mach hd S F Bowser & Co, bds 138 Smith.

Crance James, laborer, res 508 Hanna.

Crance Pritchard, laborer, res 80 Thomas.

Crandall Annie, attendant School for Feeble Minded Youth

Crane Mrs Bedelia M, res 21 Buchanan.

Crane Edward J, brakeman, res 154 Smith.

Crane Eugene T, finisher Ft Wayne Organ Co, bds 21 Buchanan.

Crane George D, Law, Abstracts and Accountant, 36 E Berry, res 305 W Jefferson.

Crane Harvey E, electrical engineer, 36 E Berry, bds 305 W Jefferson.

Crane John, brakeman, rms 2 Baker.

Crane Mrs Mary, bds 303 Hanna.

Crane Theresa R, bds 21 Buchanan.

Cranston Alice (wid John), res 28 Marion.

Cranston Elizabeth A, milliner, bds 28 Marion.

Cranston James J, engr L E & W R R, bds 28 Marion.

Cranston John W B, fireman, bds 28 Marion.

Cranston Margaret E, dressmaker, 28 Marion, bds same.

Crantz, *see also Crance and Krantz.*

Crantz Franklin, brakeman, res 312 E Creighton av.

Crathers Martha, bds E B Lepper.

Cratsley Frank C, propr Home Restaurant, 99 Calhoun, res 123 Edgewater av.

Craw, *see also Krqh.*

Craw Edward L, Real Estate, Loans and Insurance, 24 and 25 Bass Blk, res 198 W Wayne.

Craw George R, registry clk P O, bds 198 W Wayne.

Craw Sarah B, bds 198 W Wayne.

Crawford Albert H, paperhanger L O Hull, res 11 Walnut.

Crawford Benjamin F, plasterer, res 96 Montgomery.

Crawford D Frank, removed to Pittsburg, Pa.

Crawford Eugene N, apprentice Bass F & M Wks, bds 66 Melita.

Crawford Frederick E, plumber S F Bowser & Co, bds 42 Pontiac.

Crawford Henry B, winder Ft Wayne Electric Corp, res e s Sherman 2 n of Huffman.

Crawford John, helper Penn Co, bds 66 Melita.

Crawford John T, real estate, res s w cor Edgewater av and Oneida.

Crawford Joseph, engineer Fort Wayne Electric Mnfg Co, bds 5 Hamilton.

Crawford Lizzie (wid John P), bds 440 W Main.

Crawford Martin, helper Penn Co, res 66 Melita.

Crawford Nelson J, winder Fort Wayne Electric Corp, res 66 Huestis av.

Crawford Noah H, actionmkr Ft Wayne Organ Co, res 41 Miner.

Crawford Richard, painter, res n w cor Brooklyn av and Ontario.

Crawford Samantha (wid Montgomery), bds 386 E Washington.

Crawford Samuel M, laborer, res 47 Elmwood av.

Crawford Sarah S (wid Montgomery), nurse, 386 E Washington, bds same.

Crawford Thomas, appr Ft Wayne Sentinel, bds 66 Melita.

Crawford Thomas B, janitor, bds 46 Burgess.

Crawford Wm A, mach hd Ft Wayne Furn Co, res 73 W 3d.

Crayton Elizabeth, res 135 Broadway.

Cream John J, brakeman, bds 264 Calhoun.

Cregg, *see Cragg.*

Creiger Angeline, opr S M Foster, bds 24 Oliver.
Creigh Annie, cook E F Heine, rms 278 Calhoun.
Creigh Michael, engineer Penn Co, res 110 Force.
Creigh Peter F, saloon, 12 Chicago, res same.
Creighton Av public School, s w cor E Creighton and Holton avs.
Creiter Conrad, res 107 Wallace.
Cresco Bathing Institute, Dodge & Keller Proprs, cor W Washington and Broadway. Tel 335.
   (*See right side lines and p 93.*)
Cressler Alfred D, pres and genl mngr Kerr Murray Mnfg Co, res 141 W Berry. Tel 153.
Cressler Alfred S jr, student, bds 141 W Berry.
Cressler Anna S, bds 82 E Berry.
Crick Reuben W, carpenter, res 161 W De Wald.
Crick Wm T, student, bds 161 W De Wald.
Crider Anna (wid Jacob), bds 49 Elm.
Crighton David K, draughtsman Ind Mach Wks, res 37 Home av.
Crighton Francis J, student, bds 49 Brackenridge.
Crighton Thomas J, clk Western Gas Cons Co, bds 230 E Creighton av.
Crighton Wm, master mechanic Kerr Murray Mnfg Co, res 49 Brackenridge.
Crighton Wm H, draughtsman Ft Wayne Electric Corp, res 228 Fairfield av.
Crim Cyrus M, mngr Standard Wheel Co, res 445 Calhoun
Crim Walter H, student, bds 445 Calhoun.
Crimmans Dennis J, fireman Penn Co, res 47 E Butler.
Crimmans Maggie, laundress Hotel Rich.
Crippen Jennie O, bds 337 Harrison.
Crist, *see also Christ.*
Crist John, brakeman G R & I R R, res 105 John.
Crist Layman, blacksmith, res 84 Maumee rd
Criswell Ivy P, student, res 8 Marion.
Critz Albert, clk Meyer Bros & Co, rms 14 Calhoun.
Croff Abraham, shoemaker, bds 42 Wallace.
Cromwell Joseph W, lumber, res 224 W Berry.
Crone, *see also Krohn.*
Crone Henry A, lab Ft Wayne Electric Corp, bds 81 Brackenridge.
Cronin Sarah, domestic 177 W Wayne.
Croninger Edward, lab Penn Co, res 116 Hanna.
Crosby Edwin G, mach Wabash R R, res 20 South Wayne av.

Crosby Elbert W, engr N Y, C & St L R R, res 100 W 3d.
Crosby Ella S, stenogr Breen & Morris, bds 558 Calhoun.
Crosby Etta, bds 111 W De Wald.
Crosby Frederick V, clerk, bds 558 Calhoun.
Crosby George T, mach Wabash R R, res 111 W De Wald
Crosby Grace E, draughtswoman C E Kendrick, bds 111 W De Wald.
Crosby Helen I, stenogr Breen & Morris, bds 558 Calhoun.
Crosby Hiram O, res 558 Calhoun.
Crosby Mabel G, bds 111 W De Wald.
Crosby Mary E, bds 111 W De Wald.
Crosby Richard A, printer, Ft Wayne News, bds 558 Calhoun.
Crosby Wm G, machinist, bds 111 W De Wald.
Crouse, *see also Cruse, Krauhs and Kruse.*
Crouse Benjamin, laborer, res 206 W Superior.
Crouse Charles D, clk, bds 18 Mary.
Crouse Charles R, lab, res Begue s w cor Liberty.
Crouse Clinton M, teamster Standard Oil Co, res 117 Boone.
Crouse David, lab, Hoffman Bros, res 18 Mary.
Crouse George H, baker, B Gutermuth, res 36 Wilt.
Crow Benjamin A, truckman, Penn Co, res 13 Belle.
Crow Phoebe, dress mkr, bds 34 Wall.
Crowe Albert B, teacher High School, bds 26 Clay.
Crowe Rev James B, res 26 Clay.
Crowe John M, Lawyer, 34 E Berry, res 26 Clay.
Crowl Mrs Hattie, attendant School for Feeble Minded Youth.
Crowley Margaret, died May 21, 1894.
Crowley Margaret (wid Richard), bds 85 W Butler.
Croxton Milton E, packer, res 98 Gay.
Croxton Worthington A, traveling agt, res 215 W Wayne.
Croy David E, engineer, res 96 Wabash av.
Croy Harry, laborer, bds 158 Horace.
Croy Wesley V, car bldr Penn Co, res 158 Horace.
Crull, *see also Krull.*
Crull Rev August, teacher Concordia College, res same.
Crummitt Joseph H, barber, 147 Hanna, res 181 Madison.
Cruse, *see also Crouse, Krauhs, Kraus and Krouse.*
Cruse Charles A, tuck pointer, bds 76 E Pontiac.
Cruse Demetrius A, tuck pointer. res 76 E Pontiac.
Crutchfield Joseph T, helper Bass F & M Wks, res 6 Hoffman.
Crye Mrs Mary, bds 75 Scott av.

Culbertson Frank V, mngr R G Dun & Co, 35-36 Pixley
   & Long Bldg, res s e cor Hoagland av and Allen.
Culbertson Harry R, solicitor R G Dun & Co, bds s e cor
   Hoagland av and Allen.
Cull, *see also Kuhl and Kull.*
Cull Catherine (wid Cornelius), res 27 Taylor.
Cull Dennis W, wood carver, bds 27 Taylor.
Cull James J, machinist, bds 27 Taylor.
Cull Mary (wid Edmund), res 94 Chicago.
Cull Thomas, engineer, bds 27 Taylor.
Cullen James, candymkr B W Skelton Co, bds 209 Lafay-
   ette.
Cullen Michael, laborer, bds 498 W Main.
Cullen Patrick J, brakeman Penn Co, res 154 Walton av.
Culler George W, res 34 W Superior.
Culver John M, carpenter, res 58 Ferguson av.
Culver Wm M, finisher Ft Wayne Organ Co, res 34 Miner
Cummerow George F R, reporter, bds 121 W Superior.
Cummerow Mamie A, bds 121 W Superior.
Cummerow Otto F, res 121 W Superior,
Cummerow Rudolph M, saloon, 276 Calhoun, res 122 W
   Butler.
Cummings Anna (wid Rhody), res 77 Douglas av.
Cummings Charles L, collector, bds 29 Grand.
Cummings Elmer E, carpenter, res 29 Stophlet.
Cummings Francis E, opr Wabash R R, bds 77 Doug-
   las av.
Cummings Jeremiah, brakeman, bds 78 Murray.
Cummings Josephine, opr Troy Steam Laundry, bds 84
   Fairfield av.
Cummings Mary (wid Michael). laundress Troy Steam
   Laundry, res 84 Fairfield av.
Cummings Mary C, tailoress, bds 77 Douglas av.
Cummings Nellie, seamstress, bds 84 Fairfield av.
Cummings Owen, saloon, 268 Calhoun, res 34 Bass.
Cummings Philip, finisher Ft Wayne Furn Co, bds 34 W
   Superior.
Cummings Thomas J T, insurance agt, res 29 Grand.
Cummins Mrs Abigail, bds Allen Co Orphans' Home.
Cunningham Bertha, res n s Baltes 1 e of Spy Run av.
Cunningham Edward, bds 305 Lafayette.
Cunningham Mrs Ida B, res 305 Lafayette.
Cunningham Kate, domestic 52 Brackenridge.
Cunningham Patrick F, boilermkr Wabash R R, res 23
   W Lewis.

Cunningham Robert R, supt construction Star Iron Tower Co, res 31 2d.

Cunz Charles, res 90 Maumee rd.

Curbrugg John, helper, res 21 John.

Curdes Louis F, Real Estate, Loans and Insurance, 3 and 4 Pixley and Long Blk, res 45 W Creighton av. (*See p* 115).

Currall John, laborer Penn Co, res 10 Erie.

Curran Bridget (wid Michael), bds 312 Lafayette.

Curran Catherine, cook, bds 312 Lrfayette.

Curran John F, brakeman, bds 117 Hanna.

Curran Margaret, bds 312 Lafayette.

Curran Michael, painter Olds Wagon Wks, res 312 Lafayette.

Curran Michael F, conductor. res 397 Hanna.

Curran Thomas, brakeman G R & I R R, bds 209 Lafayette.

Current Charles S, laborer Penn Co, bds s s Pioneer av 1 e of New Haven av.

Current Samuel W, switchtender, res 101 Pennsylvania.

Current Sylvanus S, car bldr Penn Co, res s s Pioneer av 1 e of New Haven av.

Current Wm A, conductor, res 35 Eliza.

Currie Martha, cook McKinnie House, rms same.

Currier Burleigh, electrician Ft Wayne Electric Corp, bds 341 E Wayne.

Currier Charles A, tel opr W U Tel Co, res 133 W Wayne.

Currier Charles H, tel opr W U Tel Co, res 341 E Wayne.

Currier John L, tel opr W U Tel Co, res 136 Wells.

Currier Leah G, clk S F Bowser & Co, bds 341 E Wayne.

Curry Denesia S (wid Wm T), res 302 Harrison.

Curry James, gasfitter Kerr Murray Mnfg Co, res 75 Dawson.

Curry Mrs Melissa D, housekeeper, 3 Centre.

Curtice John F, Loans, Investments, Real Estate, Oil and Gas Propertys. Propr Leedy Mineral Springs, Rooms 1, 2, 3, and 4 Tri-State Bldg, res 142 Montgomery. (*See front cover and p 89.*)

Curtin Josie H, bds 11 Grand.

Curtis Charles L, clk Peoples' store, bds 121 E Main.

Curtis Erastus R, res 23 Eliza.

Curtis Grant D, asst supt Adams Ex Co, res 152 E Berry.

Curtis Harry J, lather, bds 23 Eliza.

Curtis Harvey, bell boy New Aveline House.

Curtis Herbert, lather, bds 74 E Columbia.

Curtis Jennie (wid Jeremiah), res 74 E Columbia.

Curtis Lawrence, helper, bds 74 E Columbia.
Curtis Levi L, bds 23 Walnut.
Curtis Maggie D, dressmaker, bds 23 Eliza.
Curtis May, domestic 87 W Wayne.
Curtis Samuel H, truckman Penn Co, res 23 Walnut.
Cushing Timothy J, engr G R & I R R, res 17 E Creighton av.
Custer House, Gerson Scherzinger Propr, 16 and 18 W Main. (*See page 85.*)
Cutler Elmer L, asst foreman Standard Wheel Co, res 34 Walton av.
Cutler Wm M, grocer, 268 E Wayne, res same.
Cutler Wm N, polisher Standard Wheel Co, bds 268 E Wayne.
Cutshall Frank H, clk Ft Wayne Gas Co, bds 2 Monroe.
Cutshall Jessie M, bds 51 N Calhoun.
Cutshall Joseph H, watchman H B Phillips, res 266 W Jefferson.
Cutshall Theodore M, wheelmaker, bds 2 Monroe.
Cutshall Wm H, carpenter, res 2 Monroe.
Cutshall W S, clk Penn Co, bds 23 E Williams.
Cutshall Wills C, fireman Penn Co, res 142 Barr.
Cypher Rufus, fireman David Tagtmeyer, res 87 Ewing.

D

Daas Abdullah S, notions, 303 Lafayette, res same.
Dager Maggie, domestic, 306 Calhoun.
Dahl, *see also Dale.*
Dahl Per, music teacher, res 16 Rockhill.
Dahman John W, molder, res 115 John.
Dahms Frank, bds s e cor Pontiac and Alexander.
Dahms John, laborer, res s e cor Pontiac and Alexander.
Daib Ada L, bds 58 Division.
Daib Eliza S (wid John), res 58 Division.
Daib Freda W C, bds 58 Division.
Daib Lydia, bds 58 Division.
Daib Martin O, student, bds 58 Division.
Dailey, *see also Daley.*
Dailey Ephraim P (MacDougal & Co), res 145 Edgewater av.
Dailey George M, harnessmkr A L Johns & Co, bds 50 Maumee rd.
Dailey John A, laborer, bds 194 W De Wald.
Dailey Louis G, clk Penn Co, res 297 E Lewis.

Dailey Thomas J, driver Engine Co No 4, res 50 Maumee rd.

Dailey Wm H (Smith & Dailey), res 37 Bass.

Daily Fish Market, Daniel Gorman Propr, Dealer in Fish, Oysters and Game in Season, 17 W Main, res 16 same. Tel 541.

Dale, *see also Dahl.*

Dale James M, tel opr N Y, C & St L R R, res 4 Jackson.

Daler Louis P, watchman Penn Co, res n s Maumee rd 1 e of Edsall av.

Daley, *see also Dailey.*

Daley John, machinist, res 351 Lafayette.

Daley Kate, domestic 54 Hanna.

Daley Michael conductor, res 77 Hoagland av.

Dalman David, bds 116 W Williams.

Dalman Edwin F, bds 368 Fairfield av.

Dalman Frederick, bds 116 W Williams.

Dalman Ivy L, milliner, bds 171 Wells.

Dalman John, res 368 Fairfield av.

Dalman Robert, fish peddler, res 90 E Main.

Dalrymple Charles W, bartender J W Hosler, rms 11 W Columbia.

Dalton Edmund, carp Ft Wayne Electric Corp, res 32 Wilt.

Dalton Edward J, student, bds 58½ W Williams.

Dalton Frankie, bds Maysville rd, e of city limits.

Dalton James, laborer, res 58½ W Williams.

Dalton James, stripper Bourie, Cook & Co, bds 87 Richardson.

Dalton John E, timekeeper Ft Wayne Electric Corp, bds 32 Wilt.

Dalton Katie, stripper, bds 87 Richardson.

Dalton Katie H, bds 32 Wilt.

Dalton Lizzie, bds Maysville rd e of city limits.

Dalton Mary, dressmaker, bds 58½ W Williams.

Dalton Mary C, bds 32 Wilt.

Dalton Timothy J, fireman Penn Co, res 28 Wallace.

Dalton Wm, cigarmkr, bds 75 Richardson.

Dalton Wm F, woodturner, bds 58½ W Williams.

Daly John, painter, rms 72 Barr.

Daly Mary C (wid Wm G), res 120 Ewing.

Daman Wm J, molder, res 115 John.

Dame Rolla L, billposter Ft Wayne City Bill Posting Co, rms rear New Aveline House.

Dammeier Louise E J, bds 63 Douglas av.

14

Dammeier Wm E H jr, driver Himan Goldstine, res 63 Douglas av.

Dammeyer Anna, bds 213 Hanna.

Dammeyer August, laborer, res 213 Hanna.

Dammeyer August jr, lab Standard Wheel Co, bds 213 Hanna.

Dammeyer Carl C H, blacksmith, res 201 Ewing.

Dammeyer Frederick H, helper, bds 213 Hanna.

Dammeyer Henry E, lathe hand Ind Mach Wks, bds 201 Ewing.

Damon Charles D, teamster, bds 314 Buchanan.

Damon Charles E, fireman, res 314 Buchanan.

Damon Clara A, teacher, bds 314 Buchanan.

Danahy, *see also Denehy.*

Danahy Cornelius, tinner G H Heit, bds 13 Brandriff.

Danahy Jeremiah, insurance agt, res 13 Brandriff.

Danahy Nellie, bds 13 Brandriff.

Danehy James, grocer, 8 Hoagland av, res 4 Bass.

Danehy Michael, painter, 12 Bass, res same.

Danehy Philip P, clk James Danehy, bds 4 Bass.

Daniel Albert, student, bds 70 W Jefferson.

Daniels Rana A (wid Samuel S), res 115 W Washington.

Dannecker Rev Henry P, pastor Evangelical Lutheran St John's Church, res 212 W Washington.

Dannenfelser George J, clk, res 148 Clinton.

Danner George W, helper Bass F and M Wks, res 11 St Martin's.

Danner Robert M, condr G R & I R R, res 129 Montgomery.

Dannler Frederick, laborer, res 41 E Superior.

Danse Alphonse M, bds 128 Fairfield av.

Danse Leopold O, removed to Pittsburg, Pa.

Danz, *see Denz.*

Darby Hudsell B, stenographer, bds 106 Fairfield av.

Darker George U, time kpr Bass F and M Wks, bds 77 W Butler.

Darker Martha E (wid Wm), res 77 W Butler.

Darling Joseph L, piano tuner, bds 15 E Wayne.

Darmond Jules, lab Penn Co, bds s s Coombs 1 w of New Haven av.

Darroch Austin M, bds Custer House.

Darroch A M, res 153 Jackson.

Darroch Hugh M, bds 153 Jackson.

Darroch Josie, seamstress, bds 153 Jackson.

Darroch J Wm, driver, bds Custer House.

Darrow Elizabeth, bds 196 Calhoun.

Darrow James R, boarding house, 196 Calhoun.
Darrow Margaret J (wid Milton W), bds 17 Holman.
Dart Harry E, engineer, res 214 Calhoun.
Dartnell Ernest W, clerk Penn Co, bds 15 E De Wald.
Dascomb Thomas H, bkkpr Ft Wayne Electric Corp, bds 50 Douglas av.
Daseler Charles H, painter, bds 117 Madison.
Daseler Christian L, clk Penn Co, res 59 Nirdlinger av.
Daseler Dora S, bds 117 Madison.
Daseler Frederick C, carpet weaver, bds 211 Madison.
Daseler Frederick G, serg of police, res 185 Lake av.
Daseler George H, clk Hartman & Bro, bds 117 Madison.
Daseler Henry C, electrician Penn Co, res 117 Madison.
Daseler Henry J, boilermkr L E & W R R, bds 324 Hanna
Daseler Louisa S, bds 117 Madison.
Daseler Minnie (wid Conrad C), res 211 Madison.
Daseler Sophia E, bds 117 Madison.
Dau Frederick, res 19 Charlotte av.
Dau Frederick jr, carpenter, bds 19 Charlotte av.
Dau Gust, carpenter, bds 19 Charlotte av.
Daugherty, see also Dougherty.
Daugherty Alfred, res 227 Wells.
Daugherty George B, engineer, res 68 W 3d.
Daugherty James, shoemkr John G Zuber, res 80 Chicago.
Daugherty May, teacher Hanna School, bds 23 Douglas av.
Daunth Clara, domestic 116 W Main.
Daus Mary, domestic 102 Madison.
Davenport Edward N, carp S F Bowser & Co, res n e cor Oliver and Buchanan.
David Frederick C, coremkr, res 226 Gay.
Davidson Charles, fireman N Y, C & St L R R, bds 335 W Main.
Davidson May, dressmkr, 74 Walton av, bds same.
Davidson Wm B, machinist, bds 19 Bass.
Davies Anna G, bds 8 Fulton.
Davies Rev George E, pastor Bethany Presbyterian Church, res 432 W Main.
Davies John, clk Wm Hahn & Co, res 8 Fulton.
Davies Mabel C, clerk, bds 8 Fulton.
Davies Ormonde C, clk Root & Co, bds 8 Fulton.
Davis Alfred A, carpenter, res 90 E Lewis.
Davis Amos, agent, bds 28 Lake av.
Davis Amy, clerk, bds 90 E Lewis.
Davis Belle, rms 226 Calhoun.
Davis Blanche A, stenographer, bds 345 W Washington.

Davis Charles A, slater, bds 96 E Lewis.
Davis Charles E, binder Empire Box Factory, res 386 E Wayne.
Davis Christine. bds 28 Lake av.
Davis Delbert C, bkkpr Ft Wayne Electric Corp, res 44 W Wayne.
Davis Edward T, foreman frght house Penn Co, bds 209 Barr
Davis Edwin, barber, res 48 W 3d.
Davis Edwin G, engr Standard Wheel Co, bds 323 E Wayne.
Davis Eli, coachman 138 E Berry.
Davis Eliza (wid Amos), res 28 Lake av.
Davis Mrs Elizabeth, res 76 E Columbia.
Davis Lieut Ellis, U S Army, bds McKinnie House.
Davis Frank E, bds 40 Douglas av.
Davis Frank L, engr N Y, C & St L R R, res 112 Boone.
Davis Frank V, engr N Y, C & St L R R, bds 345 W Washington.
Davis Frederick M, mach hand, bds 22 Murray.
Davis Gail N, bds 58 Leith.
Davis George P, brakeman Penn Co, bds 109 Brackenridge.
Davis Grace M, bds 253 W Creighton av.
Davis Harry S, feeder Ft Wayne Newspaper Union, bds 308 E Wayne.
Davis Miss Hattie A, res 33 Grand.
Davis John C, brakeman, res 200 Francis.
Davis John J, brakeman N Y, C & St L R R, bds 345 W Washington.
Davis John J, car inspr Penn Co, res 191 E Lewis.
Davis John S, trav agt, bds 126 Harrison.
Davis Joseph, brakeman G R & I R R, res 136 Buchanan.
Davis Joseph B, mngr Lincoln Tea Co, res 44 Scott av.
Davis May, bds 13 Smith.
Davis Oscar, truckman Penn Co, res 58 Leith.
Davis Robert B, bookkeeper, res 117 Taylor.
Davis Sarah E, bds 44 Scott av.
Davis Thomas A, letter carrier P O, res 306 E Wayne.
Davis Thomas J, student, bds 44 Scott av.
Davis Vill Roy, condr N Y, C & St L R R, res 345 W Washington.
Davis Warren, bds 38 Baker.
Davis Wesley T, engr Olds Wagon Wks, res 308 E Wayne.
Davis Wilbur E, yard master Penn Co, res 40 Douglas av.

Davis Willard T, helper Ft Wayne Electric Ry Co, res Spy Run av n e cor Baltes.

Davis W H, died March, 95.

Dawkins Ellen A, res 50 W Superior.

Dawkins Sheldon, driver W H Brown, res 222 Lafayette.

Dawkins Wm H, lab Penn Co, res 524 E Lewis.

Dawsey Frederick, carpenter, bds 230 Harmer.

Dawson Alverda J, mach Penn Co, bds 105 E Washington.

Dawson Amanda M (wid John W), res 140 E Berry.

Dawson Andrew J, condr Penn Co, res 51 E Superior.

Dawson Hon Charles M, Judge Superior Court, office Court House, res 287 W Wayne. Tel 532.

Dawson Ellen (wid Michael), res 46 Chicago.

Dawson G Wallace, musical merchandise 27 W Main, res 187 E Jefferson.

Dawson Jennie E, bds s e cor Griffith and Pearl.

Dawson John W, engr Paragon Mnfg Co, res s e cor Griffith and Pearl.

Dawson Ronald, student, bds 287 W Wayne.

Day Amelia, bds 147 W Superior.

Day Anna C, bds 147 W Superior.

Day Henry D, res 147 W Superior.

Day John, brakeman, res 94 Oliver.

Deady Emmett A, mach S F Bowser & Co, bds 28 E Taber.

Deagan Christina, milliner, bds 52 E Leith.

Deagan Edward, helper, res 52 E Leith.

Deagan Edward jr, tinner, bds 52 E Leith.

Deagan John J, blacksmith, res 111 Hanna.

Deagan Joseph A, boilermkr, bds 52 E Leith.

Deahl, *see also Deihl and Diehl.*

Deahl Amanda P, bds 67 Barthold.

Deahl Edward H, carpenter, bds 67 Barthold.

Deahl Frederick, condr N Y, C & St L R R, res 165 High.

Deahl Joseph A, caller N Y, C & St L R R, bds 67 Barthold.

Deahl Samuel S, brakeman N Y, C & St L RR, bds 67 Barthold.

Deal Sarah (wid Peter K), res rear 20 W Lewis.

Dean Charles (col'd), helper Penn Co, bds 49 Hayden.

Dean Harvey (col'd), porter, rms 54 Chicago.

Dean Harvey, bds 237 Clay.

Dean Hattie M, bkkpr Louis Wolf & Co, bds 69 Garden.

Dean Mrs Jennie, bds 90 E Main.

Dean Nancy, bds 237 Clay.

Dean May, housekeeper East Yard Hotel.

Dean Robert, teamster, bds 61 E Main

Deardorff Herbert, attendant School for Feeble Minded-Youth.
DeArmitt Carrie B, bds 48 Wells.
DeArmitt Charles, clk F W DeArmitt, bds 48 Wells.
DeArmitt Frank W, shoes, 20 Calhoun, res 48 Wells.
DeArmitt Jennie E, bds 48 Wells.
Deatrick Maurice, brakeman, res 37 Elm.
DeCamp Wm H, barber, 136 Broadway, bds 266 W Jefferson.
Deck Frank, plumber, res 459 Lafayette.
Deck John, tailor S J Robacker, res 478 Hanna.
Decker John C, res 206 High.
Decker Mary, supervisoress School for Feeble Minded-Youth.
Dedier Kate (wid August E), cook, rms 288 Calhoun.
Dedolph Wm, laborer, res 133 Franklin av.
Dedrick Wm E, conductor Ft Wayne Electric Ry Co, res w s Euclid av 2 s of Creighton av.
Deem Mrs Annie, res 225 Hanna.
De Frain Francis, carpenter Penn Co, res 2 Erie.
Defreeze Anna, seamstress, bds 120 Ewing.
Degitz Charles, laborer, res 202 John.
Degitz Charles, res 15 Colerick.
Degitz Charles, driver Zoeller & Merz, bds 72 E Leith.
Degitz Charles A, helper Bass F & M Wks, bds 137 Force.
Degitz Frank, lab Bass F & M.Wks, bds 26 John.
Degitz Frank, laborer, res 72 E Leith.
Degitz Frank jr, helper Kerr Murray Mnfg Co, bds 72 E Leith.
Degitz Gustave, helper, bds 137 Force.
Degitz Joseph, molder Bass F & M Wks, bds 137 Force.
Degitz Lizzie, seamstress, bds 137 Force.
Degitz Louis, bds 15 Colerick.
Degitz Theresa, seamstress, bds 137 Force.
Degrattery Elizabeth (wid James), res 67 Hayden.
De Hart Abraham, res 43 Wall.
De Hart Wm, letter carrier P O, bds 147 Union.
De Haven Harrison D, res 73 Cass.
De Haven Martha E, bds 73 Cass.
De Haven Perry N, res 175 Columbia av.
De Haven Sarah A (wid Abram B), res 56 Nelson.
Dehm, see Diehm and Diem.
Dehne Ernst, patternmkr Penn Co, res 190 E Lewis.
Deibel, see also Dibble.
Deibel Maggie M, bds 133 Holman.
Deihl, see also Deahl.

Deihl Fred G, student, bds 49 Harmer.
Deihl Hugh M, air brake mkr, res 49 Harmer.
Deininger Joseph E, laborer, res 168 E Taber.
Deininger Joseph E jr, shoemkr App Bros, bds 168 E Taber
Deister Deidrich A, porter G E Bursley & Co, bds 215 W Main.
Deister Emil, mach Bass F & M Wks, bds 310 Harrison.
Deister Otto, fireman N Y, C & St L R R, bds 215 W Main
Deitsch Rosalie (wid Moritz), propr Mergentheim's Bazaar, res 84 W Washington.
De Lagrange Frank J, mach hd Anthony Wayne Mnfg Co, res 68 Lasselle.
De Lagrange Frank J E, clk Old Fort S & E Co, bds 68 Lasselle.
De Lagrange Justin F, clerk J H Hartman, bds 68 Lasselle
Delaney Rev Joseph F, rector St Patrick's Church, res n w cor De Wald and Harrison.
Delano Edward A, rms 28 Chicago.
Delano Elizabeth D (wid Thomas), res 116 Wells.
Delaware Insurance Company of Philadelphia, Pa, Edward Seidel Agt, 52½ Calhoun.
De Lay Andrew, asst yardmaster N Y, C & St L R R, res 102 St Mary's av.
Dell Wm, appr C W Bruns & Co, bds Reformed Orphan's Home.
Demond Miner, res 55 Baker.
Denbow Darlen B, condr N Y, C & St L R R, bds 324 W Main.
Denehy, *see also Danahy.*
Denehy Cornelius, laborer, res 70 Force.
Denehy Frank J, lab Standard Wheel Co, bds 70 Force.
Denehy Jeremiah, insurance agt, bds 13 Brandriff.
Denehy Philip, appr Bass F & M Wks, bds 70 Force.
Denges Frederick C, lab Standard Wheel Co, res 65 Buchanan.
Denges Wm, carpenter, res 12 Oliver.
Denio Dwight V, clk Windsor Hotel.
Denk Rev Rudolph J, asst St Mary's German Catholic Church, res 142 E Jefferson.
Denman George E, engr Ft Wayne Artificial Ice Co, rms 5 Cass.
Denner Joseph, res 415 W Main.
Denney Elmer E, res 108 Broadway.
Dennis Albert, helper, res 116 Hayden.
Dennis John C, laborer, res 80 Gay.

Dennis Mary (wid Wm), boarding house, 127 Holman.
Dennis Michael, laborer, res 153 Putnam.
Dennis Pearl, domestic County Poor Farm.
Dennis Rosa M, bds 157 Holman.
Dennis Wm, teamster, res 509 E Washington.
Dennison Daisy L, bds 320 Broadway.
Dennison Gail, bds 320 Broadway,
Dennison John, repair shop, 119 Harrison. rms 15 W Washington.
Dennison Phoebe (wid John). res 320 Broadway.
Denny John A, res 65 Charles.
Denny Watts P (Chapin & Denny), res 275 W De Wald. (*See page 2.*)
Deno Ellen (wid Andrew), bds 45 Gay.
Deno Mrs Ellen, res 419 W Main.
Deno Henry, laborer, bds 419 W Main,
Denzel John, framemkr Keil & Keil, res 398 E Lewis.
Depler James, bds 50 John.
Depler John W, polisher Olds Wagon Wks, res 50 John.
Depner Anna, domestic 36 Montgomery.
Depner George. porter, bds 108 Hugh.
Depot Drug Store, H F Beverforden prop, 286 Calhoun, tel 286.
Depotty Bessie, ironer F L Jones & Co, bds 83 W DeWald.
De Potty John, caller, res 179 Hanna.
Deppeller Ida A, bds rear 204 W Superior.
Deppeller Lucinda, cook, res 204 W Superior.
Deppeller Mary J, seamstress, rms 72 Barr.
Deppeller Rudolph, phys, 32 E Columbia, rms same.
Deppen Benadina, (wid August), res 326 E Washington.
Deppen John H, bkkpr Western Lime Co, bds 326 E Washington.
Derbin, *see Durbin.*
Derheimer Catherine, bds 177 E Jefferson.
Derheimer Edward, plumber Martin F Noll, bds 177 E Jefferson.
Derheimer Joseph, res 177 E Jefferson.
Derheimer Joseph W, clk, bds 177 E Jefferson.
De Ricard Karl, res 24 E Washington.
Desmond James L, blacksmith, res 66 Howell.
Dermitt *see McDermott.*
Derome Solomon R, res 14 Murray.
DesPrez August, mach Western Gas Cons Co, res 58 Smith.
Des Prez Josephine, bds 73 Lasselle.

Des Prez Rosa, bds 73 Lasselle.
Des Prez Victor, watchman Penn Co, 73 Lasselle.
Des Prez Victorine, bds 73 Lasselle.
Dessauer Carrie, bds 90 W Main.
Dessauer Jacob, clk B Lehman, bds 90 W Main.
Dessauer Louis S, clk Louis Wolf & Co, bds 90 W Main
Dessauer L & Co, (Isaac Trauermann), cigar mnfrs, 23 Calhoun.
Dessauer Yetta (wid Louis), res 90 W Main.
Desser Francis, bds 132 Lafayette.
Dessler Jennie C, tailoress, bds Spy Run av n e cor Baltes.
Detering Amelia, domestic 280 W Wayne.
Detering Gustave, laborer, bds 324 E Jefferson.
De Turk Frank J, clk Eckart Pkg Co, bds 38 Buchanan.
De Turk Lebanon (De Turk & Schnitker), res 38 Buchanan.
De Turk & Schnitker (Lebanon De Turk, Christian F Schnitker), saloon, 72 E Main.
Detzer August J, mngr The Century Chemical Co, rms 15 Douglas av.
Detzer Edward N, bkkpr First National Bank, res 168 W Jefferson.
Detzer Gustave G, asst cash White National Bank, rms 15 Douglas av.
Detzer Mrs Laura G (Lehman Book and News Co), res 15 Douglas av.
Detzer Lottie, bds 260 Calhoun.
Detzer Martin, drugs, 260 Calhoun, res same. Tel 269.
Detzer Paul, student, bds 260 Calhoun.
Deuell Allen L, driver Eckart Pkg Co, res 196 E Jefferson.
Deuter Michael J, stonecutter Keller & Braun, res 103 High.
Deutchel Andrew, carbldr Penn Co, res 6 Huffman.
Deutschmann Bernhard, japanner, res 146 Taylor.
Devaux David, watchman, res 41 Wagner.
Devaux Frank, lab Penn Co, res 143 Oliver.
DeVilbiss Jason G, mach Wabash R R, bds 194 W DeWald.
DeVilbiss Thomas D, chairman Public Wks, res 265 E Creighton av. Tel 505.
Devine Grace (wid Robert J), res 132 Monroe.
Devitt Patrick J, condr N Y, C & St L R R, bds 71 Boone.
Devlin Georgia W, bds 24 South Wayne av.
Devlin James, bds 212 Fairfield av.
Devlin Robert J, fireman Wabash R R, bds 24 South Wayne av.
Devlin Wm, watchman, res 24 South Wayne av.
De Wald Anna M, clk M Frank & Co, bds 404 Calhoun.

De Wald Catherine (wid Anthony), bds 143 E Wayne.
De Wald Ella, bds 404 Calhoun.
De Wald Elizabeth M, bds De Wald sq.
De Wald George (George De Wald & Co), res De Wald sq. Tel 123.
De Wald George L, clk Geo De Wald & Co, bds De Wald sq.
De Wald George & Co (George De Wald, Effingham T Williams, Amelius J Lang, Robert W T De Wald), Wholesale and Retail Dry Goods and Notions. Columbia n e cor Calhoun. Tel 112.
De Wald Henry, res 141 Barr.
De Wald Lucy, clk N De Wald, bds 404 Calhoun.
De Wald Mary, seamstress, bds 404 Calhoun.
De Wald Nicholas, grocer, 406 Calhoun. res 404 same.
DeWald Robert W. T (George DeWald & Co), res 270 W Wayne.
DeWald Sophia, clk Siemon & Bro, bds 404 Calhoun.
DeWald square, E DeWald, near Hanna.
Dewey Charles M, laborer, res 7 Duck.
Dewey Mrs Mary E, res 7 Duck.
DeWitt Cynthia, bds 40 Pearl.
DeWitt Lorenzo B, laborer, res 40 Pearl.
Dexter Wm, engr Penn Co, res rear 16 Brackenridge.
Dexter Wm G (Miner & Dexter), bds 29 Brackenridge.
Diamond, see also Dimon.
Diamond Adolph, mngr Pottlitzer Bros, res 99 E Wayne.
Dibble Fay W, brakeman, res 150 Horace.
Dick Elizabeth H (wid Daniel), res 89 W Butler.
Dick John, brakeman N Y C & St L R R, res 21 Boone.
Dick Mary E, teacher Hoagland School, bds 89 W Butler.
Dick Ralph W, student, bds 89 W Butler.
Dicke Frederick H, grocer, 29 Smith, res same.
Dicke Henry, grocer, 119 E Lewis, res 192 same.
Dickerson Andrew F, porter Ft Wayne Newspaper Union, res 69 Melita.
Dickerson Jefferson, res 19 Lafayette.
Dickerson Louise J (col'd), bds 21 Melita.
Dickerson Sarah A (col'd), (wid Andrew), res 21 Melita.
Dickey Helen J, bds 586 Calhoun.
Dickey Joseph H, peddler, res 14½ Melita.
Dickey Robert, res 596 Calhoun.
Dickinson Ada, waitress New Aveline House.
Dickinson Mamie, bds 130 E Berry.
Dickinson Philemon, mngr D H Baldwin & Co, 98 Calhoun, res 130 E Berry.

Dickman, *see also Dieckman.*
Dickman Henry W, pension atty, 13 E Main, rms 45 same
Dickmeier Charles, helper Bass F & M Wks, res 99 Gay.
Diekmeier Henry, blacksmith, res 123 Gay.
Dickmeyer Ferdinand, blacksmith, res 86 Swinney av.
Dickmeyer Mary T, bds 168 Greeley.
Dickmeyer Wm, watchman Root & Co, res 168 Greeley.
Dickmeyer Wm, driver Wm H Oetting, bds 382 E Lewis.
Dickson, *see also Dixon.*
Dickson James M, engineer, res 503 Calhoun.
Dickson John G, fireman N Y, C & St L R R, res 63 Elm.
Dickson Robert, policeman, bds New Aveline House.
Didie Jefferson, engineer, bds 199 Broadway.
Didier August, painter, bds 410 E Wayne.
Didier Emeline (wid Frank), res 410 E Wayne.
Didier Francis X, saloon, 71 E Columbia. res same.
Didier Henry, clerk, bds 410 E Wayne.
Didier James. car bldr Penn Co, res 347 E Creighton av.
Didier John L A, plumber J S Hines, bds 104 Maumee rd.
Didier Joseph C, clk Sherman Levauway, rms 66 E
  Columbia.
Didier Julian J W, wood shaver S D Bitler, res 40 Schick
Didier Julian F, harnessmkr, bds w s Spy Run av 5 n of
  bridge.
Didier Wm H, harnessmkr, res w s Spy Run av 5 n of
  bridge.
Didierjohn Joseph, broom mnfr. 102 Maumee rd, res 104
  same.
Didierjohn Louis A, plumber, bds 104 Maumee rd.
Didierjohn Mary E, bds 104 Maumee rd.
Didierjohn Rose, dressmkr, bds 104 Maumee rd.
Didion Amelia M, boxmkr G W Winbaugh, bds 242 E
  Lewis.
Didion Martin, teamster Peter A Moran, bds 201 E Wayne
Didion Martin A, watchman, res 242 E Lewis.
Didion Olivet J, opr Hoosier Mnfg Co, bds 242 E Lewis
Didion Otto E, clerk, bds 242 E Lewis.
Diebold Albert J, harnessmkr A L Johns & Co, bds 68
  Boone.
Diebold Catherine (wid Joseph G), res 275 E Washington.
Diebold Emma E, patternmkr, bds 275 E Washington.
Diebold Henry, baker B W Skelton Co, res 68 Boone.
Diebold Henry A, clk H G Sommers, bds 275 E Washington
Diebold Mary E, seamstress, bds 275 E Washington.
Diebold Wm H. bds 68 Boone.

Dieckmann, *see also Dickman.*
Dieckmann Henry, carpenter, res 85 Lillie.
Diedrick Catherine C (wid John), res 20 Ohio.
Diehl, *see Deahl and Deihl.*
Diehm George, lab, res w s Lafayette 3 s of Grace.
Diehm Henry, lab, bds w s Lafayette 3 s of Grace.
Diek Agnes, domestic 105 W Berry.
Diek John B, finisher Ft Wayne Organ Co, rms 490 Fairfield av.
Diek Mary (wid John), res 65 Stophlet.
Diek Mary R, dressmaker, bds 65 Stophlet.
Diek Mary S (wid Harmon), res 95 Clay.
Diem Charles, res 87 Madison.
Dierkes Anthony J. mach Ft Wayne Electric Corp, res 7 Clark.
Dierkes August, brakeman, bds 94 Lasselle.
Dierkes Catherine (wid Frederick E), res 72 Barthold.
Dierkes Edward J, laborer, bds 72 Barthold.
Dierkes Theresa G, stenographer, bds 72 Barthold.
Dierstein Amelia S, dressmaker, bds 105 Fairfield av.
Dierstein Frederick C. bartender A F Bolman, bds 105 Fairfield av.
Dierstein Frederica L (wid Christian), res 2 Fairfield av.
Dierstein George C, upholsterer, bds 2 Fairfield av.
Dierstein Henry G, bartender F Schmueckle, res 72 Baker.
Dierstein Mary F, bds 2 Fairfield av.
Dierstein Minnie, opr Hoosier Mnfg Co, bds 105 Fairfield av
Dierstein Philip C, upholsterer, bds 105 Fairfield av.
Dierstein Samuel W, laborer, bds 105 Fairfield av.
Dierstein Wilhelmina (wid Samuel), res 105 Fairfield av.
Dieterich Charles F, pres Ft Wayne Gas Co, res New York.
Diether Charles F, bds 267 W Wayne.
Diether Edward, mach hd Louis Diether & Bro, res 128 Griffith.
Diether John H (Louis Diether & Bro), res 167 W Superior.
Diether Louis (Louis Diether & Bro). res 267 W Wayne. Tel 312.
Diether Louis & Bro (Louis and John H Diether), Dealers in Rough and Dressed Lumber and Shingles ; Mnfrs and Dealers in Sash, Doors, Blinds and Mouldings ; All Kinds of Factory Work ; Office and Yards bet City Mills and Gas Works on E Superior. Tel 111 ; Factory 100 Pearl. Tel 78. (*See right side lines.*)

Diether Wm A, clk Louis Diether & Bro, res 179 W Superior.
Diffenderfer Harry C, painter, res 19 Wall.
Diffenderfer Isabella A (wid Benjamin A), bds 33 W De Wald.
Diffenderfer Wm A, bkkpr Mossman, Yarnelle & Co, res 33 W De Wald.
Diggins Charlotte (wid Wm G), res 76 W Creighton av.
Digison Joseph G, barber C B Schmuck, bds 47 Bass.
Dildine Frank, editor in chief Fort Wayne Sentinel, res 88 W Jefferson.
Dilgart Frank, butcher, bds 15 Pearl.
Dille Bessie I, artist, 27 Lavina, bds same.
Dille Joseph H, artist, 27 Lavina, res same.
Dillingham Ida R, nurse Hope Hospital.
Dillon J Edwin N, stenogr Penn Co, bds 161 Webster.
Dillon Lena L, bds 161 Webster.
Dillon Martha (wid James H), res 161 Webster.
Dills Charles S, traveling agent, res 123 Columbia av.
Dills Thomas J, physician, 26 W Wayne, res 241 W Berry.
Dimon, *see also Diamond.*
Dimon John, moved to Hartford, Conn.
Dinekas Frederick, florist G W Vesey, res 28 Park av.
Dinger Henry P, driver Powers & Barnett, res 22 W Jefferson.
Dinger John T, bartender T J Schuhler, rms 93 W Superior
Dingman Hiram, res n s Humphrey 1 w of Glasgow av.
Dingman Scott W, traveling agt, res 229 W De Wald.
Dinius Bert W, apprentice, bds 127 W Williams.
Dinius Sylvester, lumberman, res 127 W Williams.
Dinkel John C, carp John Suelzer, res 65 Wabash av.
Dinklage Herman L, brakeman, res 30 John.
Dinklage Margaret (wid Henry), bds 271 E Washington.
Dinklage Mary (wid Herman), res 30 Gay.
Dinklage Patrick O, conductor, bds 30 Gay.
Dinklager Bernard, laborer, bds n s New Haven av 3 e of Edsall av.
Dinklager Cora A (wid Anthony), res 20 Ohio.
Dinklager Elizabeth (wid Bernard), res n s New Haven av 3 e of Edsall av.
Dinklager Josephine, domestic w s Spy Run av 1 n of Edna.
Dinnen James M, physician, 67 W Wayne. res 69 same. Tel 56.
Dirks Albert, laborer, res rear 122 Buchanan.

218 R. L. POLK & CO.'S

Disbro Frank W, clk Coverdale & Archer, res 177 Wells.
Dishong C, res 101 Fletcher av.
Dishong Morris, res rear 45 W Main.
Disler I Willis, huckster, res e s Piqua av 4 s of Rudisill av.
Dissen Amelia, seamstress, bds 59 John.
Dissen August, clerk, bds 59 John.
Dissen Mary, spool winder, bds 59 John.
Dissen Valentine, res 59 John.
Disser Joseph P, upholsterer Penn Co, res 132 Lafayette.
Distel Edward, traveling agt, bds 394 Force.
Distel John W, printer, res 394 Force.
Ditmars Emmet A, mach Penn Co, res 7 Victoria av.
Dittmann Charles, laborer, bds 2 Reed.
Dittmann Charles F, helper Bass F & M Wks, res 10 Gay.
Dittmann Hermann, molder, bds 10 Gay.
Dittmann Wm F, laborer, res 2 Reed.
Dittmann Wm jr, bds 2 Reed.
Dittoe Albert J (Dittoe's Grocery Co), res 195 E Wayne.
Dittoe Albert V, clk C B Woodworth & Co, bds 195 E Wayne.
Dittoe Charles W (Dittoe's Grocery Co), trav agt, bds 195 E Wayne.
Dittoe Loretta A, bds 195 E Wayne.
Dittoe Mary C, cashier Dittoe's Grocery Co, bds 195 E Wayne.
Dittoe's Grocery Co, (Albert J and Charles W Dittoe), Grocers, 72 Calhoun. Tel 152.
Dix Frank J, electrician Jenney E L & P Co, bds n w cor 7th and Lafayette.
Dix Hugh T, driver engine Co No 3, bds 99 Calhoun.
Dix Seth J, res n w cor 7th and Lafayette.
Dixon, *see also Dickson.*
Dixon George, teamster Ft W Lumber Co, res 12 Ida av.
Dobberkau Frederick, car bldr Penn Co, res 5 Eliza.
Dobler Frank, student, bds 154 John.
Dobler Theodore, clk Penn Co, res 154 John.
Dochterman Marcellus H, condr L E & W R R, res 41 E 3d.
Docter Allen W, driver C L Centlivre Brewing Co, res 2 Charlotte av.
Docter Matthias W, teamster G E Bursley & Co, res 22 Oliver.
Docter Minnie, opr S M Foster, bds 2 Charlotte av.
Docter Wm, carpenter, bds 22 Oliver.

Dodane Amede L, Propr Bloomingdale Fruit House, Fine Groceries, 92 Wells, res same.

Dodane Justine (wid Frank), bds n w cor Spy Run av and Randolph.

Dodane Theodore C, reporter The Journal, bds 72 Wells.

Dodez E Wright, dentist, bds 113 W Wayne.

Dodez Gustavus C, res 113 W Wayne.

Dodge Arthur, Veterinary Surgeon, 19 and 21 W Washington, res 143 W Berry.

Dodge Charles, cabinetmkr Ft Wayne Furn Co, bds 34 W Superior.

Dodge Curtain T, motorman, bds 237 Barr.

Dodge Samuel W, clk Harmon House.

Dodge Wm A (Dodge & Keller), Physician, 92 and 96 Broadway, res 108 Barr.   Tel 335.

Dodge & Keller (W A Dodge, M D, A J Keller), Proprs Cresco Bathing Institute, cor W Washington and Broadway.   Tel 535.   (*See right side lines and page 93.*)

Doecher John, fireman Penn Co, bds 324 Calhoun.

Doehle Annie, carpet weaver S Reehling, bds 77 Hayden.

Doehle John, laborer, res 77 Hayden.

Doehring Mrs Rachel F, res n s New Haven av 3 e of Summer.

Doehrman Anna W, domestic 118 Montgomery.

Doehrman Charles E, car bldr Penn Co, res s s Chestnut 3 w of Warren.

Doehrmann Frederick W, carpenter, res 39 Nirdlinger av.

Doehrmann Henry, lab Penn Co, res 156 E Creighton av.

Doehrmann Henry, tailor J G Thieme & Son, res 160 Rockhill.

Doehrmann John C, helper J C Winte, bds 216 Fairfield av.

Doehrmann Lizzie M, cook Wm Seidel & Bro, bds 112 Eliza.

Doehrmann Wm, baker J H Schwieter's, bds 156 E Creighton av.

Doehrmann Wm, grocer 36 Barr, res 339 E Washington.

Doelker Caroline (wid Jacob), res 63 E Superior.

Doelker Wm, teamster, bds 63 E Superior.

Doell Henry, janitor, bds 64 Summit.

Doell Wm, blacksmith, res 64 Summit.

Doelling Ernest W, car repr N Y C & St L R R, bds 184 Greeley.

Doenges Christian, carp, 126 Maumee rd, res same.

Doenges Frank H, mach hd Anthony Wayne Mnfg Co, bds
   413 E Washington.
Doenges Frederick. laborer, res 65 Buchanan,
Doenges Frederick J, carriage mkr City Carriage Wks,
   res 413 E Washington.
Doenges Herman (C Franke & Co), res 24 Oliver.
Doenges Louis, carpenter, res 59 Winter.
Doenges Peter, carp S F Bowser & Co, res 129 Eliza.
Doenges Philip, res 11 Winch,
Doenges Philip jr, carpenter, bds 11 Winch.
Doenges Wm, lab Penn Co, res e s Roy, 1 n of Chestnut.
Doerfel Lena, domestic Orphans' Home of the Reformed
   Church.
Doermann, see Doehrmann.
Doermer Anna, rms 240 W Washington.
Doermer Lyda, coremkr Ft Wayne Electric Corp, rms 240
   W Washington.
Doermer Peter, res cor New Haven and Pioneer avs.
Doescher John, fireman Penn Co, rms 324 Calhoun.
Doggett John E, bds 18 Cass.
Doings, see Douings.
Dolan Albert L, helper Horton Mnfg Co, bds 8 Runnion av.
Dolan Alice, former, bds 8 Runnion av.
Dolan Charles, engr Horton Mnfg Co, res 8 Runnion av.
Dolan Edward A, bartender Stephen Drew, bds 316 W
   Main.
Dolan George F, helper Horton Mnfg Co, bds 8 Runnion av.
Dolan Joseph J, cigarmkr C A Tripple, bds 58 Walton av.
Dolan Margaret, bds 58 Walton av.
Dolan Mary, opr F L Jones & Co, bds 72 W 3d.
Dolan Mary E (wid John), res 58 Walton av.
Dolan Mary E, laundress, bds 74 W 3d.
Dold Anton, porter L Heilbroner, bds 21 Barthold.
Dolin George B, carpenter, res 153 Wells.
Dolin J Frank, bds 474 Broadway.
Dolin Laura, bds 474 Broadway.
Dolin Sherman, res 474 Broadway.
Donahoe Peter S, flagman, res 16 Smith.
Donahue, see also Donohue.
Donahue Daniel J, laborer, bds 44 Brandriff.
Donahue Ellen (wid Florence), res 44 Brandriff.
Danahue Ellen, clerk, bds 44 Brandriff.
Donahue Patrick W, engr N Y, C & St L R R, res 289 W
   Main.
Donaldson Alexander W, barber, bds 23 Poplar.

Donaldson Anna F, bkkpr Golden & Patterson, bds 23 Poplar.
Donaldson Clara, waitress Hotel Rich,
Donaldson Ebenezer R, insurance, res 23 Poplar.
Donaldson Edmonia A (wid Matthew K), res 21½ Poplar.
Donaldson Matthew K, died Sept 29, 1894.
Dondero Anthony, res 14 Lafayette.
Dondero George, fruits, 16 Calhoun, res same.
Dondero Pililip, fruits, 15 E Main, res same.
Donges Wm F, carpenter, res 12 Oliver,
Donhour Lizzie, rms 238 W Wayne.
Donivan John W, conductor, res 20 W Williams.
Donley John M, shoemkr Wm Rockhill, rms 57 W Superior.
Donlon Wm A, bartender Hotel Rich, rms 210 Calhoun.
Donnell Edward R, appr Robert Spice, bds 80 Walnut.
Donnell Eva, milliner, bds 80 Walnut.
Donnell Wm, plater F W Electric Corp, res 80 Walnut.
Donnell Wm B, winder F W Electric Corp, bds 80 Walnut.
Donnelly Amelia (wid Harry), bds 131 Griffith.
Donnelly Claudia, vocalist, bds 131 Griffith.
Donnelly Gertrude M, domestic 106 W Berry.
Donohue see also Donahue.
Donohue James T, lab Penn Co. bds 39 Walnut.
Donohue Thomas, hostler Penn Co, res 39 Walnut.
Donovan, see Donivan.
Dooley Wm M, res 16 Park av.
Doolittle Mrs Rebecca A, bds 34 W Main.
Doolittle Willis, real estate, 34 W Main, res 75 Organ av.
Doran Wm, brakeman, bds Harmon House.
Doriot Frank S, stenogr Penn Co, bds 58 Charles.
Doriot Harry W, brakeman, bds 58 Charles.
Doriot Julius, molder Bass F & M Wks, res 58 Charles.
Dormer James D, bartender New Aveline House, rms same.
Dornberg Wm, grocer, s s Pioneer av 1 e of New Haven av, res same.
Dornte August, mach Penn Co, res 198 Hanna.
Dornte August F, mach hd Penn Co, res 45 Hayden.
Dornte Edward H W, mach hd Penn Co, res 161 E Washington.
Dornte Emma, domestic 26 Douglas av.
Dornte George F, car repr Penn Co, res 69 Shawnee av.
Dornte Henry F, carp Fort Wayne Electric Corp, res 230 W Washington.
Dornte Lena, bds 274 E Lewis.

15

Dornte Wm, laborer, res 274 E Lewis.

Dorr Everett K, trav agt, res 91 E Washington.

Dorsey Wm M (col'd), cook, res 51 W Superior.

Dorwin Margaret, teacher School for Feeble-Minded Youth.

Doswell Charles A. custodian of parks, res 88 N Harrison.

Doswell George W, florist, 85 Calhoun, res W Main, nr Lindenwood Cemetery.

Doswell Henry J, asst supt Lindenwood Cemetery, bds J H Doswell.

Doswell John H, supt Lindenwood Cemetery, res same.

Dothage Sophia E (wid Ernest H), res 23 Wilt.

Doty, see also Doughty.

Doty Amelia A (wid Willis P), dressmaker, 91 Madison, bds same.

Doty James C, coachman C W Fulton.

Doty Richard E, engr Penn Co, res 352 Hanna.

Doty Wm, engr Penn Co, res 26 E Leith.

Double Bertha M, bds 29 E Main.

Double, Jennie A, bds 29 E Main.

Double John W, feed stable 14 Pearl, and restaurant 29 E Main, res 29 E Main.

Doud Wallace E (Everett & Doud), res 228 W Washington.

Dougall Allen H (Miller and Dougall), res 321 E Wayne.

Dougall Arthur H, clk Ft Wayne Electric Corp, bds 321 E Wayne.

Dougall John T, city editor Daily News, bds 321 E Wayne.

Dougherty, see also Daugherty.

Dougherty Catherine (wid Christopher), res 320 Lafayette.

Dougherty Samuel W, timber buyer, res 51 Euclid.

Doughman Newton D (Randall & Doughman), prosecuting attorney elect, res 243 Broadway.

Doughty, see also Doty.

Doughty Edith, domestic 16 Douglas av.

Doughty Grace, bds 152 Force.

Doughty Will L, clk Seavey Hardware Co, res 152 Force.

Doughty Wm H, bds 152 Force.

Douglas Joseph A, saloon, 284 Calhoun, res 399 same.

Douglas Robert F, asst passenger and ticket agt Wabash R R, bds 399 Calhoun.

Douglas Warren J, brakeman, bds 53 Thomas.

Douglass Hannah C (wid Wm B), bds 262 W Jefferson.

Douglass Wm V, Real Estate, Loans and Insurance and Agt Merchants Despatch Transportation Co, 3 Schmitz Blk, res 262 W Jefferson.

Douings Ella, bds 52 E 3d.

Douings Lavina, domestic 141 W Berry.
Douings Nellie, bds 52 E 3d.
Douings Sarah A (wid Henry), res 52 E 3d.
Dowd Mary, clk Mc Kinney House, rms same
Dowie Garnet L, bds 84 Taylor.
Dowie Wm A, boilermaker, res 84 Taylor.
Downer George, brakeman N Y, C & St L R R, res 6 Orchard.
Downes Charles E, brakeman, bds 269 E Creighton av.
Downey Charles S, brakeman N Y, C & St L R R, res 72 Boone.
Downing Myron, trav agt Fox br U S Baking Co, bds The Randall.
Downing Wm W, barber Wm H De Camp, bds 266 W Jefferson.
Downs Mary, domestic 156 W Jefferson.
Doyle Addie H, seamstress, bds 96 E Lewis.
Doyle Anna F, bds 237 Madison.
Doyle Annie G, seamstress, bds 96 E Lewis.
Doyle Catherine (wid Patrick), res 96 E Lewis.
Doyle Daniel M, trav agt G E Bursley & Co, res 47 Home av.
Doyle Dudley (Kennelly & Doyle), res 308 E Creighton av.
Doyle James, wheelmaker, res 202 Hanna.
Doyle James C, res 425 W Main.
Doyle John H, mach hd Ind Mach Wks, bds 237 Madison.
Doyle John P, brakeman. res 6 Melita.
Doyle John W, teamster Weil Bros & Co, res 290 E Wayne
Doyle Joseph T, machinist, bds 237 Madison.
Doyle Luella, bds 6 Melita.
Doyle Mary (wid Patrick), res 38 Baker.
Doyle Matilda L, seamstress, bds 96 E Lewis.
Doyle Minnie A, seamstress, bds 96 E Lewis.
Doyle Thomas, engr Penn Co, bds 66 Nelson.
Doyle Thomas, patternmkr Ind Mach Wks, res 237 Madison.
Draeger Charles P, teacher Grace School, bds 260 Gay.
Dragoo Grant U, conductor, res 134 Horace.
Drake Bert, laborer, bds 282 W Main.
Drake Charles A, cook, res 94 Barr.
Drake Elam R, laborer, res 282 W Main.
Drake Frederick J, genl delivery clk P O, bds The Randall.
Drake Gabriel A (col'd), cook, rms 128 Chicago.

Drake John L, brakeman N Y C & St L R R, res 282 W Main.

Drake Thomas F, engineer Penn Co, res 151 Wallace.

Drake Ray L, fireman N Y C & St L R R, bds 33 St Mary's av.

Draker Frank J, teamster, res 134 W 3d.

Draker John, lumber, res e s Spy Run av, 3 n of Riverside av.

Dratt John A, saloon, 51 E Main, res same.

Drayer L Park, city bacteriologist and city chemist, 9 E Wayne, bds 47 W Wayne.

Drebert Frank, carpenter, 91 W De Wald, res same.

Drebert Mary C, bds 91 W De Wald.

Dreibelbiss Abstract of Title Company The, John Dreibelbiss Pres, Robert B Dreibelbiss Sec and Treas, 25 Court. Tel 516.

Dreibelbiss Anna K (wid John P), res 35 Walnut.

Dreibelbiss Christian G, gardener, res 1½ miles s of city limits.

Dreibelbiss Conrad W, grocer, 246 W Main, res same.

Dreibelbiss Edward D, tel opr Penn Co, bds 134 W De Wald.

Dreibelbiss John, pres The Dreibelbiss Abstract of Title Co, res 17 Holman.

Dreibelbiss Myrtie, bds 210 W Superior.

Dreibelbiss Robert B, lawyer and sec and treas The Dreibelbiss Abstract of Title Co, 25 Court, res 63 W Jefferson. Tel 516.

Dreir, *see also Dreyer and Dryer.*

Dreier Loretto, bds 178 W Berry.

Dreier Wm H (Dreier & Bro), vice pres Wayne Knitting Mills, res 178 W Berry.

Dreier & Bro (Wm H Dreier), Druggist, 10 Calhoun. Tel 197.

Driesbach Catherine E, seamstress, bds 20 W Superior.

Dreisbach Levy, clk J H Notestine, res 20 W Superior.

Drerup John, coachman, 135 E Berry.

Dressel Henry F, carpenter, res 155 Holman.

Dressel John A, laborer, bds 158 Montgomery.

Dressel Mary T (wid George), res 158 Montgomery.

Dressel Rosa F, bds 158 Montgomery.

Dressel Sadie M, clk Root & Co, bds 158 Montgomery.

Dressel Valentine J, brakeman, bds 158 Montgomery.

Dresser Herman, taxidermist, rms 74 Barr.

Drew Stephen A, saloon, 319 W Main, res 316 same.

Drew Wm E, carpenter, res 291 W Main.

Drewett Wm, canvasser, res 122 Clay.
Drewett Wm H, laborer, res 7 Savannah.
Dreyer, *see also Dryer.*
Dreyer August, clk C F Lahmeyer, bds 67 Union.
Dreyer Conrad, shoemaker Charles Stellhorn, res 133 Union
Dreyer Henry F W, laborer, res 36 Charles.
Dreyer Wm F H, helper Penn Co, res 191 Madison.
Driftmeier Wm H, electrician, res 138 E Main.
Driftmeyer August F, watchman Hoffman Bros, res 190 W Main.
Driftmeyer Edward H, clerk, bds 190 W Main.
Driftmeyer Emma L, bds 190 W Main.
Driftmeyer Ernest D, res 154 Madison.
Driftmeyer Frederick H, lab Hoffman Bros, bds 190 W Main.
Driftmeyer Lillie B, bds 190 W Main.
Driftmeyer Louisa M, bds 84 Van Buren.
Drinkwitz Paul, cigar mnfr, 21 E Main, res same.
Driscoll Timothy, brakeman N Y, C & St L R R, bds 79 Boone.
Driver George, brakeman N Y, C & St L R R, rms 320 W Main.
Driver Samuel C, laborer, res n s Jesse 1 w of High.
Droegemeyer Charles F, decorator, res 35 Buchanan.
Droegemeyer Clara, bds 173 Ewing.
Droegemeyer Henry G, helper Horton Mnfg Co, bds 173 Ewing.
Droegemeyer John, bartender Martin Lill, rms 214 Calhoun
Droegemeyer John A, clk Princess Cash Store, res 173 Ewing.
Droegemeyer Robert F, messenger, bds 173 Ewing.
Droegemeyer Theodore F, lab Ft Wayne Elec Corp, bds 173 Ewing.
Droegemeyer Walter C, cigarmaker, bds 173 Ewing.
Droegemeyer Wm J, laborer, bds 173 Ewing.
Droste Christina S, bds 438 Broadway.
Droste Diedrich, plasterer, res 438 Broadway.
Droste Emma, domestic 485 Harrison.
Droste Lizzie H, domestic 425 Broadway.
Druhot Augustina (wid Joseph C), res 28 Force.
Druhot Charles E, molder Bass F & M Wks, bds 28 Force.
Druhot Clara E, bds 28 Force.
Druhot Frank C, molder Bass F & M Wks, res 28 Force.
Druhot John F, molder Bass F & M Wks, res 4 Monroe.
Druhot Joseph N, molder Bass F & M Wks, res 155 Wallace.

Drummond Arthur E, plumber C W Bruns & Co, bds 203 W De Wald.

Drummond Charles A, barber John H Kabisch, bds 203 W De Wald.

Drummond Charles L, journalist, res 358 E Washington.

Drummond Estella B, student, bds 203 W De Wald.

Drummond Harris E, printer Ft Wayne Sentinel, res 290 E Washington.

Drummond Hiram S, driver Scott Bros, bds 203 W De Wald.

Drummond Sylvester, plasterer, res 203 W De Wald.

Drury Mrs Lyle M, cash Rocker Washer Co, bds 150 Clinton.

Drury Michael M, calker A Hattersley & Sons, res 106 Francis.

Dryer, *see also Drier and Dreyer.*

Dryer Charles R, res 160 Thompson av.

Dryer Minnie, domestic, 54 E Wayne.

Duber Albert, laborer, res 98 E Columbia.

Dubois Katie, domestic 290 Fairfield av.

Dudenhoefer Anna (wid Philip G), bds 123 Maumee rd.

Dudenhoefer Anna, opr S M Foster, bds 401 E Washington.

Dudenhoefer George P (City Carriage Wks) res 336 E Wayne.

Dudenhoefer Mary, bds 336 E Wayne.

Dudley Sarah (wid Maurice), res 226 High.

Duemling Herman, professor Concordia College, res 441 E Washington.

Duemling Herman A, physician, 94 Calhoun, res 200 E Jefferson. Tel 419.

Duerr Jacob, carpenter, res 119 Fairfield av.

Duesler John S, wagonmaker, res 103 Cass.

Duesler Bert J, clk F C Cratsley, bds 103 Cass.

Duff Wm, waiter Jackson & Giles, rms 89 W Berry.

Duffy James E, clk Princess Cash Store, bds 410 E Wayne.

Duffy Mary, opr Hoosier Mnfg Co, bds 95 W Superior.

Duffy Thomas H, bartender J F Getz, res 102 W 3d.

Dugan Anna C, bds 50 Chicago.

Dugan Lizzie J, bds 50 Chicago.

Dugan Savannah (wid Marshall), dressmaker, res 50 Chicago.

Duke David M, lab Ft W E Ry Co, res 36 Hough.

Duke Leslie W, machine hand, bds 36 Hough.

Dukeman Samuel, janitor, res 333 E Washington.

Dull Anna, domestic 34 W Main.
Dull Daniel J, lab Ft W E Ry Co, res 18 Hamilton.
Dull John A, driver Pearse & Poff, res 1 Railroad.
Dull Milda M, bds 1 Railroad.
Dun R G & Co, The Mercantile Agency, F V Culbertson Mngr, 35, 36 and 37 Pixley-Long Bldg, Tel 329.
Dunann Elizabeth E (wid Jefferson J), bds 216 W Jefferson.
Dunann George L, engr N Y, C & St L R R, res 216 W Jefferson.
Dunbar Maggie J, domestic 138 W Main.
Dunbar Samuel, lab Penn Co, bds w s Spy Run av opp Leo gravel rd.
Duncan James, ins agt, bds 39 W Washington.
Duncan Thomas E, electrician Ft Wayne Electric Corp, res 407 Broadway.
Duncker Ernest, butcher, res 165 Erie.
Dunfee Alice M, bds n w cor Calhoun and 3d.
Dunfee Emet W, foreman Olds Wagon Wks, res 20 Lake av.
Dunfee Harry E, bds n w cor Calhoun and 3d.
Dunhan A Eugene, conductor, res 26 Van Buren.
Dunkle Carnia C, fireman N Y, C & St L R R, res 21 Michael av.
Dunlap Wm, plumber, res 15 Lafayette.
Dunlop Abbie M, bds 313 Hanna.
Dunlop Andrew W, res 313 Hanna.
Dunn Margaret, dressmaker, 6 Brandriff, bds same.
Dunn Robert, laborer, res 55 E Superior.
Dunn Wm, machinist, res 6 Brandriff.
Dunne Kathleen H, baths 49-51 Pixley and Long Bldg, res same.
Duplein Catherine (wid Joseph), res 16 Barthold.
Duplein George, bds 16 Barthold.
Dupler Roy L, hostler, bds 493 Calhoun.
Dupont Emma M, domestic 287 W Wayne.
Dupree Angus, traveling agt, res 54 Division.
Dupree Pearl V, bds 54 Division.
Durbin John W, bds 92 Franklin av.
Durbin Robert D, res 132 E Taber.
Durbrow Charles W, teamster Charles F Muhler & Son, res 50 N Calhoun.
Durbrow Lydia (wid James), res 22 N Calhoun.

Durfee Calvin F, fireman N Y, C & St L R R, bds 95 Fulton.
Durfee George A, trav agt Moellering Bros & Millard, res 39 W Butler.
Durfee Wm R, res 285 W Washington.
Durgin Cora A, teacher Westminster Seminary, bds 257 W Main.
Durnell Addie, teacher Hamilton School, bds 29 Duryea.
Durnell Alfred S, tinner Penn Co, res 294 E Jefferson.
Durnell Chester, engr Penn Co, res 49 W De Wald.
Durnell Herman A, engr Penn Co, res 27 Duryea.
Durnell Jane (wid George), res 60 Burgess.
Durnell Louis, res 29 Duryea.
Durnell M Harry, engr Penn Co, res 84 W De Wald.
Durnell Thomas, laborer, res e s Spy Run av 3 n of canal.
Durnell Tillie M, bds 294 E Jefferson.
Duryee George F, student, bds n w cor Fisher and Holton av
Duryee George W, baggageman G R & I R R, res n w cor Fisher and Holton av.
Dustman George G, butcher, res s s Dwenger av nr city limits.
Dustman Mary A, seamstress, bds 16 Purman.
Dwelly Charles W, machinist, res 20 McClellan.
Dwelly Frank W, appr The Journal Co, bds 20 McClellan.
Dwenger Albert, cook Ft Wayne Club, rms 28 E Wayne.
Dwyer Charlotte, milliner, bds 492 W Main.
Dwyer Joseph, clerk, bds Hoffmann House.
Dyche Alvina L (wid George), res 110 W Main.
Dyche Harriet B, bds 110 W Main.
Dyer Charles F, laborer, bds 22 Randolph.
Dyer Thomas, engr Penn Co, res 273 W Jefferson.
Dyer Thomas W, press feeder Ft Wayne Newspaper Union, bds 273 W Jefferson.
Dykes Agnes, bds 182 E De Wald.

E

Eade Henry, teamster, bds Frederick Wesson.
Eakin, see also Aiken
Eakin Margaret (wid Joseph S), bds 264 W De Wald.
Earhart James, engr, bds 292 W Main.
Earl Freeman M, sawyer L Rastetter & Son, res 54 Ferguson.
Earl Mattie, res 168 Hayden.
Earl Nora, domestic 231 W Wayne.

Earl Wm, laborer, bds 54 Ferguson.

Easley Charles P, carpenter, res 64 Home av.

Easley Sarah A (wid John), bds 64 Home av.

East End Bottling Works, The Hermann Berghoff Brewing Co Proprs, e s Grant av nr E Washington. (*See right top lines*).

East German School, in Harmer School bldg.

East Yard Hotel, James Gardner, Propr, Walton av and P, Ft W & C Ry.

Eastwood Henry C, clk Arcade Music Store, res cor St Joseph boulevard and Oneida.

Eaton Eliza, rms 225 E Wayne.

Ebel, *see also Abel and Habel.*

Ebel Louis F, painter Olds Wagon Wks, res 166 John.

Eberhardt, *see also Eberhart.*

Eberhardt Wm E, molder Bass F & M Wks, res 125 Cass.

Eberline Harry A, clk Ft W Gas Co, bds 86 E Jefferson.

Eberline Mrs Sophia, dressmkr, 86 E Jefferson, res same.

Eberly Annie M (wid Daniel), res 40 E 5th.

Eberly Edith, bds 40 E 5th.

Ebert, *see also Hebert.*

Ebert Adam, sawyer Horton Mnfg Co, res 127 Franklin av.

Ebert Edward C, conductor, res 43 Hugh.

Ebert Frank D, brakeman, res 88 Greene.

Eberwein Christian, res 96 Walton av.

Ebey Mary (wid Andrew), bds 225 W Main.

Ebner Caroline B, bds 145 E Lewis.

Ebner George, car bldr Penn C, res 192 Lafayette.

Ebner Jacob L, laborer, bds 192 Lafayette.

Ebner John J, driver Moellering Bros, bds 145 E Lewis.

Ebner Joseph G, laborer, bds 145 Lafayette.

Ebner Lorenz, car bldr Penn Co, res 145 E Lewis.

Ebner Veronica G, tailoress, bds 145 E Lewis.

Eby Amos M, res w end of Ontario.

Echelberry George, laborer, res w s Osage 1 n of Main.

Echelberry Ulysses G, brakeman, rms w s Osage 1 n of Main.

Eckart Annie M, bds 91 E Wayne.

Eckart Anton, gate keeper Penn Co, res 282 Broadway.

Eckart Blk, s e cor Main and Harrison.

Eckart Charles, laborer, bds 135 Madison.

Eckart Electric Co (Henry and Frederick Eckart), N Harrison nr L S & M S Ry depot.

Eckhart Elizabeth (wid Fred), res 91 E Wayne. Tel 411.

Eckart Frank A, clerk, bds 141 Madison.
Eckart Frederick, died August 7, 1894.
Eckart Frederick (Fred Eckart Packing Co, Eckart Electric Co) res 442 W Main.
Eckart Fred Packing Co, Frederick and Henry Eckart props, 35 W Main. Tel 291.
Eckart Harry A, helper Seavey Hardware Co, bds 141 Madison.
Eckart Henrietta, bds 91 E Wayne.
Eckert Henry (Fred Eckart Packing Co, Eckart Electric Co) bds 91 E Main.
Eckart Lucy, bds 91 E Wayne.
Eckart Wm S, laborer, bds 75 E Jefferson.
Eckart Wm W, brick setter, res 141 Madison.
Eckelburger Samuel, lab Penn Co, res 123 Taber.
Eckels Elizabeth E, asst librarian Public Library, bds 57 Riverside av.
Eckels Harry C, inspr C U Tel Co, res 55 Riverside av. Tel 180.
Eckels James M, carpenter, res 57 Riverside av.
Eckels Willis J, bkkpr Hoffman Bros, res 115 Cass.
Eckenrod David N, foreman Ft Wayne Gazette, res 170 W Jefferson.
Eckenrod Myra C, bds 170 W Jefferson.
Ecker, *see Acker, Aker and Eicher.*
Eckerle Addie, bds n w cor Spy Run av and Edna.
Eckerle Albert, brewer C L Centlivre Brewing Co, res n w cor Spy Run av and Edna.
Eckerle Frank L, cutter Hoosier Mnfg Co, bds n w cor Spy Run av and Edna.
Eckerle Hattie, domestic 60 Barr.
Eckert David S, mngr J C Eckert, bds 19 W Williams.
Eckert John C, cigar mnfr, David S Eckert mngr, 20–22 E Wayne.
Eckert John C, died April 6, 1895.
Eckert John C jr, bds 19 W Williams.
Eckert Rachel A (wid John C), res 19 W Williams.
Eckert Wm E, foreman J C Eckert, res 168 Creighton av.
Eckley Eliza A (wid Peter), bds 186 Ewing.
Eckmeier Charles, res 33 Duryea.
Eckrich Peter, meats, 5 Smith, res 7 same.
Eddy Ola R, bds 57 Rivermet av.
Edelman John J, mach Penn Co, res 71 Charles.
Edgar Bert W, porter Hotel Rich.

Edgell Joseph, blacksmith, 13 Lafayette, res 143 Fairfield av.

Edgerton Alfred P, res 154 W Berry.

Edgerton Clara, bds 87 W Wayne.

Edgerton Clement W, Administrator Estate of J W Edgerton, Bicycles and Real Estate, 57 W Main, res 87 W Wayne.

Edgerton Dixon (Bittinger & Edgerton), bds 44 Archer av.

Edgerton Hannah W (wid Joseph K), res 87 W Wayne.

Edgerton Harry H jr, type writers, bds 324 E Wayne.

Edgerton Joseph K (est of), C W Edgerton administrator; real estate, 57 W Main.

Edgerton Sarah (wid James), res 21 W 4th.

Edison Mutual Telegraph Co, O L Perry mngr, Wayne Hotel.

Edler Angeline (wid Frank), res 55 Madison.

Edmonds Delbert, shipping clk S Bash & Co, bds 21 Cass.

Edmonds Gertrude, bds 21 Cass.

Edmonds Minnie, clk A Mergentheim, bds 21 Cass.

Edmonds Wm, buyer S Bash & Co, res 21 Cass.

Edmunds Frank W (Keller, Edmunds & Law, Electric Construction Co), bds 150 Ewing.

Edmunds Harry M, telegraph opr, bds 150 Ewing.

Edmunds Mary (wid James), died Sept 24th, 1894.

Edsall Charles W, cigarmaker, bds 334 W Washington.

Edsall Clarence W, County Auditor, Office Court House, res s s Maumee rd 1 n of Walton av.

Edsall Frank, brakeman, bds 61 Oliver.

Edsall Grace B, bds 334 W Washington.

Edsall Jasper, lab Ft Wayne Electric Corp, res 61 Oliver.

Edsall Manford S, clk Root & Co, bds C W Edsall.

Edsall Sarah A, domestic, 101 E Berry.

Edsall Simon, farmer, res s s New Haven av 2 e of Edsall av.

Edsall Tecumseh, brakeman, bds 61 Oliver.

Edsall Wm E, engineer, res 334 W Washington.

Edsall Wm S jr, clk County Auditor, bds s s Maumee rd 1 w of Walton av.

Edwards Albert J, baggageman, res 12 Orchard.

Edwards Emery E, gluer Ft W Organ Co, res 42 Bass.

Edwards Frank, motorman Ft W E Ry Co, res 150 Taber.

Egan Mary C, milliner, 128 Calhoun, res same.

Egertson Wm, res w s Oneida 1 s of Rivermet av.

Egg Charles B, molder Ft Wayne Electric Corp, res 58 W Wayne.

Eggemann John W, day distributing clk P O, res 20 W Jefferson.
Eggemann Laura M, bds 20 W Jefferson.
Eggemann Matilda, bds 20 W Jefferson.
Eggemann Peter J, shoemaker, 17 E Main, res 20 W Jefferson.
Eggert Martha, domestic 83 Smith.
Eggert Tillie, domestic De Wald Square.
Eggiman Peter J, clk N Y, C & St-L R R, res 209 High.
Eggimann Charles F, candymkr, bds 74 E Pontiac.
Eggimann Conrad, clk Penn Co, res 74 E Pontiac.
Eggimann Daniel C, laborer, bds 33 Walnut.
Eggimann Edward D, mach hd Ft Wayne Electric Corp, bds 74 E Pontiac.
Eggimann Frederick E, died Nov 29th, 1894.
Eggimann Mamie A, bds 74 E Pontiac.
Eggimann Mary (wid Frederick E), res 33 Walnut.
Egner Gertrude, domestic 220 W Washington.
Egner Nellie, domestic 149 Griffith.
Egner Thomas, died May 19th, 1894.
Ehinger Adolph, plasterer, res 73 Riverside av.
Ehinger Charles, lab Hoffman Bros, res 4 Herman.
Ehinger Charles C, bds 4 Herman.
Ehinger Emma M, clk Louis Wolf & Co, bds 112 Clay.
Ehinger Felix, laborer, rms 104 E Wayne.
Ehinger Frank O, mngr Lathrop & Co, res 66 Monroe.
Ehinger Joseph, helper Wabash R R, res 153 W 3d.
Ehinger Louisa (wid Norman), res 176 E Lewis.
Ehinger Mary, dresmaker, bds 276 E Jefferson.
Ehinger Othman, car bldr Penn Co. res 112 Clay.
Ehinger Regina (wid John), res 204 Madison.
Ehinger Theresa M, laundress, bds 4 Herman.
Ehle August N, cigar mnfr 178 Broadway, res 180 same.
Ehle Augusta (wid Frederick E), res 171 Rockhill.
Ehle Edward T, mason, bds 199 Broadway.
Ehle Frank cigarmkr A N Ehle, bds 180 Broadway.
Ehle Frederick E, died Oct 1, 1894.
Ehle Henry C, bricklayer, res 73 Stophlet.
Ehle Mary S, bds 171 Rockhill.
Ehle Michael, res 224 W Creighton av.
Ehrhardt Martha, domestic 190 W Berry.
Ehrhardt Mary, domestic 204 W Berry.
Ehrhart Lehnert, sausage mkr F Eckart Pkg Co, res 49 Archer av.
Ehrman Carrie C, seamstress, bds 175 Van Buren.

Ehrman Charles F (Ehrman & Geller), bds 475 Van Buren.

Ehrman Coleman, res 146 E Jefferson.

Ehrman Edward J, bkkpr Wm Kaough, res 157 Montgomery.

Ehrman Elizabeth, tailoress, bds 175 Van Buren.

Ehrman Fredericka, bds 175 Van Buren.

Ehrman & Geller (Charles F Ehrman, Charles C Geller), barbers, 12 W Main.

Ehrmann Alvina C. laundress, bds 163 Taylor.

Ehrmann Caroline (wid Matthias), res 134 Greeley.

Ehrmann Carrie C, laundress, bds 163 Taylor.

Ehrmann Charles, Mnfr of and Dealer in Buggies, Platform, Spring and Farm Wagons, 149 W Main, res 339 W Jefferson. (*See left side lines..*)

Ehrmann Charles H, washer Herman Berghoff Brewing Co, bds s s Chestnut, 4 e of Sumner.

Ehrmann Emily, bds C H Ehrmann.

Ehrmann Emma, opr S M Foster, bds 134 Greeley.

Ehrmann Frederick C, collarmkr A Racine, res 36 W 4th.

Ehrmann Charles W F, laborer, bds 153 Taylor.

Ehrmann George J, painter Fleming Mnfg Co, bds 42 Elm.

Ehrmann Hermann, with Charles Ehrmann, bds 339 W Jefferson.

Ehrmann John F, molder Bass F & M Wks, bds s s Chestnut 4 e of Summer.

Ehrmann John G W, contractor, res 42 Elm.

Ehrmann John M, car bldr Penn Co. res s s Chestnut 2 w of Lumbard.

Ehrmann J Henry, res 153 Taylor.

Ehrmann Lizzie C, starcher F L Jones & Co, bds 339 W Jefferson.

Ehrmann Louise P, domestic 60 W Main.

Ehrmann Michael, laborer, res 24 Huffman.

Ehrmann Michael, mach Bass F & M Wks, res 17 Taylor.

Ehrmann Minnie, opr S M Foster, bds 134 Greely.

Ehrmann Minnie M, bds s s Chestnut 4 e of Summer.

Ehrmann Minnie R, bds 339 W Jefferson.

Ehrmann Paulina M, seamstress, bds 153 Taylor.

Ehrmann Wm C, helper Ft Wayne Electric Corp, bds 153 Taylor.

Ehrsam Otto, laborer, bds 46 E Columbia.

Ehrstein Edward F, tel opr N Y, C & St L R R, bds 266 W Jefferson.

Eib Kate E, domestic County Jail.

Eichel Andrew, brewer C L Centlivre Brewing Co, res 50 Randolph.
Eichel Charles J, lab Bass F & M Wks, res 497 E Wayne.
Eichelberger Samuel, lab Penn Co, res 123 E Taber.
Eicher, *see also Acker and Aker.*
Eicher Ida, laundress F L Jones & Co, bds 108 Huffman.
Eicher Gotttieb, res 108 Huffman.
Eicher Gustav, porter McDonald & Watt, bds 40 Monroe.
Eichmann George, fitter Ft Wayne Gas Co, bds Hoffmann House.
Eichmeyer Charles L, car bldr Penn Co, res 33 Duryea.
Eickhoff Bernard H, candymaker, res 72 W 4th.
Eickhoff Charles A, machinist, res 270 Webster.
Eickhoff Frank R, lab Ft Wayne Electric Corp, bds 270 Webster.
Eickhoff Minnie, domestic 93 W Wayne.
Eickhoff Wm, lab Ft Wayne Pneumatic Novelty and Model Wks. res 137 John.
Eifel John, lab Bass F & M Wks, res 18 Gay.
Eiler John W, machinist, bds 154 Madison.
Einsiedel Andrew J, blacksmith, res 69 Stophlet.
Einsiedel Fritz, sheet iron wkr Wabash R R, bds 18 Zollars av.
Eisen David, peddler. res 201 Hanna.
Eisennacher August C. cash A Mergentheim, bds 197 Taylor.
Eisennacher Frederick, gluer L Rastetter & Son, res 197 Taylor.
Eisenring Rev Thomas, chaplain St Joseph Hospital, res same.
Eising John, car bldr Penn Co. res 73 Force.
Eising John jr, clk Anthon Wayne Mnfg Co, bds 73 Force.
Eiter Augustus, coremkr Ind Mach Wks, bds 22 John.
Eiter Frank, molder Kerr Murray Mnfg Co, res 24 John.
Eiter Henry, molder Kerr Murray Mnfg Co, res 38 Hough
Eiter Joseph, molder, bds 22 John.
Eiter Maggie (wid Peter), res 22 John,
Eiter Mary, bds 24 John.
Eitzinger Andrew C, molder, bds w s Winter 2 s of Pontiac.
Eitzinger George, molder Bass F & M Wks, res 53 Gay.
Eitzinger Rose (wid George), res w s Winter 2 s of Pontiac
Eix August, bds 60 W Washington.
Eix A Frederick, blacksmith, res 197 Hanna.
Eix Ernest, laborer Bass F & M Wks, res 159 Hayden.

Eix Frederick C, sexton, res 60 W Washington.
Eix Henry, lab Bass F & M Wks, res 189 Madison.
Eix John, helper, bds 189 Madison.
Eix Lottie, domestic 61 Douglas av.
Eix Lottie, seamstress, bds 235 Harmer.
Eix Minnie, bds 197 Hanna.
Eix Minnie (wid August), res 163 E Jefferson.
Eix Sophia (wid August), bds 60 W Washington.
Ek George, fireman Penn Co, res 326 Hanna.
Elbert Anthony, lab Bass F & M Wks, res 374 E Washington.
Elder Cynthia, bds 45 Savilla av.
Eldred Danford P, engr Penn Co, res 24 Baker.
Eldred Frankie, bds 24 Baker.
Eldridge Anna B, clk F L Jones & Co, bds 138 Union.
Eldridge Nettie, clk F L Jones & Co, bds 138 Union.
Elett Herman H, truckman Penn Co, res 228 W Superior.
Elias Tillie, bds 351 E Wayne.
Elion Charles J, molder Bass F & M Wks, res 93 Smith.
Ell Adam J, laborer, res 22 Hough.
Ell Frederick, died May 20 1894.
Ell George F, cabmkr F W Furn Co, bds 22 Hough.
Ellenwood Clifton A, conductor, res 69 Lasselle.
Ellenwood Cloyd C, fireman Penn Co, res 131 Wallace.
Ellenwood George W, baggageman L E & W R R, res 24 Cass.
Ellenwood O Rodney, engr Penn Co, res 185 Hanna.
Ellenwood Warren D, brakeman Penn Co, bds 185 Hanna.
Ellert Benoit, Propr New Aveline House Barber Shop, 71 Calhoun, res 67 Elmwood av.
Ellert Benoit G, clk Kuhne & Co, bds 67 Elmwood av.
Ellert Louis A, barber Benoit Ellert, bds 67 Elmwood av.
Elligsen Henry G, res 19 Clark.
Elliott Alexander, brakeman, rooms 96 Boone.
Elliott Benjamin H, policeman, res 88 Thomas.
Elliott Enoch W (col'd), engineer, res 153 High.
Elliott Fennimore F, engineer, res 70 Boone.
Elliott Frank W, laborer, res 31 Wagner.
Elliott Leota M, bds 57 W Butler.
Elliott Lida, dressmkr School for Feeble Minded Youth.
Elliott Loyal D, condr N Y, C & St L R R, res 82 W 4th.
Elliott Margaret J (wid George W), bds 82 W 4th.
Elliott Nelson D, blacksmith, bds 57 W Butler.
Elliott Samuel B, patternmkr Ft Wayne Electric Corp, res 57 W Butler.

Elliott Walter L, laborer, bds 57 W Butler.
Elliott Wilfred, brakeman, bds 57 W Butler.
Ellis George (Skaf & Ellis). res 123 Fairfield av.
Ellis Margaret E (wid Robert), res 127 Oliver.
Ellison Elizabeth C (wid George C). res 367 E Wayne.
Ellison George R, machinist, bds 2 Emily.
Ellison James, laborer, res 32 Thompson av.
Ellison John T, teamster, bds 2 Emily.
Ellison Richard E, engineer, res 2 Emily.
Ellison Thomas E, Lawyer, 23 and 24 Bank Blk,
    res 167 W Wayne. Tel 214, res 318.
Ellsworth Hannah (wid Augustine), bds 17 Lincoln av.
Elser Charles V, yd brakeman Penn Co, res 322 W Main.
Elser Clement, switchman, bds Hyer House.
Ely George W, res 108 E Berry.
Elzie Rose, domestic Harmon House.
Emanuel German Lutheran Church, s s Jefferson nr Union.
Emanuel German Lutheran School, n e cor Wilt and Union.
Emanuel Miss Julia E, clk Meyer Bros & Co, bds 47 W
    Washington.
Embrey Eliza A (wid Louis S), bds 326 Broadway.
Embry Edward J, paperhanger, res 193 Calhoun.
Embshoff George F, car checker Wabash R R, bds 15
    Summit.
Eme Claude F (Eme & Son), res 175 E Wayne.
Eme Julius, carpenter, res 183 E Lewis.
Eme Julius J (Eme & Son), res 93 Montgomery.
Eme & Son (Claude F and Julius J), insurance, 1-2 Foster
    Blk.
Emerick Henry, laborer, res 183 Madison.
Emerick Jacob, laborer, res 226 Gladstone.
Emerson Charlotta M, bkkpr Karn Bros, bds 11 Harrison.
Emerson Margaret E (wid Almeron), res 11 Harrison.
Emerson Nellie, bds Hyer House.
Emery George H, trav agt Lawyer's Co-operative Pub-
    lishing Co, 32 Bass Blk, bds 145 Griffith.
Emery Henry, res 183 Madison.
Emery John W (S B Thing & Co), res Troy, N Y.
Emme Wm, car bldr Penn Co, res 141 Montgomery.
Empie Anna E, bds 164 Broadway.
Empie Lizzie N, bds 164 Broadway.
Empie Thomas B, contractor, 164 Broadway, res same.
Empire Box Factory and Book
    Bindery, Bank Blk. (*See right top lines*).

Empire Flour Mills, John Orff propr, nr W Main st bridge. Tel 93.

Empire Line (Fast Freight), Angus McPherson Agent, 26 Court. Tel 49.

Employers' Liability Assurance Corporation Ld of London, England, Charles B Fitch agt, 26 Bass Blk.

Emrick August, watchman Penn Co, res 363 E Lewis.

Emrick Emmett V, Lawyer, 33 E Main, bds New Aveline House.

Emrick Frederick, messenger Penn Co, bds 58 Force.

Emrick Louisa, bds 363 E Lewis.

Ench, *see also Ensch.*

Endinger George, laborer, res s w cor Chestnut and Warren,

Endinger Henry J, laborer, bds s w cor Chestnut and Warren.

Endres Susan (wid Rudolph), bds 204 Lafayette.

Engelbrecht Henry B, carpenter, res 156 Union.

Engelking Charles H, helper Penn Co, bds 172 Ewing,

Engelking Diederich F, lab, res 148 Broadway.

Engelking Edward, bell boy The Randall.

Engelking Eliza A (wid Henry D), res 172 Ewing.

Engelking Frederick, lab Penn Co, bds 148 Broadway.

Engelking Henry C, mach hd, res n w cor Sherman and Aboit.

Engelking Louisa (wid Henry), res 125 High.

Engelking Louisa M, bds 172 Ewing.

Engelking Lulu, bds 128 High.

Engelking Sophia, bds 75 Harrison.

Engelking Wm, bds 25 High.

Engine House No 1, 89 E Main.

Engine House No 2, Wallace bet Clay and Lafayette.

Engine House No 3, 66 W Washington. Tel 301.

Engine House No 4, 70 and 72 Maumee rd.

Engine House No 5, e s Broadway 2 s of Lavina.

Engine House No 6, n w cor Wells and 3d.

Engle Alexander (Engle & Stenson), res 178 Greeley.

Engle Edward J, helper Keller Dental Co, bds 35 Taylor.

Engle George, farmer, res e s Muncie R R, 1½ miles s of city limits.

Engle Gertrude, opr S M Foster, bds 35 Taylor.

Engle John F, lab Hoffman Bros, bds 178 Greely.

Engle John F, lab, res w s Piqua av 3 s of Rudisill av.

Engle John M, bds 179 W De Wald.

Engle Seldon D, helper F Schanz, res 235 E Wayne.

Engle Wm, res 35 Taylor.

Engle Wm, cabtmkr Ft Wayne Furn Co, res 179 W DeWald

Engle Wm A, helper, bds 178 Greely.

Engle & Stenson (Alexander Engle, Morris A Stenson), meats, 228 W Main.

Englert Kate, bds 68 Maumee rd.

Englert Lena, bds 134 Francis.

Englert May, bds 58 Oliver.

English Lutheran Church of the Redeemer, W Washington n w cor Fulton.

English Wm, brakeman, res 119 Force.

English Wm J, laborer, res 10 Oliver.

Engmann Anna, dressmaker, 133 E Jefferson, bds same.

Engmann John, carp L Rastetter & Son, bds 133 E Jefferson

Engmann K August (K A Engmann & Co), res 133 E Jefferson.

Engmann K A & Co (K August Engmann), Organ Builder and Tuner, 133 E Jefferson. (*See left side lines.*)

Engst Ernest, bds 231 Barr.

Enkhausen Herman, bds 382 E Lewis.

Ennis Asenath (wid John A), res 49 W Jefferson.

Ens Catherine, cook 103 W Berry.

Ensch Adam, lab Ft Wayne Electric Corp, bds 150 Suttenfield.

Ensch Jacob, lab Ft Wayne Electric Corp, bds 150 Suttenfield.

Ensch John, lab Penn Co, res 9 Caroline.

Ensch John H, finisher Standard Wheel Co, bds 150 Suttenfield.

Ensch Margaret (wid Matthew), res 150 Suttenfield.

Ensch Mary A, bds 9 Caroline.

Ensch Matthias, polisher Standard Wheel Co, res 89 Pontiac.

Enslen Columbus E, fireman Penn Co, res 108 W DeWald.

Lnslen Frank M, fireman Penn Co, bds 139 Fairfield av.

Enslen Wm M, physician 286 Calhoun, res 139 Fairfield av. Tel 365.

Entemann Christian, saloon 11-13 E Main, res 149 W Berry.

Entemann Ernest E, mngr C Entemann, bds 149 W Berry.

Entradacker Sebastian, car bldr Penn Co, res 72 Hayden.

Enz Ernest, lab, bds 100 Montgomery.

Enz Frederick, molder Bass F & M Wks, bds 224 Gay.

Enz Mrs Katie, res 224 Gay.

Enz Wm, molder Bass F & M Wks, bds 224 Gay.

Epotty Bessie E, bds 83 W De Wald.
Epple Charles, candymkr, bds 188 Fairfield av.
Epple Christian, lab, res 40 Taylor.
Epple David, lab, res 1 Pine.
Epple Edward, apprentice, bds 188 Fairfield av.
Epple George, student, bds 188 Fairfield av.
Epple Gottlieb, Agent Schaller Bros, Cincinnati Beer, 188 Fairfield av, res same.
Epple Gottlieb P, mason, bds 188 Fairfield av.
Epple Rosa M (wid John), res 40 W Allen.
Epple Wm, cabinetmkr, bds 1 Pine.
Epple Wm. mach hd Ft Wayne Electric Corp, bds 188 Fairfield av.
Epps Wm H, brakeman N Y C & St L R R, bds 75 Boone.
Epstein Babat (wid Meyer), died Oct 13th, 1894.
Epstein Hart (Epstein & Sons), 18 Calhoun.
Epstein Samuel H (Epstein & Sons), 18 Calhoun.
Epstein Simon (Epstein & Sons), 18 Calhoun.
Epstein & Sons (Hart, Samuel H and Simon), clothing, hats, caps and furnishing goods, 18 Calhoun.
Equitable Life Assurance Society of New York, W S Buck Gen'l Mngr, 52½ Calhoun.
Erb John F, car bldr Penn Co, res 170 Francis.
Erdel Emma, domestic John Orff.
Ericson Eric G, civil engr Penn Co, res 425 Broadway.
Erickson Emil, wood carver, rms 36 Miner.
Erickson Frank L, brakeman Penn Co, bds 142 Wallace.
Erickson Furniture Co The, John Erickson Mngr, Mnfrs of Special Furniture, 152 Pearl. (See p 95.)
Erickson James E, condr Penn Co, res 88 E Berry.
Erickson John, Mngr The Erickson Furniture Co, res 43 Miner. (See p 95.)
Erickson Marguerite B, bds 84 E Berry.
Erickson Mary A (wid John Q), res 142 Wallace.
Erickson May, bds 142 Wallace.
Erickson May, bds 43 Miner.
Erickson Richard W, clk O R Kelsey, bds 43 Miner.
Erington Samuel (W L Stevenson & Co), bds 136 Broadway.
Erlenbaugh Elizabeth, domestic 107 W Berry.
Erlenbaugh Maud, domestic 107 W Berry.
Ernest Andrew, laborer Wabash R R, res 25 Brandriff.
Ernest Joseph, section hand Wabash R R, bds 110 Chicago.

R. L. POLK & CO.'S

Erni Catherine, opr Troy Steam Laundry, bds 15 Pearl.
Erni Louis, engineer Wm Geake, bds 15 Pearl.
Ernsting Charles H, res 16 Clark.
Ernsting Charles H jr, laborer, res 121 Wells.
Ernsting Christian, helper Kerr Murray Mnfg Co, res 54 Gay.
Ernsting Dorothea, bds 121 Wells.
Ernsting Wm C, bds 16 Clark.
Ersig Dorothy (wid Wm), res 129 Monroe.
Ersig Emma H, teacher Harmer School, bds 129 Monroe.
Ersig Katharine A, teacher Clay School, bds 129 Monroe.
Ersig Wm A, horseshoer Wm Geary, res 123 Wilt.
Ertel George, molder C M Menefee, res 53 John.
Ertel Henry C, switchtndr Penn Co, res w s Lillie 2 s of Milan.
Ertel John, hostler 146 Maumee rd.
Ertel Louis, janitor Schmitz Blk, res 177 Erie.
Ertel Louis B, laborer, bds 177 Erie.
Ertle Bernhard, died March 4, 1895.
Ervin House, John Ervin propr, 12 Harrison.
Ervin John, propr Ervin House, res same.
Ervin Joseph F, moved to Boise City, Idaho.
Ervin Belle, bds 134 Calhoun.
Ervin Rose, student, bds 134 Calhoun.
Erwin Maria E (wid Joseph T), res 39 Indiana av.
Erwin Mary C, bkkpr F C Parham, bds 39 Indiana av.
Erwin Richard K jr, carp, res s s Rebecca 1 e of G R & I, R R.
Esch Emma (wid August), bds 45 Grand.
Escott Wm T, steamfitter Robert Ogden, bds 293 W Jefferson.
Essig Adam P, died July 7, 1894.
Essig Charles O, business manager Ft Wayne Sentinel, res 39 E Superior.
Essig Susanna (wid Adam P), bds 39 E Superior.
Essinger Charles W, waiter Oscar Wobrock, rms 181 Suttenfield.
Essinger Emil G, waiter Oscar Wobrock, rms 181 Suttenfield.
Essinger John, res 181 Suttenfield.
Essinger Maggie A, bds 181 Suttenfield.
Esslauer Mary, domestic 388 Fairfield av.
Estill Emma F (wid James A), bds 21½ Poplar.
Estry Albert G, condr Penn Co, res 432 Broadway.
Estry Elwood T, conductor, res 52 Thomas.

Etchey Edward M, barber C B Schmuck, bds 37 Wefel.
Etchey Elizabeth, laundress, bds 37 Wefel.
Etchey Frank, res 37 Wefel.
Etchey Frank H, candymaker Fox br U S Baking Co, bds 37 Wefel.
Etchy Michael, clk F M Smith & Co, res 8 Elmwood av.
Etzel Mary, seamstress, bds 173 W Jefferson.
Etzold Christina (wid Wm), res 46 Douglas av.
Etzold Emil, trimmer S Freiburger & Bro, bds 46 Douglas av.
Etzold Frederick A, helper Horton Mnfg Co, bds 110 Webster.
Etzold Gustave C, machinist, bds 46 Douglas av.
Etzold Henry J, shoemaker, 110 Webster, res same.
Etzold Minnie M, bds 46 Douglas av.
Etzold Wm, died April 7, 1894.
Etzold Wm C, clk Horton Mnfg Co, res 44 Boone.
Eubanks Cora (wid John), res over 41½ W Berry.
European School of Music, 16 Rockhill.
Evangelical Lutheran St John's Church (German), W Washington s e cor Van Buren.
Evangelical Lutheran Zions Church, s e cor Hanna and E Creighton av.
Evans Amos S, pres Hoosier Mnfg Co, res San Jose, Cal.
Evans Anna C (wid Josiah), res 22 E De Wald.
Evans Barbara B (wid John K), res 110 W Superior.
Evans Bennett B, agent, bds 110 W Superior.
Evans Bertrand W, bkkpr Rhinesmith & Simonson, bds 22 E De Wald.
Evans Blk, 28 and 30 E Berry.
Evans David E, brakeman N Y, C & St L R R, res 83 Broadway.
Evans Edwin, res 174 W Wayne.
Evans Eva M, rms 83 Calhoun.
Evans Frank D (Geiger & Evans), bds 141 Lafayette.
Evans George P, sec Hoosier Mnfg Co and Sperry Pelton Mnfg Co, res 225 W Berry. Tel 380.
Evans Gordon M, clk City Comptroller, bds 22 E DeWald.
Evans Harry, traveling agent, res 398 E Washington.
Evans Henry J, foreman Ft Wayne Electric Corp, res 144 Union.
Evans Ira P, supt Rhinesmith & Simonson, res 109 W Washington.
Evans Irving D, draughtsman Kerr Murray Mnfg Co, bds 22 E De Wald.

Evans Miss Jennie L, asst The Public Library, bds 22 E De Wald.

Evans Jesse (Hirt & Evans), res 5 N Clinton.

Evans John B, teamster, res 142 Madison.

Evans John M, deputy comptroller, res 22 E De Wald.

Evans John P, treas Hoosier Mnfg Co and Sperry Pelton Mnfg Co, res 126 E Main. Tel 356.

Evans Josiah O, bkkpr S Bash & Co, res 22 E De Wald.

Evans Lydia M (wid Nathan), bds 200 WBerry.

Evans Mary T, bds 174 W Wayne.

Evans Maurice, student, bds 126 E Main.

Evans Oliver F, traveling agt Hoosier Mnfg Co, res 95 E Berry.

Evans Raleigh B, condr G R & I R R, res 62 E Williams.

Evans Regina C (wid Joseph A), res 141 Lafayette.

Evans Robert D, student, bds 109 W Washington.

Evans Wm A, traveling agt. bds 45 E 3d.

Evans Wm C, engr N Y C & St L R R, bds 52 Runion av.

Evarts Charles E, photo printer F R Barrows, bds 104 Wells.

Evarts Emma R, bds 104 Wells.

Evarts George C, candymaker, bds 104 Wells.

Evarts Nancy (wid Gilbert C), res 104 Wells.

Evarts Sarah M (wid Gilbert C), bds 6 Orchard.

Eveland Mary (wid Samuel H), bds 24 Boone.

Everett Charles E (Everett & Doud), insurance agent, Old National Bank Bldg, res 24 W Creighton av. Tel 253, res 503.

Everett Percy F, bds 39 W Washington.

Everett Samuel, butcher, bds 105 Barr.

Everett Wm E, engr L E & W R R, res 63 Huffman.

Everett & Doud (Charles E Everett, Wallace E Doud), real estate, Old National Bank Bldg. Tel 253.

Evergreen Terrace, Creighton av s w cor Shawnee av.

Everhart, see also Eberhardt.

Everhart Elizabeth (wid Alfred), res 46 Lavina.

Evers Henry, mason 199 John, res same.

Evers James H, motorman Ft W E Ry Co, res 41 W Lewis.

Evers John, bricklayer, res 323 Hanna.

Evers John H, bricklayer, bds 323 Hanna.

Evers Lizzie C, bds 323 Hanna.

Evers Michael, barber J A Stier, bds 323 Hanna.

Eversole Oscar P, General Agt Mutual Life Insurance Co of Indiana, Rooms 1, 4 and 12 W Wayne, res 192 E Wayne.

Everson Fidelia (wid John), bds 232 W Washington.
Eville Thomas E jr, clk A Copinus, bds 120 Harrison.
Ewald Albert, boilermkr, bds 309 Lafayette.
Ewald Charles P, helper, bds 309 Lafayette.
Ewing Aaron, laborer, res 35 Force.
Ewing Block, s w cor Harrison and Main.
Ewing Mary C (wid George), res 115 W Main.
Exner Robert, lab P, Ft W & C Ry, res e s Lumbard 2 n of Chestnut.
Ey Minetta, domestic 40 W Washington.
Eylenberg John H, tel opr W U Tel Co, res 76 Baker.

F

Fabian Adolph, carpenter, res 81½ Smith.
Fabian Julius W, laborer, res 133 E Lewis.
Fabin Lizzie, domestic The Wayne.
Fahling Frederick, laborer, res 148 Maumee rd.
Fahling Henry, bds 148 Maumee rd.
Fahlsing Angust K, boilermkr, res 87 Barthold.
Fahlsing Charles W, removed to Auburn, Ind.
Fahlsing Christina (wid Frederick W), bds 67 Barthold.
Fahlsing Frederick, transfer agent, res 36 Baker.
Fahlsing Frederick W, helper Olds' Wagon Wks, res 9 Sturgis.
Fahlsing John, lab Ft Wayne Electric Corp, bds 9 Sturgis.
Fahlsing Minnie S, opr C U Tel Co, bds 334 E Washington.
Fahlsing Wm C F, bailiff, res 334 E Washington.
Fahner Wm F, laborer, res n s Penn 1 e of Dubois.
Fahnestock James, bookkeeper, rms 169 W Jefferson.
Fair Charles S, student, bds 39 E Williams.
Fair Joseph, lab, res n s Cochran 1 w of Coombs.
Fairbank Clark, General Agt Penn Mutual Life Insurance Co of Philadelphia, Pa, 19 Court, res 115 E Berry. Tel 521.
Fairfield Anna M, prin Hamilton School, res 66 W DeWald.
Fairfield Charles, res n s County rd 2 w of County Poor Farm.
Fairfield Cyrus K, real estate, res 7 Belle av.
Fairfield George W, toolmkr Ft Wayne Electric Corp, res 398 Broadway.
Fairfield John D, carpenter, res w s Hillside 2 s of Eliza.
Falconer John, blksmith Ft Wayne Iron Wks, res 71 W Williams.
Falconer Martha E, bds 71 W Williams.

Falconer Richard, mach Wabash R R, bds 71 W Williams.
Falger Elizabeth (wid Peter), res 173 W Jefferson.
Falk Charles (Charles Falk & Co), res 181 W Berry.
Falk Charles & Co (Charles Falk), Wholesale Notions, 23 W Main. Tel 337.
Falk Leopold (Falk & Lamley), res 181 W Berry.
Falk & Lamley (Leopold Falk, Moses E Lamley), whol liquors, 17 E Columbia.
Falls Olive. bds 163 W Wayne.
Falls Daniel M, tallow, e end Dwenger av, 1 mile e of limits, res 163 W Wayne.
Falvy Daniel, boilermkr N Y, C & St L R R, res 42 Boone.
Falvy John F, appr Ind Mach Wks, bds 42 Boone.
Falvy Mary A, machine opr, bds 42 Boone.
Fankhauser Frederick, laborer, bds 22 Euclid av.
Fankhauser Sarah (wid Andreas), res 22 Euclid av.
Fanz August, lab Penn Co, res 128 Madison.
Farbar Christina, domestic 166 E Berry.
Farks Edward H, lab Penn Co, res 200 Force.
Farnan Dancing Academy, Foster Blk.
Farnan Mary (wid Owen), bds 25 Foster Blk.
Farnan M Della, pianist, bds 25 Foster Blk.
Farnan Owen, laborer, res cor Oneida and Eden Park av.
Farnan Stella I, dancing teacher, bds 25 Foster Blk.
Farnsworth Wm F, clk S A Karn, bds 36 Wilt.
Farra Joseph, laborer, res 23 Cochran.
Farrand Mrs Emma, rms 356 Calhoun.
Farrand Mrs Wilhelmina, res 356 Calhoun.
Farrell Edward, carpenter, bds 119 Fairfield av.
Farrell John, laborer, res e s Webster 1 n of Cour.
Fast Mrs Ella, student, bds 119 W Washington.
Father's Medicines, H H Haines, Proprietor, 24 E Washington.
Faudree. *see also Votrie.*
Faudree John M, tank inspr, res s s Jesse 4 e of Runnion av.
Faught Anna, retoucher F Schanz, bds 123 W Williams.
Faulks, *see Foulks.*
Faust, *see also Foust.*
Faust Adam, barber, res 129 Union,
Faust Benjamin, driver City Trucking Co, res 148 W Main.
Faust Peter, bds 148 W Main.
Favery Catherine, dressmaker, bds 102 Webster.
Fay, *see also Fey.*

Fay Montford W, pres and treas M W Fay Warehouse Co and merchandise broker, 135 Calhoun. Tel 334, rms 115 E Berry. Tel 521.

Fay M W Warehouse Co, M W Fay Pres and Treas, H C Rockhill Sec, Storage and Commission, 135 Calhoun, Warehouse s e cor Francis and Hayden. Tel 334.

Fay Stephen V, laborer, bds 28 E Columbia.

Feanza Christ, res 15 Smith.

Feaser Amos, lab Hoffman Bros, res 60 Riverside av.

Fechter, *see Feichter and Feuchter.*

Feddem Emil, lab Penn Co, res 81 Hayden.

Federspiel John B, foreman Ft Wayne Electric Corp, res 145 Shawnee av.

Fee Frank F, lumber, 181 W Wayne, res same. Tel 364.

Fee Loretta (wid Thomas W), bds 27 E Washington.

Feeny John H, tinner, res 63 W Pontiac.

Feeny Miranda, dressmaker, 63 W Pontiac, res same.

Fehling August H, laborer, res 87 Madison.

Fehling Frederick H, grocer, 324 Broadway, res 56 South Wayne av.

Feichter, *see also Feuchter.*

Feichter Jacob H, carpenter, res 200 Metz.

Feidler, *see also Fiedler.*

Feigel Caroline C (wid Charles), domestic Hope Hospital.

Feipel Frank, grocer, 122 Madison, res 131 Monroe.

Feist Katie, cook J H Bass.

Feist Lena, bds 30 Madison.

Feist Louis J, merchant tailor, 226 Lafayette, res same.

Feistkorn Charles A, clk D N Foster, res 14 Liberty.

Feldheiser Andrew, motorman Ft W E Ry Co, res 14 Melita

Felger Clara L, opr S M Foster, bds 172 John.

Felger Elizabeth (wid Peter), bds 173 W Jefferson.

Felger John, bds 172 John.

Felger Julia A, domestic 126 E Main.

Felger Mary, clk B Gutermuth, bds 79 Cass.

Felger Matilda M, bds 172 John.

Felger Rosanna (wid Jacob), died Sept 16, 1894.

Felker Elizabeth J, bds 315 W Jefferson.

Felker Forrest J, contractor, rms 143 Fairfield av.

Felske Charles H, mach Wabash R R, res 50 Walnut.

Felt Adolph, carpenter, res 12 Caroline.

Felt Emma, seamstress, bds 102 Franklin av.

Felt Frank, teamster, res 102 Franklin av.

Felt Frederick P, cigarmkr J C Eckert, res 35 Douglas av.

Felt John, painter, bds 343 E Creighton av.

Felt Mabel, former Wayne Knitting Mills, bds 102 Franklin av.

Felt Warren B, teamster, res 68 Putnam.

Felton W, helper Penn Co, res 12 Oak.

Felts Charles E, brakeman, res 23 Erie.

Felts George F, Lawyer, 34 E Berry, res 229 W Creighton av.

Felts Herman W, supt County Poor Farm, res same.

Felts Mrs Lillian D, res 43 Grand.

Felts Mary, bds 23 Erie.

Fenker Conrad, farmer, res e s Walton av nr Pontiac.

Fenker Herman R, carp Penn Co, res s e cor Chestnut and Summer.

Fenker Rudolph G, carp, res w s Lumbard 2 n of Chestnut.

Fenton Richard, machinist, bds 91 Force.

Ferber Henry, carpenter, res 269 E Lewis.

Ferckel Adam, molder Bass F & M Wks, res 324 Hanna.

Ferckel Bertha (wid Martin), res 188 Ewing.

Ferckel Charles A, clerk, bds 188 Ewing.

Ferckel Emma, clk Root & Co, bds 188 Ewing.

Ferckel Louisa M, bkkpr A Copinus, bds 188 Ewing.

Ferckel Martin, died Sept 9th, 1894.

Ferckel Martin J, cutter S Freiburger & Bro, bds 188 Ewing.

Ferckel Otto H, trimmer S Freiburger & Bro, bds 188 Ewing.

Ferckel Wm F, clk Pixley & Co, bds 188 Ewing.

Ferguson, *see also Firguson*

Ferguson Amelia E, bds 82 W Berry.

Ferguson Anna, dressmaker, bds 302 W Jefferson.

Ferguson Elmer E, helper Penn Co, bds 231 Lafayette.

Ferguson George E, mach hd Ft Wayne Organ Co, rms 226 Calhoun.

Ferguson George W, laundry man School for Feeble Minded Youth, res n s Griswold 2 e of bridge.

Ferguson Gertrude T, bds 82 W Berry.

Ferguson Helen J, bds 82 W Berry.

Ferguson James H, blacksmith, res 231 Lafayette.

Ferguson John (Ferguson & Palmer Co), res 203 W Berry. Tel 468.

Ferguson John K (Ferguson & Palmer Co), res 93 W Main. Tel 241.

Ferguson John T, printer Fort Wayne Sentinel, res 372 E Wayne.

Ferguson Joseph E, finisher Ft Wayne Organ Co, res 303 Winter.

Ferguson Matthew A, comnr Allen Co, res Lima Plank rd 2 miles n of city limits.

Ferguson May, bkkpr Singer Mnfg Co, bds 24 McClellan.

Ferguson Minnie E, bds 203 W Berry.

Ferguson Orville B. brakeman Penn Co, bds 301 Calhoun.

Ferguson Samuel T, brakeman, res 98 Boone.

Ferguson Thomas A, bds 82 W Berry.

Ferguson Thomas W, tinner Seavey Hardware Co, res 24 McClellan.

Ferguson Tena, domestic 300 W Main.

Ferguson Walter O, helper Penn Co, bds 231 Lafayette.

Ferguson Wm G, physician, 82 W Berry, res 138 Walton av.

Ferguson Wm T, physician, 82 W Berry, res same.

Ferguson & Palmer Co (John Ferguson, Earl Parmer, John K Ferguson), Manufacturers of and Dealers in Hardwood Lumber and Piling ; Railroad Supply a Specialty, 1 and 2 Pixley and Long Bldg.

Feriter Albert R, mach Wabash R R, bds 32 Brandriff.

Ferner David A, bds 83 E Berry.

Fernwalt Harry G, laborer, bds 324 Calhoun.

Ferrell Nicholas, clk E F Heine, res 278 Calhoun.

Ferris Frank C, brakeman, res 111 John.

Ferris Jennie, cook New Aveline House.

Ferris Wm A, bds 111 John.

Fessenden Charles E, clk B W Skelton Co, res 128 Fairfield av.

Fessenden Eva A, dressmaker, bds 128 Fairfield av.

Fessenden Fred, printer, bds 128 Fairfield av.

Fetters Andrew, driver, res 130 Wells.

Fetters John, machine hand, bds 37 Maumee rd.

Fetters Martin, turner Standard Wheel Co, res 37 Maumee rd.

Fetters Mary (wid John), bds 37 Maumee rd.

Fetters Wm H, mach hd Penn Co, res 12 Oak.

Feuchter, *see also Feichter*.

Feuchter Matthias, blksmith Penn Co, res n w cor Eagle and Taylor.

Feulner Anthony, hub stamper, res 33 Lasselle.

Feulner Eva, plater, bds 33 Lasselle.

Feulner Margaret (wid Frank), bds 33 Lasselle.

Feustel Adolph J, barber, bds 2 Riverside av.

Feustel Edward, clk F P Mensch, bds 2 Riverside av.

Feustel George O, plumber A Hattersley & Sons, bds 2 Riverside av.

Feustel Henry A, bartender H S Latham, rms 6 E Columbia.
Feustel Sophia D (wid August), res 2 Riverside av.
Fey, *see also Fay.*
Fey Conrad, harnessmkr A L Johns & Co, bds 108 Erie.
Fey Jacob, lab Penn Co, res 108 Erie.
Fey John, laborer, bds 108 Erie.
Fey Katie, seamstress, bds 108 Erie.
Fey Maggie, domestic 49 Pixley & Long Bldg.
Fickel George W, County Recorder, office Court House, res 332 W Washington.
Ficker Mary E (wid Eugene B), res 97 Pearl.
Fidelity Benevolent Association, Carl Sauer pres, Dr John Schilling vice pres, A L Schroeder sec, 7and 9 Pixley & Long Bldg.
Fiedler Bernhardt, helper, bds 75 Smith.
Fiedler Charles, solicitor, bds 75 Smith.
Fiedler Emil E, painter Olds Wagon Wks, bds 75 Smith.
Fiedler Ida, domestic 133 W Washington.
Fiedler Oswald E, painter Olds Wagon Works, bds 75 Smith
Fiedler Theresa (wid Charles), res 75 Smith.
Fiedler Wilhelm, lab, res n s Coombs 1 w of New Haven av.
Fieldbleat Samuel, clothing, 76 Barr, res same.
Fields Mrs James S, res 84 Barr.
Fields Wm J, cigarmkr H W Ortmann, res 180 Griffith.
Figel Albert G, fireman, bds 121 Wells.
Figel Caroline C (wid Charles), res 12 Clark.
Figel Charles S, res 8 Oakland n e cor Spring.
Figel Clara M, domestic 87 Cass.
Figel Edward J, wiper L E & W R R, res 49 N Calhoun.
Figel Frederick C, clk J C Figel, res 56 Wells.
Figel Fredericka M, bds 49 N Calhoun.
Figel Henry, teamster, res w s Spy Run av 5 n of canal bdge
Figel John C, grocer, 54 Wells, res 16 Cass. Tel 284.
Figel Wm, tailor, res 89 Maumee rd.
Fike Cyrus W, transfer agt Powers & Barnett, res 57 Huestis av.
Filley Julia (wid Robert), bds 154 E Berry.
Filley Nettie, music teacher, 154 E Berry, bds same.
Filley Wm S, res 251 E Washington.
Findlay, Fort Wayne and Western Ry, (Tangent Line), C M Bissell General Manager, J H Russell General Freight and Passenger Agent, C H Roser Comptroller, A B Merriam Auditor, A S Johnson Chief Train Dispatcher, Tri-State Bldg. Tel 255.

Findlay Frederick T, engr Wabash R R, res 230 W De Wald
Fink Caroline M, bds 176 E Jefferson.
Fink Frank H, foreman, res 176 E Jefferson.
Fink Frank J, molder Bass F & M Wks, bds 176 E Jefferson.
Fink Frederick F, lab Penn Co, res 138 Fairfield av.
Fink Frederick H, mach Penn Co, res 31 Duryea.
Fink George B, conductor, res 212 Walton av.
Fink John B, barber, 56 E Main, rms same.
Fink John H, lab Standard Wheel Co, bds 138 Fairfield av.
Fink John W, foreman A.L Johns & Co, res 136 Barr.
Fink Mary E, clerk, bds 176 E Jefferson.
Finkhouse Frederick, motorman, bds 121 Greene.
Finlayson John L, mach Penn Co, bds 207 E Wayne.
Finn Mary A, bds 39 W Washington.
Finnegan Edward D, condr G R & I R·R, res 21 Hamilton.
Finnell James, condr Penn Co, res 29 W De Wald.
Finney Cecelia M, wrapper Fox br U S Baking Co. bds 18 Melita.
Finney James H, lab Ft Wayne Electric Corp, bds 18 Melita.
Finney Lawrence E, laborer, bds 14 Huffman.
Finney Michael A, watchman, res 18 Melita.
Finney Wm, insurance agt, res 14 Huffman.
Finze Christian, bartender, res 15 Smith.
Firestine Lyman, teamster Electric L & P Co, res 27 Randolph.
Firgusson, *see also Ferguson.*
Firgusson John, laborer, res 112 John.
Firks Albert T, lab Hoffman Bros, res 152 Greeley.
Firks August, painter, bds 24 Huron.
Firks Frederick W, lab Hoffman Bros, res 24 Huron.
First Baptist Church, n s W Jefferson bet Harrison and Webster.
First National Bank, Capital $300,000, Surplus $175,000, John H Bass Pres, M W Simons Vice-Pres, Lem R Hartman Cash, Wm L Pettit Asst Cash, 73–77 Calhoun. Tel 134.
First Presbyterian Church, n e cor E Washington and Clinton.
First Regiment Light Artillery Band and Orchestra, Gart Shober bandmaster, 7 E Main.
First United Brethren Church, s e cor E Lewis and Harmer
Firth Frederick, agent, res 111 Wells.
Fischer, *see also Fisher.*

250   R. L. POLK & CO.'S

Fischer Anna M (wid John), res 66 Charles.
Fischer Anna M, domestic, rms 77 E Berry.
Fischer Annie C, bds 85 E Berry.
Fischer Anton, cabinetmkr, res 483 Fairfield av.
Fischer Anton jr, blksmith Penn Co, bds 483 Fairfield av.
Fischer Brenda W, bds 182 W Creighton av.
Fischer Catherine (wid Michael), res 85 E Berry
Fischer Charles F, cabinetmkr, bds 483 Fairfield av.
Fischer Christopher, helper Penn Co, res 49 Hugh.
Fischer Dorothy E, bds 85 E Berry.
Fischer Edna A, draughtswoman, bds 182 W Creighton av
Fischer Edward H, mach hd Ft Wayne Organ Co, bds 483 Fairfield av.
Fischer Frank W, tailor H C Meyer, bds 324 Calhoun.
Fischer George, painter Olds Wagon Wks, bds 66 Charles.
Fischer Henry E, civil engineer, 96 Barr, rms same.
Fischer Herman E, clerk, res 182 W Creighton av.
Fischer Nicholas, lab Bass F & M Wks, res 14 Force.
Fischmann David, shoemkr, 322 Calhoun, res 9 Brandriff.
Fischmann Samuel, shoemkr, 17½ W Main, res same.
Fish Emma (wid George), boarding house, 231 Calhoun.
Fisher, *see also Fischer.*
Fisher Anna, domestic 59 E Berry.
Fisher Benjamin, fresco artist, res 108 Howell.
Fisher Benjamin F, traveling agent, res 16 Columbia av.
Fisher Bros (Max B, Samuel S and Edwin J); whol paper 125 Calhoun. Tel 33.
Fisher David C, Real Estate, Insurance, Loans and Notary Public, 32 E Berry, res 26 W Wayne. Tel 46.
Fisher Della, domestic Union House.
Fisher Edwin J (Fisher Bros), bds 229 W Wayne.
Fisher Ella M, bds 41 St Martin's.
Fisher Ellen C, tailoress, bds 131 W Washington.
Fisher Ellis B, brakeman G R & I R R, bds 301 Calhoun.
Fisher Frank, res 324 Calhoun.
Fisher Frank, bds 51 Home av.
Fisher Frederick C, mach Ft Wayne Organ Co, res 126 Hoagland av.
Fisher George, carpenter, res 131 W Washington.
Fisher George H, bds 131 W Washington.
Fisher Henrietta A, tailoress, bds 131 W Washington.
Fisher Henry, attendant Dodge & Keller, rms 94 Broadway.
Fisher Hugh F, traveling agt, res 66 Lake av.
Fisher Jacob, died Jan 28, 1895.
Fisher Jacob, baker B W Skelton Co, res 285 Webster.

Fisher John, laborer, res 309 Hanna.
Fisher John, laborer, res 419 W Main.
Fisher Jonathan H, machinist, res 41 St Martin's.
Fisher Martin L, laborer, bds 7 Duck.
Fisher Max B (Fisher Bros), res 227 W Wayne.
Fisher May, teacher, bds 64 Chicago.
Fisher Regina, bds 269 E Washington.
Fisher Robertson J, treas Bass F & M Wks. res 151 W Berry. Tel 43.
Fisher Samuel S (Fisher Bros), res 229 W Wayne.
Fisher Wesley M, gunsmith, res 332 E Wayne.
Fisher Wm F, coppersmith Penn Co, res 143 Holman.
Fisk Lillian, teacher Miner St School, bds 217 W De Wald.
Fisk May L, sub teacher Public Schools, bds 217 W De Wald.
Fisk Wm W, clk J M Miller. res 217 W De Wald.
Fissel Charles F, clk A R Hills, bds 61 Archer av.
Fissel George J, conductor, bds 61 Archer av.
Fissel Philip, teamster. J M Miller, res 61 Archer av.
Fitch Charles B. General Insurance Agent, 26 Bass Blk. res 52 Brackenridge.
Fitch Clarence M, truckman Penn Co, res 75 Douglas av.
Fitch Delmer C, solr C B Fitch, bds 121 E De Wald.
Fitch Eugene, agent, bds 121 E De Wald.
Fitch Kelsey D, student, bds 83 W De Wald.
Fitch Mary E (wid Nathaniel H), res rear 5 Brandriff.
Fitch Mason J, driver Am Ex Co, res 49 Maumee rd.
Fitch Monroe W, solr C B Fitch, res 131 E De Wald
Fitch Nathaniel H, watchman Penn Co, res 75 Douglas av.
Fitch Otis B, shoes, 52 Calhoun, res 407 same.
Fitch Wm S, clk Penn Co, res 83 W De Wald.
Fitzgerald Alice A, clerk, bds 8 Orchard.
Fitzgerald Mrs Ellen, boarding house, 39 W Washington.
Fitzgerald Ellen M (wid Peter), res 113 Holman.
Fitzgerald Frank, lab F Hagan, res 8 Orchard.
Fitzgerald Frank, painter, bds 58 Walton av.
Fitzgerald Helen, domestic 3 Eliza.
Fitzgerald James, saloon, 55 E Main, res same.
Fitzgerald John, sec Old Fort Spice and Extract Co, 29 E Columbia.
Fitzgerald Lillian M, opr Hoosier Mnfg Co, bds 113 Holman.
Fitzgerald Marguerite, seamstress, bds 8 Orchard.
Fitzgerald Michael. Agt Keeley Brewing Co, Chicago, Ill, 355 Lafayette, res same.

Fitzgerald Wm T, removed to Akron, O.
Fitzgibbon Charlotte A, rms 134 W Berry.
Fitzgibbon Margaret (wid Michael), res rear 94 Baker.
Fitzgibbon Michael E, ins agt, rms 134 W Berry.
Fitzpatrick Hattie, dressmaker F Julliard, bds 385 E Wayne
Fitzpatrick James B, student, bds 46 Bass.
Fitzpatrick John, watchman, res 46 Bass.
Fitzpatrick Margaret E, clk People's Store, bds 46 Bass.
Fitzpatrick Mary E, bds 46 Bass.
Fitzsimmons Henry A L (Martin & Fitzsimmons), bds 12 Harrison.
Fitzsimons Arthur N, mngr Fleming Mnfg Co, res 202 W Wayne.
Flack Charles R, watchman, res 100 Wabash av.
Flack Cyrus I, fireman Olds Wagon Wks, res 315 Harrison.
Flagle Milton G, engineer L E & W R R, res 37 E 3d.
Flaig Engelbert, lab Penn Co, res s s Manford opp Siemon.
Flaig George J, lab Penn Co, rms 36 Miner.
Flanigan Michael, engineer, bds 80 Baker.
Flaugh Christian, traveling agt, rms 56 E Wayne.
Fleckenstein Elizabeth M (wid John G), res 99 Barr.
Fleckenstein Henry E, bartender H A Wiebke, res 4 Riverside av.
Fledderman Elizabeth (wid John G), res 49 Madison.
Fleischmann Eva T (wid Henry), res 30 Huffman.
Fleischmann John M, lab Ind Machine Wks, bds 30 Huffman
Fleischmann & Co, Compressed Yeast, Theo Thorward Agent, s w cor Berry and Harrison.
Fleming Agnes, waitress New Aveline House.
Fleming Artemis, waitress New Aveline House.
Fleming Block, e s Calhoun bet Washington and Jefferson.
Fleming Erin, teacher School for Feeble-Minded Youth.
Fleming Helen F (wid Wm), res 261 W Berry. Tel 3.
Fleming Jane, bds 61 Cass.
Fleming John J, lab C L Centlivre Brewing Co, bds 121 N Harrison.
Fleming Manufacturing Company, Charles Pape Propr, Manufacturers of Road Graders and Street Ry Snow Plows, 78 High. Tel 83. (*See left bottom lines*).
Fleming Mary C, teacher School for Feeble-Minded Youth.
Fleming M Celeste, bds 261 W Berry.
Fleming Roderick, stonecutter George Jaap, res Washington Township.
Fleming Sadie M, student, bds 261 W Berry.

Fleming Sarah, res 61 Cass.
Fleming Wm A, student, bds 261 W Berry.
Fleming Wm H (Rockhill Bros & Fleming), res 106 W Berry.
Fleming Wm J, motorman Ft W E Ry Co, res 38 Bass.
Fletcher Charles P, res 124 E Berry.
Fletcher Harry P, clk Golden & Patterson, bds 26 W Wayne.
Fletcher John F, removed to Chicago, Ill.
Fletcher Josiah F, Livery, 32 Barr, res same. (*See page 99.*)
Fletcher Loretta, opr S M Foster, bds 89 Erie.
Fletcher Mrs. Margaret A, dressmkr 47 Barr, res same.
Fletcher Stephen G, res 89 Erie.
Fletcher Thomas (col'd), brakeman, rms 72 Murray.
Fletter Charity (wid James N), bds 47 Coombs.
Fletter Charles, brakeman, res 437 Lafayette.
Fletter Henry A, res 101 Taylor.
Fletter Ida M, bds 101 Taylor.
Flick Clara B, florist, 33 W Berry, bds 132 Thompson av. Tel 467, res 455.
Flick George W, florist, 132 Thompson av, res same.
Flickinger John W, policeman, res 400 W Main.
Flinn, *see also Flynn.*
Flinn Charles M (C M Flinn & Bro), res 11 Cass.
Flinn C M & Bro (Charles M and Theodore C), horseshoers, 21 N Harrison.
Flinn George A, traveling agent, bds 101 Cass.
Flinn Louisa (wid George N), res 101 Cass.
Flinn Theodore C (C M Flinn & Bro), bds 101 Cass.
Flinn Wm W, laborer, bds 101 Cass.
Flochmann Anna, bds 152 Ewing.
Flood John, bell boy New Aveline House.
Florence Thomas, mach hd Ft Wayne Organ Co, res 93 Shawnee av.
Florent Charles, mach Bass F & M Wks, res 67 Grand.
Florent Emil, clk N Leykauf, bds 67 Grand.
Florent Mary F, bds 67 Grand.
Flutter May M, domestic M P Wefel.
Flynn, *see also Flinn.*
Flynn Anthony, grocer, 253 E Lewis, res same.
Flynn Peter, (Ward & Flynn), res 292 Calhoun.
Fogle Cora A, bds 45 E 3d.
Foellinger Adolph, drugs, 174 Broadway, res 32 Lavina. Tel 648.

Foellinger Augusta M, clk C Foellinger & Co, bds 441 Fairfield av.

Foellinger Blk, 34 and 36 Calhoun.

Foellinger Christopher (C Foellinger & Co), res 441 Fairfield av.

Foellinger C & Co (Christopher and Martin C), shoes, 15 W Main.

Foellinger Jacob, bds 441 Fairfield av.

Foellinger Lizzie M, bds 441 Fairfield av.

Foellinger Louis F, clk S B Thing & Co, res 273 W DeWald.

Foellinger Martin C (C Foellinger & Co), res 441 Fairfield av.

Foerster, see also Foster.

Foerster Conrad, car repr Penn Co, res 581 E Washington.

Foerster Henry, motorman Ft. W E Ry Co, res 579 E Washington.

Fogle, see Vogel.

Foley Annie, bds 236 W Jefferson.

Foley Bartholomew, finisher Ft Wayne Organ Co, bds 176 Greeley.

Foley Bertha C, bds 28 Poplar.

Foley Cecilia C, prin McCulloch School, bds 236 W Jefferson.

Foley George S, finisher Ft Wayne Organ Ce, res 28 Poplar.

Foley Jennie, clk Geo DeWald & Co, bds 236 W Jefferson.

Foley Jeremiah, laborer, bds 176 Greely.

Foley John, watchman, res 236 W Jefferson.

Foley John W, carpenter, res 101 Barr.

Foley Laura M, bds 101 Barr.

Foley Mary (wid Jeremiah), res 176 Greeley.

Foley Matthew, laborer, bds 176 Greeley.

Foley Thomas J, tel opr Penn Co, bds 236 W Jefferson.

Foley Timothy, wiper Penn Co, res 24 Poplar.

Foley Timothy, lab N Y, C & St L R R, res 176 Greeley.

Foley Timothy P, boilermkr Bass F & M Wks, bds 20 Murray.

Foley Timothy S, varnisher, bds 28 Poplar.

Foley Wm, laborer, bds 176 Greeley.

Folkening, see Volkening.

Folkner, see Falconer.

Follett Lynn D, removed to Chicago, Ill.

Folmer, see also Vollmer.

Folsing, see Fahlsing.

Folz, see Volz.

Foncannon Oliver P, paperhanger, res s s Wagner 1 e of Spy Run av.

Foncannon Oliver P, timber buyer. res w s Glasgow av 5 s of E Washington.
Fonderwell Minnie, cook The Wayne.
Fonner John B, stenogr Morris, Bell, Barrett & Morris, res 87 W Jefferson.
Foohey Hannah E, bds 60 Brackenridge.
Foohey John M, clerk, bds 60 Brackenridge.
Foohey Maggie. opr S M Foster, bds 60 Brackenridge.
Foohey Michael J, clerk, bds 60 Brackenridge,
Foohey Timothy, res 60 Brackenridge.
Foohey Timothy jr, clerk, bds 60 Brackenridge.
Foote Mrs Helen M, res 118 Fulton.
Forbing Frank, lather, bds 159 Hanna.
Forbing Harry, condr Ft W E Ry Co, bds 159 Hanna.
Forbing John, real estate, 28 Bank Blk, res 385 Hanna.
Forbing Mrs Martha, res 159 Hanna.
Forche August. carpenter, rms 188 Calhoun.
Forche Joseph carp L E & W R R, res 5 Emily.
Ford Andrew J, engr Penn Co, res 76 E Williams.
Ford James E, molder Bass F & M Wks, bds 216 E Wayne.
Ford John J, special delivery P O, bds 216 E Wayne.
Ford Wm E (col'd), barber, 230 Lafayette, res same.
Ford Wm O, foreman S M Foster, res 216 E Wayne.
Fordham Carrie (wid Edward), housekeeper 45 Locust.
Fordham Louis, brickmaker, res 556 Hanna.
Fordney George M, molder Bass F & M Wks, res 197 Montgomery.
Forrer Emma, teacher School for Feeble-Minded Youth.
Forrest Joseph E. laborer, res 55 W Williams.
Fortmeyer Mary, dressmaker, bds 113 Brackenridge.
Fortriede Louis, shoes, 19 Calhoun. res 212 E Wayne.
Fort Wayne Artificial Ice and Cold Storage Co, Ronald T Mc Donald Pres, Cecilius R Higgins Sec and Treas, Ice Manufacturers, n e cor Wells and Lake Shore Ry. Tel 87 and 469.
Fort Wayne Beef Co, B F Rousseau Mngr, Receivers of Swifts' Chicago Dressed Beef, Mutton, Lamb, Veal, Pork and Provisions, 4 and 6 Calhoun. Tel 281.
Fort Wayne Board of Underwriters, C E Graves, sec and treas, 28 Bass Blk.
Fort Wayne Book Bindery (Mennonite Book Concern), J Welty Mngr, 25 Court. (*See left bottom lines.*)

Fort Wayne Brass Works, A Hattersley & Sons Proprs, 48 E Main. (*See embossed line front cover.*)

Fort Wayne Business College, G W Lahr pres, Calhoun n w cor Berry.

Fort Wayne Catholic Circulating Library and Association, n e cor Calhoun and Lewis.

Fort Wayne City Band, 70 Calhoun, prof Philip Keinz leader

Fort Wayne, Cincinnati & Louisville R R, *see* Lake Erie & Western R R.

Fort Wayne City Bill Posting Co, C B Woodworth mngr, 1 New Aveline House Blk. Tel 16.

Fort Wayne City Directory, John Andrews Manager, 38 Bass Blk.

Fort Wayne Club The, S R Alden Pres, James H Fry Sec, J W White Treas, 71 and 73 Harrison. Tel 475.

Fort Wayne College of Medicine, C B Stemen dean, W W Barnett sec, 160 W Superior. Tel 449.

Fort Wayne Commercial Exchange, G E Bursley pres, W L Carnahan vice-pres, F L Smock sec, E H McDonald treas, 29 and 30 Bass Blk. Tel 528.

Fort Wayne Conservatory of Music, Charles F W Meyer Director, Bank Blk.

Fort Wayne Cycling Club, Frank S Lightfoot pres, F W Urbahns sec, A L Randall treas, 54 W Wayne.

Fort Wayne Dispatch, James Mitchell propr, 88 Clinton.

Fort Wayne District Telegraph Company, R T McDonald Pres. Edward Gilmartin Vice-Pres, W P Breen Treas, C R Higgins Sec and Mngr, 15 W Columbia. Phones 233 and 240.

Fort Wayne Driving Club, H C Rockhill sec, 30 E Main.

Fort Wayne Electrical Construction Company, (P E Cox, Charles J Sosenheimer, Murray U Smith), Isolated Electric Light Plants, 176 Calhoun. Tel 219.

Fort Wayne Electric Corporation, R T McDonald Pres, C S Knight Vice-Pres, Charles C Miller Sec and Treas, Broadway s e cor G R & I R R. Tel 57.

Fort Wayne Electric Railway Company, J H Bass Pres, M S Robison Vice-Pres and Treas, J M Barrett Sec, L D McNutt Supt, Office Main s e cor Court, Power House cor Clinton and Chestnut. Tel 229.

Fort Wayne Freie Presse, Fort Wayne Freie Presse Co publrs, 24 Clinton. Tel 233.

Fort Wayne Freie Presse Company, Publishers of Fort Wayne Freie Presse, Carl Schilling Pres, Louis F Curdes Sec, John Schilling Treas, Carl Sauer Mngr, 24 Clinton. Tel 522.

Fort Wayne Furniture Co, D N Foster Pres, P A Randall Vice-Pres, W E Mossman Sec, E B Caldwell, Treas and Manager, Folding Bed Manufacturers, e end Columbia. Tel 252.

Fort Wayne Gas Co, Charles F Dieterich Pres (N Y), Henry C Paul, Asst to Pres, E J Jerzinanowski Vice-Pres (N Y), A B Proal, Treas (N Y), F E W Scheimann Sec, G Max Hofmann Supt, 50 Clinton and 9 Court. Tel 107.

Fort Wayne Gazette, Daily and Weekly, N R Leonard Propr, 41 E Berry. Tel 36.

Fort Wayne Glove and Mitten Co, S Freiburger & Bro props, 35 E Columbia.

Fort Wayne Grays' Armory, Anderson Hall, n w cor Broadway and Jefferson.

Fort Wayne Harrison Telephone Co, George P Haywood Pres, E G Leysenski Vice-pres, W P Breen Treas, E H Andrews Sec, I N Wood Promoter, White Bank Bldg.

Fort Wayne Iron Works, Mnfrs of Engines, Boilers and Band Saw Mills, Office and Works, s e cor Superior and Harrison. Tel 82.

Fort Wayne Journal (daily), The Journal Co Proprs, 30 E Main. Tel 18.

Fort Wayne Land & Improvement Co, R T McDonald pres, pres, D N Foster vice-pres, Aaron B Howey sec, Geo W Pixley treas, 3 and 4 Pixley & Long Bldg. Tel 216.

Fort Wayne Loan and Collecting Agency, J F Schell & Co Proprs, 21 and 22 Pixley & Long Bldg. (See add in classified collecting agts.)

Fort Wayne Lumber Co, (Augustus C Beaver, Montgomey G Beaver, Volney Parks), Dealers in Pine Lumber, Lath and Shingles, Mouldings, Sash, Doors and Blinds, Yard and Office, 391 Broadway. Tel 224.

Fort Wayne Mercantile Accident Association, Organized December, 1892, George A Durfee Pres, Charles F Falk, Vice-Pres, W S Buck Sec and Treas, 3 Arcade. (See back cover and page 4.)

258   R. L. POLK & CO.'s

Fort Wayne Music Co (Harry A Achenbach), Music and Musical Instruments, 34 E Berry.

Fort Wayne News (daily and weekly), W D Page Propr, n w cor Washington and Clinton. Tel 120,

Fort Wayne Newspaper Union (eastern branch Chicago Newspaper Union), John E Cramer pres, George A Strong sec and treas, Charles D Tillo resident mngr, 76–80 Clinton. Tel 137.

Fort Wayne Omnibus, Baggage and Carriage Line, Powers & Barnett proprs, 12–24 E Wayne. Tel 26.

Fort Wayne Organ Co, Stephen B Bond pres, Arthur S Bond sec, treas and supt, office and factory Fairfield av n e cor Organ. Tel 59.

Fort Wayne Pneumatic Novelty and Model Works, Henry C Miller Manager, Experimental work in all its branches, Pneumatic Music Leaf Turner a Specialty, 139 John.

Fort Wayne Postal Telegraph Co, R T McDonald Pres, Edward Gilmartin Vice-Pres, W P Breen Treas, C R Higgins Sec, C E Stetler Mngr, 15 W Columbia. 'Phones 233 and 240.

Fort Wayne Power Co, Jacob S Goshorn supt, w s Spy Run av 2 n of Burgess.

Fort Wayne Relief Union, Mrs E H McDonald pres, Miss Helen Moffat sec and supt, 144 Pritchard.

Fort Wayne Rifle Armory, Randall Hall.

Fort Wayne Roofing and Paving Co, 152 W Main. Tel 316.

Ft Wayne Sængerbund Hall (new building), Paul Richter pres, August Langhorst sec, Gottlieb Unger treas, 51 and 53 W Main.

Fort Wayne Safety Valve Works, E B Kunkle & Co proprs, 87 Barr.

Fort Wayne Sentinel (Daily and Weekly), A K Hackett Propr. 107 Calhoun. Tel, Counting-Rooms 173, Editorial Rooms 650.

Fort Wayne Steam Laundry, W B Phillips Propr, 46 W Main. (*See left side lines.*)

Fort Wayne Steam Stone Works, Keller & Braun Proprs, 84-98 Pearl. Tel 116. (*See right bottom lines.*)

Fort Wayne Variable Saw Mill Feed Co, Henry C Zollinger pres & sec, Louis C Zollinger, treas, Walter G Burns, genl mngr, Charles Bowman supt, 15 and 17 E Superior.

Fort Wayne Water Works, office City Hall.

Fort Wayne Weekly Journal, The Journal Co Props, 30 E Main. Tel 18.

Foskett John, mach Ft Wayne Furn Co, bds 34 W Superior.

Fosler Christian, section foreman, res 76 Taylor.

Fosler Christina M, bds 76 Taylor.

Fosler Edith P, bds 76 Taylor.

Fosler Frank M, fireman, bds 76 Taylor.

Fosler George, condr Wabash R R, bds 76 Taylor.

Fosler Mamie, clk Lincoln Tea Co, bds 76 Taylor.

Fosler Mary J, packer, bds 76 Taylor.

Foss Frederick H, farmer Institution farm.

Foster, *see also Foerster.*

Foster Almond, car bldr Penn Co, rms 361 Lafayette.

Foster Andrew, Merchant Tailor, 15 W Wayne, res 150 Griffith. (*See left top lines.*)

Foster Blk, 15 and 17 Court.

Foster Catherine P, clerk, bds 292 E Lewis.

Foster David N, pres D N Foster Furniture Co, Ft Wayne Furniture Co and Ft Wayne Land and Improvement Co, res 98 E Berry.

Foster D N Furniture Co, David N Foster Pres, L G Hamilton Sec, Wm J Kettler Treas, Furniture and Carpets, 11 and 13 Court. Tel 235.

Foster Frederick W, clk Penn Co, bds 292 E Lewis.

Foster Harriet S (wid Dr John L), bds 98 E Berry.

Foster Henry A, train despatcher Penn Co, res 172 Columbia av.

Foster James A, clk Hoosier Mnfg Co, bds 172 Columbia av.

Foster John, section hd Penn Co, bds 41 Nirdlinger av.

Foster Dr John L, died May 25th, 1894.

Foster Lydia T (wid Wm T), res 292 E Lewis.

Foster Nathaniel H, clk Penn Co, bds 292 E Lewis.

Foster Sadie, bds 292 E Lewis.

Foster Samuel M, shirt waist mnfr, n end Lafayette, res 96 E Berry. Tel 428.

Foulke Frank E, foreman Ft Wayne Furn Co, res 3 Duryea.

Foulkes Albert G, policeman, bds 83 E Berry.

Foulks George H, fireman Penn Co, res 19 Baker.

Foulks Morgan, motorman Ft W E Ry Co, bds 53 Baker.

Fournier Frank A, laborer, res 13 Purman.

Fournier Frank E, molder Bass F & M Wks, res 89 Lasselle.

Fournier Joseph P, molder bds 13 Purman.

Fournier Louis J, laborer, bds 13 Purman.

Fournier Lucy A, bds 13 Purman.

Fousnought George A, helper, res 365½ E Lewis.

Foust, see also Faust.

Foust Effie, domestic 40 McClellan.

Foust Henry, lab Standard Wheel Co, bds 186 Harmer.

Foust Henry, traveling agt, res 165 Columbia av.

Foust J Elton, clk John Langard, res w s Spy Run av 4 n of bridge.

Foust Peter, laborer, res 84 Chicago.

Foust Peter, laborer, res 129 Oliver.

Fowler Benjamin E, watchman Muncie crossing, res 1 e of same.

Fowler Clara, bds 40 E Washington.

Fowler George S, railroad supplies, res 234 W Berry.

Fowler Harriet W, bds 234 W Berry.

Fowler Harry, switchman, bds 36 Hayden.

Fowler Wm A, janitor School for Feeble Minded Youth, res n s Hicksville State rd, 2 w of St Joe Gravel rd.

Fowles John W, Importer and Merchant Tailor, Good Fit and Good Goods at Reasonable Prices, 64 Barr, res same. (*See left side lines.*)

Fox, *see also Fuchs.*

Fox Albert C, gardener, res n s Miller 1 w of Brooklyn av.

Fox Andrew J, fireman G R & I R R, res 55 E De Wald.

Fox August L, with Fox br U S Baking Co, res 71 Walnut. Tel 515.

Fox Bakery U S Baking Co, Louis Fox, Mngr, Cracker and Candy Mnfrs, 145–149 Calhoun. Tel 183.

Fox Catherine, opr S M Foster, bds 495 E Washington.

Fox Catherine J, clk M Frank & Co, bds 85 Brackenridge.

Fox Celia S (wid Cicero), dressmaker, bds 180 E Lewis

Fox Charles G, plumber, 80 Taylor, res same.

Fox Charlotte A, bds 112 Van Buren.

Fox Clemens A, clerk, bds 46 W Superior.

Fox Edward S, helper Penn Co, bds 85 Brackenridge.

Fox Elsworth, mach Ft Wayne Electric Corp, bds 112 Van Buren.

Fox Frank E, mach Penn Co, res 369 Calhoun.

Fox George T, bookkeeper. bds 71 Walnut.

Fox Gilbert L, driver Adams Ex Co, res 43 W Lewis.

Fox Henry, wagonmkr Olds Wagon Wks, res w s Walton av 6 s of Pontiac.

Fox Henry A, express, res 140 Howell.

Fox Hiram, res 43 W Lewis.

Fox James J, res 85 Brackenridge.

Fox James T, machinist, bds 85 Brackenridge.

Fox Jehiel. conductor. res 514 Broadway.

Fox John R, mach S F Bowser & Co, res 112 Van Buren.

Fox Joseph H, clk J V Fox, bds 46 W Superior.

Fox Joseph V, restaurant 25 E Main, res 46 W Superior.

Fox Josephine, opr S M Foster, bds 85 Brackenridge.

Fox Katie E (wid John J), bds 24 Charles.

Fox Lewis, mngr Fox Bakery, U S Baking Co, res 102 W Wayne. Tel 212.

Fox Louis, student, bds 112 Van Buren.

Fox Martin L, painter, res 62 Elm

Fox Mary A, clerk. bds 85 Brackenridge.

Fox Michael K, fireman Penn Co, rms 36 Baker.

Fox Minnie M, bds 112 Van Buren.

Fox Mollie A, clk A Mergentheim, bds 85 Brackenridge.

Fox Nellie M, opr S M Foster, bds 85 Brackenridge.

Fox Robert, bds 102 W Wayne.

Fox Roe, bds 102 W Wayne.
Fox Walter E, mach Western Gas Const Co, bds 112 Van Buren.
Fox Wm R, bds 127 W Wayne.
Fox Wm W, grocer 325 W Main. res 327 same.
Foxhuber, *see Fuchsber.*
Foxon John, opr Wayne Knitting Mills, bds 12 Park av.
Fraikin John J, mach Bass F & M Wks, bds 144 Wallace.
Fraikin Oscar J, machinist, res 144 Wallace.
Fraine, *see also Frane.*
Fraine John, helper Penn Co, bds 48 Charles.
Fraine Prosper C, plasterer, 48 Charles, res same.
France, *see also Franz.*
France Abraham, transfer agt, res 110 Shawnee av.
France Addie, student, bds 39 Duck.
France Amasa S, teamster, res w 3 Home 2 n of P. F W & C Ry.
France Belle, bds 110 Shawnee av.
France Earl, bds 39 Duck.
France Elizabeth A, res 39 Duck.
France Frank E, bartender The Randall, bds same.
France George, res 39 Duck.
France Harry F, justice of the peace, 13 E Main, res 600 Calhoun.
France James E K (Colerick & France), res 496 Harrison.
France Jesse W, trucker Wabash R R, bds 110 Shawnee av
France Joseph S, carpenter, res 16 Purman.
France Lulu, bds 39 Duck.
France Mace S, section hd Penn Co, res w s Home 2 n of Wayne Trace.
France Phillip L, mach Penn Co, res 83 Home av.
France Wm, driver, res 247 E Washington.
France Wm N, lab Hoffman Bros, bds 39 Duck.
France Wm O, laborer, res 247 E Washington.
Francis Wm H, dining car conductor, rms 331 Calhoun.
Frane, *see also Fraine.*
Frane Charles, helper Bass F & M Wks, bds 30 Lasselle.
Frane Joseph, mach hd Anthony Wayne Mnfg Co, rms 224 Francis.
Frane Margaret (wid Xavier), res 371 Lafayette.
Frane Pauline, bds 371 Lafayette.
Frank Ellen (wid Francis J), res 142 E Wayne.
Frank George A, train dispatcher Penn Co, res 60 W De Wald.
Frank George W, carpenter, bds 142 E Wayne.

Frank Henry W, coachman, res rear 107 W Berry.
Frank John T, fireman, rms 429 W Main.
Frank Josephine, tailoress, bds 60 W De Wald.
Frank Marx (M Frank & Co), res 82 W Washington.
Frank Mendel, Grocer, Meat Market, Flour and Feed, 208 Hanna and 45 Hough. res 206 Hanna.
Frank Minnie, bds 82 W Washington.
Frank M & Co (Marx and Theodore Frank), Dry Goods and Carpets, 60 Calhoun. Tel 407.
Frank R y, bkkpr M Frank, bds 206 Hanna.
Frank Theodore (M Frank & Co), res 192 W Wayne.
Frank Wm T, painter, bds 142 E Wayne.
Franke August H, asst engr Ft Wayne Water Wks, res 154 N Clinton.
Franke Charles (Wiegmann & Franke), res 129 Taylor.
Franke Charles, shoemkr. L P Huser, res 206 W Jefferson.
Franke Christian (Christian Franke & Co), res 364 E Lewis.
Franke Christian & Co (Christian Franke, Charles Rodenbeck, Herman Doenges), carpenters 364 E Lewis.
Franke Edward G, bkkpr C L Centlivre Brewing Co, res 153 Spy Run av.
Franke Elizabeth, opr Hoosier Mnfg Co, bds 22 Wiebke.
Franke Frederick, rag peddler, res 22 Wiebke.
Franke Frederick jr, horse trader, bds 8 Wiebke.
Franke Henry, laborer, res 19 Barthold.
Franke Henry, laborer, bds 22 Wiebke.
Franke Henry jr, cabinetmaker, bds 19 Barthold.
Franke Henry C (H C Franke & Son), res 408 E Washington.
Franke Henry F (H C Franke & Son), bds 408 E Washington.
Franke H C & Son (Henry C and Henry F), Practical Sanitary Plumbers, Steam and Gas Fitters, 68 Barr. (*See p 111*).
Franke H Franz, carpenter, 43 Hugh, res 362 E Lewis.
Franke John B; sec and treas The B W Skelton Co, res 276 W Washington.
Franke John H. mach Penn Co, res 366 Hanna.
Franke John H jr, laborer Penn Co, bds 366 Hanna.
Franke Julian F, clk The Dreibelbiss Abstract of Title Co, bds 366 Hanna.
Franke Maria L, bds 19 Barthold.
Franke Wm H, car bldr Penn Co, res 152 Eliza.
Frankel Louis (Heller & Frankel), res 187 W Berry.
Frankenstein Max L, druggist, 120 Barr, res same. Tel 100

Frankhauser Frederick, appr Penn Co, bds 22 Euclid av.

Franking Anthony, bds 134 Madison.

Franking Margaret (wid Bernard), res 134 Madison.

Franklin Hotel, Mendel Frank propr, 43 Hough.

Franklin School, n e cor Franklin av and Huffman.

Franks August, mngr C Entemann, res 67 Maumee rd.

Franks Minnie, domestic 324 W Washington.

Franz, *see also France.*

Franz Charles W, helper Kerr Murray Mnfg Co, bds Windsor Hotel.

Franz George. cigarmkr F J Gruber, res 88 Dawson.

Franz Mary A (wid George), propr Windsor Hotel, res 302 Calhoun.

Franz Wm P, bds Windsor Hotel.

Frary Frank, mach Wabash R R, res 19 Brooklyn av.

Frase Beniah F, electrician, bds 70 W 3d.

Frase H Washington, fireman N Y, C & St L R R, bds 70 W 3d.

Frase Lucinda O, opr Troy Steam Laundry, bds 70 W 3d.

Frase Mary E (wid Charles), res 70 W 3d.

Frase Mary S, bds 70 W 3d.

Frase Sarah E, opr Troy Steam Laundry, bds 70 W 3d.

Fratenburgh Abraham A, trimmer Jenney E L & P Co, res 5 Riverside av.

Fratenburgh Frederick, bds 4 Emily.

Frauenfelder Clara N, milliner, bds n e cor Hanna and Eckart lane.

Frauenfelder Edward, mach hd Ft Wayne Organ Co, bds n e cor Hanna and Eckart lane.

Frauenfelder Jacob, car bldr Penn Co, res n e cor Hanna and Eckart lane.

Frauenfelder Wm H, cabtmkr Ft Wayne Organ Co, bds n e cor Hanna and Eckart lane.

Frech Christina (wid Henry), res 205 Broadway.

Frech Henry, laborer, res 9 Romy av,

Frech Wm, carp L Rastetter & Son, bds 205 Broadway.

Frecke Augusta (wid Henry), res 175 Lafayette.

Frederick Christine (Widow Jacob), Propr Railroad Restaurant, 264 and 266 Calhoun, res same. (*See page 95.*)

Frederick John W, machinist, res 415 Lafayette.

Frederick Samuel. mach Ind Mach Wks, res 164 Wells.

Frederick Wm R, Mngr Mrs C Frederick, res 266 Calhoun.

Frederickson Annie B, bds 44 Hoagland av.

Frederickson Catherine (wid Jacob), res 44 Hoagland av.
Frederickson Jennie, waitress Arlington Hotel.
Frederickson Mary E, bds 44 Hoagland av.
Frederickson Sarah J, bds 44 Hoagland av.
Frederickson Wm, motorman, res 61 Grant av.
Fredrick John, fireman, res 100 N Harrison.
Free Methodist Church, E Creighton av bet Thomas and Holton av.
Freeby Mrs Agnes, dressmkr 317 Harrison, res same.
Freeby George H B, clk Wabash R R, res 317 Harrison.
Freeman Bertha, music teacher, bds w s Spy Run av 1 n of Elizabeth.
Freeman Elizabeth L, teacher, bds 139 W Main.
Freeman Henry R, teller First Nat Bank, res w s Spy Run av 1 n of Elizabeth.
Freeman Julia R (wid Newton B) res w s Spy Run av 1 n of Elizabeth.
Freeman Mary E, principal Franklin School, bds w s Spy Run av 1 n of Elizabeth.
Freeman Mary M, janitress, res 127 Harrison.
Freer Jennie (wid John W), res 19 Cass.
Freer Laura A, dressmaker 19 Cass, res same.
Freese, see also Freize.
Freese August, Dealer in Wines and Liquors 57 E Main, res 178 W Creighton av. Tel 174. (*See left top lines.*)
Freese Charles F (Freese & Ranke), res 177 W Washington.
Freese Frederick, bds 182 Metz.
Freese Frederick, grocer, 405 E Washington, res 403 same.
Freese Sophia A (wid Wm), bds 177 W Washington.
Freese Wm, teamster Kerr Murray Mnfg Co, res 182 Metz
Freese Wm A, miller, bds 177 W Washington.
Freese & Ranke (Charles F Freese, Wm F Ranke jr), Druggists, 88 Calhoun.
Freiburger Anthony C, mach E B Kunkle & Co, bds 103 Gay
Freiburger Bernhard, foreman J B White, res 28 Charles.
Freiburger Gette (wid Simon), res 95 W Berry.
Freiburger Henry, helper, bds 28 Charles.
Freiburger Herman (S Freiburger & Bro), bds 91 W Berry
Freiburger Ignatius, foreman J B White, res 152 W Jefferson.
Freiburger Joseph (S Freiburger & Bro), bds 91 W Berry.
Freiburger Joseph J (Freiburger & Suelzer), res 103 Gay.
Freiburger Leopold (S Freiburger & Bro), res 91 W Berry
Freiburger Louis I, clk Wm Hahn & Co, bds 28 Charles.

Freiburger Peter F, driver Hook and Ladder Co No 1, res 31 Barr.

Freiburger Simon, died July 8, 1894.

Freiburger S & Bro (Leopold, Herman and Joseph), leather and findings and proprs Ft Wayne Glove and Mitten Co, 35 E Columbia.

Freiburger & Suelzer (Joseph J Freiburger, John Suelzer), Proprs South Side Hardware Co, 364 Calhoun.

Freimuth, see also Friemuth.

Freimuth August, lab Ft Wayne Electric Corp, res 83 Broadway.

Freinstein George, clk Wm Hahn & Co, res 217 E Washington.

Freistroffer Building, 41 W Main.

Freistroffer Henry, horseshoer, 41 W Main, res same.

Freistroffer Simon, real estate, 5-6 Bank Blk, res 5 Liberty

Freitag, see also Friday.

Freitag August, laborer, res 142 South Wayne av.

Freitag Lottie E, bds 142 South Wayne av.

Freitag Wm H. clerk, bds 142 South Wayne av.

Freize, see also Freese.

Freize John, driver City Trucking Co, bds 154 Harrison.

Fremion August, brickmkr, bds 510 Hanna.

Fremion Frank (Fremion & Vollmer), res 17 Harrison.

Fremion John, laborer, res s s Wiebke 6 e of Lafayette.

Fremion Joseph, res 510 Hanna.

Fremion Joseph E, brickmkr. res 575 Hanna.

Fremion & Vollmer (Frank Fremion, Frederick C Vollmer), mineral water bottlers, 9 Harrison.

French Albert S, collector Singer Mnfg Co, res 31 Pixley & Long Bldg.

French Ella M, bds 134 Harrison.

French Evangella (wid Charles G), res 134 Harrison.

French George E, printer The Journal, bds 65 W Superior

French Maria C (wid R Morgan), bds 148 E Washington.

French Mary J (wid Samuel C), res 65 W Superior.

French Nellie B, asst dentist S B Brown, bds 65 W Superior.

Frenking Anthony, laborer, res 134 Madison.

Frenking Margaret (wid Bernard), bds 134 Madison.

Frentzel John A N, picture frames, 191 Calhoun, res 14 Chicago.

Freund Wm H, asst supt City Parks, res 33 E 3d.

Frey, see also Fry.

Frey George, cook C Entemann, res 91 Maumee rd.
Fricke Mrs Augusta, res 175 Lafayette.
Fricke Christian D, bds 91 Huestis av.
Fricke Frederick W, carpenter, res 91 Huestis av.
Fricke Joseph, gardener, res Griswold av n w cor Parnell.
Fricke Mary L, domestic 137 E Washington.
Fricke Richard, physician, 9 E Wayne, res same.   Tel 358.
Friday, *see also Freitag.*
Friday August L, truckman, bds 1 Brandriff.
Friday Henry A, machinist, bds 1 Brandriff.
Friday Louis A, teamster, bds 1 Brandriff.
Friday Sophia E (wid Henry A), res 1 Brandriff.
Fridley Louis F, trucker Wabash R R, res 70 Gay.
Friederich, *see Frederick.*
Friedlich Isaac (Mautner & Friedlich), res Milwaukee, Wis.
Friedline John W, miller, res 493 E Wayne.
Friedman Charles, clk Meyer Bros & Co, res s e cor
    Thomas and Maud.
Friedman Frank, molder Bass F & M Wks, res s e cor
    Thomas and Maud.
Friedman Lizzie, seamstress S M Foster, bds s w cor
    Fisher and Holton av.
Friedman Matthias, bds Frank Friedman.
Friedman Ralph A, driver A Copinus, bds Hoffmann House.
Friedman Wendelin, lab, res s w cor Fisher and Holton av.
Friemuth, *see also Freimuth.*
Friemuth Charles, boilermkr, res 152 High.
Friend Alfred I (A I & H Friend), bds 35 W Washington.
Friend A I & H (Alfred I & Henry), clothing, 62 and 64
    Calhoun.
Friend Helen V (wid Jonathan T), dressmaker, bds 248 St
    Mary's av.
Friend Henry (A I & H Friend), res 172 W Wayne.
Friend Isadore, specialist for cure of stuttering, room 3
    Tri-State Bldg, bds 35 W Washington.
Friend Jacob, clk A I & H Friend, res 35 W Washington
Friend Stella, bds 35 W Washington.
Friend Wm, actor, bds 35 W Washington.
Fries Charles W, blacksmith, res 10 Thomas.
Frisbie Rosa E, seamstress, bds s s Spring 1 w of St
    Mary's av.
Frisbie Mrs Susan, res s s Spring 1 w of St Mary's av.
Frisby Frank H, car bldr Penn Co, res 60 Miner.
Fritch Ralph, helper, bds 129½ W 3d.
Fritz August, carpenter, bds 60 Barthold.

Fritz Mary, domestic 79 Boone.
Froelick Charles F, res 66 Nelson.
Frohmuth Adolph G, removed to Chicago, Ill.
Frohmuth Gustav H, removed to Chicago, Ill.
Frohmuth Emma P M, bds 33 N Calhoun.
Frohmuth John, bds 31 Prince.
Frohmuth John jr, helper L E & W R R, res 33 N Calhoun.
Frohmuth John M F, res 95 Buchanan.
Frohmuth Mrs Mary, res 31 Prince.
Frohmuth Theodore, cigarmkr, bds 95 Buchanan.
Fronefield Edith, bds 28 W Superior.
Fronefield Reuben, res 28 W Superior.
Frost Benjamin, res 313 Calhoun.
Fruit House and Great Tea Depot, J B White, propr, 95–97 Calhoun and 8–12 E Wayne.
Fruth Henry, laborer, res 25 Clark.
Fry. *see also Frey.*
Fry Charles F, laborer, bds 52 John.
Fry Charles F, turner Standard Wheel Co, rms 27 Lillie.
Fry Charles J, clk Mossman, Yarnelle & Co, bds 61 Maud.
Fry Clara H, bds 37 E 3d.
Fry Frank J, bds 132 W Main.
Fry Henry W, teamster, res 256 E Washington.
Fry Jacob, truckman Penn Co, res 52 John.
Fry James H, chief clk Penn Co, bds Ft Wayne Club.
Fry James M, brakeman, res 53 Euclid av.
Fry John, helper Fleming Mnfg Co, res 1 Pape av.
Fry John N, waiter Fort Wayne Club, rms 56 E Wayne.
Fry J Louis, driver J H Welch, res 13 Duryea.
Fry Margaret (wid Joseph), boarding house, 32 Chicago.
Fry Mary, bds 256 E Washington.
Fry Mary (wid Jacob), bds 321 Harrison.
Fry Wm M, laborer, bds 256 E Washington.
Fry Jerome B, condr G R & I R R, res w s Harrison 1 s of Killea av.
Fryer Clarence E, bds 52 Hendricks.
Fryer Frank H, drugs, 83 Wells, res 88 same.
Fryer Lewis E, foreman Fort Wayne Electric Corp, res 52 Hendricks.
Frygy Deyb, clk Salem Bashara, rms 43½ E Columbia.
Fuchs, *see also Fox.*
Fuchs Albert, laborer, bds 100 Greely.
Fuchs Amelia, domestic, rms 104 E Main.
Fuchs Francis J, bds 13 Force.

Fuchs Frederick, laborer Weil Bros & Co, bds w s Walton av 5 s of Pontiac.

Fuchs George, laborer, res 167 E Jefferson.

Fuchs Michael, laborer, bds e s Smith 1 s of Pontiac.

Fuchs Rosina (wid Adam), bds 88 Hayden.

Fuchshuber Augustus F, died August 4th, 1894.

Fuchshuber Charles F, student, bds 100 W Williams.

Fuchshuber George M, coremkr Bass F & M Wks, res 224 Gladstone.

Fuchshuber G Philip, teamster P Quicksell, res 58 Pritchard.

Fuchshuber John L, watchman Penn Co, res 100 W Williams

Fuchshuber Margaret, domestic 83 Broadway.

Fuchshuber Matilda B, bds 100 W Williams.

Fuelber Anselm, city editor Indiana Staats Zeitung, res 23 E Creighton av.

Fuelling Frederick H, heater Bass F & M Wks, res 138 Eliza.

Fuelling Lissette E, bds 231 W Washington.

Fuelling Lisette M (wid Frederick), res 231 W Washington.

Fuhrman Wm C J, carpenter, res 50 W Leith.

Fulford James, mach hd Penn Co, res 224 Hugh.

Fuller Anna, domestic 68 W Berry.

Fuller Lena, bds 108 Buchanan.

Fuller Louise L (wid Job R), res N Calhoun opp jail.

Fuller Patrick F, condr G R & I R R, res 108 Buchanan.

Fullerton Bauer, fireman N Y, C & St Louis R R, bds 335 W Main.

Fullgraben Emil, clerk, bds 26 Wall.

Fullmer Charles L, molder Bass F & M Wks, res 106 Gay

Fulton Ancel M, fireman Hoffman Bros, res 188 W Superior

Fulton Charles W, Livery and Boarding Stable, 18 W Wayne, res 36 same. Tel 53.

Fulton David R, driver W B Phillips, bds 36 W Wayne.

Fulton James N, prin Ft Wayne Bus Coll, rms 121 Harrison.

Funk Jacob, dairy, Maysville rd e of city limits, res same.

Funk Michael, brewer C L Centlivre Brewing Co, res 24 Centlivre av.

Furian Frederick, lab Bass F & M Wks, res 56 Hayden.

Furian Wm, candymkr Fox br U S Bkg Co, bds 71 Ohio.

Furlong Ella M, seamstress, bds 213 Madison.

Furlong George H, brakeman N Y, C & St L R R, bds 31 Boone.

18

Furlong James, fireman N Y, C & St L R R, rms 368 W Main.
Furlong John W, helper, bds 408 Calhoun.
Furlong Thomas A, shoemkr J W Graham, bds 17 Grand.
Furney Dora, domestic 283 W Berry.
Furney Henry S, driver City Trucking Co, res 157 Harrison.
Furste Alice M C, clk People's Store, bds 73 E Berry.
Furste Elizabeth B (wid Francis L), res 73 E Berry.
Furste George A, clk Pfeiffer & Rousseau, res 209 E Wayne.
Furste John H, clerk, bds 73 E Berry.
Furste Mary C A, bkkpr Ohnhaus & Monahan, res 73 E Berry.
Furthmiller Albert, car rpr Penn Co, res 176 Hanna.
Furthmiller Freeman, lab Penn Co, res 110 Buchanan
Futter Charles T, barber D R Benninghoff, res 416 Clinton.
Futter Joseph O, barber Edward Schele, bds 85 Baker.
Futter Martin, finisher, res 85 Baker.

G

Gable, see also Goebel.
Gable Charles F, lab Bond Cereal Mills, bds 169 John.
Gable George F, machinist, bds 74 Lillie.
Gable Georgie, bds 40 Madison.
Gable Henry A, clk M W Fay, bds 74 Lillie.
Gable Mary (wid Christian), res 40 Madison.
Gable Peter, farmer, res Lake av, e of city limits.
Gable Philip, mach Bass F & M Wks, res 74 Lillie.
Gable Siebert, fireman Penn Co, res 137 Force.
Gaddis Margaret A (wid James), res 45 Grand.
Gaertner Bernhard H, teacher St John's Lutheran School, bds 25 W Washington.
Gaetje John, res 92 Montgomery.
Gaff Ella, clk W F Geller, bds 98 Broadway.
Gaffney Edward F, fireman, bds 263 Webster.
Gaffney Frank C S, clk J B White, bds 42 W Williams.
Gaffney Kate A, bds 42 W Williams.
Gaffney Mamie A, bds 263 Webster.
Gaffney Margaret E, clk Root & Co, bds 263 Webster.
Gffney Mary (wid Edward), res 263 Webster.
Gaffney Mary G, clk People's Store, bds 263 Webster.
Gaffney Sadie E, bds 42 W Williams.
Gaffney Wm, clk J B White, res 42 W Williams.

Gage Joseph E, broommaker R Gage, bds 320 W Main.
Gage Robert, broommaker, 318 W Main, res 320 same.
Gaide Carl J W, watchmkr Trenkley & Scherzinger, res 26 W Wayne.
Gailey Ferdinand, carpenter, res 231 Force.
Gailey James, bds 32 E Leith.
Gailey Joseph A, truckman Penn Co, res 5 W Leith.
Gailey Lizzie, domestic 47 Douglas av.
Gailey Wm A, porter Adam's Ex Co, res 32 E Leith.
Gale Clara, bds 69 Columbia av.
Galer Chauncey D, cabtmkr Ft Wayne Furn Co, res 42 Wagner.
Gales Grace S (col'd), bds 23 Holman.
Gales Simon (col'd), laborer, res 23 Holman.
Gallagher Daniel, laborer, res 32 W Williams.
Gallagher Edward D, traveling agt, res 295 W Jefferson.
Gallagher James, clerk J B White, bds 32 W Williams.
Gallagher John, fireman, bds 32 W Williams.
Gallagher Wm, fireman G R & I R R, bds 32 W Williams.
Galland Edmund F, fireman Standard Wheel Co, bds 25 Lasselle.
Galland Henry, lab Penn Co, res 191 Hanna.
Galland Matilda, bds 191 Hanna.
Gallivan Thomas H, brakeman, bds Lake Shore Hotel.
Gallmeier Emma, domestic 54 E Wayne.
Gallmeier Ernest, res e s Force 2 n of 10th.
Gallmeier Ernest, carpenter, res 69 Maumee rd.
Gallmeier Frederick, carpenter, bds 136 Francis.
Gallmeier Frederick W, policeman, res 61 Maumee rd.
Gallmeier Louis, packer Olds' Wagon Works, res n e cor Force and 10th.
Gallmeier Louisa, bds 136 Francis.
Gallmeier Louisa, seamstress, bds e s Force 2 n of 10th.
Gallmeier Minnie, trimmer, bds e s Force 2 n of 10th.
Gallmeier Otto, clk H B Lahmeyer, bds 61 Maumee rd.
Gallmeier Sophie, seamstress, bds e s Force 2 n of 10th.
Gallmeier Wm, bds e s Force 2 n of 10th.
Gallmeier Wm, carpenter, res 136 Francis.
Gallmeier Wm F, coachman 301 Fairfield av.
Gallmeyer Conrad W, Flour and Feed 53 E Main, res 68 Organ av. Tel 373.
Gallmeyer Sophia, domestic 52 E Jefferson.
Galloway Bert W, driver City Trucking Co, bds 159 Harrison.
Gamble Mary A, domestic 85 Brackenridge.

272   R. L. POLK & CO.'S

Gamrath Charles F W, clk Miller Bros, bds 374 W Main.
Gamrath Hiesner, bds 374 W Main.
Gamrath Marie G, clk F Barrett & Co, bds 374 W Main.
Gamrath Wm, laborer, res 374 W Main.
Gangwer Emily (wid James), res 71 Boone.
Gannon George H, laborer, res 75 E Jefferson.
Gans Carrie, opr S M Foster, bds 42 High.
Gans Joseph, mach hd Penn Co, bds 42 High.
Gans Lizzie C, opr S M Foster, bds 42 High.
Gans Louis, res 42 High.
Gans Michael, apprentice Penn Co, bds 42 High.
Ganser August A, laborer, bds 66 W 5th.
Ganser F Joseph, mach, bds 66 W 5th.
Ganser Jacob, baker The Wayne, res 66 W 5th.
Ganth, see Genth.
Ganzer Stephen, grocer 254 E Lewis, res same.
Garard Manasseh G, miller Mayflower Milling Co, res 45 Wagner.
Gard Brookfield, Physician and Orificial Surgeon and Electro-Therapeutic Baths, 13 W Wayne, res same. Tel 245.
Gard Mrs Margaret C, res 27 Lillie.
Gardella Andreas, fruits, 234 Calhoun, res 88 Montgomery.
Gardella Jacomin, clk G Dondero, bds 16 Calhoun.
Gardner Anthony, molder Bass F & M Wks, bds 435 Hanna
Gardner Branson L, removed to Lynn, Ind.
Gardner DeMott C, foreman news room Ft Wayne News, res 309 Harrison.
Gardner Frances A (wid Frank), bds 144 Holman.
Gardner Frederick W, painter, res 35 Charles.
Gardner Harry R, agt Prudential Ins Co, bds 106 Barr.
Gardner Henry J, brakeman, res 155 Clay.
Gardner James, propr East Yard Hotel, res same.
Gardner James R, conductor, bds 155 Clay.
Gardner Maude E, bkkr A Bruder, bds 155 Clay.
Gardner Melvin R, lineman C U Tel Co, res 178 Oakland.
Gardner Rosa (col'd), bds 53 Elizabeth.
Gardt Henry, barber, 271 Hanna, bds Gottlieb Mueller.
Gardt Henry jr, removed to Cincinnati O.
Gardt Peter, laborer, bds 271 Hanna.
Gardt Stephen J, molder Bass F & M Wks, bds 271 Hanna.
Garlow George A, brakeman N Y, C & St L R R, rms 84 Boone.
Garman, see also Gorman.
Garman Howard L, bds Peter Gable.

Garman John W, jeweler, 203 Calhoun, res same.
Garmire Robert B, messenger Penn Co, bds 200 E Washington.
Garmire Sarah J (wid Jacob), res 200 E Washington.
Garrison Anna, bds n s New Haven av 4 w of Lumbard.
Garrison Annie W, waitress Grand Central Hotel.
Garrison C Lee, teacher School for Feeble-Minded Youth.
Garrison John H, painter, res n s New Haven av 5 e of Summer.
Garrison Major F, engr G R & I R R, bds 49 Baker.
Garrison Mary (wid Albert), res 18 Colerick.
Garrison Robert H, molder, bds n s New Haven av, 5 e of Summer.
Garta Emma (wid James), res 290 Maumee rd.
Garta John A, bds 290 Maumee rd.
Gartley Ada L, opr C U Tel Co, bds 150 Taber.
Gartley Bertie E, opr C U Tel Co, bds 150 Taber.
Garver Alfred L, helper, res 40 Bass.
Garver John E, removed to Chicago, Ill.
Garvey May F, bds 26 Douglas av.
Garvey Patrick H, watchman Penn Co, bds 26 Douglas av.
Gaske Frederick, tailor, bds 143 Buchanan.
Gaskell Robert W, fireman, bds 33 St Mary's av.
Gaskill Abijah M, helper L E & W R R, res 16 W 3d.
Gaskill Charles M, removed to Hartford City, Ind.
Gaskill Edward H, driver C J Ulmer, res 142 Erie.
Gaskill Frank C, laborer, bds 159 Huffman.
Gaskill Harrison W, lab L Diether & Bro, bds 1 Osage.
Gaskill Ira J, lab Penn Co, bds 68 W Jefferson.
Gaskill Kyle, vet surg, 5 Harrison, res 159 Huffman.
Gaskill Leonard M, lab Standard Wheel Co, res 69 McCulloch.
Gaskill Malcolm P, painter Penn Co, bds 67 Franklin av.
Gaskill Nehemiah O, laborer, res 175 St Mary's av.
Gaskill Wm, res 67 Franklin av.
Gaskill Wm L, helper Hoffman Bros, bds 213 W Superior
Gaskins Annette A, teacher Clay School, bds 188 W Creighton av.
Gaskins Catherine (wid Joseph), res 188 W Creighton av.
Gaskins Charles E, stampmkr Aldine Ptg House, bds 188 W Creighton av.
Gaskins Harry M, lab Penn Co, res 188 W Creighton av.
Gaskins Joseph E, collector Aldine Ptg House, bds 188 W Creighton av.

Gaskins Mary E, bds 188 W Creighton av.
Gaskins Maude A, student, bds 188 W Creighton av.
Gaspar Peter, laborer, res n e cor Lumbard and Chestnut.
Gassert Frederick J, flagman, bds 208 Smith.
Gassert Nicholas, helper Penn Co, res 130 Gay.
Gassert Nicholas jr, bds 130 Gay.
Gatchell U Grant, brakeman, res 24 Euclid.
Gates Abraham, res 326 Harrison.
Gates George, cigarmkr F J Gruber, bds 86 Barr.
Gates Horatio S, clerk Penn Co, res 57 W De Wald.
Gates Watt C, clk A Mergentheim, bds 153 Jackson.
Gates Wm H, engineer Penn Co, res 412 Clinton.
Gauntt Forest G, miller Mayflower Milling Co, res 404 Broadway.
Gauspohl Henry, helper, res 5 Oak.
Gavin Frank W, physician, 4 Tri-State Bldg, bds 311 E Wayne. Tel 188.
Gavin James A, janitor-in-chief Public Schools, res 311 E Wayne.
Gavin Robert, miller City Mills, res 8 Harmer.
Gawvehn August F, tailor J G Thieme & Son, res rear 144 Erie.
Gay Eliza R (wid Enos), bds Selina Barnum.
Gay John, grocer, res 151 Gay.
Gay Millard F, lab Penn Co, res 23 Euclid.
Gay Monroe W, clerk Ind Furn Co, res 105 E Main.
Gaylord Frank H, farmer, bds 265 Hanna.
Gaylord James E, rag buyer, res 67 Hayden.
Gaylord Meda, bds 156 Greeley.
Gaylord Rosa A, bds 265 Hanna.
Gaylord Sylvester, sawyer James Wilding, res 265 Hanna.
Geake Belle M, teacher Clay School, bds 293 W Jefferson.
Geake Charles H, apprentice Wm Geake, bds 142 W Jefferson.
Geake Clara E, res 293 W Jefferson.
Geake Edward C, stonecutter, bds 293 W Jefferson.
Geake Marina J, teacher Washington School, bds 293 W Jefferson.
Geake Maud A, clk F M Smaltz, bds 293 W Jefferson.
Geake Walter G H, stonecutter, bds 293 W Jefferson.
Geake Wm, Steam Stone Works and Dealer in Cut and Ornamental Stone, 76-82 Pearl, res 142 W Jefferson. Tel 94. (*See left bottom lines and page 81.*)
Geake Wm C, draughtsman, bds 142 W Jefferson.
Gearhart, *see also Gerhard.*

Gearhart Charles R, saw filer Hoffman Bros, bds 95 Putnam.
Gearhart Edward L, saw filer Hoffman Bros. bds 95 Putnam
Gearhart Wm S, res 95 Putnam.
Geary Charles, contractor, 192 Griffith, res same.
Geary Charles T, butcher E Rich, res 132 W Main.
Geary Edward, saloon, 192 Griffith, res same.
Geary Ellen, seamstress, rms 96 E Jefferson.
Geary Elizabeth, bds 132 W Main.
Geary John G, driver H P W Brinkroeger, bds 132 W Main.
Geary Lula, seamstress, bds 2 Brookside.
Geary Wm, horseshoer, 5 Harrison, res 230 High.
Gebele Adeline C, bds 57 W Berry.
Gebele Mary K, bds 67 Harrison.
Gebert Alfred, clk Hotel Arlington, bds same.
Gebert Frank (Ryan & Gebert), bds 107 E Columbia.
Gebert John L, fireman Penn Co, res 250 E Lewis.
Gebert Mrs Nellie, cook Hotel Arlington, bds same.
Gebfert Louis H, meats 100 W Main, res same.
Gebhard see also Gephardt.
Gebhard Caspar, gardener, res s s Miller 3 w of Brooklyn av.
Gebhard Charles W, molder, bds 25 Liberty.
Gebhard George, harnessmkr G H Kuntz, res 25 Liberty.
Gebhard Henry F, lab Penn Co, bds 166 Maumee rd.
Gebhard Theodore, candymaker, bds 172 Maumee rd.
Gebhard Wm, mason, res 172 Maumee rd.
Gebhard Wm F, mach Bass F & M Wks, res 98 Maumee rd.
Gebhardt David, lab, res s s French 9 w of Webster.
Gebhart Edward J, bartender C Muehlfeith, bds 40 Wells.
Gebhart Edward J, farmer, res 1½ m s of city limits.
Gebhart John, saloon s s Bluffton rd 1 w of County Poor Farm, res same.
Geerer Catherine (wid John J), res 49 W Jefferson.
Geerer Charles F, traveling agt, bds 49 W Jefferson.
Geerer Florence M, clk Miss E O Hanna, res 49 W Jefferson.
Geerer Susan, bds 49 W Jefferson.
Geerken Charles F, driver Globe Spice Mills, res 32 Eliza.
Geerken Ernest, janitor, res 52 E Pontiac.
Geerken Ethel G, bds 139 Holman.
Geerken Frederick C, caller G R & I R R, bds 38 Eliza.
Geerken Frederick H, mach Penn Co, res 38 Eliza.

Geerken Henry, boilermkr Penn Co, res 139 Holman.
Geerken Louisa (wid George), bds 80 Montgomery.
Geerken Louise D, bds 38 Eliza.
Geerken Ora M, bds 139 Holman.
Gehle Ferdinand, carpenter, res 336 Force.
Gehring Andrew J, foreman, res 206 W Creighton av.
Gehring Augusta, bds 206 W Creighton av.
Gehring Jacob C, appr Wabash R R, bds 72 Brackenridge.
Gehring Mary K, bds 206 W Creighton av.
Gehring Paul, mach Bass F & M Wks, res 73 Huestis av.
Gehring Wm F, cigarmkr F W Ropa, bds 206 W Creighton av.
Gehrke, see also Gerke.
Gehrke Louis G, foreman Pottlitzer Bros, res 105 W Williams.
Geib Louis F, conductor, bds 440 W Main.
Geiger Catherine (wid Herman), bds 265 E Wayne.
Geiger Charles J, bookbinder, 125 E Jefferson, res same.
Geiger Emilia, bds 125 E Jefferson.
Geiger Frank J (Geiger & Evans), res 51 W Williams.
Geiger Joseph, laborer, bds 100 Putnam.
Geiger Wm, agt Adams Express Co, res 31 Lavina.
Geiger Wm, laborer, bds 100 Putnam.
Geiger & Evans, (Frank J Geiger, Frank D Evans), saloon, 294 Calhoun.
Geisdorfer Ferdinand J, tanner, res Washington Township ½ miles n of Centlivre Brewery.
Geise Henry, car repr Penn Co, res 179 John.
Geiseking, see also Giesking.
Geiseking Dietrich, farmer, bds 129 Wells.
Geisman Charles, driver H J Ash, res 140 Force.
Geisman Elizabeth (wid Jacob), res 40 Locust.
Geisman George G, switchman Wabash R R, bds 40 Locust.
Geisman John, cutter Paragon Mnfg Co, bds 40 Locust.
Geisman Adolph, treveling agt, res 101 E Berry.
Geiss Julia (wid Jacob), res 78 Barr.
Geiss Louis J, insurance agt, res 106 W Superior.
Geistdoerfer Bros (Frederick C and Wm J), saloon, Hicksville State rd n w cor Malcolm av.
Geistdoerfer Frederick C (Geistdoerfer Bros), res Hicksville State rd n w cor Malcolm av.
Geistdoerfer Wm J (Geistdoerfer Bros), bds Hicksville State rd n w cor Malcolm av.
Geller Charles C (Ehrman & Geller), res 186 Griffith.

Geller George, helper Penn Co, res 126 Union.
Geller Gottlieb, saloon 53 W Main, res 53 Stophlet.
Geller Louisa, domestic 285 W Wayne.
Geller Louise. domestic 212 W Washington.
Geller Minnie M, removed to Huntington, Ind.
Geller Theodore, gardener, res 93 Huffman.
Geller Theodore H, baker J H Meyer, bds 93 Huffman.
Geller Wm F, Baker, 98 Broadway, res same. Tel 163.
Gellert Max E, sheet iron wkr Penn Co, res 513 Harrison.
Genth Michael, helper Bass F & M Wks, res 36 John.
George Ensign C, painter, res 49 E Main.
George Eugene C, bartender Russell George & Son, res 49 E Main.
George J Lewis, removed to Lansing, Mich.
George Milo L (Russell George & Son), res 49 E Main.
George Russell N (Russell George & Son), res 49 E Main.
George Russell & Son (Russell N and Milo S), saloon, 49 E Main.
Georiz, *see Goeriz*.
Gephart Carrie, domestic 50 W Washington.
Gepfert Christian, bds 377 Lafayette.
Gephardt, *see also Gebhardt*.
Gephardt Frank, lab Penn Co, res n s Pennsylvania av, 4 e of Wayne trace.
Gephart Valentine, gardener, res s s Baker av 2 e of Hillside av.
Gephart Wm, mach hd L Rastetter & Son, bds 5 Walnut.
Gerard, *see also Garard and Girard*.
Gerard Antoine, helper Penn Co, res 92 Lillie.
Gerard Benoit, brakeman, res 91 Lillie.
Gerard Catherine L, stenographer Ft Wayne Electric Corp, bds 92 Lillie.
Gerard George J, caller Penn Co. bds 92 Lillie.
Gerard Wm, mach Bass F & M Wks, res 353 E Lewis.
Gerard Wm E, removed to North Webster, Ind.
Gerardin Hippolyte, res 65 Pixley & Long Bldg.
Gerardin Joseph P, press feeder The Journal, bds 65 Pixley & Long Bldg.
Gerber Conrad, driver Geo De Wald & Co, res 114 Erie.
Gerberding Alma, bds 69 E Jefferson.
Gerberding August, sand, res 103 Erie.
Gerberding Bertha, bds 69 E Jefferson.
Gerberding Edward. teacher St Paul's German Lutheran School, res 69 E Jefferson.

Gerberding Henry A, contractor, 103 Erie, bds same.

Gerberding Rudolph, teamster, bds 103 Erie.

Gerberding Rudolph E (Gerberding & Miller), res 331 E Lewis.

Gerberding Walter R, clk Penn Co, rms 85 Monroe.

Gerberding & Miller (Rudolph E Gerberding, Frederick Miller), Druggists and Chemists, 120 Calhoun Tel 305.

Gerdes Henry, bricklayer, bds 88 Home av.

Gerdes Herman, laborer, res 6 Oak.

Gerdes Mathias, laborer, bds 6 Oak.

Gerding Bros (Herman C and John P), livery, 66 Harrison. Tel 187.

Gerding Herman C (Gerding Bros), res 10 McClellan.

Gerding John P (Gerding Bros), res 122 John.

Gerding Wm E (Gerding & Aumann Bros), res 365 Hanna.

Gerding & Aumann Bros (Wm E Gerding, Wm H and Henry F Aumann). Hardware, Furnaces and Tinware; Tin, Copper, and Sheet Iron Workers, also Slate, Asphalt and General Roofers, 115 Wallace, Tel 389. (See top edge and p 85).

Gerdom Henry E, yard foreman Bass F & M Wks, res 160 Smith.

Gerdom Herman W, molder, res 46 John.

Gerhard, see also Gearhart.

Gerhard Wm J, machinist, res 353 E Lewis.

Gering, see Gehring.

Gerke, see also Gehrke.

Gerke Anna W, bds 174 Hanna.

Gerke Charles W, bkkpr Ft W E Ry Co, res 15 Suttenfield

Gerke Christina (wid Henry), bds 15 Suttenfield.

Gerke Dora (wid Henry J), res 25 Summit.

Gerke Elizabeth, seamstress, bds 25 Summit.

Gerke Fred C, clerk H G Wiegmann, bds same.

Gerke Henry C, salesman Moellering Bros & Millard, res 174 Hanna.

Gerke Henry J, died May 26, 1894.

Gerke Henry W, clerk R M S, res 3 McClellan.

Gerke John F, carpenter, bds 25 Summit.

Gerke Louis, slater, bds 15 Suttenfield.

Gerke Louis H, clerk R M S, res 5 McClellan.

Gerke Louisa, ironer Troy Steam Laundry, bds 15 Suttenfield.

Gerke Sophia, opr Wayne Knitting Mills, bds 15 Suttenfield.

Gerlach Emil, lab Bass F & M Wks, res e s Winter 1 s of Pontiac.
Gerlach Gustave, painter Olds Wagon Works, bds Emil Gerbach.
Gerbach Mary E, domestic 407 Calhoun.
Germain Rosswell M, engineer N Y, C & St L R R, res Illinois rd beyond limits.
German Evangelical Church, n e cor Clinton and Holman.
German Lutheran Cemetery, see Concordia Cemetery.
German Lutheran Cemetery (St John's), Bluffton rd 3 miles s w of city.
German Lutheran School, cor W Washington and Van Buren
Gerow Teles D, grocer, 108 Fairfield av, res 25 Grand.
Gerrardot Mary, domestic 84 W Creighton av.
Gerson Leah, domestic 142 W Berry.
Gerwig Mary (wid Louis), res 18 Liberty.
Geske Frederick, tailor, bds 145 Buchanan.
Geske Henry, laborer, bds 145 Buchanan.
Gessler Albert F, butcher Fred Eckart Pkg Co, res 23 Madison.
Gessler Jennie, res e s Spy Run av 4 n of Baker av.
Getts Mrs Elmira, bds 168 W Jefferson.
Getty Annie F, tailoress, bds 27 Buchanan.
Getty Christopher, res 73 Buchanan.
Getty Frank, dairy, w s Hanna 10 s of Pontiac, res same.
Getty George, clk A Hirsh & Co, res 27 Buchanan.
Getty Lydia A, music teacher, res 180 W Jefferson.
Getty Mary, bookkeeper, bds 27 Buchanan.
Getty Philip J, driver Fox U S Baking Co, res 75 Buchanan
Getz, see also Goetz.
Getz Edward, rms 144 E Berry.
Getz John C, shoemaker, rear 184 Fairfield av, res cor Fulton and Jefferson.
Getz Joseph F, saloon, 3 E Main, res 93 W Jefferson.
Geye Francisca (wid Henry), bds 151 Hugh.
Geye Henry J, removed to Huntington, Ind.
Geye Herman F W, clerk, res 274 John.
Geye Pauline L M, domestic 137 W Wayne.
Gibford Angela W (wid Abram), bds 224 Lake av.
Gibford Catherine (wid David), bds 331 Calhoun.
Gibford Harry W, clk O B Fitch, res 224 Lake av.
Gibson Agnes S, bds 38 Oak.
Gibson Charles A, helper, bds 38 Oak.
Gibson Daniel, laborer, bds 192 Smith.
Gibson Edward D, laborer, bds 192 Smith.

280   R. L. POLK & CO.'S

Gibson Frank, traveling agent, res 13 Hamilton.
Gibson Frank P, brakeman, bds 13 Hamilton.
Gibson Frederick A, carpenter, bds 38 Oak.
Gibson George B, brakeman. res 137 Buchanan.
Gibson Jennie (wid Wm), res 157 St Mary's av.
Gibson John, laborer, res 192 Smith.
Gibson John D, laborer, bds 192 Smith.
Gibson Joseph, driver City Trucking Co, bds 159 Harrison.
Gibson Lena S (wid Charles), res rear 59 W Williams.
Gibson Louisa, domestic 131 Griffith.
Gibson Mary, res e s Piqua av, 2 s of Rudisill av.
Gibson Mary J (wid Frank), res 38 Oak.
Gibson Rose A, dressmaker, bds 38 Oak.
Gibson Sarah A (wid Theodore), bds 137 Buchanan.
Gick Frederick H C, clk A W Stace, bds 292 E Wash-
   ington.
Gick George, clk Pickard Bros, res 292 E Washington.
Gick Louis W, clk H J Ash, res 66 Erie.
Gick Wm H F, clk Ft Wayne Iron Wks, bds 292 E
   Washington.
Gidley John A, mach Ft Wayne Electric Corp, res 28 Pine
Gidley Rebecca (wid Wm), res 20 Pine.
Gidley Richard A, boilermaker, res 23 Brandriff.
Gierhart John, bds 485 E Washington.
Giesking, see also Geiseking.
Giesking Henry, wagonmkr. bds 23 Jones.
Giestdoerfer, see Geistdoerfer.
Giffen Clarence, lab Ft Wayne Electric Corp, bds 41 Taylor
Giffin Robert E, fireman Penn Co, res 41 Taylor.
Gifford Clark, bartender Ft Wayne Club, rms 94 Calhoun.
Gift Bert S, printer, bds 51 Hugh.
Gilb Nicholas M, cigarmkr Bourie. Cook & Co, res 176 Metz
Gilbert Charles W, real estate, res 220 Lake av.
Gilbert Gertrude R, bds 246 W Washington.
Gilbert Grace G, bds 305 E Lewis.
Gilbert Harry N, saloon, 226 Calhoun, res 61 Brackenridge
Gilbert John, res 246 W Washington.
Gilbert John V, trav agt, res 268 E Lewis.
Gilbert May, dressmaker, bds 268 E Lewis.
Gilbert Rille, lab, res w s Hillside av 2 n of Baker av.
Gilbert Walter S, trav agt B W Skelton Co, bds 305 E
   Lewis.
Gilby John, mach hd Star Iron Tower Co, res 69 Garden.
Gilchrist Elizabeth H (wid Wm L), bds cor Spy Run av
   and Prospect av.

Gilchrist Kate, teacher, rms 60 W Berry.
Giles Addison A (Jackson & Giles), res 41 E Creighton av
Gill Lawrence, laborer, bds 55 Barr.
Gill Fintie, domestic 100 W Berry.
Gillen Bernard, fireman Penn Co, bds 353 Lafayette.
Gillespie Asa E, student, bds 242 E Wayne.
Gillespie Mrs Susannah L, bds 242 E Wayne.
Gillespie Wm R, brick mason, res 44 W 3d.
Gillette Edwin A, machinist, res 30 Wilt.
Gillette Horace, barber J Fitzgerald, bds same.
Gilliom Emma E (wid Henry), res 17 W Lewis.
Gilliom Emma L, teacher International Business College,
   bds 43 Douglas av.
Gilliom Julia, seamstress, res 181 Jackson.
Gilliom Leonora D, stenographer, bds 17 W Lewis.
Gilliom Zella M, bds 17 W Lewis.
Gillus Rosina (wid Wm), bds 55 Madison.
Gilman Charles A, tinner S F Bowser & Co, bds 130
   Thomas.
Gilmartin Edward, lumber, n e cor Holman and Clinton,
   res 31 W Williams. Tel 144.
Gilmartin Edward T, student, bds 31 W Williams.
Gilmartin Helen M, bds 31 W Williams.
Gilmartin Mamie A, bds 31 W Williams.
Gilmartin Michael, lineman, bds 20 Murray.
Gilmartin Michael J, bkkpr E Gilmartin, bds 31 W
   Williams.
Gimpel Clara J, opr Hoosier Mnfg Co, bds 119 Taylor.
Gimpel Henry, coremkr Bass F & M Wks, res 119 Taylor.
Gimpel Minnie H, clk Louis Wolf & Co, bds 119 Taylor.
Ginder John A, brakeman, res 22 Baker.
Gindlesparger Ida, bds 8 Ewing.
Gindlesparger Jacob, agent, res 8 Ewing.
Gindlesparger Mead A, fireman Engine Co No 4, bds 18
   McClellan.
Ginty Michael O, conductor, res 104 Brackenridge.
Ginz J F, bds 14 Lafayette.
Girard, see also Garard and Gerard.
Girard Frank, helper Penn Co, bds 518 E Lewis.
Girard Nicholas, car repairer Penn Co, res 518 E Lewis.
Girardot Alphonse M, clk Morgan & Beach, res 57 E
   Superior.
Gladbach Gottfried, car bldr Penn Co, res 17 Grace.
Gladbach Joseph, carp P H Wyss, res 230 Force.

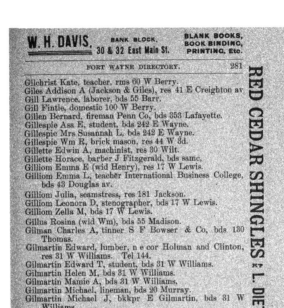

Gladieux Francis C. salesman Wm Kaough, res 51 E
Superior.
Glah Henry, laborer, res 587 E Washington.
Glaser Bertha, bds 195 Hanna.
Glaser Edward F, baker, 195 Hanna, res same.
Glaser Edward K, lather, bds 195 Hanna.
Glaser Frank, agent, bds 195 Hanna.
Glaser John E, baker E F Glaser, bds 195 Hanna.
Glasgow Adam, engr N Y, C & St L R R, bds 231 W Main
Glass Lena E, bds 244 W De Wald.
Gleason John E, engineer, res 29 Duck.
Gleitz Herman, toolmkr Ft Wayne Electric Corp, res 670
Broadway.
Glenn Burr, clerk, bds 67 W De Wald.
Glenn Carrie, student, bds 67 W De Wald.
Glenn Grace C, teacher Bloomingdale School, bds 67 W
De Wald.
Glenn Robert W, removed to Chicago, Ill.
Glenn Wm M, engineer Penn Co, res 67 W De Wald.
Glessner Charles H, paperhanger Heine & Israel, bds 65
W 4th.
Glessner Cora I, opr S M Foster, bds 65 W 4th.
Glessner Mrs Harriet M, res 65 W 4th.
Glessner Maude C, opr S M Foster, bds 65 W 4th.
Glickman Jacob, removed to South Bend, Ind.
Glissmann Christian G, helper Wabash R R, res 82 Swin-
ney av.
Globe Spice Mills, H C Berghoff, Propr, Spice
and Flouring Mills, 73-79 E Columbia. Tel 139.
Glock Otto J, helper Ft Wayne Newspaper Union, bds 156
Wallace.
Glocke Herman, laborer, res 205 Gay.
Gloeckle Anna (wid John), res 50 Columbia av.
Glosop Wm, bds 326 Hanna.
Glover Frank, brakeman G R & I R R, rms 16 Chicago.
Gloyd Louis L, clk Penn Co, res 410 Clinton.
Glusenkamp Amelia, opr Wayne Knitting Mills, res 397
W Main.
Glusenkamp Frederick, blksmith L E & W R R, res
51 W 5th.
Glusenkamp Frederick H, bkkpr Ind Mach Wks, bds 397
W Main.
Glusenkamp Louisa C, knitter, bds 397 W Main.
Glusenkamp Louise E, seamstress S M Foster, bds 51 W 5th
Glusenkamp Wm H, wiper L E & W R R, res 397 W Main.

Glutting Andrew F (Glutting, Bauer & Hartnett), res s e cor Fulton and Washington.
Glutting, Bauer & Hartnett (Andrew F Glutting, Kajetan J Bauer, Murray Hartnett), real estate, 55 Clinton. Tel 263.
Glutting Elizabeth F, res 15 W Washington.
Glutting John J, agent, bds 15 W Washington.
Gmeiner Anna M, bds 63 High.
Gmeiner Charles, engr L E & W R R, res 50 W 4th.
Gmeiner Michael F, lab L E & W R R, bes 50 W 4th.
Gnau John, laborer Penn Co, res 15 Wabash av.
Gnau Martin, lab Penn Co, res 69 Oliver.
Gnau Peter, helper Penn Co, res 13 Force.
Goba Bertha, domestic 25 Broadway.
Gocke Anthony, bds 162 Griffith.
Gocke August C, clk B R Noll, bds 162 Griffith.
Gocke Augustus A, laborer, res 91 Grant av.
Gocke Clara J, bds 162 Griffith.
Gocke Edward F, helper, bds 91 Grant av.
Gocke Frank A, traveling agt, res 325 E Wayne.
Gocke Frank M, bds 325 E Wayne.
Gocke Louis C, laborer, res 200 E De Wald.
Gocke Louis H, 17 Bass Blk, res 80 Brackenridge.
Godfrey James P, engr Wabash R R, res e s Brooklyn av 1 s of Ontario.
Godown Mary D, bds 115 E Berry.
Goebel, see also Gable.
Goebel Christina (wid Peter), res 219 Lafayette.
Goebel Frank A, clerk, bds 219 Lafayette.
Goebel Frederick, musician, res 32 W Main.
Goeglein Abraham, policeman, res 83 Smith.
Goeglein Andrew J, helper Kerr Murray Mnfg Co, res 200 Taylor.
Goeglein Frederick, coremkr Bass F & M Wks, res 44 Taylor.
Goeglein George J, harnessmaker F Hilt, bds 28 Jones.
Goeglein Henry, trucker Penn Co, res 86 Gay.
Goeglein Jacob, laborer, res 28 Jones.
Goeglein Mrs Lizzie, mid wife, 86 Gay, res same.
Goeglein Minnie, bds 200 Taylor.
Goeglein Minnie, domestic 27 W Berry.
Goeglein Rosa, bds 200 Taylor.
Goeglein Rosa C, bds 130 E Lewis.
Goehren Joseph (Langhals & Goehren), res 320 E Washington.

Goehringer John, laborer, res 161 Force.

Goehringer Selma M, tailoress, bds 161 Force.

Goens Sadie, domestic 35 W Lewis.

Goeriz Anna (wid Adolphus), res 104 E Wayne.

Goeriz Charles F, molder F H Borcherding, res 104 E Wayne.

†Goers August W, helper, res 85 Shawnee av.

Goers Margaret, domestic 192 W Wayne.

Goers Wm, painter Penn Co, bds Weber Hotel.

Goertz Theodore, harnessmkr, res 68 E Pontiac.

Goethe Frances, domestic 493 Calhoun.

Goette Frederick, coremkr Bass F & M Wks, res 113 Gay

Goetty Mary, opr Wayne Knitting Mills, bds 27 Buchanan

Goetze, see also Getz.

Goetz Hubert, engineer Ft Wayne Iron Wks, res 55 Maumee rd.

Goetze Herman, saloon, 31 Clinton, res same,

Goetze Herman, helper, bds 5 Eliza.

Goff James O, tel opr L S & M S Ry, res 410 Clinton.

Goheen Ada, rms 250 W Jefferson.

Gohl Dena (wid Thomas), bds 175 Lafayette.

Goings Arthur, driver City Trucking Co, bds 159 Harrison

Goings Frank J, laborer, res 125 Walton av.

Goings Wm (col'd), waiter The Wayne, rms 93 E Lewis.

Goings Wm H, bds Windsor Hotel.

Gokey Joseph, res 52 Hugh.

Gokey Lavinia, bds 52 Hugh.

Goldammer Charles, cigarmaker L Bender, res 336 Hanna

Goldberg Benjamin, mngr Weil Bros & Co, res 335 E Wayne.

Goldberg Jacob, tailor, 232 Calhoun, res same.

Goldberger Maurice, junk dealer, res 419 E Washington.

Golden Annie, bds 32 Smith.

Golden Anthony W, clk Golden & Patterson, res 175 E Wayne.

Golden Bridget (wid Patrick), died August 24th, 1894.

Golden Catherine, winder Ft Wayne Electric Corp, bds 38 Melita.

Golden Edward J (Golden & Patterson), res 177 W Wayne.

Golden Frank, laborer, res 99 Wagner.

Golden John, brakeman, res 195 Hayden.

Golden John J, fireman G R & I R R, bds 38 Melita.

Golden Lizzie B, res 29 Melita.

Golden Margaret (wid Thomas), res 38 Melita.

Golden Mary, bds 38 Melita.
Golden Patrick E, conductor, res 32 Smith.
Golden Samuel W, watchman Barber Asphalt Paving Co, res Wabash R R 2 w of Broadway.
Golden Thomas F, clk Catholic Knights of America, res 38 Melita.
Golden & Patterson (Edward J Golden, Reuben S Patterson), Clothing, Hats and Furnishing Goods, 56 Calhoun.
Goldstine Harry (Goldstine & Pearlman), res 76 Canal.
Goldstine Himan, 2d hd store, 246 Calhoun, res 61 Douglas av.
Goldstine Samuel J, agt Metropolitan Life Ins Co, bds 61 Douglas av.
Goldstine & Pearlman (Harry Goldstine, Sam J Pearlman), 2d hd goods, 82 Barr.
Goleeke George, cutter D S Redelsheimer & Co, bds 167 E Jefferson.
Goleeke John, wrapper Summit City Soap Wks, bds 167 E Jefferson.
Goleeke Veronica, bds 167 E Jefferson.
Gollmer Emil, laborer, res 195 Jackson.
Gollmer Robert, clk C O Lepper, bds 197 Jackson.
Gombert Frederick, butcher, res 421 E Washington.
Gombert Frederick J, meats, 100 Maumee rd, bds 421 E Washington.
Gombert John, bds 421 E Washington.
Gomoll Julius, laborer, res 293 Winter.
Gongaware Zachariah N, bds 81 Brackenridge.
Good Daniel (Seibert & Good), res Pittsburg, Pa
Good Eli W, mngr Seibert & Good, res 151 E Jefferson.
Good Mary A, cash Seibert & Good, bds 151 E Jefferson.
Gooden Isaac (Bowersock & Gooden), res 19 W 3d.
Goodenough George, engineer, bds 215 W Jefferson.
Goodes Eliza A, dressmaker, res 202 Ewing.
Goodfellow Bros (James F and Wm H), saloon 274 Calhoun.
Goodfellow James F (Goodfellow Bros), res 274 Calhoun.
Goodfellow Wm H (Goodfellow Bros), res 74 E De Wald.
Goodman Charles, U S gauger, bds 139 E Jefferson.
Goodman Harry T, stonecutter Wm Geake, bds 202 W Superior.
Goodman Joseph, laborer, res 105 Fletcher av.
Goodman Katie (M & K Goodman), res 139 E Jefferson.
Goodman Mary (M & K Goodman), res 139 E Jefferson.

19

Goodman M & K (Misses Mary & Katie), notions 1E 39 Jefferson.

Goodman Wm, foreman Wm Geake, res 202 W Superior.

Goodrich Wm L, clk Search & McCormick, rms 55 E Berry.

Goodsell Harry R, died Dec 2d, 1894.

Gordon Alice A, opr S M Foster, bds 57 Wells.

Gordon Clifford H, plumber Indiana School for Feeble-Minded Youth, res s w cor Griswold and Parnell avs.

Gordon C Edward, student, bds 16 E Leith.

Gordon Daniel D, stereotyper Ft Wayne Newspaper Union, res 609 Calhoun.

Gordon Eugene B, printer Ft Wayne Sentinel, res 345 E Washington.

Gordon George P, baggage agt Penn Co, res 16 E Leith.

Gordon Guy H, bds 11 McLachlan.

Gordon Horace J, appr Ft Wayne Sentinel, bds 345 E Washington.

Gordon Hugh K, baggageman Penn Co, res 375 E Washington.

Gordon James S, clk Penn Co, res 16 E Leith.

Gordon James W, inspector Ft Wayne Gas Co, res 11 McLachlan.

Gordon J George, fireman G R & I R R, res 348 Broadway

Gordon Samuel E, gas inspector Ft Wayne Gas Co, res Leith n w cor Harrison.

Gordon Wm D, traveling agt, bds 16 E Leith.

Gordon Wm H, watchman, bds 375 E Washington.

Gorgan Wm, printer, res 226 Calhoun.

Gorham Charles D, Division Superintendent N Y, C & St L R R, Odd Fellows Bldg, res 103 W Berry.   Tel 124.

Gorman, see also Garman.

Gorman Catherine (wid Wm), res 74 Melita.

Gorman Daniel, Propr Daily Fish Market, 17 W Main, res 16 same. Tel 541.

Gorman Dennis, bkkpr Catholic Knights of America, bds 67 Harrison.

Gorman Mary, bds 74 Melita.

Gorman Thomas, helper Kerr Murray Mnfg Co, bds 74 Melita.

Gorrell Albert C, bds 12 Wilt.

Gorrell Jennie E (wid Jesse O G), res 12 Wilt.

Gorrell John T, helper Seavey hardware Co, bds 12 Wilt.

Gorrell Mamie E, bds 12 Wilt.

Gorrell Maud E, bds 12 Wilt.

Gorrol John, bds 71 Hamilton.

Gorsline Homer A, clk Heller & Frankel, res 124 South Wayne av.

Gorsline Mrs Maria B, bds 124 South Wayne av.

Gorsline Sylvester L, watchman, rms 288 Calhoun.

Gosda August, helper, res 44 Smith.

Goshorn Frederick, foreman Fort Wayne Water Power Co, res n e cor Spy Run and Riverside avs.

Goshorn Jacob S, Superintendent Water Power Co, res 386 E Washington. Tel 394.

Goshorn Jennie, domestic 205 W Berry.

Goshorn Jennie F, bds 205 Thompson av.

Gorshorn John T, artist, bds 205 Thompson av.

Goshorn Maggie, teacher, bds 205 Thompson av.

Goshorn Margaret L, clk Lehman Book & News Co, bds 386 E Washington.

Goshorn Wm H, supt bridges Allen co, rms 15 Douglas av

Goslee Samuel M, yd brakeman Penn Co, res 81 Brackenridge.

Gotsch Christian C, clk Morgan & Beach, res s s Griswold av 3 e of bridge.

Gotsch Laura (wid Julius), bds s s Griswold av 3 e of bridge.

Gotta Conrad C, tailor, res s s Pontiac 1 w of Wayne Trace.

Gotta John B, bds 339 Lafayette.

Gotta Michael, stonemason, res 2 Liberty.

Gotty Christopher, res 73 Buchanan.

Gould Carroll C, stenographer Ft Wayne Electric Corp, bds 86 W De Wald.

Gould Eliza E (wid Solomon), bds 177 Griffith.

Gould James A, clk Ft Wayne Electric Corp, bds 86 W DeWald.

Gould Theodore H, engr Penn Co, res 86 W De Wald. Tel 443.

Gould Wm A, mach Ft Wayne Electric Corp, bds 86 W De Wald.

Gouty Alvin C, caller Penn Co, bds 248 Calhoun.

Gouty Benjamin F, engr Wayne Knitting Mills, res 73 Howell.

Gouty Birdie, dressmkr, 227 W Superior, bds same.

Gouty Emma, bds 252 Calhoun.

Gouty James M, carp, res 227 W Superior.

Gouty Louis E, laborer, bds 227 W Superior.

Gouty Thomas A, pawnbroker, 252 Calhoun, res same.

Gouty Wm F, (Steger-Gouty Cycle Co), bds 252 Calhoun.

Gove Wm H, inspr Olds Wagon Wks, res 52 E Williams.

Government Building, s e cor Berry and Clinton.

Gowans John F, mach Western Gas Const Co, bds 92 Force.

Gowen Angeline, domestic 154 Greeley.

Gowen Henry W, carp L Diether & Bro, res 83 Richardson.

Grable John, engineer Penn Co, res 97 Baker.

Grable Samuel A, yardmaster N Y. C & St L R R, res 152 W Wayne.

Grace German Evangelical Lutheran Church, s e cor Gay and Pontiac.

Grace John, conductor G R & I R R, rms 210 Calhoun.

Grace Reformed Church, s s E Washington bet Barr and Lafayette.

Graden John, laborer, bds 46 E Columbia.

Grady Emma S, bds 38 Lillie.

Grady John F, brakeman Penn Co, bds 38 Lillie.

Grady Mary (wid Henry), res 38 Lillie.

Graeter Wm F, sec and treas Ind Furn Co, res 50 E De-Wald.

Graf Barbara (wid John), bds 18 Buchanan.

Graf Philip, Groceries, Dry Goods, Queensware and Sample Room, 335 and 337 Lafayette, res 401 Same. Tel 336. (*See right side lines.*)

Graffe Carrie M, bds 178 Ewing.

Graffe Charles F (C F Graffe & Co), res 186 Ewing.

Graffe Clara J, ironer Troy Steam Laundry, bds 26 W Jefferson.

Graffe C F & Co (Charles F Graffe), hardware, 132 Calhoun.

Graffe Daisy A, bds 26 W Jefferson.

Graffe Edward J, tinner, res 163 Clinton.

Graffe Frederick M, jeweler H C Graffe, res 138 W Wayne

Graffe George W, engraver C F Graffe & Co, bds 186 Ewing.

Graffe Henry C, pres Jenney Electric Light Co, jeweler, s e cor Calhoun and Columbia, res 156 W Jefferson. Tel 287, res 158.

Graffe Julian B, helper Ft Wayne Gas Co, bds 26 W Jefferson.

Graffe Mary E (wid George W), res 26 W Jefferson.

Graffe May E, bds 156 W Jefferson.

Graffe Regina C, res 178 Ewing.

Graffe Wm H, clk C F Graffe & Co, bds 186 Ewing.

Grage Emma. inspr Paragon Mnfg Co, bds 133 Wallace.

Grage Frederick, expressman, 185 W Jefferson, res same.

Grage Henry F, trav agt Geo De Wald & Co, res 99 E Berry.

Grage Sophia M, bds 185 W Jefferson.

Grage Wm A, clk A H Staub, res 68 E 2d.

Grage Wm H, watchman, res 133 Wallace.

Graham Belle, clk Root & Co, bds 89 Montgomery.

Graham George E, painter Penn Co, res 632 Calhoun.

Graham George W, laborer, res 14 Summit.

Graham Harry H, lab Ft Wayne Electric Corp, bds 52 Grace av.

Graham Howard M, printer Daily News, bds 14 Summit.

Graham James A, foreman Penn Co, res 230 E Lewis.

Graham James E, Abstracts of Titles, Lawyer, Real Estate, Loans and Insurance, 26 Bank Blk, res 405 Hanna.

Graham James N, carp J M Henry, bds 405 Hanna.

Graham John W, shoemaker, 17 Grand, res same.

Graham L Maude, stenogr and notary J E Graham, bds 405 Hanna.

Graham Mattie B, student, bds 230 E Lewis.

Graham M Jennie, notary public, 405 Hanna, res same.

Graham Samuel D, carp Ft Wayne Electric Corp, res 52 Grace av.

Graham Wm F, clk Penn Co, res 23 Van Buren.

Grahl Clemens W, teacher St Paul's German Lutheran School, res 6 Summit.

Grahl Theodore F, teacher Emanuel German Lutheran School, bds 6 Summit.

Gramlich John, laborer, bds 199 Broadway.

Grand Army of the Republic Hall, over 80½ Calhoun.

Grand Central Hotel, S A Bradley propr, 101 Calhoun.

Grand Clara E (wid George), stenographer U H Stewart, bds 352 Hanna.

Grand Rapids Fire Ins Co, of Grand Rapids Mich, Charles B Fitch agt, 26 Bass Blk.

Grand Rapids & Indiana Railroad, Operating Cincinnati, Richmond & Ft Wayne R R, P S O'Rourke Supt. R B Rossington, Freight Agt, John E Ross Ticket Agt, Offices and Depots with Pennsylvania Co, cor Clinton and Railroad. Passenger Depot Tel 211, Freight Depot Tel 108. (See inside back cover)

Granger Claude E, bds 19 E Jefferson.

Granger Frank T, brakeman, res 295 Buchanan.

Granger Horace G, chief clk Wabash R R, bds 202 W Washington.

Granneman Anna, bds 235 Webster.

Granneman Emma S, clk E C Rodenbeck, bds 235 Webster.

Granneman Henry C, clk C B Woodworth & Co, res 237 Webster.

Granneman Karl H, expressman, res 235 Webster.

Grant Daniel D, blksmith A Vogely, res 113 Madison.

Grant Ernest, bds 244 Smith.

Grant Florence J, stripper G Reiter, bds 113 Madison.

Grant Frederick, brakeman G R & I R R, res 109 Greene.

Grantz Ernst, laborer, bds Washington House.

Grashoff Frank, driver J B White, res 201 Calhoun.

Graue Frederick H, bricklayer. res 86 Home av

Graue Mary (wid George), housekeeper 99 W Jefferson.

Graves Charles E, sec Board of Underwriters, 23 Bass Blk, res 79 Griffith.

Gray, see also Grey.

Gray Calvin S, trav agt J A Armstrong & Co, rms 44 Harrison.

Gray Charles, express messenger, bds Lake Shore Hotel.

Gray George P, waiter J T Connolly, rms 175 Wells.

Gray James P, condr Penn Co, res 90 W Williams.

Gray Jennie M, bds 230 E Wayne.

Graybill Luther C, laborer, res e s Chute 2 n of Oak.

Greaney Conrad J, helper Bass F & M Wks, res 413 Lafayette.

Greaney Dennis S A, actionmkr Ft Wayne Organ Co, bds 66 E DeWald.

Greaney Michael J, molder Bass F & M Wks, bds 66 E De Wald.

Greaney Patrick J, finisher Ft Wayne Organ Co, bds 66 E De Wald.

Greaney Wm J, finisher, bds 66 E De Wald.

Greaney Wm M, laborer, res 66 E De Wald.

Grebe Frederick, cigarmaker, res 165 Rockhill.

Greek Candy Manufactory, Angelo Kutche Propr, 154 Calhoun. (See page 107.)

Greek Charles W, lab Hoffman Bros, res 217 W Superior.

Greek Frederick, res 39 Huestis av.

Greek John W, teamster, res s s Organ av 2 e of Broadway

Greek Wm T, teamster, res 561 Broadway.

Green Addie, domestic, bds 100 Walton av.

Green Mrs Albina, dressmkr, res 69 Baker.

Green Charles, electrician Ft Wayne Electric Corp, bds 25 W Washington.
Green Mrs Cora, bds 150 W Wayne.
Green Dallas F (Green & Probasco), res 128 Lafayette.
Green Emma L (Emma L and Lettia M Green), bds 179 Jackson.
Green Emma L and Lettia M, dressmkrs, 179 Jackson.
Green Frank (col'd), laborer, bds 100 Walton av.
Green George W, brakeman, res 40 E Butler.
Green Henry S (col'd), laborer, bds 100 Walton av.
Green Hugh W, res 179 Jackson.
Green John H (col'd), janitor Ft Wayne Electric Corp, res 37 Grand.
Green Lettia M (Emma L and Lettia M Green), bds 179 Jackson.
Green Lewis H, printer Ft Wayne News, res 79 Riverside av.
Green Lillie B, domestic 123 W Williams.
Green Malcolm A, carriage trimmer City Carriage Wks, bds 139 W Main.
Green Margaret (wid Johnson), bds 84 E Berry.
Green M Frances (wid Seth R), physician, 139 W Main, res same.
Green M Gertrude, bds 139 W Main.
Green Noah (col'd), laborer, res 100 Walton av.
Green Sarah (col'd), laundress, bds 100 Walton av.
Green Seth F, clk G E Bursley & Co, bds 139 W Main.
Green Wm H, sewing machines, 76 Lafayette. res same.
Green & Probasco (Dallas F Green and Wm J Probasco), jewelers, 3 Arcade Bldg.
Greenawalt George L, Physician and Surgeon, 151 E Wayne, res same. Tel 189.
Greene Mrs Ella, res 73 High.
Greene Frank R, switchman, bds 6 Orchard.
Greene Laura E, binder, bds 32 Home av.
Greene Louisa A M (wid Frank R), res 9 Duck.
Greene Richard B, carver J M Henry, res 32 Home av.
Greene Thomas C, engr Hoffman Bros, res 228 St Mary's av.
Greene Walter A, laborer H H Schroeder, bds 9 Duck.
Greene Wm H, teamster Kilian Baker, bds 73 High.
Greener, see also Greiner.
Greener John, laborer, res 119 Eliza.
Greenewald Clara, clerk, bds 11 Fairfield av.
Greenewald David D, jeweler, 132½ Broadway, res 11 Fairfield av.

Greenewald Esther E, milliner, 132½ Broadway, bds 11 Fairfield av.

Greenewald Marquis, physician. 11 Fairfield av. res same.

Greenick Abraham A, fireman Penn Co, res 139 E DeWald.

Greenick Arthur, bds 139 E De Wald.

Greenick Charles W, machinist, bds 139 E De Wald.

Greenlun Carrie M, bds 92 Oliver.

Greenlun Helsel J, conductor, res 65 Maud.

Greenlun Herbert C, fireman Penn Co, res 92 Oliver.

Greenlun Mrs Libbie, bds 92 Oliver.

Greensfelder Aaron, salesman J B White, bds 95 Ewing.

Greensfelder Gustav, res 95 Ewing.

Greensfelder Josias, bkkpr J B White, bds 95 Ewing.

Greensfelder Mollie, bds 95 Ewing.

Greenslade Walter E, brakeman, rms 71 Boone.

Greenwich Ins Co of New York The, Charles B Fitch agt, 26 Bass Blk.

Greer, *see also* Grier.

Greer Anna L, milliner, bds 20 Erie.

Greer Charles E, clk Seavey Hardware Co, bds 20 Erie.

Greer Clara M, stenographer, bds 20 Erie.

Greer Elizabeth M (wid James), res 1 Division.

Greer Frank J, clk Penn Co, res 52 E De Wald.

Greer Mrs Frank J, artist, 52 E De Wald, res same.

Greer James A, clk P O, bds 1 Division.

Greer James L, harnessmkr A L Johns & Co, bds 20 Erie.

Greer John, res 36 Walnut.

Greer John, saloon, 178 Calhoun, res 84 Brackenridge.

Greer John J, policeman, res 54 Walnut.

Greer John W, carpenter, res 20 Erie.

Greer Thomas jr, clk County Auditor, rms 37 Baker.

Greer Wm, fireman Wabash R R, bds 84 Brackenridge.

Gregg Anna (wid James S), res 176 E Wayne.

Gregg Frederick M, student, bds 176 E Wayne.

Gregg Stella M, bds 176 E Wayne.

Greibel, *see Griebel.*

Greiner, *see also Greener.*

Greiner Christopher, lab Bass F & M Wks, res 273 Gay.

Greiser Wm M, lab Wabash R R, res 65 Shawnee av.

Grennell, *see Grinnell.*

Grenneman Wm H, switchman, res 280 W Main.

Grenzenbach August, helper Penn Co, res 12 Wiebke.

Grenzenbach Heinrich F, laborer, res 22 Jane.

Grenzenbach John, painter, bds s e cor Calhoun and Marshall.

Gresham Frederick H (col'd), porter, res 39 Grand.

Gresham Isaac (col'd), waiter The Wayne, rms 95 E Lewis.

Gretzinger Emelia A (wid Jacob), res 75 Home av.

Gretzinger Jacob J, died March, 1895.

Greve John C, clerk, bds n s Cochran 2 w of Coombs.

Greve Joseph F, carpenter, res 22 Cochran.

Grewe Frederick C, cigarmkr F W Ropa, res 165 Rockhill.

Grewe Wm, carpenter, res 383 E Wayne.

Grey, *see also Gray.*

Grey Gestie E, dressmaker, bds 230 E Wayne.

Grey Jennie M, dressmaker, bds 230 E Wayne.

Grey John W, contractor, 230 E Wayne, res same.

Grey Justina E, marker Paragon Mnfg Co, bds 230 E Wayne.

Grey Wm J, brakeman G R & I R R, bds 230 E Wayne.

Gribben Charles O, carpenter, bds 24 Douglas av.

Gribben Esther J, bds 24 Douglas av.

Gribben John F, mach Ft Wayne Electric Corp, bds 24 Douglas av.

Gribben Louis J, clk Ward & Flynn, bds 24 Douglas av.

Gribben Mary J (wid James), res 24 Douglas av.

Grice Jessie V, res 163 E Wayne.

Grieb Andrew, lather, bds 30 Cochran.

Grieb John, tailor, rms 182 E Lewis.

Grieb John, asst yard master Penn Co, res Huntington rd south of city limits.

Griebel Adolph L, business mngr Indiana Staats Zeitung, res 211 W Berry.

Griebel Annie L, bds 157 W 3d.

Griebel Caroline E, opr Troy Steam Laundry, bds 157 W 3d.

Griebel Charles (Griebel & Pask), res 346 E Washington.

Griebel Christian, laborer, res w s Eagle 2 s of Taylor.

Griebel Edward R C, lab Ft Wayne Electric Corp, bds Christian Griebel.

Griebel Elizabeth C, ironer Troy Steam Laundry, bds 157 W 3d.

Griebel Flora, bds 178 W Superior.

Griebel George, laborer, bds 157 W 3d.

Griebel George C, driver, bds 181 Taylor.

Griebel Louis (W J Griebel & Co), res 58 E Jefferson.

Griebel Louis, wheelmkr Paul Mnfg Co, bds 157 W 3d.

Griebel Wm G, coilarmkr Bayer Bros, res 36 2d.

Griebel Wm J, helper Horton Mnfg Co, bds 181 Taylor.

Griebel Wm J (Wm J Griebel & Co), res 178 W Superior.

Griebel Wm J & Co (Wm J and Louis Griebel), furniture, 87 E Main.

Griebel & Pask (Charles Griebel, George W Pask), Marble Yard, 74 and 76 W Main.

Grier Edna E, bds s w cor Pontiac and Oliver.

Grier Elias, mach hd, res 96 Lasselle.

Grier Joseph H, res s w cor Pontiac and Oliver.

Grier Viola L, bds s w cor Pontiac, opp Oliver.

Grieser A P Henry, carpenter, res 88 Wall.

Griffin David H, fireman Penn Co, rms 23 Baker.

Griffin Edward, barber, bds 100 Montgomery.

Griffin Henry, engineer, bds 517 Harrison.

Griffin Leonidas R, student, bds 3 Pine.

Griffin Nora, attendant School for Feeble-Minded Youth.

Griffin Thomas T, inst mkr Ft Wayne Electric Corp, res 3 Pine.

Griffith Catherine, stenographer, bds 81 W Washington.

Griffith Chauncey L, draughtsman, bds 77 W Williams.

Griffith David S, clk People's Store, res 135 Holman.

Griffith Edward E, brakeman, rms 36 Baker.

Griffith Godfrey R, bds 135 Holman.

Griffith James A, engr N Y, C & St L R R, bds 357 W Main.

Griffith James M, carpenter, res 82 W De Wald.

Griffith John, bds 42 W Main.

Griffith John C, porter, rms 101 Calhoun.

Griffith Kate, rms 81 W Washington.

Griffith Levi, contractor, 77 W Williams. res same. Tel 531

Griffith Margaret, seamstress, bds 81 W Washington.

Griffith May M, bds 135 Holman.

Griffith Nellie M, bds 77 W Williams.

Griffiths Ada M, teacher Washington School, bds 348 W Washington.

Griffiths A, Hardware, 110 Broadway, res 348 same

Griffiths Eliza M (wid Edwin), bds 164 Broadway.

Griffiths Wm E, mngr A Griffiths, res 348 W Washington.

Griley Michael A, fireman N Y, C & St L R R, res 123 High.

Grim John F, butcher, res 90 Fairfield av.

Grime Edward, policeman, res 186 Montgomery.

Grimes Charles A, clk Root & Co, res 146 E Wayne.

Grimes Charlotte C, student, bds 146 E Wayne.

Grimm Flora U (wid John G), res 107 Wilt.

Grimm Mrs Mary, res 17 Walnut.

Grimm Nellie, bds 17 Walnut.

Grimm Paul G, lab Mayflower Milling Co, bds 17 Walnut.
Grimm Theresa E, dressmkr 107 Wilt, bds same.
Grimme Ferdinand, carpenter, res 229 Madison.
Grimme Frank J, switchman Wabash R R, res 227 Madison.
Grimme Frederick, car bldr Penn Co, bds 229 Madison.
Grimme Gerhard B (J H Grimme & Sons), res 162 Griffith.
Grimme James C, tailor, bds 2 McClellan.
Grimme John C (J H Grimme & Sons), res 2 McClellan.
Grimme John H (J H Grimme & Sons), res 83 Brackenridge.
Grimme John P, plumber, bds 229 Madison.
Grimme J H & Sons (John H, Gerhard B, and John C) merchant tailors, 108 Calhoun.
Grimme Rose M, bds 229 Madison
Grindle Alfred, Architect and Superintendent 34–37 Bass Blk, res 15 Clay. Tel 513.
Griner Christian F, brickmkr, res e s Gay 1 s of No 343.
Griner Mary, bds 56 Walnut.
Grinnell Melinda W (wid Hiram W), bds 372 Fairfield av.
Grismer Libbie, knitter, bds 320 W Main.
Griswold Crawford, foreman Penn Co, res 165 W De Wald.
Griswold Ethel D, bds 165 De Wald.
Grodzik Henry R, band leader School for Feeble-Minded Youth, bds 26 Lake av.
Groman Carl, coachman w s Spy Run 1 n of Elizabeth.
Groman Celia, dressmaker, bds 104 Webster.
Groman Joseph, painter, bds Ervin House.
Gronau Frank J, painter. bds Louis Gronau.
Gronau Frederick W, Carriage Painter, rear 89 E Superior, res n s Pittsburg 2 e of Lumbard. (See p 107.)
Gronau Louis, mach hnd Penn Co, res n e cor Lumbard and Pittsburg.
Gronau Wm F W, salter F Eckart Pkg Co, res 112 Hanna
Grosh Henry, car bldr Penn Co, bds 503 Hanna.
Grosh Henry, carpenter, res 503 Hanna.
Grosh Martha K, presser Hoosier Mnfg Co, bds 503 Hanna.
Grosh Minnie (wid John), bds 503 Hanna.
Grosjean August, bds n e cor Duck and Clinton.
Grosjean Frank J, agent, res 127 Cass.
Gross Augusta H J, bds 241 W Jefferson.
Gross Rev Charles, pastor Emanuel Lutheran Church, res 241 W Jefferson.
Gross Charles jr, student, bds 241 W Jefferson.

Gross Charles H, bds 163 Van Buren.
Gross Charles T, clk Ind Furn Co, res 29 Lillie.
Gross Emanuel M, bds 29 Lillie.
Gross Emma L, dressmaker, bds 255 E Lewis.
Gross Frank Y, insurance agt, bds 228 Calhoun.
Gross Frederick, bds 163 Van Buren.
Gross Gottlieb, barber F W Brown, bds 163 Van Buren.
Gross Harry, polisher Ft Wayne Furn Co, bds 24 Wilt.
Gross Lodema H (wid Thomas), res 255 E Lewis.
Gross Martin C, auditor Ft Wayne Electric Corp, res 167 W Washington.
Gross Pauline (wid Frederick), res 163 Van Buren.
Gross Wm O (Gross & Pellens), res 159 W Washington.
Gross & Pellens (Wm O Gross, Joseph B Pellens), Druggists' and Barbers' Supplies, 94 Calhoun. Tel 185.
Grosse Max, printer Ft Wayne Freie Presse, res 66 Oakley.
Grosshoff Frank, driver, res 200 Calhoun.
Grossenbacher Frederick, helper Penn Co, res 116 Fairfield av.
Grosvenor Charles V, clerk C W Edgerton, bds 64 Burgess.
Grosvenor Harry, res 64 Burgess.
Grosvenor Harry M, lab Hoffman Bros, bds 64 Burgess.
Grosvenor Herbert J, student, bds 64 Burgess.
Grosvenor Wm C, appr Robert Ogden, bds 64 Burgess.
Grosvenor Wm H, lab, bds 64 Burgess.
Grote Annie, domestic 227 W Wayne.
Grote Caroline C (wid Charles W), res 245 W Washington.
Grote Frederick H, carpenter, bds 69 Wilt.
Grote Herman H, lathe hd Ind Mach Wks, bds 69 Wilt.
Grote Minnie C, bds 120 Harrison.
Grothaus Anna B, domestic 162 Holman.
Grothaus Frances R, bds 194 E Wayne.
Grothaus George H, bds 194 E Wayne.
Grothaus Henry, laborer, res 208 Monroe.
Grothaus Henry F, res 194 E Wayne.
Grothaus Joseph F, blksmith Penn Co, bds 194 E Wayne.
Grotholtman Henry A (H A Grotholtman & Co), res 28 E 4th.
Grotholtman H A & Co (Henry A Grotholtman, John H Meyers) contractors, 48 W Jefferson.
Grout Wm H, conductor G R & I R R, res 37 Huestis av.
Grove James S, teamster Kilian Baker, bds 109 E Superior

Grove Maxwell J, boiler inspr Penn Co, res 25 W Butler.
Groves Edward E, butcher, res 523 E Wayne.
Groves Oscar, conductor, res 38 Lasselle.
Grubb Charles E, fireman N Y, C & St L R R, bds D T Grubb.
Grubb Daniel T, engr F Y, C & St L R R, res w s Leesburg rd, opp G R & I R R Dock.
Grubb Frederick, fireman, bds w s Brookside n of W Main
Grubb Miles O, fireman N Y, C & St L R R, bds 98 Boone.
Gruber Andrew J, collector Ft Wayne Sentinel, bds 108 Jackson.
Gruber August C, coppersmith Penn Co, res 64 Walnut.
Gruber Bertha, bds 108 Jackson.
Gruber Carrie M, packer G E Bursley & Co, bds 18 Wilt.
Gruber Charles J, saloon, 101 Broadway, bds 108 Jackson.
Gruber Clementina, dressmkr E A Waltemath, bds 108 Jackson.
Gruber Edward J, sawyer Ft Wayne Organ Co, res 157 College.
Gruber Edward J, cigarmkr F W Ropa, bds 18 Wilt.
Gruber Frank J, boilermkr Bass F & M Wks, res 48 E De Wald.
Gruber Frank J, Cigar Manufacturer, 110 Calhoun, res 178 W Washington. Tel 310.
Gruber Ignatz, boiler washer Penn Co, res 83 Force.
Gruber Jacob J, patternmkr Bass F & M Wks, res 68 Hugh.
Gruber John V, helper Wabash R R, res n s Guthrie 1 e of Thompson av.
Gruber Joseph A, bartender, res 108 Jackson.
Gruber Joseph E, cigarmkr C A Tripple, bds 108 Jackson.
Gruber Joseph L, Hardware, Nails, Cutlery, House Furnishing Goods, 140 Fairfield av, res 21 Brackenridge. Tel 350.
Gruber Josephine (wid Valentine), bds 157 College av.
Gruber Michael J, res 18 Wilt.
Gruber Michael J jr, cigarmkr F J Gruber, bds 18 Wilt.
Gruber Veronica, bds 18 Wilt.
Gruber Veronica M, opr S M Foster, bds 157 College.
Grueb, *see Grubb.*
Gruenert Frederick J, brakeman, bds 129 Horace.
Grummon Fowler, agent, res 189 E Jefferson.
Grummon Fred M, stenographer, bds 189 E Jefferson.
Grund Effie G, bds 256 W De Wald.

Grund John H, shaver S D Bitler, res 24 Schick.

Grund Mrs Mary, bds 155 Holman.

Grund Philip R, blacksmith, res 256 W De Wald.

Guardian Medical and Surgical Institute, Brookfield Gard, mngr, 13 W Wain.

Guebard John F, brakeman N Y, C & St L R R, res 344 W Main.

Gucib Louis F, brakeman N Y, C & St L R R, bds 21 Ewing.

Guendling Rev Charles B, asst pastor Cathedral Immaculate Conception, res 172 Clinton.

Guenther Clara, wrapper Keller Dental Co, bds 11 Maumee rd.

Guenther Emma, wrapper Keller Dental Co, bds 11 Maumee rd,

Guenther Henry, barber, res 11 Maumee rd.

Guenther Stephen A, mach hd Olds Wagon Wks, bds 60 Miner.

Guerin Helen J, bds Peter Guerin.

Guerin Katie J, bds Peter Guerin.

Guerin Peter, res e s Brooklyn av 1 n of Poor Farm.

Guethe Joseph, cabinetmaker, res 88 W 4th.

Guffin Elmer, barber 94½ Barr, bds 100 Montgomery.

Guiff Fannie, domestic 127 W Wayne.

Guild Albert D, bkkpr Ft Wayne Electric Corp, res 372 Fairfield av. Tel 203.

Guild Charles G, sec and mngr Jenney Electric Light and Power Co, 43 E Berry, res 171 same. Tel 459.

Guild Helen T, librarian Emerine J Hamilton Library, bds 372 Fairfield av.

Guillaume James, carpenter, res 58 Wells.

Guillaume Julia, opr S M Foster, bds 181 Jackson.

Guise Joseph, laborer, bds 9 Clay.

Guldlin Olaf N, pres The Western Gas Construction Co, res 11 Webster. Tel 508.

Guldner Reuben, bds 53 Baker.

Gulka John W F, laborer, res 145 Buchanan.

Guller Herman, bottler, bds 509 E Washington.

Gumbert Henry, watchman Penn Co, res 192 Jackson.

Gumbert Henry P C, clk A Griffiths, bds 192 Jackson.

Gumpper Charles H (Neireiter & Gumpper), bds 269 W Washington.

Gumpper Christian C, res 241 Webster.

Gumpper Frederic C, student, bds 241 Webster.

C. P. TINKHAM, D. D. S. 21, 22, 23, 24 Arcade Block, West Berry Street, FORT WAYNE, IND.
Office Telephone   Residence Telephone

FORT WAYNE DIRECTORY.   299

Gumpper Jacob D, grocer, 240 Calhoun, res 16 E De Wald. Tel 67.

Gumpper John F, brickmason, res 46 Home av.

Gunder Emanuel, collarmkr Aime Racine, res 223 Wells.

Gunder Henry, res 215 Wells.

Gunder Millie, domestic 51 Maple av.

Gundlagh Edward J, fireman, bds 250 E Lewis.

Gunkel Cecilia, bds 40 Nirdlinger av.

Gunkel Otto, tinner, bds 40 Nirdlinger av.

Gunkel Otto F, tinner, bds 40 Nirdlinger av.

Gunkel & Son (Otto & Otto F), tinners, 38 Nirdlinger av.

Gunkler John P, cabinetmaker, res 34 E Leith.

Gunther, see also Guenther.

Gunther Charles H, heater Bass F & M Wks, bds 207 E Wayne.

Gunther Rudolph, brewer, res 47 Buchanan.

Gusching Jacob, frt handler L S & M S Ry, res 137 Wells.

Gusching Joseph, res 150 Holman.

Gusta, see Gorsda.

Gustin Jennie. domestic 442 W Main.

Gutermuth Benjamin, baker, 29 W Columbia, res 155 Broadway.

Gutermuth Casper, turner Jacob Klett & Sons, res 39 W Jefferson.

Gutermuth Elizabeth (wid John G), res s w cor Wells and Huffman.

Gutermuth Emma S, teacher Mc Culloch School, bds 39 W Jefferson.

Gutermuth George J, sawyer Hoffman Bros, res s w cor Wells and Huffman.

Gutermuth Jeannette M, bds 155 Broadway.

Gutermuth John G, bds 51 Maple av.

Gutermuth John G, watchman, res 15 Edna.

Gutermuth Valentine, Cloaks and Furs, 52½ Calhoun, res 51 Maple av.

Guth Henry P, pipeman Engine Co No 6, res 85 Wells.

Guth Margaretta, domestic 42 W Washington.

Guthe Joseph, cabinetmaker, res 88 W 4th.

Gutmann Pius, laborer, res 187 Gay.

Guy Ida, laundress, res 14 Lafayette.

Guy John F, brakeman, bds 14 Lafayette.

H

Haag Adam S, carpenter, res 201 Taylor.
Haag Charles (Brunner & Haag), res 155 Van Buren.
Haag George A, tailor A Foster, bds 155 Van Buren.
Haag Gottlieb L, stonecutter Keller & Braun, res 153 W Main.
Haag John G, clk H Mariotte, res 13 Ida.
Haag Louisa (wid John), bds 329 W Washington.
Haag Louise, tailoress, bds 155 Van Buren.
Haag Mary, bds 155 Van Buren.
Haag Mary, domestic 66 Wilt.
Haag Wm, lab Ft Wayne Electric Corp, res 329 W Washington.
Haak Charles, tailor W C Cleary, bds 172 Ewing.
Haak Robert, foreman, bds 112 Broadway.
Haas, see also Hass and Hess.
Haas Jacob, helper Bass F & M Wks, res 206 Madison.
Haas Joseph, lab Bass F & M Wks, bds 110 W Leith.
Haas Louis H, clk Freight House Penn Co, res 108 Hugh.
Haas Simon, lab Bass F & M Wks, res 10 W Leith.
Haas Wm J, asst cashier Penn Co, res 16 South Wayne av.
Haase Frank L, lab Penn Co, res 54 Liberty.
Haase Hannah, dressmaker Krull Sisters, bds 54 Liberty.
Habbert J Heinrich, messngr Wabash R R, res 5 Jones.
Habbinger Harry, removed to Bellevue, O.
Habecker Alice M (Lehman Book and News Co), prin Miner st School, bds 23 Douglas av.
Habecker Annie G, teacher Clay School, bds 23 Douglas av
Habecker Charles W, painter, res 39 Buchanan.
Habecker Elias, carpenter, res 23 Douglas av.
Habecker Frank E, printer Ft Wayne News, res 55 Madison.
Habel Charles J, machinist, res 164 Taylor.
Habel John G, machinist, res 172 Taylor.
Habel Pauline, seamstress, bds 172 Taylor.
Habel Wm C, laborer, bds 164 Taylor.
Haberkorn Amelia A, bds 130 Harrison.
Haberkorn Augusta, bds 130 Harrison.
Haberkorn Emma, bds 130 Harrison.
Haberkorn Emil F, mach Penn Co, res 130 Harrison.
Haberkorn Henry, machinist, res 234 Hoagland av.
Haberkorn Hulda C, tailoress G Stauffer, bds 130 Harrison
Haberkorn Theodore H, mnfr air brakes, res 71 Douglas av
Habig August, lab Bass F & M Wks, res 59 Lasselle.
Habig Hubert, bartender T J Baker, res 31 Clinton.

Hachmann Frederich H, contractor, s w cor Reynolds and Summer, res same.

Hachmeier Henry, bricklayer, res 66 Stophlet.

Hackett Blk, e s Calhoun, bet Wayne and Washington.

Hackett Edward A K, Propr Fort Wayne Sentinel, 107 Calhoun, res 207 W Berry. Tel 191.

Hackett Elizabeth. bds 346 W Washington.

Hackius Adolph C G, clk Ft Wayne Electric Corp, bds 71 Brackenridge.

Hackius F Wm, clk Root & Co, bds 71 Brackenridge.

Hackius Gustave L, treas Kerr Murray Mnfg Co, res 427 Calhoun.

Hackius Lena M, bds 71 Brackenridge.

Hackius Mary A (wid Andrew), res 71 Brackenridge.

Haddix Lawrence O, car bldr Penn Co, res 271 E Creighton av.

Haddon Alfred, city sol Ft Wayne Sentinel, rms 53 W Lewis

Hadley Arthur L, electrician Ft Wayne Electric Corp, bds 149 Griffith.

Hadsell Cyrus M, meats, 20 Indiana av, res same.

Haenel August H, motorman Ft W E Ry Co, res 52 Hamilton.

Haenel Wm A, engr N Y, C & St L R R, res 244 W Main.

Haensch, see also Hench.

Haensch August, truckman Penn Co, res s s Eckart lane 1 e Hanna.

Haertig Ernest, opr Wayne Knitting Mills. res 38 Watkins.

Haeseler Hermann, foreman Wayne Knitting Mills, bds 10 Runnion av.

Haffner, see also Heffner.

Haffner Edward H, died September 15, 1894.

Haffner Emma, clerk, bds 30 Madison.

Haffner Frederick C, baker, bds 30 Madison.

Haffner George M, mangr Mary Haffner, bds 30 Madison.

Haffner Lawrence, mach Kerr Murray Mnfg Co, res 39 E De Wald.

Haffner Mary (wid Christian), baker, 105 E Lewis, res 30 Madison.

Haffner Rose M, clk Mrs Mary Haffner, bds 30 Madison.

Hagan Edward C, barber E Sterling, bds 46 Harrison.

Hagan Mary C (wid Frank), dressmaker, res 46 Harrison.

Hagan Minnie, bds 82 W Main.

Hagan Robert W, teamster F S Tinkham, res 82 W Main.

Hagan Thomas W, 2d hd goods 64 E Columbia, res 114 N Harrison.

20

Hagan Wm, helper Ft Wayne Iron Wks, res 105 W Butler.
Hage Wm, agent, bds 113 Barr.
Hagedorn Ernest E, lab, bds 24 Pine.
Hagedorn Mrs Hattie, laundress Model Hand Laundry, res 24 Pine.
Hagedorn Herman, foreman Penn Co. res 24 Pine.
Hagedorn Herman E, helper Model Hand Laundry, bds 24 Pine.
Hagedorn Jessie A, folder, bds 24 Pine.
Hagedorn Mary M C, bds 24 Pine.
Hagemann Anna H, bds 188 Broadway.
Hagemann Elizabeth, bds 188 Broadway.
Hagemann Frederick W, cigarmkr H W Ortmann, res 165 Jackson.
Hagemann Henry, laborer, bds Washington House,
Hagemann Henry W, molder Bass F & M Wks, res 37 John.
Hagemann Henry W, trav agt Root & Co, bds 188 Broadway
Hagemann John H, gardener, bds s w cor Edsall av and Wabash R R.
Hagemann Joseph H, gardener s w. cor Edsall av, and Wabash R R, res same.
Hagemann Louis E, clk Root & Co, bds 188 Broadway.
Hagemann Louisa (wid Charles), seamstress, res w s Spy Run av 3 n of bridge.
Hagemann Wm F, res 188 Broadway.
Hagemann Wm F, cigarmkr, res 165 Jackson.
Hagen Frederick, bds 364 E Lewis.
Hager Gottlieb O L. clk Stahn & Heinrich, bds 216 Francis.
Haggenjos Gustavus, porter Peter Certia, bds Spy Run av n of city limits.
Hagist Adolph G, paperhanger, res 73 Canal.
Hagist Emilie, bds 433 E Washington.
Hagist Henry, cigarmkr L Bender, bds 433 E Washington
Hagist John G, laborer, res 433 E Washington.
Hagist Mary, clk, bds 433 E Washington.
Hahn Albert G, bkkpr Prudential Ins Co, bds 157 W Main
Hahn August, coremkr, res 72 Swinney av.
Hahn Frederick A. lab Hoffman Bros, bds 157 W Main.
Hahn Henry, coremaker Bass F & M Wks, res 215 John.
Hahn John, oiler Penn Co, res e s Lumbard 1 n of Wabash R R.
Hahn Mary E, bds e s Lumbard 1 n of Wabash R R.
Hahn Minnie M, bds 157 W Main.
Hahn Wm (Wm Hahn & Co), res 208 W Berry.

Hahn Wm, Saloon, 148 W Main, res 157 same.
Hahn Wm & Co (Wm Hahn), dry goods, 28 Calhoun.
Hahnel Anton T, opr Wayne Knitting Mills, res 25 Elm.
Haiber Carrie E, bds 64 Wells.
Haiber Charles F, meats, 122 Wells, res 124 same.
Haiber Frederick, Dealer in Real Estate, and Notary Public, 64 Wells, res same.
Haiber George W, grocer, 378 Hanna, res same.
Haiber John, butcher, rms 108 Clinton.
Haiber Lawrence, meats, 15 High, res 64 Wells. Tel 320.
Haiber Wm B, clerk, bds 64 Wells.
Haifley Joseph D, moved to Ossian, Mich.
Haiges Wm, blacksmith Olds Wagon Wks, res 327 E Washington.
Hail George S, agt Prudential Ins Co, res 60 E Pontiac.
Hail Martha A (wid John B), bds 20 Savilla av.
Haines, see also Hanes and Haynes.
Haines Clarence, bds 1 Lincoln av.
Haines Henry H, Propr Father's Medicines, 24 E Washington, res same.
Haines C H, res 1 Lincoln av.
Haines Jerome, laborer, res 18 Barthold.
Haines Morris M, fly finisher Ft Wayne Organ Co, res 183 Fairfield av.
Haines Rosa, bds 1 Lincoln av.
Hake, see also Hecke.
Hake Christena (wid Frank), saloon, 26 Wells, res same.
Hake Frank, died December 12, 1894.
Hake Frank jr, died December 25, 1894.
Hake Lena, bds 28 Wells.
Hake Sibyl (wid Elias), died October 6, 1894.
Hale Annie, seamstress D S Redelsheimer & Co, bds 134 Harrison.
Hale Lillian M, stenogr Smith Credit Rating Co, bds 146 W Main.
Hale Mary, chambermaid G H Seabold.
Hale James C, laborer, res 146 W Main.
Haley, see also Healy.
Haley Daniel P, motorman Ft W E Ry Co, res 69 E Creighton av.
Haley John P, brakeman Penn Co, bds 150 E Taber.
Haley Joseph A, engr N Y, C & St L R R, res 132 Wells.
Haley Joseph M, student, bds 132 Wells.
Haley Margaret, opr S M Foster, bds 51 Baker.
Hall Albert H, laborer, res 5 Winch.

Hall Beverly, res s w cor Spy run av and Elizabeth.
Hall Charles, laborer, res 5 Winch.
Hall Charles W, mach Penn Co, rms 100 Harrison.
Hall Edward W, sawyer Standard Wheel Co, res 49 Lillie.
Hall Edwin A, res 529 Broadway.
Hall Ella (wid Ernest B), res 118 W Creighton av.
Hall Elmira, chambermaid Arlington Hotel.
Hall Elsie A (wid Wm), teacher Miner St School, bds 23 Douglas av.
Hall Emerson V, medical student, res 197 W Superior.
Hall Frank C, brakeman, res 70 Taylor.
Hall James E, contractor, res 254 W Creighton av.
Hall John C, traveling agt, res 369 Lafayette.
Hall John S, sawyer Standard Wheel Co, bds 150 Walton av.
Hall John W, lab Ft Wayne Electric Corp, res 14 Zollars av
Hall Mark C, stock buyer, res 219 E Wayne.
Hall Marshall S, bds 23 Douglas av.
Hall May, asst G E Johnson, bds 23 Douglas av.
Hall Miranda P (wid Samuel P), bds 167 W Wayne.
Hall Samantha B (wid Silas), res 64 Chicago.
Hall Thomas N, conductor, res 21 Lavina.
Hall Wm, blacksmith, res 150 Walton av.
Hall Wm A, foreman Fort Wayne Times, res 38 Harrison.
Halleck Wm H, switchman, res cor Lillie and Milan.
Haller Adolph, butcher J W Suelzer, res 34 Elm.
Haller Freida, bds 366 Calhoun.
Haller Gottlieb (Klotz & Haller), Wall Paper, Paints, Oils, etc, 362 Calhoun, and Meat Market, 366 Calhoun and 277 Hanna, res 366 Calhoun. Tel 222.
Haller Samuel, with Wm Haller, bds 231 Barr.
Haller Wm, Pork Packer and Propr Wholesale and Retail Meat Market, Dealer in Choice Fresh and Smoked Meats, 107 E Lewis, res same.
Halliday Frank (col'd), res 76 E Columbia.
Hallien Nellie, milliner, bds 194 W Superior.
Halos Lizzie, domestic 134 W Main.
Halstein Henry D, clerk, res 178 E Washington.
Halverstott Clinton W, driver Adams Express Co, res 307 W Washington.
Hambrock Frederick H, mach hd Olds Wagon Wks, res 16 Jane.
Hambrock Frederick J, laborer, res 20 Jane.
Hambrock Henry C, clerk L F Limecooly, bds 20 Jane.
Hambrock Matilda, tailoress, bds 20 Ja e.

Hambrock Wm J, clk Princess Cash Store, res 598 Lafayette.

Hamburg Harry F, asst supt Prudential Ins Co, res 13 W Wayne.

Hamil Alice L, teacher Bloomingdale School, bds 114 Clinton.

Hamilton Agnes, bds A H Hamilton.

Hamilton Allen, mach Penn Co, res 19 Holman.

Hamilton Allen, student, bds A H Hamilton.

Hamilton Andrew H, res s w cor Clinton and Lewis.

Hamilton Bridget (wid John), res 155 W Wayne.

Hamilton Catherine, bds Andrew H Hamilton.

Hamilton Catherine S, bds Peter Hamilton.

Hamilton Charles J, brakeman, rms 337 W Main.

Hamilton Emerine J Library (2300 Volumes), Margaret V Hamilton Pres and Sec, 23¼ W Wayne.

Hamilton Emma L, teacher High School, bds Robert J Hamilton.

Hamilton Frances C, prin Hoagland School, bds 151 W Wayne.

Hamilton Frederick R, bds n s Bluffton rd 1 w of river bridge.

Hamilton George, laborer, res 122 Maumee rd.

Hamilton Homestead, n e cor Clinton and Lewis.

Hamilton House, Wm H Jones propr, 103 W Berry.

Hamilton James M, student, bds 19 Holman.

Hamilton James O, brakeman Penn Co, res 57 Force.

Hamilton Jane A, seamstress. res 235 E Wayne.

Hamilton Jessie, bds A H Hamilton.

Hamilton Joseph, brakeman N Y, C & St L R R, rms 84 Boone.

Hamilton Joseph A, driver J B White, res 38 Summit.

Hamilton L G, sec D N Foster Furn Co, res Lafayette, Indiana.

Hamilton Margaret, pres and sec Emerine J Hamilton Library, res s e cor Clinton and Lewis.

Hamilton Montgomery, res n w cor Montgomery and Clinton.

Hamilton National Bank, (Capital $200,000; Surplus $250,000), Charles McCulloch Pres, John Mohr jr Cashier, Charles W Orr Asst Cashier, Frank H Poole 2d Asst Cashier, 44 Calhoun. Tel 162.

Hamilton Peter, boilermkr Wabash R R, res w s Hanna 4 s of Pontiac.

Hamilton Robert J, gardener, res n s Bluffton rd 1 w of river bridge.

Hamilton Robert J jr, ticket clk N Y, C & St L R R, res 122 Greeley.

Hamilton School, n e cor Pontiac and Clinton.

Hamilton Taber, student, bds A H Hamilton.

Hamilton Wm G, Helper Bass F & M Wks, bds Peter Hamilton.

Hamilton Wm J, head sawyer Standard Wheel Co. res 407 Clinton.

Hamlet Jesse E, brakeman, rms 94 Calhoun.

Hamm Alexander, ress 99 Maumee rd.

Hamm Andrew, res 134 Lafayette.

Hamm Andrew, driver, L P Scherer, res 9 Ohio.

Hamm Henry, driver, rms 9 Ohio.

Hamm John, hostler, res 140 Lafayette.

Hamm Louisa, bds 134 Lafayette.

Hammell Alleyne, seamstress, bds 48 Oliver.

Hammer Charles W, coremkr Bass F & M Wks, res 59 Gay.

Hammer Ernest, lab Bass F & M Wks, res 59 Gay.

Hammer Ernestina (wid Ehregott), bds 59 Gay.

Hammer Herman F, lab F & M Wks, bds 59 Gay.

Hammerle Edward, helper, bds 297 W Main.

Hammerle Otto, molder Ind Mach Wks, bds 300 W Main.

Hammerle Xavier, saloon 197 W Main, res 299 same.

Hammil Mrs Catherine, res 254 W Jefferson.

Hammond Martin E, laborer, res 195 Barr.

Hammond Thomas G, porter Home Billiard Hall, res 9 Indiana av.

Hammond Wm D, brakeman G R & I R R, rms 56 Pixley and Long Bldg.

Hamus Paul A Z, supt of agents, res 261 E Creighton av.

Hanagan John, lab Hoffman Bros, res 406 W Main.

Hanam Allie J, boarding house, 17 Simon.

Hanam Harry A, brakeman Penn Co, res 17 Simon.

Hanauer George W, engr Ft Wayne Gas Co, res cor Monroe and Montgomery.

Handenchild John, helpr Penn Co, res 277 Webster.

Handenchild Sophie, bds 277 Webster.

Handschiegel Antoine, laborer, res 171 Madison.

Handy Wm, section hd, res 10 Huron.

Hanefeld Carrie, domestic 166 W Wayne.

Hanefield Cord H, carp, res 168 Suttenfield.

Hanefeld Tenie, domestic, bds s s Chestnut 2 e of Summer.

Haneferd Mary, domestic 130 E Berry.
Hanes, *see also Haines and Haynes.*
Hanes Charles W, student, bds 142 Fairfield av.
Hanes Grant, removed to Plymouth, Ind.
Hanes Jonathan, carp Rhinesmith and Simonson, res 142 Fairfield av.
Haney Mary, bds 29 E De Wald.
Hankel Christine C, domestic 197 W Wayne.
Hankens Bernard, brickmason, res 141 Suttenfield.
Hanker Anna, bds 217 E Wayne.
Hanker Charles, barber, bds 217 E Wayne.
Hanker Clara, milliner, bds 217 E Wayne.
Hanker Hulda, dancing teacher, res 217 E Wayne.
Hanker Laura, seamstress, bds 217 E Wayne.
Hanks Mary, seamstress, bds 116 Jackson.
Hanley Alice A, domestic 57 W Berry.
Hanley Anthony, machinist, res 25 Elm.
Hanley Ella, bds 146 Wallace.
Hanley Ellen (wid James H), res 43 Baker.
Hanley Emily, bds 146 Wallace.
Hanley James, bds 43 Baker.
Hanley James J, clk car dept Penn Co, res 275 Hanna.
Hanley Mrs James J, notions, 275 Hanna, res same.
Hanley John F, messenger, bds 43 Baker.
Hanley Maggie, bds 43 Baker.
Hanley Maggie, bds 146 Wallace.
Hanley Paul J, foreman Penn Co, res 146 Wallace.
Hanna A Newton, clerk, res 4 Fulton.
Hanna Elizabeth C (wid Henry C), res 135 E Berry.
Hanna Emma O, milliner, 84 Calhoun, bds 332 W Jefferson
Hanna Henry C, lawyer 8 and 9 Bank Blk, bds 135 E Berry. Tel 214.
Hanna Homestead, E Lewis opp Division.
Hanna Hugh T, res Hanna Homestead.
Hanna John L, clk Penn Co. res 402 Broadway.
Hanna Joseph T, clk W L Carnahan & Co, res 285 E Wayne.
Hanna J Thomas, real estate, 8 and 9 Bank Blk, res 266 W Wayne. Tel 214.
Hanna Marguerite C, bds 288 W Berry.
Hanna Martha E (wid Samuel T), res 288 W Berry.
Hanna Mary, bds 288 W Berry.
Hanna Mrs Mary G, milliner, bds 1 Division.
Hanna Oliver S (Nuttman & Co), res 130 W Berry.

Hanna Robert B, lawyer, 8 and 9 Bank Blk, bds 135 E
    Berry. Tel 214.
Hanna School, s w cor Hanna and Wallace.
Hannen George W, lab Rhinesmith & Simonson, res 122
    Wilt.
Hannen Wm E, clerk, bds 122 Wilt.
Hanrahan Timothy, laborer, res rear 20 Bass.
Hans Adam, blksmith Olds Wagon Wks, res 18 Charles.
Hans Bruno, died April 19, 1895.
Hans Charles A (Winkelmeyer & Hans), res 253 Broadway
Hans Herman, carpenter, bds 53 Hugh.
Hans Minnie, clerk, bds 53 Hugh.
Hans Rudolph, tinner, bds 53 Hugh.
Hans Theresa (wid Carl) res 53 Hugh.
Hansch Carl, bds s s Eckart lane 1 e of Hanna.
Hansel Peter, res 37 Miner.
Hansen Henry F, carpenter, bds 162 Holman.
Hansen Peter, res 10 Oak.
Hanson Albert P C, blksmith Olds Wagon Wks, res 309
    Lafayette.
Hanson Carrie S, bds 31 Summit.
Hanson Clark, truckman Penn Co, res 15 Ida.
Hanson Elizabeth (wid Joseph), bds J H Doswell.
Hanson Frank, electrician, bds 17 W Lewis.
Hanson Lillie, domestic Allen Co Orphans' Home.
Hanson Richard C, steamfitter A Hattersley & Sons, res 31
    Summit.
Hanson Thomas F, electrician Ft Wayne Electric Corp,
    bds 17 W Lewis.
Hanson Wm E, mach Ft Wayne Iron Wks, bds 31 Summit.
Happ Joseph A, helper Bass F & M Wks, bds 89 Summit.
Happ Nicholas, stonemason, rms 89 Summit.
Happ Wm, stonemason, bds 89 Summit.
Harber, see also Haiber, Harper and Herber.
Harber August A, clk M H Wefel, bds 390 Hanna.
Harber Joseph W, fireman N Y, C & St L R R, bds 390
    Hanna.
Harber Louis, mach hd Olds Wagon Wks, bds 97 John.
Harber Maggie, dressmaker, bds 97 John.
Harber Margaret T (wid Nicholas), res 150 Broadway.
Harber Mary T, seamstress, bds 97 John.
Harber Peter, mach Penn Co, res 390 Hanna. Tel 405.
Harber Peter M, meats, s s Buchanan 1 e of Force, bds
    390 Hanna.
Harber Valentine, helper, res 97 John.

Herdendorf Charles. lab Penn Co, res 169 Gay.
Hardendorf Eugene R, traveling agent, bds 113 W Wayne.
Hardendorf Louise, opr Wayne Knitting Mills. bds 30 St Mary's av.
Hardendorf Minnie, domestic 225 W Wayne.
Hardendorf Theodore, policeman, res 13 Barthold.
Hardesty Adeline P (wid Philip W), bds 126 Eliza.
Hardesty Wm H, removed to Cleveland, Ohio.
Harding Christian, brakeman, res 38 Smith.
Harding Daniel L, insurance, 28 Bank Blk, res 254 W De Wald. Tel 214, res 294.
Harding Frank, rms 28 Smith.
Harding Joseph, laborer, res 393 E Wayne.
Harding Nellie M, bds 393 E Wayne.
Harding Perry, laborer, bds 42 W Main.
Harding Robert F, bkkpr Ft Wayne Electric Corp, res 176 W Creighton av.
Hardung, *see also Hartung.*
Hardung Amelia, dressmaker, rms 23 W Lewis.
Hardung Charles J, clk Frederick Hardung, bds 207 Madison.
Hardung Clara, bks 207 Madison.
Hardung Frederick, Fashionable Merchant Tailor, 35 E Main cor Clinton, res 207 Madison. (*See right top lines.*)
Hardwick Joseph, supt Eckart Electric Co, bds 136 E Berry
Harges August H P, helper Fleming Mnfg Co, bds 329 E Washington.
Harges Theodore C, carriagemkr City Carriage Wks, bds 329 E Washington.
Harges Wm F, blacksmith, res 327 E Washington.
Harkenrider, *see also Hergenrather.*
Harkenrider Henry J, policeman, res 449 Hanna.
Harkenrider John, laborer, bds 115 John.
Harkenrider Joseph, restaurant, 61 E Main, res same.
Harkenrider Wm W, lab Bass F & M Wks, res 76 Buchanan.
Harkins Wm H, dep collr of customs P O Bldg, res Portland, Ind.
Harlan Perry C, clk L E & W R R, bds 40 E 5th.
Harland Henry, coremkr Bass F & M Wks, bds 181 Gay.
Harmer School, n w cor Harmer and Jefferson.
Harmeyer Cyrus L, bds 17 Gay.
Harmeyer Mrs Elizabeth, domestic James Munn.

Harmeyer Frederick W, foreman L Diether & Bro, res 87 W Superior.

Harmeyer Henry J, motorman, res 25 Hamilton.

Harmeyer John F, collector, res 194 Lafayette.

Harmeyer Wm, collector. bds 17 Gay.

Harmon, *see also Harman and Herrmann*.

Harmon Cora B, bds 70 Douglas av.

Harmon Daniel. propr Harmon House, 282 Calhoun.

Harmon House, Daniel Harmon Propr, 282 Calhoun.

Harmon Samuel W, res 70 Douglas av.

Harmony Hall, 20 W Berry.

Harmon John, fireman N Y, C & St L R R, bds 323 W Main.

Harner Frank, dining car conductor, rms 331 Calhoun.

Harnischfeger Joseph, carp Gustave Lauer, bds 78 Buchanan

Harnischfeger Josephine, bds 78 Buchanan.

Harnischfeger Mary, opr Hoosier Mnfg Co, bds 78 Buchanan

Harnischfelger Peter, wiper Penn Co, res 78 Buchanan.

Harnung Charles removed to San Francisco, Cal.

Harper, *see also Haiber. Harber and Herber.*

Harper Anna L (wid James), res 46 Monroe.

Harper Benjamin F, Attorney at Law, Rooms 10 and 11 Pixley & Long Bldg, res New Aveline House.

Harper Eliza (wid John), res 365 W Main.

Harper Elmer J, conductor N Y, C & St L R R, bds 75 Boone.

Harper James B, Lawyer, 12 and 13 Bank Blk. res 76 E Washington. Tel 214.

Harber Lorenzo V, motorman Ft W E Ry Co, bds 365 W Main.

Harper Mary, domestic 213 W Berry.

Harper Oliver J, carver, res 86 Walton av.

Harper W Paul, bds 46 Monroe.

Harper Wm W, condr N Y, C & St L R R, rms 96 Boone

Harries Bertha L, clerk, bds 63 W Jefferson.

Harries Lydia M, clk Allen County Loan & Savings Assn, bds 63 W Jefferson.

Harries Mary (wid John H), res 63 W Jefferson.

Harries Wm G, lab Ind Mach Wks, res 226 Walton av.

Harris, *see also Herres.*

Harris Charles T, driver City Trucking Co, bds 163 Clinton.

Harris Dorothy M, bkkpr, bds 182 E Jefferson.

Harris Ella F, physician. 148 Calhoun, res same.

Harris Elwood E, teamster, res 182 E Jefferson.

Harris Emmett V, Lawyer, 19 Bass Blk, res 56 Huestis av.

Harris George L, mach Penn Co, res 108 Hanna.

Harris Guy, trav agt S Bash & Co, res Lima, Ind.

Harris Henry E, molder Penn Co, res 157 Taylor.

Harris Joseph D, mach Penn Co, rms 127 E Washington.

Harris Joseph D jr, apprentice, bds 126 Harrison.

Harris Lyman P, physician, 148 Calhoun, res same.

Harris Philip G, medical student, bds 137 W Superior.

Harris Samuel, tel opr G R & I R R, rms 38 Brackenridge

Harrison Bertha E, bds 22 Charles.

Harrison George A, brakeman N Y, C & St L R R, bds 354 W Main.

Harrison Harry N, bartender The Wayne, bds same.

Harrison Ida M, bkkpr S M Foster, bds 22 Charles.

Harrison John (col'd), foreman, res 275 E Wayne.

Harrison John (col'd), laundryman School for Feeble-Minded Youth.

Harrison Josephine S, bkkpr S M Foster, bds 213 Barr.

Harrison Louisa (col'd), seamstress, bds 275 E Wayne.

Harrison Maude A, bkkpr S M Foster, bds 213 Barr.

Harrison Michael A, hostler, bds 37 Taylor.

Harrison Robert H, foreman Penn Co, res 22 Charles.

Harrison Viola, bds 22 Charles.

Harrison Wm, mach Penn Co. res 213 Barr.

Harrison Wm H, res 145 Fairfield av

Harrod Daniel V, carpenter, bds 67 W Main.

Harrod George W, detective, res 67 W Main.

Harrod Horatio S, turnkey County Jail, bds same.

Harrod Marion, traveling agt, rms 179 Clinton.

Harrod Minnie, bds 67 W Main.

Harrod Morse, physician and county coroner, 44 Maumee rd, res same. Tel 500.

Harsh, *see also Hersh, Hirsh and Hursh.*

Harsh George G, conductor N Y, C & St L R R, res 266 W Jefferson.

Harshman John N, laborer, res 200 Thomas.

Hart Agnes, opr Wayne Knitting Mills, bds George C Hart.

Hart George C, dairy, e s Thomas 1 s of Pontiac, res same.

Hart Herbert E, driver Pearse & Poff, res 8 Huron.

Hart Henry M, mach, res 109 Wallace.

Hart Henry M, mach Kerr Murray Mnfg Co, bds 58 W Wayne.

Hart James S, flagman, res 50 Runnion av.

Hart John C, car bldr Penn Co, res 99 Hugh.

Hart Lewis D, lab Standard Wheel Co, bds 27 Indiana av.
Hart Nellie, bds 50 Runnion av.
Hart Wm P, flue cutter, res 20 Charles.
Harter Alida A, bds 12 Huffman.
Harter George A, cabtmkr, res w s Winch 1 n of Wabash R R
Harter George M, lab Hoffman Bros, res 12 Huffman.
Harter Joseph, blacksmith, 170 W Main. res same.
Harter Philip, clk Geo De Wald & Co, res 202 W Washington.
Hartigan James, engr N Y. C & St L R R, bds 376 W Main
Hartle Wm M, driver Ft Wayne Beef Co, res 129½ W 3d.
Hartley Nelson L, painter, res 13 Zollars av.
Hartley Wm E, condr G R & I R R, bds 38 Baker.
Hartman Bros (Joseph and Henry), boats, w s Spy Run av nr St Joseph river.
Hartman Charles A, bookkeeper. bds 244 W Washington.
Hartman Clement, clk J H Hartman, bds 273 Hanna.
Hartman Elizabeth, domestic 148 E Washington.
Hartman Eva, bds 273 Hanna.
Hartman Fannie T, draughtswoman C E Kendrick, bds 65 Maple av.
Hartman Fred S, student. bds 241 W Wayne.
Hartman Frederick, res 62 Wall.
Hartman George B, clk R M S, res 244 W Washington.
Hartman Henry (Hartman & Bro), res 63 E Wayne.
Hartman Homer C, Lawyer and Solicitor of Patents, 31 Arcade Bldg, res 65 Maple av.
Hartman Hugh H, stenographer, bds 65 Maple av.
Hartman Jacob (Hartman & Ankenbruck), res 272 E Washington.
Hartman John, porter Grand Central Hotel.
Hartman John F, bds 62 Wall.
Hartman John G, mgr Hartman Bros, bds 344 E Wayne.
Hartman John H, grocer. 273 Hanna, res same. Tel 322.
Hartman Joseph H (Hartman & Bro), bds 344 E Wayne.
Hartman Joseph R, fireman N Y, C & St L R R, bds Jackson opp Stevens.
Hartman Lee F, student, bds 241 W Wayne.
Hartman Lem R, cashier First National Bank, res 241 W Wayne. Tel 456.
Hartman Philip, helper Bass F & M Wks, res 398 Force.
Hartman Philip C, molder Bass F & M Wks, bds 398 Force
Hartman Stephen, laborer, res 11 Rumsey av.
Hartman S Brenton, dentist, 1 and 2 Schmitz Blk, res 536 Broadway.

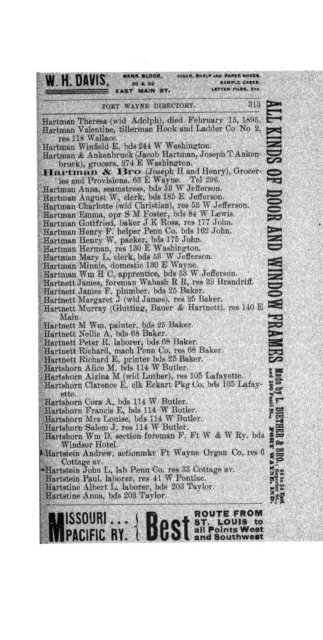

Hartman Theresa (wid Adolph), died February 15, 1895.

Hartman Valentine, tillerman Hook and Ladder Co No 2, res 118 Wallace.

Hartman Winfield E, bds 244 W Washington.

Hartman & Ankenbruck (Jacob Hartman, Joseph T Ankenbruck), grocers, 274 E Washington.

Hartman & Bro (Joseph H and Henry), Groceries and Provisions. 63 E Wayne. Tel 296.

Hartman Anna, seamstress, bds 53 W Jefferson.

Hartman August W, clerk, bds 185 E Jefferson.

Hartman Charlotte (wid Christian), res 53 W Jefferson.

Hartman Emma, opr S M Foster, bds 84 W Lewis.

Hartman Gottfried, baker J K Ross, res 177 John.

Hartman Henry F, helper Penn Co, bds 162 John.

Hartman Henry W, packer, bds 175 John.

Hartman Herman, res 130 E Washington.

Hartman Mary L, clerk, bds 53 W Jefferson.

Hartman Minnie, domestic 130 E Wayne.

Hartman Wm H C, apprentice, bds 53 W Jefferson.

Hartnett James, foreman Wabash R R, res 32 Brandriff.

Hartnett James F, plumber, bds 25 Baker.

Hartnett Margaret J (wid James), res 25 Baker.

Hartnett Murray (Glutting, Bauer & Hartnett), res 140 E Main.

Hartnett M Wm, painter, bds 25 Baker.

Hartnett Nellie A, bds 68 Baker.

Hartnett Peter R, laborer, bds 68 Baker.

Hartnett Richard, mach Penn Co, res 68 Baker.

Hartnett Richard E, printer bds 25 Baker.

Hartshorn Alice M, bds 114 W Butler.

Hartshorn Alzina M (wid Luther), res 105 Lafayette.

Hartshorn Clarence E, clk Eckart Pkg Co, bds 105 Lafayette.

Hartshorn Cora A, bds 114 W Butler.

Hartshorn Francis E, bds 114 W Butler.

Hartshorn Mrs Louise, bds 114 W Butler.

Hartshorn Salem J, res 114 W Butler.

Hartshorn Wm D, section foreman F, Ft W & W Ry, bds Windsor Hotel.

Hartstein Andrew, actionmkr Ft Wayne Organ Co, res 6 Cottage av.

Hartstein John L, lab Penn Co, res 33 Cottage av.

Hartstein Paul, laborer, res 41 W Pontiac.

Hartstine Albert L, laborer, bds 203 Taylor.

Hartstine Anna, bds 203 Taylor.

Hartsuff Isabelle M (wid Wm D), res 235 W Jefferson.
Hartung, *see also Hardung.*
Hartung Casper, painter, bds 11 Gay.
Hartup Alonzo C, mason, res 96 Metz.
Hartwell Harlow A. meats, 430 Calhoun, rms 302 Harrison.
Hartwig, *see also Hertwig.*
Hartwig Herman H (C Shiefer & Son), res 99 E Main,
Hartzell James D, bartender J A Douglas, res 34 W Butler.
Hartzler Arthur, music teacher, 27 Broadway; bds same.
Hartzler Elizabeth (wid Adam), res 27 Broadway.
Hartzler Le Roy, train despatcher N Y, C & St L R R,
    bds 27 Broadway.
Hartzog John W, barber Browand & Heldt, res 51 Hugh.
Harvey Estelle B, stenogr Western Gas Constr Co, bds 26
    W Williams.
Harvuot Charles W, clk Ft Wayne Club, rms 38 Bracken-
    ridge.
Harvuot Harry B, clk J C Hinton, rms 38 Brackenridge.
Hasel Julius J, laborer, res 36 Brandriff,
Hasel Michael, bds 36 Brandriff.
Haseltine Frank, trav agt, rms 48 Brackenridge.
Haskell George W, painter. res 48 Lillie.
Haskell Harry L, bds 48 Lillie.
Haskell James M, clerk, res 415 Calhoun.
Haskell James M jr, bds 415 Calhoun.
Haslem Alfred E, supt Prudential Life Ins Co of America,
    bds 120 Harrison.
Haslup James A, mach hd Penn Co, res 163 Hanna.
Hass, *see also Haas and Hessert.*
Hass Jacob M, mach Ft Wayne Iron Wks, bds 181 Calhoun.
Hass Jacob W, res 228 Calhoun.
Hassard, *see also Hazzard and Hessert.*
Hassard Edward E. laborer, bds 26 Dubois.
Hassard Elizabeth (wid George), res 26 Dubois.
Hassard George, died June 26th, 1894.
Hassard Henry, laborer, bds 56 Hugh.
Hassard Henry, spoke turner, bds 37 Maumee rd.
Hassard John, spoke turner, bds 37 Maumee rd.
Hassel George, cabtmkr Ft Wayne Furn Co, res 22 Wefel.
Hasser Walter G, electrical engineer Ft Wayne Electric
    Corp, bds 25 W Lewis.
Hassinger Martha A, housekeeper 62 Greene.
Hassler Bessie H, stenogr Ft Wayne Organ Co, bds 209
    Barr.
Hassler Herman, dyer, bds 5 Taylor.

Hassler Kositt D, driver F L Jones & Co, res 102 W
    Superior
Hastings Ethel, starcher W B Phillips, bds 92 Oliver.
Hastings Jennie, cook Weber Hotel.
Hasty Della B, seamstress, bds 110 Grant av.
Haswell Burton S, carver, bds 50 Oliver.
Haswell George I, cabinetmkr, res 50 Oliver
Hatch Anthea B, bds 246 Hoagland av.
Hatch Arthur A, engr F L Jones & Co, bds 266 W Jef-
    ferson.
Hatch D Julia, domestic 24 W Washington.
Hatch Elizabeth (wid John E), res e s Brooklyn av 3 s of
    river.
Hatch Wm E, saloon, 1 N Calhoun, rms 2 Baker.
Hatfield Albert A, mach hd Hoffman Bros, res 15 Elm.
Hatfield Jacob, lab Jacob Klett & Sons, res 194 Metz.
Hatfield Jennie, stenogr Mossman, Yarnelle & Co, bds 91
    W Superior.
Hatfield Lida M, bds 29 Indiana av.
Hatfield Lincoln, laborer, res 5 Fulton.
Hathorne Edward J, with Ft Wayne Electric Corp, bds
    The Wayne.
Hattendorf Anthony, driver Philip Graf, bds 491 Lafayette
Hattendorf Caroline W (wid Wm), res 30 St Marys av.
Hattendorf Christian E, removed to Indianapolis, Ind.
Hattendorf Henry G, lab Hoffman Bros, res 7 Herman.
Hattendorf Minnie, bds 30 St Marys av.
Hattendorf Wm F, driver, bds 30 St Marys av.
Hattersley Alfred (A Hattersley & Sons), res 173 W
    Wayne. Tel 37.
Hattersley Alfred I (A Hattersley & Sons), res 147 E
    Berry.
Hattersley A & Sons (Alfred, Willis, Byron E &
    Alfred I), Plumbers, Steam and Gas Fitters, 48 E Main.
    Tel 129. (See embossed line front cover.)
Hattersley Byron E (A Hattersley & Sons), res 131 E
    Main.
Hattersley Kathryne C, bds 173 W Wayne.
Hattersley Willis (A Hattersley & Sons), res 60 E Wash-
    ington.
Hauck, see also Hawk and Houck.
Hauck August, carp H A Grotholtman & Co, bds 66 Erie.
Hauck Bertha, bds 111 Griffith.
Hauck Grace, bds 111 Griffith.
Hauck Gussie C, stenogr J F Rodabaugh, bds 111 Griffith.

Hauck John J, teacher St Paul's German Catholic School, res 111 Griffith.

Hauckmaer August, lab Bass F & M Wks, bds 25 Wall.

Haudenschild Jacob, laborer, res e s Franklin av 3 s of Huffman.

Haudenschild John, laborer, bds Jacob Haudenschild.

Haudenschild John jr, helper, res 277 Webster.

Hauk Adam, shoemaker, n e cor Lafayette and Buchanan, res 9 Buchanan.

Hausbach Jacob, asst foreman Bass F & M Wks, res 112 W De Wald.

Hausbach Joseph, lab Huser & Blomenberg, bds 117 W De Wald.

Hausbach Michael, mach Wabash R R, res 181 W De Wald

Hausbach Nicholas, res 105 Mechanic.

Hauser, *see also Houser.*

Hauser Henry, dairy, res w s Hanna 8 s of Pontiac, res same.

Hauss Daniel F, pipefitter A Hattersley & Sons, res 107 Broadway.

Hauss David H, laborer, bds 8 McClellan.

Hauss Frederick F, florist Markey Bros, bds 8 McClellan.

Hauss Mrs Laura A, Hair Store and Dress and Cloak Making, 105 Broadway, res 107 same. (*See p 113*).

Hauss Susan (wid David), res 8 McClellan.

Hautch George A, saloon, 375 W Main, res same.

Hautch Mary (wid Simon), bds 375 W Main.

Hautch Peter, painter, bds 375 W Main.

Havens Ada, telephone opr, bds 44 Monroe.

Havens Frank E, cutter Paragon Mnfg Co, bds 44 Monroe.

Havens Isaac B, traveling agt, res 73 Maumee rd.

Havens Nathaniel, shoemkr C F Benze, res 53 Maumee rd.

Havens Stella, chief opr Central Union Tel Co, bds 53 Maumee rd.

Haverley Anthony, died May 21st, 1894.

Haverley Burgie, seamstress, bds 194 E Jefferson.

Haverley Elizabeth (wid Anthony), dressmaker, 194 E Jefferson, res same.

Haverley George N, blacksmith Penn Co, res 106 Hayden.

Haverley Jennie, tailoress, bds 194 E Jefferson.

Haverley Margaret, clk Peoples' Store, bds 8 E Main.

Havert Alphonso, switch tender Penn Co, res 146 Holman.

Havert Louis J, brakeman, bds 119 Holman.

Havert Mary M (wid Theodore), res 119 Holman.

Havice Samuel H, physician, 38 W Wayne, res same. Tel 410.

Hawk, *see also Hauck.*

Hawk Benjamin, attendant County Poor Farm.

Hawk Rufus, attendant School for Feeble-Minded Youth.

Hawkey Minnie (wid Wm A), res 440 W Main.

Hawkey Wm A, died June 21st, 1894.

Hawkins Carrie, opr S M Foster, bds 40 Marion.

Hawkins Edward, cigarmkr M A Schele, bds cor Jefferson and Archer av.

Hawley, *see Howley.*

Hawthorn£on Idella A (wid Arthur), res 38 Harrison.

Hay, *see also Hey.*

Hay Frank, conductor, rms 331 Calhoun.

Hay Wm T, clerk, bds 469 Harrison.

Hayden Elizabeth (wid Isaac), res 537 Broadway.

Hayden Frederick J, real estate, 68 Barr, res Hanna Homestead.

Hayden John R, bds 68 Thompson av.

Hayden John W, lawyer, 31 W Berry, res 68 Thompson av

Hayden Park, e s Harmer bet Maumee rd and E Jefferson.

Hayden Thomas, laborer, bds 83 Maumee rd.

Hayes, *see also Hays.*

Hayes Bridget (wid Dennis), res 73 Melita.

Hayes Cornelius B, fireman Penn Co, res 204 Francis.

Hayes Dennis, bds 204 Francis

Hayes Dennis T. yardmaster Wabash R R, res 31 Colerick.

Hayes Ellen (wid Thomas D), res 25 Colerick.

Hayes Elmore E, condr Ft W E Ry Co, res 138 Horace.

Hayes Frederick, res 132 Shawnee av.

Hayes Frederick J, mantel setter, bds 194 Lafayette.

Hayes Harry M, machinist, bds Windsor Hotel.

Hayes James J, condr G R & I R R, res 354 Hanna.

Hayes James J, engineer Penn Co, res 136 Fulton.

Hayes John H, carpenter, res 132 Shawnee av.

Hayes J Thomas, switchman Wabash R R, bds 73 Melita.

Hayes Margaret, bds 73 Melita.

Hayes Thomas D, lab Horton Mnfg Do, bds 113 Mechanic.

Hayes Wm, appr Penn Co, bds 111 Wallace.

Haynes, *see also Haines and Hanes.*

Haynes Clara D, bds 38 W Williams.

Haynes Clarence L, clk Penn Co, bds 36 W Williams.

Haynes Dollie M, stenogr Smith Credit Rating Co, bds 36 W Williams.

Haynes Franklin, mach hd Penn Co, res 36 W Williams.

21

Hays, *see also Hayes.*

Hays Charles A, justice of peace, 15 W Main, res 15 Rebecca.

Hays John, laborer, bds 209 Lafayette.

Hays Wm H, condr Penn Co, res 131 Fairfield av.

Hazen Italy, teacher, rms 238 W Wayne.

Hazer Lillian, bds 134 E Main.

Hazzard, *see also Hassard and Hessert.*

Hazzard Al, Propr National Cigar Factory, Wholesale Dealer in and Manufacturer of the "National" and "Royal" Five Cent Straight, 11 E Main, res 37 Marion.

Hazzard Louis N, res 39 Marion.

Heacock Leonora, laundress School for Feeble-Minded.

Headford Samuel, patternmkr, res 171 Erie.

Healy, *see also Haley.*

Healy Alfred, printer The Journal, rms 226 Calhoun.

Healy Timothy, printer Monday Morning Times, bds 226 Calhoun.

Healy Retta, dressmkr 72 Barr. rms same.

Heany Anna M (wid Anthony), res 25 W 5th.

Heany Frank, barber Charles Hoenig, bds 25 W 5th.

Heany Isaac, sawyer Hoffman Bros, bds 25 W 5th.

Hearlihie Ellen (wid Thomas), res 48 Baker.

Hearlihie Thomas M, clk Shepler & Noble, bds 48 Baker.

Heath Stephen A, county assessor Court House, bds 29 E Main.

Heathman Bradley, bds 5 Koch.

Heathman Charles B, mach hd L Rastetter & Son, bds 5 Koch.

Heathman David, horseshoer John Jackson, res 5 Koch.

Heathman E Lee, painter, bds 5 Koch.

Heathman Homer H, mach hd Rastetter & Sons, bds 5 Koch.

Heathman H Franklin, clk F M Smith & Co, bds 5 Koch.

Heaton Dr Charles E, Propr Postoffice Drug Store 36 E Berry, res 65 Columbia av. Tel 309, res 438.

Heaton Luella, opr C U Tel Co, bds 65 Columbia av.

Heaton Owen N (Vesey & Heaton), res 260 Hoagland av.

Heaton Pearl J, bds 260 Hoagland av.

Hebbison George M, real estate, res 28 W Williams.

Hebert, *see also Ebert.*

Hebert Alice M, bds 73 Thomas.

Hebert Elizabeth, bds 73 Thomas.

Hebert Emma M, teacher Hanna School, bds 73 Thomas.

Hebert Oliver, engr Penn Co, res 73 Thomas.
Hebrew Cemetery, w of Lindenwood Cemetery.
Heche Cecelia S, res 8 Erie.
Hechler George, helper Bass F & M Wks, bds 40 Lillie.
Hechler Mary (wid Frederick), res 40 Lillie.
Hecht Edward, bell boy The Randall.
Hecht Wm, clk Stephen Ganzer, bds 194 E Wayne.
Heck Christian, lab Wm Geake, bds 191 Oakland.
Heck Christina, domestic 16 E Washington.
Heck Ernest J, appr Wm Geake, bds 191 Oakland.
Heck Louis C, cigarmaker, res 49 W Washington.
Hecke, *see also Hake.*
Hecke Catherine, opr, bds 152 E Washington.
Hecke Herman C, teamster, bds 152 E Washington.
Hecke John, polisher, bds 152 E Washington.
Hecke Rosa (wid Herman), res 152 E Washington.
Hecker Katharine C (wid Philip), res 134 E Main.
Heckert Clara S, stenogr Fox br U S Baking Co, bds 81 E Jefferson.
Heckert Florence S, milliner, rms 81 E Jefferson.
Heckler Charles W, hostler, bds 15 Pearl.
Heckler Elmer C, plumber, bds 15 Pearl.
Heckler George, boarding house, 15 Pearl.
Heckman Wm C, asst supt R M S, res 46 W Wayne.
Heckmann Annie, bds 59 Brackenridge.
Hedekin Elizabeth, bds 94 W Wayne.
Hedekin House, J W Swaidner propr, 25 Barr.
Hedekin Julia, bds 94 W Wayne.
Hedekin Marie, bds 156 W Wayne.
Hedekin Mary C. bds 94 W Wayne.
Hedekin Thomas B, vice-pres White National Bank, res 94 W Wayne.
Hedges Bailey S, engr Penn Co, res 151 Holman.
Hedges John P, traveling agt, res 384 W Main.
Hedges Mary (wid Edward), bds 52 E 3d.
Hedges Thomas J, watchman Penn Co, res 323 W Main.
Heersche Herman, car bldr Penn Co, res 131 Monroe.
Heffelfinger Arthur I, agent, bds 71 Cherry.
Heffelfinger Edith, opr Wayne Knitting Mills, bds 71 Cherry.
Heffelfinger Emma, bds 71 Cherry.
Heffelfinger John M, clerk, res 71 Cherry.
Heffelfinger Robert, driver Pfeiffer & Rousseau, bds 71 Cherry.
Heffert Mrs Elizabeth, bds 231 Barr.

Heffert John, laborer, res 231 Barr.
Heffert Mary A, bds 231 Barr.
Heffner, *see also Haffner*.
Heffner Zachariah T, car bldr Penn Co, res 365 Lillie.
Hege Wm P, agt Prudential Ins Co, bds 113 Barr.
Heger Ernst W, clk Stahn & Heinrich, bds 140 Francis.
Heger George M, clk J B White, res 140 Francis.
Heger George W F, lab Ft Wayne Electric Corp, bds 140 Francis.
Heger Gottlieb O L, clerk, bds 140 Francis.
Hegerfeld Charles W, butcher C G Zickgraf, rms 23 Smith.
Hegerfeld Christian W, clk F H Fehling, res 354 Broadway.
Hegerfeld Louis, bartender W F A Hollenbeck, res 87 Wall.
Hegerhorst Christian J, Cabinetmaker, 114 and 116 Fulton, res same. (*See card in classified Cabinetmakers.*)
Heibler, *see also Hibler*.
Heibler Jane P (wid George W), bds 51 Hendricks.
Heid, *see Heit and Hite.*.
Heidenreich Annie, bds 23 W 4th.
Heidenreich Henry, tinner, bds 23 W 4th.
Heidenreich Henry C, laborer, res 25 Taylor.
Heider Albert H, bricklayer, res 87 Wall.
Heider Wm jr, tailor, bds 33 Canal.
Heider Wm H, bricklayer, res 33 Canal.
Heier Elizabeth, opr Troy Steam Laundry, bds 107 Force.
Heier Mary M, tailoress, bds 107 Force.
Heikowski, *see Hikowski*.
Heilbroner Abraham, res 62 W Main.
Heilbroner Carrie, bds 56 W Wayne.
Heilbroner Louis, saloon 18 W Berry, bds 56 W Wayne. Tel 147.
Heilbroner Louis A, clk Isadore Lehman, bds 62 W Main.
Heilbroner Samuel A, shoemkr 27 Pearl, res 56 W Wayne.
Heine, *see also Heiny*.
Heine Augusta, mender Wayne Knitting Mills, bds 52 Douglas av.
Heine Charles W, res 500 Hanna.
Heine Christian, res 134 Force.
Heine Edward H, student, bds 167 Hanna.
Heine Ernest F, restaurant 278 Calhoun, bds 52 Douglas av.
Heine Frederick C (Heine & Israel), res 139 Wallace.
Heine Frederick C, bkkpr Tri-State Bldg & Loan Assn, bds 52 Douglas av.
Heine Frederick C, plater Kellar Dental Co, bds 167 Hanna.

Heine Frederick W, carp Penn Co, res 52 Douglas av.
Heine Gottlieb, student, bds 52 Douglas av.
Heine Gottlieb W, helper Fleming Mnfg Co, res 7 Pape av.
Heine Henry, carp J F Tielmann, bds 424 Broadway.
Heine Henry F A, engr The Herman Berghoff Brewing
Co, res 87 Grant av.
Heine Henry W G, boilermkr Penn Co, res 141 Wallace.
Heine John C, boilermaker, res 98 Madison.
Heine John H, lab Penn Co, bds 97 Pennsylvania.
Heine Minnie, domestic 41 1st.
Heine Wm, mach hd Penn Co, res 307 Maumee rd.
Heine Wm C, boilermkr Wabash R R, res 100 Madison.
Heine Wm F, laborer, res 167 Hanna.
Heine Wm F, tinner Gerding & Aumann Bros, bds 139
Wallace.
Heine Wm F jr, hoop maker S D Bitler, bds 167 Hanna.
Heine Wm M, clk Penn Co, res 167 Hanna.
Heine & Israel (Frederick C. Heine. Charles
Israel), Painters and Wall Paper, 123 Broadway.
Heingartner Emma M, bds 155 W Main.
Heingartner Frederick, helper bds 155 W Main.
Heingartner Jennie E, bds 155 W Main.
Heingartner Sybilla (wid Martin), res 155 W Main.
Heingartner Wm D, bds 155 W Main.
Heinlen, see also Henline.
Heinlen Arthur W, mach, bds 128 W Butler.
Heinlen Wm J, res 128 W Butler.
Heinrich J R, Druggist, 210 Calhoun, cor Douglas
av, bds 185 E Jefferson.
Heinrich Louis A (Stahn & Heinrich), res 185 E Jefferson.
Heinroth Catherine (wid Andrew), bds. 60 E Washington.
Heintzelman Andreas, baker J H Schwicters, res 26 Orchard
Heiny, see also Heine.
Heiny Maggie, bds 122 E Wayne.
Heiny Nicholas, res 122 E Wayne.
Heinz Gustav, glass-blower, res 36 Wefel.
Heir Christian. res 107 Force.
Heisener Wm F, carpenter, res 68 Wilt.
Heisiner Josephine, domestic Lake Shore Hotel.
Heising Agnes, domestic 88 N Harrison.
Heistel Amandus, laborer, res 49 South Wayne av.
Heisner, see also Hisner.
Heisner Anna (wid Wm F), bds 374 W Main.
Heit, see also Hite.
Heit Alexander, butcher C F Haiber, res 74 Wells.

Heit Amos, foreman C F Muhler & Son, res 129 W DeWald

Heit Anthony W, trav agt Fox Bakery U S B Co, res 39 W Creighton av.

Heit Catherine, wrapper Keller Dental Co, bds 74 Wells.

Heit Charles F J, salesman McDonald & Watt, res 129 W De Wald.

Heit Christopher, trav agt Fox Br U S B Co, res 42 E De Wald.

Heit Edward P, mach hd Olds Wagon Wks, bds 129 W De Wald.

Heit Eliza (wid John), bds 243 W Washington.

Heit Frank C, grocer, 167 E Jefferson, res same.

Heit George H, tinner, 378 Calhoun, bds 129 W De Wald.

Heit Helen, opr S M Foster, bds 74 Wells.

Heit Joseph J, trav agt Fox Br U S Baking Co, bds 190 Griffith.

Heit Josephine (wid Anthony), res 190 Griffith.

Heit Lena F, bds 74 Wells.

Heit Lillian, bds 74 Wells.

Heit Matilda, bds 74 Wells.

Heit Wm, cabinetmkr, res 21 Nirdlinger av.

Heitwinkel Henry, bds 43 Charles.

Heitzler Joseph W, brakeman, res 48 Walter.

Heitzler Margaret (wid Joseph), bds 48 Walter.

Helbig Carl E, tinner Pickard Bros, res 64 Hugh.

Heldt Barbara (wid John M), died Sept 4th, 1894.

Heldt Elizabeth M, bds 182 E Wayne.

Heldt John M (Browand & Heldt), bds 182 E Wayne.

Helener F Harry, clk Wm Kaough, res 56 E Columbia.

Heley Arthur, candymkr, bds 340 E Wayne.

Helfer Charles F, barber, bds 176 Suttenfield.

Helfer Leopold, tailor S Fieldbleat, res 176 Suttenfield.

Helfrich Christian, marble cutter Brunner & Haag, bds 199 Broadway.

Helfrich Wendell, storekpr Penn Co, rms 199 Broadway.

Heliker Frank A, student, bds 46 Mc Clellan.

Heliker Wm, engr Penn Co. res 46 Mc Clellan.

Hellberg Frederick W, lab Standard Wheel Co, res Gay s w cor 9th.

Hellberg Mary S, opr Hoosier Mnfg Co, bds Gay s w cor 9th.

Helle Andrew, laborer, res 74 Murray.

Helle Anna, domestic 100 Broadway.

Helle Wm, carpenter, res 99 Wall.

Heller Adah M, stenogr Ft Wayne Newspaper Union, bds 32 W Washington.

Heller Flora A, bds 32 W Washington.

Heller George F, inspr Ft Wayne Gas Co, res 1 Sturgis.

Heller George W (Heller & Frankel), bds 107 E Washington.

Heller John C, clk County Recorder, bds 32 W Washington

Heller Lee T, bds 32 W Washington.

Heller Leonora, bds 107 E Washington.

Heller Louise C, teacher Hanna School, bds 32 W Washington,

Heller Mahlon, res 58 E Williams.

Heller Pauline (wid Jonas), res 107 E Washington.

Heller Philip A, clerk, bds 58 E Williams.

Heller Thomas S, agr imp, 25 Wells, res 32 W Washington.

Heller Wm D, cabinetmaker, res 84 St Mary's av.

Heller Wm M, bds 32 W Washington.

Heller & Frankel (George W Heller, Louis Frankel), Clothing, 42 Calhoun.

Helling Frederick jr, agent, res 189 Griffith.

Helling Frederick W, res 83 W Washington.

Helling John F W, driver Ft Wayne Art Ice Co, res 58 N Harrison.

Hellings Joel A, restaurant, 59 E Berry, rms 77 same.

Hellings Mary (wid James A), bds 59 E Berry.

Hellwig Bertha, seamstress, bds 6 Edgerton.

Hellwig Frederick, lab Penn Co, res 222 John.

Hellwig Julia (wid Emil), res 6 Edgerton.

Helmer Fannie (wid Henry), housekeeper 7 Duryea.

Helmick George C, cabtmkr Ft Wayne Furn Co, bds 54 Begue.

Helmick John H, died December 12, 1894.

Helmkamp Henry, carpenter, bds 16 Harrison.

Helmkamp John C, saloon, 16 Harrison, res same.

Helmke Charles C, bds 13 Douglas av.

Helmke Edward jr, cabtmkr K A Engmann, res 212 Calhoun,

Helmke Frederick W E, shoes, 212½ Calhoun, res 13 Douglas av.

Helmke Gustav, bds 13 Douglas av.

Helmke Herman, shoemkr F W E Helmke, res 212½ Calhoun.

Helver Burt A, brakeman N Y, C & St L R R, bds 371 W Main.

Hemhardt Charles F, car bldr Penn Co, bds 158 Wallace.

Hench, *see also Haensch.*

Hench George R, foreman Ft Wayne Sentinel, res 45 Elmwood av.

Hench Samuel R, lawyer, 31 E Main, bds New Aveline Hotel.

Henderson Alexander, engr Wabash R R, bds 499 Calhoun.

Henderson Andrew R, res 115 E Wayne.

Henderson Angeline M (wid Wm D), res 86 E Main.

Henderson David, watchman. Powers & Barnett, res 62 Madison.

Henderson Eliza C (wid Edgar), res 59 Huestis av.

Henderson Fred O H (col'd), bds 84 W Main.

Henderson Harry, brakeman, bds Lake Shore Hotel.

Henderson Harry, messenger the Journal Co, bds 149 Barr.

Henderson Henry, car inspector, res 126 E Lewis.

Henderson Henry C, mach E B Kunkle & Co, res 149 Barr.

Henderson Milton J, driver Powers & Barnett, bds 62 Madison.

Henderson Samuel C, foreman Penn Co, res 17 W Creighton av.

Henderson Wm D, Flour and Feed, 69 E Columbia, res 84 Columbia av. Tel 144.

Henderson Wm E, porter Bass F & M Wks, res 299 Hanna.

Hendler Joseph, mach hd Olds Wagon Wks, bds 157 Holman

Hendricks Maude F, teacher Hoagland School, bds 154 Harrison.

Hendrix Frederick C, mach hd S F Bowser & Co, bds 46 Oliver.

Hendrix George A, foreman Olds Wagon Wks, res 46 Oliver

Hengsteler Charles F, shoemaker, 115 Broadway, rms same

Hengsteler Martin, blksmith Bass F & M Wks, res 222 Gay.

Henkel, *see also Hinkel.*

Henkel Ferdinand, car bldr Penn Co, res 83 Shawnee av.

Henkenius August, laborer, bds 71 Huffman.

Henkenius Cecilia, seamstress, bds 92 E Jefferson.

Henkenius Christina F (wid Frank), res 71 Huffman.

Henkenius Clemens A, laborer, res 333 Hanna.

Henkenius Frank, car rpr Penn Co, res 92 E Jefferson.

Henkenius George J, grocer 243 St Mary's av, res same.

Henkenius Peter, candymkr Fox br U S Baking Co, res 16 Columbia av.

Henker Anna S, bds 217 E Wayne.

Henker Charles F, barber Benoit Ellert, res 217 E Wayne.

Henker Clara R, milliner, bds 217 E Wayne.

Henker Hulda teacher. bds 217 E Wayne.
Henker Laura I, opr S M Foster, bds 217 E Wayne.
Henker Wm, bds 217 E Wayne.
Henker Wm C, mach hd Penn Co, res 20 Charles.
Henley Albert, laborer, res 5 Runnion av.
Henline, see also Heinlen.
Henline Christian, clerk, bds 65 Barthold.
Henline John H, carpenter, res 18 Wefel.
Henline Samuel, carpenter, res 65 Barthold.
Henline Wm D, carpenter, res 36 Pritchard.
Henneger Anna, domestic n s 6th 1 e of N Clinton.
Henneger Louise E, domestic 11 Huffman.
Hennessy Timothy, lab N Y, C & St L R R, bds Lake Shore Hotel.
Henninger Gottfried, laborer, res 5 Romy av.
Henry Alma, domestic 39 W Washington.
Henry August, shoemaker, 24 Barr, res same.
Henry Carroll B, bds 331 W Jefferson.
Henry George A, shoemaker, bds 244 E Creighton av.
Henry Jacob, Dealer in Illuminated Marriage Certificates, Death Memorials, Books, Oil Paintings, Pictures, Frames and Stationery, 338 Hanna, res same.
Henry James C, tel opr, bds 331 W Jefferson.
Henry James M, carpenter, 161 W Jefferson, res 39 Grace av. Tel 307.
Henry John A, carpenter, bds 312 Harrison.
Henry John M, carpenter, res 331 W Jefferson.
Henry John W, shoes, 249 Calhoun, res 244 E Creighton av.
Henry Julius A, helper Penn Co, res 14 Oak.
Henry Louis G, shoes, 244 E Creighton av, bds same.
Henry Mattie (wid Thomas), bds 139 Francis.
Henry Robert A, carp J M Henry, res 272 W Jefferson.
Henry Wm H, truckman Penn Co, res 312 Harrison.
Henschen Edward, driver Engine Co No 6, rms same.
Henschen Ernest H, coremkr Bass F & M Wks, res 242 E Jefferson.
Henschen George H, mach hd, bds n s Chestnut 2 w of Warren.
Henschen Henry F, driver C H Waltemath & Sons, bds 325 Lafayette.
Henschen Henry G, car repr Penn Co, res n s Chestnut 2 w of Warren.
Henschen J Henry, clk E H Coombs, res 164 Ewing.
Henschen Wm, student, bds 242 E Jefferson.
Henschen Wm R, helper Penn Co, res 222 Francis.

Henscil Delcena (wid Albert), bds 84 Richardson.
Hensel Albert G, harnessmaker, bds 37 Gay.
Hensel Frank, bricklayer, bds 37 Miner.
Hensel Frederick Wm, mach Bass F & M Wks, res 37 Gay.
Hensel Louis, laborer, bds 37 Miner.
Hensel Peter, Contractor and Builder, 37 Miner, res same.
Hensel Peter jr, died Nov 10th, 1894.
Hensel Wm F H, pipeman Engine Co No 6, res 103 Wells.
Hensler Adam, lab Bass F & M Wks, res w s of Abbott, 4 s of Pontiac.
Hensler Ervine, lab Penn Co, res 24 Walnut.
Henstock Arthur S, patternmkr Ft Wayne Electric Corp, rms 37 Baker.
Henze Elizabeth, milliner, bds 102 Wells.
Henze Minnie, hairdresser, bds 102 Wells.
Henze Wm, saloon 20 Clinton, res 102 Wells.
Hepner Emma, domestic 76 E Washington.
Herber, *see also Haiber. Harber and Harper.*
Herber Frederick E, carbldr Penn Co, res 495 E Washington.
Herber Garret P, carp, res n s Hugh 1 e of Walton av.
Herber Jacob N, carpenter, bds 9 Liberty.
Herber John F, carpenter, res 9 Liberty.
Herber Nicholas, bds 162 Taber.
Herbert, *see also Ebert.*
Herbert Wm J, clk F, Ft W & W Ry, bds 46 E Jefferson.
Herbrook Robert F, forman Model Hand Laundry, bds 125 W Williams.
Herbst Otto P (Geo Motz & Co), bkkpr Hamilton National Bank, res 344 E Lewis.
Herderhorst Ernest, carpenter, res 50 Hugh.
Hergenrader H John, laborer, bds 43 Wall.
Hergenrader Michael, plasterer, res 43 Wall.
Hergenrather, *see also Harkenrieder.*
Hergenrather Joseph, mach hd Rhinesmith & Simonson, bds 89 Wagner.
Hergenrather Margaret (wid Joseph), res 89 Wagner.
Hergenrather Wm, mach hd, res 76 Murray.
Hergenrother Joseph, bricklayer, res 389 E Washington.
Hering, *see also Herring.*
Hering Harry D, clk Ft W Electric Corp, rms 165 Griffith
Hering W Frank, printer The Journal, bds 105 Lafayette.
Herman, *see also Harmon and Herrmann.*
Herman Blanche, bds 8 Mechanic.

Herman David, brakeman. rms 36 Baker.
Herman John A, carp John Suelzer, res 22 W Allen.
Herman John H, engr Empire Mills, res 40 Boone.
Herman John L, winder, bds 40 Boone.
Herman Nicholas, lab Penn Co, res 54 Thomas.
Hermans Henry H, shoes, 376 Calhoun. res same.
Hermeler Delia L, opr. bds 100 Mechanic.
Hermeler Henry, mach hd Hoffman Bros, res 100 Mechanic
Hermeler Henry F, sawyer, bds 100 Mechanic.
Hermeler Sophia D, bds 100 Mechanic.
Herminghuysen Frank, laborer, bds 419 W Main.
Hermsdorfer George A, grocer, 279 W Jefferson, res 281
  same.
Hermsdorfer Sarah E (wid Frederick), bds 44 W Williams.
Herr Charles, laborer, res 590 Lafayette.
Herr Sarah M (wid George), res 61 W 5th.
Herres, *see also Harris*.
Herres Mathew, lab Penn Co, res w s Euclid av 1 w of
  Mercer.
Herrick Ruth (wid Wm), res n s Ruth 1 w of Spy Run av.
Herrin Jeremiah, tinner S F Bowser & Co, res 250 E
  Creighton av.
Herring, *see also Hering*.
Herring Howard L, newstand, 1 Railroad, bds 386 Calhoun
Herring Isaac J, lather, res 40 E Jefferson.
Herring John P. conductor, res 267 E Creighton av.
Herring Lottie I, domestic Jacob Funk.
Herrington Blk. e s Fairfield av bet Williams and Bass.
Herrington Minnie, domestic 29 Duryea.
Herrmann. *see also Herman and Harmon*.
Herrmann George, res 82 Walton av.
Herrmann George jr, meat market, 84 Walton av, res 76
  same.
Herrmann Michael J, died March 3d, 1894.
Herrold Daniel J, driver Am Ex Co, res 78 Lake av.
Hersh, *see also Harsh, Hirsch and Hursh*.
Hersh Joseph W, agent, res n s Prospect av 2 e of Spy
  Run av.
Hershey Fannie A (wid Christian), bds 329 W Main.
Hertwig, *see also Hartwig*.
Hertwig Ernest P, carpet weaver, 42 Eliza, res same.
Hertwig Freda, dressmaker, bds 42 Eliza.
Hesemeyer Augusta, seamstress, bds 15 Lavina.
Hesemeyer Henry, brickmason, res 15 Lavina.
Hesemeyer Matilda, milliner, bds 15 Lavina.

Hess, *see also Haas and Hass.*
Hess Alice M, bds 51 Elizabeth.
Hess Bertha E, student, bds 132 E Creighton av.
Hess Charlotte (wid Jacob), res s w cor Lafayette and Leith.
Hess Jacob C, switchman, bds 33 Gay.
Hess John, expressman, res 38 Wefel.
Hess John R, removed to Maysville, Ind.
Hess Laura, cook McKinnie House.
Hess Maggie K, bds 38 Wefel.
Hess Mary E, bds 38 Wefel.
Hess Nicholas W, carriagemkr, res 51 Elizabeth.
Hess Philip E, appr Penn Co, bds 132 E Creighton av.
Hess Philip J, mach Pann Co, res 132 E Creighton av.
Hess Wm J, mach Rocker Washer Co, res 29 N Calhoun.
Hesser Walter G, clerk, bds 25 W Lewis.
Hessert, *see also Hassard and Hazzard.*
Hessert Bernard, teamster, res 162 W Superior.
Hessert Edward G, clk Karn Bros, bds 162 W Superior.
Hessert George, teamster, res 218 W Superior.
Hessert John B, teamster, bds 162 W Superior.
Hester Kate (wid James), bds 33 St Mary's av.
Heth Emma, bds 2 Erie.
Heth Tillie, bkkpr Moellering Bros & Millard, bds 2 Erie.
Hetrick Jacob, physician, 10 Calhoun, res 160 E Wayne. Tel 436.
Hetrick Jacob A, clk People's Store, res 214 E Jefferson
Hettler Albert, brakeman, bds 61 Lasselle.
Hettler Christopher F, lumber agt, res 99 E Lewis.
Hettler Clara, bds 61 Lasselle.
Hettler Gottleib, sewer bldr, res 84 Charles.
Hettler Mrs Harriet, res 61 Lasselle.
Hetzel Mathias, lab Penn Co, res 204 Lafayette.
Heuer Christian, helper, res 107 Force.
Heuer Ernest G, boilermakr Wabash R R, res 33 Summit.
Heuer Frederica (wid Herman), bds 164 Griffith.
Heuer Martin, agent, rms 39 W Berry.
Heuer Wm F, boilermaker, bds 107 Force.
Hewes, *see also Hughes.*
Hewes James C, foreman Penn Co, res 142 E Lewis.
Hewitt George W, conductor, res 294 Hanna.
Hewitt Marshall, mach hd Ft Wayne Furn Co, bds 294 Hanna.
Hey, *see also Hay.*
Hey August M, jeweler F J Voirol, bds 60 Buchanan.
Hibbins Thomas H, slater, res 85 Swinney av.

Hibbins Wm J, messenger Penn Co, bds 85 Swinney av.

Hibernia Hall, White Blk.

Hibinger John D, conductor N Y, C & St L R R, res 279 W Main.

Hibler, *see also Heibler.*

Hibler Anthony, mason, res e s Lafayette 3 s of Grace.

Hibler Bernard, teamster, res w s Lafayette, 2 s of Grace.

Hibler Bernard A, motorman Ft W E Ry Co, res 6 Bass.

Hibler Henry G, helper, res 578 Lafayette,

Hibler Louis, helper Penn Co, res 55 Grand.

Hickey Morris L, engr L E & W R R, bds Lake Shore Hotel.

Hickman Cora B, clk Princess Cash Store, bds 84 Van Buren.

Hickman Daniel, expressman, res 195 Sherman.

Hickman Edward A, lab Hoffman Bros, res 197 Sherman.

Hickman Eugene, condr Ft W E Ry Co, res 170 Montgomery.

Hickman James H, res 84 Van Buren.

Hickman John C, mach Penn Co, res 49 Indiana av.

Hickman John W, carpet weaver, 171 Broadway, res same.

Hicks Wm, laborer, res s s French 2 w of Webster.

Hieber, *see Hueber.*

Higbee Elmer J, condr N Y, C & St L R R, res 16 Huron.

Higginbotham John F, mach hd Ft Wayne Electric Corp, bds 39 W Washington.

Higgins Cecilia W, bds 166 E Berry.

Higgins Cecilius R, Sec and Treas Fort Wayne Artificial Ice Co, Sec and Mngr Fort Wayne District Tel Co, Agent Fort Wayne Harrison Tel Co, res 166 E Berry, Tel 469.

Higgins Clara M, domestic 90 W Main.

Higgins Emmitt M, bds 143 E Jefferson.

Higgins Frank P, engr Penn Co, res 143 E Jefferson.

Higgins Maggie J, bds 143 E Jefferson.

High School, E Wayne bet Calhoun and Clinton.

Higley Mrs Martha J, res 38 Taylor.

Hikel Wm, notions, 121 Fairfield av, res same.

Hikowski Florentine (wid Ferdinand), res 211 John.

Hikowski Hannah, domestic 203 W Wayne.

Hilbrecht Clara, stenogr Dreibelbiss Abstract of Title Co, bds 61 Clinton.

Hilbrecht Henry, res 228 W Jefferson.

Hilbrecht Henry jr, chief Fire Department, office Central Station, res 61 Clinton.

Hilbrecht Louisa S, bds 228 W Jefferson.
Hild Albert D, painter Henry Hild. bds 159 Van Buren.
Hild Emma W, seamstress, bds 159 Van Buren.
Hild Henry, Sign and Carriage Painter, 149 W Main, res 159 Van Buren. (See p 115).
Hild Otto G, collr C U Tel Co. bds 159 Van Buren.
Hildebrand Charles H, mach hd Anthony Wayne Mnfg Co, bds 215 Madison.
Hildebrand Wm H, res 234 W Washington.
Hildebrandt Felix, polisher, bds 74 Nelson.
Hildebrandt Frederick, res 215 Madison.
Hildebrandt Louisa (wid Julius), res 74 Nelson.
Hildenbrand Howard F. mngr Fort Wayne Club, rms 70 Harrison.
Hildinger Caroline B, domestic 91 E Washington.
Hildinger Jacob F, bds n e cor Chestnut and Lumbard.
Hildinger Jacob J, lab Penn Co, res n e cor Lumbard and Chestnut.
Hile Frederick, hostler F H Myers, rms 62 E Wayne.
Hiler Clara, rms 33 Madison.
Hiler John B, contractor, res n s Killea av 2 e of Hoagland av
Hiler Lena E, teacher, bds n s Killea av 2 e of Hoagland av.
Hilgeman Lena, opr S M Foster, bds 111 Wall.
Hilgeman Wm, carpenter. res 111 Wall.
Hilgemann Clara, bds 28 Locust.
Hilgemann Ernest R, car inspr, res 559 Broadway.
Hilgemann Florence W, mach, bds 128 Locust.
Hilgemann Franklin H, clerk, bds 121 W Jefferson.
Hilgemann Frederick, laborer, res 66 Smith.
Hilgemann Frederick G. lab. res n e cor Locust and Pine.
Hilgemann Frederick H, helper Bass F & M Wks, bds 66 Smith.
Hilgemann Frederick W, carp, res 399 E Washington.
Hilgemann Gustave F, hoseman Engine Co No 2, rms same.
Hilgemann Henry, res 91 W Jefferson.
Hilgemann Henry F. carp 355 E Lewis, res same.
Hilgemann Henry F, grocer 121 W Jefferson, res same.
Hilgemann Henry W, carp Bass F & M Wks, res 42 W Allen.
Hilgemann Jacob W, lab Ft Wayne Electric Corp, bds 215 W Main.
Hilgemann John F, winder, bds 28 Locust.
Hilgemann Louisa (wid August), res 81 Force.
Hilgemann Louise domestic 151 W Berry.
Hilgemann Louise K, bds 219 E Washington.

Hilgemann Matilda, opr Hoosier Mnfg Co, bds 66 Smith.
Hilgemann Wm, helper Anthony Wayne Mnfg Co, bds 66 Smith.
Hilgemann Wm J, carp, res 216 E Washington,
Hilker, *see also Hilleke.*
Hilker Anna H, opr S M Foster, bds 114 Fairfield av.
Hilker Anthony H, carpenter, bds 69 Summit.
Hilker Anthony J, boilermkr Wabash R R, bds 114 Fairfield av.
Hilker August, laborer, res 114 Fairfield av.
Hilker Catherine E, bds 114 Fairfield av.
Hilker Charles A, cupola tender Bass F & M Wks, res 231 John.
Hilker Charles C, helper, bds 231 John.
Hilker Charles D W, carp Penn Co, res 137 Francis.
Hilker Charles F, foreman Jacob Klett & Sons, res 37 Erie
Hilker Diedrich F W, mach hd Olds Wagon Wks, res 63 Buchanan.
Hilker Frank C, mach hd Jacob Klett & Sons, bds 69 Summit.
Hilker Frederick, died January 12th, 1895.
Hilker Herman, brakeman, res 219 John.
Hilker Herman H, clk J B White, res 4 Huffman.
Hilker Mary (wid Harmon H), res 69 Summit.
Hilker Minnie, bds 231 John.
Hilker Wm C, molder Bass F & M Wks, res 227 John.
Hilker Wm F, driver Powers & Barnett, res 175 W Washington.
Hill Amelia, waitress New Aveline House.
Hill Andrew, res 55 Hendricks.
Hill Anna M B, bds 64 W 3d.
Hill Arthur L, died January 3, 1895.
Hill Barbara (wid Valentine), bds 186 Monroe.
Hill Charles A, salesman D H Baldwin & Co, res 188 Griffith
Hill Charles L, Musical Merchandise, 38 Clinton, res 27 Prospect av.
Hill Mrs Cornelia A, res 28 Douglas av.
Hill David, driver L Diether & Bro, res 64 W 3d.
Hill Edith M, bds 64 W 3d.
Hill Edward C, engr Engine Co No 1, res 26 Douglas av.
Hill Frank H, clk Louis Wolf & Co, bds 90 W 4th.
Hill Frank W, fireman N Y, C & St L R R, bds 309 W Washington.
Hill George, mach hd Penn Co, res 2 Erie.
Hill Harriett L, bds 28 Douglas av.

Hill John D, helper L Diether & Bro, bds 64 W 3d.
Hill Louis H, mach hd L Diether & Bro, res s w cor St Mary's av and Aboit.
Hill Mandeville E, stopmaker Ft Wayne Organ Co, res 407 Fairfield av.
Hill Martha (wid John), res 174 Hayden.
Hill Minnie E, opr S M Foster, bds 35 W 4th.
Hill Onslow G, res 316 W Jefferson.
Hill Richard S, designer Ft Wayne Organ Co, res 59 W De Wald.
Hill Robert H (col'd), waiter The Wayne, rms 71 Monroe.
Hill Thomas, res 23 W Butler.
Hill Wm E, removed to Chicago, Ill.
Hill Wm M, foreman S F Bowser & Co, res 130 Thomas.
Hill Wm W, weighmaster N Y, C & St L R R, res 309 W Washington.
Hille August, carp H A Grotholtman & Co, bds 106 Wall.
Hille Henry J, helper Wabash R R, res 256 W Jefferson.
Hille J Henry, baggageman Wabash R R, res 106 Wall.
Hille Louise, bds 256 W Jefferson.
Hille Wm, helper Bass F & M Wks, bds 106 Wall.
Hilleke, see also Hilker.
Hilleke Henry, helper Penn Co, res 44 Hendricks.
Hilliard Anna (wid Robert M), res 5 Wall.
Hilliard May, teacher School F M Y, bds same.
Hilliker Wm H, engineer, res 46 McClellan.
Hills Annie R (wid Francis M), notions, 9 E Main, res 17½ same.
Hills Henrietta, opr Hoosier Mnfg Co, bds 55 Hendricks.
Hills Henry, lab L Rastetter & Son, bds 55 Hendricks.
Hills Leslie W, clk A R Hills, bds 17½ E Main.
Hills Lorenzo V, expressman, bds w s Warren 1 s of Wabash R R.
Hills Sarah E (wid Ambrose A), res n w cor Chestnut and Summer.
Hilt Catherine F, housekeeper 26 Baker.
Hilt Frederick, harness, 18½ E Columbia, res 26 Baker.
Hilt Sarah, bds 26 Baker.
Hilton Charles S, supt Ft Wayne Electric Corp, res 67 Walnut.
Himbert John E, expressman, bds 14 Lavina.
Himbert John F, lab L S & M S Ry, bds 106 Chicago.
Himbert John M, saloon, 53 Wells, res same.
Himbert Louisa A, tailoress, bds 14 Lavina.
Himbert Michael, res 14 Lavina.

Himbert Wm, coachman, res 24 Van Buren.
Hinch Henry, baker L P Scherer, res 84 Summit.
Hindle Edward W, brakeman N Y, C & St L R R, bds 10 St Mary's av.
Hindle Jane C (wid Henry), res 10 St Mary's av.
Hiner Edward S, barn man, bds 24 Harrison.
Hines Adolphus J, policeman, res 47 Walnut.
Hines Alma, waitress The Randall.
Hines Alta M, bds 47 Walnut.
Hines John, clk J S Hines, bds 379½ W Main.
Hines John S, Plumber. Steam and Gasfitter, 379 W Main, res 379½ same. Tel 512. (*See right top lines.*)
Hines Lucien M, painter, res 116 W Williams.
Hines Mattie, laundress Hyer House.
Hines Philip, carpenter, res 6 Short.
Hines Richard O, student, bds 47 Walnut.
Hines W R (J W Wilding & Co), res Indianapolis, Ind.
Hinkel, *see also Henkel.*
Hinkel Ernest, knitter, bds 29 Boone.
Hinkle Catherine (wid Henry), res 9 Elm.
Hinkle Dora, bds 9 Elm.
Hinkle Mary E, bds 9 Elm.
Hinton Alice F, bds 30 Baker.
Hinton Johanna (wid Samuel), res 30 Baker.
Hinton John C, restaurant 270½ Calhoun, res same.
Hinz Charles, laborer, res 235 Force.
Hinz Ernest, butcher F Boes, bds 235 Force.
Hipp Carl O B, press feeder Aldine Printing House, bds Windsor Hotel.
Hipp Edward F, car bldr Penn Co, res 154 Suttenfield.
Hippenhamer John W, ins agt, res 170 Brackenridge.
Hippenhamer Mrs Rosa E. dressmaker, 170 Brackenridge.
Hire Edna F, bds 6 Prospect av.
Hire Elias, farmer, res 6 Prospect av.
Hire Elma, bds 6 Prospect av.
Hirons A R, res 16 Clay.
Hirsch, *see also Harsh,. Hersh and Hursh.*
Hirsch Bertha, clk Louis Wolf & Co, bds 70 W Jefferson.
Hirsch Caroline S (wid George), housekeeper 164 Ewing.
Hirsch David, mngr R Deitsch, bds 84 W Washington.
Hirsch Hannah (wid Leopold), res 70 W Jefferson.
Hirsch Henry, baker, res 62 Summit.
Hirsch Louis, clk Pottlitzer Bros, bds 70 W Jefferson.
Hirschberg Rev Samuel, rabbi Temple Achduth Veshalom, rms 134 W Berry.

22

Hirschfelder Anna, opr Wayne Knitting Mills, bds 240 E Wayne.

Hirschfelder Caroline (wid Michael), res 240 E Wayne.

Hirschfelder Catherine (wid Lucas), res 362 E Wayne.

Hirschfelder Frank, bottler The Hermann Bergboff Brew-Co, bds 274 E Wayne.

Hirschfelder Henry, bricklayer, res 244 Erie.

Hirschfelder Joseph, bds 362 E Wayne.

Hirschfelder Mary, former, bds 240 E Wayne.

Hirschfelder Matilda, seamstress, bds 362 E Wayne.

Hirschmann John, carp, res e s Victoria av, 1 s of Piqua av.

Hirschmann Louisa, bds e s Victoria av 1 s of Piqua av.

Hirsh Adolph (A Hirsh & Co), res 146 W Berry.

Hirsh A & Co (Adolph Hirsh, Joseph Kirchheimer, Charles Nathan), Wholesale Papers, Twines. Paper Bags and Wood Dishes, 23 East Columbia. Tel 66.

Hirsh Maud, bds 146 W Berry.

Hirst Frederick, foreman Western Gas Const Co, res 103 Greene.

Hirst James E, foreman Ind Mach Wks, res 232 W Washington.

Hirst Richard G, mach Western Const Co, bds 103 Greene.

Hirt Jacob (Hirt and Evans), res 5 N Clinton.

Hirt Minnie, domestic 84 W Washington.

Hiser Samuel A, engr G R & I R R, res 123 W Williams.

Hislop Catherine (wid Robert), res n s New Haven av 4 W of Lumbard.

Hisner, see also Heisner.

Hisner Annie, finisher Wayne Knitting Mills, bds 186 Gay.

Hisner Charles, teamster E Gilmartin, bds 186 Gay.

Hisner Charles H jr, clk Golden & Patterson, bds 186 Gay.

Hisner Frederick W, student, bds 186 Gay.

Hisner Wm F, carpenter, res 68 Wilt.

Hitchcock Frank A, clk Penn Co, res 48 Hugh.

Hitchcock Wm, conductor, res 139 Francis.

Hitchcock B F, condr F, Ft W & W R R, bds 193 Lafayette

Hite, see also Heit.

Hite Adam, lab, res w s St Mary's av 1 s of Putnam.

Hite Adelia J, bds 157½ Wells.

Hite Andrew K (Hite & Son), res 182 Oakland.

Hith Fredick (Hite & Son), bds 182 Oakland.

Hite Georgia A, opr S M Foster, bds 157½ Wells.

Hite Harvey T, engineer. res 157½ Wells.

Hite Oscar, laborer, res n w cor Putnam and Oakland.

Hite Samuel H, lab Ft Wayne Organ Co, res 611 Calhoun.

Hite & Son (Andrew K and Frederick), contractors, 182 Oakland.

Hitzeman Charles F, clk Ft W E Ry Co, res 62 Hugh.

Hitzeman Christian C, clk Geo De Wald & Co, res 290 W Washington.

Hitzeman George J, grocer, 47 Maumee rd, res 24 Summit.

Hitzeman Kate L, clk G J Hitzeman, bds 24 Summit.

Hitzeman Sophia K, dressmkr, bds 24 Summit.'

Hitzemann Bertha, domestic 45 W Main.

Hitzemann Charles F, press feeder Ft Wayne Newspaper Union, bds 36 Lavina.

Hitzemann Conrad, teamster, bds 28 Liberty.

Hitzemann Ernest F, finisher Ft Wayne Organ Co, res'119 Wall.

Hitzemann Frederick, res 36 Lavina.

Hitzemann Frederick H D, bds 36 Lavina.

Hitzemann Frederick J, tailor G H Hitzemann, res 58 Huffman

Hitzemann Gottlieb, tailor, 133 Broadway, res 49 Wilt.

Hitzemann Gottlieb H jr, clk C F Reinkensmeier, bds 49 Wilt.

Hitzemann Henry C, clk Pfeiffer & Schlatter, res 48 Stophlet.

Hitzemann Herman W, clerk, bds 49 Wilt.

Hitzemann Louise W (wid Henry C), matron Concordia College. res same.

Hitzemann Mary, bds 36 Lavina.

Hitzemann Minnie, bds 36 Lavina.

Hitzemann Minnie S, opr Wayne Knitting Mills, bds 49 Wilt

Hitzemann Sophia W M, domestic 150 Montgomery.

Hitzemann Sophie, domestic 96 W Wayne.

Hively Jennie, seamstress, bds n s E Lewis 1 e of Barr.

Hively Lucinda (wid Francis), res n s Lewis 1 e of Barr.

Hoadley Annie C, clk J A Armstrong & Co, bds 115 W Washington.

Hoadley Jennie, hairdresser Mrs F Malloy, res 115 W Washington.

Hoadley May, dressmaker, bds 115 W Washington.

Hoagland Merica E, bds 106 W Berry.

Hoagland School, n w cor Hoagland av and Butler.

Hobbs Charles I, truckman Penn Co, res 34 Eliza.

Hobbs Eva, seamstress, bds 75 W Lewis.

Hobbs Frank H, driver Smith & Dailey, res 56 Ferguson av

Hobbs Julia B (wid Reuben), res 75 W Lewis.

Hobbs Oscar L, music teacher, 164 Madison, res same.

Hobbs Reuben, carpenter, res 75 W Lewis.
Hobbs Wm, cook Windsor Hotel.
Hobbs Wm H, lab A Kalbacher, bds Windsor Hotel.
Hoben Ellen M, res 66 W Main.
Hoben James, laborer, res 12 Winch.
Hobrock Anna M, bds 94 Fairfield av.
Hobrock August C, mach Robert Ogden, bds 94 Fairfield av
Hobrock Carrie (wid John H), res 94 Fairfield av.
Hobrock Carrie E, clk M Frank & Co, bds 94 Fairfield av.
Hobrock Edward L, clk Penn Co, bds 94 Fairfield av.
Hobrock Henry, lab Olds Wagon Wks, bds 601 Gay.
Hobrock John H, bds 27 Baker.
Hobrock J Herman, clk Penn Co, res 100 Fairfield av.
Hobrock Martin H, helper Penn Co, bds 168 Ewing.
Hobrock Wm H, furnace tender Penn Co, res 134 E De
    Wald.
Hoch Emanuel, driver Engine Co No 2, res 105 Wallace.
Hoch George, butcher Wm Hoch jr, bds 313 Lafayette.
Hoch Henry, fireman Penn Co, bds 321 Lafayette.
Hoch Wm, Meat Market 121 Wallace, First Class
    Saloon, 313 Lafayette, res 313 Lafayette.
Hoch Wm jr, mngr Wm Hoch, bds 313 Lafayette.
Hochmann Frederick jr, laborer, bds s w cor Reynolds and
    Summer.
Hochstetter Augusta, bds 15 Sturgis.
Hochstetter Minnie, bds 15 Sturgis.
Hochstetter Wm G. res 15 Sturgis.
Hochstraser Elizabeth (wid John), res n w cor Spy Run av
    and Edna
Hochstraser John W, bottler C L Centlivre Brewing Co,
    bds n w cor Spy Run av and Edna.
Hochstraser Mamie J, bds n w cor Spy Run av and Edna.
Hockaday Deborah (wid Samuel), res 80 Chicago.
Hockemeyer Amelia, bds 115 Madison.
Hockemeyer Charles F, printer, bds 317 W Washington.
Hockemeyer Christina, opr Wayne Knitting Mills, bds 115
    Madison.
Hockemeyer Emma H, tailoress, bds 317 W Washington.
Hockemeyer Henry, brickmason, res 115 Madison.
Hockemeyer Henry, carp H A Grotholtman & Co, res 30
    Chute.
Hockemeyer Henry, laborer, bds 174 Francis.
Hockemeyer Lizzie S, clk Seavey Hardware Co, bds 317
    W Washington.

Hockemeyer Mary (wid Charles), res 317 W Washington.
Hockemeyer Minnie, domestic 127 E Washington.
Hockemeyer Minnie, tailoress, bds 317 W Washington.
Hockemeyer Sophia W L, bds 148 Broadway.
Hockemeyer Sophie, domestic 75 Wilt.
Hodges Henry F, engr G R & I R R, res 58 Oliver.
Hoefler Harry R, rms 214 Calhoun.
Hoeffner, see Haffner and Heffner.
Hoelke Mrs Leonora, bds 214 W Jefferson.
+Hoelle Jacob, helper Bass F & M Wks, res 56 Grace.
Hoelle Martin, lab Bass F & M Wks, res 194 Taylor.
Hoeltje Hannah M, domestic 216 W Berry.
Hoeltje Henry C, cigarmkr F J Gruber, res 44 Michigan av
Hoeltje Louisa (wid August), bds 44 Michigan av.
Hoeltje Mary R, bds 44 Michigan av.
Hoemig Charles, barber, 118 Wells, res 33 E 4th.
Hoemig Nellie M, bkkpr Pfeiffer & Rousseau, bds 33 E 4th
Hoenick Charles, pressfeeder Ft Wayne Newspaper Union,
  bds 2 Elm.
Hoeppner Charles, laborer Penn Co, res 160 Gay.
Hoeppner Charles jr, blacksmith, s w cor Gay and Creigh-
  ton av, bds 160 Gay.
Hoeppner Frederick, helper Penn Co, res 253 Gay.
Hoeppner Philip, laborer, bds 160 Gay.
Hoeppner Wm, laborer, bds 160 Gay.
Hoewischer Frederick A, carp Rhinesmith & Simonson,
  res 92 Chicago.
Hoewischer Martha M, seamstress, bds 92 Chicago.
Hoewischer Mary, shirtmkr P G Kuttner, bds 92 Chicago.
Hofer Andrew, butcher, res 61 Lake av.
Hofer Anna, bkkpr F P Mensch, bds 61 Lake av.
Hofer A Edward, removed to Muncie, Ind.
Hofer Charles G, clk A R Hills, bds 61 Lake av.
Hofer John, laborer, bds 500 W Main.
Hofer John, peddler, res 151 Broadway.
Hofer Robert, blksmith City Carriage Wks, bds Hedekin
  House.
Hofer Rosa, clk A R Hills, bds 61 Lake av.
Hofer Theobald, real estate, 38 Bank Blk, res 140 Cass.
Hoff Mary, died Dec 1st, 1894.
Hoffer Celia L, clk Wm Hahn & Co, bds 37 Cass.
Hoffer Frederick, molder, bds s s Putnam 1 w of Frank-
  lin av.
Hoffer John, mach Star Iron Tower Co, res 14 W 3d.
Hoffer John G, carpenter, res 37 Cass.

Hoffer Lena, domestic 25 W Lewis

Hoffman, *see also Huffmann*

Hoffman Adam J, molder Bass F & M Wks, bds 31 Force.

Hoffman Alois, stonemason, res 417 E Lewis.

Hoffman Amelia, bds s w cor Jenison and Reid.

Hoffman Augusta F, seamstress, bds s w cor Reed and Jenison.

Hoffman A Ely (Hoffman Bros and J R Hoffman & Co), pres Hoffman Lumber Co, res 188 W Wayne. Tel 13.

Hoffman Barbara, opr Hoosier Mnfg Co, bds 31 Force.

Hoffman Bros (A Ely and Wm H), Lumber Manufacturers. 200 W Main. Tel 61. (*See right bottom lines.*)

Hoffman Catherine, bds 200 W Berry.

Hoffman Cynthia A, clk Root & Co, bds Hamilton Homestead.

Hoffman Daniel, painter, res s w cor Reed and Jenison.

Hoffman Ellen S, bds 52 W Creighton av.

Hoffman Emily, bds 200 W Berry.

Hoffman Frederick E, student, bds 200 W Berry.

Hoffman George, wagonmkr, res cor Montgomery and Clinton.

Hoffman Henry, butcher, res 252 Erie.

Hoffman Henry A, Contractor and Builder, res 52 W Creighton av.

Hoffman Henry C H, clerk, bds s w cor Reed and Jenison.

Hoffman Jacob R (J R Hoffman & Co), res Charleston, W Va

Hoffman John F, carp P H Wyss, res 32 Walton av.

Hoffman John N, carpenter, res 194 Smith.

Hoffman J R & Co (Jacob R, A Ely and Wm H Hoffman), Manufacturers Patent Band Saw Mills, 200 W Main. (*See right bottom lines.*)

Hoffman Kate, domestic 100 Calhoun.

Hoffman Lizzie (wid Charles), res 121 Ewing,

Hoffman Louise M, domestic 322 Fairfield av.

Hoffman Lumber Co, A Ely Hoffman Pres, Wm H Hoffman Vice-Pres, John W Sale Sec and Treas, Hardwood Lumber and Logs, 200 W Main. Tel 61. (*See right bottom lines.*)

Hoffman Margaret (wid John A), res 31 Force.

Hoffman Minnie, bds 188 W Wayne.

Hoffman Mollie, clk J H Brimmer, bds cor Montgomery and Clinton.

Hoffman Nicholas, porter J B White, res 51 Force.

Hoffman Peter E G, painter D Hoffman, bds s w cor Reed and Jeneson.

Hoffman Susan C (wid J Francis), librarian The Public Library, City Hall, res 132 E Main.

Hoffman Urban S, clk Root & Co, res 8 Riverside av.

Hoffman Wm H (Hoffman Bros and J R Hoffman & Co), vice-pres Hoffman Lumber Co, res 200 W Berry. Tel 92.

Hoffmann Charles, car bldr Penn Co, res 518 E Washington.

Hoffmann Charles A, Wholesale and Retail Dealer in Cider, Apple Wine and Cider Vinegar, and Propr Hoffmann House, 183–187 Calhoun. (*See p 87.*)

Hoffmann George, laborer, res 35 Maumee rd.

Hoffmann House, Charles A Hoffmann Propr, 183–187 Calhoun. (*See p 87.*)

Hoffmann Martin C H, carp, res s s Zollars av 5 w of Metz.

Hoffmann Mary R, domestic s w cor Clinton and Washington.

Hoffmeister Henry, cooper, res 12 W 3d.

Hofmann G Adolph, lab Bass F & M Wks, res 165 Hayden.

Hofmann G Max, vice-pres Phoenix Building and Savings Union and supt Ft Wayne Gas Co, res 429 Broadway. Tel 292.

Hogan Catherine (wid Michael), res 58 Prince.

Hogan Edward P, mach hd Anthony Wayne Mnfg Co, bds 176 Fairfield av.

Hogan Elizabeth M, bds 176 Fairfield av.

Hogan Frank J, city agt, bds 176 Fairfield av.

Hogan Hugh P, mach Penn Co, bds 94 Baker.

Hogan Hugh T, foreman Penn Co, bds 94 Baker.

Hogan Jane (wid Samuel), bds 93 Ewing.

Hogan John P, plumber A Hattersley & Sons, bds 176 Fairfield av.

Hogan J Dennis, machinist, res 22 Murray.

Hogan Margaret M, bds 94 Baker.

Hogan Mary, bds 176 Fairfield av.

Hogan Mary T (wid Timothy), res 11 Grand.

Hogan Michael, fireman. bds 58 Prince

Hogan Patrick, watchman, res 176 Fairfield av.

Hogan Stephen A, laborer. res 93 Ewing.

Hogan Stephen D, bartender J Benedict, bds 93 Ewing.

Hogan Wm S, bds 176 Fairfield av.

Hoham Fred D, Druggist, 298 Calhoun, res 484 Harrison.

Hoham George K, clk F D Hoham, bds 484 Harrison.

Hoham Wm H, night clk Police Headquarters, bds 298 Calhoun.

Hohan Bertha, student, bds 52 W Washington.

Hohmann Elizabeth E, clk Siemon & Bro, bds 175 High.

Hohmann Emily E, dressmaker, bds 175 High.

Hohmann Franklin, tailor, res 175 High.

Hohmann Henry H (Hohmann & Swaidner), res 248 Calhoun

Hohmann Josephine, bds 175 High.

Hohmann & Swaidner (Henry H Hohmann, Edwin J Swaidner), barbers, 248 Calhoun.

Hohmeyer, see Homeyer.

Hohnhaus Amelia S (wid Wm J), bds 63 Wall.

Hohnhaus Dora L, bds 63 Wall.

Hohnhaus George, died February 19, 1894.

Hohnhaus Mrs George, res s e cor Hanna and Eckart lane.

Hohnhaus Peter G, cabinetmaker, res 63 Wall.

Hohnhaus Wm G F, helper Ft Wayne Organ Co, bds s.e cor Hanna and Eckart lane.

Hohnhausen George P, mason Bass F & M Wks, bds 83 Taylor.

Hohnhausen Magdalena (wid Nicholas), res 13 Wall.

Hohnholz Conrad, clk J R Heinrich, rms 201 Calhoun.

Hohnholz Herman, cigar mnfr, 135 Wallace, res 226 W Jefferson.

Hoke Anna, forelady Fox br U S Baking Co, bds 42 W Butler.

Hoke Charles L, lab Penn Co, res 60 Prince.

Hoke Mary, opr S M Foster, bds 185 Lafayette.

Holder Chichester, lawyer, 13 E Main, res 14 Purman.

Holdsworth Emma A C, bds 157 Ewing.

Holdsworth Maud E, clk Louis Wolf & Co, bds 157 Ewing.

Holdsworth Nathan B, patents 157 Ewing, res same.

Holibaugh Adelbert G, trav agt, res 47 Pixley & Long Blk.

Holl Charles, butcher Eckart Pkg Co, bds 165 Erie.

Hollan Joseph, lab Bass F & M Wks, bds 87 Force.

Holland Henry, laborer, bds 94 Montgomery.

Holland Margaret (wid Patrick), bds 228 W Creighton av.

Holland Richard, carpenter, res 15 Euclid av.

Holland Willard A, hatter, res 94 Barr.

Holland W Tiffin, traveling agt, rms 94 Calhoun.

Hollandsworth Richard J, motorman, res 14 Wall.

Hollenbacher Arthur J, cutter S Freiburger & Bro, bds 141 Francis.

Hollenbacher Frederick C, bds 141 Francis.

Hollenbacher Louis C, city weighmaster, res 141 Francis.
Hollenbeck Amelia, bds 443 E Washington.
Hollenbeck Anna, bds 443 E Washington.
Hollenbeck Frederick G, res 273 Webster.
Hollenbeck Wm F A, saloon, 144 Calhoun, res 443 E Washington.
Hollencamp Mrs Edith, bds 13 Clark
Hollinger Alfred, laborer, bds 76 E Columbia.
Hollinger Eli B, laborer, res 76 E Columbia.
Hollinger Elizabeth (wid Daniel), bds 76 E Columbia.
Hollinger Harry W, packer Pottlitzer Bros, bds 76 E Columbia.
Hollinger May, domestic 18 Maiden lane.
Hollinger Wm, lab C L Centlivre Brewing Co, res 76 E Columbia.
Hollister A Judson (Hollister & Son), res 104 W Williams.
Hollister Clara J, cash A Mergentheim, bds 104 W Williams
Hollister Edwin J (Hollister & Son), res 82 W Williams.
Hollister Ida, cash B Lehman, bds 104 W Williams.
Hollister & Son (A Judson and Edwin J), cigar mnfrs, 104 W Williams.
Hollmann August, carpenter, res 394 E Washington.
Hollmann Charles F E, lab Olds' Wagon Wks, bds 312 Broadway.
Hollmann Frederick H, carpenter, res 312 Broadway.
Hollmann John H, bds 312 Broadway.
Hollmann Wm C, laborer, res 384 E Lewis.
Hollmann W F Henry, janitor Concordia College, res same.
Hollomon Ella, domestic 261 W Wayne.
Hollopeter Henry J, laborer, res 121 Hayden.
Holloway Joseph H, physician, res 102 Calhoun.
Holly John S, conductor N Y, C & St L R R, res 41 Boone.
Holly Lillian, finisher Wayne Knitting Mills, bds 41 Boone.
Holmes Abiram T, engr Penn Co, res 189 Barr.
Holmes Alice L, bds 106 Fairfield av.
Holmes Anna B, clerk, bds 106 Fairfield av.
Holmes Carrie E, clk, bds 106 Fairfield av.
Holmes Charles W, section hd Penn Co, res Pennsylvania av n e cor Bond.
Holmes Frank L, barber Frederick Miller, res 273 W Main.
Holmes Simon, carpenter, res 106 Fairfield av.
Holmes Wm A, clk R G Dun & Co, bds 106 Fairfield av.
Holmes Wm P, laborer, res 82 Home av.
Holsworth, see also Holzworth.
Holsworth Addison, res 158 W Wayne.

Holsworth Edith, teacher Harmer School, bds 158 W Wayne
Holsworth Frank P, clerk, bds 158 W Wayne.
Holsworth John A, carp, res s s Richardson 1 w of canal feeder.
Holt Wm J, floor mngr Princess Cash Store, res 245 E Wayne.
Holtermann Frederick J, laborer, res 169 Gay.
Holtermann Katie, bds 169 Gay.
Holtermann Minnie, domestic Concordia College.
Holton, *see also Houlton.*
Holton Avenue School, s w cor Holton and Creighton avs.
Holton Harry E, bkkpr Ft Wayne Club, bds same.
Holtzman Daniel W, laborer, bds 337 W Main.
Holtzman Samuel M, cooper Standard Oil Co, res 337 W Main.
Holverstott Charles H, winder Ft Wayne Electric Corp, res 519 Broadway.
Holverstott Clinton W, driver Adams Ex Co, res 307 W Washington.
Holverstott Flora B, bds 30 Bass.
Holverstott Wm Z, lab Ft Wayne Electric Corp, res 30 Bass.
Holycross Edward J, laborer, res 90 E Main.
Holzborn Adolph O, opr Ft Wayne Gas Co, res 20 Scott av
Holzhauer Arthur C, helper Keller Dental Co, bds 20 Gay.
Holzhauer Henry, helper Bass F & M Wks, res 507 Hanna.
Holzhauer Lizzie A, domestic 16 E De Wald.
Holzwarth, *see also Holsworth.*
Holzwarth Christian E, brakeman G R & I R R, res 69 Oakley.
Holzwarth George A, keymkr Ft Wayne Organ Co, res 6 College av.
Holzwarth George J, bds 319 Harrison.
Holzwarth John A, laborer, res s s Richardson 1 w of Canal feeder.
Holzwarth Lisetta A, domestic 93 W Main.
Holswarth Lizzie C, domestic 49 W Creighton av.
Holzworth Alfred, laborer, res Polk nr St Marys av.
Holzworth Kate, opr Hoosier Mnfg Co, bds 99 E Washington.
Home Billiard Hall, L A Centlivre Propr, H B Monning Mngr, 20 W Berry. Tel 89.
Home Restaurant, F C Cratsley propr, 99 Calhoun.
Homeyer Carrie L, clk Seibert & Good, bds 57 High.
Homeyer Ernest C, engr Globe Spice Mills, res 50 South Wayne av.

Homeyer Frederick A, driver E C Becker, bds 164 W De Wald.

Homeyer Frederick C, teamster Ft Wayne Organ Co, res 164 W De Wald.

Homeyer F Wm, watchman, res 57 High.

Homeyer Henry C D, mach Wabash R R, res 160 W De Wald.

Homeyer John, moved to Cecil, O.

Homeyer Louise C, clk E C Becker, bds 164 W De Wald.

Homeyer Otto H, driver J C Peters & Co, bds 160 W De Wald.

Homeyer Theodore W, student, bds 160 W De Wald.

Homsher Benjamin F, engr Penn Co, res 255 Webster.

Homsher Bessie A. bds 255 Webster.

Homsher Frank B, portrait artist 508 Calhoun, res same.

Homsher Minnie F, teacher, bds 255 Webster.

Honaker David, florist 25 W Berry, res same.   Tel 482.

Honaker S Bettie, bds 25 W Berry.

Hondheim, see also Hontheim.

Hondheim Jacob, carpenter, res 31 Pine.

Hondheim Jacob jr, laborer, bds 31 Pine.

Honeck, see also Ohneck.

Honeck Clara, bds 157 Montgomery.

Honeck Conrad, printer, bds 17 Elm.

Honeck Conrad, sawyer L Rastetter & Son. res 42 Pritchard.

Honeck Emma, bds 151 Montgomery.

Honeck Fredericka S, tailoress, bds 17 Elm.

Honeck Henry C, carpenter, res 151 Montgomery.

Honeck Henry C, laborer, res 17 Elm.

Honeck Wm, helper, bds 17 Elm.

Honeck Wm F, carpenter, bds 151 Montgomery.

Honeck Wm F, driver Pickard Bros, res 85 Winch.

Honeck Wm H, padmaker A L Johns & Co, bds 17 Elm.

Honeick Herman, carpenter, res 165 Madison.

Honeick Sophie, candymkr J H Meyer, bds 39 Hough.

Honeiser Jacob, cellarman Charles A Hoffmann, rms 74 Barr.

Honold Sibylla, cook Custer House.

Hontheim, see also Hondheim.

Hontheim John J, mach Wabash R R, res 12 McClellan.

Hontheim Michael, erecter Kerr Murray Mnfg Co, res 57 Taylor.

Hontheim Michael M, plumber, res 121 Baker.

Hontheim Peter T, blksmith Kerr Murray Mnfg Co, res 69 Taylor.

Hood Charles A, clk Root & Co, res 177 Griffith.

Hood Emily M, stenogr R G Dun & Co, bds 34 Garden.

Hood John O, fireman N Y, C & St L R R, bds 130 W 3d.

Hood Martha B (wid George), res 130 W 3d.

Hood Mary H, bds 34 Garden.

Hood Robert, meats, 98 Barr, res 25 W Lewis.

Hood True, bell boy The Wayne, bds 130 W 3d.

Hood Wm E, sec and treas The W L Carnahan Co, res 247 W Berry.

Hood Wm E jr, trav agt, bds 247 W Berry.

Hoog John, organ bldr, bds 133 E Jefferson.

Hook Nicholas, laborer, res 207 Spy Run av.

Hook and Ladder Co No 1, Central station, E Main.

Hook and Ladder Co No 2, Wallace, bet Clay and Lafayette

Hooper Edna M, milliner, bds 60 E Pontiac.

Hooper John G, stock manager. rms 143 W Berry.

Hooper Samuel T, engr N Y, C & St L R R, res 133 W Superior.

Hoopingarner George C, carpenter, res 210 Fairfield av.

Hoopingarner Wm H, painter, 192 Metz, res same.

Hoormann Diedrich C, coremkr Bass F & M Wks, res 112 Eliza.

Hoormann Henry F C, coremkr Bass F & M Wks, res 115 Eliza.

Hoosier Mnfg Co, Amos S Evans Pres, George P Evans Sec, John P Evans Treas, Mnfrs Overalls, Pants and Linen Duck Goods, 28 and 30 E Berry. Tel 330.

Hoosier Steam Laundry, W B Phillips Propr, 191 Calhoun. Tel 382. (*See left side lines.*)

Hoot Mary, waitress New Aveline House.

Hoover Abraham, car bldr Penn Co, res 91 E Lewis.

+Hoover Lizzie, bds 39 Grace av.

Hop Lee, laundry, 180 Calhoun, res same.

Hope Hospital, Nancy Mayhew supt, s w cor Barr and Washington. Tel 157.

Hopkins Zelous, carpenter, res 30 Huron.

Hoppe Adolph F C, mach hd Paul Mnfg Co, bds 20 Wall.

Hoppe Clara W, seamstress Ella H Kenlin, bds 20 Wall.

Hoppe Dora A (wid Henry W), res 20 Wall.

Hoppe Edwin G, clk People's Store, bds 20 Wall.

Hoppe Herman, packer City Mills, res 10 Franklin av.

Hoppe Paul T, clk Ft Wayne Electric Corp, bds 20 Wall.

W. H. DAVIS, BANK BLOCK, 30 & 32 East Main St. BLANK BOOKS, BOOK BINDING, PRINTING, Etc.

FORT WAYNE DIRECTORY. 345

Hoppel Bert C, driver B W Skelton Co, bds 96 Montgomery.
Hoppel George, res 54 E 3d.
Hoppel Lottie, bds 54 E 3d.
Hoppel Martin V B, porter G E Bursley & Co, res 131 W 3d.
Hopper Alice, domestic 29 W Lewis.
Horman Minnie (wid George), bds 17 Summit.
Hormann Frederick H, blksmith Fleming Mnfg Co, res 8 Pape av.
Hormann Henry C, patternmkr Bass F & M Wks, bds 155 Madison.
Hormel Augusta E, student, bds 16 McClellan.
Hormel George, teacher Emanuel German Lutheran School, res 16 McClellan.
Hormel Herman C, student, bds 16 McClellan.
Horn Ferdinand H, laborer, res 482 Hanna.
Horn Frederick W, helper, res 35 Smith.
Horn Frederick W jr, cigarmkr, bds 35 Smith.
Horn John L, wagonmaker, res w s Hillside av 1 s of Eliza
Horn Wm H F, mach hd Anthony Wayne Mnfg Co, bds 482 Hanna.
Horner Louis E, fireman, bds 27 Grand.
Horner Peter, heater Bass F & M Wks, res 97 Oliver.
Horning Emma (wid Peter), died Nov 27th, 1894.
Horning Sophia, domestic 35 W Washington.
Hornung Max, engr Penn Co, res 28 Taber.
Horstman, see also Hostman.
Horstman Annie M, laundress, bds 7 Oak.
Horstman Caroline, seamstress, bds 23 Maumee rd.
Horstman John B, plasterer, res 7 Oak.
Horstman John B jr, laborer, bds 7 Oak.
Horstman Louis F, Carriage Trimming, 9 E Superior, res same. (See p 99).
Horstman Lydia, laundress, bds 7 Oak.
Horstmann Alfred M, tailor F H Horstmann, bds 64 Baker.
Horstmann Amalie, opr S M Foster, bds 64 Baker.
Horstmann Cecilia, bds 203 Hanna.
Horstmann Charles, laborer, res 227 John.
Horstmann Frank B, laborer, bds 203 Hanna.
Horstmann Frederick H, tailor, 360½ Calhoun, res 64 Baker
Horstmann George H, student, bds 203 Hanna.
Horstmann Gustav, car repr Penn Co, res 121 Alliger.
Horstmann Henry C, carp Penn Co, res 203 Hanna.
Horstmann Henry G, helper Penn Co, bds 203 Hanna.

346 R. L. POLK & CO.'s

Horstmann Joseph, bell boy The Randall, bds 7 Oak.
Horstmann Wm, contractor, 121 Alliger, res same.
Horstmeier Frederick, carpenter, res 25 Wall.
Horstmeyer August C, printer The Journal, bds 197 Ewing.
Horstmeyer Charles H, clerk, bds 197 Ewing.
Horstmeyer Emma, bds 30 Savilla av.
Horstmeyer Frederick W, mach hd Ft Wayne Furn Co, res 69 Dawson.
Horstmeyer Henry, cabinetmaker, res 30 Savilla av.
Horstmeyer Henry L, machinist, bds 197 Ewing.
Horstmeyer Lewis, laborer, res 244 Beaver av.
Horstmeyer Lizzie L, bds 244 Beaver av.
Horstmeyer Martha, bds 197 Ewing.
Horstmeyer Mary B, bds 244 Beaver av.
Horstmeyer Wilhelmina (wid Frederick), bds 80 Swinney av
Horstmeyer Wm, carp Wabash R R, res 197 Ewing.
Horstmeyer Wm, laborer, res 49 Gav.
Horstmeyer Wm H, boilermaker Wabash R R, bds 197 Ewing.
Horton George E, switchman, res 236 W Main.
Horton Harry, laborer, bds 284 E Jefferson.
Horton John C, res 368 W Main.
Horton Julius C, jeweler H Mariotte, res 100 E Jefferson.
Horton Mnfg Co, Henry C Paul pres, Wm A Bohn sec and treas, John C Peters mngr, mnfrs washing machines, w s Osage n of Boone. Tel 273.
Hose Charles, pastry cook G H Seabold, rms 78 Barr.
Hose Co No 1, Central Fire Station.
Hose Co No 2, Wallace bet Clay and Lafayette.
Hese Co No 3, W Washington bet Harrison and Webster.
Hosenfeld Marie (wid August), bds s e cor Chestnut and Summer.
Hosey Wm J, mach Penn Co, res 131 E Washington.
Hosier Charles, paperhanger J H Brimmer, res 150 Wells.
Hosier Clifford, mach hd Penn Co, bds 173 Hayden.
Hosier Joseph H, conductor, res 421 E Washington.
Hosler Abraham L, carpenter, res 431 Lafayette.
Hosler Calvin, transfer agt, res 60 Hamilton.
Hosler George J, brakeman N Y C & St L R R, bds 22 Boone.
Hosler Jennie, domestic 166 W Berry.
Hosler John W, saloon 11 W Columbia, rms same.
Hosler Roxie, opr S M Foster, bds 6 Kansas.
Hossmann Rosa E, domestic 141 W Superior.
Hostemann John D, laborer, res 7 Oak.

Hostemeyer, *see Ostemeier.*

Hostman, *see also Horstman.*

Hostman Charles W, clk D J Spencer, bds 86 W Jefferson.

Hostman Christian F, hackman, res 86 W Jefferson.

Hostman Frederick A, clk F Eckart Pckg Co, res 88 W Jefferson.

Hostman John F, carpenter, bds 86 W Jefferson.

Hostman Louis A, bds 86 W Jefferson.

Hotel Arlington, M S Wickliffe Propr, 107 and 109 E Columbia.

Hotel Emery, L R Singleton Propr, 2 Cass. (*See page 348.*)

Hotel Rich, Brown & Purcell proprs 206 and 208 Calhoun. Tel 226.

Houck, *see also Hauck.*

Houck Adam B, carp Rhinesmith & Simonson, res 469 Lafayette,

Houck Jacob H, carp Rhinesmith & Simonson. res 374 Lafayette.

Houck Robert C, cashier Wabash R R, bds 374 Lafayette.

Houder Martin L, conductor, res 96 Boone.

Hough, *see also Huff.*

Hough Frank L, clk Ft Wayne Electric Corp, res 128 W Butler.

Hough Wm M, ticket clerk L S & M S Ry, res 194 Wells.

Hougham Ira D, teamster, res 93 Fairfield av.

Houghton Alice, bds 198 W De Wald.

Houghton Charles F, agt Prudential Ins Co, bds 58 Oakley

Houlihan Bridget, milliner, bds 93 W Williams.

Houlihan James J, bkkpr Morgan & Beach, bds 93 W Williams.

Houlihan Johanna, bds 93 W Williams.

Houlihan John J. laborer, res 93 W Williams.

Houlihan Josephine, bds 93 W Williams.

Houlihan Michael J, bookkeeper, bds 93 W Williams.

Houlton Roger R, music teacher, 224 E Jefferson, res same

Hous Frederick G, brakeman, res 36 Euclid av.

House James A, brakeman N Y, C & St L R R, res 328 W Main.

House John S, traveling agt, res 52 Huestis av.

Houser, *see also Hauser.*

Houser Caroline, bds 97 Cass.

Houser Charles, fireman, res s s Rebecca 1 w of Tyler av.

Houser Charles H A, fireman N Y, C & St L R R, bds 329 W Main.

348   R. L. POLK & CO.'S

Houser Christina, dressmkr F M Lehr, bds John Houser.
Houser Clara, opr S M Foster, bds 97 Cass.
Houser David E, machinist, res 13 Ida av.
Houser Elizabeth A, seamstress, bds 278 E Jefferson.
Houser George, farmer, bds John Houser.
Houser John, farmer, res s s Wells 1 n of St Vincent Orphan Asylum.
Houser John, lab Bass F & M Wks, res 257 Hanna.
Houser John A, traveling agt. res 135 Lake av.
Houser Mrs Lizzie, attendand School for F M Y.
Housh John E, foreman Archer Ptg Co, res 40 Home av.
Howard Arthur M, fireman N Y, C & St L R R, bds 72 Brackenridge. Tel 425.
Howard Christian E, carpenter, res 8 Ida av.
Howard Jane (wid Charles), bds 149 Howard.
Howard Marvin P, laborer, bds 55 Grand.
Howe Delia, physician School for F M Y.
Howe Horatio A, confectioner, 85 Calhoun, res 84 same.
Howe John, lab Ft Wayne Electric Corp, bds 47 Wilt.
Howe Nelson, plater Ft Wayne Electric Corp, res 47 Wilt.
Howell Charles A, machinist, res 39 Miner.
Howell Grace C, bkkpr Keller Dental Co, bds 39 Miner.
Howenstein Charles, lab John Weber & Son, bds 91 W Main.
Howenstein Franklin, photographer, res 255 W Wayne.
Howenstein John C, bds 255 W Wayne.
Howenstein Julius, lab John Weber & Son, bds 91 W Main.
Howey Aaron B, sec Ft Wayne Land and Improvement Co, res 67 Wilt.
Howey May A (wid Isaac), res 225 W Washington.
Howey Wm T, bartender, res 196 Ewing.
Howley Bernard C, brakeman, bds 313 Calhoun.
Howley Kate, waiter St James Hotel.
Howley Katie A, opr S M Foster, res 17 Brandriff.

Howley Martin, boilermaker, bds 313 Calhoun.
Howley Rosa E, bds 17 Brandriff.
Howrand Bernard, contractor, 107 Swinney av, res same.
Hoy J Harry, appr Penn Co. rms 127 E Washington.
Hubbard Alvin L, grocer, 9 N Calhoun, res 3 E Superior.
Hubbard Clara N, domestic 109 Glasgow av.
Hubbard Clifford S, clk A L Hubbard, rms 7 N Calhoun.
Hubbard George K, H B Smitley mngr, bee hives, 277 Harrison.
Hubbard John H, laborer, res 48 Penn.
Hubbard Sidney G, barber, 21 W Columbia, res 14 Cass.
Hubbard Willis, photogr, 8 Euclid av, res same.
Huber Andrew J, mach hd Penn Co, res 212 Lafayette.
Huber Bertha, seamstress Hoosier Mnfg Co, bds 276 E Washington.
Huber Caroline (wid George), bds 212 Lafayette.
Huber Charles, saloon, 46 E Columbia, res same.
Huber Frederick, lab Jacob Klett & Sons, res 276 E Washington.
Huber Johanna, seamstress, bds 276 E Washington.
Huber John, laborer, res 423 E Lewis.
Huber John F, tillerman Hook and Ladder Co No 1, rms same.
Huber John G, fireman Penn Co, res 442 Lafayette.
Huber Katie T, bds 212 Lafayette.
Huber Matilda A, seamstress, bds 276 E Washington.
Hubler John C, clk R M S, res 115 W De Wald.
Hubler Wm H, teamster. res 446 Hanna.
Hubner Charles J, helper, res 147 Buchanan.
Hudgel R Daniel (F P Wilt & Co), res 271 W Jefferson.
Hudry Anna (wid Nicholas), res 186 Montgomery.
Hudry Rosella C, bds 186 Montgomery.
Hudson, *see also Hutson.*
Hudson Charles R, roaster G E Bursley & Co, res 24 W 5th
Hudson Elmer E, student, bds 119 W Williams.
Hudson Hamilton, watchman, res 119 W Williams.
Hudson Lillian J, bds 119 W Williams.
Hue Constant L, fireman N Y, C & St L R R, bds 64 Elm.
Hueber Isadore, driver Ft Wayne Art Ice Co, res 9 Huffman.
Hueber Barbara (wid Tobias), bds 42 W 4th.
Huebner Charles C F, lab Bass F & M Wks, res 147 Buchanan.
Huebner John H, janitor, res 163 Webster.
Huebner Reinhardt, res 32 Lillie.

23

Huefner, *see Hoeffner.*
Huelf Johanna S, opr S M Foster, bds 52 W 4th.
Huelf Savilla (wid David), res 52 W 4th.
Huestis Alexander C, died January 23, 1895.
Huestis Bertha S, bds 205 W Berry.
Huestis Charles D C, res 205 W Berry.
Huff *see also Hough.*
Huff Cortland, switchman, bds 5 Brandriff.
Huff Hiram, watchman, res 5 Brandriff.
Huff Udney, conductor, res 81 Smith.
Huffmann, *see also Hoffman.*
Huffmann Ira D, driver City Trucking Co, res 116 Fairfield av.
Huge Agnes, domestic 76 W Berry.
Huge Bertha, domestic 340 W Jefferson.
Hugh James E, physician, 240 E Creighton, res same.
Hughes, *see also Hewes.*
Hughes Annie A, tailoress, bds 25 Walnut.
Hughes Bertha B, bds 25 Walnut.
Hughes Emma, bds 25 Walnut.
Hughes Francis M. clk Penn Co, bds 25 Walnut.
Hughes Grant U S, mngr Ind Furn Co, res 116 W Washington.
Hughes James, cabinetmkr Ft Wayne Furn Co, res 53 Elmwood av.
Hughes James E, engr N Y, C & St L R R, bds 25 Walnut
Hughes Jennie, opr Hoosier Mnfg Co, bds 53 Elmwood av
Hughes John L, attendant School for F M Y, rms 54 E Washington.
Hughes John W, tel opr N Y, C & St L R R, bds 190 W Berry.
Hughes John R, removed to Cincinnati, O.
Hughes Joseph, died August 28th, 1894.
Hughes Margaret, seamstress, bds 117 Hanna.
Hughes Mary (wid James), res 25 Walnut. Tel 346.
Hughes Mary A (wid Edwin), res 117 Hanna.
Hughes Michael J, mach Penn Co, bds 25 Walnut.
Hughes Leah E, domestic 202 Thomas.
Hughes Mervin E, clk L P Sharp, bds 53 Elmwood av.
Hughes Nora B (wid Joseph), bds 240 W Berry.
Hughes Rose A, bds 117 Hanna.
Hughes Sarah, bds 117 Hanna.
Hughes Thomas, canvasser, bds 61 Meridian.
Hughes Thomas E, removed to Danville, Ill.
Hughes Viola J, opr Hoosier Mnfg Co, bds 53 Elmwood av

Hughes Wm P, canvasser, r s 61 Meridian.
Huguenard August C, res 152 High.
Huguenard August F, blacksmith, res 63 Hugh.
Huguenard Frank A, letter carrier P O, bds 63 Hugh.
Huguenard Frank C, laborer, bds 152 High.
Huguenard Julius C, grocer, 107 Maumee rd, res same.
Huguenard Lou, bds 63 Hugh.
Huguenard Victor A, feed barn, 62 E Superior, res 61 same.
Huguenard Wm, helper Algier Mnfg Co, bds 305 Hanna.
Huhn Amand, bes 70 Swinney av.
Huhn August, coremkr Bass F & M Wks, res 70 Swinney av
Huhn Edward, laborer, bds 236 Smith.
Huhn Frank, died August 7, 1894.
Huhn Frederick, stonecutter Keller & Braun, res 51 Nird-
    linger av.
Huhn Frederick E, wiper Penn Co, res 236 Smith.
Huhn Henry, stonecutter Keller & Braun, res 68 Walnut.
Huhn Pius, bds 282 Broadway.
Hnkerkus Nicholas, bds 141 Barr.
Hulburd Loyal P, Agent American and Na-
    tional Express Cos, 24 E Main, res 69 Columbia av.
    Tel 141, res 518.
Hulburt, see Hurlbut.
Hull Elizabeth (wid Wesley), bds 201 W Wayne.
Hull Grace E, bookkeeper, bds 201 W Wayne.
Hull Lewis O, Wall Paper, Paints and Painting,
    Artists' Material. 90 Calhoun, res 201 W Wayne.
    Tel 285. (See back cover.)
Hull Sylvester W, wall paper, paints, oils and decorations,
    27 Clinton, res 247 E Lewis. Tel 250.
Hulse Edwin M, stenogr Ft Wayne Electric Corp, bds 228
    Fairfield av.
Hulse Wm L, mach Penn Co, res 228 Fairfield av.
Hulse Wm S, electrician, res 228 Fairfield av.
Humbel John, lab Hoffman Bros, res 52 W Butler.
Humbert James J, laborer J F Fletcher, bds 47 Barr.
Humbrecht Annie J, bds 42 W 3d.
Humbrecht August, with I & G Sommers, res 42 W 3d.
Humbrecht Henry G, cigarmaker, bds 42 W 3d.
Humbrecht H George, cigar mnfr, 42 W 3d, res same.
Humcke Diedrich, laborer, res 225 John.
Hume Anna P (wid Roderick R), bds 407 Calhoun.
Hume James H, plasterer, res 101 Huffman.
Hume Wm T, street car condr, res 35 E Williams.
Hummel John G, teamster, res 192 E De Wald.

Hummel Magdalena (wid John), bds 15 Suttenfield.
Humphrey George B, mailing clk P O, bds 301 E Washington.
Humphrey Hanna (wid John M), res 38 Brackenridge.
Humphrey James A, tie agt Penn Co, res 16 E Taber.
Humphrey Janet A, bds 16 E Taber.
Humphrey Jennie, bds 171 W Berry.
Humphrey Jessie L, teacher Washington School, bds 171 W Berry.
Humphrey Louise M (wid George), res 171 W Berry.
Humphrey Lucina W (wid Noah), res 19 Madison.
Humphrey Marshall B, appr Penn Co, bds 38 Brackenridge.
Humphrey Matthew, bds 171 W Berry.
Hundley Rev Adolphus A, pastor Christ's Evangelical Lutheran Church, res 33 E Butler.
Hunsche August, laborer, res s s Eckart lane 1 e of Hanna.
Hunsche Frederick H, carpenter, res 65 Elizabeth.
Hunsche Henry, clerk, bds 65 Elizabeth.
Hunsche Henry J, mach hd L Diether & Bro, res 41 Wells
Hunsche Katie E, opr S M Foster, bds 65 Elizabeth.
Hunsche Mary, domestic 100 E Washington.
Hunsche Wm, lab G Reber, bds same.
Hunt Albert F, hostler J T Hunt, bds 329 Spy Run av.
Hunt Mrs Belle, attendant School for F M Y.
Hunt Bertha R, domestic 149 E Berry.
Hunt Charles E, brakeman, res 142 Holman.
Hunt Charles S, trav agt G E Bursley & Co, res 44 McClellan.
Hunt Edward, res 168 Harmer.
Hunt Edward J, fireman, bds 4 E Butler.
Hunt Edward P, train dispatcher Penn Co, rms 188 Calhoun.
Hunt Frederick, flagman, bds 324 Calhoun.
Hunt Harry H, engr N Y, C & St L R R, bds 352 W Main
Hunt Hoag H, driver City Trucking Co, bds 159 Harrison.
Hunt Hoyt B, General Agt Northwestern Mutual Life Insurance Co of Milwaukee, Wis, 5-6-7 Trentman Bldg, res 24 W Washington. (*See left top lines and page 353*).
Hunt John E, fireman G R & I R R, res 4 E Butler.
Hunt J Thomas, sale stable 329 Spy Run av, res same.
Hunt Leonard, telegraph operator, rms 188 Calhoun.
Hunt Lincoln R, train dispatcher Penn Co, rms 188 Calhoun.

The Northwestern Mutual Life Insurance Company,

Organized 1857.
A Purely Mutual
Company . . .

H. L. PALMER, President.
J. W. SKINNER, Secretary.
H. B. HUNT, General Agent.

Cash Assets January 1, 1895, $73,324,694.13   Liabilities, $59,178,578.19.

Surplus. $14,146,115.94.

No Fluctuating Securities.

Over 98 per cent. of Reserve Invested in First Mortgage Bonds.
Percentage of Death Loss to Mean Amount at Risk 1894,-0.82,
Increase of Surplus in Four Years Over 100 Per Cent.
Increase of Surplus During 1894, $2,946,544.94.

Compare figures on this most important point with any other company.

Issues All Kinds of Popular and Approved Policies, including Installments,
Annuities, Renewable Terms, etc.

Loans 90 per cent. of Cash Value of Policies at 6 per cent.

Its Dividends to Policy Holders are Unequaled.

It is the only Company which has in recent years printed
tables of current cash dividends for the information of the public.
The Northwestern has done this for twenty-four consecutive years.

Hunt Louis R., brakeman. bds 142 Holman.
Hunt Patrick, teamster, res 6 Smith.
Hunt Thomas R. laborer. bds 6 Smith.
Hunt Wm L, brakeman N Y, C & St L R R, bds 46 Elm.
Hunt Wm P, lab, bds 6 Smith.
Hunter Agatha P, bds 222 W Wasbington.
Hunter Albert D, fireman Penn Co, bds 250 E Lewis.
Hunter Edward J, lab G H Seabold, bds 22 W Main.
Hunter Eugene W, sec and treas Wayne Oil Tank Co, rms
35 W Lewis.
Hunter George F, teamster, bds 75 W Jefferson.
Hunter James L, res 153 Hayden.
Hunter James W, master transportation G R & I R R, res
26 McClellan.
Hunter John C, res 222 W Washington.
Hunter John L, broom mnfgr, 153 Hayden, res same.
Hunter Lewis C, County Treasurer (elect), Office Court
House, res 269 W Wayne.
Hunter Matilda C, bds 153 Hayden.
Hunter Una B, bds 222 W Washington.

Hunter Wm C, steamfitter Robert Ogden, res 74 Barr.

Hunter Wm S, traveling agt, res 36 W 3rd.

Huntine, see Hondheim and Huntheim.

Hunting Frederick S, chief engr Ft Wayne Electric Corp, res 330 W Washington.

Hunting Harlan H, lab, bds 134 W Creighton av.

Hunting Wm, lab Ft Wayne Electric Corp, bds 330 W Washington.

Hunting Wm H, fireman Olds' Wagon Wks, res 134 W Creighton av.

Huntoon Ludean P, supply clk N Y, C & St L R R, res 216 W Superior.

Huntsman Elizabeth A (wid Israel), res 55 W Williams.

Huntsman Vina, dressmkr 164 Montgomery, bds same.

Huntsman Wallace W, saloon 80 Barr, res same.

Hunziker Jacob, saloon, 25 Force, res same.

Hurd Oscar D, carpenter, bds 207 Metz.

Hurlbut Belle N, bds 105 W Superior.

Hurlbut Cora M, bds 105 W Superior.

Hurlbut Edward S, clk Olds' Wagon Wks, res 83 Wilt.

Hurlbut Fannie M, bds 83 Wilt.

Hurlbut Mrs Hattie, res 105 W Superior.

Hurlbut Myrtle, finisher, bds 105 W Superior.

Hurlbut Wm R, fireman N Y, C & St L R R, bds 83 Wilt.

Hurley Daniel J, asst foreman Penn Co, res 46 E Butler.

Hurley Grant R, brakeman, res 20 Euclid av.

Hurley John, horseshoer Wm Geary, bds 72 Cass.

Hurley Maggie M (wid Michael), bds 374 Calhoun.

Huron Mrs Alice G, bds 265 John.

Hursh, see also Harsh, Hersh and Hirsch.

Hursh Anna (wid Samuel C), bds 348 Broadway.

Hursh Elizabeth, nurse, res 11 Fairfield av.

Huser Albert (Huser & Blomenberg), res 89 W De Wald.

Huser Louis P, Justice of Peace and Shoes, Justice Office 9 Foster Blk, Store 178 Broadway, res 167 Jackson.

Huser Mary (wid George), bds 89 W De Wald.

Huser & Blomenberg (Albert Huser, Christian Blomenberg), Livery, Sale and Boarding Stable, Hacks and a Variety of Turnouts Always Ready, 201 Fairfield av.   Tel 381.

Hushour Louis B, brakeman G R & I R R, res 16 Chicago.

Huston Gertrude B, bds 266 E Lewis.

Huston Harry M, train dispatcher Penn Co, res 266 E Lewis.

Huston Hattie M, bds 266 E Lewis.
Huston John H, laborer, res 382 W Main.
Huston Nancy A (wid James G), bds 266 E Lewis.
Hutchinson Mrs Blanche I, seamstress, bds 130 W 3d.
Hutchinson Frank, painter, res 44 Hoagland av.
Hutchinson Mahlon R, patternmkr Bass F & M Wks, res 444 Lafayette.
Hutchinson Oliver G, tanner, res 294 W Main.
Hutchison Alonzo M, plasterer, res 37 W Williams.
Hutchison Elmer E, truckman, bds 213 Lafayette.
Hutchison John H, traveling agt, res 247 W Washington.
Hutchison Mrs Rebecca, music teacher, res 247 W Washington.
Hutchison Van Rensselaer, produce buyer, res 213 Lafayette.
Hutker Hattie, pastry cook, The Wayne.
Hutsel John, res 200 W Washington.
Hutson, see also Hudson.
Hutson Belle, seamstress, rms 145 Rockhill.
Hutson Charles N car bldr Penn Co, res 104 Gay.
Hutzell Daniel, saloon, 378 W Main, res 276 same.
Hutzell Valentine G, caller, N Y, C & St L R R, bds 376 W Main.
Hutzell Joseph C, student, bds 376 W Main.
Hutzell Mary C, bds 376 W Main.
Huxley Frank S, engineer, res 114 Boone.
Huxoll August, grocer 92 Barr, res 171 Harmer.
Huxoll August jr, clerk, bds 171 Harmer.
Huxoll Frederick W, clk August Huxoll, bds 171 Harmer.
Hyde Wesley, bds 51 Oakley.
Hyer House, Mary M Hyer propr, 231 Calhoun.
Hyer Mary M (wid Edward A), propr Hyer House, 231 Calhoun.
Hyman Arthur F, bds 338 Calhoun.
Hyman Edward A, clk C E Heaton, bds 338 Calhoun.
Hyman Philip H, res 338 Calhoun.
Hyman Philip H jr, clk, bds 338 Calhoun.

I

Iba Elizabeth (wid Wm), res 129 Fairfield av.
Iba Floretta, bda 129 Fairfield av.
Iba George S, fireman Ft Wayne Pumping Station, res N Clinton 1 n of bridge.
Ibel Charles J, agt Met Life Ins Co, bds 1 Emily.
Ibel Louisa M, domestic 56 W Wayne.

Ickes Louis E, clk The Wayne, bds same.

Iiams Elmer O, carpenter, res 161 Barr.

Iliff David H, res 30 Winch.

Imbody Adam, foreman Ft Wayne Organ Co, bds 79 W De Wald.

Imbody Clara C, bds 79 W De Wald.

Imbody Daniel, molder. res 51 Hendricks.

Imbody Dorothy (wid Harrison), res 79 W De Wald.

Imbody Henry A, brakeman N Y, C & St L R R, res 166 Broadway.

Imbody Lottie, bds 79 W De Wald.

Immel Amelia, bds 568 E Washington.

Immel Edward A H, painter, bds 568 E Washington.

Immel John, janitor Jefferson School, res 63 McClellan.

Immel John C, bottler, bds 568 E Washington.

Immel Louise (wid Henry), res 568 E Washington.

Immel Walter H, shipping clk Herman Berghoff Brewing Co, bds 568 E Washington.

Imswiler Wm H, foreman, res 40 Killea av.

Indiana Farmers' Savings and Loan Association, Hon R S Peterson Pres, Decatur, Ind, Hon R C Bell Vice-Pres, Wm Miller Treas, C E Rhoades Sec, H P Moses Asst Sec, over 32 E Berry. Tel 493.

Indiana Furniture Co, John V Reul pres, Wm F Graeter sec and treas, 166 Calhoun. Tel 359.

Indiana Insurance Co of Fort Wayne, John H Jacobs pres, John E Beahler sec, 22 Bank Blk.

Indiana Oil and Land Co, (Capital $15,000), J H Grier Sec and Treas, 3-4 Tri-State Bldg.

Indiana Machine Works, John C Peters pres, John M Landenberger sec, treas and mngr, mnfrs woodworking and road making machinery, e s Osage n of Main. Tel 125.

Indiana School for Feeble-Minded Youth, Alexander Johnson Supt, n s Hicksville State road bet Parnell av and St Joe Gravel road. Tel 242.

Indiana Staats Zeitung (Daily and Weekly), Indiana Staats Zeitung Co, Proprs, 37 E Columbia. Tel 119.

Indiana Staats Zeitung Co, publishers Indiana Staats Zeitung, and job printers, 37 E Columbia.

Indiana Stamp Co, E W Cook, Sec, 37 W Berry.

Indiana State Gazetteer, R L Polk & Co Publishers, 38 Bass Blk.

Ingram Albine P, special examiner U S Pension Office, res 211 E Wayne.

Ingst Ernest, bds 100 Montgomery.

Inman Charles W, paperhanger, res 66 Riverside av.

Inman Samuel D, baggeman G R & I R R, bds Harmon House.

Innes Tillie, res w s N Calhoun 2 n of Locust.

Inteman Wm, cabtmkr Ft Wayne Furn Co, bds 34 W Superior.

International Business College, T L Staples propr, Schmitz Blk.

Irelan Albert W, lab Standard Wheel Co, bds 110 John.

Ireland Susanna (wid Aaron), res 90 Maumee rd.

Irey Anna E, (wid Alfred K), res 126 Harrison.

Irey Elma, bds 126 Harrison.

Irey Frank J, traveling agent, bds 126 Harrison.

Irey Sarah (wid Wm), bds 126 Harrison.

Irion, see also Arieon.

Irion Jacob, coremkr Bass F & M Wks, res 228 John.

Irish Edwin C, engineer N Y, C & St L R R, res 285 W Jefferson.

Irmscher Max, bricklayer, res 37 Eliza.

Irvin Anna R (wid Robert), res 68 W Butler.

Irwin Frank F, agt Prudential Ins Co, bds 145 Broadway.

Irwin Frank W, genl mngr Singer Mnfg Co, res 239 E Jefferson.

Irwin George B, real estate, res 240 W De Wald.

Irwin George H, brakeman, bds 145 Broadway.

Irwin George U, bds 241 W Main.

Irwin John S, M D, L L D, Superintendent Public Schools, Office Central Grammar School, res 241 W Main.

Irwin Kate, bds 39 Duck.

Irwin Mary, clk and librarian Public Schools, bds 241 W Main.

Irwin Mary A (wid Robert), res 119 W Washington.

Irwin Michael, res 39 Duck.

Irwin Nellie J, clk Lathrop & Co, bds 119 W Washington.

Irwin Rebecca, bds 68 W Butler.

Irwin Wm J, boilermaker, res 37 Wilt.

Israel Charles (Heine & Israel), res 130 Union.

Israel Henry, blksmith Olds Wagon Wks, res 121 Broadway.

Israel Wm. driver The Herman Berghoff Brewing Co, res n s New Haven rd 2 e of Lumbard.

Iten Frank, Inspector City Water Wks, res 51 Buchanan.

Iten John C, meat market 13 Begue, res same.

Ivins Leon A, asst ticket agt P F W & C R R and G R & I R R, bds New Aveline Hotel.

J

Jaap George, General Contractor and Builder, Cut and Ornamental Stone a Specialty, n s L S & M S R R Tracks w of Wells, res 180 Wells. Tel 390. (*See opposite page.*)

Jabas Emil. brickmason, res 361 E Lewis.

Jabas L Emil, bricklayer, bds 361 E Lewis.

Jackson Albert E (col'd), waiter Ft Wayne Club, rms 84 W Main.

Jackson Allen P, foreman S F Bowser & Co, res 82 South Wayne av.

Jackson Anthony A, laborer. res 101 Franklin av

Jackson Augustus B (Jackson & Giles), res 99 W Superior.

Jackson Brownell, helper Penn Co, res 106 Hayden.

Jackson Cullen R, lab Olds' Wagon Wks, bds 82 South Wayne av.

Jackson Clara, cook School F M Y.

Jackson Daniel W, condr F W E Ry Co, res 86 South Wayne av.

Jackson Edward, hostler J C Brinsley, bds 25 W Columbia.

Jackson Effie A, bds 82 South Wayne av.

Jackson Frank B, mach Western Gas Const Co, res 459 Calhoun.

Jackson Grace, student, bds 55 Brackenridge.

Jackson Harry, porter, bds 106 Hayden.

Jackson Ira C, bds 82 South Wayne av.

Jackson John. horseshoer 81 E Columbia, res 14 Lafayette.

Jackson John A, brakeman N Y C & St L R R, bds 197 W Superior.

Jackson John C, horseshoer John Jackson, bds 14 Lafayete.

Jackson John J, opr S M Raines. rms 60 Clinton.

Jackson John M, adv solr Ft Wayne Sentinel, res 346 W Washington.

Jackson Kirby, engr Penn Co, res 55 Brackenridge.

Jackson Mary, bds 197 W Superior.

Jackson Mary A (wid Wm), bds 20 E De Wald.

Jackson Sampson, res 197 W Superior.

Jackson Thomas W, supt maintenance of ways, Penn Co, res 297 Fairfield av.
Jackson Wm, watchman, res 216 Broadway.
Jackson Wm A, driver Princess Cash Store, bds 216 Broadway.
Jackson Wm H, carpenter, res 50 McClellan.
Jackson & Giles (Augustus B Jackson, Addison A Giles), Restaurant, 92 Calhoun.
Jucobs Alfred A, clk Standard Oil Co, bds 315 W Main.
Jacobs Andrew, grocer 360 Broadway, res 42 Stophlet.
Jacobs Bros (George H and Christopher C), bakers, 62 E Main.
Jacobs Caroline (wid Peter), res 116 Madison.
Jacobs Carrie, bds 60 Swinney av.
Jacobs Charles, meats, 197 E Washington, res 116 Madison.
Jacobs Charles V, clk M Frank & Co, bds 297 W Washington.
Jacobs Charles W, res 297 W Washington.
Jacobs Christopher C (Jacobs Bros), res 62 E Main.
Jacobs Mrs Clara, res 110 W Creighton av.

Jacobs David, foreman City Trucking Co, res 45 1st.

Jacobs Edwin E, trucker Wabash R R, res 82 W Lewis.

Jacobs Elmer E, cooper, res 6 Jackson.

Jacobs Felinda (wid John), bds 125 Harrison.

Jacobs George (Jacobs & Conklin), res 207 W Main.

Jacobs George H (Jacobs Bros), res 62 E Main.

Jacobs Gustave, flagman N Y, C & St L R R, res 38 Watkins.

Jacobs Harry N, trav agt Falk & Lamley, bds The Randall.

Jacobs Henry, mach hd Penn Co, res 115 Hayden.

Jacobs Henry, driver, res 19 Richardson.

Jacobs James (Jacobs & Neuhaus), res 159 Harrison.

Jacobs John, res w s Spy Run av 1 n of canal bridge.

Jacobs John H, pres Indiana Ins Co of Ft Wayne, res Washington township.

Jacobs John W, clerk, res 245 Clay.

Jacobs Lizzie, bds 297 W Washington.

Jacobs Mary E, res 171 E Wayne.

Jacob's Shoe Store, Isidor Lehman propr, 17 Calhoun.

Jacobs Sophia, clk L P Scherer, bds 297 W Washington.

Jacobs Thomas, driver City Trucking Co, res 125 Harrison

Jacobs Wm F, baker Jacobs Bros, bds 62 E Main.

Jacobs Wm L, brakeman, res 317 Hanna.

Jacobs & Conklin (George Jacobs, Guy Conklin), Pianos and Organs, 34 E Berry.

Jacobs & Neuhaus (James Jacobs, Frank Neuhaus), Proprs City Trucking Co, 19-21 W Washington. Tel 122.

Jacobsen Siebert, clk Princess Cash Store, bds 25 W Washington.

Jacobson Rosalie (wid Victor), res 136 W Wayne.

Jacoby Arthur E, stenogr Penn Co, bds 76 Lake av.

Jacoby Charles, teamster, res 86 Montgomery.

Jacoby George, res 78 Murray.

Jacquart Mrs Mary, res 18 Liberty.

Jaebker August, tire setter Olds' Wagon Wks, res 41 Summit.

Jaeckel Morris K F, lab Penn Co, res 105 Force.

Jaeckel Richard M, cigarmkr L Bender, bds 105 Force.

Jaeger, *see also Yager and Yeager.*

Jaeger Amelia (wid Nicholas), res 75 W Washington.

Jaeger August, carpet weaver, n w cor Franklin av and Aboit, res same.

Jaeger Christian, bartender Oetting & Co, res 72 Organ av

Jaeger Henry J, laborer, bds n w cor Franklin av and Aboit.

Jahn. *see also John and Johns.*

Jahn Ernest O, laborer, res 89 Force.

Jahn Frederika (wid Nicolaus), res 145 Rockhill.

Jahn Herman, painter Olds' Wagon Wks, res 84 Buchanan

Jahn Jacob C (J C Jahns & Co), res 21 Hough.

Jahn J C & Co (Jacob C Jahn), plumbers, 123 E Lewis.

Jahns Mrs Elizabeth M, res 30 Nirdlinger av.

Jahns Sophia M, pkr G E Bursley & Co, bds 30 Nirdlinger av

James Eliza (wid Elisha), res 215 St Mary's av.

James Frank, died August 23, 1894.

James Frank B, helper Penn Co, res 97 Eliza.

James Hiram L, painter, res 101 Lake av.

James Jesse M, carpenter, res 157 Shawnee av.

James Maggie, bds 45 1st.

James Wm, laborer Robert Spice, bds 127 Fairfield av.

James Wm H, teamster, res 161 Shawnee av.

Jamey Emil, engr Penn Co, res 85 Greene.

Jamey Frank M, helper Bass F & M Wks, bds 85 Greene.

Jamey Frederick, laborer, res 535 E Wayne.

Jamey Joseph P, elevator opr Louis Wolf & Co, bds 85 Greene.

Jamison George D, pipefitter A Hattersley & Sons, res 75 Douglas av.

Janorschke Frank, cabinetmaker Ft Wayne Furn Co, res 61 Wagner.

Jansen, *see also Jensen and Johnson.*

Jansen George, laborer, res 63 St Martin's.

Jansen Herman, painter Olds' Wagon Wks, bds 63 St Martin's.

Jarrett Cyrenius F, clerk, res 65 W Williams.

Jarrett Daisy V, bds 65 W Williams.

Jarrett James B, laborer, bds 65 W Williams.

Jasper Elizabeth (wid Rudolph), res 49 W Washington.

Jasper Frederick, carp Penn Co, bds 49 W Washington.

Jasper George W, fireman Engine Co No 3, res 51 W Washington.

Jasper W Frederick, carpenter, res 201 W Superior.

Jauch Albert J, mngr H Berghoff Brewing Co saloon, 582 E Washington, res 578 same.

Jautz, *see also Yautz.*

Jautz Charles L, car repairer, res 115 High.

Jautz Christian, gardener, bds 3 Polk.

Jautz George A, bds 115 High.

Jautz Louis F, clk J H Rahe, bds 115 High.
Jaxtheimer Alexander W (L Jaxtheimer & Son), bds 291 E Wayne.
Jaxtheimer Leonard (L Jaxtheimer & Son), res 291 E Wayne.
Jaxtheimer L & Son (Leonard and Alexander W), merchant tailors, 29 E Berry.
Jay Albert R, car bldr Penn Co, res 232 Walton av.
Jay Mary L, teacher High School, bds 38 W Wayne.
Jeager, *see Jaeger, Yager and Yeager.*
Jeaumougin Frank C, driver J B White, res 165 Clinton.
Jefferds Oliver W, res 131 E Main.
Jefferies Wm F, trav agt. bds 49 Miner.
Jefferies Wm T, City Clerk, office City Hall. res 7 Mc Clellan.
Jefferson Clifford, laborer, bds 173 Hayden.
Jefferson D Ristori, elocutionist, 49 W Berry, bds same.
Jefferson Lewin F, car repr Penn Co, res 173 Hayden.
Jefferson School, s w cor Jefferson and Griffith.
Jehl Eugene, helper Wabash R R, res 23 Lasselle.
Jehl Virgil, baker W F Geller, res 41 Force.
Jenkins Jose (col'd). domestic 87 E Jefferson.
Jenkins Mary R, rms 114 Clinton.
Jenkinson Emma B, embroiderer, bds 219 W Washington.
Jenkinson Wm E, bkkpr Jenney E L & P Co, res w s Harrison 2 s of Killea av.
Jenne Camera Mnfg Co, C R Jenne Inventor and Mngr, Frederick C Jenne Sec, 16 W Columbia. (*See p 99.*)
Jenne Chauncey R, Mngr Jenne Camera Mnfg Co, Dealer in Hercules Stump Blasting Powder, 16 W Columbia, res 98 N Harrison.
Jenne Edward C, cabinetmkr Jenne Camera Mnfg Co, bds 98 N Harrison.
Jenne Frank L, clk Jenne Camera Mnfg Co, bds 98 N Harrison.
Jenne Frederick C, sec Jenne Camera Mnfg Co, bds 98 N Harrison.
Jenness Charles H, foreman Rocker Washer Co, res 343 E Wayne.
Jenness Ethel K, sub teacher Public Schools, bds 343 E Wayne.
Jenny Ernest, watchman Ft Wayne Electric Corp, res 87 Home av.

Jenney Electric Light & Power Co, Henry C Graffe Pres, R T McDonald Vice-Pres, George W Pixley Treas, Charles G Guild Sec and Mngr, 43 E Berry, Power House cor Spy Run and Burgess avs. Tel office 298, works 279.

Jennings Clement V, condr G R & I R R, res 509 E Lewis.

Jennings Frederick, fireman, bds 40 E 5th.

Jennings George T, fireman G R & I R R, bds 113 Barr.

Jennison Samuel W, musician, bds 149 Griffith.

Jensen, *see also Jansen and Johnson.*

Jensen Hans P, blksmith Bass F & M Wks, res 124 John.

Jensen Lizzie, domestic The Wayne.

Jensen Mary, domestic The Wayne.

Jenson Abbie J (wid John), res 19 Cass.

Jenson Emma, clerk, bds 20 Cass.

Jenson James O, horsedealer, bds 19 Cass.

Jenson Wm A, steward The Wayne, res 20 Cass.

Jeretzky Anna, domestic 112 E Wayne.

Jeretzky Anton, lab Bass F & M Wks, res 29 Liberty.

Jerke Frederick, teamster Wm Miller, bds same.

Jerome Charles E, fireman N Y C & St L R R, res 64 Boone.

Jerzmanowski E J, vice-pres Ft Wayne Gas Co, res New York City.

Jesse Wm J F, carpenter Bass F & M Wks, res 148 Erie.

Jewell Mrs Elizabeth, res n w cor Calhoun and 3d.

Jeurgens Wm, carpenter School F M Y.

Jewel House, David E Maxwell propr, 225 Calhoun.

Jewell Mrs Elizabeth, res n w cor Calhoun and 3d.

Jewell Frank, sargeant of police, res 319 W Washington.

Jobst, *see Yobst.*

Jockel Leonard, stonemason, res 6 Liberty.

Jockers Lillie E, bds 46 Cass.

Jocquel John J, bds 168 Calhoun.

Jocquel Louis, books, 168 Calhoun, res same.

Jocquel L Charles, appr Penn Co, bds 168 Calhoun.

Johann Andrew H, baker Fox br U S Baking Co, bds 248 E Jefferson.

Johann Catherine, presser S M Foster, bds 248 E Jefferson.

Johann Frank S, candymkr Fox br U S Baking Co, bds 248 E Jefferson.

Johann George N, mach hd Ft Wayne Furn Co, res 155 W Superior.

Johann Mary A (wid Andrew), res 248 E Jefferson.

Johann Peter, helper, res 42 Wallace.

Johann Theresa R, bds 248 E Jefferson.
John, *see also Jahn and Johns.*
John Robert, engr N Y, C & St L R R, res 398 W Main.
Johnell Benjamin, laborer, bds 535 E Wayne.
Johnell Henry J, lab N Y, C & St L R R, res 137 High.
Johnell Lawrence W, section hand, res 155 High.
Joho John, lab City Mills, bds 28 E Columbia.
Johns, *see also Jahn and John.*
Johns Alfred L (A L Johns & Co), res 283 W Berry, Tel 497.
Johns Alfred S, res 308 W Washington.
Johns A L & Co (Alfred L Johns), whol saddlery hardware, 49–53 E Columbia, Tel 400.
Johns Julius, molder, bds 56 Miner.
Johns Malley J, bds 308 W Washington.
Johns Pauline (wid Charles), res 56 Miner.
Johns Wm, mach hd Penn Co, bds 56 Miner.
Johnson, *see also Jansen and Jensen.*
Johnson Alexander, Superintendent Indiana School for Feeble-Minded Youth, res same.
Johnson Alfred S, chief train dispatcher F, Ft W & W Ry, res 39 Brackenridge.
Johnson Alice, bds 210 W Superior.
Johnson Andrew J, lumber, res 40 Marion.
Johnson Mrs Annie, res 261 Hanna.
Johnson August, coremaker Bass F & M Wks, bds 157 Holman.
Johnson Augusta, bds 33 Lincoln.
Johnson Augustine, engr Penn Co, res 203 Barr.
Johnson A Lincoln, lab Ft Wayne Electric Corp, res 154 W De Wald.
Johnson Barney, helper Bass F & M Wks, res 87 Holman.
Johnson Benjamin F, constable, 23 E Main, res 254 E Jefferson.
Johnson Bessie, bds 198 W De Wald.
Johnson Byron J, carp S F Bowser & Co, res 24 Oliver.
Johnson Charles E, painter, res 167 High.
Johnson Charles E, planer Ind Mach Wks, res 43 Boone.
Johnson Charles W, mach hd Penn Co, res 2 Brookside.
Johnson Clarence F, Gas Fitter, res 101 Fletcher av.
Johnson Clarissa D (wid Henry C), bds 173 Griffith.
Johnson Cynthia C (wid Edward), bds 167 High.
Johnson Della, bds 5 Boone.
Johnson Edward S, brakeman, bds 158 Harmer.

Johnson Elbe C, painter Fleming Mnfg Co, res 21 St Mary's av.

Johnson Mrs Eliza, matron Ind School for F M Y.

Johnson Eliza A, domestic 19 W Williams.

Johnson Elsie M, bds 231 W Jefferson.

Johnson Emmet E, lab Hoffman Bros, res 5 Boone.

Johnson E May, bds 133 W Wayne.

Johnson Fannie L (wid Alva), bds 54 E Washington.

Johnson Fenton M, dining car conductor, rms 331 Calhoun

Johnson Frank M, traveling agt, res 173 Wells.

Johnson Frank O, fireman Penn Co, res 15 W Leith.

Johnson Frederick, bds 319 Hanna.

Johnson George E, Dentist, 2d floor 74 Calhoun, rms 4th floor same,

Johnson Mrs George E, Dressmaking and Stamping, 79 W Main, res same.

Johnson George M, machinist, res 39 W Williams.

Johnson George W, laborer, bds 145 Ewing.

Johnson Rev Harry M, pastor Trinity (M E) Church, res 158 Wells.

Johnson Honry, laborer, bds 136 W De Wald.

Johnson Henry, helper Bass F & M Wks, bds 43 Gay.

Johnson Henry E, inspr Penn Co, res 217 John.

Johnson Henry F, bds 319 Hanna.

Johnson Isaac, conductor, bds 146 Walton av.

Johnson Johanna B (wid Gerhard F), res 319 Hanna.

Johnson John H, Cement Contractor, above 68 E Columbia, res same. (See p 99.)

Johnson John W, mach hd Penn Co, res 136 W De Wald.

Johnson Joseph, well borer, bds Union House.

Johnson Josiah, lab Penn Co, bds 19 Indiana av.

Johnson Lillian, seamstress, bds 104 Hanna.

Johnson Loren H, oil peddler, res 31 Baker.

Johnson Louisa, domestic, rms 72 Barr.

Johnson Mrs Lucinda, res 356 Calhoun.

Johnson Mable W, bds 231 W Jefferson.

Johnson Maggie, domestic 172 W Wayne.

Johnson Marcus R, toolmkr Ft Wayne Electric Corp, res 231 W Jefferson.

Johnson Marion B, bds 24 Oliver.

Johnson Margaret, res 203 Barr.

Johnson Margaret (wid Jacob), res 214 John.

Johnson Mary, bds 136 W De Wald.

Johnson Mary E, drawing teacher, 26 Schmitz Blk, bds 287 W Wayne.

24

Johnson Mary M, laundress, res 41 Monroe.

Johnson Mrs Minnie, domestic 144 Holman.

Johnson Mrs Mollie E, res cor Jesse and Archer av.

Johnson Myrtle, music teacher, 31 Baker, bds same.

Johnson Olive, bds 16 W 3d.

Johnson Ollie (wid Albert), milliner, 60 Maumee rd, res 381 E Washington.

Johnson Oscar B, clk Penn Co, res 250 E Jefferson.

Johnson Oscar E, died November 28, 1894.

Johnson Peter H, blksmith Ft Wayne Electric Corp, res 73 Shawnee av.

Johnson Rose B, teacher Ft Wayne Conservatory of Music, bds 58 W Berry.

Johnson Susan E (wid James), bds 386 E Washington.

Johnson Theodore, laborer, bds 41 Duck.

Johnson Walter F, bkkpr Bond Cereal Mills, res 9 W De Wald.

Johnson Wesley H, trucker L S & M S Ry, res 32 Wefel

Johnson Wm H, res 145 Ewing.

Johnson Wilmer B, res 6 Burgess.

Johnston David D, incubator, res 120 Boone.

Johnston Edward R, principal School for F M Y, res same

Johnston Glenn W, brakeman N Y, C & St L R R, bds 120 Boone.

Johnston Mathew E, blacksmith, res w s Hanna 7 s of Pontiac.

Johnston Monroe, janitor School for F M Y, res s e cor 4th and Sherman.

Johnston Wm, plumber, res 246 E Creighton av.

Johnston Winnie E, stenogr Randall & Doughman, bds 157 E Berry.

Johnstonbaugh Emory E, e gr Jenny E L & P Co, res 184 Wells.

Joly, see also Jully.

Joly Frank, clerk John Langard, res 105 Lake av.

Jones Ambrose F, res 301 Harrison.

Jones Arthur L, medical student, bds 112 Wells.

Jones Belle M (wid Maurice L), res 121 E Main.

Jones Benjamin F, finisher, bds 63 W Butler.

Jones Catherine (wid John), bds 22 John.

Jones Catherine (wid Paul), res 51 Oliver.

Jones Charles, peddler, res n e cor Winter and Hayden.

Jones Charles, clk Ft Wayne Electric corp, res 110 Brackenridge.

Jones Charles E, student, bds 63 W Butler.

Jones Charles M, chief clerk Penn Co, res 116 Force.
Jones Charles M (col'd), janitor, bds 31 Pearl
Jones Charles P, cleaner Pantitorium, bds 59 Maumee rd.
Jones Cora E C (wid Robert M), milliner, rms 312 Calhoun.
Jones Daisy, domestic 34 Douglas av.
Jones Daisy I, bds 28 Douglas av.
Jones David, laborer, bds 57 Barr.
Jones David W, res 21 E Leith.
Jones Edward (col'd), barber H H Stites, res 19 Melita.
Jones Edward A, plumber, bds 112 Wells.
Jones Edward S, engr G R & I R R, res 83 W Butler.
Jones Emma A (wid Levi M), res 152 E Berry.
Jones Emma R, clk Princess Cash Store, bds 30 Pine.
Jones Eva J, bds 63 W Butler.
Jones Evan, bds John N Christie.
Jones Frederick W, driver Powers & Baneroft, res 149 Griffith.
Jones Fremont L (F L Jones & Co), res 246 Hoagland av.
Jones F L & Co (Freemont L Jones, Ogden Pierce), Proprs Troy Steam Laundry, 48 and 50 Pearl. Tel 160. (*See left bottom lines.*)
Jones George A, trav agt Seavey Hardware Co, res 28 Erie.
Jones George W, Real Estate, Loans, Insurance, Abstracts of Title, Notary and Collections, 9 and 11 W Main, res 146 Jackson.
Jones Harry A, trav agt M L Jones, bds 121 E Main.
Jones Harvey P, foreman F L Jones & Co, bds 21 E Leith.
Jones Hattie, bds 149 Griffith.
Jones Hattie (wid Heber F), res 131 W Jefferson.
Jones Henry, engr Penn Co, res 47 E De Wald.
Jones Henry P, conductor, res 51 Oliver.
Jones Isaac, brakeman, res 41 Smith.
Jones James, engr N Y, C & St L R R, bds 361 W Main.
Jones Jasper W, commissioner Allen County, bds Columbia House.
Jones John, cigarmkr A Hazzard, bds 112 Wells.
Jones John, mach Wabash R R, res 63 W Butler.
Jones John, switchman, bds 76 Taylor.
Jones John L, hostler, bds 63 W Butler.
Jones Joseph H, physician, 320 W Jefferson res same.
Jones Levi M, died August 4, 1894.
Jones Lillie, bds 112 Wells.
Jones Lloyd, clk J B White, res 112 Wells.
Jones Mary (col'd), bds w s Savannah 1 n of Pontiac.
Jones Mary E, bds 63 W Butler.

Jones Mary E, dressmaker, bds 30 Pine.
Jones Mrs Mary O, died July 1, 1894.
Jones Maurice L, photographers' supplies, 44 Calhoun, res 222 W Wayne. Tel 267, res 472.
Jones Oliver S, foreman, bds 63 W Butler.
Jones Sarah A, bds 21 E Leith.
Jones Silas C, express, bds 266 E Creighton av.
Jones Thomas, truckman, res 30 Pine.
Jones Wells, laborer, bds 367 E Wayne.
Jones Wilburn (col'd), coremkr Bass F & M Wks, bds 299 Hanna.
Jones Wm, brakeman G R & I R R, bds 28 Chicago.
Jones Wm (col'd), laborer, bds 68 Murray.
Jones Wm, printer, bds 112 Wells.
Jones Wm D, propr New Aveline House, s e cor Calhoun and Berry.
Jones Wm H, lab City Water Wks, res 37 Buchanan.
Jones Wm H, propr Hamilton House, 103 W Berry.
Jones Wm M, solicitor, bds 28 Chicago.
Jones Wm R, driver, bds 30 Pine.
Joost Albert, music teacher, 132 W Jefferson, res same.
Joost Clara, teacher, bds 132 W Jefferson.
Jordan, *see also Jourdain.*
Jordan Aloys (Jordon Bros), res 19 Harrison.
Jordan Anthony (Jordon Bros), rms 67 Harrison.
Jordan Bros (Anthony and Aloys), saloon, 19 Harrison.
Jordan George S, engr L E & W R R, res 33 W 4th.
Jordan Joseph F, mach Bass F & M Wks, res 409 E Lewis.
Jornod Ernest A, mach hd Anthony Wayne Mnfg Co, bds 401 E Washington.
Jose Fredericka (wid Edward), res w s Franklin av 2 n of Putnam.
Joseph Benjamin E, Manager New York and London Etectric Assn, 101 E Wayne, res same. (*See card in classified deformity apparatus.*)
Joseph Catherine (wid David), res 101 E Wayne.
Joseph Maude, bds 101 E Wayne.
Joss Mrs Elizabeth B, bds 189 W Berry.
Josse Charles P, oil peddler, res 154 High.
Josse Elizabeth M, bds 132 Wells.
Josse Frederica (wid Edward), res 126 Franklin av.
Jourdain, *see also Jordan.*
Jourdain Celestin J, grocer, 98 Maumee rd, res 94 same.
Jourdain Louis J, clk C J Jourdain, bds 94 Maumee rd.
Jourdain Mary F, bds 94 Maumee rd.

Journal Co The, H C Rockhill Pres and Genl Mngr, A J Moynihan Sec and Treas, Publishers Fort Wayne Daily and Weekly Journal and Journal of the Medical Sciences, 30 E Main. Tel 18.

Journal of the Medical Sciences, 30 E Main.

Joy Fannie, res n s Locust 1 w of N Calhoun.

Joy Josephine M (wid Victory), res 105 E Main.

Joyce Albert, clk S Schwier and Son, res 128 E De Wald.

Judt Charles H, lab Olds' Wagon Wks. bds 67 Lillie.

Judy David L, mach Penn Co, res 24 E Williams.

Judy George H, foreman Penn Co, res 23 E Williams.

Judy Lloyd W, mach Penn Co, bds 55 Grand.

Judy Oscar B, blksmith Penn Co, res 60 Hugh.

Juengel Clara W, bds 413 Hanna.

Juengel Hannah J, bds 413 Hanna.

Juengel Rev Henry, pastor German Evangelical Lutheran Church, res 413 Hanna.

Juengel Lena R, dressmaker, bds 413 Hanna.

Juengel Paul O, bds 413 Hanna.

Juergensen Frederick K, messenger Old National Bank, res s s Griswold av 1 e of bridge.

Juergensen Helen H, bds s s Griswold av 1 e of bridge.

Juergensen Marie A, bds s s Griswold av 1 e of bridge.

Juergensen Peter K, clk Morgan & Beach, res s s Griswold av 1 e of bridge.

Juillerat Marie, opr S M Foster, bds 32 Charles.

Julliard Frances M, dressmaker, res 70 W Washington.

Jully, see also Joly.

Jully Clara, domestic 259 W Wayne.

Jully George, teamster, bds 112 St Mary's av.

Jully Louis, barber, 114 St Mary's av, res 112 same.

Jnlly Sophia A, domestic 132 W Jefferson.

Jump Edward, painter J H Brimmer, res rear 70 Charles.

Junge Clemens J, painter, 179 Taber, res same.

Junge Henry, bds 179 Taber.

Junghaus Edwin F R, carpenter, bds 516 Harrison.

Junghaus George, cabtmkr Ft Wayne Furn Co, res 516 Harrison.

Jungles W Frederick, fireman Penn Co, res 37 Eliza.

Junk Agnes, opr Hoosier Mnfg Co, bds 74 E Leith.

Junk Beecher W, res 395 Broadway.

Junk Gertrude (wid Nicholas), res 74 E Leith.

Junk Jacob, lab Penn Co, res 74 E Leith.

Junk Joseph, lab Penn Co, res 26 Killea av.

Junk Lizzie, clerk, bds 74 E Leith.

Junk Matthias, cabinetmaker, bds 74 E Leith.
Junk Peter, helper Penn Co, res s e cor Monroe and Wallace.
Junod Alfred, butcher, bds 28 E Columbia.
Just, *see Yost.*

K

Kaade Anna, bds 71 Swinney av.
Kaade August, helper Wabash R R, res 71 Swinney av.
Kaade Emma, bds 71 Swinney av.
Kaade Ferdinand, lab Ft Wayne Electric Corp, res 533 Broadway.
Kaade Herman E, machinist, bds 71 Swinney av.
Kaade John, molder Bass F & M Wks, res 135 Union.
Kaade Wm, coremkr Bass F & M Wks, res 65 Wall.
Kaag Annie, opr Wayne Knitting Mills, bds cor Spring and Oakland.
Kaag Charles F W, bkkpr M F Kaag, bds 45 Cass.
Kaag Lilian E, clk Peoples Store, bds 283 W Jefferson.
Kaag Mathias F, Crockery, Glassware, Lamps, Chandeliers, Etc, 5 E Columbia, res 45 Cass. Tel 447. *(See left bottom lines.)*
Kabisch Catherine, bds 182 Fairfield av.
Kabisch Franz R (Kabisch & Son), res 182 Fairfield av.
Kabisch Frederick C (Kabisch & Son), res 180 W De Wald.
Kabisch Jeannette, domestic 106 W Washington.
Kabisch John H, barber, 137½ Fairfield av, res 106 W Butler.
Kabisch Rudolph F, butcher, res 182 Fairfield av.
Kabisch & Son (Franz R and Frederick C), meats, res 156 Fairfield av.
Kaeck Elizabeth, domestic 73 Barthold.
Kable Lena, domestic Lake Shore Hotel.
Kaeck Peter, died March 23, 1895.
Kaeck Wm, grocer, 244 St Mary's av, res same.
Kaestel, *see also Casteel and Kestel.*
Kaestel Wolfgang, stonecutter Keller & Braun, bds 51 Carson av.
Kahl Wendelin, molder, res 48 Buchanan.
Kahnlein, *see Koehnlin.*
Kahoe Wm, engr Penn Co, res 6 Monroe.
Kahogan Mrs Laura, domestic 270½ Calhoun.
Kain Wm, lab Olds' Wagon Wks, res Wayne township.
Kaiser, *see also Kayser, Keyser and Kiser.*
Kaiser Anna, dressmaker, bds 12 Force.

Kaiser Anton H, clk East Yards Penn Co, res 127 Madison.
Kaiser Charles, blacksmith Wabash R R, res 34 W Allen.
Kaiser Charles L, leader Wayne Orchestra and plasterer, res 130 Shawnee av.
Kaiser Christian D E, planer Ind Mach Wks, bds 186 E Lewis
Kaiser Conrad C, millwright, res 43 Cass.
Kaiser Edward, lab N Y, C & St L R R, bds 82 Wilt.
Kaiser Ernest, laborer. bds 229 John.
Kaiser Ernst, mach hd Penn Co, res 186 E Lewis.
Kaiser Frederick E, boilermkr Wabash R R, res 148 Force.
Kaiser Frederick F, boilermaker. bds 148 Force.
Kaiser Henry D, removed to Indianapolis, Ind.
Kaiser John, helper Penn Co, res 244 Putnam.
Kaiser John, lab Penn Co, res 12 Force.
Kaiser J Henry, lab Penn Co, res 360 E Lewis.
Kaiser Leonora W S, seamstress, bds 186 E Lewis.
Kaiser Lizzie, tailoress, bds 148 Force.
Kaiser Louise, bds 34 W Allen.
Kaiser Mary, bds 43 Cass.
Kaiser Minnie, bds 148 Force.
Kaiser Rudolph, driver Brenzinger Baking Co, res 30 Madison.
Kaiser Rudy, driver, res 132 Monroe.
Kaiser R, res 123 Monroe.
Kaiser Wm C, appr Ft Wayne News, bds 34 W Allen.
Kaiser Wm G, patternmkr Western Construction Co, res 20 E De Wald.
Kalaus Joseph, bottler L Brames & Co, res 287 E Washington.
Kalbacher, see also Kohlbacher.
Kalbacher Anton, Flour and Feed, 296 Calhoun Dry Goods and Groceries, 13 and 15 Grand, res 234 E Wayne. Tel 69.
Kalbacher Edward H, clk A Kalbacher, bds 234 E Wayne.
Kalbacher Kate M, bkkpr A Kalbacher, bds 234 E Wayne.
Kalbacher Theresa U, bds 234 E Wayne.
Kalbus Charles H, laborer, bds 153 Archer av.
Kalbus John M, laborer, res 153 Archer av.
Kaler, see also Kaylor. Kehler, Keller, Koehler and Kohler.
Kaler Charles P, condr N Y, C & St L R R, res 235 W Washington.
Kaliker Jacob, laborer, bds 62 Buchanan.
Kalkman Frederick, founder Bass F & M Wks, res s s Manford 2 w of Hartman.
Kallen Kate, opr Wayne Knitting Mills, bds Peter Kallen.

Kallen Louisa S, bds Peter Kallen.

Kallen Matilda H, bds Peter Kallen.

Kallen Peter, head sawyer Hoffman Bros, res n e cor Richardson and Rumsey av.

Kallen Sophia K, opr Wayne Knitting Mills, bds Peter Kallen.

Kallenbach George, wiper Penn Co, res 40 Charles.

Kallor Emma, seamstress Ella M Roush, bds 26 High.

Kalteyer Victor, inspr Ft Wayne Gas Co, res 221 E Wayne.

Kamm Alma, bds 512 E Lewis.

Kamm Julius, tinner Gerding & Aumann Bros, bds 512 E Lewis.

Kamm Oswold W, helper A Vogely, bds 512 E Lewis.

Kamm Wm, engr Mayflower Milling Co, res 512 E Lewis.

Kammer Henry, truckman Penn Co, res 95 Walton av.

Kammer Louis, wagonmkr Olds' Wagon Wks, res 93 Walton av.

Kammeyer Diedrich, lab, res 80 Swinney av.

Kammeyer Ernst C, clk Dittoe's Grocery Co, bds 57 Baker.

Kammeyer Ferdinand, carpenter, bds 302 Hanna.

Kammeyer Henrietta, domestic 188 W Wayne.

Kammeyer Henry C, laborer, bds 87 St Mary's av.

Kammeyer Henry W, laborer, res 87 St Mary's av.

Kammeyer Sophia L R, bds 87 St Mary's av.

Kampe, *see also Kemp and Komp.*

Kompe Charles A, bds 306 W Jefferson.

Kampe Christian J, clk E H Coombs, res 217 W Jefferson.

Kampe Ernest G, bkkpr S Bash & Co, res 18 Union.

Kampe Gustav J, teacher Emanuel G L School, res 306 W Jefferson.

Kampe Otto F, upholsterer P E Wolf, bds 168 Ewing.

Kampf, *see also Kempf.*

Kampf Ernest G, cabinetmaker, res 26 Cass.

Kampf Ernest J, bds 26 Cass.

Kamphues Henry L, butcher, res 250 Erie.

Kamphues Mary (wid Joseph), bds 44 Hendricks.

Kanaga Francis J, conductor, res 86 W Williams.

Kanaga Lee A, conductor, res 88 W Williams.

Kane, *see also Cain and Cane.*

Kane Alfred L, bds 88 W Berry.

Kane Blk, s s Main bet Calhoun and Harrison.

Kane Charles M, clk J M Kane, bds 88 W Berry.

Kane Daniel W, clk J M Kane, res 439 Broadway.

Kane Hanna (wid James), died April 12, 1895.

Kane James M, bazaar, 24 Calhoun, res 88 W Berry.
Kane John, motorman Ft W E Ry Co, bds 41 W Lewis.
Kane John P, conductor, res 504 Hanna.
Kane Mary, rms 46 W Berry.
Kane Mary, domestic 190 W Wayne.
Kane Patrick H, cigars, The Wayne, res 50 W Berry.
Kane Rosa, domestic 190 W Wayne.
Kane Stella C, bds 50 W Berry.
Kanenman Annie, domestic 82 W Washington.
Kanne August F, painter, res 9 Emily.
Kanne Frederick H, city agt Fisher Bros, res 170 Madison.
Kanney John, Contractor in Stone and Brick Work, Public Buildings, Court Houses and Churches a Specialty. Stone Abutments and Piers, Cisterns, Sewers and Chimneys, Correspondence Solicited, Office 5 Bass Blk, res 35 Maumee rd. (*See page 79.*)
Kanning Frederick L, actor, rms 59 E Wayne.
Kenning Henry C, bricklayer, res 68 Stophlet.
Kanning Henry F, blksmith E B Kunkle & Co, bds 99 Madison.
Kanning Henry W, trav agt Eckart P Co, res 98 W Main.
Kanning Lizzie, domestic 268 W Washington.
Kanning Louisa A, bds 59 E Wayne.
Kanning Sophia (wid Louis), res 99 Madison.
Kanning Sophia M (wid Wm), furnished rooms, 59 E Wayne.
Kanning Wm F, letter carrier P O, res 59 E Wayne.
Kaough Elizabeth, bds 166 Montgomery.
Kaough Margaret (wid Nicholas), bds 166 Montgomery.
Kaough Richard, engineer, res 166 Montgomery.
Kaough Wm, Agricultural Implements, 54 and 56 E Columbia, res 166 Montgomery.
Kappel Henry, real estate, res 182 E Washington.
Kappel Henry J, helper Penn Co, res 349 E Lewis.
Kappel Herman G, clk Geo De Wald & Co, res 43 Columbia av.
Kappel John H, Physician and Surgeon, 180 E Washington, res same. Tel 543.
Karbah, *see Carbaugh.*
Karbasch, *see Kerbach and Kirbach.*
Karber, *see also Kerber.*
Karber Frederick, molder Bass F & M Wks, bds 44 John.
Karber George D, carp, res 120 Fletcher av.
Karber James H, carpenter, res 44 Glasgow av.
Karber Wm E, watchman Winch & Son, bds 120 Fletcher av
Karg George A, laborer, res 39 Duck.

Kariger Joseph P, clerk, bds 187 Harmer.
Kariger Samuel, res 187 Harmer.
Karkhoff Joseph F, lab Penn Co, res 14 McLachlan.
Karn, see also Kern and Kirn.
Karn Bros (Joseph and Kaim), meats, 16 W Main. Tel 166.
Karn Elias, res 126 Ewing.
Karn Joseph (Karn Bros), res 133 W Washington.
Karn Kaim (Karn Bros), bds 126 Ewing.
Karn Samuel A, pianos, 9 E Columbia, res n s Rivermet av
    4 e of St Joseph boulevard.
Karns, see also Cairns.
Karns Mrs Barbara E, dressmkr, 123 Harrison, res same.
Karns Ellis A, cigarmkr, bds 123 Harrison.
Karns Wilson C, photographer, bds 123 Harrison.
Karp Helena (wid Ludwich), bds 223 Walton av.
Karten Rose, bds 515 E Washington.
Kartholl Caroline (wid Joseph), res 112 Clay.
Kartrey Kunigunda (wid John), res 104 E Wayne.
Kasbaum Charles, gardener, res 58 Spy Run av.
Kassel, see Castle and Kestel.
Kassens Jacob, lab Penn Co, res 521 E Lewis.
Kasten Louis C (Kasten & Kohlmeyer), res 116 W Jefferson.
Kasten & Kohlmeyer (Louis C Kasten, Edward Kohl-
    meyer), cigar mnfrs, 130 Calhoun.
Kathner Edward, painter, bds 197 Barr.
Kathner Guido, painter, res 90 Wagner.
Katt August C, bicycles, 37 W Berry, res 69 same.
Katt Claus, stone mason, res 41 Maumee rd.
Katt Gustave E, collector, bds 41 Maumee rd.
Katzenwadel Jacob, cooper The Herman Berghoff Brewing
    Co, res 60 Huffman.
Kaudder Christian, baker S H Schwieters, res 58 W 5th.
Kauder Benjamin, lab Wabash R R, res 131 E Taber.
Kauffman Harry St C, tel opr, bds 262 W Berry.
Kauffman John B, cook, res 179 W Washington.
Kauffman Julia M C, opr Hoosier Mnfg Co, bds 163 Taber.
Kauffman Kate (wid Christian), res 163 Taber.
Kauffman Mary, domestic 150 Force.
Kauffman May, bds 163 Taber.
Kaufmann Valentine, helper, res 564 Lafayette.
Kauter, see Kaudder.
Kavanaugh, see also Cavanaugh.
Kavanaugh Elizabeth M, bds 103 Fairfield av.
Kavanaugh Thomas, clk J O Caswell, bds 205 Calhoun.
Kavanaugh Thomas C, blksmith, res 103 Fairfield av.

Kay, *see also Key.*
Kay Mrs Amanda E, res 194 W De Wald.
Kay John, brakeman N Y, C & St L R R, rms 98 Boone.
Kaylor, *see also Kalor, Kehler, Keller, Koehler and Kohler.*
Kaylor Elmer, bds 249 E Washington.
Kaylor Joseph, laborer, res 21 W 4th.
Kaylor Lyman, res 23 Lillie.
Kaylor Mary A (wid Peter), bds 249 E Washington.
Kaylor Peter, lab Ft Wayne Gas Co, res 249 E Washington
Kaylor Reuben, laborer, bds 28 W 3d.
Kaylor Wm H. laborer, res 28 W 3d.
Kaylor Wm W, butcher, bds 249 E Washington.
Kayser, *see also Kaiser, Keyser and Kiser.*
Kayser Anthony A, harnessmkr. bds 346 E Wayne.
Kayser Anton, tailor, res 252 W Jefferson.
Kayser August, mach Ft W E Corp, bds 101 Wall.
Kayser Charles E H. cigarmkr F J Gruber, bds 346 E
   Wayne.
Kayser Christian H, painter Penn Co, res 353 Lillie.
Kayser Ernest. packer Pottlitzer & Bros, res 101 Wall.
Kayser Ferdinand, lab Ft W E Corp, bds 101 Wall.
Kayser Frederick, tailor, 42 Harrison, res same.
Kayser Frederick C, springmkr Ft W Furn Co, res 295
   W Wayne.
Kayser Frederick D, shoemaker, res 346 E Wayne.
Kayser George E, mach Ft Wayne Electric Corp, bds 252
   W Jefferson.
Kayser Mary J, dressmaker, bds 252 W Jefferson.
Kayser Minnie L, dressmaker, bds 252 W Jefferson.
Kayser Oscar, lab Penn Co, res 334 Force.
Kayser Theodore S, clk Isadore Lehman, bds 252 W Jef-
   ferson,
Kayser Wm (Kayser & Baade), res 220 W Jefferson.
Kayser Wm D, printer, bds 346 E Wayne.
Kayser Wm D C, tailor Frederick Kayser, bds 42 Harrison.
Kayser & Baade (Wm Kayser, Henry C Baade),
   General Store, 129–133 Broadway. Tel 181.
Keagle Leah, res 369 Jesse.
Kearns, *see also Cairns.*
Kearns Bridget (wid Thomas), bds 143 E De Wald.
Kearns Dennis, conductor, bds 143 E De Wald.
Kearns Thomas, died May 21, 1894.
Kebeckel Wm, coachman 290 Fairfield av.
Kee Mank, laundry, 104 Broadway, res same.
Keech Edward J, engr Engine Co No 5, res 59 Hendricks.

Keefe, *see also* O'Keefe.
Keefe Alice M, bds 326 Maumee rd.
Keefe Edward, res 326 Maumee rd.
Keefe Edward C, section hand, bds 326 Maumee rd.
Keefe Mary (wid Cornelius), res 43 Baker.
Keefe Zoe F, bds 326 Maumee rd.
Keefer, *see also Keever and Kiefer.*
Keefer Christian, stonecutter Keller & Braun, res 275 W Jefferson.
Keefer Edward J, machinist, bds 275 W Jefferson.
Keefer Emma L, bds 275 W Jefferson.
Keefer George H, asst supt Prud Ins Co, res 278 E Lewis.
Keefer John, bricksetter, res e s Lafayette 1 s of Grace.
Keefer Minnie, bds 278 E Lewis.
Keegan Abbie C, bds 147 W Washington.
Keegan Hugh G, student, bds 147 W Washington.
Keegan Patrick H, engr Penn Co, res 147 W Washington.
Keel, *see also Keil, Kiel and Kyle.*
Keel Mrs Aurora C, milliner, 22 W Berry, res 24 same.
Keel Chester, bds 24 W Berry.
Keel Ellen, bds 24 W Berry.
Keeler Joseph W, conductor, res 36 Thomas.
Keeley Brewing Co, Michael Fitzgerald agt, 355 Lafayette.
Keeley Wm F, fireman G R & I R R, res 45 Baker.
Keen Zebulon, bds 73 Dawson.
Keener Katie, domestic 254 W Wayne.
Keenan Daisy, domestic County Jail.
Keeran Wm H, res 64 Lake av.
Kees, *see also Kiess.*
Kees Christopher, stenogr Julius Nathan & Co, bds 35 Wilt.
Kees Frank, watchman, res 35 Wilt.
Kees John, boilermkr Wabash R R, bds 35 Wilt.
Keever, *see also Keefer and Kiefer.*
Keever David, res s s Richardson 3 e of Rumsey av.
Keever Edwin, saloon, 44 E Calumbia, res same.
Keever Elizabeth (wid David), res w s Spy Run av 3 n of Burgess av.
Keever George, bartender Wm Miller, res w s Spy Run av 2 s of Randolph.
Keffer, *see also Keefer and Kiefer.*
Kegelmann Charles (J Kegelmann & Son), bds 553 E Wayne.
Kegelmann Julius J (Kegelmann & Son), res 553 E Wayne.
Kegelmann & Son (Julius & Charles), Mattress Manufacturers and Patent Feather Renovator, 551 E Wayne.

Kegg Emanuel S, carpenter, res 116 W Butler.
Kegg Lillian M (wid Wm A), bds 116 W Butler.
Kegg Nancy L (wid Emanuel S), boarding, 113 Barr.
Kehler, see also Kalor, Kaylor, Keller, Koehler and Kohler.
Kehler Daniel B, trav agt, bds Spy Run av n e cor Prospect av.
Kehler Franklin H, helper, bds n e cor Spy Run av and Prospect av.
Kehler George A, foreman, res 158 Harmer.
Kehler Joseph W, attendant. res 7 Prospect av.
Keil, see also Keel and Kyle.
Keil Amy J, bds 145 W Superior.
Keil Benjamin F, student, bds 139 W Superior.
Keil Frederick W (Keil & Keil), res 145 W Superior.
Keil Jacob H (Keil & Keil), bds 139 W Superior.
Keil Luther H, clk Keil & Keil, bds 41 Cass.
Keil Mary A, bds 145 W Superior.
Keil Sadie S, bds 145 W Superior.
Keil & Keil (Jacob H and Frederick W), Wall Paper, Pictures, Mouldings and Curtains, 106 Calhoun.
Keim, see also Kime.
Keim Clara, seamstress, bds 40 Pearl.
Keim Daniel, feed stable, 40 Pearl, res same.
Keim Emma J, seamstress, bds 40 Pearl.
Keim Solomon D, laborer, bds 40 Pearl.
Keintz John, died August 2, 1894.
Keintz Rachael (wid John), res 293 Hanna.
Keinz Philip, saloon, 307 Lafayette, res same.
Keiser, see Kaiser, Kayser, Keyser and Kiser.
Kelker Anthony, engr G R & I R R, res 174 Griffith.
Kelker Charles A, barnman W H Brown, bds 69 Holman.
Kelker Harry O, engineer Penn Co, bds 174 Griffith.
Kelker John H, teamster W H Brown, bds 69 Holman.
Kelker Margaret A. bds 88 Chicago.
Kelker Matilda M, bds 250 E Wayne.
Kelker Mattie, bds 16 W Lewis.
Kelker Orlo L, bartender Home Billiard Hall, res 139 Columbia av.
Kelker Samuel G, clk L S & M S Ry, bds 16 W Lewis.
Kelker Samuel S, engineer Penn Co, res 16 W Lewis.
Kelker Thomas J, caller, bds 16 W Lewis.
Kelker Wm C, engineer G R & I R R, res 89 Baker.
Kelker Wm P, carpenter, res 250 E Wayne.
Kell Alice, waitress 25 W Wayne.
Kell Fred J, music teacher, 54 E Washington, bds same.

Kelleher Hannah, waiter McKinnie House, rms same.
Kelleher Mary, waiter McKinnie House, rms same.
Keller, *see also Kalor, Kaylor, Kehler, Koehler and Kohler.*
Keller Abraham, laborer, res 71 Monroe.
Keller Albert J, upholsterer Pape Furn Co, res s s Putnam 1 w of Franklin av.
Keller Andrew J (Dodge and Keller; Keller, Edmunds & Law Electric Construction Co), Druggist, 96 Broadway, res 83 Brackenridge. Tel 335.
Keller Caspar, helper, res 11 Gay.
Keller Dental Co The, Josiah O Keller mngr, 93 Barr.
Keller Edmund W, brakeman Penn Co, res 76 Montgomery.
Keller, Edmunds & Law Electric Construction Co (A J Keller, F W Edmunds, Henry J Law), Electric Bells, Batteries, Gas, Electric and Combination Fixtures, 4–14 Schmitz Blk. Tel 262.
Keller Edward S, clerk F X Keller, bds 7 Boone.
Keller Elizabeth (wid Charles), res rear 224 W Main.
Keller Edward W, bds 312 Harrison.
Keller Frank X, druggist, 332 W Main, res 7 Boone. Tel 473.
Keller Frederick, bds 54 Fletcher av.
Keller George W, clk W D Henderson, res e s Spy Run av 2 n of Riverside av.
Keller Harry D, printer The Journal, bds 156 E Wayne.
Keller Henry (Keller & Braun), res 141 W Superior.
Keller Jacob, mach hd Bass F & M Wks, res 295 Maumee rd
Keller James W, foreman The Journal, res 156 E Wayne.
Keller John F, car inspr. res 19 Taylor.
Keller Josiah O, mngr Keller Dental Co, res 154 E Berry.
Keller Le Roy, stenogr Keller Dental Co, bds 154 E Berry.
Keller Mary (wid Sebastian), died September 11, 1894.
Keller Mattie J (wid Frederick E), dressmkr, 47 W Superior, res same.
Keller Morris J, car repairer, res 17 Melita.
Keller Oliver R, clerk, bds e s Spy Run av 2 n of Riverside av.
Keller Oliver R, driver W D Henderson, bds G W Keller.
Keller Paul, helper Keller & Braun, res 75 Wall.
Keller Pharis M, brakeman, res 54 Fletcher av.
Keller Wm B, lab Standard Wheel Co, bds 19 Indiana av.
Keller Wm E, laborer, res n s Ruth 1 w of Spy Run av.
Keller & Braun (Henry Keller, Charles G Braun), Props Ft Wayne Steam Stone Works, 84–98 Pearl. Tel 116. (*See right bottom lines.*)

Kellermann Frederick, lab Bass F & M Wks, res e s Lillie 1 n of Wabash R R.
Kellermeier Henry E, carpenter, res 90 Stophlet.
Kellermeier Wm, coachman 113 W Berry.
Kellermeyer Christian H, driver F P Wilt & Co, res 191 Taylor.
Kelley, *see also Kelly.*
Kelley Anna E (wid Michael), res 171 Clinton.
Kelley Cleona M (wid John M), res 160 Walton av.
Kelley Frank, fireman N Y, C & St L R R, bds 82 Madison.
Kelley Hugh, coachman 252 W Wayne.
Kelley John, laborer, bds 57 Prince.
Kelley John B, grocer 26 E Columbia, res same.
Kelley Maggie, domestic 84 Brackenridge.
Kelley Sarah (wid John H), bds 100 W Berry.
Kelley Sarah (wid Daniel), res 57 Prince.
Kelley Wm C, clk J B Kelley, bds 26 E Columbia.
Kelley Wm F, carpenter, res 79 W 3d.
Kellogg John H, engr Penn Co, res 175 Harrison.
Kelly, *see also Kelley.*
Kelly Andrew J, laborer, bds 20 Brandriff.
Kelly Anna, seamstress, bds 313 Harrison.
Kelly Catherine, bds 9 Walnut.
Kelly Christopher, constable, res 82 Madison.
Kelly Clara B, cook, rms 288 Calhoun.
Kelly Deborah A, opr Hoosier Mnfg Co, bds 20 Brandriff.
Kelly Dennis, truckman Wabash R R, bds 55 Grand.
Kelly Elizabth (wid John J), bds 162 Wells.
Kelly Johanna (wid John), res 81 Hoagland av.
Kelly John, boilermkr Penn Co, res 313 Harrison.
Kelly John jr, bds 313 Harrison.
Kelly John J, laborer, bds 81 Hoagland av.
Kelly Louis P, helper Penn Co, bds 55 Grand.
Kelly Margaret, bds 9 Walnut.
Kelly Margaret (wid Thomas), bds 106 W 3d.
Kelly Mary A, opr S M Foster, bds 81 Hoagland av.
Kelly Patrick, laborer, bds 81 Hoagland av.
Kelly Patrick J, watchman Penn Co, res 9 Walnut.
Kelly Patrick J jr, laborer, bds 9 Walnut.
Kelly Richard, brakeman, bds 20 Brandriff.
Kelly Robert E, engr L E & W R R, res 106 W 3d.
Kelly Timothy, res 20 Brandriff.
Kelly Timothy jr, laborer, bds 20 Brandriff.
Kelly Wm B, brakeman, res 223 Lafayette.
Kelly Wm C, fresco artist, res s s Jesse 2 e of Runnion av.

Kelpin Charles, laborer, bds 253 Gay.
Kelpin Louis, wiper, res s s Pontiac 1 w of Smith.
Kelsey Alfred N, trav agt, res 492 W Main.
Kelsey Bertha, clk A Mergentheim, bds 16 Jones.
Kelsey Charles, laborer, bds 133 Baker.
Kelsey Charles B, res 45 Indiana av.
Kelsey Elias M, meat market, 504 Broadway, res 22
    Savilla av.
Kelsey Elizabeth A (wid Samuel), bds 42 Brandriff.
Kelsey Frank W, propr Model Hand Laundry. 137. Fair-
    field av, res 3 Michigan av.
Kelsey Laura B, bds 133 Baker.
Kelsey Oscar R, grocer, 506 Broadway, res same.
Kelsey Mrs Sarah A, res 133 Baker.
Kelsey Walter D, driver, res 24 Harrison.
Kelsey Wm A, barber, 6 Pearl, res 38 Wilt.
Kelsey Wm H, res 425 W Main.
Keltsch Adam, lab Kerr Murray Mnfg Co, res 40 Jones.
Keltsch Nicholas, cabinetmkr, res 49 Barthold.
Kelty John B, brakeman, bds 275 E Creighton av.
Kelty Patrick, foreman, res 275 E Creighton av.
Kelty Thomas, laborer, bds 275 E Creighton av.
Kemler Mrs Ella M, res 71 Hamilton.
Kemp, *see also Kampe and Komp.*
Kemp Charles M, hoseman Engine Co. No 2, rms same.
Kemp Cornelius W, carpenter, res 95 Riverside av.
Kemp Edgar, baking powder mnfr, 169 E Wayne, res same.
Kemp Herbert L, trav agt Mossman, Yarnelle & Co, bds
    169 E Wayne.
Kemp Martin W, foreman Penn Co, res 303 E Lewis.
Kempf, *see also Kampf.*
Kempf Anna M, bds 7 High.
Kempf Charles F, laborer, res 140 Fairfield av.
Kempf John W, carpenter, res 97 Eliza.
Kempf Wm, laborer, res 17 High.
Kempf Wig H, pressfdr Ft Wayne Newspaper Union, bds
    17 High.
Kendall Wallace E, winder Ft Wayne Electric Corp, res
    114 Jackson.
Kendrick Charles E Architect, 20 and
    21 Schmitz Blk, bds 21 W De Wald.
Kendrick Harriet B, clk Wabash R R, bds 21 W De Wald.
Kendrick Louise, bds 21 W De Wald.
Kendrick Wm G, res 21 W De Wald.
Kenlin Mrs Ella H, dressmkr, res 205 W Jefferson.

Kenlin Henry J, barber, res 205 W Jefferson.
Kenlin Mary, seamstress, bds 57 Hendricks.
Kennedy Eliza, bds 22 W De Wald.
Kennedy John J, engineer, res 80 Boone.
Kennedy John J jr, bds 80 Boone.
Kennedy Jonathan R, plasterer, res 217 John.
Kennedy Martin J, bartender, bds 12 Chicago.
Kennedy Philip S, saloon, 341 W Main, bds 80 Boone.
Kennedy Wm, laborer, bds 42 W Main.
Kennel Silvia, bds 266 Calhoun.
Kennelly Jeremiah, lab Penn Co, res 56 Baker.
Kennelly Michael E (Kennelly & Doyle), res 319 E Creighton av.
Kennelly & Doyle (Michael E Kennelly & Dudley Doyle), grocers, 319 E Creighton av.
Kenner Celia A, forewoman, bds 26 Murray.
Kennerk John, res 26 Murray.
Kennerk John jr, teamster, bds 26 Murray.
Kennerk Wm A, bds 26 Murray.
Kenning, *see Kanning.*
Kensill Annie B, bds 173 Holman.
Kensill Emma, bds 173 Holman.
Kensill George W, engr Penn Co, res 148 Clay.
Kensill George W jr, engr Penn Co, res 30 Suttenfield.
Kensill Harry M, student, bds 173 Holman.
Kensill John C, boilermaker, res 173 Holman.
Kensill John C, engineer, res 204 Hanna.
Kent Charles S, clk W R Frederick, bds same.
Kentner Etta P, seamstress, bds 221 W Main.
Keoline Catherine, domestic 1 Sturgis.
Keopf, *see Koepf.*
Kepler John H, brakeman, bds 26 Gay.
Kepler Joseph H, brakeman N Y, C & St L R R, rms 72 Boone.
Kepler Louisa (wid John G), res 26 Gay.
Keplinger Claude J, clk Penn Co, bds 118 Force.
Keplinger Edward A, real estate, res 62 Alliger.
Keplinger Frank E D, assistant postmaster, bds New Aveline Hotel.
Keplinger George F, bds 118 Force.
Keplinger Harry A, cash White National Bank, res 49 W Creighton av.
Keplinger Jacob A, engr Penn Co, res 118 Force.
Keplinger Maud B, clk S F Bowser & Co, bds 118 Force.
Kerbach, *see also Kirbach.*

25

Kerbach Louis, yd foreman Wm Moellering & Son, res 78 Force.

Kerber, *see also Karber.*

Kerber Emil, laborer, res 44 John.

Kerber Frederick, laborer, bds 44 John.

Kerlin Wm L (Kerlin & Bloom), res 388 E Wayne. Tel 397

Kerlin & Bloom (Wm L Kerlin, Nathan W Bloom), Undertakers and Embalmers, 101 Calhoun. Tel 362.

Kern, *see also Karn.*

Kern Anna, domestic 80 Rivermet av.

Kern Jacob, car bldr Penn Co, bds 22 W Main.

Kern Jacob J, with Ft Wayne Gas Co, res 107 W Washington.

Kern Mary, domestic 106 E Berry.

Kern Mary J, bds 64 Harrison.

Kern Samuel, fireman N Y, C & St L R R, bds 323 W Main

Kern Wm C, student, bds 107 W Washington.

Kernan John, laborer, rms 18 W Wayne.

Kerns, *see Cairns, Karn, Kearns and Kirn.*

Kernz Ernst, dyer Wayne Knitting Mills, bds Washington Hotel.

Kerp Joseph W, clk Gottlieb Haller, res 372 Calhoun.

Kerr, *see also Carr.*

Kerr Clara M, clerk, bds 155 Ewing.

Kerr Montgomery T, clk Wm Lawson, bds 156 Rockhill.

Kerr Murray Mnfg Co, Alfred D Cressler Pres and Genl Mngr, G Adolph Schust Sec, Gustave L Hackius Treas, Mnfrs Gas Works Machinery, Gas Holders and Gray Iron Castings of all Descriptions, n e cor Calhoun and Murray. Long Distance Tel 95.

Kerr Walter C, tel opr N Y, C & St L R R, bds 353 E Wayne.

Kerr Wm J, pension attorney, 13 E Main, res 156 Rockhill.

Kerr Wm W, clk P O, bds 19 E Jefferson.

Kesler, *see also Kessler.*

Kesler Abraham J, phys, 286 Calhoun, res 156 Wallace.

Kessens Christian, polisher, bds 363 E Washington.

Kessens Jacob, laborer, res 521 E Lewis.

Kessens John V, bds 363 E Washington.

Kessens Lena, opr Hoosier Mnfg Co, bds 363 E Washington.

Kessens Mary, operator, bds 363 E Washington.

Kessens Tracey, operator, bds 363 E Washington.

Kessens Wm, teamster, res 363 E Washington.

Kessler, *see also Kesler.*

Kessler Simon H, molder Bass F & M Wks, res 359 E Lewis.

Kessmann Bernard, clk Zoeller & Merz, res 330 Harrison.

Kestel, *see also Castle and Kaestel*.

Kestel Louis E, helper Penn Co, bds 117 Madison.

Kestel Paul P, mach, Berry n w cor Barr, res same.

Kester, *see also Koester*.

Kester Morris R, clk Freiburger & Suelzer, res 59 W Butler.

Ketcher John, res 23 Charles.

Ketker Elizabeth S (wid Frederick), res 18 Lavina.

Ketker Frederick W, motorman, res 219 Lake av.

Ketker Frederica S, seamstress, bds 18 Lavina.

Ketker Rosa L, seamstress, bds 18 Lavina.

Ketker Sophia M, seamstress, bds 18 Lavina.

Kettern Peter, laborer, res 13 Euclid av.

Kettler Conrad F, supt letter carriers postoffice, res 205 E Jefferson.

Kettler Eliza (wid Conrad), res 205 E Jefferson.

Kettler Emma M, bds 90 E Wayne.

Kettler E Harry, news boy, bds 90 E Wayne.

Kettler Mary, clerk, bds 205 E Jefferson.

Kettler Wm J, treas D N Foster Furn Co, res 90 E Wayne.

Key, *see also Kay*.

Key Mrs Anna E, seamstress, res 16 Francis.

Key Clayton H, wheelmaker, bds 29 E Main.

Key Wm S (col'd), porter, bds 21 Melita.

Keys, *see Kees and Kiess*.

Keyser, *see also Kaiser, Kayser and Kiser*.

Keyser Grace E, bds 66 Glasgow av.

Keyser Jacob M, real estate, res 66 Glasgow av.

Keyser John, laborer, res 244 Putnam.

Keyser Wm, res n s Humphrey 1 e of Wabash av.

Keyser Wm A, painter, bds 66 Glasgow av.

Keystone Blk, s w cor Calhoun and Columbia.

Kibiger Edward C, clerk, bds 105 Barr.

Kibiger Emanuel, laborer, bds 105 Barr.

Kibiger George J, teamster, rms 415 W Main.

Kibiger John F, hostler, bds 105 Barr.

Kibiger Louisa (wid George), res 105 Barr.

Kickley, *see also Kikley*.

Kickley Arthur E, bds 100 Baker.

Kickley Charles M, mach Wabash R R, res 230 Fairfield av.

Kickley Ida J, bds 100 Baker.

Kickley Joseph C, fireman Wabash R R, res 100 Baker.

Kidd John, stonecutter Wm Geake, res 3 Liberty.

Kidd Kate, dressmkr, bds 150 Clinton.
Kiefer, see also Keefer and Keever.
Kiefer Adolph, driver C L Centlivre Brewing Co, res s s Griswold av 3 e of St Joseph River.
Kiefer Charlotte C, clk G A Kiefer, res 210 Spy Run av.
Kiefer Christian, clk P F Kiefer, rms 16 Wilt.
Kiefer Christian F F, carp, bds 58 Pritchard.
Kiefer Edward, carpenter, bds 11 Zollars av.
Kiefer Frederick, planer Horton Mnfg Co, res 8 Zollars av.
Kiefer George A, grocer, 210 Spy Run av, res same.
Kiefer Henry F, car bldr Penn Co, res 273 E Creighton av.
Kiefer Julius G, foreman C L Centlivre Brewing Co, res 70 Elizabeth.
Kiefer Mary, bds 8 Zollars av.
Kiefer Phillip F, grocer, 16 Wilt, res 181 W Jefferson.
Kiefer Susan M, mach opr, bds 8 Zollars av.
Kiefhaber Frederick J, winder Ft Wayne Elec Corp, res 22 Pritchard.
Kiefhaber George J, res 168 Van Buren.
Kiel, see also Keel, Keil and Kyle.
Kiel Edward F, student, bds 264 Webster.
Kiel Frederick W, mach hd Ft W O Co, bds Wm C Kiel.
Kiel Henry C, clk Ft Wayne Electric Corp, bds 264 Webster.
Kiel Henry F, policeman, res 264 Webster.
Kiel Mary S, bds 264 Webster.
Kiel Wm C, lab, res n s Eckart lane 4 e of Hanna.
Kieley, see Keeley.
Kienzle Charles, bartender, bds 21 E Main.
Kienzle Christian, teamster, res 105 Huffman.
Kienzle Christian J, candymkr W F Geller. bds 105 Huffman.
Kiep Theodore, laborer, res 254 E Jefferson.
Kiep Wm, soap maker, res 137 E Washington.
Kiermaier Michael, tailor, res 178 Gay.
Kiermaier Michael jr, painter, bds 178 Gay.
Kierspe Charles F, mach Wabash R R, res 39 Locust.
Kierspe Ellen S, bds 39 Locust.
Kierspe Frederick W, carver Ft W O Co, res 346 Broadway
Kierspe George J, bkkpr Root & Co, res 298 W Main.
Kiesling Ferdinand W, baker Brenzinger Co, bds 255 Broadway.
Kiesling John N, carpet weaver, 212 Broadway, res same.
Kiess, see also Kees.
Kiess John F, storekpr Ft W Elect Corp, res 73 Wilt.

Kiger Perry A, relief agent N Y, C & St L R R, res 113 Baker.

Kikley, *see also Kickley.*

Kikley P Isadore, conductor, res 53 W De Wald.

Kiley Bridget, seamstress, bds 33 Colerick.

Kiley Dennis T, lab Ft W Elect Corp, bds 33 Colerick.

Kiley John, engineer, bds 33 Colerick.

Kiley Margaret L, seamstress, bds 33 Colerick.

Kiley Mary (wid Thomas)) res 33 Colerick.

Kilgore Wm R, fireman Penn Co, res 11 W Butler.

Killday Hugh, helper Kerr Murray Mnfg Co, bds 301 Calhoun.

Killen George G, blksmith Penn Co, res 329 E Creighton av.

Killen Maud M, dressmaker, bds 333 E Creighton av.

Killen Wm A, bkkpr G E Bursley & Co, bds 333 E Creighton av.

Killen Wm G, blksmith Penn Co, res 333 E Creighton av.

Kilpatrick Harry E, engr L S & M S R R, res 142 Cass.

Kilpatrick James, foreman Wabash R R, bds Windsor Hotel.

Kilpatrick Oscar D, engr L S & M S R R, res 38 E 5th.

Kimball Clara A, clk Louis Wolf & Co, bds 82 Baker.

Kimball Eliza M (wid Samuel W), bds 118 Fulton.

Kimball George B, clk W L Carnahan Co, rms 87 E Jefferson.

Kimball Laura A, res 175 Rockhill.

Kimball Mary E, bds 175 Rockhill.

Kimble Charles, engineer, res 44 Wall.

Kimble John, laborer, res 60 E Columbia.

Kime, *see also Keim.*

Kime Franklin C, brakeman G R & I R R, res 104 South Wayne av.

Kime Wm T, barber, res 282 John.

Kimmel Bishop S, packer, bds 266 Beaver av.

Kimmel Carrie B, bds 73 Wall.

Kimmel Charles, helper Ft Wayne Organ Co, bds 172 Indiana av.

Kimmel Frank E, res s w cor Leslie and Milan.

Kimmel Jacob C, lab Ft Wayne Organ Co, res 63 Home av.

Kimmel John J, farmer, res 266 Beaver av.

Kimmel Kate, bds 266 Beaver av.

Kimmel Kinzey, conductor, res 73 Wall.

Kimmel Loren P, student, bds 73 Wall.

Kimmel Milo, mach hd Ft W Furn Co, bds 266 Beaver av.

Kimmel Milton G, engr Ft W O Co, res 172 Indiana av.

Kincade Frank A, trimmer, bds F B Kincade.

Kincade Frank B, res Hicksville State rd 3 w St Joe Gravel rd.

Kinder Anna F, bds 159 Taber.

Kinder Michael, carp Gustave Lauer, res 157 Taber.

Kinder Paul P, carp, res 105 Brackenridge.

Kindt Wm P, lab Ft Wayne Electric Corp, res 172 W Jefferson.

King Albert H, res s e cor Packard and South Wayne av.

King Arthur L, draughtsman Ft Wayne Electric Corp, res 45 Savilla av.

King Caroline M, bds 25 E Washington.

King Charles, clk Bass F & M Wks, bds 125 Montgomery.

King Cyrus, res 174 Taylor.

King Edward, student, bds 125 Montgomery.

King Eliza M (wid George E), res 125 Montgomery.

King Elton J, electr Ft Wayne Electric Corp, bds 45 Savilla av.

King Frank W, cutter S M Foster, res 47 Harmer.

King Ida C, seamstress, bds 125 Montgomery.

King John E, brakeman, bds 271 E Washington.

King Jonathan T, harnessmkr, res 45 Harrison.

King Josiah, 4 Foster Blk, res 28 Wilt.

King Josiah D, lab Penn Co, res 320 Maumee rd.

King Marion C, mngr Standard Oil Co, res 27 Prospect pl

King Sarah J, bds 25 E Washington.

King Victor, car inspr L E & W R R, res 271 E Washington.

King Wm L, trav agt, rms 22 W Berry.

King Winnie H, bds 320 Maumee rd.

Kingdon Richard H, clk J P Ross & Co, bds Columbia House.

Kinkead Joel H, helper Penn Co, res 79 W 3d.

Kinley Christian, cellarman C A Hoffmann, bds 143 Francis.

Kinley George, mason, bds 101 Barr.

Kinley Paul O, upholsterer Penn Co, res 31 John.

Kinnaird Alexander, scale inspr, bds 25 W Williams.

Kinnaird Mary W, bds 25 W Williams.

Kinnaird Louis S, bds 25 W Williams.

Kinnaird Robert, mach Wabash R R, res 25 W Williams.

Kinnan John W, messenger Penn Co, bds 392 Calhoun.

Kinnan Martha A (wid John M), res 392 Calhoun.

Kinney Laura, domestic Columbia House.

Kinnick Henry, porter 24 E Wayne.
Kinnie George A, printer The Journal, bds 104 Barr,
Kinnie John E, laborer, bds 123 W De Wald.
Kinnie Michael, lab Penn Co, res 123 W De Wald.
Kinsey Ida M. bds 75 Riverside av.
Kintz, *see also Koontz and Kuntz.*
Kintz Ambrose W, mason, res 149 Archer av.
Kintz Carl, lab Olds' Wagon Wks, rms 226 Calhoun.
Kintz Daniel W, bricklayer, bds 52 E 3d.
Kintz Frank A, bds 149 Archer av.
Kintz Henry, engr C L Centlivre Brewing Co, res 9 Edna.
Kintz John, car bldr Penn Co, res 11 Lillie.
Kintz John, teamster C L Centlivre Brewing Co, res w s Spy Run av 2 n of Edna.
Kintz John G, laborer, bds w s Piqua av 2 s of Rudisill av
Kintz Laura M, opr S M Foster, bds 11 Lillie.
Kirbach, *see also Kerbech.*
Kirbach Anna L, seamstress, bds 159 Gay.
Kirbach Ernest F, lab Olds' Wagon Wks, res 159 John.
Kirbach Frank F, pumpmkr S F Bowser & Co, bds 159 John.
Kirbach Frederick, mason, res 159 Gay.
Kirbach Louisa A, bds 149 Gay.
Kirbach Max W, cigarmkr C A Wilhelm, bds 159 John.
Kirbach Paul G, cigarmkr, bds 159 John.
Kirback Wm F, carp Paul Mnfg Co, bds 159 Gay.
Kirby Mary A (wid Michael), res 44 E Williams.
Kirby Michael, engineer Penn Co, bds 27 Baker.
Kirchefer Herman A, Fresco Painter and Decorator, 12 Arcade Bldg. res 114 Force. (*See p 93.*)
Kirchheimer Joseph (A Hirsh & Co), rms 144 E Berry.
Kirchheimer Sigmund, clk A Hirsh & Co), rms 144 E Berry
Kirchner Albert, bds 40 Lasselle.
Kirchner Caroline, bds 161 Eliza.
Kirchner Catherine S, bds 16 Nirdlinger av.
Kirchner Elenora, bds 161 Eliza.
Kirchner Elizabeth M, milliner, bds 16 Nirdlinger av.
Kirchner Ernst F, laborer, res 161 Eliza.
Kirchner Gottlieb W, lab Hoffman Bros, res 16 Nirdlinger av.
Kirchner Peter A, bds 40 Lasselle.
Kirchner Rosina E (wid Charles E), res 44 Oak.
Kirchner Wm G, clk F G Schneider, bds 16 Nirdlinger av.
Kirk Louis C, car bldr Penn Co. res 64 Greene.
Kirkendall Claudia, clk Princess Cash Store, bds 44 Webster

Kirkendall James M, laborer, res 16 Barthold.

Kirkham Fannie, clk People's Store, bds 31 W Columbia.

Kirkham Ida B, waiter Wm Kirkham.

Kirkham Lillie M, waiter Wm Kirkham.

Kirkham (Mary (wid John), bds 253 W Creighton av.

Kirkham Wm, restaurant, 31 W Columbia, res same.

Kirkhoff Caroline (wid Frederick), res 131 Jackson.

Kirkhoff Eliza C, dressmkr, bds 131 Jackson.

Kirkpatrick Charles A L. clk R M S, res 38 Michigan av.

Kirn, see also Karn and Kern.

Kirn John M, cabinetmkr Ft W O Co, res 82 Walnut.

Kirn Michael J, engr Bass F & M Wks, res 5 Grace.

Kirpach Julia, domestic 91 W Berry.

Kiser, see also Kaiser, Kayser and Keyser.

Kiser Byron A, bds 70 W Wayne.

Kiser Charles, opr Wayne Knitting Mills, bds 38 Watkins.

Kiser Charles S, patternmkr, bds 70 W Wayne.

Kiser David W, lab Penn Co, res 194 Gay.

Kiser Ellis, civil engineer, bds 70 W Wayne.

Kiser Isaac G, plasterer, rms 492 W Main.

Kiss Ernest J, foreman Bass F & M Wks, bds 218 Broadway.

Kitselman Wm B, condr N Y, C & St L R R, res 87 Wilt.

Kittley Mrs Ottilie, tailoress School for F M Y.

Klaas, see Claus.

Klaehn W Robert (Scheumann & Klaehn), res 171 W Superior.

Klaffei Charles, bartender G Ortleib, res 148 Ewing.

Klapper Frederick, lab, res w s Spy Run av 1 s of toll gate.

Klaren Matthias, lab F Eckart Pkg Co, res 65 Melita.

Klausner Paul, knitter, rms 38 Watkins.

Klebe Anna, finisher, bds 146 Franklin av.

Klebe Bertha E, opr, bds 146 Franklin av.

Klebe Henry J, harness, 36 Clinton, res 23 Wilt.

Klebe Maggie A, opr, bds 146 Franklin av.

Kleber John, driver J H Meyer, bds 96 Calhoun.

Kleber Sebastian R, engr N Y, C & St L R R, res 297 Hanna. Tel 383.

Klee, see also Kley.

Klee Annie, domestic 121 W Jefferson.

Klee John, bell boy The Randall.

Klee John J, painter L E & W R R, res 378 E Washington.

Klee Verona, bds 378 E Washington.

Kleeberg Paul A, brickmaker, res 53 Winter.

Kleekamp Franklin H, Lawyer 5 and 6 Bank Block, res 196 Calhoun.

Kleemeier Carrie, opr bds 10 Nirdlinger av.

Kleemeier Clara L, bds 10 Nirdlinger av.

Kleemier Dietrich, tailor 197 Calhoun, res 10 Nirdlinger av.

Kleemeier Dora J, opr, bds 10 Nirdlinger av.

Kleemeier Louis J, apprentice, bds 10 Nirdlinger av.

Klein, see also Cline and Kline.

Klein Frederick A, teacher Zion's Lutheran School, res 417 Hanna.

Klein George F. lab Wabash R R, bds 19 Summit.

Klein John, packer Paragon Mnfg Co, bds 143 W Wayne.

Klein Joseph, lab, rms 74 E Columbia.

Klein M Magdalina (wid Charles). janitress, res 8 Marion.

Klein Richard, furrier 20 E Washington, res same.

Kleinegees Ada C, bds 153 Harrison

Kleinegees Henrietta (wid Adolph), res 153 Harrison.

Kleinmiller Henry C, res 55 Madison.

Kleinrichert Francis A, car bldr Penn Co, res 313 E Creighton av.

Kleinrichert Josephine (wid John), res 19 Wall.

Kleinrichert Lawrence C, conductor, res 19 Wall.

Kleinsorge Herman, res 164 High.

Kleinsorge Louisa C, seamstress, bds 164 High.

Kleinsorge Minnie D, tailoress, bds 164 High.

Kleinsorge Wm H, clerk, bds 164 High.

Kleint August G, patternmkr Ft W Elec Corp, res 92 Dawson.

Klenke Conrad F, helper, res 58 W Lewis.

Klenke Emma (wid August), bds w s Broadway s of city limits.

Klenke Frederick, car bldr Penn Co, res 239 Barr.

Klenke Henry, car bldr Penn Co. res 411 E Lewis.

Klenke Henry G, clerk, bds 239 Barr.

Klenke Sophia, bds 239 Barr.

Klepper, see also Kloepper.

Klepper Charles, car bldr Penn Co, res 92 Oliver.

Klepper Charles W, mach hd Penn Co, bds 92 Oliver.

Klepper Minnie, domestic w s Spy Run av 3 n of Edna.

Klepper Minnie, clk Abraham Mick, bds 92 Oliver.

Klepper Minnie. domestic 77 W Wayne.

Klepper Sadie M, domestic 53 Hendricks.

Klepper Sophie, stamper, bds 19 Wilt.

Klerner George, saloon, 166 E Washington, res 109 Wells.

Klett Jacob (Jacob Klett & Sons), res 328 Broadway.

Klett Jacob & Sons (Jacob, John A and Wm B), lumber, 52–66 Pearl. Tel 370.

Klett John A (Jacob Klett & Sons), bds 328 Broadway.

Klett John G, clk Jacob Klett & Sons, bds 328 Broadway.

Klett Mary R, bds 328 Broadway.

Klett Wm B (Jacob Klett & Sons), bds 328 Broadway.

Kley, see also Klee.

Kley Carrie D, clerk, bds 336 W Main.

Kley Elizabeth K, clk Root & Co, bds 336 W Main.

Kley Frederick, res 336 W Main.

Hley Frederick G, cooper C L Centlivre Brewing Co, res 69 Elizabeth.

Kline, see also Cline and Klein.

Kline Anna M, bds 118 E Berry.

Kline Barbara, bds 224 St Mary's av.

Kline Bernard, res n s Miller 2 w of Brooklyn av.

Kline Carl W, lab, res Pennsylvania av nr Home.

Kline Charles W, saloon, 242 Calhoun, res same.

Kline Edward, mngr Masonic Temple, res 64 Madison.

Kline Frederick, bds 120 Chicago.

Kline Harry C, clk J Kline, bds 118 E Berry.

Kline Harry E, blksmith, bds 120 Chicago.

Kline Mrs Ida, bds 38 E Butler.

Kline Jacob, grocer, 30 E Columbia, rea 118 E Berry.

Kline John, bds 224 St Mary's av.

Kline John, laborer, bds 194 E Lewis.

Kline Joseph, res 224 St Mary's av.

Kline Laura W (wid John), rms 39 Brackenridge.

Kline Madge R, stenogr Ind Mach Wks, bds 362 W Main.

Kline Matilda D, bds 118 E Berry.

Kline Milton F, car bldr Penn Co, res 120 Chicago.

Kline Peter, clk Isaac Wile & Co, res 32 E 5th.

Kline Peter, shoemkr, bds 273 W Jefferson.

Kling Peter, laborer. res 213 John.

Klingel Eva B (wid John M), bds 76 Lasselle.

Klingel John M, coremkr Kerr Murray Mnfg Co, res 76 Lasselle.

Klingenberger Emma, opr S M Foster, bds 265 E Creighton av.

Klingenberger George, res s s Wiebke 2 e of Lafayette.

Klingenberger George B, molder Bass F & M Wks, res 287 Hanna.

Klingenberger Joseph, watchman, res 265 E Creighton av.

Klingenberger Joseph M, driver, res 32 Cochran.

Klingerberger Justin C, carp Penn Co, res 113 Force.

Klingenberger Susan, bds 265 E Creighton av.
Klingenberger Wm L, lab, bds 265 E Creighton av.
Klingenberger Xavier, helper, bds 285 Hanna.
Klingensmith Esther (wid Abraham), bds 432 Broadway.
Klingenstein Frederick, lab Ft W Elect Corp, bds 135 Fairfield av.
Klinger Allen W, timber, res 174 Huffman.
Klinger James E, 2d-hd goods, 67 E Columbia, bds 56 Charles.
Klinger John A, Hack, Livery, Feed and Sale Stable, 91 and 93 E Columbia, res 112 E Main. Tel 48. (*See page 103.*)
Klinger Joseph, lab Ft W Elec Corp, res 16 Guthrie.
Klinger Wm E, stone cutter George Jaap, bds 67 E Columbia.
Klingmann Albert M, molder Bass F & M Wks, bds 373 Lafayette.
Klingmann George W, driver Engine Co No 3, res 68 W Washington.
Klingmann John, stockman, bds 150 Smith.
Klingmann Wm, molder Bass F & M Wks, res 373 Lafayette.
Klinke, *see Klenke.*
Klinkel Michael, condr G R & I R R, res 36 Lillie.
Klinkel Wm M, clk S B Thing & Co, res 198 W Superior.
Klinkenberg G Wm, clk O G Klinkenberg, bds New Aveline House.
Klinkenberg Otto G, druggist, 33 E Berry, res 25 E Washington. Tel 188.
Klinkenberger John, car bldr Penn Co, res 285 Hanna.
Klinkenberger John jr, car bldr Penn Co, bds 285 Hanna.
Klippert George, baker, 393 Lafayette, res same.
Kloepper, *see also Klepper.*
Kloepper Henry, helper Wabash R R, res 19 Wilt.
Kloepper Henry C, boilermkr Wabash R R, res 113 Wall.
Kloepper Susan, stamper, bds 123 Wall.
Kloepper Wm K, teamster, res 93 John.
Klomp Mae, bds 48 Scott av.
Klomp Mamie, domestic 250 W Creighton av.
Klomp Wm, mach hd Ft W Organ Co, res 48 Scott av.
Klotz Catherine J, bds 546 Calhoun.
Klotz Daniel (Klotz & Haller), res 546 Calhoun.
Klotz Daniel F, painter Olds' Wagon Wks, bds 9 Buchanan.
Klotz Frank G, dry goods, 372 Calhoun, bds 546 same.
Klotz Herman, laborer, res s w cor Calhoun and Johns av.

Klotz Joseph F, painter Olds' Wagon Wks, bds Herman Klotz.
Klotz Minnie, bds 546 Calhoun.
Klotz & Haller (Daniel Klotz, Gottlieb Haller), coffee roasters, 362 Calhoun.
Klug Elizabeth, bds 190 Hanna.
Klug Gregor, shoes, 194 Hanna, res 190 same.
Klug Henry J, clk G Klug. bds 190 Hanna.
Klug John A, clk, bds 190 Hanna.
Klug Joseph G, removed to Lima, O.
Klug Kate, clerk, bds 190 Hanna.
Klug Martin, carpenter, res 293 E Wayne.
Klug Nicholas, grocer 196 Hanna, bds 190 same.
Klug Lena, domestic 246 W Berry.
Klug Wm, laborer, res 7 Duck.
Kluger Joseph, lab Ft Wayne Elect Corp, res n s Cottage av 1 w of Indiana av.
Klumpe Catherine (wid Hubert), bds 37 Colerick.
Kluppel Gerhardt J, carpenter, bds 77 Smith.
Kluppel John G, mason. res 77 Smith.
Kluppel Sophia M, clk J Loos, bds 196 E De Wald.
Klusmann Dora, bds 229 John.
Klusmann Frederick J, laborer, res 229 John.
Kluzinski Frank, res 113 High.
Klyser Wm, res n s Humphrey 1 e of Wabash av.
Knaack Caroline (wid Frederick), res 39 Elm.
Knaack Charles L, laborer, bds 39 Elm.
Knab, see Knob.
Knapp Frederick J, laborer, res 72 Gay.
Knapp Nicholas, laborer Penn Co, bds 69 Charles.
Knase Charles, painter, res 49 Taylor.
Knecht Catherine E, bds 260 E Jefferson.
Knecht Frank J, florist 301 E Wayne, res 27 Erie.
Knecht John, florist F J Knecht, bds 48 Barr.
Kneese August H, laborer, res 70 Packard av.
Knepper Emma B, dressmaker, res 104 Hanna.
Knepper Wm J, lab N Y, C & St L R R, res 71 St Mary's av.
Knewoeller Fred, bds 277 Webeter.
Kniepstein Dora, domestic 266 W Jefferson
Kniepstein Louise, domestic 266 W Jefferson.
Kniffen Ambrose E, brakeman, res 69 Smith.
Knight Asa L, clerk, bds 328 E Jefferson.
Knight Charles S, helper A Hattersley & Sons, bds 31 Randolph.

Knight Charles S, vice-pres Ft W Elec Corp, res 160 Spy Run av. Tel. 208.

Knight Elizabeth, bds e s Spy Run av 5 n of Prospect.

Knight Embra A, car bldr Penn Co, res cor Smith and Wallace.

Knight J Cheney, electrician Ft W Elec Corp, bds 150 Spy Run av.

Knight John H, fireman Penn Co, res 52 Baker.

Knight Matilda E, teacher Hoagland School, bds 15 E De Wald.

Knight Sarah J (wid Noel), res 31 Randolph.

Knight Thomas H, foreman L E & W R R, res 121 N Harrison.

Knight Williard C, clk Ft W Elec Corp, bds 160 Spy Run av

Knight Wm H, foreman Penn Co, res 15 E De Wald.

Knights of Labor Hall, Bank Blk.

Knisely Ellen M, domestic 9 Harrison.

Knisely Loren D, student, bds 50 Walnut.

Knisely Ora F, student, bds 50 Walnut.

Knisely Wm H, finisher. res 113 Mechanic.

Knob George, laborer, res 263 Hanna.

Knob Louis, wiper Penn Co, bds 263 Hanna.

Knob Magdalena, bds 263 Hanna.

Knobel Gottlieb, shoemaker, 110 Well-, res 30 same.

Knoche August D, polisher Olds' Wagon Wks, res 96 Oliver

Knoche Frederick A, carp S F Bowser & Co. bds 112 Thomas.

Knoche Henry T, teamster Olds' Wagon Wks, res 110 Thomas.

Knoche Johanna M, dressmaker, bds 112 Thomas.

Knoche John P, laboror, bds 111 Wilt.

Knoche Peter C, laborer, res 112 Thomas.

Knock Charles L, painter Ind Mach Wks, bds 39 Elm.

Knock Wm F, policeman, res 179 Metz.

Knoder George W, painter Penn Co, res 130 Madison.

Knoeder Frederick, lab, res 104 E Wayne.

Knoedler Henrietta (wid Frederick), res 851 Broadway.

Knoedler Henry, laborer, res 246 Erie.

Knoll George W, lab Ft W Elec Corp, bds 15 Miner.

Knoll Harry H, laborer, bds 15 Miner.

Knoll Wm H, mach Wabash R R, res 15 Miner.

Knothe Charles F, foreman Ft W Elec Corp, res 103 Brackenridge.

Knothe Charles H, mach Ft W Elec Corp, bds 103 Brackenridge.

Knothe Julia, bds 103 Brackenridge.
Knothe Julius, bds n e cor Liberty and Canal.
Knox Thomas E. watchman Star Iron Tower Co, res 43 Elizabeth.
Knuth Henry, fireman, res 79 Putnam.
Knuth Mary, opr Hoosier Mnfg Co, bds 79 Putnam.
Koby Joseph M, painter, res 66 Walton av.
Koby Louisa, domestic 132 W Wayne.
Koby Viola M, bds 66 Walton av.
Koch, *see also Cook and Kocks.*
Koch Anna, domestic 137 Edgewater av.
Koch Anthony F, laborer, res 57 W Lewis.
Koch Benedict, res 261 Hanna.
Koch Bernard, engr E B Kunkle & Co, bds 119 Lafayette.
Koch Charles, shoemkr C Buesking, bds 301 Hanna.
Koch Charles A, carp Bass F & M Wks, res 146 E Creighton av.
Koch Charlotte (wid Charles), bds 134 Force
Koch Christian, rimmer, res rear 72 Brackenridge.
Koch Christian H W, clk C Brase, bds rear 72 Brackenridge.
Koch Elizabeth (wid Christian F), res 45 W Jefferson.
Koch Elizabeth (wid John W), bds 119 Lafayette.
Koch Frederick J, blacksmith, res 112 Griffith.
Koch Gottlieb C, appr Lahmeyer Bros, bds 57 W Lewis.
Koch Harlan B, teamster, bds 112 Griffith.
Koch Harry B, driver, bds 112 Griffith.
Koch Henry, cigarmaker, res 9 Duryea.
Kock Henry A, helper Olds' Wagon Wks, bds rear 72 Brackenridge.
Koch John, polisher, bds 119 Lafayette.
Koch John A, clk Root & Co, bds 33 W Washington.
Koch John B, ironwkr Kerr Murray Mnfg Co, res 85 Force.
Koch John B, res 119 Lafayette.
Koch John D C, cigarmkr, bds rear 72 Brackenridge.
Koch Julius, laborer, res 47 Oliver.
Koch Katherine (wid Charles), res 33 W Washington.
Koch Lizzie, domestic 282 W Wayne.
Koch Minnie S, clerk, bds 57 W Lewis.
Koch Minnie, bds 119 Lafayette.
Koch Sebastian, laborer, bds 85 Force.
Koch Sophia (wid Anthony), bds 58 W Lewis.
Koch Theodore C, cigarmkr, bds rear 72 Brackenridge.
Koch Wm, trimmer Olds' Wagon Wks, bds 119 Lafayette.
Koch Wm, coremkr Bass F & M Wks, res 220 Force.

Koch Wm, car builder Penn Co, res 148 Taylor.
Koch Wm C, trimmer L F Horstman, bds 57 W Lewis.
Koch Wm J, student, bds 112 Griffith.
Kocher David, coachman W H Hoffman, res 213 W Superior.
Kocher John, carpenter, 130 Greeley, res same.
Kocher Leota, seamstress S M Foster, bds 130 Greeley.
Kocher Mary (wid Michael), bds 132 Greeley.
Kocher Maude, presser S M Foster, bds 132 Greeley.
Kocher Michael, carpenter, res 132 Greeley.
Kocher Wm F, driver, bds 132 Greeley.
Kocks, *see also Cox.*
Kocks Annie E, bds 27 High.
Kocks Frank C, painter, res St Joseph boulevard nr Baker av.
Kocks Frank J, machine hand, res 27 High.
Kocks Henry B, shoemaker, 60 Wells, res 20 W 4th.
Kocks John B, sawyer Hoffman Bros, res 174 E Lewis.
Kocks Mary E, bds 27 High.
Koeble Charles J, roofer Gerding & Aumann Bros, res 140 Wallace.
Koeble Eva (wid George J), bds 15 Grace.
Koegel Emma, bds 54 Lavina.
Koegel George C, machinist, bds 54 Lavina.
Koegel John C, watchmkr, 173 Broadway, bds 54 Lavina.
Koegel Mary (wid Christian), res 54 Lavina.
Koegel Mary E, bds 54 Lavina.
Koehl, *see also Cole and Kuhl.*
Koehl Adam, coremkr Penn Co, res 111 E Creighton av.
Koehl Anna (wid Adam), bds 111 E Creighton av.
Koehl Jacob, stonecutter Keller & Braun, res 125 E DeWald.
Koehl John, lab Penn Co, res 132 E Taber.
Koehl Michael, stonecutter Keller & Braun, res 493 Lafayette.
Koehl Wendelen, molder Bass F & M Wks, res 48 Buchanan
Koehler, *see also Kalor, Kaylor, Kehler, Keller and Kohler.*
Koehler Frederick C, lab John A Koehler, bds same.
Koehler Henry, died December 9th, 1894.
Koehler Henry, foreman L P Scherer, res 150 Eliza.
Koehler John A, brick mnfr, w s Lafayette e s of Wiebke, res same.
Koehler John M, lab John A Koehler, bds same.
Koehler Louis, lab, res e s Piqua av opp Rudisill av.
Koehler Michael A, lab, res s s French 7 w of Webster.

Koehler Paul, brick mnfr, n e cor Rudisill and Hoagland avs, res n w cor Rudisill and Webster.
Koehlinger Gustav A, clk Louis Wolf & Co, res 10 Riverside av.
Koehlinger Henry C, bds 16 Maiden lane.
Koehlinger Mrs Johanna L, boarding house, 16 Maiden lane
Koehlinger Philip, rms 3 Winch.
Koehn, *see also Cohen, Coon, Kohn and Kuhn.*
Koehn August, clk W L Waltemath, bds 217 E Jefferson.
Koehn Edward W, mach Ind Mach Wks, res 370 W Main.
Koehn Wm F, shoemkr, res 217 E Jefferson.
Koehnle Cresence, opr, bds 202 Francis.
Koehnlein Andrew. car repr Penn Co, res 114 Gay.
Koehnlein Emma B, opr S M Foster, bds 57 Hendricks.
Koehnlein Henry J, barber, bds 205 W Jefferson.
Koehnlein John M, motorman Ft W E Ry Co, bds 5 Sturgis
Koehnlein Julia C, bds 57 Hendricks.
Koenamann Catherine (wid Frederick), res 21 McLachlan.
Koenemann Frederick W, lab, bds 32 Colerick.
Koenemann Herman A, clk Root & Co, bds 32 Colerick.
Koenemann John, Vault Cleaning, Odorless Excavating Process, No Filth, No Odor, No Discomfort, 32 Colerick, res same.
Koenemann Wm, carpenter, bds Washington House.
Koenig Anna, domestic 141 E Berry,
Koenig Anna E, seamstress, bds w s Union 1 s of P, Ft W & C Ry.
Koenig Charles F C, clerk, bds 335 E Washington.
Koenig Charlotte (wid Wm), res 335 E Washington.
Koenig Christian F, grocer, 90 Harmer, res 187 Madison.
Koenig Rev Edward, pastor St Paul's Church, res 95 Griffith.
Koenig Frederick A, clerk, res 332 E Washington.
Koenig Frederick H, saloon, 52 W Main, res same.
Koenig Henry A, carpenter, res 48 Oak.
Koenig John N, lab L Rastetter & Son, res 34 Union.
Kocnig Lizzie, domestic 153 Spy Run av.
Koenig Minnie A, bds 77 Douglas av.
Koenig Theresa, church goods, 181 Calhoun, bds 95 Griffith.
Koenig Wilhelmina M (wid August C), res 77 Douglas av.
Koenig Wm jr, boilermaker, res 332 E Jefferson.
Koenig Wm F, laborer, bds 335 E Washington.
Koepf Henry F, flagman N Y, C & St L R R, bds 325 W Washington.

Koepf Jacob E, bds 17 Howell.
Koerber, *see also Kerber.*
Koerber Frederick. watchmkr H C Graffe. res 203 High.
Koerber Frederick jr, appr H C Graffe, bds 203 High.
Koerber Robert, stripper John C Eckert, bds 203 High.
Koers Christopher, barnman Herman Berghoff Brewing Co, res 116 Erie.
Koester, *see also Kester.*
Koester Martin A, draughtsman Penn Co, res 168 Harmer.
Koffmehl Jacob, carp Bass F & M Wks, res 278 E Washington.
Kohen, *see Cohen, Coon Koehn, Kohn and Kuhn.*
Kohlbach, *see also Kuhllach.*
Kohlbach Anna, knitter, bds 100 Richardson.
Kohlbach Gustav W F, lathe hd Ind Mach Wks, bds 100 Richardson.
Kohlbach John, lab, res 100 Richardson.
Kohlbach Wm, fireman N Y, C & St L R R, res 33 Boone.
Kohlbacher, *see also Kolbacher.*
Kohlbacher Adam, lab Penn Co, res 65 Force.
Kohlbacher John H, bds 159 E Tabor.
Kohlenberg Frederick, clk Princess Cash Store, bds 130 John.
Kohlenberg Fredreca, domestic 17 Brackenridge.
Kohler, *see also Kaler, Kaylor, Kehler, Keller and Koehler.*
Kohler Andrew J, engr Wabash R R, bds 461 Calhoun.
Kohler Catherine A (wid Daniel), res 461 Calhoun.
Kohler Katherine A, bkkpr S F Bowser & Co, bds 461 Calhoun.
Kohler Uriah H, fireman Penn Co, bds 461 Calhoun.
Kohlhepp Moritz, res n e cor New Haven and Edsall avs.
Kohli Ernst, res e s Edsall av 1 n of New Haven av.
Kohlman, *see also Coleman and Coolman.*
Kohlman Edward A, laborer, bds 9 Marion.
Kohlman Elizabeth (wid Conrad), res 9 Marion.
Kohlman John, res s e cor Rumsey av and Richardson
Kohlman Valentine, lab N Y, C & St L R R, bds 9 Marion
Kohlman Veronica, bds 9 Marion.
Kohlmann Dorothea (wid John), res 90 E Lewis.
Kohlman Henry, laborer, bds 90 E Lewis.
Kohlmeyer Christian, cigarmaker, bds 58 South Wayne av.
Kohlmeyer Christian H, carpenter, res 100 Summit.
Kohlmeyer Christina, bookkeeper, bds 58 South Wayne av.
Kohlmeyer Edward (Kasten & Kohlmeyer), res 58 South Wayne av.

398   R. L. POLK & CO.'S

Kohlmeyer Edward C, molder Ft W Elec Corp, res 123 Wall.
Kohlmeyer George E, cigarmkr Bourie, Cook & Co, bds 58 South Wayne av.
Kohlmeyer Henry, helper Wabash R R, res 21 Jones.
Kohlmeyer Henry C E, clerk, bds 58 South Wayne av.
Kohlmeyer Henry W, painter Heine & Israel, bds 21 Jones
Kohlmeyer John C, cigarmaker, bds 58 South Wayne av.
Kohlmeyer Minnie, knitter, bds 21 Jones.
Kohn, see also Cohen, Coon, Koehn and Kuhn.
Kohn Charles, meats, 42 Maumee rd, res same.
Kohn Fannie E, teacher Harmer School, bds 42 Maumee rd
Kohn Nathan, clerk, bds 42 Maumee rd.
Kohn Rosa E, teacher Clay School, bds 42 Maumee rd.
Kohr Nicholas, truckman Penn Co, res 43 Shawnee av.
Kohrmann Andrew, tailor, res 314 E Wayne.
Kohrmann Bros (John J and Henry M), grocers 94 Broadway. Tel 58.
Kohrmann Henry M (Kohrmann Bros), bds 215 W Superior.
Kohrmann Henry W, bkkpr White National Bank, res 136 Lake av.
Kohrmann John J (Kohrmann Bros), bds 215 W Superior.
Kohrmann Mary A (wid John B), res 215 W Superior.
Kohte Ernest H, molder Bass F & M Wks, res 192 Montgomery.
Kolb, Caroline (wid George A), res 16 Belle av.
Kolb Edward H, clk J B White, bds 83 Montgomery.
Kolb John A, car bldr Penn Co, res 83 Montgomery.
Kolb Kate, bds 16 Belle av.
Koldewey Sophia, domestic 83 W Main.
Kolkmann Frederick, laborer, res w s Manford 1 e of Pontiac.
Kollock Fred N, res 231 W Berry.
Kollock John K, bds 231 W Berry.
Kolthoff Frederick W, lab Wabash R R, res 23 Wall.
Kolthoff Louise, bds 23 Wall.
Kolthoff Mary, milliner, bds 23 Wall.
Kolthoff Wm F C, clk H N Ward, bds 23 Wall.
Komp, see also Kamp and Kemp.
Komp Daniel, real est, 38 Bank Blk, res s s Pontiac 5 w of Webster.
Komp Sarah D, bds s s Pontiac 5 w of Webster.
Konow Christina (wid Christopher), bds 26 Wall.
Konow Herman, teacher Emanuel G L School, res 26 Wall.

Koomler Eugene A, res s s New Haven av nr Edsall av.
Koons, *see also Koontz and Kuntz.*
Koons Andrew, engr Penn Co, res 212 Francis.
Koons Andrew E, appr Penn Co, bds 212 Francis.
Koons Carrie, bds 212 Francis.
Koons Ella, bds 212 Francis.
Koons Emma, cash J B White, bds 1 Prospect av.
Koons George, farmer, res 205 Thompson av.
Koons Henry, teamster, res n s Prospect av 1 e of Spy Run av.
Koons Ida E, dressmkr, bds n s Prospect av 1 e of Spy Run av.
Koons Lida M, presser S M Foster, bds 205 Thompson av.
Koons Mary E, cash J B White, bds n s Prospect av 1 e of Spy Run av.
Koons Ollie H, bds 205 Thompson av.
Koontz, *see also Kintz and Kuntz.*
Koontz Frank N, brakeman, rms 133 Holman.
Koontz John B, groom, bds 22 W Main.
Koontz Wm F, brakeman Penn Co, res 238 Walton av.
Koop Christian F, bds 91 Smith.
Koop Frederick H W, molder Bass F & M Wks, res 53 Buchanan,
Koop Henry C, teamster Bass F & M Wks, res 91 Smith.
Koop Sophia, opr S Freiburger & Bro, bds 53 Buchanan.
Koopmann Henry F, boilermkr Wabash R R, res 23 Jones
Koorsen George H, turner, res 76 Gay.
Koorsen Henry, mach hd Penn Co, bds 80 Smith.
Koorsen John B, laborer, res 94 Force.
Koorsen John M, laborer, res 80 Smith.
Kopp, *see also Cope.*
Kopp John H, mach Bass F & M Wks, res 31 Lillie.
Kopp Joseph, bds 177 Jackson.
Kopp Louis C, machinist, res 290 Hanna.
Kopp Michael, lab Bass F & M Wks, res Lillie s e cor Creighton av.
Kopp Wm F, bds Lillie s e cor Creighton av.
Koppenhaver Mary (wid Uriah W), boarding house, 74 W Main.
Koppenhaver Wilson, barber, bds 150 Fulton.
Koppenhoefer Frederick, meats, 205 Lafayette, res 65 Stophlet.
Korn August, grocer, 194 Broadway, res 60 Nirdlinger av
Korn Carrie, clk John Korn, bds 136 Fairfield av.
Korn Frederick, butcher G Hermann, res 83 Walton av.

Korn John, Groceries, Provisions and Meat Market; Choice Teas and Coffees a Specialty, 134 and 136 Fairfield av, res same.

Korn Philip, clk John Korn, bds 136 Fairfield av.

Korn Rosa, domestic 75 Lafayette.

Korte Christian E, farmer, res w s Broadway s of city limits.

Korte E Frederick W, teamster Rhinesmith & Simonson, res 74 Walnut.

Korte Frederick (Korte & Son), res 65 Maumee av. (*See p 111.*)

Korte Wm, molder Bass F & M Wks, res 101 Smith.

Korte Wm H (Korte & Son), res 48 Walton av. (*See p 111.*)

Korte & Son (Frederick and Wm H), Carpenters, Contractors and Builders, Jobbing Neatly and Cheaply Done; Shop and res 65 Maumee av. (*See p 111.*)

Kortum Henry, lab Bass F & M Wks, res 39 Hough.

Kos Henry, trav agt Julius Nathan & Co, bds Hotel Rich.

Koselitz Gustav, lab Weil Bros & Co, res 14 Cedar.

Kover Edward W (Kover & Son), bds O J Kover.

Kover Obadiah J (Kover & Son), res s w cor Howell and Rumsey av.

Kover & Son (Obadiah J and Edward W), fresco painters, s w cor Howell and Rumsey av.

Krack, *see also Krock.*

Krack Anselm, contractor, res 132 Maumee rd.

Krack Benedict, laborer, bds 132 Maumee rd.

Krack George J, painter Olds' Wagon Wks, bds 132 Maumee rd.

Kraeger Wilhelmina (wid Charles), bds 3 Summit.

Kraft Annie C, domestic 329 W Washington.

Kraft Charles H, molder Ind Mach Wks, res 23 Koch.

Kraft Christina H, domestic 191 Taylor.

Kraft Conrad F, foreman, res 271 W Washington.

Kraft Frederick C, molder, res 70 Hugh.

Kraft Frederick J, boilermkr Penn Co, res 333 E Lewis.

Kraft Frederick W, carpenter, res 317 Lafayette.

Kraft Henry, helper Bass F & M Wks, res 372 E Washington.

Kraft Henry, molder, bds 333 E Lewis.

Kraft Henry F, appr Wabash R R, bds 271 W Washington.

Kraft Henry F, cellerman The Herman Berghoff Brewing Co, bds 372 E Washington.

Kraft Herman, helper, bds 333 E Lewis.

Kraft Louisa, bds 317 Lafayette.
Kraft Minnie H, dressmaker, bds 271 W Washington.
Kraft Minnie, bds 317 Lafayette.
Kraft Minnie H, seamstress, bds 333 E Lewis.
Kraft Sophia L, tailor G Scheffler, bds 271 W Washington.
Kraft Tena, bds 271 W Washington.
Kraft Wm C, cash Geo De Wald & Co, bds 313 Lafayette.
Krah, *see also Craw.*
Krah Christian F, mason, res 159 Griffith.
Krah Emma, bds 159 Griffith.
Krah Henry J, bricklayer, res 82 Wilt.
Krah Henry W, foreman Ind Staats Zeitung, rms 37 E Columbia.
Krah Minnie, bds 159 Griffith.
Krah Wm H, driver, bds 159 Griffith.
Krahn Frank, watchman, res rear 73 High.
Krainowitz Abraham, laborer, bds 587 E Washington.
Kramer, *see also Cramer.*
Kramer Adam, watchman, res 81 Greene.
Kramer Alfred A, painter, 163 John, res same.
Kramer Bernard E, clerk, bds 49 Madison.
Kramer Bernard J, bkkpr The Herman Berghoff Brewing Co, res 49 Madison.
Kramer Christian C, clk Root & Co, res 380 E Wayne.
Kramer Christian C, street sprinkler, res 108 W Jefferson.
Kramer Conrad, painter Penn Co, res 3 Summit.
Kramer Edith, bds 350 E Wayne.
Kramer Edith, domestic 47 W Lewis.
Kramer Elizabeth C, bds 465 Lafayette.
Kramer Ernest, sign painter, 90 E Main, res 156 Shawnee av
Kramer Frederick, painter Penn Co, res 126 John.
Kramer Frederick E, laborer, res 117 Wall.
Kramer Frederick J, driver J Jacobs, bds 55 E Main.
Kramer Frederick W, clerk, bds 380 E Wayne.
Kramer George, tinner J H Welch, res 19 Elizabeth.
Kramer Gottlieb H, laborer, res 19 Huron.
Kramer Hattie, opr S M Foster, bds 245 W De Wald.
Kramer Henry, laborer, bds 140 Runnion av.
Kramer Henry C, bookkeeper, bds 49 Madison.
Kramer John A, cutter Hoosier Mnfg Co, res 7 Riverside av
Kramer John G, clk J B White, res 17 Pritchard.
Kramer Joseph C, pressfeeder The Journal, bds 44 Madison.
Kramer Lena, domestic 107 W Williams.
Kramer Lottie, bds 245 W De Wald.
Kramer Louis A, clerk C L Rastetter, bds 49 Madison.

Kramer Louis C, porter J B White, bds 126 John.
Kramer Mamie M, dressmkr, 92 Hanna, res same.
Kramer Martin, foreman, res 245 W De Wald.
Kramer Matthias. roofer, res 465 Lafayctte.
Kramer Mrs Minnie D, res 92 Hanna.
Kramer Peter, res s e cor Spy Run av and Ruth.
Kramer Rickie, opr Troy Steam Laundry, bds 71 E Main.
Kramer Rosina (wid Frederick), bds 59 Indiana av.
Kramer Wm C, car builder Penn Co, res 21 Summit.
Kramer Wm F, molder Bass F & M Wks, res 350 E Wayne.
Kramer Wm F jr, harnessmkr, bds 350 E Wayne.
Kranichfeld Theodore F, sawyer Hoffman Bros, res 230 W Superior.
Krantz, see also Crance and Crantz.
Krantz Anton, wiper Penn Co, res 257 Hanna.
Krantz Casper, washer Penn Co, res 257 Hanna.
Kranz Peter, painter, res 94 Summit.
Kranzman Mary, domestic 55 E Jefferson.
Kranzman Wm H, printer Ft Wayne Gazette, bds 139 Holman.
Krapf David. clk Morgan & Beach, res 212 E Lewis.
Kratzmann John, laster App Bros. bds 14 Force.
Kratzmann Simon, shoemkr I Lehman, res 14 Force.
Kratzsch Bros (Emil R & Herman), millinery, 114 Calhoun.
Kratzsch Charles R, clk Sam, Pete & Max, res 91 Baker.
Kratzsch Dora, clk Kratzsch Bros, bds 53 E Lewis.
Kratzsch Eleanor (wid Herman), bds 15 W Wayne.
Kratzsch Emil R (Kratzsch Bros), bds 55E Lewis.
Kratzsch Frederick C, clk Root & Co, bds 168 Greeley.
Kratzsch Herman (Kratzsch Bros). res 55 E Lewis.
Krauhs, see also Crouse, Cruse and Kruse.
Krauhs Carl C, shoemkr, 169 Jackson, res same.
Krauhs Catherine, seamstress, bds 169 Jackson.
Krauhs Dora M, bds 169 Jackson.
Krauhs Frederick J, mach Kerr Murray Mnfg Co. res 83 Swinney av.
Krauhs John C, barber. bds 169 Jackson.
Krauhs John H, shoemkr G Spiegel, bds 169 Jackson.
Krauhs J Charles, foreman, res 61 Shawnee av.
Kraus Charles L, switchman, res 74 Walton av.
Kraus George, baker, res 36 Wilt.
Kraus George M, res 104 Hanna.
Kraus Wm R, lineman, bds rear 104 Hanna.
Krause Amelia (wid Ferdinand), res rear 34 Cochran.
Krause Paulina, domestic 416 Fairfield av.

Krauskopf Henry, trucker Penn Co, res 42 Oak.
Krauskopf Mary A (wid Henry), bds 114 W Main.
Kraut Henry, laborer, bds 57 John.
Krauter John, blksmith, bds 16 Gay.
Kreager Frank D, clk Princess Cash Store, bds 154 Harrison.
Kreager Hannah M (wid Carrie P), boarding, 154 Harrison
Krebs Edward, foreman Olds' Wagon Wks, res 68 Masterson.
Krebs Frederick G, cigarmkr Lahmeyer Bros, bds Weber Hotel.
Kreckmann Anna M, opr Hoosier Mnfg Co, bds 123 Eliza
Kreckmann Clara W E, seamstress, bds 123 Eliza.
Kreckmann Frederick W, horseshoer, bds 123 Eliza.
Kreckmann Jacob L, boilermaker, bds 377 E Washington.
Kreckmann Michael, painter 123 Eliza, res same.
Kreckmann Mildred J, opr, bds 123 Eliza.
Kreibaum Frederick, wall paper, 90 Barr, res same.
Krentz Anton, laborer, res 8 Force.
Kress Amos, mach hd Olds' Wagon Wks, bds 51 Nirdlinger av.
Kress Catherine, waiter, bds 10 Zollars av.
Kress Edward, bds 346 Broadway.
Kress Frank, winder, bds 517 Broadway.
Kress George J, lab Horton Mnfg Co, res 10 Zollars av.
Kress Jacob, driver, bds 10 Zollars av.
Kress Jacob W, coachman 72 W Wayne.
Kress John, wagonmkr, res 112 W Butler.
Kress John N, lab Ft W Elec Corp, res 517 Broadway.
Kress Joseph, laborer, bds 346 Broadway.
Kress Kate M, waiter Custer House.
Kress Michael, res 29 Pine.
Kress Minnie M, bds 10 Zollars av.
Kress Philip J, laborer, bds 29 Pine.
Kress Theodore, tinner, 12 Huffman, res same.
Kress Walter B, lab Ft W Elec Corp, res 372 Broadway.
Kress Wm A, lab Ft Wayne Elec Corp, res 153 Union.
Kresse Charles A, carp Wabash R R, res 6 Fox.
Kressler George F, mach hd, bds Euclid nr Walton av.
Kretsinger Constantine, mach hd Penn Co, res 47 Baker.
Kretsinger Henry (Kretsinger & Angevine), res 1 Piqua av.
Kretsinger John R, foreman Penn Co, res 303 Hanna.
Kretsinger & Angevine (Henry R Kretsinger, Wm E Angevine), real est, 10 Vordermark Blk, 32 Calhoun.
Kreutzer Charles, cigarmkr, res 277 E Jefferson.

Krider A Jay, bartender, bds 223 Calhoun.
Kridler Jesse S, paperhanger, bds 22 N Calhoun.
Krieg Barney, driver M F Kagg, res 99 Cass
Krieg Frederick, grocer 372 Broadway, res 39 Huestis av.
Krieg George, laborer, res 34 Wefel.
Krieg George, sausage mnfr, s s Rudisill av 3 e of Calhoun, res same.
Krieg John, laborer, bds 34 Wefel.
Krieg Michael, butcher, res 533 E Wayne.
Krieg Wm, laborer, bds 34 Wefel.
Krimmel Carrie, bds 55 Douglas av.
Krimmell Charles A T (Root & Co), res 55 Douglas av.
Krimmell Christian, car bldr Penn Co, res 55 Douglas av.
Krimmell John Wm, cigarmkr J C Eckert, bds 55 Douglas av.
Krimmell Julius, piano tuner, bds 55 Douglas av.
Kring Frank N, painter Penn Co, rms 250 Calhoun.
Kritzmann Valentine, carp, res w s Abbott 2 s of Manford.
Krock, *see also Krack.*
Krock Anna, bds 416 E Wayne.
Krock Anna C, domestic, bds 364 E Wayne.
Krock George J, lab Bass F & M Wks, res 364 E Wayne.
Krock John J, carpenter, res 416 E Wayne.
Krock Josephine, domestic 151 E Wayne.
Krock Mary, bds 416 E Wayne.
Krock Mary C, opr HoosieryMnfg Co, bds 364 E Wayne.
Kroener Frederick W, laborer, res 30 Brandriff.
Kroener Fredericka K, bds 80 Oakley.
Kroesch Frederick, blksmith Bass F & M Wks, res 136 John
Kroesch Frederick C, clk J B White, bds 136 John.
Kroesch Henry C, boilermkr, bds 136 John.
Krohn, *see also Crone.*
Krohn August, truck bldr Penn Co, bds 220 Smith.
Krohn Charles C, saloon, s w cor Washington and Glasgow av, res same.
Krohn Louisa (wid Henry), res 49 W 4th.
Krohn Wm G, saloon, 30 W Main, res same.
Krohne Herman H L, res 96 E Jefferson.
Krokenberger Jacob, laborer, res 137 Suttenfield.
Krokenberger Jacob jr, blksmith, res 449 Lafayette.
Krokenberger John, laborer, bds 137 Suttenfield.
Krokenberger Rosa, domestic 90 E Washington.
Krolen Frank, res rear 73 High.
Krominaker Annie, domestic 39 W Washington.
Kromm Curtis L, lab N Y, C & St L R R, res 146 High.

Kromm Moses, res n e cor Home and Pennsylvania avs.
Kronmiller Charles, helper Penn Co, bds 566 Hanna.
Kronmiller Edward F, plumber A Hattersley & Sons, bds 43 Taylor.
Kronmiller Elizabeth, milliner, bds 566 Hanna.
Kronmiller George, carpenter, res 38 Koch.
Kronmiller George, farmer, res 566 Hanna.
Kronmiller George A, brakeman G R & I R R, bds 43 Taylor.
Kronmiller George H, painter, bds 566 Hanna.
Kronmiller George N, washer Penn Co, res 43 Taylor.
Kronmiller Henry W, student, bds 43 Taylor.
Kronmiller Kate, bds 566 Hanna.
Kronmiller Louie S, operator, bds 43 Taylor.
Kronmiller Matilda, seamstress, bds 43 Taylor.
Kronmiller Peter, cook G Ortlieb, rms 31 Calhoun.
Kropp Frank J, trucker L S & M S Ry, res 96 W 3d.
Kropp Louis, fireman L E & W R R, res 88 N Harrison.
Krot, see Kraut.
Krouse, see Crouse, Cruse, Krauhs and Kruse.
Kruckeberg Frederick, clk G J Hitzeman, res 17 Summit
Krudop Anna M, stenogr J M Robinson, bds 25 W Jefferson.
Krudop Charles F, carpenter, 151 Hugh, res same.
Krudop Charlotte M (wid John B), res 25 W Jefferson.
Krudop Frederick, driver, bds 25 W Jefferson.
Krudop George H, coal and wood, n e cor Francis and Hayden, res 9 Eliza. Tel 135.
Krudop H Gottlieb, mach hd, res 13 Wall.
Krudop John E, teamster, res 287 Barr.
Krudop Wm F, lab Penn Co, bds 157 Holman.
Krueckemeyer Henry, upholsterer, 52 Barr, res 139 Montgomery.
Krueckemeyer Mary, bds 141 Montgomery.
Krueckemeyer Rudolph, car bldr Penn Co, bds 139 Montgomery.
Krueger August C, bkkpr Siemon & Bro, bds 150 Ewing.
Krueger Charles J, car bldr Penn Co, res 122 Fletcher av.
Krueger Louisa, domestic 9 Webster.
Krueper August E, traveling agt, res 53 Cass.
Krull, see also Crull.
Krull Bernard J, harnessmaker, bds 266 E Washington.
Krull Henry F, clk R L Krull, bds 266 E Washington.
Krull Lena (Krull Sisters), bds 266 E Washington.
Krull Rudolph (Joseph Weick & Co), res 266 E Washington.

Krull Rudolph L, jewelry, 128 E Washington, bds 266 same.

Krull Sisters (Maggie Weick, Lena Krull), milliners, 268 E Washington.

Kruse, *see also Crouse, Cruse and Krauhs.*

Kruse August, laborer, bds 169 Gay.

Kruse August F, machine hd, res 20 Pine.

Kruse August H, tailor Charles Kruse, bds 35 Elm.

Kruse Charles, Merchant Tailor. 39 Harrison, res 35 Elm.

Kruse Charles H, lab Penn Co, bds 161 Montgomery.

Kruse Christian, gardencr, Lake av, e of city limits, res same.

Kruse Ferdinand, helper Bass F & M Wks, res 115 Gay.

Kruse Frederick G, hoop mkr S D Bitler, bds 415 E Wayne.

Kruse Frida, labeler The Herman Berghoff Brewing Co, bds 415 E Wayne.

Kruse Henry C, helper Penn Co, res 161 Montgomery.

Kruse Henry F, carpenter, res 415 E Wayne.

Kruse Henry W, clk J B White, bds 67 E Jefferson.

Kruse Henry W, cutter C Kruse, bds 35 Elm.

Kruse Henry W, engr Penn Co, res 185 Hayden.

Kruse Lizzie M, bds 161 Montgomery.

Kruse Louis F, oil peddler, res 386 E Lewis.

Kruse Louisa S, bds 35 Elm.

Kruse Wm, painter, bds 172 Francis.

Kruse Wm C, clk O B Fitch, res 412 E Washington.

Kruse Wm F, contractor, 67 E Jefferson, res same.

Kruse Wm F, molder E B Kunkle & Co, bds 161 Montgomery.

Kucher Anna (wid John J), res 39 Savilla av.

Kucher Gustav N, stenogr, bds 39 Savilla av.

Kucher Herman, clk Penn Co, res 468 Harrison.

Kucher Martha, bds 39 Savilla av.

Kucher Nathaniel G, clk Penn Co, bds 39 Savilla av.

Kucher Ottilia, bds 39 Savilla av.

Kucher Otto E, clk Penn Co, bds 39 Savilla av.

Kucher Paul C, bds 39 Savllla av.

Kucher Theodore N, machinist, bds 39 Savilla av.

Kucher Theophilus J, stenogr Penn Co, bds 39 Savilla av.

Kuckuck Charles A, fireman Bass F & M Wks, res 150 John.

Knelling Rev John, pastor Salem Reformed German Church, res 83 Clinton.

Knelling Martha, bds 83 Clinton.

Knelling Theophilus, civil engr, res 176 E Washington.

Kuentzel Frank J, mach, res 136 Wallace.
Kuhfuss F Julius, mach Wabash R R, bds 18 Colerick.
Kuhl, *see also Cull and Kull.*
Kuhl Edward G, clerk, bds 89 Greene.
Kuhl Martin H, coremkr Bass F & M Wks, res 89 Greene.
Kuhl Otto, clerk, bds 89 Greene.
Kuhl Rudolph, coremkr C M Menefee,, bds 89 Greene.
Kuhlbach, *see also Kohlbach.*
Kuhlbach Elizabeth (wid Wm), bds 119 Lafayette.
Kuhlbach Wm F, driver The Herman Berghoff Brewing
    Co, res 497 E Washington.
Kuhn, *see also Cohen, Coon, Koehn and Kohn.*
Kuhn Emil, coremkr Bass F & M Wks, res 206 Gay.
Kuhn Wilhelm, lab, res s s Wiebke 4 e of Lafayette.
Kuhne Charles W, lawyer, 19 Court, rms 144 E Berry.
Kuhne Frederick W (Kuhne & Co), res 124 W Jefferson.
Kuhne H Richard, with Kuhne & Co, bds The Randall.
Kuhne Paul F, with Kuhne & Co, rms 124 W Jefferson.
Kuhne & Co (Frederick W Kuhne), The Abstract
    Office, Insurance, Loan, Real Estate and Steamship
    Agents, 19 Court.
Kuhner Valentine, laborer, res 283 Hanna.
Kuhns, *see also Koons, Koontz and Kuntz.*
Kuhns John M, bkkpr G E Bursley & Co, res 360 Fair-
    field av.
Kukuck Dorothea (wid Louis), res 181 Jackson.
Kukuk Frank, laborer, bds 162 Madison.
Kukuk Joseph, shoemaker, res 162 Madison.
Kull, *see also Cole, Cull and Kuhl.*
Kull Christina (wid Gottlieb), res 105 Huffman.
Kull Dora M (wid George F), res e s Franklin av 2 n of Lake.
Kull Edward F, helper, bds 143 W 3d.
Kull John, hostler L E & W R R, res 143 W 3d.
Kull Louisa W, bds D M Kull.
Kumfer Owen, carpenter, res 96 Smith.
Kummer Albert R, machinist, res 114 E Creighton av.
Kummer Catherine, domestic 181 W Berry.
Kummer Frederick C, painter Olds' Wagon Wks, rms 226
    Calhoun.
Kummer Emma, bds 114 E Creighton av.
Kummer Lucinda, domestic 185 W Berry.
Kummerant Frank A. blacksmith, res 290½ Hanna.
Kuner Andrew, carp Olds' Wagon Wks, bds 25 Force.
Kunkle Blanche M, bds 138 E Wayne.
Kunkle Erastus B (E B Kunkle & Co), res 138 E Wayne.

Kunkle Ella A, bds 138 E Wayne.
Kunkle Eva H, bds 138 E Wayne.
Kunkle E B & Co (Erastus B Kunkle, Wm D Bostick), Proprs Fort Wayne Safety Valve Works, 87 Barr. Tel 423.
Kuntz, *see also Kintz and Kootz.*
Kuntz Charles E, candymkr Fox Br U S Baking Co, res 98 N Harrison.
Kuntz Elizabeth (wid Peter), res 550 Calhoun.
Kuntz Eva (wid Adam), res 21 Buchanan.
Kuntz Frank B, harnessmkr, 14 Pearl, res 5 Cass.
Kuntz George, died May 17th, 1894.
Kuntz George H, harnessmkr, 11 Harrison, res 227 W Washington.
Kuntz Mary (wid Jacob), bds 268 W Jefferson.
Kuntz Samuel, saloon, 548 Calhoun, res 550 same.
Kunz Sophia, bds 95 W Berry.
Kuper, *see also Cooper.*
Kuper Annie (wid John), res 37 Colerick.
Kuper Hubert, laborer, bds 37 Colerick.
Kutche Angelo, Propr Greek Candy Manufactory, 154 Calhoun. (*See p 107.*)
Kutsch August, brakeman, res 52 Buchanan.
Kuttner G Joseph, car bldr Penn Co, res 237 E Jefferson.
Kuttner Peter G, Shirt Manufacturer, 144 Calhoun, res 253 E Washington. (*See left side lines.*)
Kyle, *see also Keel, Keil and Kiel.*
Kyle Abraham P, brakeman, res 72 Chicago.
Kyle Allen C, brakeman, res 226 Francis.
Kyle Dale W, brakeman G R & I R R, bds 72 Chicago.
Kyle Ethel B, bds 72 Chicago.
Kyle Robert V, lab L E & W R R, bds Lake Shore Hotel.
Kyle Wm D, res 101 Rivermet av.
Kyler Louis M, engr Ind Mach Wks, res 42 Brandriff.

L

Labbe Joseph, fireman Penn Co, res 198 Madison.
Labbe Joseph P jr, clk F C Heit, bds 198 Madison.
Labeck Peter J, machinist, bds St James Hotel.
LaBoub Julian, laborer, res 21 Pritchard.
Lackey Ephraim, carpenter, res 28 Savilla av.
Lackey Melvin, car bldr Penn Co, res 28 Gay.
Lackey Thomas, laborer, bds 28 Savilla av.
Lacklin Charles L (col'd), cook The Wayne, res 50 Leith.
Lacklin John, fireman, bds 69 E Main.

Lacroix Julia, domestic, bds 78 E Columbia.
Lacy Harry P, laborer, bds 184 W Main.
Lacy Michael R, engr Penn Co, res 163 Montgomery.
Ladd Frank B, phys, 411 W Main, res same.
Ladd Myrtle, bds 273 W Jefferson.
Lade Sophia P (wid Max G), bds 98 Harrison.
Laemmermann Adolph, cellerman The Herman Berghoff Brewing Co, bds 497 E Wayne.
Laemmle, *see also Leammle.*
Laemmle George J, broommkr, bds 284 M Main.
Laemmle Jennie S (wid David), res 284 W Main.
Laemmle Johanna (wid John), res 295 W Main.
Laemmle Margaret, bds 284 W Main.
Laepple Christian, carpenter, res 208 Webster.
Lafever, *see Lefever.*
LaFrance Henry, res 294 W Jefferson.
LaFrance Minnie, domestic 208 W Berry.
Lagemann Augusta, bds 47 St Martin's.
Lagemann Frederick C, laborer, bds 45 St Martin's.
Lagemann Frederick R W, boilermaker, bds 47 St Martin's.
Lagemann Henry, boiler inspr Penn Co, res 47 St Martin's
Lagemann Henry, stonemason, res 49 Summit.
Lagemann Henry E, laborer, bds 45 St Martin's.
Lagemann Henry H W, shipping clk, bds 47 St Martin's.
Lagemann Rudolph F, laborer, res 45 St Martin's.
Lagemann Sophia, bds 49 Summit.
Lagemann Wm, helper Penn Co, bds 45 St Martin's.
Lagemann Wm F, bds 47 St Martin's.
Lahey Bridget, domestic School for F M Y.
Lahmeyer Annie, bds 51 Stophlet.
Lahmeyer Bros (John G D and Henry B), Manufacturers of Tiger Cigar, Factory 72 E Main.
Lahmeyer Caroline (wid Daniel), bds 87 Union.
Lahmeyer Charles, bds w s Lillie 3 s of Milan.
Lahmeyer Charles F, Grocer, 108 Broadway, res 67 Union. Tel 177,
Lahmeyer Christian J, carp, res 51 Stobhlet.
Lahmeyer Christian L, driver, bds 51 Stophlet.
Lahmeyer Frederick, bds 64 W Williams.
Lahmeyer Frederick, molder, bds Henry Lahmeyer.
Lahmeyer Frederick C, ins agent, res 64 W Williams.
Lahmeyer Henry, res w s Lillie 3 s of Milan.
Lahmeyer Henry jr, molder, bds Henry Lahmeyer.
Lahmeyer Henry B, (Lahmeyer Bros), bds 61 W Lewis.

Lahmeyer John G D, (Lahmeyer Bros), bds 61 W Lewis.
Lahmeyer John H, patternmkr Penn Co, res 61 W Lewis.
Lahmeyer Louis, molder, bds Henry Lahmeyer.
Lahmeyer Louisa, bds Henry Lahmeyer.
Lahmeyer Martha M, dressmkr, bds 51 Stophlet.
Lehmeyer Mary, bds 64 W Williams.
Lahmeyer Wm H, molder Bass F & M Wks, res 212
    Walton av.
Lahr, see also Laier and Lehr.
Lahr George W, pres Ft W Bus College, res 41 Grace av.
Laibe Frank J, lab Penn Co, res 19 Fletcher av.
Laibe Frank J jr, bottler Herman Berghoff Brewing Co,
    bds 19 Fletcher av.
Laibe Mary E labler Hermann Berghoff Brewing Co, bds
    19 Fletcher av.
Laible Catherine (wid Christian F), res 96 W De Wald.
Laible Christian, died Aug 2, 1894.
Laible Paul L, bds 96 W De Wald.
Laier, see also Lahr, Lauer and Lehr.
Laier Adam, laborer, res 15 Caroline.
Laier John, painter Olds' Wagon Wks, res 73 Buchanan.
Laier Joseph, painter, bds 134 Warsaw.
Laier Matthias, laborer, res 134 Warsaw.
Lake Erie & Western R R, freight office cor 1st and L S
    & M S Ry, pass depot cor Cass and L S & M S Ry
    Tel 104.
Lake Shore Hotel, John B Lassus Propr, 2 Cass.
Lake Shore & Michigan Southern Ry, E S Philley freight
    and ticket agent, pass depot junction Cass and
    Wells, freight depot cor 1st and Railroad. Tel 104.
Lakeside Baseball grounds, Lake av, nr limits.
Lakeside Park, n s Maumee river e of Columbia st bridge.
Lakeside School, 85 Lake av,
Lakeside Street Railroad Co, R D McDonald, H J Miller,
    A D Guild, Directors, J D McDonald Supt, office The
    Wayne.
Lallow Charles P, carpenter, res 596 Calhoun.
Lallow Jennie, attendent County Poor Farm,
Lallow Louis J, carpenter, res 61 W Pontiac.
Lamar Adam, apprentice Penn Co, bds 21 Eliza.
Lamar Eve, stenographer, bds 21 Eliza.
LaMaster George W, clk H W Mordhurst, bds 33 W
    Washington.
Lamb Annie, bds 103 W Williams.
Lamb David, machinist, res 103 W Williams.

Lamb George A, fireman Penn Co, res 215 W Jefferson.
Lamb Joseph, laborer, rms 121 W Jefferson.
Lamb Lottie M, stenographer, bds 215 W Jefferson.
Lamb W Samuel, motorman, res 52 Maumee rd.
Lamb Wm T, trav agt S F Bowser & Co, res 71 W Wayne.
Lambert Frederick H, artist F Schanz, res 153 W Washington.
Lambert Jennie, cook F C Cratsley, rms 288 Calhoun.
Lambert Norris W, regulator Ft W Organ Co, res 226 Calhoun.
Lamley Moses E (Falk & Lamley), res 128 W Wayne.
Lamley Reada, bds 128 W Wayne.
Lamont, see Lomont.
Lampke, see also Lemke.
Lampke Conrad, porter Mossman, Yarnelle & Co, res 128 Madison.
Lancaster Charles J, molder, res 67 W Butler.
Lancaster Clara B (wid Nelson W), res 45 Elm.
Lancaster Eliza A (wid John), bds 228 E Creighton av.
Lancaster Grace E, bds 45 Elm.
Lancaster Lewis M, clerk N Y, C & St L R R, bds 45 Elm
Landenberger, see also Latenberger.
Landenberger Frederick G, clk Horton Mnfg Co, res 175 W Superior.
Landenberger John M, sec, treas and mngr Ind Mach Wks, bds 290 Fairfield av.
Landerman, see Lanterman.
Landgraf Elizabeth (wid John), res 164 Gay.
Landgraf Eva, domestic 401 Lafayette
Landgraf John H, painter Olds' Wagon Wks, bds 164 Gay.
Landgraf Mary A, opr Hoosier Mnfg Co, bds 164 Gay.
Landis Lydia, domestic 227 E Lewis.
Lane Chester F, A B, prin Central Grammer School, res 55 Maple av.
Lane John W, piano tuner Arcade Music Store, res 209 W Jefferson.
Lane Maud C, bds 13 Zollars av.
Lane Mendel, porter, bds 209 W Jefferson.
Lane Wm M, sawyer, res 28 Murray.
Lang, see also Long.
Lang Amelius J (Geo De Wald & Co), res 304 W Washington
Lang Anna (wid George), res 30 Wells.
Lang Anna, bds 4 Marion.
Lang Aurora L, stenogr A Hattersley & Sons, bds 25 W Butler.

412   R. L. POLK & CO.'S

Lang Bertha, bds 17 Hensch.
Lang Charles W, stenogr V Gutermuth, bds 304 W Washington.
Lang Christian, engr Keller & Braun, res 17 Hensch.
Lang D Ernest. bds 124 Harrison.
Lang Edward F M, student, bds 165 Ewing.
Lang Frances, bds 75 W Butler.
Lang Frederick C, bds 304 W Washington.
Lang Gustav A, lab Keller & Braun, res 17 Hensch.
Lang Ida, bds 4 Marion.
Lang John, packer M F Kaag, res 4 Marion.
Lang Leonard. engineer, res 75 W Butler.
Lang Margaret J, clk Peoples Store, bds 165 Ewing.
Lang Rose. bds 75 W Butler.
Lang Rose, stenogr Wabash R R, bds 4 Marion.
Lang Wm, bds e s Piqua av 2 s of Calhoun.
Lang Wm, engineer Keller & Braun, bds 17 Hensch.
Lang Wm P, caller Penn Co, bds 165 Ewing.
Langard Clara, bds 70 E Columbia.
Langard John, grocer, 70 E Columbia, res same.
Langard Louis, bds 70 E Columbia.
Langard Victorine (wid Joseph), res 70 E Columbia.
Lange August H D, bds 327 Calhoun.
Lange Christian C (John H Lange & Son), bds 327 Calhoun
Lange Herman, clk Moellering Bros & Millard, res 316 Clay.
Lange John H (John H Lange & Sons), res 327 Calhoun.
Lange John H & Sons (John H, Christian C and John W), grocers, 327 Calhoun.
Lange John W (John H Lange & Sons), bds 327 Calhoun.
Lange Lizzie, dressmkr, bds 30 Pritchard.
Lange Louis, baker J H Lange & Sons, bds 327 Calhoun.
Lange Mary, bds 327 Calhoun.
Lange Minnie, clerk, bds 327 Calhoun.
Lange Minnie, tailoress G Scheffler, bds 30 Pritchard.
Lange Sophia, bds 30 Pritchard.
Lange Wm, clk Root & Co, res 30 Pritchard.
Lange Wm E, laborer, res 28 Brackenridge.
Lange W Herrmann, clk V Gutermuth, res 334 W Jefferson.
Langenfeld John A, clk J B White, res 67 Charles.
Langer Charles, regulator Ft W Gas Co, res 139 W 3d.
Langhals John J (Langhals & Goehren), res 8 Oak.
Langhals & Goehren (John J Langhals, Joseph Goehren). merchant tailors, 13 Maumee rd.

Langhorst August W. saloon, 51 E Main, cigar mnfr, 79 E Washington, res 51 E Main.

Langohr Amelia (wid John), res 129 Wells.

Langohr Andrew J, Baker and Confectioner, 142 Broadway, res same.

Langhor Anna B. tailoress, bds Christian Griebel.

Langhor Charles W, saloon 144 Broadway, res 142 same.

Langhor Clara M, clk A J Langhor, bds 142 Broadway.

Langhor Henry C, lab Ft W Elec Corp, bds 142 Broadway.

Langhor John W (Sommers & Langhor), res 32 W 4th.

Langhor Louis E. packer Ft W Furn Co, res 212 Fairfield av.

Langson Miriam (wid Richard), res 72 Madison.

Langtry Walter, vet surg 5 N Harrison, res e s 'Spy Run av 6 n of Riverside av. Tel 367.

Lanigan James F, engineer, bds 67 Melita.

Lanigan John P, laborer, bds 67 Melita.

Lanigan Patrick, gateman Penn Co, res 67 Melita.

Lanigan Thomas J, night agt Adams Ex Co, bds 69 Grand.

Lankenau Catherine (wid Frank), res 84 W Jefferson.

Lankenau Christian, clk M Frank & Co, res 70 Union.

Lankenau Clara K, domestic 225 W Berry.

Lankenau Wm J, clerk Root & Co, res 40 Wilt.

Lannon, see also Lennon.

Lannan Anna (wid Wm), res 103 W Washington.

Lannan August P, blacksmith, bds 103 W Washington.

Lannan Edward, died March 28. 1895.

Lannann James E, bartender, bds 47 Douglas av.

Lansdown Agnes E, bds J A Lansdown.

Lansdown Harry, stenogr Penn Co, bds w s Rumsey av 1 n of Nickel Plate.

Lansdown Job A, car bldr Penn Co, res w s Rumsey 1 n Nickel Plate.

Lansing Bertha, laundress, rms 37 W Berry.

Lanterman Frank E, printer, bds 63 E Berry.

Lanternier August, gardener 133 Walton av, res same.

Lanternier Clara, bds 133 Walton av.

Lanternier Edmund, barber, bds 133 Walton av.

Lanternier Louis J. laborer, bds 133 Walton av.

Lantz, see Lentz and Lintz.

Lapp Mrs Alzina, res 71 McCulloch.

Lapp Annie (wid Valentine), res 107 Wall.

Lapp Charles, molder Ft W Elec Corp, bds 52 W Williams

Lapp Clara J, clk G Haller, bds 52 W Williams.

27

Lapp Henry, lieut of police, res 52 W Williams.
Lapp Henry J, res 34 Stophlet.
Lapp John, clk J C Peters, res 107 Wall.
Lapp Valentine C, bds 107 Wall.
Larimore Mrs Alice, res 111 Howell.
Larimore Charles W, fireman Penn Co, res 35 E De Wald.
Larimore Eli, motorman Ft W E Ry Co, bds 154 Harrison
Larimore George W, paper hanger L O Hull, rms 15 Cass.
Larimore James, fireman Penn Co, res 77 E Williams.
Larimor Levi B, engr N Y, C & St L R R, res 148 Wells.
Larimore Mary E, bds 158 Horace.
Larimore Thomas J jr, fireman, res 77 E Williams.
Larrabee Thomas, wiper Penn Co, res 74 E Lewis.
Larson Michael L, conductor, bds 80 Baker.
La Rue Charles M, train despatcher Penn Co, res 213 W De Wald.
Larwill John S, office 9 W Main, res 93 E Berry.
Larwill Othniel H, - treas Wayne Knitting Mills, res 21 W Creighton av. Tel 353.
Lassfalls Wm, shoemkr B Novitzky, bds 145 Holman.
Lassus John B, Propr Lake Shore Hotel, 2 Cass, res 8 same.
Latenberger, *see also Landenberger.*
Latenberger Peter, foreman Olds' Wagon Wks, res 81 Shawnee av.
Latham Harry S, saloon, 6 E Columbia, res same.
Latham Maria L (wid Joseph), bds 182 Broadway.
Latham Maud B, student, bds 36 E Washington.
Lathrop Elias L (Lathrop & Co), res 125 E Main.
Lathrop J Madge, bds 125 E Main.
Lathrop & Co (Perry A Randall, Elias L Lathrop), glass and china; 17 Court.
Latta Charles S, well digger, res 20 Purman.
Lau, *see also Law and Low.*
Lau Julian, bds 122 Calhoun.
Lau Margaret J, millinery, 31 E Main, res 122 Calhoun.
Lau Mary, res 122 Calhoun.
Lau Thomas, bkkpr Fox br U S Baking Co, res 437 Calhoun.
Laubach Blanche W, bds 127 E Washington.
Laubach Gertrude L, bds 127 E Washington.
Laubach Lula A, bds 127 E Washington.
Laubach May W (wid Amandus J), res 127 E Washington.
Laubscher John H, laborer, res 25 Lasselle.
Lauderberg Charles G, machinist, res 157 St Mary's av.

Lauer, *see also Lahr, Laier and Lehr.*
Lauer Anna, bds 289 E Washington.
Lauer Mrs Anna K, dressmkr, bds 70 E Jefferson.
Lauer August, bds 348 Hanna.
Lauer Barbara (wid Paul), res 70 E Jefferson.
Lauer Christina, opr S M Foster, bds 70 E Jefferson.
Lauer Edward, molder, bds 153 E Lewis.
Lauer Elizabeth, dressmkr, 70 E Jefferson, bds same.
Lauer Emily, bds 278 E Washington.
Lauer Frank, driver J C Huguenard, bds 116 Maumee rd.
Lauer Frank P, car inspr Penn Co, res 46 Gay.
Lauer Frederick, molder Bass F & M Wks, res 133 Erie.
Lauer Frederick, molder, bds 166 Smith.
Lauer Gregory, carpenter, 101 Maumee rd, res same.
Lauer Gustave, contractor, 159 E Taber, res same.
Lauer Henry, brick mason, res 153 E Lewis.
Lauer Henry, car bldr Penn Co, res 129 Lafayette.
Lauer Henry, cigarmkr, bds 298 E Washington.
Lauer Henry, laborer, res 248 Erie.
Lauer Henry C, barber, 562 E Washington, bds 289 same.
Lauer Henry P, barber John Lauer, bds 70 E Jefferson.
Lauer John, barber 154 Barr, bds 70 E Jefferson.
Lauer John G, laborer, bds 101 Maumee rd.
Lauer John G, student, bds 226 E Lewis.
Lauer Joseph, carpenter, res 131 Erie.
Lauer Joseph, laborer, res 98 Harrison.
Lauer Julia, janitress P O, res 153 E Lewis.
Lauer Justin, carpenter, res 226 E Lewis.
Lauer Lizzie M, seamstress, bds 129 Lafayette.
Lauer Margaret, domestic 27 E Washington.
Lauer Martie K, bds 159 E Taber.
Lauer Mary, domestic 166 Smith.
Lauer Mary A (wid Ferdinand), res 126 Chicago.
Lauer Mary C, forelady Paragon Mnfg Co, bds 289 E Washington.
Lauer Michael, carp C Wermuth, res 198 Gay.
Lauer Michael, car bldr Penn Co, res 77 Erie.
Lauer Minnie, domestic, bds 160 Smith.
Lauer Minnie, domestic 324 Calhoun.
Lauer Nicholas, stone mason, res 202 Gay.
Lauer Nicholas J, carp Justin Lauer, bds 226 E Lewis.
Lauer Paul, helper Bass F & M Wks, bds 153 Clay.
Lauer Peter, laborer, bds Washington House.
Lauer Peter, laborer, bds 289 E Washington.
Lauer Peter, mach hd Penn Co, bds 126 Chicago.

Lauer Peter, molder, res 75 Madison.
Lauer Sarah R (wid John A), res 34 Oliver.
Lauer Sophia (wid Conrad), res 116 Maumee rd.
Lauer Wm C, laborer, bds 166 Smith.
Lauer Wm M, porter J B White, res 280 E Lewis.
Lauer Wm P, lab Bass F & M Wks, res 766 Smith.
Lauferty Alexander S, res 75 W Berry.
Lauferty Betty (wid Isaac), died April 17th, 1895.
Lauferty Samuel A, rms 105 W Wayne.
Laughlin, see also Loughlin.
Laughlin Charlton, packer City Mills, res 344 E
    Washington.
Laughlin Frank, bell boy, bds 332 Lafayette.
Laughlin James, laborer Penn Co, bds 326 Hanna.
Laughlin John, engr County Jail, rms 69 E Main.
Laughlin Michael, engr Penn Co, res 332 Lafayette.
Laughlin Mollie E, bds 332 Lafayette.
Laumann, see also Lohman and Lohrman.
Laumann Herman J, carpenter, res 127 W 3d.
Laumann Minnie A, dressmaker 127 W 3d, res same.
Laumann Rudolph H, carpenter, res 125 W 3d.
Launsbury James B, carpenter, bds 104 Barr.
Laurent, see also Lourent.
Laurent August C, saloon, 62 E Columbia. res same.
Laurents Alexander, butcher, res 414 E Wayne.
Laurentz, see also Lorenz.
Laury Hannah, chambermaid New Aveline House.
Lauterberg Charles G, mach L E & W R R, res 157 St
    Mary's av.
Lautzenheiser Almond, mach Rocker Washer Co, res 77
    Eliza.
Laux Wm, opr Wayne Knitting Mills, res 241 St Mary's av
Lavack, see Leveck.
Lavanway Charles J, clk H T Stapleford, res 47 E Columbia
Lavanway Frank, res rear 86 Barr.
Lavanway Luke, broker, res 28 Cochran.
Lavanway Sherman, grocer, 66 E Columbia, res same.
Law, see also Lau and Low.
Law Charles D, supt Western division Penn Co, rms
    McKinnie House.
Law David, res 302 W Washington.
Law Herbert J (Keller, Edmunds & Law Electric Con-
    struction Co), bds 302 W Washington.
Lawrence, see also Laurents.
Lawrence Alexander, engineer, res 34 Hayden.

Laws Benjamin (col'd), waiter The Wayne, rms 93 E Lewis
Lawson Wm, mdse broker, 22 Schmitz Blk, res 45 Home av
Lawton Harry, bds 3 Centre.
Layer, *see Laier and Lauer.*
Laylander John, fireman, bds 354 W Main.
Layman, *see also Lehman, Lohman and Luhmann.*
Layman Edna, student, bds 114 Howell.
Layman George, res 114 Howell.
Layman Nora, domestic 54 E Wayne.
Lazzarini Amadeo, saloon, 37 Barr, res same.
Leach Edward, carp Penn Co, res 64 Eckart lane.
Leach James, clk J B White, bds 83 Lasselle.
Leach John T, boilermkr Penn Co, res 83 Lasselle.
Leach Mabel, bds 64 Eckart lane.
Leach Mary, stenogr School for F M Y, bds 83 Lasselle.
Leach Porter F, trav agt Bass F & M Wks, bds The Wayne
Leach Rebecca J (wid John), res 166 W De Wald.
Leach Walter, molder, res 138 Force.
Leach Wm G, boilermkr Penn Co, res 56 Burgess.
Leachman Mrs Julia, attendnt School for F M Y, bds same
Leader Wm J, laborer, res 501 Lafayette.
Leammle, *see also Laemmle.*
Leammle Adeline (wid Charles J), res 25 Poplar.
Leammle John W, student, bds 25 Poplar.
Leammle Josephine, domestic J V Fox.
Leammle Josephine L, bds 25 Poplar.
Learmonth Robert, chief clk Penn Co, res 242 W Berry.
Leary Daniel, bds Hoffmann House.
Leary James T, clk Penn Co, res 151 E Berry.
Lease Abraham L, carpenter, res 157 Wells.
Lease John B, engr Penn Co, res 186 Monroe.
Lebrecht Frederick, lab Bass F & M Wks, res 237 Force.
Lebeck Peter Y, mach Bass F & M Wks, bds St James
    Hotel.
Lechler Franklin L, clk V Gutermuth, bds 324 W Jef-
    ferson.
Lechler Harry M, agt Singer Mnfg Co, res 324 W Jefferson
Lechler James A, lab Ft W Elec Corp, res 165 Broadway.
Lee Arnold A, engineer Jenney E L & P Co, res 1½ River-
    side av.
Lee Charles W, car bldr Penn Co, bds 381 Hanna.
Lee George H, pensioner, bds Union House.
Lee Jeffrey J, car bldr Penn Co, res 22 Madison.
Lee John, driver J Jacobs, bds 55 E Main.
Lee John O, died January 12, 1895.

Lee John S. fireman, res 322 Broadway.

Lee Louis H, laborer, res s s French 3 w of Webster.

Lee Margaret (wid Israel), res 88 E Lewis.

Lee Maurice J, mach Penn Co, res 381 Hanna.

Lee Samuel, bds 170 Huffman.

Lee Samuel S, carp, res 170 Huffman.

Lee Sarah C, rms 63 W Superior.

Lee Sophia C (wid Israel), boarding, 120 Harrison.

Leeper, see also Lepper.

Leeper Rev James L, pastor Second Presbyterian Church, res 24 W Washington.

Leeper Joseph J, engr Penn Co, res 159 Montgomery.

Leese A Lincoln, brakeman, res 162 Brackenridge.

Leeser Amelia A, bds 14 Wall.

Leeser Emma J, housekeeper, bds 6 Summit.

Leeser Mary M (wid Charles H), res 14 Wall.

Leeser Pauline A H (Borgmann & Leeser), bds 14 Wall.

Leeuw Andrew, appr The Journal, bds 368 E Washington.

Leeuw Edward, shoemkr App Bros, res 368 E Washington.

Leeuw John H, clerk, bds 368 E Washington.

Lefever Calvin W, carp S F Bowser & Co, res 29 Grace av.

Lefever Lillie M, seamstress, bds 31 Walton av.

Lefever Philip E, carpenter, res 31 Walton av.

Leffel Burton, switchman Penn Co, rms 27 Baker.

Leffers John, molder Bass F & M Wks, res 71 Summit.

Le Gras August, meats, 106 Spy Run av, res same.

Le Gras Emile F, clerk, bds 106 Spy Run av.

Le Gras John L, clk A Le Gras, bds 106 Spy Run av.

Le Gras Julia (wid Joseph), housekeeper 172 Clinton.

Le Gras Margaret (wid John L), bds 106 Spy Run av.

Lehman, see also Layman, Lohman and Luhman.

Lehman Ada M (wid Samuel H), res 44 W Washington.

Lehman Benjamin, Clothing, 34 and 36 Calhoun, bds The Wayne.

Lehman Book and News Co (Eugenia H Lehman, Laura G Detzer, Alice M Habecker), Books, Stationery, Newspapers and Periodicals, 81 Calhoun.

Lehman Charles L, cigar mnfr, 290 Hoagland av, res same

Lehman Conrad, contr, 618 Calhoun, res same.

Lehman Eugenia H (Lehman Book and News Co); res 44 W Washington.

Lehman Fidelia, dressmkr. bds 48 Mc Clellan.

Lehman Frank, sawyer Standard Wheel Co, res 520 E Lewis.

Lehman Henry, lab Penn Co, res 520 E Lewis.
Lehman Isidor, Propr of The Jacobs' Shoe Store, 17 Calhoun, res 138 W Main.
Lehman Jacob laborer, bds 520 E Lewis.
Lehman Jacob J, res 290 Hoagland av.
Lehman Julius, molder Bass F & M Wks, res 48 Force.
Lehman Lena, bds 520 E Lewis.
Lehman Lotta M, milliner, bds 618 Calhoun.
Lehman Louis, laborer, bds 520 E Lewis.
Lehman Magdalena (wid Jacob), res 618 Calhoun.
Lehman Oliver W, helper Penn Co, res 283 Webster.
Lehmann Anna, bds 222 E Washington.
Lehmann Charles, molder, res 166 E Creighton av,
Lehmann Emma, bds 222 E Washington.
Lehmann Frederick, helper, res 102 Gay.
Lehmann John, brewer C L Centlivre Brewing Co, res 26 Randolph.
Lehmann John C, painter, res 222 E Washington.
Lehmann John D, res n w cor Huron and Mechanic.
Lehmann Louise, bds 222 E Washington.
Lehmann Olive, domestic School for F M Y.
Lehmann Samuel O, paper hanger, res 72 Walnut.
Lehmcuhly Wm H, hammersmith Bass F & M Wks, res 49 W Williams.
Lehmkuhle, see also Limecooly.
Lehmkuhler Casper, helper Penn Co, res 324 Hanna.
Lehmkuhler John H, clk L Fortriede, bds 233 Calhoun.
Lehnemann, see also Lenemann.
Lehrman Mary, res 75 W Lewis.
Lehmeke Leonard C, brakeman N Y, C & St L R R, rms 320 W Main.
Lehmeke Otto E, brakeman N Y, C & St L R R, res 51 Elm.
Lehnert, see also Lennart and Leonard.
Lehnert Barbara (wid Henry), res 344 Broadway.
Lehnert Henry C, painter, 344 Broadway, bds same.
Lehnert Martin G, painter, bds 344 Broadway.
Lehr, see also Lahr and Laier.
Lehr Charles F, engr Penn Co, res 152 E Lewis.
Lehr Eliza A, clk Charles Falk & Co, bds 67 Cass.
Lehr Frankie E, dressmkr, 67 Cass, res same.
Lehr Georgia, bds 152 E Lewis.
Lehr Hannah (wid Justus J), res 67 Cass.
Lehr George P, wiper Penn Co, bds 74 Montgomery.
Lehr John G, bds w s Harrison 2 s of Killea av.
Leib Henry, plasterer, res 81 Madison.

Leibmann, *see Liebmann.*
Leichner Anna, bds 35 Douglas av.
Leichner Carrie, bds 132 W Williams.
Leichner Charles, helper, bds 132 W Williams.
Leichner Christina (wid John), res 35 Douglas av.
Leichner Conrad, lab Bass F & M Wks, res 370 E Lewis.
Leichner Emma, bds 370 E Lewis.
Leichner George J, hostler C A C Meyers, bds 35 Douglas av
Leidolf Conrad S, janitor High School, res 391 E Wayne.
Leidolf Frederick, insurance agt, bds 92½ Walton av.
Leidolf Henry, groom, res 571 W Washington.
Leight, *see Light.*
Leikauf, *see also Leykauf.*
Leikauf Mrs Barbara A, furnished rooms, 86 E Wayne.
Leikauf Frank N, pork packer, res 162 E Lewis.
Leikauf Henrietta, bds 86 E Wayne.
Leikauf Henry, butcher, res 105 Erie.
Leikauf John, butcher, bds 536 E Wayne.
Leikauf John J, res s e cor Parnell and Carson avs.
Leinker, *see also Linker.*
Leinker Charles F, truckman, bds 19 Marion.
Leinker Christopher H, cabinetmkr, res 19 Marion.
Leinker Ernst, laborer, bds 19 Marion.
Leinker Louisa A, bds 19 Marion.
Leinker P Henry F, carpet layer, bds 19 Marion.
Leinker Wm H, cigarmkr, bds 19 Marion.
Leischel Gustave, helper Bass F & M Wks, bds 26 John.
Leisering Herman C, baker, bds 223 Fairfield av.
Leising Mrs Dorothy, died June 7th, 1894.
Leising Peter J, check boy New Aveline House.
Leitz Clara A, seamstress, bds 11 Jones.
Leitz Edward H, bartender U Stotz, bds 11 Jones.
Leitz Herman, clk G W McAllister, res 123 Home av.
Leitz Joseph P, carp Ft W Elec Corp, res 11 Jones.
Leize Gottlieb, res n s Grace 2 e Calhoun.
Leland Harry, stage mngr, bds 244 W Washington.
Lemay David, ins agt, res 132 Madison.
Lemke, *see also Lampke.*
Lemke Charles, laborer, res 17 Custer av.
Lemmelet Celestine, brewer C L Centilvre Brewing Co, res 7 Edna.
Lemmle Mrs Adeline, res 23 Poplar.
Lenemann, *see also Linnemann.*
Lenemann John A, laborer, bds 1 Fair.
Lenemann Katie, opr Wayne Knitting Mills, bds 1 Fair.

Lenemann Rose (wid John), res 1 Fair.
Lenfesty Solon W, conductor, res 107 Gay.
Lenhard Clemens, lab B Kline, bds same.
Lenington Monroe, teamster, res 65 Home av.
Lenk John, cellarman Herman Berghoff Brewing Co, res 89 Grant av.
Lennamier Wm, blksmith J F Zurbuck, bds 387 W Main.
Lennart, see also Lehnert and Leonard.
Lennart John E, foreman Penn Co, res 366 E Washington.
Lennart John P, bkkpr Kerr Murray Mnfg Co, bds 366 E Washington.
Lennart Mary, bds 366 E Washington.
Lennart Wm J, stenogr S C Lumbard, res 364 E Washington.
Lennon, see also Lannon.
Lennon Edwin J (Belger & Lennon), res 22 McClellan.
Lenocker Ella, bds 194 E Lewis.
Lenocker John J, condr Penn Co, res 194 E Lewis.
Lenocker Sadie, bds 194 E Lewis.
Lentz, see also Lintz.
Lentz Frederick, springmkr Penn Co, res 92 Baker.
Lentz Louisa (wid Wm), res 152 Holman.
Lenz Charles F, molder, bds 78 Oliver.
Lenz Charles J, helper Horton Mnfg Co, bds 20 Mary.
Lenz Emma L, dressmaker, bds 20 Mary.
Lenz Ernest L, mach hd Penn Co, res 99 Brackenridge.
Lenz Frederick, meats, 170 Hanna, res 172 same.
Lenz Henry L, clk C H Buck, bds 99 Brackenridge.
Lenz John H, lab Bass F & M Wks, res 78 Oliver.
Lenz Joseph, helper Penn Co, res 21 Gay.
Lenz Wm, bottler L Brames & Co, bds 78 Oliver.
Lenz Wm, harnessmkr, bds 20 Mary.
Lenz Wm F, car bldr Penn Co, res 20 Mary.
Lenz Wm H, clk Bass F & M Wks, res 99 Brackenridge.
Leonard, see also Lehnert and Lennart.
Leonard Clara (wid Samuel), res 272 W Washington.
Leonard Elmer (W and E Leonard), U S commissioner, res s e cor Spy Run av and Leo Gravel rd.
Leonard Harriet E, prin Jefferson School, bds 155 W Wayne.
Leonard James H (Seavey Hardware Co), res 272 W Washington.
Leonard Jefferson, foreman Nelson Leonard, bds same.
Leonard Kate, bds 272 W Washington.
Leonard Mary J, clk People's Store, bds 71 W Superior.

Leonard Mary J, stenogr Rocker Washer Co, bds 188 W De Wald.

Leonard Minnie E, bkkpr Ft Wayne Gazette, bds 128 E Wayne.

Leonard Nathan R. Propr Fort Wayne Gazette, 41 E Berry, res 128 E Wayne.

Leonard Nelson, brick mnfr, s e cor Spy Run av and Leo Gravel rd, res same.

Leonard Park M, physician, 188 W DeWald, res same.

Leonard Smith E, clk Pacific Tea Co, bds 19 E Jefferson.

Leonard Thomas, engr N Y, C & St L R R, bds 45 Boone

Leonard Wm A, gunsmith, 71 W Superior, res same.

Leonard Wm A jr, paperhanger, bds 71 W Superior.

Leonard Wilmer (W & E Leonard), res 218 W De Wald.

Leonard W & E (Wilmer and Elmer), lawyers 25 Bank Blk. Tel 214

Lepper, *see also Leeper.*

Lepper Charles L, painter. bds 324 E Washington.

Lepper Charles O, drugs 66 W Jefferson, res same.

Lepper Edmund B, engr Engine Co No 4, res n e cor Oak and Chute.

Lepper Elizabeth (wid Christian), res 324 E Washington.

Lepper Elizabeth (wid Wm), bds 421 E Washington.

Lepper Frederick, patternmkr Penn Co, res 443 E Wayne.

Lepper Frederick H W, clk C E Heaton, res 324 E Washington.

Lepper Henry C, lab Ft W Elec Corp, bds 71 Huestis av.

Lepper Henry W, clk Geo De Wald & Co, res 43 Harmer.

Lepper Jennie, seamstress, bds 242 E Jefferson.

Lepper Louis H, truckman Penn Co. res 65 Lillie.

Lepper Louise (wid Henry), res 242 E Jefferson.

Lepper Mary, domestic 90 E Wayne.

Lepper Peter, mach hd Penn Co, bds 186 Francis.

Lepper Susan, domestic 338 Calhoun.

Lepper Wm. mach hd Penn Co, res 214 Francis.

Lepper Wm H, carpenter, res 9 Zollars av.

Lepple Gottlieb, laborer Penn Co, res 17 Duryea.

Lerch Annie, bds 360 Force.

Lerch Archibald, mach W Gas Const Co, bds 401 Clinton.

Lerch Casper, died Nov. 29th, 1894.

Lerch Frank, grocer 360 Force, res same.

Lerch Henry. helper Penn Co. res 241 Force.

Lerch Joseph, shoemkr 127 Fairfield av, res 401 Clinton.

Lerch Mary, clk F Lerch, bds 360 Force.

Lerch Minnie (wid Casper), res 121 Force.

Lerch Wm M, mach Bass F & M.Wks, res 353 E Wayne.
LeRoy John B, res New Haven av cor Rex.
Lesley Frank G, brakeman, res 335 Hanna.
Lett Sidney, fireman Penn Co, bds 36 Baker.
Leu John, traveling agt, bds Weber Hotel.
Leuschner Herman, cabtmkr Ft W Organ Co, res 106 South Wayne av.
Leuthner Barbara, res 278 E Jefferson.
Leutwyler Wm, meats. 536 Calhoun, res same.
LeVan Simon P, contractor, res 19 Archer av.
Leveck John. helper Kerr Murray Mnfg Co, res s s Piqua av s city limits.
Levenberger Clara, milliner, bds 43 Force.
Levenberger John H, car repr N Y, C & St L R R, res 43 Force.
Levenberger Lizzie. seamstress, bds 43 Force.
Levi August, res 116 W Main.
Levi Belle, bds 116 W Main.
Levi Carl, clk A I & H Friend, bds 116 W Main.
Levi Henry, cook, G H Seabold, res 3 Harrison.
Levi Lucy (col'd) (wid Henry), res 51 W.Superior.
Levine Isaac, pedler, res 85 Maumee rd.
Levington Samuel, ticket broker, 85 Calhoun, res 76 W Jefferson.
Levistein Ida, bds 75 W Berry.
Levy Abraham (Levy Bros), res 88 Barr.
Levy Bros (Abraham and Moses), clothing, 72 and 88 Barr.
Levy Moses (Levy Bros). res 88 Barr.
Lew, see Leu.
Lewis Bayless A, laborer, res 83 Baker.
Lewis Bessie, bds 56 Riverside av.
Lewis Clara F (wid Wm E), died April 17th, 1895.
Lewis Dominick, fruits, res 68 Riverside av.
Lewis Edgar F, apprentice, bds 83 Baker.
Lewis Edwin W, Wholesale and Retail Oysters and Fish 38 Harrison, res 20 Savilla av. Tel 451.
Lewis Elsie M, bkkpr Robert Ogden, bds 83 Baker.
Lewis Frank, printer Archer Ptg Co. res 56 Riverside av.
Lewis Frank W, fireman Penn Co. res 57 Charles.
Lewis Gertrude, domestic 267 W Wayne.
Lewis James D, Druggist, 434 Calhoun, res same. Tel 280.
Lewis John W, gasfitter Robert Ogden, res 73 Baker.
Lewis Jonathan, res 142 W Main.
Lewis Laura A (wid Levi), bds 600 Calhoun.

Lewis Mary A (wid David), res 38 Clinton.
Lewis Mary H, teacher, bds 251 W Main.
Lewis Mary J (wid Sylvester L), res 60 Grant av.
Lewis Mrs Matilda, attendant School F M Y.
Lewis Moses W (col'd), waiter Ft Wayne Club, rms 84 W Main.
Lewis Nellie (wid Vernon L), housekpr 34 Douglas av.
Lewis Rissa C, dressmkr 142 W Main, res same.
Lewis Wm, engineer, res 216 W De Wald.
Lewis Wm E, clk A Copinus, res 250 W Creighton av.
Lexington Restaurant, Owens & Welsh Proprs, meals 20 cts, 7 Harrison. (*See p 105.*)
Leykauf, *see also Leikauf.*
Leykauf Henry N, plumber A Hattersley & Sons, res 149 Union.
Leykauf John N, brakeman, res 66 E Pontiac.
Leykauf Nicholas, grocer 209 Broadway, res 147 Union.
Libbing Louis J, clk A Kalbacher, res 63 Baker.
Libeck Peter, machinist, bds St James Hotel.
Library Hall, n e cor Calhoun and Lewis.
Lichtenwalter Albert L, barber, res 136 Jackson.
Lichtenwalter A Elmer, lab Ft W Elec Corp, bds 185 Jackson.
Lichtenwalter George, mach hd, res 372 E Lewis.
Lichtenwalter J Leary, lab Ft W Elec Corp, res 185 Jackson.
Lichtenwalter Orrin J, res 185 Jackson.
Lichtenwalter Sarah (wid Solomon M), res 260 E Lewis.
Lichtenwalter Solomon M. died Dec 2d, 1894.
Lichtenwalter Wallace A, barber, 32 E Columbia, rds 260 E Lewis.
Lichtenwalter Wm M, clerk, res 19 Elm.
Lichtle Paul, bds n s Ruth 2 w of Spy Run av.
Lichtle Peter P, lab, res n s Ruth 2 w of Spy Run av.
Lichtle Rosa A, domestic 110 Chicago.
Lichtsinn Henry, lab Penn Co, res 34 Charles.
Lichtsinn Henry, teamster, res 382 E Washington.
Lichtsinn Henry W F, student, bds 382 E Washington.
Lichtsinn Johanna (wid Wm J), res 15 Summit.
Lichtsinn Lena, bds 15 Summit.
Lichtsinn Wm A, student, bds 15 Summit.
Lichty Judith, bkkpr Ft W Bk Bindery, bds 130 Wells.
Lickly Newton A, sawyer, res 318 Hanna.
Liddell Hattie (wid Wm), domestic The Randall.
Liebe Edith, domestic, bds 172 Suttenfield.

Liebe Ida, domestic Concordia College.
Liebenguth Albert, molder Bass F & M Wks, res 22 Gay.
Liebenjans, see Lubbenjans.
Liebig Charles, mason, 1 Tam, res same,
Liebig Edith, bds 1 Tam.
Liebig Emil C, laborer, bds 1 Tam.
Liebman Ernest F, contractor, 106 W Wayne, res same.
Liebman Minnie F, bds 166 W Wayne.
Liebmann Anna B, bds 109 Barr.
Liebmann August, cutter Hoosier Mnfg Co, bds 109 Barr.
Liebmann Oscar, bds 109 Barr.
Liebmann Rienhold E, shoemkr, res 109 Barr.
Liebmann Sophia E, bds 109 Barr.
Liebmann Wm G, cigarmkr H W Ortman, bds 109 Barr.
Liedtke John J, porter Meyer Bros & Co, res 110 High.
Lieter Minnie, opr Wayne Knitting Mills, bds 118 Madison.
Ligget Bros (James and Robert A), Livery, Sale and Feed Stables, 5 and 7 N Harrison. (See p 101). Tel 258.
Ligget Grace B, bds 10 Columbia av.
Ligget James (Ligget Bros), Superintendent of Police, City Hall, res 10 Columbia av.
Ligget Phraortes C, clk M J Blitz, bds 10 Columbia av.
Ligget Robert A (Ligget Bros), res 73 Wells.
Liggett Frank, brakeman N Y, C & St L R R, bds 235 W Main.
Liggett James M, motorman Ft W E Ry Co, res 285 Harrison.
Light Hattie E, opr S M Foster, bds 130 E Lewis.
Light John W, truckman, res 130 E Lewis.
Light Louis C, laborer, bds 130 E Lewis.
Light Wm J, truckman, bds 130 E Lewis.
Lightfoot Frank S, treas Rock Run Iron and Mining Co, rms 46 W Berry.
Likley George B, engineer, res 183 W Jefferson.
Lile, see also Lyle.
Lile Alfred, laborer, res 7 Winch.
Lill Martin, saloon, 150 Calhoun, bds 149 E De Wald.
Lill Peter, watchman, res 147 E De Wald.
Lilley Merritt B, brakeman, res 153 Hanna.
Lillieh Melvin J, tailor, 409 Lafayette, res same.
Lillie John S, brakeman, bds 153 Hanna.
Limbach Charles H, res 59 Grant av.
Limbach Herman, blacksmith, res 79 Wall.

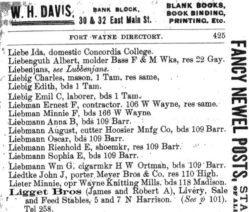

Limbach Otto C, harnessmkr Mrs A C Corneille, bds 59 Grant av.

Limecooly, *see also Lehmkuhler.*

Limecooly Charles G, clerk, res 28 Stophlet.

Limecooly Frederick R, res 453 Lafayette.

Limecooly Henry J, cigarmkr, bds cor John and Pontiac.

Limecooly Louis F, grocer, 562 Calhoun, res same.

Limecooly Mary S L, bds 453 Lafayette.

Limecooly Wm F, grocer, 260 W Creighton av, res same.

Lincoln Caroline B (wid Edmund), res 22 W Butler.

Lincoln Charles, lab Penn Co, res 117 Holman.

Lincoln Elizabeth C, stenogr L M and H W Ninde, bds 22 W Butler.

Lincoln Etta, opr S M Foster, bds 47 Lillie.

Lincoln George W, peddler, res 47 Lillie.

Lincoln Mary B, teacher, bds 22 W Butler.

Lincoln Tea Co, J B Davis mngr, 50 Harrison.

Lincoln Theodore, mach Wabash R R, res 94 W Creighton av.

Lindeman, *see also Linnemann.*

Lindeman Frederick H, clk W H Schultz, bds 106 Wilt.

Lindeman Gottlieb, appr Penn Co, bds 106 Wilt.

Lindeman Henry L, bkkpr, bds 106 Wilt.

Lindeman John H, carpenter Penn Co, res 106 Wilt.

Lindeman Mary, bds 106 Wilt.

Lindeman Wm, machinist, bds 106 Wilt.

Lindemann Charles H, stripper, bds 152 Rockhill.

Lindemann Clara D, dressmkr, bds 81 Wilt.

Lindemann Daniel, teacher, res 81 Wilt.

Lindemann Edward J, clk Penn Co, bds 134 Montgomery.

Lindemann E Wm, mason, res 152 Rockhill.

Lindemann Frederick, foreman, res 161 Rockhill.

Lindemann George H, lab Bass F & M Wks, bds 152 Rockhill.

Lindemann Gustave C F, carp, bds 404 E Washington.

Lindemann Harry J, brakeman, bds 134 Montgomery.

Lindemann Henry F, upholsterer P E Wolf, bds 404 E Washington.

Lindemann John, helper Bass F & M Wks, res 21 Charles.

Lindemann Julius M, cutter S M Foster, bds 152 Rockhill.

Lindemann Mary E, stenogr, bds 81 Wilt.

Lindemann Matilda, music teacher, bds 81 Wilt.

Lindemann Oscar A H, engineer, res 410 E Washington.

Lindemann Robert E, tinner, bds 161 Rockhill.

Lindemann Theodore, molder Ind Mach Wks, bds 81 Wilt.

Lindemann Wm R, carpenter, res 404 E Washington.
Lindenberg Anna E, bds 55 Stophlet.
Lindenberg Christian, mach Ft W Iron Wks, res 146 Union.
Lindenberg Christian W, clk Old National Bank, bds 146 Union.
Lindenberg Frederick, bricklayer, res 55 Stophlet.
Lindenberg Fred W, clk A Riethmiller, bds 55 Stophlet.
Lindenberg John F, bkkpr J Wilding, bds 146 Union.
Lindenberg Louise, dressmkr, bds 55 Stophlet.
Lindenberg Minnie, bds 55 Stophlet.
Lindenberg Sophia, bds 55 Stophlet.
Lindenberg Wm F, bkkpr J Wilding, bds 146 Union.
Lindenwood Cemetery, J H Doswell supt, Huntingdon rd ¼ mile w of city limits.
Lindenwood Cemetery Assn, O P Morgan pres, C A Wilding secy and treas, J H Doswell supt, cor Berry and Court.
Lindlag Jacob J, res 115 Brackenridge.
Lindlof Oscar F, electrician Ft W Elec corp, bds 79 W De Wald.
Lindlof Wm A, electrician Ft W Elec Corp, bds 18 McClellan.
Lindner Andrew, shoemkr L Fortriede, res 89 Putnam.
Lindsey Charles , W, constable 13 E Main, res 223 Lafayette.
Lindsey Gertrude, stenogr Zollars & Worden, bds 223 Lafayette.
Lindsey James E, eng N Y, C & St L R R, res 74 W 3d.
Lindsley Louis C, tel opr N Y, C & St L R R, rms 89 Brackenridge.
Lindsley Percy M, meats 89 Harmer, res 262 E Jefferson.
Line Ada, domestic 30 Douglas av.
Line Albert W, clk Louis Wolf & Co, res 244 E Washington
Lingle Mrs Jennie, res 55 E Superior.
Linhardt Ernst, lab L Rastetter & Son, res 180 Metz.
Lininger Alice (wid Frank), dressmkr, bds 294 E Creighton av.
Linninger Ollie M, tailoress, res 6 Van Buren.
Link Adam, agent, res 102 E Main.
Link Anna M (wid George), res 236 E Jefferson.
Link Benjamin, oil pedler, res 137 John.
Link Carrie R, bds 236 E Jefferson.
Link Frederick, stonecutter Kellar & Braun, res 116 Chicago
Link Henry J, cashier Root & Co. bds 236 E Jefferson.
Link John, padmkr A L Johns & Co, bds 11 Mary.

428

Link Mary, operator, bds 11 Mary.
Link Mary (wid Thomas), res 11 Mary.
Link Wm B, foreman N Y, C & St L R R. res 7 Cass
Linker, *see also Leinker.*
Linker Carrie, domestic 206 W Wayne.
Linker Christine (wid Henry E), res 46 W Berry.
Linker Florence, bds 46 W Berry.
Linker Henry E, lab Penn Co, bds 382 E Lewis.
Linker John V, trav agt the Herman Berghoff Brewing Co, res 90 Wells.
Linker Katherine, bds 46 W Berry.
Linker Louis W, barber H C Lauer, bds 66 Grant av
Linker Minnie, bds 66 Grant av.
Linker Valentine, watchman The Herman Berghoff Brewing Co, res 66 Grant av.
Linnemann, *see also Lenemann and Lindemann.*
Linnemann Bernard, cabinetmkr, res 183 Oakland.
Linnemeier Caroline, domestic 121 W. Main.
Linnemeier Conrad D W, packer Root & Co, res 60 W Berry.
Linnemeier Deidrich, hostler Concordia College.
Linnemeier Herman, helper Bass F & M Wks, bds 174 Francis.
Linnemeier Minnie, domestic Concordia College.
Linnemeier Minnie, domestic 121 W Main.
Linnemeier Mrs Minnie S, midwife, 174 Francis, res same
Linnemeier Wm, porter, res 174 Francis.
Linsky Thaddeus, laborer, res 5 Fisher.
Lintner Andrew J, shoemkr, res 89 Putnam.
Linton Alice F, bds 13 Chestnut.
Linton John H, car repr, res 143 Francis.
Linton Samuel, res 13 Chestnut.
Lintz, *see also Lentz.*
Lintz Anthony W, foreman Ft W E Ry Co, res 34 Baker.
Lion Fire Ins Co of London, Eng, C B Fitch agt, 26 Bass Blk.
Lipes Alexander F, printer Ft W Newspaper Union, bds 256 W De Wald.
Lipes Anna M, teacher Hanna School, bds 389 Calhoun.
Lipes Charles J, packer J A Armstrong & Co, res 15 E Creighton av.
Lipes David D, res 301 E Lewis.
Lipes John M, foreman Keller Dental Co, res 48 Michigan av.
Lipes Margaret N (wid George), bds 74 Douglas av.

Lipes Robert F, physician, 74 Douglas av, bds same.
Lipes Ulyssis G, physician, 41½ W Berry, res same.
Lipsett Wm E, conductor, res 76 E Butler.
Lish Carl, brakeman G R & I R R, bds 224 Calhoun.
Lischy Aaron, notary public, 551 E Washington, res same.
List Emma, opr S Freiburger & Bro, bds 395 E Washington.
List John J, carpenter, res 395 E Washington.
Litique Josephine, domestic 277 W Wayne.
Litot Edward L, boilermkr, bds 338 W Main.
Litot George A, res s w cor Spy Run av and Randolph.
Litot George J, lineman Jenney E L & P Co, bds George A Litot.
Litot Joseph V, clerk, res 107 N Harrison.
Litot Mary M, bds George A Litot.
Little, see also Lyttle.
Litt George O, propr Choctaw Medicine Co, res 15 Maple av
Litt George W, res 15 Maple av.
Little Albert H, laborer, res 75 Scott av.
Little Giant Water Works, Elijah Neff patentee, Charles Pape mngr, 78 High. Tel 83.
Little Grace A, dressmaker, bds 194 E Jefferson.
Little Mrs Hattie, chambermaid The Randall.
Little Henry A, res 75 Scott av
Little Horatio A, truckman Penn Co, res 75 Scott av.
Little John L, lab Olds' Wagon Wks, res 56 W Williams.
Little Wm, mach Rocker Washer Co, bds 29 Calhoun.
Little Wm R, traveling agent, res 402 Broadway.
Littlejohn David M, appr Wabash R R, bds 19 Poplar.
Littlejohn James W, student, bds 19 Poplar.
Littlejohn Jennie, domestic 23 Douglas av.
Littlejohn John G, mach Wabash R R, bds 19 Poplar.
Littlejohn Wm, blacksmith Wabash R R, res 19 Poplar.
Livelsberger Elizabeth (wid John A), res 242 E Wayne.
Lloyd, see also Loyd.
Lloyd Allen, ins agt, bds 264 W Washington.
Lloyd Ernest F, sec Western Gas Const Co, bds 11 Webster.
Lloyd Gordon W, treas Western Gas Const Co, res Detroit, Mich.
Lloyd Isabel R, prin Hanna School, bds 141 E Berry.
Lloyd John, laborer, res 167 Van Buren.
Lloyd Rev John P, res 141 E Berry.
Lloyd Thomas J, mach, res 264 W Washington.
Lloyd Thomas M, clk Geo De Wald & Co, bds 141 E Berry.
Loag Anna R (wid George W), bds 103 W Berry.

Loarine Joseph, helper Olds' Wagon Wks, bds 59 W Superior.

Lobdell John D, motorman, res 3 Brookside.

Lochner David, mach A L Johns & Co, bds 75 W 3d.

Lochner Henry D, carp West Gas Const Co, res 55 Oliver.

Locke Elenora, rms 317 Calhoun.

Lockhart Clara A, domestic, bds 577 Calhoun.

Lockhart Flora M, dressmaker, bds 577 Calhoun.

Lockhart Henry E, laborer, res 218 John.

Lockhart Rose L, dressmaker, bds 577 Calhoun.

Lockhart Wm A, laborer, res 577 Calhoun.

Loebert Frederick C, flue cleaner Penn Co, res 216 John.

Loeffler Wm M, steamfitter A Hattersley & Sons, res 189 E Wayne.

Loesch George H, Druggist and Chemist, 96 Barr, res 52 W Washington.   Tel 232.

Logan Elizabeth M, bds 42 Baker.

Logan Felix G, clerk Shepler & Noble, bds 42 Baker.

Logan John C, brakeman G R & I R R, res 314 Harrison.

Logan John H, blacksmith, bds 42 Baker.

Logan Lot A, engineer P O, res 314 Harrison.

Logan Margaret V, seamstress, bds 42 Baker.

Logan Thomas J, deputy clk U S Court, res 168 E Jefferson

Logan Wm H, brakeman G R & I R R, res 11 Duryea.

Logan Wm L, horseshoer, res 42 Baker.

Logan Wm L jr, stenogr C K of A, bds 42 Baker.

Logue Frank H, tel opr N Y, C & St L R R, res 211 W Jefferson.

Lohman, see also Layman, Lehman and Luhmann.

Lohman Joseph, traveling agt, res 98 W Berry.

Lohmann Johann, laborer, res n w cor Walton av and Pontiac.

Lohmeyer, see also Lahmeyer.

Lohmeyer Wm, res 67 Lillie.

Lohrman, see also Laumann and Lohman.

Lohrman Wm, engineer Penn Co, bds 154 John.

Lohse Richard F, mach opr, res 38 Watkins.

Lombard, see also Lumbard.

Lombard Edith L, bds 16 Colerick.

Lombard Joseph, insurance agt, res 16 Colerick.

Lombard Louis F, brakeman, res 120 Buchanan.

Lombard Mary A, bds 16 Colerick.

Lommatzsch Herman, helper Bass F & M Wks, res s s Buchanan n e cor John.

Lomont Alexander E, waiter, bds 23 Pritchard.
Lomont Louisa F (wid Virgil'P), res 23 Pritchard.
Lomont Mary E, bds 135 W 3d.
Lomont Mary P (wid Francis), res 135 W 3d.
Lomont Mollie, cook, bds 23 Pritchard.
Lonergan Cecilia A. milliner, bds 166 Harmer.
Lonergan Charles J, brakeman G R & I R R, res 185 Monroe.
Lonergan James E, binder Ft W Sentinel, res 16 Erie.
Lonergan John C, brakeman, res 185 Monroe.
Lonergan John V. machinist, res 166 Harmer.
Lonergan Margaret J (wid Thomas), bds 185 Monroe.
Lonergan Wm J, machinist, bds 487 Harmer.
Loney Alexander J, baggageman, res 124 W Williams.
Loney Ella, seamstress, bds 211 Fairfield av.
Loney George, carp Bass F & M Wks, res 211 Fairfield av.
Loney James W, laborer, bds 211 Fairfield av.
Loney Neil M, student, bds 124 W Williams.
Long, *see also Lang and Lange.*
Long Charles, engr N Y, C & St L R R, bds 39 Elm.
Long Claude H, advance agt. rms 77 E Berry.
Long Emma L (wid Charles A), res 232 E Jefferson.
Long Frank, carriage trimmer, res 125 Walton av.
Long Frank E, brakeman, res 285 W Main.
Long Frank E, laborer, res 180 Gay.
Long Gordon W, engr, res 14 Barthold.
Long Harry M, umbrella mnfr, 97½ Calhoun, res 74 Baker
Long; Ida, domestic, 81 Weils.
Long Jacob, teamster D Tagtmeyer, res 131 W 3d.
Long Jacob E. brakeman, res 95 Greene.
Long James B (Wayne Printing Co), res 77 E Berry.
Long Mrs James B, dressmkr 77 E Berry, res same.
Long John E, engineer Penn Co, res 19 Pine.
Long Joseph F, brakeman N Y, C & St L'R R, res 16 Breck.
Long Leo, music teacher 134 Calhoun, bds same.
Long Mason (The Mason Long Publishing Co), res 104 Columbia av.
Long Mason Publishing Co (Mason Long), 17 Pixley & Long Bldg.
Long Nancy V (wid John C W), bds 77 Dawson.
Long Pearl B, tel opr, bds 232 E Jefferson.
Long Roma J, stenographer The Anthony Wayne Mnfg Co, bds 232 E Jefferson.

Long Viola, domestic, rms 246 Calhoun.
Long Wm, lab Penn Co, bds 89 Putnam.
Longacre Bertha L, teacher, bds 29 Garden.
Longacre Carrie S (wid Milton P), res 29 Garden.
Longan Benjamin, driver E Rich, bds 15 Pearl.
Longfield Edward J, solicitor D C Fisher, bds 67 Charles.
Longfield John, clerk, res 67 Charles.
Longhenry Wm S, fireman Penn Co, res 84 Madison.
Longsworth Frank L, fireman, res 48 Runnion av.
Lonsberry James B, patternmkr Bass F & M Wks, bds 104 Barr.
Loomis Annie E (wid Harry H), bds 132 Montgomery.
Loos Anna, bkkpr C Loos, bds 419 Lafayette.
Loos Henry C, grocer 421 Lafayette, res 419 same.
Loos Henry C-jr, erecter Kerr Murray Mnfg Co, bds 419 Lafayette.
Loos John, clk Henry Loos, bds 419 Lafayette.
Loos Joseph, grocer 172 W Main, res 196 E De Wald.
Loos Mary A, bds 419 Lafayette.
Loos Matilda P, bds 419 Lafayette.
Loos Ulrich, clk H C Loos, bds 419 Lafayette.
Lóose, see Lohse.
Lopshire Abraham L, engr G R & I R R, res 13 St Martins.
Lopshire Austin H, propr Union House, 49 W Main.
Lopshire H Vincent, bodymkr Olds' Wagon Wks, res 7 Grace av.
Lorain Josephine, domestic 160 Spy Run av.
Lordier August F, res 537 E Wayne.
Lordier Clara P, bds 37 Baker.
Lordier Felix, section hand, bds Lake Shore Hotel.
Lordier Frank J, asst bkkpr C L Centlivre Brewing Co, bds 537 E Wayne.
Lordier Michael J, plumber Seavey Hardware Co, bds 37 Baker.
Lordier Philip J, bell boy, bds 37 Baker.
Lordier Philip, shoemkr, 35 Baker, res 37 same.
Lorent Josephine, dressmaker, bds 63 Hugh.
Lorenz, see also Laurents and Lawrence.
Lorenz Carrie, knitter, bds 227 St Mary's av.
Lorenz Charles, wire worker, res 227 St Mary's av.
Lorenz Edith, bds 227 St Mary's av.
Lorenz George, florist, bds 227 St Mary's av.
Lorenz Ida, laundress, bds 227 St Mary's av.
Lorenz Joseph, laborer, res 80 Oliver.

Lorenz Mary, knitter, bds 227 St Mary's av.
Lorenz Siefert. laborer, bds 145 Holman.
Loring Rev Wilson T, pastor Free Methodist Church, res 268 E Creighton av.
Lorton Jesse D, condr Ft W, F & W R R, res 143 E Wayne.
Lose Cyrus J, foreman The Journal, res 41 Douglas av.
Lose Levi H, carp Penn Co, res 43 Douglas av.
Lotz Charles A, painter, bds 21 Calhoun.
Lotz Ernst, helper L Rastetter & Son, bds 37 Breck.
Lotz George C, butcher F Eckart Pkg Co, res 37 Breck.
Lotz John H, tailor, 416 E Washington, res same.
Lotz Philip, restaurant 21 Calhoun, res same.
Lotz Rosa, bds 9 Herman.
Lotz Wm J, appr Ind Mach Wks, bds 37 Breck.
Loucks Amos H, carp G Young, res 342 W Jefferson.
Loucks Nora M, opr S M Foster, bds 317 Calhoun.
Loughlin, *see also Laughlin.*
Loughlin Alonzo, sawyer Ft W Organ Co, bds 608 Calhoun
Lourent, *see also Laurent.*
Lourent Frank J, Propr Nickel Plate Restaurant, Nickel Plate Passenger Depot, res 1 N Calhoun.
Lourent Frederick, bartender F Schele, bds Nickel Plate Restaurant.
Louthain Mrs Sadie, dressmaker, res 17 Baker.
Louthan George L, condr Penn Co, res 45 John.
Louttit George W, lawyer, 19 Court, res 68 W Creighton av
Loutzenheiser, *see Lautzenheiser.*
Lovall Mrs Harriett, bds 37 Erie.
Love John, brakeman, bds 108 Buchanan.
Love Wm, laborer, res 321 Force.
Lovejoy Belle (wid George), bds 193 Ewing.
Lovekin Sadie E, bds 70 W Williams.
Loveless Walter H, physical director Y M C A, res 249 W Washington.
Low, *see also Lau.*
Low David W, mach Ft W Elec Corp, bds 164 Brackenridge
Lowe George W, res 280 W Washington.
Lown Gilbert L, car bldr Penn Co, res 124 Baker.
Lowrey Lottie C, clk J B White, bds 71 W Wayne.
Lowry Anna A, china, 10 W Berry, bds 92 same.
Lowry Charlotte C, clerk, bds 92 W Berry.
Lowry Fanny M, teacher Miner St School, bds 123 Edgewater av.

Lowry Margaret (wid James W), dressmaker, 80 W Creighton av, res same.
Lowry Mary, nurse School for F M Y.
Lowry Robert, lawyer, 52½ Calhoun, res 92 W Berry. Tel 289.
Loyd, *see also Lloyd*.
Loyd George, res s s Maumee rd 2 e of Edsall av.
Loyd Thomas W, conductor, res 435 E Washington.
Lubbenjans Annie, seamstress, bds 127 Monroe.
Lubbenjans Minnie, seamstress, bds 127 Monroe.
Luc Joseph, res rear 196 Hanna.
Luc Lena, seamstress S M Foster, bds 196 Hanna.
Lucas Charles, teamster, bds 117 Hanna.
Lucey Daniel cook C Entemann, bds 36 Union.
Lucey Timothy, laborer, res w s Union 1 n of Wall.
Luckey Elizabeth (wid John), bds 58 Maumee rd.
Luckey Henry, driver J E Klinger, bds 67 E Columbia.
Luckey Jacob, driver L Diethen & Bro, res 1 Lake.
Lucker Martha, domestic 186 W Berry.
Ludington James A, mach Penn Co, bds 65 Baker.
Ludwick Jasper, lab N Y, C & St L R R, res 11 Marion.
Ludwig Alfred, stripper, bds 224 John.
Ludwig Elsie, knitter, bds 224 John.
Ludwig Gustave T, molder Bass F & M Wks, bds 224 John.
Ludwig Louis F, coremkr Bass F & M Wks, res 224 John.
Ludwig Max, knitter, bds 224 John.
Ludwig Michael, knitter, bds 224 John.
Luegring Anthony, tinner, res 16 Cedar.
Luessenhop Louis, baggageman Wabash R R, res 175 W De Wald.
Luethi Alexander, tailor 13 Harrison, res 22 Orchard.
Luethi Frederick C, tailor A Luethi, res 19 Guthrie.
Lugenbuehl John, tailor S J Robacker, res 91 Franklin av.
Luhmann, *see also Layman and Lehman*.
Luhmann August C, painter City Carriage Wks, bds 59 Canal.
Luhmann Ernest H, carpenter, bds 447 E Wayne.
Luhmann Frederick C, printer, bds 447 E Wayne.
Luhmann Frederick D, laborer, res 447 E Wayne.
Luhmann Frederick H, tailor G Schmidt, res 77½ Hoagland av.
Luhmann Henry C, cutter J G Thieme & Son, res 51 Maumee rd.
Luhmann Minnie, milliner, bds 447 E Wayne.
Luhmann Wm C, carpenter, res 71 Canal.

Luhmann Wm F, tailor, res 59 Canal.
Luhrmann, *see also Lohrmann.*
Luhrmann Christian. teamster, res 213 W Washington.
Luhrmann Henry C, mach Wabash R R, bds 213 W Washington.
Luhrmann Mary (wid Wm), domestic 133 E Berry.
Luhrmann Leona A L, domestic C A Hoffmann.
Luhrs Charles, lab Standard Wheel Co, res 255 Gay.
Lukens Alfred B, clerk M W Fay, bds 236 W Berry.
Lukens Alfred T, bkkpr Ft Wayne News, res 236 W Berry.
Lukens Clara M, bds 236 W Berry.
Luley Anna, bds 279 Hanna.
Luley Anthony B, bkkpr Pickard Bros, bds 171 E Jefferson.
Luley Edward P, student, bds 171 E Jefferson.
Luley Frank J, foreman Bass F & M Wks, res 171 E Jefferson.
Luley Frank P, foreman Ft W Iron Wks, res 256 E Jefferson.
Luley Henry W, pattern maker. bds 171 E Jefferson.
Luley Jacob J, machinist, bds 171 E Jefferson
Luley John, mach Western Gas Const Co, bds 279 Hanna.
Luley Joseph M, molder Ind Mach Wks, bds 279 Hanna.
Luley Joseph J, molder Bass F & M Wks, res 171 E Jefferson.
Luley Magdalena (wid Philip), res 279 Hanna.
Luley Philip F, engr Wayne Oil Tank Co, bds 279 Hanna.
Luley Wm J, molder Ind Mach Wks, res 30 E 3d.
Lumbard, *see also Lombard.*
Lumbard Constance, bds 137 W Wayne.
Lumbard Effie, teacher Washington School, bds 164 W Wayne.
Lumbard Frank S, clk S C Lumbard, bds 137 W Wayne.
Lumbard Georgie, bds 137 W Wayne.
Lumbard Mary A (wid Sanford), res 164 W Wayne.
Lumbard Sidney C, Insurance, Real Estate and Loans, 3 Aveline House Blk, res 137 W Wayne. Tel office 221, res 11.
Lund Caroline H, bds 172 W Creighton av.
Lund Catherine W, stenographer, bds 172 W Creighton av.
Lund Henry M, Mantels, Fire Places and Tiling, 172 W Creighton av, res same.
Lundy Wm, peddler, bds 109 Glasgow av.
Lunger Frank, pipe liner, bds 40 E Jefferson.
Lunn James, laborer, res 40 E Jefferson.

Lunz George H, lab Penn Co, res 281 W Jefferson.
Lupke Gustave O, laborer, res 71 Gay.
Lupton Lawson P, clk W R Frederick, bds 266 Calhoun.
Lupton Patrick C, engr G R & I R R, rms 292 Calhoun.
Lusch Lizzie, cook F C Cratsley, bds 78 Barr.
Luther Maggie, laundress School for F M Y.
Lutheran Church of the Redeemer, n w cor Washington
     and Fulton.
Luthy Lena, domestic 138 E Wayne.
Luttmann Wm C, helper, res 85 Holman.
Lutze Julia F (wid John H), toll gate keeper Huntington
     toll gate, res same.
Lutze Lida, domestic 32 W Washington.
Lutze Philip, bds 21 Calhoun.
Lydick Frank, lab Olds' Wagon Wks, bds 43 Hugh.
Lydolph Eliza (wid Frederick), bds 99 E Main.
Lyle, see also Lile.
Lyle John, laborer, bds 7 Winch.
Lyle John G, blksmith Bass Wks, res 328 E Jefferson.
Lyman Charles H, toll gate keeper Bluffton rd res county
     farm.
Lyman Laura J, bkkpr F L Jones & Co, bds 48 E 4th.
Lyman Walter F, blksmith City Carriage Wks, res 164
     Hayden.
Lynch Catherine, cook Grand Central Hotel.
Lynch Edward J, fireman G R & I R R, bds 284 Harrison.
Lynch Frank J, wheelmaker, bds 322 Lafayette.
Lynch James, fireman, bds 33 St Mary's av.
Lynch Jeremiah C, engineer N Y, C & St L R R, rms 14
     St Mary's av.
Lynch John, blacksmith, res 322 Lafayette.
Lynch John, laborer, res 152 Shawnee av.
Lynch John J, coppersmith Penn Co, bds 284 Harrison.
Lynch Julia A, bds 284 Harrison.
Lynch Mary A (wid Matthias), res 284 Harrison.
Lynch Nellie, bds 322 Lafayette.
Lynch Thomas J, fireman, bds 284 Harrison.
Lynch Wm J, laborer, bds 284 Harrison.
Lyne Rebecca W (wid Wm), res 111 W Jefferson.
Lynn George W, watchman, bds 40 E 5th.
Lynn Martha (wid Lewis), bds 24 W Wayne.
Lyon Gertrude D, opr F L Jones & Co, bds 10 Ewing.
Lyons Charles F, clk N Y, C & St L R R, bds 40 Harrison.
Lyons Mrs Jennie R, res over 40 Harrison.
Lyons Robert J, engr Penn Co, rms 65 Baker.

Lyttle, *see also Little.*
Lyttle Benjamin L, helper Wabash R R, res 43 Locust.

Mc

McAdam Robert W, clk F. Ft W & W Ry, bds 39 Brackenridge.
McAfee James T, driver L H McAfee, bds 3 Wells.
McAfee L Harry, livery, 1 Wells, res 3 same.
McAfee Mary E (wid Wm J), milliner, 3 Wells res same.
McAfee Samuel, blksmith Penn Co. res 148 E Creighton av.
McAllister George W, grocer 500 Broadway, res 45 Huestis av.
McAllister Jessie E, bds 45 Huestis av.
McAllister Kate M, bkkpr, bds 45 Huestis av.
McArdle Thomas P, conductor, res 72 Thomas.
McBennett Francis, contr, 410 Lafayette, res same.
McBennett Frank J, removed to Bay City, Mich.
McBride Brenton, laborer, res 12 Custer av.
McBride George C, storekpr Penn Co, res 374 Calhoun.
McBride John C, res 169 Harrison.
McCaffery Arminda M (wid Wm), res 4 Jenison.
McCaffery Wm H, machinist, bds 4 Jennison.
McCaffrey David F, bds 16 Walnut.
McCaffrey John F, brakeman, bds 16 Walnut.
McCaffrey Mary (wid Cormick), res 16 Walnut.
McCaffrey Thomas J, bds 16 Walnut.
McCague James, lab M Bisson, res Jefferson twp.
McCain Emma D, bds 378 Calhoun.
McCain Mrs Emma J, res 378 Calhoun.
McCain John B, bds 378 Calhoun.
McCain Margaret A (wid Wm), bds 132 E Berry.
McCall John O, laborer, res 51 Baker.
McCall Joseph C, waiter, rms 29 Grand.
McCall Julia, knitter, rms 58 W Lewis.
McCanahy Mrs Bertie, asst School for F M Y.
McCann John, contr, 65 Grand, res same.
McCann Margaret, opr S M Foster, bds 65 Grand.
McCann Mary B, opr S M Foster, bds 65 Grand.
McCann Simon J, laborer, bds 65 Grand.
McCann Timothy J, molder Kerr Murray Mnfg Co, bds 65 Grand.
McCarthy Alice, knitter, bds 494 W Main.

McCarthy Andrew, laborer, bds 494 W Main.
McCarthy Ann J (wid Andrew), res 494 W Main.
McCarthy Anna C, clk People's Store, bds 3 Colerick.
McCarthy Catherine, bds 27 Bass.
McCarthy Daniel S, appr R Spice, bds 154 W Superior.
McCarthy Dennis, engr N Y, C & St L R R, res 154 W Superior.
McCarthy Dennis S, hostler Penn Co, res 27 Bass.
McCarthy Ellen, bds 3 Colerick.
McCarthy James, laborer, bds 231 Barr.
McCarthy James J, laborer, bds 494 W Main.
McCarthy John C, engr Penn Co, res 73 E De Wald.
McCarthy John F, mach hd Penn Co, bds 494 W Main.
McCarthy Maggie, housekeeper 311 E Creighton av.
McCarthy Mary, bds 3 Colerick.
McCarthy Mary (wid John), bds 7 Colerick.
McCarthy Michael, engr N Y, C & St L R R, res 165 W Superior.
McCarthy Patrick, res 3 Colerick.
McCarthy Richard A, brakeman, res 311 E Creighton av.
McCarthy Timothy S, engr Penn Co, res 27 Bass.
McCarthy Wm, removed to Chicago, Ill.
McCarty Ida, domestic 103 W Berry.
McCaskey George W, Physician and Surgeon, 107 W Main, res same. Tel 140.
McCausland Mrs Eva, bds 144 Pritchard.
McCausland John W, phys, 191 Lafayette, res 268 E Lewis. Tel 351.
McCaughey Wm F, gen sec Y M C A, res 251 W Washington
McClain, *see also McLain.*
McClain Anna, domestic 91 E Lewis
McClain Catherine, bds 91 Ewing.
McClain Hannah, bds 91 Ewing.
McClain Mary (wid Robert), res 91 Ewing.
McClellan Estella, stenogr S F Swayne, bds 28 E Williams.
McClellan Hattie, bds 28 E Williams.
McClellan Wm, bicycle repr, 59 E Columbia, bds 28 E Williams.
McClellan John A, brakeman, res 6 Thomas.
McClellan John Q, engr P, Ft W & C Ry, res 28 E Williams.
McClelland Frankie, bds n s Baltes 1 e of Spy Run av.
McClelland Jennie O, asst clk of the Boards. bds 15 Cass.
McClelland Samuel W, barber H H Stites, bds 15 Cass.
McClelland Wm H, clk Morgan & Beach, res 15 Cass.
McClintock Elizabeth (wid John). bds 69 Holman.

1

McClintock James E, lab Hoffman Bros, res 17 Wefel.
McClintock Sherman, driver L H McAfee, res 101 Putnam.
McClish Clara B, domestic 104 Barr.
McClure Andrew, res 20 Douglas av.
McClure David B, mach hd Hoffman Bros, res 225 W Main.
McClure Della, clerk, bds Andrew McDaniel.
McClure Hiram W, tailor, res 425 Calhoun.
McClure Jessie A, bkkpr Keller Elec Constr Co, bds 225 W Main.
McClure John H, clk Ft W Beef Co, res 424 E Wayne.
McClure Mary, prin Clay School, bds 126 E Wayne.
McClure Mary E, teacher Hoagland School, bds 20 Douglas av.
McClure Rosser, trav agt S F Bowser & Co, res 336 W Washington.
McClure Stella, bds Andrew McDaniel.
McCollem Anna E, seamstress, bds 225 W Superior.
McCollem Harry A, bds 225 W Superior.
McCollough Mary, rms 14 Chicago.
McComb John (col'd), porter The Randall, res 31 Grand.
McConnell Andrew, res 90 Force.
McConnell Charles, clerk, bds 183 W Superior.
McConnell Ettie M, bds 90 Force.
McConnell Joseph L, res 183 W Superior.
McConnell Mary T (wid August W), res 17 Ross.
McConnell Thomas, hostler, bds 266 E Washington.
McCormick Ada M, bds 2 Zollars av.
McCormick Firman C, student, bds 2 Zollars av.
McCormick George B, condr N Y, C & St L R R, res 14 Jackson.
McCormick James N (Search & McCormick), res Toledo, O.
McCormick Pearl R, student, bds 2 Zollars av.
McCormick Thomas H, Physician, 6 White Bank Blk, res 2 Zollars av. Tel 184.
McCormick Thomas H jr, student, bds 2 Zollars av.
McCormick Wm. carpenter, res 20 Stopblet.
McCormick Willis W, inspector, bds 317 Harrison.
McCoy Charles, lab, res Lake av e of limits.
McCoy George, farmer, res Lake av e of limits.
McCoy John W, mach Penn Co, res 60 Park av.
McCracken Bessie E, teacher, bds 271 W Wayne.
McCracken Fred C. student, bds 271 W Wayne.
McCracken Harvey M, railroad contr, res w s Spy Run av 1 n of Elizabeth.
McCracken James K, res 271 W Wayne. Tel 4.

McCracken Maud, society editress Ft Wayne Sentinel, bds 271 W Wayne.

McCrimmon Anna G (wid Samuel), res 46 E Jefferson.

McCrory George S, res 77 Lafayette.

McCulloch Alfred G, laborer, bds 230 Harmer.

McCulloch Charles, pres Hamilton National Bank, res 122 W Wayne. Tel 283.

McCulloch Jennie, bds Maggie McCulloch.

McCulloch John Ross, teller Hamilton National Bank, bds 122 W Wayne.

McCulloch Kate M (wid Samuel), res 230 Harmer.

McCulloch Maggie, toll gate keeper, res w s Spy Run av opposite Leo Gravel rd.

McCulloch Mary B, bds 107 W Berry.

McCulloch Park, e s Broadway bet Wabash and Penn R Rs.

McCulloch Robert A, night distributing clerk P O, bds 230 Harmer.

McCulloch School, n w cor McCulloch and Eliza.

McCullough Thomas P, Physician, Office Hours 7 to 9 a m. 2 to 3 p m and 7 to 8 p m, 180 Harrison, res 34 Douglas av, Tel 200.

McCumsey Ansel M, laborer, res 47 E De Wald.

McCune Andrew, mach hd Olds' Wagon Wks, bds 64 Baker.

McCune George H, bds 86 Organ av.

McCurdy Andrew R, clk Geo De Wald & Co, res 45 E 3d.

McCurdy George, clk W L Carnahan Co, bds 45 E 3d.

McCurdy John S, Dentist 21 W Berry, res s e cor Harrison and 3d.

McCutcheon Frederick D, sec, treas and mngr Brenzinger Bread Baking Co, rms 47 Douglas av.

McDaniel Alexander, justice of the peace, res 61 Elizabeth.

McDaniel Andrew, lab, res s e cor Lynn av and Bush.

McDaniel Frank, conductor, res 269 E Creighton av.

Mc Daniel George R, press feeder The Journal, bds 61 Elizabeth.

Mc Daniel Nellie, bds Andrew Mc Daniel.

Mc Dermott James, res 317 Calhoun.

Mc Dermut Willis, moved to Chicago.

Mc Dole Henry G, mach hd Penn Co, res 73 Home av.

Mc Donald Charles J, blacksmith. bds 11 Grand.

Mc Donald Donald, student, bds 280 W Wayne.

Mc Donald Emmet H (Mc Donald & Watt). res 280 W Wayne. Tel 130.

Mc Donald Esther, bds 252 W Wayne.

Mc Donald John, helper Fleming Mnfg Co, res 231 Wells.

Mc Donald John D, mngr Lakeside St Ry, bds 110 E Wayne.

Mc Donald John G, Plumber and Gasfitter, 17 N Calhoun, res same.

Mc Donald John W, asst supt Met Life Ins Co, bds 17 N Calhoun.

Mc Donald Margaret H (wid Archibald J), res 182 E De Wald.

Mc Donald Mary (wid David), bds S C Driver.

Mc Donald Oren C, apprentice, bds 17 N Calhoun.

Mc Donald Oscar, candymaker, bds 17 N Calhoun.

Mc Donald Patrick J, clk City Water Wks, res 131 Griffith.

Mc Donald Perry, yd brakeman Penn Co, res 92 Thomas.

Mc Donald Ronald T, pres Ft Wayne Artificial Ice Co, Ft Wayne Dist Tel Co; vice-pres Jenney Electric Light and Power Co, and Ryan Trucking Co, treas and mngr Ft Wayne Electric Corp, treas Star Iron Tower Co, pres Ft Wayne Land and Improvement Co, res 252 W Wayne. Tel. 50

Mc Donald Sarah M, bds 182 E De Wald.

Mc Donald Thomas E, engr Penn Co, res 527 Calhoun.

Mc Donald Vinie, domestic 26 Clay.

Mc Donald & Watt (Emmet H Mc Donald, Wm H Watt), whol grocers, 141 and 143 Calhoun. Tel 209.

Mc Donell Charles J, bds 11 Grand.

Mc Donell Helen, milliner, bds 11 Grand.

Mc Donell May A, bds 11 Grand.

Mc Donnell John M, clk N Y, C & St L R R, res 20 Van Buren.

McDonnell Oliver P, switchman, rms 92 Thomas.

McDonough Anthony, clk Root & Co, res 13 E Williams.

McDonough Hannah J (wid James), bds 250 W Creighton av

McDorman John E, blksmith Penn Co, res 193 Calhoun.

McDougall, see also MacDougal.

McDougall Celia, domestic School for F M Y.

McDougall Ella, cook County Poor Farm.

McDougall's Blk, n w cor Calhoun and Berry.

McDowell Wm, brakeman, res 12 Huron.

McElfatrick Charles L, mach Penn Co, res 166 Hanna.

McElfatrick John E, carpenter, bds 103 W Main.

McElfatrick Lena C, clk S F Bowser & Co, bds 219 Madison

McElfatrick Mrs Mary A, boarding, 103 W Main, res same

McElfish George W, park attdt, res 360 W Washington.

McEvoy Francis G, student, bds 135 Lafayette.

McEvoy James B, student, bds 135 Lafayette.

McEvoy James H, train disp G R & I R R, res 135 Lafayette.

McEvoy John C, clk Ft W News, bds 135 Lafayette.

McFee Daniel T, engr N Y, C & St L R R, res 321 Jefferson.

McFee Margaret (wid Wm), bds 330 W Jefferson.

McFeely Jackson H, painter Fleming Mnfg Co, res 182 Breck.

McFerran Benjamin H, clk Penn. Co, res 34 W Jefferson.

McFerran George H, fireman N Y, C & St L R R, res 97 Wilt.

McFerran Jane (wid Milton L), res 345 W Jefferson.

McFerran S Milton, engraver, 31 Schmitz Blk, res 345 W Jefferson.

McGary Michael, brakeman Penn Co, res 182 John.

McGaw Anna R, bds 169 W Jefferson.

McGaw Cassius H, winder, bds 169 W Jefferson.

Mc Gaw Emily A (wid Thomas), res 169 W Jefferson.

Mc Gee, see also Mc Kay and Mc Kee.

Mc Gee Elizabeth, bds 175 Clinton.

Mc Gee Mrs Irene, bds 175 Clinton.

Mc Gee Maria, res 175 Clinton.

Mc Gee Martha, clk A Mergentheim, bds 175 Clinton.

Mc Gee Patrick, condr G R & I R R, res 264 E Creighton av.

Mc Gee Thomas S, engr Penn Co, res 279 W Creighton av

Mc Ginnis Alvin O, laborer, bds 76 Barr.

Mc Ginnis Daniel, roofer, res 76 Barr.

Mc Ginnis Grace, bds 76 Barr.

Mc Ginnis Thomas V, fireman, res 3 Pape av.

Mc Govern Andrew, driver City Trucking Co, bds 159 Harrison.

Mc Govern Edward, driver City Trucking Co, bds 159 Harrison.

Mc Govern Sarah, laundress The Randall.

Mc Gowan John, died July 7th, 1894.

Mc Gowan Mary (wid Hugh), bds 151 Barr.

Mc Grady Charles E, barn man, res 25 Calhoun.

Mc Grady Mrs Eliza, res 91 W Washington.

Mc Grady John D, washer Powers & Barnett, bds 59 W Superior.

Mc Grath Wm H, res 221 W Wayne.

Mc Guire, see also Maguire.

Mc Guire Bessie W, bds 16 Baker.

Mc Guire Frank N, fireman G R & I R R, res 117 W De Wald.

McGuire Herbert F, student, bds 86 Dawson.
Mc Guire Owen E, switch tndr Penn Co, res 16 Baker.
Mc Guire Peter F, fireman Penn Co, res 86 Dawson.
McGuire Thomas, engr G R & I R R, bds Hotel Rich.
McGushin Patrick, engr N Y, C & St L R R, bds 33 St Mary's av.
McHenry J Wm W, brakeman, res 84 Baker.
Mc Hugh James E, phys 240 E Creighton av, res same.
McIntyre John H, fireman Penn Co, res 154 Taber.
McIntyre Sarah, domestic 221 W De Wald.
McKay, see also McGee and McKee.
McKay Christina, bds 134 W Main.
McKay David, steward J H Bass, Brookside.
McKay Florentine B, mach hd Fleming Mnfg Co, res 6 Pape av.
McKay James M (G E Bursley & Co), res 97 Lake av.
McKay Nellie M, teacher Clay School, bds 97 Lake av.
McKay Roy, bds 6 Breck.
McKeag Agnes T, dressmkr, bds 149 Fairfield av.
McKeag Ellen, teacher High School, res 149 Fairfield av.
McKean, see also McKeon.
McKean Anna M, stenogr T E Ellison, bds E W McKean.
McKean Elizabeth (wid Wm T), res w s Spy Run av, 3 s of Ruth.
McKean Hugh W S, mach Ft W I Wks, bds E W McKean.
McKean John L, engr C L Centlivre Brewing Co, bds E W McKean.
McKean Milton H, bkkpr J C Peltier, bds E W McKean.
McKean Sarah E, teacher, bds E W McKean.
McKee see also McGee and McKay.
McKee Annie, seamstress, bds 170 W Washington.
McKee George W, solicitor, res 425 E Lewis.
McKee Horace, teamster, bds 156 Greeley.
McKee Jefferson F, lab Hoffmann Bros, res 13 Pape av.
McKee John L, lab Hoffman Bros, res 71 W 3d.
McKeeman David C, carpenter, res 51 Prince.
McKeeman Wm, contr, 91 Organ av, res same.
McKelly Alice J (wid James), res 324 Calhoun.
McKendry Anna M, bds 36 Masterson.
McKendry Charles A, fireman G R & I R R, bds 36 Masterson.
McKendry Daniel, asst city engineer, res 36 Masterson.
McKendry Daniel J, bkkpr Fisher Bros, res 361 E Wayne.
McKendry James B, bkkpr, bds 36 Masterson.
McKenzie Caleb I, painter, res 148 Smith.

McKenzie Edward, barber, bds 83 Buchanan.
McKenzie George, mach Wabash R R, res 121 Butler.
McKenzie John L, carpenter, bds 148 Smith.
McKenzie John W, bds 121 W Butler.
McKenzie Mariette, bds 39 W Washington.
McKeon, see also McKean.
McKeon Charles M, clerk, bds 152 W Wayne.
McKeon James, bds 152 W Wayne.
McKering Dennis L, foreman, res 48 Centre.
McKinley Anna, bds 93 Wagner.
McKinley Otis, pressman Ft W Sentinel, bds 141 Cass.
McKinley Perry, motorman Ft W E R R Co, res 141 Cass.
McKinley Raymond E, bds 141 Cass.
McKinley Reginald, teamster, bds 141 Cass.
McKinney Charles N, lineman P, Ft W & Chicago Ry, res
    72 E Williams.
McKinnie House, Wm M McKinnie propr, Penn depot.
    Tel 103.
McKinnie Joseph, clk McKinnie House, rms same.
McKinnie Wm M, Propr The Wayne and McKin-
    nie House, res The Wayne.
McLachlan, see also MacLachlan and McLaughlin.
McLachlan Annie J, stenogr Seavey Hardware Co, bds 160
    E Wayne.
McLachlan Jane (wid Neil), res 66 W Creighton av.
McLachlan Jessie, bds 158 W Berry.
McLachlan John B, machinist, rms 261 E Creighton av.
McLachlan Mary E (wid James C), res 160 E Wayne.
McLachlan Nancy C, bds 66 W Creighton av.
McLachlan Wm, trav agt Ft W I Wks, res 158 W Berry.
McLain, see also McClain.
McLain Benoni P, res 23 Prospect av.
McLain Charles J, bkkpr S C Lumbard, res 132 W
    Creighton av.
McLain Zeruiah E, teacher Bloomingdale School, bds 23
    Prospect av.
McLaughlin, see also McLachlan.
McLaughlin Aaron, driver City Trucking Co, bds 159
    Harrison.
McLaughlin Eugene F, winder Ft W Elec Corp, res 83
    Taylor.
McLaughlin Henry C, watchman, res 32 Oak.
McLaughlin James, bds 241 W De Wald.
McLaughlin John, fireman N Y, C & St L R R, bds 352
    W Main.

McLaughlin John L, res 241 W De Wald.
McLaughlin Mary, bds 241 W De Wald.
McLaughlin Mary A (wid James), bds 151 Barr.
McLaughlin Mary C, bds 103 W Washington.
McLaughlin Thomas J, clerk R M S, res 373 Hanna.
McLaughlin Wm, coremkr Bass F & M Wks, bds 16 Gay.
McLaughlin Wm, stenogr, bds 241 W De Wald.
McLean, see also McClain and McLain.
McLeish Duncan tool inspr Penn Co, res 7 Liberty.
McLeish Francis M, clerk J B White, res 3 Liberty.
McLeod Will S, bkkpr A L Johns & Co, bds 25 W Lewis.
McLetchie Hattie M (wid John), res 262 E Wayne.
McLetchie Hugh, commission, bds 254 Clinton.
Mc Mahan John W, coachman, res 66 W Butler.
Mc Mahan Sophia, bds 273 W Main.
Mc Mahan Wm, laborer, bds 66 W Butler.
Mc Mahon Sylvester, condr Penn Co, res 324 Broadway.
Mc Mahon Wm M, teamster, res 152 Holman.
Mc Maken Dorothy (wid Gettys), res 104 Cass.
Mc Maken Frank A, plumber R Spice, res 19 N Calhoun.
Mc Maken Lizzie, bds 104 Cass.
Mc Manigal George M, clk Penn Co, bds 10 Highland.
Mc Manigal Harry, bds 10 Highland.
Mc Manigal James L, waiter, bds 10 Highland.
Mc Manigal Mahala (wid Josiah), res 10 Highland.
Mc Millan Edward, switchman Wabash R R, bds 60 Chicago.
Mc Millan John V, foreman L E & W R R, res 36 E 5th.
Mc Millen Harry M, bds Mary A Mc Millen.
Mc Millen Mary A (wid James B), res n s Richardson 2 w Runnion av.
Mc Mullen Henry, day clk Police headquarters, res 199 Oakland.
Mc Mullen James, engr Penn Co, res 73 Charles.
Mc Mullen John, contr, 70 Charles, res same.
Mc Mullen Lizzie, domestic The Wayne.
Mc Mullen Mary (wid Michael), bds 410 Lafayette.
Mc Mullen Maud, laundress Mc Kinnie House.
Mc Nair Mary E (wid Charles), bds 138 W De Wald.
Mc Nally Charles J, molder, bds 69 Grand.
Mc Nally Emmet, lab Ft W Furn Co, bds 69 Grand.
Mc Nally John J (J J Mc Nally & Co), bds 110 E Wayne.
McNally John J & Co (John J McNally), Insurance and Investments, 33 Bass Blk, 77 Calhoun. (See adv next page.)

29

John J. McNally & Co.,

INSURANCE AND INVESTMENTS,

Fire,	Loans,
Life and	Mortgages
Accident	and other
Insurance,	Investments.

None but First Class Insurance Companies Represented

33 BASS BLOCK, FORT WAYNE, INDIANA.

McNally Mary A (wid John), res 69 Grand.
McNally Robert E, laborer, bds 69 Grand.
McNally Wm A, laborer, bds 69 Grand.
McNamara Frank, teamster. bds s e cor Organ and Fair-
field avs.
McNamara John, laborer, bds 174 Greeley.
McNamara John, motorman Ft W E R Co, bds 48 Walter.
McNamara John, section hd, res 46 Runnion av.
McNamara J Boyd, bds s e cor Organ and Fairfield avs.
McNamara John J, bds e s Runnion av 5 s of canal feeder.
McNamara John W, solicitor Ft Wayne Sentinel, res 226
Calhoun.
McNamara Peter, foreman, res 9 Runnion av.
McNamara Thomas, laborer, res 194 Broadway.
McNamara Wm J, teamster, res s e cor Organ and Fair-
field avs.
McNaught Duncan, stone cutter Wm Geake, res 63 W 5th.
McNearney Julia, bds 66 McClellan.
McNearney Mary, matron Penn Co, bds 66 McClellan.
McNearney Thomas, lab Penn Co, res 66 McClellan.
McNulty Frank J, appr Bass F & M Wks, bds 247 Webster.

McNulty John, plumber A Hattersley & Sons, res 247 Webster.
McNulty Margaret, milliner, bds 247 Webster.
McNulty Mary (wid Anthony), res 11 Grand.
McNulty Wm, died May 7th, 1894.
McNutt Henry T, mach, bds 505 Calhoun.
McNutt Lorenzo D, supt Ft W E Ry Co, res 505 Calhoun.
McNutt Norian V, bds 505 Calhoun.
McNutt Williard C, painter Ft W E Ry Co, res 229 W DeWald.
McOscar Amos J, removed to Chicago, Ill.
McOscar Edward J, Physician, office hours 8 a m, 2 to 3 and 7 to 8 p m, 29 W Jefferson, res same. Tel 230.
McOscar Mary S (wid John), res 29 W Jefferson.
McPhail Janet A, teacher Jefferson School, bds 192 Ewing.
McPhail Laura (wid Wm), res 185 Ewing.
McPhail Margaret M, prin Bloomingdale School, bds 192 Ewing.
McPhail Mary R, bds 192 Ewing.
McPhail Wm, mach. res 192 Ewing.
McPherson Angus, Agent Empire (Fast Freight) Line, 26 Court, rms 28 Schmitz Blk. Tel 49.
McQuarrie Allan, res 28 Home av.
McQuillan Thomas H, mngr White Sewing Mach Co, 19 W Wayne, bds 175 Lafayette.
McQuiston Allan P, res Washington twp.
McQuiston Benjamin J, trustee Washington Twp, 19 Bank Blk, res Washington Twp.
McQuiston Jane, bds 70 Wells.
McQuiston May, nurse, bds 43 2d.
McQuistion John, res 70 Wells.
McQuiston Leona B, bds 43 2d.
McQuiston Wilson, bkkpr, res 43 2d.
McVey John H L, bds 3 De Groff.
McVey Margaret, seamstress, bds 3 De Groff.
McVey Mary, seamstress, bds 3 De Groff.
McVey Michael, res 3 De Groff.
McWhirter Lucile, teacher, bds 48 W Leith.
McWhorter Court O, printer Archer Prtg Co, bds 57 W 3d.
McWhorter John W, cooper, res 57 W 3d.
McWhorter Lawrence L, printer Ft W Gazette, bds 57 W 3d.
McWhorter Minnie M, clk, bds 57 W 3d.
McWhorter Wm A, printer Aldine Prtg House, bds 57 W 3d.

M

Mac Dougal. *see also Mc Dougall.*
Mac Dougal Catherine M, bds 143 W Wayne.
Mac Dougal John, res 143 W. Wayne.
Mac Dougal Michael C (Mac Dougal & Co), res 151 Wayne.
Mac Dougal & Co (Michael C Mac Dougal, Ephraim P Dailey), proprs Paragon Mnfg Co, 87 and 89 E Columbia.
Mack Catherine, domestic 137 W Wayne.
Mack Elizabeth E, dressmkr, 274 Webster, res same.
Mack Regina (wid Frederick), bds 274 Webster.
Mackie, *see Mc Kay and Mc Kee.*
Mac Lachlan, *see also Mc Lachlan.*
Mac Lachlan Andrew F, trav agt Mc Donald & Watt, res 306 W Washington.
Mac Laughlin, *see Mc Lachlan and Mc Laughlin.*
Mac Tavish Angus, tailor John Rabus, bds Columbia House
Madden Amanda (wid Allen), res 104 E Wayne.
Madden Clifford, bds 88 E Columbia.
Madden Jacob, night inspr Jenney E L & P Co, res n e cor Lake and Franklin.
Madden James D, plumber, 39 Baker, res same.
Madden John, laborer, res 210 Calhoun.
Madden John, merchant police, res 88 E Columbia.
Madden Martin G, baker Fox br U S Bkg Co, bds 88 E Columbia.
Madden Michael P, bartender, res 73 Brackenridge.
Madden Nicholas, laborer, res 195 Hayden.
Madden Virginia, bds 104 E Wayne.
Madden Wm K, truckman Penn Co, res 6 Kansas.
Maddox Joseph, helper, res 68 Howell.
Maddox Rachel D (wid John), bds e s Sherman 2 n of Huffman.
Maddux Wm A, carp N Y, C & St L R R, res 133 Sherman.
Madison Wm J, mach Penn Co, res 38 E Butler.
Maer, *see also Maher, Maier Mayer Meier Meyer and Myers*
Magers, *see also Majors.*
Magers Charles J, lab Ft W Elec Corp, bds 90 Maple av.
Magers Esther, coremkr Ft W Elec Corp, bds 90 Maple av.
Magers Frank X, coachman P A Randall, res 90 Maple av.
Magers John F, winder Ft W Elec Corp, bds 90 Maple av.
Magner Clara, bds 67 W Butler.
Magner Clara, domestic 141 W Berry.

Magner Edwin, helper Penn Co, bds 68 Gay.
Magner Eli, painter J H Brimmer, bds 196 Hanna.
Magner Eli E, res s s Pennsylvania 1 e of Wayne Trace.
Magner Oliver, helper Penn Co, bds 68 Gay.
Magnus Ellen F, bds 124 Buchanan.
Magnus Wm F, lab Penn Co, res 124 Buchanan.
Maguire, see also McGuire.
Maguire Anna (wid Edward), res 338 W Main.
Maguire Anna M, bds 338 W Main.
Maguire Frederick J, student, bds 64 McClellan.
Maguire John B, postal clerk, res 64 McClellan.
Maher, see also Maier, Mayer, Meier, Meyer and Myers.
Maher Edward J, finisher Ft W Organ Co, res 76 Charles.
Maher James L, finisher Penn Co, bds 76 Charles.
Mahl, see also Mehl.
Mahl Frank, teamster, bds 6 Dwenger av.
Mahoney James A, died April 17th, 1895.
Mahoney Kate, domestic 42 Maumee rd.
Mahoney Mary, domestic 144 W Berry.
Mahoney Neal, helper, bds 56 Smith.
Mahrt Conrad, harnessmkr F Hilt, res 42 Pritchard.
Mahurin Marshall S (Wing & Mahurin), res 388 Fairfield
    av.   Tel 487.
Maibucher Joseph, grocer 162 Montgomery, bds same.
Maier, see also Maher, Mayer, Meier, Meyer and Myers.
Maier Frederick H, printer, bds 94 Wells.
Maier Sigmund, clk Weil Bros, res 193 E Washington.
Mailand, see also Mayland.
Mailey, see also Maley.
Mailey Annie, bds 270 Harrison.
Mailey Bessie, seamstress, bds 276 W Jefferson.
Mailey Katie, seamstress, bds 270 Harrison.
Mailey Patrick, watchman N Y, C & St L R R, res 270
    Harrison.
Maines Charles C, condr Penn Co, res 218 Walton av.
Maines Henry C, bkr Fox br U S Bkg Co, res 154 Har-
    rison.
Maines Laura, bds 218 Walton av.
Maisch Anna, bds 172 Gay.
Maisch August C, bds 172 Gay.
Maisch Mrs Catherine, res 266 Gay.
Maisch Jacob, janitor, res 172 Gay.
Major David H, helper Wabash R R, res 57 Smith.
Major David W, cigarmkr M A Schele, bds 57 Smith
Major Ella M (wid James), res 143 Horace.

Major Roxena, clk Seibert & Good, bds 57 Smith.
Major Trevor J, helper, bds 57 Smith.
Majors see also Magers.
Majors Mrs Adda, dressmaker, 13 E Williams, res same.
Majors Phoebe (wid John), res s s w 4th 2 e of Sherman.
Majors Thomas J, foreman Bourie & Cook, res 358 Calhoun.
Majors Walter, laborer, bds Phoebe Majors.
Makepeace Augustus K, condr Nickel Plate, res 71 W 4th.
Malcolm Ina, bds 246 W De Wald.
Malcolm Maude M, bds 44 W Williams.
Malcolm Sherman E, real estate, res 44 Williams.
Maley, see also Mailey.
Maley Bridget (wid Patrick), bds 15 Brandriff.
Maley John J. laborer, bds 14 Brandriff.
Malle Mary (wid Henry), res 187 E Jefferson.
Malle Wm, asst Schone & Veith, res 187 E Jefferson.
Malloy Frances (wid Wm), milliner 12 Arcade Bldg, res The Randall.
Malnowski Gustave, lab Bass F & M Wks, res 65 John.
Malone Bridget (wid Patrick), bds 111 Wallace.
Malone John, condr G R & I R R, res 171 Montgomery.
Malone Patrick E, engineer Penn Co, res 111 Wallace.
Malone Peter, grocer 167 Broadway, res same.
Malone Rose, dressmkr 111 Wallace, bds same.
Malone Thomas, condr G R & I R R, rms 303 Calhoun.
Maloney Frank, fireman N Y, C & St L R R, bds 33 St Mary's av.
Malone Michael, watchman Penn Co, res 1 Thomas.
Malzer Hermann, laborer, res 24 Erie.
Manary John C, carp Penn Co, res 103 W Washington.
Mandeville Jacob H, stenogr S Bash & Co, res 170 Maumee rd.
Manet Adeline (wid Edward), res 214 Madison.
Manet C Edward, barber 329 Spy Run av, res 240 Madison.
Manet Edward, laborer, bds 28 E Columbia.
Manett Mrs Matilda, bds 100 Montgomery.
Mangan Bridget (wid Patrick), res 3 Walnut.
Mangan Thomas J, brakeman, res 38 Hendricks.
Mangels Anna, domestic Concordia College.
Mangels Elizabeth, tailoress, bds 63 Maumee rd.
Mangels Mary (wid Claus), res 63 Maumee rd.
Manier August F, clk Princess Cash Store, bds 165 Clinton.
Manier Frank, helper Penn Co, res 144 Holman.
Manier Joseph P, rim maker, res 135 Thomas.

Manier Minnie J, bds 144 Holman.
Mann Clyde D, brakeman G R & I R R, bds 425 Calhoun.
Mann George E, motorman, res 67 Grant av.
Mann Isaac N, truckman Penn Co, res 30 Eliza.
Mann James G, shoes, 25 Calhoun, rms same.
Manion Wm J, electrician, rms 37 Baker.
Mannheimer Isaac, trav agt, res 237 W Wayne.
Manning, see also Monning.
Manning Thomas F, foreman N Y, C & St L R R, res 276 W Jefferson.
Mannix Frank J, machinist, bds 10 Holman.
Mannix Mamie, bds 10 Holman.
Mannix Thomas, mail agt Wabash R R, res 10 Holman.
Mannix Wm T, clk County Treas, res 39 Edgewater av.
Mannok Charles, cigarmkr, res 4 Elm.
Mannor Wm A, switchman, res 92 Wilt.
Mannweiler Christian, res 23 Duryea.
Mannweiler Herman, boilermkr, bds 23 Duryea.
Mannweiler Mary A (wid Martin), bds 174 Fairfield av.
Manok John, boilermkr Penn Co, res 509 E Washington.
Manon Wm A, clk Mossman, Yarnelle & Co, res 197 E Jefferson.
Mansdofer Annie, domestic 411 W Main.
Manstoeffer Charles, lab, res nr Orphans Home of the Reformed Church.
Manth Albert F W, clk Gross & Pellins, bds 56 Buchanan.
Manth Jeannette (wid Julius), res 56 Buchanan.
Manth Louis P, clk Meyer Bros & Co, bds 56 Buchanan.
Manth Louisa (wid Ephraim), bds 108 Maumee rd.
Manuel Alice R, bds 190 Brackenridge.
Manuel Francis J, clk People's Store, res 190 Brackenridge
Manuel Frank A, letter carrier P O, res 17 W Lewis.
Manuel Josephine J, clk County Recorder, bds 50 Douglas av.
Manuel Julius P, clk Sam, Pete & Max, res 223 W Jefferson.
Mapes Benjamin, laborer, rms 26 Harrison.
Maple Charles E, brakeman Penn Co, res 7 Winter.
Maple Wm B, laborer, res 66 Murray.
Marahrens Charles, lab Bass F & M Wks, res 36 Smith.
Marahrens Charles H, lab Ft W E Corp, bds 36 Smith.
Marc Charles, laborer 107 Fletcher av.
Marc Charles D, laborer, bds 107 Fletcher av.
Marchant S David, mach Penn Co, res 301 Hanna.
Marchel, see also Marshall.
Marchel Peter, gardener, n e cor New Haven and Lumbard.

Marhanke Augusta (wid Frederick), res 145 High.
Marhenke Christian, switchtender Penn Co. res 110 Madison
Marhenke Christian H, butcher, rms 110 Madison.
Marhenke Frederick H, cigarmkr, bds 110 Madison
Marhenke Mary, opr S M Foster, bds 110 Madison.
Marhenke Wm F, clk C W Schuler, bds 110 Madison.
Mariotte Benjamin (Mariotte Bros), res 266 Hoagland av.
Mariotte Bros (George and Benjamin), pawnbrokers, 20 W
    Main.
Mariotte George (Mariotte Bros), res w s Brooklyn av 1 n
    of Wabash R R.
Mariotte Horace, pawnbroker, 20 E Columbia. res 142 W
    Washington.
Markey Andrew J, ins agt, res 286 Broadway.
Markey Bros (Edd J and Willis J), florists, s e cor Jeffer-
    son and Ewing. Tel 41.
Markey Edd J (Markey Bros), res 109 W Jefferson.
Markey Eliza (wid Lawrence). res 344 Calhoun.
Markey Frank L, stenogr Vesey & Heaton, bds 109 W
    Jefferson.
Markey Frederick F, driver U S Exp Co, res 196 W
    Superior.
Markey Georgina, bds 286 Broadway.
Markey Hattie, bds 109 W Jefferson.
Markey Lawrence, died July 10th, 1894.
Markey Mary E, teacher Clay School, bds 286 Broadway.
Markey Nellie L, teacher Bloomingdale Schools, bds 286
    Broadway.
Markey Richard F, bkkpr First National Bank, res 414
    Calhoun.
Markey Willis J, Markey Bros, bds 111 W Jefferson.
Markley Daniel, agent, res 102 South Wayne av.
Markley Jennie E, bds 102 South Wayne av.
Marks Charles Q, brakeman, res 208 Walton av.
Marks Cora A, milliner, bds J J Marks.
Marks Cyrus C, laborer, bds J J Marks,
Marks John J, lab K Baker, res s w cor Sherman and
    Aboit.
Marks Maggie S, dressmkr, bds J J Marks.
Marks Margaret, domestic 37 Brackenridge.
Marks Philip W, laborer, bds J J Marks.
Marks Simon L, barber, 213 Lafayette, bds 264 E Wash-
    ington.
Marks Simon P, engine inspr Penn Co, res 264 E
    Washington.

Marks Wilbert T, mach Penn Co, res 367 Lafayette.
Maroney Michael, engr N Y, C & St L R R, res 29 W 4th
Maroney Thomas, bds 29 W 4th.
Marquardt Catherine (wid John), bds 117 E Lewis.
Marquardt Daniel A, clk Penn Co, bds 238 E Jefferson.
Marrott Frank, bds 11 Lavina.
Marsch Jacob G, cigarmkr A C Baker, bds 172 Gay.
Marschner Hugo, knitter, res 391 W Main.
Marsh Mrs Bertha, res 77 W 3d.
Marsh Charles W, engr Penn Co, rms 219 Lafayette.
Marshall, see also Marchal.
Marshall George, helper, res w s Turpie 1 s of Pontiac.
Marshall Peter, laborer, bds 89 Hanna.
Martin Alexander A, saloon 24 E Columbia, res same.
Martin Alice (wid Bernard), res 52 Baker.
Martin Allen, plumber E Martin, bds 359 Hanna.
Martin Allen G, ex messr, res 263 E Washington.
Martin Alonzo, painter, res 89 Hanna.
Martin Alvin L, Livery, Boarding, Hack and Coupe Line, Clinton n e cor Nickel Plate R R, res 14 Clinton. (See p 97.)
Martin Anna M (wid Lambert), res 206 W Washington.
Martin Annie G, trimmer, bds 235 E Washington.
Martin Anthony D, clerk Penn Co, res 191 Griffith.
Martin August C, laborer, res 111 N Harrison.
Martin Bernard H, brakeman, bds 4 E Butler.
Martin Bertha, domestic 99 E Wayne.
Martin Charles F, inspr Jenney E L & P Co, bds 12 Riverside av.
Martin Charlotte, bds 225 Broadway.
Martin Christian, driver, bds 225 Broadway.
Martin Christian F, laborer, res 73 John.
Martin Dennis, lab Penn Co, bds 58 Prince.
Martin Diederich, janitor E Luth School, res 57 Wilt.
Martin Edgar S, cigarmkr, rms 59 E Main.
Martin Edward, flagman Penn Co, rms 22 Baker.
Martin Edward, helper, res 235 E Washington.
Martin Edward, brakeman Penn Co, rms 226 Calhoun.
Martin Elizabeth, operator, bds 206 W Washington.
Martin Emma, res 115 W Superior.
Martin Emmett, Plumber, Steam and Gas Fitter, Hydrants, Sinks, Bath Tubs, Electric Wiring and Fixtures, etc, also Dealer in Sewer Pipe, cor Hanna and Buchanan, bds 359 Hanna. Tel 379.
Martin Frank, bds 359 Hanna.

Martin Frank, lab, Ft W E Corp, bds 46 Wall.
Martin Frank J, finisher, bds 111 N Harrison.
Martin Frederick, truckman Penn Co, res 73 John.
Martin George, removed to Chicago.
Martin Henry W, letter carrier P O, res 126 Smith.
Martin Jacob L, died April 9 1895.
Martin Mrs Jacob L, res 21 Euclid av.
Martin James E, bkkpr E Martin, bds 359 Hanna.
Martin James L, painter, bds w s Spy Run av 4 n of bridge
Martin John H painter, bds 89 Hanna.
Martin John L, stripper, bds 111 N Harrison.
Martin John W, teamster Jenney E L & P Co, bds 12 Riverside av.
Martin John W (Martin & Fitzsimmons), bds 25 W Jefferson.
Martin Leonard, lab Ft W Elec Corp, bds 46 Wall.
Martin Lester, fireman, bds 57 Barr.
Martin Lincoln, watchman C L Centlivre Brewing Co, res Centlivre's Park.
Martin Lottie, clerk, bds 225 Broadway.
Martin Louis E, clk Wm Hahn & Co, res 53 Hendricks.
Martin Mrs Margaret, boarding house, 89 Hanna.
Martin Mary T (wid John), res 12 Riverside av.
Martin Minnie, bds 57 Wilt.
Martin Minnie A. seamstress, bds 12 Riverside av.
Martin Paul, lab Penn Co, res w s Lumbard 1 n of Chestnut
Martin Rosa, domestic 15 Cass.
Martin Terence, blksmith Penn Co, res 359 Hanna.
Martin Victor, lab Penn Co, res Chestnut nr Lumbard.
Martin Wm, house mover, 225 Broadway, res same.
Martin Wm, motorman Ft W Elec Ry Co, res 2 Randolph.
Martin Wm E, mach hd, bds 15 Savannah.
Martin Wm F, engr Ft W Newsppr Union, bds 73 John.
Martin Wm H, lab Ft W Elec Corp, res 110 Chicago.
Martin Wm W. polisher Olds' Wagon Wks, res 63 Winter.
Martin & Fitzsimmons (John W Martin, Henry A L Fitzsimmons), Merchant Tailors 172 W Jefferson. (See p 107.)
Martz, see also Merz.
Martz Christian, physician, res 15 W Jefferson. Tel 195.
Martz Mary A (wid John G), res 27 E Creighton av.
Martz Susie, dressmkr 27 E Creighton av, res same.
Masbaum Anthony car bldr Penn Co, res 177 Madison.
Masbaum George G, res 221 E Washington.
Masel John, carpenter, bds 162 Huffman.

Masel Lena D, bds 162 Huffman.
Masel Martin, fireman, res 162 Huffman.
Masel Wm B, painter Paul Mnfg Co, bds 162 Huffman.
Mason David L, fireman Penn Co, res 353 Lafayette.
Mason Edward. laborer, bds 36 W 3d.
Mason George W, clerk, bds 353 Lafayette
Mason Melville A, dentist, 26 W Wayne, res 30 Lake av.
Mason Richard A, bds 406 Clinton.
Mason Sidney A, brakeman, bds 353 Lafayette.
Mason Walter A, hostler, 82 W Berry
Masonic Temple, n e Clinton and Wayne.
Masonic Temple Association, A Hattersley pres, W W.
    Rockhill sec, H W Mordhurst treas. proprs Masonic
    Temple, n e cor Clinton and Wayne.
Masonic Temple Theatre, F E Stouder and N S Smith
    lessees and mngrs, s e cor Wayne and Clinton. Tel 392
Masterson Ellis H, car repairer, res 391 E Washington.
Maston Jesse L, motorman, res 499 E Washington,
Mathews, *see also Matthews.*
Mathews John, laborer. res 53 E Main.
Mathia John, barnman, res 91 W Washington.
Mathieu Charles J, lab Bass Wks, bds Joseph Mathieu.
Mathieu Joseph, carp, res n s New Haven ave, nr Summer.
Mathis Eugene T, janitor Y M C A, res Main w of limits.
Mathis Lillian A. clk County Recorder, bds 391 Hanna.
Mathy Bernard G. malster C L Centlivre Brewing Co, bds
    n w cor Spy av and Edna.
Matott Charles T, conductor, res 129 Horace
Matsch Anna A S, student, bds 165 E Creighton av.
Matsch Catherine (wid Wm), res 82 Montgomery.
Matsch J Christopher, clk Bass F & M Wks, res 165 E
    Creighton av.
Matson Addie H (wid Harry). bds 59 Erie
Mattern Christian, foreman Hoffman Bros, res 12 Huron.
Mattes Jacob, watchman Penn Co, res 31 Julia.
Mattes Joseph, blksmith, 310 W Main, res 332 same.
Mattes Nicholas, laborer, res 59 Greene.
Matthews Daniel, conductor G R & I R R, rms 210 Calhoun
Matthews John (col'd); res 66 Murray.
Matthias Charles W, condr Ft W E Ry Co. bds 612 Calhoun
Matthias George H, laborer, res 8 Force.
Matthias John, laborer, res 612 Calhoun.
Matthias Theresa, bds 612 Calhoun.
Matz Frederick, fireman N Y, C & St L R R, bds 68 W
    Jefferson.

Mauck Francis M, conductor, res 61 Maud.
Maughan Thomas, fireman N Y, C & St L Ry, bds 71 Boone
Maul George, clk T Koenig, bds 95 Griffith.
Maulow Frederick, laborer, bds 67 John.
Maurer, *see also Mowrer.*
Maurer Gottlieb, laborer, res 179 Oakland.
Maurer Henry P, mattress mnfr, res 589 E Washington.
Maurer Jacob, lab Hoffman Bros, res 132 Franklin av.
Maurer Jacob, watchman Concordia College, res 587 E Washington.
Mauth Louis W P, clk Meyer Bros & Co, bds 59 Buchanan.
Mauthe John, laborer, res 537 E Washington.
Mauthe Martin, bartndr, res s e cor Spring and Sherman.
Mauthe Mary B, domestic 110 W Main.
Mautner Isadore (Mautner & Friedlich), res 171 W Wayne.
Mautner & Friedlich (Isadore Mautner, Isaac Friedlich), clothing, 58 Calhoun.
Maxwell David E, propr Jewel House, 225 Calhoun.
Maxwell Edward, lab Ft W Electric Corp, rms 45 Grand.
Maxwell Frank B, brakeman N Y, C & St L R R, res 11 Boone.
Maxwell Wm, teamster, res 181 Oakland.
Maxwell Wm D, carpenter, res 35 St Martin's.
May Mary, domestic The Randall.
May Patrick, bds 18 Cass
Mayer, *see also Maher, Maier, Meier, Meyer and Myers.*
Mayer Barbara, domestic 45 W Creighton av.
Mayer Bernard, butcher, res 118 Maumee rd.
Mayer Charles, mach Ft W Elec Corp, res 148 Taylor.
Mayer Charles E, painter, bds 6 Force.
Mayer Elenora (wid Louis), bds 47 E Lewis.
Mayer Frederick, stone mason, res 21 Barthold.
Mayer Gottlieb, laborer, res 104 St Mary's av.
Mayer Jacob G, Nice Hotel and Saloon, 6 Force, res same. (*See p 91.*)
Mayer Julia (wid Andrew), res 29 W Wayne.
Mayer Lawrence, res 47 E Jefferson.
Mayer Louis, clk A I & H Friend, bds 119 Brackenridge.
Mayer Mary, bds 47 E Jefferson.
Mayer Moses, clerk, bds 119 Brackenridge.
Mayer Pauline, with C A Hoffmann, 183 Calhoun.
Mayer Sophie, bds 47 E Jefferson.
Mayer Theodore, res 119 Brackenridge.
Mayer Ward B, trav agt. res 86 E Washington.

Mayflower Milling Co, C S Bash pres, J W Orr sec and treas, H E Bash genl mngr, 18 and 20 W Columbia. Tel 63.
Mayhew Allen, laborer, res n s Hicksville State rd 1 w of St Joe Gravel rd.
Mayhew Gertrude D, stenogr Ft W Elec Corp, bds 271 W Wayne.
Mayhew Grace, ironer W B Phillips, bds 428 E Wayne.
Mayhew Mary, nurse Hope Hospital.
Mayhew Mary E, stenogr Penn Co, bds 271 W Wayne.
Mayhew Nancy, supt Hope Hospital, res same.
Mayland August F, lab Ft W E Corp, bds 236 W Washington.
Mayland Ernst, bds 87 Maumee rd.
Mayland Henry F, lab Wm Geake, bds 236 W Washington
Mayland Louisa S, bds 236 W Washington.
Mayland Mary (wid Frederick), res 236 W Washington.
Mayland Pauline, dressmaker, res 55 Wilt.
Mayland Sophia D, bds 236 W Washington.
Mayo Wm A, bds 13 Marion.
Mayo Wm J, res 13 Marion.
Mayor's Office, City Hall. Tel 340.
Meads Zachariah (col'd), brakeman, rms 70 Murray.
Meckel Lulu, clerk, bds 55 Lake av.
Meckel Matilda (wid George). res 192 Taylor.
Meddaline Aman, pensioner, bds 230 W Main.
Medsker, see also Metker.
Medsker Emma M, bds 70 Baker.
Medsker Isaac N, trav agt, bds 473 Lafayette.
Medsker James R, mach Penn Co, res 70 Baker.
Medsker J Harry, trav agt Fisher Bros, res 236 Hoagland av.
Meegan Thomas, clk Penn Co, rms 110 E Berry.
Meehan Charles F, brakeman, bds 28 Brandriff.
Meehan Ella H, bds 28 Brandriff.
Meehan Frances C, tailoress, bds 260 E Jefferson.
Meehan James, laborer, bds 28 Brandriff.
Meehan James P, laborer, bds 260 E Jefferson.
Meehan Joseph N, molder, res s s Maumee rd e Lumbard.
Meehan Maggie, domestic Hotel Rich.
Meehan Margaret, bds 28 Brandriff.
Meehan Margaret (wid James), res 28 Brandriff.
Meehan Mary, tailoress, res 180 E Wayne.
Meehan Mary M (wid Lawrence), bds G D Ohneck,
Meehan Michael, res 260 E Jefferson.
Meehan Wm, lab Standard Wheel Co, bds 28 Brandriff.

Meek Charles W, tel opr N Y, C & St L R R, res 114 W Washington.
Meek Wm H, laborer, res 13 Monroe.
Meeks Elijah W, lawyer, 126 Eliza, res same.
Meeks U S Grant, winder Ft W Elec Corp, res 284 Broadway.
Meese Benjamin I, brakeman, res 117 Greene.
Meese John P, res w s Lafayette 1 n of Piqua av.
Mehl, see also Mahl.
Mehl Amos K, letter carrier P O, res 21 Elizabeth.
Mehl Frank W, clk Geo De Wald & Co, bds 225 Lafayette
Mehl George J, machinist, bds 225 Lafayette.
Mehl Mary (wid John), res 225 Lafayette.
Mehnert Louis, Blacksmith and Wagonmaker, 93 E Superior, res 69 same. (See p 101.)
Meier, see also Maher, Maier, Mayer, Meyer and Myers.
Meier Amelia, bds 99 Wilt.
Meier Annie, bds 310 Harrison.
Meier August, lab Penn Co, res 88 Stophlet.
Meier Caroline M, dressmaker, bds 99 Wilt.
Meier Charles F, gardener, bds 99 Wilt.
Meier Christina (wid Bernard), bds 20 W Jefferson.
Meier Ferdinand, blksmith, 123 Wallace, res 120 same.
Meier Henry, mattressmkr, res 167 Erie.
Meier Henry C, driver A Kalbacher, bds 310 Harrison.
Meier Henry E, carp Penn Co, res 310 Harrison.
Meier Leonard J, lab Ft W Gas Co, res 39 Franklin av.
Meier Louisa, tailoress, bds 99 Wilt.
Meier Louis H, tailor 99 Wilt, res same.
Meier Mary A, tailoress, bds 99 Wilt.
Meier Rosie (wid Frederick W), died Jan 27, 1895.
Meier Sophie C, tailoress, bds 99 Wilt.
Meier Wm F, bds 99 Wilt.
Meierding Catherine (wid Christian), res 418 E Washington
Meierding Christian H, bookkpr L Brames & Co, bds 418 E Washington.
Meierding Lizzie, seamstress, bds 418 E Washington.
Meiland Christopher, lab Penn Co, bds 310 Harrison.
Meiney Henry, died Oct 13, 1894.
Meinz Eva, bds 31 Pine.
Meinzen August D, removed to New Haven, Ind.
Meinzen Frederick H, clerk bds Wm Munzen.
Meinzen Henry, bricklayer, res 241 Madison.
Meinzen Henry W, Pharmacist-Druggist and All Kinds of Toilet Supplies, 64 Maumee av, rms same. Tel 426.

Meinzen Wm, sexton, Concordia Cemetery, res n s Maumee rd 3 w of Grand av.
Meinzen Sophia, bds Wm Meinzen.
Meiser Benjamin, res 33 Wagner.
Meiser Bessie L, retoucher F F Barrow's, bds 33 Wagner.
Meiser Elsie, teacher, bds 33 Wagner.
Meisner, *see also Misner.*
Meisner Carrie, knitter, bds 172 Greeley.
Meisner Christina (wid Jacob), res 172 Greeley.
Meister Helen, domestic 211 E Wayne.
Meister Henry T, laborer, res 80 Liberty.
Melcher James M, mach Ft W E Corp, bds 199 Broadway.
Melching Albert W, deputy sheriff Allen County, res 18 N Harrison.
Melching Charlotte (wid Wm), res 41 High.
Melching Wm, apprentice, bds 18 N Harrison.
Mellinger Christian, shoemkr 107 Walton av, res same.
Mellinger Joseph F, bds 107 Walton av.
Mellinger Wm E, bds 107 Walton av.
Melsheimer Lewis, printer Ft W Sentinel, bds 121 E Main.
Melsheimer Martha (wid Dr Charles T), bds 207 E Berry.
Melsheimer Shaphat D, tel editor Ft W Sentinel, res 357 E Wayne.
Melzer Herman, laborer, res 24 Erie.
Mendenhall Farla, bds 113 Lafayette.
Mendenhall Isaac, clk, res 113 Lafayette.
Menebrecker Martha, opr S M Foster, bds 199 W Superior.
Menebrecker Matilda (wid Henry), res 199 W Superior.
Menefee Charles M (Menefee & De Vilbiss), Brass and Iron Founder, 135 and 137 Oliver, res 202 Thomas. *(See next page.)*
Menefee Harry B, molder C M Menefee, res 204 Thomas.
Menefee Jennie, domestic New Aveline House.
Menefee Oscar F, molder C M Menefee, bds 202 Thomas.
Menefee & De Vilbiss (Charles M Menefee, Thomas D De Vilbiss), Safety Cistern and Well Cover Mnfrs, 135 and 137 Oliver.
Mennewisch Edward, blksmith Penn Co, res 20 Hough.
Mennewisch Frederick, car bldr Penn Co, res 186 Francis.
Mennewisch Frederick W, mach Penn Co, res 230 Francis.
Mennewisch Henry, heater Bass F & M Wks, res 289 Hanna
Mennewisch Henry C, helper Penn Co, bds 20 Hough.
Mennewisch Wm T, laborer, bds 20 Hough.

Mennonite Book Concern, Fort Wayne
    Book Bindery. (*See left bottom lines.*)
Mensch Emil C, knitter, res 44 Elm.
Mensch Ferdinand B, clerk, bds 45 E 4th.
Mensch Franklin P, grocer, 26 Calhoun, res 45 E 4th.
    Tel 256.
Mensing August E, lab Wilkens Bros, res 191 Jackson.
Mensing Charles, laborer, res 3 Mary.
Mensing Frederick, painter, bds 3 Mary.
Mensing Sophia, knitter, bds 3 Mary.
Mensing Wm J, cutter D Redelshimer & Co, bds 3 Mary.
Menze Bernadina (wid Henry), died March 14th, 1895.
Menze Charles H, tailor, bds 338 E Washington.
Menze Frederick, coremaker, res 108 Eliza.
Menze Minnie, domestic 282 W Washington.
Menze Wm, laborer, rms 86 Barr.
Menze Wm C, tailor, res 338 E Washington.
Mercer Hannah (wid David), bds 38 E 5th.
Merchant Maggie, domestic 139 W Main.
Merchants Despatch Transportation
    Company, W V Douglass Agt, 3 Schmitz Blk.
Meredith Adoniram J, carpenter, rms 63 W Superior.
Meredith Frank, conductor, rms 98 Boone.
Mercer Ellis, laborer, res 2 Franklin av.
Mergel Reinhard, res 456 Calhoun.
Mergel Rink T, mngr C Entemann, res 482 Calhoun.
Mergentheim Alexander, millinery, 38 Calhoun, res 84
    W Washington.
Mergentheim Morton, student, bds 84 W Washington.
Mergentheim's Bazaar, Mrs Rosalie Deitsch propr, 38
    Calhoun.
Mergott Emily K, dressmaker, bds Fox av.
Meriam Ann J (wid Cyrenius), res 174 E Creighton av.
Meriam Mason S, foreman Penn Co. res 56 Division.

Merillat John P, carpenter, res 63 Boone.
Merillat Joseph P, grocer, 408 Calhoun, res 48 McClellan.
Merillat Moses J, clk, bds 48 McClellan.
Meriwether James R, res 169 W Wayne, Telephone 369.
Merklein Frederick, lab, res 192 Taylor
Merkler Anton, lab Penn Co, res 69 Buchanan.
Merkler Catherine, bds 69 Buchanan.
Merlet Matthew, lab Penn Co, bds 307 E Washington.
Merrell Ellen D (wid E D); music teacher, res 26 Chute.
Merrell Frank R, printer, bds 26 Chute.
Merriam Arthur B, auditor F, Ft W & W Ry, bds 241 W Berry.
Merriett Charles F, engineer N Y, C & St L R R, res 72 W 3d.
Merriett John T, engineer, bds 69 W 4th.
Merriman George W, trav agt, res 31 Wefel.
Merriman, Oscar, lab Penn Co, res 179 Hanna.
Merritt George W, cond Ft W E Ry Co, bds 231 Barr.
Mertens, *see also Martin.*
Mertens Emma L, domestic 240 W Berry.
Mertens Frederick, tailor J G Thieme & Son, res 77 Liberty.
Mertens Frederick C, upholster P E Wolf, bds 77 Liberty.
Mertens Minnie, domestic 69 W Wayne.
Merz, *see also Martz.*
Merz Albert, tinner, res 25 Pine.
Merz George A, carpenter, bds 196 E Lewis
Merz Gertrude, knitter, bds 196 E Lewis.
Merz, Joseph, died March 10, 1895.
Merz Lena, domestic 137 E Berry.
Merz Louis (Zoeller & Merz), res 125 W DeWald.
Merz Mary, domestic 41 W Main.
Merz Nicholas, carpenter, res 125 W De Wald.
Merz Peter, carpenter. res 196 E Lewis.
Merz Peter B, car builder, bds 196 E Lewis.
Merz Theodore, bartndr Zoeller & Merz, res 37 Pine.
Mesing Charles F, bkr H H Barcus, bds 238 Calhoun.
Mesing Emma, domestic 270 W Wayne.
Messerschmidt John M, lab Bass F & M Wks, res 117 Eliza
Messerschmidt Mary (wid John), res 42 Liberty.
Messerschmidt Wm K, baker, bds 42 Liberty.
Messick Della, bds 106 Barr.
Messmann Rev Anthony, rector St Peter's German Catholic Church, res 90 St Martin's.
Metcalf Samuel C, phys, 109 W Superior, res same.

Metcalf Samuel S, brakeman, res 46 Hugh.
Metcalfe Eva C, bds 9 W De Wald.
Metcalfe John, clk Penn Co, res 55 Force.
Metcalfe Wm E, clk S M Foster, bds 33 Madison.
Metker, see also Metzger.
Metker Benjamin, brakeman, res 241 E Washington.
Metker Bernhard, stone mason, res 198 Lafayette.
Metker Emma, seamstress, bds e s Comparet 2 s of E
    Wayne.
Metker John A, painter City Carriage Wks, bds 30 Coch-
    rane.
Metker Joseph, helper, Bass, res rear 347 E Washington.
Metker Joseph, Plastering Contractor, rear cor
    Washington and Comparet, res same. (*See p 109.*)
Metker Joseph jr, bds 3 Comparet.
Metropolitan Life Insurance Co of New York, P S Boltz
    supt, 1 and 2 White Bank Blk.
Metsch Frederick Wm, painter, res 186 Metz.
Metsker, see also Medsker.
Metsker Allan W, foreman Wabash R R, res 552 Broadway
Mettey Mrs Elizabeth, res s s Wagner 2 e of Spy Run av.
Metting Wm C, conductor, res 17 Sturgis.
Mettler Anna, opr S M Foster, bds 5 Liberty.
Mettler Bernard, cigarmkr A C Baker, bds 198 Madison.
Mettler Catherine, opr S M Foster, bds 5 Liberty.
Mettler Catherine (wid Peter), res w s Spy Run 2 s of
    Ruth.
Mettler Clara E, bds 609 Calhoun.
Mettler John, clk M Frank & Co, bds C Mettler.
Mettler John A, barber, W Wilder, bds 609 Calhoun.
Mettler Joseph, wheelmkr, bds 609 Calhoun.
Mettler Matthias, cabtmkr, res 276 E Jefferson.
Mettler Matthias, cutter Hoosier Mnfg Co, bds C Mettler.
Mettler Peter, saloon, 91 Harmer, res same.
Mettler Peter J, coachman, res rear 235 Spy Run av.
Metty Edna, domestic 38 St Mary's av.
Metty Elizabeth (wid Frederick), res 18 Wagner.
Metz Hermann, knitter, bds 308 W Main.
Metzger, see also Metker.
Metzger Elizabeth (wid Andrew), res 40 Brackenridge.
Metzger Harry M, Clerk Allen Circuit Court,
    Office Court House, res 280 W Berry.
Metzler Charles, lab Penn Co, res 163 E Taber.
Metzler Leo, tailor, 324 Lafayette, res same.
Metzner Jasper, condr G R & I R R, res 358 Hanna.

Metzner Louis, fireman G R & IR R. bds 50 Buchanan.
Meyer, *see also Maher, Maier, Mayer, Meier and Myers.*
Meyer Adolph, res 188 W Berry.
Meyer Alice, domestic 142 W Berry.
Meyer Anna L, bds 175 W DeWald.
Meyer Anna M (wid John), bds 443 E Wayne.
Meyer Anna M E, bds 26 Oak.
Meyer Anselma G, stripper. bds 76 N Harrison.
Meyer Anthony G (Meyer Bros), ice 62 Buchanan.
Meyer August, mach hd Bass Wks, bds 66 Alliger.
Meyer Bros (Anthony G and Louis J), ice 62 Buchanan.
Meyer Bros & Co (Christian F G and John F W Meyer), Wholesale and Retail Druggists, Paints, Oils, Toilet Articles and Baking Powder Mnfrs, 14 Calhoun and 9 Columbia. Tel 159.
Meyer Bruno, molder Bass F & M Wks, res 127 Gay.
Meyer Caroline, bds 118 W Jefferson.
Meyer Caroline (wid Gottlieb). res 118 W Jefferson.
Meyer Carrie C, domestic 240 W Berry.
Meyer Charles, carpenter Penn Co, res 149 Ewing.
Meyer Charles. helper Olds' Wagon Wks, res 71 Wilt.
Meyer Chàrles F, machinist Penn Co, res 337 Force.
Meyer Charles F W, Director Ft Wayne Conservatory of Music, Bank Blk, res s s Pontiac 4 w of Webster.
Meyer Charles H, painter Heine & Israel, bds 127 Gay.
Meyer Charles L, lab C L Centlivre Brewing Co, bds 76 N Harrison.
Meyer Charles W, clk Kayser & Baade, bds 149 Ewing.
Meyer Charles W, packer McDonald & Watt, res 154 W Jefferson.
Meyer Christena, domestic 66 Douglas av.
Meyer Christian, helper Olds' Wagon Wks, bds 61 Stophlet
Meyer Christian F G (Meyer Bros & Co), res St Louis, Co.
Meyer Clara H, student, bds s s Pontiac 4 w of Webster.
Meyer Clara M, seamstress, bds 127 Gay.
Meyer Conrad, watchman Ft Wayne Iron Wks, res 84 Wall.
Meyer Rev C F Wm, pastor Lutheran church of the Redeemer, (English) res 79 Brackenridge.
Meyer Diedrich, res 22 W Wayne.
Meyer Diedrich H, molder Bass F & M Wks, res 41 Gay.
Meyer Emma F, bds 127 Gay.
Meyer Engel (wid Wm.), bds 148 Clinton.
Meyer Frank H, res 76 W Washington.
Meyer Frank J, gunsmith J Trautman, res 138 Maumee rd.

Meyer Frederick, boilermkr Bass Wks, res 5 Summit.
Meyer Frederick, clk C F Lahmeyer, bds 131 Jackson.
Meyer Frederick, collector, bds 328 E Wayne.
Meyer Frederick, lab Penn Co, res 191 Wallace.
Meyer Frederick C W, helper Penn Co, res 16 Rockhill.
Meyer Frederick H, saloon, 8 Calhoun, res 97 W Main.
Meyer Frederick W, lab J S Hines, res 381 M Main.
Meyer Frederick W, molder Bass Wks, res 60 Gay.
Meyer Fredericka, bds 188 W Berry.
Meyer George. laborer, res 39 Wells.
Meyer George E, servant R Swinney.
Meyer George L (Miller & Meyer), res 155 Ewing.
Meyer George M, molder, res 254 E Washington.
Meyer Gustav, lab, res 50 Taylor.
Meyer Gustave E, bds 66 Alliger.
Meyer Hannah, stenog Pottlitzer Bros, bds 188 W Berry.
Meyer Henrietta, bds 100 Harrison.
Meyer Henry, carriage trimmer, bds 76 W Washington.
Meyer Henry, hostler 96 W Berry
Meyer Henry, whitewasher, res 200 E Lewis
Meyer Henry C, lab Penn Co, res 294 W Jefferson.
Meyer Henry, Merchant Tailor, 12 E Berry, res
103 Columbia av. (*See clasified Merchant Tailors.*)
Meyer Henry C, merchant tailor, 44 Harrison, res 281 W
Washington.
Meyer Henry F, bkkpr Paul Mnfg Co, bds 129 E Lewis.
Meyer Henry H, laborer, bds 149 Ewing.
Meyer Henry J, with Meyer Bros & Co, bds The Wayne.
Meyer Henry J jr (Wm Meyer & Bro), res 42 W
Washington.
Meyer Henry W, draughtsman, res 179 W Jefferson.
Meyer Henry W, foreman Bass F & M Wks, res 26 Oak.
Meyer Herman, res e s Hanna 3 s of Eckart Lane.
Meyer Jacob, trav agt Pottlitzer Bros, bds 188 W Berry.
Meyer John, barber, bds 76 W Washington.
Meyer John, helper, bds e s Compcret 2 s of E Wayne.
Meyer John, laborer, bds Washington House.
Meyer John F W (Meyer Bros & Co), res 290 Fairfield av.
Tel 282.
Meyer John H, confectioner 96 Calhoun, res same.
Meyer Joseph, laborer, bds 419 W Main.
Meyer Lena, res 100 Harrison.
Meyer Lizzie, bds 76 W Washington.
Meyer Lizzie D, bds 396 E Wayne.
Meyer Louis G, sawyer D Tagtmeyer, res 76 N Harrison.

Meyer Louis J, Meyer Bros, bds 62 Buchanan.
Meyer Louise, res 100 Harrison.
Meyer Maggie, domestic 84 Columbia av.
Meyer Margaretta (wid Wm), res 152 Union.
Meyer Martha, bds 149 Ewing.
Meyer Martin, laborer, bds 16 Maiden Lane.
Meyer Mary, bds 200 E Lewis.
Meyer Mary (wid Ernest), bds 51 Maumee rd.
Meyer Mary A, domestic 241 W Main.
Meyer Mary H (wid John H), res 519 E Lewis.
Meyer Minnie, dressmaker, bds 396 E Wayne.
Meyer Morris B, furnishings, 9 Harrison, res 37 W Main.
Meyer M Louisa, bds s s Pontiac 4 w of Webster.
Meyer Otto C, clk Gross & Pellens, bds 254 E Washington
Meyer Otto H, boxmkr, bds 127 Gay.
Meyer Otto J, cabinetmkr F W Furn Co, bds 519 E Lewis
Meyer Paul A, lab Ft W Elec Corp, bds 337 Force.
Meyer Peter, lab City Mills, bds 187 E Lewis.
Meyer Rachel, bds 188 W Berry.
Meyer Robert, cutter J G Thieme & Son, bds 53 E Wayne
Meyer Sophia, domestic 26 E De Wald.
Meyer Theodore G, clerk, bds 118 W Jefferson.
Meyer Theodore W H, plasterer, res 61 Stophlet.
Meyer Wilhelmina (wid Henry), bds 41 Gay.
Meyer Wm jr (Wm Meyer & Bro), res 40 W Washington.
Meyer Wm C, clk Eckart Pkg Co, res 32 Charles.
Meyer Wm C, lathe hd Ind M Wks, bds 396 E Wayne.
Meyer Wm D, res 129 E Lewis.
Meyer Wm F, res 405 Webster.
Meyer Wm F, carpenter, res 144 Taber.
Meyer Wm F, instrument maker, bds 337 Force.
Meyer Wm H C, tailor, res 396 E Wayne.
Meyer Wm L, bds 148 Clinton.
Meyer Wm & Bro (Wm jr and Henry J jr), furnishings,
    80 and 80½ Calhoun.
Meyer Yette, res 100 Harrison.
Meyers Bernard, coremkr, res 256 E Wayne.
Meyers Carrie, domestic 132 Fairfield av.
Meyers Catherine (wid Frederick), bds 416 Clinton.
Meyers Charles A C, livery, 176 Harrison, bds 45 W
    Washington. Tel 466.
Meyers Charles C, bookkeeper, res 128 W Main.
Meyers Charles F F, clk Root & Co, res 45 W Washington
Meyers Ernst C, laborer, bds 91 Force.
Meyers Ethel W, bds 45 W Washington.

Meyers Frank, farmer, County Poor Farm.

Meyers Frederick C, foreman Bass F & M Wks, res 198 E De Wald.

Meyers Frederick G, Groceries, Provisions, Notions, Flour and Feed, 181 E Lewis, res same.

Meyers George, clerk Arlington Hotel.

Meyers Harry W, bds 45 W Washington.

Meyers Henrietta, domestic 50 W Superior.

Meyers Henry C, res 91 Force.

Meyers Henry C, carpenter, res 183 E Lewis.

Meyer Henry F, car repairer, res 71 Oakley.

Meyers John E, laborer, bds 357 E Washington.

Meyers John F H, clk F G Meyers, bds 181 E Lewis.

Meyers John H, died October 12, 1894.

Meyers John H (H A Grotholtman & Co), res 138 Harrison.

Meyers Leander H, foreman C L Centlivre Brewing Co, res 22 Randolph.

Meyers Louise (wid Frederick), bds 198 E De Wald.

Meyers Margaret (wid Ferdinand), res 165 Ewing.

Meyers Mary, waiter Ervin House.

Meyers Sophia J, domestic 229 W Jefferson.

Meyers Wm, died August 15th, 1894.

Meyers Wm, died October 5th, 1894.

Meyers Wm H, saloon 207 Lafayette, res same.

Meyett James, spoke grader, bds 108 Wallace.

Michael Herman, real est 19 Court, res 373 Calhoun.

Michael John C, bds w s Victoria av, 2 s of Piqua av.

Michael Phenie, bds 373 Calhoun.

Michael Wm, lab N-Y, C & St L R R, res 107 Mechanic.

Michaelis Charles D, cigarmkr A Hazzard, res 115 College

Michaelis Charles, upholsterer, res 297 W Jefferson.

Michaelis Herman, cigarmaker, bds 115 College.

Michaelis Mrs Kate, bds 115 College.

Michel Adam, laborer, res 48 Taylor.

Michel Andrew, pressman Ind Staats Zeitung, res 404 E Wayne.

Michel Charles J, trav agt G E Bursley & Co, bds 151 Ewing.

Michel Charles L, barber, bds 404 E Wayne.

Michel Frank J, watchman Ind M Wks, res 130 Cass.

Michel Frederick G, mach Western Gas Const Co, bds 130 Cass.

Michel George, stone carver, res 116 Jackson.

Michel George, wagonmkr A Vogely, res 517 E Lewis.

Michel George H, carpenter, bds 517 E Lewis.
Michel John M, planer Ind M Wks, bds 130 Cass.
Michel Joseph B, machinist, bds 130 Cass.
Michel Lewis H, stripper, bds 517 E Lewis.
Michel Maggie, milliner, bds 517 E Lewis.
Michel Melissa (wid Lewis), bds 252 Clinton.
Michel Minnie, seamstress, bds 404 E Wayne.
Mick Abraham C, grocer, 283 E Creighton av, res 62 Greene.
Mick Arthur E, clerk, bds 62 Greene.
Middendorf Bernard, contr, res 276 E Wayne.
Middendorf Herman, brewer C L Centlivre Brewing Co, res s s Griswold av 2 e of the bridge
Middendorf Herman H, mason, bds 276 E Wayne.
Middleton Ambrose E, lab, res 397 Lafayette.
Middleton Bertha B, bds 397 Lafayette.
Middleton George A, lab, res 320 Hanna
Middleton Louis L, lab, bds 320 Hanna.
Middleton Matilda M, bds 397 Lafayette.
Middleton Sylvester O, late Wabash R R, bds 320 Hanna
Mieland Christian, lab Penn Co, bds 310 Harrison.
Miesing Laura, domestic 239 W Berry.
Miesse Harry, legal d'pt G R & I R R, bds The Wayne.
Mikesell Arthur L. phys, 32 Calhoun, res same.
Miles Arthur, lab, res 28 Huron.
Miles Caroline, bds 221 W Washington.
Miles David, lab, res 105 Wells.
Miles Helene, milliner, bds 221 W Washington.
Miles Harriette L, bds 221 W Washington.
Miles John, lab, bds 221 W Washington.
Miles Mary H, milliner, bds 221 W Washington.
Miles Sarah A (wid Charles), res 221 W Washington.
Miles Thomas J, bds 105 Wells.
Miles Wm, music teacher, 134 Calhoun, res same.
Miles Wm B, lab, bds 105 Wells.
Milroy, Harry, bds s s Bluffton rd, nr Poor Farm.
Millard Charles D, machinist, res 24 Euclid.
Millard Robert (Moellering Bros & Millard), res 320 W Washington.
Miller, *see also Moeller, Mueller, Muhler and Muller.*
Miller Abbie B, bds 78 Barr.
Miller Adolph, house boy The Wayne.
Miller Albert A, mach hand, bds 169 E Washington.
Miller Albert F, carp Penn Co, res 185 Suttenfield.
Miller Albert W, condr Penn Co, res 56 E De Wald.

Miller Albert W, student, bds 5 Guthrie.
Miller Alice, stenogr Keller Dental Co, bbs 29 Bass.
Miller Aloysius (Miller Bros), res 114 Spy Run av.
Miller Alvina (wid Charles T), res 96 Wilt.
Miller Amelia, bds 36 E De Wald.
Miller Andrew, fireman Penn Co, res 122 Wallace.
Miller Anna, domestic 269 W Wayne.
Miller Anna E, bds s s Columbia av 1 w bridge.
Miller Anna M, bds 125 Cass.
Miller Annie, bds 55 W Williams.
Miller Annie L, sub teacher Public Schools, bds 161 Harmer
Miller Annie M, bds 222 W Creighton av.
Miller Anthony, clk Pottlitzer Bros, bds 63 Wells.
Miller Anton, mach Ft W Elec Corp, res 46 Wall.
Miller Arthur W, bottler Herman Berghoff Brewing Co,
　　bds 26 Walton av.
†Miller Asenath (wid Wm), bds 23 Miner.
Miller August, gunsmith, res 5 Frederick.
Miller Benjamin, clerk, bds 446 W Main.
Miller Bertha B, bds 161 Harmer.
Miller Bros (Wm and Alois), junk, 94–98 E Superior.
Miller Carl L, clerk, bds 125 Cass
Miller Casper, tray agt G E Bursley & Co, res 161 Har-
　　rison.
Miller Cash A, clk J M Miller, res 295 W Berry.
Miller Catherine (wid John J), bds 44 Wells.
Miller Charles, carpenter, res 5 Sturgis.
Miller Charles, clerk, bds 8 Summit.
Miller Charles, patternmkr Bass Wks, res 63 Charles.
Miller Charles, porter, bds 306 Harrison.
Miller Charles A, motorman Ft W E Ry Co, res 34
　　Scott av.
Miller Charles C. sec and treas Ft Wayne Electric Corp.
　　res 182 W Jefferson.
Miller Charles E, optician, bds 71 W Wayne.
Miller Charles F W, lab City Mills, res 10 Lavina.
Miller Charles G, bds 20 Marion.
Miller Charles H, guns, 20 W Main, res 446 same.
Miller Charles H,, laborer, bds 26 Walton av.
Miller Charles J, tailor, res 10 Erie.
Miller Charles L, treas Old Fort Spice and Extract Co,
　　res 115 W Washington.
Miller Charles O, cabinetmkr, bds 513 Broadway.
Miller Charles S. painter, res 139 John.
Miller Charles W, painter S W Hull, bds 67 E Main.

Miller Chauncey O, carriage painter, res 23 Miner.
Miller Christian, clerk, res 9 Force.
Miller Christian, horseshoer F Becker, bds 306 Harrison.
Miller Christina, bds 20 Marion.
Miller Clara E, milliner, bds 513 Broadway.
Miller Clara M, bds 10 Lavina.
Miller Clarence C, fireman Penn Co, bds 493 Calhoun.
Miller Claude C. res 101 Lafayette.
Miller Clement E, clk J B White, res 38 Hendricks.
Miller Conrad, fireman, res 106 Boone.
Miller Conrad, laborer, res rear 31 Smith
Miller Cornelius A. foreman Ft W Gas Co, res 18 Stophlet
Miller Cortez D, clk Seavey Hardware Co, bds 120 Harrison.
Miller Cyrus E, carpenter, res 25 Lincoln av.
Miller Daniel, carpenter, bds 122 South Wayne av.
Miller Daniel M, res 82 E Berry.
Miller David E, laborer, bds 81 Lillie.
Miller Dell, fireman, res 313 E Washington.
Miller Dolly, bds 267 E Creighton av.
Miller Dora, student, bds 5 Guthrie.
Miller Edward, barber J Munich, bds 43 Nirdlinger av.
Miller Edward, printer Archer Ptg Co. res 74 Montgomery
Miller Edward C, died February 22, 1894.
Miller Edward C, clk A B White, bds 70 Erie.
Miller Edward R, bds 131 W Jefferson.
Miller Edwin W, agent, res 16 Lincoln av.
Miller Elmer M, lab Olds' W Wks, bds 392 Calhoun.
Miller Emily, bds 36 E De Wald.
Miller Emma, milliner, bds 29 Bass.
Miller Emma, seamstress. bds 54 Elm.
Miller Ernest, laborer, res 49 W Williams.
Miller Erwin, clk McDonald & Watt, res 314 E Jefferson
Miller Esther (wid James B), bds 333 Harrison.
Miller Flora E. stenographer, bds 131 W Jefferson.
Miller Frank, book keeper, bds Daniel Rehm.
Miller Frank H, clk Ft W Gas Co. bds Eliza s e cor Parnell av.
Miller Frank H, driver, bds 54 Elm.
Miller Frank J, driver, bds 202 W Creighton av.
Miller Frank P. teamster, res w s Winter 1 s of Pontiac.
Miller Frank S. janitor City Hall, res 201 E Jefferson.
Miller Frank X, blacksmith Penn Co, res 51 Grand.
Miller Fred, clk Seavey Hardware Co, bds 190 W Main.

Miller Fred (Gerberding & Miller), Pres and Treas Builders' Lime Association, Office 257 Calhoun, also Contractor and Builder, Office 8 Summit, res same. (*See right bottom lines and p 103.*)

Miller Frederick, wiper Penn Co, res 49 Gay.

Miller Frederick A, apprentice, bds 16 Locust.

Miller Frederick C, engr Herman Berghoff Brewing Co, res 62 Grant av.

Miller Frederick C, laborer Penn Co, res 5 Force.

Miller Frederick C, mason, bds 8 Summit.

Miller Frederick D, barber 331 W Main, res 64 Elm.

Miller Frederick F, carp Ft W Elec Corp, res 42 Walnut.

Miller Frederick J, Druggist, 327 Lafayette, res same. Tel 266.

Miller Frederick M, clk Penn Co, res 56 W De Wald.

Miller Frederick N, condr Ft W Elec Ry Co, bds 50 Grant av.

Miller F Wm, laborer, res 16 Locust.

Miller F Wm jr, helper, bds 16 Locust.

Miller George, clerk, res 26 Walton av.

Miller George, slater, res 29 Buchanan.

Miller George A, engr Penn Co, res 124 E De Wald.

Miller George E, clerk, bds 197 E Jefferson.

Miller George E, mach hd Fleming Mnfg Co, bds 49 W 4th

Miller George F, clk Dreier & Bro, bds 314 E Wayne.

Miller George F, lab Penn Co, res 71 Lasselle.

Miller George F, patternmkr Bass F & M Wks, res 172 Harmer.

Miller George P, lab Penn Co, bds 26 Walton av.

Miller George S (Miller & Dougall), notary public 4 Foster Blk, res 275 E Jefferson.

Miller George T, mach Wabash R R, bds s s Columbia 1 w bridge.

Miller George W, phys, 19 E Washington, res same.

Miller Gilbert C, teamster, res 269 W Creighton av.

Miller Gilbert S, clk F C Parham, res 238 W Wayne.

Miller Glo, bds 70 Erie.

Miller Grover, fireman N Y, C & St L R R, bds 71 Boone.

Miller Gustav H, mach opr, res 9 Park av.

Miller Harry D, carriagemkr, res 273 E Jefferson.

Miller Harvey D, car bldr Penn Co, res 205 Metz.

Miller Mrs Hattie, seamstress, bds 82 Hanna.

Miller Henrietta, died Sept 7th, 1894.

Miller Henry, clk M L Frankenstein, rms 399 W Main.

Miller Henry, driver Brenzinger Bkg Co, res 49 Gay.

Miller Henry C, laborer, res 55 W Williams.
Miller Henry C. Manager Ft Wayne Pneumatic Novelty and Model Works, res 139 John.

FORT WAYNE PNEUMATIC
Novelty and Model Works.

Pneumatic Music Leaf Turner a Specialty.

The Pneumatic Music Leaf Turner

Will turn an unlimited number of leaves without adjusting every separate leaf to it, as has to be done with the most of other turners, which is very troublesome and takes a lot of time when you haven't the time to spare.

You simply put your folio on the Turner like any ordinary music rack and the Turner will do the rest. Unbound sheet music is bound in the rack by a simple clasp binder and can be turned the same as folios.

The Turner is entitled to its name for it is operated throughout with air. Air not only turns the arm but also grasps the leaves by suction. It has hardwood (3 ply veneered) frame, well finished, with trimmings nickel plated, which makes it very neat and handsome.

NOTE:—We guarantee the Turner to do its work satisfactory, and will replace any defect there may be in it free of charge if notice is given within one month.

For Further Information address the Inventor and Manufacturer,

H. C. MILLER,

No. 139 John Street,   Fort Wayne, Ind.

Miller Henry G, cabtmkr Ft W O Co. res 621 Fairfield av.
Miller Henry J, bkkpr Ft W Elec Corp, res 268 W Washington. Tel 52.
Miller Henry J, clk H Wellman, bds 18 McClellan.
Miller Henry J, trav agt Mossman, Yarnelle & Co, res 36 E De Wald.
Miller Henry L, paper hanger, bds 122 South Wayne av.
Miller Henry M, painter, res e s Calhoun 4 s of Marshall.
Miller Herman A, blksmith Ind Mach Wks, res 16 Barthold
Miller Herman F W, mason, res 416 Hanna
Miller Herman J, clk J B White, bds 18 McClellan.
Miller Herman W, mason, bds 8 Summit.
Miller Ida, bds 29 Bass.
Miller Ida, bds 114 Spy Run av.
Miller Isaac, grocer, 428 Calhoun, res same.
Miller Jacob J, hoop mkr S D Bitler, res 242 Erie.
Miller Jacob, brakeman G R & I R R, res 224 Calhoun.

Miller James B, fireman N Y, C & St L R R, bds 329 Elm
Miller James E, phys, 327 Lafayette, res same. Tel 372.
Miller James G, porter J B White, res 52 Runnion av.
Miller James M, lab, res n s Jesse 1 e of Runnion av.
Miller John, cigarmaker, bds 306 Harrison.
Miller John, clk Princess Cash Store, res 75 W 3d.
Miller John, coachman J H Bass, Brookside.
Miller John, laborer, bds 231 Barr.
Miller John, teamster, res 312 Lafayette.
Miller John A, res 222 W Creighton av.
Miller John A, clk I Miller, bds 18 Oak.
Miller John A, hoop mkr S D Bitler, bds 242 Erie.
Miller John C, Physician, 96 Broadway, res same.
Miller John D, res 8 Wheeler.
Miller John E, barber, bds 215 W Main.
Miller John E, boiler maker, res 49 W Williams.
Miller John E, carpenter, res 81 Litlie.
Miller John E, lab F W Elec Corp, res 29 Bass.
Miller John E, sanitary insp, res 333 Harrison.
Miller John H, condr G R & I R R, res 1 Michigan av.
Miller John H, laborer, res 54 Elm.
Miller John H, machinist, res 20 Marion.
Miller John J, clk Metro Life Ins Co, bds 8 Edgerton.
Miller John M, Furniture, 50 and 52 E Main, res 52 E Jefferson.
Miller John S, apprentice, bds 296 E Washington.
Miller John S, foreman G Young, res 5 Guthrie.
Miller John W, bds 5 N Clinton.
Miller Joseph, carp G Lauer, res 202 W Creighton av.
Miller Joseph, fireman N Y, C & St L R R, rms 329 W Main.
Miller Joseph, wood turner, bds 43 Nirdlinger av.
Miller Joseph A, res 122 South Wayne av.
Miller Joseph D, bds 60 E Williams.
Miller Joseph F, engineer, res 202 W Creighton av.
Miller Joseph F, trav agt Fox Br U S Baking Co, res 419 Calhoun.
Miller Joseph L, engineer, res 105 Wilt.
Miller Julius, car bldr Penn Co, bds 53 Hugh.
Miller J Louis, boilermkr Penn Co, res 274 Webster.
Miller J Wm, carpenter, res 28 Lincoln av.
Miller Kate, bds 306 Harrison.
Miller Lena, domestic 51 W Berry.
Miller Levi H. plasterer, res 222 Broadway.

Miller Levi H jr, laborer, bds 222 Broadway.
Miller Lizzie (wid Charles), boarding, 326 Hanna.
Miller Lizzie, domestic 68 W Berry.
Miller Lizzie L, bds s s Columbia 1 w of Bridge.
Miller Louis C, conductor, res 105 Gay.
Miller Louis D, appr Wabash R R, bds 10 Lavina.
Miller Louis J, res 63 W Williams.
Miller Louis L, trav agt Root & Co, bds St James Hotel.
Miller Louisa, laundress McKinnie House.
Miller Louisa M (wid Samuel), res 70 Erie.
Miller Martin C, bds 82 Hanna.
Miller Mary (wid Samuel), res 82 Hanna.
Miller Mary A, bds 78 Barr.
Miller Mrs Mary E, dressmkr, 101 Lafayette, res same.
Miller Mary L, bds 111 Wilt.
Miller Mary M, bds 179 Clinton.
Miller Mattie, bds 62 Grant av.
Miller Michael, res 224 W Washington.
Miller Naomi, ironer W B Phillips, bds 82 Hanna.
Miller Nathaniel C (Miller & Dougall), pension attorney, 4 Foster Blk, res 273 E Jefferson.
Miller Nicholas, car repr Penn Co, res 296 E Washington.
Miller Orria V, bds 18 Stophlet.
Miller Oscar D, bookkeeper, bds 70 Erie.
Miller Oscar L, florist B L Auger, bds 16 E Washington.
Miller Otto, lab Miller Bros, res 134 Warsaw.
Miller Paul, laborer, res rear 31 Smith.
Miller Paul, teamster, res 8 Edgerton.
Miller Phillip, baker School for F M Y, res 201 Ewing.
Miller Rachel, trimmer, bds 219 E Wayne.
Miller Ray, bds Maysville rd e of limits.
Miller Richard, gardener, 391 Fairfield av.
Miller Richard C, shoemaker, res 65 Clinton.
Miller Richard H, mach opr, res 243 Force.
Miller Robert, driver Pfeiffer & Rousseau, bds 122 South Wayne av.
Miller Robert A, conductor, bds 323 W Main.
Miller Robert K, clerk, bds 122 South Wayne av.
Miller Rosa, domestic 124 E Berry.
Miller Ruches C, barber, 78 Barr, res same.
Miller Samuel, brakeman, bds 36 Hough.
Miller Seraphine C, (Fort Wayne Pneumatic Novelty and Model Works), res 139 John.
Miller Simon, feed barn, 5 N Clinton, res same.
Miller Sophia (wid Wm), res 305 Calhoun.

Miller S Ollie, bds 82 Hanna.

Miller Theodore N, tinner A Griffiths, res 64 Wall.

Miller Ulrich M, tinner, bds 101 Lafayette

Miller Walter D, engr N Y, C & St L R R, res 70 W Main.

Miller Webster, teamster D Tagtmeyer, bds Union House.

Miller Wm (Miller Bros) res Lima Plank rd, Washington twp.

Miller Wm, Brick Manufacturer, e s Hanna s of city limits, res same (*see p 97*.)

Miller Wm, dairyman, res s s Spring 1 e of Runnion av.

Miller Wm, lab, res 18 Oak.

Miller Wm (col'd), porter Benoit Ellert, res 43 Hayden.

Miller Wm, saloon, w s Spy Run av nr St Joseph river bridge, res same.

Miller Wm, treas Indiana Farmers' Savings and Loan Association, res 169 E Washington.

Miller Wm C, laborer, res s s Jesse 3 e of Runnion av.

Miller Wm F, finisher Ft W Or Co. res 3 Grace av.

Miller Wm F, laborer, res s s Columbia 1 w of bridge.

Miller Wm G, barber, bds 374½ Calhoun.

Miller Wm G, helper Wabash R R, res 55 Melita.

Miller Wm G. varnisher, res 29 Wall.

Miller Wm G, (Miller & Meyer), res 164 Montgomery.

Miller Wm J, pedler, res 5 N Clinton.

Miller Wm L, meats 317 W Main, res 66 Elm.

Miller Wm M, fireman, res 268 E Lewis.

Miller Wm M, plasterer, res 152 E Wayne.

Miller Wm W, clerk, bds 122 South Wayne av.

Miller Willis, teamster K Baker, bds 109 E Superior.

Miller & Dougall (Nathaniel C Miller, Allan H Dougall), Real Estate, Insurance, Abstracts and Pensions, 4 Foster Blk.

Miller & Meyer (Wm G Miller, George L Meyer), Billiard and Sample Room 104 Calhoun.

Millet Wm C, traveling agt, rms 149 Barr.

Millholen Henry, cigarmaker, res 181 E Washington.

Millhouse John W. clerk, bds 165 Force.

Millhouse Samuel, carp Penn Co, res 165 Force.

Millhouse S Charles, porter G E Bursley & Co, bds 165 Force.

Mills Arthur E, fireman G R & I R R, res s s W Leith 1 w of Calhoun.

Mills Bluford A, attendant School F M Y.

Mills Charles J, lab Wabash R R, res 130 Gay.

Mills Charles T, plumber A Hattersley & Sons, bds 97 Riverside av.
Mills Frank E, clk Ft W Elec Corp, bds 57 Garden.
Mills George J, mach, bds 95 W Superior.
Mills Grant, laborer, res 188 W Superior.
Mills Henry W, filer, bds 678 Broadway.
Mills Horatio T, mach Penn Co, res 180 Griffith.
Mills Jessie E, bds 678 Broadway.
Mills John B, lab Ft W Elec Corp, bds 57 Garden.
Mills Joseph L, fireman N Y, C & St L R R, bds 35 Shawnee av.
Mills Morton J, helper G Abdon, bds 97 Riverside av.
Mills Percival E, car bldr Penn Co, res 57 Garden.
Mills Theodore H, painter, res 97 Riverside av.
Mills Thomas, mach Wabash R R, res 35 Shawnee av.
Mills Wm, mach Ft Wayne Elec Corp, res 678 Broadway.
Mills Wm H, cutter, bds 180 Griffith.
Milton Maude, dressmkr, 30 E Columbia, rms same.
Miner Blk, n e cor Clinton and Main.
Miner Bros (Wm E and George E), real est, 26 Court.
Miner Charles S, bds 62 Douglas av.
Miner Charles W (Miner & Dexter), bds 62 Douglas av.
Miner Daniel, mach hd Olds' Wagon Wks, res e s Calhoun 7 s of Marshall.
Miner Estella, clk Miner & Dexter, bds 62 Douglas av.
Mines George E (Miner Bros), bds 62 Douglas av.
Miner James M, laborer, bds D Miner.
Miner John J, machinist, res 219 Broadway,
Miner Leora, teacher Hoagland School, bds 62 Douglas av.
Miner Samuel R, barber, 378½ W Main, res 407 same.
Miner Sarah (wid Byron D), res 62 Douglas av.
Miner Silas, teamster, bds 219 Broadway.
Miner Street School, s w cor Miner and DeWald.
Miner Wm E (Miner Bros), res n s High, Wayne Heights.
Miner & Dexter (Charles W Miner, Wm G Dexter), photographers, 44 Calhoun.
Mineral Magnetic Well Sanitarium, Dr C B Stemen mngr and lessee, w s Home av 3 s of Pennsylvania.
Minneker Henry G, mach Olds' Wagon Wks, bds 80 Montgomery.
Minnerley Joel M, driver L Wolf & Co, res 158 W Main.
Minnich, *see also Munich.*
Minnich Charles R, laborer, bds 152 N Harrison.
Minnich Frank, helper Penn Co, bds 389 E Lewis.
Minnich Harry F, painter, rms cor Wheeler and Runnion av

Minnich James W, asst supt S F Bowser & Co, res 165 Edgewater av.
Minnich May, bds 52 N Harrison
Minnich Philip, helper Penn Co, res 27 Chute.
Minnich Philip, watchman Eckart Pkg Co, res 52 N Harrison.
Minnich Philip J, blksmth, res s s W 4th 2 w of Barthold.
Minnich T Orlan, ins agt, bds 441 Broadway.
Minot Jane (wid Samuel), res 50 W Superior.
Minser Austin A, painter, res 221 W Superior.
Minser Charles H, fireman N Y, C & St L R R, res 222 W Superior.
Minser Edward W, driver Hoffman Bros, bds 220 W Superior.
Minser Eva, bds 220 W Superior.
Minser George W, driver Hoffman Bros, res 220 W Superior.
Minser H Mitchell, painter, bds 220 W Superior.
Minskey Abraham, trav agt Pottlitzer Bros, bds 302 E Wayne.
Minskey Samuel, grocer, 302 E Wayne, res same.
Mintch Martin, baggage agt G R & I R R, res 37 Taylor.
Minto Archibald O, clk J B White, bds 126 Harrison.
Mischo Catherine (wid Michael), res 158 Broadway.
Mischo Catherine, dressmkr 33 Pritchard, bds same.
Mischo Catherine (wid Nicholas), res 33 Pritchard.
Mischo John A, mach hd Kerr Murray Mnfg Co, bds 33 Pritchard.
Mischo Julia D, domestic 246 W Berry.
Mischo Mary, seamstress, bds 158 Broadway.
Mischo Minnie F, bds 33 Pritchard.
Misner, see also Meisner.
Misner Clarence E, fireman Penn Co, res 54 E Williams.
Misner Florence M, bds 311 Lafayette.
Misner George W, painter, res 39 E Williams.
Misner Harry O, bds 311 Lafayette.
Misner James A, engr Penn Co, res 311 Lafayette.
Missler Frederick, knitter, res 38 Watkins.
Mitchell Archibald (Beadell & Co), res Norwich, Conn.
Mitchell Frank, janitor Ft Wayne College of Medicine, res same.
Mitchell George A, ins agt, rms 179 Clinton.
Mitchell James, propr Ft W Dispatch, rms 88 Clinton.
Mitchell James W, coachman A E Hoffman, res 209 W Superior.

Mitchell John C, laborer, res 82 Maumee rd.
Mitchell Wm, engineer, res 27 Edgewater av.
Mittag George, bkr Brenzinger Bread Co, res 24 W Jefferson.
Mitten J Wilmer, master mechanic L E & W R R, res 29 2d.
Mock James B, mach Wabash R R, res 165 Hoagland av.
Mittendorf. *see Middendorf.*
Model Hand Laundry, Frank W Kelsey Propr, 137 Fairfield av.
Moderwell, *see also Motherwell.*
Moderwell Hiram C, Local Freight Agent N Y, C & St L R R, res 93 W Wayne.
Moderwell Jay M, coal, e s Wells, 1 n of W Superior. res 53 W Superior.
Moderwell Mrs Martha J, sub teacher Public Schools, res 53 W Superior.
Moelich Christian, bds 11 Boone
Moeller, *see also Miller, Mueller, Muhler and Muller.*
Moeller Christian A, carpenter, res 239 Madison.
Moeller Emma, opr, bds 215 W Main.
Moeller Ernest H, clerk, bds 21 N Calhoun.
Moeller Frederick, teamster, res 60 Division.
Moeller Frederick E, wiper L E & W R R, bds 21 N Calhoun.
Moeller Gustave H, clk M Frank & Co, bds 215 W Main.
Moeller Henry E, res 215 W Main.
Moeller Herman, wiper L E & W, R R, res 21 N Calhoun
Moeller Ida E, knitter, bds 215 W Main.
Moeller Margaret L, teacher, bds 16 Rockhill.
Moeller Wm H, candy maker, Fox br U S Bkg Co, bds 21 N Calhoun.
Moellering August H F, tailor Thieme Bros, bds 57 E Lewis.
Moellering Bros & Millard (Wm F & Henry F Moellering. Robert Millard), Wholesale Grocers, 10 & 12 W Columbia. Tel 126.
Moellering Charles B, (W L Moellering & Bro), res 57 E Lewis.
Moellering Charles E (Wm Moellering & Son). bds 120 Montgomery.
Moellering Clara L, bds 120 Montgomery.
Moellering Edward H, clk Wm Moellering & Son, bds 120 Montgomery.
Moellering Helena M, domestic 241 Broadway.

31

Moellering Henry A, mach Penn Co, res 57 E Lewis.
Moellering Henry F (Moellering Bros & Millard), res 120 Montgomery.
Moellering Mary, bds 57 E Lewis.
Moellering Matilda S, bds 120 Montgomery.
Moellering Sophia, bds 120 Montgomery.
Moellering Wm (Wm Moellering & Son, Wm Moellering & Co), Brick Manufacturers, 53–59 Murray, res 120 Montgomery. Tel,198.
Moellering Wm & Co (Wm and Wm H F Moellering), brick mnfrs 53–59 Murray, brickyards w s Hoagland av s of Rudisill av. Tel 198.
Moellering Wm F (Moellering Bros & Millard), res 118 Montgomery.
Moellering Wm H F (Wm Moellering & Co, res w s Hoagland av s of Rudisill av.
Moellering Wm L (Wm L Moellering & Bro), res 100 E Washington.
Moellering Wm L and Bro (Wm L and Charles B Moellering), Druggists, 191 Lafayette. Tel 47.
Moellering Wm & Son (Wm and Charles E), General Contractors and Dealers in Building Material 53 and 59 Murray. (*See back bone and p 83.*)
Moering Emma N, bds 181 Monroe.
Moering Henry J, res 181 Monroe.
Moering Jane, domestic 252 W Wayne.
Moering Lillie, domestic 252 W Wayne.
Moering Margaret, bds 181 Monroe.
Moering Wilhelmina, bds 181 Monroe.
Moffat Rev David W, Pastor First Presbyterian Church, res 126 E Berry.
Moffat Helen, bds 126 E Berry.
Moffat Mary, bds 126 E Berry.
Moffat Samuel C, city editor Ft W Gazette, bds 126 E Berry.
Moffett Mrs Carrie, nurse 12 Zollars.
Mogalle Julius, lab Penn Co, bds 83 Shawnee av.
Mohl George, watchman, res 529 E Lewis.
Mohl Philip, butcher, rms 78 Barr.
Mohler Orion E, managing editor Ft W Gazette, bds 120 Harrison.
Mohr, *see also Moore.*
Mohr Frank X, collr Hamilton National Bank, bds Clinton s w cor Washington.

Mohr Helen, student, bds s w cor Clinton and Washington
Mohr John, bds s w cor Clinton and Washington.
Mohr John jr, cash Hamilton National Bank and sec Olds' Wagon Wks, res s w cor Clinton and Washington. Tel 486.
Mohr Louis (Mohr & Sosenheimer), res 53 E Washington.
Mohr Rose. bds 53 E Washington.
Mohr & Sosenheimer (Louis Mohr & Charles J Sosenheimer), Real Estate, Loans and Insurance 19 W Wayne.
Molboe Anna, teacher, bds 16 Rockhill.
Moler Wm, laborer, res rear 224 W Main.
Moliton Leonard, watchman Standard Wheel Co, res 69 Charles.
Mollet Henry L, carpenter, res 56 Walnut.
Mollman Wilbert G. brakeman, bds 71 Boone.
Molnovski Wilhelmina (wid Wilhelm), res 237 Force.
Molone, see Malone.
Moloney, see Maloney.
Mommer Benjamin H, dentist 76 Calhoun, bds 126 W Main
Mommer Charles J, molder Bass F & M Wks, bds 172 E Lewis.
Mommer Edward J, barber, bds 199 Broadway.
Mommer Emma E, bds 133 W Main.
Mommer John, mach Ft Wayne Iron Wks, res 172 E Lewis
Mommer John W, molder Kerr Murray Mnfg Co, res 6 McClellan.
Mommer Joseph jr, shoes, 76 Calhoun, res 133 W Main.
Mommer J Franklin, clk Joseph Mommer jr, res 99 W Washington.
Mommer Mary C, bds 133 W Main.
Mommer Wm J, molder Bass F & M Wks, bds 172 E Lewis
Monahan, see also Moynihan.
Monahan Cornelius, student, bds 6 Kansas.
Monahan Dennis (Ohnhaus & Monahan), res 65 E Jefferson.
Monahan Frank G, bkkpr Falk & Co, bds 65 E Jefferson.
Monahan Helen C (wid Daniel), res 6 Kansas.
Monahan John J, boilermkr Wabash R R, res 102 Webster.
Monahan Joseph E, plumber. bds 6 Kansas.
Monahan Mary A, stenogr Weil Bros & Co, bds 6 Kansas.
Monday Morning Times, Gart Shober propr and publr, 45 E Berry. Tel 525.
Mong George E, painter, res 76 Riverside av.
Mong George V, student, bds 76 Riverside av.
Mongey Ernest, res s s Coombs 1 w of New Haven av.

Mongovan Edith, bds 414 Calhoun.
Mongovan Ella, bds 414 Calhoun.
Mongovan Emma, bds 414 Calhoun.
Mongovan Frank, city salesman B W Skelton, res 321 Harrison
Mongovan Thomas C, tool dresser Wabash R R, res 607 Calhoun.
Mongovan Wm E, engr G R & I R R, res 291 Harrison.
Monk Wm F, clk J G Raab, rms 18½ E Columbia.
Monnier Frank, laborer, res 35 Duck.
Monnier Joseph, helper Bass F & M Wks, res 343 Gay.
Monnier Rosa, bds 35 Duck.
Monnier Seraphin, laborer, res 243 Clay.
Monning, see also Manning.
Monning Agnes W, bds 143 E Wayne.
Monning Henry B, mngr Home Billiard Hall, bds 143 E Wayne.
Monning John B, deputy clk Allen County, office Court House, res 29 Hanna.
Monning Mary M, clk J T Dills, bds 143 E Wayne.
Monning M Agnes (wid Henry), res 143 E Wayne.
Monper Matthias, barber 24 W Main, res 287 same.
Monroe Angie (wid Wm), res 92 Franklin.
Monroe Elizabeth (wid George W), boarding, 20 Murray.
Monroe Eugene C, motorman Ft W Elec Ry Co, res 99 Summit.
Monroe Louis, laborer, bds 20 Murray.
Monroe Robert J, coremkr, bds 20 Murray.
Monsdoerfer Charles F, blacksmith, bds 90 Chicago.
Monsdoerfer Emma (wid Ernest), res 90 Chicago.
Montgomery David M, brakeman, bds 65 Baker.
Montgomery Ella, bds 65 Baker.
Montgomery Emma (wid Wm), res 235 Barr.
Montgomery George M, mach E B Kunkle & Co, bds 235 Barr.
Montgomery J Edna, seamstress, bds 65 Baker.
Montgomery Noah, laborer, res 65 Baker.
Monwiller Mary, domestic 256 Fairfield av.
Mood Moses, carpenter, bds 46 Force.
Moody Edward, driver Engine Co No 1, res 86 E Main.
Moolman Wm, brakeman N Y, C & St L R R, bds 75 Boone.
Moon Clara (wid Christopher), res 231 Barr.
Moon Maud M, bds 145 Holman.
Moon Myrtle M, bds 145 Holman.

Mooney Florence (wid Wm), res over 23 Hough.
Mooney Isaac N, condr F, Ft W & W Ry, res 213 Fairfield av.
Mooney Isabella (wid Enos T), res 213 Fairfield av.
Mooney John, engr Penn Co. res 275 E Lewis.
Mooney John M, watchman, res 91 W Main.
Mooney John P, laborer, bds 91 W Main.
Mooney Mary E, laundress, bds 23 Hough.
Moore, see also Mohr.
Moore Abbie E, designer, bds 147 Griffith.
Moore Amber W, laborer, bds 191 St Mary's av.
Moore Chester L, mach hd Olds' W Wks, bds 27 St Martin.
Moore David H, engr Penn Co, res 27 St Martin's.
Moore Edward, bds 8 Hoagland av.
Moore Elias B, molder Penn Co, bds 147 Griffith.
Moore Eliza L (wid J M), res 191 St Mary's av.
Moore Frances C (wid Wm H), bds 485 Harrison.
Moore Francis, clk Ft W Dispatch, bds 113 Holman.
Moore Francis, collector, bds 56 Smith.
Moore Frank S, butcher, bds 23 Suttenfield.
Moore George, engr N Y, C & St L R R, res 57 Elm.
Moore George W, fireman, bds 71 Melita.
Moore Jacob, section hd, res 56 Smith.
Moore James, laborer Penn Co, res 8 Hoagland av.
Moore James C, foreman Hoffman Bros, res 214 Metz.
Moore Jasper, lab Horton Mnfg Co, bds 119 St Mary's av
Moore Mabel E, seamstress, bds 147 Griffith.
Moore Margaret (wid John), bds 8 Hoagland av.
Moore Mary H (wid Thomas C), bds 13 Walnut.
Moore Maud M, stenographer, bds 620 E Wayne.
Moore Maud (Maud and Zula Moore), bds 183 Jackson.
Moore Maud and Zula, Dressmakers 183 Jackson. (See p 115.)
Moore Nathan, brakeman, res 168 Brackenridge.
Moore Olie B, clk Empire Line, bds 27 St Martin's.
Moore Pearl W, bds 100 Wabash av.
Moore Samuel C, condr G R & I R R, res 23 Suttenfield.
Moore Sarah, bds 168 Brackenridge.
Moore Stanley A, stockman, bds Summit City Hotel.
Moore Thomas J, laborer, res 251 Webster.
Moore Vern F, clerk, bds 183 Jackson.
Moore Wm, laborer, bds 191 St Mary's av.
Moore Wm H, lab Ft W Elec Corp, res 6 Brookside.
Moore Wm H, lab Wabash R R, res 13 Walnut.

Moore Wm W, laborer, res cor Pearl and Webster.
Moore W Claude, bds 183 Jackson.
Moore Zula (Maud and Zula Moore), bds 183 Jackson.
Moran Celia, bds 435 Hanna.
Moran Dominick C, wood carver, res 113 W Williams.
Moran D Clifford J, wood turner, bds 113 W Williams.
Moran Edward P, plumber, bds 435 Hanna.
Moran Eliza (wid Wm), res 435 Hanna
Moran Louisa, bds 435 Hanna.
Moran Peter A, ice dealer, 201 E Wayne, res same.
Moran Rachel A (wid Peter), bds 201 E Wayne.
Mordhurst Henry W, drugs, 74 Calhoun, res same. Tel 32.
Morell Adolph, lab Ft W Elec Corp, bds 255 Broadway.
Morell Frank, molder, bds 40 Killea av.
Morell Henry, clk C Schiefer & Son, res 255 Broadway.
Morell Mary (wid Christian), res e s Brooklyn av 2 s of
     Ontario.
Morey, *see also* *Murray*.
Morey Louisa A (wid Edwin), res 438 Fairfield av.
Morey Marian S, bds 438 Fairfield av.
Morey Seldon S, mngr U Press Assn, bds 438 Fairfield av.
Morgan Blanche, bds n s Baltes 1 e of Spy Run av.
Morgan Elmer E, phys, 159 E Lewis, res same.
Morgan Frank M, mach Bass F & M Wks, bds 184 E Jef-
     ferson.
Morgan George W, oil dealer, res 184 E Jefferson.
Morgan Joseph P, conductor, res 111 W Williams.
Morgan Mathew (col'd), res n e cor Maud and Holton av.
Morgan Nannie C (wid John), bds 209 Lafayette.
Morgan Oliver P (Morgan & Beach), vice-pres Old National
     Bank, res 40 E Washington. Tel 276.
Morgan Paul (col'd), molder Ind M Wks, bds M Morgan.
Morgan & Beach (Oliver P Morgan, Frederick
     Beach), Wholesale and Retail Shelf Hardware 19–21
     E Columbia. Tel 131. (*See back cover*).
Moring, *see also* *Moering*.
Moring August J, helper Bass F & M Wks, res 36 Summit
Moring John E, clk Ft W E Corp, res 51 St Martin's.
Moritz August, clk V Moritz, bds 29 Calhoun.
Moritz Charlotte, bds 79 W Berry.
Moritz Elizabeth (wid Peter), bds 79 W Berry.
Moritz Harry L, trav agt, res 160 W Washington.
Moritz Jennie, clk, bds 29 Calhoun.
Moritz John M, res 79 W Berry.
Moritz Vincent, fruit, 26 E Main, res 29 Calhoun.

Morrey Albert R, driver Morgan & Beach, res 59 Maumee av.

Morris, Bell, Barrett & Morris (John and Samuel L Morris, Robert C Bell, James M Barret), Lawyers, 36 E Main.   Tel 29.

Morris Clara, bds 24 Harrison.

Morris Edward J, lab, res 15 Poplar.

Morris James C, brakeman G R & I R R, res 233 Webster

Morris James C, mach hd, bds L W Morris.

Morris James Jr, brakeman G R & I R R, bds 233 Webster

Morris John (Morris, Bell, Barrett & Morris), res 77 Maple av.

Morris John Jr (Breen & Morris), bds 77 Maple av.

Morris Lizzie (wid John), res 56 Chicago.

Morris Lewis W, contr, res s s Killea av 1 w of Calhoun.

Morris Mary, res 77 Maple av.

Morris Mary C, bds 233 Webster.

Morris Samuel L (Morris, Bell, Barrett & Morris), res 282 W Washington.

Morris Stephen, bookkeeper Old National Bank, res 340 W Jefferson.

Morris Thomas, appr Wabash R R, bds 6 Lavina.

Morris Wm P, brakeman N Y, C & St L R R, res 322 W Main.

Morris Wm P, engr N Y, C & St L R R, res 172 W Superior.

Morrissey Michael F, mach Ind M Wks, res 393 W Main.

Morrison M Harry, blacksmith Penn Co, res 41 E Butler.

Morrow Eliza, domestic 164 Harrison.

Morrow Wilhelmina, domestic 278 W Berry.

Morsch Catherine, bds 69 Wall.

Morsch John N, watchman, res 69 Wall.

Morsch Mary, bds 69 Wall.

Morse Emma D, teacher Westminster Seminary, bds 251 W Main.

Morse Frank W, master mechanic Wabash R R, bds The Wayne.

Morton Club, Odd Fellows' Hall.

Morton Harry A, barber, bds 101 Lafayette.

Morton Stella, bds 435 Hanna.

Morton Thomas, moved to Montpelier, Ind.

Morton Wm H, truckman Penn Co, res 24 Killea av.

Morvilius Frank W, cigarmaker, res 48 Barr.

Moser Ambrose, stonecutter Keller & Braun, bds 157 W Main.

Moser Catherine (wid John G), res 108 W Creighton av.

Moser Fritz, laborer, res 92 John.

Moser John G, died September 23, 1894.

Moser Stephen, lab Bass F & M Wks, res 310 E Wayne.

Moses Annette, compiler, bds 244 W De Wald.

Moses Homer P, asst sec Indiana Farmers' Savings and
Loan Association, res 244 W De Wald.

Mosher George, engr G R & I R R, rms 298 Calhoun.

Mosher S J, veneerer Ft Wayne Furn Co, bds 34 W
Superior.

Mospens Charles A, agent, res 65 Brackenridge.

Moss Frederick T, watchman, res 5 Hoagland av.

Moss James W, supt Ft W Furn Co, bds 34 W Superior.

Moss Martin H, molder Bass F & M Wks, res 341 Gay.

Moss Wm, mach Wabash R R, res 122 Fairfield av.

Mosshammer Jacob, coremkr, res 154 Holman.

Mosshammer John M, laborer, bds 109 Barr.

Mosshammer Louisa (wid August), res 144 E Washington.

Mossman Ethel D, bds 328 W Washington.

Mossman Paul B, clk Mossman, Yarnelle & Co, bds 328
W Washington.

Mossman Louisa, bds 99 E Lewis.

Mossman Stella D, student, bds 328 W Washington.

Mossmann Wm E (Mossman, Yarnelle & Co), sec Ft W
Furn Co, res 328 W Washington. Tel 344.

Mossman, Yarnelle & Co (Wm E Moss-
man, Edward F Yarnelle, Weidler S Sponhauer),
Wholesale Iron and Heavy Hardware, 38-42 E Main.
Tel 115.

Mote John R, photogr, 188 Columbia av, res same.

Moten Mary (col'd), bds 70 Murray.

Moten Moses (col'd), engr Kerr Murray Mnfg Co, res 70
Murray,

Motherwell, see also Moderwell.

Motherwell Annie G, opr S M Foster, bds 141 High.

Motherwell Frank, bds 141 High.

Motherwell Henry, tinner C F Graffe & Co, bds 141 High.

Motherwell John E, watchman L Diether & Bro, res 141
High.

Motherwell J Edward, tinner C F Graffe & Co, res 107 John

Motherwell Margurite, seamstress, bds 141 High.

Motherwell Michael, printer, bds 141 High.

Motherwell R Alice, seamstress, bds 141 High.

Motherwell Wm, bartender, bds 141 High.

Motsch Fritz, boarding house 518 Fairfield av.

Motz George (George Motz & Co), res 30 2d.
Motz George jr, clerk, bds 30 2d.
Motz George & Co (George and John G A Motz and Otto Herbst), Real Estate and Insurance 47 W Main. (*See classified Insurance Agents.*)
Motz John G A (George Motz & Co), cigars 47 W Main, bds 30 2d.
Mounsir Ada, clk M Frank & Co, bds 50 Brackenridge.
Mounsir Nelson D, bartender, rms 12 Chicago.
Mowrer, *see also Maurer.*
Mowrer Maud, domestic 166 W Wayne.
Moyer John, res 42 St Mary's av.
Moyer Mrs Sabra, rms rear 45 W Main.
Moynihan, *see also Monahan.*
Moynihan Andrew J, sec and treas The Journal Co, bds McKinnie House.
Mudd George W, removed to Springfield, Ill.
Muehlfeith Charles, saloon 10 W Main, res 40 Wells.
Muehlfeith Robert B, malster C L Centlivre Brewing Co, res 38 Wells.
Mueller Charles M, tailor J G Thieme & Son, res 140 High.
Mueller Rev Francis X, asst St Paul's Church (German), res 95 Griffith.
Mueller Frank R, teamster, bds Gottlieb Mueller.
Mueller Gottlieb, laborer, bds 6 Force.
Mueller Gottlieb, teamster, res s s 7th 1 e of Wells.
Mueller Henry, baker W F Geller, bds 140 High.
Mueller Henry, horseshoer Louis Schwartz, res 19 Michael av.
Mueller John G, finisher, bds 49 Barthold.
Mueller Louisa E, tailoress, bds Gottlieb Mueller.
Mueller Pauline E, bds Gottlieb Mueller.
Mueller Theodore, helper Fleming Mnfg Co, res Adams township.
Muesing Lucetta (wid Christian), bds s w cor Reed and Jennison.
Muhlenbruch Charles F, driver Pape Furniture Co, bds 17 Breck.
Muhlenbruch Charles G, packer, res 250 E Washington.
Muhlenbruch Dietrich, mach Ft W Elec Corp, bds 150 Ewing.
Muhlenbruch Deidrich C G, cabtmkr Penn Co, res 213 E Jefferson.
Muhlenbruch Frederick, lab Penn Co, bds 213 E Jefferson

Muhlenbruch Frederick G, clk S Freiburger & Bro, res 238 E Washington.

Muhlenbruch Gustave D, clk J B White, bds 238 E Washington.

Muhlenbruch Henry, mason, res 148 Greeley.

Muhlenbruch Louisa J, dressmkr. bds 238 E Washington.

Muhlenbruch Mina, mach opr, bds 213 E Jefferson.

Muhlenbruch Otto R G, clk, bds 238 E Washington.

Muhlenbruch Wm, wagonmkr Fleming Mnfg Co, res 17 Pape av.

Muhlenbruch Wm C C, clk Pape Furniture Co, bds 238 E Washington.

Muhler August T, bkkpr Hamilton National Bank, bds 166 W Wayne.

Muhler Bernard C (Chas F Muhler & Son), bds 166 W Wayne.

Muhler Catherine E, bds 166 W Wayne.

Muhler Charles F (Charles F and Bernard C), res 166 W Wayne. Tel 210.

Muhler Charles F & Son (Charles F & Bernard C), lime, 7 N Calhoun. Tel 179.

Muhler Edward F, bds 166 W Wayne.

Muhler Howard J, clerk. bds 129 W Main.

Muhler Mrs Mary E, cashier. bds 129 W Main.

Muir John J, draughtsman Ft W Elec Corp, rms 134 W Berry.

Muirhead Alexander, mach Wabash R R, res 513 Calhoun.

Muirhead John W, driver P E Cox, bds 513 Calhoun.

Muirhead Laura D, teacher Holton Avenue School, bds 513 Calhoun.

Muirhead Margaret F, teacher Miner School, bds 513 Calhoun.

Mulcahy Richard, laborer, res 58 Spy Run av.

Mulcahy Wm J, blksmith, bds 58 Spy Run av.

Muldary Andrew J, res 207 John.

Muldary Mary, knitter, bds 207 John.

Muldoon Angeline, bds 280 E Lewis.

Muldoon Charles, res over 35 W Main.

Muldoon Margaret (wid Patrick), res 280 E Lewis.

Muldoon Wm, grocer, 212 Fairfield av, bds same.

Mulharen Thomas, grocer, 117 Fairfield av, res 115 same.

Mull Nathan, huckster, res 41 Harmer.

Mullahy Annie (wid Wm), res 12 Colerick.

Mullahy Frank S, printer Ft Wayne Sentinel, bds 12 Colerick.

Mullahy John F, plumber R Ogden, bds 12 Colerick.
Mullahy Wm F, clk Penn Co, bds 12 Colerick.
Mullen Daniel D, engr Bond's Cereal Mills, bds 140 Barr.
Mullen George, engr N Y, C & St L R R, bds 335 W Main.
Mullen Henry, mach hd Ft W Furn Co, bds 57 Barr.
Mullen John F, carpenter, res 140 Barr.
Mullen Reuben, hostler C J Ulmer, res 90 E Main.
Muller, see also Miller, Moeller, Mueller and Muhler.
Muller Caroline, domestic 313 Lafayette.
Muller Herman, coremkr Bass F & M Wks, res 110 Eliza.
Mullins Johanna (wid Patrick), bds 117 Fairfield av.
Mulqueen Elizabeth (wid John W), res 83 E Berry
Mulqueen Stella, bds 83 E Berry
Mumford Robert E, lab City Trucking Co, res 96 Ewing
Mundt Ernest W, electrician Penn Co, res 44 Baker.
Mundt Frederick H, appr R Spice, bds 44 Baker.
Mungen Charles C, clk E H Coombs, bds 123 E Main.
Mungen Grace E, clk L Wolf & Co, bds 123 E Main.
Mungen John J, street commissioner, res 123 E Main.
Mungen Lynne M, stenogr Star Iron Tower Co, bds 123 E Main.
Mungen W Wallace, dentist, 2 E Columbia, rms same.
Mungovan Edward, bds 414 Calhoun.
Mungovan Thomas jr, bds 414 Calhoun.
Munich, see also Minnich.
Munich John, barber, 372 Calhoun, res 128 W Williams.
Munn James, farmer, res n of School for F M Y.
Munsdorfer, see Monsdoerfer.
Munson Charles A, bds 22 W Wayne.
Murbach Sadie, opr S M Foster, bds 37 Maumee rd
Murdock F E, teacher School Feeble Minded Youth.
Murphy Amos W, painter, res 281 W Main.
Murphy Barney, laborer, res 39 Duck.
Murphy Caroline, bds 53 Force.
Murphy Catherine (wid Francis J, res 55 E Williams.
Murphy Catherine, teacher, bds 55 E Williams.
Murphy Dennis C, switchman, res 33 Bass.
Murphy Edward W, bds 138 Holman.
Murphy Elizabeth, bds 55 E Williams.
Murphy Frank A, engr N Y, C & St L R R, res 14 St Mary's av.
Murphy Genevieve, mach opr, bds 16 Park.
Murphy George, gardener, res 11 Colerick.
Murphy George H, caller N Y, C & St L R R, bds 281 W Main.

Murphy James F, lab Penn Co, bds 195 Barr.
Murphy Johanna (wid Dennis), res 7 Colerick.
Murphy John, mach Ft W Elec Corp, res 138 Holman.
Murphy John, candymkr, bds 72 South Wayne av.
Murphy John H, painter, bds 53 Force.
Murphy John J, carp Wabash R R, res 72 South Wayne av.
Murphy John W, brakeman N Y, C & St L R R, bds 281 W Main.
Murphy Kate A, domestic 216 W Wayne.
Murphy Margaret I, teacher Bloomingdale School, bds 55 E Williams.
Murphy Mary F, stenogr L Wolf & Co, bds 55 E Williams.
Murphy Michael M, engineer, res 151 Fairfield av.
Murphy Minnie, bds 138 Holman.
Murphy M E, res 284 Harrison.
Murphy Nicholas, condr G R & I R R, bds 151 Fairfield av.
Murphy Nicholas J, appr Wabash R R, bds 151 Fairfield av
Murphy Patrick, watchman, res 54 Melita.
Murphy Patrick J, brakeman, bds 138 Holman.
Murphy Rose, bds 354 Hanna.
Murphy Samuel C, foreman, res 53 Force.
Murphy Sarah E, bds 53 Force.
Murphy Thady, lab Standard Wheel Co, bds 231 Calhoun.
Murphy Thomas J, machinist, bds 138 Holman.
Murphy Thomas J, switchman, bds 20 Van Buren.
Murphy Wm, laborer, bds 209 Lafayette.
Murphy Wm A, winder Ft W Elec Corp, res 207 Broadway
Murphy Wm E, conductor, bds 138 Holman.
Murphy Wm H, laborer Penn Co, bds 53 Force.
Murray, *see also Morey.*
Murray David, blcksmith Wabash R R, res 409 Broadway
Murray Eliza, waitress J C Hinton, res 270½ Calhoun.
Murray James, plumber, res 423 E Washington.
Murray John, cabtmkr L Diether & Bro, res 282 E Washington.
Murray Joseph V, fireman N Y, C & St L R R, bds 30 Runnion av.
Murray Mary A, tailoress A Foster, bds 39 W Washington
Murray Nellie M, bds 15 Baker.
Murray Newton, lineman, res 36 Clinton.
Murray Ophelia M (wid Americus W), res 15 Baker.
Murray T H, baggageman G R & I R R, bds Harmon House.
Mussmann Catherine (wid John), res 231 E Wayne.

Mutual Life Insurance Company of Indiana, Home Office Indianapolis, Ind, Oscar P Eversole Genl Agt, Dept Office rms 1–4, 12 W Wayne. (*See right side lines.*)

Mutual Life Insurance Company of N Y, H L Palmer Dist Mngr, 32 E Berry. Tel 46.

Myers, *see also Maher, Maier Mayer Meier and Meyer.*

Myers August H, carpenter, res 42 St Mary's av.

Myers Catherine (wid Frederick). res 416 Clinton.

Myers Charles, rms 110 Calhoun.

Myers Charles A, laborer, bds 88½ Madison.

Myers Charles F, res 66 Douglas av.

Myers Darwin S, clk Ft W Elec Corp, res 40 Michigan av.

Myers Emma C, dressmaker, bds 66 Douglas av.

Myers Frederick H, livery, 62 E Wayne, res 106 Webster. Tel 302.

Myers George, cigar mnfr, 66 Maumee rd, res same.

Myers George S, laborer, res 109 Holman.

Myers George W, rms 110 Calhoun.

Myers Henry C, fireman, bds 66 Douglas av.

Myers Henry J, carp Kerr Murray Mnfg Co, res 185 Lafayette.

Myers Margaret (wid Ephraim), bds 88 Wells.

Myers Martin, laborer, res 16 Maiden lane.

Myers Mrs Mary A, res 109 Holman.

Myers Maude, domestic w s Spy Run av 3 s of Ruth.

Myers Nelson, helper Horton Mnfg Co, bds n s High nr St Mary's av.

Myers N Louis (col'd), porter The Wayne, rms 84 W Main.

Myers P J Henry, chief clk Superintendent's office N Y, C & St L R R, res 485 Harrison.

Myers Sherman H, flagman Penn Co, res 308 Harrison.

Myers Wm, blksmith Penn Co, res 87 Grant av.

Myers Wm, traveling agent, bds 71 Melita.

Myers Wm F, vet surg, 62 E Wayne and 114 Webster, res 66 Douglas av. Tel 77.

Myers Wm H, bkkpr Hamilton National Bank, bds 165 Griffith.

Myers Wm H, phys, 157 W Wayne, res same. Tel 39.

Myers Wm M, laborer, bds 109 Holman.

Myron Frank, bds St James Hotel.

N

Naber August, bartndr T J Baker, bds 198 Broadway.

Nablo Ephraim, clk Geo De Wald & Co, rms 49 W Berry.
Nagel Frederick, watchman Wabash R R, res 99 W Jefferson.
Nagel Joseph M (Nagel & O'Ryan), bds 35 1st.
Nagel Kate, tailoress bds 35 1st.
Nagel Lawrence, cigarmkr W A Bayer, bds 35 1st.
Nagel Minnie J, bds 35 1st.
Nagel Xavier, wagonmkr Chauvey Bros, res 35 1st.
Nagel & O'Ryan (Joseph M Nagel, James O'Ryan), horseshoers, 50 Barr.
Nahrwold, see also Norwald.
Nahrwold Charles, carpenter, res 97 Eliza.
Nahrwold Charles. plasterer. res 265 E Lewis.
Nahrwold Charles F, mach hd Penn Co. bds 267 E Lewis.
Nahrwold Christian, plumber J C Jahn & Co, bds 147 E Lewis.
Nahrwold Christian C, boilermkr Bass Wks, res 147 E Lewis.
Nahrwold Conrad, carp Penn Co, res 267 E Lewis.
Nahrwold Diedrich, carp Bass F & M Wks, res 164 Smith.
Nahrwold Diedrich W, molder Bass F & M Wks, res 212 Smith.
Nahrwold Emma H, clk Rehling & Stegner, bds 29 Wilt.
Nahrwold Ernest F, car repr Penn Co, res 413 E Lewis.
Nahrwold Frank, bds 29 Wilt.
Nahrwold Frederick, lab Penn Co, res 25 Wilt.
Nahrwold Frederick C, boilermkr Wabash R R, bds 25 Wilt.
Nahrwold Frederick W, molder Bass F & M Wks, res 122 Force.
Nahrwold Henry E F, mach hd Horton Mnfg Co, bds 29 Wilt.
Nahrwold Henry F, clk Root & Co, bds 147 E Lewis.
Nahrwold Hermina C, seamstress, bds 25 Wilt.
Nahrwold John E, trimmer Olds' W Wks, bds 383 Lafayette.
Nahrwold Louisa, seamstress, bds 25 Wilt.
Nahrwold Louise E, tailoress, bds 147 E Lewis.
Nahrwold Minnie, bds 29 Wilt.
Nahrwold Minnie, domestic 16 Cass.
Nahrwold Minnie E, tailoress, bds 147 E Lewis.
Nahrwold Sophia, domestic 46 Superior.
Nahrwold Wm, bds 164 Smith.
Nahrwold Wm, sawyer Olds' Wagon Works, res 383 Lafayette.

Nahrwold Wm F, supt Horton Mnfg Co, res 29 Wilt.
Nash Daisy L, trimmer, bds 173 Griffith.
Nash Edna (wid Frederick E), res 117 Griffith.
Nash Frederick E, died Jan 3, 1895.
Nash Henry C, blksmith Olds' W Wks, res 72 Hamilton.
Nash Louis H, clerk, bds 173 Griffith.
Nassenstein Wilhelm, carpenter, res 38 E Pontiac.
Nathan Charles (A Hirsh & Co), res 142 W Berry.
Nathan Julius (Julius Nathan & Co), res 142 W Berry
Nathan Julius & Co (Julius Nathan, Max Rubin), whol liquors, 137 Calhoun. Tel 270.
Nathan Knim, finisher, bds 312 W Main.
National Cash Register Co, E B Wilson Sales Agent, 31 Bass Blk.
National Cigar Factory (Al Hazzard propr), 11 E Main.
National Express Co, Loyal P Hulburd Agt, 24 E Main. Tel 141.
National Life Ins Co of Montpelier, Vt, C B Fitch, genl agt, 26 Bass Blk.
Nave George W, res 38 South Wayne av.
Nave Isaac, res 302 Harrison.
Naylor John F, clk Wabash R R, bds 63 Brackenridge.
Neal, see also Neil and O'Neil.
Neal Caleb J, driver W F Geller, res 112½ Broadway.
Neale George E, rms 249 W Washington.
Nease Ulysses S, laborer, rms 146 Broadway.
Neasel Harry J, condr Ft W E Ry Co, res 70 Charles.
Nebelhour John F, mach Penn Co, bds 169 Brackenridge.
Nebraska School, s e cor Boone and Fry.
Neeb August J, candymkr Fox br U S Baking Co, res s s Poplar 1 e of Fox.
Neeb Catherine (wid George), res 54 Oakley.
Neeb Emma C, dressmaker, bds 54 Oakley.
Neeb John, laborer, bds 59 Walnut.
Neeb John G, laborer, res 60 Walnut.
Neeb Louis G, carver Ft W O Co, bds 54 Oakley.
Neeb Wm G, clk Fox br U S Bkg Co, bds 54 Oakley.
Needham Edward F, boilermkr Wabash R R, res 122 Fairfield av.
Nees, see also Kneese and Neise.
Nees Albert, student, bds 28 Schick.
Nees Bertha, opr S M Foster, bds 28 Schick.
Nees Eliza, tailoress, bds 28 Schick.
Nees Henry B, sheet iron wkr, res 28 Schick.
Nees Henry C C, cabtmkr Penn Co, res 28 Schick.

Neese Emma, res 21 W 4th.
Neff August, lab Penn Co, bds 323 W Main.
Neff John H, res 461 W Main.
Neff John H, harnessmkr, bds 100 Greeley.
Neff Rebecca (wid Enoch), bds 461 W ..ain.
Neff Wm F, lab K Baker, res 100 Greeley.
Neher Anna, opr, bds 12 Francis.
Neher Elizabeth (wid Joseph), rms 14 Francis.
Neher Frank, spoke mkr, bds 12 Francis.
Neher John V (Cramer & Neher), res 111 Pontiac.
Neher Joseph, shoemkr, 12 Francis, res same.
Neher Joseph, died June 25th, 1894.
Nehrenz Henry, prin T G L School, rms 166 Barr.
Neibel John, helper Penn Co, res 32 W Butler.
Neidermeyer, see Niedermeyer.
Neidhammer, see Niedhammer.
Neidhart Joseph, cabtmkr, res 60 Madison.
Neidhart Rosa, opr S M Foster, bds 60 Madison.
Neidhart Theresa, opr S M Foster, bds 60 Madison.
Neidhofer Mary F, bds 61 St Martin's.
Neil, see also Neal and O'Neil.
Neiman, see also Nieman.
Neiman Louis J, driver Engine Co No 2, res 112 Wallace.
Neimeyer Christina M, domestic 135 E Berry.
Neireiter Amanda, bds 92 Wilt.
Neireiter Amanda, domestic 18 Union.
Neireiter Conrad (Neireiter & Gumpper), res 269 W Washington.
Neireiter Eva A (wid Casper B), res 46 W Lewis.
Neireiter Jessie M, bds 46 W Lewis.
Neireiter Rebecca (wid John), res 92 Wilt.
Neireiter Wm, actionmkr F W Organ Co, bds 111 Wall.
Neireiter & Gumpper (Conrad Neireiter, Charles H Gumpper), real est, 76 Calhoun.
Neise, see also Kneese and Nees.
Neise Mrs Addie, bds 149 Barr.
Neiswonger, see also Niswonger.
Neiswonger Ella, dressmaker, rms 62 W Lewis.
Neizer Wm J, tinner Penn Co, bds St James Hotel.
Nelligan Ellen, bds 23 W Lewis.
Nelligan John, res 23 W Lewis.
Nelligan Mary, bds 23 W Lewis.
Nelson Caroline (wid John R), bds 59 Wilt.
Nelson Charles A, printer, bds 59 Wilt.
Nelson Elizabeth (wid Elmore C), res 60 W Wayne.

Nelson Eva, bds 103 W Berry.
Nelson Eva T, bds 262 W Berry.
Nelson Gustave L, bds 101 Taylor.
Nelson Helen E (wid De Groff), res 262 W Berry.
Nelson Henry, actionmaker, res 4 Killea av.
Nelson Ingerd (wid Nelse), bds 116 Home av.
Nelson Rev James S, res 395 Calhoun.
Nelson John, cabtmkr Ft W Organ Co, res 116 Home av.
Nelson J Fremont, trav agt, res 57 Rivermet av.
Nelson Louis A, res s s Rudisill av 4 w of Piqua av.
Nelson Mark A, pressman Ft W Newspaper Union, res 59 Wilt.
Nelson Rena B, bds 395 Calhoun.
Nelson Stella, bds 395 Calhoun.
Nelson Thomas, lab W Gas Const Co, res 36 Edgerton.
Nelson Thomas R, res 256 E Wayne.
Nemeyer Louis, lab Ind M Wks, bds 2 Elm.
Nerhood Fiana, dressmkr, bds 43 E Butler.
Nerhood James J, carpenter, bds 103 High.
Nerhood Matilda, nurse 43 E Butler, bds same.
Nerhood Matthias, barnman, res 103 High.
Nern Conrad, laborer, res 1 Coombs.
Nern Conrad E, lab L E & W R R, res 173 Erie.
Nern John, laborer, bds 1 Coombs.
Nern Katie, bds 1 Coombs.
Nern Lena, clerk, bds 1 Coombs.
Nern Minnie, bds 1 Coombs.
Nesbit David E, foreman, res 163 Clinton.
Ness, *see Kneese.*
Nessel Christina (wid Michael), res 463 Lafayette.
Nessell John G A, bds 463 Lafayette.
Nessel Lill e S, seamstress, bds 463 Lafayette.
Nessel Minnie I S, seamstress, bds 463 Lafayette.
Nessler John, bds w s Lumbard 1 s of Wabash R R.
Nestel Adolph G, shoemkr, 117 E Lewis, res 187½ Lafayette
Nestel Charles, bds 22 Scott av.
Nestel Charles W, bds 243 W Creighton av.
Nestel Charles W and Eliza S, Lilliputian Artists, Known as Commodore Foote and Fairy Queen, 243 W Creighton av.
Nestel Daniel, Propr South Broadway Nursery, Real Estate and Veterinary Surgeon, res Evergreen Terrace, 243 W Creighton av.
Nestel Daniel jr, painter, res 22 Scott av.
Nestel Edward P, painter, 115 E Lewis, res 187 Lafayette.

Nestel Eliza S, bds 243 W Creighton av.

Nestel John, laborer, bds 111 Pontiac.

Nestel Oscar W, res 274 W Jefferson.

Nestel Philip, tanner, res 187 Lafayette.

Nestel's Blk, s w cor Broadway and W Jefferson.

Nester Martin, driver engine Co No 1, 89 E Main, rms same

Nettlehorst Charles C, lab Wabash R R, res 193 Wallace.

Neu Herman, laborer, res s e cor Fisher and Thomas.

Neu Joseph, res 42 Lasselle.

Neu Joseph jr, driver Root & Co, bds 42 Lasselle.

Neuenschwander Isaac M. res 73 Columbia av.

Neuenschwander Matilda, clk Geo DeWald & Co, bds 73 Columbia av.

Neufer John M, drugs, 544 Calhoun, res same. Tel 435.

Neufer Leonard, hostler Wabash R R, res 419 Calhoun.

Neufer Rose M, clk People's Store, bds 419 Calhoun.

Neuhaus Frank (Jacobs & Neuhaus), bds 159 Harrison.

Neuhaus Frank G, carpenter, res 61 Huffman.

Neuhaus Lucy, bds 61 Huffman.

Neuhaus Reinhard H, shoemkr, rear 40 Harrison, res s e cor St Mary's av and Margaret.

Neuhaus & Jacobs (Frank A Neuhaus, James Jacobs), proprs City Trucking Co, 19, 23, W Washington.

Neukamm George, Propr Washington House, 121 and 123 Calhoun. (See right bottom lines.)

Neukamm John, lab, bds w s Walton 5 s of Pontiac.

Neukamm John, dairy, e s Smith 1 s of Pontiac, res same.

Neumann, see also Newman.

Neumann Albert A, lab City Mills, bds 158 Taylor.

Neumann August F, laborer, res 63 John.

Neumann Clara V, opr, bds 158 Taylor.

Neumann Gertrude, laundress Hotel Rich.

Neumann John, lab Bass Wks, res 480 Hanna.

Neumann J Matthias, laborer, res 167 E Creighton av.

Neumann Lizzie, domestic 70 Thomas.

Neumann Louis D, carp Olds' W Wks, res 70 Thomas.

Neumann Maggie, opr, bds 167 E Creighton av.

Neumann Matthias P, messenger, bds 167 E Creighton av

Neumann Peter, box mkr, bds 167 E Creighton av.

Neumann Peter, hostler, bds 44 W Leith.

Neumann Victoria (wid August), res 158 Taylor.

Neumann Walter, laborer, bds 158 Taylor.

Neumann Wm, lab Bass Wks, bds 99 Broadway.

Neumann Wm, mach hd, res 62 Lillie.

Neumeier Adam, grocer, 381 E Lewis, res same.

Neuroth Charles, student, bds 160 Taylor.
Neuroth Louis F, foreman Wabash R R, res 160 Taylor.
Neuroth Mary, dressmaker, bds 37 Stophlet.
New Aveline House, W D Jones Propr, s e
    cor Calhoun and Berry. Tel 30.
New Catholic Cemetery, Hicksville State rd, 2¼ miles e of
    Columbia bridge.
New York, Chicago & St Louis R R,
    (Nickel Plate), Charles D Gorham Division Supt,
    Melvin C Baker District Passenger and Ticket Agt, H
    C Moderwell Freight Agt; Passenger Depot Calhoun
    nr Superior; Freight Depot Harrison nr Superior;
    Tel. Ticket Office 507, Freight Office 132. (*See back
    fly leaf*).
New York Life Insurance Co, Wm P
    Cooper Special Agent, 33 E Berry. Tel 188. (*See
    adv next page.*)
New York and London Electric Assn,
    B E Joseph Mngr, Magneto-Conservative Apparatus
    and Electric Physicians, 101 E Wayne. (*See adv in
    classified Deformity Apparatus.*)
Newcomer Christian, res 145 Griffith.
Newell Hans, gardener, res 46 Park av.
Newell Lydia A, bds 12 Erie.
Newell Nellie I, teacher Hoagland School, bds 79 Doug-
    las av.
Newell Sarah E, bds 79 Douglas av.
Newell Sarah H (wid Charles D), res 79 Douglas av.
Newhouse Henry D, grocer, 2 Lincoln av.
Newhouse Mary L, clk People's Store, bds 31 1st.
Newhouse Nellie M, dressmaker, bds 17 Brandriff.
Newhouse Wm E, condr Ft W E Ry Co, res 17 Brandriff.
Newhouse Mrs Wm E, dressmkr, 39 Melita, res same.
Newingham W J, car bldr Penn Co, res 230 E Lewis.
Newland Fannie, seamstress, bds 95 Smith.
Newland Henry F, engr Hoosier Mnfg Co, res 38 E 3d.
Newton Charles H, Local Freight Agent
    Wabash R R, Freight Agent F, Ft Wayne & Western
    Ry, res 56 Douglas av.
Newton Frederick C, bds 103 W Berry.
Newton Reuben F, clerk, bds 103 W Berry.
Newton Reuben W, clk Beuret & Co, bds Hamilton House
Nicholas George M, res 2 Brookside.
Nicholas Mattie, domestic School F M Y.
Nicholas Richard, laborer, bds rear 198 Lafayette.

Nicholas, *see also Nickels.*
Nichols Emanuel M, waiter O Wobrock, rms 220 Calhoun.
Nichols John, laborer, rms 8 Orchard.
Nichols John, physician 1 Riverside av, res same.
Nichols Mrs Julia, nurse School F M Y.
Nicholson James, condr N Y, C & St L R R, res 107 Jackson.
Nicholson Alice M, bds 140 Holman.
Nicholson Fanny, bds 140 Holman.
Nicholson John M, brakeman, res 140 Holman.
Nicholson Maud E, bds 140 Holman.
Nicholson Sarah (wid John M), bds 140 Holman.
Nichter Elizabeth K, opr S M Foster, bds 34 Hendricks.
Nichter Frances M, bds 34 Hendricks.
Nichter George J, barber 99 Broadway, res 118 Baker.
Nichter Helen, bds 48 Hendricks.
Nichter Henry J, clk Geo De Wald & Co, bds 48 Hendricks
Nichter John J, carp L Diether & Bro, res 62 Walnut.
Nichter Joseph, lab Wabash R R, res 34 Hendricks.
Nichter Otto, molder, res 48 Hendricks.
Nichter Peter P, mach Wabash R R, res 22 Nirdlinger av.

Nickel Plate Depot, N Y, C & St L R R, M C Baker District Passenger and Ticket Agt, Calhoun nr Superior.

Nickel Plate Restaurant, Frank J Lourent Proprietor, Nickel Plate Pass Depot. Tel 412.

Nickell Andrew J, engr G R & I R R, res s e cor Simons and Winter.

Nickell John F, engr G R & I R R, res 130 W Washington

Nickels, *see also Nichols.*

Nickels Alexander W D, laborer, bds Wm Nickels.

Nickels James W, bds Wm Nickels.

Nickels Wm, res s e Piqua av 1 s of Marshall.

Nickels Wm C, clk J B White, bds Wm Nickels.

Nickerson Christopher C, lab, res 290 Harrison.

Nickerson Ezra, truckman, res 81 Home av.

Nickerson John, teamster Kilian Baker, res 93 E Columbia

Nickerson Lorenzo H, teamster, res 35 Ewing.

Nickey Alfred J, condr Ft W Elec Ry Co, bds 493 Calhoun

Nickolid Forest E, fireman G R & I R R, bds 396 Clinton.

Nicodemus Charles moved to Roanoke, Ind.

Nicole Frederick, lab Penn Co, res n s Chestnut 1 e of Lumbard.

Nicole James H, jeweler, res n s New Haven av 6 e of Summer.

Nicole Laura, dishwasher O Wobrock.

Nicole Netta, domestic Lake Shore Hotel.

Nicole Nimrod, laborer, bds J H Nicole.

Niebergall Charles A, bds 201 E Washington.

Niebergall Fredrick W, bds 201 E Washington.

Niebergall Henry S, grocer 201 E Washington, res same.

Niebergall H Louisa, clerk, bds 201 E Washington.

Niebur Henry, laborer, res 75 Force.

Niebur John, laborer, res 24 Lillie.

Niebur Mathilda M, domestic 184 Calhoun.

Niedermeyer Frederick, molder Bass F & M Wks, bds 24 Lasselle.

Niedermeyer Joseph, helper Bass F & M Wks, res 30 Lasselle.

Niedermeyer Paul, res 24 Lasselle.

Niedermeyer Paul jr, molder Bass Wks, bds 24 Lasselle.

Niedermeyer Peter, molder Bass F & M Wks, bds 24 Lasselle.

Niedhammer Alma W (wid George), res 158 Madison.

Niedhammer George H, mach, bds 158 Madison.

Niedhammer Hervey C, clk N Y, C & St L R R, bds 158 Madison.

Niedhammer Sibyl A, clk People's Store, bds 158 Madison.

Nieman, see also Neiman.

Nieman Anna, opr Hoosier Mnfg Co, bds 23 Maumee rd.

Nieman Benjamin, clerk, bds 2 Liberty.

Nieman Bernard, res 272 E Washington.

Nieman Clara, bds 272 E Washington.

Nieman Edith, dressmkr, bds 23 Maumee rd.

Nieman Edward, lab J Weick & Co, bds 23 Maumee rd.

Nieman John C, lab Hoffman Bros, res 186 W Main.

Nieman John, watchman Ft W Gas Co, res 23 Maumee rd.

Nieman John jr, painter, bds 23 Maumee rd.

Nieman Mary (wid Theodore), died August 3d, 1894.

Nieman Theresa, seamstress, bds 2 Liberty.

Niemann Gottlieb, res 68 Brackenridge.

Niemann Gottlieb F jr, moved to Indianapolis, Ind.

Niemann Henry D, grocer, 148 Calhoun, bds 68 Brackenridge. Tel 408.

Niemann Lizzie, bds 68 Brackenridge.

Niemann Wm F, photo printer, bds 68 Brackenridge.

Niemeyer, see also Neumeyer.

Niemeyer Christian C, res n e cor New Haven and Summer.

Niemeyer Emily, bds 155 Madison.

Niemeyer Ernest F, clk Geo DeWald & Co, bds 155 Madison

Niemeyer Henry C, clk Geo De Wald & Co, bds 155 Madison.

Niemeyer Henry J, res 155 Madison.

Niemeyer Louis H, clk Pixley & Co, res 153 Madison.

Niemeyer Minnie, domestic 164 W Berry.

Niemeyer Wm A, teamster, bds 155 Madison.

Niepoth Henry A, painter Wabash R R, res 62 Oakley.

Niermann Anna (wid Harman), res 112 Erie.

Niermann August C, lab, bds 13 Hoagland av.

Niermann Herman, died May 23rd, 1894.

Niermann Martin H, cigar mkr, res 26 Guthrie av.

Niermann Mary (wid Martin), res 13 Hoagland av.

Nieschang Charles C F, phys, 298 Calhoun, res same

Niesz B Ellen, bds 37½ W Berry.

Nieter Frederick H, boilermkr, res 118 Madison.

Nieter Henry C, carpenter, res 51 Holton av.

Nieter Louisa J S, bds 118 Madison.

Nikolai Dora E, dressmkr, bds 396 Clinton.

Nikolai Forest E, fireman G R & I R R, bds 396 Clinton.

Nill Conrad, lab, res 13 Clark.

Nill George E, shoemkr, 191 Broadway, res 36 Wall.
Nill R Barbara (wid Conrad), bds 32 W Washington.
Nill Wm H, mach Bass Wks, bds 36 Wall.
Nille Emma, bds 29 W Wayne.
Nimrod Hall, 54 E Main.
Nimtz Charles, lab Olds' W Wks, bds 106 High.
Nimtz David, polisher Olds' W Wks, res 67 John.
Nimtz Pauline, seamstress, bds 67 John.
Ninde Benjamin F (Ninde & Ninde), office Tri-State Bldg, res 187 W Wayne. Tel 293.
Ninde Daniel B, lawyer, bds 416 Fairfield av.
Ninde Elizabeth M C (wid Frederick F), bds 241 W Berry.
Ninde Ethel M, bds 187 W Wayne.
Ninde Henry W (L M & H W Ninde), bds 416 Fairfield av
Ninde James W, bds 278 W Berry.
Ninde Lindley M (L M & H W Ninde), res 416 Fairfield av Tel 366.
Ninde L M & H W (Lindley M and Henry W), lawyers, 42 W Berry. Tel 215.
Ninde Rebecca H, res 187 W Wayne.
Ninde Wm M (Ninde & Ninde), office Tri-State Bldg, res 187 W Wayne.
Ninde & Ninde (Wm M and Benjamin F), Lawyers, Tri-State Bldg. Tel 368.
Nisely Wm H, laborer, res 113 Mechanic.
Niswonger George D, clk E W Lewis, res 170 W Washington.
Niswonger Henry W, phys 33 Calhoun, res same.
Niswonger Roland C (R C Niswonger & Co), rms 33 Calhoun.
Niswonger R C & Co (Roland C Niswonger), real estate, 33 Calhoun.
Nitzsche Emil, lab Bass F & M Wks, res 43 Smith.
Nix Charles, molder, bds 80 E Jefferson.
Nix Elizabeth M, dressmaker, bds 80 E Jefferson.
Nix Flora M, dressmaker, 80 E Jefferson. bds same.
Nix Henry, shoemkr P J Eggemann, res 32 Clinton.
Nix John, laborer, bds 80 E Jefferson.
Nix Joseph, shoemkr P J Eggemann, res 255 E Wayne.
Nix Matilda, domestic 186 W Berry.
Nix Solina L, milliner, bds 80 E Jefferson.
Nix Sophia C, teacher Holton School, bds 80 E Jefferson.
Nix Valentine, shoemaker 80 E Jefferson, res same.
Nixon Jessie L, dressmaker, bds 80 W 3d.
Nixon Roger S, butcher, res 84 N Harrison.

Noack Henry, baker G Klippert, bds same.
Noble Alfred D, electrician, bds 62 W Williams.
Noble Bros (Charles E and Wm K), lumber, office Baldwin, Ind.
Noble Carrie B, bds 62 W Williams.
Noble Charles E (Shepler & Noble and Noble Bros); bds 33 Brackenridge.
Noble Charles M, turner, res Pittsburg s e cor Bond.
Noble Edward D, fireman, res 103 Wallace.
Noble Frank E, traveling agt, res 62 W Williams.
Noble Henry, physician, res 24 Winch.
Noble Hubert E, adv sol Ft W Gazette, res 409 Calhoun.
Noble James E, trav agt Bass F & M Wks, res 33 Brackenridge.
Noble Jane R (wid Wm), bds 58 W Pontiac.
Noble John E, electrician, bds 62 W Williams.
Noble Sarah E (wid Lester B), bds 45 Savilla av.
Noble Wm H H, mach Penn Co, res 86 E Lewis.
Noble Wm K (Noble Bros), bds 33 Brackenridge.
Nobles Mrs Cynthia, res 59 Grant.
Nobles Melinda, mach operator, bds 59 Grand.
Nobles Perry C, driver, bds 59 Grand.
Noecker James L, brakeman P, Ft W & C Ry, res 42 E Butler.
Noecker Mary (wid Ferdinand), res 49 Baker.
Noecker Maud, bds 49 Baker.
Noecker Millie E, bds 49 Baker.
Noelsler John, res w s Lumbard 3 n of Chestnut.
Noftzger Arthur, bds 382 Fairfield av.
Nogal Frank J, bds 89 Montgomery.
Nogal Leslie H, tinner, res 89 Montgomery.
Nohe Edward G, tailor G Stauffer, res 26 Nirdlinger av.
Nohe John, mach Ind Mach Wks, res 19 Nirdlinger av.
Nohe Rosina (wid Joseph), res 40 Hendricks.
Nohe Veronika, bds 40 Hendricks.
Nohe Wm, janitor, res 21 Nirdlinger av.
Nolan Charles D, mach Penn Co, bds 328 Lafayette.
Nolan Mrs Emma, domestic 22 Chicago,
Nolan Eugene, bell boy, bds 328 Lafayette.
Nolan James M, res 38 Chicago.
Nolan John, saloon, 330 Lafayette. bds 328 same.
Nolan John A, mach, bds 24 Charles.
Nolan John H, mach Penn Co, res 328 Lafayette.
Nolan Michael, engr Penn Co, res 24 Charles.
Nolan Nellie, bds 328 Lafayette.

Nolan Rosa A, milliner, bds 328 Lafayette.
Noll Albert J, clerk, res 30 Edgerton.
Noll Albert J, clerk B R Noll, bds 97 W Wayne.
Noll Alfred F, clk J A Armstrong & Co, res 229 W Jefferson,
Noll Alphonse A, res 117 E Wayne.
Noll Anton, mason, bds 88 W Lewis.
Noll A, lab Penn Co, res 290 Walton av.
Noll Barbara (wid Martin F), res 129 E Jefferson.
Noll Benjamin C, cook, bds 109 Barthold.
Noll Benedict R., Druggist, 128 Broadway Tel 9, and 10 E Columbia Tel 84, res 97 W Wayne.
Noll Catherine, opr S M Foster, bds 45 Harmer.
Noll Catherine H, bds 97 W Wayne.
Noll Charles A, bds 22 Brackenridge.
Noll Charles J, agt Met Life Ins Co, res 115 Barthold.
Noll Clement J, carpenter, bds 88 W Lewis.
Noll Clement W, clk J A Armstrong & Co, res 229 W Jefferson.
Noll Edward A, hat maker, bds 22 Brackenridge.
Noll Edward M, Music Teacher, Studio and Residence 68 Clay. (*See adv p 103*.)
Noll Ella, bds Wm Noll.
Noll Emma C, clk U W Noll, bds 11 Simon.
Noll Ferdinand, helper Wabash R R, res 49 Nirdlinger av.
Noll Frank J, res 227 W Jefferson.
Noll Frank J, bkkpr Fisher Bros, bds 229 W Jefferson.
Noll Frederick A, bds 22 Brackenridge.
Noll George, student, bds 97 W Wayne.
Noll Grace M, bds 22 Brackenridge.
Noll John F, Boots and Shoes, 22 Clinton, res same.
Noll John G, trav agt, res 45 Harmer.
Noll Louise, bds 22 Brackenridge.
Noll Martin A, bookkeeper F Eckart, res 22 Brackenridge.
Noll Martin F, plumber, 129 E Jefferson, res same.
Noll Martin W, clerk, bds 229 W Jefferson.
Noll Mary, died December 10, 1894.
Noll Nettie E, domestic, bds 11 Simon.
Noll Nicholas J, lithogr, bds 109 Barthold.
Noll Peter, painter Penn Co, res 129 E Jefferson.
Noll Theresa A, bds 129 E Jefferson.
Noll Mrs Theresa C, res 109 Barthold.
Noll Upton W, grocer, 338 E Creighton av, res 11 Simon.
Noll Will W, clk B R Noll, bds 97 W Wayne.
Noll Wm H, brakeman, res 325 E Creighton av.

Noll Wm H, stone cutter, bds 45 Harmer.
Noll Wm H, watchman, res e s Leesburg 2 n of N Y, C & St L R R.
Nommay Edward E, stripper, bds 52 Spy Run av.
Nommay Philomena (wid Frank), bds w s Spy Run av 5 n of bridge.
Nones Mary L, (wid Benjamin J), bds 57 Douglas av.
Nonnemaker Andrew, moved to Atlanta, O.
Noonan David, laborer, res 41 Duck.
Noonan Josephine (wid David), bds 25 Barr.
Nordeen August, action mkr, bds 116 Home.
Norman Frank A, bkkb Ft W Beef Co, bds 120 Harrison.
North David V, engr engine Co 2, res 110 Wallace.
North Side Park, e s N Clinton between 5th and 7th.
Northan Sarah, bds 14 Barthold.
Northrop James L, engr N Y, C & St L R R, res 177 St Mary's av.
Northrop Rev Stephen A, pastor First Baptist Church, res 141 W Wayne.
Northwestern Mutual Life Insurance Co, H B Hunt Genl Agent. 5-6-7 Trentman Bldg. (*See left top lines p 353.*)
Norton John, patternmkr Bass F & M Wks, bds 158 Wallace.
Norton Nevada, res 15 Maple av.
Norton Susan B (wid John T), res 396 Clinton.
Norwald, *see also Nahrwold.*
Norwald Frederick, carpenter, bds 81½ Smith.
Norwald John E, mach Olds' W Wks, bds 383 Lafayette.
Norwald Joseph W, mach Olds' W Wks, res 77 Lasselle.
Norwald Leasatta (wid Diedrick), res 67 McCulloch.
Norwald Wm, laborer, bds 67 McCulloch.
Norwald Wm C, mach Olds' W Wks, res 383 Lafayette.
Notestine Claud, student, res 15 Harrison.
Notestine Frank, student, bds 15 Harrison.
Notestine Joseph H, Saloon, Groceries and Provisions, 15 and 17 Harrison, res 15 same.
Notestine Maud, student, bds 15 Harrison.
Notestine Wm M, fireman Penn Co, bds 38 Baker.
Novitski Joseph, shoemkr 267 Hanna, bds same.
Novitsky Barnet, Shoemaker and Umbrella Repairer. 213 Calhoun, res 145 Holman.
Nowek Edith, mach opr, bds 236 John.
Nowek Edward, carpenter 236 John, res same.
Nowek Hilda, dressmaker, bds 236 John.

Nowek Ida, bds 236 John.
Noze Christian F, coremkr Bass F & M Wks, res 12 Pine.
Nugent Lyman D, lab Standard Wheel Co, res 41½ W Berry.
Nulf Almira (wid Philip), res 137 Fletcher av.
Nulf Clarence M, brakeman, res 1 Reed.
Null Elizabeth (wid Jacob), bds 120 W Butler.
Null Wm T, car bldr Penn Co, res 94 Winch.
Nunamaker Dora M. bds 264 W Washington.
Nunemaker Cyrilus A, baggage master, res s e cor Clinton and Suttenfield.
Nusbaumer Sarah, dressmaker, bds 92 Force.
Nussbaum Bertha, operator, bds 35 Eliza.
Nussbaum G Joseph, clk G E Bursley & Co, bds 235 Spy Run Av.
Nussbaum Peter, foreman C L Centlivre Brewing Co, res 235 Spy Run av.
Nussbaum Matilda, bds 235 Spy Run av.
Nussbaum Tracy, domestic 202 E De Wald.
Nussbaum Victor, bds 35 Elizabeth.
Nussmann Anthony E, harnessmkr 40 Maumee rd, bds 231 E Wayne.
Nussmann Catherine (wid John), res 231 E Wayne.
Nussmann Josephine B, clk, bds 231 E Wayne.
Nutting Mrs John C, bds 113 W Wayne.
Nuttman Caroline L (wid Joseph D), Nuttman & Co, res 130 W Berry.
Nuttman & Co (C L Nuttman, Oliver S Hanna), Bankers 32 E Main.
Nyboer John H, carp Penn Co, res 414 Hanna.
Nye Lewis S, res 208 W Superior.
Nyland Henry, mach Bass F & M Wks, res 95 Smith.
Nyland John H, laborer, bds 95 Smith.

O

Oakley Chauncey B, Mayor, Office City Hall, res 240 W Main. Tel 462.
Oakley Louisa, bds 104 E Lewis.
Oaks Sarah (wid Sumner), res 78 E Williams.
Obenchain Otis C, baggagemaster, res 75 Baker.
Ober Jacob, clerk, rms 32 Calhoun.
Oberley Louisa, domestic 229 W Berry.
Oberlin Lydia (wid Wm), bds 114 Howell.
Oberlin Otto H, clk Dan Campbell, rms 228 Calhoun.
Oberwitte Gustave, saloon, 64 E Main, res same.

Obey David, engr N Y, C & St L R R, bds 323 W Main.
O'Brien, *see also Bryan.*
O'Brien Catherine A, clk People's Store, bds 134 Fulton.
O'Brien Frank, fireman, res 54 Jackson.
O'Brien Frank K, mach Penn Co, bds 22 Charles.
O'Brien James E, bkkpr O'Brien & Rolf, bds 134 Fulton.
O'Brien Jane (wid Thomas), res 134 Fulton.
O'Brien Jennie J, bds 134 Fulton.
O'Brien John D, clk C E Everett, bds 225 W Washington.
O'Brien John H (O'Brien & Rolf), bds 134 Fulton.
O'Brien Martin, engr N Y, C & St L R R, bds 134 Fulton
O'Brien Michael, engr Penn Co, res 23 W Butler.
O'Brien Nancy (wid Dennis), res 225 W Washington.
O'Brien Patrick, helper Penn Co, bds 91 Buchanan.
O'Brien Robert E, clerk, bds 225 W Washington.
O'Brien Thomas J, clk, bds 134 Fulton.
O'Brien Wm P, laborer, bds 225 W Washington.
O'Brien & Rolf (John H O'Brien, Albert F J Rolf), Sanitary Plumbers, Steam and Hot Water Heating, 122 Broadway.
O'Callahan, *see also Callahan.*
O'Callahan Wm A, laborer, bds 83 W Williams.
O'Callahan Wm G, janitor Hoagland School, bds 83 W Williams.
Ocker Martin T, engr N Y, C & St L R R, bds 323 W Main.
O'Connell Agnes, bds 97 E Jefferson.
O'Connell Catherine (wid Daniel), res 259 Webster.
O'Connell Charles A, bartndr, bds 97 E Jefferson.
O'Connell Dennis, laborer, res n s Jesse 2 e of of Runnion av
O'Connell Edith, bds 259 Webster.
O'Connell Edward J, clerk Penn Co, res 482 Harrison.
O'Connell Frances A, bds 259 Webster.
O'Connell Hugh, plumber H C Franke & Son, bds 97 E Jefferson.
O'Connell James, foreman Ft W Furn Co, res Leo rd n of toll gate.
O'Connell John, clk Home Billiard Hall, res 97 E Jefferson.
O'Connell Thomas J, mach Penn Co, bds 259 Webster.
O'Connell Thomas P, brakeman, res 34½ John.
O'Connell Wm, fireman, bds 97 E Jefferson.
O'Connor, *see also Conners and Connors.*
O'Connor Alice M, bds 138 Fulton.
O'Connor Belle, bds 114 Clinton.
O'Connor Bernard S, res 127 W Wayne.
O'Connor Bridget (wid Jeremiah), res 198 Madison.

O'Connor Charles, painter, res 51 Melita.
O'Connor Dennis, lab Penn Co, res 16 Poplar.
O'Connor Elizabeth (wid Bernard), res 156 W Wayne.
O'Connor Ellen, bds 138 Fulton.
O'Connor Ellen, seamstress, bds 46 Baker.
O'Connor Jeremiah, blksmith Penn Co, res 46 Baker.
O'Connor Johanna, student, bds 46 Baker.
O'Connor John, helper Penn Co, res 138 Fulton.
O'Connor Julia, domestic 46 W Wayne.
O'Connor Louise M (wid Stephen), bds 104 Barr.
O'Connor Mamie, waitress The Randall.
O'Connor Mary, bds 46 Baker.
O'Connor Mary A (wid Joseph M), res 114 Clinton.
O'Connor Mary J, clk, bds 138 Fulton.
O'Connor Stephen J, news agt, bds 104 Barr.
O'Connor Wm F, tel opr W U Tel Co, bds 104 Barr.
O'Connor Wm F, helper Penn Co, bds 138 Fulton.
O'Day John S, laborer, res 48 Lillie.
Odd Fellows' Building, n e cor Calhoun and Wayne.
Odd Fellows' Hall, 20 W Berry.
Oddou Emma L, bds 74 W 5th.
Oddou Franklin E, driver Am Ex Co, res 133 Barr.
Oddou Joseph F (Louis Oddou & Co), res 48 E Columbia.
Oddou Louis A (Louis Oddou & Co), bds 48 E Columbia.
Oddou Louis & Co (Louis A and Joseph F Oddou), gro-
cers 48 E Columbia.
Oddou Peter, carpenter, res 74 W 5th.
Oden Cora L, dressmaker, bds 353½ Calhoun.
Odendahl Henrietta, domestic 322 Fairfield av.
O'Donnell John F, Saloon, 11 Harrison, res
same.
O'Dowd Thomas J, porter Hotel Rich.
Oechtering Antoinette, housekeeper 142 E Jefferson.
Oechtering Rev John H, pastor St Mary's German Catho-
lic Church, res 142 E Jefferson.
Oehler Annie, domestic 100 W Jefferson.
Oelschlaeger Edward F, bkkpr C W Bruns & Co, bds 66
Baker.
Oelschlaeger Emma, cook J H Bass Brookside.
Oelschlaeger Frederick, tailor, 66 Baker, res same.
Oelschlaeger Lena, bds 66 Baker.
Oertel Herman F, coremkr Bass Wks, res 89½ r'orce.
Oestermann, *see Ostermann.*
Oestermeier Charles, tailor, 48 E Leith, res same.
Oetting Emma, bds 169 Holman.

506 R. L. POLK & CO.'S

Oetting Ferdinand D (Oetting & Co), saloon, 214 Fairfield
    av, res 67 Shawnee av.
Oetting Frederick, grocer, 127 Eliza, res same.
Oetting Henry, clk, bds 67 Shawnee av.
Oetting Henry, stone mason, res 374 E Lewis.
Oetting Louis F, teamster, bds 66 Douglas av.
Oetting Minnie, bds 67 Shawnee av.
Oetting Wm H, Contractor and Dealer in Sewer
    Pipe and Tile, 382 E Lewis, Res same, Yard cor Ohio
    and Hugh.
Oetting & Co (Ferdinand D Oetting), saloon, 125 Broadway
Ofenloch Catherine M, clk Kratzsch Bros, bds 32 Force.
Ofenloch Edward P, clk M Frank & Co, bds 130 Francis.
Ofenloch Elizabeth, bds 32 Force.
Ofenloch Frank, butcher E Rich, bds Hoffman House.
Ofenloch Louisa, clk, bds 32 Force.
Ofenloch Michael, painter Ft W Elec Corp, res 130
    Francis.
Ofenloch Peter A, grocer, 365 Lafayette, bds 32 Force.
Ofenloch Valentine, grocer, 30 Force, res 32 same.
Offerle Joseph, lab Bass F &M Wks, res 112 Hanna.
Offerle Lawrence, brewer C L Centlivre Brewing Co. res
    32 Randolph.
Offner John, mach Wabash R R, res 46 Miner.
Ogden Robert, Plumber, Steam and Gas Fitter,
    Natural Gas Fitter, Dealer in Iron, Lead Pipe, Sheet
    Lead, Hydrants, Bath Tubs, Pumps, Brass Goods, Etc,
    26 E Berry, res 64 Barr. Tel 192. (*See embossed line
    back cover and in classified Plumbers.*)
Ogier Thomas, engr N Y, C & St L R R, res 429 W Main
Ogle John J, phys, 57 Holton av, res same, Tel 332.
O'Hara Alice, waitress Hotel Rich.
O'Hara Katie, waitress Hotel Rich.
O'Hare John, brakeman N Y, C & St L R R, bds 312 W
    Main.
O'Harra John D, lab Wabash R R, res 8 Fox.
O'Harra Marion T, bds 8 Fox.
O'Hearn Catherine (wid John), res 188 E Washington.
O'Hearn James B, laborer, bds 188 E Washington.
O'Hearn Mary (wid James), res 23 Colerick.
O'Hern Wm, lineman G R & I R R, res 65 E DeWald.
Ohio Farmers Insurance Co, Leroy, Ohio, 25 Court.
Ohler Dena, waiter Hedekin House.
Ohlfest Otto, lab N Y, C & St L R R, bds 74 W Main.
Ohlinger John B, res New Haven av n w cor Lumbard.

Ohneck, *see also Honeck.*
Ohneck Albert M, painter Penn Co, res 49 E Butler.
Ohneck Edward G, bds n s Carson av 1 e of Parnell.
Ohneck George A, lab L E & W R R, res 39 N Calhoun.
Ohneck George D, trav agt C L Centlivre Brewing Co, res n s Carson av 1 e of Parnell av.
Ohneck John, painter, res 58 W Williams.
Ohneck Velma M, dressmkr, bds G D Ohneck.
Ohnhaus Frank J, trav agt, bds 197 E Jefferson.
Ohnhaus John E, insurance, bds 197 E Jefferson.
Ohnhaus Louis (Ohnhaus & Monahan), res 169 E Berry.
Ohnhaus Scholastica (wid John E), res 197 E Jefferson.
Ohnhaus & Monahan (Louis Ohnhaus, Dennis Monahan), furnishing goods, 86 Calhoun.
Ohse Henry, lab Penn Co, bds s s Pontiac 1 e of Abbott.
Ohse John, molder Bass F & M Wks, res s s Pontiac 1 e of Abbott.
Oilar George H, draper D N Foster Furniture Co, bds 5 Monroe.
O'Keefe Edward, winder, bds 280 E Washington.
O'Keefe Patrick, section hand, res 280 E Washington.
Okonkowski Ralph, bkkpr C W Cook, rms 50 E Columbia
Old Fort Chemical Co, Wm T Brackenridge mngr, insect exterminater mnfrs, over 16 W Berry.
Old Fort Mnfg Co, Newton D Daughman pres, Perry A Randall treas, Miss Alice M Beugnot sec, mnfrs wood pulleys, office 9 Bass Blk, factory, Eaton, Ind.
Old Fort Spice and Extract Co, Jordan D Williams pres and treas, Charles L Miller vice-pres, John Fitzgerald sec, 29 E Columbia.
Old National Bank (Capital $350,000; Surplus, $125,000), Stephen B Bond Pres, Oliver P Morgan Vice-Pres, Jared D Bond Cash, James C Woodworth Asst Cash, s w cor Calhoun and Berry.
Old National Bank Building, s w cor Calhoun and Berry.
Olds Caroline, bds 107 W Berry.
Olds Charles, watchman W Gas Const Co, res 131 E De Wald.
Olds Charles L, with Star Iron Tower Co, res 324 W Washington.
Olds Egbert C, fireman, bds 139 Lake av.
Olds Eugene H, supt Olds' Wagon Wks. bds 107 W Berry.
Olds Fred G, mach Penn Co, res 293 Harrison.
Olds Harry J, agent, bds 131 E De Wald.

Olds Henry G, pres Olds' Wagon Wks, res 107 W Berry. Tel 90.

Olds John D, lumber buyer, res 139 Lake av.

Olds Noble G, purchasing agt Olds' Wagon Wks, bds 107 W Berry.

Olds' Wagon Works, H G Olds Pres, S C Lumbard Vice-Pres, John Mohr jr Sec, W H Olds Treas, Mnfrs Farm and Spring Wagons, s s Murray bet Calhoun and Lafayette. Tel 34.

Olds Wm H, treas Olds' Wagon Wks, res 480 Fairfield av. Tel 480.

O'Leary Edward, res n s Pennsylvania 5 e of Wayne Trace.

O'Leary Elizabeth (wid Timothy), res 171 W Berry.

O'Leary Ethel M, bds 32 Hugh.

O'Leary James, foreman Penn, res 32 Hugh.

O'Leary Mary C (wid Wm P), res 39 E Butler.

Olinske Christian, loborer, res 49 Smith.

Olive James, helper Wabash R R, res 35 Bass.

Olive James jr, mach Wabash R R, bds 35 Bass.

Olive Rachel, bds 35 Bass.

Olmstead George I, brakeman N Y, C & St L R R, res 213 W Main.

Olmstead Wm W, clk Wabash R R, res 253 W Wayne.

O'Meara J Patrick, express messenger, res 402d.

O'Neil, *see also Neal, Neil and Neill.*

O'Neil Daniel J, engr L E & W R R, res 341 W Washington.

O'Neil Edward, bds 341 W Washington.

O'Nell Robert J, fireman, rms 84 Brackenridge.

O'Neill John, laborer, bds 29 Colerick.

O'Neill Mrs Margaret, res 29 Colerick.

O'Neill Michael, lab Ft W Elec Corp, bds 29 Colerick.

O'Neill Patrick, clk Penn Co, bds 29 Colerick.

O'Neill Sarah, waitress The Randall.

O'Neill Sarah, laundress, bds 29 Colerick.

Opatz Frank A, blksmith Penn Co, res 187 Montgomery.

Oppelt—Bly Kittie, millinery, 156 Calhoun, res same.

Oppelt George, barber B Ellert, bds 26 W Washington.

Oppelt Joseph, helper Griebel & Pask res 26 W Superior.

Oppenhamer Margaret S, (wid Samuel), res 105 Lafayette.

Oppenhamer Wm A, elev clk Bass Blk, bds 105 Lafayette

Oppenheimer Abraham, res 54 W Berry.

Oppenheimer Frederick cigars, 17 W Main, bds 54 W Berry

Oppenheimer Jacob, clothing, 68 E Columbia, res 109 E Colnmbia.

Oppenlander Charles O, cabtmkr, bds 70 Packard av.

Oppliger Annie M (wid Daniel), res 72 E Pontiac.
Oram Ernest, brakeman G R & I R R, rms 210 Calhoun.
Ordway Arilla D, architect, 12 Schmitz Blk, res 144 Columbia av.
Orff Charles E, supt Empire Mills, bds John Orff.
Orff George E, trav agt S M Foster, bds 78 W Creighton av
Orff Henry, music teacher, res 78 W Creighton av.
Orff John, propr Empire Flouring Mills, W Main st. bridge, res junction Columbia City and Huntington rds
Orff John R, miller, res 55 Orchard av. Tel 93.
Orff Mary E, teacher Hoagland School, bds 78 W Creighton av.
Orff Robert E, student, bds 78 W Creighton av.
Ormiston James, res w s Lafayette 1 s Wiebke.
Ormiston Lewis, res w s Piqua av 4 s Rudisill av.
Ormiston L Francis, lab, bds Lewis Ormiston.
Ormiston Mark, lab. res s s Rudisill 3 w of Piqua av.
Ormiston Ruében, lab, bds Lewis Ormiston.
Ormiston Rose, domestic w s Spy Run av 2 n of Edna.
Ormiston Rufus P, res w s Piqua av 3 s Marshall.
Ormsby Mrs Jennie R, elocutionist 18 Arcade, res 51 W Berry.
O'Rourke Anna H, bds 62 Wilt.
O'Rourke Catherine M, teacher, bds 235 E Lewis.
O'Rourke Charles T, clk O G Klinkenberg, bds 62 Wilt.
O'Rourke Clement, lab Seavey Hdw Co, bds 235 E Lewis.
O'Rourke David, brakeman, bds Hotel Rich.
O'Rourke Hon Edward, Judge Circuit Court, office Court House, res 134 E Washington.
O'Rourke Gracie, bds 30 McClellan.
O'Rourke Ella, domestic The Wayne.
O'Rourke Helen, bds 134 E Washington.
O'Rourke Jeremiah W, conductor, res 395 Hanna.
O'Rourke John, conductor, res 235 E Lewis.
O'Rourke John B, plumber R Spice, bds 235 E Lewis.
O'Rourke, John C traveling agt, res 62 Wilt.
O'Rourke Julia. H, bds 235 E Lewis.
O'Rourke Julian, messr Dist Tel Co, bds 185 Montgomery
O'Rourke Loretto, bds 185 Montgomery.
O'Rourke Marie M, bds 62 Wilt.
O'Rourke Mary (wid Michael), res 185 Montgomery.
O'Rourke Patrick S, supt G R & I R R, res 30 McClellan.
O'Rourke Thomas, lab Penn Co, bds 134 E Washington.
O'Rourke Wm S (Robertson & O'Rourke), supreme sec C K of A, 27 and 28 Bass Blk, res 26 Douglas av.

510   R. L. POLK & CO.'S

Orphans Home of the Reformed Church, 1½ miles e of limits.
Orr Charles L, laborer, bds 39 Wabash av.
Orr Bessie, bds 39 Wabash av.
Orr Charles W, Agent Ætna Insurance Co, Hartford, Conn; Asst Cashier Hamilton National Bank, res 312 W Washington.   Tel 109.
Orr Clark, bds 79 Griffith.
Orr Edwin G, laborer, bds 112 Mechanic.
Orr James A, clk Ft W Gas Co, res 36 W Butler.
Orr James H, res Baker Homestead, Baker av.
Orr John W, sec and treas Mayflower Milling Co, res 28 W Butler.
Orr Joseph A, teamster, res 49 Orchard av.
Orr Joseph H, teller First National Bank, res 21 W Butler.
Orr Mrs Margaret, res 283 W Jefferson.
Orr Michael, sand, res 112 Mechanic.
Orr Michael F, laborer, bds 112 Mechanic.
Orr Rezin, res 1 Dawson.
Orr Robert W, butcher, res 39 Wabash av.
Orrock Wm W, lumber inspr, res 466 Calhoun.
Orth Christian, painter S F Bowser & Co, res 27 Julia.
Ortlieb Amelia M, bds 125 W Jefferson.
Ortlieb George A, clk County Auditor, bds 125 W Jefferson.
Ortlieb George J, saloon, 31 Calhoun, res 125 W Jefferson
Ortlieb Wm F, clk J Elec L & P Co, bds 125 W Jefferson
Ortman Grace E, dressmaker, bds 318 E Wayne.
Ortman Wm H, clk Penn Co, res 18 W Creighton av.
Ortmann Anna E, stenogr C B Fitch, bds 22 W Superior.
Ortmann Carrie L, bds 22 W Superior.
Ortmann Henry R, cigarmkr, res 318 E Wayne.
Ortmann Henry W, cigar mnfr 26 Clinton, res 22 W Superior.
Ortmann Minnie L, teacher Franklin School, bds 22 W Superior.
O'Ryan, *see also Ryan.*
O'Ryan Ann, dressmaker. bds 50 Baker.
O'Ryan James (Nagel & O'Ryan), bds 50 Baker.
O'Ryan John, engr Penn Co, bds 50 Baker.
O'Ryan Katherine, bds 50 Baker.
O'Ryan Patrick, watchman. res 50 Baker.
Osborn Charles, lab Olds' W Wks, bds St James Hotel.

Osborn James L, engr S F Bowser & Co, bds 87 Thom-
asetta.
Osborn John C, foreman S F Bowser & Co, res 87 Thom-
asetta.
Osborn Merlin C, lightning rods, res 2 E Butler.
Osborn Minnie, cook School F M Y.
Osborné Percy R, bkkpr Ft W Furn Co, bds 231 W Berry
Osenbaugh Elizabeth, bds 15 Simon.
Osenbaugh George, brakeman G R & I R R, res 15 Simon
Osenbaugh Isaac, res s s Pioneer av 3 e of Walter av.
Osenbaugh John H, bds 28 Wallace.
Osenbaugh Peter, bds 15 Simon.
Oser Josephine, housekeeper 142 E Jefferson.
O'Shaughnessy, *see also Shaughnessy.*
O'Shaughnessy Charles J, appr S Hines, bds 46 Runnion av
O'Shaughnessy George, bds 26 Murray.
O'Shaughnessy John J, finisher, bds 46 Runnion av
O'Shaughnessy Lila, opr, bds 46 Runnion av.
O'Shaughnessy Nora C, housekpr 143 W Wayne.
Ossaforth Bernard, helper Penn Co, res 68 Force.
Ossaforth Margaret, bds 68 Force.
Osseforth Mary A, domestic 297 Hanna.
Osterheld Caroline (wid Frederick), bds 126 Gay.
Osterheld Lena, bds 126 Gay.
Osterheld Louis, tailor, res 126 Gay.
Ostermann George L, O (Ostermann & Co), res 307 E
Washington.
Ostermann John, res w s Euclid av 3 s E Creighton av.
Ostermann John H, lab Hoffman Bros, res 320 E Wayne.
Ostermann Lambert, died August 19th, 1894.
Ostermann & Co (George L Ostermann), tinners, e s Har-
Harmer 1 n of e Washington.
Ostmann August, res 113 Wilt.
Ostmann Emma (wid Charles), bds 328 Harrison.
Ostmann Wilhelm F, fireman N Y, C & St L R R, bds 113
Wilt.
Ostermeyer Mennie, domestic 29 W Jefferson.
Ostermier Frederick, lab Bass F & M Wks, res 99 Smith.
Ostermier Henry, machinist, bds 99 Smith.
Oswald Annie, bds 56 Smith.
Oswald Fedelis, bds 47 Melita.
Oswald Joseph, lab Bass Wks. res 56 Smith.
Oswalt Henry, res n e cor Hicksville and St Joe Gravel rds
Otis Eugene, conductor, res 26 Fisher.
Otis Thomas F, laborer, res rear 200 Lafayette.

Ott Albert, packer, bds 7 Romy av.
Ott Frank S (Ott & Son), res 7 Romy av.
Ott Frederick, lab L Rastetter & Son, bds 7 Romy av.
Ott John O (Ott & Son), bds 7 Romy av.
Ott & Son (Frank & John Ott), painters, 7 Romy av.
Otten John, lab Penn Co, bds 141 E Washington.
Otten Louis, lab Bass F& M Wks, res 72 Summit.
Otten Lucas, tinner Klotz & Haller, res 34 Gay.
Otten Lucas jr, tinner, bds 36 John.
Otten Ludemila C, seamstress, bds 141 E Washington.
Otten Luke G, clerk R Lowry, bds 141 E Washington.
Otten Mary R (wid Otto H), res 141 E Washington.
Otten Nicholas, laborer, res 44 Force.
Otten Rose, domestic 90 St Martin's.
Otten Theodore, tinner Klotz & Haller, bds 34 Gay.
Otten Theresa M, seamstress, bds 34 Gay.
Ottenweller John H, teamster, res St Joseph boulevard nr
    Baker av.
Overholt David, fireman, bds 250 E Lewis.
Overley Daniel, lab, res w s Hanna 1 n of Wayne Trace.
Overley Didymus, plasterer, res 13 Custer av.
Overley Harry S, truckmkr, bds Daniel Overley.
Overmyer Frank B, brakeman, res 146 Walton av.
Owen Wm R, turner Ft W O Co, res 310 W Washington.
Owens Alice (wid Peter, Owens & Welsh), res 29 W
    Columbia.
Owens Edward P, clk Owens & Welsh, rms 29 W
    Columbia.
Owens James P, helper Penn Co, bds 29 W Columbia.
Owens Margaret, domestic 187 W Wayne.
Owens Michael J, barber 102 Maumee rd, res 168 same.
Owens Owen, conductor, res 277 E Creighton av.
Owens & Welsh (Alice Owens, Mrs Ella Welsh),
    Proprietors Lexington Restaurant, Short Orders
    served at all hours, Day or Night, 7 Harrison.
    (See p 105.)

P

Pace Della (wid David), res 260 Clinton.
Pacific Express Co Charles B Beaver Agent,
    79 Calhoun. Tel 416.
Paff Andrew J, turner Paul Mnfg Co, res 66 Elizabeth.
Paff Ellsworth, lab, bds 66 Elizabeth.
Page Amelia, domestic 29 Lillie.
Page Hannah L, domestic 177 W Wayne.

Page Josephine, clk Ft W News, bds 316 E Jefferson.
Page Wm D, Propr Ft Wayne News, 19 E Main. Tel 120. Res 316 E Jefferson. Tel 213.
Page Wm G, helper Penn Co, res 54 W Williams.
Pageler Frederick J, clerk, res 177 Montgomery.
Pageler Henry H, clerk, res 198 E Lewis.
Pageler John A, grocer 215 E Lewis, res same.
Pahl, *see also Paul and Pohl.*
Pahl Sophia, bds 106 Force.
Pahl Wm, mach Bass F & M Wks, res 106 Force.
Palmer Albert D, contr 63 W Pontiac, res same.
Palmer Earl (Ferguson & Palmer Co), res 273 W Wayne Tel 534.
Palmer Frank E, trav agt, res 19 Lincoln av.
Palmer Henry L, fireman N Y, C & St L R R, bds 71 Boone.
Palmer Horace L, District Mngr Mutual Life Ins Co of N Y, 32 E Berry, bds New Aveline House. Tel 46.
Palmer James V, car bldr Penn Co, res 22 E Leith.
Palmer John F, carp Olds' W Wks, res 65 W Pontiac.
Palmer John W, engr N Y, C & St L R R, res 8 Lavina.
Palmer Joseph, carp, res 181 St Mary's av.
Palmer V Leo, lathe hd Ind M Wks, bds 8 Lavina.
Palmer Wm, hammersmith Bass Wks, res 180 E Taber.
Pankoka Frederick, laborer, res 39 Hough.
Panne Minnie, domestic 142 Montgomery.
Pantitorium Co, L H Winegar Mngr, Clothes Repairing and Employment Bureau, 16 Arcade Bldg. Tel 465.
Pantlind Henry E, asst J C Peltier, res 26 Wagner.
Pantlind Mrs Martha, res 12 Wagner.
Papathcky Stavro, asst A Kutche, bds 154 Calhoun.
Pape, *see also Pepe and Pope.*
Pape Amelia, bds 56 St Mary's av.
Pape Charles, propr Fleming Mnfg Co, pres Peter's Box & Lumber Co, res 56 St Mary's av.
Pape Charles G, clk Peter's Box and Lumber Co, bds 56 St Mary's av.
Pape Furniture Co (E Clarence Shell, Adam C Buettel), Mnfrs of and Dealers in Fine Furniture, 28 and 30 E Berry.
Pape Louisa, bds 56 St Mary's av.
Pape Sophia, bds 56 St Mary's av.
Pape Wm, real estate, res 151 High.

Pape Wm C, lumber, res 47 High.
Pape Wm C H C, paperhanger, bds 151 High.
Pappert Amand J, cigar mkr. bds 18 McClellan.
Pappert Wm F, molder Bass M Wks, res 49 John.
Paragon Mfg Co (MacDougal & Co proprs), waists, 87-89 E Columbia.
Pardee Katherine (wid W McK), res 277 W Wayne.
Pardoe Samuel J, res 265 John.
Parent, *see also Parrant.*
Parent Charles, bds 41 Monroe.
Parent Charles N, lab J A Klinger, bds 112 E Main.
Parham Charles H, bds 113 Poplar.
Parham Edna M, bds 113 Poplar.
Parham Frederick C, agtl impls, 29 and 31 Barr, res 113 Poplar.
Parisoe Emma F, seamstress, rms 58 E Jefferson.
Parisoe Mary, seamstress, rms 58 E Jefferson.
Parisot Alexander J, bkkpr Kerr Murray Mnfg Co, res 74 Buchanan.
Parisot Clara H J, bds 322 Hanna.
Parisot Edward F, res s w cor Lafayette and Pontiac.
Parisot Joseph, checkman Wabash R R, res 322 Hanna.
Park Park Place Reservoir, E Creighton av and Lafayette.
Parker Annie, mach opr, bds 6 Wheeler.
Parker Charles, watchman City Trucking Co, res 39 Grand
Parker Charles A, brakeman, res 161 Gay.
Parker Charles W, lab Hoffman Bros, res 210 W Superior
Parker Dora E, bds 6 Wheeler.
Parker Edgar H, deputy auditor Allen Co, res 5 N Calhoun
Parker Eli, laborer, bds 42 W Main.
Parker Emma V, bds 161 Gay.
Parker Frederick, fireman, rms 84 Brackenridge.
Parker Grant, lab, bds 181 Fairfield av.
Parker James, laborer, res 6 Wheeler.
Parker John W, bds 6 Wheeler.
Parker Lilly F, finisher, bds 161 Gay.
Parker Mabel R F, bds 181 Fairfield av.
Parker Oliver P, teamster, res 181 Fairfield av.
Parker Pearl M, student, bds 5 N Calhoun.
Parker Wm, bds 210 W Superior.
Parks Jennie, seamstress, bds 220 E Wayne.
Parks Volney (Fort Wayne Lumber Co), res 812 Broadway.
Parmelee Robert H (Pixley & Co), res Bloomington, Ill.
Parnin Clementine C (wid August), res 214 E Wayne.

Parnin Emma, seamstress S M Foster, bds 214 E Wayne.
Parnin Frank, baggagemaster N Y, C & St L R R, res 85 Barthold.
Parnin John B, electrician Jenney E L & P Co, bds 214 E Wayne.
Parnin Joseph E, moved to Indianapolis.
Parnin Louis, brakeman, bds 214 E Wayne.
Parnin Mary, seamstress, bds 214 E Wayne.
Parr Charles J, car inspr L S & M S R R, res 90 W 4th.
Parr Frederick C, plumber, bds 29 E Main.
Parrant, *see also Parent.*
Parrant Annie E, bds 149 Walton av.
Parrant Frank A, section hd, bds 149 Walton av.
Parrant John B, barber, bds 149 Walton av.
Parrant Joseph F, clerk, bds 149 Walton av.
Parrant Julian, lab Penn Co, res 335 E Creighton av.
Parrant Peter J, painter, bds 149 Walton av.
Parrant Sophie A (wid Frank E), res 149 Walton av.
Parrish Abram C, laborer, res 316 Broadway.
Parrish John L, engr Penn Co, res 16 W Williams.
Parrish Stephen E, engr Paul Mnfg Co, res 12 Cass.
Parrish Theodore G, fireman, bds 16 W Williams.
Parrish Wm A, bds 16 W Williams.
Parrot Frank, meats 60 E Main, res same. Tel 325.
Parrot George J, photographer 62 Calhoun, bds 27 Oak.
Parrot John, lab, bds 27 Oak.
Parrot Louis A, strip grader Standard Wheel Co, res 20 Francis.
Parrot Peter J, res 27 Oak.
Parry, *see also Perrey and Perry.*
Parry Emma A, bds 337 W Washington.
Parry Gale T, traveling agt W L Carnahan Co, res 230 W Washington.
Parry George W, erecter Kerr Murray Mnfg Co, res 331 Harrison.
Parry Joseph W, condr G R & I R R, res 27 W Butler.
Parry J Edgar, traveling agt, bds 27 W Butler.
Parry Laura E, teacher, bds 27 W Butler.
Parry Wm S, lab, bds 271 Webster
Parry Wm S, traveling agt W L Carnahan Co, res 337 Washington.
Paschall Arla W, bkkpr Arcade Music Store, bds 282 Webster.
Paschall Rev John W, pastor Simpson M E Church, res 282 Webster.

516   R. L. POLK & CO.'S

Pask George W (Griebel & Pask), res 67 Brackenridge.
Pask Grace, bds 67 Brackenridge.
Passino Agnes H, dressmaker, bds 19 Jane.
Passino Alpha A, actionmkr Ft W O Co, bds 19 Jane.
Passino Amos J. stenogr Penn Co, bds 19 Jane.
Passino Frank, iron wkr Kerr Murray Mnfg Co, bds 19 Jane.
Passino George, res 201 John.
Passino Joseph P, machinist, res 405 Lafayette.
Passino Julia R, bds 405 Lafayette.
Passino Peter, brakeman, res 19 Jane.
Passino Sophia, student, bds 19 Jane.
Pattee David T, flagman, res 204 Walton av.
Pattee Lee, teamster, res s s New Haven av 1 e of Roy.
Pattee Wm H, carriage painter, res 197 High.
Patten, see also Patton.
Patten Nellie F, clk C B Flick, bds 132 Thompson av.
Patterson Collins C, painter, bds 15 Elizabeth.
Patterson Emma, domestic Harmon House.
Patterson Emma L, dressmaker, bds 32 Baker.
Patterson Frank, barber John Brunskill, bds 124 E Lewis
Patterson Hannah E (wid George W), res 248 Calhoun.
Patterson Helen (wid Henry), bds 30 Douglas av.
Patterson Homer M, motorman, res 103 Wells.
Patterson James W, harnessmkr F Hilt, res 124 E Lewis.
Patterson Jesse F, despatcher Penn Co, bds 126 E Wayne.
Patterson Mary F (wid Jesse F), bds 126 E Wayne.
Patterson Reuben S (Golden & Patterson), rms 158 W Berry.
Patterson Robert B, res 32 Baker.
Patterson Thomas A, clk Smith Credit Rating Co, res 50 Brackenridge.
Patterson Thomas R, laborer, bds 104 E Wayne.
Patterson Virgil J, laborer, bds 105 John.
Patterson Warren C, brakeman, res 61 Thomas.
Patton, see also Patten.
Patton George D, trav agt, res 47 Coombs.
Patton Helen, operator, bds 58 Brackenridge.
Patton Jesse, patrolman, res 180 Ewing.
Patton Mary, dishwasher New Aveline House.
Patton Wm S, contr. 58 Brackenridge, res same.
Pauken Nicholas, tailor, res 13 Elizabeth.
Paul, see also Pahl and Pohl.
Paul Alvina M, bds 45 High.
Paul Benjamin F, laborer, bds 25 Barr

Paul Charles, helper Ft W Gas Co, bds 45 High.
Paul Charles A. sec Paul Mnfg Co, bds 38 W Jefferson.
Paul Christian W, engr City Mills, bds 84 E 4th.
Paul Clara, bds 119 W Wayne.
Paul Elizabeth, bds 38 W Jefferson.
Paul Emil, molder, bds 45 High
Paul Ernest, policeman, res 412 Hanna.
Paul Ferdinand. mach Olds' Wagon Wks, bds 296 Harrison.
Paul Frederick, clerk, res 298 Harrison.
Paul Frederick, mach hd Penn Co, res 296 Harrison.
Paul Gustav H, painter, bds 45 High.
Paul Henry, pres Horton Mnfg Co, Paul Mnfg Co, Wayne Knitting Mills, and asst to pres Ft Wayne Gas Co, res 119 W Wayne. Tel 91.
Paul Lena, bds 296 Harrison.
Paul Mnfg Co, Henry C Paul pres, Wm Paul jr vice pres and treas, Charles A Paul sec, mnfrs wood pulleys, cor 6th and N Calhoun. Tel 402.
Paul Minnie (wid Charles), res 45 High.
Paul Wm, res 38 W Jefferson.
Paul Wm jr, vice pres and treas Paul Mnfg Co, res Calhoun s e cor DeWald.
Pauley Edward J, saloon, 204 Calhoun, res 26 Colerick.
Pauley James, helper Penn Co, bds 76 W Williams.
Pauley Johanna, bds 76 W Williams.
Pauley John J, night clk New Aveline House, res 357 E Washington.
Pauley Mary E, bds 76 W Williams.
Pauley Thomas, blksmith Penn Co, res 76 W Williams.
Paulison Samuel M, res s s Leith 3 w of Calhoun.
Paulsen Augusta, domestic 241 W Berry.
Paulsen Frederick W, coremkr Bass F & M Wks, res 148 Walton av.
Paulsen Wm, coachman 261 W Berry.
Paulson Henry, carpenter, bds 66 Baker.
Paulucci Marion, teacher, bds 88 E Lewis.
Paulus Frank D, res 49 E Jefferson.
Paund Anna (wid Salathie), bds 135 Wells.
Payne Edward I, condr Ft W Elec Ry Co, bds 62 Hamilton.
Payne Elmer E. condr Ft W Elec Ry Co, bds 62 Hamilton
Payne Emma. helper Randall Hotel.
Payne Ernest A, laborer, bds 62 Hamilton.
Payne Frank D, res rear 152 W Main.
Payne Henry E, carp, bds s w cor Pearl and Fulton.

518 R. L. POLK & CO.'S

Payne John H, clk Morgan & Beach, res 337 E Wayne.
Payne Joseph W, coachman C L Centlivre, bds w s Spy Run av 3 n of Edna.
Payne Samuel, lab Ft W Elec Ry Co, res 2 Hanover.
Payne Mrs Sarah J, bds 62 Hamilton.
Payne Seymour, lab E Martin, res 243 Webster.
Payton Alfred B, laborer, res 332 W Main.
Payton Edward T, laborer, bds 74 St Mary's av.
Payton F Phillip, bds 74 St Mary's av.
Payton John I, driver W H Brudi & Bro, res 2 Huffman.
Payton Joshua, truckman Penn Co, res 64 E Pontiac.
Payton Wm B, laborer, res 74 St Mary's av.
Pealer E Wilson, contr, res s s E Leith 3 e of Lafayette.
Pearl Minnie, seamstress, rms 305 Lafayette.
Pearlman James, laborer, res 76 Canal.
Pearlman Joseph, bds 76 Canal.
Pearlman Sam J (Goldstine & Pearlman), res 44 Harmer.
Pearlman Wm, bds 76 Canal.
Pearse, see also Pierce.
Pearse Frank D, bartndr The Wayne, res 74 Calhoun.
Pearse James W (Pearse & Poff), res 22 Chicago.
Pearse & Poff (James W Pearse, James H Poff), Livery Stable 18 and 20 Holman. Tel 76.
Pearson, see also Pierson and Pirson
Pearson John C, engr Penn Co, res 130 E Taber.
Peck Solon L, res 148 W Wayne.
Peckham Bertha R, bds 244 W Creighton av.
Peckham John W, winder Ft W Elec Corp, bds 244 W Creighton av.
Peckham Maud, dressmaker, bds 244 W Creighton av.
Peckham Wm T, res 244 W Creighton av.
Peek Henry, carp Bass F & M Wks, res 20 Jones.
Peek Henry jr, mach Bass F & M Wks, bds 20 Jones.
Pegenauer Wm, res 102 N Harrison.
Pegg Allen R, lab Ft W Elec Corp, bds 84 Fairfield av.
Pegg Edward B, laborer, bds 84 Fairfield av.
Pegg Mrs Helena A, res 84 Fairfield av.
Pegg Loren B, barber, res 12 Zollars av.
Peiser Jacob, peddler, res 56 Force.
Pelkey Jennie G, bds 122 Wells.
Pelkey Jonas A, mach hd Paul Mnfg Co, res 122 Wells.
Pellaton Louis, lab, res n s Chestnut 2 e Lumbard.
Pellens Joseph B (Gross & Pellons), res 176 W Washington.
Peltier James C, Funeral Director and Embalmer, 17 W Wayne, res 137 E Berry. Tel 25. Tel res 20.

Peltier Louis, asst J C Peltier, res 49 E Lewis.
Peltier Wm H W, collector J C Peltier, bds 137 E Berry.
Pelton Leander, supt Sperry. Pelton Mnfg Co, res 79 Boone
Pelz August, wiper Penn Co, res 40 Lasselle.
Pelzer Frederick, section foreman, res 41 Nirdlinger av.
Pelzinger Charlotte A (wid Frederick L), res s s Pontiac opp Warsaw.
Pembleton Charles, mach opr, res 14 Runnion av.
Pembroke Ellen, bds 19 Colerick.
Pembroke Mary, cook Oscar Wobrock.
Pembroke Michael, laborer, res 19 Colerick.
Pembroke Nora, cook Oscar Wobrock.
Pembroke Patrick F, condr G R & I R R, res 68 Melita.
Pembroke Thomas, laborer, bds 19 Colerick.
Pence Allie M, bds 32 Marion.
Pence Catherine L, bds 268 E Wayne.
Pence Frank C. clk M L Jones, bds 32 Marion.
Pence Sarah E (wid Robert H), res 32 Marion,
Pence Wm A, clerk, bds 268 E Wayne.
Penke Rudolph, coremkr Bass F & M Wks. res 87 Greene
Penman Robert P (James Kennedy & Co), Glasgow, Scotland, res 30 Douglas av.
Penn Mutual Life Insurance Co of Philadelphia, Clark Fairbank Agent, 19 Court
Penningroth August C, mach. res 274 E Lewis.
Pennsylvania Co, Operating P, Ft Wayne & C Ry, Offices e s Clinton bet Railroad and Holman; Passenger Depot Calhoun and Railroad; Freight Depot cor Calhoun and Railroad.
Penny Warren E, trav agt, bds 252 Clinton.
Pens Charles W, wood worker, rms 1 Indiana av.
Pens Henry D, res 107 High.
Pens Louisa A, bds 107 High.
People's Store, Beadell & Co Proprs, Dry Goods, Notions and Men's Furnishings, 20 and 22 E Berry. Tel 313.
Pepe, *see also Pape and Pope.*
Pepe Albert C, clerk Dittoe's Grocery Co, res 254 W Washington.
Peppers John L, janitor Y M C A (R R dept), res 212 Metz.
Peppers Minnie, bds 212 Metz.
Pequinot Abel, lab, res s s Chestnut 3 w of Lumbard.
Pequinot Gu-tine, bds A Pequinot.
Pequinot Nora, domestic 99 E Main.

Perkins Daisy, domestic 114 W Main.

Perkins Lafayette B, laborer, res 126 Home av.

Perkins Laura E, domestic 287 W Berry.

Perrett, see also Parrot.

Perrett Maria (wid Richard), res 155 Wallace.

Perrett Matilda, bds 155 Wallace.

Perrey, see also Parry and Perry.

Perrey Adele (wid Joseph J), res 2 Oak.

Perrey Edward F, traveling agt, res 2 Oak.

Perrey Emma, dressmaker, bds 2 Oak.

Perrey Flora, opr S M Foster. bds 2 Oak

Perrey Frank J (Perrey & Siebold), res 127 Union.

Perrey Julian J, horseshoer Perrey & Siebold, bds 2 Oak.

Perrey & Siebold (Frank J Perrey, Christian W Siebold), Horseshoers 5 Pearl.

Perriguey C Frank, res rear 41 Webster.

Perriguey Felix, brick mnfr. res 187 W Superior.

Perriguey Frank, lab. bds 187 W Superior.

Perriguey Isabella C, bds 187 W Superior.

Perriguey Julian A, res 12 Sturgis.

Perriguey Peter, res e s Lumbard 2 n of New Haven av.

Perriguey Theodore F, lab, bds 187 W Superior.

Perrin Ella (wid Ashley C), res over 107 E Main.

Perrin Hiram J, res 138 Broadway.

Perrin John W, pressman Ft W Sentinel, res 32 E 4th.

Perrin Mattie, seamstress, bds 15 W Williams.

Perrine Anna E (wid Wm), res 58 Chicago.

Perrine Van Buren, hardwood lumber, 9 Webster, res same. Tel 523.

Perry, see also Parry and Perrey.

Perry Alfred C, car bldr Penn Co, res 473 Lafayette.

Perry Bradley, mason, res 187 Montgomery.

Perry Clara I. seamstress, bds 35 Marion.

Perry Edward H, brakeman, bds 35 Marion.

Perry Everett L, hostler C L Centlivre Brewing Co, bds n w cor Spy Run and Edna.

Perry Frank F, engr G R & I R R, res 186 Clay.

Perry Franklin L, deliverer, bds 35 Marion.

Perry John, bds w s Spy Run av n w cor Edna.

Perry Madison, painter Olds' Wagon Wks, bds 108 Gay.

Perry Oscar L, mngr Western Union Telegraph Co. 2 New Aveline House Blk, res 79 W De Wald.

Perry Philip, painter Olds' Wagon Wks. res 108 Gay.

Perry Wm W, carpenter, res 35 Marion.

Perry Zelma G, opr S M Foster, bds 35 Marion.

Peters Box and Lumber Co, Charles Pape Pres, Treas and Genl Mngr, W H Murtaugh Vice-Pres, Carl F Siemon jr. Sec, Mnfrs Hardwood Lumber and Furniture, Office 78 High. Tel 83

Peters Carrie, domestic 98 Broadway.

Peters Ernest, bds 4 Grant.

Peters Fred C, clk J C Peters & Co, bds 232 W Wayne.

Peters Frederick, butcher, res 79 Force.

Peters Frederick, helper, res 219 W Superior.

Peters Frederick H, laborer, bds 216 E Washington.

Peters Jacob, cabtmkr Penn Co, res 30 Sherman.

Peters Jacob, res n e cor Franklin av and Putnam.

Peters Jacob, laborer, res 110 Riverside av.

Peters John C (J C Peters & Co), pres Indiana Machine Wks, mngr Horton Mnfg Co, lumber mnfrs, w s Osage n of Main, res 232 W Wayne.

Peters J C & Co (John C Peters), hardware, 7 E Columbia. Tel 484.

Peters John H, clk W Doehrmann, bds 216 E Washington.

Peters Lewis, cash A Mergentheim, bds 219 W Superior.

Peters Thomas, engr N Y, C & St L R R, res 80 Boone.

Peters Tillie K, tailoress, bds 30 Brandriff.

Peters Wm, student, bds 232 W Wayne.

Peterson James J, res s s Pennsylvania av 2 e of Wayne Trace.

Petgen Charles, lab Ft W Elec Corp, bds 95 Baker.

Petgen Daniel, coppersmith Penn Co. bds 9 Hough.

Petgen Frank A, flagman, res 95 Baker.

Petgen Frank H, bartender, bds 64 Melita.

Petgen Nicholas, checkman Wabash R R, res 64 Melita.

Petgen Nicholas, helper Bass F & M Wks, res 9 Hough.

Pettelark Louise, domestic The Wayne.

Pettit Benjamin F, draughtsman Ft W Elec Corp, bds 221 W De Wald.

Pettit Caroline, domestic 246 E Lewis.

Pettit Charles A, teamster, res 6 Dwenger av.

Pettit Dayton N, plumber, bds 221 W DeWald.

Pettit Ellsworth S, mach S F Bowser & Co, res 282 Walton av.

Pettit Joseph A, teamster, bds 284 E Jefferson.

Pettit Wm L, asst cash First Nat Bank, res 221 W De Wald.

Pettit Wm L jr, bds 221 W De Wald.

Pettit Wm M, teamster, res 284 E Jefferson.

Pettit Wm V, laborer, res 20 Francis.

Petzinger Charles F, removed to Savannah, Ga.
Petzinger Charlotte A (wid Frederick L), res s s Pontiac
  2 w of Hanna.
Petzinger George W, boilermkr, bds C A Petzinger.
Pettys John H, brakeman, res 21 High.
Pevert Alfred E, bds 32 Elm.
Pevert Frank, lab Ft Wayne Elec Corp, res 32 Elm.
Pevert Joseph L, laborer, bds 32 Elm.
Pfeiffer Abbie E, bds n w cor Wells and Archer av.
Pfeiffer Charles F, Real Estate and Loans,
  6-7 Bass Blk, bds n w cor Wells and Archer av.
Pfeiffer Edward, baggeman Nickel Plate R R, res 19 Ross.
Pfeiffer Eve (wid Joseph), res 61 Elm.
Pfeiffer Frederick B, died April 20th, 1895.
Pfeiffer Mrs F B (wid Fred B), res 25 Schick.
Pfeiffer Henry (Pfeiffer & Schlatter), res 148 W Berry.
Pfeiffer Henry G, asst bkkpr Pfeiffer & Schlatter, bds 148
  W Berry.
Pfeiffer John C, res n w cor Wells and Archer av.
Pfeiffer John N (Pfeiffer & Rousseau), res 50 Columbia av.
Pfeiffer Louis M, engr Penn Co, res 44 Gay.
Pfeiffer Sophia S, bds J C Pfeiffer.
Pfeiffer Thomas, lab N Y, C & St L R R, res 96 Franklin av
Pfeiffer & Rousseau (John N Pfeiffer, R Daniel Rousseau),
  grocers, 40-44 W Berry.   Tel 378.
Pfeiffer & Schlatter (Henry Pfeiffer, Christian
  C Schlatter), Builders' Hardware, Cutlery, Tools,
  Farm Implements and Sewing Machines, 38 and 40 E
  Columbia.   Tel 86.   (*See left side lines.*)
Pfeller Max, mach opr, bds 38 Watkins.
Pfenning Maggie, domestic 420 Hanna.
Pfisterer Aloysius, mason, res 82 Putnam.
Pfisterer Henry L, laborer, bds 82 Putnam.
Pfisterer John J, laborer, bds 82 Putnam.
Pfisterer Rosa, bds 82 Putnam.
Pflaumer Wm H, condr Ft W E Ry Co, res 44 Charles.
Pfleger Carrie L (wid Holt), res over 35 W Main.
Pfleger Charles W, laborer, bds Windsor Hotel.
Pfleger Harry, packer, bds over 35 W Main.
Pfleiderer Etta, bds 536 E Wayne.
Pfleiderer Jacob, butcher, res 536 E Wayne.
Pfleiderer Louise, bds 536 E Wayne.
Pfleiderer Wm, night clk J T Connolly, rms 536 E Wayne.
Pfleiger Joseph, express, res 4 Mary.
Pfleiger Mary A. bds 4 Mary.

Phebous James T, laborer, bds 37 Duck.
Phelps Clara, teacher Jefferson School, bds 258 W Wayne
Phelps Jennie, domestic The Wayne.
Phelps Jennie E, bds 7 Monroe.
Phelps John W, conductor, bds 149 Rockhill.
Phelps Minnie M, bds 7 Monroe.
Phelps Nellie F, bds 7 Monroe.
Phelps Whitcomb, phys, 7 Monroe, res same.
Philharmonic Club, 138 Calhoun.
Phillabaum Ann J (wid John M), res 168 Francis.
Phillabaum Frank D, clk G E Bursley & Co, bds 43 Wells
Phillabaum Sarah T (wid David), res 43 Wells.
Phillabaum Wm, lab, bds n s Griswold 2 e of bridge.
Philley Eli S, agt L S & M S and L E & W Rys, junction
　　Cass and Wells, res 40 Brackenridge.
Philley Emily, dressmaker, rms 50 W Superior.
Philley Hiram A, clk Penn Co, res 5 Victoria av.
Phillips Caroline W (wid Barnhard), res 121 W Main.
Phillips Catherine (wid Michael), bds 251 Webster.
Phillips Charles S, motorman Ft W E Ry Co, res 80 Baker
Phillips Edith L, student, bds 70 Jackson.
Phillips Frank B, bkkpr Bass F & M Wks, bds 121 W
　　Main.
Phillips George, feed yard, 80 E Columbia, res same.
Phillips John, laborer, res 74 Barthold.
Phillips John, switchman Wabash R R, bds 251 Webster.
Phillips Luella, res 14 Francis.
Phillips Lucy A (wid John J), res 70 Jackson.
Phillips Patrick H, laborer, bds 251 Webster.
Phillips Mrs Sarah, rms 104 E Wayne.
Phillips Warren B, Propr Hoosier and Fort
　　Wayne Steam Laundries, rms 159 W Main. (*See left
　　side lines.*)
Phillips Willis H, foreman W B Phillips, res 159 W Main.
Phipps John A, conductor, res 60 Thomas.
Phipps Oren A, laborer, res 157 Hayden.
Phipps Robert, patrolman, res 5 Park av.
Phœnix Building and Savings Union, Dr Carl Schilling
　　pres, G Max Hofmann vice-pres, Henry C Berghoff
　　treas, J F Bickel sec, Wm H Shambaugh atty, T N
　　Roach supt of agencies, 39 and 40 Bank Blk.
Piatt Cyrus H, fireman Penn Co, res 232 Harmer.
Piatt Maud, milliner, bds 232 Harmer.
Pichon Alexander, bds 329 E Wayne.
Pichon George, carpenter, bds 17 W Lewis.

524   R. L. POLK & CO.'s

Pichon Joseph J, carpenter, res 108 W 3d.
Pichon Marguerite, bds 329 E Wayne.
Pickard Artemus W, bkkpr Ft W Iron Wks, res 102 E Washington.
Pickard Bros (Peter E, Thomas D, and Harry R), Stoves and Furniture, 12 and 14 E Columbia. Tel 206.
Pickard Harry R (Pickard Bros), bds 106 E Washington.
Pickard Peter E (Pickard Bros), res 142 E Berry.
Pickard Thomas D (Pickard Bros), res Chicago, Ill.
Pickard Thomas R, supt foundry dept, Bass F & M Wks, res 106 E Washington. Tel 299.
Pickel George L, laborer, bds 15 Lafavetie.
Pidgeon Charles T (J A Armstrong & Co), rms 44 Harrison
Pidgeon Frank, bartender, bds 64 Melita.
Pidgeon John, fireman G R & I R R, res 58 Melita.
Pidgeon Nicholas, clk, res 64 Melita.
Piehl John G F, driver, bds J J Piehl.
Piehl Peter J F, carp, bds John J Piehl.
Piehl John J, junk, res s s Pioneer av 2 e of Fletcher av,
Piepenbrink Albert J, engr Jenney Elec L and P Co, res 19 Clark.
Piepenbrink Charles, res w s Lumbard 1 n of Wabash R R
Piepenbrink Clara L, bds C Piepenbrink.
Piepenbrink Christian, deputy County Treasurer, res 35 Elmwood av.
Piepenbrink Conrad, bds 522 E Lewis
Piepenbrink Conrad D, res 48 W Washington.
Piepenbrink Edith, domestic 96 E Washington.
Piepenbrink Ernst, res Lynn s w cor Lumbard.
Piepenbrink George D, letter carrier P O. bds 48 W Washington.
Piepenbrink Henry C, res 84 Lillie.
Piepenbrink Louis, condr Ft W Elect Ry Co, res 522 E Lewis.
Piepenbrink Mary, bds 522 E Lewis.
Piepenbrink Otto, laborer, bds 33 Elmwood av.
Piepenbrink Wm C, lab Penn Co, res 82 Lillie.
Pieper Casper, res 155 Wells.
Pieper Clara M, domestic 242 W Wayne.
Pieper Florentina, bds 155 Wells.
Pieper Frederick C, carpenter, res 214 W Jefferson.
Pieper John F, mach Wabash R R, res 113 Brackenridge.
Pieper Sophia, dressmkr, bds 113 Brackenridge.
Pierce, *see also Pearse.*
Pierce Alfred R, res 94 W Jefferson.

Pierce Andrew W, painter, res 160 Greeley.
Pierce Austin (wid Frank J), bds 171 Wells.
Pierce Clara B (wid Thomas M), bds 256 Fairfield av.
Pierce Clarence, fireman, bds 49 Baker.
Pierce Edward, engr N Y, C & St L R R, bds 17 Boone.
Pierce Everett G, mach Penn Co, res 245 E Lewis.
Pierce Harry W, dentist 191 Lafayette, bds 245 E Lewis.
Pierce Odgen (F L Jones & Co), res 240 Hoagland av.
Pierce Odgen jr, brakeman, bds 240 Hoagland av.
Pierce Robert B, bds 240 Hoagland av.
Pierce Robie, bds 94 W Jefferson.
Pierre Charles J, propr Pierre's Department Store, res s w cor Wells and 2d.
Pierre's Department Store, Charles J Pierre Propr, Dry Goods, Gent's Furnishing Goods, Notions, Glassware and Groceries, s w cor Wells and 2d.
Pierre Joseph M, mngr P Pierre, res 173 Van Buren.
Pierre Peter, dry goods, 168 Broadway, res 254 W Washington.
Pierson, *see also Pearson and Pirson.*
Pierson Calvin J, engr Penn Co, res 155 Hanna.
Pierson Ulietta D (wid John), res 153 Hanna.
Pietz J Ferdinand, meat market, 224 Lafayette, res s s Bluffton rd 3 w of river bridge.
Pifer Jacob, porter D F Comparet, bds 74 E Columbia.
Pike Albert, mach opr, res 12 Park av.
Pike James E, cutter L Diether & Bro, res 34 Walton av.
Pillars Charles, bds 183 W Superior.
Pilliod Frank X, wagonmaker L Mehnert, res 87 Wagner.
Pinney Charles A, conductor, res 132 Montgomery.
Pio Mary, domestic 85 Lake av.
Pion Charles, waiter F J Lourent, bds 18 Randolph.
Pion John, lab Penn Co, res 8 Oliver.
Pion Lewis, carp C L Centlivre Brwg Co, res 18 Randolph
Pipenbrink Henry P, bartender, res 97 Cass.
Piper Charles, slater Gerding & Aumann Bros, bds Summit City Hotel.
Piper Margarette (wid John), bds 142 E Lewis.
Pirson, *see also Pearson and Pierson.*
Pirson Christian, res 4 Eliza av.
Pirson Jacob B, carp S F Bowser & Co, res 4 South Wayne av.
Pisano Martin, shoemkr, res 21 Force.
Pittner Kate B, domestic 173 W Wayne.

Pittsburg, Fort Wayne & Chicago Ry (Operated by Penn Co), R B Rossington Freight Agent, Offices and Freight Depot e s Clinton bet Holman and Railroad. Tel 108.

Pittsburg, Ft Wayne & Chicago and Grand Rapids & Indiana Ry, passenger depot, cor Calhoun and Railroad. Tel 211.

Pitzlin Paul, athlete, bds 138 E Berry.

Pixley George W (Pixley & Co), Pres Tri-State Building and Loan Association, Treas Ft Wayne Land and Improvement Co, Treas Jenney Electric Light Co, res 96 W Wayne. Tel 343.

Pixley George W jr (Pixley & Co), res Utica, New York.

Pixley Henry D (Pixley & Co), res Utica, New York.

Pixley & Co (Henry D, George W and George W Pixley jr, Charles E Read and Robert H Parmelee.) Clothing, Men's Furnishings, Etc, 16 and 18 E Berry. Tel 490.

Pixley & Long Bldg, 16 and 18 E Berry.

Plank Charles E, bds rear 168 High.

Plank Jacob A, carpenter, res 41 Pine.

Plank John, mach hd, res rear 168 High.

Plank Josephine T, opr F L Jones, bds 237 St Mary's av.

Planting Peter, draughtsman W Gas Const Co, rms 100 E Jefferson.

Pleasants Amelia (col'd) (wid Simon), bds 100 Indiana av.

Pledger George C, laborer, res 141 Wells.

Plettner Mary, bds 320 Hanna.

Pleus Herman, lab Hoffman Bros, bds 27 High.

Pleuss Emil, moved to Berne, Ind.

Pliett Albert, helper Bass Wks, bds 206 John.

Pliett Bertha, domestic 99 E Wayne.

Pliett Christina (wid Charles), res 206 John.

Pliett Edward J C, molder Bass F & M Wks, bds 206 John.

Plock, *see also Block.*

Plock Bernard, fireman Penn Co, res 204 W Jefferson.

Plock Edward J, finisher Ft W Furn Co, bds 204 W Jefferson.

Plock Henry, removed to Chicago, Ill.

Plock Herman H, foreman Ft W Furn Co, bds 34 W Superior

Plogsterth Adam, res n s New Haven av opp Pioneer av.

Plogsterth Emma, bds Adam Plogsterth.

Plogsterth Fred, bds 147 Madison.

Plogsterth Wm H, trav agt Root & Co, res 300 E Creighton av.

Ploor Margaretta (wid Christian), res rear 96 E Jefferson.

Plumadore Ella (wid Wm), res 40 Madison.

Plumadore Horton A, cigar mnfr, 104 Calhoun, rms 40 Madison.

Plumadore Marshall N, teacher of music, 49 Douglas av, res same.

Plummer Annie, domestic 264 E Creighton av.

Plybon Charles C, brakeman, bds 53 Oliver.

Plymouth Congregational Church, Jefferson s e cor Harrison

Poch August F, bds 26 Stophlet.

Poch Bertha A, domestic 192 W Wayne.

Poch Bruno E, student, bds 26 Stophlet.

Poch Emil F, carpet weaver, bds 26 Stophlet.

→ Poch Emma A, domestic 77 Maple av.

Poch Moritz E, carpet weaver, 26 Stophlet, res same.

Pocock Elias, laborer, bds Union House.

Pocock Major, fireman Penn Co, rms 226 Calhoun.

Pocock Robert E, bartndr, rms 226 Calhoun.

Poetsch Agnes T (wid Frederick C), res 32 Pritchard.

Poetsch Magdalena M, shirtmkr, bds 32 Pritchard.

Poff James H (Pearse & Poff), res 22 Chicago.

Pohl, see also Pahl and Paul.

Pohl Dina, bds 36 Buchanan.

Pohl Dinah, seamstress, bds 102 Smith.

Pohl Elizabeth (wid John G), res 36 Buchanan.

Pohl Henry A, helper Penn Co, bds 36 Buchanan.

Pohl J George, died January 4, 1895.

Pohlmann Christian, carpenter, res 144 Greeley.

Pohlmeyer Frederick C, bricklayer, res 57 Baker.

Poinsoette Jacob, cellarman The Herman Berghoff Brewing Co, res 85 Grant av.

Poinsoette Joseph, bds 52 Gay.

Poirson Frank J, driver Hook and Ladder Co No 2, bds 124 Wallace.

Poirson Peter F, Real Estate, Loans and Broker, 12 Bank Blk, rms 70 E Columbia. Tel 214.

Poiry Jessie J, clk C J Welker, bds 329 E Lewis.

Poiry Peter, carp Penn Co, res 329 E Lewis.

Polhamus Albert H, foreman Penn Co, res 73 Dawson.

Polhamus Albert Z, supt S F Bowser & Co, res 250 E Creighton av.

Polhamus Grace A, bds 73 Dawson.

Polhamus John C, fireman Penn Co, res 71 W Butler.

Polhamus John G, fireman Penn Co, res 144 Horace.

Polhamus May L, stenogr Ft Wayne Elec Corp, bds 73 Dawson. Tel 514.

Polhamus Wm H, fireman Penn Co, res 25 Julia.

Police Headquarters, Barr bet E Wayne and Berry. Tel 38

Polk R L & Co, John Andrews Resident Mngr, Publishers Ft Wayne Directory, 38 Bass Blk.

Pollitz Frederick H, laborer, res 236 Gay.

Pollitz Mary, domestic 106 E Main.

Pollitz Sophia, domestic 167 E Berry.

Pollock Frank, carpenter, res 71 Dawson.

Polsen Michael, lab Penn Co, res 36 Force.

Polston Anna, domestic 12 Marion.

Polston Cora, domestic 12 Marion.

Pomper Herman, carpet weaver, res 229 Lafayette.

Pomper Max, printer Freie Presse, bds 229 Lafayette.

Pomper Otto O, cigarmkr, bds 229 Lafayette.

Pomper Richard E, cigarmkr, bds 229 Lafayette.

Pomroy Wm J W, paperhanger Siemon & Bro, res 193 High.

Ponsot Emil, butcher, res 491 E Wayne.

Pool Charles, watchman Penn Co, res 192 Walton av.

Pool Francis J, teamster, res Rudisill av nr Beaver av.

Poole Emery O, mach Wabash R R, res 43 Lavina.

Poole Frank H, 2d asst cash Hamilton National Bank, res 487 Calhoun.

Pope, *see also Pape and Pepe.*

Pope James F, train dispatcher N Y, C & St L R R, res 76 Columbia av.

Popp, *see also Bopp.*

Popp Adam, carpet weaver, res 110 Boone.

Popp Anna, domestic 80 Barr.

Popp August, bartender, bds 96 W De Wald.

Popp Charles A, saloon, 88½ Barr, res same.

Popp Christopher, clerk, bds 88½ Barr.

Porsch Amelia, bds 142 W 3d.

Porsch G Benjamin, mach Ind M Wks, res 17 Burgess.

Porsch Johanna R (wid Wm), res 142 W 3d.

Porsch John, mach L E & W R R, bds 142 W 3d.

Porteous John (Beadell & Co), res Norwich, Conn.

Porter Bertha M, bds 233 Lafayette.

Porter Charles P, clk Wabash R R, bds w s Spy Run av 1 n of Ruth.

Porter Elizabeth (wid Humphrey), res 39 Lavina.

Porter Hiram, contr, res n e cor Koch and Putnam.

Porter Hiram jr, bds n e cor Koch and Putnam.

Porter John, condr, res 200 W Superior.
Porter Lizzie (wid John N), res 51 Columbia av.
Porter Mattie (col'd), bds 48 Hayden.
Porter Miles F, Physician and Sec Pension
Examining Board, 47 W Wayne, res same. Tel 2.
Porter Oliver F, agent, res 25 Baker av.
Porter Richard L, res 620 E Wayne.
Porter Samuel H, clk Seavey Hdwe Co, res 267 E Jefferson.
Porter Sarah E (wid Henry), res 233 Lafayette.
Post Bernhard L, saloon, 308 W Main, res same.
Post Office, s e cor Berry and Clinton. Tel 220.
Post Office Drug Store, Dr C E Heaton propr, 36 E Berry.
Tel 309.
Postal Telegraph Co, C E Stetler mngr, 15 W Columbia.
Potter Mrs Elizabeth, res 130 W Creighton av.
Potter Francis J, teamster, res 93 Wagner.
Potter Frank E, frt handler Wabash R R, bds 130 W
Creighton av.
Potter George E, engr N Y, C & St L R R, res 151 W
Wayne.
Potter George L, supt motive power Penn Co, res 148 E
Washington. Tel 345.
Potter Horatio, polisher, bds 152 E Wayne.
Potter John, cabinetmkr Penn Co, res 131 Sherman.
Potter John F, helper Seavey Hdwe Co, bds 247 W DeWald
Potter Joseph L, res 130 W Creighton av.
Potter Levi N, brakeman, res 359 W Main.
Potter Matilda, bkkpr Pape Furn Co, bds 247 W DeWald
Potter Millie A (wid Orange), res 152 E Wayne.
Potter Phillip L, real estate, 28 Bank Blk, res 142 Jackson
Potter Raymond S, polisher, bds 152 E Wayne.
Potter Royal, bds 152 E Wayne.
Potter Thomas, cabinetmkr Penn Co, res 247 W DeWald.
Potterfield Thomas E, painter, res 45 Hayden.
Potthoff Wm (Ankenbruck & Potthoff), res 172 E Wash-
ington.
Pottlitzer Anna C, bds 50 W Wayne.
Pottlitzer Bros Fruit Co, Leo Pottlitzer pres, Isidore
Pottlitzer sec, Herman Pottlitzer treas, Adolph Dia-
mond mngr, produce, 8 and 10 Harrison. Tel 243.
Pottlitzer Herman, treas Pottlitzer Bros, res Lafayette, Ind
Pottlitzer Isidore I, sec Pottlitzer Bros, bds 50 W Wayne.
Pottlitzer Leo, pres Pottlitzer Bros, res Lafayette, Ind.
Pottlitzer Seelig, res 50 W Wayne.
Potts Charles H, brakeman Penn Co, bds 42 Bass.

Fort Wayne Wagon.

L. O. ZOLLINGER & BRO.,
SOLE MANUFACTURERS,
15 EAST SUPERIOR STREET.

530   R. L. POLK & CO.'S

Potts David, lab F, Ft W & W Ry, bds 119 Boone.
Potts Dayton C, brakeman, res 349 W Main.
Potts Emanuel, clk Ind Furn Co, bds 119 Boone.
Poulson Britton, patternmkr, res 108 Spy Run av.
Poulson Elmer, cabinetmaker, bds 108 Spy Run av.
Powell Granville, res 42 W Main.
Powell Henry, laborer, bds 42 W Main.
Powell Isaac B, lab L E & W Ry, res 39 Wefel.
Powell John M, laborer, res 8 Barthold.
Powell Lillie R M, bds 8 Barthold.
Powell Randall, boarding, 42 W Main.
Powers Emmet M (Powers & Barnett), res Kansas City, Mo.
Powers James, mach hd Rhinesmith & Simonson, bds 214 Fairfield av.
Powers & Barnett (Emmet M Powers, Abraham G Barnett), Proprs Ft Wayne Omnibus, Baggage and Carriage Line, 12-24 E Wayne.   Tel 26.
Powers John A, res 156 E Wayne.
Poyneer George W, died June 27th, 1894.
Poyser Caroline E (wid Henry J), res 47 Miner.
Poyser George E, mach Wabash R R, res 77 Wall.
Poyser Hiram, foreman Wabash R R, res 566 Broadway.
Poyser Wm F, patternmkr Wabash R R, res 234 Fairfield av
Prange August, carver Ft W O Co, bds Broadway s of limits
Prange Charles W, teamster, res 15 Suttenfield.
Prange Christian, carpenter, res 109 Wall.
Prange Elizabeth, domestic 54 E Main.
Prange Ferdinand, painter, res 143 Union.
Prange Frederick F, teamster, res 185 E Taber.
Prange Henry, helper Fleming Mnfg Co, res 588 Calhoun.
Prange Sophia, domestic 260 W Wayne.
Pranger Charles F, clk D J Shaw, bds 286 E Jefferson.
Pranger Edward H, bds 226 E Washington.
Pranger Harry, lab Ft W Elec Corp, bds 236 W Washington.
Pranger Harry F, car bldr Penn Co, bds 226 E Washington.
Pranger John H, carp, res 226 E Washington.
Pranger Mary R, bds 226 E Washington.
Pranger Thelka (wid Conrad), res 206 E Washington.
Pranger Wm, tinner, res 206 E Washington.
Pranger Wm F, farmer, res w s Broadway, 1½ miles s of city limits.
Pranger Wm F jr, bds W F Pranger.
Pratt Benjamin D, brick mason, res 58 Thomas.

Pratt Hannah (wid George H), bds 58 Thomas.
Pratt Nellie, bds 58 Thomas.
Pratt Walter, brick mason, bds 58 Thomas.
Pregler Louis, tailor J O Cashman, bds 201 Hanna.
Prentice Wilson, trav agt A L Johns & Co, bds 46 E Jefferson.
Pressler Albert G, appr Ft W Iron Wks, bds 52 W De Wald.
Pressler Mrs Amelia, res 344 E Washington.
Pressler Charles F, mach L G Scholze, bds 344 E Washington.
Pressler Clara, domestic 25 W Washington.
Pressler Edith A, bds 334 E Washington.
Pressler Edward C, carpenter, bds 52 W De Wald.
Pressler Emma J, bds 52 W De Wald.
Pressler George, contr, 52 W De Wald, res same.
Pressler John, bds Grand Central Hotel.
Pressler John A, plumber, bds 344 E Washington.
Pressler Lillian S, bds 52 W De Wald.
Pressler Rose, bds 344 E Washington.
Pressler Williard E, printer The Journal, res 14 Riverside av
Price Wm B, blksmith, n s Pioneer av 2 e of Winch, res s w cor Greene and Winter.
Prill August, molder Bass F & M Wks, res 88 Hayden.
Prim David A, brakeman Penn Co, res 169 E Creighton av.
Prince Charles A, fireman Penn Co, res 118 Hanna.
Prince Isaac, car inspr L E & W R R, res 44 W 5th.
Princess Cash Store, Arthur C Angove and Arthur C Jr, Proprietors, 111–119 Calhoun. Tel 314.
Princess Roller Skating Rink, W Main, s e cor Fulton.
Prindeville Maurice J, condr Penn Co, rms 228 Calhoun.
Printis Patrick, laborer, res 97 Baker.
Prior W A (S B Thing & Co), res Boston, Mass.
Pritchard Loda, bds 199 E Washington.
Pritchard Myrtle, stenographer, bds 199 E Washington.
Pritchard Samuel, lab Bond Cereal Mills, res 199 E Washington.
Pritchard Thomas, molder Bass F & M Wks, res 13 Holton av.
Pritchard Thomas jr, mach Bass Wks, bds 13 Holton av.
Proal A B, treas Ft W Gas Co, res New York City.
Probasco Wm J (Green & Probasco), res 76 Lafayette.
Probst Edward L, res 148 Holman.
Procuniar Charles E, laborer, res 505 E Washington.
Proegler Alma, bds 161 Griffith.

Proegler Carl, Physician, 128 Broadway, res 161 Griffith. Tel 9.

Proegler Jennie, bds 161 Griffith.

Provines Ann (wid John S), res 68 Lake av.

Provines Lena M, stenogr Ft Wayne Elec Corp, bds 68 Lake av.

Prows Joseph T, ins agt, bds 104 Barr.

Prudential Life Ins Co of America, A E Haslam supt, 2 3 and 4 Bass Blk.

Public Library, Ft Wayne, Ind, City Hall.

Puddy Charles, clk Root & Co, res 133 E Main.

Puff Adolph, painter, 341 Hanna, bds same.

Puff Bros (Robert C and Edwin C), shoes, 339 Hanna, saloon, 340 same.

Puff Charles B, shoes, 134 Maumee av, res same.

Puff Edwin C (Puff Bros), res 341 Hanna.

Puff Mary T, bds 341 Hanna.

Puff Richard M, bartender Puff Bros, bds 341 Hanna.

Puff Robert C (Puff Bros), res 341 Hanna.

Puff Theresa (wid Charles), died August 2, 1894.

Puls August, mason, res 150 Union.

Puls Caroline (wid August), bds 150 Union.

Pulver Bertha M, bds 419 W Main.

Pulvermueller Henrietta, res 57 John.

Purcell Frank E, trav agt Pottlitzer Bros, res 48 E 4th.

Purman Algernon A, lawyer, 1 and 2 Foster Blk, res 259 W Wayne.

Purman Ronald R, student, bds 259 W Wayne.

Purman Theodosia, bds 259 W Wayne.

Putman Charles H, lather, bds 230 Harmer.

Putman George C, car bldr Penn Co, res 230 Harmer.

Putt John, farmer, res 15 Zollars av.

Putt John jr, bds 15 Zollars av.

Pyke Charles W, ins solicitor, res 144 E Berry.

Pyke Frank H, chief clk N Y, C & St L R R, bds 144 E Berry.

Pyle Mary A, teacher High School, bds 50 W Washington

Pyle Minerva (wid Isaac N), res 37 Duck.

Pyles Jennie, rms 163 Clinton.

Pyor Joseph, lab Bass F & M Wks, res 163 Hayden.

Q

Qualls Valentine A, res 7 Duck.

Quicksell Harry M, Agt Star Union Line (Fast Freight), 3 and 4 Trentman Bldg, res 227 W

Quackenbush, E N, Dist Agt Mutual Benefit Life Ins C Newark, N J, rms 69 Pixley & Long Blk.

Quicksell Peter, wood 196 Jackson, res 16 Jones.
Quicre Emil, truckmkr, res n s New Haven av 4 e of Lumbard.
Quidor George, engr N Y, C & St L R R, res 219. W Wayne.
Quidor Martha J (wid Nathan K), res 150 W Wayne.
Quidor Sidney C, painter, bds 150 W Wayne.
Quillinan James J, clk Penn Co, res 153 Broadway.
Quillinan Nellie C, bds 23 Colerick.
Quillinan Thomas E. winder Ft W Elec Corp, bds 23 Colerick.
Quince James A, bkkpr Klett & Son, res 513 Broadway.
Quince Mrs Nancy, dressmkr 513 Broadway, bds same.
Quinlan Anna, domestic 251 W Main.
Quinlan Rev John R, asst pastor Cathedral Immaculate Conception, res 172 Clinton.
Quinlan Marie, waitress Randall Hotel.
Quinn Bridget (wid Thomas), bds 13 E Williams.
Quinn Catherine C, milliner, bds 157 W De Wald.
Quinn Daniel, fireman Bass F & M Wks. res 44 Chicago.
Quinn Edward J, bailiff Superior Court. res 42 Chicago.
Quinn Elizabeth, milliner, bds 157 W De Wald.
Quinn Elizabeth L, seamstress, bds 141 Lafayette.
Quinn James D, brakemann Penn Co, bds 141 Lafayette
Quinn James E, engr N Y, C & St L R R, res 243 W Washington.
Quinn James E, heater Penn Co, res 141 Lafayette.
Quinn Louisa (wid Patrick), res 90 Thomas.
Quinn Maggie, milliner, bds 157 W De Wald.
Quinn Mary A, bds 42 Chicago.
Quinn Mary C, wrapper, bds 44 Chicago.
Quinn Mary E, milliner 175 Fairfield av, res 157 W De Wald.
Quinn Michael, lab Wabash R R, res 157 W De Wald.
Quinn Michael S, mach Wabash R R, bds 157 W De Wald
Quinn Nellie A, wrapper. bds 42 Chicago.
Quinn Patrick, blksmith Wabash R R, res 122 Chicago.
Quinn Thomas F, bds 42 Chicago.
Quinn Thomas J, engr Penn Co, bds 15 Bass.
Quinn Thomas J, puller Ft W Elec Corp, bds 44 Chicago.
Quivey Harry A, flagman, bds n w cor Winter and Pontiac
Q and O Club, 41½ W Main.

R

Raab Catherine, milliner, bds 175 E Washington.

Raab Mrs Christina, milliner 175 E Washington, res same.
Raab Eliza (wid John), res 112 W Jefferson.
Raab Emma R, bds 112 W Jefferson.
Raab Frederick, laborer, res 175 E Washington.
Raab John G, porkpacker, 18 E Columbia, res 112 W Jefferson.
Raab Josie, milliner, bds 175 E Washington.
Raab Mary E, bds 112 W Jefferson.
Raab Mona, milliner, bds 175 E Washington.
Raab Tillie C, bkkpr J G Raab, bds 112 W Jefferson.
Rabbitt Jackson W, carpenter, res 53 Thomas.
Rabel Christian, res 105 Beaver av.
Rabel George W, candymkr, bds John Rabel.
Rabel John, shoemaker, 80 Fairfield av, res Brooklyn av s of Ontario.
Rabel Wm J, flagman, res 224 Walton av.
Rabus Charles F, clk J Rabus, bds 156 W Washington.
Rabus Edward, student, bds 156 W Washington.
Rabus George A, fireman L E & W R R, res 50 W 3d.
Rabus George J, cutter J Rabus, bds 156 W Washington.
Rabus Gustave A, cutter J Rabus, res 284 W Berry.
Rabus John, Merchant Tailor, 16 W Berry, res 156 W Washington.
Rabus John F, foreman W H Davis, res 54 W 3d.
Rabus Louisa, bds 156 W Washington.
Rabus Magdalene (wid Matthias), res 56 W 3d.
Rabus Mary, bds 156 W Washington
Rabus Wm F, student, bds 156 W Washington.
Race John L, res 66 Cass.
Race Olive L, bds 66 Cass.
Race Walter H, clk N Y, C & St L R R, bds 66 Cass.
Racht Albert, brakeman, res 25 Jane.
Racht Joseph, res 23 Killea av.
Racht Joseph L, truckman Wabash R R, res 25 Jane.
Racine Aime, horse collar mnfr, 13 1st, res 27 Cass.
Racine Annie G, bds 34 Cass.
Racine August L, bds 86 W Jefferson.
Racine Bessie P, stenogr Kuhne & Co, bds 90 Lake av.
Racine Claude, helper Hoffman Bros, bds 124 Cass.
Racine Frederick L, collarmkr 36 Cass, res 34 same.
Racine Grace, bds 34 Cass.
Racine Hermann J, bartender F P Rosselot, bds same.
Racine Jacob F, collarmkr A Racine, res 124 Cass.
Racine John F, carpenter, rms 32 E Columbia.

Racine Virgil L, condr Ft W Elec Ry, res n s New Haven av 5 e of Lumbard.
Racklan Anna, operator, bds 12 Park av.
Racklan Ernest R, operator, bds 12 Park av.
Rademacher Right Rev Joseph, D D, Bishop Diocese of Ft Wayne, res 172 Calhoun.
Rader Mrs Anna, res 37 Fairfield av.
Rader Hannah, opr S M Foster, bds 231 Barr.
Radofski Stanislaus, lab Bass F & M Wks, res 25 Force.
Radtke Herman R, teamster, res 51 Locust.
Radtke Louis, lab Penn Co, res 18 Nirdlinger av.
Raeder Belle (wid Peter), bds 203 Barr.
Raedy, *see also Raidy.*
Raedy Ella M, bds 80 Hoagland av.
Raedy John J, laborer, bds 80 Hoagland av.
Raedy Maggie C, bds 80 Hoagland av.
Raedy Mary A, bds 80 Hoagland av.
Raedy Wm, lab Wabash R R, res 80 Hoagland av.
Raedy Wm M, laborer, bds 80 Hoagland av.
Ragan Charles K, hostler F H Myers, res 62 E Wayne.
Ragan Charles R, bds 154 Greeley.
Ragan Wm H, laborer, bds 203 Lafayette.
Rager Adelbert J, music teacher, 102 E Jefferson; res same.
Rahdert Anna, domestic 174 W Wayne.
Rahdert Sophia, domestic 119 W Wayne.
Rahe August, grocer, 65 Gay, res same.
Rahe Mrs Catherine, dressmkr, 241 Broadway, res same.
Rahe Clara, clerk, bds 65 Gay.
Rahe Edward C H, painter, bds 223 E Jefferson.
Rahe Elizabeth, clerk, bds 65 Gay.
Rahe Ella H R, clk J H Meyer, bds 223 E Jefferson.
Rahe Emma M A, seamstress, bds 223 E Jefferson.
Rahe Frank H, cigar mnfr, 103 Broadway, res 241 same.
Rahe Henry K, mason, res 223 E Jefferson.
Rahe J Henry, furniture, 34 Clinton, res 161 Broadway.
Rahe Sophia, bds 161 Broadway.
Rahe Wm C, clerk, bds 65 Gay.
Rahe Wm F, clerk Fox Br U S Baking Co, res 22 E Taber.
Raiber George, help Penn Co, res 67 Wagner.
Raidy, *see also Raedy.*
Raidy David, engr Penn Co, res 20 Bass.
Raidy John, lab Ft W Elec Corp, bds 20 Bass.
Raidy Peter J, train disp Penn Co, res 336 Harrison.
Raidy Sarah, coremkr Ft W Elec Corp, bds 20 Bass.

Raifsnyder Alfred, asst yd master Penn Co, res 26 W Williams.

Railroad Restaurant, Mrs C Frederick Propr, 264 and 266 Calhoun. (*See p 95.*)

Raimboeuf Edward, helper Penn Co, res 64 Force.

Raines Charles R (col'd), cook Hotel Rich, res 111 Hayden.

Raines Solomon M, baths 60 Clinton, res 111 Hayden.

Rambo Benjamin W, jeweler 19 W Wayne, res 124 W Washington.

Rambo Ilion K, jeweler B W Rambo, bds 124 W Washington.

Ramer August O, bottler Herman Berghoff Brewing Co, bds 52 Wabash av.

Ramer Eva (wid August), res 52 Wabash av.

Ramey Mary E, bds 18 Cass.

Ramey Ora M, tel opr L S & M S Ry, res 18 Cass.

Ramey Sarah E (wid Edward), died August 4, 1894.

Ramm Anton, lab Bass F & M Wks, res 229 Gay.

Ramm Anton A, laborer, bds 229 Gay.

Ramm Emil A, laborer, bds 229 Gay.

Ramm Lena, opr Hoosier Mnfg Co, bds 38 Gay.

Ramm Louis, helper, res 38 Gay.

Ramsay Bertha V, teacher, bds 165 High.

Ramsay Helen (wid Peter), res 260 W Creighton av.

Ramsey Andrew, broommaker, bds J Ramsey.

Ramsey Freeman, res 319 Harrison.

Ramsey Jennie (wid Elihu B), furnished rooms 66 W Main

Ramsey Joseph, broommkr, res n e cor Brooklyn av and Ontario.

Randall Alfred L, Propr Randall Cycle Co, 31 W Berry, res 28 Maple av. (*See right top lines and page opp.*)

Randall Charles H, traveling agt, res 72 Douglas av.

Randall Cycle Co, A L Randall Propr, Bicycles, Supplies and Repairs, 31 W Berry. (*See right top lines and p opp.*)

Randall Frank M, city engineer Office City Hall, res 326 Broadway.

Randall Irvin, moved to N Y,

Randall Perry A (Randall & Doughman; Dick Townsend & Co; Lathrop & Co), pres Ryan Trucking Co, sec Star Iron Tower Co, res 58 Maple av. Tel 98.

Randall The, Dick Townsend & Co Proprietors, Harrison w end Columbia. Tel 323.

Randall & Doughman (Perry A Randall, Newton D Doughman), Lawyers, 5-9 Bass Blk.

Raney John H, fireman N Y, C & St L R R, res 10 Mary.

Rank Eli, bds 83 Broadway.

Rank John A, dyer, bds 175 Erie.

Rank Margaret (wid John), res 175 Erie.

Rank Richard H, bds 83 Broadway.

Ranke Emma, bds 127 W Washington.

Ranke Frederick, student, bds 127 W Washington.

Ranke Henrietta L (wid Frederick), bds 127 W Washington.

Ranke Henry, saloon, 37 Calhoun, rms same.

Ranke John, fireman N Y, C & St L R R, bds 335 W Main

Ranke J Henry, student, bds 127 W Washington.

Ranke Louisa E, bds 127 W Washington.

Ranke Wm F (Ranke & Yergens), res 127 W Washington.

Ranke Wm F jr (Freese & Ranke), bds 127 W Washington

Ranke & Yergens (Wm F Ranke, Wm Yergens), stave mnfrs, s e cor Superior and Griffith.

Rankin Christian, lab, res 168 Smith.

Rankin Frederick, bds 57 Barr.

Ranney Henry R, laborer, bds 217 E Washington.

Ransbottom Charles W. lather, bds 58 Riverside av.

Ransbottom Jasper F, plaster, res 58 Riverside av.

Ransbury Elmer W, clk Arcade Music Store, rms 40 Madison.

Ransom Lyman H, trav agt, bds 26 E Washington.

Ransom Newell H, clk Mossman, Yarnelle & Co, res cor St Joe Boulevard and Oneida.

Rapp, see also Rupp.

Rapp Frederick G, lab Ft W Elec Corp, bds 34 Taylor.

Rapp Henry C, clk Fox Br U S Baking Co, bds 34 Taylor

Rapp Henry F, lab Fisher Bros, res 19 Boone.

Rapp John N, bds 37 Stophlet.

Rapp Philip J, helper Wabash R R, res 37 Stophlet.

Rapp Wilhelmina (wid Wm), res 34 Taylor.

Rapuzzi Louis, fruits 172 Calhoun, res same.

Raquet Charles C, mach Ft W Elec Corp, bds 9 N Calhoun

Raquet Charles H, winder Ft W Elec Corp, bds 60 Barthold.

Raquet Emma, domestic 226 High.

Raquet Emma A, bds 60 Barthold.

Raquet Peter, gunsmith; res 60 Barthold.

Raquet Rosa. opr S M Foster, bds 44 W 5th.

Raquet Wm G, bottler, bds 60 Barthold.

538. R. L. POLK & CO.'S

Rarig Edward H, lab Paul Mnfg Co, bds 116 High.
Rarig Elijah A, brakeman, res 116 High.
Rasmus Jacob M, agt Met Life Ins Co, rms 246 Calhoun.
Rastenburg Charles, painter Olds' Wagon Wks, res 6 Oliver.
Rastenburg Frank, painter J H Brimmer, bds 42 John.
Rastenburg Frederick G, painter Olds' Wagon Wks, bds 42 John.
Rastenburg Frederick W, laborer, res 42 John.
Rastenburg Rudolph, painter Olds' Wagon Wks, res 52 John.
Rastetter Carl L, druggist 305 E Washington, res 321. Tel 171.
Rastetter Helen, bds 246 Broadway.
Rastetter Louis (Louis Rastetter & Son), res 246 Broadway
Rastetter Louis & Son, (Louis and Wm C), Manufacturers of Buggy Bows and Bicycle Wood Rims, s w cor Broadway and P, Ft W & C Ry. Tel 341.
Rastetter Wm C (Louis Rastetter & Son), bds 246 Broadway.
Rathburn Mrs Dora, nurse School for F M Y.
Rathert Albert, butler J H Bass, Brookside.
Rathert Christian A, blksmith Ft W Elect Corp, res 74 Home av.
Rathert Emma, domestic 210 W Wayne.
Rathert Frederick, bricklayer, res 51 Wilt.
Rathert Frederick jr, painter, bds 51 Wilt.
Rathert Gustav, bds 13 Summit.
Rathert Henry W, drugs 96 Wells, res cor Clinton and 6th.
Rathert John H, boilermkr, res 13 Summit.
Rathert Louisa, opr, bds 13 Summit.
Rathert Mary, domestic 416 Fairfield av.
Rathert Sophie, bds 51 Wilt.
Rathert Sophie S L, seamstress, bds 74 Home av.
Rathot Henry C, helper Penn Co, res 212 E Washington.
Ratliff Andrew M, section hd, rms 59 W Superior.
Ratzraff Frederick, laborer, res 9 Winter.
Ratzraff Martha, bds 9 Winter.
Rau Casper, res 299 E Washington.
Rau Wilhelm, bds 299 E Washington.
Rauch Abraham C, dentist, 48 Harrison, res 171 Wells.
Rauch Centennial C, seamstress, bds 110 John.
Rauch Clara I, clerk, bds 171 Wells.
Rauch Horatio S, painter, bds 171 Wells.

Rauch Ora D, seamstress, bds 110 John.
Rauch Wm, agent, res 110 John.
Rauen Matthias, carp Penn Co, res 186 Taylor.
Rauh George F, mach Fleming Mnfg Co, res 21 Belle av.
Rauh Gustav A, plasterer, res 49 Cass.
Rauh Gustav A jr, tailor, res 57 Cass.
Rauh Matthias, trav agt, bds 49 Cass.
Rauh Mattie E, bds 49 Cass.
Rauh Pauline A, bds 49 Cass.
Rauh Philip J, barber, bds 49 Cass.
Rauner Aloysius, blksmith Penn Co, res s s Eliza av 2 e of
  Hillside av.
Rauner Frances J, bds 16 E Williams.
Rauner George, carp Wayne Oil Tank Co, res w s Spy Run
  av 3 n bridge.
Rauner George, laborer, res 144 Force.
Rauner Joseph F, painter, res 126 Wilt.
Rauner Mary (wid Joseph), res 51 Taylor.
Raven Lena, bds 49 Walter.
Ray Edgar, bartender Ft Wayne Club, rms 46 W Berry.
Ray John D, bds 33 Monroe.
Ray Matilda (wid John W), res 33 Monroe.
Rayhouse Gideon I Z, real estate 9 Foster Blk, res 28
  Jones.
Rayhouse Wm E, condr, res 28 Jones.
Rayhouser Addie T, stenogr Wabash R R, bds 47 Hues-
  tis av.
Rayhouser Josephine (wid Gedliah), res 116 Fulton.
Rayhouser Rufus C F, printer 34 E Berry, res s w cor St
  Joe Gravel rd and Charlotte av.
Rayl John W, foreman, res 19 Lasselle.
Raymond Viola (wid Sidney), bds 186 W Berry.
Raymond Viola, starcher W B Phillips, bds 37 Wefel.
Raymond Blanche, ironer W B Phillips, bds n w cor Sum-
  mit and McCulloch.
Raypole Edward W, barber, bds 83 E Berry.
Raypole John E, butcher E Rich, res 86 W Lewis.
Read, see also Reed.
Read Abbie W (wid James M), res 149 Rockhill.
Read Asahel J, res 27 E Washington.
Read Charles E (Pixley & Co), res 137 Edgewater av.
Read Henry A, vet surg, 62 Harrison, res 64 same. Tel 14
Read James M, clk Penn Co, bds 179 Clinton.
Read Julia (wid Moses), bds 179 Clinton.
Ready, see Raedy nnd Raidy.

Reamer, *see Ramer.*

Reamsnider Amelia, domestic 200 W Berry.

Rear James E, paperhanger, bds 105 Taylor.

Rear Jesse M, painter, res 107 Taylor.

Rear Nicholas N, wood wkr Olds' W Wks, res 105 Taylor.

Reardon Elizabeth, bds 129 Broadway.

Reardon Elizabeth (wid James), res 129 Broadway.

Reardon Timothy J, brakeman N Y, C & St L R R, bds 129 Broadway.

Reaser Cornelius A, laborer, res 92 Smith.

Reaser Faith B, bds 92 Smith.

Reaser Frank M, barber, 230 W Main, res same.

Reaser Harry D, bds 92 Smith.

Reaser John J, lab, res n s Jesse cor Rumsey av.

Reaser Lillian M, bds 92 Smith.

Reaser Ray C, bds 92 Smith.

Reber, *see also Reiber.*

Reber Anna, bds George Reber.

Reber George, res Reed's rd 2 m s of city limits.

Reber George jr, bds George Reber.

Reber John, lab Ft W Elec Corp, res 71 W Pontiac.

Reber Maggie, bds George Reber.

Rebmann Anna, clk A Mergentheim, bds 197 E Lewis.

Rebmann Charles, harnessmkr A L Johns & Co, bds 197 E Lewis.

Rebmann John, molder, bds 197 E Lewis.

Rebmann Louis, molder Bass F & M Wks, bds 197 E Lewis.

Rebmann Lizzie, bds 197 E Lewis.

Rebmann Michael, butcher, res 197 E Lewis.

Rebmann Wm, tailor, bds 197 E Lewis.

Reckeweg Ferdinand, laborer, res 106 Eliza.

Reckeweg Sophia, domestic e s Spy Run av 4 n of Riverside av.

Redding Mrs Caroline, res 68 W Jefferson.

Redding John T R, helper, bds 68 W Jefferson.

Redding Louis, switchman, bds 68 W Jefferson.

Redding Wm H, salesman, res over 193 Lafayette.

Reddington Lizzie, waitress The Randall.

Reddington May, waitress The Randall.

Redelsheimer David S (D S Redelsheimer & Co), res Monroeville, Ind.

Redelsheimer D S & Co (David S Redelsheimer), overall mnfrs, 37 and 39 W Main.

Redelsheimer Sigmund, died April, 1895.

Redinger Charles, laborer, bds 143 Fairfield av.
Redinger Rachael (wid Henry), res 143 Fairfield av.
Redman Elmer E, cook J T Connolly, res 57 W Wayne.
Redrup Charles E, teamster, res 79 E Columbia.
Redwood Elizabeth, bds 171 E Wayne.
Redwood Frederick, Bkkpr Louis Deither & Bro, res 171 E Wayne.
Reed, *see also Read.*
Reed Arthur A, storekpr Bass F & M Wks, bds 230 Harmer.
Reed Bert C, student, bds 25 W Washington.
Reed Clement C, mach Bass F & M Wks, bds 230 Harmer
Reed Delia, bds 148 E Lewis.
Reed Edward H, clk New Aveline House, bds same.
Reed Ellen, bds 148 E Lewis.
Reed Elva, laborer, bds 24 Fulton.
Reed Eva E, bds 1 Brookside.
Reed Frank L, bookkeeper, bds 25 W Washington.
Reed Henry, laborer, bds 1 Brookside.
Reed Herbert L, fireman N Y, C & St L R R, res 434 W Main.
Reed James E, lineman Jenney E L & P Co, bds 25 W Washington.
Reed James W. lab Hoffman Bros, res 24 Fulton.
Reed Mrs Jennie, domestic 106 Barr.
Reed Jennie (wid Wallace W), boarding 25 W Washington
Reed John C, mach hd, bds 75 Spy Run av.
Reed John J, clk S Lavanway, res 37 Barr.
Reed John M, lab D Tagtmeyer, res 72 Pearl.
Reed Louis, mnfr printers' stock, res 529 Calhoun.
Reed Louis C M, clk The Journal Co, bds 529 Calhoun.
Reed Mary, res 259 E Washington.
Reed Mary (wid Wm B), res 148 E Lewis.
Reed Sylvanus S, laborer, res 1 Brookside.
Reed Wm D, helper, res 302 Hoagland av.
Reehling, *see also Rehling and Reiling.*
Reehling Caroline, dressmkr, bds 97 Madison.
Reehling Conrad, engr G R & I R R. res 127 Wallace.
Reehling Elizabeth, dressmaker, bds 97 Madison.
Reehling Emma F, dressmaker, bds 97 Madison.
Reehling Henry F, Mach Bass F & M Wks, bds 127 Wallace
Reehling Jacob J, car bldr Penn Co, res 129 Walton av.
Reehling John, watchman, bds 249 Gay.
Reehling Katherine (wid Conrad), res 97 Madison.
Reehling Mary S, bds 127 Wallace.

35

Reehling S, Proprietor Chicago Carpet and Rug Factory, n w cor Wells and Superior, res 222 Madison.

Reehling Wm V, mach Ft W Elec Corp, bds 97 Madison.

Reeps Magdalena (wid Charles F W), res 158 W DeWald.

Reeps Sophia F. dressmaker, bds 158 W DeWald.

Reese Augusta, seamstress, bds 131 Montgomery.

Reese Charles, Deputy Collector Internal Revenue, res 131 Montgomery.

Reese Charles E, bkkr Herman Berghoff Brewing Co, bds 131 Montgomery.

Reese Clara, teacher, bds 131 Montgomery.

Reese Frederick C, foreman Herman Berghoff Brewing Co, res 44 W Leith.

Reese F George, brakeman N Y, C & St L R R, bds 312 W Main.

Reese George H, bolt cutter Bass F & M Wks, res 60 Wall.

Reese Jacob, foreman, bds 146 Walton av.

Reese Lyman B B, barber Fort Wayne Club, res 5 Marion.

Reese Wm A, lab Wabash R R, res cor Webster and Brackenridge.

Reffelt Charles H, upholsterer, res 96 Clay.

Reffelt Flora A, stenogr, bds 235 Madison.

Reffelt Mary C, bds 235 Madison.

Reffelt Wm C. brakeman N Y, C & St L R R, rms 84 Boone.

Reffelt Wm R, carpenter, res 235 Madison.

Regedanz Charles, clk Meyer Bros & Co, res 59 Wells.

Regel Henry E, mach Bass F & M Wks, bds 153 Madison.

Regel Hermann, mach Bass F & M Wks, res 168 Hanna.

Regel Mary (wid Henry E), res 153 Madison.

Regenauer Wm, carp, res 102 N Harrison.

Rehling, see also Reehling and Reiling.

Rehling Charles F, bds 161 E Lewis.

Rehling Emma H, bds 136 E Lewis.

Rehling Ernest, (Rehling & Stegner), res 161 E Lewis.

Rehling Ernest C, mach Wabash R R, res 184 John.

Rehling Frederick H, boilermkr Wabash R R, res 193 John.

Rehling Frederick L, bds 127 John.

Rehling Henry K, boilermkr Wabash R R, res 136 E Lewis.

Rehling John, watchman Kerr Murray Mnfg Co, bds 249 Gay.

Rehling Louis E, blksmith Penn Co, res 127 John.

Rehling Wm J, fireman Penn Co, res 375 Hanna.

Rehling & Stegner (Ernest Rehling and Charles A Stegner), dry goods, 193 Lafayette.
Rehm, *see also Roehm.*
Rehm Barbara (wid Christian J), res 247 W Washington.
Rehm Daniel, gardener, res s e cor Parnell av and Eliza av.
Rehm Daniel, bartender, bds 18 McClellan.
Rehm Elizabeth (wid Peter), res rear 41 Wells.
Rehm Herman F, winder Ft W Elec Corp, res 24 Scott av
Rehm Phillip, painter G Haller, res 169 Pontiac.
Rehm Wm C F, laborer, bds Daniel Rehm.
Rehnen Catherine, bds 38 Force.
Rehnen Edward D, blksmith, bds 38 Force.
Rehnen Henry bricklayer, res 38 Force.
Rehorst Elizabeth, bds 218 E Jefferson.
Rehorst Frederick D, cabinetmkr, res 218 E Jefferson.
Rehrer Collins S, foreman Ft W Elec Corp, res 36 Huestis av.
Rehrer Robert W, helper Ft W Elec Corp, res 56 Hendricks.
Rehrer W Stuart, winder Ft W Elec Corp, res 410 Broadway.
Reiber. *see also Reber.*
Reiber George J, helper Penn Co. bds 53 Wagner.
Reichard, *see also Richard.*
Reichard Henry L, printer Ft W Gazette, bds 28 Clinton.
Reichardt Henry L, teamster, bds 91 Madison.
Reichardt John, boilermkr Wabash R R, res 180 John.
Reichardt Frederick, bds 91 Madison.
Reicheldefer Joseph E, supervisor School for F M Y.
Reichert Fredericka, domestic 24 W Berry.
Reid, *see Read and Reed.*
Reidel, *see Riedel.*
Reidmiller Charles, saloon 20 Harrison, res same.
Reidt Bernard J, engr G R & I R R, res 54 Summit.
Reidt Henry B, laborer, bds 54 Summit.
Reidt John, bds e s Lafayette 2 n of Pontiac.
Reidt John H, cigarmaker, bds 521 Lafayette.
Reidt John H, laborer, bds 54 Summit.
Reidt Wm J, laborer, res 407 E Wayne.
Reifel Elizabeth, dressmaker, bds 54 Nirdlinger av.
Reiff Mary (wid George), bds 5 Grace.
Reifine Jonathan, lab Robert Ogden, res 16 Cochran.
Reihl, *see also Riehl.*
Reike, *see also Rieke.*
Reildorf Annie, domestic 143 W Wayne.

Reiling, *see also Reehling, Rehling.*
Reiling Adolph G, laborer, bds 446 W Main.
Reiling Dorothea (wid August), res 446 W Main.
Reiling Emilie, clerk, bds 446 W Main.
Reiling Frederick R, letter carrier P O, res 147 Rockhill.
Reiling George C, joiner Ranke & Yergens, bds 111 Wilt.
Reiling Margaret (wid Frederick), res 111 Wilt.
Reiling Meinhard F, engr Engine Co No 1, res 51 Barr.
Reily Col F A, res 63 Riverside av.
Reilly, *see also Riley.*
Reilly Daniel J, foreman Fox Br U S Baking Co, res 521 Calhoun.
Reilly Peter, engr Penn Co, res 169 Harmer.
Reilly Robert M, stenogr N Y, C & St L R R, bds 487 Harrison.
Reimann, *see Riemann.*
Reincke Frederick, molder Bass F & M Wks, bds 27 Smith.
Reincke John, coremaker, res 316 Buchanan.
Reineke Frederick J, Director and Mngr Reineke's Orchestra, 70 Calhoun and Upholsterer 41 E Main, res 119 E Main. (*See p 115.*)
Reinemeyer Frank P, butcher, bds 169 Rockhill.
Reinemeyer John D, blksmith Penn Co, res 169 Rockhill.
Reiner Anna, bds 152 E Taber.
Reinewald Ernst, wrapper, bds 390 E Wayne.
Reinewald Henry F, butcher, res 353 E Washington.
Reinewald Henry W, clk R M S, bds 328 Harrison.
Reinewald Henry W, laborer, res 390 E Wayne.
Reinewald John M, foreman Olds' Wagon Wks, res e s Calhoun 3 s of Marshall.
Reinewald Lizzie M, opr S M Foster, bds 390 E Wayne.
Reinewald Mrs Mary A, dressmkr 353½ Calhoun, res same.
Reinewald Mary H, dressmaker, bds 228 Harrison.
Reinewald Rudolph C, clk Ft W Gas Co, res 353½ Calhoun.
Reinewald Wm, cigarmkr, bds 12 Harrison.
Reinewald Wm F, res 328 Harrison.
Reinewald Wm H, molder Ind M Wks, res 94 Wilt.
Reinhardt, *see also Rinehart.*
Reinhardt Amelia (wid Herman L), seamstress Orphans' Home of the Reformed Church.
Reinhart Adam A, clk Golden & Patterson, res 154 E Jefferson.
Reinhart Anna M (wid Matthias), res 258 E Washington.
Reinhart John, fireman Penn Co, res 485 Lafayette.

Reinhart John A, student, bds 258 E Washington.
Reinhart Mary R, tailoress, bds 258 E Washington.
Reinhart Laura R, bds 258 E Washington.
Reinhart Stephen, laborer, bds 94 Buchanan.
Reiniche Frank A, bds 68 Lasselle.
Reiniche Joseph H, bds 68 Lasselle.
Reiniche Louise J, laundress W B Phillips, bds 68 Lasselle.
Reiniche Mary A, starcher W B Phillips, bds 68 Lasselle.
Reinkensmeier Christian F, Grocer, 124 Broadway, res 175 Griffith. Tel 317.
Reinkensmeier Henry A G, clk C F Reinkensmeier, bds 175 Griffith.
Reinking Adeline. domestic 407 Webster.
Reinking Albert F, boilermaker Wabash R R, bds 54 Miner
Reinking Amelia B, tailoress, bds 54 Miner.
Reinking Bertha (wid Wm G), res 54 Miner.
Reinking Diederich, res 46 Stophlet.
Reinking Diederich, fireman Bass F & M Wks, bds 41 Gay
Reinking Ernst G. contr, res 59 Brackenridge.
Reinking Frederick, hose man Hose Co No 1, rms same.
Reinking Louisa E, dressmaker, bds 54 Miner.
Reinking Wm F, car bldr Penn Co, res 159 E Creighton av
Reinking Wm G, laborer Ft W Elec Corp, bds 54 Miner.
Reis Clara M, bds 365 E Washington.
Reis Philip, tailor, res 365 E Washington.
Reiter, *see also Rider.*
Reiter Anna, seamstress S M Foster bds 105 Wallace.
Reiter Charles H, driver Root & Co, bds 148 Taylor.
Reiter Christina (wid Wm), res 148 Taylor.
Reiter Conrad A, res 105 Wallace.
Reiter Emma, bds H C Reiter.
Reiter Frederick, bds H C Reiter.
Reiter Frederick, buyer, res cor Columbia and N Y, C & St L R R.
Reiter Fred C, clk Seavey Hdw Co, bds 49 Wall.
Reiter George, cigar mnfr, 30 Calhoun, res same.
Reiter Henry C, mach Bass F & M Wks, res s e cor Edsall av and Wabash R R.
Reiter Henry C, porter The Randall, bds same.
Reiter Henry F, mach, res 130 Horace.
Reiter Henry F, trav agt, bds 54 Wall.
Reiter John H, driver, res 54 Wall.
Reiter Louis, driver, bds H C Reiter.
Reiter Louis, helper Wabash R R, bds 143 Union.
Reiter Louise, bds 54 Wall.

Reiter Mary C, bds 148 Taylor.
Reiter Mrs Mary J, bds 66 McClellan.
Reiter Minnie E, bds 436 W Main.
Reiter Pauline, bds 49 Wall.
Reiter Sophia, domestic The Wayne.
Reiter Winfield S, bds 30 Calhoun.
Reiter Wm, carpenter Wabash R R, res 49 Wall.
Reiter Wm, helper Bass F & M Wks, bds 143 Union.
Reiter Wm C, student, bds 148 Taylor.
Reitnouer, *see also Ridenour*.
Reitnouer Jacob F, driver, bds 140 Beaver av.
Reitnouer Jeremiah B, bds 140 Beaver av.
Reitnouer Margaretta (wid Peter S), bds 140 Beaver av.
Reitze John B, removed to res Los Angelos, Cal.
Reitze Maggie, opr S M Foster, bds 117 W DeWald.
Reitze Mrs Minnie C, milliner, 164 Calhoun, res same.
Reitze Wm F, teller Old National Bank, res 109 Lake av.
Rekers, *see also Riker*.
Rekers Anna E, bds 110 W Washington.
Rekers Benjamin, clk G Rekers, bds 201 Wells.
Rekers Catherine (wid B John), res 121 W Washington.
Rekers Charles E, bartender, bds 110 W Washington.
Rekers Clemens A, res 110 W Washington.
Rekers Clemens A jr, clk B Lehman, res 109 Baker.
Rekers Edward C, fresco painter, bds 201 Wells.
Rekers Frank H R, cutter C J Romeis, bds 313 W Washington.
Rekers Gerhard, grocer, 116 W Washington, res 201 Wells.
Rekers Henry G V, finisher Ft W Organ Co, res 121 W Washington.
Rekers H Benjamin, clerk, bds 201 Wells.
Rekers Josephine, clerk, bds 201 Wells.
Rekers Lizzie, bds 313 W Washington.
Relue, *see Rhelue*.
Remmert Charles F, student, bds 157 W Washington.
Remmert Herman, laborer, res 30 W 3d.
Remmert Herman jr, mach Bass F & M Wks, bds 30 W 3d
Remmert Herman J, foreman Kerr Murray Mnfg Co, res 157 W Washington.
Remmert John H, died March, 1895.
Remmert Mrs John H, res 36 Marion.
Remmert John M, bds 157 W Washington.
Remmert Joseph, laborer, bds 30 W 3d.
Remmert Joseph M, helper, bds 215 Madison.

Remmert May U, stenogr Wing & Mahurin, bds 157 W Washington.
Rempis Charles C. clk H H G Upmeyer, bds 106 Hanna.
Rempis J Frederick, traveling agent, res 106 Hanna.
Rempis Wm, clk Siemon & Bro, bds 106 Hanna.
Remus Amelia E, bds 442 Broadway.
Remus Julius E, contr 442 Broadway, res same.
Renaud Emile, died August 5th, 1894.
Renfrew Benton B, mach hd Kerr Murray Mnfg Co, bds 32 Lavina.
Renfrew Richard K, mach Kerr Murray Mnfg Co, res 32 Lavina.
Renfrew Robert G, mach hd, res 64 Glasgow av.
Renier Anna, bds 192 Buchanan.
Renier Anthony, barber, bds 192 Buchanan,
Renier John, agt Singer Mnfg Co, res 192 Buchanan.
Renier Joseph F, barber, bds 192 Buchanan.
Renningroth August C, mach Wabash R R, res 274 E Lewis
Rensberger Alpheus D, carpenter, res 73 Winter.
Rensman Bernard, grocer, 120 Fairfield av, res same.
Rensman Bernard C, pattern mkr Kerr Murray Mnfg Co, bds 120 Fairfield av.
Rensman Clara, clk Wm Hahn & Co, bds 120 Fairfield av.
Rentschler Carrie, bds 48 Wall.
Rentschler Catherine, bds 48 Wall.
Rentschler Charles F, confectioner, 138 Broadway, res same.
Rentschler David W, lab Horton Mnfg Co, bds 48 Wall.
Rentschler George D, mach hd Olds' W Wks, bds 48 Wall.
Rentschler Harriet (wid David), res 48 Wall.
Rentschler Julia, opr W U Tel Co, bds 48 Wall.
Rentschler Lottie, domestic 141 W Wayne.
Rentschler Philip J, mach hd Old's W Wks, res 89 Wall.
Renz Adam, book agt, res 257 E Washington.
Renz Alexander J, clk Geo DeWald & Co, bds 257 E Washington.
Repine Earl H, car cleaner Penn Co, bds 30 Hugh.
Repine Jesse M, bds 30 Hough.
Repine John, yd master Penn Co, res 30 Hough.
Repine Wm, messgr Dist Tel Co, bds 30 Hough.
Repp, *see Rapp.*
Resner, *see Roesener.*
Rettig Rev John, Supt Orphans Home of the Reformed Church, 1½ miles n e of city limits.
Reul John V, pres Ind Furn Co, rms 28 Douglas av.

Reuss John B, (C L Centlivre Brewing Co), res
 w s Spy Run av 3 n of Edna.
Reuter Henry, knitter, res 58 Elm.
Revert Henry, asst W F Geller, bds 42 St Mary's av.
Revert Mary, bds 42 St Marys av.
Rexroth Edward K, stenographer, res 20 Michigan av
Rexroth Margaret, opr S M Foster, bds 20 Michigan av.
Reynolds, *see also Runnels.*
Reynolds Mrs Anis, res 222 Lafayette.
Reynolds Charles, bds 26 E Wayne.
Reynolds Charlotte E L (wid Elihu L), notions, 120
 Broadway, res same.
Reynolds Edward F, laborer, bds 222 Lafayette
Reynolds Florence (wid Frank), milliner, res 26 E Wayne
Reynolds Homer B, train dispr Penn Co, res 256 Clinton.
Reynolds Mary, cook J T Connolly, rms 94 W Superior.
Reynolds Nettie M, bds 94 W Superior.
Reynolds Peter, fireman G R & I R R. rms 37 Baker.
Reynolds Robert A, yd brakeman Penn Co, bds 146 Wal-
 ton av.
Reynolds Sterling, printer Archer Ptg Co, bds 40 Madison
Reynolds Wm, laborer, bds Union House.
Reynolds Wm E, dining car condr, res 331 Calhoun.
Reynolds Wm J, confectioner, bds 75 Douglas av.
Rhein Anna E, starcher W B Phillips, bds John W
 Rhein.
Rhein Charles, bds 60 Wall.
Rhein Christian C, lab Wabash R R, res 84 Swinney av.
Rhein Frederick, bds 62 Wall.
Rhein George E, mach, bds John W Rhein.
Rhein Gustav, laborer, res 5 Mary.
Rhein Jacob, carpenter, bds 11 Mary.
Rhein John W, farmer, res s e cor Alexander and Franklin
Rhein Philip, laborer, bds 5 Mary.
Rhelue Grant, laborer, bds 55 Wabash av.
Rhelue Newton, teamster, res 55 Wabash av.
Rhine Christian, helper Penn Co, res 141 Union.
Rhine George E, helper Penn Co, bds cor Creighton av
 and Winter.
Rhine Sarah M (wid Calvin), res cor Indiana and Organ avs
Rhine Wm, helper Kerr Murray Mnfg Co.
Rhinehart, *see also Reinhart and Rinehart.*
Rhinehart Calvin S, lab Fisher Bros, bds 42 Force.
Rhinehart Isaac W, spoke turner, res 42 Force.

Rhinesmith George, clk Rhinesmith & Simonson, bds 231 W Wayne.

Rhinesmith John (Rhinesmith & Simonson), pres The Anthony Wayne Mnfg Co, res 231 W Wayne.

Rhinesmith Susan, bds 231 W Wayne.

Rhinesmith & Simonson (John Rhinesmith, James H Simonson), Mnfrs Sash. Doors, Blinds and Dealers in Lumber and Shingles, s w cor Lafayette and Wabash R R. Tel 27.

Rhoades Albert H, driver, bds 186 W Main.

Rhoades Carlos E. sec Indiana Farmers' Savings and Loan Association, res 167 E Berry.

Rhoades Daniel W, fireman Penn Co, res 247 Walton av.

Rhoades George (col'd), laborer. res 232 Lafayette.

Rhoades George N, conductor, res 302 E Creighton av.

Rhoades Harry L, bds 239 Walton av.

Rhoades Mary (wid Samuel). bds 27 Oliver.

Rhoades Maud X, student, bds 302 E Creighton av.

Rhoades Owen E, cigarmkr, bds 247 Walton av.

Rhoades Wesley D, fireman Penn Co, res 296 Hanna.

Rhodenbaugh Arthur, barber, 377 E Washington, res 33 Summit.

Rhodenbaugh Elizabeth (wid Peter), res 32 Oak.

Rhodenbaugh Frank I, brakeman, res 40 Oliver.

Rhodes Alexander, teamster, res 131 Holman.

Rhodes Cassius A, bds 53 Charles.

Rhodes Chapman (col'd), brakeman, res 292 E Wayne.

Rhodes Charles H (col'd), hostler, bds 292 E Wayne.

Rhodes Elmer E, baker, res 6 Gay.

Rhodes Frank M, printer, res 131 Holman.

Rhodes James W (col'd), waiter Ft Wayne Club, rms 292 E Wayne.

Rhodes John (col'd), waiter The Wayne, rms 292 E Wayne.

Rhodes Lulu, bds 85 W Superior.

Rhodes Milton A, woodworker, res 53 Charles.

Rhodes Oscar M, brakeman G R & I R R, bds 104 Barr.

Rhodes U Grant, fireman Penn Co, bds 131 Holman.

Riblet Frank E, trav agt Root & Co, res 483 Harrison.

Riblet Hiram F, bds 483 Harrison.

Rice Albert, bds 22 Lasselle.

Rice Alfred, bds 22 Lasselle.

Rice Barbara, bds 22 Lasselle.

Rice Charles E, blksmith Penn Co, bds e s Lafayette 4 s of Grace

550 R. L. POLK & CO.'S

Rice Daniel W, brakeman N Y, C & St L R R, res 3 Center.

Rice Ida P, opr S M Foster, bds 98 W Superior.

Rice Mrs Johanna, res 22 Lasselle.

Rice Mary (wid Benjamin F), res 20 Winch.

Rice Nettie E, clk W B Phillips, bds 98 W Superior.

Rice Rev Perry J, pastor First Church of Christ, res 201 W Jefferson.

Rice Samuel, lab, res s s French 4 w of Webster.

Rice Samuel E, printer, bds 105 Lafayette.

Rich Bessie, bds 29 W Lewis.

Rich Della C, bds 29 W Lewis.

Rich Edwin (E Rich & Son), res 29 W Lewis.

Rich E & Son (Edwin and Frank J), meats, 94 Barr (Tel 406), 254 Calhoun (Tel 433) and 22 Harrison (Tel 432).

Rich Frank J (E Rich & Son), bds 29 W Lewis.

Rich Jennie, bds 368 Fairfield av.

Rich Lota E, bds 29 W Lewis.

Rich Sanford, res 35 W Lewis.

Richard, *see also Reichard.*

Richard Benjamin, carpenter, res 49 Walnut.

Richard Charles E, mach hd, bds 412 E Wayne

Richard David, bds 148 Smith.

Richard Eliza J (wid Henry L), res 25 Euclid av.

Richard Frank H, bds 25 Euclid av.

Richard George C, teamster, res 205 E Wayne.

Richard Harriet (wid John B), res 101 Wallace.

Richard James C, mach Olds' Wagon Wks, res 88 Lasselle.

Richard Nora, bds 25 Euclid av.

Richard Olive A, clk S F Bowser & Co, bds 101 Wallace.

Richard Peter, grocer, s e cor Lake av and Old Fort, res same.

Richard Philip T, machinist, res 412 E Wayne.

Richard Samuel, mach hd S F Bowser & Co, bds 101 Wallace.

Richard Wm, clk Peter Richard, bds same.

Richard Wm H, pressman Ft W Gazette, bds 412 E Wayne.

Richards Andrew K, mach Penn Co, res 60 E Williams.

Richards Catherine (wid Wm C), seamstress, res 596 Calhoun.

Richards Christ G, molder, res 46 Lillie.

Richards Estella, bds 60 E Williams

Richards George C, truckman, res 203 E Wayne.

Richards George W, carp P H Wyss, res 162 Oliver.

Richards Joseph, clerk, bds 263 Calhoun.
Richards Joseph M, bds 60 E Williams.
Richards Lewis D, condr, res 86 Chicago.
Richards Orion F, bds 60 E Williams.
Richards Robert F, restaurant, 253 Calhoun, res same.
Richards Sylvester W, watchman, res 266 W DeWald.
Richards Wm H, clk L Oddou & Co, res 60 E Williams.
Richardson Frank L, claim agt Penn Co, bds McKinnie House.
Richardson Hannah (wid Thomas), res 171 Hayden.
Richardson Mrs Ida M, cash D N Foster Furn Co, bds 101 E Berry.
Richardson James A, policeman. bds 171 Hayden.
Richardson Leala, domestic 23 W DeWald.
Richardson M A, sample mkr Ft Wayne Furn Co, bds 34 W Superior.
Richason Mattie, domestic 20 Francis.
Richey Alta L, bds 87 W Main.
Richey Amos, bkkpr Old National Bank, bds 87 W Main.
Richey Effie B, teacher, bds 87 W Main.
Richey F, lab Standard Wheel Co.
Richey Nellie M, clk Root & Co, bds 87 W Main.
Richey Nora, domestic 277 E Creighton av.
Richey Otho R, check clk Penn Co, bds 89 Baker.
Richey Sarah E (wid Amos), res 87 W Main.
Richlin Joseph A, helper Bass F & M Wks, bds 147 E De Wald.
Richter Bernard D, tinsmith, res 29 E 3d.
Richter Christliebe (wid Traugott), bds 29 Boone.
Richter Emil P, turner Horton Mnfg Co, bds cor W Main and Runnion av.
Richter Emil R, turner Horton Mnfg Co, bds 20 Jessie.
Richter Erhart B, bds 20 Jesse.
Richter Erich J B, Grocer and Saloon, 227 Lafayette, res same.
Richter Ernst, laborer, res n e cor De Groff and Polk.
Richter Max E, wagonmkr, res e s De Groff 2 n of Polk.
Richter Paul O, letter carrier P O, res 78 Jesse.
Rickel Charles H, bds 76 Canal.
Rickel Wm, lab Penn Co, res 76 Canal.
Ridenour, see also Reitnouer.
Ridenour Jackson W, tel opr, rms 37 W Berry.
Ridenour Orford H, tel opr, rms 37 W Berry.
Rider, see also Reiter and Ryder.

Rider Frank A, master mechanic Bass F & M Wks, res 23 W DeWald.

Rider John, teamster, bds 73 Holman.

Ridley John A (col'd) (Roberts & Ridley), res 7 Summit.

Riebs Katherine, domestic F P Rosselot.

Riedel Amanda M, opr, bds 229 Force.

Riedel Catherine, domestic 126 W Washington.

Riedel Christian H, laborer, bds 238 Force.

Riedel John, teacher St Paul's G L School, res s s Griswold av 5 e of the bridge.

Riedel George J, watchman, res 229 Force.

Reidel John M, mach Penn Co, bds 229 Force.

Riedel John M E, Architect, 3d Floor Schmitz Blk, cor Calhoun and Washington, res s s Griswold av 5 e of the Bridge. (*See front cover*).

Riedel Maggie, domestic 68 W Washington.

Riedel Martha, bds John Riedel.

Riedel Mary, opr, bds 229 Force.

Riedel Wm P, draughtsman J M E Riedel, bds s s Griswold av 5 e of bridge.

Riedmiller, *see also Riethmiller.*

Riedmiller August, cigarmkr G Reiter, bds 139 Taylor.

Riedmiller Catherine (wid John M), res 215 Taylor.

Riedmiller Charles, saloon, 20 Harrison, res same.

Riedmiller John M, city agt C L Centlivre, res 101 Taylor.

Rieg Alois, helper Keller & Braun, res 257 Huffman.

Reig Anton, contractor, res 100 Putnam.

Riegel Alois R (Riegel & Bougher), res 12 Calhoun.

Riegel Theresa J, bds 12 Calhoun.

Riegel & Bougher (Alois R Riegel, Frank E Bougher), saloon, 12 Calhoun.

Riehl Edward, painter Wabash R R, res 13 Grace.

Riehl Wm, lab Ft W E Corp, res 104 Fletcher av.

Rieke Anna, opr S M Foster, bds 20 Home av.

Rieke Edward J, carver Ft W O Co, bds 20 Home av.

Rieke Henry G, carp Penn Co, bds 20 Home av.

Rieke Henry S, died February 8th, 1895.

Rieke Kate (wid Henry), res 20 Home av.

Rieke Theodore W, bds 20 Home av.

Rieke Wm C, mach Ft W O Co, bds 20 Home av.

Rieman Calvin K, packer S M Foster, bds 157 E Berry.

Riemann Augustus, clk, bds 31 Maumee rd.

Riemann Elizabeth J, operator, bds 31 Maumee rd.

Riemann Joseph, knitter, res Washington twp.

Riemann Mary G, knitter, bds 31 Maumee rd.

Riemann Regina E (wid August), res 31 Maumee rd.
Riemen Joseph H, barber J H Crummitt, res 113 Hanna.
Rietdorf Carl, teamster, bds 103 Erie.
Rietdorf Elizabeth, seamstress, bds rear 125 Shawnee av.
Rietdorf Ernst C, cabtmkr Ft W O Co, res 125 Shawnee av
Rietdorf Frederick, tailor G Scheffler, bds 5 Eliza.
Rietdorf Margaret, domestic 75 W Berry.
Rietdorf Wilhelmma (wid Ernest J), res rear 125 Shawnee av.
Riethmiller, see also Riedmiller.
Riethmiller August, grocer 139 Taylor, res 318 Broadway
Riethmiller August C, cigarmaker, bds 139 Taylor.
Riethmiller Barbara (wid George), res w s Eagle 3 s of Taylor.
Riethmiller George, truckman Penn Co, res 139 Taylor.
Riethmiller Lena, knitter, bds 139 Taylor.
Riethmiller Lizzie, bds Barbara Riethmiller
Riethmiller Mary, bds 139 Taylor.
Riethmiller Mrs May, bds 20 Lafayette.
Riethmiller Wm J, grocer 184 Fairfield av. res same.
Rifles Armory, Randall Hall.
Riker Edward G, bkkpr Fox Br U S Baking Co, res 80 Lake av.
Riker Elmira (wid Elanson), res 49 W Jefferson.
Riley, see also Reilly.
Riley Jennie, opr S M Foster, bds 113 Barr.
Riley John, bds 113 Barr.
Riley Julia A (wid Wm H), bds 113 Barr.
Riley Julia, bds 113 Barr.
Riley Laban J, laborer, res 59 W 5th.
Riley Nettie. bds 113 Barr.
Riley Tillie, waitress The Randall.
Riley Mrs Thomas A, bds 87 E Berry.
Rincker Joseph, lab Bass F & M Wks, res 52 Gay.
Rinehart, see also Reinhardt.
Rinehart Louisa M (wid John A), res 48 E Pontiac.
Rinehart Martin A (M Rinehart & Co), bds 48 E Pontiac.
Rinehart M & Co (Martin A Rinehart, Joseph F Zurbuch), grocers, 546 Calhoun.
Rinehart Wm A, blksmith. 356 Broadway, res 296 same.
Rinehart Wm A, blksmith, bds 48 E Pontiac.
Ring Albert R, clk L S & M S Ry. res 158 Lake av.
Ring John, laborer, bds 32 Runnion av.
Ripley Elizabeth (wid Franklin), (Colmey & Ripley), bds 11 Suttenfield.

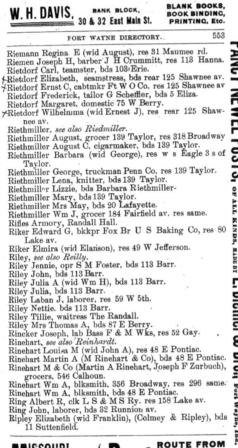

554 R. L. POLK & CO.'S

Rippe Mrs Adelia, res 4 Madison.
Rippe Charles E, livery, 111 Broadway, res 232 W Jefferson. Tel 96.
Rippe Charles H, foreman Bass Wks, res 79 Oakley.
Rippe Christian (C Rippe & Son), res 91 Wilt.
Rippe Christian H, stair bldr L Deither & Bro, res 89 Wilt.
Rippe C & Son (Christian and Frederick C), livery, 86 Broadway. Tel 453.
Rippe Emma, dressmaker, bds 89 Wilt.
Rippe Frederick, Vice-Pres Builders' Lime Association, Contractor and Builder, 176 Madison, res same. (*See right bottom lines and p 91.*)
Rippe Frederick C (C Rippe & Son), res 184 W Jefferson.
Rippe Frederick W, carpenter Wabash R R, res 125 Wall.
Rippe Frederick W, helper Olds' Wagon Wks, bds 56 Wall.
Rippe Gesina, domestic 186 W Berry.
Rippe Henry C, helper, bds 9 Jones.
Rippe Henry C, stenogr P, Ft W & C R R, bds 176 Madison.
Rippe Lizzie M, bds 176 Madison.
Rippe Louis, bds 176 Madison.
Rippe Lulu C, clk M Frank & Co, bds 89 Wilt.
Rippe Sadie C, tailoress, bds 89 Wilt.
Rippe Sophia, died October 7th, 1894.
Rippe Wilhelmina (wid Wilhelm), res 9 Jones.
Rippe Wm, carpenter, res 56 Wall.
Rippe Wm F, clk Peter Pierre, bds 56 Wall.
Rissing Clara, seamstress S M Foster, bds J H Rissing.
Rissing John F, tinner A K Staub, bds J H Rissing.
Rissing John H, cabinetmkr D N Foster Furn Co, res St Joseph Boulevard nr Baker av.
Rissing Mary M, forelady S M Foster, bds J H Rissing.
Ritcha Edward J, bds 42 Wells.
Ritcha Jennie (wid Silas), res 42 Wells.
Ritchart James M, fireman G R & I R R, res 17 Lasselle.
Ritchey John E, bds 56 E Columbia.
Ritter Bertha, teacher East German School, bds 116 E Creighton av.
Ritter Catherine, stenogr Colerick & France, bds 189 E Washington.
Ritter Cyrus R, wagonmkr, res 118 N Harrison.
Ritter Jacob J, mach Penn Co, res 116 E Creighton av.
Ritter Minnie, bds 87 E Jefferson.

Ritter Nellie A, bds 116 E Creighton av.

Ritterskamp Charles H, tailor, bds Ervin House.

Ritzius Albert H, cabinetmkr Ft W Organ Co, res 344 Calhoun.

Ritzius Wm H, cabinetmkr Ft W Organ Co, res 492 Fairfield av.

Rivers Charles W, painter, res 51 E Superior.

Rivers Sarah (wid Charles), bds 51 E Superior.

River View Farm Co, office Broadway and P, Ft W & C Ry, Incorporated 1892. Capital, $100,000 ; R T McDonald, H J Miller, A D Guild, Directors.

Rix Mrs Alice, res 103 Wells.

Roach, *see also Roche.*

Roach T Newton, supt of Agencies Phœnix Building and Savings Union, res 138 Wells.

Robacker Mrs Cora, res 214 Calhoun.

Robacker Frank F, Mngr City Steam Dye House, 11 W Jefferson, bds 214 Calhoun. (*See p 10.*)

Robacker Samuel J, Steam Dye Works, 45 E Main, res same.

Robb Wm, brickmason, res 24 W 4th.

Robbe Alphouse F, mngr Fremion & Vollmer, res 151 Wells.

Robbins Charles E, collr First Nat Bank, rms 46 W Berry.

Robbins Cyrus A, dispatcher Penn Co, res 160 Lake av.

Robbins Herbert E, Agt Remington Standard Type Writer, 32 Bass Blk, rms 29 E Washington.

Robbins John V, clk Heller & Frankel, res 39 Hugh.

Robbins Laura, attendant School F M Y.

Robbins Mrs Nellie I, bds 173 W Wayne.

Robbins Norman, bds 50 McClellan.

Robbins Oscar B, cash F Eckart Pkg Co, bds 50 McClellan.

Roberts A Frances, bds 6 Ida av.

Roberts Charles, upholsterer, 101 Walton av, res 105 same

Roberts Frank J, brakeman G R & I R R. bds 107 Wallace

Roberts George I, brakeman. res 124 W Butler.

Roberts Harry, carriage painter, res 37 W Berry.

Roberts Joseph H (Roberts R Ridley), (col'd), res 53 Elizabeth.

Roberts Mary, domestic Hedekin House.

Roberts Stephen J, carpenter, res 6 Ida av.

Roberts Wm, teamster, bds 15 Pearl.

Roberts Wm H, trav agt, bds 134 Calhoun.

Roberts & Ridley (col'd) (Joseph H Roberts, John A Ridley), barbers, 21 Harrison.
Robertson Alice A, bds 231 Webster.
Robertson Annie, bds 179 W Berry.
Robertson Annie, domestic 328 W Washington.
Robertson Charles, appr Penn Co, bds 231 Webster.
Robertson Edward B, checker N Y, C & St L R R, res 126 Cass.
Robertson Harry G, clk Peoples' Store, res 6 Madison.
Robertson Henry H, helper Penn Co, bds 231 Webster.
Robertson J Henry, blacksmith, res 231 Webster.
Robertson Louisa L (wid Wm G), res 86 Brackenridge.
Robertson Louise, bds 179 W Berry
Robertson Mabel, teacher Washington School, bds 179 W Berry.
Robertson Margaret M, bds 86 Brackenridge.
Robertson Robert S (Robertson & O'Rourke), res 179 W Berry.
Robertson Robert S jr, inspector, bds 179 W Berry.
Robertson Wallace G, clerk, bds 86 Brackenridge.
Robertson Walter W, laborer, bds 86 Brackenridge.
Robertson & O'Rourke (Robert S Robertson, Wm S O'Rourke), Lawyers, 21 and 22 Bass Blk.
Robinson Catherine B, bds 95 E Main.
Robinson Elijah, lab S Bash & Co, res 168 Huffman.
Robinson Elmer B, barber, rms 160 E Wayne.
Robinson Frank W, painter, res 6 Short.
Robinson Harry F, clk A L Johns & Co, res 6 Fulton.
Robinson Isabella B (wid David A), bds 95 E Main.
Robinson James M, Lawyer, Main, s w cor Calhoun, res 95 E Main. Tel 509.
Robinson J Scott, hostler J C Brinsley, res 36 Cass.
Robinson Lorah Z, bds 160 E Wayne.
Robinson Ludville M, res 160 E Wayne.
Robinson Oscar E, bds 160 E Wayne.
Robinson Wm L, molder Bass Wks, res 30 Euclid av.
Robinson Otto V, brakeman, res 98 Wagner.
Robinson Wm L jr, molder Bass Wks, bds 30 Euclid av.
Robinson Wm L, timber buyer, res 23 Prospect av.
Robison Frederick H, res 59 W 5th.
Robison Lydia S (wid Thomas I), res 50 W Superior.
Robison Martin S jr, vice-pres and treas Ft W Elec Ry Co, rms 28 Schmitz Blk.
Robitalli Wm, agent, res 2 Madison.
Roche, *see also Roach.*

Roche Catherine, dressmaker, bds 60 Baker.
Roche David, laborer, bds 20 Murray.
Roche David J, brakeman, res 7 Walnut.
Roche James, helper Penn Co, res 60 Baker.
Roche James P, died October 30th, 1894.
Roche John H, binder G W Winbaugh, rms same.
Roche Katie, domestic 278 Calhoun.
Roche Margaret, ironer W B Phillips, bds 167 Van Buren
Roche Mary E, bds 167 Van Buren.
Roche Nellie, student, bds 167 Van Buren.
Rocholl Anna A, clk Princess Cash Store, bds 99 Barr.
Rocholl Bertha C, clk J B White, bds 99 Barr.
Rocholl Mrs Mary, nurse 99 Barr, bds same.
Rocholl Matilda O (wid Morris A), res 99 Barr.
Rocholl Valentine C, blacksmith, bds 99 Barr.
Rock L Erastus, clk People's Store, res 74 E Williams.
Rockeman Christian H, fireman, bds 292 Hanna.
Rocker Washer Co, Frank Alderman mngr, 5 White Bank
 Bldg.
Rockford Ins Co of Rockford, Ill, 25 Court.
Rockhill Bros & Fleming (Wright W, Jesse B, Hugh M,
 and Howell C Rockhill and Wm H Fleming), horse
 breeders, ½ mile w of city limits, office 30 E Main.
Rockhill Emily (wid Wm), res 295 W Wayne.
Rockhill Howell C (Rockhill Bros & Fleming), sec M W
 Fay Warehouse Co, pres and genl mngr The Journal,
 res 163 W Main.
Rockhill Hugh M (Rockhill Bros & Fleming), res John
 Orff Homestead.
Rockhill Jessie B (Rockhill Bros & Fleming), res Elmwood
 farm, ½ mile w of city limits.
Rockhill Sadie M, bds 198 W Wayne
Rockhill Wm, Propr The Bargain Store, Cloth-
 ing, Furnishing Goods, Boots and Shoes, s w cor
 Harrison and Main, res same.
Rockhill Wright W (Rockhill Bros & Flem-
 ing), Postmaster, res 198 W Wayne.
Rockinfield George W. rms 41 Douglas av.
Rockstroh Emil, carpenter, res 192 W DeWald.
Rodabaugh Charity D (wid Adam), bds 309 Harrison.
Rodabaugh Franklin L, trav agt, res 23 Walton av.
Rodabaugh Isaiah F, brakeman, res 45 Gay.
Rodabaugh John F, lawyer, 7 Foster Blk, bds 25 W Wash-
 ington. Tel 437.
Rodabaugh Rose, bds 286 W Washington.

36

Rodabaugh Thomas J, foreman Penn Co, res 286 W Washington.
Rodeheaver Mrs Delilah, bds 612 E Wayne.
Rodeheaver Flora, stenogr Root & Co, bds 515 E Lewis.
Rodeheaver Horace S, hostler N Y, C & St L R R, res 8 Hendricks.
Rodeheaver Lillian M, bds 8 Hendricks.
Rodeheaver Wm H, res 515 E Lewis.
Rodemann Charles L, tinner, bds 292 Harrison.
Rodemann Elizabeth H, seamstress, bds 292 Harrison.
Rodemann John W, cigarmkr, res 292 Harrison.
Rodemeier Anna, operator, bds 325 E Washington.
Rodemeier Frederick, driver, res 325 E Washington.
Rodemeier Frederick jr, motorman, bds 325 E Washington
Rodemeier Henry, clk M Detzer, bds 325 E Washington.
Rodenbeck Anna, dressmkr 210 E Jefferson, bds same.
Rodenbeck Anna C, domestic 132 E Main.
Rodenbeck August, car bldr Penn Co, bds 173 Harmer.
Rodenbeck Bernardina (wid Charles), res 157 Eliza.
Rodenbeck Bernardina C, seamstress, bds 157 Eliza.
Rodenbeck Carrie, starcher W B Phillips, bds 210 E Jefferson.
Rodenbeck Catherine E, bds 168 E Lewis.
Rodenbeck Charles (C Franke & Co), res 157 Eliza.
Rodenbeck Charles H, helper Penn Co, res 201 Madison.
Rodenbeck Christian, cabtmkr Penn Co, res 513 E Lewis.
Rodenbeck Christina, domestic 119 E Wayne.
Rodenbeck Conrad, helper Penn Co, res 168 E Lewis.
Rodenbeck Diedrich F, trimmer, res 13 Hough.
Rodenbeck Diana, steamstress, bds 129 Eliza.
Rodenbeck Emma, seamstress, bds 210 E Jefferson.
Rodenbeck Emma C, hair goods, 29 E Washington, bds 67 Madison.
Rodenbeck Frederick G, clk Root & Co, bds 513 Lewis.
Rodenbeck Frederick H, clk Root & Co, bds 67 Madison.
Rodenbeck Frederick H, boilermkr, res 210 E Jefferson.
Rodenbeck Hannah (wid Wm), res 67 Madison.
Rodenbeck Henry C, blksmith Bass F & M Wks, res 345 E Lewis.
Rodenbeck John W, carpenter, bds 513 E Lewis.
Rodenbeck Kate, domestic 155 Clay.
Rodenbeck Louis D, appr Kerr Murray Mnfg Co, bds 168 E Lewis.
Rodenbeck Louisa M, bds 168 E Lewis.
Rodenbeek Mena, domestic 119 E Wayne.

Rodenbeck Minnie, domestic 188 W Wayne.
Rodenbeck Sophia, domestic 92 W Berry.
Rodenbeck Wm, car repr Penn Co, bds 20 Home av.
Rodenbeck Wm F, boilermaker, bds 168 E Lewis.
Rodenbeck Wm F, tinner Wabash R R, res 18 Jones.
Rodenbeck Wm G F, car repr Penn Co, bds 513 E Lewis.
Roderick Martha, bds 106 Wells.
Rodermand John, section hand, res 66 Oliver.
Rodewald Catherine (wid Frederick), bds 574 E Washington.
Rodewald Frank F, bartender, res 58 South Wayne av.
Rodewald Herman C, carpenter, res 169 John.
Rodewald John H, fireman, bds 169 John.
Rodgers, *see also Rogers.*
Rodgers Harry S, machinist, rms 24 Oliver.
Rodgers Josephine (wid Samuel), res 69 Huffman.
Roebuck Asa, lab S F Bowser & Co, res 19 Purman.
Roebuck Asa jr, mach hd, bds 19 Purman.
Roebuck Homer E, candymaker Fox Br U S Baking Co, bds 19 Purman.
Roebuck Willis T, motorman, res 19 Penn.
Roeger Charles, saloon 26 W Main, res same.
Roeger Frederick H, bds 26 W Main.
Roeger Wm A C, carpenter, bds 26 W Main.
Roehling, *see Reehling, Rehling, Reiling.*
Roehm, *see also Rehm.*
Roehm Hattie B (wid Emanuel), music teacher, res 58 W Berry.
Roehrs Henry, expressman, res 261 W Jefferson.
Roehrs Susie M, milliner, bds 261 W Jefferson.
Roelle Frank G, res 16 W Jefferson.
Roelle Jacob, mach Wabash R R, res 404 Clinton.
Roelle Rose, clk Brenzinger Bread Baking Co, bds 16 W Jefferson.
Roembke, *see also Rombke.*
Roembke Anna, bds 100 Smith.
Roembke August, truckman, res 75 Wilt.
Roembke August H, clerk, bds 118 Union.
Roembke Charles, carpenter, bds 50 Smith.
Roembke Ernest, fireman Penn Co, res 100 Smith.
Roembke Frederick H, fireman N Y, C & St L R R, res 100 Wilt.
Roembke Frederick, grocer, 55 Wall, res 57 same.
Roembke Frederick W, constable, res 81 Wall.
Roembke F Wm, clk B Lehman, bds 57 Wall.

Roembke Henry, blksmith L E & W R R, res 243 Madison.
Roembke Henry A, janitor Court House, res 118 Union.
Roembke Henry F, helper Wabash R R, res 127 Wall.
Roembke Herman, clerk, bds 118 Union.
Roembke Minnie, bds 57 Wall.
Roembke Minnie L, housemaid J H Bass, Brookside.
Roembke Sophia, died Dec 23, 1894.
Roembke Sophia C, bds 57 Wall.
Roembke Wm H, lab Bass F & M Wks, bds 100 Smith.
Roemmerman Henry F W, res 143 Broadway.
Roemmerman Henry J, engineer, bds 143 Broadway.
Roepke Charles W, res s s Packard, 1 e of Indiana.
Roepke Frederick A, lab Bass Wks, res 64 Walton av.
Roepke Paul A, helper, bds 64 Walton av.
Roesener Christian H, carpenter Penn Co, res 21 Savilla av.
Roesener C H Frederick, clk Seavey H Co, res 35 Stophlet.
Roesener C H Frederick jr, printer, bds 35 Stophlet.
Roesener Frederick, laborer, bds 133 Union.
Roesener Frederick, coremkr Bass Wks, res 208 John.
Roesener Henry F C, driver Pottlitzer Bros, res 32 Stophlet.
Roesener Louise C W, bds 35 Stophlet.
Roesener Mary D (wid Frederick H), res 356 Broadway.
Roesler Agatha (wid Henry), bds 116 W Jefferson.
Roesler Wilhelm, knitter, res 38 Watkins.
Roftenberg Charles, bds 42 John.
Rogers, see also Rodgers.
Rogers Agnes, domestic 83 Brackenridge.
Rogers Alexander P, teamster, bds 224 Madison.
Rogers Edgar D, trav agt, res 517 Harrison.
Rogers Edith, domestic 68 Thompson av.
Rogers Edward E, res 43 E DeWald.
Rogers Mrs Elizabeth, chambermaid St James Hotel.
Rogers Elmer H, engr Penn Co, res 459 Lafayette.
Rogers Mrs Emma, seamstress, bds 143 Holman.
Rogers Frank, conductor, res 207 E Lewis.
Rogers Fitz G, bds 82 Lake av.
Rogers Herbert A, printer, Ft Wayne News, bds 126 Harrison.
Rogers H Orlando, res 186 Francis.
Rogers Mrs Isabella, housekeeper 113 W Berry.
Rogers James, supt of bridges, res 40 Garden.
Rogers Lydia, bds 207 E Lewis.
Rogers Mary (wid Wm H), rms 157 E Washington.
Rogers Mary E, bds 64 E Jefferson.

Rogers Millie, domestic 28 Maple av.
Rogers Thomas C, sec Allen County Loan and Savings Association, res 64 E Jefferson.
Rogers Warren, brakeman G R & I R R, res 8 Gay.
Rogers Wm H, mach C Bowman, bds 39 1st.
Rogerson Robert, engr N Y, C & St L R R, rms 22 Boone
Rogge August, janitor P, Ft W & C Ry, res 268 W Jefferson.
Rogge Frederick W, watchman N Y, C & St L R R, res 16 Jackson.
Rogge Fredericka (wid Wm), res 52 McClellan.
Rogge Fredericka E, bds 52 McClellan.
Rogge Gustave F, lab Ft W Elec Corp, bds 52 McClellan.
Rogge Minnie A, bds 16 Jackson.
Rogge Sophie R, seamstress, bds 16 Jackson.
Rogge Wm, died August 27, 1894.
Rogge Wm F, clerk, bds 214 W Superior.
Rogge Wm G, lab Hoffman Bros, res 214 W Superior.
Rohan, see also Rowan.
Rohan Edward G, finisher Ft W Organ Co, bds 386 Fairfield av.
Rohan Frank J, finisher Ft W Organ Co, bds 386 Fairfield av.
Rohan John H, foreman Ft W Organ Co, res 386 Fairfield av.
Rohan Lottie E, clk V Gutermuth, bds 386 Fairfield av.
Rohan Wm H, bkkpr White National Bank, bds 386 Fairfield av.
Rohker Theo, pastry cook The Randall.
Rohlfing Augustus, watchman Penn Co, res 232 Force.
Rohlfing Edward, lab, res s s Pontiac 2 w of Wayne Trace
Rohlfing Wm, lab, Penn Co, bds Edward Rohlfing.
Rohlman Charles F, driver, bds 184 Ewing.
Rohlman Elizabeth (wid Wm), res 184 Ewing.
Rohlman Frederick W, helper Penn C, bds 184 Ewing.
Rohlman George W, fireman, res 84 Boone.
Rohlman Henry, painter, res 91 W Jefferson.
Rohlman John H, clerk, bds 184 Ewing.
Rohrbach Charles, laborer Penn Co, res 97 Summit.
Rohrbach John, porter Mossman, Yarnelle & Co, res 123 Erie.
Rohrbach John G, stripper, bds 123 Erie.
Rohrbach Louis J, spoke turner, bds 438 E Wayne.
Rohrer Frank H, bds 36 Wells.
Rohrer Jacob, collarmkr A Racine, bds 36 Wells.

Rohrer John. laborer, res 36 Wells.
Rohrer John jr, painter, bds 36 Wells.
Rohrer Wm, helper Bass F & M Wks, res 111 Cass.
Rohyans Christian, driver Engine Co No 6, res 13 E 3d.
Rohyans John N, clk P, Ft W & C R R, res 401 E Lewis.
Rohyans Wm G, helper Penn Co, res 521 Lafayette.
Rolape Angeline (wid John), bds 100 St Joe boulevard.
Rolf Albert F J (O'Brien & Rolf), bds 35 Hendricks.
Rolf August W, bds 49 Wall.
Rolf Clara L, tailoress, bds 35 Hendricks.
Rolf Elizabeth M, milliner, bds 35 Hendricks.
Rolf Ernst H, teacher, res 35 Hendricks.
Rolf Frederick A, bricklayer, res 53 Wall.
Rolf Frederick H, lampmkr Ft Wayne Elec Corp, bds 49 Wall.
Rolf Wilhelmina L S (wid Conrad), died June 28th, 1894.
Rollens Richard R, teamster. res 97 Hugh.
Roller Emma, domestic 34 W Superior.
Rollins Anna (wid Wm), bds 84 Baker.
Rollins Edward W, printer Aldine Ptg House, res 84 Baker.
Rollins Wm E, removed to Mansfield, O.
Rolshausen Henry, cigarmaker, res 16 Purman.
Romary August, painter, bds 106 Spy Run av.
Romary Charles C J, blacksmith City Carriage Wks, bds 128 Erie.
Romary Clara, bds 128 Erie.
Romary Elenora, bds 128 Erie.
Romary Joseph A, clk Morgan & Beach, res 129 Erie.
Romary Joseph J, clk Morgan & Beach, res 128 Erie.
Romary Julia, domestic 172 Clinton.
Rombke, see also Roembke.
Rombke Amalie, seamstress, 68 Madison.
Rombke Ella, seamstress, bes 68 Madison.
Rombke Henry, cabtmkr, res 68 Madison.
Rombke Herman E, painter, res 97 Buchanan.
Rombolt Lena (wid Gottlieb), res 55 Wilt.
Romeis Charles J, tailor, 118 Calhoun, res 199 W Wayne.
Romick John W, painter, res 13 Boone.
Rominger Carl, coachman w s Spy Run av 1 n of Elizabeth.
Romy Charles M, painter 140 Maumee rd, res same.
Romy Edward, res n e cor Wiebke and Lafayette.
Romy Louis C, lab Penn Co, bds 140 Maumee rd.
Romy Louis H, conducter, res 91 Gay.

Romy Robert L (Romy and Bobilya), res 3 miles w on Romy Gravel rd.

Romy and Bobilya (Robert L Romy, Louis J Bobilya), real estate, 22 Bank Blk. Tel 214.

Rondot Augusta, domestic J P Rosselot.

Rondot Charles A, stoker Ft Wayne Gas Co, res 8 Mary.

Rondot Eugene, lineman, res 2 Huffman.

Rondot Joseph E, res 44 Summit.

Rondot Millie E, bds 40 W Superior.

Rondot Sophia M, seamstress, bds 40 W Superior.

Roney Julia (wid John), bds 62 Wilt.

Ronk Wm E, conductor, res 57 E DeWald.

Roos, see also Ross.

Roos Dorothy (wid George), res 377 E Washington.

Root Adeline M (wid Valorius), bds 33 Grace av.

Root Darwin S (Vandorn Root & Co), rms 106 E Berry.

Root Hortense V, cash Ft W Gas Co, res 33 Grace av.

Root John H, helper, res 322 E Jefferson.

Root Lewis B (Root & Co), res New York City.

Root Vandorn (Vandorn Root & Co), res Clear Lake, Ind.

Root Vandorn & Co (Vandorn and Darwin S Root) hardwood lumber, 106 E Berry. Tel 393.

Root & Company (Lewis B Root, Ernest C Rurode, Wm H Brady, Charles A T Krimmel), Wholesale and Retail Dry Goods, 46 and 48 Calhoun. Tel 288.

Ropa Carl W, spoke maker, bds 116 John.

Ropa Frederick W, cigar mnfr, 173 Broadway, bds 27 Wall.

Ropa Frederick W, mach hd Penn Co, bds 116 John.

Ropa George C, lab Ft W E Corp, bds 27 Wall.

Ropa Henry W, removed to New York, N Y.

Ropa Lizzie, domestic 61 W Berry.

Ropa Wm, market master, res 27 Wall.

Ropa Wm C, lab Standard Wheel Co, bds 116 John.

Ropa Wm F, clk A I & H Friend, bds 27 Wall.

Ropp Mrs Josephine H, bds 70 Harrison.

Rorison Brainard, with Ft W E Corp, bds New Aveline House.

Rosa Henry A, blksmith, res 93 Summit.

Rosa Louisa (wid Anthony), bds 93 Summit.

Rosabaum Nettie, bds 87 Duck.

Rosch Paul, knitter, rms 391 W Main.

Roscher Sophia M (wid Diedrich W), res 310 W Jefferson.

Rose Anthony C, bartndr C H Rose, res 286 E Jefferson.

Rose Charles W, grocer, 156 Griffith, res 154 same.   Tel 81.

Rose Charles W, brakeman, bds 345 W Main.

Rose Christian B, clk Sam, Pete & Max, res 26 Lavinia.

Rose Christian H, saloon, 77 E Wayne, res same.

Rose Haswell D, engr Penn Co, res 270 Hoagland av.

Rose Henry, fireman N Y, C & St L R R, rms 103 W Main.

Rose Henry A, blksmith G Biemer, bds 28 Lavina.

Rose Wm, res 19 Summit.

Rose Wm F, helper Anthony Wayne Mnfg Co, bds 19 Summit.

Rosenberger Anthony, cigarmkr, bds 134 Wallace.

Rosenberger Charles, res 231 Force.

Rosenberger Charles, painter Penn Co, res 134 Wallace.

Rosenberger Charles J, finisher, bds 134 Wallace.

Rosenberger Edward J, mach hd, bds 134 Wallace.

Rosenberger Frank C, painter Penn Co, res 52 Charles.

Rosenberger Wm, mach Olds' W Wks, res 76 Murray.

Rosenthal Charles D, trav agt C Falk & Co, bds 60 W Main.

Rosenthal Eli, meats, cor St Joseph boulevard and Columbia av, bds 105 W Wayne.

Rosenthal Emanuel M, clk Geo DeWald & Co, bds 60 W Main.

Rosenthal Emma, clk A Mergentheim, bds 60 W Main.

Rosenthal Ephraim, horse dealer, res 60 W Main.

Rosenthal Isaac M, physician, 96 W Berry, res same. Tel 237.

Rosenthal J Milton, student, bds 96 W Berry.

Rosenthal Louis S, butcher, bds 105 W Wayne.

Rosenthal Mary (wid Martin), bds 17 Custer av.

Rosenthal Maurice I, physician, 96 W Berry, res same.

Rosenthal Max, cigarmkr, res 105 W Wayne.

Rosenthal Minnie, bds 96 W Berry.

Rosenthal Minnie, clk Geo DeWald & Co, bds 60 W Main.

Rosenthal Moses, saloon, 240 Lafayette, res 165 Holman.

Rosenthal Samuel, clk A Mergentheim, bds 60 W Main.

Rosenwinkel Hugo J, printer Ind Staats Zeitung, bds 41 Maumee rd.

Roser Charles H, comptroller F, Ft W & W Ry, bds The Randall.

Rosler Wilhelm, knitter, res 38 Watkins.

Ross, *see also Roos.*

Ross Celia, milliner, bds 266 E Washington.

Ross Charles, packer Olds' Wagon Wks, bds 324 Lafayette.

Ross Edward C, cigars, The Randall, bds same.

Ross George A, Physician and Surgeon ; Office Hours 7.30 to 8.30 a m, 1.30 to 3.30 and 7 to 8 p m, Tri-State Bldg, rms same. Tel 28.

Ross Gertrude, waitress New Aveline House.

Ross James P (J P Ross & Co) and propr Columbia House, res 25 W Columbia.

Ross Jessie, bds Columbia House.

Ross John, bds 18 Brackenridge.

Ross John E, ticket agt P, Ft W & C Ry and G R & I R R, res 403 Calhoun.

Ross Judson K, baker 27 W Columbia, res 143 Lake av.

Ross J P & Co (James P Ross), grocer, 25 W Columbia.

Ross Martha (wid Donald), res 18 Brackenridge.

Ross-Lewin Edward A, contractor, res 63 Columbia av.

Ross-Lewin Ida L, bkkpr Ft W Furn Co, bds 63 Columbia av.

Ross Orion Q, asst ticket agt P, Ft W & C Ry and G R & I R R, bds New Aveline House.

Ross Richard C, condr N Y, C & St L R R, res 208 High.

Ross Samuel, cigarmaker, bds 48 Barr.

Ross Wilbert A, letter carrier P O, res 210 W Superior.

Ross Willie A, bds Columbia House.

Ross Wm, clerk, res 101 Wilt.

Ross Wm M, tel opr Penn Co, bds 18 Brackenridge.

Rossbach Charles, res 5 Sturgis.

Rossell, *see also Russell.*

Rossell Eva E, bds 239 W Berry.

Rossell Joseph A, traveling agt W L Carnahan Co, res 239 W Berry.

Rossell Louis A, bds 239 W Berry.

Rosselot Catherine (wid Peter), res 16 Barthold.

Rosselot Charles A, plumber A Hattersley & Sons, bds 101 Riverside av.

Rosselot Frederick P, saloon 28 E Columbia, res same.

Rosselot Henry A, agent, bds 101 Riverside av.

Rosselot Julia A (wid Louis), res 101 Riverside av.

Rosselot Lucy S, bds 101 Riverside av.

Rosselot Peter, trimmer Jenney E L & P Co, res 85 Putnam.

Rossington Anna, bds 179 Clinton.

Rossington Charles H, clerk The Randall, bds same.

Rossington Richard, truckman Penn Co, res 129 E Washington.

Rossington Rodolphus B, Local Freight Agent Penn Co and G R & I R R. Office cor Clinton and Railroad, res 181 Clinton. Tel 415.

Rossington Wm W, clerk Penn Co, res 228 E Lewis.

Rossman Jane (wid August), bds 24 Erie.

Rost, *see also Rust.*

Rost Anna, bds 38 Charles.

Rost August, appr Penn Co, bds 38 Charles.

Rost Emil M, fireman Penn Co, bds 38 Charles.

Rost Herman, mach hd Bass F & M Wks, res 33 Buchanan

Rost John D, heater Penn Co, res 38 Charles.

Rost Otto, mach hd, bds 38 Charles.

Rost Wm H, stripper, bds 38 Charles.

Rostenburg, *see Rastenburg.*

Roth August, clk Penn Co, res 65 Scott av.

Roth Bernard, lab Bass F & M Wks, res 20 Force.

Roth Carrie A, bds 131 W Main.

Roth Catherine, milliner, bds 20 Force.

Roth Clara, bds 20 Force.

Roth Emma S, bds 131 W Main.

Roth Ernest C, stonecutter Keller & Braun, bds 131 W Main.

Roth John B, tinner, res 505 Hanna.

Roth Mary A, opr S M Foster, bds 20 Force.

Roth Matilda S, bds 131 W Main.

Roth Nicholas J, pattern mkr Bass Wks.

Roth Peter B, molder, bds 20 Force.

Roth Susanna (wid Frederick), res 131 W Main.

Rothenberger Frederick G, iron wkr Penn Co, res 181 Griffith.

Rothenberger George, res 190 Ewing.

Rothgeb Carrie S, domestic 443 E Lewis.

Rothschild Aaron, res 190 W Wayne.

Rothschild Benjamin (Rothschild & Bro), bds 144 W Berry

Rothschild Charles J, student, bds 152 W Washington.

Rothschild Henry, res 152 W Washington.

Rothschild Ida (wid Bernhard), bds 138 W Main.

Rothschild Joseph, trav agt, bds 68 W Berry.

Rothschild Nathan, bds 144 W Berry.

Rothschild Otto D, clk M Frank & Co, bds 68 W Berry.

Rothschild Sadie, bds 68 W Berry.

Rothschild Solomon (Rothschild & Bro), res 68 W Berry.

Rothschild & Bro (Solomon and Benjamin), loan agents, 1 Bass' Blk.

Rouen, *see Rauen.*

Roush Ella M, dressmaker, 75 Lafayette, bds same.

Roush Etta F, bds 75 Lafayette.

Roush George W, teamster, bds 75 Lafayette.

Roush Mary C (wid John), res 75 Lafayette.

Rousseau Benjamin F, mngr Ft Wayne Beef Co, res 47 Columbia av.

Rosseau R Daniel (Pfeiffer & Rosseau), res 37 W Berry.

Roussel Anna, domestic 108 E Wayne.

Roussel Francis J, bkkpr, bds Columbia House.

Roussey Amanda, seamstress, rms 25 Hough.

Roussey Lena, seamstress, rms 25 Hough.

Roussey Louise, opr S M Foster, bds 71 Columbia.

Roux Charles F, butcher, res 68 Walton av.

Roux Emilie, bds 500 E Wayne.

Roux George, wholesale meats, 500 E Wayne, slaughter house n end Glassgow av, res 500 E Wayne.

Rouzer Cassius M, letter carrier P O, res 55 Boone.

Rouzer Charlotte M, stenogr Ind Farmers' Savings and Loan Assn, bds 55 Boone.

Rouzer Harry E, clk N Y, C & St L R R, bds 55 Boone.

Rowan, *see also Rohan.*

Rowan Barbara A (wid Benjamin C), bds 76 E Washington.

Rowan David P, student, bds 228 W Creighton av.

Rowan James E, brakeman, bds 247 Walton av.

Rowan James W, conductor, res 228 W Creighton av.

Rowan Mark H, brakeman, res 247 Walton av.

Rowan Mark W, printer Archer Ptg Co, bds 247 Walton av.

Rowan Katie, bds 247 Walton av.

Rowe Dessie, opr S M Foster, bds 37 Fairfield av.

Rowe Grace, bds 234 Harmer.

Rowe Mary, bds 187 W Wayne.

Rowe Mrs Mary M, res 294 W Washington.

Rowe Mrs Melissa A, res 234 Harmer.

Rowe Nicholas B, meats, 189 Broadway, res 294 W Washington.

Rowe Wm, carpet layer, res 21 Francis.

Rowland Lindley F, agent Wood Harvester Co, bds The Randall.

Rowley Bridget, cook McKinnie House.

Roy Ida, opr S M Foster, bds 72 E Williams.

Roy John B, farmer, res n s New Haven av 5 e of Lumbard.

Roy Justin Y, bartender The Randall, bds same.

Royce Erank H, bds 459 Lafayette.

Royhans John N, clerk, res 401 E Lewis.

Rubel Charles, cigarmkr, res 26 Hough.

Rubin Eliza (wid Edward), bds 140 W Main.

Rubin Max (Julius Nathan & Co), res 140 W Main.

Ruby Aday C, lab Hoffman Bros, res 27 W 4th.

Ruch Mrs Clara I, milliner, 339 W Main, res same.

Ruch Franklin J, plumber Penn Co, res 59 E DeWald.

Ruch Samuel. truckman Penn Co, res 339 W Main.

Ruchel Charles F W, asst cash Root & Co, bds 209 E Lewis

Ruchel Wm, General Carpenter, Contractor and Builder, 209 E Lewis, res same.   (See p 97.)

Rucker Charles, laborer, bds Union House.

Ruckle Marshal M, condr N Y, C & St L R R, res 342 W Main.

Rudert Barbara (wid George), res 482 W Main.

Rudert Edward, butcher, res 406 W Main.

Rudisill Eliza C, bds w s Spy Run av 1 n of Elizabeth.

Rudisill Sarah (wid Frank), bds 259 St Mary's av.

Rudolph Alvin, carpenter, bds 160 Huffman.

Rudolph Charles, upholsterer, bds 160 Huffman.

Rudolph Christina (wid Charles), bds 104 Huffman.

Rudolph Gangolph, carpenter, 160 Huffman, res same.

Rudolph Josephine M. seamstress, bds 216 E Lewis.

Rudolph Sophie, domestic Montgomery Hamilton.

Rudolph Sophia M (wid Frank), res 58 Huffman.

Rudolph Wm, res 7 Short.

Rudolph Wm L, pressman The Journal, res 228 Columbia av.

Rue Frank E (col'd), cook, res 73 Grand.

Rufner Samuel. conductor, res 329 Hanna.

Rugg Isabella C (wid Samuel L), res s s New Haven av 2 e of Edsall av.

Ruggaber Mary K. bds 310 E Wayne.

Ruhl Charles, lab C L Centlivre Brewing Co, res e s Hillside av 2 n of Baker av.

Ruhl Wm D, physician, 45 W De Wald, res same

Rumboldt, see Romboldt.

Rumez Minnie, bds 214 Calhoun.

Rumler James T, clk People's Store. bds 315 Harrison.

Rump Clara M, milliner. bds 29 Lavina.

Rump Ernst F, carpenter, res 29 Lavina.

Rump Ernest H, carpenter, res 44 South Wayne av.

Rump Frederick A, bottler, bds 29 Lavina.

Rump Frederick J, carpenter, res 42 South Wayne av.

Rump Fredericka M, bds 29 Lavina.

Rump Mary E, domestic 149 W Washington.

Rump Minnie, domestic 320 W Washington.

Rumrill Anna, attendant School for F M Y.

Rumrill Nancy M (wid Wm), bds 407 ½ E Lewis.

Rumsey Helen E (wid Henry B), res 159 E Wayne.

Rumsey Julia, bds 159 E Wayne.

Rund Theresa, waitress The Randall.

Rundel Charles B, tinner A H Staub, bds 22 W Jefferson.

Rundel Martin A, cigarmaker, bds 22 W Jefferson.

Rundel Martin E, engr, res 22 W Jefferson.

Runnels Minnie F, domestic 17 Holman.

Rupert Frank, rms 63 Baker.

Rupert Harry E, lab Ft W E Corp, bds 129 W Williams.

Rupert Ira, res 234 W De Wald.

Rupert John E, mach Ft W Elec Corp, bds 129 W Williams.

Rupert Lydia M (wid David), res 129 W Williams.

Rupley Bridget (wid Jacob), res 148 Fairfield av.

Rupley George R, mach Wabash R R, bds 148 Fairfield av.

Rupley Mary, waitress, rms 77 E Berry.

Rupley Mary A, bds 148 Fairfield av.

Rupp, *see also Rapp.*

Rupp John, blacksmith, e s n Barr 2 n of Superior, res Penn n w cor Dubois.

Rupp John, helper Penn Co, res 113 E Creighton av.

Rupp Philip, engr Penn Co, res 149 E DeWald.

Rupp Regina, seamstress, bds 113 E Creighton av.

Rupp Theresa, seamstress, bds 113 E Creighton av.

Rupp Wm H, blksmith J Rupp, bds same.

Ruppel Carrie C, opr S M Foster, bds 20 Locust.

Ruppel Charles, clerk, bds 21 Francis.

Ruppel Clement J, driver Princess Cash Store, bds 20 Locust.

Ruppel Emma, packer B W Skelton Co, bds 20 Locust.

Ruppel Eva, finisher, bds 389 E Washington,

Ruppel Fabian, bricklayer, res 20 Locust.

Ruppel Flora, bds 20 Locust.

Ruppel Henry, yardman The Wayne.

Ruppel John P, peddler, res 264 E Wayne,

Ruppel Josephine, bds 258 E Wayne.

Ruppel Katherine (wid Paul), res 258 E Wayne.

Ruppel Lena, opr S M Foster, bds 389 E Washington.

Ruppel Paul, died July 26th, 1894.
Ruppel Theresa M, fore woman Hoosier Mnfg Co, bds 578
    Lafayette.
Ruppel Wm W, motorman Ft W E Ry Co, res 63 Grand.
Rurode Emma, bds 76 W Berry.
Rurode Ernest C (Root & Co), res 76 W Berry.
Rurode Vallet, bds 76 W Berry.
Rush Margaret R (wid George), res 79 Boone.
Rush Wm H (Wilkins R Rush), res 28 Cass.
Rusher Francis M, stenogr D N Foster Furn Co, bds 29 E
    Williams.
Russell George H, wood carver, res 139 Thomas.
Russell George O, clk J B White, res 31 Cass.
Russell Harry O, removed to Toledo, O.
Russell James, machinist, bds 104 Barr.
Russell Jerome H, general freight and passenger agt F,
    Ft W & W R R, bds The Randall.
Russell John T, machinist, res 118 Thomas.
Russell Louis, janitor, res 172 Rockhill.
Russell Mary, seamstres, bds 28 Rockhill.
Russell Thomas G, cigarmkr F J Gruber, res 120 Butler.
Russell Victor E, clk R G Dun R Co, bds 31 Cass.
Russman Wm, fireman Rhinesmith & Simonson, bds 209
    Lafayette.
Rust, *see also Rost.*
Rust Henry F C, truckman, res 150 Ewing.
Rustenberg, *see Rastenburg.*
Ryan, *see also O'Ryan.*
Ryan Agnes B, bds 118 Barr.
Ryan Andrew, helper Penn Co, res 16 Bass.
Ryan Anna H, bds 118 Barr.
Ryan Mrs Catherine, res 83 Hoagland av.
Ryan Catherine (wid John), res rear 164 Indiana av.
Ryan Charles J, Attorney at Law, 6 Upstairs
    Arcade Bldg, bds 121 E Washington.
Ryan Christopher W, porter The Wayne, rms 89 W Berry
Ryan Cornelius M (Ryan & Gebert), res 58 E Columbia.
Ryan Daniel, Lawyer, 7 Upstairs Arcade Bldg, res
    121 E Washington.
Ryan Edith, bds 121 E Washington.
Ryan Edward J, lab, bds 83 Hoagland av.
Ryan Ellen, bds 320 Lafayette.
Ryan Frank J, painter Bass Wks, res 212 Fairfield av.
Ryan George J, student, bds 164 Harrison.
Ryan Henry P, student, bds 121 E Washington.

O. P. TINKHAM, ══ **DENTIST.** ══ 21, 22, 23, 24 ARCADE BLOCK, West Berry Street, Fort Wayne, Ind. — Office Telephone   Residence Telephone

FORT WAYNE DIRECTORY. 571

Ryan Jacob J, plumber Ryan & Surrell, bds 121 E Washington.

Ryan James, cabtmkr Ft W O Co, res 175 E Pontiac.

Ryan James A, fish 152 Calhoun, res 30 E Leith.

Ryan Jane M, seamstress, bds 9 Clay.

Ryan Jeremiah J, clk J D Gumpper, bds 282 Harrison.

Ryan John B, deputy sheriff, bds 118 Barr.

Ryan John B, fireman, res 330 Calhoun.

Ryan John J, coppersmith Penn Co, bds 83 Hoagland av.

Ryan Lawrence J, carpet layer L Wolf & Co, res 2 Baker.

Ryan Mrs Louisa, bds 66 Howell.

Ryan Margaret A, seamstress, bds 282 Harrison.

Ryan Margaret M (wid James W), res 164 Harrison.

Ryan Mary, chambermaid Hotel Rich.

Ryan Mary, domestic 13 Elm.

Ryan Mary A (wid Michael), bds 214 Fairfield av.

Ryan Mary C, bds 83 Hoagland av.

Ryan Michael J, fireman Penn Co, res 332½ Calhoun.

Ryan Michael S, car builder Penn Co, res cor Wheeler and Runnion av.

Ryan Oscar D (Ryan & Surrell), bds 121 E Washington.

Ryan Patrick, brakeman G R & I R R, bds 266 Calhoun.

Ryan Patrick, custodian P O, res 118 Barr.

Ryan Patrick H, fireman Penn Co, res 210 Lafayette.

Ryan Patrick J, finisher Ft Wayne Iron Co, bds 34 W Superior.

Ryan Paul P, bds 30 Runnion av.

Ryan Philip F, lumber inspector, res 163 Harmer.

Ryan Susan, res 181 Jackson.

Ryan Thomas, commission, res 406 Clinton, Tel 127.

Ryan Trucking Co, P A Randall Pres, R T McDonald Vice Pres, E W Cook Sec, John A Coy Mngr, Storage and Packing, 19–23 Wells. Tel 429. (*See right top lines and p 95.*)

Ryan Wm B, watchman, bds 37 Barr.

Ryan Wm C, lawyer, 7 up stairs Arcade Bldg, res 121 E Washington.

Ryan Wm H, helper Penn Co, res 282 Harrison.

Ryan and Gebert (Cornelius M Ryan, Frank Gebert), saloon, 58 E Columbia.

Ryan & Surrell (Oscar D Ryan, Howard Surrell), plumbers, 41 W Berry.

Ryder David, fruits, 228 Calhoun, res same.

Ryder Frank J, brakeman Penn Co, res 206 Walton av.

Ryder Simon J, foreman, res 119 Boone.

Rygowski Wadislow, helper, rms 21 Force.
Rys Charles J, cigar mkr, rms 59 E Wayne.
Ryus Victor V, brakeman G R & I R R, bds 145 E De Wald.
Ryus Wm H, machinist, res 145 E De Wald.

S

Saalfrank Wm, driver L P Scherer, res 95 Maumee rd.
Sabin Ebenezer, bds 106 Fairfield av.
Sabin Wm F, tuner Ft W O Co, rms 114 W Williams.
Sachreiter Mrs Anna, res 570 Hanna.
Sachreiter Mathias, bds 570 Hanna.
Sachreiter Peter, bds 570 Hanna.
Sack Augusta (wid Wm), res 55 Walter.
Sack Virginia (wid Jacob), res 56 Madison.
Sadler Mrs Samuel, rms 611 Calhoun.
Saengerbund Hall, 51 and 53 W Main.
Saffen Birdie, bds 390 E Washington.
Saffen Francis S, mach Bass F & M Wks, res 103 Madison
Saffen George B, molder Bass F & M Wks, res 387 E Washington.
Saffen Samuel D, teamster, bds 42 Walter.
Saffen Thomas D, mach Ft W Iron Wks, res 47 E Superier
Saffen Thomas W R, mach Ft W Iron Wks, res 42 Walter
Saffen Wm R, lineman, res 68 Maumee rd.
Safford Frank K (G E Bursley & Co), bds 210 W Wayne.
Safford Lucy K (wid Jonas P), res 210 W Wayne.
Sage Arthur E, teamster, res 13 Custer av.
Sahner, see also Sayner and Zauner.
Sahner Barbara (wid Marcus), res 431 W Washington.
Sailer, see also Saylor.
Sailer August G, baker, res 68 Smith.
St Augustin's Academy for girls, s e cor Calhoun and Jefferson.
St Hair Gertrude R, bds 139 E Lewis.
St Hair Wm S, blacksmith, res 139 E Lewis.
St James Hotel, J D Brown Propr, 233 and 235 Calhoun.
St John's German Lutheran School, Jacob Stumpf principal, W Washington s e cor Van Buren.
St John's German Reformed Church, s e cor W Washington and Webster.
St Joseph Hospital, Broadway, s w cor Main.
St Mary's German Catholic School (for boys), s w cor E Jefferson and Lafayette, (for girls), s e cor E Jefferson and Lafayette.

St Mary's Hall, s w cor Lafayette and Jefferson.
St Patrick's Catholic Church, n w cor De Wald and Harrison.
St Patrick's Catholic School, n e cor De Wald and Webster
St Paul's German Catholic Church, n e cor Griffith and W Washington.
St Paul's German Catholic School, s e cor Griffith and W Washington.
St Paul's German Lutheran Church, w s Barr bet Jefferson and Lewis.
St Paul's German Lutheran School, n e cor Barr and Madison.
St Paul's M E Church, s w cor Walton and Selden.
St Peter's German Catholic Church, Warsaw bet St Martin's and De Wald.
St Peter's School (German Catholic), s s St Martin's bet Warsaw and Hanna.
St Vincent Orphan Asylum, e s Wells opp Archer av.
Sakrente Constantina, helper Angelo Kutche, bds 154 Calhoun.
Sale H Brooke, clk Hoffman Bros, bds 323 W Wayne.
Sale Jessie J, bds 203 W Wayne.
Sale John W, sec and treas Hoffman Lumber Co, res 203 W Wayne. Tel 277.
Salem German Reformed Church, e s Clinton bet Wayne and Berry.
Salga Henry C, laborer, res 197 Jackson.
Salge Carrie, domestic 142 Berry.
Salge Christena M (wid Christian C), res 151 Rockhill.
Salge Lena, domestic 286 W Wayne.
Salge Frederick H, laborer, bds 151 Rockhill.
Salge Louisa S, bds 151 Rockhill.
Salimonie Mining and Gas Co, succeeded by Ft Wayne Gas Co.
Sallier Emma C, bds 40 Hough.
Sallier Francis X, oil peddler, bds 40 Hough.
Sallier Justine (wid Francis), res 40 Hough.
Sallot James F, res 164 E Lewis.
Sallot Victor A, agent, res 4 Summit.
Salmon Catherine (wid Michael R), bds 18 Chicago.
Salmon Daniel T, clk Penn Co, bds 42 McClellan.
Salmon John, bookkpr, bds 42 McClellan.
Salmon Margaret (wid Daniel), res 42 McClellan.
Salmon Margaret E, seamstress, bds 18 Chicago.
Salter James A, clerk, bds 46 Burgess.

37

574   R. L. POLK & CO.'S

Salter Lizzie, clk F L Jones, bds 46 Burgess.
Salter Mary A (wid John), bds 85 Swinney av.
Salter Wm, conductor, res 46 Burgess.
Saltzgaber Douglas D, trav agt. res 208 W Creighton av.
Salzmann Wm, photogr, 164 Calhoun, res same.
Sam, Pete & Max, Mautner & Friedlich Proprs, Clothing, Etc, 58 Calhoun.
Samesky Charles, laborer, bds 112 Mechanic.
Sampson Charles T, clk E Shuman, bds 83 Holman.
Sampson Louis, hostler A L Martin, bds 14 Clinton.
Sampson Mollie (wid Charles), bds 60 Chicago.
Sams John W, laborer Penn Co, res 17 Baker.
Sams Wm, carpenter. res s w cor Chestnut and Summer.
Samse Caroline (wid Wm), bds e s Spy Run av 5 n Riverside av.
Samuels John M, jeweler 270 Calhoun, bds St James Hotel
Sanborn Emelia A. bds 7 Prospect av.
Sanburn Amanda M (wid Amos H), bds 87 W Jefferson.
Sanburn John W. engineer, bds 10 Pritchard.
Sander Caroline, bds 86 W Washington.
Sander Catherine (wid Ernest), res rear 103 W Jefferson.
Sander Charles W, clk Siemon & Bro, res 187 Griffith.
Sander Henry F. driver patrol wagon, res 39 Madison.
Sander Lena, bds 86 W Washington.
Sander Wm, res 86 W Washington.
Sanders, *see also Saunders.*
Sanders Clara E, bds 200 Hanna.
Sanders John G, painter Penn Co, res 200 Hanna.
Sanders Loren P, cigarmkr, res 471 Lafayette.
Sanders Robert. saloon 70 Barr, res same.
Sanders Wm F, clk People's Store. res 103 W Jefferson.
Sandkuhler Henry, coremkr Bass F & M Wks. res 234 Gay
Sandmyer Wm, laborer, bds 1 Brookside.
Sands John H, teamster, res 114 E Berry.
Sanford Charles A, conductor, rms 201 Calhoun.
Sanford John S, hacker, bds 8 Wiebke.
Sanford Philip, machine hand. res 8 Wiebke.
Sarber Charles W, student, bds 197 W Superior.
Sarber Thomas J. brakeman, res 28 John.
Sargent, *see also Serjeant.*
Sargent Archibold W, cigarmkr, bds 322 E Wayne.
Sargent Thomas P, teamster, res 16 Marion.
Sargent Wm, res 14 Marion.
Sargent Wm jr, blacksmith, res 322 E Wayne.

Sarnighausen John D, propr and editor-in-chief Indiana Staats Zeitung, 37 E Columbia, res same. Tel 119.
Sarrazen August, lab Penn Co. res 58 Force.
Sarrazen August, lab Penn Co. res 305 Hanna.
Sarrazen Carrie M, clk F L Jones, bds 37 Barr.
Sarrazen Emil C, laborer, res n s Coombs, 2 w of New Haven av.
Sarrazen George E, helper Penn Co, res 34 Smith.
Sarrazen Hattie, domestic 295 Buchanan.
Sarrazen Joseph A, harnessmkr A L Johns & Co, bds E C Sarrazen.
Sarrazen Julian E, lab, res e s Lumbard 2 n of Wabash R R.
Sarrazen Josephine, domestic 140 E Main.
Sarrazen Mary (wid Joseph), res 37 Barr.
Sarrazen Pauline, domestic 22 E Washington.
Satterthwaite Almira (wid Charles), bds 197 W Wayne.
Sauer Carl, Pres Fidelity Benevolent Association, Insurance, 9 Pixley & Long Bldg, Mngr Ft W Freie Presse, res 283 Edgewater av.
Sauer Emma M, student, bds 170 Barr.
Sauer Gottlieb M, condr N Y, C & St L R R, res 2 N Fulton.
Sauer Rev Henry G, pastor St Paul's Luth Church, res 170 Barr.
Sauer Wm A, bds 31 Walton av.
Sauertieg Frederick, cooper Herman Berghoff Brewing Co. res 531 E Main.
Sauerwein Barbara (wid Ernest), res 58 Barthold.
Sauerwein Ernest S H, mach hd L E & W R R, res 8 Franklin
Sauerwein Frank E, lab Wabash R R, res 56 Barthold.
Saunders, *see also* Sanders.
Saunders Benjamin, bds 164 Broadway.
Saunders Clara, domestic 131 E Main.
Saunders Grace T, bds 55 W Lewis.
Saunders Joseph B, machinist, res 55 W Lewis.
Saurbaugh Marion A. bartender, res 86 W 4th.
Saurers Laura, domestic 27 Prospect av.
Saurs David F, lab, res 38 South Wayne av.
Saurs James T, engineer, res 226 Fairfield av.
Saurs Samuel P, engr, bds 226 Fairfield av.
Sauser Louis, jeweler, 188 Calhoun, res same.
Sauter Mrs Mary, res 12 Lafayette.
Savercool Edward M, trav agt S F Bowser & Co, bds 44 St Joseph boulevard.

Savio Edward A, calker, bds 59 Euclid av.
Savio Frank A, res 59 Euclid av.
Savio Frank A jr, removed to Kansas City, Mo.
Savio John W, bds 59 Euclid av.
Savio Louis, brakeman, bds 59 Euclid av.
Savio Sarah J, bds 59 Euclid av.
Sawtelle Henry P, res 161 Shawnee av.
Sawyer Abeline E (wid Oscar L), bds 330 W Washington.
Sawyer Charles S. engr Wabash R R, res 74 Dawson.
Sayles Charles W, lab, res s s New Haven av 2 W of Coombs.
Saylor George B, trav agt, res 17 Lincoln av.
Saylor Jacob K, res n s New Haven av 3 E Pioneer av.
Sayner, *see also Sahner and Zauner.*
Sayner Cora M, bds 106 W Williams.
Sayner Henry, fireman Penn Co, res 106 W Williams.
Scanell Hannah, laundress Hope Hospital.
Scanlon Thomas M, commissioner. res 40 Wagner.
Scantling Catherine (wid Wm C), boarding house, 181 E Wayne.
Scantling Charles W, bds 181 E Wayne.
Scantling Kate, bds 181 E Wayne.
Scantling Wm H, clerk, res 70 W Main.
Scarlet Bertha P, bds 375 Jesse.
Scarlet Chester, plasterer, res 375 Jesse.
Scarlet Chester, real est 27 Bank Blk. res 56 N Harrison.
Scarlet Malinda (wid Henry O), bds 375 Jesse.
Scarlet Reuben W, packer Ft W O Co, res 40 Miner.
Scarlet Rose E, bkkpr Coverdale & Archer, bds 56 N Harrison.
Schaaf Jacob, laborer, res 5 Zollars av.
Schaaf Sarah C, teacher West German. School, res 177 E Lewis.
Schaaf Wm G, teamster, bds 851 Broadway.
Schaar Adolph, inst mkr Ft W Elec Corp, res 28 Scott av.
Schaber Albert W, stonecutter Keller & Braun, res 95 Wall.
Schacher J Charles, molder Bass F & M Wks, res 80 Wall.
Schacher Christopher F, clk A Karn, bds 41 Stophlet.
Schacher George, lab L Rastetter & Son, bds 41 Stophlet.
Schacher Leonard, died April 17, 1895.
Schacher Wm H, tinsmith, bds 41 Stophlet.
Schack Augusta (wid Wm), bds 55 Walter.
Schack George H. mach Bass F & M Wks, res 231 Madison
Schack George W A, clk Root & Co, bds 231 Madison.
Schack Mary, bds 265 E Lewis.

Schack Wm, carpenter, res 55 Walter.
Schade Mary, domestic 53 W Wayne.
Schadel Eugene, harnessmkr, res 226 Lake av.
Schaden Peter W, lawyer, 19 Bank Blk, res 349 W Jefferson.
Schaefenacker Christian F, baker, rms 62 E Main.
Schaefenacker Frederick, truckmkr Penn Co, res s s Chestnut 5 e of Summer.
Schaefenacker Jacob F, truck bldr, res 60 Smith.
Schaefer, *see also Scheffer, Shafer and Shaffer.*
Schaefer Augusta C, milliner, bds 26 Wilt.
Schaefer Charles H, helper Penn Co, bds 314 Buchanan.
Schaefer Charles T, clk J B White, bds 26 Wilt.
Schaefer Christian F, carpenter, res n s Poplar 1 e of Fox
Schaefer Elizabeth, opr Hoosier Mnfg Co, bds 193 Montgomery.
Schaefer Emilie, dressmaker, bds 26 Wilt.
Schaefer Ferdinand. car bldr Penn Co, res 159 Rockhill.
Schaefer George, blksmith Fleming Mnfg Co, res 259 Gay
Schaefer Jacob, helper Penn Co, res 84 Summit.
Schaefer John H W, grocer 1 s of 143 w 3d, res same.
Schaefer Reinhard, clk Siemon & Bro, bds 26 Wilt.
Schaefer Wm, mach Ft W Elec Corp, bds 26 Wilt.
Schaefer Wm E, mach hd Penn Co, res 26 Wilt.
Schaehtele John, fireman N Y, C & St L R R, rms 33 St Mary's av.
Schafer Alfred, helper C H C Bradtmueller, res 77 Spy Run av
Schafer Amelia, dressmkr, bds 90 St Mary's av.
Schafer Christian F W, bartender, bds n e cor Main and Clay.
Schafer Clara L, seamstress, bds Clay n e cor Main.
Schafer Edward, clk J B White, bds 314 Lafayette.
Schafer Frank H. helper Penn Co, bds 186 Francis.
Schafer Frederick C, teamster P A Moran, bds n e cor Clay and Main.
Schafer Frederick J, clk Geo De Wald & Co, bds 90 St Mary's av.
Schafer F Wm, boilermkr Penn Co, res 193 Montgomery.
Schafer George, helper Penn Co, bds 193 Montgomery.
Schafer Henry C, asst bkkpr G E Bursley & Co, res 90 St Mary's av.
Schafer Henry L, trimmer Olds' W Wks, bds n e cor Clay and Main.
Schafer John, res 314 Lafayette.

Schafer John G, barber, res 316 Lafayette.
Schafer Joseph, upholsterer D N Foster, bds 314 Lafayette
Schafer Lizzie, seamstress, bds 193 Montgomery.
Schafer Mary L (wid Christian), res Clay n e cor Main.
Schafer Wm, helper Penn Co, res 167 Holman.
Schafer Wm G, coachman, bds Clay n e cor Main.
Schaffer Christian J, car bldr Penn Co, res 105 Wall.
Schaffer George, res 169 Broadway.
Schaich Annie. domestic 132 W Wayne.
Schaich Christian, res 2 Hillside av.
Schalbar Oscar, res 204 Gay.
Schalk Emma, asst, bds 168 W Main.
Schalk Otto J, blksmith, bds 168 W Main.
Schalk Rosa E, bds 168 W Main.
Schallenberger Stephen, foreman Penn Co, res 418 Lafayette.
Schaller Bros, Cincinnati Beer, Gottlieb Epple Agent, 188 Fairfield av.
Schane Catherine M, bds 305 Harrison.
Schane Henry C, painter A W Mnfg Co, bds 305 Harrison.
Schane Joseph E, laborer, bds 305 Harrison.
Schane M Catherine (wid John R), res 305 Harrison.
Schane Rudolph H. bds 305 Harrison.
Schank, *see also Schenk and Shank.*
Schank Emil G, real estate, res 173 Madison.
Schank Mary A C (wid Louis), bds 155 W Superior.
Schanz Felix, photogr 112 Calhoun, res 447 E Washington
Schaper Wm, harness, 20 N Harrison, res same.
Schaphorst Edward J, clerk, bds 10 Orchard.
Schaphorst Emma C, bds 128 W 3d.
Schaphorst Frederick H, carriagemkr, bds 10 Orchard.
Schaphorst Frederick H W, butcher L Haiber, bds 128 W 3d.
Schaphorst Frederick J, car bldr Penn Co, res 128 W 3d.
Schaphorst Harry H, elev opr. bds 150 W 3d.
Schaphorst Henry, carp Penn Co, res 10 Orchard.
Schaphorst Henry W, bds 128 W 3d.
Schaphorst John H, clk Siemon & Bro. bds 150 W 3d.
Schaphorst Sophia, housekeeper 108 E Berry.
Schaphorst Wm, carp L E & W R R, res 150 W 3d.
Schaphorst Wm C J, packer K Dental Co, bds 150 W 3d.
Schaphorst Wm P, clk Golden & Patterson, bds 10 Orchard
Schapp Jacob. laborer, bds 64 E Jefferson.
Schapper Christian, farmer, bds Wm Miller.

Scharf Carrie, domestic 271 W Wayne.
Scharf Charles A, tinner, res 202 Madison.
Scharf Louisa, domestic 271 W Wayne.
Scharf May, bds 202 Madison.
Scharmann Anna E (wid Philip), res 43 Walnut.
Scharmann Philip, teacher, res 73 Oakley.
Schaumann Amelia, milliner, bds 321 Calhoun.
Scheele, *see also Schele.*
Scheele August, clk H Scheele, bds 400 Hanna.
Scheele Emma, dressmkr, bds 400 Hanna.
Scheele Emma, seamstress, bds 174 E Creighton av.
Scheele Henry, clk H Scheele, bds 400 Hanna.
Scheele Henry, grocer 400 Hanna, res same.
Scheele Martin H, clk J D Lewis, bds 400 Hanna.
Scheele Mary S, bds 400 Hanna.
Scheele Wm M, shoes 352½ Calhoun, res 60 W Williams.
Scheer, *see also Scheerer and Scherer.*
Scheer Elizabeth. bds 94 Wall.
Scheer Elizabeth, domestic 124 W Jefferson.
Scheer Wm, truckman Penn Co, res 94 Wall.
Scheer Wm F, clk Penn Co, bds 94 Wall.
Scheffer, *see also Schaefer, Schafer, Shafer and Shaffer.*
Scheffer John E, clk A Bruder, bds 402 Calhoun.
Scheffer John H, res 402 Calhoun.
Scheffler Gustav, tailor 48 W Main, res 198 Ewing.
Schefman Louis, huckster, res 109 Glasgow av.
Schegel Gottlieb, lab, res s s French 1 w of Webster.
Schegman John F, bds 35 E Jefferson.
Scheib Edward J, stockkpr J B White, bds 165 Harmer.
Scheib John, carpenter Penn Co, res 165 Harmer.
Scheid Frank, mach Penn Co, bds 100 E Lewis.
Scheid George A, appr Penn Co, bds 129 E De Wald.
Scheid Peter J, foreman Penn Co, res 129 E De Wald.
Scheidel, *see Shidel.*
Scheiman, *see also Scheuman and Shuman,*
Scheiman Charles F, printer The Journal. bds 129 Taylor
Scheiman Christian D, helper, bds 256 W Jefferson.
Scheiman Ernest D, substitute P O, res 37 E Williams.
Scheimann Charles J, bkkpr Ft W O Co, bds 86 E Jefferson
Scheimann Dora, bds 86 E Jefferson.
Scheimann Frederick E W, sec Ft W Gas Co, res 298 E
  Jefferson.
X Scheimann Frederick W, carpenter, res 15 Grace.
Scheimann Lizzie, domestic 144 Taber.
Scheimann Sophia (wid Frederick), res 86 E Jefferson.

Scheimann Wm F, mach hd, res 6 Zollars av.
Scheimann Wm H, bkkpr Pfeiffer & Schlatter, bds 86 E Jefferson.
Schele Amelia, bds August Schele.
Schele Arnold J, cigarmkr, bds August Schéle.
Schele August, contr, n s Wayne Trace 2 e of New Haven av
Schele Bernard H, trav agt, bds August Schele.
Schele Blanche, bds w s Lumbard 2 n of Chestnut.
Schele Catherine (wid John B), bds 286 E Wayne.
Schele Clarence A, bds s s Pioneer av 1 e of Walton av.
Schele Clemens, cigar mnfr, 26 Harrison, res 244 E Washington.
Schele Edward, barber, 156½ Calhoun, bds A Schele.
Schele Frank, saloon, 14 Harrison, res 180 W Superior.
Schele Henry, lab, res s s Pioneer av 1 e of Walton av.
Schele John H, saloon, 26 Harrison, res 286 E Wayne.
Schele Louise, bds August Schele.
Schele Martin A. cigar mnfr, 35 W 4th, res same.
Schell, see also Shell.
Schell Ella, domestic 143 Lake av.
Schell Frank K, clk Penn Co, res 113 E Washington.
Schell Jeremiah F (J F Schell & Co), Attorney at Law, 22 and 23 Pixley & Long Blk. bds 181 E Wayne. (*See adv in classified collecting agents and loan agents.*)
Schell J F & Co (Jeremiah F Schell), Proprs of Ft Wayne Loan and Collecting Agency, 22 and 23 Pixley & Long Blk. (*See adv in classified collecting agents and loan agents.*)
Schell Myron J, trav agt, res 102 Fairfield av.
Schellhammer Amelia, domestic 109 W Berry.
Schellhammer Amelia (wid Robert), res w s Walton av 2 s of Pontiac.
Schellhammer Charles, molder Bass F & M Wks, bds w s Walton av nr Pontiac.
Schellhammer Robert C, boilermkr, res 8 Thomas.
Schelper Oscar, lab Ft W Elec Corp, res 204 Gay.
Schenk, see also Schank and Shank.
Schenk Charles, bender L Rastetter & Son, bds 11 Caroline.
Schenk Elizabeth, domestic 95 E Jefferson.
Schenk John, laborer, bds 46 E Columbia.
Schenk Kate, domestic 123 Edgewater av.
Schenk Peter, mach Penn Co, res 56 E 3d.

Schenkel Peter, mason, res 128 Franklin av.

Scherer, *see also Scheer.*

Scherer Amelia H (wid John). res 12 Erie.

Scherer Andrew, laborer, res 56 Hugh.

Scherer Catherine, teacher, bds 50 Oakley.

Scherer Charles W. Groceries, Provisions, Notions and Dry Goods, 56 Walton av, res same.

Scherer Frederick, cabtmkr Penn Co, res 95 E Washington.

Scherer Henry P, res 95 Maumee rd.

Scherer Henry T, driver L P Scherer, res 95 Maumee rd.

Scherer Herman, helper Bass Wks, bds 353 E Lewis.

Scherer John C. mach Ft W O Co, res 37 Walnut.

Scherer John H, clk Hartman & Bro, res 464 E Wayne.

Scherer Louis, res 28 Lillie.

Scherer Louis P, Baker and Confectioner, 99 Maumee av. res 50 Oak. Tel 388.

Scherer Louis T, sawyer Ft W O Co, bds 50 Oakley.

Scherer Margaret (wid Frederick), res 50 Oakley.

Scherer Wm F. tinner, bds 95 E Washington.

Scherfenberg F Emil, cigar mkr, res 95 Eliza.

Scherman Herman, clk H H G Upmeyer, bds 422 E Washington.

Scherman John, cigar mkr, bds 422 E Washington.

Scherman Theresa (wid John), res 422 E Washington.

Scherzinger Gerson, Propr Custer House, 16 and 18 W Main. (*See p 85.*)

Scherzinger Primus (Trenkley & Scherzinger), rms 78 Calhoun.

Scheuck Lora, domestic 405 E Washington.

Scheumann, *see also Schieman and Shuman.*

Scheumann Amelia. bds 321 Calhoun.

Scheumann Bernardina. bds 321 Calhoun.

Scheumann Christian, cabt mkr Penn Co, res 315 E Washington.

Scheumann D F Wm, cigar mkr, bds 315 E Washington.

Scheumann Edward F, bkkpr First National Bank, bds 16 W Butler.

Scheumann Edward F H, clerk, bds 315 E Washington.

Scheumann Frederick H (Scheumann & Klaehn), res 321 Calhoun. Tel 186.

Scheumann Lisette, domestic Concordia College.

Scheumann Minnie, clk, bds 315 E Washington.

Scheumann Otto W, clk Bass Wks, bds 16 W Butler.

Scheumann Theodore H, draughtsman, bds 16 W Butler.

Scheumann Wm D, molder Bass Wks, res 16 W Butler.
Scheumann & Klaehn (Frederick H Scheumann, W Robert Klaehn), undertakers 39 W Main. Tel 228.
Schick George, professor Concordia College, res same.
Schick Gertrude, teacher, bds Concordia College.
Schick Minnie, domestic 95 E Berry.
Schiefer Christian (C Schiefer & Son), bds 99 E Main.
Schiefer C & Son (Christian Schiefer, Herman H Hartwig), shoes 8 E Columbia.
Scheifer Dietrich, tinsmith Wabash R R, res 20 Lavina.
Schiefer Mrs Elizabeth, bds 206 Spy Run av.
Schiefer Ernst, bds 314 Lafayette.
Schiefer Evangeline, bds 206 Spy Run av,
Schiefer Lillian A, bds 20 Lavina.
Schiefer Paul, clk Henry Dicke, bds 20 Lavina.
Schiefer Wm C, mach Wabash R R, res 20 Lavina.
Schiefer Wm D, clerk, res 206 Spy Run av.
Schieferstein Albert, lab, res n w cor Main and Runnion av
Schieferstein Frederick, lab Penn Co, res 59 Winter.
Schieferstein Henry, gardener, bds 500 W Main.
Schieferstein Phillip, butcher, res 500 W Main.
Schieferstein Phillip jr, lab, bds 500 W Main.
Schieferstein Wm R, blksmith 146 W Main, res 500 same.
Schiemer Annie, bds 51 W Lewis.
Schiemer Frank, Wines, Liquors and Cigars 41 Harrison, res 51 W Lewis.
Schiemer Frank jr, clk A Mergentheim, bds 51 W Lewis.
Schifferly Conrad, agent, res 512 Harrison.
Schiffle Elizabeth, domestic 312 E Jefferson.
Schiffly Louise, domestic 44 Brackenridge.
Schild Jesse S, machinist, res 18 Emily.
Schilling Agnes L, bds 255 W Jefferson.
Schilling Anna E, domestic 102 W Wayne.
Schilling Mrs Camilla, res e end Howell.
Schilling Carl, phys, pres Phœnix Building and Savings Union, n w cor Washington and Barr, res 112 E Wayne. Tel 101.
Schilling Frank J, clk, bds 255 W Jefferson.
Schilling Frank X, stonecutter Wm Geake, bds 255 W Jefferson.
Schilling Hannah, bds Camilla Schilling.
Schilling John, clk S A Aurentz, bds 255 W Jefferson.
Schilling John, phys, 7 Pixley & Long Bldg, bds 112 E Wayne. Tel 272.
Schilling Mary B, res 88 W Washington.

Schilling Mary E, milliner, bds 255 W Jefferson.
Schilling Theresa, bds 313 W Washington.
Schimmele George, teamster Keller & Braun, res 253 Huffman.
Schimmelpfennig Gustave, res 239 Force.
Schimming Sophia (wid Henry), bds 199 W Superior.
Schirmeyer Albert J, mach. bds 127 E Jefferson.
Schirmeyer Anthony J, laborer. res 20 Fairfield av.
Schirmeyer Bertha A, bds 127 E Jefferson.
Schirmeyer Charles W, bds 20 Fairfield av.
Schirmeyer Leo G, bds 127 E Jefferson.
Schirmeyer Louis, clk Sam Pete & Max, res 127 E Jefferson
Schirmeyer Oscar W, cigarmkr, bds 127 E Jefferson.
Schirmeyer Otto A, bkkpr Root & Co, bds 127 E Jefferson.
Schisler, see Shisler.
Schlagel, see also Schlegel.
Schlagel Christina, domestic 480 Fairfield av.
Schlagel John, carpenter, res 72 Lillie.
Schlatter, see also Schlotter.
Schlatter Catherine B, retoucher, bds 337 E Wayne.
Schlatter Charles, res 25 Smith.
Schlatter Christian C (Pfeiffer & Schlatter), res 111 E Wayne.
Schlatter David D, clk Pfeiffer & Schlatter, res 72 Elizabeth.
Schlatter Noah W, draughtsman Kerr Murray Mnfg Co, res 63 E Jefferson.
Schlaudroff John P, finisher Horton Mnfg Co, res 187 Taylor.
Schlaudroff Louis, expressman, res 507 E Lewis.
Schlaudroff Louis C, humane officer, res 24 Michigan av.
Schlaudroff Louis P, laborer, bds 507 E Lewis.
Schlaudroff Theodore, expressman, bds 187 St Mary's av.
Schleabacker George, street sprinkler, res 91 Madison.
Schlegel, see also Schlagel.
Schlegel Adam J, janitor, res 51 W Main.
Schleinkofer John W. laborer, res 59 Force.
Schlenker Bertha D, bds 1 Bass.
Schlenker George, machinist, bds 199 Broadway.
Schlesinger Nanette (wid Nathan), bds 109 E Washington.
Schlie Christian H, car cleaner, res 25 Savilla av.
Schliebitz Frederick W, watchmkr, bds Custer House.
Schlink Charles J, printer, bds 27 Brandriff.
Schlink Frank H, barber, 109 E Lewis, res 60 Maumee rd
Schlink George A, driver, bds 30 Madison.

Schlink John, wood worker, res 27 Brankriff.
Schlink John H, blksmith, 363 Calhoun, bds 27 Brandriff.
Schlink Wm E, laborer, bds 27 Brandriff.
Schlotter, *see also Schlatter.*
Schlotter Alexander, winder Ft W Elec Corp, res 118 W DeWald.
Schmahl Paul, molder Bass F & M Wks, res 38 John.
Schmalz, *see also Smalz,*
Schmalz Caroline, bds 56 Masterson.
Schmalz Charles, tailor, 56 Masterson, res same.
Schmalz Elizabeth, bds 56 Masterson.
Schmalz Mary, bds 56 Masterson.
Schmalzriedt Sophia (wid George), bds 157 Force.
Schmeling Agnes, tailoress, bds 187 Hayden.
Schmeling Albert G, boilermkr Bass Wks, res 400 E Lewis
Schmeling C F George, res 187 Hayden.
Schmeling Fred C, laborer, bds 187 Hayden.
Schmeling Gertrude A M, bds 187 Hayden.
Schmeling Herman, spoke turner, res 187 Hayden.
Schmeling Wm G, appr, bds 187 Hayden.
Schmenk K Gerard, lab Ft W Elec Corp. res 70 Wilt.
Schmenk Ida A. dressmkr, bds 70 Wilt.
Schmenk Lillie D, dressmkr, bds 70 Wilt.
Schmetzer Adolph C, mach. res 240 W Washington.
Schmetzer August, lab Ft W Elec Corp, bds 240 W Washington.
Schmetzer Della M, bds 240 W Washington.
Schmetzer Frederica H, bds 240 W Washington.
Schmetzer John G, cigarmkr, bds 240 W Washington.
Schmetzer Michael F, Township Trustee (elect), res 240 W Washington.
Schmid, *see also Schmit and Smith.*
Schmid August, lab Bass F & M Wks, res 47 Melita.
Schmid Joseph, baker Concordia College, res 29 Schick.
Schmid Lorenz, car bldr Penn Co, res 130 E De Wald.
Schmidt Alice, bds 33 Wilt.
Schmidt Anna, domestic 97 Walton av.
Schmidt Anna M, tailoress, bds 148 Eliza.
Schmidt Augustus M, yardmaster Wabash R R, res 216 E Jefferson.
Schmidt Charles. clk Penn Co, res 318 E Jefferson.
Schmidt Charles, lath hd Ind Mach Wks, bds 142 Erie.
Schmidt Charles, mach Wabash R R, res 173 Fairfield av.
Schmidt Charles, saloon, 130 Chicago, res 132 same.

Schmidt Charles J, foreman F J Schmidt, bds Bluffton rd 1 w of river.
Schmidt Conrad, res rear 281 E Washington.
Schmidt Edward L, driver, bds 33 Wilt.
Schmidt Elizabeth (wid Peter S), res 29 St Martin's.
Schmidt Elizabeth A, bds 148 Eliza.
Schmidt Emma M, shirtmkr P G Kuttner, bds 29 St Martin's.
Schmidt Franz S, lath hd Ind Mach Wks, res 49 Winter.
Schmidt Frank S, clerk, bds w s Hanna 9 s of Pontiac.
Schmidt Frederick, res n s Bluffton rd 1 s of Poor Farm.
Schmidt Frederick H, clk Rudolph Siemon, bds 130 Smith
Schmidt Frederick J, car bldr Penn Co, res 19 Euclid av.
Schmidt Frederick J, Saloon and Dealer in Ice, Gravel and Sand, Bluffton rd 1 w of River, res same. (See p 91.)
Schmidt Frederick S, mach, res w s Hanna 9 s of Pontiac.
Schmidt Frederick W C, mason, res 130 Smith.
Schmidt George, car repr Penn Co, res n w cor Eagle and Taylor.
Schmidt Gottfried, tailor 70 E Main, res 75 Monroe.
Schmidt Helena (wid John W), bds 231 Madison.
Schmidt Henry, saloon 179 Calhoun, res same.
Schmidt Henry G, car bldr Penn Co, bds 58 Force.
Schmidt Henry R, clerk, bds 44 E Williams.
Schmidt Herman, laborer, bds 127 Eliza.
Schmidt Jacob, lab Bass F & M Wks, res 148 Eliza.
Schmidt Jacob A, machinist, bds 33 Wilt.
Schmidt Jacob J, laborer, res 33 Wilt.
Schmidt John, laborer, res 142 Erie.
Schmidt John, mason, res 82 Alliger.
Schmidt John, wagonmkr Olds' Wagon Wks, bds 192 Taylor.
Schmidt John F, car builder, res 19 Euclid av.
Schmidt Joseph, pres Concordia College, res same.
Schmidt Katie, domestic 123 E Main.
Schmidt Louis, laborer, res 53 Walton av.
Schmidt Louis W, res 244 W Washington.
Schmidt Ludwig S, lab Gerding & Aumann Bros, res 93 Howell.
Schmidt Martin, clk, res Spy run av n e cor Butler.
Schmidt Margaret (wid John), bds 233 John.
Schmidt Mary, bds 168 W Main.
Schmidt Mary E, shirtmaker P G Kuttner, bds 29 St Martin's.

Schmidt Peter C, res 135 Van Buren.
Schmidt Peter S, died August 28, 1894.
Schmidt Philip, saloon 168 W Main, res same.
Schmidt Regina A (wid Andrew J), bds 90 Wilt.
Schmidt Theodore, appr S Reehling, bds 168 W Main.
Schmidt Wm, clk Morgan & Beach, res 127 Erie.
Schmidt Wm F, bds Bluffton rd 1 w of River.
Schmidt Wm F, blksmith, res 324 Force.
Schmidt Wm F, file cutter, bds 211 W Main.
Schmidt Wm H, laborer, res 72 Oliver.
Schmidt Wm J, cigarmkr A N Ehle, res 95 Swinney av.
Schmeider August, laborer, res 160 Smith.
Schmieder Max, molder C M Menefee, bds 160 Smith.
Schmieders George H, cigarmkr W A Bayer, bds 282 W
    Jefferson.
Schmieders Mary (wid Frederick), res 282 W Jefferson.
Schmieman Gustav, trav agt Moellering Bros & Millard,
    res 181 Ewing.
Schmieman Louis A, stenogr G E Bursley & Co, bds
    181 Ewing.
Schmit, *see also Schmid and Smith.*
Schmit John, laborer, res 89 Force.
Schmit John P, laborer, bds 89 Force.
Schmit Julia, bds 89 Force.
Schmitt Adam P, molder Bass F & M Wks, res 28 John.
Schmitt Charles, car repr Penn Co, res 169 Eliza.
Schmitt Clara, bds 16 Gay.
Schmitt Eva M (wid Pancreas), res 22 Clark.
Schmitt George O, stone mason, res 16 Gay.
Schmitt George V, laborer, bds 22 Clark.
Schmitt Jacob, laborer, res 129 Taber.
Schmitt Jacob, lab Ft W E Corp, bds 28 Killea av.
Schmitt John, laborer, bds 379 E Lewis.
Schmitt John E, sec hd Penn Co, bds 28 Killea av.
Schmitt John J, laborer, res 28 Killea av.
Schmitt Joseph, laborer, bds 16 Gay.
Schmitt Joseph B, sect hd Penn Co, res 25 Killea av.
Schmitt Peter, mach hd, bds 28 Killea av.
Schmitz Block, n w cor Calhoun and Washington.
Schmitz Henrietta (wid Dr Charles), bds 262 W Jefferson.
Schmitz Philip, laborer, bds 212 John.
Schmitz Theodore, res 212 John.
Schmitz Theodore jr, laborer, res 212½ John.
Schmoe Louis H, shoemkr L Fortriede, res 161 Ewing.

Schmoe Louis H jr, city agt Fox for br U S Baking Co, res 111 Baker.

Schmoll, *see also Small.*

Schmoll George A, foreman Penn Co, bds 78 Force.

Schmoll Gottlieb, wiper Penn Co, res 78 Force.

Schmoll Katie, bds 447 E Washington.

Schmoll Louise, bds 78 Force.

Schmoll Margaret M, milliner, bds 78 Force.

Schmoll Theresa, clk F Schanz, bds 78 Force.

Schmuck, *see also Smock.*

Schmuck Asa C, janitor, res e s Spy Run av 5 n of Riverside av.

Schmuck Charles B, barber, 101 Fairfield av and 21 Grand, res 47 Bass.

Schmuck Francis, barber C B Schmuck, bds 14 Huron.

Schmuck Mary, res 14 Huron.

Schmueckle Frederick, saloon, 24 E Berry, res same.

Schmueckle Frederick L, stenogr Penn Co, bds 339 Broadway.

Schnabel Henry, shoemkr School for F M Y, bds same.

Schnee J Joseph, saloon, 354 Calhoun, res same.

Schneider, *see also Snider and Snyder.*

Schneider Adam, grocer, 173 High, res same.

Schneider Andrew M, lab, res s s Richardson 2 e of Rumsey av.

Schneider Catherine, bookbinder, bds 136 Cass.

Schneider Catherine (wid John), res 102 Putnam.

Schneider Christian, lab Penn Co, bds 102 Putnam.

Schneider Christian, laborer, res 111 Putnam.

Schneider Conrad, laborer, bds 11 Gay.

Schneider Frank E, clerk, bds 81 W Washington.

Schneider Frederick G, cigar mnfr, 104 Webster, res 25 Foster Blk.

Schneider Gottleib F, tailor, res 52 Wells.

Schneider Henry F, lab Ranke & Yergens, bds 52 Wells.

Schneider Henry J, foreman Fleming Mnfg Co, res 108 High.

Schneider J, car bldr Penn Co, res 136 Cass.

Schneider John, laborer, res 105 Putnam.

Schneider John M, janitor, res 81 W Washington.

Schneider Kate, domestic 14 St Mary's av.

Schneider Lillia R, bds 104 Webster.

Schneider Lizzie, domestic The Randall.

Schneider Louis, driver Powers & Barnett, bds 81 W Washington.
Schneider Mary, domestic 167 Clinton.
Schneider Mary E, bds 104 Webster.
Schneider Mary F, Dancing Academy, res 25 Foster Blk.
Schneider Matthias, express, res 324 E Wayne.
Schneider Matthias, laborer, bds 106 Chicago.
Schneider Maurice, res s s Richardson 2 e Rumsey av.
Schneider Wm, deputy sheriff, res 104 Webster.
Schneider Wm, engr The Wayne, res 79 Hayden.
Schneider Wm, laborer, bds 102 Putnam.
Schneider Wm H, cigarmkr F G Schneider, res 97 Wall.
Schneider Wm H, music teacher, 4 N Fulton, res same.
Schneider Wm H, porter, res 212 W Washington.
Schneider Wolfgang, laborer, res 79 Hayden.
Schnelker Mrs Adeline A, res 64 Maumee rd.
Schnelker Agnes M, milliner, bds 64 Maumee rd.
Schnelker Elizabeth A, clk H H G Upmeyer, bds 257 E Wayne.
Schnelker Henry, mason, res 257 E Wayne.
Schnelker Henry F, clk Dreier & Bro, bds 64 Maumee rd.
Schnelker Herman J, driver, res 17 Colerick.
Schnelreider Martin, car bldr Penn Co, bds 50 Smith.
Schnetzler Clementina, domestic, bds 228 Lafayette
Schnetzler John W, barber Edward Schele, bds 165 Clinton
Schnieders Anna E, clk Root & Co, bds 193 Barr.
Schnieders Bernard H, shoemkr 193 Barr, res same
Schnieders Clement H, clk Moellering Bros & Millard, res 151 Barr.
Schnieders Joseph W, clerk, bds 193 Barr.
Schnieders J Bernard, wrapper L Wolf & Co, bds 193 Barr
Schnieders Mary E, clk Root & Co, bds 193 Barr.
Schnitker Charlotte O, domestic 187 W Wayne.
Schnitker Christian F (De Turk & Schnitker), res 13 High
Schnitker Emma, domestic 167 W Wayne.
Schnitker Wm C, helper Fleming Mnfg Co, bds 200 Hanna
Schnor John N, lab Standard Wheel Co, res 297 Maumee rd
Schnor Tobias, carp, res 297 Maumee rd.
Schnoesberger Andrew, res 156 E Jefferson.
Schnorberger Charles, clk M Frank & Co, bds 95 Montgomery.
Schnorberger Mrs Mary, res 95 Montgomery.
Schoch August F, tailor 41½ W Main, res 46 2d.
Schoch Edward F, clk A F Schoch, bds 46 2d.

Schoch Frank G, moved to Chicago.
Schoch Marguerite, bds 484 Harrison.
Schoch Wm F, cutter A F Schoch, res 46 N Harrison.
Schoedel Jacob, brewer C L Centlivre Brewing Co, res 51 Carson av.
Schoen, *see also Schone*.
Schoen Gustave H, carp S F Bowser & Co, bds 76 Maumee rd.
Schoen Oswald H, barber C A Shidel, bds 76 Maumee rd.
Schoen Wm F, carpet weaver, 76 Maumee rd, res same.
Schoenbein Alice (wid Wm B), rms 162 E Wayne.
Schoene Catherine M, res 305 Harrison.
Schoene Henry T, bds 305 Harrison.
Schoene Joseph W, mach hd Olds' Wagon Wks, bds 305 Harrison.
Schoene Rudolph H, bds 305 Harrison.
Schoenfeld Louisa M, bds 59 Stophlet.
Schoenfeld Wm H, truckman, res 59 Stophlet.
Schoenherr Albert J, car repr Penn Co, res 109 Smith.
Schoenherr August, laborer, res 135 Erie.
Schoenherr C Oscar, knitter, res 178 Oakland.
Schoenherr Paul, janitor, res 178 Oakland.
Schoenle Joseph, molder Bass Wks, bds w s Lumbard 3 n of Chestnut.
Schoenle Theresa, bds w s Lumbard 3 n of Chestnut.
Schoenlein Annie M, domestic 74 Douglas av.
Schoenlein Charles B, tailor, res 350 W Main.
Schoenlein John A, tailor, res 348 W Main.
Schoenlein Paul C, paperhanger, bds 350 W Main.
Schoepke Hattie, domestic 273 W Wayne.
Schoepke Wm, helper Penn Co, res John nr Creighton av.
Schoepke Wm H, painter Penn Co, res 89 Shawnee av.
Schoerpf Cecelia K, seamstress, bds 242 E Wayne.
Schoerpf John, plumber, res 242 E Wayne.
Schof John V, barber John Munich, bds 180 Fairfield av.
Schof Joseph J, tinner, bds 180 Fairfield av.
Schof Valentine, painter, res 180 Fairfield av.
Schof Wm F, lab Ft W Elec Corp, bds 180 Fairfield av.
Schofield Charles B, machine hand, res 10 Pape av.
Scholze Louis G, propr Columbia Machine Works, 54 E Columbia, res 8 Erie.
Schomburgh Henry, carp, res 86 Smith.
Schone, *see also Schoen*.
Schone Henry H (Schone & Veith), res 227 E Washington. Tel 304.

Schone & Veith (Henry H Schone, Frank Veith), Undertakers and Embalmers, 53 E Berry. Tel Office 377, res 304. (*See p 113.*)

Schoonover Louis, brakeman, bds 20 Charles.

Schoonover Owen R, foreman Wabash R R, res 71 Melita.

Schopf John, cigarmkr John C Eckert, res 408 E Wayne.

Schoppman Charles L, helper, bds 215 Hanna.

Schoppman Emma, bds 215 Hanna.

Schoppman Frederick W, bartndr, bds 215 Hanna.

Schoppman John R, laborer, bds 215 Hanna.

Schoppman Louisa, bds 215 Hanna.

Schoppman Minnie M, bds 215 Hanna.

Schoppman Wm, bds 141 E Lewis.

Schoppman Wm, saloon, 209 Hanna, res same.

Schoppman Wm H, lab, bds 215 Hanna.

Schoppmann John A W, res 105 Madison.

Schoppmann Lottie, domestic 138 W Wayne.

Schoppmann Minnie, domestic 251 W Washington.

Schoppmann Philip, boilermkr, res 41 Eliza.

Schorr John, res s s Eliza 2 e of Hillside av.

Schotemeyer Elizabeth G K, bds 82 Oakley.

Schotemeyer Fredericka H, tel opr Wabash R R, bds 82 Oakley.

Schotemeyer Henry H, bds 82 Oakley.

Schotemeyer Henry L, student, bds 82 Oakley.

Schotemeyer Herman J, car inspector, res 82 Oakley.

Schotemeyer Herman W, student, bds 82 Oakley.

Schotemeyer Wm H, car inspr, res 4 Killea av.

Schott George J, res 260 W Berry.

Schott Julia C, bds 260 W Berry.

Schott's Block, n w cor Barr and Washington.

Schowe Frederick R, mason, res 86 Oakley.

Schrader, *see also Schroeder.*

Schrader A Lillian, bds 14 Rockhill.

Schrader Carrie B, teacher, bds 14 Rockhill.

Schrader Henry C (Schrader & Wilson), res 14 Rockhill.

Schrader Herman H, bds 121 Force.

Schrader L Gertrude, bds 14 Rockhill.

Schrader Omah, nurse Hope Hospital.

Schrader Wm, bricklayer, res 33 Hough.

Schrader W Frank, phys Hope Hospital, res same.

Schrader & Wilson (Henry C Schrader, Edward M Wilson), Insurance, Real Estate and Notaries Public, 7 Court. Tel 21.

Schrag John, brakeman N Y, C & St L R R, bds 98 Boone

Schrage Christian, tailor, res 57 Huffman.
Schrage Emma, bds 55 Lillie.
Schrage Mary A (wid August), res 55 Lillie.
Schramm Clara, bds Edward Connett.
Schramm Elenora (wid John), bds 5 Oak.
Schramm Francis, res 26 Wallace.
Schramm Frank, mach Penn Co, res 79 Oliver.
Schramm Frank G, plasterer, res 41 Summit.
Schramm Henry F, clk W L Moellering & Co, bds 86 Madison.
Schramm John T, laborer, bds 86 Madison.
Schramm Laura, bds 5 Oak.
Schramm Martin, clk Princess Cash Store, res 86 Madison
Schramm Martin F, boilermkr, bds 86 Madison.
Schramm Peter M, tailor, bds 86 Madison.
Schramm Wm D, lab Bass Wks, res 133 Fletcher av.
Schrantz Adeline (wid Edward J), res 49 Melita.
Schrantz Alfred J, laborer, bds 49 Melita.
Schrantz Delia M, opr, bds 49 Melita.
Schrantz Edward P, driver, bds 49 Melita.
Schrantz Frank C, engr Ft W Furn Co, bds 49 Melita.
Schrantz Frona M, bds 49 Melita.
Schrantz Mrs Mary, bds 49 Melita.
Schranz Bernhard, bds 564 Lafayette.
Schranz Lena, domestic 314 Clay.
Schranz Louis, candymkr, bds 546 Lafayette.
Schreck Charles, contr, 131 Baker, res same.
Schreiber Augusta E, dressmkr, 58 W 3d, bds same.
Schreiber John, lab Paul Mnfg Co, bds 58 W 3d.
Schremser Catherine L, domestic 200 W Berry.
Schremser Henry, clerk, bds 57 John,
Schremser John, helper Penn Co, res 57 John.
Schreve, see Shreve.
Schrod John, bds cor Francis and Hugh.
Schroeder, see also Schrader.
Schroeder Albert, press feeder Ft W Newspaper Union, bds 19 Miner.
Schroeder Andrew L, sec Fidelity Benevolent Assn, res 136 Maumee rd.
Schroeder Anna, bds 21 Charles.
Schroeder Bros (Louis S C and Charles J H), mngrs Broadway Theater, 97 Broadway.
Schroeder Charles H, laborer, bds 597 Calhoun.
Schroeder Charles J H (Schroeder & Sons), res 181 W Washington.

Schroeder Charles L, turner, rms 597 Calhoun.
Schroeder Christian, lab Ft W Elec Corp, bds 58 Gay.
Schroeder Christian L (Schroeder & Sons), res 119 W Superior.
Schroeder Dora, domestic 120 Harrison.
Schroeder Edmund, car bldr Penn Co, res 58 Gay.
Schroeder Edward G, clk Sam, Pete & Max, bds 58 Gay.
Schroeder Eliza M (wid Louis), res 19 Miner.
Schroeder Ferdinand, capt Hook and Ladder Co No 1, rms same.
Schroeder Ferdinand H, laborer, res 88 Summit.
Schroeder Florencé K, bds 597 Calhoun.
Schroeder Frederick, lab Olds' Wagon Wks, bds Winter s of limits.
Schroeder Frederick, teacher, bds 170 E Jefferson.
Schroeder Frederick L, laborer, bds 597 Calhoun.
Schroeder George, tailor, res 170 E Jefferson.
Schroeder Henry, res w s Walton av 8 s of Pontiac.
Schroeder Henry F, laborer, res 106 St Mary's av.
Schroeder Henry H, feed, e s N Calhoun opp jail, res same
Schroeder Henry J, res e s N Calhoun, opp jail.
Schroeder John, coachman 137 W Wayne.
Schroeder John, lab Penn Co, res 21 Charles.
Schroeder John S, electrician Central Fire Station, res 31 Edgewater av.
Schroeder Louis C, teamster, res 106 St Mary's av.
Schroeder Louis S C (Schroeder & Sons), res 109 Broadway
Schroeder Margaret E (wid John F), res 597 Calhoun.
Schroeder Martha (wid Christopher), res 163 E Jefferson.
Schroeder Theodore, bds 19 Miner.
Schroeder Wilhelmina, bds 33 Hough.
Schroeder Wm, laborer, res 131 Eliza.
Schroeder & Sons (Christian L, Lewis S C, Charles J H), real est, 97 Broadway.
Schroeder's Block (new), 97-105 Broadway.
Schroeder's Blk (old), s e cor Broadway and W Washington
Schroeder's Hall, 97-105 Broadway.
Schtinzer Anna, domestic 115 W Main.
Schu John, painter, 594 Lafayette, res same.
Schubert C August, grocer, 230 Gay, res same.
Schubert Gottfreid, dyer Gust Schubert, bds 65 E Main.
Schubert Gust, Dyer and Clothier, 65 E Main, res same. (See p 111.)
Schuck Albert E, clk Heller & Frankel, res 42 E Pontiac.
Schuck Dora A, clk J O Seibert, bds 42 E Pontiac.

Schuck Louis, switchman Penn Co, bds 35 John.
Schuck Mary (wid Louis), res 42 E Pontiac.
Schuckman Anna M, bds 211 E Washington.
Sohuckman Anna M, clk Root & Co, bds 105 E Washington
Schuckman Clements H, packer Globe Spice Mills, bds 211 E Washington.
Schuckman Edward, tailor, bds 211 E Washington.
Schuckman Elizabeth, clk, bds 211 E Washington.
Schuckman Elizabeth C (wid John G), res 105 E Washington.
Schuckman Francis M, clk, bds 211 E Washington.
Schuckman George, clerk, bds 105 E Washington.
Schuckman Henry J, clerk, bds 105 E Washington.
Schuckman Laura C, bds 105 E Washington.
Schuckman Mary E (wid Henry), res 211 E Washington.
Schueler Mary (wid George), res 54 W Creighton av.
Schuerger Frederick, lab. res 16 Zollars av.
Schuff Charles C, fireman N Y, C & St L R R, bds 323 W Main.
Schug John H, clerk, bds 19 W 3d.
Schulder Max, Practical Grinder, Razors and Shears a Specialty, 52 Barr, rms 139 Montgomery.
Schuhler Frank X, insurance, 25 Court, res 107 Wells. Tel 516.
Schuhler John. car bldr Penn Co, res 306 Hanna.
Schuhler Theodore J, saloon, 35 W Columbia, rms 3 Harrison.
Schuler Constantine W, grocer, 302 E Washington, bds 268 E Jefferson.
Schuler Kittie A, bds 268 E Jefferson.
Schuler Mary A, opr, bds 268 E Jefferson.
Schuler Matthias, watchman Penn Co, res 268 E Jefferson.
Schulke Louis, lab Bass F & M Wks, res 143 Buchanan.
Schulte Adolph, res 139 E DeWald.
Schulte Ernest H, carp Bass Wks, res 216 E Washington.
Schulte Fredericka, knitter, bds 205 High.
Schulte Herman F, cigarmkr G F Sorge, bds 205 High.
Schulte John H, pumpmkr, res 133 Thomas.
Schulte Mrs Marie G, Milliner, 332 Calhoun, res 139 E DeWald.
Schulte Theodore, clk Fox Br U S Baking Co, bds 139 E DeWald.
Schulte Wm, trav agt S Bash & Co, res 205 High.
Schultheis August A, bds 211 E Jefferson.
Schultheis Louis P, clk A Kalbacher, bds 211 E Jefferson.

594   R. L. POLK & CO.'S

Schultheis Pius, porter, res 211 E Jefferson.

Schultz, *see also Shultz.*

Schultz Carrie, bds 298 E Lewis,

Schultz Edward, brakeman N Y, C & St L R R, bds 312 W Main.

Schultz Elizabeth (wid Wm), res 71 John.

Schultz Frederick H, molder, res 29 Gay.

Schultz Gustave, boilermkr, bds 71 John.

Schultz Henry, agent, bds 71 John.

Schultz Henry, plasterer, res 298 E Lewis.

Schultz Lizzie, bds 52 John.

Schultz Martha, domestic Hannah Homestead.

Schultz Sophia, opr Hoosier Mnfg Co, bds 71 John.

Schultz Sophia, bds 298 E Lewis.

Schultz Wm H, Druggist and Chemist ; Dealer in Foreign and Domestic Chemicals, Paints, Perfumery, Toilet Articles ; Prescriptions Compounded Day and Night, 142 Fairfield av, res 106 same. Tel 223.

Schultz Wm H J, mach Ft W Elec Corp, res 181 Metz.

Schulz Adolph F, saloon 199 Broadway, res same.

Schulz Charles, laborer, res 240 Smith.

Schulz Christopher H, mach Bass Wks, bds 152 Horace.

Schulz Frederick, contr 140 Francis. res same.

Schulz Frederick C, molder Bass Wks, bds 162 Gay.

Schulz Frederick J, clk A Schulz, bds same.

Schulz Henry F, foreman, res 162 Gay.

Schulz Herman, mason, res 38 Hugh.

Schulz John. res 65 Pixley-Long Bldg.

Schulz Martha E, bds 140 Francis.

Schulz Wm C, peddler, res 152 Horace.

Schulz Wm F, bds 162 Gay.

Schulze Charles H, clk O B Fitch, bds 397 Webster:

Schumacker, *see also Shoemaker.*

Schumacher John, haybaler H T Stapleford, bds 47 E Columbia.

Schumaker Anna (wid Joseph), res 179 Calhoun.

Schumaker Christian (wid Adam), res 23 Baker.

Schumaker M Josephine, bds 23 Baker.

Schuman Herman A, blksmith Bass Wks, res Lima Plank rd.

Schumm Minnie, domestic 176 W Washington.

Schuricht Herman, coremkr Bass F & M Wks, res 15 Oak.

Schust F Harry, engineer Engine Co No 6, rms same.

Schust George A, fireman Pumping Station, res 188 Wells

Schust G Andrew, carpenter. res 182 Wells.

Schust G Adolph, sec Kerr Murray Mnfg Co, res 38 W Creighton av.

Schust Julia J, stenographer, bds 182 Wells.

✗ Schust Louis H, mach Kerr Murray Mnfg Co, res 56 Home av.

Schust Michael J, patternmaker, res 230 W Jefferson.

Schust Paulina C, music teacher, bds 182 Wells.

Schuster, *see also Shuster.*

Schuster Barbara, bds 156 Taylor.

Schuster G Wm, car inspector. res 18 W Allen.

Schuster Henry G, carpenter Penn Co, res 156 Taylor.

Schuster Henry W, clerk J B White, bds 18 W Allen.

Schuwerk August, res 531 E Wayne.

Schwab Catherine (wid John), res 392 E Wayne.

Schwab G Martin, fireman. res 39 Lasselle.

Schwab John A F, wood shaver S D Bitler, res 395 E Wayne.

Schwabe Julius F, patternmkr Bass Wks, res 59 Summit.

Schwabe Richard J, clk L Fortriede, bds 59 Summit.

Schwager John, carpenter, res 30 Cochran.

Schwager Peter S, bds 30 Cochran.

Schwake Henry G, student, bds 73 Oakley.

Schwake Henry, died Sept 7th, 1894.

Schwake Wilhelmina F (wid J Henry), res 73 Oakley.

Schwalm Elizabeth (wid George), bds 143 Erie.

Schwaninger Peter, lab Hoffman Bros, res 90 Franklin av

Schwanz Mary C, bds 130 University.

Schwanz Matthias, carpenter, res 130 University.

Schwarberg Christian H, confectr B W Skelton Co, res 163 Madison.

Schwartz Charles A, harnessmkr Mrs A C Corneille, res 442 E Wayne.

Schwartz Christian, plasterer, res 113 Boone.

Schwartz Christian jr, painter, bds 113 Boone.

Schwartz Edith, bds 542 Calhoun.

Schwartz Emma, waitress The Randall.

Schwartz Frederick, harnessmaker, res 42 W Butler.

Schwartz George, res 350 Broadway.

Schwartz George L, slate roofer, res 21 Pine.

Schwartz George M, car inspector Penn Co, res 36 Taylor

Schwartz Henry, laborer, bds 113 Boone.

Schwartz Henry C, engr Penn Co, res 330 Harrison.

Schwartz Henry F, Plastering Contractor, 542 Calhoun, res same. (*See p 115*,)

Schwartz Johanna (wid John A), res 104 W Butler.

Schwartz Louis, horseshoer, 84 Barr, res 102 Madison.
Schwartz Louisa, bds 42 W Butler.
Schwartz Rosa, bds 42 W Butler.
Schwartz Sophia, milliner, bds 542 Calhoun.
Schwarz Carl, principal West German School, res 20 E Washington.
Schwarz Caroline C, bds 20 E Washington,
Schwarz Emma, bds 233 John.
Schwarz Eveline L, domestic 187 W Berry.
Schwarz Wm F, laborer. res 233 John.
Schwarze E Sophia, student, bds 15 St Mary's av.
Schwarze Henry C F, carp L Diether & Bro, res 15 St Mary's av.
Schwarze Louis H, stenogr, bds 15 St Mary's av.
Schwarze Sophia (wid Wm), tailoress, bds 197 Lafayette.
Schwarzkopp F Joseph, mach Ft W Elec Corp, res 65 W 5th
Schwarzkopp Louis, lab Ft Wayne Elec Corp, res 67 Wells.
Schwedler John, lab, bds Washington House.
Schwegman Clara A, bds 35 E Jefferson.
Schwegman Gustav A, bkkpr Old Nat Bank, res 35 E Jefferson.
Schwegman John F, plumber C W Bruns & Co, bds 35 E Jefferson.
Schwegman Lydia L, bds 23 E Jefferson.
Schwegman Matilda (wid Herman R), res 35 E Jefferson.
Schwegman Paul H, mngr Root & Co, bds 35 E Jefferson.
Schwehn Anna D E, bds 18 Orchard.
Schwehn Conrad, helper. res 18 Orchard.
Schwehn Conrad J, clk Ft Wayne Gas Co, res 128 Union.
Schwehn Henry C, clk Ft W E Ry Co, bds 178 Gay.
Schwehn Henry W, bds 18 Orchard.
Schwehn Johanna D E, bds 18 Orchard.
Schwehn John, blacksmith, res 178 Gay.
Schweigel Diederich, helper, bds 173 Gay.
Schweigel Ernst F, painter, bds 173 Gay.
Schweigel Frederick A, carpenter, res 173 Gay.
Schweigel Ida. bds 173 Gay.
Schweis Louis P, laborer, res 24 Clark.
Schweringen. *see Sweringen.*
Schwier Amelia, bds Pontiac s w cor Thomas.
Schwier Charles (Charles Schwier & Son), res 174 Montgomery.
Schwier Charles & Son (Charles and Wm C), grocers, 176 Montgomery.   Tel 174.
Schwier Frederick W, bds 33 Barr.

Schwier Henry C, boilermkr Bass Wks, res s w cor Thomas and Pontiac.

Schwier Henry F, student. bds 186 E Jefferson.

Schwier Theodore C. bkkpr Builder's Lime Assn, bds H C Schwier.

Schwier Wm, horseman Engine Co No 1, res 33 Barr.

Schwier Wm C (Charles Schwier & Son), res 174 Montgomery.

Schwier Wm F, res 186 E Jefferson.

Schwieters Catherine A, cash J B White, bds 151 Ewing.

Schwieters Charles F, driver, rms 41 E Columbia.

Schwieters Frank W, driver, rms 41 E Columbia.

Schwieters Herman. res 151 Ewing.

Schwieters John H, baker, 41 E Columbia, res 64 W Wayne.

Schwieters Rose R, bds 151 Ewing.

Schwind Albert, engr N Y, C & St L R R, bds 70 Boone.

Schwind Clara, opr Wayne Knitting Mills, bds 61 Elm.

Schwind Ernest. opr Wayne Knitting Mills, bds 61 Elm.

Schwind Gustav. opr Wayne Knitting Mills, res 20 Huron.

Schwind Minnie, opr Wayne Knitting Mills, bds 61 Elm.

Schwind Oscar, opr Wayne Knitting Mills, bds 20 Huron.

Schwind Otto, opr Wayne Knitting Mills, bds 20 Huron.

Schwind Richard, opr Wayne Knitting Mills, res 20 Huron.

Schwind Tracy (wid August), rms 61 Elm.

Scofield Clara, dressmaker, bds 453 Webster.

Scott Alice. teacher School for F M Y.

Scott Amanda O, bds 24 Murray.

Scott Annie (col'd), domestic, bds 275 E Wayne.

Scott Arza W, motorman, res 466 E Wayne.

Scott Bros (Stephen D and Michael C), meats, 352 Broadway.

Scott Carl S, brakeman N Y, C & St L R R, bds 52 Runnion av.

Scott Mrs Catherine J, res 24 Murray.

Scott Charles (col'd), waiter, bds 275 E Wayne.

Scott Charles E, packer A Copinus, bds 24 Murray.

Scott Chloe M, domestic 207 W Berry.

Scott Clara A, bds 24 Murray.

Scott Edwin D, student, bds 304 Harrison.

Scott George M, motorman Ft W Elec Ry Co, rms 42 Glasgow av.

Scott George, mach Penn Co, res 241 E Lewis.

Scott George F, brakeman Penn Co, bds 266 Calhoun.

Scott George T, clk Penn Co, res 241 E Lewis.

Scott James, molder Bass F & M Wks, res 241 E Lewis.
Scott Jefferson W, packer Olds' W Wks, bds 122 Ewing.
Scott Jennie, bds 75 E Butler.
Scott Jennie G, bds 122 Ewing.
Scott Jessie W, bds 122 Ewing.
Scott John G, car bldr Penn Co, res 122 Ewing.
Scott Martin E, painter, bds 122 Ewing.
Scott Mattie H, bds 122 Ewing.
Scott Michael C (Scott Bros), res 168 Taylor.
Scott Stephen D (Scott Bros), res 364 Broadway.
Scott Wm L, engr Penn Co, res 75 E Butler.
Scott Wm M, res n s Jesse 2 e of Rumsey av.
Scoville Seth S, engineer, res 95 W De Wald.
Screen Bessie, domestic 326 W Main.
Screen John, laborer, res 18 Wheeler.
Screen Katje, stamper, bds 18 Wheeler.
Screen Lillie, knitter, bds 18 Wheeler.
Screen Patience (wid George), res 7 Wheeler.
Scribner Judson L, mach Western Gas Const Co, res 117 Greene.
Scully John, lab Penn Co. res 208 Smith.
Scully Patrick J, helper Penn Co, bds 208 Smith.
Seabold, see also Seibold, Seybold and Siebold.
Seabold Adam, brakeman, res 22 Huron.
Seabold Adeline (wid John), res 74 Barthold.
Seabold Christian, teamster, res 211 W Main.
Seabold Edward W, waiter G H Seabold, bds 22 W Main.
Seabold George H, feed stable 15 Pearl, restaurant 22 W Main, res same
Seabold George H jr, mngr G H Seabold, bds 71 W 3d.
Seabold Henry, engr Penn Co, res 6 Hendricks.
Seabold H J, bds cor St Joe boulevard and Onedia.
Seabold John, farmer. res 92 Hayden.
Seabold John A, laundryman, rms 191 Calhoun.
Seabold Louis K, clk Siemon & Bro, bds 211 W Main.
Seabold Maud A, waiter H G Seabold, bds 22 W Main.
Seabold Sarah (widow Christian), res 24 W Main.
Seabold Sophia M, waiter G H Seabold, bds 22 W Main.
Seabold Theodore W, clk F M Smaltz, bds 211 W Main.
Seabrease Agnes A, bds 167 W Berry.
Seabrease Rev Alexander W, rector Trinity Episcopal Church, res 167 W Berry.
Seabrease Alexander W Jr, Bkkpr The W L Carnahan Co, bds 167 W Berry.
Seacrist Harvey, bds 223 Calhoun.

Seacrist Sophia (wid August), res 223 Calhoun.
Sealy Albun, brakeman, bds 252 Clinton.
Seaman Claudia R, domestic 29 E Main.
Seaney Bertha, trimmer Seaney Millinery Co, bds 158 Calhoun.
Seaney John W (Seaney Millinery Co), res Ridgeville, Ind
Seaney Millinery Co (John W and Ora E Seaney), 158 Calhoun Tel 360.
Seaney Ora E (Seaney Millinery Co), res 158 Calhoun.
Seaney Thomas H, condr N Y, C & St L R R, bds 10 Ewing.
Search S Cleophas, conductor, res 63 W Main.
Search Wm N (Search & McCormick), rms 55 E Berry.
Search & McCormick (Wm N Search, James W McCormick), billiard hall, 55 E Berry.
Sears Nannettie (wid Leonard), res 132 Broadway.
Seaton John, died August 17th, 1894.
Seaton Margaret H (wid John), res 91 W Superior.
Seaton Robert L, conductor, res 279 Webster.
Seaton Sophia, bds 91 W Superior.
Seaton Wm D, clerk P O, bds 279 Webster.
Seavey Amy R (wid Gideon W; Seavey Hardware Co), res Ann Arbor. Mich.
Seavey Hardware Co (Mrs Amy R Seavey, George W Stilson, James H Leonard), Wholesale and Retail Hardware, Tinware Mnfrs, Plumbers, Steam and Gas Fitters, 19 and 21 W Main. Tel 149.
Secaur Mary, domestic 167 W Berry.
Sechler Milo H, dispatcher G R & I R R, bds 316 Calhoun.
Second Presbyterian Church, s s W Berry bet Ewing and Webster.
Second U B Church, s w cor Boone and Fry.
Seedse Thomas, res s w cor Brooklyn av and Ontario.
Seeger, *see also Segur.*
Seeger Frederick H, cabinetmkr, res s s Chestnut 2 w of Warren.
Seehausen Gustav, clk Kerr Murray Mnfg Co, bds 285 W Berry.
Seekell Cora B (wid Chauncey T), clk V Gutermuth, bds 79 W Main.
Seele Henry A, mach hd Olds' Wagon Wks, res 30 Nirdlinger av.
Seelig Charles, baker Fox Br U S Baking Co, bds John Seelig.
Seelig Conrad, clk G W Wilson & Sons, bds John Seelig.

Seelig Henry, clk Fox Br U S Bkg Co, res 20 Summit.
Seelig John, gardener Lake av e of city limits, res same.
Seelig John jr, clk Fox Br U S Bkg Co, bds John Seelig.
Seelig Lizzie, bds John Seelig.
Seely Albert J, cabtmkr J M Miller, res 72 W Williams.
Seely Albert J jr, appr Penn Co, bds 72 W Williams.
Seely Almon W, brakeman Penn Co, bds 195 Sherman.
Seely Etta, dressmkr, bds 72 W Williams.
Seemann, see also Sieman.
Seemann Charles, fnshr H Mnfg Co, res 395 W Main.
Seemann Conrad, expressman, res 19 Jones.
Seemann Louisa, opr, bds 395 W Main.
Seemann Wm C, foreman Horton Mnfg Co, bds 395 W
　　Main.
Seemeyer Caroline A, bds 118 W Jefferson.
Seemeyer Caroline L (wid Gottlieb), bds 118 W Jefferson.
Seemeyer Theodore G, stockkeeper The W L Carnahan
　　Co. bds 118 W Jefferson.
Seffel Burton, switchman, bds 217 Baker.
Segur, see also Seeger.
Segur Charles A, clk Mossman, Yarnelle & Co, res 312 E
　　Wayne.
Seibert, see also Siebert.
Seibert Charles H, laborer, bds 106 W Creighton av.
Seibert Francis M, carpenter, res 38 Walnut.
Seibert George D, truckman Penn Co, res 29 Hugh.
Seibert Harry W, laborer, bds 106 W Creighton av.
Seibert Henry W, truckman Penn Co, res 115 Force.
Seibert John C, wood carver, bds 106 W Creighton av.
Seibert John O (Seibert & Good), res Grand Rapids, Mich
Seibert & Good (John O Seibert, Daniel Good), Notions,
　　91 Calhoun.
Seibold, see also Seabold, Seybold and Siebold.
Seibold Andrew, boilermkr Wabash R R, res 77 Huestis av
Seibold Catherine (wid Gottlieb), bds 173 W DeWald.
Seibold Charles, student, bds 173 W DeWald.
Seibold Charles F, stop mkr Ft W O Co, res 173 W De
　　Wald.
Seibold Jacob, res 18 Miner.
Seibold John J, lab Bass Wks, res 35 Huestis av.
Seibold Joseph A, cabinetmkr Ft W O Co, res 61 Home av
Seibold Lydia, bds 18 Miner.
Seibold Minnie, domestic 126 W Main.
Seibold Olive M, bds 107 Cass.
Seibt Charles B, lab, res e s Lafayette 1 s of Grace.

Seibt Charles W H, mach Bass Wks, bds Charles B Seibt.
Seibt Louis, mach Bass F & M Wks, bds 95 Buchanan.
Seibt Minnie B, teacher Miner School, bds Charles B Seibt
Seibt Rosa, dressmkr, bds e s Lafayette 1 s of Grace.
Seidel's Block, 52, 52½ and 54 Calhoun.
Seidel Conrad, helper Kerr Murray Mnfg Co, res 86 Hayden.
Seidel Elizabeth, bds 86 Hayden.
Seidel Edmund (Wm Seidel & Bro), bds 52½ Calhoun.
Seidel Edward, Insurance and Loans 52½ Calhoun, res same.
Seidel Frederick, lab, res 18 Zollars av.
Seidel John, sheet iron wkr Kerr Murray Mnfg Co, bds 86 Hayden.
Seidel Otto, ins solr Edward Seidel, bds 52½ Calhoun.
Seidel Wm C (Wm Seidel & Bro), res 107 E Main.
Seidel Wm & Bro (Wm and Edmund), Bakers and Confectioners, Ice Cream Mnfrs, Restaurant and Caterers 116 E Main. Tel 239,
Seifert Lawrence, bds 27 Force.
Seiler August G, res 68 Smith.
Seitz Charles J, res over 71 Holman.
Seitz David A, carpenter, res 10 Elm.
Seitz John H, bds 10 Elm.
Selbst Josephine, opr S M Foster, bds 110 W De Wald.
Selbst Marianna (wid Jacob), res 37 Charles.
Selby Vinnie, printer The Journal, bds 32 Calhoun.
Selix Patrick, bds 81 Barthold.
Selkmann John A, mach hd Ft W O Co, res 178 W De Wald.
Selle Gustave A, clk L F Curdes, bds 45 W Creighton av.
Sellers John A, motorman, res 225 Lake av.
Sellers Joseph A, died September 14, 1894.
Sellers Thomas J, mach hd Rhinesmith & Simonson, bds 108 Wallace.
Semotan Frederick, fresco artist, res 22 Mary.
Sepp, *see Zepp.*
Seralian Mihran K, Portrait Artist and Teacher of European School of Art, 14 Schmitz Blk, bds 215 W Jefferson.
Serjeant, *see also Sargent.*
Serjeant James E, harnessmkr Calhoun n e cor Duck, res 106 Wells.
Seroczynski Andrew, sexton St Patrick's Church, bds 395 Lafayette.

Seroczynski Helena A, tailoress, bds 395 Lafayette.
Seroczynski Thomas, laborer, res 395 Lafayette.
Serva Amos A, winder Ft W Elec Corp, rms 29 W Jefferson.
Sesseman Mary (wid Wm), res 52 Elm.
Sesseman Wm, died September 17, 1894.
Sessions Frank L, electrical engr Ft W Elec Corp, res 58 Douglas av.
Sessler Annie J, bds 61 Grand.
Sessler Charles E, brakeman, bds 61 Grand.
Sessler Clara B, bds 61 Grand.
Sessler Dora J, bds 61 Grand.
Sessler Harry, printer Ft W Gazette, res 143 Wells.
Sessler Harry E, student, bds 61 Grand.
Sessler John L, printer Ft W Gazette, bds 113 Barr.
Sessler Mary E, cigarmkr Kasten & Kohlmeyer, bds 61 Grand.
Sessler Peter, buyer, res 61 Grand.
Seward Albert R, moved to Hudson, Ind.
Sewell Frederick R, bartender L H Young, bds 36 E Columbia.
Seybold, see also Seabold, Seibold and Siebold.
Seybold Wm, tuner Ft W Org Co, res 158 W De Wald.
Seyfert Rufus, laborer, res 87 Ewing.
Seys Charles D, carpenter, res 30 W Butler.
Shafer, see also Schaefer, Schafer, Schaffer, Scheffer.
Shafer Aaron V, saw filer Standard Wheel Co. bds 20 Ohio
Shafer Franklin P, laborer, bds 122 W Washington.
Shafer John R, clk Empire Mills, res 122 W Washington.
Shafer Joseph, agent, rms 303 Calhoun.
Shaffer Allen C, blacksmith, res 77 Riverside av.
Shaffer Freeman S, fireman G R & I R R, res 230 Walton av.
Shaffer Henry L, brakeman, res 131 Horace.
Shaffer James B, truckman, bds 67 Hayden.
Shaffer Wm, coachman 252 W Wayne.
Shambaugh Wm H, lawyer, 10 Bank Blk, res 108 E Wayne. Tel 214.
Shanahan Mary, housekeeper The Wayne.
Shandall Wm, driver Dittoe's Grocery Co, bds 195 E Wayne.
Shank, see also Schank and Schenk.
Shank Jacob, cigarmkr H A Plumadore, res 69 W 4th.
Shannon George A, helper Penn Co, res 299 Harrison.

Shannon Samuel P, contr, res e s Piqua av 1 s of Rudi-
   sill av.
Shannon Wm, carp, bds S P Shannon.
Shannon Wm J, agt Prudential Ins Co, res 33 Monroe.
Shapland Harry T, clk Pantitorium Co, res 178 Hanna.
Sharp Carrie B, prin Westminster Seminary, res 251 W
   Main.
Sharp Charles (col'd), hostler 445 Calhoun.
Sharp Charles (col'd), janitor Standard Wheel Co, rms same
Sharp Henry, res 25 Jackson.
Sharp John, harness maker, res 27 Elm.
Sharp John W, bds 85 Lake av.
Sharp Lewis P, sewing machines 12 E Berry, grocer cor
   St Joe boulevard and Columbia av, res 85 Lake av.
Sharp Lot F, policeman, res 246 Calhoun.
Sharp Ralph P, clk Coverdale & Archer, res 176 W
   Superior.
Sharp Wesley J, bds 85 Lake av.
Shaughnessy, *see also O'Shaughnessy.*
Shaughnessy Wm E, mach hd Ft W Furn Co, res 4
   Colerick.
Shaver Ora B, bds 173 W Superior.
Shaver Martin V, engr N Y, C & St L R R, res 173 W
   Superior.
Shaw Albert P, conductor, bds 23 Smith.
Shaw Charles H, painter Smith & Lee, res 74 W 4th.
Shaw Charles S, brakeman N Y, C & St L R R, rms 33
   Elm.
Shaw David J, grocer, 75 E Wayne, res same.   Tel 31.
Shaw Frank W, painter Smith & Lee, bds 74 W 4th.
Shaw Maude, student, bds 75 E Wayne.
Shaw Nellie E, bds 74 W 4th.
Shaw Michael J, horseshoer Wm Geary, bds 72 Cass.
Shaw Thomas, helper, res 135 E De Wald.
Shaw Vincent B, res 23 Smith.
Shea Catherine, waitress The Randall.
Shea Catherine (wid Bartholomew), res 7 Walnut.
Shea Catherine A, bds 7 Walnut.
Shea Daniel E, condr N Y, C & St L R R, bds 79 Boone.
Shea Hannah, bds 7 Walnut.
Shea Hannah, domestic The Wayne.
Shea James, condr N Y, C & St L R R, bds 75 Boone.
Shea John, engineer, bds 33 St Mary's av.
Shea John S, clk Ft Wayne Gas Co, bds 421 Calhoun.
Shea Joseph, brakeman, bds 91 Gay.

Shea Joseph P, plumber O'Brien & Rolf, bds 421 Calhoun
Shea Mary F, boarding house, 33 St Mary's av.
Shea Michael F, engr Penn Co, res 421 Calhoun.
Shea Nellie, bds 91 Gay.
Shea Patrick, engr Penn Co, res 87 W Williams.
Shea Thomas, switchman, res 36 Eliza.
Shea Thomas E, laborer, res 91 Gay.
Shea Timothy, res 91 Gay.
Shea Wm H, brakeman, bds 36 Eliza.
Sheafer Burgh, clk J C Peters & Co, bds 55 Ferguson.
Sheafer Charles H, machinist, bds 36 Hayden.
Sheafer Isaac, carpenter, res 55 Ferguson.
Sheafer Martha, bds 55 Ferguson.
Sheafer Mary, dressmkr, 55 Ferguson, bds same.
Shear Adolph, instrument mkr, bds 37 Swinney av.
Shearer Lizzie, domestic 50 W Wayne.
Shearlock Henry, brakeman N Y, C & St L R R, res 66
    Burgess
Sheehan Charles S, motorman, res 78 Grant av.
Sheehan John, lab N Y, C & St L R R, bds Lake Shore
    Hotel.
Sheets Benton W, bds 28 Stophlet.
Sheets Johanna (wid Godfried), bds 28 Stophlet.
Sheets Samuel R, shoemkr, res 28 Stophlet.
Shelby Charles F, sign writer, res 235 W Main.
Sheldon, see also Shelton.
Sheldon Charles H, bleacher 57 Clinton, res same.
Shell, see also Schell.
Shell Ada, laundress, bds 105 Summit.
Shell Edward L, clerk, bds 382 Lafayette.
Shell Ella M, domestic The Randall.
Shell E Clarence (Pape Furniture Co), bds 68 W Main.
Shell George W, clerk, bds 382 Lafayette.
Shell Jacob H, driver W B Phillips, res 105 Summit.
Shell Maggie L, bds 105 Summit.
Shell M Jennie (wid Frank V), res 68 W Main.
Shell Otto, lab City Mills, bds cor Berry and Barr.
Shell Rosa (wid Alfred), res 382 Lafayette.
Shellaberger Edwin, clk J B White, res 244 Smith.
Shelley Hamilton R, brakeman, bds 51 Hayden.
Shelley James F, bds 8 Melita.
Shelley Joseph W, engr Penn Co, res 8 Melita.
Shelly Thomas J, moved to Warsaw, Ind.
Shelton, see Sheldon.
Shelton Costa C, barber B Ellert, bds 101 Lafayette.

Shelvey Harry, engineer Penn Co, res 20 Baker.
Shelvey Thomas J, boilermkr, res 5 Pine.
Shelvey Thomas M, clerk, bds 5 Pine.
Shelvey Wm H, engr Penn Co, res 20 Baker.
Shepard Abram L, conductor, res 71 Taylor.
Shepard James A, bkkpr Olds' Wagon Wks, res 519 Harrison.
Shepard Leroy M, laborer, bds 71 Taylor.
Shepard Wm S, mach Ft W Elec Corp, bds F Taylor.
Shepherd Morton E, laborer, res 48 Oliver.
Shepler Elizabeth A (wid Joseph), bds 36 Hayden.
Shepler James A (Shepler & Noble). res 48 Brackenridge.
Shepler John F, conductor, res 296 E Creighton av.
Shepler Leonzo M, brakeman, res 324 Buchanan.
Shepler & Noble (James A Shepler, Charles E Noble), whol grocers, 256 Calhoun. Tel 441.
Shepley Amanda, ironer W B Phillips, bds 37 W Superior.
Sheppard Thomas, res 189 Montgomery.
Sherbondy Edward M, fireman Wabash R R, bds 144 W De Wald.
Sherbondy Frank P, apprentice, bds 144 W DeWald.
Sherbondy George L, caller Wabash R R, bds 144 W DeWald.
Sherbondy Susannah R (wid Abraham), res 144 W DeWald.
Sherbondy Wm H, electrician Penn Co, bds 144 W DeWald.
Sheridan Catherine, janitor Bloomingdale School, res 68 W 3d.
Sheridan Frank, hostler C L Centlivre Brewing Co, bds n w cor Spy Run av and Edna.
Sheridan James, agent, res 199 Montgomery.
Sheridan John F, clk J B White, bds 199 Montgomery.
Sheridan Mary, seamstress, bds 199 Montgomery.
Sheriff's Office, Edward F Clausmeier sheriff, Court House, Tel 145.
Sherin Eliza (wid John), bds 47 W Berry.
Sherin Mary L, dressmkr, 47 W Berry, res same.
Sherman, see also Scherman.
Sherman Arthur E, canvasser, bds 16 Huron.
Sherman Margaret E, dressmaker, 33 Lincoln av, bds same.
Sherwin Millard, machinist, res 84 Force.
Shertzer B Franklin, trav agt, res 149 E Berry.
Shessel Valentine, laborer, res 21 Hensch.
Shidel, see also Scheidel.
Shidel Charles A, barber, 170 Calhoun, res 182 E Wayne.

39

Shideler Irvan P, helper Penn Co, res 320 Calhoun.
Shideler Mrs Sarah E, boarding house, 320 Calhoun.
Shiltz Rose, domestic 15 Douglas av.
Shipley Margaret (wid Joseph), res 112 Richardson.
Shipman Frank I, res 16 Hamilton.
Shirey Charles J, bds e s Piqua av 1 n of Rudisill av.
Shirey George W, grocer, e s Piqua av 2 n of Rudisill av, res same.
Shirey Henry H, lab, bds e s Piqua av 2 n of Rudisill av.
Shirey John, res s w cor Rudisill and Piqua avs.
Shirey John B, printer The Journal, rms 65 W Superior.
Shirky John A, cook New Aveline House, res 40 Webster.
Shisler George W, foreman Anthony Wayne Mnfg Co, res 443 Lafayette.
Shisler Grace M, bds 443 Lafayette.
Shivers George B, bkkpr A L Johns & Co, res 16 Monroe
Shives Chester H, mach Bass F & M Wks, res 38 Clay.
Shmenk, see Schmenck.
Shoaff Anna, bds 81 Brackenridge.
Shoaff Frederick B, bds e s Spy Run av 4 n of Riverside av.
Shoaff Frederick H, bds 12 St Mary's av.
Shoaff James B, insurance agent, res 12 St Mary's av.
Shoaff John A, photographer, res e s Spy Run av 4 n of Riverside av.
Shoaff Mary E, teacher Franklin School, bds John A Shoaff.
Shoaff Mary M (wid Samuel H), res 132 E Berry
Shoaff Oran L, fireman N Y, C & St L R R, rms 12 St Mary's av.
Shoff Uriah S, trav agt Geo De Wald & Co, res 53 Columbia av.
Shobe Albine, dressmaker, bds 69 Baker.
Shober Gart, propr Monday Morning Times 47 E Berry, res 27 Cass.
Shober Karl O L, brakeman, bds 27 Cass.
Shoemaker, see also Schumacher.
Shoemaker Lavina (wid George), res 54 Spy Run av.
Shoemaker Lizzie (wid James S), res 156 Spy Run av.
Shoemaker Mary E (wid Andrew), res 92 W Superior.
Shoemaker Rose M, waitress The Randall, bds 92 W Superior.
Shoeph Matthias, bds 199 Broadway.
Sholts Edward, brakeman, bds 312 W Main.
Shondell George J, fireman Kilian Baker, res 252 E Wayne

Shondell Louise P, seamstress, bds 207 E Wayne.
Shondell Lydia V, bds 207 E Wayne.
Shondell Mary, domestic 24 W Creighton av.
Shondell Mary M, bookbinder, bds 252 E Wayne.
Shondell Ollie R, bookbinder, bds 252 E Wayne.
Shondell Wm J, clerk, bds 207 E Wayne.
Shondell Wm M, ice peddler, res 207 E Wayne.
Shookman John, res 428 Hanna.
Shooling James, res 18 Brandriff.
Shooling Thomas, brakeman, bds 18 Brandriff.
Shoop Ernest woodworker, bds 379 Lafayette.
Shoop Fannie (wid George), bds 77 Lasselle.
Shopbeck Harry, elevator boy The Wayne.
Shordon Daniel, farm implements, 61 and 63 E Columbia, res 61 same.
Shores John W, res 15 Simon.
Shorey Amanda M (wid George), res 18 W Butler.
Shorey I Herbert, clerk Wabash R R, bds 18 W Butler.
Shorey Wm H, baggagemaster Wabash R R, res 55 W Butler.
Short Gideon H, carpenter, res 76 Howell.
Short James C, engr N Y, C & St L R R, res 98 Union.
Short Timothy E, engr N Y, C & St L R R, res 116 Boone
+Shoup Abraham, insurance agt, res 153 Home av.
×Shoup Charles T, machinist, bds 153 Home av.
Shovlin Thomas F, laborer, res 14 Brandriff.
Shrack Edward, fireman, bds 80 Baker.
Shrack Joseph, res 185 Hanna.
Shrack Viola, bds 185 Hanna.
Shreve Charles B, clk R G Dun & Co, bds 86 Lillie.
Shreve Frank E, traveling agt, bds 86 Lillie.
Shreve Louis F, car bldr Penn Co, res 86 Lillie.
Shreve Mollie E, bds 86 Lillie.
Shreve Nora A, dressmkr, bds 86 Lillie.
Shrimpton Alfred, Contractor and Builder, 152 W Main, res same.
Shroyer James M, car bldr Penn Co, res 114 Smith.
Shroyer Lottie C, bds 114 Smith.
Shroyer Martin, carpenter, res 9 Summit.
Shroyer Orville E, painter, bds 114 Smith.
Shroyer Vernit A, laborer, res 114 Smith.
Shryock Wm W, dentist, 27 W Berry, res same.   Tel 355.
Shuder Susie E, domestic 163 W Main.
Shuey Joseph S, res 496 Harrison.
Shultz, *see also Schultz.*

Shultz Jessie E, boxmkr G W Winbaugh, bds P C Shultz.
Shultz Olive B, box mkr G W Winbaugh, bds P C Shultz.
Shultz Perry C, lab, res e s Spy Run av 4 n of canal bridge.
Shulze Charles E, floorwalker Root & Co, res 397 Webster.
Shulze Elliott G, stenogr Hoffman Bros, bds 397 Webster.
Shuman, see also Sheiman and Sheuman.
Shuman Catherine F, bds 56 E Wayne.
Shuman Erastus, house furnishing goods, 43 E Main, res 56 E Wayne.
Shuman Frank G, removed to New York City.
Shunk Frank R, fireman Wabash R R, bds 3 Riverside av.
Shunk John A, student, bds 53 Gay.
Shunk Nye J, fireman L E & W R R, bds 3 Riverside av.
Shunk Therese (wid Frank), res 3 Riverside av.
Shupp Jacob, lab J M Bricker, bds 78 E Columbia.
Shuster, see also Schuster.
Shuster Charles R, painter, bds 526 E Wayne.
Shuster Cora B, bds 526 E Wayne.
Shuster Eva V, bds 526 E Wayne.
Shuster Frank J, painter, bds 526 E Wayne.
Shuster John, helper, res New Haven rd 1 e of toll gate.
Shuster Mary C, bds 526 E Wayne.
Shutsley Minnie, domestic 142 W Main.
Shutt John M, physician, res 28 Columbia av.
Sibray Mary (wid Nathan), res 230 W Wayne.
Sibray Mary E, clk Root & Co, bds 230 W Wayne.
Siebert, see also Seibert.
Siebert Charles, carpenter, res 73 Cherry,
Siebert Ida, domestic 200 W Berry.
Siebert Otto, laborer, bds 28 Huron.
Siebert Otto W, saloon 303 W Main, res same.
Siebold, see also Seabold, Seibold and Seybold.
Siebold Cora B, packer B W Skelton Co, bds 34 Pritchard
Siebold Caspar, teamster, bds 73 Barthold.
Siebold Charles W, lab L Rastetter & Son, bds 34 Pritchard.
Siebold Christian H, foreman L Rastetter & Son, res 34 Pritchard.
Siebold Christian W (Perrey & Siebold), res 32 Runnion av.
Siebold Edward F, helper Wabash R R, bds 73 Barthold.
Siebold George, coachman 154 W Berry.
Siebold Henry, blksmith Fleming Mnfg Co, bds 73 Barthold
Siebold John P, boilermkr Wabash R R, res 236 W DeWald
Siebold Margaret (wid David), res 125 Wells.

Siebold Mary E. tailoress, bds 34 Pritchard.
Siebold Samuel, mach hd, bds 73 Barthold.
Siebold Sophia (wid Bernhard), bds 7 Pine.
Siebold Wm B, frame maker Siemon & Bro, res 66 Walnut
Siebold Wm C, packer Ft W Elec Corp, res 29 Pritchard.
Siebold Wm C, teamster Peters Box and Lumber Co, res 69 Barthold.
Siegmund Herman, tailor A Luethi, res w s Abbott 1 s of Pontiac.
Siegrist Albert, appr Keller & Braun, bds 102 N Harrison
Sieling Diederich F, grocer, s w cor Pioneer and New Haven avs, res same.
Siemon, see also Seeman.
Siemon Adele E, clk A Mergentheim, bds 47 Elizabeth.
Siemon August W, clk Isadore Lehman, res 103 E Washington.
Siemon Carl F. sec Peters' Box and Lumber Co, res 142 Montgomery.
Siemon Charles A, tinner, bds 82 E Jefferson.
Siemon Charles A F, clk Rudolph Siemon, res 47 Elizabeth
Siemon Emma S, dressmkr, bds 82 E Jefferson.
Siemon Frederick J, carpenter, bds 82 E Jefferson.
Siemon Helena (wid August F), res 27 Madison.
Siemon Henry R (Siemon & Brother), res 27 Madison.
Siemon Herman T (Siemon & Brother), res 83 E Jefferson.
Siemon Otto, professor Concordia College, res same.
Siemon Paul, res 82 E Jefferson.
Siemon Rudolph, wall paper, 195 Calhoun, res 23 E Jefferson.
Siemon Walter P, bds 47 Elizabeth.
Siemon & Brother (Henry R and Herman T), Books, Stationery, Wall Paper, Pictures, Frames, Foreign Passage and Exchange, 50 Calhoun. Tel 333. (See back cover.)
Sievers Catherine, domestic 103 W Berry.
Sievers H W Louis, carpenter, res 116 High.
Sigler Edward F, lab Penn Co, res 19 Charles.
Sigrist Wm E, machine hd, res 147 High.
Sihler Carl E, dentist, 106 Calhoun, rms same.
Sill Otto, lab City Mills, bds 187 E Lewis.
Silverstein Mrs Helen, clothing, 5 E Main, res same.
Silverstein Max, agt H Silverstein, res 5 E Main.
Simmons Peter L, laborer Penn Co, res 20 E Pontiac.

Simmons Wm H, watchman School for F M Y, res 407 E Wayne.
Simon Julius, mach Penn Co, res 18 Pine.
Simon Julius C, stenogr Bass F & M Wks, bds 18 Pine.
Simon Rosa, dressmkr, bds 18 Pine.
Simons Mary, musician, rms 256 E Wayne.
Simons M Winfield, vice-pres First National Bank, res Plymouth, Ind.
Simonson James H (Rhinesmith & Simonson), sec and treas The Anthony Wayne Mnfg Co, res 61 W Berry. Tel 385
Simonton Frank, fireman Penn Co, res 310 Broadway.
Simonton George W, saloon, 163 Wells, res 162 same.
Simonton Helen, tailoress, bds 162 Wells.
Simpson Ernest C. removed to Elkhart, Ind.
Simpson Rev Franklin T, presiding elder M E Church. res 266 W Jefferson.
Simpson M E Church, Dawson s e cor Harrison.
Simms Clifford S, asst engr Penn Co, res 67 Harrison.
Sinclair Francis C, res 87 E Jefferson.
Sinclair John L, mach Penn Co, res 395 Hanna.
Sinclair Rebecca, clk V Gutermuth, bds 109 W DeWald.
Sinclair Susan S, principal Nebraska School, bds 87 E Jefferson.
Sinclair Thomas, mach Wabash R R, res 109 W De Wald.
Sinclair Thomas H, clk Penn Co, bds 109 W De Wald.
Sine Amos, engineer Penn Co, res 77 Dawson.
Sine Rosa M, bds 77 Dawson.
Sine Wm, fireman Penn Co, rms 171 Harrison.
Sinel Edward T, brakeman, res 300 Buchanan.
Sing Lee, laundry 150 Calhoun, res same.
Singer Manufacturing Co, F W Irwin General Manager, E P Thomas City Manager, Sewing Machines 12 W Wayne.
Singleton John, fireman Penn Co, bds 33 Baker.
Singleton Louis R, Proprietor Hotel Emery, 2 Cass. (See p 348.)
Singleton Michael T, sewer contractor, res 33 Baker.
Singleton Michael T jr, clerk, bds 33 Baker.
Singleton Philip J, mach Penn Co. res 27 Baker.
Singmaster Joseph M, helper Penn Co, res 177 Jackson.
Singrey Charles A, driver W B Phillips, bds 252 Hoagland av.
Singrey Frank E, clk A L Johns & Co, res 252 Hoagland av.
Sink, see also Szink and Zink.

Sink Elizabeth W (wid Elijah), bds 514 Broadway.

Sink Florence E, bds 514 Broadway.

Sinnigen Christina (wid Albert), res 26 John.

Sinnigen Henry, lab Standard Wheel Co, bds 26 John.

Sinnigen Henry S, clk The Anthony Wayne Mnfg Co, bds 22 John.

Sinnigen Lucia (wid John), res 22 John.

Sircle Emanuel J, brickmaker, res 1 Packard.

Sites Charles, teamster W H Brown, res 71 Holman.

Sites Charles E, motorman, res 31 W 4th.

Sites David, bellowsmkr Ft W O Co, res 38 Huestis av.

Sites David A, carpenter, res 10 Erie.

Sites Edward F, Dentist, 86 Calhoun, res 206 W Wayne.

Sites Emery A, mach hd Ft W O Co, res n e cor Rumsey av and Dayton.

Sites George W (Switzer & Sites), res 229 Indiana av.

Sites Henry C, Dentist, 82 Calhoun, res 15 W Lewis.

Sites Sarah (wid John), res 38 Huestis av.

Sithens Stephen G, millwright, res 127 W Superior.

Siver Emett L, Physician, Office Hours 9 to 12 a m and 1 to 4 p m. Rooms 6 and 7 Schmitz Blk, res 76 Rivermet av.

Sivits Alaska, laborer, res 13 Marion.

Skaf Hibab (Skaf S Ellis), res 123 Fairfield av.

Skaf Hibab jr, notions, 125 Fairfield av, res same.

Skaf S Ellis (Hibab Skaf, George Ellis), notions, 123 Fairfield av.

Skatulla Carl, patternmkr Western Gas Cons Co, res w s Hanna 5 s of Pontiac.

Skelley Philip S, engr, res 11 McClellan.

Skelley Wm H E, clk E C Ross, bds 11 McClellan.

Skelton Benjamin W, pres The B W Skelton Co, res 126 W Jefferson. Tel 315.

Skelton B W Co The, Benjamin W Skelton pres, Charles S Bash vice-pres, John B Franke sec and treas, manufacturing confectioners, 209 Calhoun. Tel 315.

Skelton Edmund W, clerk The B W Skelton Co, bds 126 W Jefferson.

Skelton Wanda E, clk The B W Skelton Co, bds 126 W Jefferson.

Skelton Wm W, trav agt The B W Skelton Co, res 343 W Jefferson.

Skinner Benijah C, engr Penn Co, res 367 Hanna.

Skinner Frederick C, student, bds 367 Hanna.
Skinner Nettie M, bds 367 Hanna.
Slagle Anna R (wid Levi H, res 22 Fisher.
Slagle Arthur M, fireman Penn Co, res n w cor Charles
and Clay.
Slagle Bernice, bds 64 Charles.
Slagle Cecil B, draughtsman Penn Co, bds 258 W Jefferson.
Slagle Estella I (wid John H), res 258 W Jefferson.
Slagle James A, car inspr L S & M S Ry, res 175 Wells.
Slagle Louise (wid John), bds 104 W Butler.
Slagle Nora E, bds 70 Taylor.
Slagle Wm S, engr Penn Co, res 64 Charles.
Slater Alfred, grocer, 441 Broadway, res same.
Slater Eldin, clk Alfred Slater, bds 441 Broadway.
Slater Elgin, clk Alfred Slater, bds 441 Broadway.
Slater George A, mach Penn Co, res 184 Francis.
Slater George F, medical student, bds 19 Bass.
Slater Herbert G, appr Wm Geake, bds 196 Fairfield av.
Slater John, blksmith Penn Co, res 196 Fairfield av.
Slater Joseph, foreman Bass Wks, res 19 Bass.
Slater Monroe I, wood turner, res 24 Barthold.
Slater Wm, res 9 E Superior.
Slater Wm C, student, bds 19 Bass.
Slattery Anna, domestic F J Lourent.
Slattery Emma L (wid Marmaduke M M), res 302 W
Washington. Tel 297.
Slattery Michael, laborer, res 393 Broadway.
Sleeper Frank P, engr N Y, C & St L R R, res 243½ W
Washington.
Slemmer Anna B (wid George P), res 243 E Wayne.
Sletter L, carp Penn Co, bds 46 Nirdlinger av.
Sliter Clarence, engr N Y, C & St L R R, bds 323 Boone.
Sloan Loretta H (wid Patrick), bds 213 W De Wald.
Sloat Henry W, helper Penn Co, res 45 Lasselle.
Slyer Mary (wid James), bds 85 W Main.
Small see also Schmoll.
Small John E, laborer, res 36 E Leith.
Smalley Iona A (Smalley & Allison), res 206 W Wash-
ington,
Smalley & Allison (Misses Iona A Smalley,
Mina Allison), Dressmakers 206 W Washington.
(See p 109.)
Smallwood Wm W, engr N Y, C & St L R R, bds 335 W
Main.
Smaltz, see also Schmalz.

Smaltz Francis M, dry goods 307 W Main, res 353 same. Tel 156.
Smaltz John, clk F M Smaltz, bds 353 W Main.
Smart Wm, condr N Y, C & St L R R, bds 50 Runnion av
Smead Ada A, waitress, bds 196 Calhoun.
Smead Albert, truckman, res 439 E Washington.
Smead Edith M, bds 196 Calhoun.
Smenner Charles H, lab Standard Wheel Co, res 163 Francis.
Smenner Frederick, nailer Standard Wheel Co, bds 118 Hanna.
Smenner Otto, fireman L E & W R R, res 36 E 4th.
Smenner Robert G, clk G E Bursley & Co, bds 118 Hanna
Smenner Theodore, butcher, res 60 Madison.
Smethers John H, helper Kerr Murray Mnfg Co, res 183 Lafayette.
Smethers Julia E, domestic 113 W Wayne.
Smick Manford M, contractor, res 88 W Main.
Smick Margaret A (wid Solomon S), bds 88 W Main.
Smick Wm P, contr, res 527 E Wayne.
Smith, see also Schmid and Schmit.
Smith Agnes, stenogr, bds 120 W 3d.
Smith Agnes S, student, bds 106 W DeWald.
Smith Albert E, clk L S & M S Ry, res 33 1st.
Smith Alice, domestic 167 W Washington.
Smith Andrew, finisher A Hattersley & Sons, res cor Williams and Fairfield av.
Smith Anna, bds 8 Locust.
Smith Annie B, Seamstress, bds 148 Eliza.
Smith Arthur E, bds 110 E Wayne.
Smith Bessie, domestic 169 W Wayne.
Smith Bertha E, student, bds 101 Lafayette.
Smith Bridget A (wid Millard F), res 63 Melita.
Smith Calvin L, clk Penn Co, res 44 St Joseph boulevard.
Smith Carrie (wid John M), res 86 Barr.
Smith Carrie A, sec W M M society, res 57 Pixley & Long Bldg.
Smith Casper E, engr, res 100 W Butler.
Smith Catherine (wid Charles), bds 88 W Washington.
Smith Catherine (wid Henry), bds 20 Poplar.
Smith Charles, bds 360 W Washington.
Smith Charles, molder Kerr Murray Mnfg Co, bds Windsor Hotel.
Smith Charles M, lab Standard Wheel Co, bds 5 Hamilton
Smith Charles E, student, bds 38 Clinton.

Smith Charles W, tel opr G R & I R R, res 118 W Williams.

Smith Christian D, mach hd L Rastetter & Son, res 675 Broadway.

Smith Clarence G, publr The Business Guide and cash Ft Wayne Newspaper Union, res 344 W Washington.

Smith Clarence S, cash Geo De Wald & Co, bds 344 W Washington.

Smith Claud S, bds 45 Elmwood av.

Smith Clement V, traveling agent, res 51 Douglas av.

Smith Clifton J, clerk, bds 9 Cass.

Smith Cornelius M, bds 344 W Washington.

Smith Cornelius S, Rectal Specialist, 59 and 60 Pixley & Long Bldg, res same.

Smith Credit Rating Co, Hon Robert C Bell pres, H C Rockhill vice-pres, Wm Miller treas, C E Rhoades sec, H P Moses asst sec. 32 E Berry.

Smith C Percy, stenogr, bds 44 St Joe boulevard.

Smith Daniel E, mngr Smith & Dailey, res 46 W Williams

Smith Edward, clk Kayser & Baade, bds 33 Wilt.

Smith Edward, sheet iron wkr Penn Co, res 133 Buchanan

Smith Edward (col'd), waiter The Wayne, rms 51 W Superior.

Smith Edward C, carriage mnfr, res 110 E Wayne.

Smith Edward F, machinist, bds 236 E Lewis.

Smith Edwin C (col'd) waiter, bds 277 E Wayne.

Smith Mrs Elizabeth C, bds 130 W Jefferson.

Smith Emil, laborer, bds 144 Erie.

Smith Emil H, mach hd Ind Mach Wks, bds 12 Harrison.

Smith Emily (wid Wm B), res 109 W Berry.

Smith Emma J, bds 93 Baker.

Smith Ernest D, bds Webster s e cor Taber.

Smith Esther (wid Samuel), res 53 W Lewis.

Smith Eugene B, foreman Ft Wayne Newspaper Union, res 38 McClellan.

Smith Fanny (wid Henry), res 254 Clinton.

Smith Fernando, laborer, res 8 Locust.

Smith Finley E, bds 42 E 3d.

Smith Frank, insurance agent, bds 20 Hugh.

Smith Frank (col'd), waiter, rms 51 W Superior.

Smith Frank, laborer, bds 71 McCulloch.

Smith Frank C, lab, res n s Hugh 2 e of Walton av.

Smith Frank J, printer Ft W Sentinel, bds 343 E Lewis.

Smith Fred, shoemkr, res w s Broadway 1's of toll gate.

Smith Fred M (F M Smith & Co), bds 50 W Superior.

Smith F C, painter Penn Co, res 154 Montgomery.
Smith F M & Co (Fred M Smith), hardware, 22 Calhoun. Tel 204.
Smith George, fireman Penn Co, res 45 Hurd.
Smith George B, molder, bds 343 E Lewis.
Smith George H, cigarmaker, res 63 Madison.
Smith George J, student, bds 63 Madison.
Smith George M, helper Wabash R R, res 73 Barthold.
Smith George M, lab Ft W Elec Corp, bds e s Union 1 n of Wall.
Smith George W, asst engr Ft W Water Wks, res 109 Brackenridge.
Smith Georgia A M, bds 106 W De Wald.
Smith Guy, clk W F Beneke, bds 26 Lincoln av.
Smith Guy N, clk D H Baldwin & Co, bds 219 E Wayne.
Smith Harry A, trimmer, bds 100 E Wayne.
Smith Henrietta J, bds 110 W Butler.
Smith Henry, clk Peter Malone, bds 167 Broadway
Smith Henry, engr G R & I R R, res 106 W De Wald.
Smith Henry C, clk Ft W Elec Corp, res 87 Stophlet.
Smith Henry G, clerk, bds 254 Clinton.
Smith Henry J, finisher, bds 16 Walnut.
Smith Henry R, bds 44 E Williams.
Smith Henry W, bds 106 W De Wald.
Smith Herman, laborer, bds 91 Madison.
Smith Hiram, bds 402 Broadway.
Smith Homer T, mngr United Press, 6 Bank Blk, res 41 1st
Smith Howard, fireman, bds 106 W DeWald.
Smith H Williard, appr Wabash R R, bds 106 W DeWald.
Smith Ira A, bricklayer Penn Co, res 176 Gay.
Smith Irene B, bds 109 W Berry.
Smith Jacob A, helper Ft Wayne Newspaper Union, bds 33 Wilt.
Smith James (col'd), cook The Randall, res 43 Hayden.
Smith James, machinist, res 236 E Lewis.
Smith James, rail road commissioner, res 114 W Berry,
Smith James F, carpenter, res 318 Maumee rd.
Smith James M, lab Horton Mnfg Co, res 2 DeGroff.
Smith Jennie, waiter W R Frederick, bds 226 Calhoun.
Smith John, molder Bass F & M Wks, res 343 E Lewis.
Smith John E, lab Wabash R R, bds 2 DeGroff.
Smith John J, molder Bass Wks, res 50 Force.
Smith John W, laborer, bds 15 McLachlan.
Smith Jonas, res 42 E 3d.
Smith Joseph D, car repr Penn Co, res 120 W 3d.

Smith Joseph J, well driver, bds 38 Force.
Smith J Sion, physician, 45 Elmwood av, res same.
Smith Kellie, laborer, res 38 Clinton.
Smith Lillian E, bds 77 Stophlet.
Smith Loring M (Smith & Lee), res 219 E Wayne.
Smith Lotta M, bds 344 W Washington.
Smith Mrs Maggie, res 8 Locust.
Smith Mamie A, bds 100 W Butler.
Smith Manning, clk S B Thing & Co, res 353 E Wayne.
Smith Margaret, dressmaker, bds 8 Locust.
Smith Margaret S (wid J McNutt), res 37 Douglas av.
Smith Martin, clk Baals & Co, res Spy Run av.
Smith Mary I, teacher Jefferson School, res 38 McClellan.
Smith May, bds 254 Clinton.
Smith Minnie A, seamstress, bds 2 DeGroff.
Smith Minnie P, stenogr, bds 44 St Joseph boulevard.
Smith Myra M, student, bds 110 E Wayne.
Smith Nathaniel S, lessee Masonic Temple Theater, bds 19 Lafayette.
Smith Nettie, domestic 235 Spy Run av.
Smith Nettie, laundress, rms 228 Calhoun.
Smith Persifor F, asst master mechanic Penn Co, res 199 W Wayne.
Smith Philip B, mach Bass Wks, res 152 E Creighton av.
Smith Phoebe J, bds 61 Brackenridge.
Smith Reader P, lumber, bds 37 Douglas av.
Smith Rosa, bds 7 Smith.
Smith Sadie F, clk J B White, bds 254 Clinton.
Smith Sarah J, bds 27 Oliver.
Smith Thomas B, machinist, rms 85 Lillie.
Smith Thomas C, painter Penn Co, res 154 Montgomery.
Smith U Murray (Ft Wayne Electrical Constr Co), bds 37 Douglas av.
Smith Walter C, conductor, res 9 Cass.
Smith Wilbur L, student, bds 219 E Wayne.
Smith Wilbur T, brakeman, res 6 Schick.
Smith Willard T, lumber, res 26 Lincoln av,
Smith, Wm, res 27 Oliver.
Smith Wm, laborer, res 2 De Groff.
Smith Wm A, brakeman, res s w cor Lumbard and Chestnut.
Smith Wm A, laborer, res 311 Harrison.
Smith Wm B, res s s Grace 1 e of Calhoun.
Smith Wm E, clk D N Foster Furn Co, res 141 Cass.

Smith Wm H, winder Ft W Elec Corp, res e s Union 1 n of Wall.
Smith Wm J, attendant School for F M Y.
Smith Wm J (col'd), waiter Ft W Club, rms 84 W Main.
Smith Wm L, trav agt Olds' Wagon Wks, res 93 Baker.
Smith Wm P, agt Old Fort Mnfg Co, 9 Bass Blk, res 26 Lincoln av.
Smith W Sanford, res 53 Shawnee av.
Smith & Dailey (N L Smith and Wm H Dailey), feed, 167 Fairfield av. Tel 368.
Smith & Lee (Loring M Smith), carriage mnfrs, 11 and 13 Clay. Tel 290.
Smithers, *see Smethers.*
Smitley Anna (wid Jonathan M), bds 67 E De Wald.
Smitley Christena (wid Wm), bds 53 High.
Smitley Homer B, res e s Piqua av 2 s of Marshall.
Smock, *see also Schmuck.*
Smock Frank L (G E Bursley & Co), res 164 E Berry.
Smoke Andrew, clk Princess Cash Store, bds 408 Calhoun.
Smuts George F, motorman Ft W E Ry Co, res 350 Calhoun.
Smyser Daniel F, clk S Bash & Co, bds 253 W Berry. Tel 88.
Smyser Helen T, bds 246 W Berry.
Smyser Julia, bds 246 W Berry.
Smyser Mary, teacher Washington School, bds 253 W Berry.
Smyser Mary A (wid Jacob), res 253 W Berry.
Smyser Nathan S, student, bds 246 W Berry.
Smyser Peter D, treas S Bash & Co, res 246 W Berry. Tel 88.
Smyth Robert W, draughtsman Ft W Elec Corp, res 50 Wall.
Snedeker Lee C, helper The Randall.
Snelker Mary, domestic The Randall.
Snider, *see also Schneider and Snyder.*
Snider Alberta, bds 29 Prospect av.
Snider Allen B, dentist, 48 Harrison, bds 29 Prospect av.
Snider Clyde A, appr Lahmeyer Bros, bds 505 Lafayette.
Snider George E, polisher, bds 505 Lafayette.
Snider John R, laborer, res 505 Lafayette.
Snider Lois M (wid Evan), res 29 Prospect av.
Snider Wm, bds 312 W Main.
Snively Carrie A, teacher Hoagland School, bds 76 W Creighton av.

618 R. L. POLK & CO.'S

Snively Catherine (wid Henry), res 76 W Creighton av.
Snodgrass John T, mach Ind Mach Wks, res Yellow River rd, Washington twp.
Snook Myrtle, bds 157 St Mary's av.
Snowberger Charles, clerk, bds 216 Lafayette.
Snowberger Clyde C, painter, bds 447 Calhoun.
Snowberger John, painter, res 447 Calhoun.
Snowberger Laura E, clk People's Store, bds 447 Calhoun
Snowberger Mary (wid Christian), res 216 Lafayette.
Snyder, *see also Schneider and Snider.*
Snyder Augustin J, foreman Ft W Elec Corp, res 21 Wall
Snyder Boyd W, Saloon s e cor Lafayette and Lewis, res 107 E Lewis.
Snyder Charles D, brakeman N Y, C & St L R R, bds 80 Boone.
Snyder Charles W, lab L Rastetter & Son, bds 27 Boone.
Snyder Frank E, clerk, bds 63 W Main.
Snyder George, lab Hoffman Bros, res 123 Boone.
Snyder Georgiana, opr S M Foster, bds 580 Lafayette.
Snyder Georgiana, seamstress, bds 140 Holman.
Snyder Henry J, lab F Weibel, res 44 Huestis av.
Snyder Isaac L, condr Penn Co, res 226 Calhoun.
Snyder James A, baker L P Scherer, res 83 Summit.
Snyder Jesse G, carpenter, bds 238 E Jefferson.
Snyder John, bds 123 Boone.
Snyder John, engr L E & W R R, res 136 Cass.
Snyder John H, janitor, res 23 Huffman.
Snyder Katie, bookbinder Ft W Sentinel, bds 137 Cass.
Snyder Mrs Lizzie A, bds 53 Hayden.
Snyder Louis, lab N Y, C & S L R R, res 38 Ewing.
Snyder Mary (wid Henry), res 79 W Jefferson.
Snyder Noah L, baker J H Meyer, bds 96 Calhoun.
Snyder Oscar G, fireman N Y, C & St L R R, res 200 Spy Run av.
Snyder Otto A, sheet iron worker Kerr Murray Mnfg Co, res 59 Melita.
Snyder Simon, grocer, 53 Hayden, res same.
Snyder Stella, domestic 313 Calhoun.
Snyder Wm F, carp, bds 23 Huffman.
Snyder Wm V, condr, res 133 Fairfield av.
Soest Carl, bds 360 Calhoun.
Soest Clara, domestic, bds 121 E Washington.
Soest Hannah, bds 360 Calhoun.
Soest Henry W, drugs, 360 Calhoun, res same. Tel 396.
Soest Louis S, bds 360 Calhoun.

Soest Wm, coachman 286 W Wayne.
Solberger John A, butcher, res 300 Erie.
Soldiers' Sons and Citizens Republican Club, Amos R Walters pres. A W Pierce sec, 17 Arcade.
Soliday George W, clk D N Foster Furn Co, res 432 E Wayne.
Soliday Jacob C, bds 238 E Jefferson.
Soliday John A, city licence office. res 238 E Jefferson.
Soliday Lincoln C, car. repr Penn Co, bds 238 E Jefferson.
Soliday Solomon D (Soliday & Darrow), res 29 Elizabeth.
Soliday Stella J, student, bds 29 Elizabeth.
Soliday & Barrow (Solomon D Soliday, John Barrow), 2d hd store, 71 E Main.
Solon Bernard, Farm Machinery, 55 E Columbia, res 173 Wells.
Somers, *see also Summers.*
Somers Charles E, canvasser, bds 91 W Williams.
Somers Christopher, bds Arlington Hotel.
Somers Elizabeth (wid Harrison), res 14 Walnut.
Somers Elmer E, barber, bds 14 Walnut.
Somers Harvey P, clerk, bds 99 W Williams.
Somers John W, laborer, res 99 W Williams.
Somers Preston H, clk J G Mann, bds 14 Walnut.
Somers Wm M, policeman, res 325 W Jefferson.
Somiesky Frank C, lab, bds s w cor St Mary's av and Lake
Sommer Carl, photogr, res 41 Putnam.
Sommer Josephine, bds 41 Putnam.
Sommers Charles M. teamster, bds 70 Chicago.
Sommers Emma M (wid Calvin), res 70 Chicago.
Sommers Henry G, Prescription Druggist, 35 Calhoun, res 22 E Washington. Tel 303.
Sommers Gertrude, bds 55 W Jefferson.
Sommers Henry H, mach Penn Co, res 55 W Jefferson.
Sommers John F. condr, res 58 Hendricks.
Sommers Laura (wid Peter J), res 418 Clinton.
Sommers Margaret, bds 55 W Jefferson.
Sommers Mattie, bds n s E 4th bet Wells and Cass.
Sommers Maude M, bds 70 Chicago.
Sommers Peter J, died Nov 8th, 1894.
Sommers Reinhard (Sommers & Langohr), res n s E 4th bet Wells and Cass.
Sommers & Langohr (Reinhard Sommers, John W Langohr), saloon, 118 Wells.
Sonday, *see Sunday.*
Sonne Frank, laborer, res 230 John.

620   R. L. POLK & CO.'S

Sonnenburg August, carpenter. bds 73 Oliver.
Sonnenburg August, molder Bass Wks, bds 206 Francis.
Sonnenburg Daniel, coremkr Bass Wks, res 73 Oliver.
Sonnenburg Frederick, lab Bass Wks, res 136 Force.
Sonnenburg Martha, bds 136 Force.
Sontag Louis, tailor F Hardung, bds Hoffmann House.
Sordelet August J, bds s s Zollars av 4 w of Metz.
Sordelet Charles P, clk Pfeiffer & Schlatter, res 37 E 4th.
Sordelet Ella J, bds L Sordelet.
Sordelet Emil L, laborer, bds 253 E Jefferson.
Sordelet Frank L, clk L Wolf & Co, res 60 N Harrison.
Sordelet Mrs Louisa, res s s Zollars av 4 w of Metz.
Sordelet Pauline A, bds 253 E Jefferson.
Sorg Barbara A. domestic, bds 136 Lafayette.
Sorg Charles, bds 73 Wells.
Sorg Eva (wid Joseph), res 136 Lafayette.
Sorg John H, laborer, bds 73 Wells.
Sorg John P, carp L E & W R R, res 76 Barthold.
Sorg Joseph A, mach hd Ind Mach Wks, res 63 Barthold.
Sorg George F, cigar mnfr 43 Wells, res 80 Barthold.
Sosenheimer Alice M, bds 33 E Williams.
Sosenheimer Charles J (Ft Wayne Electrical Const Co and
    Mohr & Sosenheimer), res 33 E Williams.
Sosenheimer Joseph, died May 13th, 1894.
Sosenheimer Kate (wid Benjamin), bkkpr Singer Mnfg Co,
    bds 37 Charles.
Sosenheimer Mary (wid John) bds 52 Charles,
Sottsman Archer, brakeman G R & I R R, bds 15 Chicago
Souder Charles, coachman 232 W Wayne.
Souder Daniel W, res St Joseph's rd 3 miles n of Court
    House.
South Broadway Nursery, D Nestel Pro-
    prietor, S Broadway n w cor Huestis av.
South Congregational Church, n e cor De Wald and Hoag-
    land av.
South Louis F, car bldr Penn Co, bds Weber Hotel.
South Side Hardware Co, Freiburger &
    Suelzer Props, 364 Calhoun.
South Wayne Brick Co, B S Thompson
    Mngr, w s Thompson av n of Wabash R R.
Southern Grace, bds 278 Webster.
Southern James, engr Penn Co, res 278 Webster.
Southern James J, moved to Chicago, Ill.
Sovine Charles H, blksmith, bds 2 Wells.
Sovine Emanuel, carpenter, res n s Baltes 2 e of Spy Run av

Sovine Samuel H, blksmith, n s Wells 1 s of St Mary's av, res Maysville rd.

Sowers Abraham I, motorman Ft W E Ry Co, res 44 Melita.

Sowers David J, driver L H McAfee, bds 3 Wells.

Spade Frederick, trav agt, rms 56 E Columbia.

Spain Hamilton, laborer, res 41 Wallace.

Spain Hattie, bds 41 Wallace.

Spalding, see also Spaulding.

Spalding John, bds w s Calhoun 1 s of Cour.

Spalding Lida A, teacher Hamilton School, res w s Calhoun 1 s of Cour.

Spalding Thomas R, cigarmkr F J Gruber, res 70 Rivermet av.

Spalding Willard W, dairy, w s Calhoun 1 s of Cour.

Spalding Winifred S, stenogr The Randall, bds w s Calhoun 1 s of Cour.

Spanburg John H, laborer, bds 4 Edgerton.

Spanburg Samuel R, laborer, rms 4 Edgerton.

Spangler Charles W, condr N Y, C & St L R R, res 134 Wells.

Spangler Daniel D, lineman Jenney E L & P Co, res e s Spy Run av 1 n of Randolph.

Spangler Mrs Ella, res 14 W Main.

Spangler Ephraim, carp, res 11 Duck.

Spangler George W, res 274 Hoagland av.

Spangler John, finisher Horton Mnfg Co, bds 4 Rebecca.

Spangler Nellie B, bds 374 Hoagland av.

Spanley Anna, seamstress, bds 101 Wells.

Spanley John A, elev opr, bds 101 Wells.

Spanley Louis, machinist, res 101 Wells.

Spanley Martin, grocer, 457 Calhoun, res same.

Spanley Sophia, clk C J Pierre, bds 101 Wells.

Spaulding, see also Spalding.

Spaulding Charles H, clk L P Stapleford, bds 152 E Wayne.

Spaulding Frederick H, electrician, res 18 McClellan.

Spearing Harriet E (wid Henry), res 28 Douglas av.

Speckart Adolph, bds 8 Madison.

Speckman Charles, teamster, res 3 N Harrison.

Speckman Wm D, lab. res w s Hanna 6 s of Pontiac.

Speece Samuel P, fireman Penn Co. res 339 Harrison.

Speidel Carrie, seamstress, bds 272 E Jefferson.

Speidel Frank B, molder Bass Wks, res 30 Schick.

Speidel Jacob, student, bds 20 McClellan.

40

Speidel Johanna (wid Herman), res 272 E Jefferson.

Spellman Rev Richard D, res 25 Clay.

Spencer Clyde O, coudr Ft W E Ry Co, bds 305 Harrison

Spencer Cyrus, laborer, res 5 Wall.

Spencer David J, cigars, 39 Calhoun, bds The Randall.

Spencer Milton C, laborer, bds 5 Wall.

Spencer Minnie M, bds 5 Wall.

Spencer Samuel W, lab Olds' Wagon Wks, bds 5 Wall

Spencer Wm H, driver Ft Wayne Steam Laundry, res 50 W Butler.

Spereisen Jacob A, blacksmith 165 Fairfield av, res 56 Taylor.

Sperkert Maggie (wid Casper), res 11 Caroline.

Sperr John J, laborer, res 38 Runnion av.

Sperry Charles W, pres Sperry Pelton Mnfg Co, res 489 Calhoun.

Sperry LaVon L, bds 489 Calhoun.

Sperry Maud, bds 489 Calhoun.

Sperry Pelton Mnfg Co, Charles W Sperry pres, John P Evans treas, George P Evans sec, Leander Pelton supt, mnfr broom machinery 28 and 30 E Berry.

Spice John, res 10 Runnion av.

Spice Katie (wid Herbert), bds 103 W Washington.

Spice Nellie M, bds 171 Jackson.

Spice Robert, Plumber, Gas and Steam Fitter, Pumps, Wind Mills and Drive Wells, 48 W Main and 11 Pearl, res 171 Jackson. Tel 261. (*See right bottom lines.*)

Spice W Aylmer, bkkpr Robert Spice, rms 94 W Main.

Spiegel August A, clerk, bds 36 Nirdlinger av.

Spiegel Bernhard, res 233 W De Wald.

Spiegel Carl G, clerk, res 13 Jones.

Spiegel Ernestina M, bde 36 Nirdlinger av.

Spiegel Frederick C, res 100 Broadway.

Spiegel Mrs F C, milliner 100 Broadway, res same.

Spiegel Gottfried E, grocer 100 Broadway, res 36 Nirdlinger av.

Spiegel Gustav, Boots and Shoes, 132 Broadway, res 6 Jones.

Sp ege Hanna (wid August), res 40 Wall.

Spiegel J Ernst Jr, Books, School Supplies, News Depot, Cigars, Tobacco and Candies 103 Broadway, bds 233 W De Wald.

Spiegel Sophia (wid August), res 40 Wall.

Spiegel Wm A, tuner Ft W O Co, res 315 W Jefferson.

Spielmann Jacob, lab Bass F & M Wks, bds 149 Hugh.
Spielmann Mary (wid Peter), res 149 Hugh.
Spielmann Victor, laborer, bds 149 Hugh.
Spillner Charles F, policeman, res 119 John.
Spindler August, sawyer, bds 104 Mechanic.
Spindler Emil, laborer, bds 104 Mechanic.
Spindler Henry, laborer, bds 104 Mechanic.
Spindler Jacob, lab Bass Wks, res 56 Maumee rd.
Spindler Peter, clk, bds 56 Maumee rd.
Spitler Burton A. clk Ind Furn Co, bds 66 Wells.
Spitler Ernest W, driver Ind Furn Co, bds 66 Wells.
Spitler Gertrude M. bds 66 Wells.
Spitler Levi, res 66 Wells.
Spoltman Frank, car bldr Penn Co, res 102 Smith.
Sponhauer Mrs Mary, bds 266 E Creighton av.
Sponhauer Weidler S (Mossman, Yarnelle & Co), res 43
   Union.
Sportsman's Emporium, John Trautman
   Propr, 58 E Main. (*See page 87.*)
Sprandel Mrs Margaret H, furnished rooms, 55 E Wayne.
Sprandel Wm F, attendant School for F M Y, res 55 E
   Wayne.
Sprandel Wm F jr, clk H Hartman & Bros, bds 55 E Wayne
Sprang Ella D, student, bds 136 Jackson.
Spring Beach Mineral Water, Martin
   Detzer Sole Agent, 260 Calhoun. Tel 269.
Springer Alice, opr, bds 103 Mechanic.
Springer Charles, res 346 Broadway.
Springer Clarence B, carp, bds 7 Indiana av.
Springer Elizabeth M (wid Henry L), res 563 Calhoun.
Springer Frederick W, laborer, bds 129 Walton av.
Springer Guy C. boilermkr Bass Wks, res 57½ Lassalle.
Springer Harry C, carpet weaver S Reehling, bds 563
   Calhoun.
Springer Henry B, cigarmkr, res 33 E Wayne
Springer Helen (wid Horatio), bds 10 Jackson.
Springer Lavina (wid Jacob), res 103 Mechanic.
Springer Loran, carpenter, res 7 Indiana av.
Springer Monroe, sawyer, res 7 Frederick.
Springer Ralph W, brakeman, res 10 Jackson.
Springer Samuel C, brakeman N Y, C & St L R R, res 8
   Jackson.
Sprinkle Milton O, actionmkr Ft W O Co, bds 60 W Pon-
   tiac.
Sproat Alexander D, agent, res 38 Marion.

Sproat Clarence E, mach Paragon Mnfg Co, bds 38 Marion.
Sproat Hattie, waitress, bds 263 Calhoun.
Sproat James A, laborer, bds 38 Marion.
Sproat Wm W, res n s Spring 2 w of Franklin av.
Sprong Norman A, ins agt, res 90 E Washington.
Sprouts Wm, huckster, res n s Spring 2 w of Franklin av.
Sprunger Minnie, bkbndr, bds 130 Wells.
Sprunger Wilhelmina, bkbndr Ft Wayne Book Bindery, bds 130 Wells.
Spuhler Wm H, butcher E Rich. res 9 Mary.
Spurrier Dennis D. died June 16th, 1894.
Spurrier Gertrude E, clerk, bds 141 Force.
Spurrier Melinda J (wid Dennis), res 141 Force.
Squires Grant F, helper Bass Wks, res 37 Force.
Sriner Henry C, carp, bds 67 Swinney av.
Sriner Mary E (wid John), res 67 Swinney av.
Sriner Ola, dressmaker, bds 67 Swinney av.
Stace Alfred W, grocer, 33 E Main, res 80 Erie.
Stace Arthur A, clk A W Stace, bds 80 Erie.
Stack Frederick, brakeman, res 86 Lasselle.
Stack Katie, domestic 229 W Wayne.
Stack Patrick, bds 18 McClellan.
Stacy Frank B, brakeman N Y, C & St L R R, bds 79 Boone.
Staedtler Margaret (wid Christian P), bds 207 High.
Stafford Charles, student, bds 197 W Superior.
Stafford Elmer N, asst bkkpr Pickard Bros, bds 273 E Lewis.
Stafford Martin, engr Penn Co, res 273 E Lewis.
Staffy Grace, bds 27 E 3d.
Stahl Annie, bds 260 Clinton.
Stahl Bertha, teacher Holton Avenue School, bds 127 E Main.
Stahl Charles, bds 62 N Harrison.
Stahl Charles C, lab Penn Co, bds 260 Clinton.
Stahl Charles F, clk R M S, bds 49 Charles.
Stahl Christian F, lab Penn Co, res 49 St Martin's.
Stahl C Frederick, lab Penn Co, res 49 Charles.
Stahl Emma, seamstress, bds 74 Wilt.
Stahl James M, agent, res 39 Pine.
Stahl John H, carpenter, bds 260 Clinton.
Stahl John J, student, bds 127 E Main.
Stahl L Jennie, dressmkr, bds 39 Pine.
Stahl Olie, bds 260 Clinton.
Stahl Perry I, driver, bds 260 Clinton.

Stahl Reuben, res 100 E Lewis.

Stahl Sarah J (wid John), teacher Harmer School, res 127 E Main.

Stahl Wm, bds 49 St Martin's.

Stahl Wm G, letter carrier P O, res 440 Lafayette.

Stahler Charles L, res e s Piqua av, s of city limits.

Stahlhut Charles W, driver Powers & Barnett, bds 4 Hendricks.

Stahlhut Christian W, laborer, bds 4 Hendricks.

Stahlhut Elizabeth S, bds 4 Hendricks.

Stahlhut Frederick, teamster, res 4 Hendricks.

Stahlhut Frederick C, driver Powers & Barnett, bds 4 Hendricks.

Stahlhut Henry W, mach Ind Mach Wks, bds 4 Hendricks

Stahlhut John C, capt Engine Co No 4, res 71 Maumee rd.

Stahlhut Lizzie, domestic 234 W Berry.

Stahlhut Wm, teamster, bds 535 E Washington.

Stahn George, draughtsman Penn Co, res 83 Monroe.

Stahn Oswald (Stahn & Heinrich), res 127 Montgomery.

Stahn & Heinrich (Oswald Stahn, Louis A Heinrich), Books and Stationery, 116 Calhoun.

Staiger Fredericka, domestic 159 W Washington.

Staiger Rose, domestic 241 W Jefferson.

Staley Arthur H, brakeman N Y, C & St L R R, res 313 W Main.

Stalf Leonard, laborer, res 8 Huffman.

Stalf Louis, carp Ind Mach Wks, bds 88 Hanna.

Stalker John G, res e s Brooklyn av n of Poor Farm.

Stamets Zenith H, student, rms 107 W Main.

Stammer Anna, domestic 83 E Jefferson.

Stamp Thomas, blksmith, res 28 Melita.

Stanbury Benjamin R, hoseman Hose Co No 1, res 86 E Main.

Standard Oil Co, Marion C King Mngr, Columbia City rd, Junction N Y, C & St L R R, and G R & I R R. Tel 169.

Standard Wheel Co, office and branch wks s e cor Lafayette and Wabash R R. Tel 146.

Standish Seymour, teacher Ft Wayne Conservatory of Music, res 69 Douglas av.

Staneky Harvey, lab Standard Wheel Co, bds 151 Union.

Staneky Mary (wid John), bds 151 Union.

Staneky Millard, miller Mayflower Milling Co, res 110 Chicago.

626   R. L. POLK & CO.'S

Stanford Jeremiah, lab Penn Co, res n s Eckart lane 1 e of Hanna.

Stanford John P, lab Louis Rastetter & Son, bds n s Eckart lane 1 e of Hanna.

Stanford Louis A, lab, res n s Eckart lane 1 e of Hanna.

Stanger, *see also Stenger.*

Stanger Alexander W, laborer, bds 599 Lafayette.

Stanger Henry, laborer, res 599 Lafayette.

Stanger Jacob, cooper, bds 599 Lafayette.

Stanger Katie M, domestic, bds 599 Lafayette.

Stanley Chauncey, carriage maker, res 45 Miner.

Stanley Emma, teacher Clay School, bds 45 Miner.

Stanley Grant, brakeman N Y, C & St L R R, bds 335 W Main.

Stanley Marion, bds 45 Miner.

Stanley Walter L, brakeman N Y, C & St L R R, bds 30 Runnion av.

Stanton Eliza A (wid Charles), bds 59 Maumee rd.

Stanton John W, engr W B Phillips, res 359 E Washington

Stanton Patrick S, asst supt Metropolitan Life Ins Co, bds 39 W Washington.

Stanton Wm O, fireman, bds 59 Maumee rd.

Stapff Bruno, knitter, res 72 Cherry.

Stapleford Albert E, clk N Y, C & St L R R, bds 24 Columbia av.

Stapleford Charles E, car inspr, N Y, C & St L R R, res 24 Columbia av.

Stapleford Henry T, Agent Summit City Buggy Co and National Safe and Lock Co, also Dealer in Baled Hay, Straw and Mill Feed 47 E Columbia, res 226 W Creighton av. Tel 452.

Stapleford Lucien P, auctioneer 39 E Main, res 152 E Wayne.

Stapleford Thomas R, ironwkr Penn Co, res 246 Calhoun.

Staples J Logan, fireman N Y, C & St L R R, bds 35 4th.

Staples Thomas L, Propr International Business College and School of Shorthand and Typewriting, Schmitz Blk, res 64 E Jefferson.

Stapleton Charles, teamster, res 177 Calhoun.

Stapleton James, conductor, bds Lake Shore Hotel.

Stapleton John, teamster, rms 177 Calhoun.

Stapleton Robert F, laborer, res 104 Huffman.

Star Charles, laborer, bds 63 Grand.

Star Iron Tower Co, J H Bass pres, H G Olds vice-pres, P A Randall sec. R T McDonald treas, mnfrs towers for electric lighting, foot of Wells and Nickel Plate R R. Tel 71.

Star Union Line (Fast Freight), H M Quicksell Agent, 3 and 4 Trentman Bldg. Tel 154.

Stark Mrs Caroline, bds 48 Taylor.

Stark Erasmus, laborer, res 23 Nirdlinger av.

Stark Frances, seamstress, bds 10 Force.

Stark Frank J, bartender F H Meyer, bds 10 Force.

Stark John, molder Bass Wks, bds 10 Force.

Stark John M, mach Ft W Elec Corp, res 12 Fairfield av.

Stark Martin, lab Penn Co, res 10 Force.

Starke Charles, shoemkr, res w s St Mary's av 1 n of Lake.

Starke Christian, carp Penn Co. res 158 Rockhill.

Starke Mary, domestic 232 W Wayne.

Starkel Bert, clk L S & M S Ry, bds 137 Cass.

Starkel Frank H, chief clk L S & M S Ry, res 137 Cass.

Starkel Mary, bds 137 Cass.

Starkey Frederick, boltmkr Penn Po, res 35 Orchard.

Starkey Frederick W, removed to Cleveland, O.

Starkey George S, bkkpr, bds 315 W Main.

Starkey Hannah A (wid Orlando L), res 102 E Main.

Starkey Jacob B, laborer. res 315 W Main.

Starkey Mary R, bds 35 Orchard.

Starkey Wm, bds 38 Orchard.

Starr Frederick C, trav agt, res 157 W Berry.

Staszak Anton, lab Bass Wks, res 267 Hanna.

Staub Alexander H, stoves, 15 E Columbia, res 189 Ewing

Staub George W, tinner, res 93 W Superior.

Staub Joseph J, machinist, bds 93 W Superior.

Staudacher George, res 43 Wilt.

Stauffer Emil, cutter G Stauffer, bds 66 E Williams

Stauffer Emma (wid August), attendant Orphans' Home of the Reformed Church.

Stauffer Gottlieb, merchant tailor, 214 Calhoun, res 66 E Williams.

Stauffer Paulina, bds 66 E Williams.

Staunton, *see Stanton.*

Stauter Mary I (wid John L), rms 27 E Creighton av.

Steadman Wm S, condr N Y, C & St L R R, bds 22 Boone

Stebbins James C, driver Herman Berghoff Brewing Co, bds 509 E Washington.

Stecher Charles J, lab, res 54 Buchanan.

Stecher Frederick C, clk Meyer Bros & Co, bds 54 Buchanan.
Steck Frederick, brakeman, res 86 Lasselle.
Steckbeck Wm J, cigarmkr, 110 E Creighton av, bds 447 Lafayette.
Steedley Charles F, driver, bds 36 Hayden.
Steedley James A, driver, bds 36 Hayden.
Steedley James P, junk, res 36 Hayden.
Steedley Mrs Julia, res 36 Hayden.
Steedley Wm P, molder, bds 36 Hayden.
Steele Anna, domestic 236 W Berry.
Steele Clarence D, motorman, bds 499 E Wayne.
Steele Martin, fitter Ft Wayne Gas Co, res 33 Walton av.
Steele T Johnson, stock buyer, res 69 Grant av.
Steen, see also Stein.
Steen Elizabeth (wid Joseph), res 596 Calhoun.
Steenman Mary, domestic 160 Harmer.
Steffey Alexander, lab S Bash & Co, res 62 N Harrison.
Stefler David, engr N Y, C & St L R R, bds 17 Boone.
Stege August, helper Penn Co, res 239 Smith.
Stegemeyer Catherine (wid Wm), res 88 Summit.
Stegemeyer Clara, domestic 76 W Berry.
Stegemeyer Jacob, bds e s Abbott 1 s of Pontiac.
Stegemeyer Minnie L, dressmkr, bds 88 Summit.
Steger Albert H, clk R Steger & Co, res 98 E Jefferson.
Steger Daniel G, cigarmkr, bds 159 Hanna.
Steger-Gouty Cycle Co, Steger & Gouty proprs, bicycles, 126 Calhoun.
Steger Gustav C E (Steger-Gouty Cycle Co), bds 150 Montgomery.
Steger John N, laborer, res 228 Force.
Steger Louis C G, student, bds 150 Montgomery.
Steger Rudolph (R Steger & Co), res 150 Montgomery.
Steger R & Co (Rudolph Steger), Hardware, 126 Calhoun. Tel 440.
Stegner Charles A (Rehling & Stegner), res 350 E Washington.
Stegner Peter, mach, rms 188 Calhoun.
Steib Connie, opr, bds 334 Lafayette.
Steib Jacob, molder, res 334 Lafayette.
Steib Joseph, molder, bds 334 Lafayette.
Steib Philip, cupola tender, res 334 Lafayette.
Steigerwald Eva, bds 179 Gay.
Steigerwald John, turner, res 150 Smith.
Steigerwald John A, wood turner, bds 63 Madison.

Stein, *see also Steen.*
Stein Anthony, lab, bds 44 W Butler.
Stein Arthur C, mach C F A Stein, bds 57 Winter.
Stein Barbara (wid Peter), res 122 Maumee rd.
Stein Bessie A, bds 318 Harrison.
Stein Carl, laborer. bds 53 Winter.
Stein Charles F A, General Machinist and Model Maker 57 Winter, res same. *(See p 630.)*
Stein Charles F A jr, mach C F A Stein, bds 57 Winter.
Stein Clara A, seamstress, bds 335½ Hanna.
Stein Daniel L, car bldr Penn Co, res 318 Harrison.
Stein Freda S. clk A Mergentheim, bds 25 Boone.
Stein Henry W, laborer, res 165 E Taber.
Stein Joseph N, car bldr Penn Co, res 335½ Hanna.
Stein Louisa, bds 44 W Butler.
Stein Mary V, opr S M Foster, bds 335½ Hanna.
Stein Minnie, bds 44 W Butler.
Stein Peter, molder Bass F & M Wks, res 157 Hanna.
Stein Robert J, car bldr Penn Co, res s s New Haven av 3 e of Pioneer av.
Stein Mrs Sophia, bds 25 Boone.
Stein Wilhelmina (wid Jacob), res 44 W Butler.
Stein Wm D, messgr Dis Tel Co, bds 47 Barr.
Steinacher Benjamin T, butcher, bds 112 Fairfield av.
Steinacher Edward J, butcher, bds 112 Fairfield av.
Steinacher Mrs Frances, res 112 Fairfield av.
Steinacher Frank J, clerk, bds 112 Fairfield av.
Steinacher George W, grocer, 105 Maumee rd, res 103 same.
Steinacher Henry A, candymkr, bds 112 Fairfield av.
Steinau Charles B, shoemkr, res 71 Wells.
Steinau Edward H, clk C J Pierre, bds 71 Wells.
Steinau Lillie A, clk C J Pierre, bds 71 Wells.
Steinbacher Henry X, helper Bass Wks, res 47 Lasselle.
Steinbacher John H, fireman, res 1 Walnut.
Steinbacher Veronica, bds 72 Melita.
Steinborn John L, laborer, res 223 Walton av.
Steinbrenner, *see also Stoneburner.*
Steinbrenner Frederick J, mach hd, res 271 W De Wald.
Steinbrenner Henry J, bds 271 W DeWald.
Steinbrunner Anna M, clerk, bds 24 W Williams.
Steinbrunner Catherine J, stenogr Ft W Elec Corp, bds 24 W Williams.
Steinbrunner Mamie, bkkpr, bds 24 W Williams.
Steinbrunner Robert, res 24 W Williams.

Steinbrunner Rosa, dressmkr, 24 W Williams, bds same.
Steinhaur Emanuel, meats, 109 Barthold, bds 34 E Pontiac
Steinhauser, see also Stienhauser.
Steinhauser John, lab Penn Co, res 72 Ohio.
Steinhauser Nicholas, mineral waters. 29 Miner, res same.
Steinke August R, sawyer Ft W O Co, bds 61 Oakley.
Steinke Augusta, bds 61 Oakley.
Steinke Clara, domestic 201 E Wayne.
Steinke Edward J, wiper Penn Co, res 61 Oakley.
Steinke Emil, bds 11 Gay.
Steinke Julius, laborer. res 11 Gay.
Steinke Louisa C, clk F W Wefel, bds 144 High.
Steinman Catherine (wid Jacob). died July 12, 1894.
Steinmann Abraham J, laborer, bds 230 W Main.
Steinmann John, laborer, bds 439 Broadway.
Steiss Bros (John G and Charles J F), barbers, 41 W Main
Steiss Charles J F (Steiss Bros), bds 45 Archer av.
Steiss Frederick W, cooper, bds 45 Archer av.
Steiss Gustav H, cooper, bds 45 Archer av.
Steiss John G (Steiss Bros), bds 45 Archer av.
Steiss Mary (wid John G), res 45 Archer av.
Steller Charles W, butcher, bds 208 Broadway.
Steller Conrad, lab Hoffman Bros, res 208 Broadway.
Steller Edward N, laborer, bds 208 Broadway.
Steller Rosa E, bds 208 Broadway.
Stellhorn Arminda, bds 117 Wall.
Stellhorn August, res 28 South Wayne av.
Stellhorn Charles, stationer, 146 Calhoun, res 133 W Superior.
Stellhorn Frederick W, clk F J Miller, bds 2 Griffith.
Stellhorn Frederick W, lab Ft W Elec Corp, bds 28 South Wayne av.
Stellhorn J Henry, commr Allen County, res 168 W Creighton av.
Stellhorn Lizzie F, domestic 179 W Berry.

Stellhorn Sophia (wid Henry W), bds 22 Madison.

Stellhorn Rev Theodore J C, pastor Grace German Evangelican Lutheran Church, res 260 Gay.

Stellhorn Wm, farmer, res e s Wayne Trace 1 s of R R.

Stellhorn Wm H, carpenter, bds 2 Griffith.

Stemen Christian A, condr N Y, C & St L R R, bds 63 Boone.

Stemen Christian B, dean Ft Main College of Medicine, phys 94 Calhoun, res 25 Broadway. Tel 8.

Stemen George B, phys 300 W Main, res same. Tel 321

Stemen George C, Physician 6 White's Block, res 493 Calhoun   Tel office 398, res 15.

Stemen Harriet F, physician 25 Broadway, bds same.

Stemen Margaret L, stenographer, bds 25 Broadway.

Stemmler Henry, cigarmkr F J Gruber, res 131 Wells.

Stender Henry H, laborer, res 2 Warsaw.

Stender Henry W, laborer, bds 2 Warsaw.

Stenger, *see also Stanger.*

Stenger Frank, blacksmith, res 111 Force.

Stenger Peter, Machinist and Toolmaker 18 N Ewing, res 188 Calhoun.   (*See left top lines.*)

Stenner Clara M, clk L Wolf & Co, bds 18 N Harrison.

Stenner Loretta E O, bds 18 N Harrison.

Stenson Morris A (Engle and Stenson), res 362 W Main.

Stentz Henry, cigarmaker, res 179 E Washington.

Stephan Anthony F, foreman L Deither & Bro, res 99 St Mary's av.

Stephan Augusta, bds 32 Wall.

Stephan Edward W, truckman Penn Co, res 32 Wall.

Stephan Elizabeth (wid Philip), bds 42 Stophlet.

Stephan Emily A, bds n e cor Winter and Pontiac.

Stephan Ernest F, clerk, res 230 Thomas.

Stephan Frederick W, mach Penn Co, bds n e cor Winter and Pontiac.

Stephan Ida, seamstress, bds 230 Thomas.

Stephan Julius C, clk Penn Co, res 32 Wall.

Stephan Lena A, bds n e cor Winter and Pontiac.

Stephan Wm F, draughtsman Penn Co, res n e cor Winter and Pontiac.

Stephans George A, clk Seavey Hardware Co, bds 149 W Washington.

Stephens, *see also Stevens.*

Stephens Alexander E, laborer, res e s Fletcher av 1 n of Wabash R R.

Stephens Andrew J, brakeman N Y, C & St L R R, bds 213 W Main.
Stephens James M, res 58 E Wayne.
Sterling Edward, barber, 61 E Berry, res 49 Rivermet av.
Sterling Mrs N M, bds 49 Rivermet av.
Sterling Reynolds, pressman Archer Ptg House, rms 40 Madison.
Sternberger Martin, helper Keller & Braun, res 32 W 5th.
Stetler Charles E, mngr Postal Tel Co, res 52 Spy Run av.
Stetter Frederick J, actionmkr Ft W O Co, res 35 Nirdlinger av.
Stetter John P, lab L Rastetter & Son, res 42 Nirdlinger av
Stetter Louis J, laborer, res 42 Nirdlinger av.
Stetter Mary (wid Louis), bds 42 Nirdlinger av.
Stetzer Catherine, dressmkr, bds 352 E Washington.
Stetzer Helen. dressmkr, bds 352 E Washington,
Stetzer Joseph, carpenter, res 42 Force.
Stetzer Margaret, dressmkr, bds 352 E Washington.
Stetzer Peter H, mach hd Penn Co, res 352 E Washington.
Steup Gottlieb C, fireman Engine Co No 3, res 106 W Jefferson.
Steup Henry A, bds 187 Griffith.
Steup Louis, capt Engine Co No 3, bds 106 W Jefferson.
Stevens, see also Stephens.
Stevens Arthur B, condr Penn Co, bds 320 Calhoun.
Stevens Catherine (wid Jacob), res 25 Miner.
Stevens George H, engr N Y, C & St L R R, res 106 Jackson.
Stevens George W, horseshoer, bds 163 E Jefferson.
Stevens James D, laborer, res 224 Calhoun.
Stevens John K, molder Bass Wks, res 66 Hugh.
Stevens Joseph. fireman Penn Co. bds 20 McClellan.
Stevens Joseph P, laborer, rms 224 Calhoun.
Stevens Nelson L, blksmith C Ehrmann, res 98 W Superior.
Stevens Sarah E (wid Henry), res 356 Calhoun.
Stevens Thomas, bds 173 W Wayne.
Stevens Walter W, bds 163 E Jefferson.
Stevens Wm B. teamster, rms 224 Calhoun.
Stevenson Wm L (W L Stevenson & Co), res 132 Broadway.
Stevenson Wm L & Co (Wm L Stevenson, Samuel Erington), barbers, 247 Calhoun.
Stewart Anna (wid Charles J), res 37 E DeWald.
Stewart Bessie L, clerk, bds 62 W Lewis.

Stewart Calvin M, mach hd J Klett & Sons, res 20 W 3d.
Stewart Charles, blksmith Penn Co, res 37 Hough.
Stewart Charles A, molder, bds 37 Hough.
Stewart Frank W, trav agt Root & Co, res 162 W Creighton av.
Stewart George P, train despr Penn Co, res 214 W De Wald.
Stewart John V (col'd), porter, bds 71 Monroe.
Stewart Joseph H, engr Penn Co, res 169 Montgomery.
Stewart J C, brakeman G R & I·R R, bds 352 W Washington.
Stewart Rev J M, Pastor St Paul M E Church, res 134 Walton av.
Stewart Mrs Maria, res 134 W Berry.
Stewart Martha A (wid Robert M), res 62 W Lewis.
Stewart May C, clk People's Store, bds 37 E De Wald.
Stewart U Hugh, asst to attr general, 1 and 2 Arcade Bldg, bds 157 W Berry.
Stewart Wm C, plumber Seavey Hdwre Co, bds Hoffmann House.
Stewart Wm D, clerk, res 400 E Wayne.
Stewart Wm H, res 434 E Wayne.
Sthair, see also St Hair.
Sthair Archie S, res 45 Webster.
Sthair Frank W, lab, bds Washington Twp.
Sthair George A, clk Fisher Bros, res 40 Force.
Sthair John H, tuck pointer, bds 40 Force.
Sthair Wm, collector, bds 40 Force.
Stickle Frederick, clk J B White, bds 69 Archer av.
Stickle Jacob, laborer, res 69 Archer av.
Stiefel Caroline (wid Joseph), bds 204 W Berry.
Stiegler Ottomar, knitter, bds 9 Park av.
Stienhauser, see also Steinhauser.
Stienhauser Frederick A E, wood carver, bds 31 Taylor.
Stienhauser Mary (wid Henry), res 31 Taylor.
Stienhauser Matilda, operator, bds 31 Taylor.
Stienhauser Wm J, blacksmith, res 31 Taylor.
Stier Arthur A, plumber P E Cox, bds 333 E Wayne.
Stier Mrs Catherina, milliner 32 Clinton, res 333 E Wayne
Stier Charles J, clk P E Cox, bds 333 E Wayne.
Stier Clara G, died Sept 15th, 1894.
Stier Edith T, milliner, bds 333 E Wayne.
Stier Edward A, appr Bass Wks, bds 337 E Lewis.
Stier Frank G, molder Bass Wks, res 508 E Lewis.
Stier Frederick G, molder Bass Wks, bds 337 E Lewis.

634 R. L. POLK & CO.'S

Stier George A, bartender, res 268 Calhoun.
Stier George J, res 333 E Wayne.
Stier Henry, res 106 Lafayette.
Stier Henry A, carpenter, res 94 Buchanan.
Stier Henry J, clk People's Store, res 106 Lafayette.
Stier Jacob J, foreman Bass Wks, res 337 E Lewis.
Stier John, res 188 E Washington.
Stier John A, barber 303 Hanna, res 331 same.
Stier John C, bartender, res 16 W Main.
Stier Julius J, janitor Library Hall. res 208 Lafayette.
Stier Justina, operator, bds 94 Buchanan.
Stier Sophia, bds 106 Lafayette.
Stier Wm A, saloon 135 Wallace, res 94 Buchanan.
Stierheim Estelle, stenogr S F Bowser & Co, bds 83
    Lasselle
Stierheim Frank, printer, rms 135 Madison.
Stiff George, laborer, bds 28 E Columbia.
Still Smith, machinist, res 135 Madison.
Stillgus James D (col'd), cook, res 68 Murray.
Stilson George W (Seavey Hardware Co), res 149 W
    Washington.
Stimmel Charles, fitter Ft W Gas Co, res 297 E Wayne.
Stinger Charles F, stonecutter, res 11 Oak.
Stinner Bernard A, plumber, res 92 Lake av.
Stinner John, sheet iron wkr Gerding & Aumann Bros,
    bds 92 Lake av.
Stinson Moss A, laborer, res 362 W Main.
Stirk Harry W, bkkpr E H Coombs, bds 18 Huffman.
Stirk Miriam A, bds 18 Huffman.
Stirk Samuel W, cash N Y, C & St L R R, res 18 Huffman
Stites Harvey H, barber. The Randall, rms 155 Mont-
    gomery.
Stittzworth Susan. rms 30 E Columbia.
Stock Alexander F, lab Hoffman Bros, bds 128 Greeley.
Stock George A, laborer, res 65 Wells.
Stock Martin J H, carp Horton Mnfg Co, bds 239 Madison
Stock Paul, clk H D Niemann, bds 60 Division.
Stockbridge Charles A, letter carrier P O, res 401 Web-
    ster.
Stockbridge Mary P, bds 45 Shawnee av.
Stockbridge Nathaniel P, res 45 Shawnee av.
Stockbridge Nathaniel W, trav agt, bds 401 Webster.
Stocking Alice M, bkkpr S M Foster, bds 123 Rivermet av
Stocking Henry K, res 123 Rivermet av.
Stockmann Charles H, cooper, res 44 E 4th.

Stockmann Charles P F, clk Fleming Mnfg Co, bds 44 E 4th.

Stocks George C, car repr Wabash R R, res 14 Bass.

Stockwell James S, engr G R & I R R, res 96 W Butler.

Stodel Emma (wid Gustav), saloon e s Broadway 2 s of toll gate, res same.

Stoehr Frederick, carpenter, res 502 Hanna.

Stoehr John, saloon 179 Calhoun, res same.

Stoehrel Herman, mach Wayne Knitting Mills, res 7 Park av.

Stoetzer, *see Stetzer.*

Stokes Edward M, engr G R & I R R, res 76 Brackenridge.

Stokes Granville J, driver L P Scherer, res 336 E Washington.

Stoll Amelia R, dressmaker, bds 74 Nelson.

Stoll Anna K, bds 25 2d.

Stoll Anthony J, carpenter, res 74 Nelson.

Stoll Caroline G, dressmkr 29 Wefel, res same.

Stoll Charles W, lab Ft W Elec Corp, bds 46 Walnut.

Stoll Conrad, died December 23, 1894.

Stoll Emil, cabtmkr Ft W O Co, res 135 W De Wald.

Stoll Frederick C, baker, bds 46 Walnut.

Stoll Frederick G, coppersmith Wabash R R, res 46 Walnut.

Stoll George J, appr Wabash R R, bds 46 Walnut.

Stoll Henry, res 25 2d.

Stoll Henry C, policeman, res 11 Ohio.

Stoll Martin, laborer, res 190 Smith.

Stoll Michael H, bds 74 Nelson.

Stoll Otto H, helper Bass F & M Wks, res n e cor South Wayne av and Packard av.

Stolte Charles A, motorman, res 72 Cherry.

Stone Cora M, bds 1 Riverside av.

Stone Frank, condr N Y, C & St L R R, bds 359 W Main.

Stone Lester E, paperhanger, res 420 E Wayne.

Stone Mrs Margaret E, bds 46 E Pontiac.

Stone Victoria, student, bds 154 Harrison.

Stonebraker Wm H, shaper Ft Wayne Furn Co, bds Lake Shore Hotel.

Stonebrook Thomas G, painter Penn Co, bds 73 Cass.

Stoneburner, *see also Steinbrenner.*

Stoneburner Elias, painter, res 228 Walton av.

Stoneburner Franklin E, bds 228 Walton av.

Stonecifer Benjamin F, condr L E & W R R, res 43 E De Wald.
Stonecifer Harry L, student, bds 43 E DeWald.
Stonecifer Herbert L, student, bds 43 E De Wald.
Stonehouse Louis, fireman, bds 223 Lafayette.
Stoner Arden E, brakeman, rms 405 W Main.
Stoner Daniel W, teamster, res w s Home av 3 n of Wayne Trace.
Stopher Byron M, clk Hoffman Bros, bds 278 W Jefferson
Stopher Harry C, clk Hoffman Bros, bds 278 W Jefferson
Stopher Sarah A (wid Joseph D), res 278 W Jefferson.
Stoppenhagen Charles, car bldr Penn Co, res 33 Hugh.
Stoppenhagen Christian F, moved to Friedheim, Ind.
Storch Mrs Elizabeth, nurse Concordia College, res 180 Hayden.
Storch Wilhelminie, bds 180 Hayden.
Storch Wm, bartender The Herman Berghoff Brewing Co, bds 180 Hayden.
Storms Cora, hairdresser, rms 47 Hayden.
Storms Wm (col'd), waiter, rms 12 Lafayette.
Story Harriet (wid James), res 16 W Superior.
Stotz Ulrich, saloon, 21 E Main, res 190 W Berry.
Stotzky Samuel, bds 393 E Lewis.
Stouder, see also Studer.
Stouder Frank E, mngr Masonic Temple Theater, res 148 Clinton.
Stouder Harvey F, bds n s Pioneer av 1 e of New Haven av
Stouder Henry G, engr N Y, C & St L R R, res 205 W Main.
Stouder Jacob H, res 32 E Wayne.
Stouder Jacob M, clk Pfeiffer and Schlatter, res e s Spy Run av 7 n of Riverside av.
Stouder Jennie, bds 32 E Wayne.
Stouder Leon D, janitor Masonic Temple Theater, bds 32 E Wayne.
Stouder May M, bds 30 W Williams.
Stouder Wallace W, mach hd Olds' Wagon Wks, res 30 W Williams.
Stouder Wm W, laborer, res 43 Elm.
Stouder & Smith (Frank E Stouder, Nathaniel S Smith), bill posters Masonic Temple Theater.
Stout George W, deputy sheriff, res 155 Lake av.
Stout Ira, pump man G R & I R R, bds 266 Calhoun.
Stout Nellie, trimmer J A Armstrong & Co, rms 89 W Berry
Stover George W, foreman, res 335 W Main.

Stow Eliakim, bds 119 E Main.
Strack Desdemona, bds 237 W Berry.
Strack Edward W, hardwood lumber, 52 Calhoun, res 237 W Berry. Tel 7.
Strack Elizabeth, bds 33 W Washington.
Strack May, dressmkr, 131 Broadway, res same.
Strack S Emma, seamstress, bds 131 Broadway.
Strader Edith, bds 109 Thomas.
Strader Isaac, driver S F Bowser & Co, res 109 Thomas.
Strader Wm A, lab S F Bowser & Co, res 109 Thomas.
Stradley Elsie (wid Stuart), housekeeper 63 Winter.
Straight Edith M (wid Wm P), dressmkr 54 E Washington, res same.
Strain Frank A, carver Ft W O Co, bds s s W Leith 1 w of Harrison.
Strain John, carver Ft W O Co. bds s s W Leith 1 w of Harrison.
Strain Maggie (wid John), res s s W Leith 1 w of Harrison
Strangemann Conrad P, carp Wm Moellering & Co, res 89 Monroe.
Strangemann Herman C, porter Gross & Pellen's, res 62 Erie.
Strasburg Carl, bds 119 Wilt.
Strasburg Christian E, bds 119 Wilt.
Strasburg Christopher F, res 119 Wilt.
Strasburg Ferdinand W, clk Root & Co, res 74 Wall.
Strasburg Fredericka, domestic 130 W Berry.
Strasburg Minnie, domestic 130 W Main.
Strasburg Wm A, mach hd L Diether & Bro, res 74 Wilt.
Strasburg Wm F, trav agt, bds 119 Wilt.
Strass Emanuel, trav agt, res 74 W Jefferson.
Strass Emma A, bkkpr M Frank & Co, bds 74 W Jefferson.
Strass Isaac, res 50 W Lewis.
Strass Julia, bds 50 W Lewis.
Strass Rebecca, (wid Samuel), died March 10, 1895.
Strass Rebecca L, bds 74 W Jefferson.
Strasser George A, machinist, bds Robert Strasser.
Strasser George J, machinist, res 40 Lillie.
Strasser Henry, clk Wm Briggemann, bds 277 E Jefferson
Strasser Henry, fireman Penn Co, res 118 Fairfield av.
Strasser Robert, res e s Winter 2 s of Pontiac.
Straub Anthony F, candymdr Fox Br U S Baking Co, rms 231 E Wayne.
Straub Charles M Z, barber, bds 206 Broadway.

41

Straub Louis A, lab Ind Mach Wks, res 239 St Mary's av.
Straughan Jesse R, civil engineer, res 87 E Berry.
Straughan Jessie L, bds 87 E Berry.
Strawbridge Charles T, buyer Bass F & M Wks, res 355 E Wayne.
Strawn Byron A, photogr, res n e cor Broadway and Organ av.
Strayer Samuel, fireman N Y, C & St L R R, bds 335 W Main.
Strebig Charles V, engr Fox Br U S Baking Co, res 97 Hayden.
Strebig Isaac F, mach hd Anthong Wayne Mnfg Co, bds 97 Hayden.
Strebig John P, removed to St Louis, Mo.
Strebig Loretta M, bds 97 Hayden.
Strebig Wm B, cooper, res 101 Hayden.
Street Arthur O, fireman N Y, C & St L R R, bds 79 Boone.
Streetmeyer Mrs Caroline, res 68 W Jefferson.
Streich Gottlieb J, laborer, bds 199 Broadway.
Streicher Anna (wid Andrew), bds 35 Wefel.
Streicher George, barber, bds 47 Wells.
Streicher John, bartender, res 35 Wefel.
Streicher Wm J, saloon, 50 W Main, res same.
Streubel August F, carp Bass Wks, res 202 Force.
Strieder Christopher J, teacher, res 166 Barr.
Strieder Clara, bds 166 Barr.
Strieder Gottlieb C, collr White National Bank, bds 166 Barr
Strieder Paul T, clerk, bds 166 Barr.
Striker Mrs Amanda, res 108 Fairfield av.
Striker Tunis V, actionmkr Ft W O Co, res 58 W Pontiac.
Stringer Charles K, clk W Gas Const Co, bds 76 W De Wald.
Stringer Elza T, trav agt, res 76 W DeWald.
Stringer Estella C, bds 76 W DeWald.
Stringer Frederick O, trav agt, bds 76 W DeWald.
Stringer Samuel T, student, bds 76 W DeWald.
Stringham Sydney L, cook Ft Wayne Club, rms 68 W Main.
Stritmatter Charles B, clk M Frank & Co, bds 132 Clinton
Stritmatter Gustave, lab Penn Co, res 45 Force.
Stritmatter John, laborer, bds 22 Cochrane.
Strobel Wm C, bartender, bds 128 Cass.
Strock Benjamin F, foreman, res 125 W Williams.
Strock Mina, bds 125 W Williams.

Strock Raphael E, appr, bds 125 W Williams.
Strode Wm J, lab Hoffman Bros, bds 152 Greeley.
Strodel Albert, cigarmkr Lahmeyer Bros, bds 42 W 4th.
Strodel Annie (wid Matthias), res 42 W 4th.
Strodel Bertha, bds 42 W 4th.
Strodel Christian G, lab L Brames & Co, bds 42 W 4th.
Strodel Frank B, clk J G Strodel, bds 111 W 3d.
Strodel George J, policeman, bds 42 W 4th.
Strodel Herman, butcher E Rich & Son, rms 111 W 3d.
Strodel John G, Dealer in Cheese and Delicacies, 13 Harrison bet Columbia and Main, res 111 W 3d.
Strodel Otto F, bartender, bds 111 W 3d.
Strohm Jacob, helper Penn Co, res 108 W Butler.
Strohm Mary (wid George), bds 108 W Butler.
Strong Frederick, laborer, bds 15 Pearl.
Strong George A, sec Ft Wayne Newspaper Union, res Chicago, Ill.
Strong Harriet E (wid Melzar B), res 258 W Wayne.
Strong Jared C, res 34 Rivermet av.
Strong Josephine M, bds 34 Rivermet av.
Strong Louisa, bds 27 Madison.
Strong Louvie E, teacher Lakeside School, bds 34 Rivermet av.
Strong Thomas M, bds w s Calhoun 1 s of Cour.
Strope Frederick J, mach Penn Co, bds 27 Baker.
Strous Mrs C R, cook W R Frederick, bds 266 Calhoun.
Strouse David W, bds 324 W Main.
Strouse James G, laborer, bds 324 W Main.
Strube Adolph F, instrmkr Ft Wayne Elec Corp, res 28 Scott av.
Strubey Mary C (wid Charles), res 81 E Jefferson.
Struchen Edward J, laborer, res 191 Hanna.
Struchen Edward J, helper, bds 191 Hanna.
Strunz Christian G, res 99 E Berry.
Struver Lizzie, bds 66 E Main.
Struver Wm, grocer, 66 E Main, res same.
Struver Wm F, packer McDonald & Watt, bds 66 E Main.
Stuart John C, brakeman N Y, C & St L R R, res 352 W Washington.
Stubbs Mary H, teacher Westminister Seminary, bds 251 W Main.
Stubnatzy Elizabeth C (wid Ernest), bds 222 E Washington
Stubnatzy Emilie, housekeeper 260 Calhoun.
Stuck Jay, clerk, bds 234 Indiana av.
Stuck Solomon K, teamster, res 234 Indiana av.

Stude Ferdinand, teamster, res Washington twp.

Studer, *see also Stouder.*

Studer's Blk, 228–232 W Main.

Studer Annie J, bds 232 W Main.

Studer Hermenius L, saloon 232 W Main, res same.

Studer Joseph, engr N Y, C & St L R R. res 84 W 3d.

Studer Louis, laborer, res 134 Eliza.

Studer Mary A (wid Bernard), bds 189 E Wayne.

Studor Agnes M, bds 11 Monroe.

Studor Jerome J, clk L Wolf & Co, res 11 Monroe.

Stueckle Jacob, laborer, res 69 Archer av.

Stuermer Augusta (wid Wm), res 108 Maumee rd.

Stults Charles E, phys 83 Wells, res 81 same.

Stults Joseph E, phys 96 Wells, res same.

Stump Eli C, stenogr and notary J B Harper, 12 Bank Blk, res 21 Michael av.

Stump Frank I, brakeman N Y, C & St L R R, bds 190 W Berry.

Stumpf Jacob, principal St John's Lutheran School, res 203 W Washington.

Stumpf Martha, teacher Bloomingdale school, bds 228 W Superior.

Stumpp Louis, car repr Penn Co, res 33 Wall.

Sturgeon Arthur T, res 110 W Jefferson.

Sturgeon Mrs Mary R, boarding house, 110 W Jefferson.

Sturgis Alida K, bds 132 Wallace.

Sturgis Louis T, phys 360 Calhoun, res 132 Wallace. Tel 545.

Sturgis Mary R (wid Wm E), bds w s Spy Run av 1 n of Elizabeth.

Sturgis Sadie L, bds 132 Wallace.

Stute Ferdinand, res s s Coombs 2 w of New Haven av.

Stute Frederick, lab Penn Co, res 69 Home av.

Stutler David, engineer, bds 79 Boone.

Stutz Emma K, bds 50 W Washington.

Stutz John A, phys 50 W Washington, res same. Tel 342.

Stutzenberger Clara, seamstress, bds 383 E Washington.

Stutzenberger Frank A, patternmkr Ft W I Wks, bds 383 E Washington.

Stutzenberger Josephine (wid Frank), res 383 E Washington.

Subkowski Christina (wid John), res 42 John.

Subkowski Emil, laborer, bds 122 Buchanan.

Subkowski Flora (wid John), rms 42 John.

Subkowski Frederick, lab Bass Wks, res 122 Buchanan.

Subkowski Henry, lab Bass Wks. res 356 Force.
Subkowski Herman, lab Bass F & M Wks. rms 42 John.
Subkowski John, helper, res 50 Gay.
Such Emil, lab Rhinesmith & Simonson, res 23 E Leith.
Sudebrink Wm, car bldr Penn Co, res 445 Hanna.
Sudebrink Wm jr, clk G W Haiber, bds 445 Hanna.
Suedhoff Emma L, seamstress, bds 210 W Jefferson.
Suedhoff Henry E, clerk, res 210 W Jefferson,
Suedhoff Louise, domestic 232 W Wayne.
Suedhoff Wm G, bds 210 W Jefferson.
Suelzer Christian, baker. bds 297½ Hanna.
Suelzer F Wm, butcher J W Suelzer. bds 297½ Hanna.
Suelzer John (Freiburger & Suelzer), contractor 420 Hanna, res same.
Suelzer John W. meats 350 Calhoun, 422 Lafayette and 281 Hanna, res 297½ Hanna.
Suelzer Joseph, butcher J W Suelzer, rms 422 Lafayette.
Suelzer Peter, teamster J Suelzer, bds 420 Hanna.
Suelzer Wm, carp J Suelzer, res 268 Hanna.
Sukup Andrew, res 27 Lasselle.
Sukup Joseph A, molder, res 126 E Creighton av.
Sukup Peter, molder Bass Wks, bds 27 Lasselle.
Sullinger Solomon W, laborer, res 152 E Wayne.
Sullivan Alphonso, appr Kerr Murray Mnfg Co, bds 2 Grant.
Sullivan Andrew P, engr Wabash R R, res 2 Grant.
Sullivan Catherine (wid John), bds 73 Melita.
Sullivan Charles P, student, bds 31 W Columbia.
Sullivan Cornelius, watchman, res 23 Taylor.
Sullivan Cornelius T, mach hd, bds 23 Taylor.
Sullivan James P, lab Penn Co, res 7 Bass.
Sullivan John F, boiler inspr Penn Co, res 30 Walnut.
Sullivan Lizzie, bds 400 Clinton.
Sullivan Maggie M, bds 400 Clinton.
Sullivan Mamie, laundress, bds 400 Clinton.
Sullivan Mary, bds 23 Taylor,
Sullivan Mary (wid Patrick), res 400 Clinton.
Sullivan Mary A (wid Thomas F), res 195 W Main,
Sullivan Mary J, bds 195 W Main.
Sullivan Mary S, clerk, bds 2 Grant.
Sullivan Margaret M, bds 195 W Main.
Sullivan Michael, mach hd Penn Co, res 118 E Creighton av
Sullivan Nathaniel, canvasser, res s s French 6 w of Webster.
Sullivan Patrick J, conductor, bds 400 Clinton.

Sullivan Patrick S, flagman, bds 23 Taylor.
Sult George W, opr Ft W Gas Co, res 97 Wagner.
Sult Prudie, bds 84 Baker.
Summerbell Mrs Alice, teacher School for F M Y.
Summers, *see also Somers.*
Summers Ann (wid John), res 331 Lafayette.
Summers Edgar J, messenger, bds 39 Elm.
Summers Ella C, bds 47 Douglas av.
Summers Frank J, student, bds 47 Douglas av.
Summers James, saloon 262 Calhoun, res 47 Douglas av.
Summers Lida, domestic e s Spy Run av 3 n of Riverside av.
Summers Lizzie, student, bds 47 Douglas av.
Summers Mary A (wid John), res 39 Elm.
Summers Orrin V, bell boy, bds 39 Elm.
Summit City Bottling Works, L Brames & Co, Proprs, 123–127 Clay. *(See p 3).*
Summit City Hotel, R J Wilson propr, 3 Railroad.
Summit City Soap Works, Gustav A Berghoff propr, 2–16 Glasgow av.
Sunday Cary D, fireman, bds 18 McClellan.
Sunday Daniel D, finisher Ft W O Co. res 486 Fairfield av
Sunderland Charles S, mach Ft W Iron Wks, res 90 Dawson.
Sunderland John W, brakeman, res 177 W De Wald.
Sunderland Joseph E, cash Wabash R R, res 329 Calhoun.
Sundermann Mrs Sophia, res 197 Lafayette.
Sunley George, died November 19, 1894.
Sunley George T, laborer, res 61 Barthold.
Sunley Wm, mach hd Hoffman Bros, bds 61 Barthold.
Superior Court (Allen County), Hon C M Dawson judge, second floor of Court House.
Supple Mary, res 48 Baker.
Surrell Howard (Ryan & Surrell), bds 101 Barr.
Suter Albert S, carp, bds 507 Broadway.
Suter Arthur, lab Ft W Elec Corp, bds 507 Broadway.
Suter Celia M, bds 507 Broadway.
Suter Edward, contr, 507 Broadway, res same.
Suter Wm, brakeman G R & I R R, bds 80 Baker.
Suter Wm E, carpenter, res 509 Broadway.
Sutley Mary B (wid Harry), res 72 Nelson.
Sutley Wm D, carpenter, res 72 Nelson.
Sutorius Christian, brickmkr, res 267 Gay.
Sutorius Gottlieb L, bds 176 Oakland.
Sutorius Jacob F, helper Keller & Braun, res 176 Oakland

Sutorius Mary A, opr, bds 176 Oakland.
Suttemeyer Henry, lab Olds Wagon Wks, res 9 Jones.
Suttenfield Asa M, lab Hoffman Bros, res 223 W Superior.
Suttenfield Bird, teamster Hoffman Bros, res 217 W Superior.
Suttenfield Wm R, hostler C L Centlivre Brewing Co, bds n w cor Spy Run av and Edna.
Sutter Louisa, domestic s w cor Wells and Putnam.
Sutter Wm H, motorman, res 4 University.
Sutterlin Reinhardt, lab Bass Wks, res 86 Stophlet.
Sutton David C, lab, res 210 W Creighton av.
Sutton John, machinist, bds 64 W 5th.
Sutton Nancy (wid Daniel T), bds 35 E 4th.
Swager John, carpenter, res 30 Cochran.
Swager Loretta, starcher W B Philips, bds 30 Cochran.
Swager Peter S, bds 30 Cochran.
Swaidner Edwin J (Hohmann & Swaidner), res 225 E Wayne.
Swaidner Jacob W, propr Hedekin House, 25 Barr.
Swaidner John L, tel opr, bds 25 Barr.
Swain, *see also Swayne.*
Swain Belle, bds 120 W Creighton av.
Swain Carl P, trav agt S F Bowser & Co, bds 53 Winter.
Swain Charles J, lab, bds 120 W Creighton av.
Swain Charlotte (wid Jackson), bds 73 W De Wald.
Swain Elizabeth (wid Caleb P), res 53 Winter.
Swain George G, student, bds G W Swain.
Swain George W, horse dealer, res cor Spy Run av and Prospect.
Swain George W, plasterer, res 120 W Creighton av.
Swain Howard F, laborer, bds 120 W Creighton av.
Swain John, blacksmith Wabash R R, bds 178 Gay.
Swain John D, contractor, res 6 Jones.
Swain Lillian L, cook, rms 120 W Creighton av.
Swank Alonzo D, winder Ft W Elec Corp, res 21 Lincoln av.
Swann Clarence S, clerk, bds 515 Harrison.
Swann John F, brakeman, bds 67 Hayden.
Swann J W Scott, trav agt, res 515 Harrison.
Swart Meinhard, hoseman Engine Co No 2, bds 38 Oak.
Swartz Joseph A, engr N Y, C & St L R R, res 259 W Jefferson,
Swartz Wm, engr Penn Co, res 19 E Williams.
Swartzel Oliver J, molder Bass Wks, bds 109 John.
Swartzel Wm J, molder Bass Wks, res 109 John.

644   R. L. POLK & CO.'s

Swayne, *see also Swain.*

Swayne Rhoda N (wid Samuel F), bds 278 W Berry.

Swayne Samuel F, lawyer, 15 W Main, res 278 W Berry. Tel 368.

Swayne Wm M, student, bds 278 W Berry.

Sweeney Alexander, laborer, res 77 E Superior.

Sweeney Charles F, engr Penn Co, res 429 Lafayette.

Sweeney Cornelius, watchman Penn Co, res 19 Brandriff.

Sweeney Kate F, music teacher. bds 421 Calhoun

Sweeney Louis D, engr Penn C, res 481 Lafayette.

Sweeney Maggie, bds 13 Brandriff.

Sweeney Philip, fireman, bds 19 Brandriff.

Sweer John H, iron wkr Penn Co, res 298 E Wayne.

Sweer John H jr, bds 298 E Wayne.

Sweet Edward R, agent, rms 85 W Superior.

Sweet Warren, agent, res 92 Wagner.

Sweetser Fannie C, bds 115 W Main.

Swegman Henry T, clk Penn Co, bds 121 E Main.

Swegman John F, plumber, bds 35 E Jefferson.

Sweringen Budd Van, phys, 26 W Wayne, res 264 W De Wald. Tel 399.

Sweringen Frank H, car inspr Penn Co, bds 197 W Wayne.

Sweringen George N, clk Penn Co, bds 197 W Wayne.

Sweringen Hiram V, phys, 96 Broadway, res 197 W Wayne. Tel 182.

Sweringen Lucinda (wid George), died Feb 28th, 1895.

Sweringen Stella M, bds 197 W Wayne.

Swigert Lena, domestic New Aveline House.

Swineheart Sherman, driver W B Phillips, res 141 Sherman.

Swinney Blk, 11-15 E Main.

Swinney Carrie, bds Rhesa Swinney.

Swinney Frank E, bds Rhesa Swinney.

Swinney Rhesa, res w end of W Jefferson.

Swinney Park, head of Washington bet St Mary's river and P, Ft W & C Ry.

Swisher Edward B, teamster, rms 37 W Berry.

Switz Maurice, machinist. res 74 Cherry.

Switzer Charles W, barber 59 Holton av, res same.

Switzer John H (Switzer & Sites), res e s Ramsey av 2 n of Dayton av.

Switzer Solomon L, barber, res 382 W Main.

Switzer & Sites (John H Switzer, Georg W Sites), novelties, 356 Calhoun.

Swope Martin G, fireman Penn Co, res 39 Lasselle.
Swyhart C E, brakeman, rms 248½ Calhoun.
Symonds Nathan W, moved to Adrian, Mich.
Syndram Charles J, hostler, bds 45 W Washington.
Szink, *see also Sink and Zink.*
Szink George A, foreman Penn Co, res 471 Harrison.
Szink Nora, bds 471 Harrison.

T

Tag Christian J, grainer, bds 99 E Washington.
Tag Katherine (wid Christian), res 99 E Washington.
Taggart Rollin C, trav agt, res 322 W Washington.
Tagtmeyer, *see also Tegtmeyer.*
Tagtmeyer David, Hardwood Lumber, Lumber Manufacturer and Dealer, n w cor Webster and Greeley, res 77 W Superior. (*See left top lines and classified Lumber.*)
Tagtmeyer Elizabeth, bds 77 W Superior.
Tagtmeyer Flora E, bds 270 W Washington.
Tagtmeyer Louis E, bds 77 W Superior.
Tagtmeyer Mamie H, bds 77 W Superior.
Tagtmeyer Sophia, bds 77 W Superior.
Tagtmeyer Theodore, bds 270 W Washington.
Tagtmeyer Wm, fireman, bds 624 Calhoun.
Tagtmeyer Wm, mach Ind Mach Wks, res 270 W Washington.
Tagtmeyer Wm H, foreman David Tagtmeyer, bds 77 W Superior.
Tait, *see also Tate.*
Tait Miss Frank, milliner, 26 E Wayne, res same.
Tait George, lab Hoffman Bros. res 16 128 Eliza.
Tait Rollin S, laborer, bds 57 Charles.
Talmage Charles H, bkkpr Scavey Hardware Co, bds 272 W Washington.
Talmage Minnie (wid Sandford), res 232 E Jefferson.
Talmage Sarah (wid Frank D), dressmkr, res 182 Calhoun.
Tancey Edward F, porter, bds 140 Fulton.
Tancey Hugh, plumber, bds 140 Fulton.
Tancey Michael, Justice of Peace Bank Blk, res 140 Fulton.
Tancey Thomas W, brakeman, bds 140 Fulton.
Tanner Elijah E, policeman, rms 265 Calhoun.
Tanner Josephine, domestic 65 W Williams.
Tapp Ferdinand, contractor 13 Ohio, res same.
Tapp Herman W, bridge bldr 68 Barr, res 227 E Lewis.
Tapp Nora M (wid Robert W), res 146 Maumee rd.

Tarman Frances S, dressmkr 83 E Wayne, bds same.

Tarmon Harry W (Baxter & Tarmon), res 33 Madison.

Tarmon Henry A, Contractor and Builder 191 Brackenridge, res 83 E Wayne. (See p 109.)

Tassler August, helper Penn Co, res s s Eckart lane 3 e of Hanna.

Tassler Frederick, lab Penn Co, res w s Home av 4 n of Wayne Trace.

Tate, see also Tait.

Tate Frank, lab F Weibel, res 7 Brookside.

Taylor Andrew, molder Wabash R R, res 84 South Wayne av.

Taylor Beal F, carpenter, res 59 Howell.

Taylor Bros Piano Co, Sam R Taylor pres, I N Taylor sec, pianos and organs 19 W Wayne.

Taylor Charles, clk Golden & Patterson, bds 110 W Jefferson.

Taylor Charles E, mach Bass Wks, res 166 Madison.

Taylor Charles N, condr L S & M S Ry, res 86 Wells.

Taylor Edgar L, Manager Central Union Telephone Co, bds 71 W Wayne, office tel 30, res tel 133.

Taylor Edward E, student, bds 407 Fairfield av.

Taylor Frank B, bds 391 Fairfield av.

Taylor George B, depty trustee Wayne Township, bds 31 Douglas av.

Taylor Hayes E, brakeman N Y, C & St L R R, res 35 Boone.

Taylor Henry C, res 131 Lafayette.

Taylor Henry J, bkkpr Hamilton National Bank, bds 131 Lafayette.

Taylor Hubert G, conductor, res 41 N Calhoun.

Taylor Isaac N, timber dealer and sec Taylor Bros Piano Co, 19 W Wayne, res 407 Fairfield av.

Taylor Jessie, bds 8 Euclid av.

Taylor John, lab Bass F & M Wks, bds 77 Hayden.

Taylor John J, stripper, bds 131 Lafayette.

Taylor Joseph M, polisher Olds' Wagon Wks, res 108 W Creighton av.

Taylor Mrs Julia B, res 31 Douglas av.

Taylor Julia M, bds 31 Douglas av.

Taylor Mrs Mahala A, res s s Howell ! w of Runnion av.

Taylor Mary (wid Philo H), bds 77 W Wayne

Taylor Mary H, bds 131 Lafayette.

Taylor Robert L, mach Bass Wks, bds M A Taylor.

†**Taylor Robert S,** Lawyer. 34 E Berry, res 391 Fairfield av. Tel 247.

Taylor Sam R, pres Taylor Bros Piano Co, piano tuner, 19 W Wayne, res same.

Taylor Samuel M, despatcher Penn Co, res 79 Holman.

Taylor Wm, bridge carp, res 17 Howell.

Taylor Wm, switchman Penn Co, res 8 Euclid av.

Taylor Wm, yd brakeman Penn Co, res 312 W Main.

Taylor Wm J, clk N Y. C & St L R R, bds 131 Lafayette

Teagarden Claude A, mach L E & W R R, bds 111 W Superior.

Teagarden Harvey J, removed to Springfield, O.

Teagarden Marion, engr, res 111 W Superior.

Teagarden Thomas D, fireman Penn Co, res 200 W Creighton av.

Teeters Sadie J (wid Richard W), bds 71 Pixley & Long Bldg.

Teeters Wm R, clerk, bds 92 W Superior.

Tefft Charles W. boarding 91 Wall.

Tegeder Aline (wid Frederick), res 68 Wall.

Tegeder Frederick. lab, res e s Lafayette 4 s of Grace.

Tegeder Frederick H, lab, bds Frederick Tegeder.

Tegeder Rosie, bds Frederick Tegeder.

Tegeder Wm H, lab, bds Frederick Tegeder.

Tegtmeyer, *see also Tagtmeyer.*

Tegtmeyer Andrew, mach Penn Co. res 77 Brackenridge.

Tegtmeyer Arthur, driver, bds 77 Brackenridge.

Tegtmeyer Charles D, mach L E & W R R, res 12 Clark.

Tegtmeyer Charles H, andymkr, bds 12 Summit.

Tegtmeyer Conrad H, foreman L Diether & Bro, res 42 Breck.

Tegtmeyer Ernest, mach Penn Co, res 82 Montgomery.

Tegtmeyer Ernest jr. mach hd, bds 82 Montgomery.

Tegtmeyer Frederick. mach. res 63 W Williams.

Tegtmeyer Frederick, lab Ft Wayne Elec Corp, bds 442 Broadway.

Tegtmeyer Frederick, lab Penn Co, res 12 Summit.

Tegtmeyer Frederick, watchman Old National Bank, res 624 Calhoun.

Tegtmeyer Frederick A, fireman G R & I R R, res 27 Jane.

Tegtmeyer Frederick H, agent, bds 12 Summit.

Tegtmeyer Frederick H, conductor, res 63 W Williams.

Tegtmeyer Hannah, mach opr. bds 42 Breck.

Tegtmeyer Henry W. carp, bds 42 Breck.

Tegtmeyer Henry W, student, bds 12 Summit.

Tegtmeyer Katie, tailoress, bds 624 Calhoun.
Tegtmeyer Lena, dressmkr, bds 42 Breck.
Tegtmeyer Lizzie C, bds 24 Wilt.
Tegtmeyer Mrs Lottie, res 3 Brandriff.
Tegtmeyer Louis F, cigarmkr, res 11 Caroline.
Tegtmeyer Mary A, bds 63 W Williams.
Tegtmeyer Wm, engr H Volland & Sons, res w s Hillside av 3 n of Baker av.
Tegtmeyer Wm, lab Ft W Elec Corp, bds 12 Summit.
Tegtmeyer Wm C, hostler C E Rippe, bds 63 W Willihms.
Telephone Exchange, Tri-State Bldg.
Telgmann John, plasterer, res 120 Eliza.
Telley Frank H, engineer, res 335 W Washington.
Telley George W, foreman Penn Co, res 43 W Williams.
Telley Thomas, engr Penn Co, res 13 W Williams.
Telley Thomas H, bds 13 W Williams.
Tellis John W, driver, res 210 W Superior.
Tellmann John W, molder, res 110 Gay.
Tellmann Minnie, domestic 105 W Berry.
Templar Harry, clk Ft W Elec Corp, res 66 Wilt.
Tennant Emma L, bds 165 W Washington.
Tennant Jewett G, trav freight agt N Y, C & St L R R, res 165 W Washington.
Tenseler Ella, domestic 167 W Berry.
Tensing Lena, domestic 88 W Washington.
Terry John F, brakeman, res 323 W Jefferson.
Terry M Eddiess, teacher, bds 323 W Jefferson.
Terry Walter T, condr N Y, C & St L R R, res 138 Howell.
Terwilleger Otis, appr Ft Wayne Gazette, bds 120 Harrison.
Tessier Melissa (wid Yoes), bds 171 Broadway.
Thaeter Frederick, res 23 Grand.
Thain Anna E, asst W W Shryock, bds 273 W Washington.
Thain Mrs Caroline, nurse, res 26 Baker.
Thain Charles C, foreman P E Wolf, res 36 Boone.
Thain George, phys, 273 W Washington, bds same.
Thain John, res 273 W Washington.
Thain John, motorman Ft W E Ry Co, res 33 Michigan av.
Thain Kate C, bds 273 W Washington.
Thain Minnie, bds 273 W Washington.
Thain Wm, painter Ft W Elec Corp, rms 65 Baker.
Thatcher Ollie, domestic, bds 25 Brandriff.
Thavenet Alexander, condr Penn Co, res 55 Huestis av.
Thavenet Uries, lab Ft W Elec Corp, bds 55 Huestis av.

Thayer Arthur, bds 114 Clinton.
Thayer Frederick, phys, 8 Short, res same.
Thayer Leonard E, trav agt, bds The Randall.
Thewis John, tailor, res 147 Union.
Thiebolt Elizabeth, seamstress, rms 57 W Superior.
Thiebolt Frederick W, clk Penn Co, bds 158 Wallace.
Thiebold George W, yd condr Penn Co, bds 158 Wallace.
Thiebolt John M, lab Penn Co, res 80 Walton av.
Thieke Henry, motorman Ft W E Ry Co, res 529 E Wayne
Thieke Herman L, laborer, res 78 John.
Thiel Frank W, stenogr Penn Co, bds 366 W Main.
Thiel Wm, wagonmkr, res 366 W Main.
Thiel Wm jr, bkkpr Keller & Braun, bds 366 W Main.
Thiele Diedrich, mach hd Penn Co, res 84 Wilt.
Thiele Diedrich H, clk J C Peters & Co, res 35 Wall.
Thiele Frederick G, clk Wm Meyer & Bro, bds 84 Wilt.
Thiele Gottlieb D, appr Kerr Murray Mnfg Co, bds 84 Wilt
Thiele Louise, bds 84 Wilt.
Thiele Minnie, domestic J H Bass, Brookside.
Thiele Wm H, lab Penn Co, bds 310 Harrison.
Thieme Andrew, flagman, bds 169 Van Buren.
Thieme Andrew C, helper J W Hickman, bds 170 Broadway
Thieme Mrs Annie, rms 317 Hanna.
Thieme Bros (John A and John G), merchant tailors, 12 W Berry.
Thieme Charles F W, bds 170 Broadway.
Thieme Ella M (wid George), asst janitress City Hall, res 76 Harmer.
Thieme Ernest, stone mason, res 53 Liberty.
Thieme Frederick J, trav agt, res 216 W Berry.
Thieme Gottlieb C (J G Thieme & Son), bds 53 E Wayne.
Thieme Fredericka (wid Andreas), res 169 Van Buren.
Thieme John, car inspector, res 51 Ferguson av.
Thieme John A, saloon, 170 Broadway, res same.
Thieme John A (Thieme Bros), res 212 W Berry.
Thieme John G (J G Thieme & Son), res 53 E Wayne.
Thieme John G jr (Thieme Bros), res 216 W Berry.
Thieme John G & Son (John G and Gottlieb C), Merchant Tailors and Clothiers, 37 and 39 E Columbia.
Thieme Leonie, bds 216 W Berry.
Thieme Matilda, bds 216 W Berry.
Thieme Mary, bds 53 E Wayne.
Thieme Theodore F, sec and mngr Wayne Knitting Mills, res 185 W Berry.

650 R. L. POLK & CO.'S

Thiesen Charles M, tinner Pickard Bros, res 78 Wells.
Thiesen John, mach hd Star Iron Tower Co, bds 78 Wells.
Thiesen Mary N, bds 78 Wells.
Thing Samuel B (S B Thing & Co, res Boston, Mass.
Thing S B & Co (John W Emery, Samuel B Thing, W A Prior), Boots, Shoes and Rubbers, 32 Calhoun.
Third Presbyterian Church, n e cor Calhoun and Holman.
Thoeny Andrew, molder C M Menefee, res s s New Haven av 1 e of Pioneer av.
Tholen Henry G, laborer, res 161 E Jefferson.
Tholen John G, molder Kerr Murray Mnfg Co, res 156 E Jefferson.
Thomas Ada, bds 250 Clinton.
Thomas Albert, student, bds 250 Clinton.
Thomas Allie, bds 250 Clinton.
Thomas Alonzo, attendant School for F M Y.
Thomas Mrs Anna, attendant School for F M Y.
Thomas Charles, appr Robert Ogden, bds 20 Breck.
Thomas Charles E, engr School for F M Y, res w s Hillside av 1 n Baker av.
Thomas Enoch P, city mngr Singer Mnfg Co, res 250 Clinton.
Thomas Harvey, car bldr Penn Co, res 55 Holton av.
Thomas Mary, domestic 111 E Washington.
Thomas Rienze, musician, bds 149 Griffith.
Thomas Samuel, stone cutter, res 20 Breck.
Thomas Walter, stone cutter, bds 20 Breck.
Thomma Jacob A, helper, res 6 Franklin av.
Thompson Adelbert, trav agt A L Johns & Co, res 283 E Washington.
Thompson Albert W, helper, res 28 Buchanan.
Thompson Annie, domestic 241 W Wayne.
Thompson Benjamin F, engr Penn Co, bds 29 E DeWald.
Thompson Byron S, Manager South Wayne Brick Co, w s Thompson av n of Wabash R R, res 447 Broadway.
Thompson Charles F, filer, bds 407 Clinton.
Thompson Charles S, conductor, bds 18 Maiden lane.
Thompson Cyrus L, electrician, bds 284 Webster.
Thompson Elizabeth (wid Benjamin F), res 29 E DeWald.
Thompson Elmer J, condr Ft W E Ry Co, res 284 Webster
Thompson Frank, cigarmkr G Reiter, res 289 Hoagland av.
Thompson Frank M, mach Baxter & Tarmon, bds 294 E Lewis.

Thompson Frank S, lab Penn Co, res 97 Lasselle.
Thompson George W, molder Bass Wks, res 246 E Lewis.
Thompson Grace P, bds 294 E Lewis.
Thompson Henry H, res 28 Buchanan.
Thompson Homer, coachman 98 E Berry.
Thompson James, laborer, res 284 Webster.
Thompson John R, brakeman, res s s Carson av 3 e of Parnell av.
Thompson John W, mach Bass Wks, bds 246 E Lewis.
Thompson John W, Propr United States Dental Assn, Office 9 E Wayne, res same.
Thompson John W, shoemkr, bds 329 E Wayne.
Thompson J Henry, electrician, res 148 E Lewis.
Thompson J Wm, lab Penn Co, res 33 Lillie.
Thompson Laughlin W, watchman Penn Co, bds 29 E De Wald.
Thompson Mary, bds 32 Oak.
Thompson Milton M, loans, res 241 W Washington.
Thompson Nelson, street supt, res 329 E Wayne.
Thompson Nelson W, supt carpenters Penn Co, res 111 Gay
Thompson Oliver H, clerk, res 161 Monroe.
Thompson Owen, carpenter, res 78 W Williams.
Thompson Philip E, laborer, bds 284 Webster.
Thompson Pierre A, bkkpr The Journal Co, bds 329 E Wayne.
Thompson Richard G, pass and ticket agt Wabash R R, res 61 Broadway.   Tel 22.
Thompson Susan (wid Jeremiah), bds 1 Emily.
Thompson Susan L, bds 474 Broadway.
Thompson Thomas, carpenter, res 78 Gay.
Thompson Thomas, molder Bass Wks, res 294 E Lewis.
Thompson Walter, helper, res 28 Buchanan.
Thompson Wm, laborer, bds 25 Barr.
Thompson Wm E, wheelmkr, bds s s Carson av 3 e of Parnell.
Thompson Wm L, watchman Penn Co, bds 19 W DeWald.
Thompson Wm W, clk G E Bursley & Co, bds 1 Emily.
Thomson Thomas A, winder Ft W Elec Corp, res 17 Miner,
Thorn John H, motorman, res 149 Holman.
Thornbery Lois N (wid Thomas), bds 17 Cass.
Thornton Della, cash E Rich, res 22½ Harrison.
Thornton Edward (col'd), brakeman, rms 70 Murray.
Thornton Josephine E, elocutionist, bds 190 W Berry.
Thornton Wm H B, wool buyer, bds 190 W Berry.
Thorp Frederick, clk Penn Co, res 189 E Washington.

652   R. L. POLK & CO.'S

Thorpe Ivan, ins agt, bds 39 W Washington.
Thorward Theo, Deputy State Oil Inspector, Office cor Berry and Harrison, res 33 Miner.
Thrasher Ulysses J, plumber Robert Spice, res e s Sherman 2 s of Putnam.
Threadgall Harry E, conductor, res 430 E Washington.
Threadgall John W, laborer, res 70 Dawson.
Throckmorton John A, blksmith, res 132 Monroe.
Throckmorton Sidney G, cigar mnfr, 14 South Wayne av, res same.
Thullen Adam, laborer Penn Co, res 72 Summit.
Thumm Jacob, clk E Shuman, rms 43 E Main.
Thurman Alfred F A, clk, bds 89 W Jefferson.
Thurman Charles W, Deputy County Treasurer, res 89 W Jefferson.
Thyen George W, bds 94 Force.
Thyen John H, car bldr Penn Co, res 94 Force.
Thyen Katie, bds 94 Force.
Thyen Mary, bds 414 Hanna.
Tibbits Sarah F (wid George E), Boarding House, 319 Harrison, res same.
Tibbles Frank E, yardmaster Penn Co, res 40 McClellan.
Tibbles John H, res 177 Griffith.
Tickenbrock Henry, butcher, bds Dwenger av n e cor Force
Tielker Frederick W, baggageman P, Ft W & C Ry, res 190 Taylor.
Tielker Louisa (wid Henry), bds 101 Wall.
Tielker Martha, opr, bds 190 W De Wald.
Tielker Mary (wid Henry), res e of Wabash R R, 1 mile s of city limits.
Tielker Sophie, domestic 391 Fairfield av.
Tielking Ella, domestic 132 E Berry.
Tiemann Anna M, bds 52 Summit.
Tiemann Frederick H, carp L Rastetter & Son, bds 424 Broadway.
Tiemann Frederick W, carp L Diether & Bro. res 83 Wall
Tiemann Henry F, carp L Rastetter & Son, res 222 Francis.
Tiemann Henry F, teamster Penn Co, bds 52 Summit.
Tiemann John F W, carp, bds 424 Broadway.
Tiemann J Frederick, carp, 424 Broadway, res same.
Tiemann Wm F, mach Penn Co, res 52 Summit.
Tiernan Agnes N, clk M Frank & Co, bds 73 Madison.
Tiernan Lucy E, bds 73 Madison.
Tiernan Mary (wid Andrew), bds 140 Fulton.

Tiernan Nellie L, bds 73 Madison.
Tiernan Thomas, car repr Penn Co, res 73 Madison.
Tierney Edward E, helper Penn Co, bds 23 Baker.
Tierney Michael C, engr Penn Co, bds 23 Baker.
Tigar Caroline (wid Thomas), bds 153 E Berry.
Tigar Wm H, division opr Penn Co, res 153 E Berry.
Tigges Anna E, opr S M Foster, bds 177 Ewing.
Tigges Carl G, driver, bds 177 Ewing.
Tigges Edward W, mach Ft W Furn Co, bds 177 Ewing.
Tigges Emma A, opr, bds 158 Greeley.
Tigges E Wm, clk Penn Co, res 177 Ewing.
Tigges Frederick R, lab L S & M S R R, res 158 Greeley.
Tigges George R, cigarmkr, bds 177 Ewing.
Tilberry Nahum, res 58 W Main.
Tilbery Robert, mach Ft W Org Co, res 34 Charles.
Tilbery Scott, carp W Oil Tank Co, res 122 W 3d.
Tilbury Mrs Belle. res 119 W Washington.
Tilbury Elizabeth J (wid Samuel), rms 21 Erie.
Tilbury Frank M, brakeman G R & I R R, res 200 Fairfield av.
Tillo Charles D, resident mngr Ft Wayne Newspaper Union, res 83 W Main. Tel 327.
Timbrook Mrs Martha, bds 32 E DeWald.
Timme Lena, dressmkr, bds 21 Erie.
Timme Mary (wid Barney), res 21 Erie.
Timmerman Grant E, cutter, bds 20 W Superior.
Timmis Alonzo D, lab Bass Wks, res 149 Wallace.
Timmis Harry, helper, bds Wm Timmis.
Timmis Wm, res n s Eckart lane 3 e of Hanna.
Timmons Barney, lab Penn Co. rms 17 Baker.
Timmons Bertha, bds 46 W Berry.
Timmons Wm W, clk Pfeiffer & Rousseau, res 46 W Berry.
Tindall Charles M, brakeman N Y, C & St L R R, res 115 Boone.
Tinkham Benjamin F, trav agt, res 24 Home av.
Tinkham Clyde P, Dentist, 24 Arcade, res 382 Fairfield av. (*See right top lines.*)
Tinkham Cora, bds 219 W Main.
Tinkham Frank S, coal, 120 W Main, res 182 W Superior.
Tinkham Harry S, asst Dr C P Tinkham, res 24 Home av.
Tinkham John P, coal. res 219 W Main.
Tinkham Melvin W, phys. 24 Arcade Bldg, bds 24 Home av
Tinkham Vergue P, bds 24 Home av.
Titus Charles, engr N Y, C & St L R R, rms 329 W Main
Titus Charles H, engineer, bds 130 Buchanan.

42

Titus Grace, bds 130 Buchanan.
Titus Myrtle, bds 32 Gay.
Titus Philip, engineer, res 32 Gay.
Titus Theodore, engr Penn Co, res 130 Buchanan.
Tobey Herbert B, Mngr S B Thing & Co, bds 164 E Wayne.
Toby Benjamin, brakeman, rcs 305 W Main.
Todd De R, lab Horton Mnfg Co, bds 156 Rockhill.
Todd George L, lab Wm Kaough, rms 56 E Columbia.
Todd George W, student, bds 93 Gay.
Todd John S, polisher Olds' W Wks, res 172 Gay.
Todd Wm H, clerk, rms 94 Calhoun.
Todd Wm W, car inspr, bds McKinnie House.
Toedtmann Christian F, clk Root & Co, bds 24 Melita.
Toedtmann Christina (wid Henry), res 24 Melita.
Toedtmann Christina L, clk People's Store, bds 24 Melita.
Toedtmann Louise M, clk Root & Co, bds 24 Melita.
Toenges Frederick W, shoes, 62 Maumee rd, res 57 same.
Toenges Henry, car bldr Penn Co, res 10 Howard.
Toensing Wm, driver, res 85 Cass.
Tolan Barry C, draughtsman, bds 62 W DeWald.
Tolan Brentwood S, archt, res 62 W DeWald.
Tolan Frank C, clk Ft Wayne Newspaper Union, bds 18 Brackenridge.
Tolan Ivon R, press feeder, bds 62 W DeWald.
Tolan Hattie, bds 62 W DeWald.
Tolan Hattie T (wid Thomas J), bds 62 W De Wald.
Toler E Jefferson, res w s Lafayette 3 n Piqua av.
Toler Jefferson V, laborer, bds E J Toler.
Tombaugh Daniel M, driver J Klett, res 38 Miner.
Tombaugh Ida E, bds 38 Miner.
Tombaugh Thomas C, laborer, res 317 Hanna.
Tombaugh Thomas M, molder Kerr Murray Mnfg Co, res 97 Lasselle.
Tombaugh Wm, laborer, bds 38 Miner.
Tomkinson Albert, plumber R Ogden, res s s Cochran 2 w Coombs.
Tomkinson Leonard, butcher School for F M Y.
Tomkinson Mrs Phoebe, laundry clk School for F M Y.
Tonne Helen, seamstress P E Wolf, bds 354 E Washington
Tonne Henry, car inspr Penn Co, res 6 Hurd.
Tonne Julius F Wm, foreman Ft Wayne Iron Wks, res 354 E Washington.
Tonne Lena, domestic Montgomery Hamilton.
Tonnelier Elizabeth (wid John B), bds 33 Pritchard.

Tons Gustave A, clk S B Thing & Co, res 50 Miner.
Tonsing Henry, blksmith Penn Co, res 97 Montgomery.
Toohey Annie, bd 43 Melita.
Toohey Edward, laborer, bds 43 Melita.
Toohey Ellen (wid Patrick), res 43 Melita.
Toohey Francis P, painter, bds 43 Melita.
Toohey Michael A, brickmkr, res 43 Melita.
Toohey Patrick, laborer, bds 43 Melita.
Tooley Walter S, laborer, bds 2 Riverside av.
Toomey Mary E, dressmkr, bds 102 Webster.
Toomey Thomas V, laborer, bds 34 W Superior.
Torrence George K, real estate 5 Arcade, res 195 W Wayne.
Tourgee Ada A, bds 60 Greene.
Tourgee Wm W, engr Penn Co, res 60 Greene.
Tousley Abner B, brakeman, res 138 Union.
Toussaint Joseph, laborer, res 152 Holman.
Tower Alexander M, mach Penn Co, res 96 E Wayne.
Tower Margaret A, res 104 E Wayne.
Towns Nelson, electr Jenney E L & P Co, bds 29 Hough.
Towns Sylvester, foreman Jenney E L & P Co, res 71 Pixley-Long Bldg. Tel 265.
Townsend Dick (Dick Townsend Co), res The Randall.
Townsend Dick & Co, (Dick Townsend, Perry A Randall) Proprs The Randall, Harrison, head of Columbia.
Towsley Edgar, laborer, res 429 E Washington.
Tracey David A, lab Penn Co, res w s Wayne Trace 1 s of P, Ft W & C Ry.
Tracey Frances A, bds J W Tracey.
Tracey Jacob W, res n s Pennsylvania 6 e Wayne Trace.
Tracey John A, lab Penn Co, res w s Adams 1 s Pontiac.
Tracey Mary M, bds J W Tracey.
Tracey Washington, shoemkr, w s Wayne Trace 3 s of R R, res same.
Tracy James H, laborer, res 4 Edgerton.
Tracy John, fireman N Y, C & St L R R, bds 33 St Mary's av.
Tracy John W, watchmkr, bds 4 Edgerton.
Trader Augustus, baker, res 3 Walton av.
Trader Clara, seamstress, bds 3 Walton av.
Trainer John W, foreman Ft W O Co, res 253 W De Wald
Trainer Roy C, actionmkr Ft W O Co. bds 253 W DeWald
Transure George, switchman, bds 357 W Main.
Trarbach Charles, laborer, res 568 Lafayette.

Trarbach Frederick, laborer, bds 568 Lafayette.
Trarbach Gustave A, helper Penn Co, res 145 E Taber.
Trau Frederick C, res w s Piqua av 1 s of Rudisill av.
Trau George, res w s Piqua av 2 s of Rudisill av.
Traub Carrie, clk M Frank & Co, bds 13 W Butler.
Traub Louis, harnessmkr, 353 Calhoun, res 13 W Butler.
Traub Louisa F, clerk, bds 13 W Butler.
Traub Ottilie, clk M Frank & Co, bds 13 W Butler.
Traub Rosa C, clk Root & Co, bds 102 W Butler.
Traub Sophia, dressmaker, bds 17 Duryea.
Trauermann Isaac (L Dessauer & Co), res 92 W Main.
Traut Elizabeth, bds 176 E Washington.
Traut Magdalena, bds 176 E Washington.
Trautman Frederick J, expressman, res 115 Wilt.
Trautman George, driver Engine No 5, rms same.
Trautman George J, clk People's Store, bds 115 Wilt.
Trautman John, Proprietor Sportsman's Emporium, 58 E Main, res 120 E Wayne. (*See adv p 87.*)
Trautman Louisa C, seamstress, bds 120 E Wayne.
Trautman Henry W, bds 120 E Wayne.
Trautman Jacob J, lab Ft W Elec Corp, bds 120 E Wayne
Trautman Wm F, lab Ft W Elec Corp, bds 115 Wilt.
Traver John H, fireman Penn Co, res 214 Calhoun.
Travers Martin, mach, res 36 Melita.
Travis Mary (wid Patrick), res 161 Holman.
Travis Peter C, conductor, res 45 W Williams.
Travis Richard M, conductor, res 35 Gay.
Traxler Daniel C, clk Adams Ex Co, res 43 Elmwood av.
Traxler Gertrude, bds 43 Elmwood av.
Traxler Gwendolin, bds 43 Elmwood av.
Traxler Wm, trav agt, res w s Spy Run av 3 n Burgess av.
Trease Lizzie, domestic 815 Broadway.
Trease Wm, condr N Y, C & St L R R, bds 368 W Main.
Trebra Elizabeth, domestic 316 E Jefferson.
Trebra Mary M, boxmkr, bds 194 Madison.
Trebra Robert W, lab Penn Co, res 194 Madison.
Treece Annie E, opr F L Jones, bds 396 Broadway.
Treece Florence A, bds 396 Broadway.
Treece George A, lab Wabash R R, bds 396 Broadway.
Treece James, lab Wabash R R, res 396 Broadway.
Treece Rose, opr F L Jones, bds 396 Broadway.
Treep Frank H, painter, bds 112 E Main.
Treffinger Wm M, lab Ft W Elec Corp, bds 18 McClellan.
Treiber John, laborer, res 87 Grant av.
Treiber Margaret, died April 20, 1895.

Tremmel August F, molder Ind M Wks, res 113 Wallace.
Tremmel Conrad, teamster, res 515 Hanna.
Tremmel John, res 34 Force.
Tremmel John, molder Ind Mach Wks, bds 515 Hanna.
Tremmel Lizzie, bds 515 Hanna.
Tremmel Phillip, conductor, bds 515 Hanna.
Trempel Jacob, car bldr Penn Co, res 232 John.
Trenam Anna M, teacher Jefferson School, bds 160 W Main.
Trenam George E, clk Star Union Line, res 160 W Main.
Trenam Mary, (wid George), res 162 W Main.
Trenary Peter B, laborer, res 14 Randolph.
Trenkley Celestine, died February 22d, 1895.
Trenkley Edward M, clerk, bds 106 W Washington.
Trenkley Emilia (wid Celestine), res 106 W Washington.
Trenkley Eugene G, clerk, bds 106 W Washington.
Trenkley Theodore A, clerk, bds 106 W Washington.
Trenkley & Scherzinger (Emilia Trenkley, Primus Scherzinger), jewelers, 78 Calhoun.
Trentman Anthony, moved to Hartford City. Ind.
Trentman August C, res 72 W Wayne.
Trentman Bernard H jr, trav agt Bourie, Cook & Co, res 567 Calhoun.
Trentman Bldg, 79-81 Calhoun.
Trentman Edward A, clk Globe Spice Mills, res 311 E Washington.
Trentman Mae E, bds 72 W Wayne.
Treseler Henry, res 152 Ewing.
Treseler Samuel, watchman, res 159 Griffith.
Tresselt Charles, bkkpr Meyer Bros & Co, res 88 E Jefferson.
Tresselt Christian (C Tresselt & Sons), res 55 E Jefferson.
Tresselt C & Sons (Christian, Oscar W, Herman C and Frederick T), Proprs City Flour Mills, cor Clinton and N Y, C & St L R R. Tel 268.
Tresselt Frederick T (C Tresselt & Sons), res 51 E Jefferson.
Tresselt Henry, car bldr Penn Co, res 137 Holman.
Tresselt Herman C (C Tresselt & Sons), res 8 Madison.
Tresselt Ida, bds 88 E Jefferson.
Tresselt Oscar W (C Tresselt & Sons), bds 55 E Jefferson.
Tresselt Ottilie, bds 88 E Jefferson.
Treuchet Alice F, bds 92 Lasselle.
Treuchet Celestin, wagon mkr Fleming Mnfg Co, res 92 Lasselle.

Treuchet Frank E, tinner J H Welch, bds 92 Lasselle.
Treuchet Joseph W, wheel mkr Olds' W Wks, bds 92 Lasselle.
Trevey Charles T, laborer, res 19 St Mary's av.
Triber Margaret (wid Henry), bds 15 N Calhoun.
Tribus Joseph, grocer, 379 E Washington, res 351 E Wayne.
Trier Anna E, bds 120 W Superior.
Trier Clara, domestic 46 W Creighton av.
Trier Edward H, clk Pfeiffer & Schlatter, bds 123 Madison
Trier Frank J, carp, bds 120 W Superior.
Trier George F, stengr, bds 120 W Superior.
Trier Henry, carp, 120 W Superior, res same.
Trier John C. clk Pfeiffer & Schlatter, res 123 Madison.
Trier Theodore, cornice mkr, bds 120 W Superior.
Trier Wm F, carpenter, bds 120 W Superior.
Triley Victoria, helper The Randall.
Trimble Clara A, bds 397 Broadway.
Trimble E Rebecca, dressmkr, bds 397 Broadway.
Trimble J Marion, baggagemaster Penn Co, res 138 E Lewis.
Trimble Samuel, carpenter, res 397 Broadway.
Trinity English Lutheran Church, s e cor E Wayne and Clinton.
Trinity Episcopal Church, W Berry s w cor Fulton.
Trinity German Lutheran School, Henry Nehrenz principal, s w cor Huffman and Oakland.
Trinity M E Church, n e cor Cass and 4th.
Trippeer Charles O, res 24 Chicago.
Tripple Charles A, cigar mnfr. 113 E Lewis, res same.
Tripple Paulina (wid Paul), res 74 Madison.
Trisch David, clk, res w s Spy Run av 3 s of Elizabeth.
Trisch David L, clerk, bds David Trisch.
Trisch Ima J. dressmkr, bds David Trisch.
Triskett Charles A, trav agt B W Skelton Co, res 29 W Butler.
Tri-State Building, E Berry bet Court and Clinton.
Tri-State Building and Loan Assn (Nos One–Two–Three), George W Pixley Pres, David N Foster Vice-Pres, C A Wilding Sec, Joseph W Bell Treas, W J Vesey Atty, Tri-State Bldg. Tel 216
Tritschler Charles, moved to Columbia City, Ind.
Tritschler John P, trav agt J Nathan & Co, res 7 Fulton.
Trosin Henry, car repr Penn Co, res 229 John.

Trout Hannah M (wid Dock), bds s s Wiebke 5 e of Lafayette.
Trowbridge Addison, res 101 Clay.
Trowbridge Charles A, laborer, bds 110 Clay.
Trowbridge Ollie L, bds 110 Clay.
Troxell Charles O, miller Globe Spice Mills res 126 E Wayne.
Troy Steam Laundry, F L Jones & Co Proprs, 48 and 50 Pearl. Tel 160. (*See left bottom lines.*)
Trudwig Herman, teamster, res 234 Force.
Truebenbach Amelia (wid Moritz L), res 312 W Main.
Truebenbach Henry, meats, 312 W Main, res same.
Truesdale Richard, fireman Penn Co, res 104 Fairfield av.
Trusler Samuel, gate keeper, res 46 Griffith.
Trythall James, hammersmith, res 43 E Butler.
Tschantz Wm H, clk, bds Columbia House.
Tubbs John P, moved to Montpelier, Ind.
Tucker Viola M (wid Arthur), res 88 E Lewis.
Tuckey Gardner J, condr, res 56 E Williams.
Tuerschmann Paul O, fireman. res 210 Gay.
Tufts James H, brakeman N Y, C & St L R R, bds 22 Boone.
Tullen A, lab Penn Co, bds 10 Summit.
Tulley Frank, engr N Y, C & St L R R, res 335 W Washington.
Tulley Thomas, fireman N Y, C & St L R R, res 33 St Mary's av.
Tumbleson Walter H, driver Powers & Barnett, rms 31 Barr.
Turman Furney (col'd), waiter, res 17½ Melita.
Turner Annie E (wid Wm W), res 225 W Superior.
Turner Clyde B, stockman J A Armstrong & Co, rms 115 E Berry.
Turner Delia A, bds 65 W Lewis.
Turner Ford W, clk C H Waltemath & Sons, bds 377 Hanna
Turner Frank C, machinist Wabash R R, bds 65 W Lewis.
Turner Frank C, coppersmith Penn Co, bds 377 Hanna.
Turner George, watchman, res 209 E Jefferson.
Turner James A, clk Levi Turner, bds 65 W Lewis.
Turner John E, condr N Y, C & St L R R, res 326 W Main.
Turner Joseph G, carpenter, res 62 Boone.
Turner Levi, grocer, 40 Harrison, res 65 W Lewis.
Turner Wm, engr Penn Co, res 377 Hanna.

Turner Wm, Seal Clk N Y, C & St L R R, bds 38 Elm.
Turner Wm S (James A Armstrong Co), rms 115 E Berry
Tustison Dell (wid Oliver), res 82 Lake av.
Tustison Nelson, lab Olds' W Wks, bds 82 Lake av.
Tustison Olive M, bds 82 Lake av.
Tuttle Alwilda J (wid Theodore F), bds 24 Wagner.
Tuttle Myron E, despatcher Penn Co, res 208 E Lewis.
Twining Nora, student, bds n e cor 7th and Lafayette.
Twining Thomas J, collections 26 Bank Blk, res Lafayette n e cor 7th.
Tyger Charles W, trav agt Charles Falk & Co, bds 69 Cass.
Tyger Morton B, clk Charles Falk & Co, bds 69 Cass.
Tyger Philip C, res 69 Cass.
Tyler Charles J, brakeman Penn Co, bds 115 Shawnee av.
Tyler Emilie A, tel opr Wabash R R, bds 302 Harrison.
Tyler Franklin A, labeler C L Centlivre Brewing Co, bds 51 N Calhoun.
Tyler Frank B, boilermkr Wabash R R, bds 115 Shawnee av.
Tyler George G, engr Ft W Water Power Co, res 51 N Calhoun.
Tyler Haidee, student, bds John Orff.
Tyler Mrs Inez, milliner 52 Oliver, bds 59 W Main.
Tyler James, carp, res 115 Shawnee av.   Tel 354.
Tyler Jennie B (wid Eugene), bds 117 Gay.
Tyler John L, special teacher writing Public Schools, res 117 Gay.
Tyler John S, driver L Brames & Co, bds 88 Hanna.
Tyler Judson S, mach S F Bowser & Co, bds 115 Shawnee av.
Tyler Percy A, conductor, res 136 Shawnee av.
Tyler Royal A, brakeman, bds 115 Shawnee av.
Tyson Caroline (wid Enos), died Sept 14th, 1894.

U

Uebelhoer Frederick, bds 169 Brackenridge.
Uebelhoer John F, tinner, res 169 Brackenridge.
Uebelhoer Louisa E (wid Philip), res 68 E Main.
Uebelhoer Roland W, jeweler, 68 E Main, bds same.
Uebelhoer Sophia, dressmkr, 68 E Main, bds same.
Ueber Joseph, fireman, res 492 W Main.
Uecker Louis, lab Weil Bros & Co, res 136 Franklin av.
Uetrecht Henry J, carp Olds' Wagon Wks, res 203 Gay.
Uhlig Charles G, molder Bass F & M Wks, bds 220 Force

Uhlrich Emil, died April 15th, 1895.
Ulenhake Henry A, ins agt, res 213 Madison.
Ulerich Emma, bds 448 Calhoun.
Ulerich Francis H, clk E Wiesmann, bds 448 Calhoun.
Ulerich Simon S, tel opr Penn Co, res 331 Lafayette.
Ulerich Sophie (wid John), res 1 Packard av.
Ulery Eliza A (wid John), res 332 W Main.
Ulmer Addie, mach opr, bds 191 Oakland.
Ulmer Christian, laborer, res 191 Oakland.
Ulmer Christian J, Propr Belmont Stables, 88 E Main, res 205 Madison. Tel 138. (*See p 97.*)
Ulmer Frederick C, driver City Mills, res 187 E Lewis.
Ulmer Gustav S, driver Adams Ex Co, res 292 W Jefferson.
Ulmer Theodore, janitor Root & Co, res e s Hillside av 3 n of Baker.
Ulrich Frederick, laborer L Rastetter & Son, bds 237 Gay
Ulrich John, lab Penn Co, res 237 Gay.
Ulrich Mary, seamstress, bds 117 Hanna.
Umstead Elizabeth (wid John), bds 381 E Washington.
Umstead Ellen, bds 381 E Washington.
Umstead Hiram D, shoes, 283 Calhoun, res 18 Murray.
Underhill Edward A, res 84 Barr.
Underhill Elliott S, solicitor C B Fitch, res 232 E Creighton av.
Underhill Harriet (wid Phineas S), matron Y M C A, bds 109 W Washington.
Underwood David W (Underwood & Brown), res 110 Shawnee av.
Underwood Samuel J, printer, bds 14 Fairfield av.
Underwood Thomas J, clk W J Barr, res 100 Riverside av.
Underwood & Brown (David W Underwood, Fred S Brown), job printers, 126 Calhoun.
Ungemach Beno C, clk D J Shaw, bds 15 Madison.
Ungemach John H, principal St Paul's Ger Luth School, res 15 Madison.
Ungemach Willo J, clk Ft W Gas Co, bds 15 Madison.
Unger Carrie M, opr Hoosier Mnfg Co, bds 277 W Creighton av.
Unger Clements L F, laborer, bds 51 Archer av.
Unger Ferdinand, sheet iron wkr, bds 277 W Creighton av
Unger Gottlieb, meter repairer Ft W Gas Co, res 51 Archer av.
Unger John, helper, bds 277 W Creighton av.
Unger John S, engr Gas Const Co, res 276 E Creighton av.

Ungerer Frederick, carp L Rastetter & Son, bds 49 Stophlet.

Ungerer George S, carpenter, res 49 Stophlet.

Ungerer George L, pressman Aldine Ptg House, bds 49 Stophlet.

Ungerer Lisetta, bds 49 Stophlet.

Ungerer Louis, mach hd, bds 49 Stophlet.

Ungerer Rose, bds 49 Stophlet.

Union Block, n w cor Main and Calhoun.

Union House, A H Lopshire Propr, 49 W Main.

Union Mutual Life Insurance Co, of Portland, Me, John W Cashman Gen'l Agt, 21 Bank Block.

Union Pacific Tea Co, R J Coulter mngr, 102 Calhoun.

United Firemen's Ins Co of Phila, Pa, C B Fitch agt 26 Bass Block.

United Presbyterian Church, Lafayette nr Pontiac.

United Press, H T Smith mngr, 6 Bank Blk.

United States Dental Ass'n, J W Thompson propr, 9 E Wayne.

United States District Court, s e cor Berry and Clinton.

United States Express, Charles B Beaver Agent, 79 Calhoun. Tel 416.

United States Internal Revenue Office, Government Bldg.

United States Pension Office, Government Bldg.

U S Baking Co, Fox Bakery, Louis Fox Mngr, Cracker and Candy Mnfrs, 145-149 Calhoun. Tel 183.

Updegraff Josephine, bds 34 Douglas av.

Updike Rev Jacob V, res 46 Huestis av.

Updike Perry O, bds 46 Huestis av.

Uplegger Albert, laborer, bds 146 Broadway.

Uplegger Carl, bds 221 St Mary's av.

Uplegger Mrs Fernanda, res 146 Broadway.

Uplegger Louis, barber 45 Wells, res 7 Marion.

Upmeyer Gustave W, clk H H G Upmeyer, res 70 Madison.

Upmeyer Herman H G, general store, 64 Clinton, bds 33 Berry.

Uran John G, condr, res 47 St Mary's av.

Uran Otis W, appr R Ogden, bds 47 St Mary's av.

Uran S Ellen, bkkpr Troy Steam Laundry, bds 47 St Mary's av.

Urbahns August E, condr, bds 328 W Jefferson.

Urbahns C Emil, train despatcher N Y, C & St L R R, res 80 W Jefferson.

Urbahns Elsebe (wid Jurden), res 328 W Jefferson.

Urbahns Detlef F U, clk trainmaster N Y, C & St L R R, bds 328 W Jefferson,

Urbahns Frederick W, train despatcher N Y. C & St L R R, res 328 W Jefferson.

Urbine James, clk. moved to Arcola, Ind.

Urbine Nora, opr S M Foster, bds 216 E Wayne.

Urtle Elida, bds 42 Miner.

Urtle Wm G, mach hd, res 42 Miner.

Usselmann John, machinist, res 72 Howell.

▽

Vachon Frank A, policeman, res 54 John.

Vachon Joseph A, laborer, bds 57 Barr.

Vachon Myrtle, bds 97 Lasselle.

Vachon Richard D, helper Bass Wks, res 88 Force.

Vachon Sylvester M, bartndr, bds 12 Calhoun.

Vachon Wm, mach hd Standard Wheel Co, res 92 Force.

Vail Michael, switchman Penn Co, bds 122 Wallace.

Vail Ralph E, moved to Hudson, Ind.

Valentine Charles F, car bldr Penn Co, res 92 Dawson.

Valentine David F, lab Ft W E Ry Co, bds 22 W Main.

Valentine Edward. carp J Suelzer. bds 193 E Taber.

Valroff August, plumber, res 73 W 4th.

Van Airns Wales, rms 228 Calhoun.

Van Allen John. lab D Gorman, res 114 E Berry.

Van Allen John H, driver Powers & Barnett, res 542 E Wayne.

Van Alstine Eleanor (wid Wm), bds 43 W DeWald.

Van Alstine Frank S, horse trainer, res 48 Columbia av.

Van Alstine Perry S, fireman Penn Co, res 58 Baker.

Vananda George A, lab Ind Mach Wks, res 101 Jesse.

Van Buskirk Aaron E, phys, 82 Calhoun, res 416 same. Tel 463.

Van Buskirk Minnie B, bds 416 Calhoun.

Vance Mrs Susan, res 226 High.

Vancura Jacob J, mach hd Ft Wayne O Co, res s s Johns av 1 e of Hoagland av.

Vandelier Simon, pensioner, bds 132. Chicago.

Vanderford Charles E, carp, res 170 W Main.

Vanderleeuw John H, clerk, bds 368 E Washington.

Van Dewater Charles, switchman, res 167 Hayden.

Van Dissen Amelia, bds 59 John.

Van Dissen August W, clk G E Bursley & Co, bds 59 John.
Van Dissen Mollie, bds 59 John.
Van Dissen Valentine, res 59 John.
Van Fleet Ralph A, trav agt, res 26 E Washington. Tel 418.
Van Gorder Charles H, engr N Y, C & St L R R, res 221 W Main.
Van Horn Albert, car repr Penn Co, bds 196 Hanna.
Van Horn George, laborer, res 261 E Wayne.
Van Horn Ollie, domestic 103 W Berry.
Van Horn Wm, lab Hoffman Bros, res 212 W Superior.
Van Housten Fannie, laundress, rms 38 Taylor.
Van Kirk Elizabeth (wid Reuben), bds 274 W Creighton av.
Van Meter Cary, brakeman N Y, C & St L R R, res 234 W Washington.
Van Meter Eugene J, res w s Home av 5 n of Wayne Trace.
Vanness Bessie E, student, bds 46 Walton av.
Vanness Cornelius O, cattle buyer, res 46 Walton av.
Van Osdale Benjamin, fireman Penn Co, res 30 Buchanan.
Van Osdale Gerhard, laborer, res 33 Gay
Van Osdale George N, fireman Penn Co, bds 30 Buchanan.
Van Osdale Harvey W, fireman Penn Co. res 135 Buchanan
Van Rooy Wm B, molder Kerr Murray Mnfg Co, res 212 W Creighton av.
Van Slyke Ira M, insurance, 106 E Berry, res same.
Van Tilburg Emmons, engr N Y, C & St L R R, res 426 W Main.
Van Tilburg Gaerie, fireman, bds 426 W Main.
Van Trump Henry A, foreman S Freiburger & Bro, res 103 Barr.
Van Vleck George W, res 63 Wells.
Van Vleet Lanie, teacher, bds 88 W Jefferson.
Van Volkenberg Frank F, trav agent, bds New Aveline House.
Van Winkle Isaac, res 174 E Berry.
Van Winkle Mary E, bds 174 E Berry.
Vardaman Charles, switchman, res 224 W Main.
Varner John A, butcher, bds 113 Hanna.
Varner Millie J, bds 113 Hanna.
Vashorn Myrtle, domestic 105 W Wayne
Vaty Wm E, mach hd Horton Mnfg Co, res 224 W Superior.

Vaughn Anna, stripper G Reiter, bds 60 Madison.
Vauris Louis L, sect foreman, res 12 Barthold.
Vegalues Henry J, carp, res w s St Mary's av, 2 s of Huffman.
Veit August, carpenter, bds 37 Wabash av.
Veit Charles, laborer, bds 37 Wabash av.
Veit Minnie, bds 37 Wabash av.
Veit Philip, res 37 Wabash av.
Veith Frank (Schone & Veith), res 50 Barr.
Veith Joseph H, night watchman, rms 265 E Wayne.
Veith Mary, bds 265 E Wayne.
Veith Peter, res 265 E Wayne.
Veith Wm, lab Penn Co, bds 265 E Wayne.
Velvick Ernest J, bds 303 Calhoun.
Velvick Fannie M, bds 303 Calhoun.
Velvick James A, carpenter, res 303 Calhoun.
Vernon Edwin E, with Ferguson & Palmer Co, res 287 W Berry.
Vernon Ida, dressmkr School for F M Y.
Vernon Jennie (wid Swift), res 88 Madison.
Vervalin Jay S, brakeman N Y, C & St L R R, bds 60 Wilt
Vesey John H, florist, 90 Thompson av, res same.
Vesey Wm J (Vesey & Heaton), res 90 Thompson av. Tel 231.
Vesey & Heaton (Wm J Vesey, Owen N Heaton), Lawers, Tri-State Bldg, cor Court and Berry. Tel 384.
Vessemann Henry, laborer, res 178 Smith.
Vesseriat Celestine C, car repairer, res 17 Boone.
Vesseriat Emma E, bds 17 Boone.
Vesseriat John, lab Ft W Elec Corp, bds 17 Boone.
Vetter Andrew, baker, 94 Wells, res same.
Vevia George E, condr Ft W Elec Ry Co, res 210 Metz.
Viberg Augusta H (wid Herman), res 487 Harrison.
Viberg Augusta, clk Ft W Com Exchange, bds 487 Harrison.
Viberg Carrie J, teacher, bds 487 Harrison.
Viberg George H, warehouseman, res 108 E Wayne.
Viberg George L, mach W Gas Constr Co, res 16 Walnut.
Viberg Mollie H, clk Geo De Wald & Co, bds 487 Harrison.
Viberg Russell S, dental student S B Brown, bds 108 E Wayne.
Vickers Percy B, trav agt B T Babbitt, bds 25 Barr.
Villig August, laborer, res e s Koch 1 s of Putnam.
Vincent Fannie (wid John), res 18 Maiden Lane.

666   R. L. POLK & CO.'S

Vincent Louis, rms 18 E Columbia.
Vining Charles H, broom mkr, res 30 Eliza.
Vining John E, teamster, res n s Dwenger av 1 e of Tons.
Violand Joseph F, carpenter, 61 Euclid av, res same.
Violand Louise P, bds 61 Euclid av.
Violand Milla (wid Louis N), res 340 E Wayne.
Vivian Simon, supt Ft W I Wks, res 32 E De Wald.
Vizard Mary, domestic The Wayne.
Vizard Thomas, laborer, bds 17 Brandriff.
Vlerebome Eliza (wid George), bds 51 Huestis av.
Vodde August C, machinist, bds 23 Richardson.
Vodde Christopher F, engineer, res 23 Richardson.
Vodde John B, finisher, bds 23 Richardson.
Vodde Rose, bds 23 Richardson.
Vodde Wm, laborer, bds 23 Richardson.
Vodde Wm H, clk J B White, bds s s Emily 1 w of Spy
    Run av.
Voelker Frederick, car repr Penn Co, res s s Chestnut 2
    w of Summer.
Voelker Lena, domestic 175 W Berry.
Vogel, see also Fogle.
Vogel Amelia, bds 456 Calhoun.
Vogel Peter, truckman, res 53 Walnut.
Vogel Veronica (wid Frank B), bds 456 Calhoun.
Vogel Wm C, tuner Ft W O Co, res 235 W Jefferson.
Vogelgesang Ferdinand, teamster, res 52 John.
Vogely Andrew, wagon mnfr, 82 Maumee rd, res 52 Oak.
Vogely Wm, helper, res 183 Metz.
Vogler Anna, seamstress, bds 103 Madison.
Vogler Julius F, mach hd, bds 383 E Wayne.
Vogtlin Henry, butcher R Hood, bds Weber Hotel.
Vohde Charles H, res 57 Home av.
Voigt Henry C P H, clk W J Barr, bds 72 Oakley.
Voigt Margaret (wid Herman Wm), res 72 Oakley.
Voigt Wm D J C, laborer, bds 72 Oakley.
Voirol Edward G, clk G E Bursley & Co, res 32 W 5th.
Voirol Frank A, watchmkr, res 244 Calhoun.
Voirol Frank J, jeweler, 244 Calhoun, res 25 Suttenfield.
Voirol John J, foreman G E Bursley & Co, bds 244 Calhoun
Voirol Joseph E, engr Penn Co, res 147 E Jefferson.
Voirol Louis J, barber E Sterling, bds 244 Calhoun.
Voirol Mary, bds 244 Calhoun.
Volkening Wm, helper Bass F & M Wks, bds 41 Gay.

Volland Charles H, clk Kayser & Baade, bds 279 W Washington.
Volland Henry (H Volland & Sons), res 3 McClellan.
Volland Henry J, res 279 W Washington.
Volland H & Sons (Henry, John G and Wm G), floor mills, 14 W Columbia.
Volland John G (H Volland & Sons), bds 279 W Washington
Volland Wm G (H Volland & Sons), bds 279 W Washington
Vollmar Antonia, bds 242 E Wayne.
Vollmer Frederick C (Fremion & Volmer), res 166 Holman
Vollmer Louisa H (wid Daniel), res 25 Van Buren.
Vollmer Wm C, caller, bds 25 Van Buren.
Vollriede Christian, watchman, res 3 Polk.
Volmerding Frederick, clk Root & Co, res 65 Hugh.
Volmerding Henry C, molder, bds 383 E Wayne.
Voltz Charles G, laborer Penn Co, res 184 Suttenfield.
Voltz Minnie, domestic, bds 184 Suttenfield.
Volz Anthony F, laborer Penn Co, res 558 Hanna.
Volz Baltza, laborer Penn Co, rms 161 E Taber.
Volz Charles, molder Bass F & M Wks, bds 19 Chestnut.
Volz Emma, opr, bds Anthony F Volz.
Volz Fannie, domestic 590 Lafayette.
Volz Frederick, bds 19 Chestnut.
Volz Henry, laborer Penn Co, res 19 Chestnut.
Volz Henry jr, molder Bass Wks, bds 19 Chestnut.
Volz John, laborer, bds 19 Chestnut.
Volz Robert, laborer, res 161 E Taber.
Von Behren Christian, coremkr, res 17 Guthrie.
Von Behren Lizzie C, bds 17 Guthrie.
Voorhees Peter, painter, res 184 Montgomery.
Voors John G, saloon, 81 Maumee rd, res 83 same.
Voors Louisa E, domestic, 20 Fairfield av.
Vordermark Henry E, stenogr Ft W E Ry Co, bds Maumee rd s e cor Walton av.
Vordermark Bldg, 42 Calhoun.
Vordermark's Grove, New Haven rd nr Toll gate.
Vordermark Henry P, res s e cor Maumee rd and Walton av.
Vordermark John W, res 301 E Washington.
Vordermark Lillian A, bds H P Vondermark.
Vore Wm A, clk Ft W Elec Corp bds 81 Rockhill.
Vorndran Casper, car bldr Penn Co, res n s New Haven av 7 e of Summer.
Vorndran Michael A, carp, res w s Spy Run av 5 n of bridge.

668   R. L. POLK & CO.'S

Vose Frank, condr dining car Penn Co, rms 331 Calhoun.
Votrie, *see also Fuudree.*
Votrie Frank J, lab, res w s Lafayette 2 s of Grace.
Votry Alexander, res 114 W Wayne.
Votry Harry A, bds 114 W Wayne.
Vreeland Daniel B, fireman N Y, C & St L R R, bds 312 W Main.
Vreeland Henry S, clk Root & Co, res 18 E Taber,
Vreeland Max, switchman, bds 312 W Main.
Vroman Frank A, brakeman N Y, C & St L R R, res 44½ Centre.
Vuillemin Julia, domestic 178 W Berry.

W

Wabash Railroad, Master Mechanic's Office cor Fairfield av and Wabash R R, Passenger and Freight Dept cor Calhoun and Wabash R R, Ticket Office Tel 6, Freight Office Tel 128.
Wacker Anton, molder Bass Wks, res s s Pontiac 1 w of Hanna.
Wade Margaret A, teacher Hanna School, bds 172 Holman
Wade Rev Ray J, moved to Bluffton, Ind.
Wadge Etta M, bds 307 E Lewis.
Wadge George, res 307 E Lewis.
Wadge Maria, bds 307 E Lewis.
Wadge Minnie, bds 143 Montgomery.
Wadge M Georgiana, teacher Harmer School, bds 307 E Lewis.
Wadge Wm, carpenter, res 143 Montgomery.
Wadington Benjamin C, painter, 323 E Lewis, res same.
Wadington Rosanna (wid Wm), res 325 E Lewis
Wadsworth Frank N, fireman G R & I R R, bds 223 Lafayette.
Waest Frances, bds 163 E Taber.
Wagenhals Rev Samuel, Pastor Trinity English Lutheran Church, res 54 E Wayne. Tel 464.
Wagman George, helper, res 102 Fletcher av.
Wagman Henry, car inspr Penn Co; res s s New Haven av 2 e of Pioneer av.
Wagman John, laborer, res 133 Franklin av.
Wagner Catherine (wid John), dressmkr, 79 W Jefferson.
Wagner Charles, laborer, bds 15 Pearl.
Wagner Charles W, helper Bass Wks, bds 441 Hanna.
Wagner Edward F, carp J Wagner, bds 45 W Butler.

Wagner Edward F, Physician and Medical Examiner Voluntary Relief Dept Penn Lines, Office East End Penn Pass Station. Res 397 Calhoun.

Wagner Eva, bds 15 N Calhoun.

Wagner Elizabeth (wid George), res 67 Lillie.

Wagner Ella, dressmkr, bds 79 W Jefferson.

Wagner Frank E, bds 72 N Harrison.

Wagner Frank M, died July 28, 1894.

Wagner Frederick, brewer C L Centlivre Brewing Co, res s e cor Eliza and Hillside avs.

Wagner George, laborer, bds 110 W Creighton av.

Wagner George, lab Hoffman Bros. bds 72 N Harrison.

Wagner George E, engr G R & I R R, res 219 E Jefferson.

Wagner Goldie A, bds 219 E Jefferson.

Wagner Gottlieb, bds 441 Hanna.

Wagner Grace M, bds 219 E Jefferson.

Wagner Harry J, clk M Birkhold, bds 45 W Butler.

Wagner Henry, inst mkr Ft W Elec Corp, rms 82 Baker.

Wagner Henry, lab Bass F & M Wks, res 60 Buchanan.

Wagner Henry E, fireman Penn Co, res 109 E Creighton av.

Wagner John, carp 45 W Butler, res same.

Wagner John B, foreman Rhinesmith & Simonson, bds 79 W Jefferson.

Wagner John C, res 72 N Harrison.

Wagner John C, pianos 27 W Main, rms 212 E Lewis.

Wagner John F, painter, bds 109 E Creighton av.

Wagner John H, fireman L E & W R R, res 72 N Harrison.

Wagner John T, real est 15 N Calhoun, res same.

Wagner John T jr, clk, bds 15 N Calhoun.

Wagner Joseph B, carp, res 114 Home av.

Wagner Julian, contr, res e s Calhoun 8 s of Marshall.

Wagner Mary S, bds 15 N Calhoun.

Wagner Philip, mach, res n s Maysville ½ mile e of city limits.

Wagner Phillip, section hand, bds 56 Smith.

Wagner Rudolph F, res 441 Hanna.

Wagner Rudolph F jr, painter, bds 441 Hanna.

Wagner Susan, bds 15 N Calhoun.

Wagner Tina, domestic 31 Douglas av.

Wagoner Louis, lab Bass Wks, res 238 Gay.

Wagoner Wm W, dispatcher G R & I R R, res 78 Brackenridge.

Wah Kee, laundry, 8 W Wayne and 224 Calhoun.

43

Waibel Albert P, clerk, res 171 Fairfield av.
Waibel Pesidus, res 226 W Washington.
Waite Etta B, domestic 20 W Superior.
Waite Florence. bds 188 Hanna.
Wahl Clara, bds 409 E Washington.
Wahrenburg Frederick. car bldr Penn Co, res 134 Union.
Wahrenburg Frederick D, clk Root & Co, bds 134 Union.
Wahrenburg Sophia, seamstress, bds 134 Union.
Wakefield Dora, bds 52 Hamilton.
Walbaum Eliza (wid Henry), res 63 Summit.
Walbaum Frederick, mach Bass Wks, bds 63 Summit.
Walbaum Henry W, molder, bds 63 Summit.
Walbaum Sophia. tailoress, bds 63 Summit.
Walbridge Burton F, switchman, bds 180 E Lewis.
Walda August. painter, bds 37 Wall.
Walda Carrie M, milliner, bds 325 W Washington.
Walda Charles, car bldr Penn Co, res 329 E Washington.
Walda Charles F W, painter, res 47 Walter.
Walda Christian C, carp H B Walda & Bro, res 137 Erie.
Walda Christian F, carpenter, res 17 Howell.
Walda Christina (wid Christian), res 325 W Washington.
Walda Christine, clk A Mergentheim, bds 325 W Washington.
Walda Clara. bds 150 E Creighton av.
Walda Frederick, tailor, 150 E Creighton av, res same.
Walda Frederick E, carp Penn Co, res 101 Summit.
Walda Frederick W, carp Penn Co, bds 150 E Creighton av
Walda George- laborer, res 20 W 3d.
Walda George, bds 37 Wall,
Walda George W, laborer, bds 174 Greeley.
Walda Gustav, painter, bds 53 Oliver.
Walda Gustav, carpenter, bds 147 Erie.
Walda Hannah, seamstress, bds 150 E Creighton av.
Walda Henry, molder Bass Wks, bds 150 E Creighton av.
Walda Henry B (Henry B Walda & Bro), office 89 E Superior, res 331 E Washington.
Walda Henry B & Bro (Henry B and Wm C), Contractors and Carpenters, Office and Shop 89 E Superior. (*See adv p 101.*)
Walda Henry C, carpenter, res 37 Wall.
Walda Henry G, painter, bds 150 E Creighton av.
Walda Herman C, painter, res 329 W Washington.
Walda Ida L, dressmaker, bds 137 Thomas.
Walda John F, watchman, res 7 Pine.
Walda Lizzie, seamstress, bds 150 E Creighton av.

Walda Matilda. seamstress, bds 147 Erie.
Walda Theodore W, carp H B Walda & Bro, bds 147 Erie.
Walda Theodore W, mach hd, bds 37 Wall.
Walda Tina, clerk, bds 325 W Washington.
Walda Wm C (H B Walda & Bro), res 26 Schick.
Walda Wm F, carpenter, res 147 Erie.
Walde Wm, carp Charles Wermuth, res 361 Lafayette.
Walde Wm jr, clerk, bds 361 Lafayette.
Waldemeyer Herman, mach opr, res 9 Park.
Waldmann Charles, helper Ind Mach Wks, bds 299 W Main.
Waldmann Charles J, boilermkr, res 39 Force.
Waldo Augustus, painter, res 187 Thomas.
Waldo Grace M, teacher Jefferson School, bds 99 E Washington.
Waldo Herman C, painter, res 329 E Washington.
Waldo Mrs Mary S, principal Harmer School, res 99 E Washington.
Waldo Susan M (wid George), bds 294 W Washington.
Waldschmidt George jr, bkkpr City Carriage Wks, bds 94 Walton av.
Waldschmidt George W, helper Penn Co, res 94 Walton av
Waldschmidt Jacob W, carp Penn Co, res 92½ Walton av.
Waldschmidt Kate, domestic 184 E Jefferson.
Waldschmidt Louis, bds 94 Walton av.
Waldschmidt Louisa M, domestic 46 Brackenridge.
Walke Frederick M, bds 55 Barr.
Walker, see also Welker.
Walker Alexander Y, trav agt, res 70 E Pontiac.
Walker Andrew, clk Penn Co, res 99 Greene.
Walker Anthony, molder Bass Wks, res s s Pontiac 1 w of Hanna.
Walker Anthony M, cabtmkr Ft W O Co, bds s s Pontiac 1 w of Hanna.
Walker Hannah, clk, bds s s Pontiac 1 w of Hanna.
Walker Jabez, laborer, res 202 High.
Walker Leonard S, res 57 Miner.
Walker Mary, waitress Ervin House.
Walker Mary, bds Anthony Walker.
Walker Matthew G, firemann Penn Co, res 278 E Jefferson.
Walker Robert, mach opr Wayne Knitting Mills, bds 12 Park av.
Walker Wm H, truckman Penn Co, bds 99 Greene.
Wallace Clarence E, engineer, bds 76 Harmer.

Wallace Daniel (col'd), waiter The Wayne, rms 23 Melita.
Wallace Emma C, stenogr C E Everett, bds 149 W Main.
Wallace Harriet E (wid Eleazer O), res 142 W Main.
Wallace James H, barber 374½ Calhoun, res 137 Suttenfield.
Wallace John, boilermkr Penn Co, res 140 E Lewis.
Wallace John C, clk forge dept Bass F & M Wks, bds 140 E Lewis.
Wallace Lulu J, stenographer, bds 140 E Lewis.
Wallies G Frederick, cabinetmkr, res 124 Harrison.
Wallin Charles E, trav agt, res 174 W Creighton av.
Walpole Frank F, car repr N Y, C & St L R R, res 10 Burgess.
Walsh, see also Welch and Welsh.
Walsh Annie E, bds 165 Gay.
Walsh John, conductor, rms 132 Montgomery.
Walsh Kate, laundress, bds 165 Gay.
Walsh Mary (wid Garrett), res 165 Gay.
Walsh Mary E, bds 85 E Jefferson.
Walsh Michael, laborer, res 167 Gay.
Walsh Michael, laborer, bds 5 Hamilton.
Walsh Michael V, clk county auditor, rms 2 E Columbia.
Walsh Nora, operator, bds 165 Gay.
Walsh Patrick H, laborer, bds 165 Gay.
Walsh Thomas, bds 398 Broadway.
Walsh Thomas, trv agt, bds New Aveline House.
Walsh Thomas, watchman Penn Co, res 231 Barr.
Waltemath Amelia, bds Henry Waltemath.
Waltemath Charles H (C H Waltemath & Sons), res 325 Lafayette.
Waltemath Charles H, cigar mkr, bds 49 Barthold.
Waltemath C H & Sons (Charles H, Wm H and Louis F), Dry Goods, Grocers, Bakers, Flour, Feed and Grain, 321–325 Lafayette. Tel 339.
Waltemath Emma A (wid Charles F), dressmaker, res 12 W Jefferson.
Waltemath Henry, car inspr, res Lake av e of city limits.
Waltemath Lena M, bds Henry Waltemath.
Waltemath Louis, pressman Ft W News, bds 259 E Lewis
Waltemath Louise F (C H Waltemath & Sons), bds 325 Lafayette.
Waltemath Louise D, res 49 Barthold.
Waltemath Louise S, clk Minnie C Reitze, bds Henry Waltemath.
Waltemath Minnie, bds 259 E Lewis.

Waltemath Sophia (wid Louis), res 259 E Lewis.
Waltemath Sophia M, tailoress, bds 49 Barthold.
Waltemath Wm, cigar maker, res 300 E Wayne.
Waltemath Wm F C, clk Penn Co, res 26 E Williams.
Waltemath Wm H (C H Waltemath & Sons), res 40 Wallace
Waltemath Wm L, Prescription Druggist; Toilet Articles, Cigars, Tobacco and Patent Medicines, s e cor E Lewis and Hanna, res same. Tel 454.
Walter Amos R, trav agt, res 274 W Creighton av.
Walter Anna W, dressmkr, bds 174 Columbia av.
Walter August G, plumber Robert Ogden, bds 149 Force.
Walter Charles F, bds 174 Columbia av.
Walter Daisy, opr S M Foster, bds 146 E Lewis.
Walter David, shoemkr 23 Barr, res 146 E Lewis.
Walter Elizabeth, bds 42 Pearl.
Walter Mrs Euphemia C, bds 487 Harrison.
Walter Eyer, phys, 18 Schmitz Blk, bds 101 Calhoun.
Walter Harry H, bds 274 W Creighton av.
Walter Jacob, res 174 Columbia av.
Walter Jacob, lab Penn Co, res 149 Force.
Walter Jennie, opr S M Foster, bds 146 E Lewis,
Walter Lillie L, seamstress, bds 146 E Lewis.
Walter Margaret (wid Frank), bds 12 Pine.
Walter Monroe, moved to Lagrange, Ind.
Walter Rosa, stenogr, bds 174 Columbia av.
Walter Wm, appr Robert Ogden, bds 149 Force.
Walter Wm B, teacher, res 147 Griffith.
Walters Claude D, bds cor Spy Run av and Elizabeth.
Walters John E. porter Lake Shore Hotel.
Walters Mary, domestic 24 W Berry.
Walters Mrs Savina, res 365 E Lewis.
Walters Wm, messgr Postal Tel Co, bds 146 E Lewis.
Waltke George C, miller Globe Spice Mills, bds 96 Madison.
Waltke John, laborer, bds 96 Madison.
Waltke Lizzie, bds 33 Grand.
Waltke Wm, lab George Jaap, res 72 Pearl.
Waltke Wm, res 96 Madison.
Walton Charles E, train master Penn Co, res 43 Brackenridge.
Walton Clinton H, supt, res 131 E Wayne.
Walton Herbert L. lab Ft W Elec Corp, bds 18½ Bass.
Walton Horace B, flagman, res 18½ Bass.
Walton Joseph R, store keeper Penn Co, res 43 Brackenridge.

Walton Mary E, bds 131 E Wayne.
Walton Wesley A, student, bds 18½ Bass.
Walton Wm W, res 13 E Wayne.
Wambach Maggie, bds 575 Fairfield av.
Wambach Mathew, bds 575 Fairfield av.
Wambach Michael, laborer, bds 575 Fairfield av.
Wambach Peter, lab Penn Co, res 575 Fairfield av.
Wampler Mattie, bds 8 Euclid.
Ward Albert O, barber, rms 386 Calhoun.
Ward Alice, bkbndr G W Winbaugh, bds 398 Calhoun.
Ward Alice C, bds 233 W Berry.
Ward Ambrose G, conductor, res 106 Wallace.
Ward Annie M, bds 233 W Berry.
Ward Catharine (wid John T), res 105 E Wayne.
Ward Charles C, engineer, bds 20 E Leith.
Ward Charles L, helper Ind Mach Wks, bds 106 Boone.
Ward Cyrus J, conductor, bds 386 Calhoun.
Ward Hattie A, seamstress, bds 269 E Jefferson.
Ward Hiram, moved to Roanoke, Ind.
Ward Horatio N, crockery, 8 W Columbia, res 233 W Berry.
Ward James, bds 13 E Williams.
Ward James (Ward & Flynn, Ward & Mahoney), rms 292 Calhoun.
Ward John, section foreman, res 50 Melita.
Ward Loren D, trav agt, res 117 Hanna.
Ward Lulu B, student, bds 40 E Pontiac.
Ward Robert, switchman L S & M S R R, res 178 Hanna.
Ward Samuel M, junk, res s s Maumee rd 1 e of Bond.
Ward Wm A, brakeman, res 40 E Pontiac.
Ward Wm H, res 20 E Leith.
Ward Wm H jr, clk J D Gumpper, bds 20 E Leith.
Ward & Flynn (James Ward, Peter Flynn), grocers, 292 Calhoun.
Ward & Mahoney (James Ward, James A Mahoney), cigar mnfrs, 140 Calhoun.
Warfield Wm E (col'd), waiter The Wayne, rms 51 W Superior.
Warner, see also Werner.
Warner Amandus, laborer, bds 69 Gay
Warner Barbara (wid Michael), bds 154 Suttenfield.
Warner Daniel, bds 13 Edna.
Warner Edward, timber buyer, bds 3 E Superior.
Warner George, helper L C Zollinger & Bro, res 13 Edna.
Warner George F, mach Penn Co, res 38 Lavina.

Warner Lena, bds 67 College.

Warner Thomas C. printer Ft W News, res 486 Harrison.

Warnock Jane (wid Cory), bds 70 Dawson.

Warren Cary L, laborer, bds 44 Centre.

Warren Ferren O, messenger, bds 44 Centre.

Warren John D, tanner, rms 294 W Main.

Warren Mrs Kate, dressmkr, res 294 W Main.

Warren Matilda C, laundress, res 44 Centre.

Warrick Ada C, clk S A Karn, bds 75 Oliver.

Warrick Charles A, fireman Penn Co, res 75 Oliver.

Warrick Lee A, solicitor E L Craw, bds 75 Oliver.

Warriner Arthur F. trav agt, res 417 Broadway

Wartenbe Amanda (wid Ephraim), res 119 Hayden.

Wartenbe Charles M, helper, bds 119 Hayden.

Wartenbe Wm E, helper Penn Co, res 128 Eliza.

Warton Floyd. bds 44 E 5th.

Warton Mathew, res 44 E 5th.

Wasemann Caroline, domestic 254 W Washington.

Washington House, George Neukamm Propr. 121 and 123 Calhoun. *(See right bottom lines.)*

Washington Richard (col'd), coachman 160 Spy Run av.

Washington School, s w cor Washington and Union.

Washington Township Toll Gate, Spy Run av s of Leo Gravel rd.

Wass Samuel L, millwright, res 290 E Creighton av.

Wass Samuel L jr, helper, bds 290 E Creighton av.

Wass Samuel W, brakeman, res 331 E Creignton av.

Wass Wm E, brakeman, res 112 Hugh,

Wasserbach Charles F, res 68 Oakley.

Wasserbach Clara. bds 68 Oakley,

Wasserbach John C, laborer, bds 68 Oakley.

Wasserbach Joseph, tailor. res 15 Charlotte av.

Waterhouse Clara E, bds w s Spy Run av 2 n of bridge.

Waterhouse Edward (Waterhouse & Anderson), res w s Spy Run av 2 n of bridge.

Waterhouse Grace, seamstress, bds 209 E Wayne.

Waterhouse John H, blksmith, res 209 E Wayne.

Waterhouse Mamie, bds 209 E Wayne.

Waterhouse & Anderson (Edward Waterhouse, Ingvar Anderson), blacksmiths, 88 E Columbia.

Waterman Andrew O, trav agt, res 46 W Creighton av.

Waterman George H, trav agt G E Bursley & Co, res 41 Home av.

Waterman John H, res 78 Organ av.

Waters Albert, student, bds 72 Cass.

Waters Clara (wid Wm B), bds 254 E Jefferson.

Waters Eva L (wid John E), bds 63 W Superior.

Waters James, bds 44 E Columbia.

Waters Mrs Julia, res 365 E Lewis.

Waters Kendall R, printer, res 360 E Wayne.

Waterworks office, cor Barr and E Berry, Tel 118.

Waters Mary E, bds 262 Webster.

Watkins John A, Carpenter and Builder, 200 Broadway, res 217 same. (*See p 107.*)

Watkins Lewis T, laborer, res 154 Greeley.

Watkins Maude, bds 163 E Jefferson.

Watkins Mrs Sarah, clairvoyant, bds 154 Greeley.

Watson Eli W, res 33 Elm.

Watson Maria (wid Henry). res 135 Madison.

Watt John, trav agt, bds 229 W Berry.

Watt Sern P, mechanical engr Bass Wks, bds 50 Brackenridge.

Watt Wm H (McDonald & Watt), res 229 W Berry. Tel 74

Watterson David W, farmer. res 66 Wells.

Watterson Wm F, condr, res 84 Richardson.

Watts Wm O, ins agt, 52 Calhoun, res Huntington. Ind.

Wavada Mary (wid Louis), res 14 Brandriff.

Way Luella, bds 93 E Columbia.

Waygood Charles, fireman Ft W Elec Corp, res 60 Home av

Wayne Anthony Mnfg Co The, *see Anthony Wayne Mnfg Co,*

Wayne Knitting Mills, Henry C Paul pres, Wm H Dreier vice-pres, Theodore F Thieme sec and mngr, O H Larwill treas, e s Park av nr W Main. Tel 488.

Wayne Oil Tank Co, Charles S Bash pres, Eugene W Hunter sec and treas, mnfrs oil tanks, 17 Lafayette.

Wayne Orchestra, Charles L Kaiser leader, office 103 Broadway.

Wayne Printing Co (James B and Harry Long), printers, 97½ Calhoun.

Wayne St M E Church, W Wayne s w cor Broadway.

Wayne The, Wm M McKinnie Propr, 17–23 W Columbia. Tel 99.

Wayne Township Office. G W Brackenridge trustee, 27 Arcade Bldg.

Wayne Township School No 6, e s Lafayette, s of Grace.

Wayne True Blues (military company), Randall Hall.

Weasman Helen, domestic 122 W Wayne.

Weatherhogg Charles R, draughtsman A Grindle, bds 15 Clay.

Weaver Arthur, driver, bds 259 St Mary's av.
Weaver Bert E. laborer, bds 259 St Mary's av.
Weaver Charles, carpenter, res 60 W 5th.
Weaver Charles W, trav agt B W Skelton Co, res 42 Huestis av.
Weaver Cornelius S, switchman, res 67 Boone.
Weaver Ellen (wid John Y), res 259 St Mary's av.
Weaver Elwood (cold), rms 51 W Superior.
Weaver Equa C, coachman, res 253 E Jefferson.
Weaver George, teamster, res 94 Montgomery.
Weaver George W, bds 62 McClellan.
Weaver Harry E, lab Ft W Furn Co, bds w s Spy Run av 2 s of Elizabeth.
Weaver Iva, clerk, bds 94 Montgomery.
Weaver John F, engr A Hattersley & Sons, res 103 Riverside av.
Weaver John F jr, plumber A Hattersley & Sons, bds 75 Riverside av.
Weaver John T, died December 26, 1894.
Weaver Le Roy, laborer, bds 259 St Mary's av.
Weaver Myrtle, domestic 111 W Superior.
Weaver Sarah, dressmkr 206 Lafayette, res same.
Weaver Theodore A, flagman, res n w cor Winter and Pontiac.
Weaver Wm E, fireman, res 10 Barthold.
Weaver Wm F, watchman Ft W Furn Co, res w s Spy Run av 2 s of Elizabeth.
Webb Andrew, brakeman N Y, C & St L R R, res 46 Centre.
Webb Arthur P, coachman 66 Lake av.
Webb Clara M, bds 305 W Washington.
Webb Marion A, trav agt Geo De Wald & Co, res 305 W Washington.
Webb Rhoda A (wid Augustus M), res 238 W Wayne.
Webber Bridget B (wid Milton), res 196 Ewing.
Webber Fannie L E, dressmkr 62 E Pontiac, res same.
Webber Frederick, draughtsman Wing & Mahurin, res 135 W Wayne.
Webber Henry J, brakeman, res 71 Buchanan.
Webber Mary E (wid Benjamin), res 62 E Pontiac.
Webber M Grace, stenogr Ft W Elec Corp, bds 196 Ewing
Weber Adam, shoemkr 213 Lafayette, res 81 Montgomery
Weber Albert, bds 283 Calhoun.
Weber Andrew, patternmkr, res 167 Clinton.
Weber Anna, domestic 123 Maumee rd.

Weber Bernard, Propr Weber Hotel, 281 and 283 Calhoun.
Weber Bernard K, helper Penn Co, res 26 Buchanan.
Weber Bertha, bds Weber Hotel.
Weber Carl J, accountant, mngr Smith Credit Co, bds 167 Clinton.
Weber Edward, clerk, res 395 E Lewis.
Weber Elizabeth (wid Peter), res 308 W Jefferson.
Weber Emily S, bkkpr Heine & Israel, bds 12 Walnut.
Weber Emma C, principal East German School, bds 12 Walnut.
Weber Ferdinand P, molder Bass Wks, res 391 E Lewis.
Weber Frank, cigarmkr, res 266 E Creighton av.
Weber Frank A, laborer, res 44 Erie.
Weber Frederick, res 55 Hugh.
Weber Frederick jr, appr Wabash R R, bds 55 Hugh.
Weber George H L, car rep Penn Co, res 124 Eliza.
Weber Helen (wid Frederick), bds 102 N Harrison.
Weber Henrietta S (wid John J), res 12 Walnut.
Weber Hotel, Bernard Weber Propr, 281 and 283 Calhoun.
Weber Jacob, helper, res 108 John.
Weber John, horse dealer, res 54 W Main.
Weber John, kettleman The Herman Berghoff Brewing Co, res 138 Warsaw.
Weber John, laborer, res 3 rear of Leikauf's Packing House.
Weber John jr, lab, bds 3 rear of Leikauf's Packing House
Weber John, molder Kerr Murray Mnfg Co, res 137 Force.
Weber John E, helper Penn Co, bds 108 John.
Weber John F, wiper Penn Co, bds 108 John.
Weber John J, lab, res n s New Haven av 4 e of Edsall av
Weber John & Son (John & Noah J), sale stables 21 Pearl
Weber Kate, bds 33 St Martin's.
Weber Louis, clk J B White, bds 108 John.
Weber Lulu C, bds 12 Walnut.
Weber Mark, planer Ind Mach Wks, bds 33 St Martin's.
Weber Mary, domestic 34 W Superior.
Weber Noah J (John Weber & Son), bds 54 W Main.
Weber Pierce, plumber A Hattersley & Sons, bds 33 St Martin's.
Weber Richard, bds 283 Calhoun.
Weber Robert, clk H W Mordhurst, bds Weber Hotel.

Weber Rose, bds 33 St Maatin's.
Weber Thekla (wid Louis), res 83 St Martin's.
Weber Theodore A, lab Ft W Elec Corp, bds 12 Walnut.
Weber Valentine, brakeman, res 202 Lafayette.
Weber Wm, cigarmkr, res 41 E 4th.
Weber Wm F, res 230 W Main.
Weberrus J Jacob, shoemaker, res 91 Wagner.
✗Webster Alfred M, bkkpr, bds 43 Indiana av.
Webster Frank P, clk F C Cratsley. bds 123 Edgewater av
✗Webster John H, clk H D Newhouse, res 43 Indiana av.
Webster John M, real estate, rms 54 E Washington.
✗Webster Lulu, bds 43 Indiana av.
Webster Wm H, fireman Penn Co, res 202 E De Wald.
Wedler Augusta, domestic 227 W Wayne.
Wedler Charles, laborer, bds 293 Winter.
Wedler Herman, laborer, res 3 Reed.
Wedler Minnie, domestic 172 W Main.
Wedler Theodore, helper Penn Co, res 41 Hayden.
Wedman Joseph, blksmith L Mehnert, bds 67 Wagner.
Weed Jane (wid Myron W), bds 46 McClellan.
Weeks Arthur B, electrician Ft W E Ry Co, res 92 W
    Creighton av.
Weeks George H, painter. res n s New Haven av 3 e of
    Lumbard.
Weeks Irene (wid John H), bds 185 Monroe.
Weeks Wm H, driver, bds n s New Haven av 3 e of Lumbard
Wefel Adolph, iron wkr Penn Co. res 21 E Washington.
Wefel Annie W, bds 168 High.
Wefel August L, removed to Connelsville.
Wefel Augusta (wid Frederick W A), res 163 High.
Wefel Charlotte (wid Frederick), res 161 High.
Wefel Edward J, helper A Hattersley & Sons, bds 21 E
    Washington.
Wefel Frederick W, grocer 142 High, res 144 same.
Wefel Frederick W A. died Oct. 4th, 1894.
Wefel Gibson, helper Penn Co, bds 21 E Washington.
Wefel John, meats 163 High, res 207 same.
Wefel John W, carp H B Walda & Bro, res 168 High.
Wefel Lizzie, bds 168 High.
Wefel Martin H. Druggist, n w cor Hanna and
    Lasselle, res same. Tel 349.
Wefel Minnie D, domestic 295 W Berry.
Wefel Wm C W, wheelmaker, bds 168 High.
Wefel Wm H, carpenter. bds 49 Wall.
✗Wegmiller John, clk Ft W Elec Corp, res 51 Home av.

Wehler Charles F, buyer Hoffman Bros, res 19 Burgess.
Wehmeyer August, clk Seavey Hdwre Co, bds 55 E Wayne
Wehnert Alma, bds 57 Wagner.
Wehnert Charles, reg opr Ft W Gas Co, res 57 Wagner.
Wehnert Frederick E, shoemkr, res 345 W Main.
Wehnert Hannah, domestic 102 W Berry.
Wehnert Johanna, domestic 102 W Berry.
Wehnert Lena, bds 283 W Main.
Wehnert Max, clk Ft W Gas Co, bds 57 Wagner.
Wehnert Wm, shoemaker, res 283 W Main.
Wehr Henry, laborer, res 391 W Main.
Wehr John, car bldr Penn Co, res 87 Putnam.
Wehrenberg Henry (Wehrenberg & Busching), res 504 E Lewis. (*See adv p 105.*)
Wehrenberg & Busching (Henry Wehrenberg, Fred Busching), Contractors and Builders, 504 E Lewis. (*See adv p 105.*)
Wehrmeister August, laborer, res 181 John.
Wehrmeister Emil C W, helper Bass Wks, bds 181 John.
Wehrmeister Robert, helper Bass Wks, bds 181 John.
Wehrs Anna M (wid Frederick), res 122 W Jefferson.
Wehrs Henry, laborer. res rear 358 E Wayne.
Wehrs Wm H, mach hd Penn Co, res 35 Hough.
Wehrs Wm J, bds 133 E Lewis.
Weibel Fred, Wind Mills, Wood and Iron Pumps, Tanks, Piping, Tubular Wells and Cistern Supplies, 18 Harrison, res 479 Broadway.
Weibel Placidus, res 226 E Jefferson.
Weichselfelder Louis, carp, bds 193 E Taber.
Weichselfelder Margaret, (wid John G), res 193 E Taber.
Weick Edward, laborer, bds 266 E Washington.
Weick Edward, teamster, bds 259 E Washington.
Weick Jacob, car bldr Penn Co, res 167 Harmer.
Weick Joseph (Joseph Weick & Co), res 259 E Washington
Weick Joseph & Co (Joseph Weick & Rudolph Krull) Livery, 87 Hanna. Tel 167.
Weick Mrs Maggie (Krull Sisters), res 259 E Washington
Weick Philip, res 62 W 4th.
Weidemeier Joseph, bds 108 College.
Weidman Michael, janitor Penn Co. res 30 Rockhill.
Weidner John, lab Penn Co, bds 337 Lafayette.
Weidner Michael G, bartndr Philip Graf, bds 337 Lafayette
Weidner Nicholas, teamster, res 118 Boone.
Weigand Henry P, contr, 58 Glasgow av, res same.
Weigel Jacob W, brakeman, res 77½ Hoagland av.

Weihe Emil, clk Meyer Bros & Co, res 328 E Wayne.
Weikart Curtis H, engr, res 94 Lillie.
Weikart Jacob J, trav agt C W Cook, res 16 Randolph.
Weikart James, salesman Dan Shordon, bds 28 E Columbia
Weikart Sarah M (wid Wm), bds 33 Randolph.
Weikart Sylvester W, driver C L Centlivre Brewing Co, res 33 Randolph.
Weikel Alfred, bds w s Lafayette 2 n of Piqua av.
Weikel Benjamin F, lab, bds 140 Runnion av.
Weikel Charles H, lab, bds 140 Runnion av.
Weikel George A, lab, res w s Lafayette 2 n of Piqua av.
Weikel Ira O, lab, bds w s Lafayette 2 n of Piqua av.
Weikel Jasper, mason, bds 140 Runnion av.
Weikel Levi (Wickliff & Weikel) res 140 Runnion av.
Weil, *see also Wile.*
Weil Abraham (Weil Bros & Co), res Chicago, Ill.
Weil Bros & Co (Abraham and Isaac), hides, 92 and 94 E Columbia. Tel 118.
Weil George, cabinetmkr, res 314 Broadway.
Weil Isaac (Weil Bros & Co), res Chicago, Ill.
Weil Jacob, res 53 W Wayne.
Weil Wm H, foreman Kerr Murray Mnfg Co, res 15 Holman.
Weiland Peter, shoemkr F W Toenges, bds 71 Summit.
Weiler Charles J, res 55 Lake av.
Weiler Martin, helper, res 133 Madison.
Weimer Charles, carp, res 144 E Creighton av.
Weimer George A, baker C H Waltemath & Sons, res 85 Buchanan.
Weimer Henry P, cond Ft W Elec Ry Co, bds 68 Baker.
Weimer John P, painter Heine & Israel, res 154 E Creighton av.
Weinrich Edward C F, rectifier, res 71 College.
Weipert Frekerick H, carpenter, res 11½ Custer av.
Weipert Michael, carpenter, res 99 Huffman.
Weipert Reinhart F, engineer, res 17 Huffman.
Weipert Herman, clk Freie Presse, bds 39 W Washington.
Weir Elmer, trav agt, bds 51 W Berry.
Weirs Mrs Sarah, domestic School for F M Y.
Weis, *see also Weiss, Wies and Wise.*
Weis Anna M, dressmkr 67 Charles, bds same.
Weis Emanuel, peddler, res 74 Maumee rd.
Weis Henrietta, bds 74 Maumee rd.
Weis Rose A, milliner, bds 67 Charles.
Weisbecker George, saloon 7 E Main, res 54 W 4th.

Weise Gustav, laborer Bass Wks, res 80 John.
Weisell Alfred T, tel opr, bds 311 W Jefferson.
Weisell David D (D D Weisell & Son), res 311 W Jefferson.
Weisell D D & Son (David D and W Ellis), dentists Foelinger Blk, 34–36 Calhoun.
Weisell Geary J, fireman N Y, C & St L R R, bds 311 W Jefferson.
Weisell W Ellis (D D Weisell & Son), bds 311 W Jefferson
Weisenburger Benjamin, res 34 W Superior.
Weisenburger Carrie, domestic 76 W Jefferson.
Weisenburger Charles, tailor, bds s e cor Wiebke and Lafayette.
Weisenberger Daniel, musician, res 44 Charles.
Weisenburger Mrs Emma, boarding house, 34 W Superior.
Weisenburger Herman, clk Lehman Book & News Co, bds s e cor Wiebke and Lafayette.
Weisenburger Valentine, laborer, res s e cor Wiebke and Lafayette.
Weisheit Henry G, horse shoer, res 92 Montgomery.
Weisman Wm, bds 39 Liberty.
Weismantel Frank A, lampmkr Ft Wayne Elec Corp, bds 7 Zollars av.
Weismantel Wm S, barber, bds 498 Broadway.
Weismer Nicholas, res 112 E Creighton av.
Weiss, *see also Weis, Wies and Wise.*
Weiss Anna, bds 6 Eckart.
Weiss Eda, mach opr, bds 47 Cherry.
Weiss Bertha, machine opr, bds 47 Cherry.
Weiss Jacob K, laborer, res s s Richardson 1 w canal feeder.
Weiss Moritz, mach opr, bds 47 Cherry.
Weisser Emanuel, hide buyer, rms 8 Calhoun.
Weist Wm M, laborer, bds 74 W Main.
Weitzell Jacob, candymkr, bds Francis B Kincade.
Weitzmann Felix T, tailor F T Weitzmann, res 207 Taylor.
Weitzmann F Theobold, Merchant Tailor, 182 Calhoun, res 182 Jackson.
Weitzmann Ida M F, bds 182 Jackson.
Weitzmann Maggie, bds 182 Jackson.
Weitzmann Max O, tailor F F Weitzmann, res 191 Jackson.
Weitzmann Paul T, tailor F T Weitzmann, bds 182 Jackson
Welbinghous Lenora (wid Henry), bds 214 W Jefferson.
Welch, *see also Walsh and Welsh.*
Welch Alfred J, student, bds 84 W Creighton av.
Welch Catherine (wid John), bds 61 Melita.
Welch Charles E, tinner J H Welch, res 124 Hoagland av.

Welch Charles H, fireman Penn Co, res 147 Fairfield av.
Welch George F, slater, bds 84 W Creighton av.
Welch Hugh, lab Penn Co, res 113 Hanna.
Welch James, laborer, bds 15 Brandriff.
Welch John, wiper Penn Co, res 15 Brandriff.
Welch John, boilermkr N Y, C & St L R R, bds 9 Marion
Welch John H, Slate, Asphalt and Tin Roofer,
   Galvanized Iron Cornice and Hot Air Furnaces, 190
   Calhoun, res 84 W Creighton av.   Tel 524.
Welch John O, mach Kerr Murray Mnfg Co, bds 84 W
   Creighton av.
Welch John S, hoseman Engine Co No 4, res 32 Oak.
Welch Matilda (wid Daniel), res 125 Walton av.
Welch Mrs Mattie, res 68 Maumee rd.
Welch Michael, barber 86 Barr, res 228 Lafayette.
Welch Michael S, baggageman, res 89 Barthold.
Welch Nicholas, yd brakeman Penn Co, bds 326 Hanna.
Welch Walter J, clk, bds 84 W Creighton av.
Welch Minnie (wid Patrick), res 228 Lafayette.
Welch Maria (wid John), res 48 Taylor.
Welding Ida, seamstress Ella M Roush, bds 137 Thomas.
Welker, *see also Walker.*
Welker Charles J, gents' furnishings 162 Calhoun. res
   same.
Welker Daniel, polisher, res 19 Huffman.
Welker George J, upholsterer P E Wolf, res 59 Wall.
Welker Henry, cabinetmkr, bds 99 Brackenridge.
Welker John M, clk Lehman Book & News Co, bds 19
   Huffman.
Welker Lewis, truckman Penn Co, res n w cor Oakland
   or Spring.
Welker Louis, clerk, bds 19 Huffman.
Welker Mary (wid Ernst), bds 99 Brackenridge.
Welklin John, truckman Penn Co, res 93 Stophlet.
Welklin Mary (wid John), res 44 Taylor.
Weller Arthur B, clk F, Ft W & W Ry, bds 39 Bracken-
   ridge.
Weller Charles W, meats, 92 W Jefferson, res same.
Weller Christopher C, tel opr, bds 121 Harrison.
Weller Elizabeth D, bds 121 Harrison.
Weller Gottlieb, butcher, bds 121 Harrison.
Weller John, res 121 Harrison.
Weller John jr, cigarmkr, bds 121 Harrison.
Weller Richard G, student, bds 121 Harrison.

Wellington Cafe The, James T Connolly
  Propr. 83 Calhoun. Tel 249. (*See right side lines.*)
Wellman Charles F, helper Penn Co, res 123 Taylor.
Wellman Elizabeth, seamstress, bds 237 Broadway.
Wellman Frederick H, clk H Wellman, bds 123 Taylor.
Wellman Henry, Undertaker, 39 W Berry. Tel
  278. res 237 Broadway. Tel 527.
Wellmann Edward, clk Keil and Keil, bds 112 Jackson.
Wellmann Frederick H, messenger Penn Co, bds 112
  Jackson.
Wellmann Sophia (wid Frederick), res 112 Jackson.
Wellmann Theodore C, special delivery clk, bds 112
  Jackson.
Wellmeier Bertha, mach opr, bds 229 W Superior.
Wellmeier Frederick, lab Hoffman Bros, res 229 W Supe-
  rior.
Wellmeier Lillie, mach opr, bds 229 W Superior.
Wellmeier Wm. barber, 180 W Main. bds 229 W Superior.
Wells Delaney E, ins agent, bds 105 E Wayne.
Wells Delphine B, principal Westminster Seminary, res
  251 W Main.
Wells Herbert, fireman Penn Co, bds 324 Calhoun.
Wells James E, mach hd Ft W O Co. res 608 Calhoun.
Wells James M, conductor, res 99 W Main.
Wells Jasper, canvasser, res 276 Walton av.
Wells Jay L, mach S F Bowser & Co, bds 100 W DeWald.
Wells Jennie, cash Sam, Pete & Max, bds 17 W Lewis.
Wells John T, laborer, res 155 Shawnee av.
Wells John W, fireman N Y, C & St L R R, res 18 Cus-
  ter av.
Wells Judson W, bookkpr S F Bowser & Co, res 100 W
  DeWald.
Wells Julian B, switchman, res 120 Union.
Wells Martin A, patternmkr Ft W Elect Corp, res 198 W
  DeWald.
Wells Mildred E, bds 100 W DeWald.
Wells Otis R, exp messr G R & I R R, rms 28 Douglas av
Wells Rachael (wid George), res 81 Grant av.
Wells Richard, blksmith, res w s Harrison 1 s of Marshall.
Wells Wm S, mach Penn Co, res 58 Park av.
Welsh, *see also Walsh and Welch.*
Welsh Celia, clerk, bds 75 E Superior.
Welsh Mrs Ella (Owens & Welsh), rms 29 W
  Columbia.
Welsh John, bds 441 Lafayette.

Welsh Kate, seamstress, bds 127 W Superior.
Welsh Mary (wid Patrick), res 75 E Superior.
Welsh Nora M, bds 441 Lafayette.
Welsh Patrick T, engr Penn Co, res 441 Lafayette.
Welsh Peter, apprentice P E Cox, rms 29 W Columbia.
Welsh Peter, bds 525 Calhoun.
Welsh Richard J, clk, bds 75 E Superior.
Welsh Thomas, driver H T Stapleford, bds 75 E Superior
Welsheimer Edith, student, bds 250 W Jefferson.
Welsheimer Tilla (wid John), res 250 W Jefferson.
Welsheimer Wm T, lawyer, res n w cor Howell and Runnion av.
Welten Bertha, clerk, bds 38 W Butler.
Welten Carrie, clk J B White, bds 38 W Butler.
Welten Henry R, laborer, bds 38 W Butler.
Welten John, mach Penn Co, res 38 W Butler.
Welten John B, laborer, bds 38 W Butler.
Welty Joel, Mngr Fort Wayne Book Bindery, 25 Court. bds 130 Wells. (*See left bottom lines.*)
Wendelen Henry, lab Bass Wks, res 347 E Washington.
Wendelen John A, molder Bass Wks, bds 347 E Washington
Wendelen Joseph J, helper Bass Wks, bds 347 E Washington
Wendelen Mary, bds 347 E Washington.
Wendell Benjamin, with U S Dental Assn, 9 E Wayne, res same.
Wenger Albert, chef Ft Wayne Club, rms 28 E Wayne.
Wenger Noah R, physician, 135 Calhoun, res 41 Huestis av
Weninger Agnes (wid Joseph), bds 212 Lafayette.
Weninger Ella (wid George), res 139 Madison.
Wenninghoff Christian, cigar mnfr, 114 W Main, res same.
Wenninghoff Elizabeth, bds 18 Fairfield av.
Wenninghoff Mamie M, bds 114 W Main.
Wenninghoff Mollie E, laundress F L Jones & Co, bds 18 Fairfield av.
Wenninghoff Rudolph H, cigarmkr, res 18 Fairfield av.
Wenninghoff Sarah H, bds 114 W Main.
Wente Wilhemina (wid Wm), res 90 Barr.
Wenzel Julius, bds 163 Francis.
Wenzler John C J, clk G H Loesch, res 96 Barr.
Werkman Ernest V, mach Penn Co, res 50 E Butler.
Werkman John C, barber, res 134 Fairfield av.
Werkman Philip E, finisher P E Wolf, res 377 Lafayette.
Werkmann Catherine, bds 161 Hayden.
Werkmann Gertrude, bds 161 Hayden.
Werkmann Kunigunde, bds 161 Hayden.

44

Werkmann Philip H, res 92 Walton av.
Werkmann Valentine, section hd Penn Co, res 161 Hayden.
Werkmann Valentine jr, lab Ft W Elec Corp, bds 161 Hayden.
Werkmann Wm F, painter, bds 92 Walton av.
Wermuth Adolph F, bds 172 Suttenfield.
Wermuth Charles, contr 172 Suttenfield, res same.
Werner, *see also Warner*.
Werner Adolph G, molder, bds 82 Gay.
Werner Ella (wid Henry C), res 101 Brackenridge.
Werner Frederick, laborer, res 6 Brookside.
Werner Joseph, baker M Haffner, bds 30 Madison.
Werner Louis, laborer, res 82 Gay.
Werner Mary (wid August), housekeeper s s Eckart lane 1 e of Hanna.
Werstein Philip H, clk Root & Co, res 16 E Williams.
Wertman Samuel L, laborer, res 237 E Wayne.
Wertsbaugher Judson S, barber 272 Calhoun, rms 330 same.
Wery, *see also Whery*.
Wery Charles, carpenter, res 190 W De Wald.
Wery Henry, contr 73 Hoagland av, res same.
Wery John H, medicine mnfr, res 132 W Williams.
Weseloh Frederick W, lab Bass Wks, res 122 Smith.
Weseloh John H, lab Olds' W Wks, bds 122 Smith.
Wesemann Emma, clk, bds 262 E Jefferson.
Wesemann Henry, laborer, res 178 Smith.
Wesemann Louise (wid Wm F), res 262 E Jefferson.
Wesemann Wm, helper Wabash R R, bds 176 Smith.
Wesener Catherine E, dressmkr, bds 159 Griffith.
Wesley John, carp, res w s Home n w cor Raymond.
Wesner Augustus, res 42 Thomas.
Wesner Lillian, seamstress, bds 42 Thomas.
Wessel Caroline (wid John), res 61 St Martin's.
Wessel Frederick A, molder Ind Mach Wks, res 64 W 4th
Wessel John, bds 401 Lafayette.
Wessel Mrs Lizetta, midwife, 42 Wells, res same.
Wessel Wm, stone mason, res 42 Wells.
Wessen James, gardener, res n s Maumee rd 1 e of toll gate.
Wessner Reinhard, baker W F Geller, res 25 Nirdlinger av
Wesson Frederick, died April 26th, 1895.
West Bert, fireman N Y, C & St L R R, bds 335 W Main.
West German School, e s Webster s of Washington.
West Sarah, domestic, bds 126 W Jefferson.

Westenfeld Mary J, domestic 399 Calhoun.
Westenfeld Wm F C, agt F C Parham, res 168 Madison.
Westerburg Alfred, tailor, bds 69 Cass.
Westermann Charles O, helper Fox br U S Baking Co, bds 368 E Lewis.
Westermann Fred, res 39 Eliza.
Westermann Harry J, engr Penn Co, res e s Harrison 1 s of Killea av.
Westermann Herman, painter, bds 368 E Lewis.
Westermann Wm C, coremkr Bass Wks, res 368 E Lewis.
Western Gas Construction Co The, O N Guldlin pres, Ernest F Lloyd sec, Gordon W Lloyd treas, mnfrs gas machinery, Buchanan bet Holton and Winter. Tel 202.
Western Lime Co, Edward M Baltes Mngr, Lime Mnfrs and Dealers, 3 N Harrison. Tel 161.
Western Union Telegraph Co, Oscar L Perry Mngr, 2 New Aveline House Blk, Branches Wayne Hotel and Penn Co depot. Tel 176.
Westhoff Wm, brick mason, res 38 Summit.
Westminster Presbyterian Church, s s W Berry 3 w of Webster.
Westminster Seminary (For Young Ladies), Miss C B Sharp and Mrs D B Wells, Principals, 251 W Main. Tel 324.
Westphal Frederick, res 173 Montgomery.
Westrumb Henry C F, gas fitter, res 415 E Washington.
Wetterman Gussie, domestic The Wayne.
Wetzel John W, teamster, res 76 Swinney av.
Wetzel Lydia, domestic 122 W Wayne.
Wetzel Margaret A, domestic 301 Fairfield av.
Wetzel Wm, laborer, res 74 John.
Weyer Anton, plumber, bds 10 Huffman.
Weyer Louis E, trav agt, bds 10 Huffman.
Weyer Martin, wiper Penn Co, res 10 Huffman.
Weygandt Lewis F, lab, res 330 Force.
Whalen John, molder A Hattersley & Sons, bds 122 E Washington.
Wheatfield Wm, res 77 Stophlet.
Wheeler Charles E, cook New Aveline House.
Wheeler Leon S, student, bds 87 Michigan av.
Wheeler Mary E (wid John), res 126 Horace.
Wheeler Nelson, res 163 W Main.
Wheeler Robert B, mach Hoosier Mnfg Co, res 37 Michigan av.

Wheeler Wm J, appr Penn Co, bds 126 Horace.

Wheelock Hannah (wid Elbridge G), bds 144 Maumee rd.

Wheelock Kent K, phys, 26 W Wayne, res 144 Maumee rd. Tel 70.

Whelan Anna, seamstress, bds 114 W Butler.

Whelan Thomas, engr N Y, C & St L R R, bds 10 St Mary's av.

Whery *see also* Wery.

Whery Mary A, Physician and Surgeon. Diseases of Women a Specialty, Office and Res 26 Madison. Tel 470

Whery Wm, bell boy The Randall.

Whery Wm P, Physician, 94 Calhoun, Res 26 Madison. Tel 185.

Whipkey Belle, presser S M Foster, bds 194 Hanna.

Whipple I Belle, domestic 46 Elm.

Whitacre Wm, foreman, bds 23 Baker.

Whitaker Joseph W, res 450 Calhoun.

Whitby Thomas, brakeman N Y, C & St L R R, bds 96 Boone.

White Bank Bldg, n w cor Clinton and Wayne.

White's Blk, s e cor Calhoun and Wayne.

White Alexander B, bds 60 Barr.

White Amanda, seamstress, bds 90 Thomas.

White Carl V, press feeder The Journal, bds 76 South Wayne av.

White Cecilia, domestic 94 W Wayne.

White Charles, painter, res 82 Barr.

White Edward, res 162 E Berry.

White Edward H, rms 214 Calhoun.

White Edwin F, laborer, res 8 Monroe.

White Enos H, boilermkr, res 76 South Wayne av.

White Eugene H, student, bds 24 Van Buren.

White George H, brakeman N Y, C & St L R R, res 293 W Main.

White George I, laborer, bds 158 Wallace.

White Grace M, bds 60 Barr.

White Harry R, butcher, res 179 Smith.

White Ira C, brakeman, res 110 W De Wald.

White James B, Wholesale and Retail Fruit House and Dealer in General Merchandise, 95 and 97 Calhoun and 8-12 E Wayne, res 60 Barr.

White James B jr, clk J B White, bds 60 Barr.

White John I, sec Bass F & M Wks, res 75 Harrison. Tel 274.

White John R, cooper, res 117 W Butler.
White John W, Pres White National Bank, res 105 W Berry.
White Joseph D, tool dresser Penn Co, res 30 Lillie.
White Lucy, bds 28 Erie.
White Maria J (wid James), bds 45 Huestis av.
White National Bank The, Capital $200,-000, Surplus $25,000 ; J W White Pres, T B Hedekin Vice-Pres, H A Keplinger Cash, G G Detzer Asst Cash, n w cor Wayne and Clinton. (See left top lines and p 95.)
- White Richard E, moved to Alliance, O.
White Roderick W, miller Empire Mills, res 24 Van Buren
White Taylor, brakeman, bds 90 Thomas.
White Walter C, clk People's Store, bds 114 Clinton.
Whitehead Arthur T, res 316 Calhoun.
Whitehouse Arthur R, clk Root & Co, bds 83 E Berry.
Whiteleather Carrie B (wid James F), res 467 Harrison.
Whiteman Emmet A, sign painter, res 233 St Mary's av.
Whiteman Harmon, laborer, res 228 Lafayette.
Whiteman Henry M, condr Ft W E Ry Co, res 35 E Butler
Whiting Rose E (wid Almon J), res 544 E Wayne.
Whitlock Mary E, seamstress, bds 170 Rockhill.
Whitlock Solomon, res 170 Rockhill.
Whitlock Wm P, gatetndr, bds 170 Rockhill.
Whitman Mary (wid Sebastian), res 220 Lafayette.
Whitmer Daniel D, res 331 Calhoun.
Whitmer Warren, tel opr, bds 331 Calhoun.
Whitmore Butler M, bellowsmkr Ft W O Co, res e s Brooklyn av 3 s of bridge.
Whitmore Edward, bds B M Whitmore.
Whitmore Edward, carp, res s s Miller 2 w of Brooklyn av.
Whitmore Uriah H, bds 95 E Berry.
Whitmore Wm F, watchman Ft W E Ry Co, bds 69 Dawson
Whitney Frank H, engr Penn Co, res 36 McClellan.
Whitney I John, sawyer Hoffman Bros, res 261 Webster.
Whitney Miranda P (wid Washington I), bds 261 Webster.
Whitney Nancy G (wid David), bds 78 Douglas av.
Whitten Charles W, brakeman, res 278 Walton av.
Whittenberger Edward S, brakeman, bds 53 Thomas.
Whittles Edith, mach opr, bds 340 W Main.
Whittles Harry R, lab N Y, C & St L R R, bds 340 W Main.
Whittles Joab, mach N Y, C & St L R R, res 340 W Main
Whittles Josephine, bds 340 W Main.

Whittles Mamie, mach opr, \bds 340 W Main.
Whittles Martha, bds 340 W Main.
Whorton Matthew, section foreman, res 46 E 5th.
Wichern John, lab, res 73 Smith.
Wichman Adolph F, mach Bass Wks, bds 112 Summit.
Wichman Agnes, cook Hope Hospital.
Wichman Albert C F, supt The Anthony Wayne Mnfg Co, res 181 E Jefferson.
Wichman Albert O, bricklayer. res 324 E Jefferson.
Wichman Henry J, appr, bds 181 E Jefferson.
Wichman Herman W, foreman Anthony Wayne Mnfg Co, res 42 Division.
Wichman John T, mach Bass Wks, res 27 Schick.
Wichman Paul J, turner A W Mnfg Co, bds 181 E Jefferson
Wick Philip, harnessmkr, res 62 W 4th.
Wickliff Benjamin H, bds 140 Runnion av.
Wickliff Peter (Wickliff & Weikel), res 140 Runnion av.
Wickliff & Weikel (Peter Wickliff, Levi Weikel), dairy, 140 Runnion av.
Wickliffe Albert P, finisher Ft Wayne F Co, res 41 Barthold.
†Wickliffe Branson, plasterer, res 50 Grace av.
Wickliffe Daisy D, stenogr Postal Tel Co, bds 226 Hugh.
Wickliffe Frank P, car bldr, res 226 Hugh.
Wickliffe John, carpenter, res 21 Phillips.
Wickliffe Michael S, propr Hotel Arlington, 109 E Columbia.
Wiebke August H, bartndr, bds 92 Barr.
Wiebke Emma C, clerk E C Becker, bds 107 W Williams.
Wiebke Florence L, bds 92 Barr.
† Wiebke Frederick, farmer, res s s Rudisill av bet Fairfield av and Broadway.
Wiebke Frederick D, farmer, bds Frederick Wiebke.
ʄWiebke Frederick W, carver Ft W O Co, bds s s Broadway 1½ miles s of city limits.
Wiebke Henry, res 92 Barr.
Wiebke Henry, sawyer, res 84 W Lewis.
Wiebke Henry, carp, res e s Leesburg rd 1 n of N Y, C & St L R R.
Wiebke Henry A, saloon, 33 Calhoun, bds 92 Barr.
Wiebke Henry F, cooper, res 84 W Lewis.
Wiebke Wm C, bartender, bds 92 Barr.
Wiebke Wm H, clk C W Rose, bds 36 Pritchard.
ʄ Wiebke Wm H, bkkpr Ft W O Co, res s s Rudisill av 2 w of Fairfield av.

Wiedbruck Anna N (wid Christian), res 90 Barr.
Wiedelmann Henry W, carp A W Mnfg Co, bds 28 Liberty
Wiedelmann John, appr H Klebe, bds 28 Liberty.
Wiedelmann Sophia (wid Wm), res 28 Liberty.
Wiedelmann Wm C, laborer, bds 28 Liberty.
Wiedemann Bertha, domestic 106 E Washington.
Wiedemann Caspar, foreman Bass F & M Wks, res 370 E Washington.
Wiedemann Charles, car bldr Penn Co, res 130 Maumee rd
Wiedemann Charles, carpenter, res 97 Greene.
Wiedemann Gertrude (wid Lauer), bds 347 Lafayette.
Wiedemann Herman, mach hd Horton Mnfg Co, res n s Rebecca 1 w of Tyler av.
Wiedemann John, carp Penn Co, res n w cor Chestnut and Warren.
Wiedemann Joseph, bds 347 Lafayette.
Wiedemann Julius H, finisher, bds n s Rebecca nr Taylor.
Wiedemann Mary, bds 347 Lafayette.
Wiedemann Ulrich, whitewasher, res 347 Lafayette.
Wiedemeier Frank, laborer, res 108 College.
Wiedemeier Joseph, tailor, bds 108 College.
Wiedmann John, car bldr, bds Pioneer av s e cor C.
Wiedmann Michael G, janitor, res 174 Rockhill.
Wiegand Elizabeth M, opr S M Foster, bds 343 Lafayette.
Wiegand Frank A, car bldr Penn Co, res 118 Eliza.
Wiegand Frank A, plumber Penn Co, bds 343 Lafayette.
Wiegand John W, driver, res 506 E Lewis.
Wiegand Joseph G, mach hd, bds 343 Lafayette.
Wiegand Otto H, draughtsman, bds 343 Lafayette.
Wiegand Otto R, clk Mariotte Bros, bds Wilhelm F Wiegand
Wiegand Sebastian, carpenter, res 343 Lafayette.
Wiegand Wilhelm F, gardener, res w s Brooklyn av 2 s of Ontario.
Wiegand Wm F, finisher Ft W O Co, res 155 E Taber.
Wiegmann Frederick H, oil dealer, res 417 E Wayne.
Wiegmann Henry G, grocer 199 Lafayette, res same.
Wiegmann Henry G, farmer, res Lake av nr city limits.
Wiegmann Herman (Wiegmann & Franke), res 399 W Main.
Wiegmann Wm H, bds Henry G Wiegmann.
Wiegmann & Franke (Herman Wiegmann, Charles Franke), carpenters, 363 Broadway.
Wiehe Lottie M, domestic 146 E De Wald.

Wiehl John, laborer, bds 324 Lafayette.
Wiemann Catherine E (wid Wm), res 102 E Lewis.
Wiemann Laura E, clerk, bds 102 E Lewis.
Wiemann Wm E, cook The Wayne, bds 102 E Lewis.
Wieneke Amelia, bds 7 Jones.
Wieneke Carl, harnessmkr, bds 7 Jones.
Wieneke Edward, lab L Rastetter & Son, res 7 Jones.
Wieneke Frederick, shoemkr, 311 W Main, bds 7 Jones.
Wieneke Herman, lab L Rastetter & Son, bds 7 Jones.
Weis, *see also* Wies, *Wise and Wyss.*
Wies Annie, opr, bds 216 Francis.
Wies Jacob, carpenter, res 216 Francis.
Wies Jesse J, painter City Carriage Wks, res n s Winter 4 w of Warren.
Wies Wm, lather, bds 216 Francis.
Wiese Henry, engr City Mills, res 367 W Main.
Wiese Henry A, clk Wayne Knitting Mills, res 403 W Main
Wiese Marie, mach opr, bds 367 W Main.
Wiesenberg August, janitor St Paul's German Lutheran Church, res 45 Hugh.
Wiesmann Eugene, meats, 214½ Fairfield av, res 448 Calhoun.
Wiesmantle Lena (wid Frank), res 108 Clinton.
Wiesmer Peter N, painter, bds 147 E DeWald.
Wiggins Almon D, brakeman, res 5 Edgerton.
Wight Adam, stone mason, res 69 Hamilton.
Wihe Minnie, domestic 144 W Wayne.
Wilbert David H, sander, res 21 E William's.
Wilbert Harry H, fireman, res 21 E Williams.
Wilbur Harvey C, clk S A Karn, bds 149 Griffith.
Wilcox Clarence H, mach Ft W Elec Corp, bds 150 Taylor
Wilcox Daniel, teamster, bds Union House.
Wilcox Florence E, bds 150 Taylor.
Wilcox George H, painter Penn Co, res 54 Oliver.
Wilcox L E, res 46 Pixley & Long Blk.
Wilcox Minnie, milliner, bds 39 W Washington.
Wilcox Pauline O (wid Isaac E), res 150 Taylor.
Wilder Amelia (wid Lyman), bds 401 Webster.
Wilder Edward C, bds 146 E Washington.
Wilder Helen E (wid Charles), bds 146 E Washington.
Wilder Lillie E, bds 78 Baker.
Wilder Wm M, barber, 203 Calhoun, res same.
Wilder Wm K, fireman Penn Co, res 146 E Washington.
Wilder Wilson W, switchman, res 78 Baker.

Wilding Charles A, sec Tri-State Building and Loan Association, res 89 Edgewater av.

Wilding Cornelia A, student, bds James W Wilding.

Wilding Emily, domestic 47 W Berry.

Wilding James, coal, 35 Murray, res 260 W Wayne.

Wilding James W (J W Wilding & Co), res Park Pl s w cor Webster.

Wilding J W & Co (James W Wilding, W R Hines), street and sewer contractors, 193 Calhoun. Tel 143.

Wilding Lillie B, bds James W Wilding.

Wildtman Jacob, coachman DeWald square.

Wile, *see also Weil.*

Wile Isaac (Isaac Wile & Co), bds Rich Hotel.

Wile Isaac & Co (Isaac Wile), whol liquors, 8 Calhoun.

Wiley George W, bartndr A C Laurent, bds 62 E Columbia.

Wiley Hattie M, clk Root & Co, bds 129 Holman.

Wiley Ochmig B, civil engr, bds O A W Wiley.

Wiley Oliver A W, farmer, res e s Savannah 1 s of Mercer.

Wiley Sarah J (wid Alexander), bds A O W Wiley.

Wilhelm Charles A, cigarmkr, res 135 Wallace.

Wilhelm Charles H, insurance, bds 12 Harrison.

Wilhelm Frank, laborer, bds 106 Chicago.

Wilhelm George W, teamster, res 12 Short.

Wilhelm John, laborer, bds 52 Gay.

Wilhelm Joseph, with Wm Haller, bds 100 Montgomery.

Wilhelm Peter, laborer, res 106 Chicago.

Wilhelm Peter jr, carpenter, bds 106 Chicago.

Wilken Elizabeth, ironer Troy Steam Laundry, bds Herman Wilken.

Wilken Herman, res s e cor Oakland and Aboit.

Wilken John H, drugs 84 Wells, bds Herman Wilken.

Wilken Mary, bds Herman Wilken.

Wilkening Charles, bds 109 Lafayette.

Wilkening Louis, jeweler 81 Calhoun, res 109 Lafayette.

Wilkens Annie, bds 116 Broadway.

Wilkens Bros (Charles. Jacob V, John H and Christian), meat market 112 Broadway. Tel 295.

Wilkens Catherine (wid Christian), res 116 Broadway.

Wilkens Charles (Wilkens Bros), bds 116 Broadway.

Wilkens Christian (Wilkens Bros), bds 116 Broadway.

Wilkens Emma C (wid Wm), res 153 Jackson.

Wilkens Jacob V (Wilkens Bros), res 202 W Jefferson.

Wilkens John H (Wilkens Bros), bds 116 Broadway.

Wilkens Mary, bds 116 Broadway.
Wilkie Joseph, car bldr Penn Co, res 27 Walton av.
Wilkins Oliver P (Wilkins & Rush), res 140 W Jefferson.
Wilkins & Rush (Oliver P Wilkins, Wm H Rush), barbers 192 Calhoun.
Wilkinson Charity (wid Thomas), res 225 E Wayne.
Wilkinson Elven, trav agt, res 68 Walton av.
Wilkinson Frank, grocer 116 Wells, res 91 Cass.
Wilkinson Frank E, bartndr John Wilkinson, bds 24 E Wayne.
Wilkinson George, mach Bass Wks, bds 117 Hanna.
Wilkinson Gertrude, bds 24 E Wayne.
Wilkinson Johanna, bds 210 Calhoun.
Wilkinson John, saloon, 24 E Wayne. res same.
Wilkinson John jr, clk J B White, bds 24 E Wayne.
Wilkinson John E, porter Adams Ex Co, res 10 Brandriff.
Wilkinson Kate, bds 210 Calhoun.
Wilkinson Mary E, waitress New Aveline House.
Wilkinson Millie A (wid Henry), res 68 Walton av.
Wilkinson Thomas A, U S Marshall, res 50 Douglas av.
Wilkinson Wm, lab Robert Spice, res 55 W 5th.
Wilkinson Wilmer W, clerk, bds 50 Douglas av.
Wilkison Michael, watchman L S & M S Ry, bds Lake Shore Hotel.
Will Frank, fireman N Y. C & St L R R, bds 26 W Jefferson.
Will Harriet L, clerk, bds 85 E Washington.
Will Nicholas, laborer, res 17 Wabash av.
Will Thomas H, blksmith Kerr Murray Mnfg Co, res 85 E Washington.
Willett Charles G, clk Dreier & Bro. res 228 High.
Willey Mrs Frances B, bds 316 E Jefferson.
Williams Abner (col'd), laborer, res Lake av nr city limits.
Williams Addie H, teacher Hanna School, bds 82 Baker.
Williams Albert C, lab S Bash & Co, res 57 Wells.
Williams Allan Hamilton, bds Hamilton Homestead.
Williams Benjamin, brick mason. res 25 Duck.
Williams Bros (Edward P, Meade C and Henry M), office 36 E Berry.
Williams Carrie, domestic 65 Brackenridge.
Williams Carrie P, bds 227 Barr.
Williams Creighton Hamilton, res Hamilton Homestead.
Williams Dan N, lumber inspr, res 89 W Superior.
Williams Daniel D, trav agt Old F S and E Co, res 130 W Main.

Williams Edward P, capitalist, 36 E Berry, res The Wayne.

Williams Effingham T (Geo DeWald & Co), res 132 E Main.

Williams Frank, driver L H McAfee, bds Union House.

Williams Harry M, printer, bds 54 Hendricks.

Williams Henry C, barber. bds 57 Wells.

Williams Henry M, Real Estate, 36 E Berry, res The Wayne.

Williams Isaac (col'd), hostler, res 78 Riverside av.

Williams James B, trav agt, res 18 VanBuren.

Williams James H, conductor, res 294 Hanna.

Williams James H, dyer S J Robacker, res 227 Barr.

Williams Jeremiah, laborer, bds 153 Union.

Williams John, switchman, res 226 W Superior.

Williams John, laborer, res 57 Wells.

Williams John A, helper Wabash R R, res 82 Baker.

Williams John C, tuner, bds 195 W DeWald.

Williams John W, brakeman N Y, C & St L R R, bds 5 Fulton.

Williams Jordan D, pres and treas Old Fort Spice and Extract Co, lawyer, 63 E Main. res 332 W Jefferson.

Williams Joseph, butcher Wm Haller, bds 100 Montgomery.

Williams Joshua J, ins agt, res 30 E DeWald.

Williams Kate, bds 30 E DeWald.

Williams Kate, dressmaker, bds 81 W Washington.

Williams Lewis S, lumber inspr Ft W O Co, res 195 W De Wald.

Williams Madge, stenogr, bds 30 E De Wald.

Williams Maggie, dressmaker, bds 81 W Washington.

Williams May, assist S B Brown, bds n w cor Harmer and Eliza.

Williams Mrs Murtie, res s s Wheeler 1 w of Runnion av.

Williams Nellie E, bds 82 Baker.

Williams Park, s s Creighton av bet Webster and Hoagland av.

Williams Samuel, bkkpr Custer House, bds same.

Williams Sarah, chambermaid New Aveline House.

Williams Thomas, blksmith Penn Co, res 236 Harmer.

Williams Thomas G (col'd), waiter. res 277 E Wayne.

Williams Wallace W, horseshoer, res 29 Union.

Williams Wm D, Insurance, Real Estate and Loans, 9 and 11 W Main, res 54 Ferguson.

Williamson Andrew J, cooper, res e s Runnion av 1 s of Nickel Plate R R.

Williamson Harry L, printer Ft W Gazette, res 129 Monroe

Williamson James S, cooper, bds A J Williamson.

Williamson Jessie A, bds A J Williamson.

Williard Ella R, teacher Jefferson School, bds 45 Madison.

Williard Mary C, teacher, bds 45 Madison.

Williard Rachael A (wid Bianchronie L P), res 45 Madison

Willis Augustus, agent, res 1 De Groff.

Willis Jennie, bds 260 Clinton.

Wills Wesley, brakeman, bds 46 Elm.

Wills Wm H, brakeman N Y, C & St L R R, res 46 Elm.

Wills Wm S, mach hd Penn Co, res 58 Park av.

Willsey Wm C, motorman Ft W E Ry Co, res 70 Dawson.

Willson Clinton R, collr First National Bank, bds 59 Oakley.

Willson Frederick M, student, bds 59 Oakley.

Willson Martin S, fireman Ft W Elec Corp, res 59 Oakley.

Willson Oscar J, clerk, res 217 W Wayne.

Willson Ralph, clk J M Robinson, bds 59 Oakley.

Willson Winifred M, bds 217 W Wayne.

Wilmot Osee L, stenogr Bass Wks, res 486 Harrison.

Wilrath Anna P, domestic 290 W Berry.

Wilrath Carrie, domestic 171 W Wayne.

Wilrath Louis, carriagemkr City Carriage Works, bds 336 E Wayne.

Wilson Adrian L, press feeder Ft Wayne News, bds 3 Railroad.

Wilson Alexander, plumber Penn Co, res 46 Park av.

Wilson Carrie A, stenogr Dr A E Bulson, bds 221 W Berry

Wilson Charles M, student, bds 238 W Creighton av.

Wilson David J, brakeman, res 216 Lafayette.

Wilson Mrs Delia F, teacher Hamilton School, res 42 Home av.

Wilson Dessie, bds 44 Huestis av.

Wilson Earl B, Sales Agt National Cash Register Co, 32 Bass Blk, res 264 W Wayne.

Wilson Edward M (Schrader & Wilson), res 290 W Berry.

Wilson Frank D, medical student, bds 13 Colerick.

Wilson Frank W, chief dispatcher G R & I R R, res 29 E. Williams.

Wilson George, saw repairing, 177 Calhoun, res 338 W Creighton av.

Wilson George C, carpenter, res 29 Indiana av.

Wilson George H (George H Wilson & Son), res 221 W Berry.

Wilson George H, truckman Penn Co, res 42 Home av.

Wilson George H & Son (George H and George W), stoves, 31 E Columbia.

Wilson George J, mach Bass Wks, res 238 W Creighton av.

Wilson George W (George H Wilson & Son), bds 221 W Berry.

Wilson Henrietta (wid Ora L), res 174 Greeley.

Wilson Henry A, agent, bds 70 Indiana av.

Wilson Hugh O, train dispatcher N Y, C & St L R R, res 39 Brackenridge.

Wilson Jacob L, bds 122 Clay.

Wilson John C, res 316 Maumee rd.

Wilson John W, teamster David Tagtmeyer, res rear 81 W Superior.

Wilson Julia B, bds 42 Home av.

Wilson Laura A, bds 221 W Berry.

Wilson Lewis W, car bldr Penn Co, res n s Chestnut n w cor Warren.

Wilson Lula E (wid Judson), nurse, res 62 W Lewis.

Wilson Mary (wid John), res 179 Clinton.

Wilson Mary C (wid Charles H), bds 189 W Superior.

Wilson Mary E, bds 304 W Washington.

Wilson Opal, domestic School for F M Y.

Wilson Richard J, propr Summit City Hotel, res 3 Railroad.

Wilson Mrs Susan, bds 71 Holman.

Wilson Talbot M, carp, res 31 Indiana av.

Wilson Thomas W, lawyer, 80 Calhoun, res 13 Colerick.

Wilson Wm E, laborer, bds 285 Webster.

Wilson Wm R, engr L Diether & Bro, res 189 W Superior

Wilson Wm R, trav agent, res 69 Grant.

Wilt Frank P (F P Wilt & Co), res 306 Calhoun.

Wilt F P & Co (Frank P Wilt, R D Hudgel), teas and tobacco, 33 E Columbia. Tel 40.

Wilton Sanford, laborer, rms 518 Fairfield av.

Wimmer Henry, coremkr Bass Wks, res 113 Eliza.

Wimmer Louise, domestic 4 Jackson.

Winans Charles V, brakeman, res 405 W Main.

Winans Sanford H, clerk, bds 137 Shawnee av.

Winans Theodore O, ins agent, res 137 Shawnee av.

Winbaugh George W, Blank Book Mnfr, Binder and Paper Box Mnfr, 13 E Main, res 105 W Jefferson. Tel 495.

Winbaugh Henrietta M, teacher Harmer School, bds
   246 E Lewis.
Winbaugh John F, printer Ft W Sentinel, bds s e cor
   Holton av and Jennison.
Winch Calvin J, res 300 Maumee rd.
Winch Fannie M, student, bds 300 Maumee rd.
Winch Homer D, trav agt, res 100 Grant av.
Winch Howard, clerk, bds 300 Maumee rd.
Winch Jessie M, stenogr Gart Shober, bds 300 Maumee rd.
Winch Mildred, bds 300 Maumee rd.
Wind John, molder, bds Windsor Hotel.
Windsor Bertha M, stenogr M L Jones, bds 27 E Butler.
Windsor Clara, bds 27 E Butler.
Windsor Hotel, Mrs Mary A Franz propr, 302 Calhoun.
Windsor Wm H, engr P, Ft W & C Ry, res 27 E Butler.
Winegar Inez E, bkkpr Pantitorium Co, bds 196 Calhoun.
Winegar Louis H, mngr Pantitorium Co, bds 196 Calhoun
Wineke Charles G, harnessmkr, bds 7 Jones.
Wineke Wm F, laborer, res 13 Nirdlinger av.
Wing John F (Wing & Mahurin), res 37 W Creighton av.
   Tel 478.
Wing Warfield, porter, bds 28 Chicago.
Wing & Mahurin (John F Wing, Marshall S Mahurin),
   architects, 41–42–43 Pixley & Long Bldg. Tel 328.
Wirges Peter, laborer, res 17 St Martin's.
Winget Fremont, foreman Penn Co, bds 114 W Creighton av
Winget Lizzie, bds 114 W Creighton av.
Winget Wm, watchman Penn Co, res 114 W Creighton av.
Wink Helena (wid John), res 55 Madison.
Wink John, brakeman N Y, C & St L R R, res 324 W Main.
Winkelmeyer Charles, driver Hose Co No 5, rms same.
Winkelmeyer Henry, bds 81 W Superior.
Winkelmeyer Henry F (Winkelmeyer & Hans), res 81 W
   Superior,
Winkelmeyer & Hans (Henry F Winkelmeyer, Charles A
   Hans), livery, 44 W Main. Tel 175.
Winkenweder Benjamin, clk J G Mann, res rear 70 Hoag-
   land av.
Winkler Charles H, baggageman P, Ft W & C Ry, res 97
   Walton av.
Winkler Charles W, foreman, res w s Hartman 1 s of Pon-
   tiac.
Winkler Elizabeth, domestic 85 Maumee rd.
Winslow Gerney F (col'd), barber, bds 7 Summit.
Winslow Lee, domestic The Wayne, rms 275 E Wayne.

Winte John C, blksmith, 216 Fairfield av, res 218 same.
Winte John D, lab Penn Co, res 342 Calhoun.
Winte Minnie, bds 342 Calhoun.
Winter Frederick, grocer, 273 Maumee rd, res 271 same.
Winter Hattie, bds 120 N Harrison.
Winter Moses, Gold and Silver Plater, 35 E Main, res 35 Home av.
Winter Stella R, teacher, bds 35 Home av.
Winter Wm H, tailor, res 120 N Harrison.
Wintermote Mary, dressmkr Indiana School for F M Y.
Winters Eliza A (wid George), res 9 Smith.
Winters Frank F, lab Penn Co, res 39 Lincoln av.
Winters John, res 80 N Harrison.
Wintle Wm G, clk People's Store, bds 5 Hamilton.
Winzlow Maggie, domestic 55 Maple av.
Wirche Katherine (wid Peter), res 174 Jackson.
Wirche Polly, bds 174 Jackson.
Wirges Peter, laborer, res 17 St Martin's.
Wirth George J, tel opr Penn Co, res 70 W Williams.
Wirts Cora, domestic 69 W Wayne.
Wise, *see also Weis and Wies.*
Wise Chester P, barnman A L Martin, bds 37 Duck.
Wise Eliza (wid Michael), res 77 Holman.
Wise Harry O, A B, teacher High School, bds 228 W Berry.
Wise Isaac B, carp Penn Co, res 13 Smith.
Wise James A, lab S F Bowser & Co, res 331 Hoagland av.
Wise John, bds 77 Holman.
Wise Platt J, deputy sheriff, res 228 W Berry.
Wise Wm, laborer, res 52 Oliver.
Wise Wm H, lab S F Bowser & Co. bds 13 Smith.
Wishart Robert G T, helper Wabash R R, res 246 W De Wald.
Wismer Nicholas jr, watchman, res 17 Purman.
Wisniewski Frank, lab Penn Co, res 74 John.
Wissel August, carp Penn Co, res n s Pioneer av 1 e of Winch.
Wisterman Fannie, music teacher, bds 58 W Berry.
Withrow Emma H (wid Finley), bds 295 W Main.
Withrow Ruell E, engr, res 295 W Main.
Witt Emma A, bookbdr Ft Wayne Book Bindery, rms 31 W Columbia.
Witte Amelia, bds 27 Charles.
Witte Catherine M, bds 49 Locust.

Witte Christian, tailor Thieme Bros, res 77 Maumee rd.

Witte Christian F, car bldr Penn Co, res 27 Charles.

Witte Christian J, Sample Room and Dealer in Fine Wines, Liquors and Cigars, 27 E Main, res 203 E Washington.

Witte Clara M, bds 49 Locust.

Witte Conrad D, clk Wm Muldoon, bds 200 Fairfield av.

Witte Dora M, dressmkr, bds 77 Maumee rd.

Witte Edward, baker, res 490 Fairfield av.

Witte Frank, watchman Fox Br U S Baking Co, res 49 Locust.

Witte Frederick, teamster Standard Wheel Co, res 77 Shawnee av.

Witte Herman, mach hd Penn Co, res 147 W 3d.

Witte Louis, molder Bass F & M Wks, res 130 John.

Witte Wilhelmina (wid Conrad D), res 200 Fairfield av.

Witte Wm, lab Ft W Elec Corp, res 59 Maud.

Witte Wm E, helper, res over 35 W Main.

Witzigreuter Charles, helper, bds 12 Elm.

Witzigreuter Ferdinand R, painter City Carriage Wks, bds 12 Elm.

Witzigreuter Max, drugs 360 W Main, res 12 Elm.

Witzigreuter Max jr, carriage painter City Carriage Wks, bds 12 Elm.

Witzigreuter Theodore G, painter, res 301 W Main.

Wobrock Oscar, restaurant 14 W Berry, res same.

Woebbeking Charles G, helper Siemon & Bro, bds 195 Broadway.

Woebbeking Christian, res 30 Lavina.

Woebbeking Christian C, molder Bass F & M Wks, bds 195 Broadway.

Woebbeking Conrad C, carpenter, 195 Broadway, res same

Woebbeking Gustave C, molder Ft W Elec Corp, bds 195 Broadway.

Woebbeking Henry C F, tailor G Stauffer, bds 195 Broadway.

Woebbeking Sophia M, bds 195 Broadway.

Woebbeking Theodore, helper, res 104 Summit.

Woebbeking Wm E, buyer J A Armstrong & Co, res 39 Wilt.

Woechenliche Freie Presse, Fort Wayne Freie Presse Co publishers, 24 Clinton.

Woehnker Frank H, helper Seavey Hardware Co, res 46 Erie.

Woehnker Fred H, driver Seavey Hardware Co. res 227 E Jefferson.

Woehnker Frederick, janitor, res 205 E Washington.

Woehnker Henry J, helper Penn Co, bds 205 E Washington

Woehnker Herman, molder, res 224 E Wayne.

Woehnker John N, bds 205 E Washington,

Woehnker Wm C, lab Globe Spice Mills, res 209 E Washington.

Woehr Frederick, upholsterer, res 204 Metz.

Woehr Wm, laborer, bds 204 Metz.

Woenker Agnes, ironer W B Phillips, bds 21 Oak.

Woenker Bernard, car bldr Penn Co, rms 73 Summit.

Woenker Christopher, laborer, res 21 Oak.

Woenker Frank, shoemkr Matthias App, res 91 Summit.

Woenker Henry, laborer. bds 21 Oak.

Wohlers Augusta, domestic 242 W Berry.

Wohlers Charlotte (wid Henry), bds 174 Francis.

Wohlers Lena, bds 32 Stophlet.

Wohlfort Emma C, forewoman Hoosier Mnfg Co, bds 389 Calhoun.

Wohlfort Martha E (wid Rosmond W), teacher Hanna School, res 389 Calhoun.

Wohlfromm Leopold, butcher N B Rowe, res 418 Broadway

Wolf, *see also Woulf and Wulf.*

Wolf Abraham, res 73 W Main.

Wolf Alfred A, hoseman, 89 E Main, res 70 same.

Wolf August, teamster. res 39 Liberty.

Wolf Bessie I, bds 354 W Main.

Wolf Bruno, blksmith Olds' Wagon Wks, res 155 Eliza.

Wolf Carrie E, bds 354 W Main.

Wolf Daniel H, carpenter, res 612 E Wayne.

Wolf Edward F, engineer N Y. C & St L R R, res 309 W Main.

Wolf Ephraim E, student. bds 354 W Main.

Wolf Frederick, helper L E & W R R, res w s Cass 1 s of 7th.

Wolf Frederick A, baker H H Barcus, bds 238 Calhoun.

Wolf Frederick H, brakeman N Y, C & St L R R, bds 71 Boone.

Wolf George, messgr Penn Co, bds n w cor Mercer and Savannah.

Wolf Henry, teamster Amelia Kraus, bds rear 34 Cochran

Wolf Jasper E, foreman Anthony Wayne Mnfg Co, res 363 Lafayette.

45

Wolf John W, lab Bass Wks, res n w cor Savannah an Mercer.
Wolf Levi A, butcher, res 354 W Main.
Wolf Louis (Louis Wolf & Co), res 204 W Berry. Tel 259
Wolf Louis & Co (Louis Wolf), Dry Goods and Carpets, 54 Calhoun. Tel 217.
Wolf Michael, laborer, res 65 Oliver.
Wolf Minnie, domestic w s Spy Run av 1 n of Elizabeth.
Wolf Otto P, clk P E Wolf, bds n e cor Liberty and Canal
Wolf Paul E, Furniture and Pres Ft Wayne Carpet Beating Wks, 33–35 Clinton, res n e cor Liberty and Canal. Tel 404, res 403.
Wolf Pauline, seamstress, bds 67 John.
Wolf Samuel, mngr Louis Wolf & Co, bds 73 W Main.
Wolf Sophia, domestic 466 Calhoun.
Wolf Wm, laborer, bds 139 Taylor.
Wolf Wm A G, teacher Zion Lutheran School, res 415 Hanna.
Wolf Wm W, clerk, bds J W Wolf.
Wolfe Emma F, bds 271 W De Wald.
Wolfe Fredrica C (wid Edmund F), bds 271 W De Wald.
Wolfe Henry R, toolmkr Ft W Elec Corp, res 406 Broadway.
Wolff Alfred A, fireman Engine Co No 1, res 70 E Main.
Wolff Bertha, domestic 202 W Washington.
Wolff C Henry, shoemkr 61 Wells, res 70 E Main.
Wolff Ella, dressmaker, bds 11 Harrison.
Wolford Dennis A, punchman Penn Co, res 48 Miner.
Wolford Lee, bds 408 Hanna.
Wolford Rush L, laborer, bds 408 Hanna.
Wolford Wm A, foreman, res 408 Hanna.
Wolfrum Adam, carpenter, bds 61 E Main.
Wolfrum John G, stenogr Penn Co, bds 92 Fairfield av.
Wolfrum John T, carpet weaver 92 Fairfield av, res same.
Wolfrum Leopold, butcher, res 418 Broadway.
Wolke Frederick A, carpenter, bds 55 Barr.
Wolke Wm, helper Keller & Braun, bds cor Hillsdale and Baker avs.
Wolke Wm F, contractor 17 Jones, res same.
Wollert Rudolph, car repr Penn Co, res 160 Force.
Wolz Mat J, finisher Ft W Furn Co, bds 34 W Superior.
Wood Alexander P, bds 286 W Wayne.
Wood Ezra, bds 122 Chicago.
Wood Frank C, clk E H Coombs, res 47 Grace av.
Wood George E, foreman Ft W E Corp, bds 103 W Berry

Wood Hester A (wid George W), res 50 W Superior.

Wood James J, electrician Ft Wayne Elec Corp, res 286 W Wayne.

Wood Jeannette L (wid Washington), bds 28 Lincoln av.

Wood Matilda M (wid Charles), res 11 Lavina.

Wood Oscar D, laborer, res 180 Gay.

Wood Paul E, toolmkr Ft W Elec Corp, bds 103 W Berry

Wood Vernie E, bds 286 W Wayne.

Wood Wm C jr, civil engr Penn Co, rms 100 Harrison.

Wood Wm E, helper Ft W Elec Ry Co, bds 122 Chicago.

Wood Wm J, foreman Standard Wheel Co, bds 101 Wallace

Woodard John, laborer, bds St James Hotel.

Woodard John, mach Ft W Elec Corp, res 233 Calhoun.

Woodruff Wm H, clk Penn Co, res 310 E Creighton av.

Woods Ada (wid Milton), clk Wm Rockhill, res 40 W Superior.

Woods Isaac N, promoter Harrison Ft Wayne Telephone Co, res 430 E Wayne.

Woods James F, harnessmkr, bds 57 Barr.

Woods Robert, laborer, bds 28 E Columbia.

Woodward Edward, removed to St Louis, Mo.

Woodward Edward J, fireman G R & I R R, bds 29 E Williams.

Woodward Grace T, stenogr, bds 106 E Main.

Woodward Harry D, bds 106 E Main.

Woodward Mrs Jennie S, teacher Clay School, res 106 E Main.

Woodward Marcus E, clk Pixley & Co, bds 106 E Main.

Woodworth Alice, bds 224 W Wayne.

Woodworth Alida T (C B Woodworth & Co), res 234 W Berry.

Woodworth Benjamin S, clk C B Woodworth & Co, bds 254 W Wayne.

Woodworth Charles B (C B Woodworth & Co), res 254 W Wayne. Tel 194.

Woodworth C B & Co (Charles B, Laura and Alida T Woodworth), dental depot 1 New Aveline House Blk. Tel 16.

Woodworth C B & Co (Charles B Woodworth), Druggists, 1 New Aveline House Blk. Tel 16.

Woodworth Edward J, lawyer, 36 E Main, bds 224 W Main.

Woodworth James C, asst cash Old National Bank, res 224 W Wayne.

Woodworth James E, boilermkr, res 26 Melita.

Woodworth Laura (C B Woodworth & Co), res 234 W Berry
Woodworth Mary (wid James), bds 26 Melita.
Wooff Joseph F, mach Penn Co, res 127 Holman.
Woolery Frank H, brakeman N Y, C & St L R R, res 12
Jackson.
Woolery Wm H, brakeman N Y, C & St L R R, bds 12
Jackson.
Woolever Orla A, bds 63 Boone.
Woolsey Ann E (wid John V), bds Harrison n e cor Allen.
Woolsey Hiram B, mach Star Iron Tower Co, res 25 W
Creighton av.
Woolsey Isaac B, bds 76 E Pontiac.
Woolsey Jay C, bds 25 W Creighton av.
Woolsey Kate V (wid Samuel), bds 92 Wilt.
Worch Louis A, optician, 101 Calhoun, res 22 W Washington. Tel 200.
Worch Louise A, dressmkr, 22 W Washington, res same.
Worden Anna (wid James R), res 209 Barr.
Worden Charles H (Zollars & Worden), res 279 Fairfield
av. Tel 504.
Worden Harry L, clk Penn Co, res 41 Hugh.
Work Alexander S, trav engineer N Y, C & St L R R,
res 250 W Jefferson.
Work Hannah M (wid Robert), res 44 Pritchard.
Work Robert C, milk, 44 Pritchard, bds same.
Work Wesley I, trav agt, res 86 E Washington.
Work Wm S, teamster, res 35 E Butler.
Workman Samuel, meats, 230 Calhoun, res 228 same.
Worman Harry W, laborer, bds 143 Force.
Worman Jacob, engr Penn Co, res 143 Force.
Worman Samuel O, flagman Penn Co, res 101 Greene.
Worman Wm H, laborer, bds 143 Force.
Wormcastle Hugh M C, lumberman, res 121 Greene.
Wormer Ella, domestic School for M Y.
Wort Alfred A, lab Ft W Gas Co, bds 122 E Main.
Wort John H, clk American Ex Co, bds 122 E Main.
Wort John M, foreman Ft W Gas Co, res 122 E Main.
Worton Matthew. section foreman L S & M S R R, res s
w corner 5th and Harrison.
Woulfe, see also Wolf and Wulf.
Woulfe Ella, waiter McKinnie House, rms same.
Woulfe Catherine, bds 36 Melita.
Woulfe James, res 28 Baker.
Woulfe John J, clk Wabash R R, bds 28 Baker.
Woulfe Marie (wid Michael). res 36 Melita.

Woulfe Richard, laborer, res 35 Melita.
Woy George, engr B W Skelton, bds 43 Wagner.
Wratel Joseph, cabinetmkr Ft W Furn Co, bds 3 Duryea.
Wray Amelia, nurse Hope Hospital.
Wren Mary M (wid Joseph), bds 64 Charles.
Wright Anna B, bds 241 W Washington.
Wright Carrie C, bds 51 W Butler.
Wright Charles E, time keeper Wabash R R, bds 51 W Butler.
Wright Charles F. cupola tndr C M Menefee, bds 77 Home av.
Wright Clara M, bds 77 Home av.
Wright Daniel, watchman Ft W O Co, res 77 Home av.
Wright Daniel, lab Penn Co, res cor Leith and McLaughlin
Wright Elmira J (wid Samuel P), res 51 W Butler.
Wright Frank F, engr, res 13 McClellan.
Wright James (col'd), waiter The Wayne, res 93 E Lewis.
Wright Jennie, coremkr Ft W Elec Corp, bds 46 Lavina.
Wright John D, finisher, res 1 McLachlan.
Wright John M, supt Barber Asphalt Paving Co, bds New Aveline House.
Wright Luther, helper Wabash R R, res 11 Colerick.
Wright Manford C, appr Wabash R R, res 51 W Butler.
Wright Mary E (wid Louis), res 46 Lavina.
Wright Mary J (wid Edward), res 157 Madison.
Wright Norval W, student, bds 67 W De Wald.
Wright Philip L, laborer, bds 77 Home av.
Wright Thomas B, bkkpr Ft Wayne Artificial Ice Co, bds 67 W De Wald.
Wright Wm U, mach hd Ft W O Co, res 59 Home av.
Wuertenberger Catherine (wid Paul), bds 26 Orchard.
Wuertenberger Ernest, collarmkr, res 26 Orchard.
Wulf, *see also Wolf and Woulfe.*
Wulf Christian, shoemkr 74 Barr, res same.
Wunderlin Gustav, florist G W Flick, res 22 Park av.
Wunderlin Wm, foreman Weil Bros & Co, res 79 Summit.
Wursthorn Anthony, res w s Walton av 3 s of Pontiac.
Wurtle Elida I, bds 52 Miner.
Wurtle Wm G, mach Ft W Elec Corp, res 52 Miner.
Wyatt Henry M, res 112 E Main.
Wyatt Isaiah, conductor, res 24 E Washington.
Wyatt Jasper N, cabtmkr Ft Wayne Furn Co, res 41 Lasselle
Wyatt Marion, painter, bds 112 E Main.
Wyatt Thomas T, waiter, bds 112 E Main.
Wybourn Christopher W, helper Penn Co, res 90 E Lewis

706 R. L. POLK & CO.'s

Wygralak Otto F, cabinetmkr, bds s e cor Rudisill av and Calhoun.
Wygralak Stanislaus, lab, res s e cor Rudisill av and Calhoun.
Wymer Bert, brakeman N Y, C & St L R R, bds 324 W Main.
Wyneken Ferdinand, clk, res rear 9 Howard.
Wysong Wm C, painter School for F M Y, res Griswold av.
Wyss, *see also Wies.*
Wyss Albrecht, cabtmkr Ft W Furn Co, res e s Harrison 2 s of Killea av.
Wyss Gerhard S, clk County Auditor, bds 195 E Lewis.
Wyss Philip H, Contractor and Builder, Oliver n e cor Emily, res same. (*See p 115.*)
Wyss Theodore, meat market, 66 Gay, res 14 Grant.

Y

Yager, *see Jaeger and Yeager.*
Yager Lizzie, bds 15 Oak.
Yagerlehner Charles, winder Ft W Elec Corp, bds 201 W Jefferson.
Yaggy Hannah, domestic 111 E Wayne.
Yahne Frank L, boarding house 106 Barr.
Yahney John H, laborer, bds 223 Lafayette.
Yanklevetch Frank, pedler, res 140 Maumee rd.
Yann George V, tuner Ft Wayne O Co, res 114 W Williams
Yant Frederick, bartndr C Muehlfeith, rms 10 W Main.
Yant Leander E, truckman Penn Co, res 30 Julia.
Yarian Isaac N, res 10 Marion.
Yarnelle Edith A, bds 282 W Wayne.
Yarnelle Edward F (Mossman, Yarnelle & Co), res 282 W Wayne. Tel 224.
Yates Andrew, laborer, bds 207 Metz.
Yates Ann (wid Wm), bds 18 Michigan av.
Yates Cora, bds 207 Metz.
Yates Edna, bds 18 Michigan av.
Yates Harry, teamster, bds 207 Metz.
Yates Ida M, bds 207 Metz.
Yates Mary (wid John), res 207 Metz.
Yates Nellie, milliner, bds 18 Michigan av.
Yates Olive L, dressmkr, bds 18 Michigan av.
Yates Wm, engineer, res 18 Michigan av.
Yates Wm L, iron wkr, bds 18 Michigan av.
Yautz, *see also Jautz.*

Yautz Conrad W, lab Wabash R R, res 25 Orchard.
Yeager, *see also Jaeger and Yager.*
Yeager Edward M, brakeman, bds 41 E 3d.
Yeager Yetta, bds 41 E 3d.
Yeakley Charles, barber, bds 20 W Superior.
Yenney Gottlieb, bds 312 E Wayne.
Yenney Mrs Mary, res 312 E Wayne.
Yenney Robert, mach hd L Rastetter & Son, res 237 Barr.
Yenni John, engr Rhinesmith & Simonson, res 314 Clay.
Yergens Gustave F, cigar mnfr, res 90 W Washington.
Yergens Sophia, domestic 160 W Washington.
Yergens Wilhelmina (wid Henry), bds 87 Montgomery.
Yergens Wm (Ranke & Yergens), res 87 W Washington.
Yergens Wm jr, painter, bds 87 W Washington.
Yergens Wm F A, fireman Wabash R R, bds 87 W Washington.
Yerick Edward H, engineer, res 64 W 5th.
Yerk Charles P, molder, res rear 21 Francis.
Yerk Charles P, molder, res 231 Harmer.
Yetter Charles, market gardener, res w s Spy Run av 8 n of Canal bridge.
Yetter Charles jr, bds C Yetter.
Yetter Millie, bds C Yetter.
Yoast, *see also Joost and Yost.*
Yoast Charles, conductor, res 399 Clinton.
Yobs Dora, bds 69 E Main.
Yobst Annie, bds 206 E Washington.
Yobst Belbine (wid Alexander), res 206 E Washington.
Yobst Bruno, res 83 Cass.
Yobst Charles B, plumber E Martin, bds 206 E Washington
Yobst Dorothea, opr S M Foster, bds 69 E Main.
Yobst Elizabeth (wid Aman), res 11 Edna.
Yobst Elizabeth M, bds 201 E Jefferson.
Yobst Elizabeth, bds 206 E Washington.
Yobst Frank H, died January 8, 1894.
Yobst F Wm, driver C L Centlivre Brewing Co, res 161 E Washington.
Yobst Grace, trimmer, bds 206 E Washington.
Yobst Henry, plumber C W Bruns & Co, bds 83 Cass.
Yobst John, clerk, res 1 Fry.
Yobst Joseph, butcher. res 57 W Williams.
Yobst Minnie K (wid Frank H), res 3 Short.
Yobst Tracy C, bds 206 E Washington.
Yobst Wm, bds 11 Edna.

708 R. L. POLK & CO.'S

Yoder W Amos F, clerk Mossman, Yarnelle & Co, res 51 Miner.
Yoest Charles, brakeman, res 399 Clinton.
Yohey Addie, canvasser, bds 19 Miner.
Yohey Charles C, lab Penn Co, bds 19 Miner.
Yohey Daisy D, bds 19 Miner.
Yohey Joseph M, res 19 Miner.
Yoho John, lab, bds 46 E Columbia.
Yokel Amelia, bds 118 W DeWald.
Yokel Annie, bds 118 W DeWald.
Yokel Louise (wid Matthias), res 118 W DeWald.
Yost, *see Joost and Yoast.*
You Adolph J, Clerk of The Administration Boards City Hall, res 22 Van Buren.
Young Alfred W, trav agt, bds 171 W Washington.
Young Almah L, clk H H Barcus, bds 31 Hough.
Young Amos, laborer, bds 66 Howell.
Young August F A, bds 58 W 3d.
Young Bessie, bds 31 Hough.
Young Birdie, stenographer, bds 31 Hough.
Young Carrie E, bds 205 Taylor.
Young Charles, bkkpr S Freiburger & Bro, res 73 Webster.
Young Charles, carpenter, res 80 Oakley.
Young Charles H, draughtsman Bass Wks, bds 130 Wilt.
Young Cora M, bds S Young.
Young Edgar S, clk N Y, C & St L R R, res 101 W Superior.
Young Edward S, lab, res n s Rebecca 1 e of G R & I R R
Young Flavius J, County Supt of Schools, 11 Bass Blk, res 787 Broadway.
Young Frank A, exp messgr, res 117½ E Wayne.
Young Fred G, attendant School for F M Y.
Young George, hostler G D Ohneck.
Young George, contractor, 367 Broadway, res same.
Young Gertrude (wid Nicholas), res 74 E Leith.
Young Harry E, machinist, bds 31 Hough.
Young Henry W, carver Ft W O Co, bds 205 Taylor.
Young Henry W A, laborer, res 93 E Columbia.
Young James R, bds 505 E Washington.
Young James S, bds 36 E Columbia.
Young James W, switchman Penn Co, bds 164 Walton av.
Young Jesse H, insurance, res 76 E DeWald.
Young John, yd condr Penn Co, res 31 Hough.
Young John B, music teacher, res 563 E Washington.

Young John T, engineer, res 99 N Harrison.
Young Joseph, laborer, res 26 Killea av.
Young Josie L, bds 563 E Washington.
Young Lena. domestic 116 Madison.
Young Lewis, well digger, res 58 W 3d,
Young Lizzie, opr S M Foster, bds 74 E Leith.
Young Lois A, bds 171 W Washington.
Young Louis, lab N Y, C & St L R R, res 205 Taylor.
Young Louis W. bartndr. bds 58 W 3d.
Young L Hiram, saloon, 36 E Columbia. res same.
Young Louise H, candymkr, bds 205 Taylor.
Young Men's Christian Association (City Dept), A H Polhamus Pres. W F McCaughey, Financial Secretary, 103–105 Calhoun. Tel 529.
Young Men's Christian Association (R R Dept). Amos Sine Chairman, J W Burns Genl Sec, 245 Calhoun.
Young Paul, laborer, res 31 Charles.
Young Paulina. bds 73 Webster.
Young Peter, shoemkr, 25 Ewing, res same.
Young Ransom (col'd), brakeman Penn Co, res 72 Murray.
Young Ruby F, bds 221 W Main.
Young Stephen. laborer, res 66 Howell.
Young Sylvester P, condr, res 525 E Lewis.
Young Tillie, domestic 312 W Washington.
Young Tillman C. painter, bds 66 Howell.
Young Winnie, bds 73 Webster.
Young Wm, clk Ft W Music Co, bds.130 Wilt.
Younk Wm, fireman, bds 324 Calhoun.
Young Wm C, stonecutter Griebel & Pask, res 171 W Washington.
Young Wm D, clerk, res 130 Wilt.
Young Wm G, fireman Ft W Elec Ry Co, res 407½ E Lewis
Young Women's Christian Assn. Mrs Harriet O Underhill matron, 25 W Wayne.
Younge John W, physician, 176 Calhoun. res 407 Webster
Younker Arley J, stripper A C Baker. bds 174 Maumee rd
Younker George W, painter, res 174 Maumee rd.
Younker Isaac C, car repr Penn Co, bds 316 E Creigh-ton av,
Yunk Gertrude (wid Nicholas), res 74 E Leith.
Yunk Jacob, laborer, bds 74 E Leith.
Yunk Mathias, cabinetmkr, bds 74 E Leith.

Yunker Charles, lab, res w s Euclid av 3 s of E Creighton av.

Z

Zagel Andrew J, teacher, res 109 Hanna.
Zagel August L, clk Stahn & Heinrich, bds 109 Hanna.
Zagel Henry C. helper, bds 109 Hanna.
Zagel Sophia L, bds 109 Hanna.
Zahn Catherine (wid Andrew), res 27 Erie.
Zahn Charles A, cigar mkr John Zern, bds 173 Hanna.
Zahn Elizabeth, milliner, bds 27 Erie.
Zahn Frederick, car bldr Penn Co, res 173 Hanna.
Zahn Matthias, cupulo tndr Ind M Wks, res 241 E Jefferson
Zahn Wm, clk Fred Lenz, bds 173 Hanna.
Zahn Wm J, butcher, bds 173 Hanna.
Zakszewski Frank, tailor J Rabus, res 124 E Madison.
Zaro George, bds 108 Clinton.
Zaro John, bds 108 Clinton.
Zartman Rev Allen K, pastor Grace Reformed Church, res 96 E Washington.
Zauner, see also Sahner and Sayner.
Zauner Amelia A, operator, bds 33 Force.
Zauner Hannah, opr S M Foster. bds 33 Force.
Zauner Henry M, engineer, bds 33 Force.
Zauner Matthias, engr Bass F & M Wks, res 33 Force.
Zegenfus Margaret (wid David), res 23 Hough.
Zeh Wm, tinner Wabash R R, res 220 Lafayette.
Zehender Katie, domestic 51 Columbia av.
Zeigenfelder Mary (wid George), bds 260 E Jefferson.
Zeisig Emil, lab Bass F & M Wks, res 58 Elm.
Zeis Sylvester S, trav agt, bds 33 Walton av.
Zeller, see also Zoeller.
Zeller Anna C, bds 98 Archer av.
Zeller Anton, mason, bds 98 Archer.
Zeller Bernadina, bds 98 Archer av.
Zeller Josephine, bds 98 Archer av.
Zeller Kilian, laborer, res 98 Archer av.
Zellers Wm, lab Penn Co, res 56 Charles.
Zelt Catherine (wid Nicholas), bds 58 Division.
Zelt Edward F, grocer 401 E Wayne, res same.
Zelt Frederick, bds 401 E Wayne.
Zelt John, grocer, 149 Gay, res 151 same.
Zelt Theodore F N, carp. res 75 Maumee rd.
Zelt Wm, clk John Zelt, bds 151 Gay.
Zelt's Hall, s e cor E Creighton av and Gay.

Zent John F, capt Engine Co No 6, rms same.
Zeperning Christian, helper, res 138 John.
Zeperning Ferdinand, cash boy, bds 138 John.
Zepp Frederick, mason, res 48 Archer av.
Zepp Frederick P, laborer, bds 48 Archer av.
Zern Gregory A, student, bds 348 Hanna.
Zern John, grocer 342 Hanna, res same.
Zern Justina (wid Xavier), res 348 Hanna.
Zern Mary, clerk, bds 348 Hanna.
Zern Matilda, bds 348 Hanna.
Zerull Augusta, mach opr, bds 94 Howell.
Zerull Herman, helper Horton Mnfg Co, res 94 Howell.
Zerull Julius W, helper, bds 94 Howell.
Zerull Minnie, domestic 154 W Superior.
Zeschoche Clara A, domestic 134 E Washington.
Zickau Frederick W, molder, res 55 John.
Zickgraf Charles G, meats 19 Grand, res 18 Gay.
Ziegler Adam G, wagonmkr Jacob A Spereisen, res 19 Maple av.
Ziegler Caroline M, bds 19 Maple av.
Ziegler Charles W, clk R Siemon, bds 19 Maple av.
Ziegler Charles W, condr N Y, C & St L R R, res 203 W Superior.
Ziegler Frank W, clk W Hahn & Co, bds 220 E Washington.
Ziegler Frederick G, foreman, res 114 Home av.
Ziegler George F, laborer, res 13 Huffman.
Ziegler George G, nailer Standard Wheel Co, res 19 Maple av.
Ziegler Henry J, laborer, bds 19 Maple av.
Ziegler John A, bds 19 Maple av.
Ziegler Sarah I (wid Jeremiah), res 220 E Washington.
Ziemendorff Charles W, porter Fox Br U S Baking Co, bds 19 Wagner.
Ziemendorff Frederick (F Ziemendorff & Son), res 19 Wagner.
Ziemendorff Frederick & Son (Frederick and Wm F), Portland, Cement and Diamond Walks, 19 Wagner.
Ziemendorff Theodore, laborer, bds 19 Wagner.
Ziemendorff Wm F (Frederick Ziemendorff & Son), bds 19 Wagner.
Zimmer Emil, painter H A Kirchefer, bds 152 Greely.
Zimmer Carpet Cleaning Co (J G Zimmer & Son), 202 St Joseph boulevard. Tel 496.

Zimmer Cyrus (Zimmer Carpet Cleaning Co), res 201 St Joseph boulevard.

Zimmer John G (Zimmer Carpet Cleaning Co), res 200 St Joseph boulevard.

Zimmer John G & Son (John G and Cyrus W), proprs Zimmer Carpet Cleaning Co, 200 St Joseph boulevard Tel 690.

Zimmer Oscar E, trav agt, res 6 N Fulton.

Zimmerly Mrs Caroline A, bds 158 Griffith.

Zimmerly Frederick J (C W Bruns & Co), res 158 Griffith.

Zimmerly Wm, res 78 Dawson.

Zimmerly Wm, letter carrier P O, res 19 Lavina.

Zimmerman Anthony, res 522 Fairfield av.

Zimmerman Augustina (wid Andrew), nurse. res 59 E Wayne.

Zimmerman Charles M. erecter Kerr Murray Mnfg Co, bds Windsor Hotel.

Zimmerman Clara, stenogr Wayne Knitting Mills, bds 522 Fairfield av.

Zimmerman Ernest H, student, bds 110 Summit.

Zimmerman George, barber M Momper, bds 17 W 5th.

Zimmerman Hannah (wid John), res 110 Summit.

Zimmerman John B, carver Ft W O Co, bds 552 Fairfield av

Zimmerman Kate, seamstress, bds 40 Pritchard.

Zimmerman Mary, forewoman Horton Mnfg Co, bds 40 Pritchard.

Zimmerman Wm, boilermkr, bds 40 Pritchard.

Zimmermann Anna, bds 77 Baker.

Zimmermann Anthony, shoemkr, res 40 Pritchard.

Zimmermann David, carpenter, res 17 W 5th

Zimmermann Denora, dressmkr, bds 77 Baker.

Zimmermann Edward, lab Ft W Elec Corp, bds 77 Baker.

Zimmermann Frank E, clerk, res 77 Baker.

Zimmermann Henry J, clk L O Hull, bds 289 W Jefferson

Zimmermann John, clerk, res 289 W Jefferson.

Zimmermann Julia J, domestic 289 Fairfield av.

Zimmermann Louisa, domestic 17 Barthold.

Zimmermann Lulu, bds 289 W Jefferson.

Zimmermann Martin F, clk Adolph Foellinger, bds 289 W Jefferson.

Zimmermann Martin S, lab C W Bruns & Co. res 294 Broadway.

Zimmermann Paul J, clk L O Hull, bds 289 W Jefferson.

Zink, see also Sink and Szink.

Zink John W, painter, res 55 Smith.

Zink Joseph, brakeman N Y, C & St L R R, bds 5 Boone.
Zinn John H, switchman, bds 9 Buchanan.
Zinn John N, meats 198 Broadway, res same.
Zion German Lutheran Church, s w cor E Creighton av and Force.
Zion German Lutheran School, s w cor E Creighton av and Force.
Zitzman Augusta (wid Edward), res 108 Maumee rd.
Zitzman Charles T, hostler L H McAfee, bds 3 Wells.
Zitzman John G, engr W H Brudi & Bros, bds 76 Wells.
Zitzman Margaret A (wid Peter), bds 179 Metz.
Zoeller, *see also Zeller.*
Zoeller Roman (Zoeller & Merz), res 370 Calhoun.
Zoeller & Merz (Roman Zoeller, Louis Merz), grocers 370 Calhoun. Tel 238.
Zollars Allen (Zollars & Worden), res 17 Brackenridge.
Zollars Charles E. student, bds 17 Brackenridge.
Zollars Clara E, bds 17 Brackenridge.
Zollars Edith A, bds 122 W Wayne.
Zollars Frank, bds 148 High.
Zollars Fred E, student Zollars & Worden, bds 17 Brackenridge.
Zollars John M, mach hd, res 148 High.
Zollars & Worden (Allen Zollars, Charles H Worden), Lawyers, 62 Calhoun cor Berry. Tel 391.
Zollinger August, saloon, 562 E Washington, res 575 same
Zollinger Battery Armory, 27 Calhoun.
Zollinger Charles, bds 17 E Superior.
Zollinger Charles C, boilermkr Wabash R R, res 170 John
Zollinger Christian F, bds 575 E Washington.
Zollinger Christian F jr, clk August Zollinger, bds 575 E Washington.
Zollinger Edward, mach hd. res 11 Calhoun.
Zollinger George H, student, bds 17 E Superior.
Zollinger Henry A, collector, bds 10 W Superior.
Zollinger Henry C (L C Zollinger & Bro), res 10 W Superior
Zollinger Henry L, car bldr Penn Po, res 172 John.
Zollinger Louis C (L C Zollinger & Bro), res 17 E Superior
Zollinger L C & Bro (Louis C and Henry C), Carriage, Wagon and Truck Mnfrs, Blacksmithing, Horseshoeing and Carriage Painting, 13–17 E Superior. (*See left bottom lines and p 89.*)
Zollinger Matilda, bds 17 E Superior.
Zollinger Wm F, carp Penn Co, res 98 Wabash av.
Zook Fannie L, student, bds 191 W DeWald.

714   R. L. POLK & CO.'S

Zook John H. painter, res 191 W DeWald.
Zorbaugh Emanuel, mach Penn Co, res 570 Broadway.
Zorbaugh Philip L, solicitor S C Lumbard, bds 570 Broadway.
Zuber Andrew F W, lab, bds e s Piqua av 3 s of Rudisill av.
Zuber Ferdinand, laborer, res 509 E Washington.
Zuber Hieronymus R, butcher, res 525 E Wayne.
Zuber Jacob J, carp, res 812 Broadway.
Zuber Jacob P, laborer, bds 812 Broadway.
Zuber John, bds 31 Pine.
Zuber John C, carp Penn Co, res 288 E Jefferson.
Zuber John G, shoes, 92 Broadway, 156 Fairfield av, res 31 Pine.
Zuber Joseph J, bds 812 Broadway.
Zuber Nicholas, plasterer, rms 58 Maumee rd.
Zuber Phillip, carpenter, res 3 Liberty.
Zuber Wm D, lab, res e s Piqua av 3 s of Rudisill av.
Zucker Anna L, teacher McCulloch School, bds 49 Walter.
Zucker Frederick, professor Concordia College, res 49 Walter.
Zumbro Anna, bds 23 Elm.
Zumbro George M, brakeman, bds 23 Elm.
Zumbro Henry, watchman F M Smaltz, res 23 Elm.
Zumbro Henry W, clk Scheumann & Klaehn, bds 23 Elm.
Zumbro Wm L, carpenter, res 59 Elm.
Zurbrugg John, helper, res 21 John.
Zurbrugg Julian, lab Penn Co, bds 21 John.
Zumbrum Minnie, helper Randall Hotel.
Zurbuch Anthony J, condr Penn Co, res 91 Buchanan.
Zurbuch F Xavier, lab, res s w cor Pontiac and Webster.
Zurbuch George, trav agt, res 315 Hanna.
Zurbuch George I, clk Geo De Wald & Co, bds Pontiac s w cor Webster.
Zurbuch Henry A, clk Louis Wolf & Co, bds Pontiac s w cor Webster.
Zurbach John C, conductor, res 187 Suttenfield.
Zurbuch Joseph F (M Rinehart & Co), res 387 W Main.
Zurbuch Peter V, clk Penn Co, res Pontiac s w cor Webster.
Zurbuch Wm J, clk Geo De Wald & Co, bds Pontiac s w cor Webster.
Zur-Muehlen Henry, clk H N Ward, res 52 W Lewis.
Zuttermeister Wm, lab Ft W Elec Corp, res 18 McClellan
Zwahlen Frank M, res 256 E Lewis.
Zwahlen Harry A, letter carrier P O, res 52 Walnut.
Zwaigler John, laborer, rms 104 E Wayne.
Zwick Mary C, domestic 353 W Main.

R. L. POLK & CO.'S
FORT WAYNE DIRECTORY.
1895-96.

CLASSIFIED BUSINESS DIRECTORY.

Names appearing under headings marked * are only inserted when specially contracted for.

ABSTRACTS OF TITLE.

Crane G D, 36 E Berry.
Dreibelbiss Abstract of Title Co The, 25 Court.
Graham J E, 26 Bank Blk.
Jones G W, 9 and 11 W Main.
Miller & Dougall, 4 Foster Blk.
The Abstract Office (Kuhne & Co), 19 Court.

ACCOUNTANTS.

Crane G D, 36 E Berry.

*ACME CEMENT PLASTER.

Moellering W & Son 53–59 Murray. (*See back bone and p 83.*)

*ADDRESSING.

Polk R L & Co, 122 LaSalle, Chicago, Ill.

AGENTS LOAN.

(*See also Loan Agents.*)

Kuhne & Co, 19 Court.
Mohr & Sosenheimer, 19 W Wayne.
Seidel Edward, 52½ Calhoun.

716   R. L. POLK & CO.'S

AGRICULTURAL IMPLEMENTS.

(See also Hardware.)

Alderman Dayton, 4 Harrison.
Cook C W, 50 and 52 E Columbia.
Heller T S, 25 Wells.
Kaough Wm, 54 and 56 E Columbia.
Morgan & Beach, 19 E Columbia. *(See back cover.)*
Parham F C, 31 Barr.
Pfeiffer & Schlatter, 38 and 40 E Columbia. *(See left side lines.)*
Shordon Daniel, 61 and 63 E Columbia.
Solon Bernard, 55 E Columbia.

*ALE AND PORTER.

(See also Bottling Works.)

Brames L & Co, 123-127 Clay. *(See p 3.)*

AMMUNITION.

See Guns and Ammunition.

AMUSEMENTS--PLACES OF.

See Theatres, Halls. Etc.

ARCHITECTS.

(See also Carpenters, Contractors, and Builders.)

Grindle Alfred, 34-37 Bass Blk.
Kendrick C E, 22 Schmitz Blk.
Ordway A D, 12 Schmitz Blk.
Riedel J M E, 3d Floor Schmitz Blk, cor Calhoun and Washington. *(See front cover.)*
Tolan B S, 62 W DeWald.
Wing & Mahurin, 41. 42 and 43 Pixley & Long Bldg.

*ARTIFICIAL STONE.

Johnson J H, 68 E Columbia. *(See p 99.)*

ARTISTS.

Dille Bessie I, 27 Lavina.

Dillo Joseph H, 27 Lavina.
Grier Mrs F J, 52 E DeWald.
Homsher F B, 508 Calhoun.
Johnson M E, 26 Schmitz Blk.
Serailian M K, 14 Schmitz Blk.

ARTISTS' MATERIALS.

Hull L O, 90 Calhoun. (*See back cover.*)
Siemon & Bro., 50 Calhoun. (*See back cover.*)
Stahn & Heinrich, 116 Calhoun.

ATTORNEYS AT LAW.
See Lawyers.

AUCTIONEERS.

Stapleford L, P, 39 E Main.

AWNING AND TENT MNFRS.

Beach F J, 290 Calhoun.
Reineke F J, 41 E Main. (*See p 115.*)

*BABY CARRIAGES.

Pfeiffer & Schlatter, 38–40 E Columbia. (*See left side lines.*)

BAKERS.

(*See also Confectioners.*)
Aurentz A C, 18 W Berry.
Barcus H H, 288 Calhoun.
Braun George, 135 Fairfield av.
Brenzinger Bread Baking Co The, 14 W Washington.
Fox Branch U S Baking Co, 145–149 Calhoun.
Geller W F, 98 Broadway.
Glaser E F, 195 Hanna.
Gutermuth Benjamin, 29 W Columbia.
Haffner Mrs Mary, 105 E Lewis.
Jacobs Bros, 62 E Main.
Klippert George, 393 Lafayette.
Lange John H & Sons, 327 Calhoun.
Langohr A J, 142 Broadway.
Ross J K, 27 W Columbia.
Scherer L P, 99 Maumee rd.

46

718　　　　　　　R. L. POLK & CO.'s

Schwieters J H, 41 E Columbia.
Seidel Wm & Bro, 111 E Main.
Vetter Andrew, 94 Wells.
Waltemath C H & Sons, 325 Lafayette.

BAKING POWDER MANUFACTURERS.

Kemp Edgar, 169 E Wayne.
Old Fort Spice and Extract Co, 63 E Main.

*BAND SAW MILLS.

Fort Wayne Iron Works, s e cor Superior and Harrison.
Hoffman Bros, 200 W Main. *(See right bottom lines.)*
Hoffman J R & Co, 200 W Main. *(See right bottom lines.)*
Peters Box and Lumber Co, The 75-105 High.

BANDS AND ORCHESTRAS.

Reineke's Orchestra, 70 Calhoun and 41 E Main. *(See p 115.)*

BANKS AND BANKERS.

First National Bank, 73-77 Calhoun.
Hamilton National Bank, 44 Calhoun. *(See front cover.)*
Nuttman & Co, 32 E Main.
Old National Bank, s w cor Calhoun and Berry.
White National Bank, n w cor Wayne and Clinton. *(See right top lines.)*

BAR GOODS.

Kaag M F, 5 E Columbia. *(See left bottom lines.)*

BARBERS.

Atchison M F, 131 Buchanan.
Benninghoff D R, 300 Calhoun.
Brown C L, 9 Maumee rd.
Brown F L, 178½ Broadway.
Brown J W, 42 E Columbia.
Brunskill J S, 318 Lafayette.

Budde J F C, 333½ Lafayette.
Clark Theodore, 352½ Broadway.
Crummitt J H, 147 Hanna.
De Camp W H. 136 Broadway.
Ehrman & Geller, 12 W Main.
Ellert Benoit, 4 New Aveline House Blk, 71 Calhoun.
Fink J B, 56 E Main.
Ford W E, 230 Lafayette.
Gardner James, cor Walton av and P, Ft W & C Ry.
Gardt Henry, 271 Hanna.
Guffin Elmer, 94½ Barr.
Hoemig Charles, 118 Wells.
Hohmann & Swaidner, 248 Calhoun.
Hubbard S G, 21 W Columbia.
Jully Louis, 114 St Mary's av.
Kabisch J H, 137 Fairfield av.
Kelsey W A, 6 Pearl.
Kime W T, s e cor E Creighton av and Gay.
Lauer H C, 562 E Washington.
Lauer John, 154 Barr.
Lichtenwalter W A, 32 E Columbia.
Manet C E, 329 Spy Run av.
Marks L, 213 Lafayette.
Miller Frederick, 331 W Main.
Miller R C, 78 Barr.
Miner Samuel, 378½ W Main.
Monper Mathias, 24 W Main.
Munich John, 352 Calhoun.
Nichter G J, 99 Broadway.
Owens M J, 102 Maumee rd.
Randall Hotel, 2 Harrison.
Reaser F M, 230 W Main.
Rhodenbaugh Arthur, 377 E Washington
Roberts & Ridley, 21 Harrison.
Schele Edward, 156½ Calhoun.
Schlink F H, 109 E Lewis.
Schmuck C B, 101 Fairfield av and 21 Grand.
Shidel C A, 170 Calhoun.
Steiss Bros, 41 W Main.
Sterling Edward, 61 E Berry.
Stevenson W L & Co, 247 Calhoun.
Stier J A. 330 Hanna.
Stites H H, The Randall.
Switzer C W, 59 Holton av.

Uplegger Louis, 45 Wells.
Wallace J H, 374½ Calhoun.
Welch Michael, 86 Barr.
Wellmeier Wm, 170 W Main.
Wertebaugher J S, 272 Calhoun.
Wilder Wm, 203 Calhoun.
Wilkins & Rush, 192 Calhoun.

BARBER'S SUPPLIES.

Gross & Pellens, 94 Calhoun.
Schulder Max, 52 Barr.

BARREL TRUCK MANUFACTURERS.

Bowser S F & Co, cor E Creighton av and
Thomas. (*See p 4.*)

BASE BALL GOODS.

Sportsman's Emporium, 58 E Main. (*See p 87.*)

*BATH ROOMS.

Dodge & Keller, cor W Washington and Broadway. (*See right side lines and page 93.*)

*BATH TUBS.

Ogden Robert, 26 E Berry. (*See embossed line back cover and classified plumbers.*)

BATHS.

(*See also Barbers.*)

Dunne K H, 49 and 51 Pixley & Long Bldg.
Dodge & Keller, cor W Washington and Broadway. (*See right side lines and page 93.*)

BATHS--ALCOHOL.

Dodge & Keller, cor W Washington and Broadway. (*See right side lines and page 93.*)

BATHS-ELECTRIC AND VAPOR.

Bower G B M, 72 Harrison.

*BATHS—ELECTRO THERAPEUTIC.

Gard Brookfield, 13 W Wayne.

*BATHS—HOT WATER.

Dodge & Keller, cor W Washington and Broadway. (*See right side lines and p 93.*)

*BATHS MINERAL.

Dodge & Keller, cor W Washington and Broadway. (*See right side lines and p 93.*)

*BATHS--SALINE.

Dodge & Keller, cor W Washington and Broadway. (*See right side lines and p 93.*)

*BATHS—SEA.

Dodge & Keller, cor W Washington and Broadway. (*See right side lines and p 93.*)

*BATHS—STEAM.

Dodge & Keller, cor W Washington and Broadway. (*See right side lines and p 93.*)

*BATHS—SULPHUR.

Dodge & Keller, cor W Washington and Broadway. (*See right side lines and p 93.*)

*BATHS TURKISH.

Dodge & Keller, cor W Washington and Broadway. (*See right side lines and p 93.*)
Raines S M, 60 Clinton.

BEE HIVE MNFRS.

Hubbard G K, 277 Harrison.

BEE SUPPLIES.

Stockbridge C A, 2 E Columbia.

Fort Wayne Wagon.　　L. O. ZOLLINGER & BRO.,
SOLE MANUFACTURERS,
19 EAST SUPERIOR STREET.

*BEER AGENTS.

Brames L & Co, 123–127 Clay. (*See p 3*).
Epple Gottlieb, 188 Fairfield av.
Fitzgerald Michael, 355 Lafayette.

BELTING AND PACKING.

Morgan & Beach, 19 E Columbia. (*See back cover.*)
Pfeiffer & Schlatter, 38 and 40 E Columbia. (*See left side lines.*)

BICYCLE WOOD RIMS.

Rastetter L & Son, s w cor Broadway and P, Ft W & C Ry.

BICYCLES AND SUPPLIES.

Columbia Machine Wks, 54 E Columbia.
Edgerton C W, 57 W Main.
Katt A C, 37 W Berry.
Krull R L, 128 E Washington.
Randall Cycle Co, 31 W Berry. (*See right top lines and p 536.*)
Steger-Gouty Cycle Co, 126 Calhoun.

BICYCLE REPAIRERS.

Randall Cycle Co, 31 W Berry (*See right top lines and p 536.*)

BILL POSTERS.

Fort Wayne Bill Posting Co, 1 New Aveline House Blk.
Stouder & Smith, Masonic Temple Theater.

BILLIARD HALLS.

(*See also Saloons.*)
Home Billiard Hall, 20 W Berry.
Miller & Meyer, 104 Calhoun.
Search & McCormick, 55 E Berry.

*BIRCH BEER MNFRS.

Brames L & Co, 123–127 Clay. (*See p 3*.)

Troy Steam Laundry HAS ALL THE MODERN MACHINERY. PRICES MODERATE.

BLACK WALNUT LUMBER.

Peters Box and Lumber Co, 79–105 High.

BLACKSMITHS.

(See also Carriage and Wagon Makers, also Horseshoers.)
Angevine G E, 35 Pearl.
Biemer George, 7 Clay.
Bradtmueller C H C, 6 Calhoun.
Edgell Joseph, 13 Lafayette.
Ehrmann Charles, 149 W Main. *(See left side lines.)*
Harter Joseph, 170 W Main.
Hoeppner Charles, s w cor Gay and Creighton av.
Mattes Joseph, 310 W Main.
Mehnert Louis, 93 E Superior. *(See p 101.)*
Meier Ferdinand, 123 Wallace.
Price W B, n s Pioneer av 2 e of Winch.
Rinehart W A, 356 Broadway.
Rupp John. e s N Barr 2 n of Superior.
Schieferstein W R, 146 W Main.
Schlink J H, 363 Calhoun.
Sovine S H, w s of Wells 1 s of St Mary's river.
Spereisen J A, 165 Fairfield av.
Vogely Andrew, 82 Maumee rd.
Waterhouse & Anderson. 88 E Columbia.
Winte J C, 216 Fairfield av.
Zollinger L C & Bro, 13 and 17 E Superior.
(See left bottom lines and p 89).
Zurbuch J F, 387 W Main.

BLANK BOOK MNFRS.

(See also Bookbinders.)
Empire Box Factory and Bookbindery, Bank Blk. *(See right top lines).*
Ft Wayne Book Bindery, Tri–State Bldg.
(See left bottom lines.)
Siemon & Bro, 50 Calhoun. *(See back cover.)*

BLEACHERS AND PRESSERS.

Sheldon C H, 57 Clinton.

BOARDING HOUSES.

Byers Mrs C E, 57 Barr.

Cassady M J, 19 E Jefferson.
Casteel Mary, 209 Lafayette.
Covault Emma, 194 Lafayette.
Darrow J R, 196 Calhoun.
Dennis Mary. 157 Holman.
Fitzgerald Ellen, 39 W Washington.
Fry Margaret, 32 Chicago.
Hamilton House. 103 W Berry.
Hanam A J, 146 Walton av.
Heckler George, 15 Pearl.
Koehlinger Mrs J L, 16 Maiden Lane.
Koppenhover Mrs Mary, 74 W Main.
Kreager H M, 154 Harrison.
Lee S C, 120 Harrison.
McElfatrick Mrs M A, 103 W. Main.
Matsch Kate, 82 Montgomery.
Mayer J G, 6 Force.
Michael Melissa, 252 Clinton.
Monroe Mrs Elizabeth, 20 Murray.
Moon Clara, 231 Barr.
O'Connor Mrs L M, 104 Barr.
Powell Randall, 42 W Main.
Reed J E, 25 W Washington.
Scantling Mrs Catherine, 138 E Berry.
Shideler Mrs S E, 320-Calhoun.
Schulz Adolph F, 199-201 Broadway.
Sturgeon M R, 110 W Jefferson.
Tefft C W, 301 Calhoun.
Tibbits Mrs Sarah F, 319 Harrison.
Weisenburger Emma, 34 W Superior.
Yahne F L, 106 Barr.

BOAT HOUSES.

Hartman Bros, w s Spy Run av nr St Joseph river bridge.

BOILER ATTACHMENTS—MNFRS.

Cook Automatic Boiler Cleaner Co, 59 E Columbia.

BOILER CLEANERS.

Cook Automatic Boiler Cleaner Co, 59 E Columbia.

BOILERMAKERS.

Bass F & M Wks, Hanna s of Wabash R R.

Ft Wayne Iron Works. s e cor Superior and Harrison.
Kerr Murray Mnfg Co, n e cor Calhoun and Murray.

BOOKBINDERS AND BLANK BOOK MNFRS.

Empire Box Factory and Bookbindery, Bank Blk. (*See right top lines.*)
Fort Wayne Book Bindery, Tri-State Bldg. (*See left bottom lines.*)
Ft Wayne Sentinel, 107 Calhoun.
Geiger C J, 125 E Jefferson.
Journal Co The, 30 E Main.
Siemon & Bro, 50 Calhoun. (*See back cover.*)
Winbaugh G W, 13 E Main.

BOOKS AND STATIONERY.

(*See also Newsdealers.*)
Goodman M & K, 139 E Jefferson.
Henry Jacob, 328 Hanna.
Lehman Book and News Co, 81 Calhoun.
Siemon & Bro, 50 Calhoun. (*See back cover.*)
Spiegel J E jr, 103 Broadway.
Stahn & Heinrich, 116 Calhoun.
Stellhorn Charles, 146 Calhoun.

*BOOT AND TOE PADS.

Horstman L F, 9 E Superior. (*See p 99.*)

BOOTS AND SHOES MNFRS.

App Bros, 46 W Main.

BOOTS AND SHOES—WHOLESALE.

Carnahan W L Co The, 13 W Jefferson.

BOOTS AND SHOES—RETAIL.

Acrolf Abraham, 174 Calhoun.
App Matthias, 106 Calhoun.
Bauer Henry, 321 Lafayette.
Benz C F, 111 Maumee rd.
Buesking Conrad, 302 Hanna.
De Armitt F W, 20 Calhoun.
Fitch O B, 52 Calhoun.

Foellinger C & Co, 15 W Main.
Fortriede Louis, 19 Calhoun.
Helmke F W E, 212½ Calhoun.
Henry J W, 249 Calhoun.
Henry L G, 244 E Creighton av.
Hermans H H, 376 Calhoun.
Huser L P, 178 Broadway.
Klug Gregor, 194 Hanna.
Lehman Isidor, 17 Calhoun.
Mann J G, 25 Calhoun.
Mommer Joseph jr, 76 Calhoun.
Noll J F, 22 Clinton.
Novitzky Barnet, 213 Calhoun.
Princess Cash Store, 111 Calhoun.
Puff Bros, 339 Hanna.
Puff C B, 134 Maumee rd.
Rockhill Wm, 37 W Main.
Scheele Wm, 352½ Calhoun.
Schiefer C & Son, 8 E Columbia.
Schnieders B H, 193 Barr.
Spiegel Gustav, 132 Broadway.
Stellhorn Charles, 146 Calhoun.
Thing S B & Co, 32 Calhoun.
Toenges F W, 62 Maumee rd.
Umstead H D, 283 Calhoun.
Zuber J G, 92 Broadway.

BOOT AND SHOE MAKERS.

Beach Henry, 375 Lafayette.
Braeuer Conrad, 358 Broadway.
Buuck Conrad, 11 W Jefferson.
Colvin Wm, 80 E Columbia.
Eggemann P J, 13 E Main.
Etzold H J, 110 Webster.
Fischmann David, 322 Calhoun.
Fischmann Samuel, 17½ W Main.
Getz J C, rear 184 Fairfield av.
Heilbronner S A, 27 Pearl.
Hengsteler C F, 115 Broadway.
Henry August, 24 Barr.
Knobel Gottlieb, 110 Wells.
Kocks H B, 60 Wells.
Lerch Joseph, 127 Fairfield av.
Lordier Philip, 35 Baker.

Mellinger Christian, 107 Walton av.
Nestel A G, 117 E Lewis.
Neuhaus R H, 40 Harrison.
Nill G E, 191 Broadway.
Nix Valentine, 80 E Jefferson.
Novitzky Barnet, 213 Calhoun.
Rabel John, 80 Fairfield av.
Rockhill Wm, s w cor Harrison and Main.
Walter David, 23 Barr.
Weber Adam, 213 Lafayette.
Wieneke Frederick, 311 W Main.
Wolff C H, 61 Wells.
Wulf Christian. 74 Barr.
Young Peter, 25 Ewing.
Zimmermann Anthony, 40 Pritchard.

BOTTLING WORKS.

(See also Mineral Water Mnfrs.)

Berghoff Herman Brewing Co The,
e s Grant av nr E Washington. *(See right top lines.)*
Brames L & Co, 123–127 Clay. *(See p 3.)*
Centlivre C L Brewing Co, n end Spy
Run av. *(See front edge and left side lines.)*
Christen John, 100 Calhoun.
Hoffmann C. A., 183–187 Calhoun. *(See p 87.)*
Summit City Bottling Works, 123–127
Clay. *(See p 3.)*

BOX FACTORIES—WOOD, PAPER AND CIGAR.

Empire Box Factory, Bank Blk. *(See right
top lines.)*
Winbaugh George, 13 E Main.

BOX MNFRS—PACKING.

Peter's Box & Lumber Co, 79 to 105
High.

*BRASS FINISHERS.

Hattersley A & Sons, 48 E Main. *(See embossed line front cover.)*

WHITE NATIONAL BANK.—Interest paid on certificate of deposit at three (3) per cent. per annum if left four (4) months. Deposits of any amount received. **Safe Deposit Boxes for rent at $5 per annum.**

728   R. L. POLK & CO.'S

BRASS FOUNDERS.

Hattersley A & Sons, 48 E Main. (*See embossed line front cover.*)
Menefee C M, 135 and 137 Oliver. (*See p 460.*)

*BRASS GOODS.

Ogden Robert, 26 E Berry. (*See embossed line back cover.*)

BREWERS.

Berghoff Herman Brewing Co The, e s Grant av nr E Wash ngton. (*See right top lines.*)
Centlivre C L Brewing Co, n end Spy Run av. (*See front edge and left side lines.*)

BREWERS' AGENTS.

Brames L & Co, 123-127 Clay. (*See adv p 3.*)
Epple Gottlieb, 188 Fairfield av.
Fitzgerald Michael, 355 Lafayette.

BRICK MNFRS.

Baltes Jacob, 5¼ miles w of city limits.
Koehler J A, w s Lafayette 2 s of Wiebke.
Koehler Paul, n e cor Rudisill and Hoagland avs.
Leonard Nelson, s e cor Spy Run av and Leo Gravel rd.
Miller Wm, e s Hanna s of city limits. (*See adv p 97.*)
Moellering Wm & Son, 53-59 Murray. (*See back cover and p 83.*)
South Wayne Brick Co, w s Thompson av n of Wabash R R.

BRIDGE BUILDERS.

Miller Fred, 8 Summit. (*See adv p 103.*)

BRIDGE CONTRACTORS.

Moellering Wm & Son, 52-59 Murray. (*See back bone and p 83.*)

BROKERS—INVESTMENT.

Curtice J F, 1-2-3-4 Tri-State Bldg. (*See front cover and p 89.*)

BROKERS—NOTE AND BOND.

Curtice J F, 1-2-3-4 Tri-State Bldg. (*See front cover and p 89.*)

Schell J F & Co, 22 and 23 Pixley & Long Blk. (*See adv in classified collecting agts, lawyers and loans.*)

BROKERS--REAL ESTATE AND LOAN.

Curtice J F, 1-2-3-4 Tri-State Bldg. (*See front cover and p 89.*)

BROKERS--TICKET.

Blitz M J, 82 Calhoun.
Levington Samuel, 85 Calhoun.

BROOM MACHINERY.

Sperry Pelton Mnfg Co, 28 E Berry.

BROOM MNFRS.

Cartwright C A, 110 Hugh.
Didierjohn Joseph, 102 Maumee rd.
Gage R, 318 W Main.
Hunter J L, 153 Hayden.

BUGGY BOW MNFRS.

Rastetter L & Son, s w cor Broadway and P, Ft W & C R R

BUGGY TOP MNFRS.

Horstman L F, 9 E Superior. (*See p 99*).

BUILDERS.

(*See Carpenters, Contractors and Builders.*)

BUILDERS' HARDWARE.

Morgan & Beach, 19 and 21 E Columbia. (*See back cover.*)

Pfeiffer & Schlatter, 38 and 40 E Columbia. (*See left side lines.*)

* BUILDER'S SUPPLIES.

Moellering Wm & Son, 53-59 Murray. (*See back bone and p 83.*)

BUILDING MATERIAL.

Builders' Lime Association, 257 Calhoun.
  (*See right bottom lines.*)
Moellering Wm & Son, 53–59 Murray.
  (*See back bone and p 83.*)
Western Lime Co, 3 N Harrison.

BUILDING AND LOAN ASSOCIATIONS.

Allen County Loan and Savings Assn, 32 E Berry
Indiana Farmers' Savings and Loan Assn, over 32 E Berry
Phœnix Building and Savings Union, 39 and 40 Bank Blk.
Tri-State Building and Loan Assn, 13 Pixley & Long Bldg

* BUSINESS ADDRESSES.

Polk R L & Co, 138 La Salle, Chicago.

BUSINESS COLLEGES.

(*See also Colleges, Schools, Etc.*)

Fort Wayne Business College, n w cor Calhoun and Berry
International Business College, Schmitz Blk.

BUTCHERS.

See Meat Markets.

* CABINET MAKERS.

Hegerhorst C J, 116 Fulton. (*See below.*)

CAMERA MNFRS.

Jenne Camera Mnfg Co, 16 W Columbia.
  (*See p 99.*)

CAR WHEEL MNFRS.

Bass Foundry and Machine Wks, Hanna s of Wabash R R.

CARPENTERS, CONTRACTORS AND BUILDERS.

(See also. Contractors also Masons.)

Bandt F W, 87 W DeWald.
Barrus Timothy, 14 Winch.
Bengs O F, 175 John.
Blystone O A, 53 High.
Bock Wm C. 35 Nirdlinger av.
Boester F H, 164 Griffith.
Borkenstein Bernhard, 222 John.
Breimeier E F H, 207 W De Wald.
Clemmer B R, 183 Fairfield av.
Doenges Christian, 126 Maumee av.
Drebert Frank, 91 W De Wald.
Feichter J H, 200 Metz.
Felker F J, 143 Fairfield av.
Franke Christian & Co, 364 E Lewis.
Franke H F, 43 Hugh.
Fricke F W, 91 Huestis av.
Geary Charles, 192 Griffith.
Grey J W, 230 E Wayne.
Griffith Levi, 77 W Williams.
Grotholtman H A & Co, 48 W Jefferson.
Henry J M, 161 W Jefferson.
Hensel Peter, 37 Miner.
Hilgemann H F, 355 E Lewis.
Hilgemann J W, 216 E Washington.
Hoffman H A, 52 W Creighton av.
Howrand Bernard, 107 Swinney av.
Kinder P P, 105 Brackenridge.
Kocher John, 130 Greeley,
Korte & Son, 65 Maumee av. *(See p 111.)*
Krudop C F, 151 Hugh.
Lallow L J, 61 W Pontiac.
Lauer Gregory, 101 Maumee rd.
Lauer Gustave, 159 E Taber.
Lauer Justin, 226 E Lewis.
Lindemann W R, 404 E Washington.
McBennett Francis, 410 Lafayette.
McKeeman Wm, 91 Organ av.
McMullen John, 70 Charles.
Miller Frederick, 8 Summit. *(See p 103.)*

Moellering Wm & Son, 53–59 Murray. (*See back bone and p 83*.)

Nowek Edward, 236 John.

Patton W S, 58 Brackenridge.

Pressler George, 52 W DeWald

Rippe Frederick, 176 Madison. (*See right bottom lines and p* 91.)

Ruchel Wm, 209 E Lewis. (*See p* 97.)

Shrimpton Alfred, 152 W Main.

Suelzer John, 420 Hanna.

Tapp Ferdinand, 13 Ohio.

Tarmon H B, 191 Brackenridge. (*See p* 109.)

Tiemann J F, 424 Broadway.

Trier Henry, 120 W Superior.

Vanderford C E, 170 W Main.

Violand J F, 61 Euclid av.

Wagner John, 45 W Butler.

Walda H B & Bro, 89 E Superior (*See p* 101.)

Watkins J A, 200 Broadway. (*See p* 107.)

Wermuth Charles, 172 Suttenfield.

Wery Henry, 73 Hoagland av.

Wiegmann & Franke, 363 Broadway.

Woebbeking C C, 195 Broadway.

Wyss P H, Oliver n e cor Emily. (*See p* 115.)

CARPET CLEANERS.

Wolf P E, 33–35 Clinton.

Zimmer Carpet Cleaning Co, 202 St Joseph boulevard.

CARPET WEAVERS.

Bayer J M, 34 Sherman.

Beck Leopold, 136 Barr.

Chicago Carpet and Rug Factory, n w cor Wells and Superior.

Claus J A, 16 University.

Cragg Charles, 121 E Taber.

Hertwig T T, 42 Eliza.

Hickman J W, 171 Broadway.

Jaeger August, n w cor Franklin av and Aboit.

Kiesling J N, 212 Broadway.

Poch M E, 26 Stophlet.

Pomper Herman, 229 Lafayette.

Schoen W F, 76 Maumee rd.

Wolfrum J T, 92 Fairfield av.

CARPETS, OIL CLOTHS, ETC

(*See also Dry Goods, also Furniture.*)

Foster D N Furn Co, 11 and 13 Court.
Frank M & Co, 60 Calhoun.
Root & Co, 46–48 Calhoun.
Wolf Louis & Co, 54 Calhoun.

*CARRIAGE MNFRS.

City Carriage Works, Main, n w cor Barr.
(*See left top lines.*)

CARRIAGE REPOSITORIES.

City Carriage Works, n w cor Main and
Barr. (*See left top lines.*)
Cook C W, 50 E Columbia.
Parham F C, 29 and 31 Barr.
Stapleford H T, 47 E Columbia.

CARRIAGE TRIMMERS.

Horstman L F, 9 E Superior. (*See p 99.*)

CARRIAGE AND WAGON MAKERS.

(*See also Blacksmiths.*)

Baker B H, 18 Lafayette.
Chauvey Bros, 35 E Superior.
City Carriage Works, n w cor Main and
Barr. (*See left top lines.*)
Ehrmann Charles, 149 W Main. (*See left side
lines.*)
Mehnert Louis, 93 E Superior. (*See p 101.*)
Olds' Wagon Wks, s s Murray bet Calhoun and Lafayette.
Smith & Lee, 11 and 13 Clay.
Vogely Andrew, 82 Maumee rd.
Zollinger L C & Bro, 13–17 E Superior.
(*See left bottom lines and p 89.*)

CARRIAGE AND WAGON STOCK.

Baker Killian, cor Superior and Lafayette.
Beuret & Co, 23 W Columbia.

CASH REGISTERS.

National Cash Register Co, 31 Bass Blk.

47

734   R. L. POLK & CO.'s

*CASTINGS--BRASS AND IRON.

Menefee C M, 135 and 137 Oliver,   (*See p 460.*)

* CEMENT.

Moellering Wm & Son, 53–59 Murray. (*See back bone and p 83.*)

CATERERS.

Seidel Wm & Bro, 111 E Main.

*CHANDELIERS.

Kaag M F, 5 E Columbia.   (*See left bottom lines.*)

CHEESE.

Strodel J G, 13 Harrison.

CHEMISTS—MANUFACTURING.

Central Chemical Co, 15 Douglas av.
Meyer Bros & Co, 14 Calhoun and 9 W Columbia.

CHILDREN'S CARRIAGES.

Pfeiffer & Schlatter, 38–40 E Columbia. (*See left side lines.*)

CIDER AND VINEGAR MANUFACTURERS.

Brames L & Co, 123–127 Clay.   (*See p 3.*)
Hoffmann Charles A, 183–187 Calhoun.   (*See p 87.*)

CHIMNEYS.

Kanney John, 5 Bass Blk.   (*See p 79.*)

CIGAR MNFRS.

Alexander S M, 7 E Main.
Baker A C, 31 E Main.
Bayer W A, 98 W Main.
Bender Louis. 168 E Washington.
Bourie, Cook & Co, 358 Calhoun.
Brandt A C, 158 Harrison.

CIGAR MNFRS.—Continued.

Campbell D A, 272 Calhoun.
Dessauer L & Co, 23 Calhoun.
Drinkwitz Paul O, 21 E Main.
Eckert J C, 20 E Wayne.
Ehle A N, 178 Broadway.
Gruber F J, 110 Calhoun.
Hazzard Al, 11 E Main.
Hohnholz Herman, 135 Wallace.
Hollister & Son, 104 W Williams.
Humbrecht H G, 42 W 3d.
Lahmeyer Bros, 72 E Main.
Langhorst A W, 79 W Washington.
Myers George, 66 Maumee rd.
National Cigar Factory, 11 E Main.
Ortmann H W, 26 Clinton.
Piumadore H A. 104 Calhoun.
Rahe F H, 103 Broadway.
Reiter George, 30 Calhoun.
Ropa F W, 173 Broadway.
Schele Clemens, 26 Harrison.
Schele M A, 35 W 4th.
Schneider F G, 104 Webster.
Sorge G F, 43 Wells.
Steckbeck W J, 110 E Creighton av.
Tripple C A, 113 E Lewis.
Ward & Mahoney, 140 Calhoun.
Wenninghoff Christian, 114 W Main.
Wilhelm C A, 135 Wallace.
Zern John, 342 Hanna.

CIGARS AND TOBACCO.

Belott G E, 82 Calhoun.
Carl John, 259 Calhoun.
Metz J G A, 47 W Main.
Oppenheimer Frederick, 17 W Main.
Reiter George, 30 Calhoun.
Ross E C, The Randall.
Spencer D J, 39 Calhoun.
Spiegel J E jr, 103 Broadway.
Wenninghoff Christian, 114 W Main.
Wilt F P & Co, 33 E Columbia.
Witte C J, 27 E Main.

* CISTERN BUILDERS.

Kanney John. 5 Bass Blk. (*See p 79.*)
Korte & Son, 65 Maumee rd. (*See p 111.*)

CISTERN AND WELL COVERS.

Menefee C M, 135 and 137 Oliver. (*See p 460.*)
Moellering Wm & Son, 53–59 Murray. (*See back bone and p 83.*)

CIVIL ENGINEERS AND SURVEYORS.

Brackenridge C S, 144 W Wayne.
Fischer H E, 96 Barr.
Goshorn J S, 386 E Washington.

* CLOAKS AND DRESS GOODS.

Beadell & Co, 20 and 22 E Berry.
Gutermuth Valentine, 52¼ Calhoun.

CLOTHES REPAIRERS.

Pantitorium Co, 16 Arcade Bldg.

CLOTHING.

(*See also Merchant Tailors.*)

Epstein & Sons, 18 Calhoun.
Fieldbleat Samuel, 76 Barr.
Friend A I & H, 64 Calhoun.
Golden & Patterson, 56 Calhoun.
Heller & Frankel, 42 Calhoun.
Hoosier Mnfg Co (mnfrs). 28 and 30 E Berry.
Lehman Benjamin. 34 and 36 Calhoun.
Levy Bros, 72 and 88 Barr.
Mautner & Friedlich, 58 Calhoun.
Oppenheimer Jacob, 68 E Columbia.
Pixley & Co, 16 and 18 E Berry.
Rockhill Wm, s w cor Harrison and Main.
Sam, Pete & Max, 58 Calhoun.
Schubert Gustav, 65 E Main. (*See p 111.*)
Silverstein Mrs Helen, 5 E Main.
Thieme J G & Son, 37 and 39 E Columbia.

COAL AND WOOD.

Krudop G H, n e cor Francis and Hayden.
Moderwell J M, e s Wells 1 n of W Superior.
Quicksell Peter, 196 Jackson.
Scheele Henry, 400 Hanna.
Tinkham F S, 120 W Main.
Wilding James, 193 Calhoun.

COLD STORAGE.

Fort Wayne Artificial Ice Co, n e cor Wells and Lake Shore R R.

COLLECTION AGENTS.

Bohen M H, 23 E Main.
Crowe J M, 34 E Berry.
Fort Wayne Loan & Collecting Agency, 22 and 23 Pixley & Long Bldg.
Schell J F & Co, 22 and 23 Pixley & Long Bldg. (*See adv. below.*)

COLLECTION AGENTS.—Continued.

Haiber Frederick, 64 Wells.
Twining T J, 26 Bank Blk.

COLLEGES, SCHOOLS, ETC.

Academy of Our Lady of the Sacred Heart, 6 miles n of Court House.
Bannister School of Music, 49 W Berry.
Concordia College, e s Schick nr Washington.
Fort Wayne College of Medicine, 160 W Superior.
Fort Wayne Conservatory of Music, Bank Blk.
Westminster Seminary, 251 W Main.

* COMMERCIAL PAPER.

Curtice J F, rms 1-2-3-4 Tri-State Bldg. (*See front cover and p 89.*)

COMMISSION MERCHANTS.

Bash S & Co, 22–24 W Columbia.
Comparet D F, 76 E Columbia.
Fay M W Warehouse Co, 135 Calhoun.
Pottlitzer Bros' Fruit Co, 8 and 10 Harrison.

CONFECTIONERS—WHOLESALE AND MANU-
FACTURING.

Batchelder J S, 29 W Main.
Fox Branch U S Baking Co, 145–149 Calhoun.
Kutche Angelo, 154 Calhoun. (*See p 107.*)

CONFECTIONERS—RETAIL.

(*See also Bakers, also Fruits.*)

Aurentz A C, 18 W Berry.
Barcus H H, 238 Calhoun.
Beach F J. 290 Calhoun.
Bussing Henry, 138 Maumee rd.
Fox J V, 25 E Main.
Howe H A, 85 Calhoun.
Kutche Angelo, 154 Calhoun. (*See p 107.*)
Meyer J H, 95 Calhoun.

CONFECTIONERS—RETAIL.—Continued.

Rentschler C F, 138 Broadway.
Ryder David, 228 Calhoun.
Voors J G, 81 Maumee rd.

CONTRACTORS.

(See also Carpenters, Contractors and Builders.)

Ahern Thomas, 83 Wagner.
Ahlersmeyer Wilhelm (mason), n e cor Winch and Pioneer av.
Barber Asphalt Paving Co, 7–8–9 Vordermark Bldg.
Beers G W (telephone), 17 and 18 Pixley & Long Blk.
Bertels John (sewers), 160 Harmer.
Bieberstein G W (carp), s s Rudisill av 2 e of Calhoun
Borgmann Wm, 200 Ewing.
Bowers David L, 57 Prospect av.
Breimeier E H F, 207 W De Wald.
Buesching Frederick (brick and stone), Lake av, nr city limits.
Colvin Elbert (mason), 83 Franklin av.
Empie T B (street and sewer), 164 Broadway.
Fort Wayne Steam Stone Works, 84–98 Pearl. *(See right bottom lines.)*
Fraine P C (plasterer), 48 Charles.
Geake Wm (cut stone), 76–82 Pearl. *(See left bottom lines and p 81.)*
Gerberding H A, 103 Erie.
Hachmann Frederick (mason), s w cor Reynolds and Summer.
Hensel Peter, stone and brick, 37 Miner.
Hiler J B, n s Killea av 2 e of Hoagland av.
Hite A K (carp), 182 Oakland.
Hite & Son, 182 Oakland.
Hoffman H A, 52 W Creighton av.
Horstmann Wm (sewer), 121 Alliger.
Jaap George, (stone) n s L S & M S R R track w of Wells. *(See p 359).*
Johnson J H, (cement), 68 E Columbia. *(See p 99.)*
Kanney John (General), 5 Bass Blk. *(See p 79.)*
Kintz A W (mason), 149 Archer av.
Korte & Son, 65 Maumee rd. *(See p 111.)*
Kruse W F (stone), 67 E Jefferson.
Lehman Conrad, 618 Calhoun.
Liebman E F, 106 W Wayne.

CONTRACTORS—Continued.

McCann John, 65 Grand.

Metker Joseph (Plastering), rear cor Washington and Compaiet. (*See p* 109.)

Miller Fred, 257 Calhoun and 8 Summit. (*See right bottom lines and p* 103.)

Moellering Wm & Son, 53–59 Murray. (*See back bone and p* 83.)

Oetting W H (Sewer), 382 E Lewis.

Pranger J H, 226 E Washington.

Remus J E, (sewer), 442 Broadway.

Rieg Anton (sewer), 100 Putnam.

Rippe Frederick, 176 Madison. (*See right bottom lines and p* 91.)

Ruchel Wilhelm, 209 E Lewis. (*See p* 97.)

Schele August (mason), n s Wayne Trace 2 e of New Haven av.

Schenkel Peter (mason), 128 Franklin av.

Schreck Charles (cement), 131 Baker.

Schulz Frederick (sewer), 140 Francis.

Schwartz H F (plastering), 542 Calhoun. (*See p* 115.)

Singleton M T (sewer), 33 Baker.

Smick M M, 88 W Main.

Smick W P, 527 E Wayne.

Suter Edward, 507 Broadway.

Swain J D (plasterer), 6 Jones.

Tapp Herman W (bridges), 68 Barr.

Walda H B & Bro, 89 E Superior. (*See p* 101.)

Wehrenberg & Busching, 504 E. Lewis. (*See p* 105).

Weigand H P (mason), 58 Glasgow av.

Wilding J W, 193 Calhoun.

Wolke W F (carp), 17 Jones.

Ziemendorff Frederick & Son, 19 Wagner.

COOPERS.

Williamson A J, e s Runnion av 1 s Nickel Plate R R.

CRACKER MNFRS.

Fox Bakery, U S Baking Co, 145–149 Calhoun.

Skelton B W Co The, 209 Calhoun.

CROCKERY AND GLASSWARE.

Graf Philip, 335 Lafayette.   (*See right side lines*)
Kaag M F, 5 E Columbia.   (*See left bottom lines.*)
Lathrop & Co, 17 Court.
Lowry Miss A A, 10 W Berry.
Ward H N, 8 W Columbia.

*CURTAINS.

Siemon & Bro, 50 Calhoun.   (*See back cover.*)

CUSHIONS AND DASHES.

Horstman L F, 9 E Superior.   (*See p 99.*)

* CUT STONE CONTRACTORS.

(*See also Stone Yards.*)

Fort Wayne Steam Stone Works, 84-98 Pearl. (*See right bottom lines.*)
Geake Wm, 76-82 Pearl. (*See left bottom lines and p 81.*)
Jaap George, n s L S & M S R R tracks, w of Wells. (*See p 359.*)
Keller & Braun, 84-98 Pearl. (*See right bottom lines.*)
Mollering Wm & Son, 53-59 Murray, (*See back bone and p 83.*)

CUTLERS AND GRINDERS.

Schulder Max, 52 Barr.

*CUTLERY.

Kaag M F, 5 E Columbia.   (*See left bottom lines.*)
Pfeiffer & Schlatter, 38-40 E Columbia. (*See left side lines.*)

DAIRIES.

Doermer Peter, cor New Haven and Pioneer avs.
Funk Jacob, Maysville rd e of limits.
Getty Frank, w s Hanna 10 s of Pontiac.
Hart G C, e s Thomas 1 s of Pontiac.
Hauser Henry, w s Hanna 8 s of Pontiac.

742 · R. L. POLK & CO.'S

Neukamm John. e s Smith 1 s of Pontiac.
Spaulding W W, w s Calhoun 1 s Cour.
Wickliff & Weikel, 140 Runnion av.
Work R C, 44 Pritchard.

DANCING ACADEMIES.

Farnan Dancing Academy, Foster Blk.

DECORATORS.

Hull L O, 90 Calhoun. (*See back cover.*)
Kirchefer H A, Arcade. (*See p 93.*)

DEFORMITY APPARATUS.

Joseph B E, 101 E Wayne. (*See adv. below.*)

DELICACIES.

Strodel J G, 13 Harrison.

DENTAL SUPPLIES.

Keller Dental Co, The, 93 Barr.
Woodworth C B & Co, 1 New Aveline House Blk.

DENTISTS.

Adams J H, 32 Lake av.
Brown S B, 15 Bank Blk.
Coyle J D, 96 Calhoun.
Hartman S B, 1-2 Schmitz Blk.
Johnson G E, 74 Calhoun.
McCurdy J S, 21 W Berry.
Mason M A, 26 W Wayne.
Mommer B H, 76 Calhoun.
Mungen W W, 2 E Columbia.
Pierce H W, 191 Lafayette.
Rauch A J, 48 Harrison.
Shryock W W, 27 W Berry.
Sihler, C E, 106 Calhoun.
Sites E F, 86 Calhoun.
Sites H C, 82 Calhoun.
Snider A B, 48 Harrison.
Thompson J W, 9 E Wayne.
Tinkham C P, 24 Arcade (*See right top lines.*)
Weisell D D & Son, 1 Foellinger Blk.
Wendell B F, 9 E Wayne.

* DIE MAKERS.

Stenger Peter, 30 N Ewing. (*See left top lines.*)

DINING ROOMS.

(*See Restaurants.*)

DIRECTORY PUBLISHERS.

Polk R L & Co, 38 Bass Blk.

DRAIN TILE.

Moellering Wm & Son, 53-59 Murray.
(*See back bone and p 83.*)

DRESSMAKERS.

Biggs Rebecca, 58 W Berry.

DRESSMAKERS—Continued.

Bitsberger Mrs E F, 102 Wallace.
Blynn Mrs H A, 155 W Wayne.
Branard Miss Anna, 78 W Main.
Brenner Mollie, 78 Wilt.
Brossard Theresa, 33 Wefel.
Corneille Clara A, 41 E Superior.
Covault Emma, 194 Lafayette.
Cramer Mamie M, 92 Hanna.
Doty Mrs A A, 91 Madison.
Eberline Mrs Sophia, 86 E Jefferson.
Engmann Anna, 133 E Jefferson.
Feeny Miranda, 63 W Pontiac.
Fletcher Mrs. M A, 47 Barr.
Fox C S, 180 E Lewis.
Freer L A, 19 Cass.
Goodes Eliza, 202 Ewing.
Gouty Birdie, 227 W Superior.
Grimm T E, 107 Wilt.
Hagan Mary C, 46 Harrison.
Hauss Mrs L A, 105 Broadway. (*See p* 113.)
Haverley Mrs Elizabeth, 194 E Jefferson.
Healy Retta, 72 Barr.
Hippenhamer Mrs R E, 170 Brackenridge.
Hitzman S K, 24 Summit.
Irwin Mrs A R, 110 W DeWald.
Johnson Mrs George E, 79 W Main.
Julliard Frances M, 70 W Washington.
Karns Mrs B E, 123 Harrison.
Keller Mrs M J, 47 W Superior.
Kenlin Mrs E H, 205 W Jefferson.
Lauer Elizabeth, 70 E Jefferson.
Laumann M A, 127 W 3d.
Lehr F E, 67 Cass.
Lewis R C, 142 W Main.
Long Mrs J B, 77 E Berry.
Lorent Josephine, 63 Hugh.
Lowry Margaret, 80 W Creighton av.
Louthain Mrs Sad'e, 17 Baker.
Majors Mrs Adda, 13 E Williams.
Milton Maude, 30 E Columbia.
Moore Maude and Zula, 183 Jackson. (*See p* 115.)
Nix F M, 80 E Jefferson.
Reehling Carrie, 97 Madison.

DRESSMAKERS—Continued.

Reinking L E, 54 Miner.
Rodenbeck Anna, 210 E Jefferson.
Roush Ella M, 75 Lafayette.
Schreiber A E, 58 W 3d.
Sherin Mary L, 47 W Berry.
Sherman M E, 33 Lincoln av.
Smalley & Allison, 206 W Washington. (*See p* 109.)
Steinbrunner Rosa, 24 W Williams.
Stewart M A, 62 W Lewis.
Stoll C G, 29 Wefel.
Straight Mrs E M, 54 E Washington.
Talmage Sarah, 182 Calhoun.
Tarman F S, 83 E Wayne.
Uebelhoer Sophia, 68 E Main.
Wagner Catherine, 79 W Jefferson.
Waltemath E A, 12 W Jefferson.
Webber F L E, 62 Pontiac.
Weis A M, 67 Charles.
Wolff Ella, 11 Harrison.
Worch L A, 22 W Washington.

DRIVE WELLS.

Spice Robert, 48 W Main. (*See right bottom lines.*)

DRUGGISTS' SUNDRIES.

Meyer Bros. & Co, 14 Calhoun.

DRUGGISTS—WHOLESALE.

Dreier & Bro, 10 Calhoun.
Meyer Bros. & Co, 14 Calhoun.

DRUGGISTS—RETAIL.

Beneke W F, 443 Broadway.
Beverforden H F, 286 Calhoun.
Bill Jacob W. 285 E Creighton av.
Brink J J, 44 Wells.
Byall C L, 238 E Creighton av.
Detzer Martin, 260 Calhoun.
Dreier & Bro, 10 Calhoun.
Foellinger Adolph, 174 Broadway.

DRUGGISTS—RETAIL—Continued.

Frankenstein M L, 120 Barr.
Freese & Ranke, 88 Calhoun.
Fryer F H, 83 Wells.
Gerberding & Miller, 120 Calhoun.
Gross & Pellens, 94 Calhoun.
Heaton C E, 36 E Berry.
Heinrich J R, 210 Calhoun.
Hoham F D, 298 Calhoun.
Keller A J, 96 Broadway.
Keller F X, 332 W Main.
Klinkenberg O G, 33 E Berry.
Lepper C O, 66 W Jefferson.
Lewis J D, 434 Calhoun.
Loesch G H, 96 Barr.
Meinzen H W, 64 Maumee rd.
Meyer Bros & Co, 14 Calhoun.
Miller F J, 327 Lafayette.
Moellering Wm L & Bro, 191 Lafayette.
Mordhurst H W, 74 Calhoun.
Neufer J M, 544 Calhoun.
Noll B R, 128 Broadway.
Rastetter C L, 305 E Washington.
Rathert H W, 96 Wells.
Schultz Wm H, 142 Fairfield av.
Soest H W, 360 Calhoun.
Sommers H G, 35 Calhoun.
Waltemath W L, s e cor E Lewis and Hanna.
Wefel M H, n w cor Hanna and LaSalle.
Wilken J H, 84 Wells.
Witzigreuter Max, 360 W Main.
Woodworth C B & Co, 1 New Aveline House Blk.

DRUGGISTS' SUNDRIES.

Meyer Bros. & Co, 14 Calhoun and 9 W Columbia.

DRY GOODS—WHOLESALE.

DeWald Geo & Co, Columbia n e cor Calhoun.
Root & Company, 46 and 48 Calhoun.

DRY GOODS—RETAIL.

Beadell & Co, 20 and 22 E Berry.

O. P. TINKHAM, 21, 22, 23, 24 ARCADE BLOCK,
West Berry Street, Fort Wayne, Ind
===DENTIST.=== Office Telephone   Residence Telephone

FORT WAYNE DIRECTORY. 747

DRY GOODS—RETAIL—Continued.

Becker A E C, 160 Fairfield av.
DeWald Geo & Co, Columbia n e cor Calhoun.
Frank M & Co, 60 Calhoun.
Graf Philip, 335 Lafayette. (*See right side lines.*)
Hahn Wm & Co, 28 Calhoun.
Hitzeman G J, 47 Maumee rd.
Kalbacher Anton, 13 and 15 Grand.
Klotz Frank, 372 Calhoun.
Mergentheim's Bazaar, 38 Calhoun.
Pierre C J, s w cor Wells and 2d.
Pierre Peter, 168 Broadway.
Rehling & Stegner, 193 Lafayette.
Root & Company, 46 and 48 Calhoun.
Saloom & Skaf, 125 Fairfield av.
Scherer C W, 56 Walton av.
Smaltz F M, 307 W Main.
Waltemath C H & Sons, 323 Lafayette.
Wolf Louis & Co, 54 Calhoun.

DUST PAN MNFRS.

Bowser S F & Co, cor E Creighton av and Thomas. (*See p 4.*)

DYERS AND SCOURERS.

Caswell J O, 205 Calhoun.
City Steam Dye House, 11 W Jefferson. (*See p 101.*)
Robacker Samuel, 45 E Main.
Schubert Gust, 65 E Main. (*See p 111.*)

ELECTRIC APPARATUS—MEDICAL.

New York and London Electric Assn, 101 E Wayne. (*See deformity apparatus.*)

ELECTRIC LIGHT AND POWER COMPANIES.

Fort Wayne Electric Corporation, Broadway s e cor Chicago.
Jenney Electric Light and Power Co, 43 E Berry.

ELECTRIC TOWER MNFRS.

Star Iron Tower Co, s end Wells on Nickel Plate R R.

748   R. L. POLK & CO.'s

ELECTRICAL CONTRACTORS AND ENGINEERS.

Crane H E, 36 E Berry.
Keller, Edmunds & Law Electric Construction Co, 4 and 5 Schmitz Blk.

ELECTRICIANS.

Keller, Edmunds & Law Electric Construction Co, 4-5 Schmitz Blk.

*ELECTROTYPES.

Benedict Geo H & Co, 175 and 177 S Clark, Chicago, Ill. (*See opp page.*)

EMBALMERS.

(*See also Undertakers.*)

Peltier J C, 17 W Wayne.
Schone & Veith, 53 E Berry. (*See p 113.*)

EMPLOYMENT OFFICES.

Pantitorium Co, 16 Arcade.

ENGINE BUILDERS.

(*See also Founders and Machinists.*)

Bass F & M Wks, Hanna s of Wabash R R.
Fort Wayne Iron Works, s e cor Superior and Harrison.
Kerr Murray Mnfg Co, n e cor Calhoun and Murray.

ENGINES—MECHANICAL.

Burns W G, 14 Bass Blk.
Cook J O, 59 E Columbia.

ENGRAVERS.

Benedict Geo H & Co, 175 S Clark, Chicago, Ill.
McFerran S M, 31 Schmitz Blk.
Winter Moses, 35 E Main.

* ENGRAVERS—BY ALL METHODS.

Benedict Geo H & Co, 175 and 177 S Clark, Chicago, Ill.

CARRIAGES AND BUGGIES,

WHOLESALE AND RETAIL.

City Carriage Works,   Cor. Main and Barr.

750   R. L. POLK & CO.'S

EXCAVATORS (VAULT CLEANING.)

Koenemann John, 32 Colerick.

EXPRESS COMPANIES.

Adams Express Co, 10 W Wayne.
American Express Co, 24 E Main.
National Express Co, 24 E Main.
Pacific Express Co, 79 Calhoun.
United States Express Co, 79 Calhoun.

EXPRESSMEN.

Allgeier Anthony, 162 Taber.
Grage Frederick, 185 W Jefferson.
Hickman Daniel, 195 Sherman.
Himbert J E, 14 Lavina.
Jones S C, 266 E Creighton av.
Roehrs Henry, 261 W Jefferson.
Trautman F J, 115 Wilt.

*FANCY GOODS.

(See also Notions.)

Beadell & Co, 20-22 E Berry.

FARM IMPLEMENTS.

(See Agricultural Implements.)

*FAST FREIGHT LINES.

Empire Line 26 Court.
Merchants' Dispatch Transportation Co, 3 Schmitz Blk.
Star Union Line, 81 Calhoun.

FEATHER RENOVATORS.

J Kegelmann & Son, 551 E Wayne.

FEED MILLS.

(See Flour Mills.)

FEED YARDS.

(See also Livery Stables.)

Bricker J M, 97 E Columbia.

Fleming Mnfg. Co. ROAD SUPERVISORS' SUPPLIES Office, 78 High Street.

FEED YARDS—Continued.

Double J W, 14 Pearl
Huguenard V A, 62 E Superior.
Keim Daniel, 40 Pearl.
Miller Simon, 5 N Clinton.
Paulison Samuel M, 20 N Harrison.
Phillips George, 80 E Columbia.
Seabold G H, 15 Pearl.
Schroeder Henry H, e s of N Calhoun opp jail.

FILES—PERMANENT.

Buchsbaum Maurice, 92–94 E Columbia. (See front cover.

FIRE BRICK AND FIRE CLAY.

Moellering Wm & Son, 53–59 Murray. (See back bone and p 83.)

* FIREWORKS—WHOLESALE.

Fox br U S Baking Co, 145–149 Calhoun.

FISH, OYSTERS AND GAME.

Carson J K, 250 Calhoun.
Gorman Daniel, 17 W Main.
Lewis E W, 38 Harrison.
Ryan J A, 152 Calhoun.

* FISHING TACKLE.

Trautman John, 58 E Main.   (See adv p 87.)

FLORISTS.

(See also Nurserymen.)

Auger B L, 16 E Washington.
Doswell G W, W Main, nr Lindenwood cemetery.
Flick Miss C B, 33 W Berry.
Flick G W, 132 Thompson av.
Honaker David, 25 W Berry.
Knecht F J, 301 E Wayne.
Markey Bros, s e cor Jefferson and Ewing.
Vesey J H, 90 Thompson av.

FLOUR MILLS.

Bond Cereal Mills, 65 E Columbia.
Brudi W H & Bro, n e cor Wells and 6th.
City Flour Mills, cor Clinton and N Y, C & St
  L R R.
Empire Flouring Mills, W Main st bridge,
Globe Spice Mills, 73–79 E Columbia.
Mayflour Milling Co, 18 and 20 W Columbia.
Volland H & Sons, 14 W Columbia.

FLOUR AND FEED.

Buff Julian, 24 Wells.
City Mills, cor Clinton and N Y, C & St L R R.
Doehrmann Wm, 34 and 36 Barr.
Frank Mendel, 41 Hough.
Graf Philip, 335 Lafayette. (*See right side lines.*)
Henderson W D, 69 E Columbia.
Kalbacher Anton, 296 Calhoun.
Korn John, 134 and 136 Fairfield av.
Smith & Dailey, 167 Fairfield av.
Stapleford H T, 47 E Columbia.
Waltemath C H & Sons, 321½ Lafayette.

FLUE LINING.

Moellering Wm & Son, 53–59 Murray.
  (*See back bone and p 83.*)

FOLDING BED MNFRS.

Fort Wayne Furniture Co, e end Columbia.

*FOREIGN, EXCHANGE AND PASSAGE AGENTS.

Siemon & Bro, 50 Calhoun. (*See back cover.*)
White National Bank, n w cor Clinton and
  Wayne. (*See left top lines and p 95.*)

*FOUNDERS—BRASS.

Hattersley A & Sons, 48 E Main. (*See embossed line front cover.*)

FOUNDERS AND MACHINISTS.

Bass Foundry and Machine Works, Hanna s of Wabash
  R R.

FOUNDERS AND MACHINISTS—Continued.

Borcherding F H, e s Barr 1 n of Superior.
Fort Wayne Iron Wks, s e cor Harrison and Superior.
Indiana Machine Wks, e s Osage n of Main.
Kerr Murray Mfg Co, Murray n e cor Calhoun.
Menefee C M, 135 and 137 Oliver. (*See p 460.*)

* FRESCO ARTISTS.

Hull L O, 90 Calhoun. (*See back cover.*)
Kirchefer H A, 12 Arcade. (*See p 93.*)

FRUITS—WHOLESALE.

Fox Bakery, U S Baking Co. 145–149 Calhoun.
Pottlitzer Bros Fruit Co. 8 and 10 Harrison.
White J B, 95 and 97 Calhoun.

FRUITS—RETAIL.

(*See also Confectioners.*)

Casso F A, 184 Calhoun.
Dondero George, 16 Calhoun.
Dondero Philip, 15 E Main.
Gardella Andreas, 234 Calhoun.
Moritz Vincent, 28 E Main.
Rappuzzi Louis, 172 Calhoun.

*FUNERAL DIRECTORS.

(*See also Undertakers.*)

Peltier J C, 17 W Wayne.

FURNACES—HOT AIR.

Carter & Son, 29 Clinton. (*See bottom edge and p 113*)
Gerding & Aumann Bros, 115 Wallace.
(*See top edge and p 85.*)
Pickard Bros, 12–14 E Columbia.
Welch J H, 190 Calhoun.

FURNISHING GOODS.

Golden & Patterson, 56 Calhoun.

FURNITURE MNFRS.

Erickson Furniture Co The. *(See p 95.)*
Fort Wayne Furniture Co, e end Columbia.
Peters Box and Lumber Co, 79–105 High.

FURNITURE DEALERS.

(See also Upholsterers.)
Baals & Co, 57 E Main.
Foster D N Furniture Co, 11 and 13 Court.
Griebel Wm J & Co, 37 E Main.
Indiana Furniture Co, 166 Calhoun.
Miller J M, 50 E Main.
Pape Furniture Co, 28 and 30 E Berry.
Pickard Bros, 12 and 14 E Columbia.
Rahe J H, 34 Clinton.
Shuman Erastus, 43 E Main.
Wolf P E, 33 and 35 Clinton.

FURNITURE REPAIR SHOPS.

Hegerhorst C J, 116 Fulton. *(See cabinet makers.)*

FURRIERS.

Klein Richard, 20 E Washington.

FURS.

Gutermuth Valentine, 51½ Calhoun.

GALVANIZED IRON CORNICES.

Gerding & Aumann Bros, 115 Wallace.
(See top edge and p 85.)
Welch J H, 190 Calhoun.

GAS COMPANIES.

Fort Wayne Gas Co, 50 Clinton and 9 Court.

GAS CONSTRUCTION COMPANIES.

Western Gas Construction Co, Buchanan, bet Holton av and Winter.

GAS ENGINES--MNFRS.

Burger Gas Engine Co, 36 E Berry.
Fort Wayne Iron Works, s e cor Superior and Harrison.

*GAS FITTERS.

Hattersley & Sons, 48 E Main. (*See embossed line front cover.*)
Hines J S, 379 W Main. (*See right top lines.*)
Ogden Robert, 26 E Berry. (*See embossed line back cover.*)
Spice Robert, 48 W Main and 11 Pearl. (*See right bottom lines.*)

GAS FIXTURES.

Hattersley A & Sons, 48 E Main. (*See embossed line front cover.*)
Spice Robert, 48 W Main and 11 Pearl. (*See right bottom lines.*)

GAS WORKS MACHINERY.

Kerr Murray Mnfg Co, Murray n e cor Calhoun.
Western Gas Construction Co The, Buchanan, bet Holton av and Winter.

GENERAL STORES.

Kayser & Baade, 129 Broadway.
Pierre C J, s w cor Wells and 2d.
White J B, 95 and 97 Calhoun.
Upmeyer H H G, 64 Clinton, 31 W Berry.

GENTS' FURNISHING GOODS.

Beadell & Co, 20 and 22 E Berry.
Epstein & Sons, 18 Calhoun.
Golden & Patterson, 56 Calhoun.
Meyer M B, 9 Harrison.
Meyer Wm & Bro, 80 Calhoun.
Monahan Dennis, 86 Calhoun.
Pierre C J, s w cor Wells and 2d.
Pixley & Co, 16 and 18 E Berry.
Rockhill Wm, s w cor Harrison and Main.

GLASS—PLATE AND ORNAMENTAL.

Pfeiffer & Schlatter, 38-40 E Columbia. (*See left side lines.*)

GLASS—WINDOW AND PLATE.

Dreier & Bro, 11 Calhoun.
Meyer Bros & Co, 14 Calhoun.
Pfeiffer & Schlatter, 38-40 E Columbia. (*See left side lines.*)

GLASSWARE.

(*See also Crockery and Glassware.*)
Kaag M F, 5 E Columbia. (*See left bottom lines.*)

GLOVE AND MITTEN MNFRS.

Fort Wayne Glove and Mitten Co, 35 E Columbia.

GRATES AND MANTELS.

Carter & Son, 29 Clinton. (*See bottom edge and page 113.*)
Hattersley A & Sons, 48 E Main. (*See embossed line front cover.*)

GREY IRON CASTINGS.

Menefee C M, 135 and 137 Oliver. (*See p 460.*)

GROCERS—WHOLESALE.

Bursley G E & Co, 129 Calhoun.
Lavanway Sherman, 66 E Columbia.
McDonald & Watt, 141 and 143 Calhoun.
Moellering Bros & Millard, 10 and 12 W Columbia.
Shepler & Noble, 256 and 258 Calhoun.

GROCERS—RETAIL.

Aekhnelt A, 567 E Washington.
Ankenbruck & Potthoff, 126 E Washington.
Archbold E B, 114 Richardson.
Aubrey Bros, 56 Thomas.
Aurentz S A, 31 W Main.
Bailer J & Son, 38 Maumee rd.

GROCERS—RETAIL—Continued.

Baugert Bonifacius, 34 Fairfield av.
Barr Wm J, 32 W Main.
Barrett F & Co, 380 W Main.
Bechtold Louis, 152 Maumee rd.
Becker A E C, 160 Fairfield av.
Bitner D W, 616 Calhoun.
Blythe S W, e s Leesburg rd, 3 n of N Y, C & St L R R.
Bowersock & Gooden, 45 W Main.
Brase A C, 73 W Jefferson.
Brauneisen Joseph, 146 Wells.
Brinkroeger H P W, 48 Harrison.
Broeking Charles, n e cor Gay and Creighton av.
Buck C H, 141 Broadway.
Burger A L, 81 Putnam.
Busching Wm, 124 Wallace.
Coverdale & Archer, 24 Harrison.
Cramer & Neher, 527 Lafayette.
Crance George, s w cor Smith and E Creighton av.
Cutler W M, 268 E Wayne.
Deneby James, 8 Hoagland av.
DeWald Nicholas, 406 Calhoun.
Dicke F H, 29 Smith.
Dicke Henry, 119 E Lewis.
Dittoe's Grocery Co, 72 Calhoun.
Dodane A L, 92 Wells.
Doehrmann Wm, 54 and 56 Barr.
Dornberg Peter, s s Pioneer av 1 e of New Haven av.
Dreibelbiss C W, 246 W Main.
Fehling F H, 354 Broadway.
Feipel Frank, 122 Madison.
Figel J C, 54 Wells.
Flynn Anthony, 253 E Lewis.
Fox Wm W, 325 W Main.
Frank Mendel, 208 Hanna.
Freese Frederick, 405 E Washington.
Ganzer Stephen, 254 E Lewis.
Gerow T D, 108 Fairfield av.
Graf Philip, 335 Lafayette. *(See right side lines)*
Gumpper J D, 240 Calhoun.
Haiber W, 378 Hanna.
Hartman J H, 273 Hanna.
Hartman & Ankenbruck, 274 E Washington.
Hartman & Bro, 63 E Wayne.
Heit C, 220 Madison.

758   R. L. POLK & CO.'s

GROCERS—RETAIL—Continued.

Henkenius G J, 243 St Mary's av.
Hermsdorfer G A, 279 W Jefferson.
Hilgemann H F, 121 W Jefferson.
Hitzeman G J, 47 Maumee rd.
Hubbard A L, 9 N Calhoun.
Huguenard J C, 107 Maumee rd.
Huxoll August, 92 Barr.
Jacobs Andrew, 360 Broadway.
Jourdain C J, 98 Maumee rd.
Kaeck Wm, 244 St Mary's av.
Kalbacher Anton, 13 and 15 Grand.
Kelley John B, 26 E Columbia.
Kelsey O R, 506 Broadway.
Kennelly & Doyle, 319 E Creighton av.
Kiefer G A, 210 Spy Run av.
Kiefer P F, 16 Wilt.
Kline Jacob, 30 E Columbia.
Klug Nicholas, 196 Hanna.
Koenig C F, 90 Harmer.
Kohrman Bros, 94 Broadway.
Korn August, 194 Broadway.
Korn John, 134 and 136 Fairfield av.
Krieg Frederick, 372 Broadway.
Lahmeyer C F, 108 Broadway.
Langard John, 70 E Columbia.
Lange John H & Sons, 327 Calhoun.
Lavanway Sherman, 66 E Columbia.
Lerch Frank, 360 Force.
Leykauf Nicholas, 209 Broadway.
Limecooly L F, 562 Calhoun.
Limecooly Wm F, 260 W Creighton av.
Loos H C, 421 Lafayette.
Loos Joseph, 172 W Main.
McAllister G W, 500 Broadway.
Maibucher J, 28 Smith.
Malone Peter, 167 Broadway.
Mensch F P, 26 Calhoun.
Merillat J P, 408 Calhoun.
Meyers F G, 181 Lewis.
Mick A C, 283 E Creighton av.
Miller Isaac, 428 Calhoun.
Minskey Samuel, 302 E Wayne.
Muldoon Wm, 212 Fairfield av.
Mulbaren Thomas, 117 Fairfield av.

GROCERS—RETAIL —Continued.

Neumeier Adam, 381 E Lewis.
Newhouse H D, 2 Lincoln av.
Niebergall H S, 201 E Washington.
Niemann H D, 148 Calhoun.
Notestine J H, 15 and 17 Harrison.
Oddou Louis & Co, 48 E Columbia.
Oetting Frederick, 127 Eliza.
Ofenloch P A, 365 Lafayette.
Ofenloch Valentine, 30 Force.
Pageler J A, 215 E Lewis.
Pfeiffer & Rousseau, 40-44 W Berry.
Pierre C J, s w cor Wells and 2d.
Princess Cash Store, 111 Calhoun.
Rahe August, 65 Gay.
Reinkensmeier C F, 124 Broadway.
Rekers Gerhard, 116 W Washington.
Rensman Bernard, 120 Fairfield av.
Richard Peter, s e cor Old Fort and Lake av.
Richter E J B, 227 Lafayette.
Riethmiller August, 139 Taylor.
Riethmiller Wm J, 184 Fairfield av.
Rinehart M & Co, 546 Calhoun.
Reembke Frederick, 55 Wall.
Rose C W, 156 Griffith.
Ross J P & Co, 25 W Columbia.
Schaefer J H W, 1 s of 143 W 3rd.
Scheele Henry, 400 Hanna.
Scherer C W, 56 Walton av.
Schneider Adam, 173 High.
Schubert August, 230 Gay.
Schuler C W, 302 E Washington.
Schwier Charles & Son, 176 Montgomery.
Sharp L P, cor St Joe boulevard and Columbia av.
Shaw D J, 75 E Wayne.
Shepler & Noble, 256 and 258 Calhoun.
Shirey G W, e s Piqua av 2 n of Rudisill av.
Sieling D F, s w cor Pioneer av and C.
Slater Alfred, 441 Broadway.
Snyder Simon, 53 Hayden.
Spanley Martin, 457 Calhoun.
Spiegel G E, 183 Broadway.
Stace A W, 33 E Main.
Steinacker G W, 105 Maumee rd.
Struver Wm, 66 E Main.

GROCERS—RETAIL—Continued.

Tribus Joseph, 379 E Washington.
Turner Levi, 40 Harrison.
Waltemath C H & Sons, 325 Lafayette.
Ward & Flynn, 292 Calhoun.
Wefel F W, 142 High.
Wiegmann H G, 199 Lafayette.
Wilkinson Frank, 116 Wells.
Winter Frederick, 273 Maumee rd.
Zelt E F, 401 E Wayne.
Zelt John, 149 Gay.
Zern John, 342 Hanna.
Zoeller & Merz, 370 Calhoun.

GUNS AND AMMUNITION.

Bornemann F C, 58 E Main.
Leonard W A, 71 W Superior.
Miller C H, 20 W Main.
Pfeiffer & Schlatter, 38 and 40 E Columbia.
   (*See left side lines.*)
Trautman John, 58 E Main. (*See p 87.*)

HAIR GOODS AND DRESSERS.

Hauss Mrs L A, 105 Broadway. (*See p 113.*)
Oppelt-Bly Kittie, 156 Calhoun.
Rodenbeck Mrs E C, 29 E Washington.

HARDWARE--WHOLESALE.

Coombs E H, 27 E Columbia.
Morgan & Beach, 19 and 21 E Columbia. (*See back cover.*)
Mossman, Yarnelle & Co, 38 E Main.
Pfeiffer & Schlatter, 38 and 40 E Columbia.
   (*See left side lines.*)

HARDWARE--RETAIL.

(*See also Stoves and Tinware.*)
Ash H J, 16 E Columbia.
Beuret & Co, 23 W Columbia.
Freiburger & Suelzer, 364 Calhoun.
Gerding & Aumann Bros, 115 Wallace.
   (*See top edge and p 85.*)

HARDWARE—RETAIL—Continued.

Graffe C F & Co, 132 Calhoun.
Griffith A, 110 Broadway.
Gruber J L, 140 Fairfield av.
Morgan & Beach, 19 and 21 E Columbia. (*See back cover.*)
Peters J C & Co, 7 E Columbia.
Pfeiffer & Schlatter, 38 and 40 E Columbia. (*See left side lines.*)
Seavey Hardware Co, 19 and 21 W Main.
Smith F M & Co. 22 Calhoun.
South Side Hardware Co. 364 Calhoun.
Steger R & Co. 126 Calhoun.

HARNESSMAKERS.
(*See Saddle and Harness Makers.*)

HATS, CAPS AND FURS.
(*See also Clothing; also Furs.*)

Golden & Patterson, 56 Calhoun.
Meyer Wm & Bro. 80 Calhoun.
Pixley & Co, 16 E Berry.

HEAVY HARDWARE.

Mossman, Yarnelle & Co, 38–42 E Main.

HEAVY TRUCKING.

City Trucking Co, 19 and 21 W Washington.
Brown W H, 73 and 75 Holman. (*See p 91.*)

HIDES, PELTS AND FURS.
(*See also Tanners.*)

Bash S & Co, 22 and 24 W Columbia.
Bloom J A, 227 Calhoun.
Weil Bros & Co, 94 E Columbia.

HORSE BREEDERS.

Rockhill Bros & Fleming, ½ mile w of city limits.

HORSE COLLAR MNFRS.

Bayer Bros, 28 Clinton.

HORSE COLLAR MNFRS—Continued.

Racine Aime, 13 1st.
Racine F L, 36 Cass.

HORSESHOERS.

(*See also Blacksmiths.*)

Becker Fred, 13 E Washington.
Ehrmann Charles, 149 W Main. (*See left side lines.*)
Flinn C M & Bro, 21 N Harrison.
Freistroffer Henry, 41 W Main.
Geary Wm, 5 Harrison.
Hoeppner Charles, s w cor Gay and Creighton av.
Jackson John, 81 E Columbia.
Mehnert Louis, 93 E Superior. (*See p 101.*)
Nagel & O'Ryan, 50 Barr.
Perrey & Siebold, 5 Pearl.
Schwartz Louis, 84 Barr.
Zollinger L C & Bro, 13–17 E Superior. (*See left top lines and p 89.*)

HOT AIR HEATING.

Carter Wm & Son, 29 Clinton. (*See bottom edge and p 113.*)

HOT WATER HEATING.

Hines J S, 379 W Main. (*See right top lines.*)
Spice Robert, 48 W Main and 11 Pearl. (*See right bottom lines.*)

HOTELS.

Columbia House, 25 and 27 W Columbia.
Custer House, 16 and 18 W Main. (*See p 85.*)
East Yard Hotel, Walton av and Penn Co.
Ervin House, 12 Harrison.
Grand Central Hotel, 101 Calhoun.
Harman House, 282 Calhoun.
Hedekin House, 25 Barr.
Hoffmann House, 183 Calhoun. (*See p 87.*)
Hotel Emery, 2 Cass. (*See p 348.*)
Hotel Arlington, 107 and 109 E Columbia.
Hotel Rich, 208 Calhoun.

HOTELS—Continued.

Hyer House, 231 Calhoun.
Jewell House, 225 Calhoun.
Lake Shore Hotel, 2 Cass.
McKinnie House, Penn Depot.
Mayer J G, 6 Force. (*See p* 91.)
New Aveline House, s e cor Calhoun and Berry.
Randall The, Harrison, w end Columbia.
St James Hotel, 233 and 235 Calhoun.
Summit City Hotel, 3 Railroad.
Washington House, 121 Calhoun. (*See right bottom lines.*)
Wayne The, 17–23 W Columbia.
Weber Hotel, 281 and 283 Calhoun.
Windsor Hotel, 302 Calhoun.

HOUSE FURNISHING GOODS.

Baals & Co, 57 and 59 E Main.
Foster D N Furniture Co, 11 and 13 Court.
Gruber J L, 140 Fairfield av.
Pickard Bros, 12 and 14 E Columbia.
Shuman Erastus, 43 E Main.

HOUSE MOVERS AND RAISERS.

Boerger C R & Bro, 194 E Washington and 312 Hanna.
Martin Wm, 225 Broadway.

ICE MANUFACTURERS.

Fort Wayne Artificial Ice Co, n e cor Wells and Lake
Shore Ry.

ICE CREAM MANUFACTURERS—WHOLESALE.

Geller Wm F, 98 Broadway.
Seidel Wm & Bro, 111 E Main.

ICE DEALERS.

Baade F H, 129 Broadway.
Fort Wayne Artificial Ice Co, n e cor Wells and Lake
Shore R R.
Moran Peter A, 201 E Wayne.
Schmidt F J, Bluffton rd 1 w of river (*See p* 91.)

764   R. L. POLK & CO.'s

INSECT POWDER MNFRS.

Old Fort Chemical Co. 16 W Berry.

INSURANCE AGENTS.

Albers & Wagner, 5 and 6 Foellinger Blk.
Baxter W F, 33 Bass Blk.
Beahler J E, 22 Bank Blk.
Buck W S, 3 Arcade Bldg. (*See back cover and p* 4.)
Boerger Gustav W, 215 E Wayne.
Boltz P S, 1 and 2 White Bank Blk.
Cashman J W, 21 Bank Blk.
Eme & Son, 1 and 2 Foster Blk.
Everett C E, Old National Bank Bldg.
Eversole O P, (Life) 12 W Wayne. (*See right side lines.*)
Cooper W P (Life), 33 E Berry. (*See p* 496.)
Curdes L F, 3 and 4 Pixley & Long Blk. (*See p* 115.)
Douglass W V, 3 Schmitz Blk.
Fairbank Clark, 19 Court.
Fisher D C, 32 E Berry.
Fitch O B, 26 Bass Blk.
Glutting, Bauer & Hartnett, 55 Clinton.
Graham J E, 26 Bank Blk.
Harding D L, 28 Bank Blk.
Hunt H B (Life). 6 and 7 Trentman Bldg. (*See left top lines and p* 353.)
Jones G W, 9 W Main.
Kuhne & Co, 19 Court.
Lumbard S C, 3 Aveline House Blk.
McNally J J & Co, 33 Bass Blk. (*See p* 446.)
Miller & Dougall, 4 Foster Blk.
Mohr & Sosenheimer, 19 W Wayne.
Motz George & Co, 47 W Main.

INSURANCE AGENTS.

Neireiter Gumpper, 76 Calhoun.
Orr C W, 312 W Washington.
Palmer H L, 32 E Berry.
Schrader & Wilson, 7 Court.
Schuhler F X, 25 Court.
Seidel Edward, 52½ Calhoun.
Torrence G K, 5 Arcade.
Underhill E S, 26 Bass Blk.
Van Slyke I M, 106 E Berry.
Watts W O, 52 Calhoun.
Williams W D 9–11 W Main.

INSURANCE COMPANIES ACCIDENT.

Employers Liability Assurance Corporation, Ld, of London, Eng. C B Fitch. agt, 26 Bass Blk.
Fidelity & Casualty, N Y, 3 New Aveline Blk.
Fort Wayne Ins Co, 22 Bank Blk.
Fort Wayne Mercantile Accident Ass'n, 3 Arcade. (*See back cover and p 4.*)
London Guarantee and Accident Company, Ld, England, 7 Court.
Preferred of N Y, 9–11 W Main.
Travelers Accident, of Hartford, Ct, 28 Bank Blk.
Travelers Life and Accident, Hartford, 3 New Aveline House Blk.

INSURANCE COMPANIES—FIRE.

Aetna, Hartford, Conn, 32 E Berry.
American, 26 Bank Blk.
American Central, 9 and 11 W Main.
American Central of St. Louis, Mo, S F Curdes agt, 3 Bank Blk.
American, New Jersey, 25 Court.
British America, 26 Bank Blk.
Buffalo German Ins Co, Edward Seidel agt, 52½ Calhoun.
Caledonian, Scotland, 1 and 2 Foster Blk.
Caledonian, Scotland, 7 Court.
Citizens of Evansville, 26 Bank Blk.
Commercial Union, 3 New Aveline House Blk.
Conneticut of Hartford, 7 Court.
Continental of New York, 7 Court.
Delaware, Philadelphia, Edward Seidel agt, 52½ Calhoun.
Fire Association, Philadelphia, 3 New Aveline House Blk.

INSURANCE COMPANIES—FIRE—Continued.

Fireman's Fund, California, 32 E Berry.
Franklin Phila, 3 New Aveline House Blk.
German American, N Y, 3 New Aveline House Blk.
Germania. N Y, 32 E Berry.
Girard, Phila, Pa, 7 Court.
Glens Falls, Glens Falls, N Y, 32 E Berry.
Glens Falls, N Y, 215 E Wayne.
Grand Rapids, C B Fitch agt, 26 Bass Blk.
Greenwich Ins Co, C B Fitch agt, 26 Bass Blk.
Hamburg-Bremen, 1 and 2 Foster Blk.
Hanover-N Y, 32 E Berry.
Hartford, 3 New Aveline House Blk.
Home. N Y, 3 New Aveline House Blk.
Imperial, of England, 3 New Aveline House Blk.
Indiana Ins Co, of Fort Wayne, 22 Bank Blk.
Indiana Underwriters, Ind, 22 Bank Blk.
Insurance Co of North America, 26 Bank Blk.
Lion Fire Ins, London, Eng, C B Fitch agt, 26 Bass Blk.
Liverpool, London and Globe, England, 3 New Aveline House Blk.
London Assurance Corp, London, Eng, 7 Court.
London and Lancashire Assurance Co, 26 Bank Blk.
Merchants of Indiana, 4 Foster Blk.
Merchants of Newark, N J, 215 E Wayne.
Michigan Fire and Marine, 1 and 2 Foster Blk.
Milwaukee Mechanics, 28 Bank Blk.
Milwaukee Mechanics, 25 Court.
National of Hartford, Ct, 22 Bank Blk.
National of Hartford, Ct, 1 and 2 Foster Blk.
New Hampshire Ins Co, 25 Court.
Newark of Newark, N J, 215 E Wayne.
Niagara of N Y, 3 New Aveline House Blk.
North British and Mercantile of England, 25 Court.
North British and Mercantile of England, 3 New Aveline House Blk.
Northern Assurance Co, London, Eng, 7 Court.
Northwestern National, 28 Bank Blk.
Orient of Hartford, Ct, 22 Bank Blk.
Palatine Insurance Co, London, England, 7 Court.
Pennsylvania, 26 Bank Blk.
Phœnix of Brooklyn, 3 New Aveline House Blk.
Phœnix of Hartford, 28 Bank Blk.
Phœnix of Hartford. Ct, 9 and 11 W Main
Prussian National of Stettin, Germ, 4 Foster Blk.

Queen of America, 3 New Aveline House Blk.
Royal of England, 3 New Aveline House Blk.
St Paul Fire and Marine, 9 and 11 W Main.
Scottish Union and National, Glasgow, 7 Court.
Sun Fire Office, London, Eng, 28 Bank Blk.
Springfield of Massachusetts, 3 New Aveline House Blk.
Traders, Chicago, Ill. 7 Court.
Underwriters, N Y, 32 E Berry.
United Firemen's, Philadelphia, Pa, 26 Bass Blk.
Washington of Indiana, 4 Foster Blk.
Western Assurance Co, Toronto, Can, 7 Court.
Westchester, N Y, 7 Court.

INSURANCE COMPANIES--GUARANTEE.

London Guarantee & Accident Co, London, Eng, 7 Court.

INSURANCE COMPANIES--LIABILITY.

Employers' Liability Assurance Corp, Ld, of London, Eng, 26 Bass Blk.
London Guarantee and Accident of England, 7 Court.

INSURANCE COMPANIES--LIFE.

Ætna Ins Co, Hartford, Conn, 312 W Washington.
Ætna Life of Hartford Conn, 134 W Berry.
Assurance Life Assn of Terre Haute, Ind, 320 Broadway.
Connecticut Mutual Life Ins Co of Hartford, Conn, 33 Bass Blk.   (*See adv p 446.*)
Equitable Life Assurance Society of N Y, 52½ Calhoun.
Metropolitan Life Insurance Co, 1 and 2 White Bank Bldg
Mutual Life Iusurance Co of Indiana, (Home Office, Indianapolis, Ind), O P Eversole Genl Agt, 12 W Wayne.   (*See right side lines.*)
Mutual of New York, H L Palmer District Mngr, 32 E Berry.
Mutual Benefit Life Insurance Co of Newark, N J, 28 Bank Blk.
Mutual Life, N Y, 32 E Berry.
National Life Insurance Co of Montpelier, Vt, 26 Bass Blk
New England Mutual, Boston, 3 New Aveline House Blk.
New York Life Insurance Co, W P Cooper Special Agt, 33 E Berry.   (*See page 496.*)

INSURANCE COMPANIES—LIFE—Continued.

Northwestern Mutual Life Insurance Co, 5, 6 and 7 Trentman Bldg. (*See left top lines and p* 353.)

Pence Mutual Life Insurance Co of Philadelphia, Clark Fairbank agt, 19 Court.

Travelers of Hartford, Conn, 215 E Wayne.

Travelers Hartford, Conn, 32 E Berry.

Union Central of Cincinnati, Ohio, Old National Bank Bldg.

Union Mutual of Portland, Me, John W Cashman General Agt, 21 Bank Blk.

INSURANCE COMPANIES--PLATE GLASS.

Lloyd's, 26 Bank Blk.

Metropolitan, 7 Court.

INSURANCE COMPANIES--STEAM BOILER.

Hartford Steam Boiler, 3 New Aveline House Blk.

INSURANCE COMPANIES—SURETY.

American Surety Co, 3 New Aveline House Blk.

INTELLIGENCE OFFICES.

Pantitorium, Arcade.

Young Women's Christian Assn, 25 W Wayne.

INTERIOR FINISH.

Erickson Furniture Co The. (*See p* 95.)

Kirchefer H A, 12 Arcade Bldg. (*See p 93*.)

INVESTMENT BROKERS.

McNally J J & CO, 33 Bass Blk. (*See p* 446.)

INVESTMENTS.

Curtice J F, Rooms 1, 2, 3 and 4 Tri-State Bldg. (*See front cover and p* 89.)

INVOICE—FILE—JOURNAL.

Buchsbaum Maurice, 92 and 94 E Columbia (*See front cover.*)

IRON FENCE MNFRS.

Bookwalter J A, 213 E Wayne.

IRON FOUNDERS.

Menefee C M, 135 and 137 Oliver.   (*See p* 460.)

IRON AND LEAD PIPE.

Ogden Robert, 26 E Berry.   (*See embossed line back cover.*)

IRON—WHOLESALE.

Mossman, Yarnelle & Co, 38–42 E Main.

IRON AND STEEL.

Beuret & Co, 23 E Columbia.
Coombs E H, 27 E Columbia.
Mossman, Yarnelle & Co, 38 E Main.

JEWELERS.

(*See Watches, Clocks and Jewelry.*)

JUNK.

Bloom J A, 227 Calhoun.
Miller Bros, 94–98 E Superior.

JUSTICES OF THE PEACE.

Bohen M H, 23 E Main
France Harry F, 13 E Main.
Hays C A, 13 E Main.
Huser L P, 9 Foster Blk.
Ryan Daniel, 23 Arcade.
Tancey Michael, 1 and 2 Bank Blk.

JOURNALS—INVOICE.

Buchsbaum Maurice, 92 and 94 E Columbia.
(*See front cover.*)

KNITTING MILLS.

Wayne Knitting Mills, e s Park av nr W Main.

LADIES FURNISHING GOODS.

Beadell & Co, 20 and 22 E Berry.

* LAMPS AND CHANDELIERS.

Kaag M F, 5 E Columbia. (*See left bottom lines.*)
Ogden Robert, 26 E Berry. (*See embossed line back cover.*)

LATH—PLASTERING.

Moellering Wm & Son, 53–59 Murray. (*See back bone and p 83.*)

LAUNDRIES.

Fort Wayne Steam Laundry, 46 W Main. (*See left side lines.*)
Hoosier Steam Laundry, 191 Calhoun. (*See left side lines.*)
Model Hand Laundry, 137 Fairfield av.
Troy Steam Laundry, 48 and 50 Pearl. (*See left bottom lines.*)

LAWYERS.

Abel J C, 3 Bank Blk.
Aiken J H, 11 W Main.
Alden S R, 18 Bank Blk.
Bittinger J R, 26 Court.
Bittinger & Edgerton, 27 and 28 Bank Blk.
Breen & Morris, 44 Calhoun.
Chapin & Denny, 13–14–15 Bass Blk. (*See front paster.*)
Clapham W E, 24 Bank Blk.
Colerick P B, Arcade Bldg.
Colerick W G, 22 Court.
Colerick & France, 5 and 6 Pixley & Long Bldg.
Crane G D, 36 E Berry.
Crowe J M, 34 E Berry.
Dreibelbiss R B, 25 Court.
Ellison T E, 23 Bank Blk.
Emrick E V, 33 E Main.
Felts G F, 34 E Berry.
Graham J E, 26 Bank Blk.
Hanna H C, 8 Bank Blk.
Hanna R B, 8 Bank Blk.

Hawthorn Howard, 122 Clay.
Harper B F, 10 and 11 Pixley & Long Bldg.
Harper J B, 12 and 13 Bank Blk.
Harris E V, 19 Bass Blk.
Hartman H C, 31 Arcade.
Hayden J W, 31 W Berry.
Hays Charles A, 13 E Main.
Hench S M, 31 E Main.
Holder Chichester, 13 E Main.
Kleekamp F H, 8 Bank Blk.
Kuhne C W, 19 Court.
Leonard W & E, 25 Bank Blk.
Louttit G W, 19 Court.
Lowry Robert, 52½ Calhoun.
Meeks E W, 126 Eliza.
Miller N C, 4 Foster Blk.
Morris, Bell, Barrett & Morris, 36 E Main.
Ninde L M & H W, 42 W Berry.
Ninde & Ninde, Tri-State Bldg.
Purman A A, 1 and 2 Foster Blk.
Randall & Doughman, 5–8 Bass Blk.
Robertson & O'Rourke, 21–22 Bass Blk.
Robinson J M, Main s w cor Calhoun.
Rodabaugh J F, 7 Foster Blk.
Ryan C J, 6 up stairs Arcade.
Ryan Daniel, 7 up stairs Arcade.
Ryan W C, 7 up stairs Arcade.
Schaden P W, 19 Bank Blk.

Shambaugh W H, 10–11 Bank Blk.
Stewart U H, 1–2 Arcade.
Swayne S F, 15 W Main.
Taylor R S, 34 E Berry.
Vesey & Heaton, 27 Court cor Berry.
Williams J D, 63 E Main.
Wilson T W, 80 Calhoun.

772   R. L. POLK & CO.'S

LAWYERS—Continued.

Woodworth E J, 36 E Main.
Zollars & Worden, 62 Calhoun.

* LEAD PIPE.

Ogden Robert, 26 E Berry. (*See embossed line back cover.*)

LEATHER AND FINDINGS.

Freiburger S & Bro, 35 E Columbia.

LETTER FILES.

Empire Box Factory, Bank Blk. (*See right top lines.*)

LIBRARIES.

Allen Co Teachers Library, 12 Bass Blk.
Apollo Musical Co, 87½ Calhoun.
City Directory Library (Free), 38 Bass Blk.
Fort Wayne Catholic Circulating Library and Association, n e cor Calhoun and Lewis.
Hamilton Emerine J Library, 23¼ W Wayne.
Public Library Fort Wayne, City Hall.
Y M C Association, 103 and 105 Calhoun.

LIME MNFRS.

Muhler Charles F & Son, 7 N Calhoun.
Western Lime Co, 3 N Harrison.

LIME, PLASTER AND CEMENT.

Builders' Lime Association, 257 Calhoun. (*See right bottom lines.*)
Moellering Wm & Son, 53–59 Murray. (*See back bone and p 88.*)
Western Lime Co, 3 N Harrison.

LIQUORS--WHOLESALE.
(*See Wines and Liquors.*)

LISTS OF NAMES.

Polk R L & Co, 122 LaSalle, Chicago, Ill.

LIVERY, SALE AND BOARDING STABLES.

Belmont Stables, 88 E Main. (*See p* 97.)
Brinsley J C, 28 Pearl.
Fletcher J F, 32 Barr. (*See p* 99.)
Fulton C W, 18 W Wayne.
Gerding Bros, 66 Harrison.
Hirt & Evans, 5 N Clinton.
Hunt J T, 329 Spy Run av.
Huser & Blomenberg. 201 Fairfield av.
Klinger J A, 91 E Columbia. (*See p* 103.)
Ligget Bros, 5 and 7 N Harrison. (*See p* 101.)
McAfee L H, 1 Wells.
Martin A L, Clinton n e cor N Y, C & St L R R. (*See p* 97.)
Meyers C A C, 176 Harrison.
Myers F H. 62 E Wayne.
Pearse & Poff, 18 and 20 Holman.
Rippe C E, 111 Broadway.
Rippe C & Son, 86 Broadway.
Seabold George. 13 Pearl.
Ulmer C J, 88 E Main. (*See p* 97.)
Weber John & Son, 21 Pearl.
Weick J & Co, 87 Hanna.
Winkelmeyer & Hans, 44 W Main.

LOAN AGENTS.

Albers & Wagner, 5 and 6 Foellinger Blk.
Craw E L, 24 and 25 Bass Blk.
Curdes L F, 3–4 Pixley & Long Bldg. (*See p* 115.)
Curtice J F, Rooms 1, 2, 3 and 4 Tri-State Bldg. (*See front cover and p* 89.)
Douglass W V, 3 Schmitz Blk.
Eversole O P, 12 W Wayne. (*See right side lines*)
Fisher D C, 32 E Berry.
Graham J E, 26 Bank Blk.
Kuhne & Co, 19 Court.
Lumbard S C, 3 Aveline House Blk.
McNally J J & Co, 33 Bass Blk. (*See p* 446.)
Motz George & Co, 47 W Main. (*See classified ins agts.*)
Rothschild & Bro, 1 Bass Blk.
Schell J F & Co, 22 and 23 Pixley & Long Bldg. (*See next page.*)
Schrader & Wilson, 7 Court.
Seidel Edward, 52½ Calhoun.
Watts W O, 4 Arcade.

DAVID TAGTMEYER, Mnfr. —of— HARDWOOD LUMBER, Railroad Stock and Export.

Corner Webster and Greeley Streets, - FORT WAYNE.

ATTORNEYS.   NOTARY PUBLIC.

Fort Wayne Loan
and Collecting Agency,

J. F. SCHELL & Co., Proprs.

Makes a Specialty of Farm, City and Personal Security Loans.

BUYS NOTES AND BONDS.

Careful Attention Given To Collecting of Notes and Accounts.

Loans Made Anywhere In Indiana and Western Ohio.

22-23 Pixley & Long Block,

Fort Wayne, - - Indiana.

LOGS.

Hoffman Bros, 200 W Main. (*See left bottom lines.*)

*LOOKING GLASSES.

Kaag M F, 5 E Columbia. (*See left bottom lines.*)
Siemon & Bro, 50 Calhoun. · (*See back cover.*)

LUMBER—HARDWOOD.

Baker Kilian, cor Superior and Lafayette.
Ferguson & Palmer Co, 1 and 2 Pixley & Long Bldg.
Hoffman Bros, 200 W Main. (*See right bottom lines.*)
Hoffman Lumber Co, 200 W Main. (*See right bottom lines.*)
Perrine Van B, 9 Webster.
Peters J C, w s Osage n of Main.
Peters Box & Lumber Co, 78 High.
Root Vandorn & Co, 106 E Berry.
Smith W P, 9 Bass Blk.

Fleming Mnfg. Co, ROAD SUPERVISORS' SUPPLIES Office, 78 High Street.

Strack E W, 52 Calhoun.
Tagtmeyer David, n w cor Webster and Greely
(*See left top lines.*)

LUMBER MNFRS.

Baker Kilian. cor Superior and Lafayette.
Diether Louis & Bro, Office and Yard bet
City Mills and Gas Wks on E Superior. (*See right side lines.*)
Fee F F, 181 W Wayne.
Ferguson Palmer Co, 1 and 2 Pixley and Long Blk.
Hoffman Bros, 200 W Main. (*See right bottom lines.*)
Peters Box & Lumber Co, 79-105 High.
Peters J C, w s Osage n of Main.
Tagtmeyer David, n w cor Webster and Greeley
(*See left top lines.*)

DAVID TAGTMEYER

. . Manufacturer of . .

Hardwood Lumber,

Railway Stock

And Export . .

Also WAGON STOCK.

Lumber Manufactured for the Trade.

N. W. CORNER

Webster & Greeley Sts.

FORT WAYNE, IND.

BOARDING AND LODGING, WASHINGTON HOUSE,
121 CALHOUN.

LUMBER DEALERS.

Baker Kilian, cor Superior and Lafayette.

Diether Louis & Bro, Office and Yard bet City Mills and Gas Wks, on E Superior. (*See right side lines.*)

Ferguson Palmer Co, 1 and 2 Pixley & Long Bldg.

Fort Wayne Lumber Co, 391 Broadway.

Gilmartin Edward, n e cor Holman and Clinton.

Hoffman Bros, 200 W Main. (*See right bottom lines.*)

Klett Jacob & Sons, 52–66 Pearl.

Peters' Box & Lumber Co, 79–105 High.

Rhinesmith & Simonson, s e cor Lafayette and Wabash R R

Strack E W, 52 Calhoun.

Taylor I N, 19 W Wayne.

Tagtmeyer David, n w cor Webster and Greeley (*See left top lines.*)

---

* LUMBER, LATH AND SHINGLES.

Diether Louis & Bro, Office and Yard bet City Mills and Gas Wks on E Superior. (*See right side lines.*)

LUMBER—PINE.

Fort Wayne Lumber Co, 391 Broadway.

MACHINISTS.

(*See also Founders and Machinists.*)

Bass F & M Wks, Hanna s of Wabash R R.

Baxter & Tarmon, 16 W Columbia.

Bowman Charles, 37 Pearl, (*See right side lines and classified saw works.*)

Stein C F A, 57 Winter, (*See p 630.*)

Columbia Machine Wks, 54 E Columbia.

Kestel P P, Berry n w cor Barr.

Stenger Peter, 18 N Ewing. (*See left top lines.*)

---

* MACHINISTS' TOOLS.

Pfeiffer & Schlatter, 38 and 40 E Columbia. (*See left side lines.*)

MAILING AND ADDRESSING.

Polk R L & Co, 122 LaSalle, Chicago.

MALSTERS.

Centlivre C L Brewing Co, n end Spy Run av. (*See front edge and left side lines.*)

MANTELS AND GRATES.

(*See also Grates and Mantels.*)

Carter Wm & Son, 29 Clinton. (*See bottom edge and p 113.*)

Hattersley A & Son, 48 E Main. (*See embossed line front cover.*)

Lund H M, 172 W Creighton av.

MARBLE AND GRANITE WORKS.

(*See also Stone Yards.*)

Aichele G F, 510 W Main.
Brunner & Haag, 124 W Main.
Griebel & Pask, 74 and 76 W Main.

MARKET GARDENERS.

Christie John N, e s Spy Run av 1 n of Centlivre Brewing Co
Fricke Joseph, Griswold av n w cor Parnell.
Hagemann Joseph, s w cor Edsall av and Wabash Ry.
Kruse Christian, Lake av e of city limits.
Lanternier A J, 133 Walton av.
Seelig John, Lake av e of city limits.
Wesson Frederick, n s Griswold av 3 e of St Joseph river.
Yetter Charles, w s Spy Run av 8 n of canal feeder bridge.

MASONS--BRICK AND STONE.

(*See also contractors.*)

Baltes Peter, 10 S Joseph boulevard.
Brinkmann H F, 177 Gay.
Evers John, 199 John.
Colvin Elbert, 83 Franklin av.
Gebhard Wm, 172 Maumee rd.
Kanney John, 5 Bass Blk. (*See p 79.*)
Korte & Son, 65 Maumee rd. (*See p 111.*)
Liebig Charles, 1 Tam.
Miller Fred, 257 Calhoun and 8 Summit. (*See right bottom lines and p 103.*)
Rippe Frederick, 176 Madison. (*See p 91.*)

778   R. L. POLK & CO.'s

MASONS—BRICK AND STONE—Continued.

Wehrenberg & Busching, 504 E Lewis.
(*See p* 105.)

MATTRESS MNFRS.

Kegelmann & Son, 551 E Wayne.
Pape Furn Co, 28 and 30 E Berry.

MEATS—WHOLESALE.

Ft Wayne Beef Co, 4 and 6 Calhoun.
Haller Wm, 107 E Lewis.
Roux George, 500 E Wayne.

MEAT MARKETS.

Aubrey F J, 129 Buchanan.
Birkhold Mattheus, 13 Highland.
Blaising J B, 269 E Washington.
Boese Frederick, 139 Force.
Briggemann Wm, 281 E Creighton av.
Cramer & Neher, 527 Lafayette.
Eckart Fred Packing Co, 35 W Main.
Eckrich Peter, 5 Smith.
Engle & Stenson, 228 W Main.
Frank Mendel, 45 Hough.
Gebfert L H, 100 W Main.
Gombert F J, 100 Maumee rd.
Hadsell C M, 20 Indiana av.
Haiber C F, 122 Wells.
Haiber G W, 212 E DeWald.
Haiber Lawrence, 15 High.
Haller Gottlieb, 277 Hanna and 366 Calhoun.
Haller Wm, 107 E Lewis.
Harber P W, s s Buchanan bet Force and John.
Hartwell H A, 430 Calhoun.
Herrmann George jr, 84 Walton av.
Hilgemann H F, 121 W Jefferson.
Hoch Wm, 121 Wallace.
Hood Robert, 98 Barr.
Huguenard J C, 107 Maumee rd.
Iten J C, 13 Begue.
Jacobs Charles, 197 E Washington.
Kabisch & Son, 156 Fairfield av.
Karn Bros, 16 W Main.

Kelsey E M, 504 Broadway.
Kohn Charles, 42 Maumee rd.
Koppenhoefer Fred, 205 Lafayette.
Korn John, 134 and 136 Fairfield av.
Krug George, s s Rudisill av 3 e of Calhoun.
Le Gras August, 106 Spy Run av.
Lenz Fred, 170 Hanna.
Leutwyler Wm, 536 Calhoun.
Lindsley P M, 89 Harmer.
Frank Mendel, 208 Hanna.
Miller Wm L, 317 W Main.
Oetting Frederick, 127 Eliza.
Parrot Frank, 60 E Main.
Pfeiffer & Rousseau, 40-44 W Berry.
Pietz J F, 224 Lafayette.
Raab J G, 18 E Columbia.
Rich E & Son, 94 Barr, 254 Calhoun and 22 Harrison.
Rosenthal Eli, cor St. Joseph boulevard and Columbia av.
Rowe N B, 189 Broadway.
Scheele Henry, 400 Hanna.
Scott Bros, 352 Broadway.
Slater Alfred, 441 Broadway.
Steinhaur Emanuel, 109 Barthold.
Suelzer J W, 422 Lafayette and 281 Hanna and 350 Calhoun.
Truebenbach H, 312 W Main.
Wefel John, 163 High.
Weller C W, 92 W Jefferson.
Wiesmann Eugene, 214½ Fairfield av.
Wilkens Bros, 112 Broadway.
Winter Frederick, 273 Maumee rd.
Workman Samuel, 230 Calhoun.
Wyss Theodore, 66 Gay.
Zickgraf C G, 19 Grand.
Zinn J N, 198 Broadway.

MEDICAL INSTITUTES.

Guardian Medical and Surgical Institute, 13 W Wayne.

MEDICINE MNFRS.

Corneille August L, 26 E Columbia.
Haines H H, 24 E Washington.
Lincoln Tea Co, 50 Harrison.

780   R. L. POLK & CO.'S

Meyer Bros & Co, 14 Calhoun.
Wery J H, 132 W Williams.

MERCANTILE AGENCIES.

Dun R G & Co, 35 and 37 Pixley & Long Bldg.
Smith Credit Rating Co, 32 E Berry.

MERCHANDISE BROKERS.

Fay M W Warehouse Co, 135 Calhoun.
Lawson Wm, 22 Schmitz Blk.

MERCHANT TAILORS.

(See also Clothing; also Tailors.)

Blondoit W H, 47 E Lewis.
Feist L J, 226 Lafayette.
Foster Andrew, 15 W Wayne. *(See left top lines.)*
Fowles J W, 64 Barr. *(See left side lines.)*
Grimme J H & Sons, 108 Calhoun.
Hardung Fred, 35 E Main.   *(See right top lines.)*
Jaxtheimer L & Son, 29 E Berry.
Kleemier Dietrich, 197 Calhoun.
Kruse Charles, 39 Harrison.
Martin & Fitzsimmons, 172 W Jefferson.
   (See p 107.)
Meyer Henry, 12 E Berry.

Meyer H C, 44 Harrison.
Rabus John, 16 W Berry.
Romeis C J, 118 Calhoun.
Scheffler Gustav, 43 W Main.

Schmidt Gottfried, 70 E Main.
Schoch A F, 41½ W Main.
Stauffer Gottlieb, 214 Calhoun.
Thieme Bros, 12 W Berry.
Thieme J G & Son, 37 and 39 E Columbia.
Weitzmann F T, 182 Calhoun.

MIDWIVES.

Buettel Mrs Dora, 234 Francis.
Goeglein Mrs Lizzie, 86 Gay.
Linnemeier Mrs M S, 174 Francis.
Wessel Mrs Lizzetta, 42 Wells.

MILL FEED.

Gallmeyer C W, 53 E Main.

MILLINERY GOODS - WHOLESALE.

Armstrong James A & Co, 31-35 W Berry.

MILLINERY GOODS AND MILLINERS.

Andrew Lizzie, 311½ W Main.
Borgmann & Lesser Misses, 137 Broadway.
Chapman Mrs M B, 150 Fairfield av.
Egan M C, 128 Calhoun.
Greenewald E E, 132½ Broadway.
Hanna E O, 84 Calhoun.
Johnson Mrs Ollie, 60 Maumee rd.
Jones C E C, 212 Calhoun.
Keel Mrs A C, 22 W Berry.
Kratzsch Bros, 114 Calhoun.
Krull Sisters, 268 E Washington.
Lau M J, 31 E Main.
Malloy Frances, 12 and 14 Arcade.
Mergentheim Alexander, 38 Calhoun.
McAfee Mrs M E, 3 Wells.
Noll A A, 140 Broadway.
Oppelt-Bly Kittie, 156 Calhoun.
Quinn M E, 175 Fairfield av.
Raab Mrs Christina, 175 E Washington.
Reitze Mrs M C, 164 Calhoun.
Ruch Mrs Clara J, 339 W Main.

782   R. L. POLK & CO.'S

Schulte Mrs M G, 332 Calhoun.
Seaney Millinery Co, 158 and 160 Calhoun.
Spiegel Mrs F C, 100 Broadway.
Stier Catherine, 32 Clinton.
Tait Frank, 26 E Wayne.
Tyler Mrs Inez, 52 Oliver.

*MINERAL LANDS.

Curtice J F, rms 1, 2, 3, 4 Tri-State Bldg. *(See front cover and p 89.)*

MINERAL WATERS.

Spring Beach Mineral Water, Martin Detzer Sole Agt, 260 Calhoun.

MINERAL WATER MNFRS.

(See also Bottling Works.)

Brames L & Co, 123–127 Clay. *(See p 3.)*
Fremion & Vollmer, 9 N Harrison.
Steinheuser Nicholas, 29 Miner.

MORTAR COLORS.

Moellering Wm & Son, 53–59 Murray. *(See back bone and p 83.)*

*MORTGAGE LOANS.

Curtice J F, rms 1-2-3-4 Tri-State Bldg. *(See front cover and p 89.)*
Eversole O P, 12 W Wayne. *(See right side lines.)*
Mc Nally J J & Co, 33 Bass Blk. *(See p 446.)*

MOULDINGS.

Fort Wayne Lumber Co, 391 Broadway.

*MUSIC LEAF TURNERS--PNEUMATIC.

Fort Wayne Pneumatic Novelty & Model Works, 139 John. *(See p 471.)*

*MUSIC SCHOOLS.

Banister School of Music, 49 W Berry.

MUSIC TEACHERS.

Adams Louisa, 111 Brackenridge.
Alexander C C, 54 E Washington.
Banister Mrs L W, 49 W Berry.
Bernhard Frederick, 104 E Lewis.
Bloomhuff Anna, 45 W Main.
Chambers Mrs Jennie C, 405 Calhoun.
Filley Nettie, 154 E Berry.
Ft Wayne Conservatory of Music, Bank Blk.
Hartzel Arthur, 27 Broadway.
Hobbs L, 164 Madison.
Houlton R R, 224 E Jefferson.
Hutchison Mrs Rebecca, 247 W Washington.
Johnson Myrtle, 31 Baker.
Johnson Rosa B, 58 W Berry.
Joost Albert, 132 W Jefferson.
Kell F J, 54 E Washington.
Krull H F, 266 E Washington.
Long Leo (vocal), 134 Calhoun.
Miles Wm, 134 Calhoun.
Noll E M, 68 Clay. (*See p* 103.)
Nonnemaker Lizzie, 150 Clinton.
Orff Henry, 78 W Creighton av.
Plumadore M N, 49 Douglas av.
Rager A J, 102 E Jefferson.
Roehm H B, 58 W Berry.
Schneider W H, 4 N Fulton.
Schust P C, 182 Wells.
Standish Theodore, 69 Douglas av.
Wisterman Fannie, 58 W Berry.

MUSIC AND MUSICAL MERCHANDISE.

(*See also Pianos and Organs.*)

Achenbach Harry, 34 E Berry.
Baldwin D H & Co, 98 Calhoun. (*See p* 93.)
Dawson G W, 27 W Main.
Fort Wayne Music Co, 34 E Berry.
Krull R L, 128 E Washington.
Siemon & Bro, 50 Calhoun. (*See back cover.*)

* MUSICIANS.

Reineke F J, 41 E Main. (*See p* 115.)

MUSTARD MANUFACTURERS.

Globe Mills, 73–79 E Columbia.

NATURAL GAS COMPANIES.

Fort Wayne Gas Co, 50 Clinton.

*NATURAL GAS FITTERS.

Ash H J, 16 E Columbia.
Franke H C & Son, 68 Barr. (*See p 111.*)
Hattersley A & Sons, 48 E Main. (*See embossed line front cover.*)
Ogden Robert, 26 E Berry. (*See embossed line back cover.*)

NEWSDEALERS.

(*See also Books and Stationery.*)
Herring H L, 1 Railroad.
Lehman Book & News Co, 81 Calhoun.
Siemon & Bro, 50 Calhoun. (*See back cover.*)
Spiegel J E jr, 103 Broadway.
Stahn & Heinrich, 116 Calhoun.

NEWSPAPERS—DAILY.

Fort Wayne Freie Presse, 24 Clinton.
Fort Wayne Gazette, 41 E Berry.
Fort Wayne Journal, 30 E Main.
Fort Wayne News, n w cor Washington and Clinton.
Fort Wayne Sentinel, 107 Calhoun.
Indiana Staats Zeitung, 37 E Columbia.

NEWSPAPERS—WEEKLY.

Fort Wayne Dispatch, 88 Clinton.
Fort Wayne Gazette, 41 E Berry.
Fort Wayne Journal, 30 E Main.
Fort Wayne News, n w cor Washington and Clinton.
Fort Wayne Sentinel, 107 Calhoun.
Indiana Staats Zeitung, 37 E Columbia.
Monday Morning Times, 47 E Berry.

NEWSPAPERS--MONTHLY.

Business Guide The, 76–80 Clinton.
Journal of the Medical Sciences, 30 E Main.

NOTARIES PUBLIC.

Burns M E. 30 E Main.
Craw Edward L, 24 and 25 Bass Blk.
Crowe J M, 34 E Berry.
Fisher D C, 32 E Berry.
Graham M J, 405 Hanna.
Haiber Frederick, 64 Wells.
Pfeiffer C F, 6 Bass Blk.
Lischy Aaron, 551 E Washington.
Randall & Doughman, 5–8 Bass Blk.
Schell J F, 22 and 23 Pixley & Long Blk. (*See adv in classified loan and collecting agts.*)
Schrader & Wilson, 7 Court.
Stump E C, 12 Bank Blk.

NOTIONS--WHOLESALE.

DeWald Geo & Co, n e cor Calhoun and Columbia.
Falk Charles & Co, 23 W Main.
Root & Co, 46–48 Calhoun.

NOTIONS--RETAIL.

(*See also Dry Goods.*)

Bashara Salem, 43½ E Columbia.
Beadell & Co, 20-22 E Berry.
Chapman M A, 106 Broadway.
Colmey & Ripley, 200 Calhoun.
DeWald Geo & Co, Columbia n e cor Calhoun.
Goodman M & K, 139 E Jefferson.
Hills A R, 9 E Main.
Kane James M, 24 Calhoun.
Mergentheim's Bazaar, 38 Calhoun.
Meyers F G, 181 E Lewis.
Ofenloch P A, 365 Lafayette.
Root & Co, 46–48 Calhoun.
Scherer C W, 56 Walton av.
Seibert & Good, 89–91 Calhoun.
Siemon & Bro, 50 Calhoun.   (*See back cover.*)
Skaf Hibab, 125 Fairfield av.
Skaf & Elils, 123 Fairfield av.

NURSERYMEN.

(*See also Florists.*)

Nestel Daniel, S Broadway n w cor Huestis av.

NURSES.

(*See also Midwives.*)

Cox Lizzie, 194 E Lewis.
Cramer Jennie, 86 E Lewis.
Crawford Mrs S S, 386 E Washington.
Nerhood Matilda, 43 E Butler.
Rocholl Mrs Mary, 77 E Butler.
Wilson Lula E, 62 W Lewis
Zimmerman Mrs Augustina, 59 E Wayne.

OCULISTS AND AURISTS.

(*See also Physicians.*)

Bulson A F Jr, 19, 20 and 21 Pixley & Long Bldg
Gard Brookfield (aurist), 13 W Wayne.

OFFICE AND BANK FIXTURES.

Erickson Furniture Co The. (*See p 95.*)

OFFICE AND STORE FIXTURES.

Walda H B & Bro, 89 E Superior. (*See p 101.*)

*OIL PUMP MNFRS.

Bowser S F & Co, cor E Creighton av and Thomas. (*See p 4.*)
Western Oil Pump Co, 57 E Columbia.

OIL TANK MNFRS.

Bowser S F & Co, cor E Creighton av and Thomas. (*See p 4.*)
Wayne Oil Tank Co, 17 Lafayette.

OIL AND GAS LANDS.

Curtice J F, 1, 2, 3 and 4 Tri-State Bldg. (*See front cover and p 89.*)

OILS.

Brinsley G C & Son, 28 Pearl.
Morgan G W, 184 E Jefferson.
Standard Oil Co, Columbia City rd and junction N Y, C St L R R.

OMNIBUS LINES.

Powers & Barnett, 16–24 E Wayne.

OPTICIANS.

Green & Probasco, 3 Arcade.
Worch L A, 101 Calhoun.

ORGAN MNFRS.

Engmann K A & Co, 133 E Jefferson. (*See left side lines.*)
Ft Wayne Organ Co, e_s Fairfield av n e cor.

ORGAN TUNERS.

Engmann K A & Co, 133 E Jefferson. (*See left side lines..*)

OVERALL MNFRS.

Hoosier Mnfg Co, 28 and 30 E Berry.
Redelsheimer D S & Co, 37 and 39 W Main.

PACKERS--BEEF AND PORK.

Eckart Fred Packing Co, 35 W Main.
Haller Wm, 107 E Lewis.
Raab John G, 18 E Columbia.

*PACKING—HOUSEHOLD GOODS.

Ryan Trucking Co, 19–23 Wells. (*See right top lines and p 95.*)

PAINTERS—CARRIAGE.

Gronan F W, rear 89 E Superior. (*See p 107.*)
Hild Henry, 149 W Main. (*See p 115.*)
Zollinger L C & Bro, 13–17 E Superior. (*See left bottom lines and p 89.*)

*PAINTERS—FRESCO.

Kirchefer H A, 12 Arcade Blk. (*See p 93.*)

PAINTERS--HOUSE AND SIGN.

Allen A S, 158 Calhoun.
Alter Jacob, 20 Wilt.
Beach August, 444 Broadway.
Bowser O J, 266 E Creighton av.
Brimmer J W, 33 W Main.
Brunner L J, 79 Swinney av.
Bugert Matthew, 176 Broadway.
Danehy Michael, 12 Bass.
Heine & Israel, 123 Broadway.
Hild Henry, 149 W Main.   (*See p* 115.)
Hoffman Daniel, s w cor Reed and Jennison.
Hoopingarner Wm H, 192 Metz.
Hull L O, 90 Calhoun.   (*See back cover.*)
Hull S W, 27 Clinton.
Junge C J, 179 E Taber.
Koby J M, 66 Walton av.
Kover & Son, s w cor Howell and Rumsey av.
Kramer A A, 163 John.
Kramer Ernst, 90 E Main.
Kreckmann Michael, 123 Eliza.
Lehnert H C, 344 Broadway.
Miller H M, e s Calhoun, 4 s of Marshall.
Nestel E P, 115 E Lewis.
Ott & Son, 7 Romy av.
Puff Adolph, 341 Hanna.
Romy C M, 140 Maumee rd.
Schu John, 594 Lafayette.
Shelby C F, 235 W Main.
Stoneburner Elias, 228 Walton av.
Wadington B C, 323 Lewis.

PAINTERS' SUPPLIES.

Heine & Israel, 123 Broadway.

PAINTS, OILS AND GLASS.
(*See also Druggists.*)

Dreier & Bro, 10 Calhoun.
Haller Gottlieb, 362 Calhoun.
Hull L O, 90 Calhoun.   (*See back cover.*)
Hull S W, 27 Clinton.
Meyer Bros & Co, 14 Calhoun and 9 W Columbia

Morgan & Beach, 19 and 21 E Columbia. (*See back cover.*)
Pfeiffer & Schlatter, 38 and 40 E Columbia. (*See left side lines.*)
Schults Wm H, 142 Fairfield av.
South Side Hardware Co, 364 Calhoun.

PAPER BOX MANUFACTURERS.

(*See Box Manufacturers—Paper.*)

PAPER—WHOLESALE.

Fisher Bros, 125 Calhoun.
Fort Wayne Newspaper Union, 76 and 80 Clinton.
Hirsh A & Co, 23 E Columbia.
Lahmeyer H B, 152 Barr.
Siemon & Bro, 50 Calhoun. (*See back cover.*)

PAPERHANGERS.

(*See also Painters.*)
Hull L O, 90 Calhoun. (*See back cover.*)
Siemon & Bro, 50 Calhoun. (*See back cover.*)

PATENT MEDICINES.

Fathers Medicine, 24 E Washington.
Lincoln Tea Co, 50 Harrison.

PATENT LAWYERS.

Chapin & Denny, 13, 14, 15 Bass Blk. (*See front paster.*)
Hartman H C, 31 Arcade.

PATENT OFFICE DRAWINGS.

Riedel J M E, 23, 24, 25 Schmitz Blk. (*See front cover.*)

PATENT SOLICITORS.

Chapin & Denny, 13, 14, 15 Bass Blk. (*See front paster.*)

PATTERN AND MODEL MAKERS.

Fort Wayne Pneumatic Novelty and Model Works, 139 John. (See adv p 471.)
Stein C F A, 57 Winter. (See p 630.)
Stenger Peter, 30 N Ewing. (See left top lines.)

PAWNBROKERS.

Gouty T A, 252 Calhoun.
Mariotte Bros, 34 W Main.
Mariotte Horace. 20 E Columbia.

PENSION CLAIM AGENTS.

Dickman H W, 13 E Main.
Kerr Wm J, 13 E Main.
Miller & Dougall, 4 Foster Blk.

PERFUME MNFRS.

Biddle C I, 169 Ewing.

PERMANENT INVOICE—FILE JOURNAL MNFRS.

Buchsbaum Maurice, 92 and 94 E Columbia.

PHOTOGRAPHERS.

Barrows F R, 23 W Berry.
Corlett J E, 71 Monroe.
Hubbard Wm V, 8 Euclid av.
Miner & Dexter, 44 Calhoun.
Mote J R. 188 Columbia av.
Parrot G J, 62 Calhoun.
Salzmann Wm, 164 Calhoun.
Schanz Felix, 112 Calhoun.

PHOTOGRAPHERS' SUPPLIES.

Jenne Camera Mnfg Co, 16 W Columbia. (See p 99.)
Jones M L, 44 Calhoun.

PHYSICIANS.

Barnett C E, 2 White Blk.

Barnett W W, 2 and 3 White Blk.
Bartele Michael, 207 E Jefferson.
Bergk Charles, 74 Calhoun.
Biddle F M, 169 Ewing.
Boswell A J, n w cor E Wayne and Barr.
Bowen G W, 12 W Main.
Bower G B M, 72 Harrison.
Bramigk Werner, 174 Broadway.
Buchman A P, 18 W Washington.
Bulson A E jr, 19, 20 and 21 Pixley & Long Bldg.
Buskirk A E, 80 Calhoun.
Caldwell James, 33 Calhoun.
Cary D B, 27 Clinton.
Chambers J D, 16 Brackenridge.
Coblentz J W, 63 Harrison.
Deppeller Rudolph, 32 E Columbia.
Dills T J, 26 W Wayne.
Dinnen J M, 67 W Wayne.
Dodge Wm A, 92-96 Broadway.
Duemling H A, 94 Calhoun.
Enslen W M, 286 Calhoun.
Ferguson W T, 82 W Berry.
Fricke Richard, 9 E Wayne.
Gard Brookfield, 13 W Wayne.
Gavin F W, 35 E Berry.
Green Mary F, 139 W Main.
Greenawalt George L, 151 E Wayne.
Greenewald Marquis, 11 Fairfield av.
Harris Ella F, 148 Calhoun.
Harris L P, 148 Calhoun.
Harrod Morse, 44 Maumee rd.
Havice S H, 38 W Wayne.
Heaton C E, 36 E Berry.
Holloway J H, 102 Calhoun.
Howe Delia, Ind School for Feeble-Minded Youth.
Hugh J E, 240 E Creighton av.
Jones J H, 320 W Jefferson.
Joseph B E, 101 E Wayne. (*See classified deformity apparatus.*)
Kappel J H, 180 E Washington.
Kesler A J, 286 Calhoun.
Ladd F B, 411 W Main.
Leonard P M, 188 W DeWald.
Lipes R F, 74 Douglas av.
Lipes U G, 146 W Wayne.

WHITE NATIONAL BANK.—Interest paid on certificate of deposit at three (8) per cent. per annum if left four (4) months. Deposits of any amount received.   Safe Deposit Boxes for rent at $5 per annum.

792   R. L. POLK & CO.'S

PHYSICIANS Continued.

McCaskey G W, 107 W Main.
McCausland J W. 191 Lafayette.
McCormick F H, 6 White Bank Blk.
McCullough T P, 180 Harrison
McHugh J E, 240 E Creighton av.
McOscar E J, 29 W Jefferson.
Martz Christian, 15 W Jefferson.
Metcalf S C, 109 W Superior.
Mikesell Arthur L, 32 Calhoun.
Miller G W, 19 E Washington.
Miller J C, 96 Broadway.
Miller J E, 327 Lafayette.
Morgan E E, 159 E Lewis.
Myers Wm H, 157 W Wayne.
Nichols John, 1 Riverside av.
Nieschang C C F, 298 Calhoun.
Niswonger H W, 33 Calhoun.
Ogle J J, 57 Holton av.
Phelps Whitcomb, 7 Monroe.
Porter M F, 47 W Wayne.
Proegler Carl, 128 Broadway.
Rosenthal I M, 96 W Berry.
Rosenthal M I, 96 W Berry.
Ross G A, 29 E Berry.
Ruhl Wm D, 45 W DeWald.
Schilling Carl, n w cor Washington and Barr.
Schilling John, n w cor Washington and Barr.
Siver E L, 5 Schmitz Blk.
Smith C S, 59 Pixley & Long Blk-
Smith J S, 45 Elmwood av.
Stemen C B, 94 Calhoun.
Stemen G B, 300 W Main.
Stemen G C, 6 White Blk.
Stemen H F, 25 Broadway.
Stults C E, 83 Wells.
Stults J E, 96 Wells.
Sturgis L T, 360 Calhoun.
Stutz J A, 50 W Washington.
Sweringen B V, 26 W Wayne.
Sweringen H V, 96 Broadway.
Thain George, 273 W Washington
Thayer Frederick, 8 Short.
Tinkham M W, 24 Arcade.
Van Buskirk A E, 416 Calhoun.

Wagner C E, Penn depot.
Walter Eyer, 18 Schmitz Blk.
Wenger N R, 135 Calhoun.
Wheelock K K, 26 W Wayne.
Whery Mary A, 26 Madison.
Whery W P, 94 Calhoun.
Younge J W, 176 Calhoun.

PHYSICIANS' SUPPLIES.

Dreier & Bro, 10 Calhoun.

PIANO TUNERS.

Darling J L, 15 E Wayne.
Krimmel Julius, 55 Douglas av.
Lane J W, 209 W Jefferson.
Noll B R, 68 Clay. (*See p* 103.)
Taylor S R, 19 W Wayne.

PIANOS AND ORGANS.

(*See also Music and Musical Merchandise.*)

Arcade Music Store, 2–6 Arcade.
Baldwin D H & Co, 98 Calhoun. (*See p* 93.)
Hill C L, 38 Clinton.
Jacobs & Conklin, 34 E Berry.
Karn S A, 9 E Columbia.
Taylor Bros Piano Co, 19 W Wayne.
Wagner J C, 27 W Main.

PICTURES AND PICTURE FRAMES.

Carroll R E, 14 E Berry.
Frentzel J A N, 191 Calhoun.
Heine & Israel, 123 Broadway.
Henry Jacob, 338 Hanna.
Keil & Keil, 106 Calhoun.
Siemon & Bro, 50 Calhoun. (*See back cover.*)

PLANING MILLS.

(*See also Sash, Doors and Blinds.*)

Diether Louis & Bro, Office and Yard bet
City Mills and Gas Works on E Superior. (*See right
side lines.*)

794 R. L. POLK & CO 'S

PLANING MILLS—Continued.

Hoffman Bros, 200 W Main. (*See right bottom lines.*)
Peters Box & Lumber Co, 79–105 High.
Rhinesmith & Simonson, s w cor Lafayette and Wabash R R.

PLASTERERS.

Ahern Thomas, 83 Wagner.
Kennedy J R, 217 John.
Metker Joseph, rear cor Washington and Comparet. (*See p 109.*)
Schwartz Henry, 542 Calhoun. (*See p 115.*)

PLATERS—GOLD AND SILVER.

Winter Moses, 35 E Main.

PLUMBERS, STEAM AND GAS FITTERS.

Abdon George, 30 Clinton.
Boehm C F, 120 Rockhill.
Bruns C W & Co, 135 Calhoun.
Cox P E, 176 Calhoun.
Fox C G, 80 Taylor.
Franke H C & Son, 68 Barr. (*See p 111*).
Hattersley A & Sons, 48 E Main. (*See embossed line front cover.*)
Hines J S, 379 W Main. (*See right top lines.*)
Jahn J C & Co, 123 E Lewis.
Johnson Clarence, 163 Webster.
Mc Donald J G, 17 N Calhoun.
Madden J C, 39 Baker.
Martin Emmett, cor Hanna and Buchanan.
Noll Martin F, 129 E Jefferson.
O'Brien & Rolf, 122 Broadway.
Ogden Robert, 26 E Berry. (*See embossed line back cover.*)
Ryan & Surrell, 41 W Berry.
Seavey Hardware Co, 19 and 21 W Main.
Spice Robert, 48 W Main. (*See right bottom lines.*)

*PLASTER.

Moellering Wm & Son, 53–59 Murray. (*See back bone and p 83.*)

ROBERT OGDEN,

Plumber, Steam and Gas Fitter,

AND NATURAL GAS,

And Dealer in Iron and Lead Pipe, Sheet Lead, Hydrants, Bath
Tubs, Pumps, Brass Goods, Etc.

REPAIRING OF ALL KINDS DONE.

26 East Berry Street, - Fort Wayne, Indiana.

* PLUMBERS' SUPPLIES.

Hattersley A & Sons, 48 E Main. (*See embossed line front cover.*)
Ogden Robert, 26 E Berry. (*See embossed line back cover.*)

POP MNFRS.

Brames L & Co, 123–127 Clay. (*See p 3.*)

PORK AND BEEF PACKERS.

(*See Packers—Pork and Beef.*)

POSTAGE STAMPS—FOREIGN AND DOMESTIC.

Indiana Stamp Co, cor Berry and Harrison.

POTASH MNFRS.

Bisson Michael, w s Glasgow av 2 n of N Y, C & St L R R.

POWDER—BLASTING.

Jenne C R, 16 W Columbia.

PRESSED AND ORNAMENTAL BRICK.

Moellering Wm & Son, 53–59 Murray. (*See back bone and p 83.*)

796   R. L. POLK & CO.'S

PRINTERS' SUPPLIES.

Bookwalter & Son, 15 W Williams.
Fort Wayne Newspaper Union, 76–80 Clinton.

PRINTERS—BOOK AND JOB.

Aldine Printing House, 63 E Berry. (*See page* 89.)
Archer Printing Co, 82 Clinton.
Fort Wayne Newspaper Union, 76–80 Clinton.
Fort Wayne Sentinel, 107 Calhoun.
Indiana Staats Zeitung, 37 E Columbia.
Journal Co The, 30 E Main.
Rayhouser R C F, 34 E Berry.
Siemon & Bro. 50 Calhoun. (*See back cover.*)
Underwood & Brown, 126 Calhoun.
Wayne Printing Co, 97¼ Calhoun.

PRINTERS—COPPERPLATE AND STEEL DIE.

Aldine Printing House, 63 E Berry. Tel 414. (*See p* 89.)
Archer Printing Co, 82 Clinton. Tel 55.

PRODUCE COMMISSION.

(*See also Commission.*)

Bash S & Co, 22 and 24 W Columbia.
Comparet D F, 76 E Columbia.
Copinus Albert, 25 E Columbia.
Pottlitzer Bros Fruit Co, 8 and 10 S Harrison.

PUBLICATIONS—GERMAN AND FRENCH.

Siemon & Bro, 50 Calhoun. (*See back cover.*)

PUBLISHERS.

Archer Printing Co, 82 Clinton.
Fort Wayne Newspaper Union, 76–80 Clinton.
Long Mason Publishing Co, 17 Pixley and Long Bldg.
Polk R L & Co, 38 Bass Blk.

PULLEY MANUFACTURERS.

Old Fort Mnfg Co, 9 Bass Blk.
Paul Mnfg Co, cor 6th and N Calhoun.

PUMP MNFRS AND DEALERS.

Abdon George, 30 Clinton.
Hattersley & Sons, 48 E Main. (*See embossed line front cover.*)
Gerding & Aumann Bros, 115 Wallace. (*See top edge and p 85.*)
Ogden Robert, 26 E Berry. (*See embossed line back cover.*)
Spice Robert, 48 W Main and 11 Pearl. (*See right bottom lines.*)
Weibel Fred, 18 Harrison.

QUEENSWARE.

Graf Philip, 335 Lafayette. (*See right side lines.*)
Kaag M F, 5 E Columbia. (*See left bottom lines.*)

*PUMPING MACHINERY.

Hattersley A & Sons, 48 E Main. (*See embossed line front cover.*)

RAILROAD CASTINGS.

Bass F & M Wks, Hanna s of Wabash R R.

*RANGES.

Carter Wm & Son, 29 Clinton. (*See bottom edge and p 113.*)
Hattersley A & Sons, 48 E Main. (*See embossed line front cover.*)

REAL ESTATE.

Abbott W T, 1 and 2 Foster Blk.
Albers & Wagner, 5 and 6 Foellinger Blk.
Boerger G W, 215 E Wayne.
Craw E L, 24 and 25 Bass Blk.
Curdes L F, 3–4 Pixley & Long Bldg. (*See p 115.*)
Curtice J F, Rooms 1, 2, 3 and 4 Tri-State Bldg. (*See front cover and p 89.*)
Doolittle Willis, 34 W Main.
Douglass W V, 3 Schmitz Blk.
Edgerton C W, 57 W Main.
Eme & Son, 1 and 2 Foster Blk.

51

REAL ESTATE—Continued.

Everett & Doud, Old National Bank Bldg.
Eversole O P, 12 W Wayne. *(See right side lines.)*
Fisher D C, 32 E Berry.
Forbing John, 28 Bank Blk.
Ft Wayne Land and Improvement Co, 12 Pixley & Long Bldg.
Freistoffer Simon, 5 and 6 Bank Blk.
Glutting, Bauer & Hartnett, 55 Clinton
Graham J E, 26 Bank Blk.
Haiber Frederick, 64 Wells.
Hanna J Thomas, 8 Bank Blk.
Hayden F J, 68 Barr.
Hayden J W, 31 W Berry.
Hofer Theobald, 38 Bank Blk.
Jones G W, 9-11 W Main.
Komp Daniel, 38 Bank Blk.
Kretsinger & Angevine, 10 Vordemark Blk.
Kuhne & Co, 19 Court.
Lumbard S C, 3 Aveline House Blk.
Michael Herman, 19 Court.
Miller & Dougall, 4 Foster Blk.
Miner Bros, 26 Court.
Mohr & Sosenheimer, 19 W Wayne.
Motz Geo & Co, 47 W Main. *(See insurance agents.)*
Neireiter & Gumpper, 76 Calhoun.
Nestel Daniel, 243 W Creighton av.
Niswonger R C & Co, 33 Calhoun.
Pfeiffer C F, 6 Bass Blk.
Poirson P F, 12 Bank Blk.
Potter P L, 28 Bank Blk.
McNally J J & Co, 33 Bass Blk, (*See p* 446.)
Rayhouse G I Z, 9 Foster Blk.
Romy & Bobilya, 22 Bank Blk.
Scarlet Chester, 27 Bank Blk.
Schrader & Wilson, 7 Court.
Schroeder & Sons, 97 Broadway.
Thorward Theo, 37 W Berry.
Torrenee G K, 5 upstairs Arcade.
Wagner J T, 45 N Calhoun.
Williams H M, 36 E Berry.

RECTAL SPECIALISTS.

Smith C S, 53 Pixley & Long Bldg.
Whery W P, 94 Calhoun.

RESTAURANTS.

Connolly J T, 83 Calhoun. (*See right side lines and front cover.*)
Cratsley F C, 99 Calhoun.
Double J W, 29 E Main.
Entemann Christian, 11 and 13 E Main.
Fox J V, 25 E Main.
Frederick Christine (Railroad Restaurant), 216 Calhoun. (*See p 95.*)
Gutermuth Benjamin, 29 W Columbia.
Harkenrider Joseph, 61 E Main.
Heine E F, 278 Calhoun.
Hellings J A, 59 E Berry.
Hinton J C, 270½ Calhoun.
Jackson & Giles, 92 Calhoun.
Kirkham Wm, 31 W Columbia.
Lake Shore Hotel, 2 Cass.
Nickel Plate Restaurant, Nickel Plate Pass Depot.
Owens & Welsh, 7 Harrison. (*See p 105.*)
Richards R F, 253 Calhoun.
Rosselot F P, 28 E Columbia.
Seabold G H, 22 W Main.
Seidel Wm & Bro, 111 E Main.
Wellington The, 83 Calhoun. (*See right side lines and front cover.*)
Wobrock Oscar, 14 W Berry.

*ROAD HOUSES.

Bercot F J, n w cor Spy Run av and Randolph.

ROAD MACHINE MNFRS.

Fleming Mnfg Co, 78 High. (*See left bottom lines.*)
Indiana Machine Works, e s Osage n of Main.

ROOFERS.

Fort Wayne Roofing and Paving Co, 152 W Main.
Gerding & Aumann Bros, 115 Wallace. (*See top edge and p 85.*)

ROOFERS—Continued.

Pfeiffer & Schlatter, 38 and 40 E Columbia.
  (*See left side lines.*)
Welch J H, 190 Calhoun.

*RUBBER GOODS.

Pfeiffer & Schlatter, 38–40 E Columbia. (*See
  left side lines.*)

RUBBER STAMP MAKERS.

Aldine Printing House, 63 E Berry. (*See
  p 89.*)

SADDLE AND HARNESS MAKERS.

Bair Allen, 134 Broadway.
Bayer Bros, 28 Clinton.
City Carriage Works, n w cor Main and
  Barr. (*See left top lines.*)
Corneille Mrs L J, 69 E Main.
Hilt Frederick, 18½ E Columbia.
Johns A L & Co, 51 and 53 E Columbia.
Klebe Henry, 36 Clinton.
Kuntz F B, 14 Pearl.
Kuntz G H, 11 Harrison.
Nussmann A E, 40 Maumee rd.
Schaper Wm, 20 N Harrison.
Serjeant J E, Calhoun n e cor Duck.
Traub Louis, 353 Calhoun.

SADDLERY HARDWARE.

Bell J W, 13 E Columbia.
Johns A L & Co, 49 and 53 E Columbia.

SAFE DEPOSIT VAULTS.

White National Bank, n w cor Clinton and
  Wayne. (*See left top lines and p 95.*)

SAFE MOVING.

Brown W A, 73 and 75 Holman. (*See p 91.*)
City Trucking Co, 19 and 21 W Washington.

SAFES.

Motz George & Co, 47 W Main.

Pfeiffer & Schlatter, 38 and 40 E Columbia.
(*See left side lines.*)
Stapleford H T, 47 E Columbia.

SAFETY VALVE MNFRS.

Kunkle E B & Co. 87 Barr.

SALOONS.

Ankenbruck F M, 267 E Wayne.
Ankenbruck & Potthoff, 126 E Washington.
Auth, J H, 138 Calhoun.
Baker F L, 34 E Calumbia.
Baker T J, 31 Clinton.
Banet L E, 72 E Columbia.
Bauss Conrad, 91 John.
Beekes Jacob, 221 Lafayette.
Beckmann G, 101 Force.
Belchin Frank, 54 E Main.
Belger & Lennon, 140 Calhoun.
Benedict, Jacob, 36 W Main.
Bercot F J, s w cor Spy Run av and Randolph.
Beverforden Rudolph, 288 Calhoun.
Bicknese F C, 86 Barr.
Biederman Gottfried, 150 Barr.
Blombach Hugo, s e cor E Creighton av and Gay.
Bolman A F, 36 Fairfield av.
Bothner J G, 136 Calhoun.
Brown G H, 60½ Calhoun.
Bruggemann Henry, 272 Hanaa.
Certia Peter, 70 Calhoun.
Chavane Joseph, 231 E Jefferson.
Christen John, 100 Calhoun.
Clark Thomas, 102 E Columbia.
Condon, 264 Calhoun.
Conway F O, 67 E Main.
Creigh P F, 12 Chicago.
Cummerow R M, 276 Calhoun.
Cummings Owen, 268 Calhoun.
Danehy James, 8 Hoagland av.
DeTurk & Schnitker, 72 E Main.
Didier F X, 71 E Columbia.
Doehrmann Wm, 54 and 56 Barr.
Douglas J H, 284 Calhonn.
Dratt J A, 51 E Main.

SALOONS—Continued.

Drew Stephen, 319 W Main.
Entemann Christian, 11 and 13 E Main.
Fehling F H, 354 Broadway.
Feipel Frank, 122 Madison.
Figel J C, 54 Wells.
Fitzgerald James, 55 E Main.
Frank Mendel, 43 Hough.
Gardner B L, 379 Lafayette.
Geary Edward, 192 Griffith.
Gebhart John, e s Broadway 1 s of Toll Gate.
Geiger & Evans, 294 Calhoun.
Geistdoerfer Bros, Hicksville rd n w cor Malcomb av.
Geller Gottlieb, 53 W Main.
George Russell & Son, 49 E Main.
Gerow T D, 108 Fairfield av.
Getz J F, 3 E Main.
Gilbert H N, 226 Calhoun.
Goetze Herman, 31 Clinton.
Goodfellow Bros, 274 Calhoun.
Graf Philip, 335 Lafayette.   (*See right side lines.*)
Greer John, 178 Calhoun.
Gruber, C J, 101 Broadway.
Hahn Wm, 148 W Main.
Hake Mrs Christena, 26 and 28 Wells.
Hammerle Xavier, 297 W Main.
Hansen Peter, 162 Holman.
Hartman J H, 273 Hanna.
Hartman & Ankenbruck, 274 E Washington.
Hartman & Bro, 63 N Wayne.
Hatch W E, 1 N Calhoun.
Hautch G A, 375 W Main.
Heilbroner Louis, 34 E Columbia.
Helmkamp J C, 16 Harrison.
Henze Wm, 20 Clinton.
Himbert J M, 53 Wells.
Hoch Wm, 313 Lafayette.
Hollenbeck W F A, 144 Calhoun.
Home Billiard Hall, 20 W Berry.
Hosler J W, 11 W Columbia.
Hubbard A L, 9 N Calhoun.
Huber Charles, 46 E Columbia.
Huntsman W W, 80 Barr.
Hunzinker J, 25 Force.
Hutzell Daniel, 378 W Main.

Huxöll August, 92 Barr.
Jackson A B, 92 Calhoun.
Jauch A J, 582 E Washington.
Jordan Bros. 19 Harrison.
Jourdain C J. 98 Maumee rd.
Keever Edwin, 44 E Columbia.
Keinz Philip, 307 Lafayette.
Kelley John B, 26 E Columbia.
Kennedy Phillip, 341 W Main.
Klerner George S, 166 E Washington.
Kline C W, 242 Calhoun.
Koenig F H, 52 W Main.
Korn August, 194 Broadway.
Krohn C C, s w cor E Washington and Glasgow av.
Krohn Wm, 30 W Main.
Kuntz Samuel, 548 Calhoun.
Langard John, 70 E Columbia.
Langohr C W, 144 Broadway.
Lassus J B, 2 Cass.
Latham H S, 6 E Columbia.
Laurent A C, 62 E Columbia.
Lazzarini Amadeo, 37 Barr.
Lill Martin. 150 Calhoun.
Limecooly L F, 562 Calhoun.
Martin A A, 74 E Columbia.
Mayer J G, 6 Force.   (*See p* 91.)
Mettler Peter. 91 Harmer.
Meyer F H. 8 Calhoun.
Meyers A H, s e cor St Joseph boulevard and Baker av.
Meyers L H, 223 Calhoun.
Meyers Wm H, 207 Lafayette.
Miller Wm. w s Spy Run av nr bridge.
Miller & Meyer, 104 Calhoun.
Muehlfeith Charles, 10 W Main.
Mulharen Thomas, 117 Fairfield av.
Neukamm George, 121 and 123 Calhoun.
   (*See right bottom lines.*)
Neumeier Adam, 381 E Lewis.
Nolan John, 330 Lafayette.
Notestine J H, 15 and 17 Harrison.
Oberwitte Gustave, 64 E Main.
O'Donnell J F, 11 N Harrison.
Oetting Frederick, 127 Eliza.
Oetting F D, 214 Fairfield av.
Oetting & Co, 125 Broadway.

SALOONS—Continued.

Ortlieb G J, 31 Calhoun.
Pauley E J, 204 Calhoun.
Popp C A, 88½ Barr.
Post B L, 308 W Main.
Puff Bros, 340 Hanna.
Randall The, Harrison head of Columbia.
Ranke Henry, 37 Calhoun.
Richter E J B, 227 Lafayette.
Riedmiller Charles, 20 Harrison.
Riegel & Bougher, 12 Calhoun.
Riethmiller August, 139 Taylor.
Riethmiller Wm J, 186 Fairfield av.
Roeger Charles, 26 W Main.
Rose C H, 77 E Wayne.
Rosenthal Moses, 240 Lafayette.
Rosselot Frederick P, 28 E Columbia.
Ryan & Gebert, 60 E Columbia.
Sanders Robert, 70 Barr.
Schele Frank, 14 Harrison.
Schele J H, 26 Harrison.
Scherzinger Gerson, 16 and 18 W Main. (*See* *p* 85.)
Schiemer Frank, 41 Harrison.
Schmid Frederick, s s of Bluffton rd 1 w of Bridge.
Schmidt Charles, 130 Chicago.
Schmidt F J, Bluffton rd 1 w of river. (*See p* 91.)
Schmidt Henry, 179 Calhoun.
Schmidt Philip, 168 W Main.
Sieling D F, s w cor Pioneer av and C.
Simonton G W, 163 Wells.
Snyder B W, 189 Lafayette.
Sommers & Langohr, 118 Wells.
Spiegel G E, 183 Broadway.
Steinacker G W, 105 Maumee rd.
Stier Wm, 135 Wallace.
Strodel Emma, e s Broadway 2 n of Toll Gate.
Stoehr John, 122 E Washington.
Stotz Ulrich, 21 E Main.
Streicher Wm, 50 W Main.
Studer H L, 232 W Main.
Summers James, 262 Calhoun.
Thieme J A, 170 Broadway.
Voors J G, 83 Maumee rd.
Ward & Flynn, 292 Calhoun.

Weber Bernard, 281 and 283 Calhoun.
Weisbecker George, 7 E Main.
Wiebke H A, 33 Calhoun.
Wilkinson Frank, 116 Wells.
Wilkinson John, 24 E Wayne.
Witte C J, 27 E Main.
Young L Hiram, 36 E Columbia.
Zern John, 344 Hanna.
Zoeller & Merz, 368 Calhoun.
Zollinger August, 562 E Washington.

SALT.

Tresselt C & Sons, cor Clinton and N Y, C & St L R R.

SAND AND GRAVEL.

Schmidt F J, Bluffton rd 1 w of river. (*See p* 91.)

SANITARIUMS.

Mineral Magnetic Well Sanitarium, w s Home av 3 s of Pennsylvania av.
Dodge & Keller, cor Washington Boulevard and Broadway. (*See right side lines and p 93.*)

* SANITARY PLUMBERS.

Franke H C & Son, 68 Barr. (*See p* 111.)
Hattersley A & Sons, 48 E Main. (*See embossed line front cover.*)
Martin Emmett, cor Hanna and Buchanan.
O'Brien & Rolf, 122 Broadway.
Ogden Robert, 26 E Berry. (*See embossed line back cover.*)

SASH, DOORS AND BLINDS.

(*See also Planing Mills.*)

Diether Louis & Bro, Office and Yard bet City Mills and Gas Wks on E Superior. (*See right side lines.*)
Fort Wayne Lumber Co, 391 Broadway.
Pfeiffer & Schlatter, 38 40 E Columbia. (*See left side lines.*)
Rhinesmith & Simonson, s w cor Lafayette and Wabash R R

SAW MILL SUPPLIES.

Fort Wayne Variable Saw Mill Feed Co, 17 E Superior.

*SAW MILLS.

(*See also Lumber Mnfrs.*)

Baker Kilian, cor Superior and Lafayette.

Hoffman Bros, 200 W Main. (*See right bottom lines.*)

Tagtmeyer David, n w cor Webster and Greeley (*See left top lines and classified Lumber.*)

SAW REPAIRERS.

Bowman Charles, 37 Pearl. (*See right side lines and below.*)

Wilson George, 177 Calhoun.

*SAW WORKS.

Bowman Charles, 37 Pearl.

*SAWS--CIRCULAR, MILL AND CROSS-CUT.

Pfeiffer & Schlatter, 38 and 40 E Columbia. (*See left side lines.*)

*SCENIC ARTISTS.

Kirchefer H A, 12 Arcade Bldg. (*See p 93.*)

*SCHOOL FURNITURE.

Siemon & Bro, 50 Calhoun.   (*See back cover.*)

SCHOOL SUPPLIES.

Siemon & Bro, 50 Calhoun.   (*See back cover.*)
Spiegel J E jr, 103 Broadway.

SCHOOLS OF MUSIC.

European School of Music. 16 Rockhill.

SCHOOLS AND COLLEGES.

(*See Colleges, Schools, Etc.*)

SECOND HAND GOODS.

Goldstine Himan, 246 Calhoun.
Goldstine & Pearlman, 82 Barr.
Hagan Thomas. 64 E Columbia.
Klinger J E, 67 E Columbia.
Soliday & Barrow, 71 E Main.
Spitler Levi, 355 Calhoun.
Stapleford L P, 39 E Main.

SEEDS.

Alderman Dayton, 4 Harrison.
Bash S & Co, 22 and 24 W Columbia.

SEWER CONTRACTORS.

Moellering Wm & Son, 53–59 Murray.
  (*See back bone and p 83.*)

SEWER PIPE.

Builders' Lime Association, 257 Calhoun.
  (*See right bottom lines.*)
Martin Emmett, cor Hanna and Buchanan.
Moellering Wm & Son, 53–59 Murray.   (*See
  back bone and p 83.*)
Oetting W H, 382 E Lewis.
Western Lime Co, 3 N Harrison.

SEWER BUILDERS.

Kanney John, 5 Bass Blk.   (*See p 79.*)

SEWER TRAPS.

Menefee C M, 135 and 137 Oliver. (*See p 460.*)
Moellering Wm & Son, 53-59 Murray. (*See back bone and p 83.*)

SEWING MACHIHES.

Green W H. 76 Lafayette.
McQuillan F H, 19 W Wayne.
Pfeiffer & Schlatter, 38 and 40 E Columbia. (*See left side lines.*)
Sharp L P, 12 E Berry.
Singer Mnfg Co, 12 W Wayne.

*SHEET IRON WORKERS.

Gerding & Aumann Bros, 115 Wallace. (*See top edge and p 85.*)

*SHINGLES.

Diether Louis & Bro, Office and Yard bet City Mills and Gas Wks, on E Superior. (*See right side lines.*)

SHIRT MNFRS.

Comparet C M, 219 Madison.
Foster S M, n end Lafayette.
Kuttner P G, 144 Calhoun (*See left side lines.*)

SHOEMAKERS.

(*See Boot and Shoemakers.*)

SIDEWALKS.

Johnson J H, 68 E Columbia. (*See p 99.*)

SIGN WRITERS.

Buckeys W T, 16 W Columbia.
Brimmer J H, 33 W Main.

SINKS AND SLOP POTS.

Menefee C M, 135 and 137 Oliver. (*See p 460.*)

SLATE ROOFERS.
(See Roofers.)

SOAP MANUFACTURERS.
Summit City Soap Works, 2–16 Glasgow av.

SODA WATER MNFRS.
(See Bottling Works.)

SPICE MILLS.
Globe Spice Mills, 73–79 E Columbia.

SPORTING GOODS.
Trautman John, 58 E Main. *(See p 87.)*
Miller C H, 20 W Main.

STAIR BUILDERS.
(See Carpenters, Contractors and Builders.)

STAMPS.
Indiana Stamp Co, 37 W Berry.

STAVE MNFRS.
Ranke & Yergens, s e cor Superior and Griffith.

STEAM DYE WORKS.
City Steam Dye House, F F Robacker Mngr. 11 W Jefferson. *(See p 101.)*
Robacker S J, 45 E Main.
Schubert Gust, 65 E Main. *(See p 111.)*

STEAM HEATING APPARATUS.
Abdon George, 30 Clinton.
Hattersley A & Sons, 48 E Main. *(See embossed line front cover.)*
Hines J S, 379 W Main. *(See right top lines.)*
O'Brien & Rolf, 122 Broadway.
Ogden Robert, 26 E Berry. *(See embossed line back cover.)*

STEAM HEATING APPARATUS—Continued.

Spice Robert, 48 W Main and 11 Pearl. (*See right bottom lines.*)

STEAMSHIP AGENTS.

Blitz M J, 82 Calhoun.
Kuhne & Co, 19 Court.
Siemon & Bro, 50 Calhoun. (*See back cover.*)

STEAMSHIP LINES.

Allan State Line, Siemon & Bro, Agents, 50 Calhoun.
American Line, Siemon & Bro, Agents, 50 Calhoun.
Anchor Line, (New York and Glasgow) Siemon & Bro, Agents, 50 Calhoun.
Anchor Line, (New York, Gibraltar and Naples) Siemon & Bro, Agents, 50 Calhoun.
Hamburg-American Packet Co, Siemon & Bro, Agents, 50 Calhoun.
International Navigation Co, Siemon & Bro, Agents, 50 Calhoun.
Netherlands Line (N. A. S. M.), Siemon & Bro, Agents, 50 Calhoun.
New York, Gibraltar & Mediterranean Line, Siemon & Bro, Agents, 50 Calhoun.
North German Lloyd, Siemon & Bro, Agents, 50 Calhoun.
Red Star Line, Siemon & Bro, Agents, 50 Calhoun
White Star Line, Siemon & Bro, Agents, 50 Calhoun.

* STENCIL CUTTERS.

Stenger Peter, 30 N Ewing. (*See left side lines.*)

*STEPLADDER MNFRS.

Bowser S F & Co, cor E Creighton av and Thomas. (*See p 4.*)

STEREOTYPERS.

Fort Wayne Newspaper Union, 76–80 Clinton.

O. P. TINKHAM,   2I, 22, 23, 24 ARCADE BLOCK,
DENTIST.   West Berry Street, Fort Wayne, Ind
   Office Telephone   Residence Telephone

FORT WAYNE DIRECTORY.   811

STOCK POWDERS.

Gallmeyer C W, 53 E Main.

STONE ABUTMENTS AND PIERS.

Kanney John, 5 Bass Blk. (*See p* 79.)

*STONE CONTRACTORS—CUT.

Fort Wayne Steam Stone Works,
84–98 Pearl, (*See right bottom lines.*)
Geake Wm, 76–82 Pearl. (*See left bottom lines and p* 81.)
Jaap George, n s L S & M S R R tracks, w of Wells. (*See p* 359.)
Johnson J H (Artificial), 68 E Columbia. (*See p* 99.)
Keller & Braun, 84–98 Pearl. (*See right bottom lines.*)
Miller Fred, 8 Summit. (*See adv p* 108.)

STONE DEALERS.

Builders' Lime Association, 257 Calhoun. (*See right bottom lines.*)

STONE QUARRIES.

Moellering Wm & Son, 53–59 Murray. (*See back bone and p* 83.)

STONE YARDS.

Fort Wayne Steam Stone Works,
84–98 Pearl. (*See right bottom lines.*)
Geake Wm, 76–82 Pearl. (*See left bottom lines and p* 81.)
Jaap George, n s L S & M S R R tracks w of Wells. (*See p* 359.)
Keller & Braun, 84–98 Pearl. (*See right bottom lines.*)
Moellering Wm & Son, 53–59 Murray. (*See back bone and p* 83.)

STORAGE.

City Trucking Co, 19 W Washington.
Fay M W Warehouse Co, 135 Calhoun.

812   R. L. POLK & CO.'S

STORAGE—Continued.

Ryan Trucking Co, 19 and 23 Wells. (*See right top lines and p 95.*)

STORM APRONS.

Horstman L F, 9 E Superior. (*See p 99.*)

STOVES AND TINWARE.
(See also Hardware.)

Ash H J, 16 E Columbia.
Baals & Co, 57 E Main.
Gerding & Aumann Bros, 115 Wallace.
  (*See top edge and p 85.*)
Pickard Bros, 12 and 14 E Columbia.
Staub A H, 15 E Columbia.
Wilson G H & Sons, 31 E Columbia.

Grindle Alfred, ^{34} Bass Blk.
Riedel J M E, 23, 24 and 25 Schmitz Blk. (*See front cover.*)

SURGICAL APPLIANCES.

Dreier & Bro, 10 Calhoun.
Meyer Bros & Co, 14 Calhoun.
Mordhurst H W, 74 Calhoun.

SURVEYORS.
(See Civil Engineers and Surveyors.)

STREET RAILROAD SNOW PLOWS.
Snow Plows

Fleming Mnfg Co, 78 High. (*See left bottom lines.*)

TAILORS.
(See also Merchant Tailors.)

Blondoit Wm H, 47 E Lewis.
Butz Frederick, s e cor Calhoun and Marshall.

Cleary Will C, 118 Harrison.
Foster Andrew, 15 W Wayne. (*See left top lines.*)
Fowles John W, 64 Barr. (*See left side lines..*)
Goldberg Jacob, 232 Calhoun.
Hardung Frederick, 35 E Main, cor Clinton. (*See right top lines.*)
Hellings J A, 59 E Berry.
Hitzemann G H, 133 Broadway.
Horstmann F H, 360½ Calhoun.
Kayser Frederick, 42 Harrison,
Kleemeier Dietrich, 197 Calhoun.
Kruse Charles, 39 Harrison.
Langhals & Goehren, 13 Maumee rd.
Lillich M J, 409 Lafayette.
Lotz J H, 416 E Washington.
Lueth A, 13 Harrison.
Martin & Fitzsimmons, 170 W Jefferson. (*See p 107.*)
Meier L H, 99 Wilt.
Meyer Henry, 12 E Berry. (*See classified merchant tailors.*)
Metzler Leo, 324 Lafayette.
Oelschlaeger Frederick, 66 Baker.
Oestermeier Charles, 48 E Leith.
Schmalz Charles, 56 Masterson.
Schmidt Gottfried, 70 E Main.
Schoch A F, 41½ W Main.
Walda Frederick, 150 E Creighton av.

TAILORS' SHEARS.

Schulder Max, 52 Barr.

TALLOW RENDERERS.

Falls D M, e end Dwenger av 1 m e of city limits.

TANNERS AND CURRIERS.

Hutchinson O G, 294 W Main.

TEAS AND COFFEES.

Pacific Tea Co, 102 Calhoun,
White J B, 95 and 97 Calhoun.
Wilt F P & Co, 33 E Columbia.

TELEGRAPH COMPANIES.

Fort Wayne District Telegraph Co, 15 W Columbia.
Fort Wayne Postal Telegraph Co, 15 W Columbia.
Postal Telegraph Co, 15 W Columbia.
Western Union Telegraph Co, 2 New Aveline House Blk.

TELEPHONE COMPANIES.

Central Union Telephone Co, Tri-State Bldg.

THEATERS, HALLS, ETC.

Fort Wayne Saengerbund Hall, 51 and 53 W Main.
Masonic Temple Theater, n e cor Wayne and Clinton.
Princess Roller Skating Rink, W Main s e cor Fulton.

TICKET BROKERS.

Blitz M J, 82 Calhoun.
Levington Samuel, 85 Calhoun.

TILE.

Oetting W H, 382 E Lewis.

* TILE FLOORS.

Carter Wm & Son, 29 Clinton. (*See bottom edge and p* 113.)
Griebel & Pask, 74 and 76 W Main.

TILE MNFRS—MANTEL.

Carter & Son 29 Clinton. (*See bottom edge and page* 113.)

TIN, COPPER AND SHEET IRON WORKERS.

Algier Mnfg Co, 252 E Lewis.
Ash H J, 16 E Columbia.
Gerding & Aumann Bros, 115 Wallace. (*See top edge and p* 85.)
Heit G H, 378 Calhoun.
Ostermann & Co, e s Harmer 1 n of E Washington.
Pickard Bros, 12 and 14 E Columbia.
Seavey Hardware Co, 19 and 21 E Main.
South Side Hardware Co, 364 Calhoun.

TINNERS' STOCK.

Ash H J, 16 E Columbia.

TINSMITHS.

Gunkel & Son, 38 Nirdlinger av.
Kress Theodore, 12 Huffman.
Ostermann & Co, e s Hanna 1 n of E Washington.

TOBACCO AND CIGARS.

(See Cigars and Tobacco.)

TOOL MNFRS.

Bowser S F & Co, cor E Creighton av and
  Thomas. *(See p 4.)*
**Fort Wayne Pneumatic Novelty &
  Model Works,** 139 John. *(See p 471.)*
Stein C F A, 57 Winter. *(See p 630.)*
Stenger Peter, 30 N Ewing. *(See left top lines.)*

TOOLS.

Pfeiffer & Schlatter, 38 and 40 E Columbia.
  (See left side lines.)

TOYS.

(See Notions.)

TRANSFER AND BAGGAGE LINES.

Brown W H, 73 and 75 Holman. *(See p 91.)*
City Trucking Co, 19 and 23 W Washington.
Fort Wayne Omnibus, Baggage and Carriage Line, 14-24
  E Wayne.

TRANSPORTATION COMPANIES.

Empire Line (fast freight), 26 Court.
**Merchants Despatch Transporta-
  tion Co,** 3 Schmitz Blk.
Star Union Line (fast freight), 3 and 4 Trentman Bldg.

TRESS HOOP MNFRS.

Bitler S D, 421 E Wayne.

TRUCK MNFRS.

Zollinger L C & Bro, 13-15 E Superior.
(See left bottom lines and p 89.)

TRUCKMEN.

Brown W H, 73 Holman. *(See p 91.)*

TRUSSES.

New York and London Electric Assn, 101 E Wayne. *(See classified Deformity Apparatus.)*

TUCK POINTERS.

Cruse C A, 76 E Pontiac.

TYPE WRITING MACHINES.

Edgerton Dixon, 37 Bank Blk.
Remington Type Writer, 12 W Wayne.
Robbins H E, 32 Bass Blk.

UMBRELLAS AND PARASOLS.

Long H M, 97½ Calhoun.
Novitzky Barnet, 213 Calhoun.

UNDERTAKERS.

Kerlin & Bloom, 101 Calhoun.
Peltier J C, 17 W Wayne.
Schone & Veith, 53 E Berry. *(See p 113.)*
Wellman Henry, 39 W Berry.

UPHOLSTERERS.

(See also Furniture.)

Kruekemerfer Henry, 52 Barr.
Reineke F J, 41 E Main. *(See p 115.)*
Roberts Charles, 101 Walton av.

*.VENEERS.

Hoffman Bros, 200 W Main. (*See right bottom lines.*)

VETERINARY SURGEONS.

Dodge Arthur, 19 and 21 W Washington.
Gaskill Kyle, 5 Harrison.
Langtry Walter, 7 N Harrison.
Myers W F, 62 E Wayne and 114 Webster.
Nestel Daniel, S Broadway n w cor Huestis av.
Read H A, 62 Harrison.

WAGONMAKERS.

(*See Carriage and Wagon Makers.*)

WAGON MANUFACTURERS.

Ehrmann Charles, 149 W Main. (*See left side lines.*)
Olds' Wagon Works, s s Murray bet Calhoun and Lafayette.
Zollinger L C & Bro, 13 and 17 E Superior. (*See left top lines and p 89*).

* WAGON STOCK.

Baker Kilian, cor Superior and Lafayette.
Ferguson Palmer Co. 1 and 2 Pixley & Long Bldg.

WAGONS.

Pfeiffer & Schlatter, 38 and 40 E Columbia. (*See left side lines.*)

WALL PAPER.

Brimmer J H, 33 W Main.
Haller Gottlieb, 362 Calhoun.
Heine & Israel, 123 Broadway.
Hull L O, 90 Calhoun. (*See back cover.*)
Hull S W, 27 Clinton.
Keil & Keil. 116 Calhoun.
Kreibaum Frederick, 90 Barr.
Siemon Rudolph, 195 Calhoun.
Siemon & Bro, 50 Calhoun. (*See back cover.*)

WAREHOUSEMEN.

Fay M W Warehouse Co, 135 Calhoun.
Ryan Trucking Co, 19-23 Wells. (*See right top lines and p 95.*)

WASHING MACHINE MNFRS.

Anthong Wayne Mnfg Co. The, s w cor Lafayette and Wabash R R.
Horton Mnfg Co, w s Osage n of Boone.
Rocker Washer Co, 5 White Bank Bldg.

WATCHES, CLOCKS AND JEWELRY.

Achenbach Harry, 34 E Berry.
Bruder August, 93 Calhoun.
Garman J W, 205 Calhoun.
Græffe H C, s e cor Calhoun and Columbia.
Green & Probasco, 3 Arcade.
Greenewald D D, 132½ Broadway.
Koegel J C, 173 Broadway.
Krull R L, 128 E Washington.
Nicole J H, s s New Haven av 6 e of Summer.
Rambo B W, 19 W Wayne.
Samuels J M, 270 Calhoun.
Sauser Louis, 188 Calhoun.
Trenkley & Scherzinger, 78 Calhoun.
Uebelhoer R W, 68 E Main.
Voirol F J, 244 Calhoun.
Wilkening Louis, 81 Calhoun.

*WATER WORKS SUPPLIES.

Ogden Robert, 26 E Berry. (*See embossed line back cover.*)

*WELL DRILLERS.

Spice Robert, 48 W Main and 11 Pearl. (*See right bottom lines.*)
Weibel Frederick, 18 Harrison.

WELL AND CISTERN SUPPLIES.

Weibel Frederick, 18 Harrison.

WHEEL MNFRS.
Standard Wheel Co, s e cor Lafayette and Wabash R R.

WHITE SAND.
Moellering Wm & Son, 53–59 Murray. (*See back bone and p 83.*)

WIND MILLS.
Spice Robert, 48 W Main. (*See right bottom lines.*)
Weibel Fred, 18 Harrison.

*WINDOW SHADES.
Heine & Israel, 123 Broadway.
Hull L O, 90 Calhoun. (*See back cover.*)
Siemon & Bro, 50 Calhoun. (*See back cover.*)

WINES AND LIQUORS—DEALER.
Freese August, 57 E Main. (*See left top lines.*)

WINES AND LIQUORS—WHOLESALE.
Falk & Lamley, 17 E Columbia.
Nathan Julius & Co, 137 Calhoun.
Wile Isaac & Co, 8 Calhoun.

WOOD DEALERS.
(*See also Coal and Wood.*)

WOOD PULLEY MANUFACTURERS.
Old Fort Manufacturing Co, 9 Bass Blk.

WOOL.
Bash S & Co, 22 and 24 W Columbia.
Weil Bros & Co, 94 E Columbia.

YEAST MNFRS.
Glaser Frank, 195 Hanna.
Fleischmann & Co, 37 W Berry.

DIRECTORY
BORROWERS

WE RECEIVE many complaints from our patrons to the effect that they are bothered so much by **BOR-ROWERS**. These parties are not the private citizen nor the stranger in the city, who steps in, looks at the Directory and goes out, but merchants, business and professional men, who need a directory every day in the year, yet who are too close-fisted to buy one.

These same individuals are the ones that borrow your Directory "just for a minute," which, in the majority of cases, means a day or perhaps a week, unless you remember that they have it and send for it.

These same borrowers will tell the Directory canvassers that he has "no use for a Directory," that he "knows everybody," and vice versa, "everybody knows him."

R. L. POLK & CO.'S

Allen County Directory.

1895-6.

Following each name are given: First, number of section upon which person resides; second, name of township; third, postoffice address.

A

Aaron Henry, 21, Pleasant, Sheldon.
Abbott, Barney, 11, Adams, New Haven.
Abbott Herman, 11, Adams, New Haven.
Able A, 22, Aboit, Fort Wayne.
Able George W, 14, Aboit, Fort Wayne.
Abney Milford, 34, Springfield, Harlan.
Acres John, 20, Lafayette, Roanoke.
AdairAlexander, 31, Madison, Hoagland.
Adair George, 19, Madison, Hoagland.
Adair John, 29, Madison, Hoagland.
Adair Philip, 1, Madison, Monroeville.
Adair Samuel, 25, Madison, Hoagland.
Adair Sloan, 31, Madison, Hoagland.
Adams Abraham, 17, Jefferson, New Haven.
Adams Charles, 28, Aboit, Aboit.
Adams Gabriel, 13, Madison, Monroeville.
Adams Isaiah, 18, Jefferson, New Haven.
Adams James, 28, Aboit, Aboit.
Adams John, 28, Aboit, Aboit.
Adams J H, Springfield, Harlan.
Adams J L, 18, Jefferson, New Haven.

Adams Seth, 18, Jefferson, New Haven.
Adams Wm, 28, Aboit, Aboit.
Adams Wm, 34, Adams, Soest.
Adams Wm C, 34, Adams, Soest.
Ahrens F, 26, Adams, Fort Wayne.
Ainsworth Wm, 34, Monroe, Monroeville.
Aix Wm, Jackson, Monroeville.
Ake Gideon, 19, Marion, Poe.
Ake Marion, 11, Pleasant, Fort Wayne.
Ake Samuel, 12, Pleasant, Fort Wayne.
Aken Charles, 3, Wayne, Fort Wayne.
Akey James, 35, Adams, Maples.
Akins James, Lafayette, Zanesville.
Albaugh Oliver, 30, Monroe, Monroeville.
Aldrick Fred, Jefferson, Maples.
Alleger J D, 18, Monroe, Monroeville.
Allen Alfred, 5-6, Scipio, Hicksville, O.
Allen Arthur, 5-6, Scipio, Hicksville, O.
Allen Ervin, 8, Washington, Wallen.
Allgier Daniel, 16, Adams, Fort Wayne.
Allgier Edward, 16, Adams, Fort Wayne.
Allschewede Christian, 25, Adams, Maples.
Altekruse Ernest A, 29, Washington, Fort Wayne.
Altekruse Frederick, 25, Lake, Arcola.
Altekruse Frederick, 29, Washington, Fort Wayne.
Ambler Christian, 33, Aboit, Fort Wayne.
Ambler John, 28, Pleasant, Sheldon.
Ambler Samuel, 28, Pleasant, Sheldon.
Ambrose Patrick, 20, Lake, Arcola.
Ambrose Wm, 20, Lake, Arcola.
Ames Frank, 33, Lake, Arcola.
Ames Fred, 33, Lake, Arcola.
Ames James, 33, Lake, Arcola.
Ames John, 33, Lake, Arcola.
Amstutz Eli, 4, Cedar Creek, Leo.
Amstutz Jacob, 6, Springfield, Harlan.
Amstutz John, 4, Cedar Creek, Leo.
Amstutz John jr, 4, Cedar Creek, Leo.
Amstutz Joseph, 30, Springfield, Harlan.
Amstutz J, 8, Cedar Creek, Collingwood.

Amstutz Peter S, 19, Springfield, Harlan.
Amy Louis, 5, Aboit, Dunfee.
Anderson Andrew, Jackson, Edgerton.
Anderson Augustus, Jackson, Edgerton.
Anderson A H, 18, Monroe, Monroeville.
Anderson Beeson, 35, Lake, Arcola.
Anderson Charles, Jackson, Edgerton.
Anderson Daniel, 35, Lake, Arcola.
Anderson James, 4, Monroe, Monroeville.
Anderson John, 36, Eel River, Wallen.
Anderson John, Jackson, Dawkins.
Anderson John, 4, Monroe, Monroeville.
Anderson Oliver, 15, Lake, Arcola.
Anderson Stephen, 34, Eel River, Wallen.
Anderson Wm, 35, Eel River, Heller's Corners.
Anderson Wm, 29-30, Eel River, Wallen.
Anderson Wm, 33, Lake, Arcola.
Anderson Wm, 3, Washington, Wallen.
Andoffer Jacob, 25, Pleasant, Poe.
Andoffer James, 25, Pleasant, Poe.
Andoffer Paul, 25, Pleasant, Poe.
Andrews Al, 36, Springfield, Harlan.
Andrews Ernest, 20, Monroe, Monroeville.
Andrews James, 11, Adams, Fort Wayne.
Andrews L, 26, Springfield, Harlan.
Andrews M F, 7, Perry, Huntertown.
Andrews Sidney D, 7, Perry, Huntertown.
Andrews S C, Jefferson, Maples.
Andrews Wm, 18-19, Milan, Thurman.
Angeo D, 35, Madison, Binger.
Ankenbrook Martin, 18, Adams, Fort Wayne.
Ankrim Richard, 15, Milan, Harlan.
Anspach Daniel, Jackson, Edgerton.
Anspach George W, 2-3, Jackson, Edgerton.
Anspach Hosea M, 1-2, Jackson, Edgerton.
Anspach L D, Jackson, Edgerton.
Anstriff R, 12, Adams, New Haven.
Antler David, 24, Lafayette, Zanesville.
Antler John W, 24, Lafayette, Zanesville.
Antrup Edward, 16, St Joseph, Fort Wayne.

Antrup Henry, 16, St Joseph, Fort Wayne.
Applegate D, 18, Cedar Creek, Collingwood.
Applegate John, 10, Maumee, Antwerp, O.
    Archer Andrew, 11, Washington, Fort Wayne.
Archer Henry, 3, Washington, Wallen.
Archer John, 33, Lake, Arcola.
Archer John, 11, Washington, Fort Wayne.
Archer John D, 29, Lake, Arcola.
Archer Oliver, 11, Washington, Fort Wayne.
Archibald A B, 10, Marion, Soest.
Archibald Frank, 36, Pleasant, Sheldon.
Argo M E, 12, Madison, Monroeville.
Armbruster Charles, Maumee, Woodburn.
Armbruster Charles G, Maumee, Woodburn.
Armbruster George, 3, Maumee, Antwerp, O.
Armbruster Samuel, 20, Maumee, Woodburn.
Armel Casper, 5, Washington, Wallen.
Armel Wm, 21, Washington, Fort Wayne.
Armstrong James, Perry, Collingwood.
Armstrong Jasper, Perry, Collingwood.
Armstrong Wm, Perry, Collingwood.
Arney Scott, 14, St Joseph, Fort Wayne.
Arnold Amos, 28, Maumee, Woodburn.
Arnold Charles, 1, Lake, Heller's Corners.
Arnold Eli, 11, Cedar Creek, Leo.
Arnold Frederick, 27, Madison, Hoagland.
Arnold George, 28, Cedar Creek, Cedarville.
Arnold Henry, 27-28, Eel River, Heller's Corners.
Arnold John J, 28, Cedar Creek, Cedarville.
Arnold Wm, 1, Lake, Heller's Corners.
Arter Joseph, Jefferson, Maples.
Asa John, 18, Adams, Fort Wayne.
Ash John, Perry, Cedarville.
Ash Wm, Perry, Cedarville.
Ashland Ambrose, 5, Maumee, Harlan.
Ashland James, 5, Maumee, Harlan.
Ashley George, 17, St Joseph, Fort Wayne.
Ashley T H, 16, St Joseph, Fort Wayne.
Askran J D, 4, Washington, Wallen.
Astbough Daniel, 25, Lafayette, Nine Mile.

Astry Isaac, 19, Springfield, Harlan.
Astry James, 17, Springfield, Harlan.
Atkins A, 16, Aboit, Fort Wayne.
Atwood Wm, 1, Milan, Harlan.
Auer August, 22, Jackson, Edgerton.
Auer Nicholas, 22, Jackson, Edgerton.
Aufelt Henry, 29, Marion, Poe.
Aulls Silas, 33, Pleasant, Sheldon.
Auman Elias, 7, St Joseph, Fort Wayne.
Aurand Daniel, 31, Jackson, Monroeville.
Austman Andrew, 8, Washington, Fort Wayne.
Auth Joseph, 5, Marion, Fort Wayne.
Auth Joseph jr, 5, Marion, Fort Wayne.
Author F, 6, Aboit, Dunfee.
Axt A, 18, Adams, Fort Wayne.
Ayres James, 30, Wayne, Fort Wayne.

B

Baade Frederick, 22, St Joseph, Fort Wayne.
Baals John, 9, Aboit, Fort Wayne.
Baals John, 16, Wayne, Fort Wayne.
Baals Samuel, 9, Aboit, Fort Wayne.
Babbitt Robert, 33, Lake, Arcola.
Bach Charles S, 2, Washington, St. Vincent.
Bacon Albert, 28, Jefferson, Maples.
Bacon Charles, 27, Jackson, Baldwin.
Bacon Charles, 32, Milan, Gar Creek.
Bacon Samuel, 28, Jefferson, Maples.
Badiac Charles, 3, Washington, Wallen.
Badiac James, 3, Washington, Wallen.
Bailey Fred, 1, Wayne, Fort Wayne.
Bailey Frederick, 6, Washington, Fort Wayne.
Bailey J C, Cedar Creek, Hursh.
Bailey Louis, 6, Washington, Fort Wayne.
Bailey Nelson, 26, Lafayette, Zanesville.
Baily Wm, Perry, Cedarville.
Bair Christian, 6, Cedar Creek, Spencerville.
Bair Simon, 6, Cedar Creek, Spencerville.

816 R. L. POLK & CO.'S

Baird David, 36, Eel River, Wallen.
Baird Ellsworth, 36, Eel River, Wallen.
Baird Robert, 36, Eel River, Wallen.
Baird Wm, 36, Eel River, Wallen.
Baker Adam, 32, Monroe, Monroeville.
Baker Albert, 20, Wayne, Fort Wayne.
Baker Alexander, 9, Maumee, Woodburn.
Baker Alexander jr, 9, Maumee, Woodburn.
Baker Cain, Maumee, Woodburn.
Baker Cain jr, Maumee, Woodburn.
Baker C, 13, Wayne, Fort Wayne.
Baker David, 26, Lafayette, Zanesville.
Baker Elam, 26, Lafayette, Zanesville.
Baker Francis, Lafayette, Zanesville.
Baker Frank, 1, Adams, New Haven.
Baker Frank, 33, St Joseph, Fort Wayne.
Baker George, 29, Monroe, Monroeville.
Baker George, 20, Wayne, Fort Wayne.
Baker Isaac, 32, St Joseph, Fort Wayne.
Baker Jacob, 25, Milan, Gar Creek.
Baker James, 29, Monroe, Monroeville.
Baker John, 35, Lafayette, Zanesville.
Baker Killian, 29, Aboit, Aboit.
Baker Killian & Son, Lafayette, Aboit.
Baker Samuel, 26, Lafayette, Zanesville.
Baker Simon S, 10, Monroe, Monroeville.
Baker Sylvanus F, 27, Monroe, Monroeville.
Baker Warner, 27, Monroe, Monroeville.
Baker Wm, 13, Wayne, Fort Wayne.
Baldwin Abel, 31, St Joseph, Fort Wayne.
Baldwin Alva J, 35, Jackson, Baldwin.
Baldwin Joseph, 27, Jackson, Baldwin.
Baldwin Joseph jr, 27, Jackson, Baldwin.
Baldwin Timothy, Jackson, Baldwin.
Ball Edward, 5, Monroe, Monroeville.
Ball John, 31, Aboit, Aboit.
Ball Patrick, 5, Monroe, Monroeville.
Ball Samuel L, 5, Monroe, Monroeville.
Ballou Edward, 33, Perry, Fort Wayne.
Ballou John, 33, Perry, Fort Wayne.

Ballou J E, Perry, Huntertown.
Ballou Paul, 33, Perry, Fort Wayne.
Ballmeyer J, 19, Madison, Hoagland.
Balls Enos, 4, Madison, Maples.
Balman James, 16, Lafayette, Myhart.
Balsinger Alfred, 20, Springfield, Harlan.
Baltemeyer Frederick, 34, Marion, Poe.
Baltemeyer L, 36, Marion, Williams Station.
Baltz Benjamin, 1-2, Eel River, Huntertown.
Baltz John, 1-2, Eel River, Huntertown.
Bamnert Charles, Jackson, Edgerton.
Bandalier Frederick, 9, Jefferson, New Haven.
Bandalier Henry L, 9, Jefferson, New Haven.
Bandalier Paul, 17, Jefferson, New Haven.
Bandalier Samuel, 12, Adams, New Haven.
Bandalier S, Jackson, Edgerton.
Banger Frederick, 11, Adams, New Haven.
Barunder James, 12, Adams, New Haven.
Baunet Joseph, 5, St Joseph, Fort Wayne.
Barclay Jeremiah, 36, Madison, Monroeville.
Barclay John, 29, Monroe, Monroeville.
Bardeman W, 33, Pleasant, Sheldon.
Bardy F, Jackson, Dawkins.
Barfield Frank, 35, Jefferson, Monroeville.
Barfield Jeremiah, 35, Jefferson, Monroeville.
Barkley Joseph, 33, Monroe, Monroeville.
Barnes J W, 20, Maumee, Woodburn.
Barnett Jacob, 33, Lafayette, Zanesville.
Barney Henry, 18, Springfield, Harlan.
Barnhard Charles, 11, Adams, New Haven.
Barnhard John, 12, Adams, New Haven.
Barnhart C W, 7, Monroe, Monroeville.
Barnhart M, 4, Adams, New Haven.
Barnhart Wm, 21, Eel River, Heller's Corners.
Barr John, 6, Cedar Creek, Spencerville.
Barrand Frank, 16, Washington, Fort Wayne.
Barrand Herbert, 16, Washington, Fort Wayne.
Barrand Joseph, 16, Washington, Fort Wayne.
Barrand Julian, 28, Lake, Arcola.
Barrett George, 2, Perry, Collingwood.

UNITED STATES MEDICAL AND SURGICAL REGISTER. Third Edition. ISSUED APRIL, 1898. Contains the Names of over 100,000 Physicians. R. L. POLK & CO., Publishers.

Barrett George W, 3, Perry, Collingwood.
Barrett James, 19, Cedar Creek, Cedarville.
Barron Amos, 6, Monroe, Monroeville.
Bartel Ham, 19, Madison, Hoagland.
Bartels Henry, 7, St Joseph, Fort Wayne.
Barthold Alex H, 5, Wayne, Fort Wayne.
Barthold Edward, 5, Wayne, Fort Wayne.
Barthold Harry, 5, Wayne, Fort Wayne.
Bartholomew Jack, 24, Springfield, Halls Corners.
Bartholomew John, 24, Springfield, Halls Corners.
Barto Amiel, 22, Jefferson, Maples.
Barto Louis, 22, Jefferson, Maples.
Barto T, 22, Jefferson, Maples.
Barton Daniel, Jefferson, Maples.
Barton R, Jackson, Edgerton.
Barva Benjamin, 19, St Joseph, Fort Wayne.
Barva Joseph, 10, Cedar Creek, Leo.
Bash Charles S, Aboit, Fort Wayne.
Bash John, Jackson, Baldwin.
Bashalier Henry, 11, Washington, Wallen.
Bashalier Louis, 11, Washington, Fort Wayne.
Basson Isaac, 11, Adams, New Haven.
Bates Alfred H, 5, Aboit, Dunfee.
Bates C, 12, Adams, New Haven.
Bates Edward, 15, St Joseph, Fort Wayne.
Bates Gary, 10, Cedar Creek, Leo.
Bates Max, 15, St Joseph, Fort Wayne.
Bathurst John, 31, Springfield, Harlan.
Bathurst Lawrence, 20, Springfield, Harlan.
Bathurst Severance, 24, Springfield, Halls Corners.
Baughman John, 33, St Joseph, Fort Wayne.
Baum Herman, 12, Adams, New Haven.
Baumgardner Samuel, 13, Aboit, Fort Wayne.
Bauserman Eugene P, 12, Milan, Harlan.
Bauserman E D, 4, Monroe, Monroeville.
Bauserman F, 4, Adams, New Haven.
Bauserman George, 4, Madison, Maples.
Bauserman Wm, 3, Madison, Maples.
Baxter D D, 32, Monroe, Monroeville.
Baxter James, 24, Lake, Arcola.

Baxter Wm, 25, Lake, Arcola.
Bayard Charles, 27, Lake, Arcola.
Bayless Frank, 14, Adams, New Haven.
Beam Finley, 24, Pleasant, Poe.
Beam John, Scipio, Hicksville, O.
Beam Milo, Scipio, Hicksville, O.
Bear George, 19-20, Eel River, Heller's Corners.
Bear Isaiah, 21, Aboit, Fort Wayne.
Bear Levi, 29-30, Eel River, Churubusco.
Bearbaum Frederick, 29, Washington, Fort Wayne.
Bearbaum Henry, 29, Washington, Fort Wayne.
Beard Milo, 31, Wayne, Fort Wayne.
Beard W, 31, Wayne, Fort Wayne.
Beatty Clark, 32, Pleasant, Sheldon.
Beaushot Louis, 6, Monroe, Monroeville.
Becker Wm, 24, Adams, New Haven.
Beckett Milton, 29-30, Eel River, Heller's Corners.
Beckman Edward, 12, Washington, Fort Wayne.
Beckman Frank, 15, Marion, Hoagland.
Beckman Fred, 1, Marion, Soest.
Beckman Henry, 25, Milan, Gar Creek.
Beckman Henry, 12, Washington, Fort Wayne.
Beskstein Henry, 29, St Joseph, Goeglien.
Beckstein John jr, 29, St Joseph, Goeglien.
Beeber Wm, 12, Aboit, Fort Wayne.
Beech Henry, Springfield, Harlan.
Beerbower Albert, 29, Scipio, Antwerp, O.
Beerbower Peter, 29, Scipio, Antwerp, O.
Beerman Charles, 36, Adams, Maples.
Behrman Louis, 25, Adams, Maples.
Behring Conrad, 20, St Joseph, Fort Wayne.
Behring Henry, 6, Madison, Maples.
Behring Henry, 20, St Joseph, Fort Wayne.
Beiber Alfred, 34, Milan, Gar Creek.
Beiber Eli, 34, Milan, Gar Creek.
Beiber John, 34, Milan, Gar Creek.
Bell Adam, Jackson, Baldwin.
Bell Charles, 12, Adams, New Haven.
Bell Eben, 23, Jefferson, Zulu.
Bell Evan, 16, Lafayette, Zanesville.

Bell Ham, 29, Monroe, Monroeville.
Bell Harvey, 12, Adams, New Haven.
Bell John, Jackson, Dawkins.
Bell Robert, 23, Jefferson, Zulu.
Bell Wm, 32, Lafayette, Zanesville.
Belot F, 1, Wayne, Fort Wayne.
Belot Jacob C, 1, Wayne, Fort Wayne.
Belot Jacquis F, 14, Perry, Leo.
Bellamy, Lorenzo D, 28, Washington, Fort Wayne.
Bellamy M E, 33, Lake, Arcola.
Benchot August, 34, Jefferson, Monroeville.
Benckman F, 32, Milan, Gar Creek.
Bender Wm, 7, Cedar Creek, Collingwood.
Benjamin Abraham, 16, Monroe, Monroeville.
Benjamin C, Jackson, Edgerton.
Benke C V, Jackson, Edgerton.
Bennett J, Jackson, Monroeville.
Bennett Newton F, 22, Eel River, Heller's Corners.
Benninghoff Benjamin, 18, Springfield, Harlan.
Bensinger Frederick, 11, Marion, Soest.
Bensinger Frederick jr, 11, Marion, Soest.
Bensinger John, 11, Marion, Soest.
Benton Frank, 5, Wayne, Fort Wayne.
Benton George F, 8, Washington, Fort Wayne.
Benton Thomas, 3, Wayne, Fort Wayne.
Benward C. P, 26, Eel River, Wallen.
Benz Adam, 19, Washington, Fort Wayne.
Bercot Claude, 15, Lake, Arcola.
Bercot Francois, 24, Wayne, Fort Wayne.
Bercot Frank, 21, Lake, Arcola.
Bercot Henry, 5, St Joseph, Fort Wayne.
Bercot Jacques, 15, Lake, Arcola.
Bercot Louis, 24, Wayne, Fort Wayne.
Bercot Louis jr, 24, Wayne, Fort Wayne.
Berg Adolph, 26, St Joseph, Goeglien.
Berg Elias, 15, Marion, Hoagland.
Berg John, 15, Marion, Hoagland.
Berg Michael, 26, St Joseph, Goeglien.
Berg Philip, 16, Marion, Fort Wayne.
Berger Frederick, 34, Madison, Binger.

Berger L, 34, Madison, Binger.
Bergman George, 8, Madison, Maples.
Berkeley Jacob, 26, Marion, Hoagland.
Berkhart John, 25, St Joseph, Goeglien.
Bernardine Jacob, 15, St Joseph, Fort Wayne.
Berneke Ernest, 31, Washington, Fort Wayne.
Berning C W, 36, Marion, Williams Station.
Berning John, 32, Madison, Binger.
Berry Eli, 10, Springfield, Harlan.
Berry Henry, 10, Springfield, Harlan.
Berry Wm, Jackson, Baldwin.
Bervase Jacob, 9, Cedar Creek, Leo.
Bethel Walter, 33, Pleasant, Sheldon.
Betz Frank, 16, Springfield, Harlan.
Betz George, 13, Springfield, Harlan.
Betz Joel, 16, Springfield, Harlan.
Betz John, 16, Springfield, Harlan.
Betz Samuel W, 11, Springfield, Spencerville.
Beugnot John, 4, Adams, New Haven.
Beuret August, 9, Jefferson, New Haven.
Bice Adam D, 6, Scipio, Hicksville, O.
Bice David, 6, Scipio, Hicksville, O.
Bickel John, 1, Adams, New Haven.
Biddell Henry, 34, Lafayette, Zanesville.
Biddler Adam, 4, Jefferson, Gar Creek.
Biddler Joseph, 4, Jefferson, Gar Creek.
Bidlack Martin, 31, Scipio, Harlan.
Bieber Allen, 1, Jefferson, Gar Creek.
Bieber Michael, Perry, Collingwood.
Bieber Nathaniel, Perry, Collingwood.
Bilderback James, 12, Adams, New Haven.
Bilderback, J W, 12, Adams, New Haven.
Biners Warren, Jackson, Baldwin.
Binkley Abraham, 13, Lake, Fort Wayne.
Binkley Levi, 13, Lake, Fort Wayne.
Birchard G, 23, Aboit, Fort Wayne.
Birchard J, 23, Aboit, Fort Wayne.
Bird Lewis, 27, Pleasant, Sheldon.
Bird Oak, 2, Aboit, Fort Wayne.
Bireline Charles, 11, Lake, Arcola.

Bireline George, 11, Lake, Arcola.
Bishop Henry, 31, Milan, New Haven.
Bishop Henry, 29, St Joseph, Goeglien.
Bishop Richard, 31, Milan, New Haven.
Bishop Wm, 18, Pleasant, Nine Mile.
Bixler Samuel, 3, Jefferson, Gar Creek.
Black George, 11, Aboit, Fort Wayne.
Black John T, 26, St Joseph, Goeglien.
Black Joseph, 18-19, Milan, Thurman.
Black L, 18-19, Milan, Thurman.
Black Wm, 26, St Joseph, Goeglien.
Blackburn Byron, 17, Jefferson, New Haven.
Blackburn John, 17, Jefferson, New Haven.
Blackburn Leroy, 19, Scipio, Fansler.
Blackburn Samuel, 17, Jefferson, New Haven.
Blackburn Sumner, 20, Scipio, Fansler.
Blakley Alvin, 1, Cedar Creek, Hursh.
Blakley Jasper, 1, Cedar Creek, Hursh.
Blakley Truman, 1, Cedar Creek, Hursh.
Blanken Wm, 12, Adam, New Haven.
Blase Charles, 29, Washington, Fort Wayne.
Blase James, 34, Lafayette, Zanesville.
Blase John, 34, Lafayette, Zanesville.
Blase Watt, 35, Lafayette, Zanesville.
Blaser F G, 16, St Joseph, Fort Wayne.
Blazing August, 12, Adams, New Haven.
Blazing Henry, 11, Adams, New Haven.
Blee James, 29, Aboit, Aboit.
Blee John, 30, Aboit, Saturn.
Bleke Charles, 6, Marion, Fort Wayne.
Bleke Charles, 31, Perry, Huntertown.
Bleke Charles, 24, Washington, Fort Wayne.
Bleke Edward, 6, Marion, Fort Wayne.
Bleke Frederick, 7, St Joseph, Fort Wayne.
Bleke Frederick, 24, Washington, Fort Wayne.
Bleke Wm, Perry, Huntertown.
Bleke Wm, 25, Washington, Fort Wayne.
Bleitcher John, 23, Lake, Arcola.
Blenn Josiah S, 26, Jackson, Baldwin.
Blessing Charles, 18, Washington, Fort Wayne.

Blessing Edward, 15, St Joseph, Fort Wayne.
Blessing Frederick, 24, Lake, Arcola.
Blessing George L, 20, Lake, Arcola.
Blessing Henry, 17, Washington, Fort Wayne.
Blessing John, 15, St Joseph, Fort Wayne.
Blessing Peter, 24, Lake, Arcola.
Blessing Wm, 24, Lake, Arcola.
Bley Abraham, 5, Pleasant, Nine Mile.
Block G, 14, Pleasant, Fort Wayne.
Bloid Rev, Lafayette, Zanesville.
Bloom Andrew, 3, St Joseph, Fort Wayne.
Bloom Martin jr, 3, St Joseph, Fort Wayne.
Bloom Martin, 9, St Joseph, Fort Wayne.
Bloser Alfred, 26, Lafayette, Zanesville.
Blue George, 28, Cedar Creek, Cedarville.
Blumm August, 32, Cedar Creek, Cedarville.
Blumm August, 20, St Joseph, Fort Wayne.
Blumm Frederick, 20, St Joseph, Fort Wayne.
Blumm Henry, Jackson, Dawkins.
Blumm Henry, 29, St. Joseph, Goeglien.
Bobay Frank, 14, St Joseph, Fort Wayne.
Bobay Gustav, 5, St Joseph, Fort Wayne.
Bobay James, 14, St Joseph, Fort Wayne.
Bobay John, 14, St Joseph, Fort Wayne.
Bobay Philip, 5, St Joseph, Fort Wayne.
Bobay Victor, 14, St Joseph, Fort Wayne.
Bobay Victor jr, 5, St Joseph, Fort Wayne.
Bobilya Eugene, 26, Madison, Hoagland.
Bode Henry, 21, St Joseph, Fort Wayne.
Bode Henry jr, 21, St Joseph, Fort Wayne.
Bodeker Wm, 25, Milan, Gar Creek.
Boehnke Frederick, 35, Madison, Binger.
Boese Edward, 14, Springfield, Harlan.
Boeuf August, 33, Lake, Arcola.
Boeuf Henry, 21, Lake, Arcola.
Boeuf Octave, 27, 200, $5005, Lake, Arcola.
Boger Albert, 9, Springfield, Spencerville.
Boger Andrew, 15, Springfield, Harlan.
Boger Charles, 9, Springfield, Spencerville.
Boger Chris, 25, Springfield, Halls Corners.

Boger Daniel D, 15, Springfield, Harlan.
Boger Franklin, 3, Springfield, Harlan.
Boger John, 8, Springfield, Harlan.
Boger Joseph, 8, Springfield, Harlan.
Boger Samuel, 14, Springfield, Harlan.
Boger Solomon, 5, Perry, Huntertown.
Boggs Hubert, 29-30, Eel River, Heller's Corners.
Boggs John, 29-30, Eel River, Heller's Corners.
Bohde Frederick, 15, St Joseph, Fort Wayne.
Bohlmann August, 22, St Joseph, Fort Wayne.
Bohlmann Henry, 22, St Joseph, Fort Wayne.
Bohlmann Martin, 2, St Joseph, Fort Wayne.
Bohrer Charles jr, 11, Aboit, Fort Wayne.
Boise Charles, 12, Adams, New Haven.
Boisnet Charles, 24, Jefferson, Zulu.
Boiteaux Frank, 3, Jefferson, Gar Creek.
Boitet Francis, 5, St Joseph, Fort Wawne.
Boitet James, 5, St Joseph, Fort Wayne.
Boitet Lester, 5, St Joseph, Fort Wayne.
Boitet Peter, 5, St Joseph, Fort Wayne.
Boland George, 13, Aboit, Fort Wayne.
Boley J, 9, Cedar Creek, Leo.
Bolinger Isaac, Jackson, Dawkins.
Bolinger Jacob, Lafayette, Aboit.
Bolinger John, 18, Pleasant, Nine Mile.
Bolinger Wash, 7, Pleasant, Nine Mile.
Bolt David, 33, Perry, Fort Wayne.
Bolterman F, 13, St Joseph, Thurman.
Bolton Henry, 5, Springfield, Harlan.
Bolton, James, 7, Scipio, Hicksville, O.
Bolton Oscar, Springfield, Harlan.
Bolyard Andrew, 2, Madison, Monroeville.
Bolyard Henry, 28, Jefferson, Maples.
Bolyard John, 28, Jefferson, Maples.
Bolyard J, Jackson, Baldwin.
Bolyard Leo, 15, Madison, Monroeville.
Bolyard Paul, 13, Milan, Harlan.
Bolyard Steven, 28, Jefferson, Maples.
Bonjour Louis, Jackson, Dawkins.
Bonnell John, 33, Lake, Arcola.

W. H. DAVIS, BANK BLOCK, 30 & 32 East Main St. BLANK BOOKS, BOOK BINDING, PRINTING, Etc.

ALLEN COUNTY DIRECTORY. 825

Bonner Benjamin, 30, Scipio, Fansler.
Book Frederick, 33, Marion, Poe.
Boone George, 31, Wayne, Fort Wayne.
Boone John, 32, Wayne, Fort Wayne.
Boone Wm, 33, Wayne, Fort Wayne.
Borden Reuben, 17, Scipio, Hicksville, O.
Bordey H, 9, Aboit, Fort Wayne.
Boschet H, 35, Pleasant, Sheldon.
Boschet Michael, 12, Lake, Arcola.
Boschet Michael jr, 12, Lake, Arcola.
Bosselman Henry, 23, Milan, Gar Creek.
Bossler A B, 2, Eel River, Ari.
Bossler A H, 3, Eel River, Ari.
Bossler Francis, 8, Pleasant, Nine Mile.
Bossler Frederick, 8, Pleasant, Nine Mile.
Bost Chris, 26, Wayne, Fort Wayne.
Boston Charles, 13, Springfield, Harlan.
Boston Dell, 7, Springfield, Harlan.
Boston Thomas, 20, Springfield, Harlan.
Boston Wm, 5, Milan, Chamberlain.
Boston Wm, 15, Springfield, Harlan.
Boston Wm, 2, Springfield, Spencerville.
Boswell John, 20, Maumee, Woodburn.
Bott John, 24, Wayne, Fort Wayne.
Botte James, 21, Jefferson, Maples.
Bottenberg David, 22, Monroe, Monroeville.
Bottenberg Jason, 22, Monroe, Monroeville.
Bottenberg Z J, 29, Monroe, Monroeville.
Botteron Frederick, 8, Milan, Chamberlain.
Botteron Henry, 8, Milan, Chamberlain.
Botteron Joseph, 8, Milan, Chamberlain.
Botteron Wm, 8, Milan, Chamberlain.
Boty Henry, 9, St Joseph, Fort Wayne.
Boty Paul, 16, St Joseph, Fort Wayne.
Bouvier George, Jackson, Monroeville.
Bouvier Peter, 33, Jackson, Monroeville.
Bowen Otto, 13, Perry, Leo.
Bower Charles, 21, Wayne, Fort Wayne.
Bower George, 21, Wayne, Fort Wayne.
Bowers Benjamin, 6, Jefferson, New Haven.

Chicago, Milwaukee & St. Paul Ry. The POPULAR LINE to the **West and Northwest.**

Bowers Daniel, 29, Lake, Arcola.
Bowers George, 28, Pleasant, Sheldon.
Bowers Henry, 15, Monroe, Monroeville.
Bowers H C, 28, Jefferson, Maples.
Bowers Jacob, 21, Monroe, Monroeville.
Bowers John, 29, Lake, Arcola.
Bowers John, 22, Monroe, Monroeville.
Bowers John, 28, Pleasant, Sheldon.
Bowers Michael, 5, Jefferson, New Haven.
Bowers Peter, 29, Lake, Arcola.
Bowers Peter jr, 29, Lake, Arcola.
Bowers Samuel, Jackson, Edgerton.
Bowers Wm, 8, Lafayette, Myhart.
Bowman Edward, 36, Lafayette, Zanesville.
Bowman Elga, 35, Lafayette, Zanesville.
Bowman George, 6, Lafayette, Aboit.
Bowman George, 7, Pleasant, Nine Mile.
Bowman George, 12, Springfield, Georgetown.
Bowman Len, 12, Springfield, Georgetown.
Bowman Lycurgis, 5, Eel River, Ari.
Bowman Philip, 35, Lafayette, Zanesville.
Bowman R M, 36, Lafayette, Zanesville.
Bowman Samuel, 36, Lafayette, Zanesville.
Bowman Sylvester, 9, Lafayette, Myhart.
Bowman Tony, 36, Lafayette, Zanesville.
Bowman Valentine, 35, Lafayette, Zanesville.
Bowman Wm, 12, Springfield, Georgetown.
Bowser Adam, 2, Madison, Monroeville.
Bowser Arthur, 7, Pleasant, Nine Mile.
Bowser Charles, 12, Washington, Fort Wayne.
Bowser Edward, 2, Washington, St Vincent.
Bowser Jack, 10, Washington, Wallen.
Bowser John, 14, Lafayette, Nine Mile.
Bowser Levi, 2, Washington, St Vincent.
Bowser Theodore, 25, Perry, Fort Wayne.
Bowser Wally, 14, Lafayette, Nine Mile.
Boyd Lee, 26, Lake, Arcola.
Boyle Edward, 8, Marion, Fort Wayne.
Brace Ellery, 6, Scipio, Hicksville, O.
Bradbury Shiard, 33, Wayne, Fort Wayne.

Bradtmiller Fred R, 21, Adams, Fort Wayne.
Bradtmiller Wm, 21, Adams, Fort Wayne.
Bradtmiller Wm jr, 21, Adams, Fort Wayne.
Braithwaite Wm, 28, Lake, Arcola.
Bramer John, 35, Milan, Gar Creek.
Brames Henry, 18, Adams, Fort Wayne.
Brames Martin, 6, Jefferson, New Haven.
Brames Wm, 18, Adams, Fort Wayne.
Brammer Henry, 12, St Joseph, Goeglien.
Brammer Wm, 12, St Joseph, Goeglien.
Brandebury George W, 7, Monroe, Monroeville.
Brandt Frederick, 30, Adams, Fort Wayne.
Branstrator Del, 28-33, Wayne, Fort Wayne.
Branstrator D, Lafayette, Nine Mile.
Branstrator George, 28, Lafayette, Zanesville.
Branstrator John, Lafayette, Zanesville.
Branstrator J, 24, Aboit, Fort Wayne.
Branstrator Wm, Lafayette, Nine Mile.
Breck Adolph, 22, Lake, Arcola.
Breneke August, 18, Maumee, Woodburn.
Brenton Elijah, 8, Jefferson, New Haven.
Brenton Richard, 8, Jefferson, New Haven.
Breont Em, 18, Jefferson, New Haven.
Brewer Conrad, 17, Madison, Hoagland.
Brewer George, 17, Madison, Hoagland.
Brewer George, 8, Madison, Maples.
Brewer Henry, 9, Madison, Maples.
Brick August, 8, Madison, Maples.
Brick Charles, 28, Adams, Soest.
Brick Christian, 28, Adams, Soest.
Brick, Henry, 36, Adams, Maples.
Brick Henry, 26, St Joseph, Boeglien.
Brick Jacob, 26, St Joseph, Goeglien.
Brick John, 28, Adams, Soest.
Brick John, 22, St Joseph, Fort Wayne.
Brick Martin, 26, St Joseph, Goeglien.
Brick Wm, 28, Milan, Thurman.
Bricker Cass, Jackson, Edgerton.
Bricker Michael E, Jackson, Edgerton.
Brickhart Ellsworth, 8, Springfield, Harlan.

2

Brickhart John, 3, Springfield, Harlan.
Briggs Jeremiah, 19, Madison, Hoagland.
Briggs Lewis, 19, Madison, Hoagland.
Brinckley D F, Jackson, Edgerton.
Brindle Daniel, 36, Lafayette, Zanesville.
Brindle Wm, 25, Lafayette, Nine Mile.
Brineshoff Albert, 10, Wayne, Fort Wayne.
Brinkhart Samuel, 2, Milan, Harlan.
Brockmeyer Henry, 32, Madison, Binger.
Brockmeyer Wm, 32, Madison, Binger.
Bronson Wm, 28, Scipio, Harlan.
Brookmeyer Henry, 11, Marion, Soest.
Brooks Albert, 8-17, Milan, Chamberlain.
Brooks Charles, 9, Milan, Chamberlain.
Brooks Delbert, 9, Milan, Chamberlain.
Brooks Edson A, 4, Milan, Chamberlain.
Brooks Thomas, 12, Adams, New Haven.
Brooks Thomas jr, 12, Adams, New Haven.
Brooks Willis, 9, Milan, Chamberlain.
Broom Charles, 1, Lake, Heller's Corners.
Broom Isaac, 31, Lake, Arcola.
Brosius H, 10, Aboit, Fort Wayne.
Brothers Charles, 35, Milan, Gar Creek.
Brothers Gideon, 35, Milan, Gar Creek.
Brothers John, 35, Milan, Gar Creek.
Brouse Wm, 29, Marion, Poe.
Brown Alexander, 35, Monroe, Monroeville.
Brown Alfred, 23, Madison, Monroeville.
Brown Amasa, 13, Lake, Fort Wayne.
Brown A C, 12, Adams, New Haven.
Brown A L, 12, Adams, New Haven.
Brown Charles, 12, Adams, New Haven.
Brown David, 21, Eel River, Heller's Corners.
Brown David, 30, Monroe. Monroeville.
Brown Drew, 35, Monroe. Monroeville.
Brown Edward, 24, Madison, Monroeville.
Brown George, 8, Springfield, Harlan.
Brown Henry, 29, Marion, Poe.
Brown Jacques. 33, Lake Arcola.
Brown James, 26, Madison. Hoagland.

Brown James A, 23, Madison, Monroeville.
Brown Jesse, 26, Madison, Hoagland.
Brown John, 35, Madison, Binger.
Brown John, 24, Madison, Monroeville.
Brown John H, 30, Monroe, Monroeville.
Brown Joseph, 26, Madison, Hoagland.
Brown Noah, Jackson, Monroeville.
Brown N P, 13, Madison, Monroeville.
Brown Orrin, 12, Adams, New Haven.
Brown Samuel, 26, Lafayette, Zanesville.
Brown Stanley, 29-30, Eel River, Heller's Corners.
Brown Stewart, 23, Madison, Monroeville.
Brown Wm, 27, Adams, Soest.
Brown Wm, 36, Madison, Monroeville.
Brown Wm, 5, Springfield, Harlan.
Brown Wm R, 30, Monroe, Monroeville.
Browning Conrad, 4, Lake, Arcola.
Browning Wm, 14, Adams, New Haven.
Bruick Adam, 6, Jefferson, New Haven.
Brudi Carl, 13, Adams, New Haven.
Brudi Frederick, 12, Adams, New Haven.
Brudi G G, 12, Adams, New Haven.
Brudi Henry, 11, Adams, New Haven.
Brudi Joseph, 12, Adams, New Haven.
Brundridge David, 28, Washington, Fort Wayne.
Brundridge Homer, 4, Springfield, Harlan.
Brundridge Isaac, 28, Washington, Fort Wayne.
Brundridge Robert, 28 Washington, Fort Wayne.
Brundridge Wesley, 28, Washington, Fort Wayne.
Brusbach Ephraim, 30, Cedar Creek, Cedarville.
Bryant Ira, 4, Jefferson, Gar Creek.
Brye Theo, 5, St Joseph, Fort Wayne.
Bubb Anthony, 21, Marion, Poe.
Bubb Edward, 29, Lafayette, Zanesville.
Buchanan Henry, 12, Adams, New Haven.
Buchfink George, 13, Lafayette, Nine Mile.
Buchfink John, 13, Lafayette, Nine Mile.
Buchfink John jr, 13, Lafayette, Nine Mile.
Buck Wm, 22, Madison, Hoagland.
Budenhoffer Louis, 10, Marion, Soest.

Bueker Ernest F, 22, Aboit, Fort Wayne.
Buettcher Ernest, 3, Wayne, Fort Wayne.
Buetters John B, 8, Adams, Fort Wayne.
Buetters J Herman, 8, Adams, Fort Wayne.
Buetters T H, 12, Adams, New Haven.
Bufferberger E, Jackson, Edgerton.
Bufferberger J, Jackson, Edgerton.
Bufferberger L, Jackson, Edgerton.
Buhler Jacob, 31, Adams, Fort Wayne, box 125.
Buhr Frederick E, 20, Milan, Thurman.
Buhr Henry, 16, St Joseph, Fort Wayne.
Bullerman Frederick, 32, St Joseph, Fort Wayne.
Bullerman Frederick jr, 32, St Joseph, Fort Wayne.
Bullerman George, 22, St Joseph, Fort Wayne.
Bump Cyrus, Lafayette, Nine Mile.
Bump Uzel, 29, Lafayette, Zanesville.
Bunch Fred, 34, Marion, Poe.
Bunch Herman, 33, Pleasant, Sheldon.
Bunn John, 33, St. Joseph, Fort Wayne.
Burgart Peter, 6, Monroe, Monroeville.
Burke Samuel, 16, Springfield, Harlan.
Burkely A, 18, Monroe, Monroeville.
Burker Fred, 23, Washington, Fort Wayne.
Burkholder David, 18-19, Milan, Thurman.
Burkholder Henry, 35, St Joseph, Goeglien.
Burnam A B, 9, Lafayette, Myhart.
Burman Fred, 31, Jefferson, Maples.
Burman Henry, 6, Wayne, Fort Wayne.
Burman Theo, 1, Marion, Soest.
Burns Patrick, 9, Monroe, Monroeville.
Burrier George, 19, Scipio, Fansler.
Burrier Isaac, 19, Scipio, Fansler.
Burrier Joseph, 13, Springfield, Harlan.
Burrier Philip, 31, Scipio, Harlan.
Burrier Wm, 19, Scipio, Fansler.
Burrier Wm, 13, Springfield, Harlan.
Burris Mack, 9, Monroe, Monroeville.
Burris Michael, 9, Monroe, Monroeville.
Burris Thomas, 9, Monroe, Monroeville.
Busche Ernest, Milan, Gar Creek.

Busche Ernest, 27, St Joseph, Goeglien.
Busche Henry, 27, St Joseph, Goeglien.
Busching Wm, 31, St Joseph, Fort Wayne.
Bush Amos L, 21, Lafayette, Myhart.
Bush Frank, 21, Lafayette, Myhart.
Bush George, 21, Lafayette, Myhart.
Bush Nathan, 17, Lafayette, Myhart.
Bush Robert, 21, Lafayette, Myhart.
Bush Wm, 15, Cedar Creek, Leo.
Bush Wm A, 21, Lafayette, Myhart.
Buskirk David, 24, Lafayette, Zanesville.
Buskirk George, 19, Pleasant, Nine Mile.
Buskirk John, 24, Lafayette, Zanesville.
Buskirk John, 26, Madison, Hoagland.
Busse Charles, 29, Milan, Gar Creek.
Busse Fred, 33, Milan, Gar Creek,
Busse Henry, 33, Milan, Gar Creek.
Butler David, 26, Lake, Arcola.
Butler George H, 25, Lake, Arcola.
Butler Henry, 12, Adams, New Haven.
Butler Ira, 6, Jefferson, New Haven.
Butler Jacob, 12, Adams, New Haven.
Butner E S, 30, Jefferson, Maples.
Butner John, 30, Jefferson, Maples.
Butt Anthony, 20, Marion, Poe.
Butt F, 23, Aboit, Fort Wayne.
Butt George, 15, Pleasant, Nine Mile.
Butt James F, 8, Maumee, Woodburn.
Butt Wm, 4, Lake, Heller's Corners.
Butts James, 20, Lake, Arcola.
Butty Frank, 15, Jefferson, Zulu.
Butty Frank jr, 15, Jefferson, Zulu.
Byall Howard, 20, Lake, Arcola.
Byers Andrew, 25, Perry, Cedarville.
Byers Emmet, 11, Milan, Harlan.
Byers Enos, 25, Perry, Cedarville.
Byers George, 5, Lafayette, Aboit.
Byers George, 13, Lake, Arcola.
Byers John, 22, Milan, Gar Creek.
Byers Samuel, 25, Perry, Cedarville.

Byers Wm, Milan, Gar Creek.
Byers Wm, 25, Perry, Cedarville.

C

Cahill John, Perry, Huntertown.
Calbatzer Aaron, 4, Washington, Wallen.
Calbatzer Emerson, 4, Washington, Wallen.
Calbatzer Frank, 4, Washington, Wallen.
Calbatzer Sherman, 4, Washington, Wallen.
Callahan Daniel, 12, Adams, New Haven.
Callahan John, 12, Adams, New Haven.
Callahan Michael, 12, Adams, New Haven.
Calvin Bowman, 6, Lafayette, Aboit.
Camp Barney, 1, Adams, New Haven.
Campbell Charles, 19, Perry, Huntertown.
Campbell George, 4, Washington, Wallen.
Campbell Isaac, 28, Eel River, Heller's Corners.
Campbell James, 8, Springfield, Harlan.
Campbell, John, 32, Cedar Creek, Cedarville.
Campbell John, 4, Washington, Wallen.
Campbell Wesley, 8, Springfield, Harlan.
Cane Delbert, Perry, Huntertown.
Cane Reuben, Perry, Huntertown.
Carder Lewis, 14, Lake, Fort Wayne.
Carder Valentine, 14, Lake, Fort Wayne.
Carey Wm, 18, Lake, Arcola.
Carey Wm jr, 18, Lake, Arcola.
Carier Preston, 34, Monroe, Monroeville.
Carl E, 29, Cedar Creek, Cedarville.
Carl Henry, 26, St Joseph, Goeglien.
Carl Thomas, 28, Perry, Fort Wayne.
Carles Horace W, 24, Pleasant, Poe.
Carles John, 24, Pleasant, Poe.
Carlton John, 1, St Joseph, Fort Wayne.
Carmelot C, 1, Wayne, Fort Wayne.
Carmon A G, 15, Lafayette, Myhart.
Carpenter Adam, 1, Madison, Monroeville.
Carpenter Andrew, 26, Lafayette, Zanesville.
Carpenter D, 3, Madison, Maples.

Carpenter Eric, 26, Lafayette, Zanesville.
Carpenter John, Jackson, Monroeville.
Carpenter John, 27, Lafayette, Zanesville.
Carpenter Joseph, 23, Lafayette, Zanesville.
Carpenter Samuel, 26, Lafayette, Zanesville.
Carpenter Smith, 23, Lafayette, Zanesville.
Carrington Andrew, 1, Springfield, Harlan.
Carrington E C, 28, Springfield, Harlan.
Carrington John, 15, Cedar Creek, Leo.
Carrington Seth, 28, Cedar Creek, Cedarville.
Cartaugh Albert, 28, Washington, Fort Wayne.
Carter Charles, 4, Washington, Wallen.
Carter E C, 11, Adams, New Haven.
Carter Wm, Jackson, Edgerton.
Cartwright A, 29, Marion, Poe.
Cartwright John, 8, Wayne, Fort Wayne.
Cartwright J, 31, Marion, Poe.
Cartwright Rollin, 31, Marion, Poe.
Cartwright Samuel, 4, Aboit, Arcola.
Cartwright Wm, 33, Lake, Arcola.
Caskell Cornelius, 8, Wayne, Fort Wayne.
Cass Wm, 9, Adams, Fort Wayne.
Cassel C, 12, Adams, New Haven.
Cassel George, 20, Monroe, Monroeville.
Cassel John, 20, Monroe, Monroeville.
Cassel Robert, 12, Adams, New Haven.
Cassenare David, 8, Wayne, Fort Wayne.
Cassidy Seaton, 32, Monroe, Monroeville.
Casteel H, 29, Pleasant, Sheldon.
Castello Michael, 1, St Joseph, Fort Wayne.
Castello Thomas, 1, St Joseph, Fort Wayne.
Castle James, 11, Adams, New Haven.
Castric L, 9, Aboit, Fort Wayne.
Cavalier Victorine, 33, Lake, Arcola.
Caxter John, 3, Maumee, Antwerp, O.
Certia Louis, 11, Adams, Fort Wayne.
Certia Peter, 11, Adams, New Haven.
Challot Israel, 9, Jefferson, New Haven.
Challot Philip, 9, Jefferson, New Haven.
Chandler John, 5, Springfield, Harlan.

Chaney John, 8, Lafayette, Aboit.
Chaney J R, Washington, St Vincent.
Chaney Otto, 34, Lafayette, Zanesville.
Chaney Wm, 33, Lafayette, Zanesville.
Chapman John, 34, Madison, Binger.
Chapman John, 20, Madison, Hoagland.
Chapman P, 12, Pleasant, Fort Wayne.
Chapman Solomon, 23, Perry, Huntertown.
Chapman Wm, 24, Madison, Monroeville.
Chapman Wm, Perry, Collingwood.
Chapman Wm, 13, Pleasant, Fort Wayne.
Charten Charles, 12, Adams, New Haven.
Chase Levi, 27-28, Eel River, Heller's Corners.
Chaussee Alfred, 36, Jefferson, Zulu.
Chaussee Amiel, 25, Jefferson, Zulu.
Chaussee Amiel jr, 25, Jefferson, Zulu.
Chaussee Charles, 30-31, Jackson, Monroeville.
Chaussee Edward, 24, St Joseph, Thurman.
Cheney George, 5, Springfield, Spencerville.
Cheney Philip, 5, Springfield, Spencerville.
Cheney Wallace, 5, Springfield, Spencerville.
Chevillot Auguste, Jackson, Monroeville.
Chester Charles, 18, Milan, Thurman.
Chotin George, 3, Wayne, Fort Wayne.
Christen Anthony, 14, Marion, Hoagland.
Christen Edward, 14, Marion, Hoagland.
Christian Henry, 34, Madison, Binger.
Christian Joseph, 9, Lake, Arcola.
Christian Oscar, 19, Perry, Huntertown.
Christman Jacques, 31, Lake, Arcola.
Christman John, 26, Pleasant, Sheldon.
Christman Louis, 27, Pleasant, Sheldon.
Christman Nicholas, 26, Pleasant, Sheldon.
Christman Peter, 34, Pleasant, Sheldon.
Christy George, 16, St Joseph, Fort Wayne.
Chriswell A O, 9, St Joseph, Fort Wayne.
Clapper Fred, 26, Washington, Fort Wayne.
Clapsattle Alfred, 27, Lake, Arcola.
Clapsattle G A, Wayne, Fort Wayne.
Clapsattle John, 27, Lake, Arcola.

Clark Enoch, 28, Aboit, Aboit.
Clark Henry, 5, Aboit, Dunfee.
Clark Howard, 26, Aboit, Fort Wayne.
Clark H, 33, Pleasant, Sheldon.
Clark James, 33, Lafayette, Zanesville.
Clark John, 14, Aboit, Fort Wayne.
Clark R, 11, Aboit, Fort Wayne.
Clark Wm, 10, Cedar Creek, Leo.
Clark Wm, 10, Maumee, Antwerp, O.
Clark Wm, 17, Wayne, Fort Wayne.
Clark Wm jr, 10, Maumee, Antwerp, O.
Classman Thomas, 34, Springfield, Harlan.
Clayton Enoch, 24, Madison, Monroeville.
Clayton John, 24, Madison, Monroeville.
Clayton Robert, 4, Eel River, Ari.
Clear Herman, 27, Washington, Fort Wayne.
Clem Adam, 27, Monroe, Monroeville.
Clem Daniel, 34, Monroe, Monroeville.
Clem George, 27, Monroe, Monroeville.
Clem Jacob, Jackson, Baldwin.
Clem Jerry, 34, Monroe, Monroeville.
Clem Noah, 33, Monroe, Monroeville.
Clem Samuel, 23, Monroe, Monroeville.
Clem Wm, 7, Monroe, Monroeville.
Clemens Frederick, 21, Wayne, Fort Wayne.
Clemens John, 21, Wayne, Fort Wayne.
Clevinger Daniel, 27, Monroe, Monroe.
Clevinger Simon, 27, Monroe, Monroeville.
Click Walter, 10, Aboit, Fort Wayne.
Clindrick Henry, 12, Washington, Fort Wayne.
Closson Leyrus, 7, Maumee, Woodburn.
Clugston S S, 9, Pleasant, Nine Mile.
Clutter Clover M, 17, Perry, Huntertown.
Clutter Wm M, Perry, Huntertown.
Coblentz Ephraim, 21, Aboit, Fort Wayne.
Coblentz F, 21, Aboit, Fort Wayne.
Coblentz Wm, 21, Aboit, Fort Wayne.
Cochoit Joseph, 20, Jefferson, New Haven.
Coleman A G, 23, Aboit, Fort Wayne.
Coleman Charles, 26, Aboit, Fort Wayne.

Coleman Ellis, 16, St Joseph, Fort Wayne.
Coleman George, 23, Aboit, Fort Wayne.
Coleman Isaiah, 16, St Joseph, Fort Wayne.
Coleman John, 23, Aboit, Fort Wayne.
Coleman Thomas, 24, Aboit, Fort Wayne.
Coleman Wm, 9, Aboit, Fort Wayne.
Collett Alfred, Jackson, Dawkins.
Collins C F G, 26, Aboit, Fort Wayne.
Collins George, 26, Aboit, Fort Wayne.
Collins Joseph, 24, Jefferson, Zulu.
Collins M, 26, Aboit, Fort Wayne.
Colter Jacques, 28, Lake, Arcola.
Colvin A, 1, Wayne, Fort Wayne.
Colvin Joseph, 1, Wayne, Fort Wayne.
Colvin W, 1, Wayne, Fort Wayne.
Comer Matthew, 35, Pleasant, Sheldon.
Comer Wm, 36, Pleasant, Sheldon.
Common John, Jefferson, Dawkins.
Como Jesse, 25, Jefferson, Zulu.
Compton Ira, 28, Lake, Arcola.
Compton R E, 21, Lake, Arcola.
Confer Benjamin, 31, Pleasant, Sheldon.
Conine Milo W, 4, Maumee, Harlan.
Conine Roscoe, 4, Maumee, Harlan.
Conklin Guy, 1, Wayne, Fort Wayne.
Connelly F M, Jefferson, Maples.
Connett Allen, 16, Wayne, Fort Wayne.
Connett David, 16, Wayne, Fort Wayne.
Connett Edward, 16, Wayne, Fort Wayne.
Connett Edward jr, 16, Wayne, Fort Wayne.
Connett George, 16, Wayne, Fort Wayne.
Connett John, 10, Wayne, Fort Wayne.
Connor Edward, 5, Monroe, Monroeville.
Connors Edward, 29, Lake, Arcola.
Connors Frank, 29, Lake, Arcola.
Conrad Peter, 9, Adams, Fort Wayne.
Conway David, 2, Milan, Harlan.
Conway Edward, 5, Maumee, Harlan.
Cook Anthony, 4, Adams, New Haven.
Cook Arthur P, 27, Lake, Arcola.

Cook Charles, 5, Washington, Wallen.
Cook C W, 12, Adams, New Haven.
Cook Eugene, 28, Cedar Creek, Cedarville.
Cook Frank, 28, Cedar Creek, Cedarville.
Cook Jacob, 4, St Joseph, Fort Wayne.
Cook Reuben, 15, Cedar Creek, Leo.
Cook Roman, 6, Cedar Creek, Spencerville.
Cook Samuel, 1, Jefferson, Gar Creek.
Cook Samuel, 10, Washington, Wallen.
Cook Theo, 4, Adams, New Haven.
Cook Wm, 10, Washington, Wallen.
Coolman George, 1, Wayne, Fort Wayne.
Coombs Henry, 16, St Joseph, Fort Wayne.
Coon Alvin, 7, Perry, Huntertown.
Copenhauer D, 1, Springfield, Harlan.
Copper Grant, 26, Aboit, Fort Wayne.
Corbat Alphone, 3, Aboit, Arcola.
Corbat Frank, 3, Aboit, Arcola.
Corbat Vandalier, 3, Aboit, Arcola.
Corbin David, 26, Eel River, Wallen.
Cordrey Francis, 1, Aboit, Fort Wayne.
Cordrey John, 1, Aboit, Fort Wayne.
Core Ephraim, 32, Lafayette, Zanesville.
Core E T, 33, Lafayette, Zanesville.
Core Henry, 20, Maumee, Woodburn.
Corelle Andrew S, 8, Wayne, Fort Wayne.
Corine Thomas, 13, Aboit, Fort Wayne.
Cork Arthur, 28, Lake, Arcola.
Corn Amos, 12, Adams, New Haven.
Corneille Frank, 22, Lake, Arcola.
Corneille Gustave, 3, Aboit, Arcola.
Corneille H, 25, Marion, Hoagland.
Corson Daniel, 27-32, Lake, Arcola.
Corson John, 15-16, Pleasant, Nine Mile.
Cortall N H, 24, Lafayette, Zanesville.
Cosgrove F K, 28, Springfield, Harlan.
Cotter Wm, 8, Lafayette, Myhart.
Cotton Othel, 29-30, Eel River, Heller's Corners.
Counsel George, 21, Washington, Fort Wayne.
Coupler Joseph, Jackson, Baldwin.

Cour August, 4, Washington, Wallen.
Courdevey Eugene, 13, Perry, Leo.
Courdevey Frank, 3, Wayne, Fort Wayne.
Courdevey Herman, 1, Wayne, Fort Wayne.
Courlardot Hippolite P, 12, Jefferson, Dawkins.
Courlardot Narcisse, 13, Jefferson, Dawkins.
Coverdale George W, 12, Lafayette, Nine Mile.
Cowell John, 22, Monroe, Monroeville.
Cox Frank, Perry, Huntertown.
Cox Thomas, 12, Washington, Fort Wayne.
Crabb George, Lafayette, Aboit.
Crabb John, Lafayette, Aboit.
Crabb Wm, 19, Lafayette, Myhart.
Crabill Benjamin, 8, Monroe, Monroeville.
Crabill David, 8, Monroe, Monroeville.
Crabill Harvey, 8, Monroe, Monroeville.
Crabill James, 33, Monroe, Monroeville.
Craig James, 15, Aboit, Fort Wayne.
Craig Thomas, 15, Aboit, Fort Wayne.
Craig Thomas, 31, St Joseph, Fort Wayne.
Cramer, see also Kramer.
Cramer Adam, 3, Washington, Wallen.
Cramer Alfred, 18, Jackson, Dawkins.
Cramer David, 8, Wayne, Fort Wayne.
Cramer H G, 28, Washington, Fort Wayne.
Cramer J E, 17, Washington, Fort Wayne.
Cramer Wm, 17, Washington, Fort Wayne.
Crank Fross, 32, St Joseph, Fort Wayne.
Crank John, 32, St Joseph, Fort Wayne.
Crates Levi, 31, Monroe, Monroeville.
Crates Perry, 31, Monroe, Monroeville.
Crawford Adam, Jefferson, Maples.
Crawford Allen, 21, Lake, Arcola.
Crawford Cary, Jefferson, Maples.
Crawford Frank, 29, Scipio, Antwerp, O.
Crawford George, 6, Aboit, Dunfee.
Crawford Wm, 20, Scipio, Fansler.
Creighton Arthur, 13, Lake, Fort Wayne.
Crickmore Henry, 28, Pleasant, Sheldon.
Crisswell W, 19, Marion, Poe.

Crouse, see also Krouse.
Crouse Frank, 18, Aboit, Dunfee.
Crouse Herman, 28, Pleasant, Sheldon.
Crouse Jesse, 18, Aboit, Dunfee.
Crouse Jesse, 19, Aboit, Saturn.
Crouse Wm, 21, Adams, Fort Wayne.
Crow Alexander, 31, Wayne, Fort Wayne.
Crow Calvin, 34, Lafayette, Zanesville.
Crow Frederick, Lafayette, Zanesville.
Crow George, Lafayette, Zanesville.
Crow James, 26, Lafayette, Zanesville.
Crow James, 18, Monroe, Monroeville.
Crow John, 28, Lafayette, Zanesville.
Crow Jonathan, 31, Wayne, Fort Wayne.
Crow Jonathan, jr, 32, Wayne, Fort Wayne.
Crow Joseph, Perry, Huntertown.
Crow Martin, 27, Lafayette, Zanesville.
Crow Willard, 18, Monroe, Monroeville.
Crow Wm, 34, Lafayette, Zanesville.
Crowder John, 34, Pleasant, Sheldon.
Crowder John jr, 34, Pleasant, Sheldon.
Crowell Samuel, 25, Springfield, Halls Corners.
Crozier Samuel, Jefferson, Maples.
Crozier Stephen, 4, Madison, Maples.
Crumm George, 3, Lake, Hellers Corners.
Cubert Fred, 12, Adams, New Haven.
Cubert Henry, 12, Adams, New Haven.
Cubert Victor, 12, Adams, New Haven.
Culver Henry, 12, Adams, New Haven.
Cummerow Henry, 17, Adams, New Haven.
Cummerow Henry, 15, Jefferson, Zulu.
Cummings Charles, 28, Springfield, Harlan.
Cummings F, 35, Springfield, Harlan.
Cummings Henry, 28, Springfield, Harlan.
Cummings Joseph D, 28, Springfield, Harlan.
Cummings Luther, 9, Springfield, Harlan.
Cummings Marion F, 4, Springfield, Harlan.
Cummings Robert, 6, Springfield, Harlan.
Cunningham Michael, 6, Aboit, Dunfee.
Cunnison Alexander, 5, Pleasant, Nine Mile.

Cunnison Charles, 4, Wayne, Fort Wayne.
Cunnison Fielden, 3, Wayne, Fort Wayne.
Cunnison George, 30, Wayne, Fort Wayne.
Cunnison James, 5, Pleasant, Nine Mile.
Curry David, Perry, Huntertown.
Cutshall Edward, 36, Eel River, Wallen.
Cutshall G W, 28, Lake, Arcola.
Cutshall Isaac, 4, Washington, Wallen.
Cutshall Jacques, 28, Lake, Arcola.
Cutshall Samuel, 36, Eel River, Wallen.
Cutshall Thomas, 4, Washington, Wallen.

D

Daffon Albert, 33, Eel River, Heller's Corners.
Daffon John, 33, Eel River, Heller's Corners.
Daffon Samuel, 31, Pleasant, Sheldon.
Daffon Wm, 17, Pleasant, Nine Mile.
Dager Peter, 24, Jefferson, Zulu.
Dalman Charles, 4, Pleasant, Fort Wayne.
Dalman James, 3, Pleasant, Nine Mile.
Dalman Jesse, 33, Wayne, Fort Wayne.
Dalman Wm, 7, Pleasant, Nine Mile.
Dalman Wm, 28, Pleasant, Sheldon.
Dalton Francis, 5, Adams, Fort Wayne.
Dames John, 18, Adams, Fort Wayne.
Damm John, 31, Springfield, Harlan.
Dammeyer Ernest, 3, Lake, Arcola.
Daniels George, 3, Maumee, Antwerp, O.
Daniels Martin, 36, St Joseph, New Haven.
Daniels Wm, 36, St Joseph, New Haven.
Daniels Wm, 7, Springfield, Harlan.
Dannenfelser Albert, 18-19, Milan, Thurman.
Danton Irwin, 5, Aboit, Dunfee.
Darby Henry, 3, Lake, Arcola.
Darling Almon, 1, Milan, Harlan.
Darling B, 12, Adams, New Haven.
Darling Conrad, 32, St Joseph, Fort Wayne.
Darling Eli, 2, Milan, Harlan.
Darling George W, 2, Milan, Harlan.

Darling Mordecai, 4, Milan, Chamberlain.
Darr Frederick, 36, Madison, Monroeville.
Darr John, 27, Madison, Hoagland.
Dassler Christian, 17, St Joseph, Fort Wayne.
Dassot Philip, 15, Jefferson, Zulu.
Dave Wm, 31, Perry, Huntertown.
Davis Columbus, 5, Pleasant, Nine Mile.
Davis John, 29, Marion, Poe.
Davis Kirk, 16, St Joseph, Fort Wayne.
Davis Louis, 26, Washington, Fort Wayne.
Davis L, 23, Monroe, Monroeville.
Davis Martin, 4, Springfield, Spencerville.
Davis Samuel, 16, St Joseph, Fort Wayne.
Davis Scott, 12, Adams, New Haven.
Dawkins Charles, 18, Jefferson, New Haven.
Dawkins Frank, 12, Jefferson, Dawkins.
Dawkins Henry, 19, Jefferson, Maples.
Dawkins James, 11, Jefferson, Dawkins.
Dawkins James G, 7, Jefferson, New Haven.
Dawkins John, 19, Jefferson, Maples.
Dawkins John, 17, Jefferson, New Haven.
Dawkins Samuel, 12, Jefferson, Dawkins.
Dawkins Will, 19, Jefferson, Maples.
Dawson Amaziah, 22, Eel River, Heller's Corners.
Day George, Jackson, Baldwin.
Daylor L, 8, Adams, Fort Wayne.
Deager Fred, 20, Jackson, Monroeville.
Deal John, 31, Marion, Poe.
Deal Joseph, 29, Marion, Poe.
Dean Ephraim, 25, Springfield, Halls Corners.
Deardorff George, 12, Adams, New Haven.
Deatsman M, 4, Scipio, Hicksville, O.
Decker Christian, 22, Aboit, Fort Wayne.
Decker Daniel, 22, Adroit, Fort Wayne.
Decker John, 5, Adams, Fort Wayne.
Decker Martin, 22, Aboit, Fort Wayne.
Decker Wm, 22, Aboit, Fort Wayne.
Deiderich Albert, 4, Milan, Chamberlain.
Deisler Wm, 16, Maumee, Woodburn.
De La Grange, 24, Perry, Cedarville.

De La Grange James, 11, Washington, Fort Wayne.
De La Grange Joseph, 6, Milan, Thurman.
De La Grange Joseph, 27, Perry, Fort Wayne.
De La Grange Julius, 27, Perry, Fort Wayne.
De La Grange Victor, 18, Cedar Creek, Collingwood.
De La Grange Victor, 10, Milan, Harlan.
De Long Eugene, 15, Eel River, Ari.
De Long Isaac, 14, Aboit, Fort Wayne.
De Long Joel, 15, Eel River, Ari.
De Long Wm, 23, Marion, Hoagland.
Demoney Joseph, 19, Lake, Arcola.
Denges Christopher, 35, Milan, Gar Creek.
Denges Christopher jr, 35, Milan, Gar Creek.
Denges Henry, 35, Milan, Gar Creek.
Denner John, 2, Aboit, Fort Wayne.
Denner M, 13, Aboit, Fort Wayne.
Dennis David, 16, Lafayette, Myhart.
Dennis Edward, 15, Lafayette, Myhart.
Dennis Frederick, 7, Monroe, Monroeville.
Dennis George, 12, Adams, New Haven.
Dennis Henry, 20, Lafayette, Roanoke.
Dennis Isaac, 30, Jefferson, Maples.
Dennis Jacob, 9, Lafayette, Myhart.
Dennis James, 15, Lafayette, Myhart.
Dennis John, 14, Adams, New Haven.
Dennis John, 18, Lafayette, Aboit.
Dennis Milton, 33, Aboit, Aboit.
Denny E, 34, Lafayette, Zanesville.
Denny Frank, 32, Pleasant, Sheldon.
Denny James, Maumee, Antwerp, O.
Denny Walter, 27, Lafayette, Zanesville.
Dentlebeck George A, 15, Lafayette, Myhart.
Denwert Henry, 17, Monroe, Monroeville.
Denzill Francis, 10, Adams, Fort Wayne.
Depew John, 6 Cedar Creek, Collingwood.
Depew Wm, 18, Cedar Creek, Collingwood.
Depperon J B, 24, Jefferson, Zulu.
Depperon Simon, 24, Jefferson, Zulu.
Deppler David, 27, Aboit, Fort Wayne.
Deppner Henry, 4, Jefferson, Gar Creek.

Deraner Alfred, 13, St Joseph, Thurman.
Derby George H, 23, Lake, Arcola.
Derby W K, 3, Springfield, Harlan.
Dest Isaac, 26, Jefferson, Zulu.
Deturk David, 8, Wayne, Fort Wayne.
Devaux Amiel, 11, Milan, Harlan.
Devaux D, 1, Wayne, Fort Wayne.
Devaux John, 24, St Joseph, Thurman.
Devaux John, Scipio, Harlan.
Devender Frederick C, 21, Cedar Creek, Cedarville.
De Vilbiss W F, 28, Washington, Fort Wayne.
Dewell Henry, 9, Adams, Fort Wayne.
De Witte Daniel, 19, Lafayette, Myhart.
Dice Henry, 22, Eel River, Heller's Corners.
Dice John, 3, Washington, Wallen.
Dice Levi, 22, Eel River, Heller's Corners.
Dicker Henry, 9, Cedar Creek, Leo.
Dickinson John, 30, Madison, Hoagland.
Dickinson Sherman, 6, Cedar Creek, Collingwood.
Dickey Diederick, 13, Aboit, Fort Wayne.
Dickey George W, Jackson, Edgerton.
Dickover Jacob, 28' Cedar Creek, Cedarville.
Didier Peter, 22, Lake, Arcola.
Didier Victor, 15, Jefferson, Zulu.
Diebold Benjamin, 36, Perry, Cedarville.
Diederich Esau, Springfield, Harlan.
Diedrich Francis, 11, Aboit, Fort Wayne.
Diedorf Otto, 5, Wayne, Fort Wayne.
Diehl George, 31, Springfield, Harlan.
Diehl John, 3, Maumee, Antwerp, O.
Diffendorfer Alfred, 4, Lake, Heller's Corners.
Diffendorfer George, 24, Lafayette, Zanesville.
Diffendorfer John, 4, Lake, Heller's Corners.
Dinger Conrad, 9, Madison, Maples.
Dinger Cornelius, 28, Jefferson, Maples.
Dinger Robert, Jefferson, Maples.
Dingman John, 31, Jefferson, Maples.
Denius H C, 19, Aboit, Saturn.
Dischon Emery, 15, Lafayette, Myhart.
Dischon John, 33, Pleasant, Sheldon.

844   R. L. POLK & CO.'S

Dischon Jonah, 33, Pleasant, Sheldon.
Dischon Thomas, 15, Lafayette, Myhart.
Disler Alva C, 9, Eel River, Ari.
Disler Pearce, 20, Cedar Creek, Cedarville.
Disler Samuel, 21, Cedar Creek, Cedarville.
Disler Timothy, 28, Cedar Creek, Cedarville.
Ditmar Henry A, 8-9, Eel River, Churubusco.
Ditzell Gerard, 31, Jefferson, Maples.
Ditzell Henry, 31, Jefferson, Maples.
Ditzell John, 31, Jefferson, Maples.
Ditzell Wm jr, 31, Jefferson, Maples.
Dobbins Henry, 30, Pleasant, Sheldon.
Dobbins Wm, 19, Pleasant, Nine Mile.
Dober John, 9, Adams, Fort Wayne.
Doctor Albert, 4, Marion, Fort Wayne.
Doctor Allen, 33, Adams, Fort Wayne.
Doctor Charles, 2, Marion, Soest.
Doctor Frederick, 2, Marion, Soest.
Doctor George, 2, Marion, Soest.
Doctor George, 10, Maumee, Antwerp, O.
Doctor Henry, 33, Adams, Soest.
Doctor Henry, 4, Marion, Fort Wayne.
Doctor Louis, 22, Marion, Hoagland.
Doctor Nathan C, 11, Maumee, Antwerp, O.
Dodane Edward, 16, Jefferson, New Haven.
Dodane Frank, 33, Jefferson, Monroeville.
Dodane Joseph, 16, Jefferson, New Haven.
Doenges Frederick, 32, Adams, Fort Wayne.
Doenges John, 32, Adams, Fort Wayne.
Dolan Edward, 31, Wayne, Fort Wayne.
Dolan Frank, 17, Wayne, Fort Wayne.
Dolan John, 18, Wayne, Fort Wayne.
Dolan Sherman, 18, Wayne, Fort Wayne.
Dolan Wm, 31, Wayne, Fort Wayne.
Dollerhite Isom, 20, Maumee, Woodburn.
Dollerhite John, 20, Maumee, Woodburn.
Donaldson Ernest, 27, St Joseph, Goeglien.
Donovan Daniel, 24, Springfield, Halls Corners.
Dore Dr, 29, Marion, Poe.
Dorsey Allen, 8, Scipio, Hicksville, O.

Dorsey Benjamin, 7, Scipio, Halls Corners.
Dorsey George, 17, Scipio, Hicksville, O.
Dorsey Linn, 7, Scipio, Halls Corners.
Dorsey Robert, 7, Scipio, Halls Corners.
Doswell John H, 3, Wayne, Fort Wayne.
Doty Alfred, 16, Milan, Chamberlain.
Doty Solomon, 17, Milan, Thurman.
Double Daniel, 11, Pleasant, Fort Wayne.
Double Wm, 11, Pleasant, Fort Wayne.
Douglass John, 18, Cedar Creek, Leo.
Douglass Joseph, 12, St Joseph, Goeglien.
Dougley Fletcher, 17, Eel River, Heller's Corners.
Dougley Lorain, 18, Eel River, Churubusco.
Dowall Alfred, 30, Aboit, Saturn.
Dowall John, 30, Aboit, Saturn.
Dowall Thomas, 30, Aboit, Saturn.
Dowdick Andrew, 5, St Joseph, Fort Wayne.
Dower August, 36, Adams, Maples.
Dower Henry H, 19, Madison, Hoagland.
Dowling Edward, 12, Adams, New Haven.
Dowling Edward jr, 12, Adams, New Haven.
Dowling John, 12, Adams, New Haven.
Downing Jeremiah B, 25, Wayne, Fort Wayne.
Downing John, 5, Maumee, Harlan.
Doyle John, 8, Jefferson, New Haven.
Doyle Martin, 8, Jefferson, New Haven.
Doyle Wm, 8, Jefferson, New Haven.
Drage Frederick, 31, Madison, Hoagland.
Drake Albert, 35, Marion, Williams Station.
Drake Edward, 35, Marion, Williams Station.
Drake Henry, 35, Marion, Williams Station.
Drake Jacob, 35, Marion, Williams Station.
Dressbach Isaac, 8, Springfield, Harlan.
Dressler August, 27, St Joseph, Goeglien.
Driver Adam, 24, Springfield, Halls Corners.
Driver David, 4, Madison, Maples.
Driver John, 4, Madison, Maples.
Driver John, 25, Springfield, Halls Corners.
Driver J W, 6, Maumee, Harlan.
Driver Louis, 4, Madison, Maples.

Driver Luther, 17, Scipio, Hicksville, O.
Driver Oscar, 4, Madison, Maples.
Driver Robert, 9, Madison, Maples.
Driver Ulysses, 4, Madison, Maples.
Driver Wm, 24, Springfield, Halls Corners.
Driver Wm, 13, Springfield, Harlan.
Driver Wm W, 7, Maumee, Harlan.
Drummeux F, 18, Jackson, Dawkins.
Drury John, 12, Adams, Fort Wayne.
Dryer Charles, 15, Washington, Fort Wayne.
Ducat John, 24, Perry, Cedarville.
Ducat Joseph, 14, Perry, Leo.
Ducat Stephen, 14, Perry, Leo.
Dudgeon Charles, 28, Scipio, Harlan.
Dudgeon Eli, 16, Jackson, Monroeville.
Duffy Charles, 17, Jackson, Monroeville.
Dukeman A, 1, Aboit, Fort Wayne.
Dukeman D, 1, Aboit, Fort Wayne.
Dukeman F, 1, Aboit, Fort Wayne.
Dulen Wm, 18, Eel River, Churubusco.
Dunfee Andrew, 36, St Joseph, New Haven.
Dunfee Elijah, 19, Perry, Huntertown.
Dunfee Isaac, 1-2, Eel River, Huntertown.
Dungarty Alvin, 29, Madison, Hoagland.
Dunn Charles, 11, Lake, Arcola.
Dunn Wm, 12, Lake, Arcola.
Dunton Allen, 33, Perry, Fort Wayne.
Dunton Anson, 19, Perry, Huntertown.
Dunton Ellis, Perry, Huntertown.
Dunton Elmer, Perry, Huntertown.
Dunton Friend, Perry, Huntertown.
Dunton George, 19, Perry, Huntertown.
Dunton Henry C, Perry, Huntertown.
Dunton Manville N, 7, Perry, Huntertown.
Dunton Sidney, 19, Perry, Huntertown.
Dunton Washington, Perry, Huntertown.
Dupont Marcellus S, 36, Perry, Cedarville.
Dush Jeremiah, 10, Monroe, Monroeville.
Dustman H, 8, Adams, Fort Wayne.

E

Eager Major, 34, Springfield, Harlan.
Eagly Jacob, 2, Milan, Harlan.
Eagy Wm, 27, Madison, Hoagland.
Ealing Adam, 21, Monroe, Monroeville.
Earlbrich Wm, 16, Adams, Fort Wayne.
Early B, 11, Aboit, Fort Wayne.
Eberle John, 28, Lake, Arcola.
Eby Andrew, 15, Milan, Harlan.
Eby Anna M, 10, Wayne, Fort Wayne.
Eby Daniel, 3, St Joseph, Fort Wayne.
Eby Eli, 15, Milan, Harlan.
Eby George, 26, Eel River, Wallen.
Eby Henry, 2, St Joseph, Fort Wayne.
Eby James, 9, St Joseph, Fort Wayne.
Eby Martin, 10, St Joseph, Fort Wayne.
Eby Robert, 9, St Joseph, Fort Wayne.
Eby Rufus, 9, St Joseph, Fort Wayne.
Eby Samuel, 26, Eel River, Wallen.
Eckelburger Frank, 9, Adams, Fort Wayne.
Eckels Benjamin, 35, Washington, Fort Wayne.
Eckels John, 8, Springfield, Harlan.
Eckels John, 35, Washington, Fort Wayne.
Edgerton Edward, 20, Maumee, Woodburn.
Edsall A, 11, Pleasant, Fort Wayne.
Edwards Lee, 12, Adams, New Haven.
Eggeman D, 22, Adams, Fort Wayne.
Eggeman Theodore, 23, Adams, Fort Wayne.
Eggeman Wm, 31, Adams, Fort Wayne.
Ehehart John, 4, Monroe, Monroeville.
Ehinger F, 4, Adams, New Haven.
Ehinger John, 4, Jefferson, Gar Creek.
Ehinger Philip, 11, Adams, New Haven.
Ehle Ernest, 9, Milan, Chamberlain.
Ehle Wm, 10, Milan, Harlan.
Ehrhausen Wm, 2, Marion, Soest.
Eicher Joseph, 12, Milan, Harlan.
Eigenberger Henry, 15, Madison, Monroeville.
Eitzinger Andrew, 13, Wayne, Fort Wayne.

Eix Christian, 29, St Joseph, Goeglien.
Eix Conrad, 29, St Joseph, Goeglien.
Elf Henry, 5, Aboit, Dunfee.
Ellenwood H, 30, Marion, Poe.
Ellert Christian, 33, Adams, Soest.
Ellert John, 5, Marion, Fort Wayne.
Ellinger Fred, 3, Marion, Soest.
Elliott Rev C M, 29, Marion, Poe.
Ellison Dean, 3, Madison, Maples.
Ellison John, 3, Madison, Maples.
Ellsworth Edward, 12, Adams, New Haven.
Elm Charles, 12, Madison, Monroeville.
Elmer Wm, 4, Maumee, Harlan.
Ely Casper, 10, Cedar Creek, Leo.
Ely David, 29, Cedar Creek, Cedarville.
Ely Edward, 31, Cedar Creek, Cedarville.
Ely Edward, 4, St Joseph, Fort Wayne.
Ely James, 17, St Joseph, Fort Wayne.
Emerick Adam, 13, Marion, Hoagland.
Emerick A J, 13, Pleasant, Fort Wayne.
Emerick Charles, 31, Perry, Huntertown.
Emerick Commodore, 13, Pleasant, Fort Wayne.
Emerick Ellis, 13, Pleasant, Fort Wayne.
Emerick Henry, 13, Marion, Hoagland.
Emerick Jacob, 13, Pleasant, Fort Wayne.
Emerick Jacob jr, 13, Pleasant, Fort Wayne.
Emerick James, 29, Marion, Poe.
Emerick John, 23, Marion, Hoagland.
Emerick John, Perry, Huntertown.
Emerick Timothy, 23, Marion, Hoagland.
Emerick Wm, Jackson, Edgerton.
Emerick Wm, 3, Madison, Maples.
Emerick Wm, 8, Perry, Huntertown.
Emmenheiser David, 29, Madison, Hoagland.
Emmenheiser James, 29, Madison, Hoagland.
Emmenheiser Joseph, 29, Madison, Hoagland.
Emmenheiser J R, Jackson, Dawkins.
Emmenheiser Stephen C, 17, Jackson, Monroeville.
Engle George, 21, Wayne, Fort Wayne.
English James, 19, Madison, Hoagland.

English John, 2, St Joseph, Fort Wayne.
English Thomas, 15, Milan, Harlan.
Enninger Mangus, 25, St Joseph, Geoglien.
Enninger Wm C, 3, Springfield, Harlan.
Ensign Arthur, Maumee, Antwerp, O.
Erdman Frederick, 17, Wayne, Fort Wayne.
Erick E W, 28, Springfield, Harlan.
Erick George, 31, Perry, Huntertown.
Erick Wm, 22, Lafayette, Zanesville.
Erickman Thomas, 33, Pleasant, Sheldon.
Ersig James, 30, Madison, Hoagland.
Ertel J, 14, Washington, Fort Wayne.
Ervin A K, 10, Aboit, Fort Wayne.
Ervin Jeremiah, 6, Washington, Fort Wayne.
Ervin Perry, 8, Washington, Wallen.
Esquires L D, Scipio, Hicksville, O.
Essig John, 20, Marion, Poe.
Essig J F, 29, Marion, Poe.
Esterline Wm J, 19, Aboit, Dunfee.
Evans Charles, Jefferson, Maples.
Evans Levi, 6, Lafayette, Aboit.
Evard Aime C, 29, Milan, Gar Creek.
Evard August, 36, Jefferson, Zulu.
Evard Clement, 31, Jackson, Monroeville.
Evard Clement, Milan, Thurman.
Evard David, 5, St Joseph, Fort Wayne.
Evard Frederick, Milan, Thurman.
Evard James, 24, St Joseph, Thurman.
Evard Julius, 7, Milan, Thurman.
Eveland Peter, 1, Adams, New Haven.
Everly John, 6, Cedar Creek, Spencerville.
Ewart David S, 10, Lafayette, Nine Mile.
Ewart Robert, 10, Lafayette, Nine Mile.
Exivery Frank, 14, Jefferson, Zulu.

F

Fagley Theo, 1, Milan, Harlan.
Fahl Charles, 19, Lafayette, Myhart.
Fahl Daniel, 19, Lafayette, Myhart.

Fahlsing Christian, 5, Wayne, Fort Wayne.
Fahlsing Conrad, 8, Maumee, Woodburn.
Fahlsing Frederick, 30, Maumee, Woodburn.
Fahlsing Frederick, 5, Wayne, Fort Wayne.
Fahlsing Frederick jr, Maumee, Woodburn.
Fair Andrew, 9, Washington, Wallen.
Fair Gabriel, 26, Eel River, Wallen.
Fair Ora, 9, Washington, Wallen.
Fairfield Charles W, 20, Wayne, Fort Wayne.
Fairfield Edmund, 35, Lake, Arcola.
Fairfield James, 35, Lake, Arcola.
Fairfield Wm, 20, Wayne, Fort Wayne.
Falk George, 11, Adams, New Haven.
Falkner Frank, 9, Maumee, Woodburn.
Falkner Joseph, Maumee, Woodburn.
Falls James, 21, Marion, Poe.
Falls Owen, 27, Marion, Hoagland.
Fansler Isaiah, 19, Scipio, Fansler.
Fantz Wm, Jackson, Baldwin.
Fark Fred, 16, St Joseph, Fort Wayne.
Fark Henry, 15, St Joseph, Fort Wayne.
Fark Louis, 15, St Joseph, Fort Wayne.
Farner Cyrus, 2, Milan, Harlan.
Farrand R S, Perry, Huntertown.
Farrell Andrew, 28, Pleasant, Sheldon.
Farrell Frank, 11, Madison, Maples.
Farrell George, 30, Pleasant, Sheldon.
Farrell James, 28, Pleasant, Sheldon.
Farrell Jonah, 33, Pleasant, Sheldon.
Farvet John, 33, Jefferson, Monroeville.
Farvet Louis, 33, Jefferson, Monroeville.
Faulkner Cyrus, 27, Perry, Fort Wayne.
Faulkner Perry, 28, Perry, Fort Wayne.
Faulkner Williard, 27, Perry, Fort Wayne.
Faust Peter, 31, St. Joseph, Fort Wayne.
Favier Claude, 15, Jefferson, Zulu.
Favier Lucas, 18, Monroe, Monroeville.
Fearman Fred, 16, Springfield, Harlan.
Fearman Zachariah, 16, Springfield, Harlan.
Federspiel Balzer, 1, Adams, New Haven.

Federspiel Bernard, 12, Adams, New Haven.
Federspiel Charles, 21, Milan, Thurman.
Federspiel Joseph, 2, Adams, New Haven.
Federspiel Michael, 31, Perry, Huntertown.
Federspiel M, 28, Milan, Thurman.
Federspiel Peter, 24, Milan, Gar Creek.
Fehling Frederick, 1, Milan, Harlan.
Feicker Elias, 21, Madison, Hoagland.
Feidler Albert, 34, Milan, Gar Creek.
Feighner Adam, 27, Lafayette, Zanesville.
Feirsone Wm, 31, Milan, New Haven.
Felger Alfred, 13, Lake, Arcola.
Felger Charles, 13, Lake, Arcola.
Felger Christian, 18, Marion, Poe.
Felger Daniel, 22, Lake, Arcola.
Felger George, 29-30, Eel River, Heller's Corners.
Felger Gottleib, 34, Milan, Gar Creek.
Felger Henry, 22, Lake, Arcola.
Felger Henry, 11, Marion, Soest.
Felger Jacob, 13, Lake, Arcola.
Felger John, 28, Lake, Arcola.
Felger John, 3, Marion, Soest.
Felger Wm, 13, Lake, Arcola.
Felger Wm C, 22, Lake, Arcola.
Fell Christian, 2, Pleasant, Fort Wayne.
Fell Frederick, 9, Pleasant, Nine Mile.
Feller Adam, 21, Monroe, Monroeville.
Fellus David, 20, Monroe, Monroeville.
Felt Wm, 1, Marion, Soest.
Fenton Frank, 32, Monroe, Monroeville.
Fenton John, 32, Monroe, Monroeville.
Ferber Conrad, 3, Marion, Soest.
Ferguson Matthew, 26, Washington, Fort Wayne.
Ferl Oswald, 26, Lafayette, Zanesville.
Ferris Warren, 8, Wayne, Fort Wayne.
Ferry Frank, 10, Wayne, Fort Wayne.
Feser L, 9, Aboit, Fort Wayne.
Feusse Henry, 6, Maumee, Harlan.
Figel Charles, 4, Madison, Maples.
Filling Frederick, 21, Madison, Hoagland.

852 R. L. POLK & CO.'S

Finker C, 18, Adams, Fort Wayne.
Firestine George, 2, Adams, New Haven.
Fisher Andrew, 31, Madison, Hoagland.
Fisher Elias, 5, Cedar Creek, Collingwood.
Fisher F F, 14, Pleasant, Fort Wayne.
Fisher Henry, 7, Eel River, Churubusco.
Fisher Henry, 20, Milan, Thurman.
Fisher Henry W, 22, Lafayette, Zanesville.
Fisher Jacob, 17, Lafayette, Myhart.
Fisher Jacob, 14, Pleasant, Fort Wayne.
Fisher John, 20, Madison, Hoagland.
Fisher Joseph, 12, Adams, New Haven.
Fisher Samuel, 21, Cedar Creek, Cedarville.
Fisher Samuel, 7, Lafayette, Aboit.
Fitch Harvey, 8, Perry, Huntertown.
Fitch Michael, 13, Lake, Fort Wayne.
Fitch Schneider, Perry, Huntertown.
Fitzgerald Henry, 6, Milan, Thurman.
Fitzgibbon August, 15, Lafayette, Myhart.
Fitzgibbon Daniel, 15, Lafayette, Myhart.
Fitzgibbon Solomon, 15, Lafayette, Myhart.
Fitzgibbon Wm, 15, Lafayette, Myhart.
Fitzsimmons George, Perry, Huntertown.
Fitzsimmons W, Perry, Huntertown.
Flaig E, 18, Adams, Fort Wayne.
Flaig Fred, 23, Lafayette, Zanesville.
Flaig Jacob, 12, Lafayette, Nine Mile.
Flanagan John, 12, Perry, Collingwood.
Flaugh Christian, 19, Lafayette, Roanoke.
Flaugh Jacob, 31, Jefferson, Maples.
Flaugh John, 19, Lafayette, Roanoke.
Flaugh Lewis, 19, Lafayette, Roanoke.
Flaugh Michael, 6, Wayne, Fort Wayne.
Flaugh M, 18, Madison, Maples.
Fleming James W, 31, Perry, Huntertown.
Fleming Oliver, 27, Washington, Fort Wayne.
Fleming Thomas, 16, Washington, Fort Wayne
Flickinger Frank, 13, Milan, Harlan.
Flickinger James, 7, Milan, Thurman.
Flickinger John, 7, Milan, Thurman.

Flickinger Levi, 18-19, Milan, Thurman.
Flickinger Lyle, 13, Milan, Harlan.
Fluthron August, 16, Jackson, Monroeville.
Fluthron John, 28, Jackson, Monroeville.
Fluthron Lewis, 28, Jackson, Monroeville.
Foellinger Christian, 29, Washington, Fort Wayne.
Fogel Elmer, 10, Eel River, Ari.
Fogel Frank, 10, Eel River, Ari.
Fogel Frank, 16, Eel River, Heller's Corners.
Fogel John, 3, Eel River, Ari.
Fogel Orin, 7, Eel River, Churubusco.
Fogel Winton, 3, Eel River, Ari.
Fogwell Alfred, 1, Lafayette, Nine Mile.
Fogwell Wm, 1, Lafayette, Nine Mile.
Folk Martin, 5, Aboit, Dunfee.
Folks Christian, 29, Pleasant, Sheldon.
Fonner David W, 34, Marion, Poe.
Fonner George, 34, Marion, Poe.
Fonner Milton, 33, Marion, Poe.
Foote Harvey B, 29, Scipio, Antwerp, O.
Foote James, 36, Springfield, Harlan.
Foote Joseph, 23, Springfield, Halls Corners.
Foote Wm, 23, Springfield, Halls Corners.
Foote Wm, 36, Springfield, Harlan.
Ford Lance, 15, Cedar Creek, Leo.
Forsyth F, Aboit, Dunfee.
Forsyth J, 7, Aboit, Dunfee.
Forsyth Wesley H, 7, Aboit, Dunfee.
Forthmiller, see Furthmiller.
Fortmeyer Fred, 13, Lake, Fort Wayne.
Fortmeyer Henry, 19, Washington, Fort Wayne.
Fosnight Henry, 4, Springfield, Harlan.
Fosnight Henry jr, 4, Springfield, Harlan.
Fosnight Hiram, 29, Sciopio, Antwerp, O.
Foster Frederick, 35, Adams, Maples.
Foster Jesse, 18, Monroe, Monroeville.
Foster Jesse jr, 21, Monroe, Monroeville.
Foster Leonard, 21, Monroe, Monroeville.
Foster Levi, 15, Monroe, Monroeville.
Foster Philip, 24, Springfield, Halls Corners.

854 R. L. POLK & CO.'S

Foster Wm, 21, Monroe, Monroeville.
Foster Wm, 16, Wayne, Fort Wayne.
Fouser Jacob H, 26, Washington, Fort Wayne.
Fox Adolph, 22, Pleasant, Sheldon.
Fox Alexander, 27, Adams, Soest.
Fox A, 15, Wayne, Fort Wayne.
Fox Frank, 27, Adams, Soest.
Fox Henry, 27, Adams, Soest.
Fox Hiram, Perry, Huntertown.
Fox Philander, 34, Lake, Arcola.
Fox Valentine, 16, Wayne, Fort Wayne.
France August, 24, St Joseph, Thurman.
France Frank, 24, St Joseph, Thurman.
France Lewis, 5, St Joseph, Fort Wayne.
France Peter, 24, St Joseph, Thurman.
France Wm, 18, Lafayette, Aboit.
Frane Eugene, 16, Aboit, Fort Wayne.
Frane W, 16, Aboit, Fort Wayne.
Frank Wm, 1, Lake, Heller's Corners.
Franke Frederick, 16, Madison, Hoagland.
Franklin James, Sciopio, Harlan.
Fratert Henry, 5, Marion, Fort Wayne.
Fratert John, 5, Marion, Fort Wayne.
Frazure Edward, 19-20, Eel River, Heller's Corners.
Frazure Henry, 31, Eel River, Heller's Corners.
Frazure Wash, 29-30, Eel River, Heller's Corners.
Frech Frank, 23, Aboit, Fort Wayne.
Frech Henry, 23, Aboit, Fort Wayne.
Fredensberg John, 18, St Joseph, Fort Wayne.
Frederick Amos, 2, Perry, Collingwood.
Frederick Frank, 7, Cedar Creek, Collingwood.
Frederick Gustave, Jefferson, Maples.
Frederick John, 9, Cedar Creek, Leo.
Frederick Samuel, 2, Perry, Collingwood.
Frederickson Chris, 7, Springfield, Harlan.
Frederickson George, 7, St Joseph, Fort Wayne.
Frederickson Peter, 2, Washington, St Vincent.
Freeman R L, 14, Eel River, Huntertown.
Freeman Wm D, 11, 60, $1265, Eel River, Huntertown.

Freese Charles, 15, Springfield, Harlan.
Freese Daniel, 14, Springfield, Harlan.
Freiberger George, 5, Pleasant, Nine Mile.
Freiberger John, 27, Pleasant, Sheldon.
Freidt Jacob, 22, Springfield, Harlan.
Freistroffer John, 4, Marion, Fort Wayne.
Freistroffer Simon, 9, Marion, Fort Wayne.
Fremion Oliver, 31, St Joseph, Fort Wayne.
Friece Charles, 4, Springfield, Spencerville.
Friedline Emanuel, 29, Monroe, Monroeville.
Friedline John D, 30, Monroe, Monroeville.
Friedline John L, 32, Monroe, Monroeville.
Friedline Otis, 30, Monroe, Monroeville.
Friedrick Fass, 3, Wayne, Fort Wayne.
Fritche Bernard, 27, Milan, Gar Creek.
Fritche Henry, 22, Milan, Gar Creek.
Fritche Julian, 26, Milan, Gar Creek.
Fritz Augustus, 2, Lake, Heller's Corners.
Fritz Charles, 1, Lake, Heller's Corners.
Fritz Daniel, 1, Lake, Heller's Corners.
Fritz Henry, 5, Washington, Wallen.
Fritz John, 2, Lake, Heller's Corners.
Fritz Michael, 11, Lake, Arcola.
Fritz Wm, 1, Lake, Heller's Corners.
Frosch Conrad, 30, Adams, Fort Wayne.
Frosch Martin, 30, Adams, Fort Wayne.
Fruechtenicht Francis, 31, Adams, Fort Wayne.
Fruechtenicht Fred, 31, Adams, Fort Wayne.
Fruechtenicht John H, 31, Adams, Fort Wayne.
Fry Albert, 10, Madison, Maples.
Fry Charles, 8, Adams, Fort Wayne.
Fry Charles, 27, Springfield, Harlan.
Fry Conrad, 17, Madison, Hoagland.
Fry Fred, Jefferson, Maples.
Fry Frederick, 19, Madison, Hoagland.
Fry George, 14, Madison, Monroeville.
Fry Henry, 2 ,Madison, Monroeville.
Fry Jacob, 3, Madison, Maples.
Fry James, Jefferson, Maples.
Fry John, 10, Madison, Maples.

Fry Martin, 10, Madison, Maples.
Fry Oscar, 28, Lake, Arcola.
Fry Philip, 16, Madison, Hoagland.
Fry Wm, 27, Springfield, Harlan.
Fuchman John, 33, Marion, Poe.
Fuchshober F, 35, Pleasant, Sheldon.
Fudge Oscar, 29-30, Eel River, Heller's Corners.
Fulger James, 11, Springfield, Spencerville.
Fulk Jacob, 6, Eel River, Churubusco.
Fulk Jacob jr, 6, Eel River, Churubusco.
Fulk John, 6, Eel River, Churubusco.
Fulkerson Samuel, 7, Washington, Fort Wayne.
Fulkison D L, 30, Cedar Creek, Cedarville.
Fuller Charles, 10, Cedar Creek, Leo.
Fulmer Jacob, 25, Milan, Gar Creek.
Fulmer James, 25, Milan, Gar Creek.
Fulmer Leonard, 25, Milan, Gar Creek.
Fulmer Wm, 25, Milan, Gar Creek.
Fultz Emanuel, 22, Lafayette, Zanesville.
Fultz G W, 29, Lafayette, Zanesville.
Fultz S, 4, Aboit, Arcola.
Funk Jacob, 9, Lake, Arcola.
Funk Joseph, 6, Adams, Fort Wayne.
Funk Leonard, 29, St Joseph, Goeglien.
Funk Matthew, 28, Jackson, Monroeville.
Funk M V B, 31, Springfield, Harlan.
Furnace Alexander, Jackson, Dawkins.
Furnace Wm, Jackson, Dawkins.
Furney Bert, 8, Springfield, Harlan.
Furney Jeremiah, 8, Springfield, Harlan.
Furnish Thomas E, 2, Cedar Creek, Spencerville.
Furthmiller Henry, 7, Jefferson, New Haven.
Furthmiller Jacob, 7, Jefferson, New Haven.

G

Gable Charles, 12, Adams, New Haven.
Gable Charles, 29, Washington, Fort Wayne.
Gable Christopher, 21, Cedar Creek, Cedarville.
Gable Daniel, 30, Jefferson, Maples.

Gable David, 25, Wayne, Fort Wayne.
Gable Jacob, 25, Wayne, Fort Wayne.
Gable Frederick, 5, Madison, Maples.
Gable Frederick jr, 5, Madison, Maples.
Gable Joseph, 12, Adams, New Haven.
Gable Joseph, 5, Madison, Maples.
Gage Anthony, 3, Wayne, Fort Wayne.
Gaily Calvin, 7, Monroe, Monroeville.
Gaily John, 7, Monroe, Monroeville.
Gake Louis, 25, Wayne, Fort Wayne.
Galer C D, 1, Wayne, Fort Wayne.
Gallane Edward, 11, Jefferson, Dawkins.
Gallane Henry, Jackson, Edgerton.
Gallmeyer Charles, 34, Marion, Poe.
Gallmeyer Diederick, 26, Milan, Gar Creek.
Gallmeyer Frederick, 33, Milan, Gar Creek.
Gallmeyer Wm, 26, Adams, Fort Wayne.
Gallope Peter, Jackson, Monroeville.
Galloway David, Maumee, Woodburn.
Gamroth George, Jackson, Edgerton.
Gans Philip, 3, Eel River, Ari.
Gariff Frank, 31, Perry, Huntertown.
Garig James, 30, Springfield, Harlan.
Garig Joseph, 17, Springfield, Harlan.
Garison Levi, 6, Eel River, Churubusco.
Garland J B, 29, Marion, Poe.
Garrett Frank, 32, Pleasant, Sheldon.
Garrett Z T, 28, Cedar Creek, Cedarville.
Garver Charles, 15, Milan, Harlan.
Garver David, 24, Milan, Gar Creek.
Garver Franklin, 24, Milan, Gar Creek.
Garver Henry, 8, Maumee, Woodburn.
Garver James, 24, Milan, Gar Creek.
Gaskill A P, 29, Lafayette, Zanesville.
Gaskill John, 22, Monroe, Monroeville.
Gatz E, 2, Cedar Creek, Spencerville.
Gault George, 23, Madison, Monroeville.
Gay J C, Perry, Huntertown.
Gaylord John, 33, Lake, Arcola.
Gearing Cornelius, 31, Lake, Arcola.

858   R. L. POLK & CO.'S

Gebb Godfrey, 12, Adams, New Haven.
Gebert Christian L, 19, Milan, Thurman.
Gehring Henry, 9, Lake, Arcola.
Gehring Peter, 10, Wayne, Fort Wayne.
Geiseking D, 33, Eel River, Heller's Corners.
Geiseking Fred W, 20, Washington, Fort Wayne.
Geiss Joseph, 16, Springfield, Harlan.
Geller Louis, 31, Perry, Huntertown.
Genth Eli, 12, Lafayette, Nine Mile.
Genth George, 23, Lafayette, Zanesville.
Genth John, 12, Lafayette, Nine Mile.
Genth John A, 15, Lafayette, Myhart.
Genth John P, 24, Lafayette, Zanesville.
Genth Wm, 24, Lafayette, Zanesville.
Genth Wm A, 9, Lafayette, Myhart.
George Frederick, 20, Adams, Fort Wayne.
Gephart Bernard, 9, Washington, Wallen.
Gephart Cassius, 16, Wayne, Fort Wayne.
Gephart Charles, 21, Wayne, Fort Wayne.
Gerding Louis, 34, Lake, Arcola.
Gerding Wm, 35, Lake, Arcola.
Gerig Andrew, 15, Cedar Creek, Leo.
Gerig Andrew, 2, Cedar Creek, Spencerville.
Gerig Christian, 17, Milan, Thurman.
Gerig David, 4, Cedar Creek, Leo.
Gerig Enoch G, 11, Milan, Harlan.
Gerig Joseph, 4, Cedar Creek, Leo.
Gerig Joseph N, 5, Cedar Creek, Collingwood.
Gerig Peter, 3, Cedar Creek.
Gerke Frederick, 26, St Joseph, Goeglien.
Gerke Frederick jr, 26, St Joseph, Goeglien.
Gerke Henry, 25, Wayne, Fort Wayne.
Gerken George, 21, St Joseph, Fort Wayne.
Gerlach Emil, 13, Wayne, Fort Wayne.
Gethart Fred jr, 14, St Joseph, Fort Wayne.
Gethart Julian, 13, St Joseph, Thurman.
Getmone Thomas, 31, Perry, Huntertown.
Getz Andrew, 10, Springfield, Harlan.
Getz Charles, 5, Wayne, Fort Wayne.
Getz Henry, 8 Wayne, Fort Wayne.

Gevers Henry, 27, Milan, Gar Creek.
Gevette Con, 18, Adams, Fort Wayne.
Ghein Walter, 5, Aboit, Dunfee.
Giant Frank, 26, Jefferson, Zulu.
Giant Joseph, 7, Jackson, Edgerton.
Giant Nicholas, 26, Jefferson, Zulu.
Gibbons John, 15, Springfield, Harlan.
Gibson Arthur, 36, Pleasant, Sheldon.
Gibson Daniel, 16, Marion, Fort Wayne.
Gibson David, 20, Marion, Poe.
Gibson Edward, 5, Marion, Fort Wayne.
Gibson Frank, 4, Monroe, Monroeville.
Gibson George, 4, Monroe, Monroeville.
Gibson Henry, 20, Marion, Poe.
Gibson Henry jr, 5, Marion, Fort Wayne.
Gibson John, 3, Monroe, Baldwin.
Gibson John, 31, Monroe, Monroeville.
Gibson Wm, 3, Monroe, Baldwin.
Gibson Wm, 36, Pleasant, Sheldon.
Giff Wm, 8, Perry, Huntertown.
Gifford Dexter, 6, Cedar Creek, Collingwood.
Gifford Russ, 23, Springfield, Halls Corners.
Gill Daniel, Jackson, Dawkins.
Gill Joseph, 15, Washington, Fort Wayne.
Gill Mack, 5, Springfield, Harlan.
Gillard Louis, 14, St Joseph, Fort Wayne.
Gillett Alvin, 1, Cedar Creek, Hursh.
Gillett Charles, 18-19, Milan, Thurman.
Gillett Tyler, 18-19, Milan, Thurman.
Gilley John, 27, Washington, Fort Wayne.
Gillyard F, 12, Adams, New Haven.
Ginger Ferd, 18, Monroe, Monroeville.
Ginther George, 7, Monroe, Monroeville.
Ginther Grant, 6, Monroe, Monroeville.
Ginther Samuel, 5, Monroe, Monroeville.
Girard Israel, 21, Jefferson, Maples.
Girard Lafayette, 4, Madison, Maples.
Girard M G, 1, Wayne, Fort Wayne.
Girard Peter, 4, Madison, Maples.
Girardin Victor, 10, Jefferson, Dawkins.

Girardot Charles, 35, Jefferson, Monroeville.
Girardot Charles C, 21, Jefferson, Maples.
Girardot Henry, 35, Jefferson, Monroeville.
Girardot Jacob, 33, Jefferson, Monroeville.
Girardot John, 35, Jefferson, Monroeville.
Girardot Joseph, 33, Jefferson, Monroeville.
Girardot Julius, 10, Jefferson, Dawkins.
Girardot Louis, 32, Jefferson, Maples
Girardot Louis, 35, Jefferson, Monroeville.
Girardot Louis, 27, Jefferson, Zulu.
Girardot Louis L, 29, Jefferson, Maples.
Girardot S, 21, Jackson, Monroeville.
Gladieaux Celestine, 24, Jefferson, Zulu.
Gladieaux Charles, 23, Jefferson, Zulu.
Gladieaux Emil, 25, Jefferson, Zulu.
Gladieaux Francois, 25, Jefferson, Zulu.
Gladieaux Louis, 21, Jefferson, Maples.
Gladieaux Louis J, 23, Jefferson, Zulu.
Gladieaux Julius, 25, Jefferson, Zulu.
Glass Wm, 9, Adams, Fort Wayne.
Glazure Nathan C, Perry, Huntertown.
Glener Wm, 11, Aboit, Fort Wayne.
Glenn Wm, Jackson, Edgerton.
Gocke August, 7, Adams, Fort Wayne.
Godfrey James P, 10, Wayne, Fort Wayne.
Goebling Rex, 12, Adams, New Haven.
Goeglien Christian, 25, St Joseph, Goeglien.
Goeglien Daniel, 27, St Joseph, Goeglien.
Goeglien George, 26, St Joseph, Goeglien.
Goeglien George jr, 25, St Joseph, Goeglien.
Goeglien Gottlieb, 26, St Joseph, Goeglien.
Goeglien Jacob, 27, St Joseph, Goeglien.
Goeglien John, 25, St Joseph, Goeglien.
Goeglien John jr, 25, St Joseph, Goeglien.
Goeglien Valentine, 27, St Joseph, Goeglien.
Goeglien Wm, 26, St Joseph, Goeglien.
Goette Conrad, 21, Madison, Hoagland.
Goetz George, 17, Adams, Fort Wayne.
Goetz John, 17, Adams, Fort Wayne.
Goetz John jr, 17, Adams, Fort Wayne.

Goff Orin, 14, Eel River, Huntertown.
Goheen Charles, 29-30, Eel River, Wallen.
Goheen Perry, 11, Lake, Arcola.
Goings James, 28, Perry, Fort Wayne.
Golden Henry, 36, Eel River, Wallen.
Goldsmith Amos, 1, Cedar Creek, Hursh.
Goldsmith Christian, 1, Cedar Creek, Hursh.
Goldsmith Henry, 1, Cedar Creek, Hursh.
Goliver Henry, 31, Pleasant, Sheldon.
Goliver James, 33, Pleasant, Sheldon.
Gollan Adam, 21, Lake, Arcola.
Gooden Robert, Maumee, Antwerp, O.
Goodes George, 35, Milan, Gar Creek.
Goodes Henry, 35, Milan, Gar Creek.
Goodes Henry jr, 35, Milan, Gar Creek.
Goodman John, 35, Washington, Fort Wayne.
Gordon James W, 6, Eel River, Churubusco.
Gordon Jasper, 6, Eel River, Churubusco.
Gordon John, 17, Eel River, Heller's Corners.
Gorman Benjamin F, 10, Perry, Collingwood.
Gorman Eli, 1, Perry, Collingwood.
Gorman Ernest, 1, Perry, Collingwood.
Gorman George, 5, Cedar Creek, Collingwood.
Gorman Jeremiah, 1, Perry, Collingwood.
Gorman Joseph E, 1, Perry, Collingwood.
Gorman Mahlon, 10, Cedar Creek, Leo.
Gorman Thomas, 29, Lake, Arcola.
Gorman Wm, 1, Perry, Collingwood.
Gorop Jefferson, 19, Jefferson, Maples.
Gorop John, 19, Jefferson, Maples.
Gorrell Allen, 13, Springfield, Harlan.
Gorrell Burt, 13, Springfield, Harlan.
Gorrell Cyrus, 1, Milan, Harlan.
Gorrell Gilbert C, 12, Adams, New Haven.
Gorrell Isaac, 13, Springfield, Harlan.
Gorrell John W, 12, Adams, New Haven.
Gorrell Milo, 17, Scipio, Hicksville, O.
Gorrell Milo D, 12, Adams, New Haven.
Gorrell Myron, Milan, Chamberlain.
Gorren Jeremiah, 6, Aboit, Dunfee.

Gotat Charles, Jefferson, Maples.
Gothe L M, 2, Marion, Soest.
Gothe Richard, 12, Adams, New Haven.
Gowan Henry, 3, Wayne, Fort Wayne.
Graber Daniel, 3, Milan, Harlan.
Graber Jacob, Milan, Chamberlain.
Graber John, 5, Milan, Chamberlain.
Graber Victor, 3, Milan, Harlan.
Grabner John, Jackson, Baldwin.
Grade Louis, 21, Jefferson, Maples.
Gradel V, 11, Aboit, Fort Wayne.
Graham Charles, 21, Wayne, Fort Wayne.
Graham E, Jackson, Edgerton.
Graham Grant, 21, Wayne, Fort Wayne.
Graham Jacob, 21, Wayne, Fort Wayne.
Graham James, 21, Wayne, Fort Wayne.
Graham Robert, 4, Eel River, Ari.
Graham Samuel, 18, Monroe, Monroeville.
Graham Wm, 21, Wayne, Fort Wayne.
Grant George, 6, Adams, Fort Wayne.
Grate Anthony, 9, Springfield, Spencerville.
Graves George J, 11, Springfield, Spencerville.
Gray Ferdinand, 26, Washington, Fort Wayne.
Grayless Charles, 18, Lake, Arcola.
Grayless George, 4, Lake, Heller's Corners.
Grayless James, 18, Lake, Arcola.
Greek Dallas, 30, Pleasant, Sheldon.
Green Chester, 22, Lafayette, Zanesville.
Green Elisha W, 12, Adams, New Haven.
Green Henry, 9, Eel River, Ari.
Green Judson, Perry, Huntertown.
Green N B, 12, Adams, New Haven.
Green Silas, 12, Adams, New Haven.
Greenawalt Charles, 8, Scipio, Hicksville, O.
Greenawalt Edward, 17, Eel River, Heller's Corners.
Greenawalt John, 8, Scipio, Hicksville, O.
Greenawalt Oliver J, 17, Springfield, Harlan.
Greenfield E, 29-30, Eel River, Heller's Corners.
Greenwell C L, 11-14, Eel River, Huntertown.

Greenwell Frank, Perry, Huntertown.
Greenwell George, 15, Eel River, Huntertown.
Greer J H, 13, Wayne, Fort Wayne.
Greer Thomas, 5, Pleasant, Nine Mile.
Greer Wm, 5, Pleasant, Nine Mile.
Gregg Austin W, Jackson, Dawkins.
Gregg Squire, 19, Lafayette, Myhart.
Gremaux Victor, Jackson, Monroeville.
Gresley John, 13, Marion, Hoagland.
Gresley John A, 27, Madison, Hoagland.
Gresley John E, 13, Marion, Hoagland.
Gresley Noah, 13, Marion, Hoagland.
Gresley Peter, 28, Madison, Hoagland.
Grider David, 2, Pleasant, Fort Wayne.
Grider Finley C, 2, Pleasant, Fort Wayne.
Grider John C, 3, Wayne, Fort Wayne.
Grider Jesse W, 2, Pleasant, Fort Wayne.
Grider Martin, 10, Pleasant, Nine Mile.
Grider Samuel, 3-4, Wayne, Fort Wayne.
Grider Wm, 2, Pleasant, Fort Wayne.
Griebel Fred, 16, St. Joseph, Fort Wayne.
Griebel George, 11, Marion, Soest.
Griebel Louis, 14, Marion, Hoagland.
Griebel Wm, 11, Marion, Soest.
Grieser Frank, 8, Marion, Fort Wayne.
Grieser Henry, 8, Marion, Fort Wayne.
Griff Frank, 12, St Joseph, Goeglien.
Griff Frank jr, 12, St Joseph, Goeglien.
Griff James, 12, St Joseph, Goeglien.
Griff Leslie, 12, St Joseph, Goeglien.
Griffin Alanson C, 2, Perry, Collingwood.
Griffin John E, 2, Perry, Collingwood.
Griffith Henry W, 18, Eel River, Churubusco.
Griffith John, 16, Monroe, Monroeville.
Griffith Louis, 34, Eel River, Heller's Corners.
Griffith Thomas, 16, Monroe, Monroeville.
Griffith Wm, 16, Monroe, Monroeville.
Grill Albert, 5, Springfield, Spencerville.

Grill Isaac, 4, Springfield, Spencerville.
Grill Jacob, 5, Springfield, Spencerville.
Grill Samuel H, 4, Springfield, Spencerville.
Grim Christian, 11-14, Eel River, Huntertown.
Grim William, Perry, Huntertown.
Grimm Charles, 4, Eel River, Ari.
Grimm Charles, 31, Jefferson, Maples.
Grimm Perry, 10, Eel River, Ari.
Griswold Edward, 5, Washington, Wallen.
Griswold George, 6, Washington, Fort Wayne.
Griswold Joseph, 5, Washington, Wallen.
Griswold R A, 5, Washington, Wallen.
Grodeaux Charles, 22, Jefferson, Maples.
Grodeaux Elias, 22, Jefferson, Maples.
Grodeaux Louis, 22, Jefferson, Maples.
Grodot Jule, 12, Jefferson, Dawkins.
Grodrian August, 8, Madison, Maples.
Grodrian Charles, 17, Madison, Hoagland.
Grodrian Charles, 6, Madison, Maples.
Grodrian Fred, 17, Madison, Hoagland.
Grodrian Louis, 8, Madison, Maples.
Grodrian Wm, 8, Madison, Maples.
Gromeaux Andrew, Lafayette, Nine Mile.
Gromeaux Arsene, 24, Jefferson, Zulu.
Gromeaux Frank, 24, Jefferson, Zulu.
Gronaur George, 6, Jefferson, New Haven.
Gronaur George, 20, Marion, Poe.
Gronmiller George, 14, Lake, Fort Wayne.
Grosh David, 21, Aboit, Fort Wayne.
Grosh Isaac, 11, Cedar Creek, Leo.
Grosjean Adolph, 1, Washington, St. Vincent.
Grosjean Aristide, 4, Washington, Wallen.
Grosjean Edward J, 12, Washington, Fort Wayne.
Grosjean Felix, 4, Washington, Wallen.
Grosjean John, 28, Lake, Arcola.
Grosjean John B, 4, Washington, Wallen.
Grosjean Julian, 28, Lake, Arcola.
Gross Curt, 20, Lake, Arcola.
Gross John, 19, Lake, Arcola.
Grotian Will, 34, Jefferson, Monroeville.

Groutman Henry, 34, Adams, Soest.
Grover Albert H, 17, Jefferson, New Haven.
Grover Frank, 20, Jefferson, New Haven.
Grover I, 17, Jefferson, New Haven.
Grover Nathaniel, 20, Jefferson, New Haven.
Grover Samuel, 17, Jefferson, New Haven.
Grover Sidney, 7, Maumee, Woodburn.
Grover Van, 17, Jefferson, New Haven.
Grubb Charles, 5, Springfield, Harlan.
Grubb Ira, 21, Springfield, Harlan.
Grubb Jacob, 16, Milan, Chamberlain.
Gruber Christian, 23, Springfield, Halls Corners.
Gruber Daniel, 30, Madison, Hoagland.
Gruber Henry, 12, Adams, New Haven.
Gruber John, 17, Lafayette, Myhart.
Gruber John, 12, Milan, Harlan.
Gruber Milton, 7, Scipio, Halls Corners.
Gruber Wm, 23, Springfield, Halls Corners.
Guerley John, 12, Adams, New Haven.
Guertlet Henry, 34, Lake, Arcola.
Guiff, see also Juiff.
Guiff Lester, 12, Milan, Harlan.
Guiff Victor, 33, Perry, Fort Wayne.
Guillaumme Florenz L, Adams, New Haven.
Guion Frank, 14, Madison, Monroeville.
Guion John, 32, Jefferson, Maples.
Gumbert Charles, 28, Adams, Soest.
Gumbert J, 33, Adams, Fort Wayne.
Gump, see also Jump.
Gump Albert, 8-9, Eel River, Ari.
Gump Calvert, Perry, Huntertown.
Gump Ernest, 10, Eel River, Ari.
Gump George, Perry, Huntertown.
Gump Jeremiah, 9-10, Eel River, Ari.
Gump Jesse, 4, Eel River, Ari.
Gump Madison, 3, Perry, Collingwood.
Gump Marion, Perry, Huntertown.
Gump Perry, 3, Perry, Collingwood.
Gunder Charles, 16, Washington, Fort Wayne.
Gunder George, 12, Adams, New Haven.

Gunder George, 16, Washington, Fort Wayne.
Gundy W H, 28, Aboit, Aboit.
Gunther Albert, 32, Springfield, Harlan.
Gunther Daniel, 32, Springfield, Harlan.
Gunther Wm, 32, Springfield, Harlan.
Gussy August, 26, Washington, Fort Wayne.
Gustin Harvey, 32, Scipio, Harlan.
Gustin James, 10, Maumee, Antwerp, O.
Gustin Marion, 32, Scipio, Harlan.
Gustin Milo, 32, Scipio, Harlan.
Gustin Oliver, 10, Springfield, Harlan.
Gutermuth Henry, 18, Pleasant, Nine Mile.
Guyer Charles, 7, Monroe, Monroeville.
Guyer Robert, 7, Monroe, Monroeville.

H

Habecker John, 17, Adams, Fort Wayne.
Habecker Martin, 17, Adams, Fort Wayne
Haddenchild John, 27, Marion, Hoagland.
Haffner John, 33, Lake, Arcola.
Haffner Moses, 33, Lake, Arcola.
Hagen John, 15, Lake, Arcola.
Hagen Wm, 15, Lake, Arcola.
Haiber Charles, Jackson, Baldwin.
Haiber John, 20, Marion, Poe.
Haifly George, 17, Springfield, Harlan.
Haifly Harvey, 18, Springfield, Harlan.
Haifly John B, 7, Springfield, Harlan.
Haifly J W, 16, Springfield, Harlan.
Haifly Simon P, 16, Springfield, Harlan.
Haifly U, 15, Milan, Harlan.
Hailer Alfred, 26, Aboit, Fort Wayne.
Haines Wm, 9, Aboit, Fort Wayne.
Haines Wm, 12, Adams, New Haven.
Haining George, 35, Eel River, Heller's Corners.
Hake Frank, 24, Marion, Hoagland.
Hake George, 14, Marion, Hoagland.
Hake Jacob, 14, Marion, Hoagland.
Hake Samuel, 19, Marion, Poe.

Hale Ellsworth, 31, Cedar Creek, Cedarville.
Hale Al, 18, Milan, Thurman.
Hall Ervin, 13, Springfield, Harlan.
Hall Francis, 26, Milan, Gar Creek.
Hall Putnam, 26, Milan, Gar Creek.
Hall Wm, 18-19, Milan, Thurman.
Hall Wm, 9, Monroe, Monroeville.
Hallien George, 19, Pleasant, Nine Mile.
Hallien John, 21, St Joseph, Ft Wayne.
Hallien Wm, 19, Pleasant, Nine Mile.
Halminger F H, 17, Aboit, Ft Wayne.
Halminger Wm, 17, Aboit, Ft Wayne.
Halter Edward, 32, Cedar Creek, Cedarville.
Halter Henry, 28, Cedar Creek, Cedarville.
Hamilton James, 28, Lafayette, Zanesville.
Hamilton John, Jackson, Dawkins.
Hamilton Michael C, 33, Lafayette, Zanesville.
Hamilton M F, 12, Adams, New Haven.
Hamilton Thomas, 22, Washington, Ft Wayne.
Hamm Adam, 15, Cedar Creek, Leo.
Hammond Charles, 31, Jefferson, Maples.
Hammond Michael, 12, Jefferson, Dawkins.
Hammond Wm, 9, Madison, Maples.
Hamshild Henry, 21-22, Milan, Thurman.
Hand George W, 29-30, Eel River, Wallen.
Hand J, 8, Scipio, Hicksville, O.
Hand Wm, 29-30, Eel River, Wallen.
Hanefeld Wm, 12, Adams, New Haven.
Hanes Perry, 5, Washington, Wallen.
Hansen Will, 15, Washington, Ft Wayne.
Harber Adam, 21, Pleasant, Sheldon.
Harber Casper, 22, Pleasant, Sheldon.
Harber Daniel, 17, Pleasant, Nine Mile.
Harber Francis, 15, Pleasant, Nine Mile.
Harber George, 16, Pleasant, Nine Mile.
Harber Gerhard, 10, Pleasant, Nine Mile.
Harber Henry, 21, Pleasant, Sheldon.
Harber Jacob, 21, Pleasant, Sheldon.
Harber James, 21, Pleasant, Sheldon.
Harber John, 15, Pleasant, Nine Mile.

Harber John Jr, 20, Pleasant, Nine Mile.
Harber Michael, 7, Pleasant, Nine Mile.
Harddarp Ira, 5, Adams, Ft Wayne.
Hardesty Bowman, 3, Springfield, Harlan.
Hardesty Edward, 29, Cedar Creek, Cedarville.
Hardesty Gilbert, 19, Cedar Creek, Cedarville.
Hardesty John, 29, Cedar Creek, Cedarville.
Hardesty Lucas, 9, Springfield, Harlan.
Harding Robert, 24, St Joseph, Thurman.
Harding John H, 18-19, Milan, Thurman.
Hare Arthur, 1, Springfield, Harlan.
Hare Charles, 3, Wayne, Ft Wayne.
Hare Gilmore, 1, Springfield, Harlan.
Hare Walter, 4, Washington, Wallen.
Hargrave H B, 11, Adams, Ft Wayne.
Hargrave Wm, 11, Adams, New Haven.
Harlow G A, 11, Adams, New Haven.
Harlow James, 12, Adams, New Haven.
Harlow Jesse, 11, Adams, New Haven.
Harlow, Joseph, 12, Adams, New Haven.
Harman George, 26, Milan, Gar Creek.
Harman Henry, 35, Milan, Gar Creek.
Harmeyer H, 14, Washington, Ft Wayne.
Harmon E, 28, Springfield, Harlan.
Harmon Fred, 3, Marion, Fort Wayne.
Harper Edward, 12, Adams, New Haven.
Harper Hamilton, 11, Jefferson, Dawkins.
Harper John, 32, Milan, Gar Creek.
Harper Joseph, Jackson, Edgerton.
Harper J W, 7, Aboit, Dunfee.
Harper Robert, 5, Jefferson, New Haven.
Harper Wm, Jackson, Edgerton.
Harper Wm, 32, Milan, Gar Creek.
Harrigan Henry, 10, Pleasant, Nine Mile.
Harrigan John, 10, Pleasant, Nine Mile.
Harrington C, 14, Adams, New Haven.
Harrington Henry, 12, Adams, New Haven.
Harris George, 5, Marion, Fort Wayne.
Harris R B, 9, Milan, Chamberlain.
Harrison Albert D, 7, Aboit, Dunfee.

Harrod C E, 19, Madison, Hoagland.
Harrod Enos, 19, Madison, Hoagland.
Harrod Joseph, 19, Madison, Hoagland.
Harrod Miles, 29, Marion, Poe.
Harrod Morgan, 19, Madison, Hoagland.
Harrold Frank, 33, Lake, Arcola.
Harrold J W, 33, Lake, Arcola.
Hart Fred, 11, Adams, New Haven.
Hart George, Jackson, Edgerton.
Hart Johnston, 16, Monroe, Monroeville.
Hart Oliver, 15, Monroe, Monroeville.
Hart Oscar, 24, Springfield, Hall's Corners.
Hart Wayne, 10, Monroe, Monroeville.
Hartell Harvey, 7, Scipio, Hall's Corners.
Harter Arthur, 12, Springfield, Georgetown.
Harter Isaac, 12, Springfield, Georgetown.
Harter Louis, 18, Wayne, Fort Wayne.
Harter Michael, 10, Cedar Creek, Leo.
Harter Perry, 18, Eel River, Heller's Corners.
Harter Perry, 19, Eel River, Heller's Croners.
Harter Wm H, 12, Springfield, Georgetown.
Hartman August, 11, Jefferson, Dawkins.
Hartman David, 16, Lafayette, Myhart.
Hartman George, 9, Adams, Fort Wayne.
Hartman George, 4, Lafayette, Aboit.
Hartman Henry, 16, Adams, Fort Wayne.
Hartman Henry jr, 16, Adams, Fort Wayne.
Hartman James, 2, Marion, Soest.
Hartman James jr, 2, Marion, Soest.
Hartman John, 11, Jefferson, Dawkins.
Hartman John, 3, Jefferson, Gar Creek.
Hartman John, 2, Marion, Soest.
Hartman Wm, 9, Adams, Fort Wayne.
Hartz John, 14, Lake, Fort Wayne.
Hartz S W, 3, Wayne, Fort Wayne.
Hartzell A M, 12, Adams, New Haven.
Hartzell Charles, 1, Springfield, Harlan.
Hartzell Elias, 27, Marion, Hoagland.
Hartzell Frank, 6, Springfield, Harlan.
Hartzell F, 15, Adams, New Haven.

Hartzell F jr, 15, Adams, New Haven.
Hartzell James, 14, Adams, New Haven.
Hartzell John, 14, Adams, New Haven.
Hartzell Warren, 11, Adams, New Haven.
Harvant Theo, 31, Jefferson, Maples.
Harvey Aaron, 1, Madison, Monroeville.
Harvey Calvin, 10, Cedar Creek, Leo.
Harvey John, Cedar Creek, Hursh.
Hass E, 28, Pleasant, Sheldon.
Hass F, 28, Pleasant, Sheldon.
Hass Henry, 22, Lafayette, Zanesville.
Hassart B, 30, Washington, Fort Wayne.
Hasselman De Witt, Jackson, Baldwin.
Hasselman Henry, Jackson, Baldwin.
Hassler Frank, 15, Cedar Creek, Leo.
Hassler Henry, 10, Cedar Creek, Leo.
Hassler John, 10, Cedar Creek, Leo.
Haswell A M, Perry, Collingwood.
Hatch Arthur, 12, Eel River, Huntertown.
Hatch Emmet, Perry, Huntertown.
Hatch F, 22, Pleasant, Sheldon.
Hatch Louis L, 23, Pleasant, Sheldon.
Hatch Newton N, Perry, Huntertown.
Hatch S B, 12, Eel River, Huntertown.
Hatfield Clarke, 11, Aboit, Fort Wayne.
Hatfield D, 22, Aboit, Fort Wayne.
Hatfield F, 19, Aboit, Saturn.
Hatfield James, 21, Washington, Fort Wayne.
Hatfield John, 13, Milan, Harlan.
Hathaway Bert, 8, Wayne, Fort Wayne.
Hathaway Frank, 9, Eel River, Ari.
Hathaway James, 22, Eel River, Heller's Corners.
Hathaway John, 8, Wayne, FortWayne.
Hathaway Joseph, 12, Adams, New Haven.
Hathaway Philip, 22, Eel River, Heller's Corners.
Hathaway N, 26, Eel River, Wallen.
Hathaway Thomas, 12, Adams, New Haven.
Hawk David, 10, Maumee, Antwerp, O.
Hawk Theo, 26, Washington, Fort Wayne.
Hawk Zachariah, 10, Maumee, Antwerp, O.

Haylett Wm, 18-19, Milan, Thurman.
Haynes Henry, 7, Aboit, Dunfee.
Haynes Patrick, 24, Aboit, Fort Wayne.
Hays Charles, 21, Lake, Arcola.
Hays Daniel, 21, Lafayette, Myhart.
Hays John, 1, Cedar Creek, Hursh.
Hays Wm, 14, Madison, Monroeville.
Hazen Martin, 9, Washington, Wallen.
Hazen Warren, 11, Adams, Fort Wayne.
Hazen Wm, 15, Eel River, Heller's Corners.
Hazer Henry, 12, Adams, New Haven.
Hazerfelt Fred, 28, Madison, Hoagland.
Hazlett Charles, 18-19 Milan, Thurman.
Hazlett John, 13, St Joseph, Thurman.
Hazlett Thomas, 12, Adams, New Haven.
Hazzard Wm jr, 8, Wayne, Fort Wayne.
Headman Mark, 35, Lake, Arcola.
Heath Kent, 18-19, Milan, Thurman.
Heath Stephen, 8, Milan, Chamberlain.
Heaton E J, 28, Marion, Poe.
Heck Joseph, 3, Monroe, Baldwin.
Heckbur Frank, 27, Pleasant, Sheldon.
Heckert David S, 2, Monroe, Monroeville.
Heckler John, Jackson, Baldwin.
Heckman Edward, 16, Maumee, Woodburn.
Heff Bernard, 23, Eel River, Heller's Corners.
Heff George, 23, Eel River, Heller's Corners.
Heff Martin, 23, Eel River, Heller's Corners.
Heffelboner Christian, 21, Lafayette, Myhart.
Heffelfinger Chaney, 16, Eel River, Heller's Corners.
Heffelfinger Jeremiah, 16, Eel River, Heller's Corners.
Heffelfinger John, 16, Eel River, Heller's Corners.
Heffelfinger Sherman, 36, Eel River, Wallen.
Heiber Charles, 4, Eel River, Ari.
Heiber George, 4, Eel River, Ari.
Heiber Herman, 16, Lafayette, Myhart.
Heiber Jacob, 3, Eel River, Ari.
Heidelbrecht Henry, Jackson, Edgerton.
Heidenrich August, 28, Washington, Fort Wayne.

Heidenrich Jacob, 28, Washington, Fort Wayne.
Heine August, 18, Jefferson, New Haven.
Heine Christian, 13, Adams, New Haven.
Heine Frederick, 17, Adams, Fort Wayne.
Heine Frederick, 19, Jefferson, Maples.
Heine Frederick jr, 17, Adams, Fort Wayne.
Heine Henry W, 18, Jefferson, New Haven.
Heintzelman Andrew, 8, Wayne, Fort Wayne.
Heintzelman John, 31, Washington, Fort Wayne.
Helle August, Jackson, Edgerton.
Hellerman Joseph, 20, Washington, Fort Wayne.
Hellworth John, 1, Adams, New Haven.
Hellworth Michael, 1, Adams, New Haven.
Helmick Christian, 31, Jefferson, Maples.
Helmick Frank, 1, Adams, New Haven.
Helmick Fred, 31, Jefferson, Maples.
Helmick H C, 18, Jefferson, New Haven.
Hemerick Andrew, 4, Springfield, Spencerville.
Hemille Frederick, 8, St Joseph, Fort Wayne.
Henderson G W, 30, Cedar Creek, Cedarville.
Henderson James A, 17, Springfield, Harlan.
Hendrick Anthony, 27, Lake, Arcola.
Hendrickson George, Lake, Arcola.
Henline George, 14, Lake, Arcola.
Henline George, 7, Washington, Fort Wayne.
Henline Michael, 13, Lake, Fort Wayne.
Henry Frank, 13, St Joseph, Thurman.
Henry James, 14, St Joseph, Fort Wayne.
Henry John, 14, St Joseph, Fort Wayne.
Henry Moses, 19, Madison, Hoagland.
Henry Peter, 13, St Joseph, Thurman.
Henry Samuel, 14, Pleasant, Fort Wayne.
Henry Wm, 14, Pleasant, Fort Wayne.
Henschen Ernst, 13, Washington, Fort Wayne.
Henschen Frederick J, 14, Washington, Fort Wayne.
Henschen Henry, 2, Aboit, Fort Wayne.
Hensil M, 13, Aboit, Fort Wayne.
Hensinger Harris, 11, Perry, Collingwood.
Hensinger John, 11, Perry, Collingwood.
Hensinger Michael, 6, Cedar Creek, Collingwood.

Herber Anthony, 16, Marion, Fort Wayne.
Herber Frank, 20, Marion, Poe.
Herber Nicholas, 21, Marion, Poe.
Herber Samuel, 6, Marion, Fort Wayne.
Herlinger J W, 35, Jefferson, Monroeville.
Herlinger W H, 35, Jefferson, Monroeville.
Herman Adolph, 26, St Joseph, Goeglien.
Herman Diedrich, 17, Marion, Fort Wayne.
Herman Henry, 17, Marion, Fort Wayne.
Herman Henry, 26, St Joseph, Goeglien.
Herman Jacob, 9, Madison, Maples.
Herman Valentine, 26, St Joseph, Goeglien.
Herman Wm, 17, Marion, Fort Wayne.
Hermick Wm, 11, Springfield, Spencerville.
Heron John, 24, Springfield, Hall's Corners.
Herrian Peter, 3, Eel River, Ari.
Herrick Andrew, 3, Springfield, Harlan.
Herrick Daniel, 7, Scipio, Hall's Corners.
Herrick De Graff, 35, Springfield, Harlan.
Herrick Frank, 1, Springfield, Harlan.
Herrick Horace, 35, Springfield, Harlan.
Herrick Scott, 18-19, Milan, Thurman.
Herrin James, 10, Cedar Creek, Leo.
Herrin John, 11, Cedar Creek, Leo.
Herrin Roth, 11, Cedar Creek, Leo.
Herrod Wm, 30, Madison, Hoagland.
Herven James, 27-28, Eel River, Heller's Corners.
Hess Charles, 3, Lake, Heller's Corners.
Hetrick M, Maumee, Woodburn.
Hettinger Emanuel, 14, Springfield, Harlan.
Hibler Barney, 27, Washington, Fort Wayne.
Hibler John, 36, Wayne, Fort Wayne.
Hibler John jr, 36, Wayne, Fort Wayne.
Hibler Michael, 27, Washington, Fort Wayne.
Hickman Edward, 17, Aboit, Fort Wayne.
Hickman W, 17, Aboit, Fort Wayne.
Higgins Charles, 9, Springfield, Harlan.
Higgins Morris, 24, Springfield, Hall's Corners.
Higgins Wales, 24, Springfield, Hall's Corners.
Higgs M, 28, Pleasant, Sheldon.

High Daniel, 29, Marion, Poe.
Highland James, 36, Jefferson, Zulu.
Hild Dayton, 1, Madison, Monroeville.
Hildebrand August, 10, Marion, Soest.
Hildebrand Wm, 9, Marion, Fort Wayne.
Hiler Sebathiel, 17, Aboit, Fort Wayne.
Hilke Lynas, 11-14, Eel River, Huntertown.
Hill Adam D, 12, Lafayette, Nine Mile.
Hill C S, 23, Monroe, Monroeville.
Hill Jacob, 5, Lafayette, Aboit.
Hill John, 12, Jefferson, Dawkins.
Hill Nathan, 24, Milan, Gar Creek.
Hiller Louis, 23, Lake, Arcola.
Hiller Wm, 23, Lake, Arcola.
Hilligass Hezekiah, 8, Perry, Huntertown.
Hilligass Jacob, 19, Perry, Huntertown.
Hilligass Robert, 8, Perry, Huntertown.
Himbert John, 17, Milan, Thurman.
Hines George W, 27-28, Eel River, Heller's Corners.
Hines Samuel, Jackson, Edgerton.
Hinnen Francis, 14, Pleasant, Fort Wayne.
Hinney Wm, 5, Jefferson, New Haven.
Hintzman Addison, 31, Lake, Arcola.
Hippenhamer Charles, 4, Washington, Wallen.
Hippenhamer George, Perry, Huntertown.
Hippenhamer Israel, Perry, Huntertown.
Hippenhamer John, Perry, Huntertown.
Hippenhamer Samuel, 4, Washington, Wallen.
Hire Augustus, 33, Lake, Arcola.
Hire Charles, 33, Lake, Arcola.
Hire Elisha, 3, Lake, Heller's Corners.
Hirkendasa James, 28, Eel River, Heller's Corners.
Hirner Fred, 33, Jefferson, Monroeville.
Hirsch Hiram, 19, Cedar Creek, Cedarville.
Hirsch John, 28, Springfield, Harlan.
Hirsch Joseph, 21, Cedar Creek, Cedarville.
Hiser Arthur, 19, Lafayette, Myhart.
Hiser Daniel, 29, Aboit, Aboit.
Hiser David, 26, Pleasant, Sheldon.
Hiser Fred, 19, Lafayette, Myhart.

Hiser George, 25, Pleasant, Poe. •
Hiser George, 4, Wayne, Fort Wayne.
Hiser Henry, 29, Aboit, Aboit.
Hiser Jacob, 4, Wayne, Fort Wayne.
Hiser John, Lafayette, Aboit.
Hiser J B, 19, Lafayette, Myhart.
Hiser Wm, Lafayette, Aboit.
Hiser Wm, 33, Wayne, Fort Wayne.
Hisner John, 5, Madison, Maples.
Hissing David, 32, Scipio, Harlan.
Hite Charles, 12, Lafayette, Nine Mile.
Hite Ernest, 36, Marion, Williams Station.
Hite George, 31, Jefferson, Maples.
Hite John, 32, Jefferson, Maples.
Hite Joseph, 1, Washington, St Vincent.
Hittinger Henry, 1, Springfield, Harlan.
Hitzeman Fred, 31, Washington, Fort Wayne.
Hitzeman Frederick, 36, Marion, Williams Station.
Hitzeman Henry, 31, Washington, Fort Wayne.
Hobbs Christian, 21, Lafayette, Myhart.
Hobbs Henry, 16, Milan, Chamberlain.
Hobbs Wm, 16, Milan, Chamberlain.
Hobson Jacob, 31, St Joseph, Fort Wayne.
Hobson Lafayette, 31, St Joseph, Fort Wayne.
Hobson Walter, 31, St Joseph, Fort Wayne.
Hockemeyer Charles, 28, Milan, Gar Creek.
Hockemeyer Charles, 25, Wayne, Fort Wayne.
Hockemeyer Frederick, 28, Adams, Soest.
Hockemeyer Frederick, 27, Madison, Hoagland.
Hockemeyer Frederick, 8, Marion, Fort Wayne.
Hockemeyer Herman, 28, Madison, Hoagland.
Hockemeyer Wm, 27, Madison, Hoagland.
Hockemeyer Wm, 30, Washington, Fort Wayne.
Hoewson H G, 11, Monroe, Monroeville.
Hoffman, see also Huffman.
Hoffman Christian, 21, Monroe, Monroeville.
Hoffman Conrad, 21, St Joseph, Fort Wayne.
Hoffman George, 21, Monroe, Monroeville.
Hoffman Henry, 22, Adams, Fort Wayne.
Hoffman John, 21, Monroe, Monroeville.

5

Hoffman Wm, 18, Cedar Creek, Collingwood.
Hoffmeyer Conrad, 32, St Joseph, Fort Wayne.
Hoffmeyer Wm, 23, Lake, Arcola.
Hogue James, Perry, Huntertown.
Hoke John H, 10, Pleasant, Nine Mile.
Hoke Warren, 10, Pleasant, Nine Mile.
Hollie Frederick, 5, Marion, Fort Wayne.
Hollopeter Avery, 13, Springfield, Harlan.
Hollopeter Charles, 28, Cedar Creek, Cedarville.
Hollopeter Charles, 22, Eel River, Heller's Corners.
Hollopeter Clarence, 21, Cedar Creek, Cedarville.
Hollopeter Cyrus, 13, Springfield, Harlan.
Hollopeter George W, 28, Cedar Creek, Cedarville.
Hollopeter Hiram, 9, Cedar Creek, Leo.
Hollopeter Hiram, Scipio, Harlan.
Hollopeter Huron, 22, Eel River, Heller's Corners.
Hollopeter H J, 34-35, Jackson, Baldwin.
Hollopeter Israel, 22, Eel River, Heller's Corners.
Hollopeter John, 8, Springfield, Harlan.
Hollopeter Marion, 15, Cedar Creek, Collingwood.
Hollopeter Martin, 17, St Joseph, Fort Wayne.
Hollopeter Matthias, 28, Cedar Creek, Cedarville.
Hollopeter Seth, 21, Cedar Creek, Cedarville.
Hollopeter Wm C, 7, Cedar Creek, Collingwood.
Hollopeter Wm H, 19, Cedar Creek, Cedarville.
Holman Edward, 7, Jefferson, New Haven.
Holman Frederick, 6, Madison, Fort Wayne.
Holman John, 6, Marion, Fort Wayne.
Holman Wm, 13, St Joseph, Thurman.
Holmes John W, 34, Eel River, Wallen.
Holmes Rolland, 6, Wayne, Fort Wayne.
Holsattle B T, 28, Jackson, Monroeville.
Holsattle Wm S, 28, Jackson, Monroeville.
Holstine John, 28, Washington, Fort Wayne.
Holt A H, 16, Lake, Arcola.
Holt Thomas, 20, Springfield, Harlan.
Holt Thomas, 24, Springfield, Hall's Corners.
Holt Wm, 10, Madison, Maples.
Holt Wm F, 17, Lake, Arcola.
Holten Dr, Perry, Huntertown.

Holverstott Wm, 33, Lafayette, Zanesville.
Holzworth Daniel, 10, Springfield, Harlan.
Holzworth John, 14, Springfield, Harlan.
Honkel John, 34, Adams, Soest.
Hood Charles, 12, Adams, New Haven.
Hood Frank, 29-30, Eel River, Heller's Corners.
Hood H Y ,3, Springfield, Harlan.
Hood Joseph, 12, Adams, New Haven.
Hood Joseph, 29-30, Eel River, Heller's Corners.
Hood Thomas, 5, Springfield, Harlan.
Hood Walter, 5, Springfield, Harlan.
Hoopingarner Solomon, 32, Lafayette, Zanesville.
Hoovel Henry, 19, Adams, Fort Wayne.
Hoovel Wm, 21, Adams, Fort Wayne.
Hoover Wm, 32, Scipio, Harlan.
Hoppe Frederick, 36, Marion, Williams Station.
Hoppe Henry, 36, Marion, Williams Station.
Hoppe Henry, 6, Maumee, Harlan.
Hopple Edward, 2, Lake, Heller's Corners.
Horn Frank, 18, Springfield, Harlan.
Horn Frank, 5, Springfield, Spencerville.
Horn George, 8, Springfield, Harlan.
Horn Henry, 15, Springfield, Harlan.
Horn Henry, 5-6, Springfield, Spencerville.
Horn John, 10, Cedar Creek, Leo.
Horn John, 21, Springfield, Harlan.
Horn Moses, 10, Cedar Creek, Leo.
Horn Nathan, Lafayette, Zanesville.
Horney W C, 15, Cedar Creek, Leo.
Houk Edwin, 11, Perry, Collingwood.
Houk John, Perry, Collingwood.
Houk John, Perry, Huntertown.
Houk Lee, 33, Madison, Bingen.
Houk Newton, 23, Madison, Monroeville.
Houk Samuel, 32, Madison, Bingen.
House Jeddish, 12, Eel River, Huntertown.
House John, 15, Springfield, Harlan.
Housemann Charles, 26, Washington, Fort Wayne.
Houser Albert, 22, Washington, Fort Wayne.
Houser Charles, 19, Madison, Hoagland.

Houser David, 29, Marion, Poe.
Houser Henry L, 20, Adams, Fort Wayne.
Houser James, 19, Madison, Hoagland.
Houser Michael, 22, Washington, Fort Wayne.
Houser Washington, 11-14, Eel River, Huntertown.
Howard A P, Jackson, Edgerton.
Howard W P, 7, Monroe, Monroeville.
Howe Estes, 4, Springfield, Harlan.
Howe Ezra, 3, Springfield, Harlan.
Howe Frederick, 19, Madison, Hoagland.
Howe George, 15, Jackson, Edgerton.
Howe George, 22, Jackson, Monroeville.
Howe John, 13, Madison, Monroeville.
Howell John, 26, Lafayette, Zanesville.
Hubbard Mikerson, 2, Washington, St Vincent.
Hubler John F, 19, Washington, Fort Wayne.
Hubler Peter, 20, Washington, Fort Wayne.
Hudson James, 8, Jefferson, New Haven.
Hudson Reuben, 8, Jefferson, New Haven.
Hue Garton, 29, Marion, Poe.
Huffman, see also Hoffman.
Huffman Edward, 2, Pleasant, Fort Wayne.
Huffman Frank, 11, Marion, Soest.
Huffman Frederick, 10, Madison, Maples.
Huffman George, 6, Madison, Maples.
Huffman George, 35, Springfield, Harlan.
Huffman George jr, 35, Springfield, Harlan.
Huffman Gideon, 35, Springfield, Harlan.
Huffman Henry, 10, Madison, Maples.
Huffman Jacob, 11, Marion, Soest.
Huffman John, 10, Madison, Maples.
Huffman John jr, 2, Madison, Monroeville.
Huffman Martin, 10, Madison, Maples.
Huffman Nicholas, 10, Madison, Maples.
Huffman Nicholas jr, 2, Madison, Monroeville.
Huguenard Alexander, 4, Washington, Wallen.
Huguenard August, 1, Aboit, Fort Wayne.
Huguenard August, 9, Washington, Wallen.
Huguenard Edward, Jefferson, Dawkins.
Huguenard Felecine, 10, Jefferson, Dawkins.

ALLEN COUNTY DIRECTORY.   879

Huguenard Felix, 9, Washington, Wallen.
Huguenard Frank, 9, Washington, Wallen.
Hull Adam, 19-20, Eel River, Hiller's Corners.
Hull Charles E, 29-30, Eel River, Heller's Corners.
Hull Henry, 19-20, Eel River, Heller's Corners.
Hull Robert, 20, Cedar Creek, Cedarville.
Hull S P, 29-30, Eel River, Heller's Corners.
Hull Timothy, 31, Eel River, Heller's Corners.
Hull Wm, 11, Monroe, Monroeville.
Humbert Frank, 9, Washington, Wallen.
Humbert George, 5, Eel River, Ari.
Humbert Jesse, 16, Jefferson, New Haven.
Humbert Joseph, 20, Jefferson, New Haven.
Hunsted Al, 1, Springfield, Harlan.
Hunt James, 10, Cedar Creek, Leo.
Hunter Cardel, Perry, Huntertown.
Hunter J C, 30-31, Perry, Huntertown.
Hurd Henry, 3, Springfield, Harlan.
Hursh Adam, 1, Cedar Creek, Hursh.
Hursh Christian, 3, Springfield, Harlan.
Hursh James, 5, Cedar Creek, Collingwood.
Hursh John W, 13, Perry, Leo.
Hursh J S, 20, Monroe, Monroeville.
Hursh Sine, 24, Perry, Cedarville.
Hursh S, 1, Cedar Creek, Hursh.
Hursh West, 24, Perry, Cedarville.
Husted George W, 3, Maumee, Antwerp, O.
Husted Louis B, 3, Maumee, Antwerp, O.
Hute F, 23, Aboit, Fort Wayne.
Hutker Bernard, 15, Milan, Harlan.
Hutler Frank, 26, Marion, Hoagland.
Hutler John, 21, Washington, Fort Wayne.
Hutler Peter, 21, Washington, Fort Wayne.
Hutson Reuben, 5, Jefferson, New Haven.
Hutton J B, 4, Eel River.
Hyatt Frank, 12, Eel River, Huntertown.
Hyde Cornelius, 36, Pleasant, Sheldon.
Hyde Emmet, Jefferson, Maples.
Hyde Frederick, 36, Pleasant, Sheldon.
Hyndman G B, 29-30, Eel River, Churubusco.

Hyndman Joseph, 19-20, Eel River, Heller's Corners.
Hyndman Nelson, 18, Eel River, Churubusco.
Hypers John, Jackson, Edgerton.

I

Idenberg Frederick, 21, Madison, Hoagland.
Idenberg Wm, 21, Madison, Hoagland.
Ikenburger Jacob, 6, Pleasant, Nine Mile.
Ipelman Henry, 5, Maumee, Harlan.
Ireland Adam, Jefferson, Maples.
Ireland Cal, Jackson, Dawkins.
Ireland E H, 32, Jefferson, Maples.
Ireland John C, Jackson, Edgerton.
Irvine Joseph, 26, Jefferson, Zulu.
Irvine Peter, 26, Jefferson, Zulu.
Irwin John, 28, Lake, Arcola.
Isbell Charles, Perry, Huntertown.
Isbey George, 9, Adams, Fort Wayne.
Isbey Lewis, 9, Adams, Fort Wayne.
Isetmore John, 21, Eel River, Heller's Corners.

J

Jackmeyer Conrad, 24, Adams, New Haven.
Jackmeyer Henry, 24, Adams, New Haven.
Jackson Albert, 8, Scipio, Hicksville, O.
Jackson Arthur, 5, Scipio, Hicksville, O.
Jackson Charles, 5, Scipio, Hicksville, O.
Jackson Henry, 11, Adams, New Haven.
Jackson John, 33, Milan, Gar Creek.
Jackson John, 18, Monroe, Monroeville.
Jackson John, 8, Wayne, Fort Wayne.
Jackson John H, 29, Lafayette, Zanesville.
Jackson Joseph, 13, Madison, Monroeville.
Jackson Marion, 5, Scipio, Hicksville, O.
Jackson Martin, 12, Eel River, Huntertown.
Jackson P W, 31, Perry, Huntertown.
Jackson Silas A, 8, Wayne, Fort Wayne.
Jackson Thomas, 28, Aboit, Aboit.
Jacob Thomas, 11, Washington, Fort Wayne.

Jacobs John, 1, Wayne, Fort Wayne.
Jacquay August, 26, Jefferson, Zulu.
Jacquay Henry, 2, Adams, New Haven.
Jacquay John, 2, Adams, New Haven.
Jacquay John B, 6, Monroe, Monroeville.
Jacquay Louis, 27, Jefferson, Zulu.
James Ellis, 3, Springfield, Harlan.
James George, 3, Springfield, Harlan.
James S V, 1, Springfield, Harlan.
James Wm, 3, Springfield, Harlan.
Jaquer Louis, 29, Jefferson, Maples.
Jarrard Wm, 35, Washington, Fort Wayne.
Jennette Jacob, 36, Zulu.
Jennette James, 36, Jefferson, Zulu.
Jennette John, 36, Jefferson, Zulu.
Jennette Joseph, 36, Jefferson, Zulu.
Jennette Peter, 36, Jefferson, Zulu.
Jennings David W, 4, Eel River, Ari.
Jennings Henry, 35, Springfield, Harlan.
Jennison Curt, 23, Marion, Hoagland.
Jennison Edward, 13, Madison, Monroeville.
Jennison O E, 23, Marion, Hoagland.
Jobs James M, 20, Maumee, Woodburn.
Jobs Wm, 17, Lafayette, Myhart.
Johns Robert, 17, Wayne, Fort Wayne.
Johnson Alfred, 9, Eel River, Ari.
Johnson Benjamin, 15, Milan, Harlan.
Johnson Charles, 34, Milan, Gar Creek.
Johnson David, 27-28, Eel River, Heller's Corners.
Johnson David, 15, Milan, Harlan.
Johnson Edward, 8, Monroe, Monroeville.
Johnson Ellsworth, 35, Springfield, Harlan.
Johnson Francis A, 31, Scipio, Harlan.
Johnson Frank, 21, Eel River, Heller's Corners.
Johnson George, 7, Eel River, Churubusco.
Johnson George, 22, Springfield, Harlan.
Johnson Henry, 31, Pleasant, Sheldon.
Johnson Isaac, 9, Lake, Arcola.
Johnson Isaac, 31, Pleasant, Sheldon.
Johnson James, 6, Jefferson, New Haven.

Johnson James, 9, Lake, Arcola.
Johnson James, 35, Springfield, Harlan.
Johnson John, 25, Lafayette, Nine Mile.
Johnson John, 31, Wayne, Fort Wayne.
Johnson John F, 31, Scipio, Harlan.
Johnson Joseph B, Maumee, Woodburn.
Johnson Louis, 36, Lafayette, Zanesville.
Johnson Luther, 19-20, Eel River, Heller's Corners.
Johnson Oscar, 31, Pleasant, Sheldon.
Johnson Perry, 21, Eel River, Heller's Corners.
Johnson Richard, 9, Maumee, Woodburn.
Johnson Sherman, 7, Eel River, Churubusco.
Johnson Wesley, 19-20, Eel River, Heller's Corners.
Johnson Wm F, Maumee, Woodburn.
Johnson Wm M, 27-28, Eel River, Heller's Corners.
Jolly Francis, 23, Perry, Huntertown.
Jolly Frank, 21, Eel River, Heller's Corners.
Jolly Louis, 32, Jefferson, Maples.
Jones Benjamin, 24, Lake, Arcola.
Jones Charles, 5, Monroe, Monroeville.
Jones David, 6, Jefferson, New Haven.
Jones Daniel, 22, St Joseph, Fort Wayne.
Jones Edward, 23, Aboit, Fort Wayne.
Jones George, 5, Monroe, Monroeville.
Jones Isaac, 18, Monroe, Monroeville.
Jones John, Jackson, Edgerton.
Jones Wm, 35, Monroe, Monroeville.
Jones Wm, 36, St Joseph, New Haven.
Jordan Edward, 31, Washington, Fort Wayne.
Jordan Frank, 5, Wayne, Fort Wayne.
Jordan George, 18, Maumee, Woodburn.
Jordan Henry, 5, Wayne, Fort Wayne.
Jordan John, 5, Wayne, Fort Wayne.
Jourdain Frank, 6, Lafayette, Aboit.
Juiff, see also Guiff.
Juiff David, 32, Perry Wallen.
Juiff Francis, 29, Perry, Wallen.
Juiff John, 6-7, Eel River, Churubusco.
Juliard Louis, 30, Wayne, Fort Wayne.
Juliard Victor, 30, Wayne, Fort Wayne.

Jump, see also Gump.
Jump Ira M, Maumee, Harlan.
Jump J R, 4, Maumee, Harlan.
Jump Oscar, 4, Milan, Chamberlain.
Junk J Paul, 8, Wayne, Fort Wayne.
Justus Lewis S, 33, Pleasant, Sheldon.
Jute H, 22, Adams, Fort Wayne.

K

Kahn Frederick, 15, Washington, Fort Wayne.
Kain Charles, 12, Adams, New Haven.
Kain Samuel, 12, Adams, New Haven.
Kain Samuel jr, 12, Adams, New Haven.
Kaiser Ernest, 28, Marion, Poe.
Kaiser Frederick, 36, Marion, Williams' Station.
Kaiser John F, 1, Marion, Soest.
Kaiser Peter, 15, Lafayette, Myhart.
Kaiser Wm, 28, Marion, Poe.
Kalager Jacob, 22, St Joseph, Fort Wayne.
Kalbman F, 18, Adams, Fort Wayne.
Kammeyer Christian, 29, Washington, Fort Wayne.
Kammeyer Frederick, 29, Washington, Fort Wayne.
Kammeyer Henry, 29, Washington, Fort Wayne.
Kammeyer Will, 29, Washington, Fort Wayne.
Kamp Matthew, 13, Adams, New Haven.
Kanary Thomas, 19, Madison, Hoagland.
Kane S, 9, Cedar Creek, Leo.
Kann Charles, 24, St Joseph, Thurman.
Kaough James, 3, Aboit, Arcola.
Kariger Andrew, 2, Milan, Harlan.
Kariger John, 19, Washington, Fort Wayne.
Kariger Morris, 2, Milan, Harlan.
Kasmere John, 10, Cedar Creek, Leo.
Katt Wm, 20, Lafayette, Roanoke.
Keck Alfred, 1, Lake, Heller's Corners.
Keck Conrad, 26, Adams, Fort Wayne.
Keck Gottlieb, 26, Adams, Fort Wayne.
Keck Jacob, 1, Lake, Heller's Corners.
Keck John, 26, Adams, Fort Wayne.

884   R. L. POLK & CO.'S

Keck Wm, 28, Cedar Creek, Cedarville.
Keefer David, 3, Springfield, Harlan.
Keener A N, 10, Springfield, Harlan.
Keener M, 1, Springfield, Harlan.
Kees Charles, 7, Maumee, Harlan.
Kees Drebert, 35, Springfield, Harlan.
Kees Hugh, 24, Marion, Hoagland.
Kees James, 35, Springfield, Harlan.
Kees Wm, Jackson, Edgerton.
Kees Wm, 8, Maumee, Harlan.
Keifer Samuel, 1, Springfield, Harlan.
Keiler A G, 19, Lake, Arcola.
Keiler George, 19, Lake, Arcola.
Keiler Louis, 33, Lake, Arcola.
Keintz Bernard, 15, Wayne, Fort Wayne.
Keintz John, 21, Wayne, Fort Wayne.
Keintz Valentine, 21, Wayne, Fort Wayne.
Keintz Valentine jr, 21, Wayne, Fort Wayne.
Kell Charles, 24, Perry, Huntertown.
Kell George, 12-13, Eel River, Huntertown.
Kell George V, 12-13, Eel River, Huntertown.
Kell Jacob, Perry, Huntertown.
Kell Solomon, 31, Perry, Huntertown.
Kellemeier John, 16, Wayne, Fort Wayne.
Kellemeier John jr, 16, Wayne, Fort Wayne.
Keller Henry, 8, Pleasant, Nine Mile.
Keller Joseph, 25, Lafayette, Nine Mile.
Keller Wm, Jackson, Baldwin.
Keller Wm, 19, Pleasant, Nine Mile.
Keller Wm N, Jackson, Monroeville.
Kelly Thomas, 33, Lake, Arcola.
Kelsey Arthur, 28, Lafayette, Zanesville.
Kelsey Atner, 29, Lafayette, Zanesville.
Kelsey Benjamin, 19, Aboit, Saturn.
Kelsey David, 19, Aboit, Saturn.
Kelsey F, 18, Aboit, Dunfee.
Kelsey Oliver, 29, Lafayette, Zanesville.
Kelsey W A, 18, Aboit, Dunfee.
Kemp George, 21, Washington, Fort Wayne.
Kender Nicholas, 31, Lake, Arcola.

Kendwick John, 26, Jefferson, Zulu.
Kenline Wm, 31, St Joseph, Fort Wayne.
Kenn George W, 3, Lake, Arcola.
Kennedy H, 10, Aboit, Fort Wayne.
Kennerk Edward J, 4, Pleasant, Fort Wayne.
Kennerk George, 10, Pleasant, Nine Mile.
Kennerk Wm, 10, Pleasant, Nine Mile.
Kennerk Timothy, 10, Pleasant, Nine Mile.
Kennert August, 15, Washington, Fort Wayne.
Kensinger Peter, 6, Cedar Creek, Spencerville.
Keplinger Charles, 33, Lafayette, Zanesville.
Keplinger J L, 23, Lafayette, Zanesville.
Keplinger Martin, 33, Lafayette, Zanesville.
Kern Charles, 15, Monroe, Monroeville.
Kern Charles, 8, St Joseph, Fort Wayne.
Kern Jacob, 15, Monroe, Monroeville.
Kern Miner, 15, Monroe, Monroeville.
Kerns Frederick, 8, Maumee, Woodburn.
Kerns Frederick jr, 8, Maumee, Woodburn.
Kerns John, 5, Springfield, Harlan.
Kerns N S, 28, Maumee, Woodburn.
Kerns Wm, 8, Maumee, Woodburn.
Kerrison John, 13, Milan, Harlan.
Kessler Robert, 26, St Joseph, Goeglien.
Kessler Robert, 5, Springfield, Harlan.
Ketchum Wm, Perry, Huntertown.
Keyser E, 36, Lafayette, Zanesville.
Keyser Jacob, 36, Lafayette, Zanesville.
Kiefer Samuel, 28, Cedar Creek, Cedarville.
Kiefer Wm, 15, Jackson, Edgerton.
Killian Charles, 18, Maumee, Woodburn.
Killian Charles, 24, Springfield, Hall's Corners.
Killian Charles, 36, Springfield, Harlan.
Killian Francis, 17, Maumee, Woodburn.
Killian George, 25, Springfield, Hall's Corners.
Killian Jacob, 24, Springfield, Hall's Corners.
Killian James, 36, Springfield, Harlan.
Killian John, 3, Maumee, Antwerp, O.
Killian Joseph, 25, Springfield, Hall's Corners.
Killian Simon, 25, Springfield, Hall's Corners.

Killian Wm, 24, Springfield, Hall's Corners.
Killian Wm, 36, Springfield, Harlan.
Killworth George, 5, Jefferson, New Haven.
Killworth Henry, 19, Adams, Fort Wayne.
Killworth Robert, 19, Adams, Fort Wayne.
Kime George W, 3, Lake, Arcola.
Kimmel Desdemona, 17, Pleasant, Nine Mile.
Kimmel Jacob, 6, Pleasant, Nine Mile.
Kimmel Newton, 28-33, Wayne, Fort Wayne.
Kimmel Robert, 17, Pleasant, Nine Mile.
King Alfred, 10, Cedar Creek, Leo.
King Asa, 25, Pleasant, Poe.
King George, 27, Aboit, Fort Wayne.
King Miles, 4, Springfield, Harlan.
King Thomas, 19, Pleasant, Nine Mile.
Kinsie Charles, 15, Springfield, Harlan.
Kinsley Daniel, 11, Springfield, Spencerville.
Kirchefer L, 22, Pleasant, Sheldon.
Kirchhoff Wm R, 31, Adams, Fort Wayne.
Kirtz Fred, 8, Springfield, Harlan.
Kiser Frederick, 7, Madison, Maples.
Kiser George, 7, Madison, Maples.
Kiser John, 16, St Joseph, Fort Wayne.
Kistler M J, 1, Perry, Collingwood.
Kistler Silas, 1, Perry, Collingwood.
Kite A, 10, Aboit, Fort Wayne.
Klaehn Frederick, 12, Aboit, Fort Wayne.
Klaehn Frederick C, 11, Aboit, Fort Wayne.
Kleber Christian, 8, Marion, Fort Wayne.
Kleinrichert John, 12, Adams, New Haven.
Kleinrichert L, 12, Adams, New Haven.
Kleist Franz, 12, Adams, New Haven.
Kline Cyrus, 28, Cedar Creek, Cedarville.
Kline Henry, 35, Marion, Williams' Station.
Kline Henry, 2, St Joseph, Fort Wayne.
Kline James, 20, Jefferson, New Haven.
Kline John, 33, Pleasant, Sheldon.
Kline John, 32, Wayne, Fort Wayne.
Klinger F, 22, Adams, Fort Wayne.
Klinger Isaac, 17, Wayne, Fort Wayne.

Klinger Jacob, 20, Monroe, Monroeville.
Klinger J, 13, Aboit, Fort Wayne.
Klinger Wm, 10, Adams, New Haven.
Klopfenstein John, 10, Cedar Creek, Leo.
Knake Wm, 29, Washington, Fort Wayne.
Knapp John R, 30-31, Scipio, Harlan.
Knapp Thomas, 16, Lafayette, Myhart.
Knapp Walter, 28, Scipio, Harlan.
Knemoeller Frederick, 4, Maumée, Harlan.
Knemoeller Frederick jr, 4, Maumee, Harlan.
Knemoeller Gottfried, 4, Maumee, Harlan.
Knemoeller John, 4, Maumee, Harlan.
Knepper D, 9, Aboit, Fort Wayne.
Knepper Joseph H, 30, Lake, Arcola.
Knepper Joseph H jr, 30, Lake, Arcola.
Knepper K, 9' Aboit, Fort Wayne.
Knepper Noah, 15, Aboit, Fort Wayne.
Knepper Reynold, 18, Lake, Arcola.
Knidlen Judd, 33, Pleasant, Sheldon.
Knight Conrad, 33, Lafayette, Zanesville.
Knight Louis, 8, Milan, Chamberlain.
Knight Louis, 17, Milan, Thurman.
Knisely Daniel, 12, Springfield, Georgetown.
Knisely David, 11, Milan, Harlan.
Knisely Roland, 2, Milan, Harlan.
Knisely Wm, Scipio, Fansler.
Kniss Frank, 12, Eel River, Huntertown.
Knoblauch Otto, 20, Maumee, Woodburn.
Knoll George, 20, Wayne, Fort Wayne.
Knoll John, 20, Wayne, Fort Wayne.
Knyoth Louis, 12, Adams, New Haven.
Knyoth Lucas, 12, Adams, New Haven.
Koch Charles, 29, Scipio, Antwerp, O.
Koch Wm, 29, Scipio, Antwerp, O.
Kockemeyer Henry, 28, Milan, Gar Creek.
Koehlen Serg, 25, Adams, Maples.
Koehlinger Christian, 11, Marion, Soest.
Koehlinger Frederick, 34, Adams, Soest.
Koehlinger George, 35, Adams, Maples.
Koehlinger George, 1, Marion, Soest.

888 R. L. POLK & CO.'S

Koehlinger Harry, 11, Marion, Soest.
Koehlinger Jacob, 11, Marion, Soest.
Koehlinger John, 13, Adams, New Haven.
Koenig C, 17, Adams, Fort Wayne.
Koenig Frederick, 27, Adams, Soest.
Koenig H, 25, Adams, New Haven.
Koerte Conrad, 14, St Joseph, Fort Wayne.
Koester Christian, 24, St Joseph, Thurman.
Kohlenberg Conrad, 24, Adams, New Haven.
Kohlenberg Wm, 24, Adams, New Haven.
Kohlmeyer Anthony, 13, Washington, Fort Wayne.
Kohlmeyer Christian, 13, Washington, Fort Wayne.
Kohlmeyer Christian, 13, Washington, Fort Wayne.
Kohlmeyer Henry, 12, Adams, New Haven.
Kohlmeyer Herman, 22, Adams, Fort Wayne.
Koons Edgar L, 4, Pleasant, Fort Wayne.
Koons J Foster, 28, Wayne, Fort Wayne.
Koons Michael, 3, Pleasant, Nine Mile.
Koop Henry, 15, St Joseph, Fort Wayne.
Koop Wm, 15, St Joseph, Fort Wayne.
Kortmeyer Wm, 26, St Joseph, Goeglien.
Krack John, 12, Adams, New Haven.
Krack J, 23, Aboit, Fort Wayne.
Krack G, 23, Aboit, Fort Wayne.
Krack Wm, 1, Adams, New Haven.
Krack Wm jr, 1, Adams, New Haven.
Krall Milton, 35, Springfield, Harlan.
Kramer, see also Cramer.
Kramer Albert, Jackson, Dawkins.
Kramer Charles, 5, St Joseph, Fort Wayne.
Kramer Charles, 31, Washington, Fort Wayne.
Kramer Charles jr, 24, St Joseph, Thurman.
Kramer Frederick, 30, Washington, Fort Wayne.
Krauskoff David, 5, Adams, Fort Wayne.
Krauskoff Henry, 5, Adams, Fort Wayne.
Krauskoff Jacob, 15, Adams, Fort Wayne.
Krauskoff John, 5, Adams, Fort Wayne.
Krauskoff Peter, 5, Adams, Fort Wayne.
Kress Henry, 10, Lafayette, Myhart.
Kress Henry, Lafayette, Zanesville.

Kress Joseph, 31, Wayne, Fort Wayne.
Krewson Matthew, 6, Monroe, Monroeville.
Krick Daniel, 26, Springfield, Harlan.
Krick Elijah, 10, Monroe, Monroeville.
Krick James A, 10, Monroe, Monroeville.
Krickenberg A, 25, Adams, Maples.
Krider Harrison, 21, Cedar Creek, Cedarville.
Krider John, 28, Cedar Creek, Cedarville.
Krider John, 4-5, Eel River, Ari.
Krider Walter, 28, Cedar Creek, Cedarville.
Krill David, 3, Wayne, Fort Wayne.
Krill Samuel, 3, Wayne, Fort Wayne.
Krill Wm, 3, Wayne, Fort Wayne.
Krim Carl, 34, Milan, Gar Creek.
Krim Gottlieb, 28, Cedar Creek, Cedarville.
Kritler Frank, 21, Cedar Creek, Cedarville.
Kritzmore V, 18, Adams, Fort Wayne.
Kroemer Christian, 8, Washington, Fort Wayne.
Kroemer H, 8, Washington, Fort Wayne.
Kroemer Wm, 8, Washington, Fort Wayne.
Kronewitz Adam, 7, Adams, Fort Wayne.
Kronimaker Wm, 2, St Joseph, Fort Wayne.
Krouder Jacob, Perry, Huntertown.
Krouse, see also Crouse.
Krouse Casmas, 34, Pleasant, Sheldon.
Krouse John, 28, Scipio, Harlan.
Krouse Wm, 23, Pleasant, Sheldon.
Kruckenberg August, 35, Adams, Maples.
Kruckerberry Christian, 20, St Joseph, Fort Wayne.
Krugh John, 17, Madison, Hoagland.
Krumlauf Cyrus, 5, Perry, Huntertown.
Krumma Christian, 13, Washington, Fort Wayne.
Krumma Frederick, 13, Washington, Fort Wayne.
Krumma Henry, 13, Washington, Fort Wayne.
Kruse Charles, 19, Washington, Fort Wayne.
Kruse Ernest, 30, Washington, Fort Wayne.
Kruse F W, 32, Washington, Fort Wayne.
Kruse Henry, 33, Milan, Gar Creek.
Kruse Wm, 27, Washington, Fort Wayne.
Kuepstine John, 20, Madison, Hoagland.

890   R. L. POLK & CO.'S

Kunkel George W, 29-30, Eel River, Huntertown.
Kunkel Nathaniel, 29-30, Eel River, Huntertown.
Kurtz Arthur, 4, Milan, Chamberlain.
Kurtz Charles, 13, Lake, Arcola.
Kurtz Henry, 4, Milan, Chamberlain.
Kurtz John, 14, Lake, Fort Wayne.
Kurtz John, 4, Milan, Chamberlain.
Kurz John, Perry, Huntertown.
Kuzmaul Michael, 4, Jefferson, Gar Creek.
Kyburg James, 15, Maumee, Antwerp, O.
Kyberg Joseph, 10, Maumee, Antwerp, O.
Kyler Frederick, 22, Adams, Fort Wayne.
Kyler Peter, 22, Adams, Fort Wayne.

L.

Lachlin Conrad, 8, Cedar Creek, Collingwood.
Lackey Homer, Perry, Huntertown.
Lackey M, 12, Pleasant, Fort Wayne.
La Croix Louis, 5, St Joseph, Fort Wayne.
Ladig John, Jackson, Edgerton.
Ladig U P, 18, Jefferson, New Haven.
La Grave O D, 28, Marion, Poe.
Lake Charles, 26, Springfield, Harlan.
Lake Chauncey, 3, Milan, Harlan.
Lake Curtis, 3, Milan, Harlan.
Lake John H, 12, Milan, Harlan.
Lake John W, 1, Milan, Harlan.
Lallow John, 14, Adams, New Haven.
Lalorde Joseph, 22, Jackson, Edgerton.
Lamar David, 26, Washington, Fort Wayne.
Lamb John, 7, Washington, Fort Wayne.
Lamblin James, Jackson, Baldwin.
Lamley Andrew, 12, Lake, Arcola.
Lamley Charles, 13, Lake, Fort Wayne.
Lamley Christian, 4, Lake, Arcola.
Lamley David, Lake, Arcola.
Lamley George, 13, Lake, Fort Wayne.
Lamont Alphonse, 10, Jefferson, Dawkins.
Lamont Charles, 10, Jefferson, Dawkins.

Lamont Frank, 16, Jefferson, New Haven.
Lamont Louis, 14, Jefferson, Zulu.
Lampe Diederich, 19, Milan, Thurman.
Lampe Herman, Milan, Chamberlain.
Lance Chris, 21, Milan, Thurman.
Lance Jacob, 9, Cedar Creek, Leo.
Lance Samuel, 18, Milan, Thurman.
Landin Henry, Milan, Thurman.
Landin Jacob, Milan, Thurman.
Landin John, 36, St Joseph, New Haven.
Landin Wm, 9, Jefferson, New Haven.
Landre Ernst, 36, Marion, Williams Station.
Landre H G, 25, Marion, Hoagland.
Landstroffer George, 14, Pleasant, Fort Wayne.
Landstroffer James, 23, Pleasant, Sheldon.
Langan Isaac, 23, Springfield, Hall's Corners.
Langden George, 12, Adams, New Haven.
Lange Frederick, 31, Adams, Fort Wayne.
Lange Henry, 31, Adams, Fort Wayne.
Langham Ancel, 31, Scipio, Harlan.
Langham James, 28, Scipio, Harlan.
Langham Jesse, 29, Scipio, Antwerp, O.
Langham John, 28, Scipio, Harlan.
Langham Wm, 29, Scipio, Antwerp, O.
Langley Gottlieb, 11, Lake, Arcola.
Langley Samuel, 13, St Joseph, Thurman.
Langley Wm, 13, St Joseph, Thurman.
Lapoliette Dr, 29, Marion, Poe.
Lapp Martin, 31, Martin, New Haven.
Lapp Valentine, 33, St Joseph, Fort Wayne.
Lapp Victor, 32, St Joseph, Fort Wayne.
Lapp Wm, 25, Wayne, Fort Wayne.
Larrimore Howard, 4, Lake, Arcola.
Larrimore James, 12, Adams, New Haven.
Larrimore Thomas, 8, Lafayette, Myhart.
Larrimore Thomas, 4, Lake, Arcola.
Latham Ralph, Perry, Huntertown.
Latham True, Perry, Huntertown.
Latham Wm, Perry, Huntertown.
Latourette Bert, 27, Eel River, Heller's Corners.

Latourette Edward, 27, Eel River, Heller's Corners.
Latourette Frank, 28, Eel River, Heller's Corners.
Latourette W H, 3, Eel River, Ari.
Lauer Martin, 25, Pleasant, Sheldon.
Laughlin James, 17, Monroe, Monroeville.
Laughlin John, 12, Adams, New Haven.
Lautz Abner, 24, St Joseph, Thurman.
Lautz Simon, 29, Milan, Gar Creek.
Lavine Frank, 12, Lafayette, Nine Mile.
Lawrence Amos, Lafayette, Zanesville.
Lawrence David, 10, Lafayette, Myhart.
Lawrence David, Lafayette, Zanesville.
Lawrence John, 30, Lafayette, Zanesville.
Lawrence Theo, Lafayette, Zanesville.
Lawyer Francis, 3, Monroe, Baldwin.
Lawyer Joseph, 3, Monroe, Baldwin.
Layman George, Lafayette, Zanesville.
Layman George, 9, Marion, Fort Wayne.
Layman Jacob, 4, Lafayette, Aboit.
Layman John, 9, Marion, Fort Wayne.
Layman Riley, 6, Lafayette, Aboit.
Leath Leren, 4, Wayne, Fort Wayne.
Leatherman Robert, Jackson, Edgerton.
Lechner Rufus, Springfield, Harlan.
Lee Edward, 31, Aboit, Fort Wayne.
Lee George, 8, Wayne, Fort Wayne.
Lee Mack, 28, Lake, Arcola.
Le Fever George, 29-30, Eel River, Wallen.
Le Fever H C, Springfield, Harlan.
Le Fevre Samuel, 31, Perry, Huntertown.
Lehneke Edward, 17, Lake, Arcola.
Lehneke Fred, 17, Lake, Arcola.
Lehrman Charles, 14, Pleasant, Fort Wayne.
Lehrman Charles F, Aboit, Fort Wayne.
Lehrman George, 23, Pleasant, Sheldon.
Leibolt T A, 4, Eel River, Ari.
Leighton Frank, Scipio, Hicksville, O.
Leighty David, 5, Cedar Creek, Collingwood.
Leininger Jacob, 27, Jackson, Baldwin.
Leininger Theobald, 32, Jackson, Monroeville.

Leininger Wm, 33, Pleasant, Sheldon.
Leinington A B, 34, Lafayette, Zanesville.
Leinington M, Jackson, Dawkins.
Leisure Charles, 5, Wayne, Fort Wayne.
Leitcher John, 6, Springfield, Harlan.
Leitz Emmet, 30, Lake, Arcola.
Lemke Charles, 3, Wayne, Fort Wayne.
Lemley Wm, 2, Lake, Heller's Corners.
Lemmon Fred, 23, Springfield, Hall's Corners.
Lemmon John, 23, Springfield, Hall's Corners.
Lemmon John S, 23, Springfield, Hall's Corners.
Lemmon Linfield, 12, Eel River, Huntertown.
Lenhart George, 4, Madison, Maples.
Lenhart H C, 14, Madison, Monroeville.
Lenhart Linius, 4, Madison, Maples.
Lenhart Orson, 4, Madison, Maples.
Lenhart Peter, 4, Madison, Maples.
Leninger E, 7, St Joseph, Fort Wayne.
Lenington Joseph, Jackson, Monroeville.
Lenker Charles, 5, Madison, Maples.
Lenker David, 5, Madison, Maples.
Lenker John, 5, Madison, Maples.
Lenker Philip, 5, Madison, Maples.
Lennon Alvin, 23, Monroe, Monroeville.
Lennon E, 23, Monroe, Monroeville.
Leonard Elmer, 26, Washington, Fort Wayne.
Leonard Jefferson, 26, Washington, Fort Wayne.
Leonard Nelson, 26, Washington, Fort Wayne.
Lepper Adolph W, 27, Adams, Soest.
Lepper Charles V, 3, Marion, Soest.
Lepper Christian, 31, Jefferson, Maples.
Lepper Christian, 16, Madison, Hoagland.
Lepper Frederick, 36, Adams, Maples.
Lepper Frederick, 3, Marion, Soest.
Lepper George, 1, Marion, Soest.
Lepper George, 12, Milan, Harlan.
Lepper Henry, 36, Adams, Maples.
Lepper Henry, 16, Madison, Hoagland.
Lepper Henry jr, 36, Adams, Maples.
Lepper John, 3, Marion, Soest.

Lepper L G, 3, Marion, Soest.
Lepper Theodore, 36, Adams, Maples.
Lerchey James, 12, Aboit, Fort Wayne.
Lerchey Simon, 12, Aboit, Fort Wayne.
Lesher George, 31, Lake, Arcola.
Lessig Ezra, Lafayette, Aboit.
Lest Emanuel, 29, Jefferson, Maples.
Lichtenwalter C C, 29, Marion, Poe.
Liggett Daniel, 18, Lafayette, Aboit.
Lilo August, 34, Eel River, Heller's Corners.
Lindeman H, 12, Adams, New Haven.
Lindemeyer F, 8, Washington, Fort Wayne.
Lindermuth Albert C, 2, Maumee, Antwerp, O.
Lindermuth Clayton A, 31, Scipio, Harlan.
Lindermuth Edward, 3, Maumee, Antwerp, O.
Lindermuth Frank, 28, Scipio, Harlan.
Lindermuth George, 4, Springfield, Harlan.
Lindermuth Vance, 28, Scipio, Harlan.
Lindon George, 6, Jefferson, New Haven.
Lindsley W C, 6, Cedar Creek, Collingwood.
Linker Henry, 17, Adams, Fort Wayne.
Linker Louis, 17, Adams, Fort Wayne.
Linton Louis, 28, Lake, Arcola.
Lipes Andrew, 29, Marion, Poe.
Lipes C, 19, Madison, Hoagland.
Lipes John M, 29, Marion, Poe.
Lipps J K, 6, Aboit, Dunfee.
Lisson George, 12, Adams, New Haven.
List Albert, 15, Eel River, Heller's Corners.
Liston C Elmort, Jackson, Edgerton.
Litchfield Edward, 11, Lake, Arcola.
Little Alfred, 4, Washington, Wallen.
Little Andrew, 8, Maumee, Woodburn.
Little Samuel, 29, Lafayette, Zanesville.
Litzenberger George, 21, Wayne, Fort Wayne.
Loar Isaac, Jackson, Edgerton.
Locheye E, 12, Adams, New Haven.
Lochner Fred, 35, Lake, Arcola.
Lochner John, 8, Cedar Creek, Collingwood.
Lochner John, 9, Cedar Creek, Leo.

Lochner Samuel, 2, Cedar Creek, Spencerville.
Lochner Wm, 8, Cedar Creek, Collingwood.
Loding Charles, Jefferson, Maples.
Loenberger Gottlieb, 14, Madison, Monroeville.
Logan Gilbert, 29, Pleasant, Sheldon.
Logan Smith, 29, Pleasant, Sheldon.
Logiet Henry, 12, Adams, New Haven.
Lohmeyer Henry, 31, Adams, Fort Wayne.
Lohmeyer Peter, 22, St Joseph, Fort Wayne.
Lohrman Henry, 35, Madison, Bingen.
Lohrman Wm, 19, Marion, Poe.
Lomen Herman, 27, Jefferson, Zulu.
Lonch Grant, 28, Aboit, Aboit.
Lonch John, 28, Aboit, Aboit.
Long Bernard, 21, Adams, Fort Wayne.
Long Cyrus, 6, Adams, Fort Wayne.
Long George, 3, Madison, Maples.
Long G W, 3, Eel River, Ari.
Long Henry, 6, Adams, Fort Wayne.
Long Jacob, 6, Lafayette, Aboit.
Long John, 3, Madison, Maples.
Long Louis, 33, Eel River, Heller's Corners.
Longacre Daniel, 10, Springfield, Harlan.
Longacre John, 31, Springfield, Harlan.
Longacre Peter, 31, Springfield, Harlan.
Longacre Samuel, 36, Cedar Creek, Harlan.
Longardner Jasper, 11, Jefferson, Dawkins.
Longardner Orlo, 11, Jefferson, Dawkins.
Longardner Wm, 11, Jefferson, Dawkins.
Loomis Barney, 19, St Joseph, Fort Wayne.
Loos Del, 8, Springfield, Harlan.
Loos George, 8, Springfield, Harlan.
Lopshire Eugene, 7, Springfield, Harlan.
Lopshire George, 12, Lafayette, Nine Mile.
Lopshire George A, 11, Lafayette, Nine Mile.
Lopshire George L, 8, Lafayette, Aboit.
Lopshire Lemuel, 7, Springfield, Harlan.
Lopshire Lewis, 7, Springfield, Harlan.
Lopshire Louis, 12, Lafayette, Nine Mile.
Lopshire Oliver, 1, Lafayette, Nine Mile.

Lopshire Wm, 9, Lafayette, Myhart.
Loraine Charles, 20, Jefferson, New Haven.
Loraine Floyd, 13, Milan, Harlan.
Loraine John, 20, Jefferson, New Haven.
Lorraine John, 12, Adams, New Haven.
Lorraine Peter, 12, Adams, New Haven.
Lortier Charles, 15, Jackson, Edgerton.
Lortier Dominick, 22, Jackson, Edgerton.
Lortier F, 5, St Joseph, Fort Wayne.
Losean John, 18, Jackson, Dawkins.
Lothamer Andrew, 22, Jackson, Edgerton.
Lothamer Joseph, 22, Jackson, Edgerton.
Lothamer Theodore, 22, Jackson, Edgerton.
Louis John, 13, St Joseph, Thurman.
Louks Harris, 4, Milan, Chamberlain.
Louks Isaac, 4, Milan, Chamberlain.
Lourch Edward, 18, Jefferson, New Haven.
Lourent Fred, 35, Lake, Arcola.
Lovine Frank, 36, Jefferson, Zulu.
Lovine Michael, 28, Jefferson, Maples.
Lowman George, 32, Marion, Poe.
Lowmiller Elroy, 26, Monroe, Monroeville.
Lowmiller John, 27, Monroe, Monroeville.
Lowry Abraham, 7, Jefferson, New Haven.
Lowry Jesse, 11, Adams, New Haven.
Lucas Wm, 12, Adams, New Haven.
Luce George, 11, Aboit, Fort Wayne.
Luce Grant, 11, Aboit, Fort Wayne.
Luckybill John, 18, Cedar Creek, Collingwood.
Ludwick Esdrus, 24, Pleasant, Poe.
Ludwig Joseph, 4, Wayne, Fort Wayne.
Luhr Herman, 32, Milan, Gar Creek.
Lumbard Joseph, 12, Adams, New Haven.
Lunn Young, 22, Lafayette, Zanesville.
Luntz George, 3, Adams, New Haven.
Luntz John, 4, Adams, New Haven.
Luntz M, 3, Adams, New Haven.
Luntz Wm, 27, St Joseph, Goeglien.
Lupkin F, 12, Adams, New Haven.
Lupkin Laborious, 25, Adams, Maples.

Lupkin Rudolph, 12, Adams, New Haven.
Luther Bert, 11, Lake, Arcola.
Luther Israel, 17, Washington, Fort Wayne.
Lutz David, 22, St Joseph, Fort Wayne.
Lutz David jr, 22, St Joseph, Fort Wayne.
Lutz Ephraim, Maumee, Antwerp, O.
Lutz Floyd, 22, St Joseph, Fort Wayne.
Lutz Frederick, 7, Pleasant, Nine Mile.
Lutz Jacob, 15, Maumee, Antwerp, O.
Lutz Samuel, 31, Marion, Poe.
Lutz Wm, 29, Marion, Poe.
Lyman Robert, Perry, Huntertown.
Lynch Thomas, 5, Lafayette, Aboit.
Lynhart D, 27, Aboit, Fort Wayne.
Lynhart W, 27, Aboit, Fort Wayne.
Lyons Dalton, Eel River, Heller's Corners.
Lyons John, 18, Springfield, Harlan.
Lyons Thomas, 29-30, Eel River, Wallen.
Lyons Samuel, 33, Eel River, Heller's Corners.
Lyons Wilmer, 33, Eel River, Heller's Corners.

Mc

McArdle Peter, 18, Monroe, Monroeville.
McBratney Henry, 9, St. Joseph, Fort Wayne.
McBride Charles, 3, Wayne, Fort Wayne.
McBride James, 22, Eel River, Heller's Corners.
McBride James, 33, Lafayette, Zanesville.
McBride Luther, 10, Eel River, Ari.
McBride Richard, Lafayette, Zanesville.
McBride Wm, 10, Eel River, Ari.
McBride Wm, 17, Lafayette, Myhart.
McCartney Wm, 9, Cedar Creek, Leo.
McCarty Dennis, 11, Adams, Fort Wayne.
McCarty Henry, 1, Eel River, Huntertown.
McCarty John, 12, Adams, New Haven.
McCarty John, 9, Eel River, Ari.
McComb David, 23, Perry, Huntertown.
McComb Edward, 23, Perry, Huntertown.
McComb James, 23, Perry, Huntertown.

McComb John, Jackson, Monroeville.
McComb John, 24, Perry, Huntertown.
McComb Martin, 31, Perry, Huntertown.
McComb Robert, Jackson, Monroeville.
McComb Thomas, 2, St Joseph, Fort Wayne.
McConaughey James, 19, Madison, Hoagland.
McConnell James, 23, Monroe, Monroeville.
McCormick Alfred, 15, Cedar Creek, Collingwood.
McCormick Joseph, 23, Jefferson, Zulu.
McCormick Monroe, 34, Eel River, Heller's Corners.
McCormick Patrick, 36, Jefferson, Zulu.
McCormick Riley, 36, Jefferson, Zulu.
McCormick Wm, 24, Lake, Arcola.
McCoy C O, 6, Adams, Fort Wayne.
McCoy George W, 6, Adams, Ft Wayne.
McCoy Thomas, 21 Lafayette, Myhart.
McCoy Thomas, 29, Lafayette, Zanesville.
McCrary David, 7, Cedar Creek, Collingwood.
McCrary James, 2, Cedar Creek, Spencerville.
McCrary Otis, 9, Cedar Creek, Leo.
McCrary Samuel, 7, Cedar Creek, Collingwood.
McCullough James, 24, Washington, Fort Wayne.
McCurdy Mack, 13, Springfield, Harlan.
McDaniels D, 23, Aboit, Fort Wayne.
McDonald Wm, 24, Lake, Arcola.
McDougal Eugene, 13, St Joseph, Thurman.
McDougal Foster, 13, St Joseph, Thurman.
McDowell Alexander, 34, Pleasant, Sheldon.
McDowell George, 34, Pleasant, Sheldon.
McDowell Wm, 28, Pleasant, Sheldon.
McDuffee Horace G, 6, Eel River, Churubuseo.
McFadden Henry, Lafayette, Zanesville.
McFadden Herbert, Lafayette, Zanesville.
McFarren Lester, 19, Lafayette, Myhart.
McFarren Martin, 19, Lafayette, Myhart.
McFarren Reuben S, 19, Lafayette, Myhart.
McGingan G B, 28, Lake, Arcola.
McGinness Dennis, 17, Lafayette, Myhart.
McGinness John, 17, Lafayette, Myhart.
McGonagh M C, 17, Monroe, Monroeville.

McGongan Wm, 33, Lafayette, Zanesville.
McGovern Charles, 11, Pleasant, Fort Wayne.
McGrath John, 32, Lake, Arcola.
McGuire Albert, Eel River, Churubusco.
McGuire Samuel, 28, Cedar Creek, Cedarville.
McIntosh Alexander F, Jefferson, Maples.
McIntosh Benjamin, 19, Madison, Hoagland.
McIntosh Benjamin jr, 29, Madison, Hoagland.
McIntosh Charles, Jefferson, Maples.
McIntosh Henry H, 30, Jefferson, Maples.
McIntosh James, 23, Monroe, Monroeville.
McIntosh John, 19, Madison, Hoagland.
McIntosh Wm, 9, Adams, Fort Wayne.
McKeag Daniel, 19, Madison, Hoagland.
McKeag George, 19, Madison, Hoagland.
McKee Robert, 29, Marion, Poe.
McKee Warren, 33, Pleasant, Sheldon.
McKeenan Alexander, 18, Madison, Maples.
McKenzie Benjamin, 29, Aboit, Fort Wayne.
McKenzie George, 29, Aboit, Aboit.
McKenzie Jacob I, 3, Milan, Harlan.
McKenzie John, 29, Aboit, Fort Wayne.
McKenzie Wm, 29, Aboit, Aboit.
McKinley James, 9, Springfield, Spencerville.
McKinnie F, 12, Adams, New Haven.
McLaren Robert, 5, Wayne, Fort Wayne.
McLesh George, Jefferson, Dawkins.
McMacken D G, 8, Wayne, Fort Wayne.
McMacken Henry C, 8, Wayne, Fort Wayne.
McMackin James, 4, Adams, New Haven.
McMackin J C, 28, Washington, Fort Wayne.
McMackin Wm B, 29, Wayne, Fort Wayne.
McMahan Marion, 33, Lake, Arcola.
McMahon Thomas, 23, Monroe, Monroeville.
McMillan Jacob, 20, Maumee, Woodburn.
McMullen Wm, 8, Maumee, Woodburn.
McQuiston Allen J, 3, Washington, Wallen.
McQuiston Benjamin, 3, Washington, Wallen.
McSorley Henry, 12, Jefferson, Dawkins.
McTigue Peter, 17, Lake, Arcola.
McWhorton H, 19, Madison, Hoagland.

M

Mack Fred, 12, Adams, New Haven.
Mack George, 12, Adams, New Haven.
Mack J G, 3, Springfield, Harlan.
Madden Dennis, 4, Washington, Wallen.
Madden Frank, 14, Milan, Harlan.
Madden W W, 4, Lake, Heller's Corners.
Maddox F, 21, Pleasant, Sheldon.
Magner Isaiah, 31, Monroe, Monroeville.
Mahoney James, 12, Adams, New Haven.
Mahoney John, 12, Adams, New Haven.
Mahoney Nail, 12, Adams, New Haven.
Main Christopher E, 14, Milan, Harlan.
Main Clarence, 5, Jefferson, New Haven.
Main Frank, 14, Milan, Harlan.
Main Jesse, 24, Milan, Gar Creek.
Maiser B, 1, Wayne, Fort Wayne.
Malcomb James, 7, Perry, Huntertown.
Malcolm John, Perry, Huntertown.
Malcolm Wm, Perry, Huntertown.
Maldena Edward, 17, Jackson, Monroeville.
Malin John, 7, Monroe, Monroeville.
Mallon Charles, 2, Pleasant, Nine Mile.
Mangus Emmet, 29, Lake, Arcola.
Manier Joseph, 28, Lake, Arcola.
Manier Michael, 28, Lake, Arcola.
Manier Robert, 28, Lake, Arcola.
Manning Amos, 9, Eel River, Ari.
Manning George, 9, Eel River, Ari.
Manning John, 9, Cedar Creek, Leo.
Manning Samuel, 18, Lake, Arcola.
Manning Wm, 9, Cedar Creek, Leo.
Manning Wm, 18, Lake, Arcola.
Manweiler John C, 4, Aboit, Arcola.
Maple Charles, Jefferson, Maples.
Maple Lewis S, Jefferson, Maples.
March John, 19, St Joseph, Fort Wayne.
Marion Edward, 19, Madison, Hoagland.
Marion John, Maumee, Woodburn.

Marker John, 9, Eel River, Ari.
Markle Daniel, 9, Springfield, Spencerville.
Markle Frank, 3, Springfield, Harlan.
Markle Ephraim, 9, Springfield, Spencerville.
Markle Jacob, 17, Springfield, Harlan.
Markle Jeremiah, 3, Springfield, Harlan.
Markle Samuel, 17, Springfield, Harlan.
Markle Wm, 3, Springfield, Harlan.
Marlett George, 8, Lafayette, Myhart.
Marquardt Aaron, 2, Madison, Monroeville.
Marquardt Adam, 14, Madison, Monroeville.
Marquardt Frederick, 1, Madison, Monroeville.
Marquardt Isaac, 1, Madison, Monroeville.
Marquardt Jacob, 11, Madison, Monroeville.
Marquardt John, 14, Madison, Monroeville.
Marquardt Philip, 11, Madison, Monroeville.
Marquit Alfred, 6, Springfield, Harlan.
Marshall George, 18, Adams, Fort Wayne.
Marshall Wesley, 33, St Joseph, Fort Wayne.
Martin Anthony, 9, Madison, Maples.
Martin August, 35, Perry, Cedarville.
Martin August jr, 35, Perry, Cedarville.
Martin Charles, 15, Cedar Creek, Leo.
Martin Charles, 14, Jefferson, Zulu.
Martin David, 16, Monroe, Monroeville.
Martin David jr, 16, Monroe, Monroeville.
Martin Delphos F, 14, Perry, Cedarville.
Martin Francis C, 14, St Joseph, Fort Wayne.
Martin George, 34, Marion, Poe.
Martin George, 14, Perry, Leo.
Martin Honora, 31, Jackson, Monroeville.
Martin Henry, 15, Madison, Monroeville.
Martin Henry, 27, Washington, Fort Wayne.
Martin Henry C, Jefferson, Maples.
Martin James, 34, Marion, Poe.
Martin Jesse, 9, Jefferson, New Haven.
Martin John, 33, Jefferson, Monroeville.
Martin John, 27, Jefferson, Zulu.
Martin Joseph, 19, Cedar Creek, Cedarville.
Martin Jules, 35, Perry, Cedarville.

artin Julian, 31, Jackson, Monroeville.
artin Oliver, 16, Monroe, Monroeville.
artin Wm, Jackson, Monroeville.
Martin Wm, 34, Marion, Poe.
Martin Wm, 14, Perry, Leo.
artin Wm, 12, Washington, Fort Wayne.
ason Frank, 35, Perry, Cedarville.
ason George, 15, Lafayette, Myhart.
ason George, Lafayette, Zanesville.
ason Henry, 12, Adams, New Haven.
ason John B, Perry, Cedarville.
ason Joseph, Perry, Cedarville.
ason Joseph jr, 21, Wayne, Fort Wayne.
ason Jules J, Perry, Cedarville.
ason Peter, 35, Perry, Cedarville.
ason Wm, Lafayette, Nine Mile.
ason Wm, Perry, Cedarville.
Mason F, 11, Cedar Creek, Leo.
Mastbaum Bernard, 22, Adams, Fort Wayne.
athias Jacob, 17, Lafayette, Myhart.
athias Louis, 17, Lafayette, Myhart.
atthews Conrad, 15, Washington, Fort Wayne.
atthews Samuel, 12, Eel River, Huntertown.
atthews Samuel jr, 11, Eel River, Huntertown.
aunet Edward, 1, Wayne, Fort Wayne.
aurer Joseph, Perry, Huntertown.   •
aurey Wm, Jackson, Edgerton.
axfield James, 9, Cedar Creek, Leo.
Maxfield Orange, 15, Cedar Creek, Leo.
Maxheimer Frank, 29, Monroe, Monroeville.
Maxheimer John, 29, Monroe, Monroeville.
Maxheimer Wm, 29, Monroe Monroeville.
axwell Abraham, 18, Eel River, Churubusco.
axwell Adam, 18, Eel River, Churubusco.
axwell Jacob, 29-30, Eel River, Heller's Corners.
ay Chester, 36, Springfield, Harlan.
May Noah, 18, Monroe, Monroeville.
May Wm, 33, Lafayette, Zanesville.
Mayer H W, 12, Adams, New Haven.
Mayhew James, 28, Cedar Creek, Cedarville.

Mayhew Joseph, 9, St Joseph, Fort Wayne.
Maynor Alexander, 17, Lake, Arcola.
Maynor James, 17, Lake, Arcola.
Mayo Frank, 27-28, Eel River, Heller's Corners.
Maze Bernard, 18, Jefferson, New Haven.
Maze John, 18, Jefferson, New Haven.
Maze Theo, 18, Jefferson, New Haven.
Mead Arthur, Jackson, Monroeville.
Mead Edward, Jackson, Monroeville.
Mead John, 34, Monroe, Monroeville.
Mead Rev, 29, Monroe, Monroeville.
Mead Thomas, 12, Adams, New Haven.
Meadow Andrew, 34, Lafayette, Zanesville.
Meadow Jacob, 34, Lafayette, Zanesville.
Means Lorain, 17, Springfield, Harlan.
Medsker Jacob, 2, Milan, Harlan.
Meeks Thomas, 14, Milan, Harlan.
Meisse John, 20, St Joseph, Fort Wayne.
Mellinger S, Perry, Huntertown.
Mendoerfer E, 27, Adams, Soest.
Menter Gottfried, 2, Abolt, Fort Wayne.
Menze A D, 12, Adams, New Haven.
Mercer Jacob, 35, Marion, Williams' Station.
Mercer Robert, 16, Madison, Hoagland.
Merchant S P, 28, Springfield, Harlan.
Merlette Richard, 28, Cedar Creek, Cedarville.
Merrillot August, 24, Jefferson, Zulu.
Merritt H M, 13, Milan, Harlan.
Messing Charles, 26, Washington, Fort Wayne.
Messing Henry, 26, Washington, Fort Wayne.
Messing Wm, 19, Washington, Fort Wayne.
Messler J, Lafayette, Nine Mile.
Metcalf John, 28, Cedar Creek, Cedarville.
Mettert Henry, 4, Maumee, Harlan.
Mettert Lewis, 32, Scipio, Harlan.
Mettert Samuel, 31, Scipio, Harlan.
Metthorn W, 19, Madison, Hoagland.
Metzger Jacob, 1, Milan, Harlan.
Meyer Barney, 9, Adams, Fort Wayne.
Meyer, see also Myers.

904   R. L. POLK & CO.'s

Meyer Christian, 2, Pleasant, Fort Wayne.
Meyer Daniel, 11, Perry, Collingwood.
Meyer Edward, 11, Perry, Collingwood.
Meyer Frank, 9, Adams, Fort Wayne.
Meyer Frank, 16, Jefferson, New Haven.
Meyer Frederick, 16, Adams, Fort Wayne.
Meyer Frederick, 2, Pleasant, Fort Wayne.
Meyer John, 9, Adams, Fort Wayne.
Meyer John J, 9, Adams, FortWayne.
Meyer Rev Joseph,, 35, Pleasant, Sheldon.
Meyer Mathias, 12, Adams, New Haven.
Meyer Rolson, 11, Perry, Collingwood.
Meyer Solomon, 11, Perry, Collingwood.
Meyer Wm, 11, Perry, Collingwood.
Meyers Andrew, 28, Cedar Creek, Cedarville.
Meyers August, 24, Jefferson, Zulu.
Meyers August, 25, St Joseph, Goeglien.
Meyers Charles, 3, Marion, Soest.
Meyers Charles, Perry, Huntertown.
Meyers Charles, 21, St Joseph, Fort Wayne.
Meyers Daniel, 2, Pleasant, Fort Wayne.
Meyers Edgar, 4, Washington, Wallen.
Meyers Edward, 23, Aboit, Fort Wayne.
Meyers Fred, 35, Adams, Maples.
Meyers Fred, 12, Adams, New Haven.
Meyers Frederick, 21, Madison, Hoagland.
Meyers Frederick, 29, Marion, Poe.
Meyers Frederick, 21, St Joseph, Fort Wayne.
Meyers Frederick, 29, St Joseph, Goeglien
Meyers Frederick, 4, Washington, Wallen.
Meyers George, 31, Madison, Hoagland.
Meyers Gustave, 24, St Joseph, Thurman.
Meyers Henry, 2, Pleasant, Fort Wayne.
Meyers Henry, 3, Wayne, Fort Wayne.
Meyers I W, Jefferson, Maples.
Meyers John, 25, St Joseph, Goeglien.
Meyers John jr, 25, St Joseph, Goeglien.
Meyers Joseph, 7, Maumee, Harlan.
Meyers J M, 2, Pleasant, Fort Wayne.
Meyers Levi, 7, Maumee, Harlan.

Meyers Louis, 21, Cedar Creek, Cedarville.
Meyers Matthias, 2, Pleasant, Fort Wayne.
Meyers Metson, 15, Cedar Creek, Leo.
Meyers Michael, Jackson, Dawkins.
Meyers M J, 1, Perry, Collingwood.
Meyers Rev, 11, Lake, Arcola.
Meyers Wm, 9, Cedar Creek, Leo.
Meyers Wm, 21, Madison, Hoagland.
Meyers Wm, 3, Marion, Soest.
Meyers Wm, Milan, Thurman.
Meyers Wm, 18, Maumee, Woodburn.
Michael L, 28, Cedar Creek, Cedarville.
Michael Rev, 27, St Joseph, Goeglien.
Michaels John, 3, Adams, New Haven.
Michaels John, 33, Lafayette, Zanesville.
Michaels Philip, 3, Adams, New Haven.
Middaugh Sidney, 23, Lafayette, Zanesville.
Middleton Thomas, Jefferson, Maples.
Mieland Charles, 21, Marion, Poe.
Milan Frederick, 35, Marion, Williams Station.
Milan Henry, 27, Marion, Hoagland.
Mildney F, 15, Jefferson, Zulu.
Mildon George, 6, Pleasant, Nine Mile.
Mildon James, 6, Pleasant, Nine Mile.
Millard Charles, 2, Aboit, Fort Wayne.
Miller Abner, Scipio, Harlan.
Miller Abraham, 14, Jefferson, Zulu.
Miller Ambrose, 5-8, Milan, Chamberlain.
Miller Amherst, 8, Milan, Chamberlain.
Miller Amherst jr, 17, Milan, Thurman.
Miller Amos, 17, Eel River, Heller's Corners.
Miller Andrew, 21, Pleasant, Sheldon.
Miller Anson, 15, Milan, Harlan.
Miller August, 20, Wayne, Fort Wayne.
Miller A, 12, Adams, New Haven.
Miller Benjamin, 36, Jefferson, Zulu.
Miller Benjamin, 28, Perry, Fort Wayne.
Miller Charles, 17, Eel River, Heller's Corners.
Miller Charles, 22, Milan, Thurman.
Miller Christian, 1, Marion, Soest.

Miller Christian, 31, Monroe, Monroeville.
Miller Christian, 32, Springfield, Harlan.
Miller C A, 11, Adams, New Haven.
Miller Daniel, 23, Monroe, Monroeville.
Miller Daniel, 32, Springfield, Harlan.
Miller Daniel D, 8, Milan, Chamberlain.
Miller David, Jackson, Monroeville.
Miller David, 8, Monroe, Monroeville.
Miller Douglass, 13, Marion, Hoagland.
Miller Edwin N, 8, Milan, Chamberlain.
Miller Elias, 35, Jefferson, Monroeville.
Miller Elijah, 14, Jefferson, Zulu.
Miller E J, 35, Jefferson, Monroeville.
Miller Frank, 10, Cedar Creek, Leo.
Miller Frank, 8, Milan, Chamberlain.
Miller Frank, 7, Milan, Thurman.
Miller Frank, 27, Pleasant, Sheldon.
Miller Frank, 13, Wayne, Fort Wayne.
Miller George, 12, Adams, New Haven.
Miller George, Milan, Thurman.
Miller George jr, Milan, Thurman.
Miller GeorgeW , 17, Eel River, Heller's Corners.
Miller Henry, 11, Adams, New Haven.
Miller Henry, 15, Milan, Harlan.
Miller Henry, 28, Pleasant, Sheldon.
Miller Herman, 9, Cedar Creek, Leo.
Miller Herman, 10, Marion, Soest.
Miller H A, 19, Madison, Hoagland.
Miller Hudson, 15, Milan, Harlan.
Miller Isa, 33, Milan, Gar Creek.
Miller Isaac, 12, Adams, New Haven.
Miller Jacob, 15, Milan, Harlan.
Miller Jacob, 33, Pleasant, Sheldon.
Miller Jacob, 32, Springfield, Harlan.
Miller Jacques, Jackson, Baldwin.
Miller James, 26, St Joseph, Goeglien.
Miller Jefferson, 36, Jefferson, Zulu.
Miller Jerome, 36, Jefferson, Zulu.
Miller Joel, 36, Cedar Creek, Harlan.
Miller John, 12, Adams, New Haven.

Miller John, 33, Pleasant, Sheldon.
Miller John, 12, Pleasant, Fort Wayne.
Miller John, 32, Scipio, Harlan.
Miller John, 32, Springfield, Harlan.
Miller John A, 20, Wayne, Fort Wayne.
Miller John H, 17, Wayne, Fort Wayne.
Miller John jr, 28, Pleasant, Sheldon.
Miller Joseph, 20, Cedar Creek, Cedarville.
Miller Joseph, 6, Maumee, Harlan.
Miller J, 27, Aboit, Fort Wayne.
Miller J E, 7, Springfield, Harlan.
Miller K, 3, Springfield, Harlan.
Miller Lewis D, 30, Madison, Hoagland.
Miller Milo, 35, Jefferson, Monroeville.
Miller Monroe, 36, Jefferson, Zulu.
Miller Newton, 25, Marion, Hoagland.
Miller Nicholas, 21, Pleasant, Sheldon.
Miller Noah, 3, Milan, Harlan.
Miller Owen W, 11, Springfield, Spencerville.
Miller Riley, 33, Milan, Gar Creek.
Miller R, 5, Monroe, Monroeville.
Miller Samuel, Eel River, Churubusco.
Miller Silas, 19, Madison, Hoagland.
Miller Wm, 25, Lake, Arcola.
Miller Wm jr, 25, Lake, Arcola.
Miller Wm, 3, Lake, Heller's Corners.
Miller Wm, 15, Milan, Harlan.
Miller Wm, 31, Monroe, Monroeville.
Miller Wm L, 11, Pleasant, Fort Wayne.
Miller W H, 2, Springfield, Spencerville.
Miller Wm, 26, Washington, Fort Wayne.
Miller Wm, 13, Wayne, Fort Wayne.
Milliman Moses, 18-19, Milan, Thurman.
Mills Charles, 34, Springfield, Harlan.
Mills James, 6, Lafayette, Aboit.
Mills George W, 9, Lafayette, Myhart.
Mills Robert, 4, Lafayette, Aboit.
Mills Samuel, 34, Springfield, Harlan.
Mills Samuel jr, 27, Springfield, Harlan.
Milwick Henry, 19, Monroe, Monroeville.

Miner Henry, 15, Monroe, Monroeville.
Miner James, 14, Monroe, Monroeville.
Miner John, 14, Monroe, Monroeville.
Miner Reuben, 14, Monroe, Monroeville.
Miner Wm, 3, Wayne, Fort Wayne.
Minnich Henry, 33, Lake, Arcola.
Minnich Henry, 4, Washington, Wallen.
Minnich John, 29, Lake, Arcola.
Minnich Julian, 18, Madison, Maples.
Minnich Nicholas, 18, Madison, Maples.
Minnich Oliver, 3, Springfield, Harlan.
Minster Henry, 17, Monroe, Monroeville.
Mintze Frederick, 15, Washington, Fort Wayne.
Miracle George, 5, St Joseph, Fort Wayne.
Miracle John, 17, Eel River, Heller's Corners.
Misner Wm, Jackson, Dawkins.
Mitchell Frank, 17, Lafayette, Myhart.
Mitchell George, 7, Springfield, Harlan.
Mitchell Philip, 27-28, Eel River, Heller's Corners.
Mitten Charles, Jackson, Baldwin.
Mitten Joseph, Jackson, Baldwin.
Mix Lyle, 12, Adams, New Haven.
Mix Thomas, 7, Jefferson, New Haven.
Mock Frank, 8, Madison, Maples.
Mock Lem, 15, Madison, Monroeville.
Moellering Charles, 25, Wayne, Fort Wayne.
Moffat H, 16, Aboit, Fort Wayne.
Mohler Charles, 16, Adams, Fort Wayne.
Mohler Jacob, 7, Washington, Fort Wayne.
Moloney John, 6, Eel River, Churubusco.
Momey Benjamin, 17, Jackson, Monroeville.
Mommer Anthony, 31, Perry, Huntertown.
Monasmith Marcus, 29, Marion, Poe.
Moninger John, 1, St Joseph, Fort Wayne.
Monn Valentine, 24, Washington, Fort Wayne.
Monnier Edward, 34, Jefferson, Monroeville.
Monnier Jule, 17, Jefferson, New Haven.
Monot Edward, 24, Jefferson, Zulu.
Monot Louis, 29, Marion, Poe.
Monroe Frank, 4, Springfield, Harlan.

Monroe Sheldon, 28, Eel River, Heller's Corners.
Montz Michael, 12, Adams, New Haven.
Mooney Charles, 6, Wayne, Fort Wayne.
Mooney Johnson, 5, Madison, Maples.
Moore Bert, 5, Aboit, Dunfee.
Moore C D, 12, Adams, New Haven.
Moore Charles, 11, Springfield, Spencerville.
Moore Daniel, 14, Adams, New Haven.
Moore David, 24, Springfield, Hall's Corners.
Moore Frank, 9, Cedar Creek, Leo.
Moore George, 11, Adams, New Haven.
Moore Henry, 7, Springfield, Harlan.
Moore John, 26, Springfield, Harlan.
Moore Lucas, 16, Washington, Fort Wayne.
Moore Matthew, 29, Scipio, Antwerp, O.
Moore Moses, 18, Scipio, Hicksville, O.
Moore Nathaniel, 23, Springfield, Hall's Corners.
Moore Robert, 26, Springfield, Harlan.
Moore Wm, 6, Lafayette, Aboit.
Moore Wm, 18, Scipio, Hicksville, O.
Moore Wm, 11, Springfield, Spencerville.
Moorehankey H, 15, Adams, New Haven.
Mopp Fred, 32, Madison, Binger.
Mopp John, 32, Madison, Binger.
Morenk A, 22, Adams, Fort Wayne.
Morey Paul, 14, Jefferson, Zulu.
Morgan Joseph D, 23, Monroe, Monroeville.
Morr John, Jackson, Baldwin.
Morrell Eleanore, 21, Wayne, Fort Wayne.
Morrison Thomas, Jackson, Edgerton.
Morrow Dennis, 24, Springfield, Hall's Corners.
Morton George A, 33, Marion, Poe.
Morton James, 6, Maumee, Harlan.
Moser Jacob, 36, Marion, Williams Station.
Moses Charles, 33, Pleasant, Sheldon.
Moses Francis, 33, Pleasant, Sheldon.
Moses George, 33, Pleasant, Sheldon.
Moses Theron, 28, Pleasant, Sheldon.
Moss Alexander, 19, Cedar Creek, Cedarville.
Moss Wm, 24, Perry, Cedarville.

Motley John, Jackson, Baldwin.
Motone Louis, 21, Jefferson, Maples.
Moudy John, 30, Cedar Creek, Cedarville.
Moudy Kirby, 30, Cedar Creek, Cedarville.
Moudy Martin, 1, Cedar Creek, Hursh.
Mourey Luther, 9, Aboit, Fort Wayne.
Moyer John, 6, Aboit, Dunfee.
Muhn John, 11, Perry, Collingwood.
Muhn Wm, 6, Cedar Creek, Collingwood.
Mulding M, 17, Jackson, Monroeville.
Muldoon Albert, 7, Marion, Fort Wayne.
Muldoon Charles, 7, Marion, Fort Wayne.
Muldoon Elliott, 12, Pleasant, Fort Wayne.
Muldoon Henry, 19, Marion, Poe.
Muldoon L, 29, Marion, Poe.
Mull Charles, Maumee, Woodburn.
Mullen Wm, Jackson, Monroeville.
Mullett John, 30, Wayne, Fort Wayne.
Mullett Peter, 30, Wayne, Fort Wayne.
Mullett Wm, 30, Wayne, Fort Wayne.
Mumma George, 32, Monroe, Monroeville.
Munch Charles, 12, Marion, Soest.
Munch Frank, 18, Madison, Maples.
Munch George, 8, Marion, Fort Wayne.
Munch Herman, 12, Marion, Soest.
Munch Jacob, 12, Marion, Soest.
Munch Wm, 18, Madison, Maples.
Mundt Wm, 19, Washington, Fort Wayne.
Mungen Charles, 21, Lake, Arcola.
Munn James, 19, St Joseph, Fort Wayne.
Murchland Abel, 4, Monroe, Monroeville.
Murchland Samuel, 22, Monroe, Monroeville.
Murphy George, 9, Cedar Creek, Leo.
Murphy James, 7, Monroe, Monroeville.
Murphy Robert, 15, Milan, Harlan.
Murphy Thomas, Jefferson, Maples.
Murphy Thomas, 7, Monroe, Monroeville.
Murray Joseph, 11, Springfield, Spencerville.
Murray Orr, 5, Wayne, Fort Wayne.
Myers, see also Meyer.

Myers C D, Jackson, Monroeville.
Myers Frederick, 31, Milan, New Haven.
Myers George B, 32, Jackson, Monroeville.
Myers George B jr, 31, Jackson, Honroeville.
Myers Henry, 14, Aboit, Fort Wayne.
Myers Henry, 31, Milan, New Haven.
Myers Israel, 8, Perry, Huntertown.
Myers John H, 31, Jackson, Monroeville.
Myers Wm, 26, Aboit, Fort Wayne.
Myers Wm, 32, Milan, New Haven.

N

Nagel Carroll, 4, Maumee, Harlan.
Nahrwald Ernest, 25, Adams, Maples.
Nahrwald F C, 24, Adams, New Haven.
Nahrwald Henry, 25, Adams, Maples.
Nahrwald L, 24, Adams, New Haven.
Nail Daniel, 29, Jefferson, Maples.
Nail John, 21, Jefferson, Maples.
Nail John W, Jefferson, Maples.
Nathan Victor, 31, Perry, Huntertown.
Neadstone John, 15, Monroe, Monroeville.
Neible Joseph, 29-30, Eel River, Heller's Corners.
Neireiter Christian, 21, Wayne, Fort Wayne.
Neireiter Daniel, 14, Marion, Hoagland.
Neireiter George, 14, Marion, Hoagland.
Neireiter John, 21, Wayne, Fort Wayne.
Neireiter Solomon, 14, Marion, Hoagland.
Neiter Herman, 31, Jefferson, Maples.
Neitert Heinrich, 31, Milan, New Haven.
Nelmer Henry, 7, Jefferson, New Haven.
Nelson Bird, 16, Lefayette, Myhart.
Nelson Charles, 19, Perry, Huntertown.
Nelson Joseph, Perry, Huntertown.
Nerbine Cass, Jefferson, Maples.
Nesbaum Edward, 18, Springfield, Harlan.
Nesboum George, 17, Springfield, Harlan.
Nesbaum James, 20, Springfield, Harlan.
Nesbaum John, 18, Springfield, Harlan.

Nesbit Isaac, 36, Jefferson, Zulu.
Nesbit Jeremiah, 2, Madison, Monroeville.
Nesbit John, 25, Jefferson, Zulu.
Nester Conrad, 9, Adams, Fort Wayne.
Nettlehurst Louis, 18, Cedar Creek, Collingwood.
Nettlehurst Louis jr, 18, Cedar Creek, Collingwood.
Neuenschwander C, 8, Cedar Creek, Collingwood.
Newhauser Christian, 6, Milan, Thurber.
Newhauser George, 18, Springfield, Harlan.
Newschwitz George, 18, Monroe, Monroeville.
Nicholson Leonard, 22, Lafayette, Zanesville.
Nicholson M C, 28, Lake, Arcola.
Niciun Wm, 32, St Joseph, Fort Wayne.
Nickelsen John, 24, Milan, Gar Creek.
Nickelson W E, 28, Lafayette, Zanesvile.
Nickey Adam, 21, Milan, Thurman.
Nickles Elias, 10, Jefferson, Dawkins.
Nicodemus A, Lafayette, Nine Mile.
Nicodemus Peter, 11, Lafayette, Nine Mile.
Niedstine Frank, 25, Madison, Hoagland.
Niemeyer Louis, 17, Adams, Fort Wayne.
Niemeyer Wm, 17, Adams, Fort Wayne.
Nieter Edward, 29, Milan, Gar Creek.
Nieter Henry, 29, Milan, Gar Creek.
Nieter Herman, 25, St Joseph, Goeglien.
Nieter Thomas, 29, Milan, Gar Creek.
Nipstine Fred, 27, Madison, Hoagland.
Nitt George, 36, Adams, Fort Wayne.
Noble Simon, 8, Adams, Fort Wayne.
Nonamaker John, 24, Lafayette, Zanesville.
Nonamaker John, 34, Monroe, Monroeville.
Nonamaker John, 22, Pleasant, Sheldon.
Noonan James A, Perry, Huntertown.
North Charles, Maumee, Woodburn.
North Harrison, 17, Maumee, Woodburn.
Norton E K, 12, Aboit, Fort Wayne.
Norton Wm, 12, Aboit, Fort Wayne.
Notestine Daniel, 32, Cedar Creek, Cedarville.
Notestine James, 3, St Joseph, Fort Wayne.
Notestine Peter, 32, Cedar Creek, Cedarville.

Notestine Wesley, 3, St Joseph, Fort Wayne.
Noyer Lynas, 18, Monroe, Monroeville.
Null Frank, 20, Jefferson, New Haven.
Null Harry, 24, Perry, Huntertown.
Null L S, 12, Adams, New Haven.
Nuttle James, 15, Milan, Harlan.
Nuttle Wm, 22, Milan, Gar Creek.

O

Oberholtzen James, 17, Springfield, Harlan.
Oberholtzen Wm, 16, Springfield, Harlan.
Oberly F, Jackson, Dawkins.
O'Briant B, 23, Monroe, Monroeville.
O'Brien Charles, 17, Washington, Fort Wayne.
O'Day Dennis, 36, Lake, Arcola.
Oddou Louis, 5, St Joseph, Fort Wayne.
Oesch Christ, 11, Milan, Harlan.
Oesch Daniel, 29, Marion, Poe.
Oesch Daniel, 11, Milan, Harlan.
Oesch John, 29, Marion, Poe.
Oetting Louis, 36, Wayne, Fort Wayne.
Oetting Wm, 4, Wayne, Fort Wayne.
Offelston John, 20, Aboit, Aboit.
Ogden Benjamin F, 25, Wayne, Fort Wayne.
O'Grady Daniel, 17, Lake, Arcola.
O'Hearn Thomas, 1, Wayne, Fort Wayne.
Ohler Jacob, 5, Cedar Creek, Collingwood.
Ohler Jacob, 24, Springfield, Hall's Corners.
Ohler Jacob, 10, Springfield, Harlan.
Ohler Jacob jr, 10, Springfield, Harlan.
Ohler John, 6, Madison, Maples.
Ohneck Benjamin, 25, Lake, Arcola.
Ohneck John, 15, Washington, Fort Wayne.
Ohrens Henry, 33, Adams, Soest.
Ohrens Henry jr, 33, Adams, Fort Wayne.
Olds Bert, 8, Adams, Fort Wayne.
Olds John, 8, Adams, Fort Wayne.
Olds John D, 12, Adams, New Haven.
Omo Frederick, 14, Springfield, Harlan.

Omo John, 14, Springfield, Harlan.
Omo Joseph H, 3, Springfield, Harlan.
Opdyke David, 18, Cedar Creek, Collingwood.
Opinger Carl, 8, Jefferson, New Haven.
Opliger A, 31, Perry, Huntertown.
Opliger Edward, 4, Washington, Wallen.
Opliger George J, 4, Washington, Wallen.
Orek Charles, 35, Eel River, Heller's Corners.
Oriel Wm, 29, St Joseph, Goeglien.
Ormiston Alexander, 8, Wayne, Fort Wayne.
Orr Wm, 20, Aboit, Aboit.
Ort Louis, 17, Maumee, Woodburn.
Osier J, 4, Aboit, Arcola.
Osterhaus Otto, 2, Marion, Soest.
Osterhaus Wm, 2, Marion, Soest.
Osterman Barney, 27, Lake, Arcola.
Oswald John F, 29, Washington, Fort Wayne.
Oswald John M, 29, Washington, Fort Wayne.
Ott George, 12, Eel River, Huntertown.
Otto Pierce, 27, Perry, Fort Wayne.
Outt Wm, 23, Lafayette, Zanesville.
Owens John, 1, St Joseph, Fort Wayne.
Overly Didymus, 3, Wayne, Fort Wayne.
Overmeyer Edward, 3, Maumee, Antwerp, O.
Overmeyer George, Maumee, Antwerp, O.

P

Packler John, 17, Madison, Hoagland.
Packler Michael, 17, Madison, Hoagland.
Page Henry, 10, Marion, Soest.
Page Wm, 4, Springfield, Harlan.
Pallman Frank, 16, St Joseph, Fort Wayne.
Palmer A, 12, Adams, New Haven.
Palmer C, 8, Aboit, Dunfee.
Palmer D, 8, Aboit, Dunfee.
Palmer Henry, 5, Pleasant, Nine Mile.
Palmer Ira, 28, Pleasant, Sheldon.
Palmer L C, 7, Scipio, Hall's Corners.
Pancake George, 32, Monroe, Monroeville.

Panks Joseph D, 16, Eel River, Churubusco.
Panks Louis, 16, Eel River, Heller's Corners.
Pape F, 27, Milan, Gar Creek.
Parcher George, 12, Adams, New Haven.
Pardner Henry, 17, Wayne, Fort Wayne.
Parker Abraham, 20, St Joseph, Fort Wayne.
Parker Bert O, 7, Perry, Huntertown.
Parker Charles, 20, St Joseph, Fort Wayne.
Parker Charles H, 9, Perry, Huntertown.
Parker Christian, 23, Eel River, Heler's Corners.
Parker Danford, Perry, Huntertown.
Parker Edward, 20, St Joseph, Fort Wayne.
Parker Edward, 12, Washington, Fort Wayne.
Parker Eli, 3, Washington, Wallen.
Parker Elmore, 23, Perry, Huntertown.
Parker George, 10, Pleasant, Nine Mile.
Parker George, 20, St Joseph, Fort Wayne.
Parker James, 20, St Joseph, Fort Wayne.
Parker John, 20, St Joseph, Fort Wayne.
Parker John, 8, Scipio, Hicksville, O.
Parker J R, 23, Monroe, Monroeville.
Parker Millard, 26, Eel River, Wallen.
Parker Nathaniel, 10, Washington, Wallen.
Parker Peter, 16, St Joseph, Fort Wayne.
Parker Sheldon, Perry, Huntertown.
Parker Stephen, 7, Perry, Huntertown.
Parker Wash, 23, Eel River, Helerl's Corners.
Parker Wm, 20, St Joseph, Fort Wayne.
Parker Wilson, Perry, Huntertown.
Parkinson John, 33, Pleasant, Sheldon.
Parks James, 16, Eel River, Heler's Corners.
Parnin Adolph, 21, Aboit, Fort Wayne.
Parnin Francis, 32, Jackson, Monroeville.
Parnin Gustave, 32, Jackson, Monroeville.
Parnin James, 21, Aboit, Fort Wayne.
Parnin James, 27, Perry, Fort Wayne.
Parnin Victor, 4, Monroe, Monroeville.
Patton Thomas, 15, Lake, Arcola.
Pauline Matthias, 8, Cedar Creek, Collingwood.
Pautson August, 12, Adams, New Haven.

Pautson Henry, 12, Adams, New Haven.
Payne Celin, 8, Aboit, Dunfee.
Payne Wm, 33, Aboit, Aboit.
Pearson Nicholas, 31, St Joseph, Fort Wayne.
Pearson Albert, 29, Scipio, Antwerp, O.
Pearson James, 19, Scipio, Fansler.
Pecken Peter, 25, Madison, Hoagland.
Peckham Capitolo, 18, Monroe, Monroeville.
Peckham Wm, 26, Madison, Hoagland.
Peirce Harry, 29, Wayne, Fort Wayne.
Peirre Frank, St Joseph, Fort Wtyne.
Peirre John, 22, St Joseph, Fort Wayne.
Peltier Solomon, 12, Adams, New Haven.
Pence Ulysses, 9, Monroe, Monroeville.
Penney Martin, 15, Lafayette, Myhart.
People John, 29, Milan, Gar Creek.
Pepe Alfred, 12, Jefferson, Dawkins.
Pepe Alexander, 1, Washington, St Vincent.
Pepe August, 22, Jefferson, Maples.
Pepe August J, 16, Eel River, Churubusco.
Pepe Ernest, 32, Adams, Fort Wayne.
Pepe Joseph, 1, Washington, St Vincent.
Pepe Jules, Jackson, Baldwin.
Pepe Jules, 1, Washington, St Vincent.
Pepe Louis, 36, Adams, Fort Wayne.
Peppler Louis, 31, Jefferson, Maples.
Pequinot August, 35, Eel River, Wallen.
Pequinot August, 1, Perry, Collingwood.
Pequinot Charles, 34, Eel River, Heller's Corners.
Pequinot Charles, 6, Washington, Fort Wayne.
Pequinot Frank, 35, Eel River, Wallen.
Pequinot James, 1, Perry, Collingwood.
Perfect John, Jackson, Edgerton.
Perkins Al, 4, Springfield, Harlan.
Perkins Daniel, 24, St Joseph, Thurman.
Perkins George W, 6, Maumee, Harlan.
Perkins Lafayette, 25, St Joseph, Goeglien.
Perkins Louis, 26, Springfield, Harlan.
Perkins Whitley, 28, Scipio, Harlan.
Perkins Wm, 6, Maumee, Harlan.

Perkins Wm, 27, Springfield, Harlan.
Pernot Constant, 18, Jackson, Dawkins.
Perrert Felix, 22, Lake, Arcola.
Perriquay Francois, Perry, Huntertown.
Perry James, 12, Perry, Collingwood.
Peters Amos, 15, Milan, Harlan.
Peters Eldridge, 11, Jefferson, Dawkins.
Peters Ernest, 29, Adams, Fort Wayne.
Peters E H, 30, Washington, Fort Wayne.
Peters John, 24, Springfield, Hall's Corners.
Peters John, 20, Springfield, Harlan.
Peters John A, 7, Springfield, Harlan.
Peters J C, 12, Madison, Monroeville.
Peters J J, 12, Madison, Monroeville.
Peters R, 30, Washington, Fort Wayne.
Peters Simon, 5, Wayne, Fort Wayne.
Peters Wm, 29, Adams, Fort Wayne.
Pettit David L, 7, Washington, Fort Wayne.
Pettit Edward, 24, Washington, Fort Wayne.
Petzold Adams, 13, Marion, Hoagland.
Pfeiffer Charles A, 3, Washington, Wallen.
Pfeiffer Charles G, 22, Washington, Fort Wayne.
Pfeiffer Edward L, 24, Washington, Fort Wayne.
Pfeiffer Frank, 22, Washington, Fort Wayne.
Pfeiffer George L, 3, Washington, Walen.
Pfeiffer W H, 22, Washington, Fort Wayne.
Phail Wm, Jackson, Monroeville.
Philley Charles H, 24, Wayne, Fort Wayne.
Philley Killian, 12, Madison, Monroeville.
Phillips Bert, 4, Washington, Wallen.
Phillips Francis, 3, Aboit, Arcola.
Phillips John, 3, Aboit, Arcola.
Phillips J A, 4, Washington, Wallen.
Phillips Wm, 4, Aboit, Arcola.
Phillips W L, Jackson, Edgerton.
Pichon Charles, 5, St Joseph, Fort Wayne.
Pichon Frank, 28, Cedar Creek, Cedarville.
Pichon John, 29, Cedar Creek, Cedarville.
Pichon Jules, 5, St Joseph, Fort Wayne.
Pieperbrink Christian, 21, Adams, Fort Wayne.

Pieperbrink Louis, 21, Adams, Fort Wayne.
Piggett Ed, 29-30, Eel River, Churubusco.
Piggett Thomas, 29-30, Eel River, Churubusco.
Piggett Wm, 29-30, Eel River, Churubusco.
Pilgrim L L, Jackson, Monroeville.
Pillars Edward, 28, Lake, Arcola.
Pine George, 9, Monroe, Monroeville.
Pio Frank, 12, Jefferson, Dawkins.
Pio Wm, Jackson, Dawkins.
Pion Frank, 24, Perry, Huntertown.
Pisson Charles, 33, Aboit, Aboit.
Plank Philip, 5, Washington, Wallen.
Plants Isaac, 29-30, Eel River, Churubusco.
Platt John, 30, Pleasant, Sheldon.
Plummer Jacob, 14, Springfield, Harlan.
Poehler Charles, 36, Wayne, Fort Wayne.
Poehler Christian, 36, Wayne, Fort Wayne.
Poehler John, 26, Aboit, Fort Wayne.
Poehler John, 32, Adams, Fort Wayne.
Poinsette Del, 24, Springfield, Hall's Corners.
Poinsette John, 16, Aboit, Fort Wayne.
Poinsette Wm, 16, Aboit, Fort Wayne.
Poisson August, 16, Washington, Fort Wayne.
Poisson Felix, 16, Washington, Fort Wayne.
Poisson Francois, Jefferson, Dawkins.
Poland Lefler C, Jackson, Edgerton.
Pollock Charles, 26, Wayne, Fort Wayne.
Pond O, 12, Adams, New Haven.
Poole James T, 31, Wayne, Fort Wayne.
Poole L R, 31, Wayne, Fort Wayne.
Poole Wm, 31, Wayne, Fort Wayne.
Poorman Matthew, 3, Monroe, Baldwin.
Poorpenny Richard, 34, Springfield, Harlan.
Popitz Frederick, 18-19, Milan, Thurman.
Popp Frederick, 31, Cedar Creek, Cedarville.
Popp Henry, 30, Cedar Creek, Cedarville.
Popp Herman, 31, Cedar Creek, Cedarville.
Popp Jacob, 30, Cedar Creek, Cedarville.
Porter Allen, 31, Perry, Huntertown.
Porter Andrew, 31, Perry, Huntertown.

C. P. TINKHAM, DENTIST.   OFFICE TELEPHONE,
                          RESIDENCE TELEPHONE,
Specialty: Teeth Extracted without Pain.   Fine Gold Crown and Bridge Work
Teeth without Plates.   Largest and Best Equipped in the State.   All Work Positively
Guaranteed.   Nos. 21, 22, 23, 24 Arcade Blk., W. Berry St., Fort Wayne, Ind.

ALLEN COUNTY DIRECTORY.   919

Porter Crawford, 7, Scipio, Hall's Corners.
Porter Daniel, 17, Scipio, Hicksville, O.
Porter James, 1, St Joseph, Fort Wayne.
Porter James F, 1, St Joseph, Fort Wayne.
Porter Oliver, 9, St Joseph, Fort Wayne.
Porter Samuel, 27, Aboit, Fort Wayne.
Porter Wesley, 9, St Joseph, Fort Wayne.
Potim Daniel, 21, Jackson, Monroevile.
Potim Henry, 21, Jackson, Monroeville.
Potter F, 1, Wayne, Fort Wayne.
Potter James, 3, Eel River, Ari.
Potts Wm, 27, Madison, Hoagland.
Powell Aaron, 28, Pleasant, Sheldon.
Powell Ephraim, 33, Pleasant, Sheldon.
Powell James, 28, Scipio, Harlan.
Powell Joseph, 28, Scipio, Harlan.
Powell Louis, 28, Scipio, Harlan.
Prange Charles, 21, Adams, Fort Wayne.
Prange Charles, 29, Washington, Fort Wayne.
Prange Christian, 21, Adams, Fort Wayne.
Prange Christian, 29, Washington, Fort Wayne.
Prange Henry, 29, Washington, Fort Wayne.
Prange H, 24, Adams, New Haven.
Prange Wm, 27, Adams, Soest.
Pratt Luther, 10, Washington, Wallen.
Preble D M, 3, Washington, Wallen.
Preston Edward, 7, Perry, Huntertown.
Preston Fred, 7, Perry, Huntertown.
Preston James, 7, Perry, Huntertown.
Preston Matthias, 2, Milan, Harlan.
Presuhn Francis, 36, Madison, Monroeville.
Price Charles, 4, Washington, Wallen.
Price Moses B, 6, Maumee, Harlan.
Price Rent, 4, Washington, Wallen.
Price Richard, 36, Springfield, Harlan.
Prill Emmet, 30, Lake, Arcola.
Prill Frank, 29, Lake, Arcola.
Prill Thomas, 29, Lake, Arcola.
Prince George, 4, Wayne, Fort Wayne.
Prince John, 3-4, Wayne, Fort Wayne.

Prince Wm, 3, Wayne, Fort Wayne.
Pring Edward, 30, Cedar Creek, Cedarville.
Pring Joseph, 31, Cedar Creek, Cedarville.
Prophet L, 16, Monroe, Monroevile.
Provines John, 9, Springfield, Spencerville.
Prusette Ernest, 6, Marion, Fort Wayne.
Pulver Frank, 24, Perry, Huntertown.
Pulver Sherman, Perry, Huntertown.

Q

Quackenbush F, 33, Pleasant, Sheldon.
Quandt Charles, 8, Madison, Maples.
Quandt Charles jr, 8, Madison, Maples.
Quandt Henry, 8, Madison, Monroeville.
Quandt Louis, 17, Madison, Hoagland.
Quinlan John, 21, Monroe, Monroeville.
Quinn Ziah, 30, Jefferson, Maples.

R

Rabb John, 19, Lake, Arcola.
Rabbit Frank, 32, Monroe, Monroeville.
Rabbit Wm, 32, Monroe, Monroeville.
Rabbit Wm jr, 32, Monroe, Monroeville.
Rablege Wm, 34, Monroe, Monroeville.
Racine August, 28, Washington, Fort Wayne.
Rahman John, Milan, Thurman.
Ramm Anthony, 13, Lake, Fort Wayne.
Ramsey James, 10, Wayne, Fort Wayne.
Ramsnyder G, 2, Adams, New Haven.
Ramsnyder John, 2, Adams, New Haven.
Rancey John, Perry, Huntertown.
Rank Ezra, 16, St Joseph, Fort Wayne.
Ranserman Dell, 31, Springfield, Harlan.
Ransom P, 15, Milan, Harlan.
Ransom S A, 15, Milan, Harlan.
Rapp Jacques, 27, Lake, Arcola.
Rapp Henry, 20, Wayne, Fort Wayne.
Rapp Louis, 26, Washington, Fort Wayne.
Rasmus Jacob, 7, Adams, Fort Wayne.

Rassgelt John, 12, Jefferson, Dawkins.
Rauh Christian, 18, St Joseph, Fort Wayne.
Rauh E, 18, St Joseph, Fort Wayne.
Rauh Gibhard, 18, St Joseph, Fort Wayne.
Rauner Isadore, 12, Pleasant, Fort Wayne.
Rawley James R, 21, Lake, Arcola.
Ray F, 33, Perry, Fort Wayne.
Ray James, 6, Monroe, Monroeville.
Ray L, 33, Perry, Fort Wayne.
Rayhouser John, 10, Adams, Fort Wayne.
Raymer Wm, 31, Aboit, Aboit.
Raymond F, Jackson, Edgerton.
Razor Peter, Jackson, Monroeville.
Reader J A, 6, Springfield, Harlan.
Reams Charles, 33, Perry, Fort Wayne.
Reams Frank, 28, Cedar Creek, Cedarvile.
Reams Oscar, 33, Perry, Fort Wayne.
Reams Wm, 33, Perry, Fort Wayne.
Reardon Joseph, Maumee, Woodburn.
Reardon J H, 9, Aboit, Fort Wayne.
Rebber Christian, 16, Adams, Fort Wayne.
Rebber Ernest, 16, Adams, Fort Wayne.
Rebber Frederick, 16, Adams, Fort Wayne.
Rebber F H, 15, Adams, New Haven.
Rebber Harry, 16, Adams, Fort Wayne.
Rebber Henry, 14, Adams, New Haven.
Rebber Louis, 16, Adams, Fort Wayne.
Recker Steven, 12, Adams, New Haven.
Recker Theo, 12, Adams, New Haven.
Recy John, 29, Lafayette, Zanesvile.
Reddin Alfred, 21, Lafayette, Myhart.
Reddin Alfred, 30, Lafayette, Zanesville.
Reddin Harvey, 21, Lafayette, Myhart.
Reddin John, 21, Lafayette, Myhart.
Reddin John, 35, Lafayette, Zanesville.
Reddin Madison, 29, Lafayette, Zanesvile.
Reddin Quincy, 29, Lafayette, Zanesville.
Reddin Sylvester, 28, Lafayette, Zanesville.
Reddin Wilson, 29, Lafayette, Zanesville.
Reed Adam, 5, Wayne, Fort Wayne.

Reed Clarence, 5, Wayne, Fort Wayne.
Reed David S, 31, Wayne, Fort Wayne.
Reed Harvey, 33, Pleasant, Sheldon.
Reed James, Jackson, Edgerton.
Reed Marion, 25, Lafayette, Nine Mile.
Reed Samuel, 29, Marion, Poe.
Reed Sylvester S, 25, Lafayete, Nine Mile.
Reed Wm, 4, Adams, New Haven.
Reeves Louis, 3, Springfield, Harlan.
Rehling Conrad, 11, Washington, Fort Wayne.
Rehling Frederick, 11, Washington, Fort Wayne.
Rehling H, 14, Pleasant, Fort Wayne.
Rehling J J, 13, Pleasant, Fort Wayne.
Reichelderfer Arthur, 1, Springfield, Harlan.
Reichelderfer Charles, 28, Springfield, Harlan.
Reichelderfer Elwood, 9, Springfield, Harlan.
Reichelderfer Francis, Maumee, Wodburn.
Reichelderfer Fred, 28, Springfield, Harlan.
Reichelderfer Henry, 1, Springfield, Harlan.
Reichelderfer Jacob, 1, Springfield, Harlan.
Reichelderfer John, 9, Springfield, Harlan.
Reichelderfer J P, 5, Springfield, Harlan.
Reichelderfer Lafayette, Springfield, Harlan.
Reichelderfer Louis, 28, Springfield, Harlan.
Reichelderfer Wm, 28, Springfield, Harlan.
Reid Wm, 5, Adams, Fort Wayne.
Reidorf Charles, 20, Cedar Creek, Cedarville.
Reidorf Ernest, 20, Cedar Creek, Cedarville.
Reilly F, 28, Pleasant, Sheldon.
Reilly Jesse, 15, Madison, Monroeville.
Reilly John, 15, Madison, Monroeville.
Reinhold Henry, 12, Perry, Collingwood.
Reinhold John, 12, Perry, Collingwood.
Reiper Gerge, 1, Wayne, Fort Wayne.
Reiter Charles, 31, Madison, Hoagland.
Reiter Daniel, 31, Monroe, Monroeville.
Reiter Deiderich, 31, Madison, Hoagland.
Reiter Herman, 31, Madison, Hoagland.
Reiter John, 6, Cedar Creek, Spencerville.
Reiter John, 32, Monroe, Monroeville.

Reiter Walter, 32, Monroe, Monreville.
Reiter Walter jr, 27, Monroe, Monroeville.
Remison James, 24, Wayne, Fort Wayne.
Remmer August, Maumee, Woodburn.
Remmer Charles, Maumee, Woodburn.
Remmy C, 7, Aboit, Dunfee.
Remmy John, 7, Aboit, Dunfee.
Remmy J F, 20, Milan, Thurman.
Remmy Robert, 7, Aboit, Dunfee.
Remus John, 31, Milan, New Haven.
Renille Adolph, 13, Jefferson, Dawkins.
Renille Henry, Jackson, Monroevile.
Renille J H, 7, Monroe, Monroeville.
Renner M, 21, Marion, Poe.
Rennert Jacob, 36, Cedar Creek, Cedarville.
Renninger Jacob, 13, Marion, Hoagland.
Repp Alonzo, 21, Springfield, Harlan.
Repp Elisha, 4, Springfield, Harlan.
Repp Levi, 15, Springfield, Harlan.
Repp Peter, 21, Springfield, Harlan.
Repp Rufus, 22, Springfield, Harlan.
Rettig John, 31, St Joseph, Fort Wayne.
Reynolds Abb, 12, Adams, New Haven.
Reynolds Adolph, 28, Monroe, Monroeville.
Reynolds Albert, 28, Monroe, Monroeville.
Reynolds C O, 28, Monroe, Monroeville.
Reynolds George M, 28, Monroe, Monroeville.
Reynolds Jefferson, 35, Jefferson, Monroeville.
Reynolds Newton, 35, Jefferson, Monroeville.
Reynolds Wm, 17, Monroe, Monroeville.
Rhea George, 9, Adams, Fort Wayne.
Rhine George, 18, Adams, Fort Wayne.
Rhine John, 18, Adams, Fort Wayne.
Rhodes A, 8, Aboit, Dunfee.
Rhodes Clarence, 19, Perry, Huntertown.
Rhodes Daniel, 20, Springfield, Harlan.
Rhodes Daniel J, 8, Aboit, Dunfee.
Rhodes Frank, 35, Pleasant, Sheldon.
Rhodes John, 28, Eel River, Heller's Corners.
Ribolet Bijah, 31, Springfield, Harlan.

924 R. L. POLK & CO.'S

Ribolet George, 31, Springfield, Harlan.
Rice Frank, 10, Eel River, Ari.
Rice Fred, 28, Pleasant, Sheldon.
Rice George, 12, Eel River, Huntertown.
Rice George, 19, Pleasant, Nine Mile.
Rice Henry, 12, Eel River, Huntertown.
Rice James, 15, Monroe, Monroeville.
Rice James, 20, Pleasant, Nine Mile.
Rice Jesse, 20, Pleasant, Nine Mile.
Rice John, 8, Lafayette, Myhart.
Rice John, 28, Pleasant, Sheldon.
Rice Newton, 19, Pleasant, Nine Mile.
Rich Amos, 12, Adams, New Haven.
Rich B L, 3, Eel River, Ari.
Rich James, 12, Adams, New Haven.
Richard Frank, 1, Adams, New Haven.
Richard J N, 18, Eel River, Churubusco.
Richard Samuel, 12, Adams, New Haven.
Richard Smith, 1, Springfield, Harlan.
Richards Allen, 4, Milan, Chamberlain.
Richards Charles, 20, Jefferson, New Haven.
Richards C E, 11, Madison, Monroeville.
Richards Daniel, 36, Perry, Cedarville.
Richards James, 20, Jefferson, New Haven.
Richards Ora, 20, Jefferson, New Haven.
Richards Ora, 4, Lake, Arcola.
Richards Wm, 29, Jefferson, Maples.
Richards Wm, 27, Jefferson, Zulu.
Richardson Albert, 35, Lake, Arcola.
Richardson Alfred, 35, Lake, Arcola.
Richardson George, 3, Wayne, Fort Wayne.
Richardson John, 19, Lake, Arcola.
Richart Francis, Milan, Gar Creek.
Richart George, Milan, Gar Creek.
Richart John, 22, Milan, Gar Creek.
Richart Joseph, 22-23, Milan, Gar Creek.
Richart Merritt, 4, Springfield, Harlan.
Richart Sherman, Milan, Gar Creek.
Richart Wm, 22, Milan, Gar Creek.
Richey Peter, 12, Adams, New Haven.

Richter Andrew J, Jackson, Edgerton.
Richter Christ, Milan, Thurman.
Richter Paul, 3, Wayne, Fort Wayne.
Rickett Edward, Perry, Huntertown.
Ridenour Adam, 22, Madison, Hoagland.
Ridenour E, 26, Monroe, Monroeville.
Ridenour Wm, 22, Madison, Hoagland.
Riley Charles, 18, Wayne, Fort Wayne.
Riley Edward, 31, Jefferson, Maples.
Riley Jacob, 31, Jefferson, Maples.
Riley John, 1, Jefferson, Gar Creek.
Rinehold Henry, Perry, Huntertown.
Rinehold Perry, Perry, Huntertown.
Ringgenberger Christian, 11, Milan, Harlan.
Ringgenberger John, 12, Milan, Harlan.
Ringgenberger Peter, 5, Milan, Chamberlain.
Ringwalt Eli, 17, Milan, Thurman.
Ringwalt George, 16, Milan, Chamberlain.
Ringwalt Wm, 16, Milan, Chamberlain.
Ringwalt Wm, 11, Springfield, Spencerville.
Risely Luther, 3, Wayne, Fort Wayne.
Ritchie Simon, 26, Springfield, Harlan.
Roach John, 3, Lake, Arcola.
Roach John, 13, Madison, Monroeville.
Roach John jr, 13, Madison, Monroeville.
Rober Alfred, 1, Jefferson, Gar Creek.
Roberts Courtland, 3, Springfield, Harlan.
Roberts Edward, 8, Springfield, Harlan.
Roberts Frank, 2, Milan, Harlan.
Roberts George W, 2, Milan, Harlan.
Roberts James, 33, Jackson, Monroeville.
Roberts John, 8, Adams, Fort Wayne.
Roberts R J, Jackson, Monroeville.
Roberts Samuel, 1, Milan, Harlan.
Roberts S A, 29, Marion, Poe.
Roberts Wm, 9, Pleasant, Nine Mile.
Roberts Wm H, 1, Milan, Harlan.
Roberts Wm S, Jefferson, Maples.
Robinette Curtis, 5, Aboit, Dunfee.
Robinette James, 5, Aboit, Arcola.

Robinette James, 6, Aboit, Dunfee.
Robinette M, 18, Aboit, Dunfee.
Robinson Adam, 23, Monroe, Monroeville.
Robinson Amasa S, 17, Monroe, Monroeville.
Robinson B, 29, Pleasant, Sheldon.
Robinson Cary, 19, Pleasant, Nine Mile.
Robinson D A, 29-30, Eel River, Churubsco.
Robinson Elijah, 29-30, Eel River, Churubusco.
Robinson Frank, 30, Lafayette, Zanesville.
Robinson Harvey, 29-30, Eel River, Churubusco.
Robinson J M, 29-30, Eel River, Churubusco.
Robinson McClaren, 29-30, Eel River, Churubusco.
Robinson Nelson, 35, Eel River, Heller's Corners.
Robinson Warren, 6, Pleasant, Nine Mile.
Robinson Wm, 22, Eel River, Heller's Corners.
Robinson Wm, Lafayette, Zanesville.
Robinson Wm, 19, Pleasant, Nine Mile.
Robinson Wm M, 29-30, Eel River, Churubusco.
Robinson W L, 1, Wayne, Fort Wayne.
Robison J J, 19, Madison, Hoagland.
Robison J J jr, 19, Madison, Hoagland.
Rockaway Charles, 8, Wayne, Fort Wayne.
Rockaway Deiderich, 13, Milan, Harlan.
Rockhill Henry, 35, Lake, Arcola.
Rockhill Wm, 33, Lake, Arcola.
Rockhill Wright, 36, Lake, Arcola.
Rodaback Jacob, 31, Jefferson, Maples.
Rodabaugh James, 9, Cedar Creek, Leo.
Rodabush George, 20, Madison, Hoagland.
Rodabush James, 20, Madison, Hoagland.
Rodabush Wm, 22, Madison, Hoagland.
Rodeck Wm, 10, Jefferson, Dawkins.
Rodenbeck Diederich, 32, Perry, Wallen.
Rodenbeck Ernest, 32, Perry, Wallen.
Rodenbeck Frederick, 23, Washington, Fort Wayne.
Rodenbeck Wm, 20, St Joseph, Fort Wayne.
Rodewell George, 4, Wayne, Fort Wayne.
Roesner Christian, 30. Maumee, Woodburn.
Rogers George, 5, Wayne, Fort Wayne.
Rogers G, 12, Adams, New Haven.

Rogers Linn M, 12, Adams, New Haven.
Rogers O S, 12, Adams, New Haven.
Rogers Wm, 25, Springfield, Hall's Corners.
Rogers W S, 12, Adams, New Haven.
Rohbaugh Minus, 6, Madison, Maples.
Rohrick John, 14, Jefferson, Zulu.
Rohrick Wm, 8, Maumee, Woodburn.
Rolfing Edward, 18, Adams, Fort Wayne.
Rolfing Wm, 18, Adams, Fort Wayne.
Rolland Frederick, 3, Harlan, Milan.
Rollands Wm, 29-30, Eel River, Heller's Corners.
Roller H B, 16, Springfield, Harlan.
Roller James, 28, Cedar Creek, Cedarville.
Roller James, 18, Pleasant, Nine Mile.
Roller John, 18, Pleasant, Nine Mile.
Romary August, 11, Cedar Creek, Leo.
Romary August, 33, Lake, Arcola.
Romine Herbert, 4, Cedar Creek, Leo.
Romley John, 6, Milan, Thurman.
Romy R L, 5, Wayne, Fort Wayne.
Rondot Eugene, 4, Washington, Wallen.
Rondot John, 4, Washington, Wallen.
Roose Herman H, Jackson, Edgerton.
Root Wm H, Perry, Wallen.
Rorse March, 29, Jefferson, Maples.
Rose Anthony F, 14, Washington, Fort Wayne.
Rose Benjamin F, 5, Scipio, Hicksville, O.
Rose Charles, 33, Adams, Fort Wayne.
Rose Christian, 7, St Joseph, Fort Wayne.
Rose Daniel B, 6, Scipio, Hall's Corners.
Rose Frank, 30, Jefferson, Maples.
Rose Frank D, 2, Adams, New Haven.
Rose Fred, Perry, Huntertown.
Rose Frederick, 7, St Joseph, Fort Wayne.
Rose James, 33, Jefferson, Monroeville.
Rose John, Milan, Thurman.
Rose Joseph, 2, Adams, New Haven.
Rose Maurice F, 27, Jefferson, Zulu.
Rose Syler, 23, Madison, Monroeville.
Rose Theo, 7, St Joseph, Fort Wayne.

Rose Washington, 3, Adams, New Haven.
Rose Wm, 33, Adams, Soest.
Ross Enoch, 27-28, Eel River, Heller's Corners.
Rosseaner F M, 17, Wayne, Fort Wayne.
Rosseaner Wm, 17, Wayne, Fort Wayne.
Rosselot Lewis, 7, St Joseph, Fort Wayne.
Rosselot Wm, St Joseph, Fort Wayne.
Rosswerm Charles, 3, Monroe, Baldwin.
Rosswerm Henry, 3, Monroe, Baldwin.
Rosswerm Jacob, 3, Monroe, Baldwin.
Rosswerm Peter, 3, Monroe, Baldwin.
Roth Daniel, 10, Springfield, Harlan.
Roth David, 20, Springfield, Harlan.
Rothgeb Chase, 8, Maumee, Woodburn.
Rothgeb C, 34, Milan, Gar Creek.
Rothgeb Henry, 1, Jefferson, Gar Creek.
Rothgeb Jesse, 1, Jefferson, Gar Creek.
Rothgeb Jesse, 34, Milan, Gar Creek.
Rothgeb Solomon, 4, Jefferson, Gar Creek.
Rothgeb Wm, 1, Jefferson, Gar Creek.
Rothgeb W S, 35, Milan, Gar Creek.
Rousseau Felix, 13, Adams, New Haven.
Rousseau F, 9, Aboit, Fort Wayne.
Rousseau John, 13, Adams, New Haven.
Roussey August, 12, Jefferson, Dawkins.
Roussey Charles, 14, Jefferson, Zulu.
Roussey Emil, 12, Jefferson, Dawkins.
Roussey Francis, 14, Jefferson, Zulu.
Roussey Francis jr, 14, Jefferson, Zulu.
Roussey John, 14, Jefferson, Zulu.
Roussey Louis, 12, Jefferson, Dawkins.
Roussey Wm, 12, Jefferson, Dawkins.
Rowe Andrew, 10, Monroe, Monroeville.
Rowe Daniel A, 10, Monroe, Monroeville.
Rowe Samuel, 10, Monroe, Monroeville.
Roy Alexander, 28, Perry, Fort Wayne.
Roy Charles, 6, Monroe, Monroeville.
Roy Charles, 28, Perry, Fort Wayne.
Roy Charles, 32, Perry, Wallen.
Roy Edward, 28, Perry, Fort Wayne.

Roy Frank, 14, Jefferson, Zulu.
Roy Jean B, 23, Jefferson, Zulu.
Roy Jefferson, 14, Jefferson, Zulu.
Roy Joseph, 23, Jefferson, Zulu.
Roy Julian, 15, Jefferson, Zulu.
Roy Louis, 29, Jefferson, Maples.
Roy Louis, 27, Jefferson, Zulu.
Roy Peter, 14, Jefferson, Zulu.
Ruan Henry, 12, Adams, New Haven.
Ruan Lawrence, 21, Lake, Arcola.
Ruble Frank, Jackson, Dawkins.
Ruby Arthur, 28, Lake, Arcola.
Ruby Edward, 28, Lake, Arcola.
Ruby Frank, 28, Lake, Arcola.
Ruch Fred, 31, Jackson, Monroeville.
Ruch George, 15, Jackson, Edgerton.
Ruch John, 15, Jackson, Edgerton.
Ruch Simon, 15, Jackson, Edgerton.
Rudisell Allison, 28, Lake, Arcola.
Rudisell I M, 31, Perry, Huntertown.
Rudisell Jacob, 25, Washington, Fort Wayne.
Rue Justin, Jackson, Baldwin.
Rue Otis, 27, Marion, Hoagland.
Ruffing Martin, 24, Milan, Gar Creek.
Ruhl Christopher, 30, Madison, Hoagland.
Ruhl John, 25, Madison, Hoagland.
Ruhl L, 24, Marion, Hoagland.
Runnells John J, 8, Perry, Huntertown.
Runnion Edward, 19-20, Eel River, Heller's Corners.
Runnion Joseph, 20, Eel River, Heller's Corners.
Runnion Thomas, 29-30, Eel River, Heller's Corners.
Rupe Joseph A, 10, Wayne, Fort Wayne.
Rupert Eli, 1, Milan, Harlan.
Rupert Isaac, 23, Springfield, Hall's Corners.
Rupert John J, Jackson, Edgerton.
Rupert M, 5, Scipio, Hicksville, O.
Rupert Oscar, 10, Springfield, Harlan.
Rupp James, 36, Lafayette, Zanesville.
Rush Henry, 23, Maumee, Antwerp, O.
Rush James, 23, Maumee, Antwerp, O.

Rushart Andrew, 35, Milan, Gar Creek.
Rushart Phillip, 4, Jefferson, Gar Creek.
Rushman John, 29, Marion, Poe.
Rushton Samuel, 12, Adams, New Haven.
Ruslige Daniel, 3, Jefferson, Gar Creek.
Russ Wm, 5, Lafayette, Aboit.
Ryan Harry, 14, Adams, New Haven.
Ryan Henry, 11, Adams, New Haven.
Ryan John, 20, Jefferson, New Haven.
Ryan John, 24, Lake, Arcola.
Ryan John, 34, Milan, Gar Creek.
Ryan Joseph, 34, Milan, Gar Creek.
Ryan Patrick, 1, Jefferson, Gar Creek.
Ryan Patrick, 34, Milan, Gar Creek.

S

Saalfrank D, 15, Marion, Hoagland.
Saalfrank Fred, 10, Marion, Soest.
Saalfrank Henry F, 15, Marion, Hoagland.
Sack Henry, 9, Marion, Fort Wayne.
Sackett C D, 19, Madison, Hoagland.
Safford Henry, 8, Milan, Chamberlain.
Safford Rufus, 9, Milan, Chamberlain.
Saiss Frederick, 3, Monroe, Baldwin.
Sales Wm, Lafayette, Nine Mile.
Salier Joseph, 4, Washington, Wallen.
Salzbrenner Charles, 3, Jefferson, Gar Creek.
Salzbrenner Frank, 3, Jefferson, Gar Creek.
Salzbrenner John, 3, Jefferson, Gar Creek.
Sams Ulrich, 33, Wayne, Fort Wayne.
Sand John, 5, Lafayette, Aboit.
Sanders Christ, 19, Springfield, Harlan.
Sanders Elmore, 29, Scipio, Antwerp, O.
Sanders John, 30, Jefferson, Maples.
Sanders Joseph, 15, Cedar Creek, Leo.
Sanders Joseph, 30, Madison, Hoagland.
Sanders Oscar, 19, Scipio, Fansler.
Sanders Samuel, 15, Cedar Creek, Leo.
Sanscotte George, 17, Jackson, Monroeville.

Sanscotte George jr, Jackson, Monroeville.
Sapp Abner, 31-32, Springfield, Harlan.
Sapp Frank, 31, Springfield, Harlan.
Sapp Samuel, 31, Springfield, Harlan.
Sargent John, 29, Marion, Poe.
Sarrazen August, 6, Washington, Fort Wayne.
Sarrazen Orzine, 32, Perry, Wallen.
Sartons Theo, 12, Lake, Arcola.
Savage Jefferson, Jackson, Monroeville.
Saviot Louis, 23, Monroe, Monroeville.
Saylor C, 15, Adams, New Haven.
Saylor Frank, 3, Maumee, Antwerp, O.
Saylor Frank, Springfield, Harlan.
Saylor Harland, Perry, Huntertown.
Saylor Lyman, Perry, Huntertown.
Saylor Wesley, Maumee, Antwerp, O.
Saynor Theo, 12, Adams, New Haven.
Scan John, 28, Monroe, Monroeville.
Scan John jr, 28, Monroe, Monroeville.
Scanels Frank, 5, Lafayette, Aboit.
Scarlett A G, 28, Washington, Fort Wayne.
Scarlett A L, 28, Washington, Fort Wayne.
Schaffer, see also Shaffer.
Schaffer Chris, 36, Wayne, Fort Wayne.
Schaffer Christian, 19, Washington, Fort Wayne.
Schaffer Frederick, 36, Wayne, Fort Wayne.
Schaffer James, 26, Madison, Hoagland.
Schaffer John, 36, Madison, Monroeville.
Schaffer John, 7, Springfield, Harlan.
Schammer Wm, 31, Madison, Hoagland.
Schantz Jacob, 29-30, Eel River, Wallen.
Schanze Amos, 25, St Joseph, Goeglien.
Schaper Charles, 20, Adams, Fort Wayne.
Schaper Christian, 19, Adams, Fort Wayne.
Schaper Frederick, 19, Adams, Fort Wayne.
Schaper Gottlieb, 17, Adams, Fort Wayne.
Scharf Fred, 10, Cedar Creek, Leo.
Scharpenberg August, 31, Jefferson, Maples.
Scharpenberg Henry, 25, Adams, Maples.
Scharpenberg Henry jr, 25, Adams, Maples.

Schears Frederick, 35, Madison, Binger.
Scheler Jacob, 11, Adams, New Haven.
Schemmershorn F, 12, Adams, New Haven.
Scherer Christian, 15, Lafayette, Myhart.
Scherer Henry, 15, Lafayette, Myhart.
Scherschel John, 6, Marion, Fort Wayne.
Scherschel Louis, 35, Milan, Gar Creek.
Scheubhole Conrad, 12, Adams, New Haven.
Schieman Edward, 36, Marion, Williams Station.
Schilling Adolph, 20, Wayne, Fort Wayne.
Schilling Charles, 8, Washington, Fort Wayne.
Schilling John, 26, Washington, Fort Wayne.
Schlatter David B, 21 Cedar Creek, Cedarville.
Schlaudroff Christian, 17, Adams, Fort Wayne.
Schlaudroff Henry, 12, Marion, Soest.
Schlaudroff John, 33, Adams, Fort Wayne.
Schlaudroff Ludwig, 33, Adams, Soest.
Schlaudroff Wm, 33, Adams, Fort Wayne.
Schlegel Henry, 32, Milan, Gar Creek.
Schlegel Jacob, 32, Milan, Gar Creek.
Schlep Frederick, 2, Aboit, Fort Wayne.
Schmid Marion, 17, Jackson, Monroeville.
Schmidt August, 10, Monroe, Monroeville.
Schmidt August, 19, Washington, Fort Wayne.
Schmidt Christian, 19, Washington, Fort Wayne.
Schmidt Gottlieb, 10, Monroe, Monroeville.
Schmidt Henry, 13, Lake, Fort Wayne.
Schmidt John, 10, Monroe, Monroeville.
Schmidt Wm, 10, Monroe, Monroeville.
Schmier H, 13, Wayne, Fort Wayne.
Schmitker A R, 12, Adams, New Haven.
Schmitker Wm, 12, Adams, New Haven.
Schneider Anthony, 36, Springfield, Harlan.
Schneider Carolus, 6, Cedar Creek, Collingwood.
Schneider Emery, 6, Cedar Creek, Collingwood.
Schneider Frederick, 27, Lake Arcola.
Schneider Frederick, 36, Springfield, Harlan.
Schneider George, 36, Springfield, Harlan.
Schneider John, 36, Springfield, Harlan.
Schneider John, 30, Washington, Fort Wayne.

Schneider Stephen, 36, Springfield, Harlan.
Schneider Wm, 36, Springfield, Harlan.
Schnelker Bernard, 12, Adams, New Haven.
Schnelker H, 12, Adams, New Haven.
Schnerles George, 6, Aboit, Dunfee.
Schnurr Jerome, 17, Wayne, Fort Wayne.
Schnurr Philip, 17, Wayne, Fort Wayne.
Schoche Charles, 2, Marion, Soest.
Schone Ludwig W, 17, Washington, Fort Wayne.
Schonnick Peter, 3, Wayne, Fort Wayne.
Schoonover Daniel, 33, Lafayette, Zanesville.
Schoppman Deiderich, 31, Madison, Hoagland.
Schoppman Louis, 32, St Joseph, Fort Wayne.
Schoppman Wm, 32, St Joseph, Fort Wayne.
Schrader Edward, 30, Adams, Fort Wayne.
Schrader Frederick, 35, Marion, Williams Station.
Schrader Henry, 35, Marion, Williams Station.
Schrader Henry jr, 35, Marion, Williams Station.
Schrader J, 35, Marion, Williams Station.
Schroeder August, 17, Marion, Fort Wayne.
Schroeder Wm, 17, Marion, Fort Wayne.
Schuckman Benjamin, 30, Madison, Hoagland.
Schuckman F, 1, Adams, New Haven.
Schuler H, 35, Pleasant, Sheldon.
Schuler John, 20, Cedar Creek, Cedarville.
Schuler Lorenz, 16, St Joseph, Fort Wayne.
Schultz Joseph, Jefferson, Maples.
Schwalm Philip, 21, St Joseph, Fort Wayne.
Schwartz Benjamin, 5, Cedar Creek, Collingwood.
Schwartz Chris, Milan, Chamberlain.
Schwartz Chris, 21, Milan, Thurman.
Schwartz Clinton, 34, Springfield, Harlan.
Schwartz Herbert, 5, Cedar Creek, Collingwood.
Schwartz John, 5, Cedar Creek, Collingwood.
Schwartz Joseph, 20, Milan, Thurman.
Scott Charles, 33, Lafayette, Zanesville.
Scott David, 33, Lafayette, Zanesville.
Scott George, 28, Lafayette, Zanesville.
Scott G, 10, Aboit, Fort Wayne.
Scott Had, 16, Monroe, Monroeville.

Scott John, 28, Aboit, Aboit.
Scott Leonidas B, 24, Madison, Monroeville.
Scott Michael, 22, Aboit, Fort Wayne.
Scott Otto, 33, Lafayette, Zanesville.
Scott Samuel, 16, Monroe, Monroeville.
Scott Sink, 25, Lafayette, Nine Mile.
Scott Wm, 24, Aboit, Fort Wayne.
Scott Wm, 27, Lafayette, Zanesville.
Scott Wm, 4, Monroe, Monroeville.
Scott Winfield S, 9, Monroe, Monroeville.
Scrines J, 4, Aboit, Arcola.
Seabold Henry, Lafayette, Nine Mile.
Seabold John, 12, Lafayette, Nine Mile.
Seabold John, 31, St Joseph, Fort Wayne.
Seaman James, 35, Lafayette, Zanesville.
Search George, 28, Aboit, Aboit.
Sears Peter, 36, Madison, Monroeville.
Seddlemeyer Henry R, 30, Adams, Fort Wayne.
Seeds Thomas, 10, Wayne, Fort Wayne.
Seffel August, 17, Washington, Fort Wayne.
Seibert F, 13, St Joseph, Thurman.
Seibold Adam, 25, Lake, Arcola.
Seidel Henry, 12, Adams, New Haven.
Seigel Reneke, 5, Washington, Wallen.
Seigel Rhinehart, 28, Monroe, Monroeville.
Seigel Rhinehart jr, 28, Monroe, Monroeville.
Selig Charles, 6, Adams, Fort Wayne.
Selig Conrad, 6, Adams, Fort Wayne.
Selig John, 6, Adams, Fort Wayne.
Selig John jr, 6, Adams, Fort Wayne.
Selking Conrad, 21, Madison, Hoagland.
Selking Conrad jr, 21, Madison, Hoagland.
Sellberg Cass, 28, Springfield, Harlan.
Sexton Wm, Jackson, Baldwin.
Shaffer, see also Schaffer.
Shaffer Daniel, 9, St Joseph, Fort Wayne.
Shaffer Gottlieb, 18-19, Milan, Thurman.
Shaffer Henry, 1, Cedar Creek, Hursh.
Shaffer Jacques, 22, Lake, Arcola.
Shaffer Judson, 6, Maumee, Harlan.

Shaffer Massey, 35, Madison, Binger.
Shaffer Reuben, Maumee, Woodburn.
Shaffer Samuel, 4, Cedar Creek, Leo.
Shaffer Valentine L, 20, Monroe, Monroeville.
Shaffer Washington, 25, Springfield, Hall's Corners.
Shaffer Wm, 29, Milan, Gar Creek.
Shambaugh Daniel, 11, Cedar Creek, Leo.
Shambaugh F, 1, Cedar Creek, Hursh.
Shambaugh John, 11, Cedar Creek, Leo.
Shank John, 20, Lafayette, Roanoke.
Shannon George, 28, Cedar Creek, Cedarville.
Sharp Wm, 1, Springfield, Harlan.
Shaughnessy Michael, 5, Adams, Fort Wayne.
Shaughnessy Michael, 18, Monroe, Monroeville.
Shaughnessy Wm, 5, Monroe, Monroeville.
Shaughnessy Wm jr, 5, Monroe, Monroeville.
Shaver John, 4, Milan, Chamberlain.
Shaver John, Perry, Huntertown.
Shaver Samuel E, 4, Milan, Chamberlain.
Shea Albert, 33, Monroe, Monroeville.
Shea Patrick, 12, Adams, New Haven.
Shea Peter, 33, Monroe, Monroeville.
Shearer Abnell, 13, Pleasant, Fort Wayne.
Shearer F, 17, Pleasant, Nine Mile.
Shearer George, 8, Pleasant, Nine Mile.
Shearer H, 17, Pleasant, Nine Mile.
Shearer John, 8, Pleasant, Nine Mile.
Sheehan Daniel, 4, Monroe, Monroeville.
Sheehan John, 8, Monroe, Monroeville.
Sheehan John jr, 8, Monroe, Monroeville.
Sheehan Thomas, 4, Monroe, Monroeville.
Sheehan Wm, 4, Monroe, Monroeville.
Sheffield L, 16, Jefferson, Zulu.
Sheldon Cyrus, 7, Eel River, Churubusco.
Shellaberger John, 33, Milan, Gar Creek.
Shellhauser Charles, 13, Wayne, Fort Wayne.
Shelner Daniel, 19, Perry, Huntertown.
Shena Patrick, 28, Aboit, Aboit.
Shepler Frank, 34, Lafayette, Zanesville.
Shepler John, 35, Lafayette, Zanesville.

Shepler Polk, 24, Lafayette, Zanesville.
Sheppleman Henry, 33, Milan, Gar Creek.
Sherding Charles, 35, Lake, Arcola.
Sherding Christian, 35, Lake, Arcola.
Sherding Fred, 35, Lake, Arcola.
Sherding Henry, 35, Lake, Arcola.
Sheridan Charles, 15, Lake, Arcola.
Sheridan James, 1, Washington, St Vincent.
Sheridan Michael, 9, Adams, Fort Wayne.
Shiffler John, 33, Eel River, Heller's Corners.
Shink George, 21, Milan, Thurman.
Shinn C, 9, Pleasant, Nine Mile.
Shinner Christian, 35, Marion, Williams Station.
Shinner Henry, 8, Monroe, Monroeville.
Shipman Frank, 1, St Joseph, Fort Wayne.
Shipman Jesse, 12, Adams, New Haven.
Shirey Jacob, 4, Springfield, Harlan.
Shirey Louis, 28, Cedar Creek, Cedarville.
Shirey Samuel, 12, Adams, New Haven.
Shirley George, 35, Jefferson, Monroeville.
Shirley H D, 28, Springfield, Harlan.
Shirley John, 3, Maumee, Antwerp, O.
Shirley Robert, 17, Maumee, Woodburn.
Shive Chester, 9, Pleasant, Nine Mile.
Shive John, 10, Pleasant, Nine Mile.
Shive Wm, 4, Pleasant, Fort Wayne.
Shoaff David, 30, Cedar Creek, Cedarville.
Shoaff D R, 29-30, Eel River, Huntertown.
Shoaff Peter, 27, Milan, Gar Creek.
Shoaff Wm, 29-30, Eel River, Huntertown.
Shoaff W Scott, 1-2, Eel River, La Otto.
Shoemaker Luther, 2, St Joseph, Fort Wayne.
Shoffman Louis, 29, St Joseph, Goeglien.
Sholts Perry, 26, Washington, Fort Wayne.
Shook Philip, 31, Marion, Poe.
Shookman Joseph, 27, Marion, Hoagland.
Shordan George, 26, St Joseph, Goeglien.
Shordan Howard, 35, St Joseph, Goeglien.
Shordan Wm, 26, St Joseph, Goeglien.
Short L, 21, Monroe, Monroeville.

Shrimp Rich, Milan, Chamberlain.
Shriver George, 4, Eel River, Ari.
Shuckman R, 31, Milan, New Haven.
Shull Charles, 19, Scipio, Fansler.
Shull John, 19, Scipio, Fansler.
Shull John, 12, Springfield, Harlan.
Shull Samuel, 32, Scipio, Harlan.
Shull Wm, 29, Scipio, Antwerp, O.
Shultz Henry, 29, Marion, Poe.
Shunk Frank, 19, Scipio, Fansler.
Shutt Edward, Springfield, Harlan.
Shutt George, 13, Eel River, Huntertown.
Shutt Mart, 3, Springfield, Harlan.
Sibel Clark, 29-30, Eel River, Wallen.
Sibel Elwin, 16, Eel River, Heller's Corners.
Sibel Ira, 16, Eel River, Heller's Corners.
Sibel Wm, 16, Eel River, Heller's Corners.
Siebolt Samuel, 33, Lafayette, Zanesville.
Siegel Philip, 7, Monroe, Monroeville.
Siegmund D, 18, Adams, Fort Wayne.
Siemon Christian, 2, Pleasant, Fort Wayne.
Sigler George, 9, Cedar Creek, Leo.
Silver John, Jackson, Edgerton.
Silvers Ed, Jackson, Dawkins.
Simero Charles, 3, Monroe, Baldwin.
Simmers Abraham, 9, Monroe, Monroeville.
Simmons David, 6, Monroe, Monroeville.
Simmons John, 22, Monroe, Monroeville.
Simms Herman, 8, Madison, Maples.
Simms Wm, 8, Madison, Maples.
Simon James, 5, Perry, Huntertown.
Simon Solomon, 5, Perry, Huntertown.
Simondorf F, 1, Wayne, Fort Wayne.
Simons Jacob, 18, Monroe, Monroeville.
Simons Wm, 18, Monroe, Monroevile.
Simonton Fred, 32, Lafayette, Zanesville.
Simonton Harry, 29, Lafayette, Zanesville.
Simonton Wm, 31, Aboit, Fort Wayne.
Simran Charles, 26, Adams, Fort Wayne.
Simran Frederick, 26, Adams, Fort Wayne.

Simran Henry, 26, Adams, Fort Wayne.
Sines Wilbur, 33, Lake, Arcola.
Skellinger S, 5, Springfield, Harlan.
Skittler James, 5, Springfield, Harlan.
Slagle Gottlieb, 33, St Joseph, Fort Wayne.
Slaten Charles, 19, St Joseph, Fort Wayne.
Slater Wm, 4, Pleasant, Fort Wayne.
Slattert Jules, 18, Jackson, Dawkins.
Slattert Louisa, 18, Jackson, Dawkins.
Slattery Arthur, 15, Monroe, Monroeville.
Slattery Michael, 15, Monroe, Monroeville.
Slattery Wm, 15, Monroe, Monroeville.
Slaughter Benjamin, 10, Cedar Creek, Leo.
Slaughter Christian, 15, Cedar Creek, Leo.
Slaughter Christian, 34, Springfield, Harlan.
Slaughter James, 10, Cedar Creek, Leo.
Slaughter John, 18, Cedar Creek, Collingwood.
Sledd Samuel D, 12, Lafayette, Nine Mile.
Slemer Philip, 22, Monroe, Monroeville.
Sloffer Henry, 12, Eel River, Huntertown.
Sloffer John, 1, Eel River, La Otto.
Slum Albert, 36, Lafayette, Zanesville.
Small Edward, 20, Jefferson, New Haven.
Small Frank, 12, Adams, New Haven.
Small Isaac, 21, Jefferson, Maples.
Small Jefferson, Maumee, Antwerp, O.
Smaltz George W, 21, Aboit, Fort Wayne.
Smiers Andrew, 9, Monroe, Monroeville.
Smiers Cal, 9, Monroe, Monroeville.
Smith Allen J, Perry, Huntertown.
Smith Andrew, 13, Lake, Fort Wayne.
Smith A, 11, Pleasant, Fort Wayne.
Smith Bert, 4, Milan, Chamberlain.
Smith Charles, 17, Lafayette, Myhart.
Smith Charles, 18, Washington, Fort Wayne.
Smith Charles H, 8, Adams, Fort Wayne.
Smith Clarence, 17, Lake, Arcola.
Smith Clement, 29, Scipio, Antwerp, O.
Smith C, 8, Aboit, Dunfee.
Smith Daniel, 26, Adams, Fort Wayne.

Smith David, 15, Eel River, Heller's Corners.
Smith Dean, 31, Eel River, Heller's Corners.
Smith D L, 1, Cedar Creek, Hursh.
Smith D P, 15, Milan, Harlan.
Smith Edward, 5, Aboit, Dunfee.
Smith Elias, 31, Monroe, Monroeville.
Smith Enoch, 30, Pleasant, Sheldon.
Smith E F, 4, Aboit, Arcola.
Smith Finley, 31, Pleasant, Sheldon.
Smith Forest, 7, Springfield, Harlan.
Smith Frank, 17, Jefferson, New Haven.
Smith Frank, 8, Marion, Fort Wayne.
Smith Frederick, 36, Springfield, Harlan.
Smith F, 5, Aboit, Dunfee.
Smith George, 30, Madison, Hoagland.
Smith George, 1, Marion, Soest.
Smith George, 18, Washington, Fort Wayne.
Smith Henry, 32, Adams, Fort Wayne.
Smith Henry, 17, Lafayette, Myhart.
Smith Henry, 8, Marion, Fort Wayne.
Smith Henry, 4, Milan, Chamberlain.
Smith Henry, 12, Perry, Collingwood.
Smith Jacob, 31, Jefferson, Maples.
Smith Jacob, Perry, Huntertown.
Smith Jacob, 29, Pleasant, Sheldon.
Smith James, 36, Lafayette, Zanesville.
Smith James, 33, Lake, Arcola.
Smith James, 31, Springfield, Harlan.
Smith John, 34, Adams, Soest.
Smith John, 36, Madison, Monroevile.
Smith John, 8, Marion, Fort Wayne.
Smith John, 8, Scipio, Hicksville, O.
Smith Jonas, 33, Pleasant, Sheldon.
Smith Joseph, 19, Lafayette, Myhart.
Smith Josiah, 6, Eel River, Churubusco.
Smith J S, 4, Lake, Heller's Corners.
Smith J T, 3, Milan, Harlan.
Smith L, 28, Springfield, Harlan.
Smith Marion, 33, Marion, Poe.
Smith Martin, 13, Aboit, Fort Wayne.

9

Smith Matthias, 2, Milan, Harlan.
Smith Merrill, 28, Springfield, Harlan.
Smith Orson, 30, Pleasant, Sheldon.
Smith Otis, 29-30, Eel River, Heller's Corners.
Smith Perry, 15, Milan, Harlan.
Smith Peter, 32, Adams, Fort Wayne.
Smith Philip, 13, Adams, New Haven.
Smith Riley, 1, Springfield, Harlan.
Smith Robert, 12, Adams, New Haven.
Smith Samuel, 16, Milan, Chamberlain.
Smith Samuel, 12, Perry, Collingwood.
Smith Samuel, Springfield, Harlan.
Smith Sherman, 6, Springfield, Harlan.
Smith S S, 22, Lake, Arcola.
Smith Walter, 33, Madison, Bingen.
Smith Wm, 26, Eel River, Wallen.
Smith Wm, Jackson, Monroeville.
Smith Wm, 5, Jefferson, New Haven.
Smith Wm, 24, Lake, Arcola.
Smith Wm, 5, Marion, Fort Wayne.
Smith Wm, 3, Springfield, Harlan.
Smith Wm, 21, Wayne, Fort Wayne.
Smith W V, 4, Eel River, Ari.
Smith W W, 32, Marion, Poe.
Smith Zachariah, 30, Pleasant, Sheldon.
Smithers Charles, 11, Lake, Arcola.
Smithers James, 16, Washington, Fort Wayne.
Smitley Ellis, 29, Scipio, Antwerp, O.
Smitley Enos, 22, Marion, Hoagland.
Smitley George, 27, Marion, Hoagland.
Smitley Sherman, 16, Washington, Fort Wayne.
Smitley Wm, 19, Madison, Hoagland.
Smodd Marion, 19, Madison, Hoagland.
Snelker H F, 12, Adams, New Haven.
Snider Jacob, 2, St Joseph, Fort Wayne.
Snider John, 35, Lake, Arcola.
Snider John, 35, Pleasant, Sheldon.
Sniel Francis, 22, Lake, Arcola.
Sniel Joseph, 22, Lake, Arcola.
Snitzler Adam, 26, Pleasant, Sheldon.

Snitzler Gust, 26, Pleasant, Sheldon.
Snitzler Peter, 26, Pleasant, Sheldon.
Snodgrass J T, 31, Washington, Fort Wayne.
Snodgrass M C, 31, Washington, Fort Wayne.
Snodgrass S W, 31, Washington, Fort Wayne.
Snurr Cornelius, 8, Lafayette, Myhart.
Snyder Anthony, 26, Springfield, Harlan.
Snyder Benjamin, 26, Jefferson, Zulu.
Snyder Bert, 18, Marion, Fort Wayne.
Snyder Charles, 2, Milan, Harlan.
Snyder Charles, 26, Springfield, Harlan.
Snyder Christian, 25, Lake, Arcola.
Snyder David, 35, Jefferson, Monroeville.
Snyder Ferry, 26, Springfield, Harlan.
Snyder George, 3, Abolt, Arcola.
Snyder George, 9, Adams, Fort Wayne.
Snyder George, 27, Springfield, Harlan.
Snyder Harris, 11, Perry, Collingwood.
Snyder Henry, 3, Aboit, Arcola.
Snyder John, 36, Adams, Maples.
Snyder John, 1, Jefferson, Gar Cleek.
Snyder John, 26, Springfield, Harlan.
Snyder Nicholas, 13, Adams, New Haven.
Snyder Philip, 12, Adams, New Haven.
Snyder P M, 29, Marion, Poe.
Snyder Samuel, 29, Lake, Arcola.
Snyder Sefare, 26, Springfield, Hall's Corners.
Snyder Solomon, 29, Marion, Poe.
Snyder Wm, Perry, Huntertown.
Snyder Wm, 11, Washington, Fort Wayne.
Snyder W, 12, Adams, New Haven.
Soest Ernest, 14, Washington, Fort Wayne.
Soest Ernest jr, 14, Washington, Fort Wayne.
Soest Frederick, 12, Washington, Fort Wayne.
Soest George, 11, Marion, Soest.
Soest Louis, 3, Marion, Soest.
Soest Wm, 2, Marion, Soest.
Soliday John jr, 11, Washington, Fort Wayne.
Solomon Charles, 15, Washington, Fort Wayne.
Solomon Christian, 2, Washington, St Vincent.

Solomon James, 7, Eel River, Churubusco.
Solon John, 21, Lake, Arcola.
Solon Michael, 21, Lake, Arcola.
Solway Charles, 16, Monroe, Monroeville.
Solway James, 22, Monroe, Monroeville.
Solway John, 16, Monroe, Monroeville.
Solway John jr, 16, Monroe, Monroeville.
Somers Christian, 36, Cedar Creek, Cedarville.
Somers Edward, 29, Marion, Poe.
Somers Eli, 36, Cedar Creek, Cedarville.
Somers Fred, 26, Pleasant, Sheldon.
Somers George, 36, Pleasant, Sheldon.
Somers Henry, 36, Pleasant, Sheldon.
Somers Levi, 25, Pleasant, Poe.
Somers Perry, 36, Pleasant, Sheldon.
Somers Simon, 21, Marion, Poe.
Sommers Ambrose, 6, Eel River, Churubusco.
Sommers George, 6, Eel River, Churubusco.
Sones Wm, 12, Springfield, Georgetown.
Sonles Wm, 29, Cedar Creek, Cedarville.
Soorat August, 13, Madison, Monroeville.
Sordelet Anthony, 1, Washington, St Vincent.
Sordelet Augustus, 15, Lake, Arcola.
Sordelet A P, Perry, Cedarville.
Sordelet Frank, 1, Washington, St Vincent.
Sordelet Jacques, 11, Jefferson, Dawkins.
Sordelet Joseph, 1, Washington, St Vincent.
Sordelet Lou, 1, Washington, St Vincent.
Sorg Anthony, 23, Marion, Hoagland.
Sorg Charles, 15, Marion, Hoagland.
Sorg George, 11, Pleasant, Fort Wayne.
Sorg Henry, 8, Marion, Fort Wayne.
Sorg John B, 8, Marion, Fort Wayne.
Sorg John W, 18, Marion, Fort Wayne.
Sorg Joseph, 18, Marion, Fort Wayne.
Sorg Michael, 22, Marion, Hoagland.
Sorg Peter, 20, Pleasant, Nine Mile.
Sorg Theo, 11, Pleasant, Fort Wayne.
Sorgen Frederick, 3, Monroe, Baldwin.
Sorgen James F, 4, Monroe, Monroeville.

Souchi John, 18, Springfield, Harlan.
Souder Daniel, 29, St Joseph, Goeglien.
Souder Jonas, 2, Cedar Creek, Spencerville.
Souder S, 26, Springfield, Hall's Corners.
Souix Horace, 5, Milan, Chamberlain.
Sours Daniel, 3, Springfield, Harlan.
Souser Oliver, 14, Milan, Harlan.
Sovine Eugene, 32, St Joseph, Fort Wayne.
Sovine Francis, 18, Monroe, Monroeville.
Sovine Frederick, 35, Eel River, Heller's Corners.
Sovine Frederick jr, 34, Eel River, Heller's Corners.
Sovine Michael, 18, Monroe, Monroeville.
Sovine Samuel, 5, Adams, Fort Wayne.
Sowers Benjamin, 6, Scipio, Hall's Corners.
Sowers Christian, 6, Scipio, Hall's Corners.
Sowers Daniel, 6, Scipio, Hicksville, O.
Span Charles, 35, Eel River, Heller's Corners.
Spanallot Henry, 20, Marion, Poe.
Spangler Frederick, 30, Marion, Poe.
Spaulding N R, 5, Monroe, Monroevile.
Spear Hugh, 30, Marion, Poe.
Spear John, 30, Marion, Poe.
Spencer Levant, 16, Milan, Chamberlain.
Spencer Wm, 5, Pleasant, Nine Mile.
Spenley Francis, 16, Wayne, Fort Wayne.
Spereisen H, 22, Adams, Fort Wayne.
Spindler George, 15, Milan, Harlan.
Spindler Wm, 16, Milan, Chamberlain.
Spittler Elias, 4, Springfield, Spencerville.
Spittler Henry, 30, Cedar Creek, Cedarville.
Spittler John, 30, Cedar Creek, Cedarville.
Spittler Morton, 29, Scipio, Antwerp, O.
Spitz George, 25, Washington, Fort Wayne.
Spitz Wm, 25, Washington, Fort Wayne.
Sprague Isaac, 23, Madison, Monroeville.
Sprague Jesse, 20, Madison, Hoagland.
Sprague Leroy, 16, Milan, Harlan.
Sprague Louis, 20, Madison, Hoagland.
Sprague Samuel, 20, Madison, Hoagland.
Sprague Randall B, 20, Madison, Hoagland.

Sprang M J, 29, Marion, Poe.
Spranger Wm, 4, Washington, Wallen.
Sprangle John, 28, Aboit, Aboit.
Sprankle J C H, 8, Wayne, Fort Wayne.
Spreier Julius, 3, Milan, Harlan.
Springer Charles, 36, Pleasant, Sheldon.
Springer Daniel, 34, Pleasant, Sheldon.
Springer Daniel, 32, Wayne, Fort Wayne.
Springer E W S, 1, St Joseph, Fort Wayne.
Springer Frederick, 33, Pleasant, Sheldon.
Springer Fremont, 17, Lake, Arcola.
Springer George, 34, Pleasant, Sheldon.
Springer Harry, 15, St Joseph, Fort Wayne.
Springer H O, 33, Pleasant, Sheldon.
Springer John, 27, Pleasant, Sheldon.
Springer L, 27, Pleasant, Sheldon.
Stahl Christian, 28, Perry, Fort Wayne.
Stahlhut Charles, 23, Lake, Arcola.
Stahlhut Wm, 23, Lake, Arcola.
Staldien Julian, 12, Jefferson, Dawkins.
Staley Bradley, 18, Maumee, Woodburn.
Staley Jacob, 18, Maumee, Woodburn.
Stalter Joel, 17, Jackson, Monroeville.
Stannon George, 10, Marion, Soest.
Stapleton George, 1, Milan, Harlan.
Stapleton Joshua, 4, St Joseph, Fort Wayne.
Stapleton Robert, 28, Cedar Creek, Cedarville.
Stapleton Wm, 4, St Joseph, Fort Wayne.
Stark Arthur, 11, Adams, New Haven.
Starling Jackson, 32, Perry, Wallen.
Starr C A, 1, Springfield, Harlan.
Starr Emery, 1, Springfield, Harlan.
Stauffer Absolom, 17, Milan, Thurman.
Stauffer David, 11, Milan, Harlan.
Steele David, 8, Cedar Creek, Collingwood.
Steen John, 25, Lafayette, Nine Mile.
Steinbecker Michael, 26, Pleasant, Sheldon.
Steinbecker Theo, 26, Pleasant, Sheldon.
Stellhorn Charles, 26, Wayne, Fort Wayne.
Stellhorn Henry, 31, Milan, New Haven.

Stellhorn Henry, 26, Wayne, Fort Wayne.
Stellhorn Henry jr, 26, Wayne, Fort Wayne.
Stellhorn Solomon, 20, Washington, Fort Wayne.
Stellhorn Wm, 8, Adams, Fort Wayne.
Stemer Charles, 20, Monroe, Monroeville.
Stemer P, 20, Monroe, Monroeville.
Stenacher James, Milan, Chamberlain.
Stephenson Charles, 3, Monroe, Baldwin.
Stephenson Don, 9, Monroe, Monroeville.
Stephenson James, 9, Monroe, Monroeville.
Stephenson J M, 4, Monroe, Monroeville.
Stephenson Wm, 34, Monroe, Monroeville.
Sterling Alexander, 25, Perry, Cedarville.
Sterling Charles E, Jackson, Dawkins.
Sterling Frank, 33, Lake, Arcola.
Sterling George, Perry, Cedarville.
Sterling James, 1, Perry, Collingwood.
Sterling John, 13, Lake, Arcola.
Sterling Wm, Perry, Cedarville.
Sterling Wm R, 13, Lake, Fort Wayne.
Stevens Wm, 28, Lake, Arcola.
Stevenson George, 3, Maumee, Antwerp, O.
Stevenson W R, 3, Maumee, Antwerp, O.
Stevick Charles, 28, Cedar Creek, Cedarville.
Stevick Jacob, 20, Cedar Creek, Cedarville.
Stevick J L, 28, Cedar Creek, Cedarville.
Stevick Samuel, 28, Cedar Creek, Cedarville.
Stevick Wm, 9, Cedar Creek, Leo.
Stevick W C, 32, Cedar Creek, Cedarville.
Stewart Benjamin, 17, Maumee, Woodburn.
Stewart Jesse, 28, Aboit, Aboit.
Stewart John, 28, Aboit, Aboit.
Stickney W J, 2, Cedar Creek, Spencerville.
Stier L, 12, Adams, New Haven.
Stineman J, Jefferson, Maples.
Stiner Eli, 28, Cedar Creek, Cedarville.
Stiver Jacob, 19, Scipio, Fansler.
Stiver John, 19, Scipio, Fansler.
Stiver Samuel, Scipio, Harlan.
Stock Rev Ferdinand, 16, Adams, Fort Wayne.

Stock Samuel, 12, Adams, New Haven.
Stock Wm, 12, Adams, New Haven.
Stock Wm jr, 12, Adams, New Haven.
Stolaker George, 10, Wayne, Fort Wayne.
Stolaker P, 10, Wayne, Fort Wayne.
Stolte Adolph, 28, Washington, Fort Wayne.
Stoltz Christian, 31, Milan, New Haven.
Stone H, 28, Adams, Fort Wayne.
Stone Thaddeus, 8, Milan, Chamberlain.
Stopher Daniel, 16, Milan, Chamberlain.
Stopher John, 1, Cedar Creek, Hursh.
Stopher John, 1, Springfield, Harlan.
Stopher Samuel, 2, Milan, Harlan.
Stopher Solomon, Maumee, Woodburn.
Stouder J H, 16, Aboit, Fort Wayne.
Stover George, 3, Wayne, Fort Wayne.
Strasser Rupert, 13, Wayne, Fort Wayne.
Straw John, Jackson, Edgerton.
Streeter Benjamin D, 2, Maumee, Antwerp, O.
Streeter John, 19, Scipio, Fansler.
Streetman H, 14, Adams, New Haven.
Strong Wm, 19, Eel River, Heller's Corners.
Strong L, 20, Eel River, Heller's Corners.
Strum John, 15, Milan, Harlan.
Strum John, 33, St Joseph, Fort Wayne.
Strum Joseph, 33, St Joseph, Fort Wayne.
Stuckey John, 10, Springfield, Harlan.
Studor S B, 10, Aboit, Fort Wayne.
Stump Jesse, 18, Lafayette, Aboit.
Stump Jonathan, 18, Lafayette, Aboit.
Stump John, Jackson, Edgerton.
Sturgeon A F, 17, Eel River, Heller's Corners.
Sturgeon J R, 18, Eel River, Churubusco.
Sturheim Arthur, 20, Monroe, Monroeville.
Sturheim Michael, 20, Monroe, Monroeville.
Suet G W, 1, Wayne, Fort Wayne.
Summers Charles, Lafayette, Nine Mile.
Sunday Frank, 10, Eel River, Ari.
Sunderland John, 8, Washington, Walen.
Sunderland Peter, 7, Washington, Fort Wayne.

Sunderland Wm, 7, Washington, Fort Wayne.
Supple Charles, 30, Aboit, Saturn.
Surface Andrew, Perry, Huntertown.
Surface Clarence, Perry, Collingwood.
Surface Cory, 6, Cedar Creek, Collingwood.
Surface George, 3, Perry, Collingwood.
Surface John, 2, Perry, Collingwood.
Surface Samuel, 2, Perry, Collingwood.
Surface Steven, 6, Cedar Creek, Collingwood.
Surface Wm, 6, Cedar Creek, Collingwood.
Surley George, 15, Lafayette, Myhart.
Sutherland Joseph, 7, Washington, Fort Wayne.
Swaidner James, 2, Springfield, Spencerville.
Swaidner James, 6, Washington, Fort Wayne.
Swaidner John, 12, Springfield, Georgetown.
Swaidner Loren, 11, Springfield, Spencerville.
Swan Emmet, 1, Springfield, Harlan.
Swank Christopher, 32, Pleasant, Sheldon.
Swank G, 16, Pleasant, Nine Mile.
Swank Mason, 16, Pleasant, Nine Mile.
Swank M, 4, Washington, Wallen.
Swank Samuel, 16, Pleasant, Nine Mile.
Swank Thomas, 16, Pleasant, Nine Mile.
Swank Thomas, 32, Pleasant, Sheldon.
Swartz Jacob, 10, Milan, Harlan.
Swartz John, 32, Cedar Creek, Cedarville.
Sweeny John, 2, Jefferson, Dawkins.
Sweeny Louis, 2, Jefferson, Dawkins.
Sweet A, 1, Wayne, Fort Wayne.
Sweet Daniel, 3, Maumee, Antwerp, O.
Sweet John, 7, St Joseph, Fort Wayne.
Sweet Julian, 3, Maumee, Antwerp, O.
Swift Alpheus, 6, St Joseph, Fort Wayne.
Swift Bayless, 6, St Joseph, Fort Wayne.
Swift C F, 5, Springfield, Harlan.
Swift Edward, 7, Springfield, Harlan.
Swift Henry, 6, St Joseph, Fort Wayne.
Swinehart E, 18, Wayne, Fort Wayne.

948 R. L. POLK & CO.'S

T

Taggert Andrew, 2, Milan, Harlan.
Tagtmeyer David, 17, Adams, Fort Wayne.
Tagtmeyer David, 29, Perry, Fort Wayne.
Tate George, 31, St Joseph, Fort Wayne.
Tate George jr, 31, St Joseph, Fort Wayne.
Taylor Arthur, Jackson, Monroeville.
Taylor A M, 24, St Joseph, Thurman.
Taylor Beal, 3, Wayne, Fort Wayne.
Taylor Charles, 18, Monroe, Monroeville.
Taylor Charles, 24, St Joseph, Fort Wayne.
Taylor Don, 18, Monroe, Monroeville.
Taylor Frank, 18, Monroe, Monroeville.
Taylor George, 20, Aboit, Aboit.
Taylor George, 27-28, Eel River, Heller's Corners.
Taylor Harry, 20, Aboit, Aboit.
Taylor Henry, 23, Eel River, Heller's Corners.
Taylor Henry, 18, Monroe, Monroeville.
Taylor H C, 18, Monroe, Monroeville.
Taylor Jacob, Wayne, Fort Wayne.
Taylor John, 32, Jackson, Monroeville.
Taylor John, 1, Madison, Monroeville.
Taylor Jolly, Jackson, Monroeville.
Taylor J M, 29-30, Eel River, Heller's Corners.
Taylor Mer, 22, Eel River, Heller's Corners.
Taylor Noah, 15, Monroe, Monroeville.
Taylor Oliver, 18, Monroe, Monroeville.
Taylor Oliver jr, 18, Monroe, Monroeville.
Taylor Thomas, 20, Monroe, Monroeville.
Taylor Wm, 19, Monroe, Monroeville.
Taylor Wilson, 24, Wayne, Fort Wayne.
Taylor Zachariah, 3, Maumee, Antwerp, O.
Taynes Wilson, 34, Lake, Arcola.
Tell Michael, 35, Lake, Arcola.
Terrian Elijah, 5, Eel River, Ari.
Terrian Orpha, 5, Eel River, Ari.
Thatcher B, Jackson, Baldwin.
Thatcher James, Jackson, Dawkins.

Theye Ferdinand, 27, Milan, Gar Creek.
Thiele Charles, 26, Pleasant, Sheldon.
Thiele Fred, 23, Lake, Arcola.
Thiele Frederick, 18, Washington, Fort Wayne.
Thiele Henry, 32, Milan, New Haven.
Thiele Henry, 26, Pleasant, Sheldon.
Thiele Louis, 18, Washington, Fort Wayne.
Thiele Michael, 28, Lake, Arcola.
Thiele Wm, 26, Pleasant, Sheldon.
Thiesman Gustave, 9, Adams, Fort Wayne.
Thiesman Henry, 9, Adams, Fort Wayne.
Thimler Charles, 9, Milan, Chamberlain.
Thimler Frank, 16, Milan, Harlan.
Thimler John, 1, Springfield, Harlan.
Thimler Levi, 10, Milan, Harlan.
Thimler Samuel, 9, Milan, Chamberlain.
Thimler Theo, 15, Milan, Harlan.
Thomas Arthur, 5, Wayne, Fort Wayne.
Thomas Benjamin, 8, Springfield, Harlan.
Thomas Charles, 5, Wayne, Fort Wayne.
Thomas Ed, Jackson, Baldwin.
Thomas F, 1, Milan, Harlan.
Thomas Herman, 27, Milan, Gar Creek.
Thomas Jemira, 8, Jefferson, New Haven.
Thomas John, 1, Milan, Harlan.
Thomas Joseph, 9, Springfield, Harlan.
Thomas J M, Jackson, Baldwin.
Thomas Levi, 4, Jackson, Baldwin.
Thomas Mahlon, 8, Maumee, Woodburn.
Thomas Matthew, 12, Adams, New Haven.
Thomas Morgan, 8, Jefferson, New Haven.
Thomas Riley, 1, Milan, Harlan.
Thomas Wm, Jackson, Monroeville.
Thomas W S, 29, Cedar Creek, Cedarville.
Thomasson Wm, Jackson, Edgerton.
Thompson Albert, 7, Maumee, Harlan.
Thompson C R, 30, Cedar Creek, Cedarville.
Thompson E L, Jackson, Baldwin.
Thompson Frank, Maumee, Woodburn.
Thompson John, 24, Milan, Gar Creek.

Thompson J J, 6, Marion, Fort Wayne.
Thompson M, 6, Aboit, Dunfee.
Thompson Samuel, 19, Perry, Huntertown.
Thompson Wm, 6, Aboit, Dunfee.
Thompson Wm, 29, Cedar Creek, Cedarville.
Thompson Wm, 7, Maumee, Harlan.
Thompson Wm, 15, Monroe, Monroeville.
Thompson Willis, Jackson, Baldwin.
Thompson W H, 5, Marion, Fort Wayne.
Thornton S A, Perry, Huntertown.
Thorp George, 7, Springfield, Harlan.
Thorp Henry, 7, Springfield, Harlan.
Thorp John, 7, Springfield, Harlan.
Thorp Joseph, 24, Aboit, Fort Wayne.
Thorp Wm, 4, Springfield, Harlan.
Thurber John, 15, Jackson, Edgerton.
Thurber Marcellus, 14, Pleasant, Fort Wayne.
Thurber Mark, 25, Pleasant, Poe.
Tielker Charles, 18, Washington, Fort Wayne.
Tielker Charles jr, 18, Washington, Fort Wayne.
Tielker Christian, 16, Wayne, Fort Wayne.
Tielker Conrad, 16, Wayne, Fort Wayne.
Tielker Conrad jr, 16, Wayne, Fort Wayne.
Tielker Frederick, 18, Washington, Fort Wayne.
Tielker Frederick W, 18, Washington, Fort Wayne.
Tielker Wm, 18, Washington, Fort Wayne.
Tielker Wm jr, 18, Washington, Fort Wayne.
Tilden Charles, 31, Perry, Huntertown.
Till Frederick, 2, Washington, St Vincent.
Till Henry, 2, Washington, St Vincent.
Till Joseph, 2, Washington, St Vincent.
Till Nicholas, 2, Washington, St Vincent.
Tillbury Charles, 27, St Joseph, Goeglien.
Tillbury James, 33, St Joseph, Fort Wayne.
Tillbury Jasper, 33, St Joseph, Fort Wayne.
Tillbury Marcus, 4, Adams, New Haven.
Tillbury Mark, 33, St Joseph, Fort Wayne.
Tillman John, 25, Jefferson, Zulu.
Tillman J S, Jackson, Baldwin.
Tilton Josiah, 24, Milan, Gar Creek.

C. P. TINKHAM. DENTIST.   OFFICE TELEPHONE, RESIDENCE TELEPHONE,
Specialty: Teeth Extracted without Pain. Fine Gold Crown and Bridge Work
Teeth without Plates. Largest and Best Equipped in the State. All Work Positively
Guaranteed.   Nos. 21, 22, 23, 24 Arcade Blk., W. Berry St., Fort Wayne, Ind.

Timbrook George, 4, Milan, Chamberlain.
Timbrook Herbert, 9, Springfield, Harlan.
Timbrook Wm, 9, Springfield, Harlan.
Timme Henry, 18, Jefferson, New Haven.
Timme Henry jr, 18, Jefferson, New Haven.
Tindall Wm, Maumee, Woodburn.
Tinkham Rev, 19, Madison, Hoagland.
Tobias F, 4, Adams, New Haven.
Todd A B, 19, Madison, Hoagland.
Todd James, 12, Aboit, Fort Wayne.
Todd James, 11, Adams, New Haven.
Todd Martin, 11, Adams, New Haven.
Todd Mills, 4, Madison, Maples.
Todd Morgan, 19, Madison, Hoagland.
Todd Wm, 24, Madison, Monroeville.
Tonkel August, 9, St Joseph, Fort Wayne.
Tonkel George, 30, Cedar Creek, Cedarville.
Tonkel Henry, 30, Cedar Creek, Cedarville.
Tonkel Henry, 4, St Joseph, Fort Wayne.
Tonkel James, 4, St Joseph, Fort Wayne.
Tonkel Wm, 30, Cedar Creek, Cedarville.
Tonot Charles, 25, Jefferson, Zulu.
Toohey Rev J M, 1, Washington, St Vincent.
Toomey Patrick, 33, Lake, Arcola.
Tope George W, 28, Lake, Arcola.
Tourney Emmet, 15, Jefferson, Zulu.
Tourney John, Jefferson, Dawkins.
Townsend Caleb, 25, Jefferson, Zulu.
Townsend George, 25, Jefferson, Zulu.
Tracy A, 18, Adams, Fort Wayne.
Tracy George, 31, Lake, Arcola.
Tracy Wash, 18, Adams, Fort Wayne.
Tracy Wm, 31, Lake, Arcola.
Trainor George, 31, St Joseph, Fort Wayne.
Trautman Daniel, 29, Aboit, Fort Wayne.
Trautman Frederick, 31, Aboit, Fort Wayne.
Trautman Jacob, 29, Aboit, Fort Wayne.
Trautman John, 31, Aboit, Fort Wayne.
Travis Daniel, 16, Lafayette, Myhart.
Trease Clement, 6, Cedar Creek, Spencerville.

952   R. L. POLK & CO.'s

Trease Dayton, 4, St Joseph, Fort Wayne.
Trease George, 32, Cedar Creek, Cedarville.
Trease Henry, 24, Perry, Cedarville.
Trease John, 29, Cedar Creek, Cedarville.
Trease Robert, 24, Perry, Cedarville.
Trease Wm, 29, Cedar Creek, Cedarville.
Treep F, 13, St Joseph, Thurman.
Trepsing B, 8, Adams, Fort Wayne.
Treuchet Frank, 12, Adams, New Haven.
Treuchet Frank jr, 12, Adams, New Haven.
Treve F, 11, Pleasant, Fort Wayne.
Treve Wm, 11, Pleasant, Fort Wayne.
Trick Francis, 2, Pleasant, Fort Wayne.
Trick George M, 9, Pleasant, Nine Mile.
Tricker G W, 10, Eel River, Ari.
Trier Herman, 29, Adams, Fort Wayne.
Trier Martin, 17, Jefferson, New Haven.
Trier Paul, 32, Adams, Fort Wayne.
Trier Peter, 27, St Joseph, Goeglien.
Trousse James, 14, Jefferson, Zulu.
Troutman Edward, 8, Madison, Maples.
Troutman Henry, 9, Marion, Fort Wayne.
Troutman Peter, 9, Marion, Fort Wayne.
Troutner John, 12, Adams, New Haven.
Truitt Thomas, 30, Jefferson, Maples.
Truman John, 5, Aboit, Dunfee.
Truman Nelson, 33, Lake, Arcola.
Tryann Julian, 21, Lake, Arcola.
Tucker Doe, 12, Eel River, Huntertown.
Tucker George, 11, Perry, Collingwood.
Tucker Isaac, 36, Eel River, Wallen.
Tucker James, 24, Wayne, Fort Wayne.
Turner Asa, 33, Aboit, Fort Wayne.
Turner Daniel, 12, Eel River, Huntertown.
Turner H K, 18, Marion, Poe.
Turner W H, 7, Marion, Fort Wayne.
Turney August, 28, Perry, Fort Wayne.
Tustison Henry, 5, Scipio, Hicksville, O.
Tustison John, 2, Adams, New Haven.
Tyler Alfred, 4, Washington, Wallen.

Tyler John, 4, Washington, Wallen.
Tyler Wm, 4, Washington, Wallen.

U

Uehlery Nelson, 23, Marion, Hoagland.
Ulen Reuben, Perry, Huntertown.
Urbine Francis, Perry, Wallen.
Urbine John, 27, Perry, Fort Wayne.
Urbine Joseph, 27, Perry, Fort Wayne.
Urbine Joseph L, 2, Washington, St Vincent.
Urbine Louis, 28, Jefferson, Maples.
Urbine Peter, 23' Jefferson, Zulu.
Urrilman John, 3, Wayne, Fort Wayne.

V

Vachon Thomas, 9, Lake Arcola.
Valentine Charles, 18, Monroe, Monroeville.
Valentine E, 21, Washington, Fort Wayne.
Valentine Jackson, 33, Eel River, Heller's Corners.
Valentine John, 1-2, Lake, Heller's Corners.
Valiot Louis, 31, Springfield, Harlan.
Van Alstine Henry, 16, St Joseph, Fort Wayne.
Van Buskirk Edward, 24, Madison, Monroeville.
Van Buskirk Joseph, 19, Madison, Hoagland.
Van Camp Henry, 9, Cedar Creek, Leo.
Van Camp James, 9, Cedar Creek, Leo.
Van Camp W, 16, Milan, Chamberlain.
Vanderan Christian, 24, St Joseph, Thurman.
Vanderan Frederick, 36, St Joseph, New Haven.
Vanderan Herman, 36, St Joseph, New Haven.
Vanderan Jacob, 36, St Joseph, New Haven.
Vanderan Jacob jr, 36, St Joseph, New Haven.
Vanderan Peter, 4, Maumee, Harlan.
Vanderlin George, 17, Jackson, Monroeville.
Vanderly John, Jackson, Dawkins.
Vanderly Louis, 24, Jefferson, Zulu.
Vandolat Benjamin, 13-14, Perry, Leo.
Vandolat Joseph, 13, Perry, Leo.

Van Hoozen Henry, 31, Aboit, Fort Wayne.
Van Hoozer J, 30, Aboit, Saturn.
Van Horn Jacob, 29, Jefferson, Maples.
Vanhorn James, 15, Madison, Monroeville.
Van Horn John, Jackson, Monroeville.
Van Horn Silas, 36, Adams, Maples.
Van Horn Wm, 15, Madison, Monroeville.
Van Horn Wm, 35, Marion, Williams Station.
Van Horn Wilson, 27, Marion, Hoagland.
Vanhouser George, 17, Aboit, Fort Wayne.
Vanhouser W, 17, Aboit, Fort Wayne.
Vanier Peter, 4, Eel River, Ari.
Vannatta Frank, 19, Perry, Huntertown.
Vannatta Jasper, 15, Cedar Creek, Leo.
Vanorden George, 17, Wayne, Fort Wayne.
Vanorden Henry, 17, Wayne, Fort Wayne.
Van Wormer Wm, 32, Lafayette, Zanesville.
Vanzile Azariah, 6, Cedar Creek, Spencerville.
Vanzile Daniel, 7, Cedar Creek, Collingwood.
Vanzile Samuel, 7, Cedar Creek, Collingwood.
Vanzile Thomas, 7, Cedar Creek, Collingwood.
Vaughn Charles, 3, Aboit, Arcola.
Vaughn Charles, 10, Aboit, Fort Wayne.
Vaughn James, 5, Aboit, Dunfee.
Vaughn Simeon, 28, Marion, Poe.
Vaughn Wm, 7, Aboit, Dunfee.
Vehrman Wm, 21, Jefferson, Maples.
Vehrman Wm jr, 21, Jefferson, Maples.
Veit Philip, 1, Madison, Monroeville.
Vetter Joseph, Jackson, Baldwin.
Vining Wash, 20, St Joseph, Fort Wayne.
Vioral Florent, Jackson, Dawkins.
Visel John, 36, Lafayette, Zanesville.
Vizard Edward, 23, Monroe, Monroeville.
Vizard Wm, 23, Monroe, Monroeville.
Vodde Bernard J, 13, Adams, New Haven.
Voetter Julius, 6, Wayne, Fort Wayne.
Voinet John, Lafayette, Nine Mile.
Voirol Samuel, Jackson, Monroeville.
Voldamer Peter, 9, St Joseph, Fort Wayne.

Volkert James, 12, Springfield, Georgetown.
Volkert Samuel, 29, Scipio, Antwerp, O.
Volland Paul, 12, Milan, Harlan.
Vollmer Frederick, 22, St Joseph, Fort Wayne.
Vollmer Louis, 22, St Joseph, Fort Wayne.
Voltz Christian, 13, Lafayette, Nine Mile.
Voltz James, 13, Lafayette, Nine Mile.
Von Cannon O, 1, Wayne, Fort Wayne.
Voors Bernard, 32, St Joseph, Fort Wayne.
Votre John, 19, Madison, Hoagland.
Vought W S, 15, Aboit, Fort Wayne.
Vreeland Francis, Jackson Edgerton.
Vreeland Wm, Jackson, Edgerton.
Vuillman James, 6, St Joseph, Fort Wayne.

W

Wade Elwood, 11, Milan, Harlan.
Wageman Andrew, 28, Washington, Fort Wayne.
Wagner Herman, 22, Adams, Fort Wayne.
Wagner Jacob, 1, Madison, Monroeville.
Wagner Jacob, 24, Wayne, Fort Wayne.
Wagner John, 14, Adams, New Haven.
Wagner Wm, 28, Pleasant, Sheldon.
Waite Geary, 9, Springfield, Harlan.
Waite George, 9, Springfield, Harlan.
Waite Warren, 8, Springfield, Harlan.
Walbold John, 32, Cedar Creek, Cedarville.
Walbold John jr, 32, Cedar Creek, Cedarville.
Walbrick John, 12, Adams, New Haven.
Walker Carl, 28, Pleasant, Sheldon.
Walker Charles, 17, Scipio, Hicksville, O.
Walker Edward F, 12, Springfield, Georgetown.
Walker E M, 10, Monroe, Monroeville.
Walker Frank, 28, Pleasant, Sheldon.
Walker Gottlieb, 2, Lake, Heller's Corners.
Walker John, 12, Springfield, Georgetown.
Walker John, 31, Springfield, Harlan.
Walker Marion, 19, Scipio, Fansler.
Walker Perry, 12, Springfield, Georgetown.

10

956   R. L. POLK & CO.'S

Walker Samuel, 19, Scipio, Fansler.
Walker Walter, 19, Scipio, Fansler.
Walker Wm, 32, Lafayette, Zanesville.
Walker Wm, 28, Pleasant, Sheldon.
Walker Wm jr, 28, Pleasant, Sheldon.
Walker W R, 10, Monroe, Monroeville.
Wall John, 11, Adams, New Haven.
Wallace Harvey, 4, Pleasant, Fort Wayne.
Wallace John, 7, Pleasant, Nine Mile.
Wallace Wm, 18, Maumee, Woodburn.
Wallace Wm, 7, Pleasant, Nine Mile.
Wallace Wm C, 23, Washington, Fort Wayne.
Walliman S, 12, Adams, New Haven.
Walman Rudolph, 21, Jefferson, Maples.
Walter George, 1, Springfield, Harlan.
Walter Henry A, 4, Springfield, Spencerville.
Walter Nicholas, Springfield, Harlan.
Waltke August, Milan, Thurman.
Waltke Frederick, 4, Maumee, Harlan.
Waltke Henry, 4, Maumee, Harlan.
Waltke Wm, 27, St Joseph, Goeglien.
Wann Charles, 25, Springfield, Hall's Corners.
Wann Daniel, 14, Springfield, Harlan.
Wann Edward, 25, Springfield, Hall's Corners.
Wann George, 24, Springfield, Hall's Corners.
Wann Samuel, 24, Springfield, Hall's Corners.
Wappes George, 3, Eel River, Ari.
Wappes John, 3, Eel River, Ari.
Warcup George, Perry, Huntertown.
Warcup John, Perry, Huntertown.
Warcup Wm, 7, Perry, Huntertown.
Ward Andrew, 12, Milan, Harlan.
Ward Mack, 35, Lafayette, Zanesville.
Warley Greeley, 1, Cedar Creek, Hursh.
Warner Albert, 6, Cedar Creek, Collingwood.
Warner Alexander, 5, Cedar Creek, Collingwood.
Warner Alfred, 28, Cedar Creek, Cedarville.
Warner Allen, 5, Cedar Creek, Collingwood.
Warner Amos, 6, Cedar Creek, Collingwood.
Warner Charles, 3, Perry, Collingwood.

Warner George, 4, Cedar Creek, Leo.
Warner George, 12, Perry, Collingwood.
Warner George, 18, Scipio, Hicksville, O.
Warner George jr, 11, Perry, Collingwood.
Warner Henry, 11, Perry, Collingwood.
Warner Howard, 18, Scipio, Hicksville, O..
Warner John, 11, Perry, Collingwood.
Warner John A, 2, Perry, Collingwood.
Warner Joseph, 11, Perry, Collingwood.
Warner Lincoln, 12, Perry, Collingwood.
Warner Perry, 7, Cedar Creek, Collingwood.
Warner Samuel, 12, Perry, Collingwood.
Warner Timothy, 12, Perry, Collingwood.
Warner Webb, 11, Milan, Harlan.
Warner Wesley, 5, Cedar Creek, Collingwood.
Warner Wm, 12, Perry, Collingwood.
Warren Wm, 25, Milan, Gar Creek.
Wassenfelder A, 1, Aboit, Fort Wayne.
Wassenfelder John, 27, Aboit, Fort Wayne.
Waters Allen, 2, Washington, St Vincent.
Waters Charles, 12, Washington, Fort Wayne.
Waters Edward, 1, Washington, St Vincent.
Waters James, 12, Washington, Fort Wayne.
Waters John, 9, Monroe, Monroeville.
Waters John, 12, Washington, Fort Wayne.
Waters John jr, 12, Washington, Fort Wayne.
Waters O P, 12, Washington, Fort Wayne.
Waters Wesley, 4, St Joseph, Fort Wayne.
Waters Wilson, 1, Washington, St Vincent.
Waterson Samuel K, 19-20, Eel River, Heller's Corners.
Watson David, 1, Cedar Creek, Hursh.
Watson John S, 10, Cedar Creek, Leo.
Watson Samuel, 1, Cedar Creek, Hursh.
Waugh John, 19, Lake, Arcola.
Weakman G, Aboit, Fort Wayne.
Weaver George, 33, Lafayette, Zanesville.
Weaver Isaac, 28, Wayne, Fort Wayne.
Weaver Jacob, 33, Lafayette, Zanesville.
Weaver James, 28, Pleasant, Sheldon.

Weaver James, 5, Springfield, Harlan.
Weaver James jr, 5, Springfield, Harlan.
Weaver Lawrence, 35, Lafayette, Zanesville.
Weaver M, 6, Pleasant, Nine Mile.
Weaver Oliver, 6, Pleasant, Nine Mile.
Webb Frank, 20, Cedar Creek, Cedarville.
Webb George, 4, Springfield, Harlan.
Webb James, 14, Springfield, Harlan.
Webb James, 9, Springfield, Spencerville.
Webb John, 24, Springfield, Hall's Corners.
Webb John, 15, Springfield, Harlan.
Webster Benjamin, 17, Pleasant, Nine Mile.
Webster Herman, 14, Jefferson, Zulu.
Webster John, 14, Jefferson, Zulu.
Webster J G, 12, Jefferson, Dawkins.
Webster N C, 15, Jefferson, Zulu.
Webster Samuel, 34, Monroe, Monroeville.
Webster Warren, 14, Jefferson, Zulu.
Webster Wm, 20, Pleasant, Nine Mile.
Weeden Bernard, 12, Adams, New Haven.
Weers Albert, 2, Milan, Harlan.
Wegeman Wm, 17, Washington, Fort Wayne.
Weich Frank, 17, Lafayette, Myhart.
Weich Joseph, 17, Lafayette, Myhart.
Weicher George, 25, Milan, Gar Creek.
Weicher Henry, 25, Milan, Gar Creek.
Weicher John, 24, Milan, Gar Creek.
Weigner Henry, 16, Madison, Hoagland.
Weipe Deiderich, 10, Marion, Soest.
Weirich John, 31, Eel River, Heller's Corners.
Weis Frank, 21, Marion, Poe.
Weise C, 15, Adams, New Haven.
Weisel John A, 1, Lake, Heller's Corners.
Weisenberger Charles, 23, Lake, Arcola.
Weisenberger Wm, 23, Lake, Arcola.
Weisse Allen, 24, Lake, Arcola.
Weisse August, 4, Maumee, Harlan.
Weisse Christian, 15, Lake, Arcola.
Weissenberg George, 14, Aboit, Fort Wayne.
Weist Charles, 8, Pleasant, Nine Mile.

Weithet Henry, 17, Adams, Fort Wayne.
Welch Thomas, 30, Aboit, Saturn.
Welking Wm, 4, Lake, Heller's Corners.
Wellbaum Aime, 5, Pleasant, Nine Mile.
Wellbaum Edward, 33, Monroe, Monroeville.
Wellbaum George, Lafayette, Nine Mile.
Wellbaum Louis, 5, Pleasant, Nine Mile.
Wellbaum Marshall, 16, Pleasant, Nine Mile.
Wellbaum Noah F, 21, Wayne, Fort Wayne.
Welling Anthony, 14, Adams, New Haven.
Welling Henry, 11, Adams, New Haven.
Welling Henry, 15, Milan, Harlan.
Wells Aaron, 18, Lake, Arcola.
Wells Bert, 29-30, Eel River, Huntertown.
Wells Charles, 31, Aboit, Aboit.
Wells David, 29-30, Eel River, Wallen.
Wells Hiram, 5, Lafayette, Aboit.
Wells Wm, Jackson, Edgerton.
Wells John, 11, Jefferson, Dawkins.
Wells John, 9, Pleasant, Nine Mile.
Wells John, 3, Wayne, Fort Wayne.
Wells Wm, 26, Eel River, Wallen.
Welph Henry, 10, Adams, New Haven.
Welph John, 8, Adams, Fort Wayne.
Welsheimer A L, 3, Lake, Heller's Corners.
Welsheimer Lucian, 19-20, Eel River, Heller's Corners
Welsheimer Otto, 3, Lake, Heller's Corners.
Welsheimer Wm, 18, Eel River, Churubusco.
Welsheimer Wm, 3, Lake, Heller's Corners.
Weltmeyer A, 12, Adams, New Haven.
Werling Frederick, 19, Jefferson, Maples.
Werling Wm, 26, St Joseph, Goeglien.
Wert Charles, 3, Pleasant, Nine Mile.
Wesling August, 20, Adams, Fort Wayne.
Wesling Herman, 20, Adams, Fort Wayne.
Wessel John, 7, Aboit, Dunfee.
West Fisher C, 5, Perry, Huntertown.
Westerfield Carl, 4, Marion, Fort Wayne.
Westerman Charles, 1, Springfield, Harlan.
Westman Dan, 7, Milan, Thurman.

Weston August, 5, Lafayette, Aboit.
Weston Fred, 5, Lafayette, Aboit.
Westphall Christian, 20, Washington, Fort Wayne.
Wettle A D, 3, Milan, Harlan.
Wetzell Henry, 3, St Joseph, Fort Wayne.
Wetzgall Wm, 10, Lafayette, Nine Mile.
Wey George, 1, Wayne, Fort Wayne.
Weyers David, 28, Madison, Hoagland.
Whartenbe Wm, 31, St Joseph, Fort Wayne.
Wheatfield Fred, 20, Madison, Hoagland.
Wheatfield Henry, 35, Madison, Binger.
Wheeler Diss, 16, Wayne, Fort Wayne.
Wheelock Eli G, 1, St Joseph, Fort Wayne.
Wherry George, 32, Monroe, Monroeville.
Whitcomb Charles, 19, Madison, Hoagland.
White August, 11, Jefferson, Dawkins.
White Brisk, 9, Washington, Wallen.
White Cooney, 36, Lake, Arcola.
White Edward, Jackson, Dawkins.
White Jonathan, 15, Eel River, Heller's Corners.
White Lawrence, 9, Washington, Wallen.
White Louis, 9, Washington, Wallen.
White Robert, 27, St Joseph, Goeglien.
White Scott, 10, Springfield, Harlan.
Whiten Charles, 18, Monroe, Monroeville.
Whitman Joseph, Springfield, Harlan.
Whitmore Chris, 32, Springfield, Harlan.
Whitney Ernest, 1, Madison, Monroeville.
Whitney Fred, 12, Adams, New Haven.
Whitney George, 28, Lake, Arcola.
Whitney Wm, 22, Jefferson, Maples.
Whittaker Eugene, 12, Adams, New Haven.
Whittemore Edward, 10, Wayne, Fort Wayne.
Whittemore Edward H, 15, Wayne, Fort Wayne.
Whittemore Merritt, 10, Wayne, Fort Wayne.
Whittern Nelson, 13, Madison, Monroeville.
Wiant Charles H, Perry, Huntertown.
Wice Charles, 4, Jefferson, Gar Creek.
Wickley Frank, 31, Lake, Arcoda.
Wickliffe Edmund, 23, Lafayette, Zanesville.

Wickliffe Francis, 28, Pleasant, Sheldon.
Wickliffe Frank, 25, Lafayette, Nine Mile.
Wickliffe Fred, 6, Lafayette, Aboit.
Wickliffe Peter, 24, Lafayette, Zanesville.
Wickliffe Ward, 6, Lafayette, Aboit.
Widdefield Mordecai, 7, Springfield, Harlan.
Widner Amos, 3, St Joseph, Fort Wayne.
Wiebke Diederich, 25, Lake, Arcola.
Wiebke Frederick, 25, Lake, Arcola.
Wiebke Wm, 25, Lake, Arcola.
Wiehe H, 23, Adams, Fort Wayne.
Wiese L, 26, Eel River, Wallen.
Wiggens Wm, 10, Wayne, Fort Wayne.
Wigman Charles, 31, St Joseph, Fort Wayne.
Wigman Frederick, 21, Madison, Hoagland.
Wigman Henry, 31, St Joseph, Fort Wayne.
Wigman Henry, 21, Madison, Hoagland.
Wigman Wm, 21, Madison, Hoagland.
Wiker John, 8, Wayne, Fort Wayne.
Wilber George, 4, Milan, Chamberlain.
Wilder Wm, 20, Lafayette, Roanoke.
Wilhelm Jacob, 20, Jefferson, New Haven.
Wilkes Noah, 28, Cedar Creek, Cedarville.
Wilkie Wm, 15, Pleasant, Nine Mile.
Wilkie Wm, 28, Pleasant, Sheldon.
Wilkins Henry, 9, Lake, Arcola.
Wilkins Wm, 9, Lake, Arcola.
Wilkinson Charles, 3, Pleasant, Nine Mile.
Wilkinson George, 19, Scipio, Fansler.
Wilkinson Jefferson, 30, Lafayette, Zanesville.
Wilkinson S, 28, Lafayette, Zanesville.
Williams Charles, 7, St Joseph, Fort Wayne.
Williams Christian, 33, Milan, Gar Creek.
Williams John, Jefferson, Maples.
Willie Henry, 12, Adams, New Haven.
Willis Franz, 12, Adams, New Haven.
Wilson A F, 30, Lafayette, Zanesville.
Wilson Daniel, 13, Springfield, Harlan.
Wilson John, 4, Eel River, Ari.
Wilson John, 4, St Joseph, Fort Wayne.

Wilson J E, 12, Adams, New Haven.
Wilson Ludwick, 21, Washington, Fort Wayne.
Wilson Thomas, 31, Lafayette, Zanesville.
Winans Frank, 18, Monroe, Monroeville.
Wince John, 18, Monroe, Monroeville.
Wince Wm, 18, Monroe, Monroeville.
Wingert Frank, 33, Lake, Arcola.
Wingert John, 33, Lake, Arcola.
Winkler Charles, 18, Adams, Fort Wayne.
Winkler Henry, 1, Jefferson, Gar Creek.
Winkler Herman, 1, Lake, Heller's Corners.
Winkler John, 1, Jefferson, Gar Creek.
Winsor Otis, 33, Lafayette, Zanesville.
Winters August, 16, Pleasant, Nine Mile.
Winters Charles, 16, Pleasant, Fort Wayne.
Winters Ernest, 4, Washington, Wallen.
Winters Jacob, 27, Jefferson, Zulu.
Winters Peter, 18, Pleasant, Nine Mile.
Wirtz Frank, 4, Milan, Chamberlain.
Wirtz John, 4, Milan, Chamberlain.
Wise John, 9, Springfield, Spencerville.
Wise Ves, 4, Springfield, Spencerville.
Wiseman Jacob, 32, Scipio, Harlan.
Wisley Isaac, 18, Monroe, Monroeville.
Wisner Benjamin, 5, Lafayette, Aboit.
Witte Ernest, 27, Marion, Hoagland.
Witte Julius, 9, Madison, Maples.
Wittefield Eugene, 35, Springfield, Harlan.
Witts Albert, 16, Eel River, Heller's Corners.
Witzgale Louis, 23, Lafayette, Zanesville.
Woebbeking Henry, 8, Maumee, Woodburn.
Woebbeking Henry jr, 17, Maumee, Woodburn.
Wolf August, 11, Adams, New Haven.
Wolf Christian, 11, Adams, New Haven.
Wolf Edward, 21, Washington, Fort Wayne.
Wolf George, 5, Jefferson, New Haven.
Wolf Gideon, 11, Adams, New Haven.
Wolf Henry, 11 Adams, New Haven.
Wolf H J, 11, Aboit, Fort Wayne.
Wolf Samuel, 4, Jefferson, Gar Creek.

Wolf Wm, 12, Adams, New Haven.
Wolford Ira, Perry, Huntertown.
Wolkerton Isaac, 8, Washington, Wallen.
Woolman Charles, Jackson, Edgerton.
Woolman Wm, Jackson, Edgerton.
Wood Comodore, 13, Eel River, Huntertown.
Wood Wm, 13, Eel River, Huntertown.
Wood Wm, 2, Marion, Soest.
Woods Alexander, 31, Pleasant, Sheldon.
Woods Clement, 32, Pleasant, Sheldon.
Woods Emery, 31, Pleasant, Sheldon.
Woods Frank, 31, Pleasant, Sheldon.
Woods George, 31, Pleasant, Sheldon.
Woods Jacob, 31, Pleasant, Sheldon.
Woods Jacob jr, 31, Pleasant, Sheldon.
Woods James, 32, Pleasant, Sheldon.
Woods John, 31, Pleasant, Sheldon.
Woods Samuel, 31, Pleasant, Sheldon.
Worden Eme, 24, Springfield Hall's Corners.
Worden Grant, 24, Springfield, Hall's Corners.
Worden W J, 31, Scipio, Harlan.
Workman Hiram, 18, Cedar Creek, Collingwood.
Workman Isaac, 3, Lake, Heller's Corners.
Wormcastle James, 29, Monroe, Monroeville.
Wormcastle Lemuel, 23, Madison, Monroeville.
Worthmer Christian, 20, Maumee, Woodburn.
Wren Reuben, 8, Springfield, Harlan.
Wright A S, 18, Monroe, Monroeville.
Wright Charles, 18, Monroe, Monroeville.
Wright Emmett, 23, Lafayette, Zanesville.
Wright George, 23, Lafayette, Zanesville.
Wright Wm, 20, Lafayette, Roanoke.
Wright Wm, 18, Monroe, Monroeville.
Wyatt Andrew, 11, Perry, Huntertown.
Wyatt Daniel, 9, Perry, Huntertown.
Wyatt Frank, 8, Perry, Huntertown.
Wyatt Jacob, Perry, Huntertown.
Wyatt James, 8, Perry, Huntertown.
Wyatt James jr, 8, Perry, Huntertown.
Wyatt Milas, 7, Perry, Huntertown.

Wyatt Spencer, 29-30, Eel River, Heller's Corners.
Wyatt Wm, 11, Jefferson, Dawkins.
Wyatt W J, 2, Cedar Creek, Spencerville.
Wyre David, 29, Monroe, Monroeville.
Wysong Harry, 20, Lafayette, Roanoke.
Wyss Frank, 16, Marion, Fort Wayne.
Wyss John, 18, Marion, Fort Wayne.
Wyss Nicholas, 13, Marion, Hoagland.
Wyss Wm, 16, Marion, Fort Wayne.

Y

Yagerleiner Wm, 12, Pleasant, Fort Wayne.
Yaggy Daniel, 10, Springfield, Harlan.
Yaggy Henry, 10, Springfield, Harlan.
Yant Cornelius, 28, Aboit, Aboit.
Yergens Andrew, 32, St Joseph, Fort Wayne.
Yergens Louis, 14, St Joseph, Fort Wayne.
Yerks James, 16, Milan, Chamberlain.
Yerkes Ora, 4, Milan, Chamberlain.
Yerks Orin, Milan, Chamberlain.
Yetter Charles, 26, Washington, Fort Wayne.
Yoder John, 8, Cedar Creek, Collingwood.
Yoder Joseph, 18, Springfield, Harlan.
Yoder R, 8, Cedar Creek, Collingwood.
Yoder Solomon, 18, Springfield, Harlan.
Youguelet Alfred, 12, Jefferson, Dawkins.
Youguelet Julius, 11, Jefferson, Dawkins.
Young Amos, 3, Wayne, Fort Wayne.
Young Andrew, Maumee, Woodburn.
Young Christian, 25, Washington, Fort Wayne.
Young Henry, 26, St Joseph, Goeglien.
Young James, 32, Lafayette, Zanesville.
Young John, 8, Lafayette, Myhart.
Young John, 3, Wayne, Fort Wayne.
Young John W, 5, Eel River, Ari.
Young Julius, 9, St Joseph, Fort Wayne.
Young Julius jr, 9, St Joseph, Fort Wayne.
Young Robert, 16, Lafayette, Myhart.
Young Samuel, 16, Lafayette, Myhart.

Young Stephen, 25, Washington, Fort Wayne.
Young S S, 18, Aboit, Dunfee.
Young Wm, 26, St Joseph, Goeglien.
Young W H, 3, Wayne, Fort Wayne.
Younger Wm, 4, Adams, New Haven.
Youse Charles, 20, Madison, Hoagland.
Youse Christian, 20, Madison, Hoagland.
Youse Christian jr, 20, Madison, Hoagland.
Youse John S, 29, Madison, Hoagland.
Youse Wm, 23, Madison, Monroeville.
Youse Wilson, 25, Madison, Hoagland.

Z

Zeddis Wm, 12, Adams, New Haven.
Zedekee George, Jefferson, Maples.
Zeis Charles, 32, Cedar Creek, Cedarville.
Zeis Elmer, 5, Springfield, Harlan.
Zeis George, 8, Springfield, Harlan.
Zeis Louis, 20, Springfield, Harlan.
Zeis Rufus, 34, Springfield, Harlan.
Zeis Samuel, 28, Springfield, Harlan.
Zentner Eman, 32, Cedar Creek, Cedarville.
Zentner James, 32, Cedar Creek, Cedarville.
Ziegler John, 20, Marion, Poe.
Ziegler Martin, 20, Marion, Poe.
Zimmer D, 22, Aboit, Fort Wayne.
Zimmer Elmer, 27, Aboit, Fort Wayne.
Zimmer Fred, 7, Springfield, Harlan.
Zimmer George, 23, Springfield, Hall's Corners.
Zimmer Martin, 26, Springfield, Harlan.
Zimmerman Bert, 28, Cedar Creek, Cedarville.
Zimmerman Charles, 28, Cedar Creek, Cedarville.
Zimmerman Eli, 10, Springfield, Harlan.
Zimmerman Elias, 18, Jackson, Dawkins.
Zimmerman Frederick, 22, Jackson, Edgerton.
Zimmerman G W, 36, Springfield, Harlan.
Zimmerman Henry, 28, Cedar Creek, Cedarville.
Zimmerman Philip, 22, Jackson, Edgerton.
Zimmerman Samuel, 21, Cedar Creek, Cedarville.

Zimmerman W D, 22, Springfield, Harlan.
Zink Paul, 3, Jefferson, Gar Creek.
Zion George N, 7, Pleasant Nine Mile.
Zollars Charles, 33, Cedar Creek, Cedarville.
Zollars George, 33, Cedar Creek, Cedarville.
Zollars Valentine, 9, Springfield, Spencerville.
Zollinger Daniel, 6, Madison, Maples.
Zollinger Valentine, 6, Madison, Maples.
Zuber Joseph, 28, Adams, Soest.
Zuber Michael, 32, Adams, Fort Wayne.
Zuber Philip, 28, Aboit, Aboit.
Zulman James, 4, Lake, Heller's Corners.
Zumber Henry, 32, Aboit, Fort Wayne.
Zurbach Francis, 1, Adams, New Haven.
Zurbach John, 1, Adams, New Haven.
Zurbrink Peter, 5, Monroe, Monroeville.

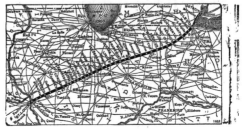